SANDERS AND YOUNG'S CRIMINAL JUSTICE

Sanders and Young's Criminal Justice

Fifth Edition

LUCY WELSH
LAYLA SKINNS
AND
ANDREW SANDERS

WITH CONTRIBUTED CHAPTERS:
CHAPTERS 2 AND 3: ALPA PARMAR
CHAPTER 6: ED CAPE

Great Clarendon Street, Oxford, OX2 6DP,
United Kingdom

Oxford University Press is a department of the University of Oxford.
It furthers the University's objective of excellence in research, scholarship,
and education by publishing worldwide. Oxford is a registered trade mark of
Oxford University Press in the UK and in certain other countries

© Oxford University Press 2021

The moral rights of the authors have been asserted

Second Edition 2000
Third Edition 2007
Fourth Edition 2010

Impression: 1

All rights reserved. No part of this publication may be reproduced, stored in
a retrieval system, or transmitted, in any form or by any means, without the
prior permission in writing of Oxford University Press, or as expressly permitted
by law, by licence or under terms agreed with the appropriate reprographics
rights organization. Enquiries concerning reproduction outside the scope of the
above should be sent to the Rights Department, Oxford University Press, at the
address above

You must not circulate this work in any other form
and you must impose this same condition on any acquirer

Public sector information reproduced under Open Government Licence v3.0
(http://www.nationalarchives.gov.uk/doc/open-government-licence/open-government-licence.htm)

Published in the United States of America by Oxford University Press
198 Madison Avenue, New York, NY 10016, United States of America

British Library Cataloguing in Publication Data

Data available

Library of Congress Control Number: 2021932708

ISBN 978-0-19-967514-2

Printed in Great Britain by
Bell & Bain Ltd., Glasgow

Links to third party websites are provided by Oxford in good faith and
for information only. Oxford disclaims any responsibility for the materials
contained in any third party website referenced in this work.

This book is dedicated to the memory of

Michael Young
(1948–1993)

Sylvia Sanders
(1921–1983)

John Wagstaffe
(1918–2002)

Paul Welsh
(1943–2019)

Contents

Preface   xi
Table of Cases   xv
Table of Statutes   xxv

1 The aims and values of 'criminal justice'   1
    1.1 The nature and structure of 'criminal justice'   1
    1.2 Guilt and innocence   8
    1.3 Adversarial and inquisitorial theories of criminal justice   11
    1.4 Recent trends in criminal justice and crime   14
    1.5 Crime control and due process   18
    1.6 The fundamental (human) rights approach   24
    1.7 Victims   33
    1.8 Promoting freedom: the overriding purpose   38
    1.9 Neoliberalism: managerialism, the rise of actuarial justice and austerity   39
    1.10 Conclusion   50

2 Stop and search   53
Alpa Parmar
    2.1 Introduction   53
    2.2 The power to stop-search   63
    2.3 Stop and search and racial discrimination   84
    2.4 Constraints and controls on the exercise of discretion   87
    2.5 The impact of stop-search powers   97
    2.6 Conclusion   107

3 Arrest   110
Alpa Parmar
    3.1 Introduction: what is an arrest?   110
    3.2 Arrest and the purposes of criminal justice   113
    3.3 The legal basis for arrest   119
    3.4 Arrest discretion and reasonable suspicion   131
    3.5 Conclusion   151

4 Detention in the police station   155
    4.1 Introduction   155
    4.2 The powers and duties of the custody officer   156
    4.3 Detention without charge   166

4.4	Deaths in custody	181
4.5	The right to legal advice	188
4.6	Conclusion	207

5 Police questioning of suspects — 210

5.1	Questioning: the drift from due process to crime control	210
5.2	Why do the police value suspect interviews?	211
5.3	The right of silence	214
5.4	Regulating police questioning	225
5.5	'We have ways of making you talk'	240
5.6	The effectiveness of interrogation tactics	262
5.7	Confessions	265
5.8	Conclusion	271

6 Non-interrogatory evidence and covert policing — 275
Ed Cape

6.1	Introduction	275
6.2	Witness and identification evidence	277
6.3	Entry, search and seizure	283
6.4	Covert policing	293
6.5	Scientific evidence	310
6.6	Conclusion	318

7 Prosecutions and constructing guilt — 322

7.1	Introduction	322
7.2	Discretion	323
7.3	Evidential sufficiency: police and CPS	328
7.4	The public interest, the police and the CPS	342
7.5	Non police-prosecution agencies	351
7.6	Organisation of the Crown Prosecution Service	355
7.7	Post charge: producing guilty pleas	356
7.8	The sentence discount principle	358
7.9	Charge bargaining	370
7.10	Do the innocent plead guilty?	380
7.11	Should plea bargaining be abolished?	382
7.12	Conclusion	386

8 Summary justice in the magistrates' court — 389

8.1	Introduction	389
8.2	Legal aid and legal representation	392
8.3	Justices' clerks and legal advisors: liberal bureaucrats?	401
8.4	Bail or jail	403
8.5	The quality and fairness of summary justice	417

8.6	Specialist magistrates	428
8.7	Conclusion	429

9 Trial by judge and jury — 431

9.1	Introduction	431
9.2	Directed and ordered acquittals—weak cases?	433
9.3	The composition of the jury	436
9.4	The verdict of the jury	444
9.5	Trial: procedure, evidence and law	454
9.6	Evaluating the jury's performance	466
9.7	Narrowing the jury's domain	474
9.8	Conclusion	477

10 Inequalities and criminal justice — 479

10.1	Introduction	479
10.2	Creating 'dangerous classes' and 'suitable enemies'	482
10.3	The construction of criminal law	487
10.4	Inequality manifested through policing	492
10.5	Inequality in charging and post charge decision-making	503
10.6	Sentencing and incarceration	505
10.7	Inequality and victimisation	508
10.8	Rights and belonging: How far can 'rights' take us?	512
10.9	Conclusion	515

11 When things go wrong in the criminal justice process — 518

11.1	Introduction	518
11.2	Democratic regulation and accountability	522
11.3	Organisational regulation and accountability	530
11.4	Legal regulatory and accountability mechanisms	551
11.5	Conclusion	596

12 Victims, the accused and the future of criminal justice — 599

12.1	Introduction	599
12.2	Taking suspects' rights seriously	600
12.3	Taking victims' rights seriously	605
12.4	Rhetoric and reality: managing the gap	622

Bibliography — 629
Index — 719

Preface

More than 10 years have elapsed since the fourth edition of this text was published in 2010. There have inevitably been many significant developments in criminal justice since that time. This book has also changed significantly in the addition of Dr Lucy Welsh and Dr Layla Skinns as authors, and the departure of Prof Richard Young from authorship, though he very kindly provided support in other forms. We (Layla and Lucy) are honoured to take up authorship of this latest edition of the book. We found earlier editions to be valuable tools as scholars ourselves, and are very grateful for Andrew's continuing support and input.

Many of the fundamentals of the subject remain the same, although many of the issues that were identified in the last edition have intensified in the wake of numerous political crises: a global lurch to the political right, austerity, Brexit and a pandemic leading to sharp recession. In the days before this preface was finalised, Prime Minister Boris Johnson himself described the criminal justice system as 'hamstrung' by the 'lefty lawyers' seeking to enforce human rights protections. A political statement of this nature is extreme to say the least, and highlights that—arguably—the criminal justice system has never been in a more precarious position.

There continues to be frequent legislative change and policy development in the field of criminal justice. Academic research in relation to some areas of criminal justice has increased (such as in relation to the use of technology) but other areas have remained under-researched (such as magistrates' courts) and we have flagged areas that we feel are in urgent need of further academic research. All criminal justice agencies have remained busy, in spite of the downturn in the crime rate, and so too have accountability bodies, often revealing failings, unequal treatment of citizens and the need for reform.

Yet the fundamentals of criminal justice, to us, remain the same. What do we mean by this? We mean, primarily, that the ideals of fairness in the black letter of the law are not matched by the realities of the way the system actually functions. The rights of the accused, and civil liberties in general, continue to be eroded at greater or lesser speed, dependent on how committed the institutions of criminal justice are to either end of the spectrum between the due process and crime control models, tempered by human rights law and what we identify as the core values of criminal justice: efficiency, justice and democracy. As has recently been brought to the fore by the Black Lives Matter movement in particular, those who are unjustifiably on the margins continue to suffer at the heavy hand of the state in a disproportionate and uneven way. Governments continue to try and justify these issues in the name of protecting victims, bringing more offenders more rapidly to justice, fighting terrorism and using resources efficiently.

Readers should decide for themselves whether the gains of these governmental policies outweigh the losses, and whether the government and agencies of criminal justice really believe their own justifications. We are clear in our views, and continue the theme of previous editions of this book: we don't think that the gains outweigh the losses, and believe that budget cuts and efficiency feature disproportionately in the aims of criminal justice, often at significant cost to the principles of justice and democracy. In the last edition of this book, it was lamented that criminal justice had not changed direction, and we continue that lament. We have included in this edition new chapters on inequality (chapter 10) and accountability (chapter 11) to really focus on the by-products of these issues, though we do additionally draw attention to them throughout this edition.

As ever, no academic subject is an exact science. We do not expect everyone to agree with us, and do not want people to feel obliged to agree simply because we are 'experts'. We'd probably be the type of legal scholars that Boris Johnson would describe as 'lefty'. We only ask that you allow your assumptions to be challenged and your intellect to be engaged. If your sense of injustice and your desire to make the world a better place, especially for those without the power to challenge those in authority is heightened, so much the better. Then—as with earlier editions of this book—make up your own minds. We do not pretend to be objective: we say what we think is wrong with the system, and where we think it should most urgently be improved. We encourage you to do the same. Studying academic subjects should not only involve learning what the rules are. Academics and students alike should evaluate those rules and ask whether they are fair, not just in how they are presented in 'the books', but also in their effects on citizens.

This edition follows a broadly similar pattern to previous editions, subject to the addition of three thematic chapters at the end. To accommodate these, previous chapters on prosecutions and the mass production of guilty pleas have been condensed into a single chapter, appeal processes have been moved into the new chapter on accountability, issues relating to victims have been inserted throughout the text rather than only being given a discrete part of a chapter, while the final chapter (chapter 12) continues to focus on victims and the future of criminal justice. As socio-legal scholars, we have written a socio-legal textbook for students. That means we go beyond the legislation and cases to examine the policy behind the law, examining whether those policies are successful, and situating them within the core values of criminal justice. To do that we necessarily look at academic and policy research on how the system works and who is affected by it—often in unintended and harsh ways. There is enough 'law' here for law students, and enough criminology for social science students. We hope that readers will get even some small sense of what it is like to be at the receiving end of criminal justice—not just as an accused person, but also as a victim, police officer and lawyer too. We hope that our inclusion of a variety of materials, many of which can be found on the Internet—if you know where to look—helps to further illuminate these realities of the system.

As in previous editions, it is impossible to cover all of the messy, interrelated sources of information and institutions that now constitute our criminal justice system. In particular, we continue to say little about sentencing and punishment, and about the youth justice system, and we refer readers to specialist texts on these subjects where appropriate. The book would be far too big if we tried to include these issues. The approach we have adopted, and particularly our examination of how core values feature in, and impact upon, criminal justice can be applied to any criminal justice topic, and we encourage readers to look into issues we do not discuss and evaluate them for yourselves. All major developments up to the Autumn of 2020 are covered. As with any text on criminal justice, the pace of change means that much detail can quickly become out of date.

Many people have helped us in so many different ways that we cannot name them all. But there are two who deserve special recognition: Alpa Parmar and Ed Cape. As the task of updating over 10 years' worth of developments in criminal justice loomed large, their input in the forms of chapters 2, 3 and 6 has been utterly invaluable and allowed us to ensure that all material has been thoroughly updated. Others who must be recognised are our partners, Vivek, Matthew and Jo, for their love and support throughout the writing process. We must also thank Carlotta Fanton at OUP for keeping faith with us and graciously putting up with inevitable delays.

Finally, the preface to the last edition of this book noted that we would be paying for the failings of banks, bankers, regulators and government for years to come. In this edition, we assess the realities and impacts of those failings thus far. Austerity and budget cuts are key features of criminal justice throughout this book. As was foretold in the last edition, we have—in an all too tragically predictable way—identified that those who were already the most disadvantaged in society, have suffered the most as a result of these problems. In the aftermath of the pandemic and Brexit, much remains uncertain about the future of criminal justice. Many wealthy people in positions of power remain largely unaccountable through the criminal justice process. We hope that reading this book will give you some insight into why this is, and why some people are more protected than others.

It's not all doom and gloom, however, and observant readers will find the occasional glimmer of hope (often brought about by those with the willingness to challenge the status quo) and even the occasional joke tucked into the pages that follow. Our sense of hope lingers on.

Andrew Sanders, Warwick
Layla Skinns, Sheffield
Lucy Welsh, Brighton
with Alpa Parmar, Oxford and Ed Cape, Bristol.

Table of Cases

A [2012] EWCA Crim 1646...488
A v United Kingdom (App No 3455/05) [2009] ECHR 301...171, 221, 241
A and B [1998] Crim LR 757...361
A and others v Secretary of State for the Home Department [2004] UKHL 56...122, 170, 181
A and others v Secretary of State for the Home Department (No 2) [2005] UKHL 71...552–553, 557
A (FC) and Others (FC) v Secretary of State for the Home Department [2005] UKHL 71...241
Abbassy v Metropolitan Police Comr [1990] 1 All ER 193...110
Abdroikov [2007] UKHL 37...437
Abdurahman [2019] EWCA Crim 2239; [2020] Crim LR 453...556, 558
Absolam (1988) 88 Cr App Rep 332...229
Adler v Crown Prosecution Service [2013] EWHC 1968 (Admin)...112
Adorian v MPC [2009] EWCA Civ 18...586
Alanov v Chief Constable of Sussex [2012] EWCA Civ 234...131
Albert v Lavin [1981] 3 All ER 878...125
Alexander and McGill [2012] EWCA Crim 2768...283
Al-Fayed v Commissioner of the Police of the Metropolis [2004] EWCA Civ 1579...175
Alford v Chief Constable of Cambridgeshire [2009] EWCA Civ 100...226, 285
Alfrey [2005] EWCA Crim 3232...571
Ali [2009] Crim LR 40...283
Al-Khawaja v UK (2012) 54 EHRR 23...25
Al-Khawaja and Tahery v UK (App No 26766/05 and 22228/06)...35, 464, 571
Alladice (1988) 87 Cr App Rep 380...191, 224, 555–556
Allan [2005] Crim LR 716...307
Allan v United Kingdom (2003) 36 EHRR 12...257
Allen v Metropolitan Police Comr [1980] Crim LR 441...586
Amado-Taylor [2000] Crim LR 618...451
Andrews (Tracey) [1999] Crim LR 156...440
Anguelova v Bulgaria (2004) 38 EHRR 31...534, 592
Argent [1997] 2 Cr App Rep 27...222–223
Armstrong v Chief Constable of West Yorkshire Police [2008] EWCA Civ 1582...285
Arrowsmith v Jenkins [1963] 2 QB 561...325
Aspinall [1999] Crim LR 741...163, 180, 194
Associated Provincial Picture Houses Ltd v Wednesbury Corpn [1948] 1 KB 223...152, 296, 326

Attorney General v Dallas [2012] EWHC 156 (Admin)...455
Attorney General v Davey; Attorney General v Bear [2013] EWHC 2317 (Admin)...455
Attorney General's Reference (No 3 of 1999) [2001] 2 AC 91...556
Attorney General's Reference (No 44 of 2000) (Peverett) [2001] 1 Cr App R 416...368, 380, 384–385
Attorney General's Reference (No 4 of 2002), *see* Sheldrake v DPP; Attorney General's Reference (No 4 of 2002)
Attorney General's Reference (No 80 of 2005) [2005] EWCA Crim 3367...367–8
Attorney General's Reference (Nos 89 and 90 of 2007) [2008] All ER (D) 69...379
Attorney General's Reference (No 3 of 2010) [2010] EWCA Crim 2055...368
Austin v United Kingdom (2012) 55 EHRR 14...127
Austin and Saxby v Commissioner of Police for the Metropolis [2009] UKHL 5; [2007] EWCA Civ 989...111, 127–128, 151
Averill v UK (2000) 31 EHRR 36...222
Azam & Others [2006] EWCA Crim 161...584

B v DPP [2008] EWHC 1655 (Admin)...87, 94
Badham [1987] Crim LR 202...286
Bailey and Smith (1993) 97 Cr App Rep 365...556
Baker v CPS [2008] EWHC 299...285
Bargery [2004] EWCA Crim 816...385
Barnes (1970) 55 Cr App Rep 100...379
Batt and Batt [1995] Crim LR 240...463
Beckford and Daley [1991] Crim LR 833...463
Beckles [2004] EWCA Crim 2766...223
Beckles v UK (2003) 36 EHRR 13...222–223
Beckles and Montague [1998] EWCA Crim 1494...462
Becouarn [2005] UKHL 55...458
Beeres v CPS West Midlands [2014] EWHC 283...269
Benham v United Kingdom (1996) 22 EHRR 293...394
Benjafield [2003] 1 AC 1099...584
Bentley (Deceased) [1998] EWCA Crim 2516; [1999] Crim LR 330...452
Berrada (1989) 91 Cr App Rep 131...452
Beswick [1996] 1 Cr App Rep (S) 343...379
Beuze v Belgium (2018) ECHR 382...243, 552
Bibby v Chief Constable of Essex [2000] EWCA Civ 113...125, 149
Billericay Justices ex p Frank Harris (Coaches) Ltd [1991] Crim LR 559...287

Birchall [1999] Crim LR 311…458
Birnie v HM Advocate [2012] SLT 935…240
Black [1995] Lexis Citation 2535, CO/877/95 (11 May 1995) QBD…64
Blackburn [2005] EWCA Crim 1349…231, 245
Blackwell [2006] EWCA Crim 2185…338
Blyth Juvenile Court, ex p G [1991] Crim LR 693…411
Boardman [2015] EWCA Crim 175…558
Booth & Anor v R [2020] EWCA Crim 575…465
Boyd (1980) 2 Cr App Rep (S) 234…360
Brady [2004] EWCA Crim 2230…270
Brannigan and McBride v UK (1993) 17 EHRR 539…170
Brennan v UK [2001] ECHR 596; (2001) 34 EHRR 507…189–191, 237
Bresa [2005] EWCA 1414…223
Brewin [1976] Crim LR 742…130
Brine [1992] Crim LR 122…268
Brogan (1988) 11 EHRR 117…122
Brogan v UK (1988) 11 EHRR 117…169
Brown [2015] EWCA Crim 1328…571
Brown (Milton Anthony) [1998] 2 Cr App Rep 364…450
Brown v Stott [2003] 1 AC 681; [2001] 2 WLR 817…27, 215
Bryant [2005] EWCA Crim 2079…448–9, 452
Bryce [1992] 4 All ER 567…305
Bubbins v UK [2005] ECHR 159…608
Bucknell v DPP [2006] EWCH 1888 (Admin)…114
Buffrey (1992) 14 Cr App Rep (S) 511…360
Burdett [2009] EWCA Crim 543…437
Button [2005] Crim LR 572…307, 556
Buzadji v Moldova (App No 23755/07) [2014] ECHR 23755/07…415

Caballero v UK (2000) 30 EHRR 643…405
Campbell v DPP [2003] Crim LR 118…190
Canale [1990] 2 All ER 187…235, 243
Cannings [2004] 1 All ER 725; Crim LR [2005] 126…313–314, 318, 566, 574–575
Castorina v Chief Constable of Surrey [1988] NLJR 180…132, 152
Chalkley and Jeffries [1998] 2 Cr App Rep 79; [1998] 2 All ER 155…117, 144, 250, 555, 570
Chall [2019] EWCA Crim 865…622
Challen [2019] EWCA Crim 916…497
Chandler [1976] 1 WLR 585…457
Chandler (No 2) [1964] 1 All ER 761…440
Chaney [2009] Crim LR 437…295
Chapman and Lauday (1976) 63 Cr App Rep 75…468
Chief Constable of Cleveland Police v McGrogan [2002] EWCA Civ 86…125
Chief Constable of Gwent v Dash [1986] RTR 41…77
Chief Constable of Hertfordshire Police v Van Colle [2008] UKHL 50; [2009] 1 AC 225…26
Chief Constable of Sussex, ex p ITF [1999] 1 All ER 129…325, 608
Chief Constable of Thames Valley v Hepburn [2002] EWCA Civ 1841…287
Christou [1992] 95 Cr App R 264; [1992] 4 All ER 559…305
Clark and Ors [2008] EWCA Crim 3221…361
Clark (Sally) [2003] EWCA Crim 1020…313–314
Clarke v Chief Constable of North Wales Police [2000] All LR (D) 477; *Independent*, 22 May, 2000…175
Clinton [2012] 2 All ER 947…487
Cole [2013] EWCA Crim 1149…283
Comerford [1998] 1 Cr App Rep 235…445
Commissioner of Police of the Metropolis (Appellant) v DSD and another (Respondents) [2018] UKSC 11…34, 328, 588, 607
Condron [1997] 1 WLR 827…222
Condron v UK (2001) 31 EHRR 1…204, 214, 216, 222–223, 570
Cooper [1969] 1 QB 267…572
Coudrat (Didier) v Commissioners of HM Revenue and Customs [2005] EWCA Civ 616…132
Cowan [1996] QB 373…215, 224, 458
Crawley [2014] EWCA Crim 1028…326, 557–558
Criminal Cases Review Commission ex p Pearson [1999] 3 All ER 498; [2000] 1 Cr App R 141…578, 581, 583
Crown Court at Birmingham, ex p Sharma [1988] Crim L R 741…559
Crown Court at Cambridge, ex p Hagi (1979) 144 JP 145…394
Crown Court at Croydon, ex p Smith (1983) 77 Cr App Rep 277…560
Crown Court at Huntingdon, ex p Jordan [1981] QB 857…559
Crown Prosecution Service v Deborah Anne Edgar (2000) 164 JP 471…371
Cullen v Chief Constable of the RUC [2003] 1 WLR 1763…588
Cullum (1942) 28 Cr App Rep 150…567
Cumming v CC Northumbria [2003] EWCA Civ 1844…132
Curry [1983] Crim LR 737…462

D [2002] 2 Cr App R 361…464
Da Silva v UK (2016) 63 EHRR 12…597, 608
Daly [2001] EWCA Crim 2643…250
Daniel v Morrison (1979) 70 Cr App Rep 142…80
Darnley [2012] EWCA Crim 1148…460
Darvell, unreported, 1992…271
Davidson v Chief Constable of North Wales [1994] 2 All ER 597…130
Davies [2004] EWCA Crim 2521…462
Davis [2008] UKHL 36…303

Davis [2016] EWHC 38...608
Davis, Johnson and Rowe [2001] 1 Cr App R 115...302, 336, 454, 570
Davison [1988] Crim LR 442...245
Dawes v DPP [1995] 1 Cr App Rep 65...110
Day [2019] EWCA Crim 935...282
Doorson v Netherlands (1996) 22 EHRR 330...450
Dover and East Kent Justices, ex p Dean (1991) 156 JP 357...411
DPP v Ara [2002] Crim LR 295; [2002] 1 WLR 815...197, 326
DPP v Avery [2002] 1 Cr App R 31...94
DPP v Evans [2003] Crim LR 338...161
DPP v Kirkup [2003] EWHC 2354...228
DPP v L [1999] Crim LR 752...111, 131, 175
DPP v Lawrence [2007] EWHC 2154 (Admin)...234
DPP v Meaden [2004] 4 All ER 75...112
DPP v Morgan [1975] UKHL 3...488
DPP v P [2007] EWHC (Admin)...563
DPP v Stonehouse [1978] AC 55...452
DPP, ex p Chaudhary [1995] 1 Cr App R 136...326
DPP, ex p Jones [2000] Crim LR 858...326
DPP, ex p Kebilene [1999] 3 WLR 972...326
DPP, ex p Lee [1999] 1 WLR 1950; [1999] 2 All ER 737...340
Dunn (1990) 91 Cr App Rep 237...235, 256
Durrant v Chief Constable of Avon and Somerset [2014] EWHC 2922 (QB)...145

E [2007] UKHL 47...171
Eastenders Cash & Carry PLC v South Western Magistrates' Court [2011] EWHC 937 (Admin)...285
Edwards [1991] 2 All ER 266, CA...583
Edwards v UK 46477/99 [2002] ECHR 303...534, 592
Edwards and Lewis v UK [2003] Crim LR 891...303
Elliot [2002] EWCA Crim 931...239
Ellis (10 June 1991)...464
Emmerson (1990) 92 Cr App Rep 284...244
Erskine v Hollin [1971] RTR 199...64

Fair Crime Contract Alliance v Legal Aid Agency (Legal Aid Procurement Challenge)...397
Fiak [2005] EWCA Crim 2381...111
Fisher v Oldham Corpn [1930] 2 KB 364...522
Fitt v UK (2000) 30 EHRR 480...303
Flannagan v Shaw [1920] 3 KB 96...563
Fogah [1989] Crim LR 141...243
Ford [1989] 3 All ER 445...440
Fox, Campbell and Hartley v UK (1990) 13 EHRR 157...122
Francis [1992] Lexis Citation 3897, CO/1434/91 (June 1992)...64
French v DPP [1996] EWHC Admin 283...64
Fulling [1987] QB 426...244–245
Funke v France (1993) 16 EHRR 297...210, 383

G [2008] UKHL 37...30
Galbraith [1981] 1 WLR 1039...433
Gerard (1948) 32 Cr App Rep 132...457
Ghaidan v Godin-Mendoza [2004] UKHL 30...25
Gibbons and Winterburn (22 June 1993)...452
Gilbert (1977) 66 Cr App R 237...217
Gill [2003] EWCA Crim 2256...556
Gillan [2004] EWCA Civ 1067; [2006] UKHL 12, HL...75, 94–95
Gillan and Quinton v the United Kingdom (4158/05) (2010) 160 NLJ 104; *The Times*, January 15, 2010...75–76, 95, 105
Gillard and Barrett (1991) 92 Cr App R 61...235
Goddard [1994] Crim LR 46...229
Gomez [1993] 1 All ER 1...465
Goodyear [2005] EWCA Crim 888...366–368, 380–381
Grafton [1993] QB 101...378
Grant [2005] EWCA Crim 1089; [2005] 2 Cr App R 28...555, 557
Grant [2006] QB 20...190
Gregory v UK (1997) 25 EHRR 577...443–444
Grey [2005] EWCA Crim 1413...573
Griffith v Jenkins [1992] 1 All ER 65...563
Guthrie v The United Kingdom (App No 22226/12) [2013] ECHR 578...446

H & C [2004] Cr App R 179...338
Halford v UK (1997) 24 EHRR 523...294
Hall (1968) 52 Cr App Rep 528...376
Hambleton [2009] EWCA Crim 13...455
Hanif and Khan v UK (App Nos 52999/08 and 61779/08) ECHR 20 December 2011...438, 443
Hanningfield v Chief Constable of Essex [2013] 1 WLR 3632...119, 175–176
Hanson [2005] EWCA Crim 824...460
Harper [1968] 2 QB 108...382
Hart [1998] Crim LR 417...467
Hart, unreported, 23 April 1998 (CA)...224
Hassan v The United Kingdom (App No 29750/09) [2014] ECHR 1145...27
Havering Juvenile Court, ex p Buckley (LEXIS 554 1983)...394, 396
Hawkes v DPP [2005] EWCA 3046...125
Hayes [2004] All ER (D) 315...381
Hayes v Chief Constable of Merseyside [2012] 1 WLR 517...121
Herbert (1991) 94 Cr App Rep 230...377–378, 560
Heron, unreported, 1993...244–245, 269
Hicks [2017] UKSC 9...136
Higgins [2003] EWCA Crim 2943...219, 243–244, 252–253, 279
Hillard [2004] EWCA Crim 837...216, 225
Hircock [1969] 1 All ER 47...448
Hirst (No 2) v UK (App No 74025/01) [2005] ECHR 681...319
HL v UK 45008/99 (5 October 2004)...32
HM Customs & Excise v Michael Atkinson and others [2003] EWHC 421...289

Hoare and Pierce [2004] EWCA Crim 784...217, 223
Holden v Chief Constable of Lancashire [1987] QB 380...589
Holgate-Mohammed v Duke [1984] AC 437; [1984] 1 All ER 1054...176, 211
Hollington and Emmens (1985) 7 Cr App Rep (S) 364...360
Holloway, R (On the application of) v Bhui and Ors [2019] EWHC 1731 (Admin)...333
Hopkins-Husson (1949) 34 Cr App Rep 47...572
Horncastle and Others v UK, ECHR 16 December 2014...464
Horne [1990] Crim LR 188...457
Horseferry Road Magistrates Court, ex p Bennett [1994] 1 AC 42...557
Hough v CC Staffordshire Constabulary [2001] EWCA Civ 39...132
Howarth v MPC [2011] EWHC 2818 (Admin)...65
Howden-Simpson [1991] Crim LR 49...242
Howell [1981] 3 All ER 383...125
Howell [2002] EWCA Crim 1; [2003] Crim LR 405...223, 239
Hsu v Metropolitan Police Commissioner [1997] 2 All ER 762...590–591
Hughes [1994] 1 WLR 876...555
Hunt [1992] Crim LR 582...229
Hussain [2005] EWCA Crim 31...584
Hussein v Secretary of State for Defence [2013] EWHC 95 (Admin)...245
Hutchings, Re application for Judicial Review (Northern Ireland) [2019] UKSC 26...475

Ibrahim [2012] EWCA Crim 837...571
Ibrahim v UK [2016] ECHR 750...236, 552, 558
Ibrahim and others v UK (2015) 61 EHRR 9; [2016] ECHR 750...29, 236, 571
Imran and Hussain [1997] Crim LR 754...203, 222, 250
IRC, ex p National Federation of Self-Employed and Small Businesses Ltd [1982] AC 617...564
Ireland v UK (1978) 2 EHRR 25...27, 181
Isa Islam, in the Matter of an Application for Bail by [2010] ACTSC 147...417
Ivey v Genting Casinos [2017] UKSC 67...465

Jalloh v Germany (2007) 44 EHRR 32...241
James [1990] Crim LR 815...379
James [1996] Crim LR 650...230
James [2018] EWCA Crim 285...578
Jarrett v CC of the West Midland Police [2003] EWCA Civ 397...133
Jasinskis v Latvia (2010) ECHR 1...534, 592
Jasper v UK (2000) 30 EHRR 1...303
Jeffrey v Black [1978] QB 490; [1978] 1 All ER 555...289
John Lewis & Co Ltd v Tims [1952] AC 676...130
Johnson [2016] EWCA Crim 191...223
Johnstone [2003] UKHL 28...9
Jones v National Coal Board [1957] 2 QB 55...447–448

K & Ors [2006] EWCA Crim 724...432
Kamara [2000] WL 664383...280, 335, 441
Kansal (No 2) [2001] 2 Cr App R 30; [2001] 3 WLR 107...584
KaraKaya [2005] EWCA 346...455
Karim [2005] EWCA Crim 533...367, 381
Kaul [1998] Crim LR 135...464
Keegan v Chief Constable of Merseyside Police [2003] EWCA Civ 936; [2003] 1 WLR 2187...288, 586–7
Keegan v UK (2007) 44 EHRR 33...288
Keenan [1990] 2 QB 54; [1989] 3 All ER 598; [1989] Crim LR 720...234, 293
Kelleher [2003] EWCA Crim 3525, CA...452
Kelly & Donnelly [2001] 2 Cr App R (S) 73...509
Kennedy [2005] EWCA Crim 685...585
Kennedy v DPP [2003] Crim LR 120...190
Kent Pharmaceuticals Ltd v Director of the SFO [2002] EWHC 3023...287
Kerawalla [1991] Crim LR 451...228
Khan [1996] 3 WLR 162...319
Khan [2008] 2 Cr App R 13...437
Khan v UK (App No 35394/97) [2001] 31 EHRR 45; [2000] Crim LR 684...294, 532, 556
Khan, unreported, 1990, CA...234–235, 254, 257
Killick [2011] EWCA Crim 1608...326, 616
King [2012] EWCA Crim 805...556
Kirk [1999] 4 All ER 698...245, 250
Kluk [2005] EWCA Crim 1331...361
Knight [2004] 1 Cr App R 9...223
Knighton [2002] EWCA Crim 2227...584
Kuimba [2005] All ER (D) 110...568
Kunle Omole [2011] EWCA Crim 1428...367
Kuruma v R [1955] 2 WLR 223...257

La Rose [2002] Crim LR 215; [2001] EWHC Admin 553...190
Lambert [2001] 2 Cr App R 511; [2001] 3 WLR 206...9, 584
Last [2005] EWCA Crim 106...359
Latif and Shazad [1996] 1 All ER 353...558
Lawless [2003] EWCA Crim 271...463
Lee [2015] EWCA Crim 971...222
Lester 63 Cr App R (S) 29...510
Lewis v Chief Constable of the South Wales Constabulary [1991] 1 All ER 206...110
Lisa Loizu [2006] EWCA Crim 1719...222
Liverpool City Magistrates, ex p McGhee [1993] Crim LR 609...394
Llewellyn [1978] 67 Cr App R 149...379
Lloyd, Ex p (1822) Mont 70...12
Looseley [2001] UKHL 53...305, 556, 558
Lubemba [2014] EWCA Crim 2064...450, 612

M, McE, Re [2009] UKHL 15...307
Macclesfield Justices, ex p Greenhalgh (1979) 144 JP 142...394
Maclean and Kosten [1993] Crim LR 687...556
Maguire (1989) 90 Cr App Rep 115...229
Maguire [1992] 2 All ER 433...313–4

TABLE OF CASES

Mahmood and Shahin [2005] EWCA Crim 1268…367
Makuwa [2006] EWCA Crim 175…9
Mansfield Justices, ex p Sharkey [1985] 1 All ER 193…408
Marper v UK [2008] ECHR 1581…602
Marsh v DPP [2007] Crim LR 162…281
Marshall v United Kingdom (App No 41571/98, 10 July 2001)…27
Martin v Watson [1996] AC 74…587
Martin, Taylor and Brown [2000] EWCA Crim 104…335
Mason [1987] 3 All ER 481; [1988] 1 WLR 139…243, 249–250, 555
Mason [2002] EWCA Crim 385; [2002] 2 Cr App R 38…556
Mattan, *The Times*, 5 March 1998…583
Maxwell [2011] 1 WLR 1837…326, 557
McCann v UK [1995] 21 ECHR 97…184
McCarthy [1996] Crim LR 818, CA…94
McDonagh [2013] EWHC 4690…238
McDonald [2007] EWCA Crim 1081…359
McFarland, Re [2004] UKHL 17…365
McFarlane [2002] EWHC 485 (Admin)…509
McFeeley v UK (App No 8317/78) (1980) 20 DR 44…181
McGarry [1998] 3 All ER 805…217
McGuiness [1999] Crim LR 318…239
McIlkenny (1991) 93 Cr App Rep 287…452, 456
McIlkenny v Chief Constable of the West Midlands [1980] 2 WLR 689…576
McInnes v HM Advocate [2010] UKSC 7…571
McKinnon v US [2008] UKHL 59…368
McManaman [2016] EWCA Crim 3…445–446
McPhee [2016] UKPC 29…255, 554
McVeigh, O'Neill and Evans v UK (1981) 25 DR 15…95, 123, 143
Mears [1993] 1 WLR 818…453
Menard [1995] 1 Cr App Rep 306…254
Metropolitan Police Commissioner, ex p Blackburn [1968] 2 QB 118…325, 523
Metropolitan Police Commissioner, ex p P (1995) 160 JP 367; (1996) 8 Admin LR 6…326, 345
Metropolitan Police Commissioner, ex p Thompson [1997] 1 WLR 1519…345
Michael and Others v Chief Constable of South Wales Police and Another [2012] EWCA Civ 981; *affirmed* [2015] UKSC 2…26, 513, 607
Michalko v Slovakia (App No 35377/05) [2010] ECHR 35377/05…405
Miller [1986] 1 WLR 1191…268, 554
Miller [1998] Crim LR 209…229, 257
Miller v Associated Newspapers Ltd [2005] EWHC 557…147
Miller v DPP [2018] EWHC 262 (Admin)…556–557
Millward [1999] Crim LR 164…467
Milton Brown [1998] 2 Cr App Rep 364…613
Mirza [2004] 1 AC 1118…444
Misick v The Queen [2015] 1 WLR 3215 PC…243, 555

Mohamed (Abdulkadir) [2020] EWCA Crim 525…454, 462
Mohidin v Commissioner of the Police of the Metropolis [2015] EWHC 2740 (QB)…139
Monnell and Morris v United Kingdom (1987) 10 EHRR 205…569
Moon [2004] EWCA Crim 2872…558
Moore (1923) 17 Cr App Rep 155…567
Moore and Burrows [2013] EWCA Crim 85…558
Morris [1984] AC 320…465
Moshaid [1998] Crim LR 420…222
Moss v McLachlan [1985] IRLR 76…125–126
Moulton v Chief Constable of the West Midlands [2010] EWCA Civ 524…586
MPC v MR [2019] EWHC 888 (QB)…132
Mullen [1999] Crim LR 561; [1999] 2 Cr App R 143…557, 570
Munden v Southampton Crown Court [2005] EWHC 2512 (Admin)…561
Murray (1996) 22 EHRR 29…189, 215–216
Murray v Minister of Defence [1988] 2 All ER 521…111, 293
Murray v UK (1996) 22 EHRR 29…191, 224, 458
Mushtaq [2005] 1 WLR 1513…554

Natsvlishvili and Togonidze v Georgia (App No 9043/05, 29 April 2014)…384
Nazham and Nazham [2004] EWCA Crim 491…365, 379
Newcastle-upon-Tyne Justices, ex p Skinner [1987] 1 All ER 349…562
Newman [2010] EWCA Crim 1566…366
Newton (1983) 77 Cr App R 13, CA…379
Northam (1967) 52 Cr App Rep 97…242

O v Crown Court at Harrow [2006] UKHL 42…417
O'Donnell v UK [2015] ECHR 16667/10…216
O'Halloran and Francis v UK [2007] ECHR 544…215
O'Hara v CC of the RUC [1997] 1 All ER 129…132
O'Hara v UK (2002) 34 EHRR 32…132
Oakwell [1978] 66 Cr App R 174…462
Odeyemi [1999] Crim LR 828…239
OP v Secretary of State for Justice [2015] 1 Cr App R 7…615
Opuz v Turkey Application No 33401/02, 9 June 2009)…513
Orange v Chief Constable of the West Yorkshire Police [2002] QB 347…607
Oransaye [1993] Crim LR 772…229, 556
Osborne [2005] EWCA Crim 3082…457
Osborne-Odelli [1998] Crim LR 902…452
Osman v UK (1998) 29 EHRR 245…184
Osman (Mustapha) v Southwark Crown Court (1999) 163 JP 725…94

Palmer [2016] EWCA Crim 2237…461
Paris, Abdullahi and Miller (1993) 97 Cr App R 99…202, 244, 248, 253, 311

Parker [1995] Crim LR 233…245, 553
Parker v CC Essex [2018] EWCA Civ 2788; [2019] 1 WLR 2238…131–132, 585
Parkes (1976) 64 Cr App Rep 25…457
Patel and Ors [2009] EWCA Crim 67…366
Paul v Chief Constable of Humberside [2004] EWCA Civ 308…117, 587
Pedro v Diss [1981] 2 All ER 59…94
Pektar [2004] 1 Cr App R 22…216
Pendleton [2001] UKHL 66; [2002] 1 WLR 72…466, 575, 584
Perkins [2013] 2 Cr App R (S) 72…622
Perren [2009] EWCA Crim 348…448
Peterborough Justices, ex p Dowler [1996] 2 Cr App Rep 561…564
Peters & Ors [2005] EWCA Crim 605…359, 361
PG v UK [2002] Crim LR 308…556
PG and JH v United Kingdom [2002] Crim LR 308…32
Pham Hoang v France (1992) 16 EHRR 53…394
Phillips [2020] Crim LR 940…558
Pintori [2007] EWCA Crim 1700, CA…437
Pitman [1991] 1 All ER 468…379
Pitts [2001] EWCA Crim 846…379
Plange v Chief Constable of South Humberside *The Times*, 23 March 1992…117
PMH [2018] EWCA Crim 2452…451
Plunkett [2013] EWCA Crim 261…307
Police Complaints Board, ex p Madden [1983] 1 WLR 447…536
Poole and Mills [2003] EWCA Crim 1753…575, 578
Popat [1998] Crim LR 825…283
Pope [2012] EWCA Crim 2241…572
Pora [2015] UKPC 9…554
Practice Direction (CA (Crim Div): Criminal Proceedings: General Matters) [2015] EWCA Crim 1567…615
Practice Direction (CA (Crim Div): Criminal Proceedings: General Matters) (Amendment No.1) [2016] EWCA Crim 97…615
Practice Note [1970] 1 WLR 663…568
Practice Note; Jury: Juror: Ground on which juror may be excused [1973] 1 All ER 240…440
PS v Germany (2000) 30 EHRR CD301; [2002] Crim LR 312…464
Public Prosecution Service v McKee [2013] UKSC 32…556
Pullar v UK (1996) 22 EHRR 391…443
Pullen [1991] Crim LR 457…229

Quaranta v Switzerland (1991) ECtHR Series A 205…394

R v A (No 2) [2001] UKHL 25; [2002] 1 AC 45; [2001] 2 Cr App R 351…25, 30, 488–489
R v Achogbuo [2014] EWCA Crim 657…566
R v AJC [2006] EWCA Crim 284…461
R v Allan [2017] Croydon Crown Court…340
R v B [2013] EWCA Crim 3…488
R v Bhambra [2008] EWCA Crim 237…229
R v Biddle [2019] EWCA Crim 86…615
R v B(J) [2009] EWCA Crim 1036…303
R v C; R v H [2004] 2 AC 134…303
R v Caley-Knowles; R v Jones (Iorwerth) [2007] 1 Cr App R 13…571
R v Cheb Miller [2007] EWCA Crim 1891…227, 243
R v Ched Evans (Chedwyn Evans) [2016] EWCA Crim 452…34, 488–489
R v Choudhery and others [2005] EWCA Crim 2598…342
R v Christopher Bristol [2007] EWCA Crim 3214…87, 94
R v Commissioner of Police of the Metropolis [2007] Crim LR 298…326
R v Cottrell and Fletcher [2008] 1 Cr App R 7, CA…584
R v Crilly [2018] EWCA Crim 168…491
R v Croydon Justices, ex p Dean [1993] QB 769…351
R v D [2008] EWCA Crim 2557…473
R v Dobson [2011] EWCA Crim 1255…4
R v Erskine; R v Williams [2009] EWCA Crim 1425…575
R v Essa [2009] EWCA Crim 43…219, 223
R v Foy [2020] EWCA Crim 270…575
R v G; R v B [2009] EWCA Crim 1207…302–303
R v Gjoni [2014] EWCA Crim 691…30, 488
R v Gore (deceased) [2007] EWCA Crim 2789…584
R v Grant-Murray and others [2017] EWCA Crim 1228…566
R v Gray and Others [2014] EWCA Crim 2372…568
R v H [2014] EWCA Crim 1555…337
R v Halliwell, unreported, Bristol Crown Court T2011/7126 (2012)…234
R v Hanif & Anor (No 2) [2014] EWCA Crim 1678…438
R v Hart and Others [2006] EWCA Crim 3239…568
R v Hendon Justices ex parte DPP [1994] QB 167…563
R v Hereford Magistrates' Court, ex p Rowlands [1998] QB 110…564
R v Hounsham & Ors [2005] EWCA Crim 1366…140
R v Hyde [2016] EWCA Crim 1031…565
R v Ibrahim, Omar, Osman and Mohamed [2008] EWCA Crim 880…249, 254, 257
R v James [1996] Crim LR 650…214
R v Jogee; Ruddock v The Queen [2016] UKSC 8…491, 567
R v Johnson and Others [2016] EWCA Crim 1613…491, 567
R v Johnson; R v Hind [2005] EWCA Crim 971…218
R v Lamaletie and Royce [2008] EWCA Crim 314…212
R v Lee [2014] EWCA Cro, 2928…566
R v Lewis [2014] EWCA Crim 48…461

R v Maya Devani [2007] EWCA Crim 1926…243
R v McCook [2014] EWCA Crim 734…566
R v Moore [2004] EWCA Crim 1624…227–278
R v Murphy [2014] EWCA Crim 1457…461
R v Neill [1994] Crim LR 441…230–231
R v O, J and S [2008] EWCA Crim 463; [2008] Crim LR 892…568
R v Ordu [2017] EWCA Crim 4…567
R v Pecco [2010] EWCA Crim 972…280
R v R and others [2016] 1 WLR 1872…558
R v Rowe [2008] EWCA Crim 2712…584
R v S(D) and S(T) [2015] EWCA Crim 662…558
R v SG [2017] EWCA Crim 617…450
R v Sullivan [2015] EWCA Crim 1565…461
R v Syed [2018] EWCA Crim 2809…558
R v Van Gelderen [2008] EWCA Crim 422…230–231
R v W [2005] Crim LR 965…30
R v W [2010] EWCA Crim 2799…243
R v Walsh (1989) 91 Cr App R 161…293
R v Wilson [2016] EWCA Crim 65…56
R v Y [2008] EWCA Crim 10…568
R (AB and CD) v Huddersfield Magistrates' Court [2014] EWHC 1089 (Admin)…293
R (Adams) v Justice Secretary [2012] 1 AC 48; [2011] UKSC 18…587
R (Allen) v Justice Secretary [2008] EWCA Civ 808…587
R (British Sky Broadcasting Ltd) v Central Criminal Court [2011] EWHC 3451 (Admin)…290
R (Cheema) v Nottingham and Newark Magistrates' Court [2013] EWHC 3790 (Admin)…287
R (Cook) v SOCA [2010] EWHC 2119 (Admin)…290
R (Dennis) v IPCC [2008] EWHC 1158 (Admin)…531, 543
R (El-Kurd) v Winchester Crown Court [2011] EWHC 1853 (Admin)…290
R (FNM) v DPP [2020] EWHC 870 (Admin); [2020] Crim LR 874…326, 617
R (Green) v PCA [2004] UKHL 6…546
R (Hewitson) v Chief Constable of Dorset Police [2003] EWHC 3296 (Admin)…286
R (Golfrate) v Crown Court at Southwark [2014] EWHC 840 (Admin)…289
R (Hicks) v Commissioner of Police of the Metropolis [2014] EWCA Civ 3…114
R (Howard League and the Prisoners' Advice Service) v The Lord Chancellor [2017] EWCA Civ 244…397
R (Lees) v Solihull Magistrates' Court [2013] EWHC 3779 (Admin)…287
R (McKenzie) v Director of the SFO [2016] EWHC 102 (Admin)…290
R (Mills) v Sussex Police [2014] EWHC 2523 (Admin)…289
R (Mullen) v Home Secretary [2004] UKHL 18…587
R (Niazi and Ors) v Home Secretary [2008] EWCA Civ 755…587
R (TL) v Chief Constable of Surrey Police [2017] EWHC 129 (Admin)…286
R (U) v Metropolitan Police Commissioner [2003] 1 WLR 897; [2003] 3 All ER 419…345
R (Virdee) v NCA [2018] EWHC 1119 (Admin)…286
R (on the application of Ajaib) v Birmingham Magistrates Court [2009] EWHC 2127 (Admin)…303
R (on the application of F) v The Director of Public Prosecutions and 'A' [2013] EWHC 945 (Admin)…4, 326
R (on the application of Guest) v DPP [2009] Crim LR 730…326
R (on the application of Gujra) v CPS [2013] AC 484…327
R (on the application of Hicks) v Commissioner of Police for the Metropolis [2017] UKSC 9…128
R (on the application of Kay) v Commissioner of Police of the Metropolis [2008] UKHL 69…128
R (on the application of Jane Laporte) v (1) Chief Constable of Gloucestershire Constabulary & Others [2006] UKHL 55…111, 126–128, 151
R (on the application of Joseph) v DPP [2001] Crim LR 489…326
R (on the application of Luke Matara) v Brent Magistrates' Court [2005] EWHC 1829…395
R (on the application of McCann) v Manchester Crown Court [2002] 4 All ER 593…5
R (on the application of Mondelly) v Commissioner of Police of the Metropolis [2006] EWHC 2370 (Admin)…143, 326
R (on the application of Nunn) v Chief Constable of Suffolk Police [2014] UKSC 37…574
R (on the application of Purdy) v Director of Public Prosecutions [2009] UKHL 45…343
R (on the application of Roberts) v Commissioner of the Police of the Metropolis [2015] UKSC 79…74, 97, 495
R (on the application of S) v CC South Yorkshire, R (on the application of Marper) v CC South Yorkshire [2004] UKHL 39…317
R (on the application of Smith) v DPP [2002] EWHC 113 (Admin)…78
R (on the application of TL) v Chief Constable of Surrey [2017] EWHC 129 (Admin)…121
R (on the application of the Law Society) v The Lord Chancellor [2018] EWHC 2094 (Admin)…397
R (on the application of the Law Society) v Lord Chancellor [2015] EWCA Civ 230…397
R (on the application of Ullah) v Special Adjudicator [2004] UKHL 26; [2004] 2 AC 323…30
R (on the application of Vickers) v West London Magistrates' Court [2004] Crim LR 63…416
R (on the application of Virgin Media Ltd) v Zinga (Munaf Ahmed) [2014] 1 WLR 2228…327
R (on the application of Warner) v Secretary of State for Justice [2020] EWHC 1894 (Admin)…577

R (on the application of WV) V CPS [2012] Crim LR 456...303
Radak, Adjei, Butler-Rees and Meghjee [1999] Crim LR 223...463
Rafferty [1998] Crim LR 433...382
Raghip, Silcott and Braithwaite *The Times*, 9 December, 1991...268, 554
Ramanauskas v Lithuania [2008] Crim LR 639...305
Ramsahai v The Netherlands (2007) (App No 52391/99, 15 May 2007)...543
Ramsden [1972] Crim LR 547...567
Rashid [2017] 1 WLR 2449...615
Rashid v CC West Yorkshire [2020] EWHC 2522 (QB)...121, 132, 285
Rawlins v Crown Prosecution Service [2018] EWHC 2533 (Admin)...125
Rees v Commissioner of Police of the Metropolis [2019] EWHC 2339 (QB)...589–590
Rees and Others v Commissioner of Police of the Metropolis [2018] EWCA Civ 1587...586, 589
Reeves v Commissioner of Police of the Metropolis [2000] 1 AC 360...607
Rehman [2006] EWCA Crim 1900; [2007] Crim LR 101...243, 556
Reid [1994] Crim LR 442...280
Reynolds [2020] 4 WLR 16...453
Riat [2012] EWCA Crim 1509...35, 464
Richardson [1999] Crim LR 563...567
Richardson v CC of the West Midlands [2011] EWHC 773 (QB); [2011] Cr App R 1...121, 175, 585
Ricketts v Cox (1981) 74 Cr App Rep 298...82
Ridehalgh v Director of Public Prosecutions [2005] EWHC 1100...231
Roberts v Chief Constable Kent [2008] EWCA Civ 1588...586
Robinson v Chief Constable of West Yorkshire [2018] UKSC 4...588, 607
Roble [1997] Crim LR 449...222–223
Rookes v Barnard [1964] AC 1129; [1964] 2 WLR 269...589
Roques v Metropolitan Police Commissioner (1997) Legal Action, September, p 23...201
Rosenberg [2006] EWCA Crim 6...222, 308
Rowe [2007] QB 975...10
Rowe and Davies v UK (2000) 30 EHRR 441...303, 338
Rowlands v Chief Constable of Merseyside Police [2006] EWCA Civ 1773...585

S v Switzerland (1991) 14 EHRR 670...189
S v UK; Marper v UK [2009] 48 EHHR 50...317, 319
Salabiaku v France (1988) EHRR 379...9
Salduz v Turkey [2008] ECHR 1542...189–190, 192
Samuel [1988] QB 615; [1988] 2 All ER 135... 190–191, 552, 555
Samuel [2014] EWCA Crim 2349...460
Sander v UK (2001) 31 EHRR 44...444

Sandor James [2015] EWCA Crim 209...450
Sang [1980] AC 402...552
Sanghera [2001] 1 Cr App R 299...292, 319
Saunders v United Kingdom (1997) 23 EHRR 313...210, 214
SC v UK [2005] Crim LR 130...615
Seckerson and Times Newspapers Ltd v UK [2012] ECHR 241...444
Secretary of State for the Home Department v AN [2009] EWCC 1966 (Admin)...171–172
Secretary of State for the Home Department v JJ [2007] UKHL 45...171
Secretary of State for the Home Department v MB and AF [2007] UKHL 46...171
Secretary of State for the Home Department v N and others [2009] UKHL 28...171
Self [1992] 3 All ER 476...129
Selvey v DPP [1968] 2 All ER 497...458
Senior and Senior [2004] 2 Cr App R 12; [2004] Crim LR 749...231, 556
Shaaban Bin Hussien v Chong Fook Kam [1970] AC 942...64, 110, 116, 131
Shamoon Ahmed v Mohammed Shafique, Kapil Arora [2009] EWHC 618...130
Shand v R [1996] 1 All ER 511...462
Shannon [2000] Crim LR 1001...305
Sheldrake v DPP; Attorney General's Reference (No 4 of 2002) [2004] UKHL 43...9
Shepherd [2019] EWCA Crim 1062...229
Shervington [2008] EWCA Crim 648...462
Shillibier [2006] EWCA Crim 793...556
Sigurdsson v Iceland (2003) 40 EHRR 15...443
Skrzypiec [2010] EWHC 1418 (Admin)...230–231, 257
Slade [1996] Lexis Citation 5011, CO/1678/96 (October 1996)...64
Smith (Wallace Duncan) [2004] EWCA Crim 631...577
Smurthwaite [1994] 1 All ER 898...304
SN v Sweden [2002] Crim LR 831...464
Snaresbrook Crown Court [2011] EWHC 3569 (Admin)...415
Sneyd v DPP [2006] EWHC 560...214, 226, 231
Somers [2003] EWCA Crim 1356...96–97, 335
Sparks [1991] Crim LR 128...230
Spencer (John) [1995] Crim LR 235; *The Times*, 13 July 1994...453
Spicer v Holt [1977] AC 987...110
Steel v UK (1988) EHRR 603...125, 140
Steele & Ors [2006] EWCA Crim 195...571, 584
Stephen Roberts [1997] Crim LR 222...257
Sunworld Ltd v Hammersmith and Fulham LBC [2000] 2 All ER 837...563
Sweeney v Westminster Magistrates' Court [2014] EWHC 2168 (Admin)...289
Sylvester [2002] EWCA Crim 1327...554

T v DPP [2007] EWHC 1793 (Admin)...217, 222
Tarrant [1998] Crim LR 342...440
Taylor v CC of the Thames Valley [2004] 1 WLR 3155...110

Teixeira de Castro v Portugal (1999) 28 EHRR 101…305
Thomas, Flannagan, Thomas and Smith [1998] Crim LR 887…464
Thompson (1961) 46 Cr App Rep 72…468
Thompson v Metropolitan Police Commissioner; Hsu v Metropolitan Police Commissioner [1997] 2 All ER 762…589–591
Togher [2001] 3 All ER 463…571
Tomlinson LAG Bulletin, May 1992, p 21…64
Torpey [2019] Crim LR 985…617
Turnbull [1977] 2 QB 224…283, 462
Turner [1970] QB 321; [1970] 2 WLR 1093…362, 365–366, 376, 380, 385
Turner [1975] Cr App R 67…304
Turner [2004] 1 All ER 1025…217
Twomey [2009] EWCA Crim 1035…446
Twomey and Cameron v the United Kingdom (App No 67318/09, 28 May 2013)…446

Underwood [2005] 1 Cr App R (S) 90…379

W [1994] Crim LR 130…554
W v Switzerland (1993) 17 EHRR 60…411
Wahab [2003] 1 Cr App R 15…554
Walker v MPC [2015] 1 Cr App R 22…110–111

Walls [2011] EWCA Crim 443…615
Wang [2005] UKHL 9…447, 452
Ward (Judith) [1993] 1 WLR 619; (1993) 96 Cr App Rep 1, CA…313–314, 338, 583
Warren v Att General for Jersey [2012] 1 AC 22…326, 555–556, 558
Webb; Simpson [2000] EWCA Crim 56…448
Webber [2004] UKHL 1…216–217, 224
Weekes (1993) 97 Cr App Rep 222; [1993] Crim LR 211…230
Weeks [1995] Crim LR 52…243
Weerdesteyn [1995] 1 Cr App Rep 405…235
Whitley v DPP [2004] Crim LR 585…190
Williams *The Times*, 6 February 1992…255
Williams [2003] EWCA Crim 3200…283
Williams [2012] EWCA Crim 2162…9
Wisdom and Sinclair (Court of Appeal, 10 December 1999, Lawtel 6/1/2000)…217
Wood [1996] 1 Cr App R 207, CA…452
Wood and Fitzsimmons [1998] Crim LR 213…463
Woolmington v DPP [1935] AC 462…9

Young [1995] 2 Cr App Rep 379…468
Younis [1990] Crim LR 425…230, 254

Zafar [2008] 2 WLR 1013…10

Table of Statutes

Access to Justice Act 1999…204, 395, 560
    s 3…192
    s 12(2)…560
    s 12(2)(b)…562
    s 17(2)…560, 562
    s 26…565
    Pt III (ss 35–53)…390
    s 36…376
    Sch 3…394
    Sch 11…418
Anti-social Behaviour, Crime and Policing Act 2014…5, 6, 114
    ss 104–105…619
    Sch 4…619
Anti-terrorism, Crime and Security Act 2001…74, 122, 159, 170, 181, 509
    Pt 4 (ss 21–32)…122, 170
    s 21(2)…122
    s 94…74
    s 117…2
Assaults on Emergency Workers (Offences) Act 2018…16

Bail Act 1976…405–406, 409–411, 415
    s 3…331
    s 3(6)…407–408
    s 3AB…409
    s 4…409
    s 4(1)…405
    s 5…331, 415
    s 6…407
    s 7…409
    Sch 1…405–406, 410
    Pt 1
        paras 2–6…406
        para 9…406
Bail (Amendment) Act 1993…415

Children and Young Persons Act 1933
    s 7…83
Confiscation of Alcohol (Young Persons) Act 1997…83
Contempt of Court Act 1981…467
    s 8…467–468, 477
Coronavirus Act 2020…17, 46, 114, 324
    Sch 21, para 15(1)…114
Coroners and Justice Act 2009…47, 407, 487
    s 1(2)…594
    s 104…615
    s 114…407, 417

    s 115(1)…407
    s 125…359
Counter-Terrorism Act 2008…171
    Pt 2…239
Counter-Terrorism and Security Act 2015…122, 172
Courts and Legal Services Act 1990…390
Crime and Courts Act 2013…7
Crime and Courts Act 2015…418
Crime and Disorder Act 1998…16, 40, 47, 59, 114, 403, 509–510
    s 5…59
    s 6…59
    s 16…114
    s 25…74
    ss 28–32…509
    s 46…424
    s 48…418
    s 51…390
    s 56…416
Crime and Security Act 2010…82, 495
Criminal Appeal Act 1907…572
Criminal Appeal Act 1964
    s 1…573
Criminal Appeal Act 1966…572
    s 5…573
Criminal Appeal Act 1968…568
    s 1(2)(b)…564
    s 2…570
    s 17…576
    s 18(3)…564
    s 23…573
    s 29…568
    s 31…564
Criminal Appeal Act 1995…562, 567, 570, 576–577
    s 9(1)…578
    s 13…577
    s 13(1)(b)…578
    s 13(1)(c)…578
    s 13(2)…578
    s 14…578
    s 16C…584
Criminal Attempts Act 1981
    s 1(1)…465
Criminal Damage Act 1971
    s 1…267
Criminal Justice Act 1967…444
    s 7…111
    s 11…218, 457
    s 13(3)…423

TABLE OF STATUTES

Criminal Justice Act 1982
 s 60...415
Criminal Justice Act 1987...439
 s 118...439
Criminal Justice Act 1988...73
 s 23...463
 ss 23–26...34
 s 37...426
 s 39...426
 s 133...587
 s 134...241
 s 139...73
 s 139B...64, 284
 s 154...410
Criminal Justice Act 2003...16, 167, 174, 179, 181, 212, 323, 338, 340, 342, 346, 358, 407, 409, 416, 436, 448, 459–463, 499, 509, 568, 571, 611, 613
 s 1...73
 s 4(4)...118
 s 4(7)...227
 s 9...179, 316
 s 10...180, 316
 s 13(1)...408
 s 14...413, 416
 s 15...416
 s 16...415
 s 19...415–416
 ss 22–27...346
 s 24...346
 s 28...371
 s 29...113
 Pt 5 (ss 32–40)...457
 s 32...338
 s 33...219
 s 34...219
 s 37...339
 s 37B(3)(b)...351
 s 39...219
 s 43...475
 s 44...446
 s 46...446
 s 51...47
 Pt 9 (ss 57–74)...448
 s 58(8)...568
 Pt 10 (75–97)...4, 446
 s 100...460
 s 101(1)(d)...460
 s 103...460
 s 103(4)...460
 s 114...462
 ss 114–136...462
 s 120(6)...463
 s 143...359
 s 144(1)...358
 s 145...509
 s 146...509
 s 154...425
 s 174(2)(d)...358
 s 306...170
 s 315...578
 s 321...436
 Sch 33...436
Criminal Justice and Courts Act 2015...7, 344, 390, 421, 455
Criminal Justice and Immigration Act 2008...16, 370, 409, 509
 s 42...584
 s 51...409
 s 52...406
 s 61...587
 s 74...509
 Sch 11...409
Criminal Justice and Police Act 2001...317, 348
 s 12...83
 s 50...290
 ss 50–70...290
 s 53...290
 s 59(5)(b)...290
Criminal Justice and Public Order Act 1994...16, 65, 80, 94, 97, 118, 203, 215–7, 219–25, 236, 250, 259, 271, 273, 416, 423, 457–8
 s 25...407, 416–417
 s 26...407, 413, 416
 s 27...331
 s 34...204, 215–218, 221, 223–225
 s 34(2)...215
 s 34(2A)...216
 s 35...215, 458
 s 35(2)...458
 s 36...215–216
 s 37...215–216
 s 38...458
 s 38(3)...215
 s 48...358, 384
 s 48(2)...361
 s 51(1)...446
 s 60...54, 73–76, 78–79, 83, 86, 94, 97, 101, 118, 127, 495
 s 60(2)...74
 s 82...9
Criminal Justice and Public Order Act 2001
 ss 1–11...348
Criminal Law Act 1967
 s 3...111
Criminal Law Act 1977
 s 15...426
Criminal Procedure and Investigations Act 1996...16, 218, 260, 338, 340–342, 423, 456–457
 s 3(1)(a)...338–9
 s 5...218, 339
 s 7A...339
 s 49...363
 ss 54–57...446

Domestic Violence, Crime and Victims Act 2004...16, 30, 497, 611

Equality Act 2006...32
Equality Act 2010...32, 258, 615
 s.149...66

TABLE OF STATUTES

Extradition Act 2003...119

Fireworks Act 2003...73

Highways Act 1959
  s 121(1)...325
Human Rights Act 1998...5, 9, 24–26, 28–30, 120, 156, 258, 294, 320, 341, 393, 405, 416, 430, 443, 512–3, 584–5, 588, 602, 607, 623
  s 7...31, 585, 607
  s 8...571, 585, 607
  s 19...28

Immigration Act 2016...79
Inquiries Act 2005...529
Intelligence Services Act 1994...307
Interception of Communications Act 1985...294
Investigatory Powers Act 2016...58, 294–298, 307–308
  s 3...295
  s 11...295
  Pt 2 (ss 15–60)...296
  s 20(5)...296
  s 23...296
  s 44...295
  s 56(1)...296
  Pt 3 (ss 60A–86)...296
  s 60A...296
  Pt 4 (ss 87–98)...296
  s 87...296
  s 138...296

Juries Act 1974...436
  s 1...436
  s 16...443
  s 17...443
Justice and Security (Northern Ireland) Act 2007...475

Knives Act 1997...74
  s 8...74

Legal Aid, Sentencing and Punishment of Offenders Act 2012 7, 16, 344, 346, 348, 393, 395, 410, 439, 509, 589
  s 17...394
  Sch 11...406

Magistrates' Courts Act 1980
  s 14...562
  s 16E...562
  s 38...369
  s 43...331
  s 108...559
  ss 111–114...3
  s 111...562
  s 111(2)...562
  s 111(4)...562
  s 111(5)...562
  s 114...562
  s 125...119
  s 128A...404
  s 142...562
Mental Health Act 1983...142, 182, 188
  s 136...114, 185, 188
Misuse of Drugs Act 1971
  s 23...65, 67, 73, 78, 85
  s 23(3)...284

Northern Ireland (Emergency Provisions) Act 1973...474

Offences Against the Person Act 1861...500
  s 47...426
Offender Management Act 2007...412
Offensive Weapons Act 1996
  s 4...64
Official Secrets Act 1911...438

Police Act 1964...531
Police Act 1996
  s 69...539
Police Act 1997...16
  Pt III (ss 91–108)...307
Police and Criminal Evidence Act 1984...14–16, 53–54, 59, 61, 64–66, 70–71, 73–74, 79, 107–108, 118–120, 131, 144, 152, 155–163, 166–167, 169–170, 176, 179, 184, 188–189, 192–193, 196, 200, 203, 207, 210–211, 219, 229–232, 234–236, 238, 241, 243, 254, 256–257, 261–262, 265, 267, 269, 271–272, 278, 284, 288–2889, 291, 329, 335, 345, 474, 529, 539, 553, 555, 588, 600, 602, 626
  s 1...53–54, 64–66, 73, 78–80, 83, 85, 90–92, 94–95, 97, 102, 105, 107, 214
  s 1(2)(b)...80
  s 1(3)...64, 73
  s 1(6)...80
  s 1(7)...64
  s 1(8)...73
  s 1(8A)...73
  s 2...87, 107
  s 2(1)...87
  s 3(6)...87
  s 2(3)(d)...87
  s 3...87, 107
  s 4...78–79, 83
  s 8...286–288, 291
  s 9...290
  s 10...290
  ss 11–13...290
  s 15...286
  s 16(4)...287
  s 16(8)...319
  s 17...119, 285
  s 17(2)...285
  s 18...285–286
  s 19...289
  s 19(2)...292
  s 19(3)...292
  s 24...116, 119–121, 152
  s 24(1)...119

TABLE OF STATUTES

s 24(5)...120–121, 152
s 24A...129
s 25...116
s 28...110
s 29...166
s 30...228
s 30(1)...254
s 30(1A)...227
s 30(7)...227
s 30(7A)...227
s 30(8)...118
s 30(10)...227–228
s 30(10A)...227
s 30A...227
s 32...285–286
s 32(1)...285
s 32(2)(a)...285
s 32(2)(b)...285
s 32(6)...285
s 33...119
s 34(2)...169
s 36...156
s 36(3)...157
s 36(4)...157
s 36(5)...157
s 37...173–177, 217, 239
s 37(2)...174
s 37(7)...174
s 38...331
s 40...167
s 40(1)...167
s 40(3)(a)–(c)...167
s 40(12)–(14)...167
s 41...167
s 41(1)...167
s 41(9)...169
s 42...168
s 42(1)...167
s 42(1)(c)...167
s 43...168
s 44...168
s 44(3)...168
s 47...331, 331
s 50A...331
s 54...179
s 55...179
s 56...158, 227–228, 588
s 56(1)...158–159
s 58...189, 198, 201, 227–228, 235, 555, 588
s 58(1)...189
s 58(4)...190
s 58(5)...189
s 58(6)(a)...189
s 58(8)...190
s 59...192
s 61...179, 316
s 62...180, 316
s 63...180, 316
s 64...317
s 67(8)...96, 585
s 67(10)...94, 585

s 76...245, 553–555
s 76(2)...244, 553
s 76(2)(b)...245
s 76(4)(a)...245, 554
s 76(8)...244
s 78...249, 251, 293, 463, 553–555, 557–559
s 78(1)...555
s 81...218
s 85...539
s 106...59
s 117...111, 586
Sch 1...290
Code of Practice A...65, 74, 80–81, 88–90, 92, 94, 102, 105, 218, 292
    para 1.1...66
    para 1.5...80
    para 2.2...65
    para 2.4...65
    para 2.5...75
    para 2.6...66
    para 2.9...81
    para 2.11...80–81
    paras 2.12–2.16...74
    para 3.1...102
    para 3.2...80, 83
    para 3.5–3.7...102
    para 4.2...87, 89
    para 4.2A...87
    para 4.10A...87
    para 4.12...81
    para 5.1...92
    para 5.3...92
    para 5.4...92
    para 5.5...92
    para 5.6...92
    para 10.2...80
    Annex A...73
    Annex C...80
Code of Practice B...284, 286–287, 289, 292–293
    para 1.3...284
    para 1.5...289
    para 3.1...287
    para 3.3...287
    para 3.4...287
    para 5.1...292
    para 5.2...292
    paras 6.4–6.8...291
    paras 7.7–7.13...290
Code of Practice C...149, 155, 156, 158–162, 168, 181, 191, 196, 200–202, 205, 216, 218, 226, 228–230, 234–235, 239–241, 243–244, 247, 257, 260, 269, 503, 588, 592
    para 1.3...214
    para 1.6(a)(i)...232
    para 1.7A...161
    para 1.13(d)...160
    para 3.1...191
    para 3.2...191
    para 3.4...229, 260

paras 3.6–3.10...187
paras 3.13–3.20...160
para 3.21...160, 191
paras 3.21–3.22B...228
para 4.1...179
para 5....158
para 5.4...159
para 5.6...158
para 5.9B...167
paras 6.1–6.15...202
para 6.1...161, 192, 235
para 6.4...161, 198
para 6.5...196, 198
para 6.5A...161
para 6.6...190, 235
para 6.6(d)...236
para 6.8...189
para 6.9–6.10...190
para 9.3A...503
para 9.3B...503
para 10.1...214, 226, 229
para 10.4...214
para 10.5...215
para 10.8...214
para 10.11...216
para 11...248
para 11.1...227–228
para 11.1(a)...229
para 11.1A...214, 221, 229, 251
para 11.2...197, 235
para 11.4...214
para 11.5...240, 242
para 11.6...239
para 11.7...164, 232, 278
para 11.8...233
para 11.9...233
para 11.10...233
para 11.11...233
para 11.13...234
para 11.15...235
para 11.17...164
para 11.18...235
para 12.2...240
para 12.3...240
para 12.4...240
para 12.5...211, 218
para 12.6...244
para 12.8...240, 244
para 15.2...167
para 15.3C...167
para 15.4...197
para 15.6...229
para 15.9–15.11...167
para 15.11A...168
para 15.11B...168
para 15.11C...168
para 16.5...239
para 16.5(a)...239
Annex A...179
Annex B...161, 235
para 1...189

Annex C...236
Annex G...240
Code of Practice D...280–283
Pt 3A...281
para 3.1...281, 283
para 3.1A(a)...281
para 3.12...281
para 3.21...281
Pt 3B...281
Pt 3C...281–282
Annex A...281
para 7...282
para 9...282
Code of Practice E...232, 278
Code of Practice F...232, 278
para 2.2...232
Code of Practice G...120–121
para 2.9...120
Police and Justice Act 2006
s 7...83
ss 7–9...129
s 11...174
Police Reform Act 2002...16, 111, 157, 546
Pt 2 (ss 9–29)...532
s 20...546
s 38...129
Sch 3...546
Sch 4...83
Police Reform and Social Responsibility Act 2011...523
s 77...41
Policing and Crime Act 2017...111, 114, 142, 165, 168, 310, 331, 533
Policing and Crime Act 2018...142
Poor Law Amendment Act 1834...482
Prevention of Terrorism (Temporary Provisions) Act 1989...121–122, 159, 170, 173
s 14...189
Prevention of Terrorism Act 2005...2, 122, 159, 171
Private Security Industry Act 2001...58
Proceeds of Crime Act 2002...5
Protection of Freedoms Act 2012...16, 476, 509
s 61...77
Prosecution of Offences Act 1985...14, 16, 323, 370, 390, 415, 568
s 18(2)...565
Public Order Act 1986...132, 140, 509–510
s 4...136
s 5...9, 10, 133, 136, 145, 234, 348
s 17...509
s 29...509

Race Relations (Amendment) Act 2000...92, 95
Racial and Religious Hatred Act 2006...509
Regulation of Investigatory Powers Act 2000...16, 294–299, 304–307, 309
Pt II (ss 26–48)...295, 306
s 26...298–299, 304, 307–308
s 26(9)...294
s 26(9)(a)...306

s 29...298
Road Traffic Act 1988...80, 215
   s 163...77–78
Road Traffic Act 1991...96

Sanctions and Anti-Money Laundering Act 2018...603
Senior Courts Act 1981
   s 28...562
   ss 29–31...563
   s 48(4)...561
   s 74...559
Serious Crime Act 2007...5, 16
   s 45...46
   s 87...74
Serious Crime Act 2015...16
   s 76...496
Serious Organised Crime and Police Act 2005...16, 120, 152, 167, 300
   ss 71–75...300
   ss 73–75...361
   s 110...116, 120, 129
   s 110(4)...121
   s 110(5)...121
   s 115...73
   ss 120–121...157
   Sch 7...167, 189
      para 43(7)...167
   Sch 8...83
Sexual Offences Act 2003...488, 614
   s 1...488
   s 1(2)...488
   s 75...488
   s 76...488
Social Security Administration (Fraud) Act 1997...354
Suicide Act 1961...343

Terrorism Act 2000...9, 29, 65, 79–80, 94, 103, 122, 159, 170, 235
   s 38B...2
   s 41...170
   s 41(1)...122
   s 43...67, 78, 83
   s 43(1)...78
   s 43A...78
   s 44...75–77, 85, 86, 95, 101, 103, 106–107
   s 44(3)...74
   ss 44–47...74
   s 45(1)...74
   s 47A...77–79
   s 57...10
   s 57(2)...9
   Sch 7...76, 78, 103
   Sch 8...170
      paras 7–9...236
Terrorism Act 2006
   s 1...122
   s 23...170
Terrorism Prevention and Investigation Measures Act 2011...6, 122, 172

Theft Act 1968...465
   s 1...73
   s 24(4)...73
Tribunals of Inquiry (Evidence) Act 1921...529

Violent Crime Reduction Act 2006...16
   s 45...84
   s 46...84
   s 48...64

Youth Justice and Criminal Evidence Act 1999...16, 279, 450, 451, 463, 500
   s 1...418
   Pt II (ss 16–63)...611
   s 28...34, 450, 613
   s 33BA...615
   s 33BB...615
   ss 35–37...614
   s 41...489, 614
   s 58...216
   s 59...214–215
   Sch 3...214–215

Statutory Instruments

Civil Procedure Rules
   Pt 54 Judicial review and statutory review...563
   r 54.5...563
Criminal Defence Service (Funding) Order 2007 (SI 2007/1174)
   Sch 4, para 1...566
Criminal Defence Service (Recovery of Defence Costs Orders) Regulations 2001 (SI 2001/856)...565
Criminal Defence Service (Recovery of Defence Costs Orders) (Amendment) Regulations 2008 (SI 2008/2430)
   reg 4...565
Criminal Legal Aid (Remuneration) Regulations 2013...337
Criminal Procedure Rules...288, 315, 341, 362–363, 367, 373, 376, 401, 404–5, 421–2, 432, 449, 456, 559, 604
   Pt 3 Case management
      r 3.2...49, 432
      r 3.2(e)...449
      r 3.9...450
   Pt 15 Disclosure...219
   Pt 19 Expert evidence...315
Criminal Practice Directions V: Evidence 16C...278
   paras 19A.4–19A.6...337
   Pt 34 Appeal to the Crown Court...559
   r 34.2(2)...560
   r 34.2(3)...560
   Pt 35 Appeal to the High Court by case stated...3, 562
   Pt 36 Appeal to the Court of Appeal: general rules

r 36.4...567
Pt 37 Appeal to the Court of Appeal against ruling at preparatory hearing...562
Pt 39 Appeal to the Court of Appeal about conviction or sentence
r 39.2...566
r 39.3(1)...566
r 39.3(1)(e)(ii)...567
r 39.3(2)...566
Pt 45 Costs
Criminal Practice Directions X: Costs
Para 3.1...560
Pt 47 Investigation orders and warrants
r 47.25...288
Consolidated Criminal Practice Directions
para 3E...612
Annex E...376
Crown Court (Recording and Broadcasting) Order 2020 (SI 2020/637)...526
Crown Court Rules 1987 (SI 1987/716)...218

Fireworks Regulations 2004 (SI 2004/1836)...73

Health Protection (Coronavirus, Restrictions) (England) Regulations 2020 (SI 2020/350) 55, 226, 324, 349
reg 10...348

Magistrates' Courts (Advance Information) Rules 1985 (SI 1985/601)...372
Magistrates' Courts (Remand in Custody) Order 1991 (SI 1991/2667)...404

Police (Conduct, Complaints and Misconduct and Appeal Tribunal) (Amendment) Regulations 2017 (SI 2017/1134)...534, 539
Police Reform Act 2002 (Standard Powers and Duties of Community Support Officers) Order 2007 (SI 2007/3202)...83

Regulation of Investigatory Powers (Juveniles) Order 2000 (SI 2000/2793)...304

European legislation

Directive 97/66/EC of the European Parliament and of the Council of 15 December 1997 concerning the processing of personal data and the protection of privacy in the telecommunications sector...294
Council Directive 2000/43/EC of 29 June 2000 implementing the principle of equal treatment between persons irrespective of racial or ethnic origin...95
Directive 2012/29/EU of the European Parliament and of the Council of 25 October 2012 establishing minimum standards on the rights, support and protection of victims of crime...616
Directive 2013/48/EU of the European Parliament and of the Council of 22 October 2013 on the right of access to a lawyer in criminal proceedings and in European arrest warrant proceedings, and on the right to have a third party informed upon deprivation of liberty and to communicate with third persons and with consular authorities while deprived of liberty...405

International instruments

European Convention for the Prevention of Torture and Inhuman or Degrading Treatment or Punishment 1989...32
European Convention on Human Rights 1950...4, 9, 24–33, 38, 65, 94–95, 122–123, 125, 153, 156, 169–170, 181, 189, 208, 215, 224, 237, 271, 294, 296, 338, 342, 350, 383, 392–394, 396, 405, 410–411, 413, 415–417, 430, 443, 463–464, 495, 556, 558, 569, 571, 585, 588, 594, 602, 608, 623
Art 2...26, 149, 184, 187, 209, 513, 534, 543, 592, 594, 608
Art 3...25, 26, 32, 158, 181, 209, 245, 328, 607
Art 5...27, 95, 111, 122, 128, 156, 171, 417
Art 5(1)...95, 122
Art 5(1)(b)...95, 123
Art 5(1)(c)...405
Art 5(2)...110
Art 5(3)...169, 405
Art 6...25, 27–28, 35, 47, 171, 189, 190–192, 201, 210, 214, 216, 236–237, 303, 305, 337, 394, 395, 405, 423, 438, 443–444, 448, 450, 463, 553, 556, 570–571, 585, 615
Art 6(1)...383, 393
Art 6(2)...9, 210, 340, 383, 405
Art 6(3)...393–394, 464
Art 6(3)(c)...189
Art 6(3)(d)...463
Art 8...26, 76, 95, 96, 105, 209, 283–284, 288, 294, 298–299, 308, 317–320, 514, 532, 556, 585–586, 602
Art 8(1)...317
Art 8(2)...317
Art 10...95–96, 126, 509
Art 11...26, 95–96, 126
Art 13...532, 571
Art 14...350, 383, 512
Art 15...27
Art 17...509
Optional Protocol to the Convention Against Torture 2002...527, 550
Universal Declaration of Human Rights 1948...24

1

The aims and values of 'criminal justice'

KEY ISSUES

- The structure of the criminal justice system
- Blurring civil and criminal boundaries
- Proving guilt and innocence: burden and standard of proof
- Adversarial and inquisitorial approaches
- Recent trends in crime and criminal justice
- Packer's 'due process' and 'crime control' models
- Police legitimacy and procedural justice
- The human rights approach to criminal justice
- Where do victims fit into these approaches?
- The managerial approach to criminal justice and austerity justice
- A unifying perspective: freedom and 'core values'

1.1 The nature and structure of 'criminal justice'

A book with a title as vague as 'criminal justice' should begin by saying what it is about. In thinking about criminal justice we all have our own images and assumptions. In this chapter we spell out our own assumptions. We also explain the theoretical framework within which we think criminal justice in England and Wales can most usefully be understood, criticised and reformed.

We see the criminal justice system as a complex social institution[1] that regulates potential, alleged and actual criminal activity within limits designed to protect people from wrongful treatment and wrongful conviction. In earlier editions of this book we focused mainly on police, prosecution and court powers and procedures in respect of *alleged* crime, resulting in either 'diversion' out of the system (e.g. through the imposition of a police or prosecution caution) or court proceedings. Recent years have witnessed some reconfiguration of criminal law and criminal justice in favour of crime pre-emption

---

[1] See further Garland D, *Punishment and Modern Society* (Oxford: Clarendon Press, 1990) p 282.

through risk management techniques,[2] alongside more diversion. It follows that while the determination of guilt and innocence is still hugely important, this must now be considered alongside the control of *potential* criminal activity through risk management devices such as dispersal and anti-social behaviour injunctions (ABIs). As we discuss in section 1.9, the increased use of diversion is also part of an agenda that introduced management techniques to encourage maximum efficiency in the criminal process. For those whose behaviour leads them into formal criminal justice processes, we see a reduction in their ability to exercise their rights. That reduction is fuelled by relentless budget cuts across all of the agencies of criminal justice, as well as an economically driven desire to increase digital working practices.

In this section we introduce some of the key issues and tensions inherent in this reconfiguration of 'criminal justice' and also discuss the key terms 'criminal' and 'justice'. First we outline the structure and core terminology of the traditional English[3] criminal process for readers unfamiliar with this jurisdiction, and explain how this relates to the organisation of this book.

1.1.1 The English criminal process

Anyone who thinks a crime may have been committed may (but need not)[4] report this to a law enforcement body. There are many enforcement bodies. First, there are 43 'local' police forces, roughly corresponding with local authority areas. Second, there are also some national police bodies such as the National Crime Agency and the British Transport Police. Third, many types of crime that would be called 'administrative offences' in some other countries—e.g. health and safety violations, pollution, tax evasion—are dealt with by specialist agencies such as the Health and Safety Executive and the Environment Agency. Fourth, some charities are able to bring prosecutions, such as the Royal Society for the Prevention of Cruelty to Animals. In addition, a lot of 'policing' is done by private security firms, which, like ordinary witnesses and victims, generally call in the police if they detect suspected crimes and want further action taken. The police may seek to find evidence of guilt through the use of powers such as stop and search (see chapter 2), arrest (chapter 3), detention and interrogation (chapters 4–5) and a variety of non-interrogative means including electronic surveillance and infiltration (chapter 6). Enforcement bodies are not obliged to prosecute even if they have overwhelming evidence of guilt. If the police do wish to prosecute, they pass the case onto the Crown Prosecution Service (CPS), except in low level traffic offences, which can be prosecuted by police court presentation officers. The CPS mostly decides whether to take matters further, and—if so—will prosecute,

---

[2] Ashworth A and Zedner L, *Preventive Justice* (Oxford: OUP, 2014). The extent to which this is merely a pendulum-like swing back to a risk management approach is debatable. See, for example, Bonner D, *Executive Measures, Terrorism and National Security: Have the Rules of the Game Changed?* (Aldershot: Ashgate, 2007).

[3] By 'English' we actually refer to England and Wales. Scotland is somewhat different, but increasingly less so as the two systems are converging.

[4] There are exceptions to this general principle. For example, s.117 of the Anti-Terrorism, Crime and Security Act 2001 (inserting s.38B into the Terrorism Act 2000) created the offence of failing to disclose to the police information thought to be of material assistance either in preventing an act of terrorism or in the apprehension, prosecution or conviction of a person for an offence involving the instigation, preparation or commission of an act of terrorism (now see the Prevention of Terrorism Act 2005). Several road traffic regulations also impose positive duties of disclosure and create offences for failure to comply.

sometimes hiring specialist lawyers (barristers) for very serious cases. Also, individual victims may prosecute in their own right.[5]

All prosecuted cases start in the lowest level of (magistrates') courts—or, where the defendant is under 18, the youth courts.[6] In this lowest tier of the criminal courts, most cases are decided by a bench of three lay magistrates supported by a legal advisor, though increasingly professional judges (once referred to as stipendiary magistrates, but now known as District Judges) decide cases alone. Very serious cases are quickly transferred out of the magistrates' court to the Crown court. Here proceedings are more formal, and there is a professional judge (and, in contested cases, a jury). The Courts are overseen by the Ministry of Justice, while the police are overseen by the Home Office.

The division of business between the magistrates' courts and the Crown court is determined by the initial legal classification of an offence as either 'summary' (triable in the magistrates' courts only), 'either-way' (triable in either the magistrates' courts or the Crown court) or 'triable on indictment only' (triable only in the Crown court). The latter two types of offence are sometimes lumped together under the label 'indictable offences'. Regardless of this classification, most prosecuted cases are uncontested, because the defendant pleads guilty.

People who are convicted of crimes may appeal to a higher court: from the magistrates'/youth courts to the Crown court (where a completely new hearing of the matter takes place) and/or the Court of Appeal; and from the Crown court to the Court of Appeal. Exceptionally, a further appeal is sometimes allowed to the Supreme Court (formerly the House of Lords). Appeals to courts other than the Crown court are generally restricted to points of law, although fresh evidence is sometimes admitted. A person wishing to appeal a point of law from the magistrates' court may do so by way of 'case stated' to the Queen's Bench Division of the High Court.[7] Once normal appeal rights are exhausted the final avenue open to the convicted defendant is to persuade an administrative body, the Criminal Cases Review Commission (CCRC), that there is some fresh evidence or argument that, if put before an appeal court, would give rise to a real possibility of the conviction being overturned. If, following investigation, the CCRC accepts that there is such a possibility the case will be referred to an appellate court for determination.

The Court of Appeal will allow an appeal where the judges think the conviction is 'unsafe'. If an appeal is lodged 'out of time', there is a further hurdle that must be passed, and that is to show that the failure to allow an appeal to be heard would amount to a 'substantial injustice'. Convictions can be 'quashed' by the Court of Appeal if a defendant is found to have been denied a fair trial, as in cases where the police fail to disclose evidence that undermined the prosecution case. Such malpractice, if adjudged severe enough, is said to render the conviction 'unsafe', and to amount to a 'miscarriage of justice', although such breaches of due process do not necessarily mean that the defendants concerned are factually innocent of the crime in question.[8] This means that there are two main types of 'wrongful conviction' (which often overlap). One is where the defendant (whether actually

---

[5] A private prosecution was launched by the parents of Stephen Lawrence, whose case has fundamentally shaped criminal procedure (see chs 2 and 12), after a public prosecution was discontinued in 1993. The private prosecution failed after identification evidence was deemed inadmissible. The defendants were eventually publicly prosecuted and convicted in 2012.

[6] Space precludes a detailed discussion of youth courts, but see further Aubrey-Johnson K et al, *Youth Justice Law and Practice* (London: Legal Action Group, 2019). For a critical analysis of youth justice, see Case S, *Youth Justice: A Critical Introduction* (London: Routledge, 2018).

[7] See ss.111–114 of the Magistrates' Courts Act 1980 and Part 35 of the Criminal Procedure Rules.

[8] See Naughton M, *The Innocent and the Criminal Justice System: A Sociological Analysis of Miscarriages of Justice* (Basingstoke: Palgrave Macmillan, 2013).

guilty or not) is convicted unfairly; in most of these cases, the lack of fair trial makes it impossible to judge whether the defendant is guilty or not. The other is where an innocent defendant is convicted (whether fairly or not). The conviction through unfair means of those perceived or known to be actually innocent is the type of miscarriage of justice that gives rise to most public concern.

Public concern can also be aroused by the acquittal of those perceived to be guilty, and some have argued that such acquittals amount to a different kind of miscarriage of justice.[9] The CPS is sometimes allowed to appeal against acquittals, especially when there is an alleged error of law, such as a refusal to let a jury hear prosecution evidence because the trial judge considers that the police lacked the legal power to secure that evidence. In rare cases, where new and compelling evidence of guilt emerges and the Director of Public Prosecutions (DPP)[10] agrees, entirely fresh proceedings can be brought against someone previously acquitted.[11] The best known example of this occurred in relation to the 2012 retrial of Gary Dobson for the 1993 murder of Stephen Lawrence.[12] Dobson was eventually convicted of the murder.

By virtue of the doctrine of precedent, the decisions of the higher appeal courts apply to all future cases with similar circumstances. In this way, the 'common law' is in a continual process of evolution.[13] Another way in which common law is created in the criminal justice area is through challenges to the decisions of state agencies ('judicial review'). For example, a victim of a crime can ask a court (usually the High Court, making this a civil, not a criminal, case) to rule on the lawfulness of a decision by the CPS not to prosecute.[14] Again, such decisions set 'precedents' that not only guide the decisions of courts, but also of enforcement agencies. Judicial review is one of a number of mechanisms that regulate the operation and policies of the criminal justice system. Others include government inspectorates and the Independent Office for Police Conduct, discussed in chapter 11.

An element of criminal justice which is often forgotten is criminal defence. Anyone arrested and taken to a police station is entitled to receive free legal advice from an accredited advisor (who is not necessarily a fully qualified lawyer) either over the telephone or in person. The state also provides funding for free legal representation in the magistrates' courts and the Crown court, subject to a means test and a merits test. The former test means that middle class defendants (a relatively small proportion of the whole, leaving motoring offences aside) generally pay for their own defence or represent themselves. The latter test means that rich and poor alike must demonstrate that there is public interest in being represented at state expense. In the Crown court, the overwhelming majority of defendants are relatively poor and face serious charges, and so are usually represented by solicitors and barristers at the state's expense. These issues are discussed throughout this book.

---

[9] Then Prime Minister Tony Blair argued that: 'It is perhaps the biggest miscarriage of justice in today's system when the guilty walk away unpunished' (cited and critiqued in Naughton M, *Rethinking Miscarriages of Justice* (Houndmills: Palgrave Macmillan, 2007).

[10] The Director of Public Prosecutions is the most senior public prosecutor and head of the CPS.

[11] Criminal Justice Act 2003, part 10.

[12] *R v Dobson* [2011] EWCA Crim 1255. A more recent example is the case of Russell Bishop, who was convicted of murder in 2018 following an acquittal in 1987 (*The Guardian*, 11 December 2018).

[13] Britain has no criminal code. Legislation has been built up piecemeal, so courts have to fill in the gaps more than in 'civil law' systems, thus creating case law (often known as 'the common law'). Moreover Britain has no constitution to guide how gaps should be filled. This also means that case law is subordinate to legislation. Even if legislation contravenes the European Convention on Human Rights, which was enshrined in the law in 1998 (see section 1.6) it is simply declared 'incompatible' rather than being rendered invalid.

[14] An example is *R (on the application of F) v The Director of Public Prosecutions and 'A'* [2013] EWHC 945 (Admin), when the claimant successfully applied to the High Court to review the CPS decision not to prosecute her husband in relation to an allegation of rape. See further examples in ch 12.

1.1.2 Civil and criminal boundary

It is difficult to provide a clear definition of the difference between 'civil' and 'criminal' matters. In general the former are dealt with in civil courts (District courts, County courts and the High Court), and are for individuals to pursue rather than the state. Many 'wrongs', such as torts (e.g. negligence) and breach of contract, are civil matters. It is not possible to prosecute or seek the state punishment of the wrongdoer, but the wronged person (the plaintiff) can sue with a view to obtaining a civil remedy, such as compensatory damages.

However the boundaries between the civil and criminal spheres are increasingly blurred. First, some matters involving civil and criminal elements are most effectively dealt with at one time. Domestic violence, in particular, may involve a crime (assault) which merits punishment but also an ongoing threat to safety necessitating a civil injunction requiring the aggressor to keep away from the family home. The shift towards crime pre-emption encourages and reinforces this blending of civil and criminal justice. Second, while criminal courts normally punish for crimes, leaving civil courts to compensate for loss,[15] at the sentencing stage criminal courts frequently order defendants to compensate victims. However, victims are reliant upon the prosecution to seek this on their behalf and are not able to participate in criminal proceedings in the way that they can in a civil claim. Third, the actions (and inactions) of the criminal justice agencies such as the police and CPS can be scrutinised in the civil justice system through judicial review (as noted earlier), or an action for professional negligence or breach of the Human Rights Act 1998.

Finally, there are important new hybrid laws. Under the Proceeds of Crime Act 2002 (consolidated by the Serious Crime Act 2007) civil courts may allow enforcement agencies to seize or retain property that is more likely than not to have been obtained criminally without having to prove anyone guilty of a crime.[16] Then there are 'civil behavioural orders' (also known as civil preventive measures (CPM)) that embody civil evidential standards, but impose restrictions on behaviour that are akin to the type of punishments imposed in criminal courts. One example of this is the ABI, which replaced the anti-social behaviour order (ASBO) as part of an overhaul of quasi criminal orders under the Anti-social Behaviour, Crime and Policing Act 2014. These differ from criminal behaviour orders (a post-conviction measure aimed at preventing future offending) in that the procedure involved is civil, not criminal.[17] This means that hearsay evidence is admissible,[18] and a lower standard of proof is required. Hendry and King have questioned the validity of such measures given that they 'illegitimately circumvent criminal law procedural protections'.[19] ABIs are intended to prevent further 'anti-social' acts by the defendant, and can include prohibitions such as curfews, or commands to avoid certain places

---

[15] Although, to muddy the waters further, civil courts sometimes award punitive damages.

[16] Millington T and Williams S, *The Proceeds of Crime* (Oxford: OUP, 2007).

[17] *R (on the application of McCann) v Manchester Crown Court* [2002] 4 All ER 593.

[18] The rule against hearsay evidence in criminal proceedings is designed to prevent a party using evidence of an out-of-court statement for the purpose of proving the truth of any fact asserted in that statement. It ensures that direct evidence is given by those with personal knowledge of the relevant matters, thus allowing cross-examination to take place, demeanour to be assessed, and so forth. See Dennis, I, *The Law of Evidence* (London: Sweet and Maxwell, 2017) part 4.

[19] Hendry J and King J, 'Expediency, Legitimacy, and the Rule of Law: A Systems Perspective on Civil/Criminal Procedural Hybrids' (2017) 11 *Criminal Law and Philosophy* 733–757, 734. See also, Pratt J, 'Risk Control, Rights and Legitimacy in the Limited Liability State' (2017) 57 *British Journal of Criminology* 1322–1339 and Demetriou, S 'From the ASBO to the Injunction: A Qualitative Review of the Anti-social Behaviour Legislation Post-2014' (2019) April *Public Law* 343–361.

or individuals. As Pratt notes, 'the pattern of risk controls has coalesced around more specific and limited areas: the presence or behaviour of certain individuals or groups thought likely to put at risk community cohesion and the quality of life of its citizens'.[20]

The replacement of the ASBO (which differed from the ABI in that breach of any condition was a crime that carried the risk of five years' imprisonment) is welcome. But the breadth of provisions that may form part of the injunction lead Duff and Marshall to the view that the prohibitions/requirements imposed on the person subject to the injunction can in fact be punitive in themselves.[21] Further, breach of the ABI is a civil contempt of court, which carries the risk of two years' imprisonment and an unlimited fine.[22]

The ABI is only one of a number of CPMs created under the Anti-social Behaviour, Crime and Policing Act 2014, which also empowers the courts to make community protection notices, public spaces protection orders, orders for the closure of premises associated with nuisance or disorder, sexual risk orders and violent offender orders. Other legislation has introduced different forms of CPM, including the terrorism prevention and investigation measures order under the Terrorism Prevention and Investigation Measures Act 2011. There are also post-conviction preventative orders, such as the serious crime prevention order and the sexual harm prevention order. Additionally, one of the first types of CPM, the restraining order, can be made against a person either without or upon conviction. The proliferation of these quasi criminal orders is representative of a governmental desire to regulate 'undesirable' behaviour, often targeting already marginalised sections of society while simultaneously creating 'low hanging fruit' that helps police to meet targets set in a system emphasising actuarial justice (section 1.9).

1.1.3 Criminal law and criminal behaviour

What is defined as criminal varies from society to society and across time, and some of the implications of this are discussed further in chapter 10. English criminal law in the twenty-first century is generally thought of as proscribing people and corporate bodies from culpably (i.e. intentionally or recklessly) acting in particularly harmful or socially undesirable ways. However, much of such behaviour is not criminalised (invasions of privacy, police abuse of suspects' rights, and the wasteful misuse of the earth's resources are examples) and many feel that much of what is criminalised should not be (examples might be smoking cannabis and swearing by football fans). Moreover, the law criminalises many forms of behaviour where the actor has acted negligently or even, in the case of some strict liability offences, where every care was taken to avoid harm. Decisions concerning which acts are to be criminalised are sometimes based on coherently expressed principles supported by an informed consensus, but more often they are the products of historical accident, political and administrative expedience, and shifting, incoherent ideological notions of the appropriate reach of the criminal law.[23]

Thus the recent lurch towards crime pre-emption is reflected in the 'general tendency to expand the boundaries of criminal liability'.[24] The Labour government of 1997–2010, with its 'tough on crime, tough on the causes of crime' stance, created a disproportionate number

---

[20] Pratt J, 'Risk Control, Rights and Legitimacy in the Limited Liability State' (2017) 57 *British Journal of Criminology* 1322–1339, 1323.

[21] Duff A and Marshall S, 'How Offensive Can You Get?' in von Hirsch A and Simester A (eds), *Incivilities: Regulating Offensive Behaviour* (Oxford: Hart Publishing, 2006) pp 80–81.

[22] Home Office, *Anti-social Behaviour, Crime and Policing Act 2014: Reform of Anti-social Behaviour Powers—Statutory Guidance for Frontline Professionals* (London: Home Office, 2017a) p 26.

[23] See further Hillyard P, Pantazis C, Tombs S and Gordon D (eds), *Beyond Criminology: Taking Harm Seriously* (London: Pluto Press, 2004).

[24] Virgo G, 'Terrorism: Possession of Articles' (2008) 67(2) *Cambridge Law Journal* 236.

of new criminal offences; nearly one for every day of its first 10 years in power. While many are either trivial or brought old laws up to date, many others criminalised previously lawful behaviour.[25] New Labour also introduced 34 statutes that had a significant impact on criminal justice and procedure, compared to only six criminal justice statutes between 1925 and 1985.[26] Most remain in force today. Since 2010 there has been a shift in the nature of new legislation, with several statutes devoted to restructuring in the criminal justice process such as the Criminal Justice and Courts Act 2015, Crime and Courts Act 2013 and the Legal Aid, Sentencing and Punishment of Offenders Act 2012. This shift is likely to have been fuelled by the austerity agenda adopted between 2010 and 2020 (section 1.9.1).[27]

Similar observations might be made about the way in which (potentially) harmful behaviours are in practice identified as criminal and responded to as such. For example, it may be that rowdy behaviour by unemployed scruffy youths will be interpreted in quite a different way to that engaged in by university students following their final examinations. One person's public disorder is another's youthful high spirits. Since the late 1800s, the people responsible for developing criminal justice policy have been drawn from a socially and educationally closed elite, with little empathy or affinity with most defendants.[28] These kinds of interpretative decisions are also influenced by shifts in ideology. Thus, for example, feminist writers and activists have raised public awareness of domestic violence to the point where many more victims and police officers now interpret what takes place within the 'private' sphere of the home as criminal.[29] And the Labour government's focus on 'anti-social behaviour' probably increased intolerance and formal reporting to the police, of people and acts previously seen as merely irritating or unconventional.[30]

Since criminal laws and perceptions of criminality are social constructs it is not surprising that much criminal justice activity reflects the interests of powerful groups and actors. There are many more criminal laws and regulatory resources aimed at harmful behaviour by individuals (particularly young people) than at harmful corporate activity, for example. And, as we shall see, benefit fraud is prosecuted (by the Department of Work and Pensions) far more frequently than is tax fraud. Much criminal justice activity supports widely held social values while at the same time compounding wider social divisions and making no concessions for the social causes of crime.[31] For example, theft laws protect poor people as well as wealthy people, but the prosecution and punishment of shoplifting has a greater impact on the poor than the wealthy, and upholds the value of private property whilst ignoring (or even reinforcing) poverty.

---

[25] Young R, 'Street Policing after PACE' in Cape E and Young R (eds), *Regulating Policing* (Oxford: Hart, 2008).
[26] Baillie A, 'Can England and Wales Afford Both Justice and the Ministry of Justice?' (Open Lecture Series University of Kent 7 December 2011).
[27] In 2019, the Chancellor declared the end of austerity, though the Shadow Chancellor expressed scepticism about that declaration. See Dearbail J, 'Chancellor Sajid Javid declares end of austerity' (2019) BBC News, 4 September. There were some (pre-Covid-19) signals that austerity was being relaxed in the form of extra investment for the police and CPS, detailed later in this chapter.
[28] McConville M and Marsh L, *The Myth of Judicial Independence* (Oxford: OUP, 2020). They further demonstrate that every single Lord Chief Justice has been a white male, and the vast majority have been Oxbridge educated. The implications of this are discussed further in ch 10.
[29] See further, Wells C, 'The Impact of Feminist Thinking on Criminal Law and Justice: Contradiction, Complexity, Conviction and Connection' [2004] *Criminal Law Review* 503.
[30] Tonry M, *Punishment and Politics: Evidence and Emulation in the Making of English Crime Control Policy* (Cullompton: Willan, 2004) p 57.
[31] Thus, measures to tackle 'anti-social' behaviour are mostly punitive, not supportive, and are generally targeted on the most disadvantaged communities: Brown A, 'Anti-Social Behaviour, Crime Control and Social Control' (2004) 43 *Howard Journal of Criminal Justice* 203; Koffmann L, 'Holding Parents to Account: Tough on Children, Tough on the Causes of Children' (2008) 35(1) *Journal of Law and Society* 113. See, more generally, Cook D, *Criminal and Social Justice* (London: Sage, 2006).

In summary, the enforcement of the criminal law upholds social order ostensibly for the benefit of all, but in reality reinforces a hierarchical social order that benefits some while disadvantaging others. In an unequal society, this is bound to be morally problematic. Consensus and conflict are thus intrinsic in all attempts at 'maintaining order' and controlling crime.

1.2 Guilt and innocence

In a democracy, state punishment can be legitimately inflicted only on those found guilty of crime. The criminal justice system insists on proof of guilt, rather than simply taking the word of the victim or the police. But proving guilt is not straightforward. If accused persons are truly criminal they will often be concerned to hide the truth. So should we always disbelieve them? Of course not—the police or prosecution witnesses may be mistaken, or they may be correct about some of the facts (for example, whether the accused punched someone) but simply not know other important details (for example, whether the punch was in self-defence). Occasionally prosecution witnesses themselves hide the truth, or even lie. Some years ago, Carl Beech accused numerous politicians of paedophile offences. The police investigation cost well over £1m. But Carl Beech had lied, and in 2019 he was jailed for 18 years.[32]

It follows that when accused persons dispute guilt it is as likely that they are innocent as guilty, unless there is evidence pointing one way or the other. And it is rare for that evidence to prove *conclusively* that someone is guilty, in the way we (often naively) expect scientific and medical tests to provide conclusive truth. The only way to completely prevent the conviction of the factually innocent would be to insist on incontrovertible proof, which would lead to very few convictions. This was recognised by the Court of Appeal in *Ward*[33] when it said that criminal justice:

> . . . should be developed so as to reduce the risk of conviction of the innocent to an absolute minimum. At the same time we are very much alive to the fact that, although the avoidance of the conviction of the innocent must unquestionably be the primary consideration, the public interest would not be served by a multiplicity of rules which merely impede effective law enforcement (at 52).

This judgment, however, fudges two key issues. No-one in their right mind would advocate a multiplicity of rules which 'merely' impeded effective law enforcement. Rules protecting suspects from wrongful conviction, harsh treatment or invasions of privacy often do impede 'effective' law enforcement, but, in a democracy, this price is seen as worth paying in order to protect the liberty and dignity of the individual suspect, and to ensure a just outcome that is beneficial to the victim and legitimacy of the process. Second, the Court of Appeal's assertion that conviction of the innocent should be kept to an absolute minimum suggests that perhaps a vast number of guilty persons should go free if necessary to achieve that goal.

Let us leave aside such rhetorical flourishes and ask to what extent is the acquittal of the innocent defendant a priority of English criminal justice in fact? The main theoretical safeguard offered to suspects in the English system of criminal justice (and also under the European Convention on Human Rights) is the presumption of innocence.

---

[32] See <https://www.theguardian.com/uk-news/2019/jul/26/carl-beech-vip-paedophile-ring-accuser-jailed-for-18-years> (accessed 20 October 2020). For another case, see Gillan A, 'Stone trial main witness admits he is habitual liar' *The Guardian*, 20 September 2001 (see <https://www.theguardian.com/uk/2001/sep/20/audreygillan> (accessed 20 October 2020). [33] (1993) 96 Cr App Rep 1.

This presumption finds expression in the principle that guilt must be proved beyond reasonable doubt. There are two aspects to this principle; first, it places the burden of proof on the prosecution; and, second, it stipulates a high standard of proof.

1.2.1 The burden of proof

Viscount Sankey LC described the burden of proof in *Woolmington v DPP*[34] as the 'golden thread' which ran throughout criminal law: 'No matter what the charge or where the trial, the principle that the prosecution must prove the guilt of the prisoner is part of the common law of England and no attempt to whittle it down can be entertained'. In recognition of parliamentary supremacy over the courts, Lord Sankey noted, however, that this common law principle was subject to statutory exceptions. These are numerous; in the mid-1990s, Ashworth and Blake calculated that 219 out of the 540 indictable offences in common use involved a shifting from the prosecution to the defence of the burden of proof in relation to some elements of the offence. For example there are many prosecutions under s.5 of the Public Order Act 1986 for using threatening, abusive or insulting words or behaviour within the hearing or sight of a person likely to be caused harassment, alarm or distress thereby. All the prosecution need prove is that defendants did as alleged (not that any alarm, etc was caused). Accused persons then escape liability only if they can prove, on the balance of probabilities, that their conduct was reasonable.

Shifts in the burden of proof, sometimes referred to as a reverse onus, never require the defendant to prove something 'beyond reasonable doubt' but only, at most, 'on the balance of probabilities'. Nonetheless, this means that a court can convict in cases where the defendant's story is as likely to be true as false. This might appear to be contrary to the European Convention on Human Rights (ECHR), Art 6(2) which states that: 'Everyone charged with a criminal offence shall be presumed innocent until proved guilty according to law'. But, following a European Court of Human Rights (ECtHR) ruling that reverse onuses did not necessarily violate the Convention,[35] the House of Lords in *Lambert*[36] stated that Art 6(2) permits a statute to place a burden of proof on a defendant, if that burden is proportionate to the aim being pursued, which must itself be legitimate. In determining these issues, a court must take account of such factors as the gravity of the conduct dealt with by the offence in question, the justification for placing a burden on the defendant, and the degree of difficulty in discharging that burden. It follows that the courts will have to proceed on a case-by-case basis, deciding for each offence whether a shift in burden is proportionate or not.[37]

Parliament has responded to the human rights era supposedly ushered in by the Human Rights Act 1998 (which made ECHR rights enforceable within the domestic court system) by stipulating that some of the more serious statutory offences which appear on their face to require the defendant to prove some matter should be read as only imposing a burden to adduce sufficient evidence to make the issue a live one. For example, when the main terrorism offences were consolidated in the Terrorism Act 2000 the opportunity was taken (in s.57(2)) to recast the offence created by s.82 of the Criminal Justice and Public Order Act 1994 (possessing an article for suspected terrorist purposes) in precisely this way. Now, if a defendant adduces evidence sufficient to raise the issue that she or he had an item in their possession for a non-terrorist purpose then an acquittal must follow unless the

---

[34] *Woolmington v DPP* [1935] AC 462 at 481–482.   [35] *Salabiaku v France* (1988) EHRR 379.
[36] *Lambert* [2001] 2 Cr App R 511. See also *Attorney General's Reference No 4 of 2002; Sheldrake v DPP* [2004] UKHL 43.
[37] See *Johnstone* [2003] UKHL 28, *Makuwa* [2006] EWCA Crim 175 and *Williams* [2012] EWCA Crim 2162. In each case, a reverse onus was upheld when the maximum penalty that could be imposed was 10 years imprisonment.

prosecution proves beyond reasonable doubt that no such purpose existed. On the other hand a number of terrorist offences were re-enacted with a shift in burden still in place. It is possible some of these reverse onus provisions will be successfully challenged, but many are undoubtedly here to stay.[38]

1.2.2 The standard of proof

If a court was allowed to find a person guilty on the balance of probabilities (the standard of proof generally applied in civil cases) then many more factually guilty persons could be successfully prosecuted, but so too could many more who were factually innocent. If, on the other hand, it was required that guilt be proven beyond any doubt at all, whether reasonable or not, then few successful prosecutions could be brought. This would protect people who were actually innocent, but would allow the vast majority of guilty suspects to escape conviction. The standard of proof required (guilt beyond reasonable doubt) amounts to a compromise between two potentially conflicting aims: to convict the guilty and acquit the innocent. The particular standard chosen expresses a preference for erroneous acquittals over erroneous convictions.[39]

The insistence that a crime or anti-social behaviour be proven 'beyond reasonable doubt' by the prosecution does little to protect defendants if that crime or behaviour is so vague or commonplace that almost anything could come within the definition. Thus s.57 of the Terrorism Act 2000 makes it an offence if the accused 'possesses an article in circumstances which give rise to a reasonable suspicion that his possession is for a purpose connected with the commission, preparation or instigation of an act of terrorism'. There is no requirement to prove that possession *was* for such a purpose but only that there is a reasonable suspicion that this is so. As we shall see in chapter 2, reasonable suspicion is an elastic concept that requires little by way of hard, objective evidence consistent with guilt. Note also that the terms 'article' and 'connected with' could hardly be broader.[40] Some might argue that breadth and elasticity is needed to enable the early disruption of activity that, if not pre-empted, might wreak large-scale death and destruction. But such pre-emptive thinking can also be seen in the definition of low-level crime and disorder. To take the ABI example again, neither the behaviour that prompts the making of the order, nor the behaviour in breach of that order need be criminal in and of itself (although sometimes it is). These problems also apply to 'behaviour liable to cause a breach of the peace' and some unambiguously criminal offences such as behaviour 'likely to cause alarm or distress'.[41] Police officers can 'prove' beyond reasonable doubt that something was 'likely' or 'liable' by stating that they believed it was likely or liable—no other witnesses are needed.

The lesson to be drawn from this section is that, rather than be taken in by oratorical claims concerning supposedly fundamental principles, one must consider in detail the actual rules and their operation. We must, in other words, be alive to the possibility that the rhetorical goals of criminal justice are not necessarily the same as the goals that are

---

[38] See further, Dennis I, 'Reverse Onuses and the Presumption of Innocence: In Search of Principle' [2005] *Criminal Law Review* 901.

[39] For a lengthy discussion and critique see Keane A and McKeown P, 'Time to Abandon "Beyond Reasonable Doubt" and "Sure"' [2019] *Criminal Law Review* 505.

[40] The courts have ruled that paper and electronic documents and records fall within the definition of an 'article': *Rowe* [2007] QB 975, but that, in the interests of legal certainty, there must be some direct connection between possession of the article and its use for terrorism: *Zafar* [2008] 2 WLR 1013. See also the preceding sub-section for an explanation of how the defendant can place a much heavier burden on the prosecution of proving that no non-terrorist purpose existed.

[41] Public Order Act 1986, s.5 (the defendant must have intended or been aware that his or her behaviour was threatening, abusive, insulting or disorderly).

actually pursued. In particular, we have seen that the recent shift towards preventive orders means that proof of guilt is not always a pre-condition of intrusive control by the agents of criminal justice.

1.3 Adversarial and inquisitorial theories of criminal justice

Evidence relating to guilt and innocence has to be gathered, put in some coherent order and then presented. This is done in accordance with rules, principles and policies of criminal procedure and evidence. There are two broad approaches to criminal justice fact-finding—the adversarial and the inquisitorial.[42] The Secret Barrister summed up what immediately springs to mind for most of us who are used to the adversarial system: '*adversarial* being a loose term for the model pitting the state against the accused in a lawyer-driven skirmish for victory played out before an impartial body of assessors … And plenty of wigs.'[43] The adversarial principle that it is for the prosecution to bring a case to court and prove guilt is a characteristic of the English system and of other common law systems such as Australia, Canada and the USA. Civil law systems, such as France or Germany, are generally said to be based on inquisitorial principles. It is also important to acknowledge that each system will also be influenced by other elements of criminal process, such as political aims and contextual factors such as the prevailing socio-political conditions, as we shall discuss in section 1.9.

In an inquisitorial system the dominant role in conducting a criminal inquiry is supposed to be played by the court.[44] A dossier is prepared to enable the judge taking the case to master its details. The judge then makes decisions about which witnesses to call and examines them in person, with the prosecution and defence lawyers consigned to a subsidiary role. In some inquisitorial systems the dossier is prepared (in serious cases) by an examining magistrate (juge d'instruction), with wide investigative powers, but more frequently this is done by the prosecutor and police.

In the 'pure' adversarial system, by contrast, the burden of preparing the case for court falls on the parties themselves. The judge (sometimes with a jury) acts as an umpire, listening to the evidence produced by the parties, ensuring that the proceedings are conducted with procedural propriety, and announcing a decision at the conclusion of the case. If the parties choose not to call a certain witness, then however relevant that person's evidence might have been, there is nothing the court can do about it. The adversarial contest in court thus resembles a game in which truth might appear to be the loser.[45] Indeed, it is sometimes said that adversarial systems focus on proof, and inquisitorial systems on truth.[46] But this is too simplistic. Both systems are concerned with establishing the facts to the required degree of certainty,[47] but they differ on the best way of achieving that end.

---

[42] 'Popular' or 'informal' justice, as found, for example, in African tribal systems, arguably represents a third broad approach. See further Vogler R, *A World View of Criminal Justice* (Aldershot: Ashgate, 2005).

[43] The Secret Barrister, *Stories of the Law and How It's Broken* (London: Macmillan, 2018).

[44] Our discussion here is of an 'ideal type' for in practice there are considerable differences between systems which are labelled 'inquisitorial': Damaska M, 'Evidentiary Barriers to Conviction and Two Models of Criminal Procedure: A Comparative Study' (1973) 121 *University of Penn Law Review* 506. See further Kessler A, 'Our Inquisitorial Tradition: Equity Procedure, Due Process, and the Search for an Alternative to the Adversarial' (2005) 90 *Cornell Law Review* 1181; Hodgson J, *The Metamorphosis of Criminal Justice* (Oxford: OUP, 2020), ch 1.

[45] See Frankel M, 'The Search for the Truth: An Umpireal View' (1975) 123 *University of Penn Law Review* 1031.

[46] See the critique of the adversarial system by a (then) Chief Constable, Pollard C, 'Public Safety, Accountability and the Courts' [1996] *Criminal Law Review* 152, and the reply by Ashworth A, 'Crime, Community and Creeping Consequentialism' [1996] *Criminal Law Review* 220.

[47] It is in this sense that 'truth' must be understood in the discussion that follows. In reality, a criminal trial focuses on whether the evidence of guilt presented meets the 'beyond reasonable doubt' test. If it does not then that is the end of the matter, and the question of whether somebody else might have committed the offence will not be examined further.

Adversarial theory holds that 'truth is best discovered by powerful statements on both sides of the question'[48] which are then evaluated by a passive and impartial adjudicator. This recognises that the events leading up to a criminal offence, and the intentions or knowledge of the parties involved, are always open to interpretation and dispute. The danger in an inquisitorial system is that whoever conducts the investigation (whether the police, a prosecutor or an examining magistrate) will come to favour one particular view of the matter, and that this will influence the construction of the dossier. Material helpful to the accused may be excluded. There is also the danger that a trial judge, having formed an initial view of the case based on a reading of the dossier, will give too much weight to evidence adduced at the trial that is consistent with the pre-existing theory, and too little to that which conflicts with it.

> In one study, two groups of professional judges were compared. They heard identical cases, but one group read the file beforehand and the other did not. All of those who read the file beforehand convicted the defendant. Only twenty-seven per cent of the others did so. The prosecutor's opinion and the documents supporting it strongly influenced prior expectations.[49]

In dossier-based systems the spoken word is so distrusted that once something is memorialised in the dossier it is hard to dislodge that later in, for example, a trial.[50] Far better, according to the adversarial theory, that the judge remain impartial throughout and allow the parties to put forward their interpretations of the facts and law in the way most favourable to them. By opening up a range of possible views, it is more likely that the 'real truth' will emerge. The arguments of counsel hold the case, as it were, in suspension between two opposing interpretations of it. While the proper classification of the case is thus kept unresolved, there is time to explore all of its peculiarities and nuances.[51]

So, while inquisitorial systems are rightly portrayed as involving a pre-eminent commitment to search for the truth, the way in which that search is conducted can shape the 'truth' that is proclaimed in court. Adversarial systems, by contrast, with their emphasis on the parties proving their case, can lose sight of the truth for different reasons: one or both of the parties might deliberately suppress relevant evidence for tactical reasons, or engage in aggressive cross-examination designed to so humiliate or confuse a witness that their evidence will be perceived as unreliable.[52] Or one party (almost invariably the defendant) might lack adequate access to the resources or expertise needed to counterbalance the arguments of their opponent.[53] In practice, there is no reliable evidence on which system is better at getting at the truth, nor is such evidence likely to be obtainable.[54]

---

[48] *Ex p Lloyd* (1822) Mont 70, 72 n.

[49] McEwan J, 'The Adversarial and Inquisitorial Models of Criminal Trial' in Duff A, Farmer L, Marshall S and Tadros V (eds) *The Trial on Trial* (Oxford: Hart, 2004) at p 64. More recently, Zuckerman discusses the problem of cognitive bias in inquisitorial systems. Such bias may shape the way investigations are conducted (Zuckerman A, 'No Justice Without Lawyers—The Myth of an Inquisitorial Solution' (2014) 33 *Criminal Justice Quarterly* 355).

[50] Hodgson J, 'Hierarchy, Bureaucracy and Ideology in French Criminal Justice' (2002) 29 *Journal of Law and Society* 227.

[51] Fuller L, 'The Forms and Limits of Adjudication' (1978) 92 *Harvard Law Review* 353 at p 383. For an accessible exploration of this point see Jackson J and Doran S, *Judge without Jury* (Oxford: OUP, 1995) ch 3.

[52] This has been a particular problem in rape trials, where the adversarial model has come under particular attack. See for example Smith O, *Rape Trials in England and Wales* (London: Palgrave, 2018); and ch 12.

[53] See generally McEwan (2004).

[54] Redmayne M, *Expert Evidence and Criminal Justice* (Oxford: OUP, 2001) p 213, n 92.

Adversarial and inquisitorial models express different conceptions of how power should be allocated in society.[55] These differences result in the adversarial model attaching less weight to the goal of reliable fact-finding than the inquisitorial model, not because that goal is seen as unimportant, but rather because of an acknowledgement that the pursuit of other important aims necessarily implies a reduced relative weighting for 'truth-discovery'.[56] The adversarial model assumes that the state is committed to proving cases against individual citizens in order to fulfil its duty of enforcing the criminal law. In order to guard against the state abusing its powerful position, safeguards must be provided. One such safeguard is an expression of the constitutional doctrine of the separation of powers: the state provides a forum in which one branch of government (the judicial, i.e. the criminal courts) considers the case built and presented by another (the executive, i.e. the police and the prosecution). The passivity of magistrates and judges required by adversarial theory can also be seen as an expression of this mistrust of official power, as can the use of lay people (juries and most magistrates) to deliver verdicts on guilt or innocence. These devices all seek, amongst other things, to guarantee the impartiality of adjudication.

The adversarial model is also sensitive to the need to ensure that prosecution evidence is collected by fair and lawful means. Adversarial systems are trial centred, in that preparation of a case for trial is a principle objective of investigation and evidence gathering. Thus, for example, defence lawyers are meant to play an active part at the investigative stage of a criminal case (advising the suspect, applying for bail, and so forth) and there are limits on the length of time suspects can be held by the police for questioning. The importance attached in an adversarial system to the integrity of the procedures followed in collecting evidence and proving guilt can also be seen in the development of rules of evidence aimed at promoting both the fairness and reliability of verdicts pronounced by a court.[57]

In inquisitorial systems, by contrast, the underlying assumption is that the state can be (largely) trusted to conduct a neutral investigation into the truth. Therefore safeguards such as passive adjudicators, a strict separation of investigative and adjudicative powers, rules of evidence and defence lawyers are seen as less important. Concerns have long been raised about the length of pre-trial detention in France.[58] Leigh and Zedner have noted that 'while nothing in French law requires the over-use of detention, a tendency to do so seems deeply ingrained in the legal culture and doubtless derives from a desire not to release a suspect until the truth has been ascertained'.[59] All too often the supposed safeguards against oppressive police practices offered by judicial or prosecution control of the investigation process is a chimera. Defence lawyers are discouraged from active defence during police interrogation.[60] According to the author of the most in-depth empirical

---

[55] See Damaska M, *The Faces of Justice and State Authority* (New Haven: Yale, 1986) and the accessible discussion by Jackson J, 'Evidence: Legal Perspective' in Bull R and Carson D (eds), *Handbook of Psychology in Legal Contexts* (Chichester: Wiley, 1995).

[56] Damaska M, 'Evidentiary Barriers to Conviction and Two Models of Criminal Procedure: A Comparative Study' (1973) 121 *University of Penn Law Review* 506 at 579–580, n 197.

[57] See generally Roberts P and Zuckerman A, *Criminal Evidence* (Oxford: OUP, 2004).

[58] Fair Trials International, *Pre Trial Detention in France* (2013), available at <https://www.fairtrials.org/wp-content/uploads/Fair_Trials_International_France_PTD_Communiqu%C3%A9_EN.pdf> (accessed 20 October 2020).

[59] Leigh L and Zedner L, *A Report on the Administration of Criminal Justice in the Pre-Trial Phase in England and Germany* (Royal Commission on Criminal Justice, Research Study no 1) (London: HMSO, 1992) p 53.

[60] Blackstock J, Cape E, Hodgson J, Ogorodova A and Spronken T, *Inside Police Custody: An Empirical Account of Suspects' Rights in Four Jurisdictions* (Antwerp: Intersentia, 2014).

study of the French system, judicial supervision does not involve a careful and impartial pursuit of alternative theories and lines of enquiry. Rather:

> The guilt of the suspect is presumed and denials are rejected. Evidence of violence committed on the suspect by the police was ignored and left for the defence to raise at court; the word of the victim or of the police was consistently preferred over that of the suspect; serious cases meant an almost automatic request for a remand in custody, even where the evidence was thin. At trial, the most serious charge which the evidence might support was preferred: the public interest demanded that nothing should risk going unpunished.[61]

The problem of abuse in the inquisitorial system, and doubts about the effectiveness of the juge d'instruction, led to the abolition of this role in Germany in 1975. Corruption amongst investigative judges led to abolition in Italy in 1988, and substantial reforms to the French system were made in 1993 and 2000. Whether adequate safeguards for suspects in France were put in place as a result of these changes seems doubtful, but attempts to abolish the system in France in 2010 were unsuccessful. Reforms to institutional arrangements are unlikely to achieve much so long as the prevailing legal culture assumes the guilt of suspects and prioritises the 'community interest' in the efficient conviction of the guilty.[62]

In order to avoid giving the impression that everything in the English adversarial garden is rosy, in the next section we supplement our account of the theoretical underpinnings of English criminal justice with a short account of its own weed-ridden history.

1.4 Recent trends in criminal justice and crime

In 1981, the Royal Commission on Criminal Procedure (the Philips Commission), originally set up because of the wrongful conviction of three youths for the murder of Maxwell Confait,[63] published its blueprint for a 'fair, open, workable and efficient' system.[64] It recommended that there should be a 'fundamental balance' in criminal justice between the rights of suspects and the powers of the police.[65] Although not all of its proposals were accepted, its report led to the Police and Criminal Evidence Act 1984 (PACE) and the Prosecution of Offences Act 1985. PACE, together with its associated Codes of Practice, provided, for the first time, a detailed legislative framework for the operation of police powers and suspects' rights. The 1985 Act created the CPS to take over the prosecution function from the police. The aim was, in part, to try to ensure that the defects in criminal procedure exposed by the 'Confait Affair'—such as undue pressure on suspects to confess, the lack of legal advice for suspects in police stations, and the absence of an independent check on police decisions—would be eliminated, thereby reducing the risk of further miscarriages of justice.

However, in the years following these Acts of Parliament, a string of both pre- and post- PACE similar cases came to light including the 'Guildford Four', the 'Maguires', the 'Birmingham Six', Stefan Kiszko, Judith Ward, the 'Cardiff Three', the 'Tottenham Three',

---

[61] Hodgson J, 'The Police, the Prosecutor and the Juge d'Instruction' (2001) 41 *British Journal of Criminology* 342 at 357. For full length treatment see Hodgson J, *French Criminal Justice* (Oxford: Hart, 2005).

[62] On the legal culture in France see Hodgson J, 'Codified Criminal Procedure and Human Rights: Some Observations on the French Experience' [2003] *Criminal Law Review* 165. For a detailed analysis of change in Britain and France in particular, see Hodgson J, *The Metamorphosis of Criminal Justice* (Oxford: OUP, 2020), ch 1.

[63] See the official inquiry into what became known as the 'Confait Affair': Report of an Inquiry into the Circumstances leading to the Trial of Three Persons on Charges arising out of the Death of Maxwell Confait and the Fire at 27 Doggett Road, London SE6 (HCP 90) (London: HMSO, 1977).

[64] Royal Commission on Criminal Procedure (RCCP), Report (Cmnd 8092) (London: HMSO, 1981) para 10.1.

[65] RCCP (1981) paras 1.11 to 1.35.

the Taylor sisters, and the 'Bridgewater Four'. Long terms of imprisonment were served by nearly all of the defendants in these cases. The causes of the miscarriages of justice varied from case to case, but common features were the suppression by the police and prosecution agencies of evidence helpful to the defence—which has remained a live issue[66]—incriminating evidence (including false confessions) secured from suspects by the police use of psychological pressure and tricks, deficiencies in the production and interpretation of expert evidence, and the distortion, manipulation and occasional fabrication of prosecution evidence (again, including confession evidence).[67] By implication, a further cause was the inadequate resources available to the defence to guard against or uncover these defects prior to conviction, which is again a matter of contemporary concern.[68] For all these reasons, the adversarial truth-discovery mechanism of hearing powerful arguments on both sides of the question had been undermined. Juries had understandably convicted on the basis of what had seemed in court to be overwhelming prosecution cases.

Some of the people involved in these cases were tried before the changes in the law ushered in by the Philips Commission,[69] but others (such as the 'Cardiff Three', where three young men were wrongly convicted of offences connected with murder of a prostitute)[70] were convicted under the new regime. Also, by July 1993, the convictions of 14 people had been quashed because of irregularities by one particular group of police officers (the West Midlands Serious Crime Squad), most of these being post-PACE cases.[71] The pressure created by these spectacular miscarriages led to the establishment of the Royal Commission on Criminal Justice (the Runciman Commission), which reported in 1993.[72] Yet the Runciman Commission advocated few major changes to the criminal process, arguing that there was no reason to believe that the 'great majority' of verdicts were 'not correct'.[73] Moreover, its recommendations taken overall favoured the interests of the police and prosecution agencies more than those of suspects.[74]

---

[66] Criminal Justice Joint Inspection, *Making it Fair: The Disclosure of Unused Material in Volume Crown Court Cases* (London: HMCPSI, 2017). Disclosure scandals came to a head in 2017 when the trial of Liam Allan, a student accused of rape, collapsed because telephone evidence had not been properly disclosed (Bowcott O, 'Solicitor for student in rape case criticises police and CPS' *The Guardian*, 30 January 2018) and again in the Post Office 'false accounting' debacle of 2020. See ch 7.

[67] For useful accounts of some of the main cases see Rozenberg J, 'Miscarriages of Justice' in Stockdale E and Casale S (eds), *Criminal Justice under Stress* (London: Blackstone, 1992) and Robins J, *Guilty Until Proven Innocent* (Hull: Backbite Publishing, 2018).

[68] See, for example, Smith T and Cape E, 'The rise and decline of criminal legal aid in England and Wales' in Flynn A and Hodgson J (eds), *Access to Justice and Legal Aid: Comparative Perspectives on Unmet Legal Need* (Oxford: Hart Publishing, 2017); Newman D, *Legal Aid Lawyers and the Quest for Justice* (Oxford: Hart Publishing, 2013); Welsh L, 'The Effects of Changes to Legal Aid on Lawyers' Professional Identity and Behaviour in Summary Criminal Cases: A Case Study' (2017) 44(4) *Journal of Law and Society* 559–585.

[69] Those tried before the introduction of PACE include the 'Guildford Four', the 'Maguires', the 'Birmingham Six', Stefan Kiszko, Judith Ward and the 'Bridgewater Four'.

[70] The real murderer was convicted in 2003, 11 years after their convictions were quashed. Three witnesses, who were bullied into giving false evidence against them, were jailed in 2008. Thirteen serving and former police officers faced charges of conspiracy to pervert the course of justice but were acquitted as a result of disclosure failings. A public inquiry into the collapse of the trial concluded, in 2017, that the trial in relation to one of the worst miscarriages of justice in English history collapsed as a result of human errors and called for revision of disclosure guidelines: *The Guardian*, 17 July 2017.

[71] Many of these cases are discussed in Kaye T, 'Unsafe and Unsatisfactory?' Report of the Independent Inquiry into the working practices of the West Midlands Police Serious Crime Squad (London: Civil Liberties Trust, 1991).

[72] Royal Commission on Criminal Justice (RCCJ), Report (Cm 2263) (London: HMSO, 1993).

[73] RCCJ (1993) para 23.

[74] For critiques see Young R and Sanders A, 'The Royal Commission on Criminal Justice: A Confidence Trick?' (1994) 15 *Oxford Journal of Legal Studies* 435; McConville M and Bridges L (eds), *Criminal Justice in Crisis* (Aldershot: Edward Elgar, 1994) and Field S and Thomas P (eds), *Justice and Efficiency? The Royal Commission on Criminal Justice* (London: Blackwell, 1994) (also published as (1994) 21 JLS no 1).

An obvious question raised by this sequence of events is whether the Runciman Commission was right to think that the framework established by PACE and the Prosecution of Offences Act 1985 was basically sound. One view is that something more than mere tinkering was needed if suspects were to be adequately protected, as indicated by continuing patterns of police malpractice and wrongful convictions.[75] An opposite view is that the mid-1980s legislation had already swung the pendulum so far in favour of safeguards for suspects that the ability of the police to bring criminals to justice had been unduly hampered, the occasional dramatic miscarriage or corruption case notwithstanding.

The latter view prevailed under the Conservative government in the years immediately following the publication of the Runciman Commission's report. Taken together, the Criminal Justice and Public Order Act 1994, the Criminal Procedure and Investigations Act 1996 and the Police Act 1997 provided the police and prosecution with important new powers and significantly reduced the rights of, and safeguards for, suspects. The Labour government in power between 1997 and 2010 dismantled suspects' rights and increased police powers at an even greater rate, such as by extending stop and search powers, amending powers to grant bail, altering disclosure provisions and creating gateways for the admissibility of evidence previously presumed inadmissible (such as that of previous convictions), all under the Criminal Justice Act 2003. The torrent of legislation on the subject includes the Crime and Disorder Act 1998, the Youth Justice and Criminal Evidence Act 1999, the Regulation of Investigatory Powers Act 2000, the Police Reform Act 2002, the Criminal Justice Act 2003, the Domestic Violence, Crime and Victims Act 2004, the Serious Organised Crime and Police Act 2005, the Violent Crime Reduction Act 2006, the Serious Crime Act 2007, the Criminal Justice and Immigration Act 2008 and numerous anti-terrorism Acts. When former Prime Minister Blair said that 'the rules of the game are changing' he was not exaggerating.

While the pace of change has slowed with more recent governments, we have continued to see concerted efforts at restructuring criminal justice and creating new offences, such as in the Legal Aid, Sentencing and Punishment of Offenders Act 2012 (LASPO). Recently, new offences of assaulting emergency service workers have been created under the Assaults on Emergency Workers (Offences) Act 2018. Such offences were previously prosecuted under existing laws regarding offences against the person, with the aggravating sentencing factor of the assault occurring against an emergency service worker (in the course of their lawful work). The governments that have followed Labour have, through the creation of such offences, responded to public concerns[76] about offenders and offending by encouraging more severe punishments for specific offences. The inclination to give priority to public protection 'reverses the post-war emphasis on protecting the criminal justice rights of individuals', and undermined ethical concerns about the state's excessive powers over its individual citizens.[77] The trend to introducing narrowly construed, very particular offences was further exemplified by the introduction of the offences of stalking under the Protection of Freedoms Act 2012 and of controlling or coercive behaviour in an intimate or family relationship under the Serious Crime Act 2015. Measures which show that governments are committed to responding to concerns about earlier failures in

---

[75] For evidence of police and prosecution malpractice of a kind likely to contribute to miscarriages of justice see chs 2–7. For accounts of the most notorious miscarriages of justice uncovered in recent times, go to <https://innocent.org.uk/miscarriage-of-justice-cases/> (accessed 28 February 2018).

[76] Whether public concerns about such behaviour are founded in evidence that suggests offending behaviour has in fact increased is contestable in light of crime rates that fell consistently until 2017. See, for example, Tonry M, 'Why Crime Rates Are Falling throughout the Western World' (2014) 43(1) *Crime and Justice*.

[77] Pratt J, 'Risk Control, Rights and Legitimacy in the Limited Liability State' (2017) 57 *British Journal of Criminology* 1322–1339, 1332.

the way offending in domestic contexts was policed and prosecuted are both overdue and welcome. But they also demonstrate that governments have continued a tendency to reactively produce voluminous amounts of criminal justice legislation. They also reveal governments' continuing commitment to punishment as deterrent as opposed to non-criminal justice responses such as education programmes. We can now add the Coronavirus Act 2020 to this list.[78]

Trends in crime are measured in two main ways. In addition to collating the crimes recorded by the police, the government also interviews large representative samples of adult householders about their experiences of victimisation in the last year to estimate roughly how many crimes are not recorded by the police (largely because many victims do not report crimes to the police). Both sets of data are published in what is now known as the Crime Survey for England and Wales (CSEW). Crime levels have tended to fall in most years since 1995, and by 2010 were around their 1981 level. Ordinarily we might expect to have seen crime rates rise as the economic recession that began in 2008 took hold. Figures for the last three months of 2008 were ambiguous, demonstrating that most 'official' crime continued to fall, apart from burglary, which rose by 4%. The 'unofficial' crime total remained stable, but personal thefts rose sharply (unlike burglary, which remained stable).[79]

Until 2017, crime rates had generally continued to fall. The police, however, recorded rises in high harm violent offending and rises were noted in some acquisitive crimes, such as burglary and vehicle-related theft. In mid-2018 violent crime, largely between young ethnic minority men in large cities such as London, had reached epidemic proportions with growing concerns about what can be done. Overall, however, eight in 10 surveyed adults did not report being the victim of any crime surveyed.[80] The crime problem, then, while always a matter of concern, provides no more reason now than it did several years ago to strengthen police powers and reduce the rights of suspects. Much the same can be said of terrorism. England and Wales has for centuries experienced occasional acts of terrorism as well as more concerted terrorist campaigns and it is arguable that the threat posed by Al-Qaeda, Islamic State and other fundamentalist groups is not qualitatively different from that, say, posed in the 1970s and 1980s by the provisional Irish Republican Army (IRA).[81] To the extent that the threat is novel (for example, the use of suicide bombers and vehicles as weapons), most of the laws passed to counter it seem unlikely to be effective, particularly given their breadth and reliance on nebulous concepts such as 'reasonableness' (see section 1.2.2). The avalanche of anti-terrorist laws passed over the last 20 years cannot be justified by the facts, however brute some of those facts are.[82]

More fundamentally, decisions about how much power to give the police and prosecution agencies can never be factually determined but rather express value choices about the appropriate goals of criminal justice, the order in which they should be prioritised, and the appropriate means to achieve them. Is there any way of clarifying the implications of such

---

[78] The new offences that were created under the Coronavirus Act 2020 are niche and will need further research to understand their impact, though there was some early indication that the public and legal experts felt the police were exercising their new powers in an excessive manner. See, for example, Henley C, 'Heavy-handed police are enforcing restrictions that do not exist in law' *The Times*, 16 April 2020.

[79] Home Office (2009c) *Crime in England and Wales: Quarterly Update to December 2008* (London: Home Office Statistical Bulletin 06/09).

[80] Office for National Statistics (2018a) *Crime in England and Wales: Year ending September 2017*, available at: <https://www.ons.gov.uk/peoplepopulationandcommunity/crimeandjustice/bulletins/crimeinenglandandwales/yearendingseptember2017> (accessed 28 February 2018).

[81] See Feldman D, 'Human Rights, Terrorism and Risk: The Roles of Politicians and Judges' (2006) *Public Law* 364 at 367–370; Bonner (2007: 8–10). For a contrary view see Greer, S 'Human Rights and the Struggle against Terrorism in the United Kingdom' (2008) 2 *European Human Rights Law Review* 163.

[82] For a measured analysis see Greer (2008).

choices and thus providing us with the normative material we need in order to come to a more rational decision about the appropriate means and ends of criminal justice?

These were the kinds of problem that, now over 50 years ago, an American writer, Herbert Packer, tackled when he developed his two models of the criminal process: due process and crime control.[83] These models have been used by many commentators on criminal justice as tools of analysis.[84] They have also been subjected to much criticism. In the next section we explain the models, and comment on their strengths and weaknesses.

1.5 Crime control and due process

Packer developed his models to illuminate what he saw as the two conflicting value systems that competed for priority in the operation of the criminal process. Neither purported to describe any specific system, and neither was to be taken as the ideal. Rather, they represented extremes on a spectrum of possible ways of doing criminal justice. Use of the models enables one to plot the position of current criminal justice practices at each stage of the criminal process, as well as to highlight overall trends.

1.5.1 Crime control

In this model the repression of criminal conduct is viewed as by far the most important function to be performed by the criminal process. In the absence of such repression, a general disregard for the criminal law would develop and citizens would live in constant fear. In order to uphold social freedom, the model must achieve a high rate of detection and conviction. But because crime levels are high and resources are limited the model depends for success on speed and on minimising the opportunities for challenge. Formal fact-finding through examination and cross-examination in court is slow and wasteful. Speed can best be achieved by allowing the police to establish the facts through interrogation. To further guarantee speed, procedures must be uniform and routine, so that the model as a whole resembles a conveyor belt in its operation.

The quality control in this system is entrusted in large measure to the police. By the application of their expertise the probably innocent are quickly screened out of the process while the probably guilty are passed quickly through the remaining stages of the process. Indeed, the model goes further in claiming that pre-trial administrative processes are more likely to produce reliable evidence of guilt than formal court procedures. The ideal mechanisms for truncating these procedures are guilty pleas. They eliminate lengthy and expensive trials. The police will thus seek to extract confessions from those whom they presume to be guilty as this makes it very difficult for the suspect to do other than admit guilt at court. For as Packer concludes of the crime control model, 'when reduced to its barest essentials and operating at its most successful pitch, it offers two possibilities: an administrative fact-finding process leading (1) to exoneration of the suspect or (2) to the entry of a plea of guilty.'[85]

The crime control model accepts that some (but not many) mistakes will be made in identifying the probably guilty and the probably innocent, and considers this a price worth paying for the efficient repression of crime. On the other hand, if too many guilty people

---

[83] Packer H, *The Limits of the Criminal Sanction* (Stanford: Stanford UP, 1968) ch 8.
[84] See, for example, McConville M and Baldwin J, *Courts, Prosecution, and Conviction* (Oxford: Clarendon, 1981) pp 3–7; Vogler R, *A World View of Criminal Justice* (Oxford: Routledge, 2016) and the first edition of this book. For refinements and other approaches see, for example, Bottoms A and McClean J, *Defendants in the Criminal Process* (London: Routledge, 1976) pp 226–232; King M, *The Framework of Criminal Justice* (London: Croom Helm, 1981) ch 2; Roach K, 'Four Models of the Criminal Process' (1999a) 89 *Journal of Criminal Law and Criminology* 671 and the rest of this book.   [85] Packer (1968: 162–163).

escaped liability, or the system was perceived to be generally unreliable (as would be the case if it was shown that innocent people were being prosecuted on a large scale) then the deterrent efficacy of the criminal law would be weakened. Limited safeguards against miscarriages of justice, including an appellate system, are therefore accepted as necessary, but primarily in order to promote confidence in the system. Confidence is promoted in part by displaying confidence in itself, so cases are regarded as closed following verdicts in all but the most compelling circumstances.

While the crime control model can tolerate rules forbidding illegal arrests or coercive interrogations (since such rules might promote reliability) those rules should not be enforced through the exclusion, in court, of illegally obtained evidence, or the quashing of convictions simply because the rules have been breached. To let the guilty go free on such technicalities undermines crime control to an unacceptable extent.

1.5.2 Due process

The due process model lacks confidence in informal pre-trial fact-finding processes. Many factors may contribute to a mistaken belief in guilt resulting in the production of unreliable evidence against the suspect. For example, witnesses to disturbing events tend to make errors in recollecting details, or may be animated by a bias that the police either encourage or will not seek to discover. Similarly, confessions by suspects in police custody are as likely to signify psychological coercion by officers convinced they have apprehended the right suspect as they are to demonstrate guilt.[86] Due process therefore insists on formal, adjudicative, adversary fact-finding processes in which the case against the accused is tested before a public and impartial court. Because of this concern with error, the due process model also rejects the crime control desire for finality. There must always be a possibility of a case being reopened to take account of some new fact that has come to light since the last public hearing. Unlike crime control, the due process model insists on the prevention and elimination of miscarriages of justice as an end in itself: 'The aim of the process is at least as much to protect the factually innocent as it is to convict the factually guilty'.[87]

Other values upheld by the due process model include the primacy of the individual citizen, and thus the complementary need for limits on official power. Controls are needed to prevent state officials exercising coercive powers in an oppressive manner even if this impairs the efficiency of the system. In certain situations, concern with abuse of power in the due process model takes precedence over reliability. Suppose, for example, that the police had illegally obtained evidence that established that a suspect had almost certainly committed a murder. The due process model would insist that the evidence be excluded at trial; if there was no other evidence of guilt, the suspect would walk free because of the procedural irregularity. It is only by demonstrating to officials that there is nothing to be gained by abusing power and breaking rules that adherence to them can be guaranteed. The due process model is also concerned with the upholding of moral standards as a matter of principle. In the belief that an important way to encourage and affirm law-abiding behaviour is by example, unlawfully obtained evidence has to be excluded.[88] To do otherwise would be to undermine the moral condemnation conveyed by a finding of guilt.[89]

---

[86] There is a wealth of literature on this issue. See, for example, Henkel L and Coffman J, 'Memory Distortions in Coerced False Confessions: A Source Monitoring Framework Analysis' (2004) 18 *Applied Cognitive Psychology* 567–588.

[87] Packer (1968: 165).   [88] Packer (1968: 231–232).

[89] In his 'reconstruction' of Packer's models, Aranella (1996: 21), points out that: 'A public trial, if fairly conducted, sends its own message about dignity, fairness, and justice that contributes to the moral force of the criminal sanction.' (Aranella P, 'Rethinking the Functions of Criminal Procedure' reprinted in Wasserstrom S and Snyder C, *A Criminal Procedure Anthology* (Cincinnati: Anderson, 1996).

The due process model also upholds the ideal of equality: that everyone should be in the same position as regards the resources at their disposal to defend against a criminal charge. Thus, whenever the system affords a theoretical right for a lawyer to advise or represent a client, the due process model insists that those who cannot afford a lawyer should be provided with one for free. Lawyers play a central part in this model since they should bring into play the remedies and sanctions which due process offers as checks against the operation of the system.

Finally, the due process model is sceptical about the morality of the criminal sanction. It notes that in practice this sanction is used primarily against the psychologically and economically impaired. To seek to condemn and deter these people for their supposedly free-will decision to breach the criminal law smacks of cruel hypocrisy, particularly when there is little attempt to rehabilitate offenders. As Packer puts it, 'doubts about the ends for which power is being exercised create pressure to limit the discretion with which that power is exercised.'[90]

At the risk of over-simplification, one can summarise the main conflict in values between the two models in the following way. Crime control values prioritise the conviction of the guilty, even at the risk of the conviction of some (fewer) innocents, and with the cost of infringing the liberties of suspects to achieve its goals. Due process values prioritise the acquittal of the innocent, even if risking the frequent acquittal of the guilty, and giving high priority to the protection of civil liberties as an end in itself. Further, whereas due process seeks to maximise adversarialism by introducing obstacles and hurdles for the prosecution to surmount at every stage, crime control seeks ways of ensuring that the adversarial contest never gets beyond the encounter between the police and the suspect in the police station. Due process and adversarial ideology thus can work harmoniously together, whereas crime control values tend to subvert adversarial procedures. Indeed, with its emphasis on trusting the police and prosecution to get at the truth in a reliable manner, the crime control model expresses some of the ideological elements which underpin the inquisitorial model. Both models employ powerful arguments and Packer himself suggested that anyone who supported one model to the complete exclusion of the other 'would be rightly viewed as a fanatic'.[91]

1.5.3 What are the goals of crime control and due process?

Some criticisms of Packer's analytical framework (and how it has been used) derive from a misunderstanding about the goals and values each model encompasses.[92] Campbell, Ashworth and Redmayne, for example, suggest that the models should be reconstructed so that crime control would be the purpose of the system, but that pursuit of this purpose should be qualified out of respect to due process.[93] Similarly Smith argues that 'the Crime Control Model is concerned with the fundamental goal of the criminal justice system, whereas the Due Process Model is concerned with setting limits to the pursuit of that goal. Due Process is not a goal in itself.'[94] These criticisms place too much weight on the labels Packer applied to his models. In particular, it is mistaken to regard the due process model as merely a negative model in which the only aim is to protect suspects. The two models share much common ground including the assumptions that the 'criminal process

---

[90] Packer (1968: 171). [91] Packer (1968: 154).
[92] For fuller discussion of abuse of Packer's models see Roberts P, 'Comparative Criminal Justice Goes Global' (2008) 28 *Oxford Journal of Legal Studies* 369 at 378–379, and the third edition of this work at pp 22–25.
[93] Campbell L, Ashworth A and Redmayne M, *The Criminal Process* 5th edn (Oxford: OUP, 2019).
[94] Smith D, 'Case Construction and the Goals of Criminal Process' (1997a) 37 *British Journal of Criminology* 319 at 335. See, to similar effect, Aranella (1996: 19), and Damaska (1973: 575).

ordinarily ought to be invoked by those charged with the responsibility for doing so when it appears that a crime has been committed' and that 'a degree of scrutiny and control must be exercised with respect to the activities of law enforcement officers,... the security and privacy of the individual may not be invaded at will'.[95] It thus follows that both models incorporate the belief that law enforcement is socially desirable[96] (because of its crime preventive effects) and both incorporate the belief that there must be some limits to the power of the government to pursue this underlying aim. The difference between the models, put simply, is about what those limits should be.

Choongh criticises Packer from an empirical standpoint, arguing that neither of his models adequately explains the experiences of a significant minority of those who are arrested and detained at the police station. For these detainees there is never any intention by the police to invoke the criminal process:

> Arrest and detention is not, for this group of individuals, the stepping stone onto Packer's conveyor belt or the first stage of an obstacle course. It represents instead a self-contained policing system which makes use of a legal canopy to subordinate sections of society viewed as anti-police and innately criminal.[97]

He argues that the police are here operating a 'social disciplinary' model, which encompasses the belief that:

> an acceptable and efficient way to police society is to identify classes of people who in various ways reject prevailing norms because it is amongst these classes that the threat of crime is at its most intense ... the police are then justified in subjecting them to surveillance and subjugation, regardless of whether the individuals selected for this treatment are violating the criminal law at any given moment.[98]

Choongh's analysis will be familiar to criminologists who have highlighted political tendencies to 'other' and 'demonise' 'undesirable' sections of society, thereby justifying intensive surveillance and control of such groups[99] (such as through the civil preventive orders discussed earlier). However, Packer was constructing ideal-type models of the criminal process, not of policing; it is not surprising that 'social disciplining' was not central in his analysis, nor that empirical evidence might reveal flaws. Policing encompasses many activities: maintaining surveillance over public space, quelling disorder, finding missing persons, directing traffic and so on. Only some of these are associated with controlling crime and even fewer are necessarily related to the formal criminal process. What Choongh's work usefully does is highlight the way in which the police sometimes use resources provided by the criminal process (such as interrogation powers) to pursue some part of the broader police mission. Nonetheless, Packer was too astute an observer to have overlooked that police powers could be used to subject whole classes of people to surveillance and subordination.[100] Thus he noted that the crime control model rejected the due process idea that arrest should only be allowed when there was reason to believe that a specific

---

[95] Packer (1968: 155–156).
[96] Note the comment by Packer (1968: 163) that the due process model 'does not rest on the idea that it is not socially desirable to repress crime, although critics of its application have been known to claim so.' See also Duff P, 'Crime Control, Due Process and "The Case for the Prosecution" ' (1998) 38 *British Journal of Criminology* 611.
[97] Choongh S, 'Policing the Dross: A Social Disciplinary Model of Policing' (1998) 38 *British Journal of Criminology* 623 at p 625.
[98] Choongh (1998: 627). See also Choongh S, *Policing as Social Discipline* (Oxford: Clarendon, 1997).
[99] See, for example, Wacquant L, *Punishing the Poor: The Neoliberal Government of Social Insecurity* (Durham: Duke University Press, 2009). These issues are discussed further at section 1.9.4.
[100] Packer (1968: 178), also noted that the criminal law itself might be so vaguely defined (e.g. vagrancy and disorderly conduct laws) as to make 'social disciplining' lawful.

individual had committed a specific crime.[101] Rather, 'people who are known to the police as previous offenders should be subject to arrest at any time for the limited purpose of determining whether they have been engaging in anti-social activities . . .'.[102] Second:

> anyone who behaves in a manner suggesting that he may be up to no good should be subject to arrest for investigation: it may turn out that he has committed an offence, but more importantly, the very fact of stopping him for questioning, either on the street or at the station house, may prevent the commission of a crime. As a third instance, those who make a living out of criminal activity should be made to realise that their presence in the community is unwanted if they persist in their criminal occupations; periodic checks of their activity, whether or not this involves an arrest, will help to bring that attitude home to them.[103]

Packer clearly linked these forms of 'social disciplining' to the ultimate goal of controlling crime. So does Choongh, albeit unwittingly.[104] The type of 'social disciplining' documented in Choongh's work highlights an important strand of crime control ideology. But it does not justify the construction of a new model of the criminal process. We will see that this element of crime control philosophy has increased since neoliberal political ideology was adopted by successive governments since the late 1970s.

We have now clarified what adherents to crime control and due process models see as the purpose of criminal justice. Whether one believes the system is (or should be) governed predominantly by due process or crime control values, the purpose of the system would (or should) remain the same: to control crime, but with some protections for suspects. Where one locates an actual criminal process on the spectrum of possibilities represented by the two models depends largely on the nature and extent of those protections.

1.5.4 English criminal justice: due process or crime control?

The English criminal system, like the American, has typically been characterised as one which emphasises adversarial procedures and due process safeguards. In terms of the formal structure we can observe these safeguards intensifying as a person's liberty is progressively constrained.[105] The least constraining exercise of police power is simple questioning of someone who is merely a citizen, not a suspect. Since the questions are not aimed at incriminating the individual no due process protections are needed, but no compulsion can be exercised either. The police are here in an information-gathering or inquisitorial mode.

As soon as the police have any reason to suspect the individual an 'adversarial' relationship is formed; the citizen becomes also a suspect. The police now have the task of collecting evidence of what they believe the suspect has done so that this can be proven to the satisfaction of the courts. To assist them in this task the law provides them with various powers and, in order to guard against the misuse of these powers, due process protections begin. In general, only if there is 'reasonable suspicion' can coercive powers be exercised to search or to arrest a suspect.[106] On arrest the suspect is usually taken to a police

---

[101] Packer (1968: 176).
[102] Packer (1968: 177). Compare with Choongh (1998: 628): 'Having arrested individuals once, this in itself becomes reason for keeping them under surveillance . . . an individual becomes permanently suspect rather than a suspect for a particular offence.'
[103] Packer (1968: 177).   [104] See Choongh (1998: 629, 632) for example.
[105] All the points made in this sub-section are discussed in later chapters, at which point supporting references are provided.
[106] Citizens can also be asked to attend police stations to be interviewed voluntarily, and the police have made greater use of voluntary attendance requests in recent years. The status of voluntary attendees is somewhat of a grey area, although many would be arrested and formally become suspects if they refused to attend voluntarily. This issue is discussed further in ch 3.

station and detained. This requires further due process justification because civil liberties are further eroded by detention and its associated procedures such as interrogation and strip-searches. Only if detention is adjudged to be 'necessary' (i.e. in a broad sense of furthering the investigation) can it be authorised. If detention is authorised, further forms of due process protection come into play, such as the right to legal advice. In order to charge and prosecute a detainee, more evidence is required and further protections are provided—vetting of the case by the CPS and a grant of legal aid to prepare a defence. In order to convict there must be yet more evidence (proof beyond a reasonable doubt). The increasingly stringent nature of these protections is in accordance with Packer's portrayal of due process as an obstacle course with each successive stage presenting impediments to carrying the citizen any further along the process. This should mean that few factually innocent persons are found legally guilty, or are carried too far down the course, but it will also mean that many factually guilty persons will be ejected from the system for lack of the required standard of evidence.

If we look at the way the system actually operates, however, it displays many features characteristic of a crime control model. Decisions to arrest and stop-search are often made on police instinct rather than reasonable suspicion,[107] and detention to obtain a confession is habitually and uniformly authorised. Perhaps most telling is the fact that the majority (approximately 70% in Crown courts,[108] and 76% in magistrates' courts[109]) of defendants who are prosecuted plead guilty and forego their right to an adversarial battle. The prosecution evidence is not tested, and 'proof' beyond reasonable doubt is constituted by the plea itself. The probability in such a system is that many more factually innocent persons will be found legally guilty, and that many more factually guilty persons will be convicted, than if the system actually operated in the formal manner described earlier. In Packer's imagery, the system operates as a conveyor belt, moving suspects through a series of routinised procedures that lead, in the vast majority of those cases that reach court, to conviction.

Packer's conclusion[110] in the American context was that the actual operation of the criminal process conformed closely to crime control, but that the law governing that process (as developed, in particular, by the US Supreme Court) expressed due process ideology. He identified a gap, in other words, between the law in books and the law in action. But as Packer himself pointed out, it was perfectly possible for the Supreme Court to change tack and develop case law that expressed crime control values, as we later address in the English context. Weisselberg argues that such a change of tack has effectively occurred in America as the Supreme Court has encouraged police practices undermining safeguards afforded to suspects.[111] If the rules themselves were in harmony with the crime control model, then there would be no need for the police to break them in order to achieve their central goal (if such it is) of repressing crime efficiently. The only gap that would then exist would be between the law in books and due process ideology.

The question of where on the spectrum between crime control and due process English criminal justice is today to be located must, therefore, take account of both the formal law as laid down in statutes and case law, and the actual operation of the system by officials

---

[107] For a thorough discussion of policing culture that highlights these issues, see Bowling B, Reiner R and Sheptycki J, *The Politics of the Police* 5th edn (Oxford: OUP, 2019).

[108] Ministry of Justice *Criminal court statistics (quarterly): July to September 2017* available at <https://www.gov.uk/government/statistics/criminal-court-statistics-quarterly-july-to-september-2017> (accessed 28 February 2018).

[109] Soubise L, 'Prosecuting in the Magistrates' Courts in a Time of Austerity' (2017) *Criminal Law Review* 847.

[110] Packer (1968: 239–240).

[111] Weisselberg C, 'Mourning Miranda' (2008) 96 *California Law Review* 1519.

operating within that legal framework. The first edition of this book, published in 1994, attempted to do this and concluded that the criminal process was far more oriented towards the crime control model than surface appearances might suggest, that there was a historical drift towards the crime control model, but that due process inspired safeguards remained, and would continue to remain, important. Subsequent events have confirmed that assessment, although the drift towards crime control has accelerated. For example, we shall see that some stop-search powers can be used lawfully even without reasonable suspicion. We will also see greater restrictions on due process rights, such as reduced access to legal aid to secure representation that can further undermine other due process rights, such as the right to silence.

Packer's models are the most enduring theoretical framework of criminal justice.[112] However, Packer's models do not identify all the major interests in the criminal process, nor all the major conflicts between them. Although still valuable, these models constitute an inadequate framework for the analysis of criminal justice. The most influential alternative is the human rights approach.

1.6 The fundamental (human) rights approach

The human rights approach starts from the position that citizens are rational, rights-bearing subjects. State power must therefore be subject to limits that respect the dignity of the individual. It follows that 'balancing' conflicting criminal justice aims and interests should not be driven by consequentialist calculations of which set of arrangements would produce the most overall benefit to society. Rather, individual rights must be assigned some special weight in the balancing process. The goal of bringing cases to effective trial in the service of crime control is authoritatively constrained by human rights principles instead of (as in Packer's models) merely compromised to a varying extent by conflicting due process principles. This philosophical position has been translated into positive law through the United Nations Declaration of Human Rights (1948) and various regional human rights instruments. For the UK, human rights law derives from the European Convention on Human Rights (ECHR).

The UK has been bound at the international level by the ECHR since 1953.[113] For over 40 years thereafter, breaches of the rights set out in the Convention could only be challenged directly before the European Court of Human Rights (ECtHR) in Strasbourg. If the Court ruled that a breach had occurred the UK was obliged to amend the offending law or practice. The recognition that this procedure was cumbersome, slow, and embarrassing to domestic political and judicial elites eventually led to the passing of the Human Rights Act 1998.[114] This requires British courts to take account of the Convention and the decisions of the European Court. If a common law precedent is found to be inconsistent with the Convention, the latter must be followed. The position with statutes is different, reflecting a concern to maintain the supremacy of Parliament over the courts. Thus, statutory provisions should be interpreted so far as is possible in accordance with the ECHR, and

---

[112] Roach K, *Due Process and Victims' Rights: The New Law and Politics of Criminal Justice* (Toronto: University of Toronto Press, 1999b).

[113] In addition, much UK criminal justice is subject to European Community law and, therefore, to judicial supervision from the European Court of Justice. See, e.g., Baker E, 'Taking European Criminal Law Seriously' [1998] *Criminal Law Review* 361, though this is unlikely to survive Brexit from January 2021.

[114] Young J, 'The Politics of the Human Rights Act' (1999) 26(1) *Journal of Law and Society* 27. Recent Conservative governments have toyed with the idea of repealing the Human Rights Act 1998 and reverting to the historical position of removing direct access to the ECtHR.

the Supreme Court (and its predecessor, the House of Lords) has repeatedly emphasised the radical and expansive nature of this interpretive obligation.[115] But if a court finds that a UK statute cannot be interpreted in accordance with the Convention, the court may make a 'declaration of incompatibility'. This does not invalidate the offending legislation. A 'fast-track' procedure allows (but does not require) Parliament to amend the incompatible legislation.[116]

If, post Brexit, the Human Rights Act 1998 is repealed, as some exit campaigners hoped, the English courts will still be bound by the principles of the ECHR, as they were between 1953 and 1998. But it will be more difficult for citizens to enforce their rights under the ECHR than it is now. The full implications of Brexit on human rights are uncertain and difficult to predict. There is likely to be a significant impact on police and judicial co-operation in relation to cross border crime,[117] and data sharing.[118] The relationship between criminal law and human rights in the post Brexit landscape will be constitutionally complex, with competing issues of sovereignty, and the benefits of cross border co-operation at stake.[119] Nevertheless, the rights enshrined in the ECHR and elaborated through decisions of the ECtHR will still provide criteria to evaluate our criminal justice system.[120] There are a number of problems with using them in this way though.

1.6.1 Vagueness and inconsistency

Many ECHR rights are vague in the sense that their scope is uncertain. Take, for example, the Art 3 prohibition of inhuman or degrading treatment. Is it degrading to be arrested in public, or to have saliva scraped from inside one's mouth, for example? This vagueness is, of course, a quality of all legal rules, since they are inevitably 'open-textured' to a greater or lesser degree.[121] Rules always require interpretation and consideration of how they are to be applied in any given situation. But, like most international treaties, ECHR rights are particularly vague (and modest in scope), reflecting the need to achieve consensus amongst states with radically different legal traditions. One consequence of this is that no-one can simply ask the ECtHR (or a domestic court) to review the compatibility of national laws with the Convention in the abstract. Rather, specific individuals have to make a case that their human rights were infringed on a specific occasion.[122] This means that judgments are sensitive to the facts of their particular cases and may not provide definitive or indicative answers to the question of whether a law or legal practice in itself might be in breach of the Convention (in other factual circumstances or all circumstances). Even under ideal

---

[115] E.g. *A (No 2)* [2001] UKHL 25, [2002] 1 AC 45; *Ghaidan v Godin-Mendoza* [2004] UKHL 30.

[116] A useful introduction to the Act and its reception is provided by Wadham J et al, *Blackstone's Guide to the Human Rights Act 1998* 4th edn (Oxford: OUP, 2007).

[117] Historically the UK has resisted calls for more integration of policing expertise, and that resistance may strengthen after Brexit with negative effects on the effective policing of crime (Weyembergh A, 'Consequences of Brexit for European Union Criminal Law' (2017) 8(3) *New Journal of European Criminal Law* 284–299).

[118] Garside R, Grimshaw R, Ford M and Mills H, *UK Justice Policy Review* vol 8 (London: Centre for Crime and Justice Studies, 2019).

[119] Mitsilegas V, 'European Criminal Law After Brexit' (2017) 28 *Criminal Law Forum* 219–250.

[120] For a full explanation of the interaction between human rights and criminal justice, see Emmerson B, Ashworth A, Macdonald A and Summers M, *Human Rights and Criminal Justice* (London: Sweet and Maxwell, 2012).

[121] Hart H, *The Concept of Law* (Oxford: Clarendon, 1961). A good example is the 'fair trial' right (Art 6): see for example, *Al-Khawaja v UK* (2012) 54 EHRR 23 discussed in Hoyano L, 'What is Balanced on the Scales of Justice? In Search of the Essence of the Right to a Fair Trial' [2014] *Criminal Law Review* 4. This is discussed further in ch 9.

[122] See Munday R, 'Inferences from Silence and European Human Rights Law' [1996] *Criminal Law Review* 370.

conditions it would take much litigation before the parameters of human rights requirements become reasonably clear. But the ECtHR is overloaded and lacks the capacity to adjudicate most applications it receives in the way it would need to in order to shape the law coherently and consistently with its earlier decisions.[123] Moreover, the Human Rights Act merely requires domestic courts to take account of (rather than regard themselves as bound by) decisions of the ECtHR. Even were this not so, the particularly open-textured nature of the Convention rights and the fact they often conflict with each other and with other important interests leaves an enormous amount of discretion to judicial elites in determining 'our human rights' and judges will naturally differ in their determinations of such issues. Uncertainty of scope, inconsistency and incoherence are thus key features of Convention rights, notwithstanding the large degree of consensus around some issues (e.g. use of physical violence to extract a confession is impermissible).

1.6.2 Human rights can be 'qualified'

While the term 'human rights' might be thought of as connoting something inviolable, this is not true of most Convention rights. The exceptions are the rights to life (Art 2) and not to be subjected to torture or inhuman or degrading treatment or punishment (Art 3). These are 'absolute' in the sense that they cannot be legitimately traded off against other rights or interests, or derogated from during times of national emergency. There is, however, a high threshold to be reached before the police will be in breach of Art 2 obligations to prevent death as a result of their negligence.[124] At the other extreme are 'qualified' rights, such as freedom of association (Art 11) and privacy (Art 8). For example, no invasion of Art 8 is allowed unless it is:

> in accordance with the law and is necessary in a democratic society in the interests of national security, public safety or the economic well-being of the country, for the prevention of disorder or crime, for the protection of health or morals, or for the protection of the rights and freedoms of others.

It is difficult to think of a law infringing a qualified right that could not be defensibly linked to the furtherance of the many 'interests' and goals of 'protection' listed here,[125] so the real question tends to be whether such an infringement is 'necessary in a democratic society'. This 'proportionality test' requires that infringements with rights must be limited and proportionate to the aim sought to be secured. Thus, a major infringement of a Convention right to secure some marginal increase in crime control should always fail this test. Whether the proportionality test is difficult for the state to satisfy in practice is debatable, however, as we shall see throughout this book. For example, in chapter 6 we show that the human rights era has made little difference to the ability of the police to invade people's privacy through the use of electronic surveillance ('bugging') devices.

---

[123] Greer S, 'Protocol 14 and the Future of the European Court of Human Rights' [2005] *Public Law* 83; Greer S, *The European Convention on Human Rights: Achievements, Problems and Prospects* (Cambridge: CUP, 2006). Also see Amos M, 'The Impact of the Human Rights Act on the United Kingdom's Performance before the European Court of Human Rights' (2007) *Public Law* 655 at 657 and 671.

[124] *Hertfordshire Police v Van Colle* [2008] UKHL 50; *Michael and Others v South Wales Police and Another* [2012] EWCA Civ 981. In the latter case, the Court of Appeal dismissed the negligence claim but upheld the Art 2 claim which would allow the Michael family to proceed to trial on that issue. Both decisions were appealed to the Supreme Court, which upheld the decision that the Art 2 claim should be allowed to proceed to trial in Strasbourg (*Michael* [2015] UKSC 2). As of April 2019 the case had not yet reached the ECtHR.

[125] '... there is hardly a case in which either the domestic courts or Strasbourg has found the state to be acting for an illegitimate aim, so broad are the specified categories': Phillipson G, 'Bills of Rights as a Threat to Human Rights: The Alleged "Crisis of Legalism"' (2007) *Public Law* 217 at 220.

1.6.3 Human rights can be 'derogated' from

Most Convention rights come somewhere between 'qualified' and 'absolute' rights. These 'strong' rights include the right to liberty and security of the person (Art 5) and the right to a fair trial (Art 6). Art 15 of the ECHR provides that, at a time of 'public emergency threatening the life of the nation' the state can take measures derogating from (i.e. in breach of) these 'strong' rights. Such measures must be 'strictly required by the exigencies of the situation'. These tests are far more easily satisfied than one might imagine given the drastic imagery they embody. Thus, in the 1970s, the UK entered a derogation in respect of the 'emergency' legislation prompted by the situation in Northern Ireland and its related breaches of the Art 5 criteria governing the legality of arrest and extended detention. The derogation was adjudged valid by the European Court on successive occasions.[126] This derogation was finally withdrawn on 19 February 2001. You might think that there would be a change in political and legal culture when the Labour government 'brought rights home' through the passing of the Human Rights Act 1998. But no: the government registered a new derogation from the Convention for its new legislation soon after (see section 3.3.3 for discussion).

The scope for derogation makes the human rights framework unstable. Several states derogated from the ECHR in order to address the Covid-19 pandemic.[127] However, even without a formal derogation, the ECtHR is still able to take into consideration the context and the provisions of international humanitarian law when interpreting and applying the provisions of the ECHR, meaning that lack of a formal derogation does not necessarily make breach of the provisions unlawful.[128] As different levels of court may differ on this question, and the conditions of the 'emergency' are bound to shift over time, this creates yet more uncertainty and inconsistency, rendering attempts to evaluate criminal justice in accordance with human right standards a speculative exercise.

1.6.4 Human rights offer little more than a minimalist safety net

Domestic courts usually interpret the ECHR in minimalist ways that do not interfere with domestic criminal justice laws and practices. Since they do not show a similar reluctance to interfere in some other areas of social policy,[129] it is difficult to attribute this minimalism to a concern with upholding parliamentary supremacy or as demonstrating deference to the supposedly specialised knowledge and skills of the Executive (although no doubt these factors play a part too). Rather, the judges' assessments of when the community interest in law enforcement outweighs human rights usually express crime control values.[130]

---

[126] *Ireland v UK* (1978) 2 EHRR 25; *Marshall v United Kingdom* (Application no 41571/98, Judgment of Court 10 July 2001). See generally Marks S, 'Civil Liberties at the Margin: the UK Derogation and the European Court of Human Rights' (1995) 15 *Oxford Journal of Legal Studies* 68.

[127] Holcroft-Emmess N, 'Coronavirus: States Derogating to Suspend Human Rights Obligations', (OxHRH Blog, 27 March, 2020) available at <http://ohrh.law.ox.ac.uk/coronavirus-states-derogating-to-suspend-human-rights-obligations/> (accessed 20 October 2020). See also European Court of Human Rights *Factsheet—Derogation in time of emergency* March 2020 Available at <https://www.echr.coe.int/Documents/FS_Derogation_ENG.pdf> (accessed 20 October 2020). At the time of writing, it is unclear whether the powers in the Coronavirus Act 2020 will require a derogation to be lodged.

[128] *Hassan v The United Kingdom* (Application no 29750/09) (2014).

[129] See recent analysis of the judiciary in McConville M and Marsh L, *The Myth of Judicial Independence* (Oxford: OUP, 2020). For brief discussion of how the judges are more willing to protect rights of a cultural nature than those which challenge political or economic arrangements, see Lustgarten L, 'Human Rights: Where Do We Go From Here?' (2006) 69(5) *Modern Law Review* 843 at 848.

[130] For an early analysis see Ashworth A, 'Criminal Proceedings After the Human Rights Act: The First Year' [2001] *Criminal Law Review* 855. See also the critique of *Brown v Stott* [2001] 2 WLR 817 by Ashworth A and Redmayne M, *The Criminal Process* 3rd edn (Oxford: OUP, 2005) p 41, which, they say, set 'the tone for many of the subsequent decisions under the Human Rights Act.'

As Ewing and Tham observe: '… the standard at which the level of rights' violations is set is now so low that even serious restraints on liberty can cross the hurdle of legality with relative ease.'[131] The government's own Department for Constitutional Affairs noted in 2006 that 'the Human Rights Act has not seriously impeded the achievement of the Government's objectives on crime, terrorism or immigration' and added that arguments 'that the Human Rights Act has significantly altered the constitutional balance between Parliament, the Executive and the Judiciary have been considerably exaggerated.'[132] As you read through this book, note where, when and why the ECtHR and domestic courts use the ECHR and HRA to limit government legislation, and make your own minds up.

Admittedly, the courts, Parliament, and all other public authorities must now incorporate the human rights framework into their decision-making.[133] But even this brief discussion of governmental and judicial decision making shows that the ECHR leaves a huge amount of room for manoeuvre. This should not be taken as implying that human rights are unimportant. They provide a legal safety-net, preventing the state from creating the kind of harsh and repressive criminal justice typical of totalitarian states. The influence of the ECHR should be seen as much in what the state has not done in the criminal justice arena as in what it has done. But while the ECHR 'safety net' must be welcomed, we must also recognise that it has little influence beyond that.

1.6.5 Human rights coverage is patchy

A further problem with using human rights as evaluative criteria is that they provide no guidance on numerous important and controversial questions such as should interrogation be judicially controlled, should juries or other lay elements always have a role in trials, and should decisions to prosecute be made by law enforcers or lawyers? Even supporters of the ECHR recognise that in many respects the protection it offers to human rights is deficient.[134] For example, it makes virtually no special provision for the rights of vulnerable groups of suspects, such as children and young people or the mentally disordered, nor is there any explicit reference to the interests of victims or witnesses. The ECtHR has made the deficiency good to some extent by stating that the Art 6 right to a fair trial applies to victims and witnesses as well as the accused (see section 1.7 and chapter 12). The ability of the human rights approach to take this kind of issue into account is a major advance on the Packer models, where the *Accused v State* spectrum has little place for victim considerations. But how far should it go? Guidance issued by the ECtHR indicates that Art 6 does not explicitly require courts to take the interests of witnesses into consideration, but that signatories' criminal proceedings should be organised in such a way that the interests of victims and witnesses are not unjustifiably impaired.[135] This seems to require some sort of case sensitive balancing act by the domestic courts, who we already know are given

---

[131] Ewing K and Tham J-C, 'The Continuing Futility of the Human Rights Act' (2008) *Public Law* 668 at 682.

[132] Department for Constitutional Affairs, *Review of the Implementation of the Human Rights Act* (2006a) available at <http://www.justice.gov.uk/docs/full_review.pdf> p 4, (accessed 5 January 2010), also cited by Ewing and Tham (2008: 691).

[133] Various mechanisms have been put in place to achieve this, e.g. a Parliamentary Joint Committee on Human Rights that assesses the implications for human rights of proposed legislation; s.19 of the Human Rights Act 1998 requires Ministers in charge of a Bill to state their view as to whether the measure is compatible with Convention rights; and some of the most controversial anti-terrorism legislation is kept under a variety of forms of extra-governmental review.

[134] See, for example, Campbell, Ashworth and Redmayne (2019).

[135] ECtHR (2018) *Guide on Article 6 of the European Convention on Human Rights*, available at <https://www.echr.coe.int/Documents/Guide_Art_6_criminal_ENG.pdf> (accessed 21 October 2020).

wide discretion and tend to uphold crime control values. While the Council of Europe has issued various Recommendations about the rights of victims,[136] we shall see that the scope and substance of victims' rights remains elusive.

1.6.6 The maximalist (legalistic) alternative and the margin of appreciation

All of this will be disappointing to those academics, practitioners and pressure groups who would like to see human rights play a much greater part in criminal justice. These 'maximalists' attempt to solve the 'no more than a safety net' and the 'patchy coverage' problems by seeking (through doctrinal argument and test-cases that draw on those arguments) to elaborate and extend the scope of the rights enshrined in the ECHR and thus (through the HRA 1998) in English law. In an unusually powerful cross-fertilisation of ideas between academic and practising lawyers, many specific legislative and common law rules in almost every area of criminal justice have been tested against the ECHR, and some detailed laws have been 'read off' from it. Cases have been decided by the ECtHR and by English courts under the HRA on, to take just a few examples, the reverse onus, drawing inferences of guilt from silence, and legislative presumptions against bail for very serious crimes.[137] Yet, as we shall see, few of these legal challenges are successful. This is because in deciding between 'maximalist' and 'minimalist' positions, the ECtHR, through its 'margin of appreciation' doctrine, subjects a state's assessment of the need to invade rights to a relatively undemanding standard of judicial review. In recent decisions, the ECtHR has emphasised that the general duty of the court to uphold the right to a fair trial will depend on the circumstances of the case, leaving domestic courts much room for manoeuvre on the basis of particular facts.[138] Even when states derogate from the ECHR the ECtHR rarely interferes, again judging that states are best placed to judge when invasions of rights are 'needed' in order to deal with an 'emergency'. Thus:

> On one level, it is impossible to regard Strasbourg rulings otherwise than as pronouncements of the very minimum protection to be afforded ... The margin of appreciation afforded to all States in all aspects of the Convention is well established ...[139]

When policy-makers draft legislation and guidance they intend it to be 'human rights compliant' in this minimalist sense. Gearty says of those elements of the Terrorism Act 2000 that did not require derogation:

> It is noteworthy that none of these concessions to human rights law involved the bald elimination (as opposed to mere procedural elaboration) of powers desired by the executive; right from the start the human rights standard set by the Act [the HRA] ... has been a relatively low one, with the consequence that only a rather undemanding jump by the executive brings its repressive practices within the zone of human rights compliance.[140]

---

[136] See Recommendation No. R (83) 7, discussed in McBride J, 'The case law of the European Court of Human Rights on victims' rights in criminal proceedings' Council of Europe, available at <https://rm.coe.int/council-of-europe-georgia-european-court-of-human-rights-case-study-vi/16807823c4> (accessed 21 October 2020), which acknowledges that coverage of the rights of victims is anything but comprehensive. See further McBride J, *Human rights and criminal procedure: the case law of the European Court of Human Rights* (Strasbourg: Council of Europe, 2018).

[137] On the reverse onus see section 1.2.1. The other examples are dealt with in chapters 5 and 8 respectively.

[138] See *Ibrahim and others v UK* [2016] ECHR 750.

[139] Ormerod D, 'ECHR and the Exclusion of Evidence: Trial Remedies for Article 8 Breaches' [2003] *Criminal Law Review* 61 at 65.

[140] Gearty C, '11 September 2001, Counter-terrorism, and the Human Rights Act' (2005) 32 *Journal of Law and Society* 18 at 21–22.

UK courts are usually (though not always) similarly minimalist.[141] By contrast, 'maximalists' want as much criminal justice law and policy as possible to be 'read off' from the ECHR. They rightly see the 'human rights compliance' approach of the policy-makers as giving them almost as much room to manoeuvre as they had before the HRA, allowing a drift towards the crime control end of the spectrum. We characterise 'maximalists' as 'legalistic' because, whenever the ECHR is open to interpretation, they attempt to argue that the law *is* what they (and, often, we) *want* it to be. But we will see throughout this book that neither courts nor governments are taken in by this.[142] Thus maximalism is unlikely to reverse the crime control trend.[143]

1.6.7 Conflicts between rights and with the priorities of the state

In its purest form a human rights framework would simply establish inviolable rights to every category of person and in every type of situation where significant freedom is threatened. This would ignore two major problems. First, the more rights there are, the more scope there is for some rights to conflict with others. Second, a real criminal justice system has to be reasonably effective in bringing cases to trial and convicting when there is strong legally obtained evidence.

Both problems are tackled in part via the hierarchy of 'absolute', 'strong' and 'qualified' rights discussed earlier. If a case involved a conflict between the right to a fair trial (strong) and to privacy (qualified) the former would trump the latter. And effectiveness can be balanced against 'qualified' rights and used to justify derogation from 'strong' rights. But what about when rights in the same position in the hierarchy clash? The classic example is when the rights of complainants to a fair trial clash with those of defendants. This first arose in the domestic courts in *A*, which concerned the prohibition of the use of sexual history evidence in rape cases: a vital element in the right of complainants to a fair trial, but arguably undermining of the defendant's right to a fair trial.[144] Although the impact of the Victims' Code created by the Domestic Violence, Crime and Victims Act 2004 on human rights appears to be negligible (see section 1.7 and chapter 12), the more rights are assigned to victims and witnesses (and maximalists, remember, seek to assign more and more rights to deserving parties) the more clashes like this there will be.

---

[141] 'It is of course open to Member States to provide for rights more generous than those guaranteed by the Convention but such provision should not be the product of interpretation of the Convention by national courts... The duty of national courts is to keep pace with the Strasbourg jurisprudence as it evolves over time...' per Lord Bingham in *R (on the application of Ullah) v Special Adjudicator* [2004] UKHL 26; [2004] 2 AC 323 at [20]. For critique see Lewis J, 'The European Ceiling on Human Rights' (2007) *Public Law* 720.

[142] See, again, Lord Bingham in *R (on the application of Ullah) v Special Adjudicator* [2004] UKHL 26; [2004] 2 AC 323 [20].

[143] This is one reason why some people argue that human rights policies, and the laws that stem from them, should be argued for at the political level rather than in the courts. See, for example, Gearty C, *Can Human Rights Survive?* (Cambridge: CUP, 2006); Campbell T, (2006) *Rights: A Critical Introduction* (London: Routledge, 2006); Munro V, 'Of Rights and Rhetoric: Discourses of Degradation and Exploitation in the Context of Sex Trafficking' (2008) 35 *Journal of Law and Society* 240.

[144] [2001] 2 Cr App R 351. The decision predictably provoked controversy amongst academics. Nicol D, 'Law and Politics after the Human Rights Act' (2006) *Public Law* 722 at 739, for example, saw the House of Lords as 'blinded by its zeal for the rights of male defendants' showing scant regard for the rights of women, 'the underprivileged majority of the population'. Hickman T, 'The Courts and Politics after the Human Rights Act: A Comment' (2008) *Public Law* 84 at 93, responded by arguing that the House 'came down fearlessly in favour of the vulnerable minority with the most immediate call on the courts for protection; namely accused persons...': Among the many later cases on the point are *W* [2005] Crim LR 965 and *Gjoni* [2014] EWCA Crim 691. See also *G* [2008] UKHL 37 for an example of a clash of Art 8 rights held by a complainant and an accused in relation to the offence of rape of a child under 13. All further discussed in ch 10.

The way human rights advocates deal with the demands of effectiveness is illustrated in Ashworth's discussion of why the principle that the innocent should be protected against wrongful conviction should not be regarded as absolute.[145] First, he acknowledges that attempts to introduce ever-more elaborate safeguards against wrongful conviction could only be achieved by diverting resources from other important social needs, such as education, health, and social security (which could themselves be described in the language of human rights). To put it bluntly, how many hospitals are we prepared to sacrifice for the sake of achieving some marginal (and unquantifiable) increase in the protection of innocent people against wrongful conviction? Second, the more elaborate safeguards against wrongful conviction became, the more difficult it might be to convict the actually guilty. Ashworth's conclusion is that the criminal process should be organised in such a way as to render the risk of wrongful conviction 'acceptably low', and that this objective necessitates research both into the sources of error and the consequences of erecting safeguards against them.[146] This leaves open the questions of what is to count as 'acceptably low', how much we are prepared to spend on achieving this, how much we are prepared to infringe the rights of victims in erecting such safeguards, and how we are to know when the actually guilty have been acquitted (and the innocent protected).

Overall, the hierarchy in the ECHR provides inadequate answers to the problems of conflicts of rights and with state priorities. As Pratt argues, there is scope for human rights to be '*redefined* according to the new framework of knowledge in which they are situated'.[147] The more maximalist the approach, the greater will be these problems. But the more minimalist the approach, the more gaps that will need to be filled. Beyond a fairly basic 'safety net' there will remain considerable room for debate over the specific content of most laws and policies, allowing a vast amount of permissible space between the crime control and due process ends of Packer's spectrum, not to mention much leeway concerning the rights of victims. We are therefore still left with the question of how to evaluate the criminal justice system.

1.6.8 Individualistic rights and legalistic remedies

A final problem is that the ECHR offers highly individualistic remedies to abuses of power. Its core method of enforcement relies on somebody pursuing a complaint about the treatment they have suffered.[148] This may not be appropriate where abuses of power are taking place against a disorganised and marginalised community as a whole, particularly where members of that community have no faith in law, lawyers or legal institutions. For in such a situation, no-one may be prepared to complain about what is happening, at least not until some considerable time has elapsed. Even then, an infringement might take years to establish; in the meantime, members of a whole community may continue to have their rights abused. Also, it is unrealistic to expect the courts, in their limited and time-pressured role of deciding individual cases, to develop research-based, principled and

---

[145] Ashworth A, *The Criminal Process* 2nd edn (Oxford: OUP, 1998a) pp 50–52.

[146] Ashworth (1998a: 51).

[147] Pratt J, 'Risk Control, Rights and Legitimacy in the Limited Lability State' (2017) 57 *British Journal of Criminology* 1322–1339, 1324.

[148] Under s.7 of the Human Rights Act 1998 those who can invoke Convention rights in legal proceedings are restricted to 'victims' of unlawful acts. This means that campaigning groups, such as Liberty do not have standing in their own right to bring proceedings. Instead, they seek to identify suitable emergent 'test cases' where they can either act on behalf of the 'victim' or intervene in the case as an interested 'third party': Maiman R, '"We've Had to Raise Our Game": Liberty's Litigation Strategy under the Human Rights Act 1998' in Halliday S and Schmidt P (eds), *Human Rights Brought Home* (Oxford: Hart, 2004).

satisfactory guidelines for, for example, law enforcement bodies on what might constitute an abusive policing method.[149] Another way of guarding against abuse is excluding from trial evidence obtained in breach of the ECHR. But much of the ECtHR's case law on remedies is 'confusing and unconvincing'[150] and UK courts do not exclude evidence that is obtained in breach of 'qualified' rights. Rights without adequate remedies are largely meaningless.

In addition to legalistic remedies such as are offered under the ECHR, we need proactive methods of guarding against systemic abuses, e.g. the committee established under the 1989 European Convention for the Prevention of Torture and Inhuman or Degrading Treatment or Punishment. The committee may visit the prisons and police stations of any member country and report on conditions that may be in breach of Art 3 of the European Convention on Human Rights. Thus, prisoners in England and Wales, a marginalised group if ever there was one, were found to be on the receiving end of practices that breached this Article.[151] In 2016, the committee made numerous recommendations to UK authorities regarding inadequate safeguards in English prisons.[152] But this does not cover all the rights supposedly protected by the European Convention. In some fields of social life regulatory agencies have been created to encourage, monitor and, more exceptionally, enforce (or assist individuals in enforcing) compliance with legal norms—for example, the Equal Opportunities Commission, the Commission for Racial Equality and the Disability Rights Commission, now brought together under the Equality Act 2006 as the Equality and Human Rights Commission (EHRC).[153] In the field of criminal justice such generic institutions are supplemented by more focused regulatory bodies such as government inspectorates and the Independent Office for Police Conduct (see chapter 11).

Regulatory bodies have grown substantially in power and importance over the last 20 years or so. As Lustgarten observes, 'human rights scholars have focused far too much on courts and the judiciary.... [T]he primary mechanism for securing what legal rights try to achieve is the harnessing of the power of state administrative institutions, not recourse to the courts to stop abuses or to goad resisting governments into taking faltering steps.'[154] Thus, in evaluating the operation of criminal justice, and in thinking about how to protect the interests embodied in human rights[155] we need to look at how regulatory bodies might most effectively encourage the police and prosecution agencies to respect rights (and what might make the latter choose to do so anyway). But we need to be realistic about this. Governments can undermine the power of regulatory bodies by starving them of resources,[156] or can control their activities by determining both their agendas and those of

---

[149] See Ashworth A, 'Re-drawing the Boundaries of Entrapment' [2002] *Criminal Law Review* 161, especially at pp 178–179. In the non-crime field see *HL v UK* 45008/99 (5 October 2004) discussed by Clements L, 'Winners and Losers' (2005) 32(1) *Journal of Law and Society* 34 at p 35.

[150] A judgment made by Ashworth in the context of ECtHR cases on the implications of breaches of Convention rights on the fairness of any subsequent trial. See his commentary on *PG and JH v United Kingdom* [2002] Crim LR 308 at 310.

[151] See further Evans M and Morgan R, 'The European Convention for the Prevention of Torture: Operational Practice' (1992) 41 *International and Comparative Law Quarterly* 590.

[152] *Council of Europe* (2017). See <https://www.coe.int/en/web/cpt/-/cpt-publishes-report-on-its-uk-visit-criticism-levelled-at-spiralling-violence-and-lack-of-safety-in-prisons-and-inadequate-safeguards-to-protect--pati?desktop=true> (accessed 21 October 2020). The UK response can be accessed on the same site.

[153] The Equality Act 2010 further consolidated anti-discrimination legislation.

[154] Lustgarten (2006: 854).

[155] For valuable essays on this theme see Galligan D and Sandler D, 'Implementing Human Rights' in Halliday and Schmidt (2004); Douzinas C, 'Left or Rights?' (2007) 34 *Journal of Law and Society* 617.

[156] Parliament created a Human Rights Commission for Northern Ireland under the Northern Ireland Act 1998. It has not been particularly successful, in part because the legal and financial resources provided to it by the government have proved inadequate: Livingstone S and Murray R, 'The Effectiveness of National Human Rights Institutions' in Halliday and Schmidt (2004). And non-police enforcement agencies have been especially badly hit by 'austerity' (see ch 7).

the agencies they are supposed to regulate. Despite these constraints, government inspectorates in the criminal justice field have uncovered problems that have led to progressive change, and some of our critique of criminal justice in subsequent chapters draws on their reports.[157] But the agenda set by successive governments does not prioritise human rights, and Prime Minister Johnson has not (yet) shown any commitment to the ECHR.[158]

1.7 Victims

We have noted that the human rights model has only occasionally and briefly dealt with the role of victims, and the due process and crime control models have little to say about them. At the time Packer was writing in the late 1960s, few criminologists gave much thought to victims. But surveys in the 1980s demonstrated their importance in reporting crime to the police, providing information on likely suspects, and acting as witnesses in prosecutions.[159] They also revealed that victims became increasingly dissatisfied with the criminal process over time.[160] Failures to keep them informed about the progress of 'their' case were felt particularly keenly. This is important from an instrumental standpoint as research also suggests that where victims perceive that the values and goals of the criminal process are insensitive to their interests, they are correspondingly less likely to come forward and participate in criminal justice.[161] This realisation led to calls for reform in police practices, pre-trial procedures and in sentencing.

Criminal justice changed slowly. The Victim's Charter, first published in 1990, was symbolically significant in setting out the services a victim could expect from various criminal justice agencies. As we shall see, the Charter and more recent developments, such as the Victims Code, make a lot of promises, but stop short of bestowing enforceable rights on victims.[162] But these 'service rights' do make a concrete contribution to the well-being of victims without undermining the rights of suspects and defendants. We shall also see that victims have also become more involved in decisions about 'their' cases. These 'procedural rights' are far more controversial. Like 'service rights' they are not generally enforceable. This is partly because the adversarial system envisages a contest between the state, representing the public interest, and the individual suspect. This structure does not easily accommodate a third party input such as that of the victim.

Are victims better served by a due process or crime control model of adversarial justice? At first sight the crime control model appears to embody a greater concern for the victim, except where it is distorted by managerialist targets. It offers the prospect of a higher rate of conviction and, by disposing of cases expeditiously through encouraging defendants to plead guilty, reduces the need for victims to come to court and give evidence.

---

[157] Look in the bibliography for reports by, for example, HM CPS Inspectorate. In the field of penal policy the HM Prisons Inspectorate has played a vital role in keeping the values of humanity and decency alive.

[158] Stone J, 'Boris Johnson refuses to commit to keeping UK in human rights convention' *The Independent*, 5 March 2020.

[159] See, for example, Hough M and Mayhew P, *Taking Account of Crime* (Home Office Research Study no 111) (London: HMSO, 1985).

[160] Shapland J et al, *Victims in the Criminal Justice System* (Aldershot: Gower, 1985). Rock P, 'Victims' Rights' in Vanfraechem I, Pemberton A and Mukwiza Ndahinda F, *Justice for Victims: Perspectives on Rights, Transition and Reconciliation* (Abingdon: Routledge, 2014).

[161] See van Dijk J, 'Implications of the International Crime Victims Survey for a Victim Perspective' in Crawford A and Goodey J (eds), *Integrating a Victim Perspective within Criminal Justice* (Aldershot: Ashgate, 2000).

[162] Davies P, 'Victims: continuing to carry the burden of justice' (2015) 76 (Summer) British Society of Criminology Newsletter.

This is particularly important in cases involving violence, children, sexual offences and other forms of assault, where giving evidence in public, particularly in cross-examination, may prove highly distressing. A clear example is rape, where the previous sexual history of the victim was in the past often treated by the courts as relevant in some general sense to the issue of consent. There have been major changes over the last 20 years, discussed further in chapters 10 and 12. However, problems remain, as illustrated in, for example, the Ched Evans case.[163] Police failures in relation to victims of sexual offences have recently been highlighted again by the Supreme Court judgment in the case of *DSD and NBV*, which found that the police had breached human rights provisions in failing to take seriously and properly investigate two allegations made against black cab rapist John Worboys.[164] This illustrates one problem with the 'crime control' model—it leaves the police to decide what are the most important crimes in which to invest time and money, and their judgements are sometimes out of step with those of the rest of us.

Understandably, some victims want to have 'their day in court' and some defendants—some of whom are innocent—refuse to plead guilty. Pressure to make the trial experience less of an ordeal for victims has thus mounted. Monitoring of the reasons for ineffective hearings was introduced in the criminal courts following a critical report by the National Audit Office in 1999.[165] This monitoring revealed that an estimated 22,000 cases failed in 2002/3 due to non-attendance of the victim or other witness. As a result the government set up the *No Witness, No Justice* project which involved the police and CPS supporting witnesses more closely through the prosecution process, including arranging pre-trial familiarisation visits to the courts, and helping with travel and child-care. The project was judged a success in reducing witness non-attendance and increasing guilty pleas,[166] but the courtroom is still a scary place for witnesses.[167]

The initiative is also one-sided. The idea that a defence witness might need help with travel or care arrangements or that their presence at court would serve the interests of justice is overlooked by both the initiative and the report. 'No witness, no justice' can thus be deconstructed as meaning 'no prosecution witness, no conviction'. Also it is not self-evident that satisfaction with the criminal justice system will be increased by using witnesses as a means to the end of extracting guilty pleas from defendants. Sometimes inroads have been made into the due process rights of the defendant in order better to protect the vulnerable victim. For example, the law now allows the admission of documentary (which includes videotaped) evidence in some cases, including where the statement is made to a police officer and the maker does not give oral evidence through fear.[168] And some victims are now allowed to give their evidence behind screens, or outside the actual trial in its entirety.[169] But, like a see-saw, as trial procedures become more just or bearable for victims, the defendant's ability to contest the prosecution case may become increasingly undermined. These special measures 'inevitably carry the risk of creating the impression that the defendant is too terrifying to be faced directly.'[170] Moreover, when evidence is admitted solely in documentary form the defence is given no opportunity to cross-examine the

---

[163] *R v Ched Evans (Chedwyn Evans)* [2016] EWCA Crim 452.

[164] *Commissioner of Police of the Metropolis (Appellant) v DSD and another (Respondents)* [2018] UKSC 11. Discussed further in ch 7.   [165] National Audit Office (1999).

[166] PA Consulting, *No Witness, No Justice—National Victim and Witness Care Project: Interim Evaluation Report* (December 2004) p 4.

[167] See Jacobson J, Hunter G and Kirby A, *Inside Crown Court* (Bristol: Policy Press, 2015) and ch 12 of this edition.   [168] See ss.23–26 of the Criminal Justice Act 1988.

[169] Section 28 Youth Justice and Criminal Evidence Act 1999; Munro V, *The impact of the use of pre-recorded evidence on juror decision-making: an evidence review* (Edinburgh: Scottish Government (Crime and Justice), 2018); and see ch 12.   [170] McEwan (2004: 61).

maker of the statement concerning its contents. This makes it less likely that defendants can win in court, and thus less likely that they will contest the matter in the first place.

Such measures have been held to be compatible with the Art 6 right to a fair trial so long as the rights of the defence are curtailed as little as possible.[171] That rider notwithstanding, it is evident that crime control and concern for victims can be made to walk hand in hand. The rhetoric of victims' rights has proved a powerful criminal justice policy-making tool, so much so that it has been argued by some that victims' rights are harnessed for crime control. Roach for example argues that a punitive model of victims' rights has emerged replicating some of the assumptions of crime control. He states: 'Victims rights have become the new rights bearing face of crime control'.[172] The rights of victims are pitted against the due process claims of defendants as if a conflict between the two were inevitable.[173]

The benefits that the due process model offers victims are more subtle than those tendered by crime control. Typical crime control techniques employed to secure guilty pleas are offers of reduced charges or reduced sentences. To take the example of rape again, charge bargaining may result in victims learning to their horror that the legal process has labelled the act in question as some lesser wrong such as indecent assault. Similarly, sentence discounts for pleas of guilty may result in convicted offenders receiving a more lenient penalty than victims consider just.[174] Due process, by contrast, opposes such strategies, making it likely that, where there are convictions, the offences proved and the sentences imposed will more accurately reflect victims' suffering—and also giving victims the opportunity to give an account to the court. Some vulnerable victims are more concerned that their story be heard and that they be taken seriously than that they be protected from the rough and tumble of an adversarial trial. Many learning disabled victims, for instance, want to make their public accusation even if the poor memory or communication skills that are a result of their disability reduce the chances of conviction.[175]

More fundamentally, with the due process model's insistence on proof of (rather than belief in) guilt, it offers superior protection to that achieved by crime control against miscarriages of justice. A wrongful conviction represents an injury to the victim (and to wider society), as well as to the defendant, because it means that the offender has not been correctly identified and convicted. When Stefan Kiszko was cleared in 1992 of the murder of Lesley Molseed after spending 16 years in prison, her father summed up the family's feelings: 'For us, it is just like Lesley had been murdered last week.' As counsel for Mr Kiszko put it: 'We acknowledge their pain in having to listen to some of the details surrounding their daughter's death and the new pain of learning that her killer has not, after all, been caught.'[176] In addition, the lengthy campaigns usually needed to bring miscarriages of justice to light must make it nigh impossible for those victimised to put their experiences behind

---

[171] For example, the ECtHR has made clear that evidence not subject to cross-examination *should not* be the sole or main evidence on which a conviction is founded, though if a conviction is based solely or decisively on hearsay evidence, this is not automatically a breach of Art 6. See further *Al-Khawaja and Tahery v UK* (Application no 26766/05 and 22228/06); *Riat* [2012] EWCA Crim 1509.

[172] Roach (1999b: 31–32).

[173] Sanders A and Jones I, ' The Victim in Court' in Walklate S (ed), *Handbook of Victims and Victimology* (Cullompton: Willan Publishing, 2012) pp 282–309.

[174] Manikis M, 'Recognizing Victims' Role and Rights during Plea Bargaining: A Fair Deal for Victims of Crime' (2012) 58 *Criminal Law Quarterly* 411; Alge D, 'Negotiated Plea Agreements in Cases of Serious and Complex Fraud in England and Wales: A New Conceptualisation of Plea Bargaining?' (2013a) 19(1) Web JCLI.

[175] Sanders A et al, *Victims with Learning Disabilities* (Oxford: Oxford Centre for Criminology, 1997).

[176] *The Guardian*, 18 February 1992. Similarly, when the three surviving members of the 'Bridgewater Four' had their convictions quashed after serving 19 years in prison, one of them observed: 'Not only have the police been devious and deceitful by getting innocent men in prison; far worse, after having a child killed the police have deceived Mr and Mrs Bridgewater': *The Guardian*, 22 February 1997.

them. And once a conviction has been quashed, reopening and solving a long-closed case is far from easy. Lesley Molseed's actual killer was finally convicted in November 2007, 32 years after her murder.

But while systems in which crime control values predominate may convict more factually innocent persons than would due process-based systems, the former model would also convict far more factually guilty persons. Overall, more victims will be able to see 'their' offenders brought to justice, albeit of a flawed kind, in a crime control-oriented system. Thus, the dilemma that Packer highlighted through the use of his two models of criminal justice exists also in relation to arguments about the treatment of victims. The claims of victims must be weighed against the competing claims of efficiency, defendants, and the need to preserve the moral integrity of the criminal process. However, in weighing the social costs of 'wrongful' convictions and acquittals against each other, it is important to remember that the interests of victims do not fall solely onto one side of the scales.

It must also be recognised that people who report alleged crimes to the police are not always victims. Shop owners have been known to burn down their own premises in order to cash in on their insurance policies. Business people have sometimes staged robberies and burglaries for the same reason, or in order to cover up earlier asset losses through their own fraud or thieving. False allegations of rape are undoubtedly rare, but they happen.[177] Our natural sympathy for victims of crime should not blind us to the fact that one of the objects of the 'adversarial model' is to discover whether prosecution witnesses, including 'victims', are telling the truth or not. A system in which complainants were treated with kid gloves (as happened in Carl Beech's case, discussed in section 1.2), or were allowed to decide the fate of suspects and defendants, would be as indefensible as one which ritually humiliated them.

In earlier sections we saw that conventional theoretical frameworks (including those of human rights) see the main purpose of criminal justice as being to control crime with due process restraints operating to a greater or lesser extent in a subsidiary fashion. Both purposes—crime control and restraints on power—can, as we have seen, work against the interests of victims. Only a 'victim centred' model of criminal justice would prioritise the interests of victims. As Cavadino and Dignan have noted, such a model has been proposed but never implemented, even experimentally.[178] Victim-centred models argue for replacing adversarial justice in which the state prosecutes citizens in the name of the public interest with civil procedures that would be initiated by victims. Its obvious weakness 'is its failure to acknowledge that an offence may have broader social implications which go beyond the personal harm or loss experienced by the direct victim'.[179] For ourselves, we do not believe that the claims of victims, powerful though they are, should be allowed to over-ride all other considerations discussed in this chapter. At present, victim concerns are increasingly thrown into the pot indiscriminately, leading to an even more tangled web of irreconcilable demands and priorities than existed hitherto. The interests of victims do need to be taken into account but in a systematic fashion.

In reality, just as most people are victims of crime at least once in their adult life, so most people also offend at some time in their lives, many people do so many times, and many are accused of this by the police. One third of all men and 9% of women born in 1953 were convicted of at least one non-Road Traffic Act offence before the age of 46.[180]

---

[177] See discussion in Hail-Jares K, Lowrey-Kinberg B, Dunn K and Gould J, 'False Rape Allegations: Do they Lead to a Wrongful Conviction Following the Indictment of an Innocent Defendant?' (2018) *Justice Quarterly*.

[178] Dignan J and Cavadino M, 'Towards a Framework for Conceptualising and Evaluating Models of Criminal Justice from a Victim's Perspective' (1996) 4 *International Review of Victimology* 153 at p 165.

[179] Ibid: 165.

[180] Prime J et al, *Criminal careers of those born between 1953 and 1978*, Home Office Statistical Bulletin 4/01 (London: Home Office, 2001).

Just think how many committed offences and got away with them, as only a small minority of reported crimes end in conviction, and reported crimes are a tiny minority of the total number of crimes committed. And who are the victims of crime? Disproportionately young working class men and members of ethnic minorities—the groups who are also disproportionately represented among convicted offenders.[181] The very people who, as victims, crime control adherents would protect are those people whose freedom would be sacrificed the next day when they are, or are suspected of, offending.

Sometimes the overlap in the two categories is complete. We refer throughout the book to the murder of Stephen Lawrence, a black teenager, in 1993. One aspect of this tragedy, and one of the reasons why the successful prosecution of the murderer took many years, was that when the police arrived they treated his friend, Duwayne Brooks, as a suspect and ignored his frantic pleas to look for the murderers in the direction he was pointing. He was later charged with numerous public disorder offences following a protest about the way the police conducted the investigation (but he was never convicted). The police eventually acknowledged his victim status, apologised for a catalogue of errors and paid £100,000 compensation. His solicitor commented 'Mr Brooks felt that because he was a young black man he was treated as a suspect and not a victim and witness.'[182] The idea that his freedom would be more or less valuable depending on which of these categories we eventually agreed he belonged to is ludicrous.

Much successful policing depends on information and co-operation from the community. Without community support the police would be even less effective than they are now. But support is not guaranteed, and most people have a deeply ingrained sense of 'fairness' and 'justice' which enables them to accept results they regard as wrong if they feel the process by which they were achieved was fair.[183] That is one reason why it is so important that the police respect the rule of law. If society divided neatly into offenders and the rest, the way offenders are treated by the police might not harm the way 'the rest' viewed the police, and their co-operation might not be jeopardised. But very large numbers of people are both occasional offenders (and even more are occasional suspects) and occasional victims. The overlap between suspect-communities and victim-communities means that if the police needs to keep the victim-community on its side, it also needs to do the same for the suspect-community. Treating suspects fairly is the best way to persuade them to respect, and thus co-operate with, the law in future. In other words, adherence to due process and the human rights of suspects and defendants can be of instrumental value in preventing and detecting crime as well as of value in itself.[184]

Over the last 10–15 years police authority has come to be thought of largely in terms of procedural justice and police legitimacy. In simple terms, police legitimacy is defined as the sense of obligation that citizens feel to obey the police and other legal authorities. However, it also more complex than this. Drawing on Beetham,[185] for example, numerous scholars have extended this understanding of police legitimacy to include more than simply an expressed consent to being policed by citizens. They also point to the importance of the normative justifiability of power, that is, whether the rules policing agents employ are premised on shared beliefs between them and policed populations, i.e. do the police

---

[181] Drake D and Henley A, '"Victims" Versus 'Offenders' in British Political Discourse: The Construction of a False Dichotomy' (2014) 53(2) *Howard Journal* 141–157. These issues are discussed further in chs 10 and 12.

[182] *The Guardian*, 10 March 2006.

[183] Tyler T, *Why People Obey the Law* (New Haven: Yale University Press, 1990).

[184] See further Young (2008).

[185] Beetham D, *The Legitimation of Power (Issues in Political Theory)* (London: Palgrave Macmillan, 1991) pp 15–16.

and citizens have a shared sense of what is right and wrong. A growing body of empirical research has shown some important links between procedural justice—that is the quality of treatment (e.g. dignity and respect), quality of decision-making (e.g. in which citizens have a voice) and trustworthiness of police motivations (e.g. whether the police are seen as trying to do their best)—and police legitimacy. In particular, it has been repeatedly shown that the fairness of encounters is what matters most to public perceptions of police legitimacy. So procedurally just treatment of citizens by the police—involving the interlinked concepts of the quality of treatment, the quality of decision-making and perceived motivations of the police—is of greater importance to police legitimacy than other things, such as assessments of police effectiveness or the favourableness of outcomes to citizens or the risk of being caught. This in turn significantly predicts the likelihood that someone will comply with the police both in the short- and long-term. However, there is also growing recognition that legality is an important, albeit non-constitutive, component of police legitimacy.[186] Beetham asserts that 'power can be said to be legitimate in the first instance if it is acquired and exercised in accordance with established rules'.[187]

1.8 Promoting freedom: the overriding purpose

In earlier editions of this book, it was argued that the point of protecting victims, offenders, and, indeed, anyone affected by crime and the justice system is primarily to protect and enhance freedom.[188] Why make it a crime to thieve or assault? Because the losses and hurts they cause are (among other things) losses of freedom—freedom to enjoy one's possessions, to walk the streets without fear, and so forth. We seek to convict thieves and violent offenders in the hope that the punishment or treatment consequent upon conviction will reduce their propensity to commit crime, and in the expectation that censuring their wrongdoing will reinforce everyone else's law-abiding instincts and behaviour. Either way the freedom of past and potential future victims should be enhanced through having their fear of crime reduced. In the same way, what is the point of protecting suspects and defendants, innocent or guilty? Again, protection is not a goal in itself, but a means to the end of promoting their freedom. And why do we insist that the police must obey the rule of law? Because their failure to do so undermines our sense that we live in a free society, where state officials cannot invade our lives in an arbitrary manner.

We are similarly committed to protecting human rights as set out in the ECHR, although we remain sceptical about maximalist attempts to elaborate and extend these rights. But we have seen that this is really a safety net approach. Like criminalising and punishing, and the protection of suspects and victims, human rights are not goals in themselves. In other words, maximising freedom requires the protection given by basic human rights, along with other rights and the suppression of crime. To put this another way, to maximise human freedom, we must value justice and fairness.

We approach the enhancement of freedom through criminal justice by arguing that it be achieved by methods that take account of the real circumstances in which they operate.

---

[186] See Tankebe J, Reisig MD and Wang X, 'A Multidimensional Model Of Police Legitimacy: A Cross-Cultural Assessment'(2016) 40 *Law and Human Behavior* 11–22; Bottoms A and Tankebe B, 'Beyond Procedural Justice: A Dialogic Approach to Legitimacy in Criminal Justice' (2012) 102(1) *Journal of Criminal Law and Criminology* 119–170; Jackson J, Huq Aziz Z, Bradford B and Tyler T, 'Monopolizing Force?: Police Legitimacy and Public Attitudes Towards the Acceptability of Violence' (2013) *Psychology, Public Policy and Law* 13–14.

[187] Beetham (1991: 16).

[188] Note here the use of the word 'primarily'. We accept that other human values are important too (such as equality, welfare and so forth). We are well aware that freedom, like human rights, is a contestable concept and can take negative or positive forms.

Due process mechanisms and crime control powers need to be sensitive to the context within which they operate. Searches of suspected drug-dealers that are carried out in such an oppressive, arbitrary and discriminatory way that they provoke widespread rioting and long-term alienation of whole neighbourhoods from the police do not enlarge freedom but undermine it. The lawful use of arrest powers in a non-discriminatory manner that cannot be shown to detect or prevent a significant amount of crime does not enlarge freedom but undermines it. Due process mechanisms that do little to protect suspects, but cause humiliation to victims or impede the police from detecting serious crime, do not enlarge freedom but undermine it. Layers of bureaucracy that add nothing to due process protections and that divert criminal justice officials from achieving legitimate goals do not enlarge freedom but undermine it.

To summarise, a freedom approach starts with the understanding that criminal justice practices are inherently coercive or involve significant invasions of privacy. However, problems such as imperfect information, the pressures of time, and personal prejudices increasingly detract from professionals' ability to finely weigh up what maximises freedom in any given situation. While adherence to rules designed to enhance freedom is likely in the long-run to promote freedom more effectively than the act-consequentialist alternative,[189] austerity measures and efficiency drives tend to encroach on the ability of those we entrust to weigh up the best interests of all the parties at any given time.

Balancing freedoms is obviously difficult, particularly as freedom is so hard to measure.[190] But it can be done. We develop this idea further at the end of the chapter, and throughout the book.

1.9 Neoliberalism: managerialism, the rise of actuarial justice and austerity

The main elements of criminal justice—the police, CPS, and the courts, and (though not covered in this book) the probation, prisons and youth justice services—are part of the public sector, financed predominantly by public revenue. The vast bulk of defence work is similarly paid for out of the public purse in the form of legal aid. Like the rest of the public sector, criminal justice has been much influenced by the 'new public management' promoted by successive governments from the early 1980s onwards.[191] The main motivating force for this programme was an ideological preference for the disciplines of the market to achieve value-for-money and control public expenditure.[192] Efficiency, effectiveness and economy became the trinity (the 'Three E's') that public sector officials were required to worship. Among the main mechanisms borrowed from the private sector in this programme were the fostering of 'consumer' power, the introduction of competition

---

[189] These ideas are worked out in more detail in the context of prosecutor behaviour in Young R and Sanders A, 'The Ethics of Prosecution Lawyers' (2005) 7(2) *Legal Ethics* 190.

[190] But it is arguably possible to measure freedom empirically: Carter I, *A Measure of Freedom* (Oxford: OUP, 1999).

[191] The phrase 'new public management' was coined by Christopher Hood, in 'A Public Management for All Seasons?' (1991) 69(1) *Public Administration* 3–19 to explain how public sector reforms in many English-speaking countries since the early 1980s emphasised explicit performance measures, outputs, and competitive private sector management styles. See further McLaughlin E and Murji K, 'The End of Public Policing? Police Reform and "the New Managerialism" ' in Noaks et al (eds), *Contemporary Issues in Criminology* (Cardiff: University of Wales Press, 1995).

[192] See the discussion by Savage S and Charman S, 'Managing Change', in Leishman et al (eds), *Core Issues in Policing* (Harlow: Longman, 1996).

in the provision of services to those 'consumers', the setting of clear objectives which would allow each service provider to be audited on their performance and (in theory) greater autonomy for local 'managers' and service-providers to enable them to be more responsive to consumer demand.

New public management has impacted on all criminal justice agencies. On coming to power in 1997 the Labour government reshaped the agenda of managerialism by promoting a wide range of programmes and devices designed above all to prevent crime and manage risk. The Crime and Disorder Act 1998 created a long list of civil preventive measures to manage risk (discussed earlier) but also, more generally, it required local authorities and the police to work together in formulating and implementing local strategies to reduce crime and disorder. Other bodies, such as probation services, health authorities and police authorities, were also required to co-operate in this endeavour. Performance targets were established to measure the extent to which local strategic objectives were achieved.

To take the police as one example, from the mid-1980s onwards chief police officers and now Police and Crime Commissioners have been obliged to formulate objectives and priorities for their force which reflect the wishes and needs of local citizens. Through their inspection work, Her Majesty's Inspectors of Constabulary Fire and Rescue Services (HMICFRS) (formerly HMIC) are required to report on how effectively chief police officers identify and respond to policing problems. Since 2015, HMICFRS has conducted annual assessments of the effectiveness, efficiency and legitimacy of police forces, known as PEEL assessments.

Many theorists have seen in such developments further evidence of the rise of what they refer to (variously) as 'the new penology', 'actuarial justice', 'the new regulatory state', the 'risk society' or 'neoliberalism'.[193] In basic terms, Stedman-Jones defines neoliberalism as 'a free market ideology based on individual liberty and limited government', which connects 'human freedom to the actions of rational, self-interested actors in a competitive market place'.[194] He defines neoliberalism as meaning less state, more personal responsibility and stress on the significance of free markets, and he connects these ideas to University of Chicago economists of the 1950s, such as Milton Friedman.

Wacquant goes deeper, defining neoliberalism as a 'transnational political project' which has four 'institutional logics': (1) 'economic deregulation'; (2) 'welfare state devolution, retraction, and recomposition'; (3) 'the cultural trope of individual responsibility'; (4) 'an expansive, intrusive, and proactive penal apparatus'.[195] That is to say there is not so much deregulation as re-regulation of economic action,[196] as well as state intervention in other areas of society, especially in relation to punishment. So rather than the state playing less of a role in citizens' lives, the state is regarded as governing 'better' through new sites and modes of governance, such as through the welfare system, crime,[197] the penal state,[198]

---

[193] There is an enormous literature associated with these terms. Accessible entry points include Braithwaite J, 'The New Regulatory State and the Transformation of Criminology' (2000) 40(2) *British Journal of Criminology* 222; Garland D, ' "Governmentality" and the Problem of Crime' in Smandych R (ed), *Governable Places: Readings on Governmentality and Crime Control* (Aldershot: Ashgate, 1999); Ericson R and Haggerty K, 'Governing the Young', in the same collection; and Feeley M and Simon J, 'Actuarial Justice: The Emerging New Criminal Law' in Nelken D (ed), *The Futures of Criminology* (London: Sage, 1994).

[194] Stedman-Jones D, *Masters of the Universe: Hayek, Friedman, and the Birth of Neoliberal Politics* (Princeton: Princeton University Press, 2012) p 2.

[195] Wacquant L, *Punishing the Poor. The Neoliberal Government of Social Insecurity* (Durham, NC: Duke University Press, 2009) pp 306–307.

[196] Harcourt B, 'Neoliberal Penality: A Brief Genealogy' (2010) 14 *Theoretical Criminology* 74, 87.

[197] Simon J, *Governing Through Crime* (Oxford: OUP, 2007) pp 4–5.

[198] Garland D, *The Culture of Control: Crime and Social Order in Contemporary Society* (Chicago: University of Chicago Press, 2001) pp 203–204.

cheap credit and debt[199] and insecurity and surveillance.[200] Harvey also emphasises the ideological quality of neoliberalism, which embeds ideas about the centrality of the market into everything we do, such that it 'becomes incorporated into the common-sense way many of us interpret, live in, and understand the world'.[201]

There has been a growing emphasis on deterring and preventing crime through the monitoring, manipulation and control of situations and populations deemed, in the aggregate, criminogenic. Garland also notes that recent crime control policies tend to be directed towards the exclusion, rather than re-integration, of those who appear to threaten the status quo in contemporary societies.[202] Private security guards, CCTV, improved car and home security devices, better street lighting, the closer regulation of 'deviant' or threatening groups (unlicensed traders, the homeless, disorderly youth, 'neighbours from hell', 'bogus' asylum seekers and so forth) all provide evidence of this pre-emptive trend. As Garland puts it: 'Whereas older strategies sought to govern crime directly, through the specialist apparatus of criminal justice, this new approach entails a more indirect form of government-at-a-distance, involving "interagency" cooperation and the responsibilization of private individuals and organizations.'[203] As ours is a textbook about the 'specialist apparatus of criminal justice' rather than about crime control in general, we will confine discussion of these new strategies to their impact on that apparatus—for instance, encouraging a crime-preventive mentality in public policing, and affecting the way in which the police use their powers ostensibly aimed at detecting individual offenders.[204]

In accordance with s.77 Police Reform and Social Responsibility Act 2011, chief constables and the then newly created (and elected) Police and Crime Commissioners (PCCs) are now required to balance local and national police priorities via the Strategic Policing Requirement.[205] The requirement for chief constables and PCCs to determine local policing priorities aimed to ensure that police forces were better equipped to deal with local need but within an overall Home Office governance framework. Funding is partially contingent on such priorities being met, which is consistent with governmental demands for efficiency that require 'higher levels of performance from public sector workers on the basis of target driven objectives'.[206] Consequently, success was redefined 'by creating performance indicators which are not concerned with the reduction of crime but the internal assessment of the performance of the organisation.'[207] By focusing on value for money, political debate about what constitutes value in specific circumstances is increasingly ignored.[208] Criticisms of the criminal justice system were not based on 'any actual

---

[199] Campbell J, 'Neoliberalism's Penal and Debtor States: A Rejoinder to Loïc Wacquant' (2010) 14(1) *Theoretical Criminology* 59–73.

[200] Lea J and Hallsworth S, 'Bringing the state back in: Understanding neoliberal security', in Squires P and Lea J (eds), *Criminalisation and Advanced Marginality: Critically Exploring the Work of Loic Wacquant* (Bristol: Policy Press, 2013).

[201] Harvey D, *A Brief History of Neoliberalism* (Oxford: OUP, 2005) p 3.

[202] Garland D, *The Culture of Control: Crime and Social Order in Contemporary Society* (Chicago: University of Chicago Press, 2001). [203] Garland (2001: 21).

[204] Indeed what Choongh sees as the 'social disciplining' by the police of problem populations (see earlier) might be better understood in terms of actuarial risk management.

[205] That Requirement was updated in 2015 in order to prioritise contemporary concerns about threats from cyber- and organised crime. See Home Office (2015) *The Strategic Policing Requirement* at <https://assets.publishing.service.gov.uk/government/uploads/system/uploads/attachment_data/file/417116/The_Strategic_Policing_Requirement.pdf> (accessed at 28 February 2018).

[206] Rawnsley A, *The End of the Party* (London: Penguin, 2010).

[207] Young J, 'Searching for a New Criminology of Everyday Life: A Review of the "Culture of Control" by David Garland' (2002) 42 *British Journal of Criminology* 228, 238.

[208] Lacey N, 'Government as Manager, Citizen as Consumer: The Case of the Criminal Justice Act 1991' (1994) 57 *Modern Law Review* 534.

deterioration in the performance of the criminal justice system, but higher expectations of what it can or should achieve.'[209] Despite this, successive governments have placed efficient case progression at the core of their cost reduction strategy. Stenson and Edwards argue that governmental preference for management techniques has diverted attention from approaches to criminal justice that emphasise welfare rights.[210] The altered approach views crime as a technical problem requiring resolution though administrative and apolitical means.

Criminal courts have not escaped this scrutiny, where a system of funding based on efficiency was introduced.[211] This is in line with Garland's comment that managerialism had become 'all pervasive',[212] affecting 'every aspect of criminal justice…performance indicators and management measures have narrowed professional discretion and tightly regulated working practice.'[213] In 2001, former senior presiding judge, Sir Robin Auld conducted a review of procedures within the criminal courts.[214] His review concluded that criminal court processes were inefficient, wasteful[215] and in need of streamlining. Bell and Dadomo noted that Auld appeared to be 'mesmerised by the idea of "efficiency" and an increased rate of conviction',[216] reflecting a desire to both reduce cost and increase crime control measures. However, schemes that focus primarily on target driven performance create conflict between the requirements of managerialism and of justice.[217]

1.9.1 Austerity justice

The last decade of government in the UK, following the economic downturn in 2008, has been characterised by the language of austerity measures and cost cutting to reduce public spending deficits across public services. Access to basic social welfare entitlements has been hugely reduced.[218] The Coalition government that succeeded Labour in 2010 inherited a criminal justice system in which reoffending rates were high and prisons were severely overcrowded. Despite this, the government still required the institutions of criminal justice to make cuts of between 25 and 33% across four years.[219]

The Coalition government initially appeared to regard rehabilitation of offenders as a form of risk management.[220] That government stated that it viewed crime as not just about numbers but also about social justice. This was, however, set against a desire to control

---

[209] Faulkner D and Burnett R, *Where Next for Criminal Justice?* (Bristol: The Policy Press, 2012).

[210] Stenson K and Edwards A, 'Policy Transfer in Local Crime Control: Beyond Naïve Emulation' in Newburn T and Sparks R (eds), *Criminal Justice and Political Cultures* (Cullompton: Willan Publishing 2004).

[211] Bell B and Dadomo C, 'Magistrates' Courts and the 2003 Reforms of the Criminal Justice System' (2006) 14(4) *European Journal of Crime, Criminal Law and Criminal Justice* 339.

[212] Garland D, *The Culture of Control: Crime and Social Order in Contemporary Society* (Chicago: University of Chicago Press, 2001) p 18.   [213] Ibid.

[214] Auld R, 'Review of the Criminal Courts of England and Wales: Executive Summary' (2001) <http://www.criminal-courts-review.org.uk/auldconts.htm> (accessed 5 October 2008).

[215] Zander M, *Cases and Materials on the English Legal System* (Oxford: OUP, 2007).

[216] Sanders A, 'Core Values, the Magistracy, and the Auld Report' (2002) 29(2) *Journal of Law and Society* 324 at 341.

[217] Bell B and Dadomo C, 'Magistrates' Courts and the 2003 Reforms of the Criminal Justice System' (2006) 14(4) *European Journal of Crime, Criminal Law and Criminal Justice* 339.

[218] Cooper V and Whyte D, *The Violence of Austerity* (London: Pluto Press, 2017).

[219] Faulkner D, 'Criminal justice and government at a time of austerity' Criminal Justice Alliance Discussion Paper (2010) available at <http://criminaljusticealliance.org/wp-content/uploads/2015/02/cjausterity3.pdf> (accessed 16 March 2018).

[220] Ministry of Justice, *Breaking the Cycle: Effective Punishment, Rehabilitation and Sentencing of Offenders* (London: The Stationery Office, 2010).

state expenditure.[221] The 2010 business plan for the criminal justice system continued to assert that the system should be simplified and made more efficient.[222] Despite Law Society concerns that, by placing emphasis on speed, the courts risk increasing the likelihood of miscarriages of justice,[223] the government pursued its desire to increase the speed at which allegations are processed in order to reduce cost. The Institute of Fiscal Studies reported that Ministry of Justice budgets fell by 29% and Home Office budgets fell by 19% between 2010 and 2015,[224] while Roberts reports an 18% decline in law and order spending between 2010 and 2014.[225] Against this background, Ward argues that neoliberalism has resulted in transformations to criminal justice that can be celebrated for modernisation and efficiency, but also criticised for reducing the delivery of criminal justice to its bare bones.[226] We can situate austerity in criminal justice through three trends: budget cuts, digitalisation and how defendants are situated in this discourse.

1.9.2 Budget cuts

The Coalition government elected in 2010 began a trend of dismantling and disinvestment in the institutions of criminal justice. Large sections of criminal justice services have been outsourced to the private security market. Although not addressed in this book, the privatisation of prisons was a major start point for this trend, when it was agreed in 1997 that all newly built prisons would be privately run.[227] By 2014, 15% of the prison population was housed in privately run prisons.[228] The pace of prison privatisation increased, parts of the Probation Service were privatised in 2014 as a result of outsourcing probation work for less serious offences to locally based Community Rehabilitation Companies, and the government-run Forensic Science Service (used at the investigative stage of the process) was dismantled in 2012. Police custody and other core policing functions have also been partially civilianised and outsourced. Roles that were formerly performed by warranted police officers are now performed by non-warranted civilians with more limited police powers, including detention officers in police custody, police community support officers engaged in neighbourhood policing and civilian investigators.[229] In some

---

[221] Silvestri A (ed), *Critical Reflections: Social and Criminal Justice in the First Year of Coalition Government* (London: Centre for Crime and Justice Studies, 2012).
[222] Office for Criminal Justice Reform, 'Working Together to Cut Crime and Deliver Justice: Criminal Justice System Business Plan 2009–2010' (2007). The Ministry of Justice also introduced the 'Stop Delaying Justice!' policy in 2012
[223] Baksi C, 'Speeding up cases "risks miscarriages"' (2012) (29 November) *Law Society Gazette* 3.
[224] Institute of Fiscal Studies 'IFS Green Budget 2015' (2015) available at <https://www.ifs.org.uk/publications/7530> (accessed 16 March 2018).
[225] Roberts R, 'Criminal justice in times of austerity' (2015) *Centre for Crime and Justice Studies* available at <https://www.crimeandjustice.org.uk/resources/criminal-justice-times-austerity> (accessed 16 March 2018).
[226] Ward J, 'Transforming "Summary Justice" Through Police-led Prosecution and "Virtual Courts"' (2015) 55 *British Journal of Criminology* 341.
[227] See, for example, Jones T and Newburn T, 'The Convergence of US and UK Crime Control Policy: Exploring Substance and Process' in Newburn T and Sparks R (eds), *Criminal Justice and Political Cultures* (Cullompton: Willan Publishing, 2012).
[228] As Robbins notes, there are significant concerns with the quality of care and rehabilitation services provided in privately run prisons, but less power to hold the prisons to account than if they were run by the state (Robbins I, 'Privatization of Corrections: A Violation of U.S. Domestic Law, International Human Rights, and Good Sense' (2006) 13(3) *Human Rights Brief* 12–16).
[229] Skinns L, *Police Custody: Governance, Legitimacy and Reform in the Criminal Justice Process* (Cullompton: Willan Publishing, 2011); Rice L, 'Junior Partners or Equal Partners? Civilian Investigators and the Blurred Boundaries of Police Detective Work' (2019) 30(8) *Policing and Society* 966–981.

cases, the staffing, management and ownership of police custody areas,[230] as well as other police functions, such as police control rooms and police station front counters, have been almost entirely outsourced to the private sector.[231]

The fragility of global markets, followed by the global economic crash in 2007–8 and the ensuing recession, together with neoliberal ideological fervour has prompted governmental cuts to police budgets and 'efficiency savings' in a bid to create a smaller, leaner and less costly public sector. The Comprehensive Spending Review (CSR) in 2010 announced a cut of central government funding for policing of £1.9 billion between 2010/11–2014/15: a 20% in police budgets. This was even though neither the National Audit Office nor HMIC were confident, at the time, that all police forces would be able to make the necessary cuts within the necessary time frame.[232] Between 1961 and 1991, the police workforce (including civilian staff) doubled from 100,000 to 200,000, eventually peaking at 300,000 in 2010. By 2013, the police workforce had dropped by 37,000 (13%).[233] Police Community Support Officers, who perform an important function in reassuring local communities, were seen as a particularly easy target, their numbers dropping fast.[234] Since September 2019 plans have been in place to recruit 20,000 new police officers, but this will still not increase the police workforce to pre-austerity levels.

Another easy target for budget cuts have been criminal defence service providers. Although operating as privately run firms (or sets of chambers of self-employed barristers), the vast majority of criminal defence services are beholden to fluctuations in government spending via the contracts that allow them to perform legally aided work. In order to be able to conduct state funded defence work, criminal defence lawyers must perform according to business models dictated by their contracts with the Ministry of Justice. Government policy towards publicly funded defence representation has long focused on reducing cost, and budget control has been a significant feature of legal aid policy since the 1990s.[235] This means that defence lawyers have long been paid on a fixed fee per case basis dependent on what stage a case reaches in court (guilty plea or trial).[236] However, recent austerity measures have exacerbated those problems. In 2010, the Ministry of Justice sought to reduce the legal aid budget by £220m by 2018. The decline of legal aid accelerated still further following the 2015 election of a Conservative government.[237] The fees that firms can claim for conducting work in the magistrates' courts were reduced by

---

[230] Skinns L, Sprawson A, Sorsby A, Smith R and Wooff A, 'Police Custody Delivery in the Twenty-first Century in England and Wales: Current Arrangements and their Implications for Patterns of Policing' (2017) 4(3) *European Journal of Policing Studies* 325–349.

[231] White A, 'Post-crisis Policing and Public–Private Partnerships: The Case of Lincolnshire Police and G4S' (2014) 54(6) *British Journal of Criminology* 1002–1022.

[232] HMIC, 'Adapting to Austerity' (2011) available at <https://www.justiceinspectorates.gov.uk/hmicfrs/media/adapting-to-austerity-20110721.pdf> (accessed 28 February 2018) 23.

[233] Cribb J, Disney R and Sibieta L, *The public sector workforce: past, present and future* IFS Briefing Note BN145 (Institute for Fiscal Studies, 2014).

[234] Hargreaves J, Cooper J, Woods E and McKee C, *Police Workforce, England and Wales, 31 March 2016* Home Office Statistical Bulletin 05/16 available at <https://assets.publishing.service.gov.uk/government/uploads/system/uploads/attachment_data/file/544849/hosb0516-police-workforce.pdf> (available at 28 February 2018).

[235] Goriely T, 'The Development of Criminal Legal Aid in England and Wales' in Young R and Wall D (eds), *Access to Criminal Justice: Legal Aid, Lawyers and the Defence of Liberty* (London: Blackstone Press, 1996).

[236] There is a wealth of evidence suggesting that such payment regimes damage lawyer/client relationships. See, for example, Newman D, *Legal Aid Lawyers and the Quest for Justice* (Oxford: Hart Publishing, 2013); Welsh L, 'The Effects of Changes to Legal Aid on Lawyers' Professional Identity and Behaviour in Summary Criminal Cases: A Case Study' (2017) 44(4) *Journal of Law and Society* 559–585.

[237] Smith T and Cape E 'The Rise and Decline of Criminal Legal Aid in England and Wales' in Flynn A and Hodgson J (eds), *Access to Justice and Legal Aid: Comparative Perspectives on Unmet Legal Need* (Oxford: Hart Publishing, 2017).

8.75% in 2014.[238] Similarly the Ministry of Justice acknowledged that fees for junior barristers working in criminal legal aid decreased by 8% between 2012 and 2016.[239] The reach of payment by fixed fee was extended to include work conducted at police stations, which had previously been paid on the basis of hourly rates. The real term decline in income is likely to be much greater than 8.75% given that there had been no increase in fee rates for 10 years preceding 2014, meaning that firms' profit margins are extremely thin. As a result, morale among defence lawyers is low.[240] They are increasingly required to pit the due process interests of their clients against the economic needs of their firms.[241]

Both issues lead defence lawyers to take more risks about conducting work not knowing whether they will be paid, which has the potential to mean that only a base level of service is provided to suspects and defendants. The Justice Committee reported that reductions in legal aid were hindering the ability of defence lawyers to conduct proper reviews of material disclosed by the CPS, raising concerns about increased potential for miscarriages of justice.[242] Service provision problems are exacerbated by dwindling recruitment into the profession: newly qualified lawyers are reluctant to take up publicly funded criminal defence work as a result of relatively low income generation and the perceived low status of the work.[243] The effects of reductions in available funding for defence lawyers include lower levels of representation, increased uncertainty about payment and consequent concerns about reduced professionalism and fragmented access to services.[244] Cape and Smith suggest that rationalisation of criminal legal aid policy, fuelled by the 2008 financial crisis, reflects the state's antipathy towards procedural justice,[245] due process and fair trial rights.[246] Against this background, the Ministry of Justice agreed, in late 2018, to conduct a review of criminal legal aid, and produced an accelerated package of proposals in early 2020,[247] about which consultation was sought. Social and public media reaction to those proposals suggest that they would do little to address crises faced by the criminal defence professions.[248]

CPS budgets, and therefore its staff, have also been steadily reduced—by 23% between 2010 and 2015.[249] Soubise demonstrated that a significant proportion of CPS work has (therefore) been delegated to less qualified members of staff, and prosecutors are offering lesser charges and plea bargains increasingly to discourage defendants from taking cases to trial.[250] This has the potential effect of persuading innocent defendants to plead guilty and is hurtful to victims who feel that their cases have not been treated with sufficient

---

[238] A further 8.75% fee cut was later abandoned in 2016 after members of The Law Society launched judicial review proceedings against the Ministry of Justice. [239] Smith and Cape (2017).

[240] Newman D and Welsh L, 'The Practices of Modern Criminal Defence Lawyers: Alienation and its Implications for Access to Justice' (2019) 48(1–2) *Common Law World Review*; Thornton J, 'Is Publicly Funded Criminal Defence Sustainable? Legal Aid Cuts, Morale, Recruitment and Retention in the English Criminal Law Professions' (2020) 40(2) *Legal Studies*.

[241] Welsh (2017). See ch 8.   [242] Garside et al (2019).

[243] The Law Society (2019a) 'Criminal Justice System in Crisis' Parliamentary Briefing.

[244] Welsh (2017).

[245] Procedural justice considerations apply across the criminal process, and incorporate the ability to effectively participate in proceedings, transparency, impartiality, confidence in consistent decision-making being treated with dignity and respect and trust in authority.   [246] Smith and Cape (2017).

[247] Ministry of Justice, *Criminal Legal Aid Review: An accelerated package of measures amending the criminal legal aid fee schemes* (2020c) available at <https://consult.justice.gov.uk/criminal-legal-aid/criminal-legal-aid-review/supporting_documents/criminallegalaidconsultationdocument.pdf> (accessed 21 October 2020).

[248] Fouzder M, 'Legal aid fees: MoJ offer to receive resounding "no"' *Law Society Gazette*, 20 March 2020; Atkinson R, 'The new legal aid settlement is an insult' *The Times*, 5 March 2020.

[249] Bowcott O, 'Crown Prosecution Service chief inspector signals concern over funding' *The Guardian*, 23 September 2015 available at <https://www.theguardian.com/law/2015/sep/23/cps-chief-inspector-kevin-mcginty-cuts-can-leave-agencies-unable-to-function> (accessed 16 March 2018).   [250] Soubise (2017).

seriousness (see section 7.9). Soubise also points out that processes of prosecution have become increasingly fragmented into a series of narrowly defined routine tasks, resulting in weak oversight of cases. Cases that are not based on robust prosecution 'are based on a partial account of the facts and could potentially lead to miscarriages of justice'.[251] One consequence is recent disclosure failings that have led to cases being abandoned and reviewed over miscarriage of justice fears (see section 7.3.3.5).[252] As these issues, alongside violent crime rates, increasingly became a cause for public concern, an investment of £85m was given to the CPS in 2019 (the defence were offered an extra £50m in the accelerated criminal legal aid review).[253] It remains to be seen whether this investment will alleviate some of the problems that we have discussed, or whether it will be funnelled towards a programme of 'modernisation'.

1.9.3 Digitalisation

The use of digital working practices to increase efficiency and reduce cost across the entire criminal justice system has been encouraged since 2012. The Ministry of Justice now has a designated Digital Director for Her Majesty's Courts and Tribunals Service. The CPS and defence have both been encouraged to use digital case management systems, in which relevant papers are exchanged using secure email systems, to make paperless working possible. Defendants can enter guilty pleas online for less serious offences so that their cases can be processed in a more automated fashion (see chapter 8). Digitalisation enables flexible working and speedy updates to files,[254] but CPS lawyers sometimes feel hindered by it.[255] It is also unclear how unrepresented, and often vulnerable, defendants are being enabled to participate in digital justice processes.[256] How confident can we be that most defendants in this situation can properly assess whether what they did really was criminal, or that they are able to fill in the online documents appropriately?

The courts have been encouraged to digitalise by making ever greater use of live link facilities, especially during the Covid-19 pandemic.[257] This means that defendants who have been remanded into custody awaiting their case will appear in court via a TV live link between the court and the prison or, in some cases, the police custody area, rather than being physically transported to the court building. This reduces prison and prisoner disruption and saves money. But defence lawyers face a dilemma about whether to be in

---

[251] Soubise (2017: 848).

[252] Criminal Cases Review Commission, *Annual Report and Accounts 2015/2016* (2016). See also Crown Prosecution Service, *Rape and serious sexual offence prosecutions—Assessment of disclosure of unused material ahead of trial* (2018d).

[253] BBC News, 'Law and order: Extra £85m for CPS to tackle violent crime' 12 August 2019. In 2020, the CPS announced it would be hiring hundreds of lawyers, which could further imbalance between defence and prosecution services.

[254] Criminal Justice Joint Inspection, *Delivering justice in a digital age* (London: CPSI, 2016).

[255] Porter A, 'Prosecuting Domestic Abuse in England and Wales: Crown Prosecution Service "Working Practice" and New Public Managerialism' (2018) 28(4) *Social & Legal Studies*.

[256] JUSTICE found that over 11 million adults in the UK lack basic digital skills (JUSTICE, 2018) *Preventing Digital Exclusion from Online Justice* available at <https://justice.org.uk/wp-content/uploads/2018/06/Preventing-Digital-Exclusion-from-Online-Justice.pdf> (accessed 1 June 2020).

[257] The Coronavirus Act 2020 broadened the availability of virtual and audio link court hearings. For discussion of the threats to transparent justice, see Townend J, 'Covid-19, the UK's Coronavirus Act and emergency 'remote' court hearings: what does it mean for open justice?' *The Justice Gap*, 30 March 2020. At April 2020, the possibility of online jury trials being conducted during the pandemic was being mooted (See 'JUSTICE pilots first ever worldwide virtual mock jury trial' at <https://justice.org.uk/wp-content/uploads/2020/04/JUSTICE-mock-virtual-trial-press-release.pdf> (accessed 21 October 2020); Mulcahy L, Rowden E and Teeder W, 'Exploring the case for Virtual Jury Trials during the COVID-19 crisis' at <https://justice.org.uk/wp-content/uploads/2020/04/Mulcahy-Rowden-Virtual-trials-final.pdf> (accessed 21 October 2020)).

court with the judge or outside the court with their client.[258] It is difficult to take instructions and build rapport with clients via video link,[259] but remaining at the police station or prison with clients reduces opportunities to negotiate with prosecutors at court. The small sample of former defendants who have been asked about their experiences of appearing via video link were concerned that they found it more difficult to communicate with their lawyers and properly participate in proceedings.[260] This undermines the right to effective participation under Art 6 ECHR.[261] It can also be difficult for lawyers to obtain case papers at short notice for video link hearings.[262] These problems 'point to issues of procedural due process rights and principles of "open justice" being weakened in some domains',[263] particularly as no one has the right to refuse an appearance via video link.[264] Those appearing via virtual court were more likely to be sent to custody than other defendants,[265] although more serious charges are more likely to be dealt with via video link.[266]

The use of virtual court facilities was extended to encourage police officers to give evidence via live links so that they do not need to leave the police station to give evidence.[267] This means that, rather than waiting at court (which is obviously an inefficient use of time), they can work in the police station. But then there is the risk of not giving the trial their full attention and for the corruption of evidence. For, while officers at court are kept in a form of sterile environment with little opportunity for collusion, there are limited safeguards available outside court. The absence of physical architectural cues about expected behaviour can affect participants' approach to virtual proceedings.[268] Using virtual court facilities also reduces costs: by late 2017, the court estate had shrunk to 350 courts from 605 in 2010, and further closures were planned (see further chapter 8).[269]

High levels of digital case transfer between parties does not necessarily mean that fewer staff are needed, because high levels of user input are required to make paper documents electronic, so costs are not reduced as much as anticipated.[270] It is, therefore, difficult to assess the true benefits of digitalisation, although virtual courts do speed cases along.[271] This appears, however, to be at the cost of fewer defendants receiving legal advice and representation (and diminished quality when it is received), and more custodial sentencing. Defendants' rights to active participation should not be sacrificed for the sake of speed, but

---

[258] Rowden E, 'Virtual Courts and Putting "Summary" Back into "Summary Justice": Merely Brief, or Unjust?' in Simon J, Temple N and Tobe R (eds), *Architecture and Justice: Judicial Matters in the Public Realm* (Farnham, Surrey: Ashgate, 2013) pp 101–113.

[259] Ward J, 'Transforming "Summary Justice" Through Police-led Prosecution and "Virtual Courts"' (2015) 55 *British Journal of Criminology* 341. See further Fielding N, Braun S and Hieke G, *Video Enabled Justice Evaluation* (2020) at <http://spccweb.thco.co.uk/our-priorities/access-to-justice/video-enabled-justice-vej/video-enabled-justice-programme-university-of-surrey-independent-evaluation/> (accessed 21 October 2020).

[260] Fielding, Braun and Hieke (2020).

[261] Gibbs P, *Defendants on video – Conveyor belt justice or a revolution in access?* (2017) Transform Justice at <http://www.transformjustice.org.uk/wp-content/uploads/2017/10/Disconnected-Thumbnail-2.pdf> (accessed 21 October 2020).

[262] Criminal Justice Joint Inspection (2016).   [263] Ward (2015).

[264] Crime and Disorder Act 1998 as amended by the Coroners and Justice Act 2009. The small sample of former defendants referred to expressed the desire to have a choice about whether or not to appear in person (Fielding, Braun and Hieke (2020)).   [265] Ward (2015).

[266] Conversely, judges involved in early virtual court hearings reported that it was more difficult to establish a sense of authority and that defendants took proceedings less seriously. See Terry M, Johnson S and Thompson P, *Virtual Court pilot: Outcome evaluation* (London: Ministry of Justice, 2010).

[267] Section 51 of the Criminal Justice Act 2003, permits the court to allow a witness who is in the UK, but outside the court building, to give evidence by live link if the court is satisfied that that is in the interests of the efficient administration of justice.

[268] Mulcahy L and Rowden E, *The Democratic Courthouse: A Modern History of Design, Due Process and Dignity* (Abingdon: Routledge, 2020).   [269] Garside et al (2019).

[270] Criminal Justice Joint Inspection (2016).   [271] Ward (2015).

unfairness to suspects and defendants is of little concern to a criminal justice process that increasingly marginalises due process rights.

1.9.4 Social justice and processes of exclusion

When considering the use of criminal justice processes to combat crime we should also consider other social needs in relation to, for instance, housing, employment, education, health, and so forth. Given that many indices of poverty (such as housing and employment problems) are related to conventional crime,[272] tackling these social problems might be more cost-effective than using the coercive powers of the state anyway.

One way of ensuring that we do not see crime in isolation from other social problems, and of highlighting the importance of social crime prevention as well as individual crime control is to look at two divergent trends in social policy: those of social inclusion and social exclusion. The exclusionary approach is one whereby: 'Crime is to be prevented by efficiency of detection, certainty of conviction and severity of punishment . . . "Criminals" are to be seen as an "enemy" to be defeated and humiliated, in a "war" in which the police are seen as the "front line"'.[273] In such discourse, the 'enemy' is also seen as causing unnecessary cost to the criminal justice system. Auld (2001) attacked 'calculating defendants' for 'wasting' resources, as did Leveson (2015), by asserting that defendants 'have no interest in improving the efficiency of the system or saving public money'.[274] Assertions of this nature further the othering of populations that are deemed criminogenic (see chapter 10), and fail to recognise that (particularly innocent) defendants are unlikely to want to increase the amount of time they must spend being processed by the system. They also provide another excuse for moving further away from due process towards more crime control measures.

As well as recasting the delivery of criminal justice processes, neoliberal governments have emphasised the importance of individual responsibility for citizens' position in society, which has created further social division and dislocation. Those who do not participate in society in accordance with a neoliberal agenda are pushed further towards the margins of society and 'othered'. While concern about victims' rights is welcome, the social dislocation caused by exclusionary discourse further polarises victims and defendants. These processes 'of de-citizenisation and ontological criminalisation provides … new discourses of nationality and citizenship'[275] because such groups are no longer seen 'as fellow "welfare citizens" with legitimate needs.'[276] Suspects and defendants have therefore been recast as 'outside society' as a result of making 'rational' choices to behave in a criminal way. This can be used to both justify severe punishment and undermine due process rights. As Nash notes, 'increasingly, it appears as if almost any risk related to public safety is not to be tolerated, thus those who put others at greater risk are by default to blame.'[277] This encouraged the use of coercive measures which threatened punitive sanctions for

---

[272] See, for example, Dorling D, Gordon D, Hillyard P, Pantazis C, Pemberton S and Tombs S, *Criminal Obsessions: Why harm matters more than crime* (London: Centre for Crime and Justice Studies, 2008).

[273] Faulkner D, *Darkness and Light: Justice, Crime and Management for Today* (London: Howard League, 1996) p 6.

[274] McConville M and Marsh L ,*The Myth of Judicial Independence* (Oxford: OUP, 2020).

[275] Lea J and Hallsworth S, 'Bringing the State Back In: Understanding Neoliberal Security' in Squires P and Lea J (eds), *Criminalisation and Advanced Marginality. Critically Exploring the Work of Loic Wacquant* (Bristol: The Policy Press, 2012) p 23. In this way, 'democracy might be characterised as tyrannical majoritarianism that allows oppression of minorities.' (Sanders A, 'Reconciling the Apparently Different Goals of Criminal Justice and Regulation: The "Freedom" Perspective' in Smith G, Seddon T and Quirk H (eds), *Regulation and Criminal Justice: Innovations in Policy and Research* (Cambridge: CUP, 2010) p 61.

[276] Lea and Hallsworth (2012: 2).

[277] Nash M, 'The Art of Deception—UK Public Protection Policy and the Criminal Justice "Crisis" of 2006' (2010) 38(3) *International Journal of Law, Crime and Justice* 79.

non-compliance with orders that required, for example those dependent on drugs or alcohol, to 'take responsibility for their actions and accept the help offered.'[278] The focus on the responsibilisation of behaviour (whereby the defendant is the maker of his or her own misfortune and responsible for the consequences and for remedying the behaviour) justifies undermining due process protections that have the potential to make prosecution more difficult.

Furthermore, the government was keen to be seen as both tough on crime and to promote speedy summary case progression in the aftermath of the five-day long 2011 city centre riots that erupted following the police shooting of Mark Duggan. As such, 'the ramping up of the penal wing of the state is a response to social insecurity, and not a reaction to crime trends.'[279] These measures have again prioritised 'efficient' working practices over traditional adversarial principles.[280] The result is that the powers of criminal justice agencies have been enlarged but vulnerable groups are left with little protection. This moves us further way from due process, and assists in promoting policies designed to encourage efficiency and save money. As criminals are increasingly viewed as undeserving of state assistance or protection from the disproportionate use of state force, protests about austerity measures undermining the right to fair trial are easily countered.

Faulkner contrasts the exclusionary rule with Locke's view that 'the end of law is not to abolish or restrain but to preserve and enlarge freedom'. On this inclusionary approach:

> Authority will not be respected if it is simply imposed: it has to be accountable and it has to be legitimate in the sense that respect for it has to be earned and justified. Consideration for others and obedience to the law are learned by explanation, discussion, experience and example ... Solutions to the problem of crime have to be sought by inclusion within the community itself – among parents, in schools, by providing opportunities and hope for young people – and not by exclusion from it.[281]

Overall, the dominant managerial impetus has been the pursuit of ever more effective, efficient and economic crime control legitimated by reference to the interests and views of the 'law abiding citizen'. However, this is at the expense of the protection of due process values and human rights, and 'target-driven' policing ends up focusing on the targets rather than the actual crime problems for which they are poor surrogates.[282] The way neoliberalism has spread 'management ideology has gradually altered the culture of criminal justice services, which have become increasingly concerned with narrowly-defined targets'.[283] An internal police inquiry into the mishandling of rape complaints provides a good example: '[police] management treated car crime as a higher priority than sex offences, because it was under pressure to meet targets for solving cases'.[284] Those who support this emphasis within managerialism would no doubt argue that targets can be tweaked to better guide performance, and that crime control and the protection of human rights are complementary. While this is theoretically possible it will not happen while the criminal process continues to operate in an exclusionary manner—failing to seek solutions from within

---

[278] Bell E, *Criminal Justice and Neoliberalism* (London: Palgrave Macmillan, 2011) p 82.
[279] Wacquant L, 'The Wedding of Workfare and Prisonfare in the 21st Century: Responses to Critics and Commentators' in Squires P and Lea J (eds), *Criminalisation and Advanced Marginality. Critically Exploring the Work of Loic Wacquant* (Bristol: The Policy Press, 2012) p 245.
[280] Criminal Procedure Rule 3.2 explicitly states that the parties are expected to co-operate and assist the court (Ministry of Justice, 'Criminal Procedure Rules' (2011) <http://www.justice.gov.uk/courts/procedure-rules/criminal> (accessed 1 June 2012).   [281] Faulkner (1996: 6).
[282] Flanagan R, *The Review of Policing: Final Report* (London: HMIC, 2008).   [283] Bell (2011).
[284] *The Guardian*, 17 March 2009. Also see *The Guardian*, 16 March 2009.

the community, and failing to show adequate respect to individual citizens, whether in the roles of suspects, defendants, witnesses or victims. This exclusionary tendency has increased alongside the rise of 'austerity justice' in our increasingly neoliberal society.

1.10 Conclusion

In this chapter we have shown that criminal justice can have several different purposes, many of which conflict with each other (and with social goals in other spheres of life) some or all of the time. There are many different values and interests at stake in criminal justice. The most important are:

- convicting the guilty;
- protecting the innocent from wrongful conviction;
- protecting victims;
- protecting everyone (innocent and guilty) from arbitrary or oppressive treatment by actors in the criminal process;
- maintaining order;
- securing public confidence in, and cooperation with, policing, prosecution and the courts;
- pursuing these goals efficiently and effectively without disproportionate cost and consequent harm to other public services.

Criminal justice is controversial, not because this list of goals is controversial, but because people differ over which are most important and which are to be given low priority. The weight to be attached to the competing factors determining the exercise of coercive state force depends partly upon the political and social outlook of the observer. Many people, especially politicians, like to pretend that all goals are equally achievable, but we have seen that this is misleading. One of the great virtues of Packer's models is that they show how hard it is to reconcile many of these purposes. However, we have seen that both models are incomplete (they do not cater for the interests of victims, in particular) and neither is normatively acceptable in itself (i.e. neither model represents an ideal to which we might aspire). We saw that the human rights perspective tries to overcome these two difficulties but that 'rights' perspectives are not the most fruitful or comprehensive ways to understand, critique or develop criminal justice.

While the conflicts that exist will never be eradicated, it is important to have a way of prioritising the different purposes of criminal justice—not just in an abstract way, but in relation to specific problems. Only then can we hope to get near achieving the best possible solutions, in terms of maximum benefits for minimum losses. Further, a rational system that applies consistent principles will be both fair and seen to be fair—which is a good thing in itself and has the added advantage of encouraging co-operation with the system and thus increasing the ability of criminal justice to control crime.

The value of the 'freedom perspective', outlined in section 1.8, is that it enables us to reconcile the apparently irreconcilable. One of us has developed this further through the elaboration of three 'core values' that flow from 'freedom':

Justice: this is procedural (e.g. having regard to human rights) but also substantive (for example, taking into account unequal access to justice due to inequality of money and power). It applies to victims just as it does as to suspects.

Democracy: thankfully we do not vote judges into their positions. But criminal justice policy results in large part from political choices and so should be formulated democratically. This does not necessarily require election manifestos. But to take into account the experiences of those subject to, as well as those responsible for, law and policy, it does require public consultation and public accountability. Without this there will be no trust. As we said earlier, being seen to be fair is nearly as important as actually being fair.

Efficiency: the 'Three Es' (i.e. including effectiveness and economy) discussed in section 1.9. The adage that 'you can't put a price on justice' is naïve. The fact is that choices have to be made about resources, and the more there are for one public good, the less there are for others. So criminal justice policy and practices cannot be measured against a counsel of perfection as then they will always fail. Moreover, to do justice the system must be reasonably speedy (efficient) and effective (reaching truthful verdicts); and the more economically the prosecution or magistrate/jury system can work, for example, the more money there should be for legal aid. Not all budget cuts and modernisations are therefore wrong. The problem is pursuing them at the expense of justice and democracy.

As we shall see in subsequent chapters, this approach can be applied to all areas of criminal justice.[285] The rest of the book will both describe the system analytically—to assess what it is trying to do and what it succeeds in doing—and elaborate our normative position.

That position, within which the freedom approach is situated, is that of an intersectionally 'inclusive' society and, within it, an inclusive way of operating criminal justice. Again, we are as concerned to see the extent to which criminal justice is, or is not, inclusive as we are to argue for inclusiveness. Here we shall see that our normative goal and the harsh reality are even farther away from each other. The social exclusionary tendencies of the criminal process reflect exclusionary tendencies within wider society that have been gathering pace over the last 40 years, from the Conservative administrations of 1979 to 1997 to the 1997 to 2010 Labour administrations (which employed inclusionary rhetoric but actually encouraged conventional paid work over inequality reduction).[286] Then, as austerity measures took hold in more recent years, the responsibility discourse was used to justify a reduction in resources given to criminal justice agencies. Suspects and defendants have become ever more excluded and designated as 'undeserving' of any protection from increasingly expansive coercive state control. The same austerity measures that increased demands for efficient case progression pushed suspects and defendants ever further away from being able to exercise their rights in meaningful ways. So, as we will see, exclusionary tactics have extended beyond the impositions of punishment for non-compliance and crept further into the actual process of criminal justice. This individualisation of social policy can also be seen in the criminal justice sphere, where the emphasis has been on remoralising or resocialising individual offenders so that they become responsible for 'reintegrating' themselves into 'law-abiding society'. Practical help and assistance to enable offenders to achieve this has been much less in evidence, as have the measures needed to tackle the conditions that generate conventional crime in the first place.[287] When offenders fail to take responsibility to stop their own offending, exclusionary measures such as tagging, curfews and prison remain the default option.[288]

---

[285] Sanders A, 'Core Values, the Magistracy, and the Auld Report' (2002) 29(2) *Journal of Law and Society* 324; at 341. Further developed in Sanders A, 'Reconciling the Apparently Different Goals of Criminal Justice and Regulation: the Freedom Perspective' in Quirk H et al, (eds) *Regulation and Criminal Justice* (Cambridge: CUP, 2010).

[286] See Levitas R, *The Inclusive Society?: Social Exclusion and New Labour* 2nd edn, (Basingstoke: Palgrave Macmillan, 2005).

[287] See Clements (2005).

[288] See Gray P, 'The Politics of Risk and Young Offenders' Experiences of Social Exclusion and Restorative Justice' (2005) 45(6) *British Journal of Criminology* 938; Wacquant (2012: 245).

It may be some time, then, before the inclusionary philosophy is applied in full to criminal justice. In the meantime, it is important to sketch out the potential of an inclusionary approach. Raising awareness of the issues at stake is a step along the road to rational reform. Packer's conclusion to his analysis of American criminal law and criminal process has received little subsequent attention. However, his final words[289] are as pertinent now as they were in the late 1960s: 'The criminal sanction is at once prime guarantor and prime threatener of human freedom. Used providently and humanely it is guarantor; used indiscriminately and coercively, it is threatener. The tensions that inhere in the criminal sanction can never be wholly resolved in favour of guaranty and against threat. But we can begin to try.' It is time we tried here too.

Further reading

BELL, E *Criminal Justice and Neoliberalism* (London: Palgrave Macmillan, 2011).

BONNER D, *Executive Measures, Terrorism and National Security: Have the Rules of the Game Changed?* (Aldershot: Ashgate, 2007).

CAMPBELL L, ASHWORTH A and REDMAYNE M, *The Criminal Process* (Oxford: OUP, 2019) chs 2 and 3.

COOK D, *Criminal and Social Justice* (London: Sage, 2006).

DRAKE D and HENLEY A '"Victims" Versus "Offenders" in British Political Discourse: The Construction of a False Dichotomy' (2014) 53(2) *The Howard Journal* 141–157.

GEARTY C, *Can Human Rights Survive?* (Cambridge: CUP, 2006).

HODGSON J, *The Metamorphosis of Criminal Justice* (Oxford: OUP, 2020) ch 1.

McCONVILLE M and MARSH L, *The Myth of Judicial Independence* (Oxford: OUP, 2020) esp. chs 8–10.

VOGLER R, *A World View of Criminal Justice* (Oxford: Routledge, 2016).

WACQUANT L, *Punishing the Poor: The Neoliberal Government of Social Insecurity* (Durham: Duke University Press, 2009).

---

[289] Packer (1968: 366).

2

Stop and search

KEY ISSUES

- The relative infrequency with which police resort to formal legal powers
- The drift from reactive peacekeeping towards proactive targeting of crime and anti-social behaviour
- Factors influencing the use of police discretion
- Stop and search powers requiring reasonable suspicion (legal and working rules)
- Stop and search powers not requiring reasonable suspicion (the pre-emptive principle writ large)
- The importance of 'consent' and the rise of 'stop and account'
- Stop and search and racial discrimination
- Do the constraints and controls surrounding the use of stop-search actually work?
- Does stop-search diminish or enhance freedom?
- Stop-search and police-community relations
- Stop-search as social exclusion

2.1 Introduction

In a textbook on criminal justice, it is natural to concentrate on the law enforcement role of the police. So this and the next four chapters look at various police powers, though we will see later in this section that the police do a lot more besides. The main power to stop and search people is provided by s.1 of the Police and Criminal Evidence Act 1984 (PACE), which is the key statute regulating police powers. The object of stop-searches is to find stolen or prohibited items, such as drugs or offensive weapons, carried by pedestrians or occupants of vehicles. PACE stop-searches require that the police reasonably suspect that such items will be found. The police have additional statutory powers that do not require reasonable suspicion. Thus they may stop vehicles (ostensibly in order to carry out routine checks) and, in certain situations, may stop anyone on foot or in a vehicle to look for weapons, or items connected with terrorism, regardless of whether they have reasonable suspicion that such items will be found. In addition, the police have developed a non-statutory practice of stopping people and asking them to account for their behaviour or presence in a particular area (so-called 'stop and account'). These kinds of stops may or may not morph into a statutory stop-search, but they always involve an attempt to search the contents of someone's mind. Finally, there are 'stops' where the police do not necessarily suspect the stopped person of anything criminal but may, for example, seek their assistance as a witness. For the sake of clarity we will reserve the term 'stop-search' for stops that involve physical searches of people's bodies and vehicles, while references to other stops should be understood as likely to involve a search for useful information.

Each year, hundreds of thousands of people are stopped by the police. In the year ending March 2019, there were 370,454 stop and searches in England and Wales conducted under s.1 of PACE and associated legislation. There were also 13,175 stop and searches under s.60 of the Criminal Justice and Public Order Act (carried out to prevent anticipated violence). Of the 383,629 total, around 16% led to an arrest, and an alternative outcome was given in another 12% of cases. The most common reason for carrying out a PACE stop and search was on suspicion of drug possession, which accounted for 61% of all stop and searches. The proportion of searches on suspicion of carrying offensive weapons was 16%, and 11% of searches were carried out on suspicion of stolen property. But in 2019 only 22% of stop and searches resulted in an outcome linked to the reason for the search. Moreover, despite a downward trend in stop and searches overall, the numbers for black, Asian and minority ethnic (BAME) groups have increased, resulting in greater disproportionality with the white population. Overall, stops of BAME individuals increased by 33,281 (34%) between 2018 and 2019. BAME people were 4.3 times as likely to be stopped as those who were white.[1]

Despite all this, formal legal powers are used relatively infrequently. Police detection rates since 2015 have shown a downward trend; for example, in 2019 only 7.8% of crimes recorded by police in England and Wales resulted in a suspect being charged or summonsed to appear in court; it was 15% in the year ending March 2015.[2] While stop and search is valued by the police,[3] to fully understand how they use street policing powers we need to begin by placing this activity in context by looking at what they do the rest of the time. This introductory discussion provides an essential building block not just for this chapter but also for those that follow on other policing powers.

2.1.1 Crime and street policing in context

In the mid-1960s, Banton made the point (subsequently confirmed by a plethora of research studies) that:

> The policeman on patrol is primarily a 'peace officer' rather than a law officer. Relatively little of his time is spent enforcing the law in the sense of arresting offenders; far more is spent 'keeping the peace' … the most striking thing about patrol work is the high proportion of cases in which policemen do not enforce the law.[4]

---

[1] *Police powers and procedures, England and Wales* (London: Home Office, October 2019). Available at <https://assets.publishing.service.gov.uk/government/uploads/system/uploads/attachment_data/file/841408/police-powers-procedures-mar19-hosb2519.pdf> (accessed 12 October 2020).

[2] *Crime Outcomes in England and Wales: year ending March 2019* (Home Office Statistical Bulletin 12/19) (London: Home Office, 2019a). Detected crimes are those that have been 'cleared up' by the police. The police may use one of several methods to count a crime as detected. These include sanctioned detections: being charged or summonsed, being cautioned, reprimanded or given a final warning, had an offence taken into consideration, received a penalty notice for disorder or received a warning for cannabis possession. Non-sanction detections which also count as detected crimes include no further action, and by local resolution.

[3] Miller J, Bland N and Quinton P, *The Impact of Stops and Searches on Crime and the Community* (London: Home Office, 2000).

[4] Banton M, *The Policeman in the Community* (London: Tavistock, 1964) p 127.

As Morgan and Newburn note, '... the police handle everything from unexpected childbirths, skid row alcoholics, drug addicts, emergency psychiatric cases, family fights, landlord-tenant disputes, and traffic violations, to occasional incidents of crime'.[5] In recent times, policing responsibilities have also widened to include migration control by tasking police officers with diverting foreign national offenders to immigration officials as soon as they identified in police stop-searches and when brought into police custody.[6] And in 2020 we can add the 'Covid-19' laws, where the police are told to encourage and persuade before enforcing.[7] Some of the disputes and fights (and all traffic violations) will involve breaches of the criminal law. But whether and when this is so will often be a matter of judgement for the officers concerned. Since, in most of these cases, 'peacekeeping' will be their main objective, the question is how best to achieve this. If the peace can be kept between the disputants by 'words of advice', as it often can, the law will only be enforced in serious cases. Research shows that patrol officers take a harsher stance when dealing with marginal populations, such as the homeless, youths 'hanging around' on the streets, and drug users.[8] Even here, however, the tendency is for the police to 'hassle' (through surveillance, questioning or 'moving people on') 'with remarkably few encounters resulting in the formal use of police powers'.[9] But if conflict continues, or there is a refusal to submit to police authority, the law can be invoked.

The fact that the police can choose whether or not to enforce the law underpins the way the criminal justice system works. Exactly the same is true of non-police agencies as well, which are discussed in chapter 7, section 7.5. This means, for instance, that the caseload of the courts is shaped not only by the way the law is enforced, but also by the way it is not enforced.

Another common observation about policing is that much of it takes place at the behest of the public. Thus police officers assigned to general patrol duties operate predominantly in reactive mode, responding to myriad and often mundane demands for service from the public. Opportunities for these officers to engage in proactive policing (using their initiative to deter, or uncover evidence of, criminal activity) occur relatively infrequently and, partly in consequence, are usually seized enthusiastically. Proactive policing is popular with the police since it fits with their self-image as skilful 'crime fighters' (see section 2.1.4). Indeed, promotion and the securing and retention of high status jobs (such as detective work)[10] still depend partly on 'activity', as measured by stops and

---

[5] Morgan R and Newburn T, *The Future of Policing* (Oxford: OUP, 1997) p 79.

[6] From 2012 onwards, police forces across the UK implemented a scheme called Operation Nexus. This formalised co-operation between the police and immigration in order to more swiftly deal with foreign national offenders by diverting them from the UK criminal justice system and instead referring them to immigration to initiate removal and deportation proceedings. Suspected foreign national offenders would be identified through stop and search and custody booking in procedures involving an immigration status check. See Parmar A, 'Policing Belonging: Race and Nation in the UK' in Bosworth M, Parmar A and Vazquez Y (eds), *Race, Criminal Justice and Migration Control* (Oxford: OUP, 2018); Parmar A, 'Policing Migration and Racial Technologies' (2019b) 59(4) *British Journal of Criminology* 938–957.

[7] The Health Protection (Coronavirus, Restrictions) (England) Regulations 2020.

[8] See, for example, Newburn et al, '"The Biggest Gang"? Police and People in the 2011 England Riots' (2016) 18(2) *Policing and Society* 205–222; Loader I, *Youth Policing and Democracy* (Basingstoke: Macmillan Press, 1996) pp 76–91; Lister et al, *Street Policing of Problem Drug Users* (York: Joseph Rowntree Foundation, 2008). See also discussion in ch 10.

[9] Lister et al (2008) p 18; on the 'Covid laws', see Grace S, Policing the coronavirus lockdown: The limits of on-the-spot fines (2020) at <https://bscpolicingnetwork.com/2020/04/02/policing-the-coronavirus-lockdown-the-limits-of-on-the-spot-fines/> (accessed 12 October 2020), and Amnesty International, *Policing the pandemic* (2020) at <https://www.amnesty.org> (accessed 12 October 2020).

[10] Detective work remains high status, in spite of the influx of civilian police staff doing this kind of work. See Rice L, 'Junior Partners or Equal Partners? Civilian Investigators and the Blurred Boundaries of Police Detective Work' (2019) 30(8) *Policing and Society* 966–981.

quality arrests.[11] As a general shift inspector put it: 'I would never demand a quota for arrests, but I do expect them to take an interest in crime, to investigate crime, and to show arrests wherever possible.'[12] Proactive stops and stop-searches enable individual officers to demonstrate measurable crime-related activity in a way which peacekeeping usually does not. In addition, there have always been specialist groups of 'proactive' officers. For example, drug, vice and serious crime squads, as well as officers engaged in order maintenance policing of low level offences (also known as 'zero tolerance' policing) are expected to take the lead in tackling their spheres of criminal activity, and therefore stop-search on their own initiative.[13] Even for the minority of stop-searches that are reactive, the nature of the police response is not predetermined. The police have to sift and interpret what they are told by the public, and they do so on the basis of their own views, experiences and priorities.

These priorities are partly set by the government, as explained in chapter 1. Thus, in the early 1990s the government decided that the 'peacekeeping' and community relations roles highlighted by Banton should no longer be prioritised on the ground that they used resources inefficiently. Police efficiency is now measured primarily in terms of crime-fighting, but instead of reactive policing, 'targeted' and 'intelligence-led' policing is encouraged.[14] This is highly proactive, in that specific offenders, offender-types, offences or geographical areas are targeted for pre-emptive police action on the basis of crime data, information from informants and so forth.

In this section we have sketched some contemporary forms of policing[15] and the drift away from reactive peacekeeping and towards proactively tackling crime and anti-social behaviour. We saw, in particular, that while 'the public' make demands on the police and shape some of what they do, the drift towards proactivity means that the police themselves, and the government, are more influential. We have stressed that the use of formal legal powers remains highly discretionary. In the next section we look more systematically at the factors influencing the exercise of police discretion.

2.1.2 Factors influencing the exercise of discretion

Crimes abound almost everywhere, yet the police have finite resources. The law is complex and is often difficult to interpret and put into practice. It follows that the police necessarily exercise discretion when deciding who to stop and who to arrest. Discretion can be defined as 'police officers' perception of the quality and nature of their authorised capacity to make choices about different courses of action or inaction'.[16] Given the volume of crime, one might expect that only the most serious offences and offenders would be selected. In reality the police spend much time on mundane crime, as this is what so many calls for service made to the police by the public concern.[17] If seriousness is not the prime

---

[11] Fitzgerald M, *Stop and Search: Final Report* (London: Metropolitan Police, 1999) ch 3; Miller et al, *The Impact of Stops and Searches on Crime and the Community* (Police Research Series Paper 127) (London: Home Office, 2000) p 17; Long J, 'Keeping PACE: Some Front Line Policing Perspectives' in Cape E and Young R (eds), *Regulating Policing* (Oxford: Hart, 2008) pp 106–108.
[12] Fielding N, *Community Policing* (Oxford: Clarendon, 1995) p 52.
[13] See Maguire M and Norris C, *The Conduct and Supervision of Criminal Investigations* (Royal Commission on Criminal Justice Research Study no 5) (London: HMSO, 1992).
[14] See Ratcliffe J, *Intelligence-Led Policing* 2nd edn (London: Routledge, 2016).
[15] For fuller assessments see McLaughlin E, *The New Policing* (London: Sage, 2007); Innes M et al, *Neighbourhood Policing* (Oxford: OUP, 2020).
[16] Skinns L, *Police Powers and Citizens' Rights* (Abingdon: Routledge, 2019) pp 22–23.
[17] Brodeur reviewed 77 studies analysing police calls for service in the US, UK, Canada or the Netherlands. In the majority of these studies, less than 33% of calls for service were crime-related: Brodeur J-P, *The Policing Web* (Oxford: OUP, 2010). On the dullness of many shifts see Pearson G and Rowe M, *Police Street Powers and Criminal Justice* (London: Bloomsbury, 2020) p 77–81.

determinant of police action, what is? The most important factors influencing the exercise of discretion, the effects of which will vary over time and from place to place, are:

Personal: where officers feel under pressure to stop-search and make arrests in order to justify themselves and enhance job prospects or to perhaps demonstrate personal power during a public stop or arrest, they may target simple cases (such as cannabis possession). Such targeting may also occur where officers are bored, where they wish to get back to the police station, or because a new recruit is encouraged to 'start at the bottom' in order to gain confidence in practical policing. And it can work the other way, as shown by observation of police practices in recent research: 'As he drives to Brandham, he speeds up to drive alongside cars that are obviously speeding. But he just warns them by glancing over and slowing down. He isn't going to stop them on the way to dinner.'[18]

Some officers also allow strong personal dislike of particular social groups to influence their decision-making. For example, racial hatred has surfaced as a motivation for stop-searches, with sometimes lethal consequences.[19] The murder of George Floyd in 2020 in the USA by police officers tragically highlighted the endemic and systemic nature of the uneven policing towards racial minorities and police brutality across the world.[20] The incident sparked further acknowledgement of racial discrimination in policing and the enduring features of colonial legacies, including calls to dramatically reform or defund the police.[21] But the USA should not be seen as exceptional or 'worse' than the UK. Figures in relation to policing and racial disproportionality are just as stark, and entrenched and individual cases of racism as egregious, in the UK both in the past and present. It is telling that the main interaction black people have with the police in Britain is through stop and search.[22] This underlines why academic analyses of policing often focus on stop and search, highlighting its crucial role as an entry point into the criminal justice system. There are many recent UK examples of the police ostensibly deciding to stop someone because they are (or are perceived to be) a racial minority. Furthermore, the nature of stop and searches when racial minorities are involved have been found to be more likely to be aggressive, involve the use of force and involve multiple forms of force and/or restraint.[23] We return to discriminatory stop-search in more detail below and again in chapter 10.

Working assumptions and working rules: working assumptions concern the way that patrol officers typically view the world around them and involve stereotypes about suspicious behaviour, people and communities. Working rules are the norms that structure police behaviour, such as the rule that those who challenge police authority ('contempt of cop') should have police power brought to bear on them in order to reassert that

---

[18] Pearson and Rowe (2020: 56).

[19] See the transcript of an undercover BBC investigation ('The Secret Policeman') at: <http://www.ligali.org/pdf/bbc_transcript_secret_policeman.pdf> (accessed 5 January 2010) and the discussion in McLaughlin (2007) ch 6.

[20] See <https://www.theguardian.com/us-news/2020/may/29/george-floyd-killing-protests-police-brutality> (accessed 3 September 2020).

[21] See <https://www.newyorker.com/news/q-and-a/how-the-federal-government-can-reform-the-police> (accessed 3 September 2020).

[22] For a useful summary of the perpetual cycle of racism in policing in the UK, see <https://www.newstatesman.com/politics/uk/2020/07/police-racism-black-people-stats-numbers-stop-search-deaths-custody-arrests> (accessed 3 September 2020). A recent British study found 'no overt discrimination' though the authors comment that 'might be a result' of their observing what the police did: Pearson and Rowe (2020: 69).

[23] Black people were almost six times more likely to have force used on them by police than white people in 2018/19 and to have multiple forms of force used. See *Police Use of Force Statistics, England and Wales, April 2018 to March 2019* (London: Home Office, 2019e).

very authority. Giving the example of a 'rude and abrasive' SUV driver, a recent study says police 'will stop a vehicle for a traffic offence but not issue a ticket if the driver passes "the attitude test"'.[24]

Procedural: offenders who have the protection of the privacy of their home or office, for instance, are less vulnerable than people on the street or in public places, where no warrants or other forms of prior authorisation for the use of policing powers are usually needed. This allows 'white collar' (i.e. business) crimes to be particularly well hidden (see further chapter 10), albeit that technological innovation and changing regulation (e.g. the so-called 'Snoopers Charter' or Investigatory Powers Act 2016), mean that Internet-based forms of 'white collar' crime may be more traceable than they once were.

Changed forms of policing: store detectives, security guards, bouncers and other forms of private police now easily outnumber the public police.[25] The Private Security Industry Act 2001 provides for the licensing of private police personnel who can then be provided with some of the powers that the public police possess in relation to relatively trivial crime. These powers are also available to another category of public quasi-police known as 'police community support officers' (PCSOs), who now play an important part in neighbourhood policing teams.[26] Despite the differences in roles between private/security police and public police, the boundaries between them are increasingly blurring.[27] Technological innovations, such as CCTV, body-worn cameras, computerised databases, digital recording and swipe card access systems have further increased the amount and effectiveness of organised surveillance (a core feature of policing) taking place in society. Some people (e.g. lower class youths)[28] and places (e.g. shopping malls)[29] are increasingly 'over-policed' while others are neglected, and new demands are being placed on the public police to take action against particular individuals identified as suspicious or anti-social by CCTV controllers or security personnel.[30] Stop-searches based on cameras that have the capacity for automatic number plate recognition are now integral to everyday policing. And police body-worn cameras were introduced to increase accountability and reduce police use of force and complaints against officers. However, the perceived benefits of body-worn cameras are by no means automatic or guaranteed.[31]

Interpretational latitude: many substantive laws (e.g. carrying an offensive weapon) are ambiguous, as are many police powers (e.g. stop-search and arrest: see later and chapter 3). Such ambiguities may deter a police officer from acting or may, conversely, allow officers to act much as they wish. Government pressure on the police to tackle low-level disorder and non-criminal activity deemed to be 'anti-social' means that the police (both public and private) now more often exercise discretion in situations of legal ambiguity.

---

[24] Pearson and Rowe (2020: 56–57).

[25] Hucklesby A and Lister S (eds), *The Private Sector and Criminal Justice* (London: Palgrave, 2017).

[26] O'Neil M, *Police Community Support Officers* (Oxford: OUP, 2019).

[27] White A and Gill M, 'The Transformation of Policing: From Ratios to Rationalities' (2013) 53(1) *British Journal of Criminology* 74–93; Button M, *Security Officers and Policing: Powers, Culture and Control in the Governance of Private Space* (Aldershot: Ashgate, 2007).

[28] Goldsmith C, 'Cameras, Cops and Contracts: What Anti-social Behaviour Management Feels like to Young People' in Squires P (ed), *ASBO Nation: The Criminalisation of Nuisance* (Bristol: The Policy Press, 2008).

[29] See, for example, McCahill M, *The Surveillance Web* (Cullompton: Willan, 2002) ch 4.

[30] See further Norris C, 'From Personal to Digital: CCTV, the Panopticon, and the Technological Mediation of Suspicion and Social Control' in Lyon D (ed), *Surveillance as Social Sorting: Privacy, Risk and Digital Discrimination* (London: Routledge, 2003); Brayne S, *Predict and Surveil* (Oxford: OUP, 2020).

[31] Ariel et al, 'Wearing Body Cameras Increases Assaults Against Officers and Does Not Reduce Police Use of Force: Results from a Multi-Site Experiment' (2018) 13(6) *European Journal of Criminology* 744–755; Rowe M, Pearson G and Turner E, 'Body-Worn Cameras and the Law of Unintended Consequences: Some Questions Arising from Emergent Practices' (2018) 12(1) *Policing* 83–90. Also see discussion in ch 12.

Organisational: some police forces adopt particular policies in relation to certain offences (e.g. a 'zero tolerance' campaign against drunken driving, vice or domestic violence; or a tolerance policy concerning the possession of 'soft' drugs). Many academics argue that individual police force policies, that emphasise some aspects of the law, and some substantive laws, more than others, are the most powerful drivers of police officer behaviour.[32]

Societal pressures: both PACE and the Crime and Disorder Act 1998 require individual police forces to consult and work with local communities in relation to policing and crime reduction,[33] with every neighbourhood in the country having its own dedicated policing team that is tasked with identifying and responding to local priorities. Wider societal pressures occur from time to time in relation to particular offences such as robbery, terrorism or knife crime, that influence police stop and search practices in particular.[34]

Political/managerial pressures: in recent times the police have been forced to respond to targets and priorities set by central government, inspectorates and the Audit Commission, causing them to focus more on some crimes and issues and less on others. As noted earlier, the overall effect of such performance targets has been to produce a shift away from peacekeeping towards 'cracking down' on disorder and crime.

2.1.3 Does law influence the police? A typology of legal rules

Law was scarcely mentioned in our account of the factors influencing police discretion in the preceding section. This is not because legal rules play no part in police officers' thinking; it is because their relationship to police actions is sufficiently complex to merit separate treatment. When the police decide to act it is usually a policy or working rule that is most directly in play, not a legal rule. Take, for example, PACE. Despite initial scepticism, many of its provisions ultimately brought the law into line with police practice or police aspirations. Thus, stop and search laws were extended by PACE from certain localities to the country as a whole, *allowing* the police to search people they think are suspicious, but not *requiring* them to do so. In part, this enabled the police to operationalise their working assumptions and rules more extensively than hitherto. Legal rules that allow the police to act more frequently in pursuit of their aspirations may be termed 'enabling rules'. In part, PACE made legal what the police were doing anyway. When the law is brought into line with pre-existing police practice the new rules are 'legitimising'.

It is no surprise to find that most 'enabling' and 'legitimising' rules embody crime control values more than due process values presented in chapter 1.

However, some PACE rules have a freedom-enhancing due process character designed to strengthen suspects' rights. These rules are intended to inhibit the police from following their working rules (or are intended to give that impression), especially where the latter embody crime control values. If legal norms succeed in this ostensible aim they are 'inhibitory rules'. If they do not they are 'presentational rules'. They create the appearance that the police are subjected to more effective legal constraint than is actually the case (see Fig 2.1).[35]

---

[32] Pearson and Rowe (2020) esp. ch 3. [33] PACE, s.106; CDA, ss.5 and 6.

[34] See, for instance: Murray et al, 'Procedural Justice, Compliance with the Law and Police Stop-and-Search: A Study of Young People in England and Scotland' (2020) *Policing and Society*. 1711756; Parmar A, 'Stop and Search in London: Counter-terrorist or Counter-productive?' (2011) 21(4) *Policing and Society* 369–382; Hall et al, *Policing the Crisis* (London: Macmillan, 1978) for an analysis of the 'mugging' scare of the 1970s.

[35] This typology builds on the terms and concepts developed by Smith D and Gray J, *Police and People in London, Vol 4* (Aldershot: Gower, 1983).

Figure 2.1 Types of legal rule and effect on police behaviour

	Rule expresses crime control values	Rule expresses due process values
Influences police	Enabling	Inhibitory
No influence on police	Legitimising	Presentational

Few legal rules are as one-dimensional as this suggests, as most originate from mixed motives and/or messy compromises. For example, as soon as a rule legitimises a police practice (such as stop-search) it is likely to encourage greater use of that practice, and so has the effect of an enabling rule. And rules that begin their life as presentational may, over time, come to develop more inhibitory qualities as a result of more effective training,[36] changes in incentive structures and so forth. Despite these complications, the typology helps us to understand the major themes of this book.

2.1.4 Cop culture

We have argued that many rules can be interpreted as the police want, and this is true of other factors influencing discretion such as community pressures. The desires of local or wider communities (which are rarely expressed with one voice and which often conflict) need to be sifted, interpreted and prioritised by the police. Similarly, offence 'seriousness' is not an objective category, and what is or is not 'anti-social behaviour', for instance, will depend in part on one's view of the world. The police world outlook—which influences the way the police handle legal rules and non-legal influences—does not simply encapsulate that of society at large. It is moulded by 'cop culture'. This is:

> rooted in constant problems which officers face in carrying out the role they are mandated to perform ... Cop culture has developed as a patterned set of understandings that help officers cope with and adjust to the pressures and tensions confronting the police.[37]

Cop culture comprises a number of related elements.[38] The most important is 'authority'. A request by an officer to stop or to answer questions is always underpinned by the unspoken threat of the use of force (e.g. stop-search or arrest), but this is only part of the *authority* of the officer. More important is the officer's symbolic role as the upholder of a (supposedly) impartial and universal law. This authority usually secures results without the need for coercion. Other related elements include a sense of 'danger', which is the officer's sense of the unpredictability of interactions with members of the public; the demand for deference from most members of the public, without which authority is undermined and order is threatened; the need, as we saw earlier, to produce 'results'; and a sense of mission to prevent 'them', the threatening 'other', from ruining things for 'us'.

---

[36] Fielding N, *Professionalising the Police: The Unfulfilled Promise of Police Training* (Oxford: OUP, 2018).

[37] Bowling et al, *The Politics of the Police* 5th edn (Oxford: OUP, 2019) p 171. The importance of police culture is contested and has been subject to much academic debate. See, e.g., Bacon M, 'Police Culture and the New Policing Context' in Fleming J (ed) *The Future of Policing* (Abingdon: Routledge, 2014); Caveney et al, 'Police Reform, Austerity and "Cop Culture"' (2020) 30(10) *Policing and Society* 1210–1225.

[38] Drawing on the work of Jerome Skolnick in *Justice Without Trial* and the notion of a police officer's working personality, these core characteristics were first articulated in Reiner R, *The Politics of the Police* (Oxford, OUP, 1985) (now see Bowling et al (2019), becoming a key point of reference in the field). For analysis of police culture with regard to race, gender and class see Loftus B, *Police Culture in a Changing World* (Oxford: OUP, 2009).

This is a dichotomous view of society that sees a relatively small section of society perpetually on the verge of revolt against the respectable majority. The sense of impending chaos and the importance of the 'thin blue line' holding it at bay permeates cop culture. This links to the police 'cult of masculinity'[39] evidenced by research conducted over several decades and 'an attitude of "on the streets we can't lose or we're finished". '[40]

Only the police know what it is really like 'out there'. If the naive, well-meaning, respectable majority knew what it was like, they would not make police officers work with one hand tied behind their backs. Thus Dixon quotes an officer saying: 'PACE was meant to protect decent people, but we don't deal with decent people.'[41] While the police see their interests and values as being those of the majority, cop culture is impatient with that majority for not realising how much it needs the police and how impractical the due process values of the 'English liberal intelligentsia'[42] are. The social isolation of officers from 'civilians' (both 'rough' and 'respectable'), and the social solidarity among officers, minimises the extent to which this view of the world is challenged. One result is, as we shall see, a very particular view of what constitutes 'suspicious' behaviour and impatience with any rules which get in the way of the 'fight against crime'. This means that legality is often sacrificed for efficiency.[43] Thus, cop culture acts as a powerful crime control engine at the heart of the machinery of criminal justice.

What we have said about 'cop culture' might lead one to believe that the police who subscribe to it see the world completely differently from the way others see it, and that cop culture is invariant. This would be a mistake. First, the differences between cop culture and that of the wider society can be overstated. For example, impatience with rules that appear to impede the fight against crime is widespread through society,[44] and governments from 1997 onwards deliberately cultivated the dichotomous notion that a minority of criminals and anti-socials will undermine 'our way of life' unless pre-emptive and punitive measures are pursued vigorously.[45] Second, there are differences within cop culture: between forces and within forces (for example between 'management cops' and 'street cops', and between different types of squad). There are differences and indeed tensions between aspects of twenty-first century cop culture and the 'cultural scripts' of a new generation of officers (especially in relation to race, gender and sexual orientation), and the 'cultural scripts' associated with 'older' officers and cop culture of the 1960s.[46]

The numbers of ethnic minority, and female police officers are growing, albeit slowly. Between 2007 and 2019, the total percentage of police officers from Asian, black, mixed and other ethnic groups only went up from 3.9% to 6.9% (chapter 10).[47] The establishment

---

[39] Silvestri M, 'Police Culture and Gender: Revisiting the "Cult of Masculinity"' (2017) 11 *Policing* 289.

[40] Westmarland L, 'Police Cultures' in Newburn T (ed), *Handbook of Policing* (Cullompton: Willan, 2008); Loftus (2009: 96–99).

[41] Dixon D, *Law in Policing* (Oxford: Clarendon, 1997) p 104.

[42] Police officer quoted by Shiner M, 'National Implementation of the Recording of Police Stops' (London: Home Office, 2006) p 51.

[43] Goldsmith A, 'Taking Police Culture Seriously' (1990) 1 *Policing and Society* 91.

[44] See Chan J, 'Changing Police Culture' (1996) 36 *British Journal of Criminology* 109.

[45] See, for example Nixon J and Parr S, 'Anti-social Behaviour: Voices from the Front Line' in Flint J (ed), *Housing, Urban Governance and Anti-Social Behaviour* (Bristol: Policy Press, 2006).

[46] Campeau H, 'Institutional Myths and Generational Boundaries: Cultural Inertia in the Police Organisation' (2019) 29(1) *Policing and Society* 69–84.

[47] Police Workforce Figures, available at <https://www.ethnicity-facts-figures.service.gov.uk/workforce-and-business/workforce-diversity/police-workforce/latest> (accessed 26 August 2020). The Home Secretary in 1999 set a target for black, Asian and mixed ethnic background individuals to make up 7% of the police force by 2009. But it should not be assumed that the dominant police culture will be broken down simply through ensuring greater socio-demographic diversity of recruits (see, for example, Cashmore E, 'The Experiences of Ethnic Minority Police Officers in Britain: Under-recruitment and Racial Profiling in a Performance Culture' (2001) 24(4) *Ethnic and Racial Studies* 642).

of groups such as the Black Police Officers Association, British Association of Women in Policing, and the Lesbian and Gay Police Association evidence and help sustain an ongoing (if painfully slow) process of 'cultural fragmentation' within the police.[48] Indeed, the culture of policing has been found to be particularly adept at withstanding the demands made of them by contemporary calls for diversity and change. Resistance and resentment characterised the attitudes towards the institutionalisation of diversity according to Loftus, who found that racial and sexual minority officers continued to be subjected to overtly derogatory comments, 'pranks' and discriminatory behaviour. This was endured by officers who wanted to succeed in their roles. Alongside the overt discrimination, minority groups were seen to have an unfair advantage in for example acquiring internal promotion because of the implementation of diversity initiatives that were regarded as tokenistic by the majority white heterosexual male police officers.[49] Recent research casts some doubt on the continued power of 'cop culture' in its racist forms, though most officers continue to divide the world they police into 'respectable' people to whose infractions they try and turn a blind eye (if fairly minor) and 'the criminal type' where similar infractions would not be tolerated.[50]

The Macpherson Report[51] published in 1999 led to a new disciplinary offence of racial misconduct. Despite the Macpherson Report representing a milestone in terms of recognition of racism within the police, later research suggested that deep changes in police culture were difficult to detect. Whilst overt racist language had been excised from the police, racist and sexist attitudes had gone 'underground'.[52] An earlier illustration of this was the undercover investigation into the police by a BBC reporter, broadcast as 'The Secret Policeman' on 21 October 2003, that showed that away from the training room (and from the canteen) a number of new recruits spoke 'privately' of their hatred of 'pakis' and five of them admitted (or boasted) that they intended to, or did, use their powers in racially discriminatory ways.[53]

One effect of police culture is to give priority to certain freedoms above others. Less value is put on the freedom involved in activities (especially those of 'them') which impinge on the freedoms of others (especially those of 'us') than is put on 'our' freedoms to be undisturbed. We shall therefore see in chapter 3, that the police prioritise public order at the expense of tolerance and the rights of unpopular minorities. The aggressive policing of demonstrations, and treatment of demonstrators as suspects, that came to the fore with the death of Ian Tomlinson in April 2009 is a stark example.[54] This leads to a tendency to over-police (and under-protect) 'police property', i.e. those who are perceived to be deviating from a 'respectable' norm.[55] Yet the opposite is true of most non-police agencies (discussed in chapter 7). The latter are very reluctant to encroach on the freedom of those whom they police. Clearly the job of law enforcement per se in an adversarial system does not produce the distinctive elements that comprise 'cop culture'.

---

[48] See Loader I and Mulcahy A, *Policing and the Condition of England* (Oxford: OUP, 2003) ch 6; Foster J, Newburn T and Souhami A, *Assessing the Impact of the Stephen Lawrence Inquiry* (London: Home Office, 2005) ch 4; McLaughlin (2007: ch 6).

[49] Loftus (2009).

[50] Pearson and Rowe (2020), esp. chs 4–6. See, especially, p 122.

[51] The Macpherson Report published in 1999 followed a public inquiry examining the Metropolitan Police Service's investigation into the racist murder of black student, Stephen Lawrence, in 1993. The Metropolitan Police Service was deemed as institutionally racist in the report and condemned for its flawed investigation of the murder.

[52] Foster J, Newburn T and Souhami A, *Assessing the Impact of the Stephen Lawrence Inquiry*, Home Office Research Study 294 (London: Home Office, 2005).

[53] See McLaughlin (2007: ch 6). See further ch 10.   [54] See, e.g., *The Guardian*, 1 May 2009.

[55] 'Police property' is a commonly-used term—including, strikingly, by former senior (black) Met Police officers (*The Guardian*, 15 June 2020).

One way of changing police practices might be to inculcate more democratic (or more inclusive) values in officers. This might be attempted through, for example, radical changes in recruitment and training practices, combined with the introduction of new performance indicators, ethical codes of conduct, a genuine commitment to working more closely with local communities, robust leadership and stronger disciplinary measures for those found to be flouting the officially espoused policies and practices.[56] Arguably, however, police values are more resistant to change than are police practices, so more emphasis should be placed on incentives, supervision and discipline.[57] Rather than getting closer to the community simply in order to glean more information from it, the police would need to engage in a continuing discussion, one involving all sections and levels of society, about the proper means and ends of policing.[58] Hope also lies in the possibility of 'generational turnover' in the police, which would allow the cultural scripts of newer and younger officers, which are currently only undercurrents in police culture, to come to the fore. As one young female officer said in recent research: 'We just have to wait for the dinosaurs to die out.'[59] In the rest of this chapter we look at how the police as presently constituted operate powers to stop and search, and at some of the social consequences.

2.2 The power to stop-search

At the time of the Royal Commission on Criminal Procedure (Philips Commission) report in 1981, the law on stop-search was confused and incoherent, having developed in an ad hoc manner. For example, there were no national stop-search powers for stolen goods or offensive weapons. On the other hand, local legislation for many big cities did allow stop-search for stolen goods.[60]

Most of these powers allowed the police to stop-search only if they 'reasonably suspected' a person of the offence in question. A major issue of concern in the 1970s and early 1980s was how far the police really were inhibited by the reasonable suspicion requirement. The early 1980s saw a number of riots in several inner-city areas where poverty and ethnic minority conflict with the police was commonplace.[61] A massive stop-search operation, 'Swamp 81', in particular, was identified as one of the 'triggers' of the Brixton riot of 1981.[62] Described by some as 'saturation policing', stop-search on this scale was manifestly not on a 'reasonable suspicion' basis.[63] Every empirical research project carried out in this period found that many stop-searches were problematic: they targeted young males (black or 'scruffy' males in particular), and were often arbitrary or based 'on grounds which police officers find it hard to specify'.[64] The Philips Commission knew that

---

[56] Evidence that such multi-layered strategies can be at least partially successful can be found in two case studies from the US and Australia respectively: Miller S, *Gender and Community Policing* (Boston MA: North Eastern University Press, 1999); Chan J, *Changing Police Culture* (Cambridge: CUP, 1997). But the success of training is limited: Fielding (2018).

[57] Pearson and Rowe (2020), who argue that 'cop culture' is therefore less a barrier to change than ineffective supervision and direction from 'above'.

[58] Loader (1996: ch 7); Crawford A, 'Reassurance Policing: Feeling is Believing' in Henry A and Smith D, (eds), *Transformations of Policing* (Aldershot: Ashgate, 2007).

[59] Campeau (2019: 81).

[60] See Royal Commission on Criminal Procedure, *The Investigation and Prosecution of Criminal Offences in England and Wales: The Law and Procedure* (Cmnd 8092–1, app 1).

[61] For discussion, see Cashmore E and McLaughlin E (eds), *Out of Order?* (London: Routledge, 1991) p 113.

[62] See further 2.5.1.

[63] Scarman Sir L, *The Brixton Disorders: 10–12 April 1981* (Cmnd 8427) (London: HMSO, 1981).

[64] Willis C, *The Use, Effectiveness and Impact of Police Stop and Search Powers* (Home Office Research and Planning Unit Paper No 15) (London: Home Office, 1983) p 15; also see Smith and Gray (1983).

stop-search was difficult to control, and was aware of the damage that these powers could do to the relationship between police and black youths in particular. It recommended a single uniform power for the police to stop-search for stolen goods or 'articles which it is a criminal offence to possess', but it also believed that 'the exercise of the powers must be subject to strict safeguards'.[65] Along with many other of the Philips Commission's proposals, these recommendations were enacted in PACE. The bundle of laws and controls that resulted contained elements of all four of the types of rule we identified earlier: the extension of the powers nationwide *legitimised* pre-existing police working practices and, by cloaking officers with legal authority, *enabled* more intensive stop and search strategies in future. At the same time, *inhibitory* elements were incorporated (with limited success, thus rendering them largely *presentational*) in the form of 'safeguards'.

As we mentioned earlier, police powers are useable far more easily in public than in private. Thus PACE stop-search powers may be used only in public places, and non-dwelling places to which the public have ready access—including public transport, and (while open to the public) museums, sports grounds, cinemas, pubs, restaurants, night-clubs, banks and shops, and even schools to search for offensive weapons.[66] Section 1 of PACE is headed: 'Power of constable to stop and search persons, vehicles, etc'. This power can best be understood as comprising three main elements: a 'reasonable suspicion' criterion, the offences to which stop and search is applicable, and the power itself.

2.2.1 Reasonable suspicion and police suspicion

2.2.1.1 The slippery concept of reasonable suspicion

Under s.1(3) of PACE police officers may only stop-search if they have 'reasonable grounds for suspecting' that evidence of relevant offences will be found; and seizure may take place only of articles which, under s.1(7), the officer 'has reasonable grounds for suspecting' to be relevant. The requirement of 'reasonable suspicion' is aimed at inhibiting the police from stopping and searching indiscriminately—or, indeed, in inappropriately discriminatory ways—without unduly fettering their ability to detect crime.

The few cases on reasonable suspicion do little to define it, other than making it clear that it may be based on material, such as hearsay, that would not necessarily be admissible in court.[67] In *Francis*, for example, suspicion was created by the suspect driving in an area known for drugs, with a passenger. The last time the driver had been stopped her passenger (a different one) had been in possession of drugs. This was held not to constitute 'reasonable suspicion'.[68] In *Slade*, on the other hand, the suspect's proximity to an address known for its drugs connections, combined with the fact that he had noticed the officer and put his hand in his pocket while smiling 'smugly', was held to constitute reasonable suspicion.[69] It would be difficult to slip a Rizla paper between the material facts of these 'reasonable suspicion' cases that nonetheless reach different conclusions.

However, demonstrators against whom there was no individual suspicion were held to be lawfully stopped and searched because there was 'intelligence' that 'people' going to

---

[65] Royal Commission on Criminal Procedure (RCCP), Report (Cmnd 8092) (London: HMSO, 1981) para 3.17.

[66] Section 4 of the Offensive Weapons Act 1996 (inserting s.139B into the Criminal Justice Act 1988), as widened by s.48 of the Violent Crime Reduction Act 2006.

[67] *Shaaban Bin Hussien v Chong Fook Kam* [1970] AC 942; *Erskine v Hollin* [1971] RTR 199.

[68] LEXIS, CO/1434/91, June 1992. *Black* CO/877/95 (11 May 1995) QBD is to similar effect. See also *Tomlinson*, reported in LAG Bulletin, May 1992, p 21 and *French v DPP* [1996] EWHC Admin 283 (27 November 1996). [69] LEXIS, CO/1678/96, October 1996.

this demonstration might have material that would cause criminal damage. As the judgment said: 'It is well recognised that the threshold for the existence of reasonable grounds for suspicion is low.'[70] Neither the PACE 'protections' nor the ECHR protected this individual or his fellow protesters, and the judgment gave no guidance on the point at which a group would be so large that it would be unreasonable to hold and search them all. The court said their right to demonstrate was unaffected as they were able to continue, but this ignores the evidence they gave that they found the police actions intimidating; this would deter many from demonstrating again.

An attempt to clarify the concept of 'reasonable suspicion' is contained in PACE Code of Practice A.[71] This Code has been revised many times, sometimes with a view to enlarging the concept of reasonable suspicion, sometimes with a view to restricting it. References in the text are to the version that came into force on 19 March 2015.[72] The core 'definition' of reasonable suspicion is contained in para 2.2:

> Reasonable grounds for suspicion is the legal test which a police officer must satisfy before they can stop and detain individuals or vehicles to search them under powers such as section 1 of PACE (to find stolen or prohibited articles) and section 23 of the Misuse of Drugs Act 1971 (to find controlled drugs). This test must be applied to the particular circumstances in each case and is in two parts:
>
> (i) *Firstly*, the officer must have formed a *genuine* suspicion in their own mind that they will find the object for which the search power being exercised allows them to search; and
> (ii) *Secondly*, the suspicion that the object will be found must be reasonable. This means that there must be an *objective* basis for that suspicion based on facts, information and/or intelligence which are relevant to the likelihood that the object in question will be found, so that a reasonable person would be entitled to reach the same conclusion based on the same facts and information and/or intelligence.

Paragraph 2.4 of the code goes on to state that reasonable grounds for suspicion should normally be linked to accurate and current intelligence or information, relating to articles for which there is a power to stop and search, being carried by individuals or being in vehicles in any locality. This would include reports from members of the public or other officers describing:

- a person who has been seen carrying such an article or a vehicle in which such an article has been seen
- crimes committed in relation to which such an article would constitute relevant evidence, for example, property stolen in a theft or burglary, an offensive weapon or bladed or sharply pointed article used to assault or threaten someone or an article used to cause criminal damage to property.

---

[70] *Howarth v MPC* [2011] EWHC 2818 (Admin), Para 34. Nothing suspicious was found.

[71] A number of Codes of Practice have been made by the Home Office under the authority of PACE. Codes of Practice are similar in effect to legislation, insofar as they must be taken into account by the courts, but they are brought into effect by statutory instrument. This makes them easy to amend in the light of experience. Code A applies not only to stop-search powers exercised under PACE, but also to those exercised under, for instance, the Terrorism Act 2000 and the Criminal Justice and Public Order Act 1994.

[72] The 2015 version of Code of Practice A can be downloaded from <https://assets.publishing.service.gov.uk/government/uploads/system/uploads/attachment_data/file/903810/pace-code-a-2015.pdf> (accessed 26 August 2020).

As with previous versions of the code, it leaves scope to identify certain groups as more suspicious than others and paragraph 2.6 acknowledges this by providing that:

> Where there is reliable information or intelligence that members of a group or gang habitually carry knives unlawfully or weapons or controlled drugs, and have distinctive clothing, tattoos etc in order to identify themselves as members of that group or gang, those identifiers can provide reasonable grounds to stop and search any person believed to be a member of that group or gang.

Reasonable suspicion can never be supported on the basis of personal factors. It must rely on intelligence or information that provides a description of a person suspected of carrying an article for which there is a power to stop and search. A person's physical appearance cannot be used as the reason for stopping and searching any individual, including any vehicle that they are driving or are being carried in. Personal factors include protected characteristics as set out in the Equality Act 2010, s.149, which are age, disability, gender reassignment, pregnancy and maternity, race, religion or belief, sex and sexual orientation or the fact that the person is known to have a previous conviction. Reasonable suspicion cannot be based on generalisations or stereotypical images of certain groups or categories of people as more likely to be involved in criminal activity. A person's religion cannot be considered as reasonable grounds for suspicion and should never be considered as a reason to stop or stop and search an individual.

Reference to not stopping someone because of their religion or belief reflects the fact that the police began to target Muslims after the terrorist atrocities of 11 September 2001 in New York and July 2005 in London.[73] It is remarkable that a legislative code of practice directs, in effect, that people should not be stopped just because they are black or Muslim, and is a rare example of the law attempting to take into account the social reality of policing on the streets. This message is amplified from the outset, for example, para 1.1:

> Powers to stop and search must be used fairly, responsibly, with respect for people being searched and without unlawful discrimination. Under the Equality Act 2010, section 149, when police officers are carrying out their functions, they also have a duty to have due regard to the need to eliminate unlawful discrimination, harassment and victimisation, to advance equality of opportunity between people who share a 'relevant protected characteristic' and people who do not share it, and to take steps to foster good relations between those persons.

That such amplification has been deemed necessary suggests that, over three decades on from the original enactment of PACE and the Codes of Practice, problems of controlling the use of police discretion have persisted. One indication that the law has proved largely ineffective in restraining the police is the enormous growth in recorded stop-searches since PACE was introduced; indeed up until 2013/14 the annual total rose and remained over one million (see Table 2.1). Since then there has been a gradual reduction in the number of stop and searches and yet since PACE first operated the arrest rate following stop-searches has remained relatively stable. However, all such statistics must be treated with caution, since they are as much a product of police recording practices that can vary over time, as actual occurrences of law-breaking.

---

[73] See, Parmar (2011); Chakraborti N, 'Policing Muslim Communities' in Rowe M (ed), *Policing Beyond Macpherson* (Cullompton: Willan, 2007); Mythen G, Walklate S and Khan T, (2009) ' "I'm a Muslim, but I'm Not a Terrorist": Victimization, Risky Identities and the Performance of Safety' 49(6) *British Journal of Criminology* 736.

Table 2.1 Recorded stop-searches (where reasonable suspicion is required) and arrest rates[74]

Year	Stop-Searches	Arrests	% of stops leading to arrest
1986	109,800	18,900	17.2
1988	149,600	23,700	15.8
1990	256,900	39,200	15.3
1992	351,700	48,700	13.8
1994	576,000	70,300	12.2
1996	814,500	87,700	10.8
1997/98	1,050,700	108,700	10.3
1999/00	857,200	108,500	12.7
2001/02	741,000	98,700	13.3
2003/04	749,400	95,100	12.7
2005/06	888,675	97,600	11
2007/08	1,053,001	120,351	11
2009/10	1,177,327	107,632	9
2011/12	1,142,909	107,592	9
2013/14	900,129	108,161	12
2015/16	382,625	60,232	16
2016/17	303,501	51,844	17
2018/19	370,454	58,251	16

Table 2.1 shows that the number of recorded stop-searches rose rapidly from the mid-1980s to the late 1990s before falling sharply at the turn of the century[75] and then steadily picked up again until 2013/14. Since then numbers of stop and searches have been falling although they rose again in 2018/19. The drop in stop and searches after 2013/14 was attributed to former Home Secretary and Prime Minister Theresa May's reining in of the power during her time in office. Her attempts to tighten the definition of reasonable suspicion and sanctions for police officers breaching the code clearly held potential for reducing the use of stop and search powers.[76] Furthermore, the relationship between the level of crime in a police force area and the level of recorded searches carried out in that area is weak, and some forces with high crime rates make relatively little recorded use of stop and search (Miller et al 2000: 13). In short, trends in the recorded use of stop-search do not appear to be driven by the amount of reasonably suspicious behaviour taking place but rather by police policies and practices.

---

[74] Source: Povey D and Smith K (eds), *Police Powers and Procedures, England and Wales 2007/08* 2nd edn (Home Office Statistical Bulletin 7/09) (London: Home Office, 2009) table 2a, and earlier bulletins in the same series, as well as *Police Powers and Procedures, England and Wales 2019* (London: Home Office). These figures largely relate to stop-search under PACE, s.1, but also s.43 of the Terrorism Act 2000, s 23 of the Misuse of Drugs Act 1971 and some other less important powers where 'reasonable suspicion' is required. Data from 2009/10 onwards includes the British Transport Police.

[75] The drop at the turn of the century appears to be a result of the high profile Macpherson Inquiry, which branded the Metropolitan Police as institutionally racist, drew attention to the damage that stop-search practices were doing to race relations and recommended tighter safeguards: Macpherson Sir W, *The Stephen Lawrence Inquiry – Report* (London: SO, 1999) recommendations 61–3. This prompted a temporary loss of confidence by the police (Fitzgerald (1999: ch 5); Fitzgerald et al (2002: 100–101); Miller et al (2000: 17)).

[76] Bowling B and Marks E, 'The Rise and Fall of Suspicionless Searches' (2017) 28(1) *King's Law Journal* 62–88.

2.2.1.2 Police suspicion, working assumptions and working rules

If the legal rules do little to constrain and structure police discretion, what does? Police officers often refer to 'instinct' and 'experience'. As Fielding observes, experience is valued, whereas 'books' or theory are not.[77] Research has repeatedly found that exhortations in probationer training to police 'by the book' are quickly overwhelmed by the more powerful influences through which traditional cop culture is reproduced, amongst which are the 'old sweats' who induct trainees into the 'realities of the street'.[78] Partly this involves learning how to deal with conflict and volatile situations. As one officer put it: 'On the street, most times, you don't have time to go through a list of reasonable grounds before stopping [and searching]. It's not like a doctor making a diagnosis: you've got this problem and you have to solve it there and then and think about it afterwards.'[79] But most stop-searches are the result of individual officer discretion (high discretion searches) rather than the result of officers acting on intelligence already received or being called to a problematic incident (low discretion searches). Thus, in the majority of stop-searches officers are not 'problem-solving' but rather proactively seeking to detect, prevent or disrupt crime and disorder.[80] This results in officers targeting those who they think offer the best prospects for achieving these ends, almost regardless of the level of individualised suspicion. The young, particularly those from ethnic minorities or lower class backgrounds, suffer particularly from such high discretion searches, but so do 'druggy-looking people',[81] the homeless, asylum seekers and other unpopular users of public space.

Just how quickly induction into the craft of street-policing can take place was exemplified by 'The Secret Policeman' programme. PC Andy Hall had served for 15 months in London but wanted to move to Manchester so had to undergo initial training again. During the course he spoke privately to a fellow probationer, PC Mark Daly, who was in fact an undercover BBC reporter. The secret recording of the conversation shows how the lessons of 'practical policing' may be taught even to probationers still in training school:

PC Hall: I would never say this in class. If you did not discriminate and you did not bring out your prejudices, you'd be a shit copper, do you know that?

PC Daly: Really?

PC Hall: If you was on the street Mark, and you wouldn't stop anyone because of their colour, because of their race, because of how they dress, because of how they thingy, you'd be a shit copper. I mean we used to drive down the road and say 'he looks a dodgy c*** let's stop him.' That is practical policing. It is mate. And nine times out of ten you're right.[82] But in training environment you can't be seen to do it because it's discrimination. It's against the equal opportunities. But when you are on the street you will fucking pick it up.

This programme was made not long after the publication in 1999 of the Macpherson Report. The latter excoriated police services for their 'institutional racism', as manifested, amongst other things, by the disproportionate stop-searching of BAME people (see section 2.3).[83] This resulted in a huge (if often misguided) reform effort to improve police

---

[77] Fielding N, *Joining Forces* (London: Routledge, 1988).
[78] For a discussion of this socialisation process and its effects see: Charman S, *Police Socialisation, Identity and Culture: Becoming Blue* (Basingstoke: Palgrave Macmillan, 2017).
[79] Cited in Fitzgerald (1999: ch 3). And see, further Pearson and Rowe (2020).
[80] Fitzgerald (1999: ch 3).
[81] An expression used by one of the officers quoted by Fitzgerald (1999: ch 2).
[82] This is an expression of confidence in police fact-finding redolent of the crime control model. It would be more accurate to say that nine times out of ten the police are wrong (see Table 2.1).
[83] Macpherson (1999: 29–30).

practice, and contributed to the virtual eradication of *openly* racist talk and action.[84] Police officers of PC Hall's ilk are thus unlikely nowadays to reveal to researchers such racially prejudiced thinking. Instead they are likely to explain their behaviour by reference to a vague concept, such as a 'hunch'.

Some generalisations that inform practical decision-making are acknowledged more openly, however. Quinton et al found that: 'The individuals who were known to the police were often targeted in stops and searches. It was common practice, on the shift briefings in each of the pilot sites, for officers to be given the details of individuals and cars which would be "worth a stop".'[85] Fitzgerald found that officers were open about their targeting of those who were 'known' to the police by virtue of their criminal record and/or their associates. As one constable put it: 'The vast majority of the people we're dealing with are the same people all the time.' This assertion was supported by Fitzgerald's analysis of search records that found that about half of those searched, who were not arrested as a result, had previous convictions or cautions. She also found that of the 589 people searched on three or more occasions within the first quarter of 1999 only two had no criminal record (Fitzgerald, 1999: ch 3). More recently, Flacks found that the rounding up of 'the usual suspects' extends to their family members too. One of the participants in the research said that having 'a name' and family members with criminal records made her a target for police stops: 'It's unfair. I think if you're known to the police, if you've got a name then they're going to harass you anyway [...] They know where I hang around, where I live, who I hang around with[...] who I'm related to. They know everything about me.'[86] As one officer said to a researcher recently, 'there's a lad worth a stop'. Being 'known' to the officer was suspicion enough.[87]

Another important factor in police suspicion is incongruity—being where one does not belong: a young male in a tracksuit, hoodie and cap in a 'posh' area, for instance,[88] or for that matter someone dressed in a dinner jacket driving around a decaying inner-city area.[89] There is an even-handedness here which is more apparent than real. The rich may seem to be equally at risk of having police power exercised against them if they spend time in poor areas as are the poor in wealthy areas. But wealthy people are less likely to be in such areas, will not be offended if the police suggest that they do not 'belong', and generally possess fewer traits (race, previous convictions and so forth) which would, when added to incongruity, lead to suspiciousness. It is also far easier for the wealthy to avoid incongruity when out of their own area (by dressing scruffily) than it is for the poor.

Membership of an ethnic minority group, especially if one is in an area with few ethnic minority people, is also important in terms of marking someone as 'not belonging'. In August 2017 Dale Semper, a black bank manager, was pulled over by police: 'They rushed up to the car, banging on the window, shouting "get out, get out of the car." They handcuffed me.' Semper recalls. He was escorted back to his home, when comments from officers started: how does someone like you afford these two cars? How can someone like you live here and be so successful? How can someone like you afford that watch, that car, this home? It was clear to Semper that by 'someone' the officers meant a black person. The police searched for firearms. None were found. He was never prosecuted.[90] This is

---

[84] Foster et al (2005: 35–40); Holdaway S and O'Neill M, 'Where has all the Racism Gone? Views of Racism within Constabularies after Macpherson' (2007) 30(3) *Ethnic and Racial Studies* 397.

[85] Quinton et al, *Police Stops, Decision-making and Practice* (Police Research Series Paper 130) (London: Home Office, 2000) pp 24–25. Scottish police similarly target the 'usual suspects' and their associates: McAra L and McVie S, 'The Usual Suspects? Street-Life, Young People and the Police' (2005) 5(1) *Criminal Justice* 5 at p 26.

[86] Flacks S, 'The Stop and Search of Minors: A "Vital Police Tool"?' (2018) 18(3) *Criminology and Criminal Justice* 364-384, 375.

[87] Pearson and Rowe (2020: 119). [88] Flacks (2018).

[89] 'I focus on people not matching area – how they dress' (officer quoted by Quinton et al (2000: 23).

[90] *The Guardian*, 22 June 2020.

only a little more extreme than countless other similar recent incidents, including in 2020 (black MP) Dawn Butler stopped (in her black friend's BMW) because 'there's people who have been coming into the area',[91] and (black civil servant) Andrea Charles-Fidelis who was stopped when falsely accused of stealing a car.[92]

What comes out of this material, as well as much other research, pre- and post-PACE, and from Australia and the USA as well as the UK, is that much police discretion is based on stereotyping and often stereotyping which subtly brings together race, class and gender.[93] This process enables rough and ready but very speedy judgements about a person's character (their 'master status') to be made on the basis of visible signs (known as 'auxiliary traits').[94] These auxiliary traits include gender, age, scruffiness, attitude to the police, previous convictions and ethnic group.

A classic example of racial stereotyping is provided by the 50-year-old Bishop of Stepney, John Sentamu who in 2010 finally expressed his anger after being stopped for the eighth time in as many years.[95] When asked why he stopped the bishop's car, the officer simply said 'Open the boot': 'He asked me what I did, and I said, "I'm the Bishop of Stepney." He said "whoops", I revealed my dog collar and he looked as if he'd just seen a ghost.' The officer immediately told the bishop he could go, refusing to say why he had stopped him. The stereotyping in this case is clear. Middle-aged men normally have a respectable master status in the eyes of the police. However, the bishop's black auxiliary trait trumped his middle-aged male auxiliary trait, giving him a 'suspicious' master status.[96] The black auxiliary trait was then trumped when his clerical collar was revealed, returning to him the 'respectable' master status he would have had, had he not been black.[97]

Research in the post-Macpherson era has confirmed the continuing firm police belief in the value of the working assumptions and rules we have outlined here.[98] As one officer declared: 'I mean I'm sure sociologists, liberal types, would say that we're employing stereotypes to make those, well yes, and it works. That's how we catch criminals.'[99] Or, to

---

[91] *The Guardian*, 9 August 2020.

[92] *The Metro*, 4 August 2020. For systematic discussions see Loader and Mulcahy (2003) pp 157–158; Equality and Human Right Commission, *Police and Racism: What has been Achieved 10 Years after the Stephen Lawrence Inquiry Report?* (London: Equality and Human Right Commission, 2009) p 24, and Hallsworth S, 'Racial Targeting and Social Control: Looking behind the Police' (2006) 14 *Critical Criminology* 293 at 301–302. Occasionally even more extreme forms of racism interact with incongruity in decision-making. Black and Asian people are evidently seen by a (hopefully tiny) minority of officers as by definition incongruous in an Anglo-Saxon England constructed as 'naturally' white. Examples of this were recorded as part of 'The Secret Policeman' documentary: 'It's fucking proactive policing, yeah, innit? He's a Paki and I'm stopping him, because I'm fucking English. At the end of the day mate, we look after our own. You know that don't you?' (PC Andy Hall).

[93] For a psychological analysis of stereotyping, and the related phenomena of prejudice and ethnocentrism see Ainsworth P, *Psychology and Policing* (Cullompton: Willan, 2002) pp 27–32; See further, for example Equality and Human Rights Commission, *Stop and Think: A Critical Review of the Use of Stop and Search Powers in England and Wales* (2010) and discussion in ch 10.

[94] The terminology is used by criminologists who adopt the 'social reaction' (or 'labelling') perspective. For an English example in this tradition see Gill O, 'Urban Stereotypes and Delinquent Incidents' (1976) 16 *British Journal of Criminology* 312.

[95] See <https://www.theguardian.com/uk/2000/jan/24/race.world> (accessed 27 August 2020).

[96] Research confirms that the trumping of a 'respectable age or class' by a 'disrespectable ethnicity' occurs quite frequently for some ethnic groups: Mooney J and Young J, 'Policing Ethnic Minorities: Stop and Search in North London' in Marlow A and Loveday B (eds), After Macpherson: Reflections on Policing after the Stephen Lawrence Enquiry (London: Russell House, 2010). Similarly black women are seen by the police as more threatening than white women: Player E, 'Women and Crime in the City' in Downes D (ed), *Crime and the City* (Basingstoke: Macmillan, 1989) pp 122–125.

[97] Off duty black police officers sometimes suffer in much the same way. For an example see Havis S and Best D, *Stop and Search Complaints: A Police Complaints Authority Study* (London: Police Complaints Authority, 2004) p 31.

[98] For example, Lister et al (2008); Shiner (2006).

[99] Police officer quoted by Shiner (2006: 53).

quote more recent research, many stops were 'based purely on a hunch, or "a sense that something is not quite right."'[100]

As mentioned earlier in the discussion about PACE, since 2010 onwards, young Asian males have become more pronounced targets for suspicion, particularly in context of the 'war on terror'. This overall and enduring pattern is reflected in figures that breakdown stop and search rates by ethnicity and are discussed later in the chapter. To give one example of how malleable stereotypes can be in adapting to more recent links between ethnic background and notions of criminality, in 2007 an officer with specialist responsibility for giving race and diversity lessons to recruits told a public meeting in Cumbria that any sightings of young Asian men in an area of the Lake District should be reported to the police, adding: 'Whilst we are told not to stereotype, the reality is that groups of young Asian males need to be checked out.'[101]

What would it take to get police officers to respect the law's requirement of reasonable suspicion? In 1995 a charitable body, NACRO, ran an experiment in one area of London in co-operation with the local police. The police were required to give a leaflet to everyone stop-searched in the area which explained their rights. No new rules were introduced, although the use of stop-search as a performance indicator in the area was stopped, and the commitment of the area's senior police to non-racist policing was emphasised. In that year, the number of stop-searches was apparently halved, at a time when stop-searches across the capital in general continued to rise. It is likely that giving out a leaflet which set out the law concentrated the minds of officers on the rules and inhibited their use of the power.[102] In a more recent trial, officers in six diverse police forces across England were randomly allocated to receive one-day training on ethnic/racial bias in stop and search, with this trial finding that whilst the training made officers more knowledgeable about stop and search regulations and reduced their stated support for ethnic/racial stereotyping, the training was too limited to impact on their stated intentions about the ethnicity/race of who they would stop and search.[103]

These experiments suggests that limited change can happen, but only with constant reinforcement and through a package of measures, not only in relation to what the rules are, but also in relation to the effects of adhering to them (or not). This is a matter of both positive reinforcement (not rewarding, through performance indicators, stops simply on a volume basis) and negative reinforcement (the threat of disciplinary action for racism and rule-breaking, and again illustrated by the police management attitude in Tottenham at the time of the experiment). Policing in general does not yet embody either form of reinforcement,[104] and so the conclusions of the authors of the NACRO study hold good in the main: 'the guidance on reasonable suspicion in the PACE Code of Practice is not clearly understood, or remembered, or put into practice … The "culture" on divisions [i.e. on the street] will have a stronger impact on probationary officers than classroom teaching

---

[100] Pearson and Rowe (2020: 101).
[101] Quoted in Equality and Human Rights Commission (2008: 19).
[102] NACRO, *Policing Local Communities: The Tottenham Experiment* (London: NACRO, 1997).
[103] Miller J, Quinton P, Alexandrou B and Packham D, 'Can Police Training Reduce Ethnic/Racial Disparities in Stop and Search? Evidence from a Multisite UK Trial' (2020) 19(4) *Criminology and Public Policy*, 1259–1287.
[104] In the wake of the Macpherson Report, the government belatedly realised the damage caused by performance indicators that emphasise quantity rather than quality (Home Office, 2005a: 12, 25, 27, 38) but as their notion of quality encompasses a strong emphasis on the intelligence-gathering function of stop-search (e.g. 27–28) and an inadequate emphasis on the precondition of individualised reasonable suspicion of a specific offence (partly a product of the mixed-message sent out by their creation of, and support for, search powers that do not carry that precondition—see next sub-section), we remain sceptical that front line police officers will change their ways.

can hope to achieve' (NACRO 1997: 41). Or to put it another way, as authors of the more recent study note, though there are grounds for cautious optimism about the benefits of training for reducing racial disparities in stop and search practices, '[g]iven the complex cultural, organizational and structural influences that likely shape these disparities, it is perhaps not surprising that a 1-day training program for police officers would not substantially ameliorate it.'[105]

The aftermath of the Macpherson Report confirms these conclusions. Macpherson's wounding critique of 'institutionally racist' stop-search practices, and the attempts to improve training and supervision in response, appear to have had the same (short-term) effect as these two experiments of concentrating officers' minds on the rules. A large-scale Home Office funded study set up to assess the impact of the Macpherson Inquiry found that:

> observed officers reported a climate in the aftermath of the Inquiry in which 'people were too afraid' to stop and search for fear of being accused of racism. This effect seemed to be particularly powerful in [the Met], where officers said the use of searches dramatically declined … It also appears that the Inquiry brought into focus officers' uncertainty and confusion about the legitimate use of their powers. As one officer explained: 'It makes police officers scared. If I saw a black youth on a street corner I would probably not search him, unless he's done something physically tangible that I have seen, I won't do it.'[106]

This, of course, is exactly what reasonable suspicion requires—something tangible. As the researchers go on to observe:

> It seems likely that because officers felt under increased scrutiny in the aftermath of the Inquiry, and that they might therefore be held to account for their actions, there were times when they realised they could not always account for their conduct. Officers reported that the perceived increase in scrutiny meant that they could no longer go on 'fishing trips' where they knew they did not have proper grounds for searching. The climate before the Inquiry appeared to have made it either acceptable and/or possible for some officers to break rules in relation to stop and search. Since the Lawrence Inquiry Report this was perceived to be more difficult.[107]

The difficulty does not appear to be insurmountable, however, as indicated by the recent rises in the stop-search figures (see Table 2.1), which have been particularly marked in the case of ethnic minorities.[108] Given the entrenched patterns of racial disproportionality evidenced in stop and search figures, it seems likely that the role of reasonable suspicion as having a safeguarding effect is fading into the background once again. We should not make the mistake,

---

[105] Miller et al (2020: 23).   [106] Foster et al (2005: 29–30).

[107] Foster et al (2005: 30). British Crime Survey data from 1999 strongly suggests that the targeting by patrol officers of black people on foot did become less pronounced at this time, although this was not true for vehicle stops: Clancy A et al, Crime, Policing and Justice: The Experience of Ethnic Minorities (London: Home Office, 2001) pp 369–382.

[108] Thus, following general and fairly even falls across the board in 1999/2000, the two years to 2001/02 saw a further overall fall in the numbers of recorded stop-searches of white people, but very significant increases for black and Asian people. The years from 2004/05 to 2006/07 are marked by large percentage increases but most noticeably for Asian people in London, reflecting the increased concern about people of Muslim faith following the July 2005 attacks on the London transport system. The upshot is that racial disparities have widened markedly over the last two decades, despite repeated exhortations from government for the police to curb 'ethnic disproportionality'. Source: annual 'Statistics on Race and the Criminal Justice System' as published by the Home Office and, now, the Ministry of Justice (available from <http://www.justice.gov.uk/publications/raceandcjs.htm> (accessed 5 January 2010) and for more recent figures <https://assets.publishing.service.gov.uk/government/uploads/system/uploads/attachment_data/file/849200/statistics-on-race-and-the-cjs-2018.pdf> (accessed 3 September 2020)).

however, of concluding that the reasonable suspicion requirement is purely presentational. That it has some inhibitory effect is indicated by the even lower arrest rates associated with stop-search powers that do not require this level of suspicion (see section 2.2.2.2).[109]

2.2.2 The offences at which stop and search is targeted

A due process theorist would argue that stop-search powers could only be legitimate if they required the police to have reasonable suspicion of a specific offence. A crime control theorist would argue that the police should be able to act whenever their suspicions, however generalised, are aroused. PACE appears at first sight to take the due process approach, but matters are not quite so simple as this, as we shall now explore.

2.2.2.1 Stop-searches requiring reasonable suspicion

Under s.1(3) of PACE, a police officer may stop and search only if 'he has reasonable grounds for suspecting that he will find stolen or prohibited articles or any article to which sub-section (8A) below applies or any firework … '. 'Stolen articles' clearly include those stolen in contravention of s.1 of the Theft Act 1968, and probably include goods obtained by handling, fraud or blackmail.[110] What is a 'prohibited article'? According to s.1(7) and (8), it is either (i) an offensive weapon or (ii) an article intended for use in burglary, theft, taking vehicles or fraud. Section 1(8A) was added by the Criminal Justice Act 1988. It allows searches for articles that, under s.139 of that Act, are unlawful if carried without a good excuse. Such articles include anything with blades or sharp points, including penknives if the blade is over three inches long. This enlarges the already extensive notion of the offensive weapon. Any item can be classed as an offensive weapon so long as it can be shown that the person possessed it with intention to cause injury. Similarly, a wide range of articles could be intended for use in committing crimes of dishonesty. The Criminal Justice Act 2003 (s.1) added items intended for use in causing criminal damage, and the Serious Organised Crime and Police Act 2005 (s.115) added prohibited fireworks,[111] to the ever-lengthening list of articles which can be the object of a stop-search. Broad as these powers are, they represent additions to (rather than replacements for) the miscellaneous powers mentioned earlier.[112] Thus, the police have long had a power to search where they reasonably suspect that a controlled drug will be found on a person or in a vehicle.[113]

2.2.2.2 Stop-searches *not* requiring reasonable suspicion

Extra powers to stop and search vehicles and pedestrians were introduced by the Criminal Justice and Public Order Act 1994 (CJPO), s.60. These can be invoked by a senior officer where the police wish to stop-search for guns, knives or other weapons as provided under PACE, s.1, but there is no individualised reasonable suspicion. This originally allowed, for

---

[109] It is likely that the growth in the use of such powers over the last decade means that some of the stop-search activity based on a weak level of suspicion which would previously have been cloaked in the authority of PACE now takes place under other legislation. This might help explain why the arrest rate for stop-searches requiring reasonable suspicion has not deteriorated as much as one might have expected in the period from 2003/04 onwards (see Table 2.1). Another explanatory factor is likely to be that arrest became a more favoured outcome given the intense pressure from the government for the police to 'bring more offenders to justice'.

[110] Assuming that the extended definition of 'stolen goods' to be found in s.24(4) of the Theft Act 1968 applies here too.

[111] That is to say, prohibited under the Fireworks Regulations (SI 2004/1836) passed pursuant to the Fireworks Act 2003.

[112] In what follows we do not attempt an exhaustive list of all stop-search powers. A score of them are set out in Annex A to PACE Code of Practice A but even this list is declared to be only of the 'main' stop and search powers.   [113] Misuse of Drugs Act 1971, s.23.

a period not normally exceeding 24 hours, the police to stop-search anyone where there is a reasonable belief *in relation to a particular locality* that 'incidents involving serious violence may take place'.[114] The Knives Act 1997 extended this power to cover situations where the senior officer (who now need only be an Inspector) has a reasonable belief that persons are carrying 'dangerous instruments or offensive weapons', again with no requirement of reasonable suspicion against any particular individuals.[115] Section 87 of the Serious Crime Act 2007 extended this again, by enabling a s.60 authorisation to be made if the authorising officer reasonably believes that an incident involving serious violence has taken place in that officer's police area, that a weapon or dangerous instrument used in that incident is being carried in any locality within that area, and it is expedient to give an authorisation to find that article. Senior officers should rely on information and intelligence when deciding to authorise searches requiring s.60 pre-condition. However, the legislation is silent on the selection of people to be searched under s.60. In practice, the police no doubt target much the same people as those stop-searched under PACE although they must adhere to PACE Code A guidance to not discriminate on the basis of a protected characteristic. Furthermore, in 2014 the Home Office published guidance to police forces on the best use of stop and search specifically to reduce the use of searches requiring an authorisation, which includes the need to seek authorisation for the use of s.60 powers by an officer from the National Police Chiefs Council.[116]

Clearly, searches *not* requiring reasonable suspicion are highly controversial powers, as without the safeguard of reasonable suspicion, abuses and harm to police community relations are even more likely than under PACE.[117] In 2015 s.60 of the CJPO was challenged in the Supreme Court; although the Court found the legislation to be compatible with the right to privacy, the case highlighted the risk of human rights violations through police enforcement of s.60.[118]

Wide-ranging powers were also provided by ss.44–47 of the Terrorism Act 2000 and the Anti-terrorism, Crime and Security Act 2001 (building on earlier anti-terrorism provisions). The police could stop any vehicle or person for the sole purpose of searching for articles of a kind that could be used in connection with terrorism 'whether or not the constable has any grounds for suspecting the presence of articles of that kind' (s.45(1)). While the 'sole purpose' restriction sounded impressive, in practice, arrests arising out of such stops were often not in connection with terrorism, leading to a huge increase in what seemed to be spurious stops. Thus, if the police searched for evidence of terrorism but found someone in possession of cannabis they could then be arrested for that offence instead. Authorisation had to be by an officer of at least the rank of Assistant Chief Constable who judged it 'expedient for the prevention of acts of terrorism' (s.44(3)); and the period could last for 28 days (renewable). Authorisation required confirmation by the Home Secretary, who had the power to set a shorter period. Like s.60 of the CJPO 1994,

---

[114] CJPO, s.60 (2). Also see Code A, paras 2.12–2.16.

[115] Knives Act 1997, s.8, amending CJPO, s.60. This also allows the 24-hour period to be extended by a further 24 hours. Section 25 of the Crime and Disorder Act 1998 extended s.60 yet further by allowing police officers to require a person to remove items which the constable reasonably suspects are designed to prevent the person's identity being revealed. See also s.94 of the Anti-terrorism, Crime and Security Act 2001 which enables an officer of at least the rank of inspector to make an authorisation relating specifically to this power to require the removal of (and/or seize) identity-concealing items.

[116] Home Office, *Best Use of Stop and Search Scheme*. Available at <https://assets.publishing.service.gov.uk/government/uploads/system/uploads/attachment_data/file/346922/Best_Use_of_Stop_and_Search_Scheme_v3.0_v2.pdf> (accessed 28 August 2020).   [117] See Parmar (2011).

[118] *R (on the application of Roberts) (Appellant) v Commissioner of the Police of the Metropolis and another (Respondents)* [2015] UKSC 79. See further ch 10.

the power was confined to an area specified in a prior authorisation by a senior officer but, unlike the s.60 power, this area could extend to an entire police force area. An authorisation could therefore cover, for example, a whole city or the whole of Northern Ireland, or even straddle a number of areas (if authorising officers were to coordinate their activities), potentially covering the whole country.

Indeed, through the litigation that has become known as *Gillan* the courts learned that the Metropolitan Police together with the Home Secretary had, since the coming into force of s.44 on 19 February 2001, adopted the practice of issuing rolling (successive) authorisations for the whole of London. The Court of Appeal upheld this practice, commenting that: 'It did no more than enable the commander in a particular area to have the powers available when this was operationally required without going back to the Secretary of State for confirmation of a particular use.'[119] Moreover, it was discovered that the Home Secretary had never refused confirmation of an authorisation or set an earlier expiry date than that established by the police.[120] In short, the capital's police had, with the connivance of the Home Secretary and the domestic courts, turned an apparently exceptional power into a routine one. It was only small comfort that when *Gillan* reached the House of Lords, Lord Bingham declared that the lack of any legal requirement of suspicion at the point of application of the power:

> cannot, realistically, be interpreted as a warrant to stop and search people who are obviously not terrorist suspects, which would be futile and time-wasting. It is to ensure that a constable is not deterred from stopping and searching a person whom he does suspect as a potential terrorist by the fear that he could not show reasonable grounds for his suspicion.[121]

This indicated that it may not be lawful for the police to stop-search everyone in a particular location under s.44, although quite which categories of person could ever be regarded as incapable of containing terrorist suspects remains unclear. In any event, the *Gillan* requirement laid down in the House of Lords that an officer must suspect someone of being a *potential* terrorist is self-evidently not a demanding one, and opened the door to the highly problematic practice of ethnic profiling.[122] Qualitative evidence of how this power was used in practice by individual officers suggests that the rationale of fighting terrorism is used by officers to stop British Asian young people with increased zeal.[123] The account given to his police authority by a senior police commander in London gives further indication:

> it's very, very flaky and I won't be at all convincing, I know that, but it would be around professional judgement, what they see around the circumstances: the behaviour of the individual and the circumstances all fall together, lead them to make a judgement. That is so flaky, you know, even I feel embarrassed saying that. But that is the truth as to what they do.[124]

---

[119] *Gillan* [2004] EWCA Civ 1067 [51]. Confirmed by the House of Lords in *Gillan* [2006] UKHL 12.

[120] *Gillan and Quinton v the United Kingdom* (Application no. 4158/05) Judgment 12 January 2010 [80].

[121] *Gillan* [2006] UKHL 12 [35]. For critical commentary see [2006] Crim LR 752.

[122] For critique, see Moeckli D, 'Stop and Search Under the Terrorism Act 2000: A Comment on *R (Gillan) v Commissioner of Police for the Metropolis*' (2007) 70(4) *Modern Law Review* 654. Code of Practice A itself acknowledges (para 2.5) that there 'may be circumstances ... where it is appropriate for officers to take account of a person's ethnic origin in selecting persons to be stopped in response to a specific terrorist threat (for example, some international terrorist groups are associated with particular ethnic identities)'. Further guidance for the police can be found in the National Policing Improvement Agency, *Practice Advice on Stop and Search in Relation to Terrorism* (London: NPIA, 2008) which emphasises (somewhat bizarrely) that 'every person searched under section 44 should be told explicitly that they are not suspected of being a terrorist' (p 14) (available from <http://www.npia.police.uk/en/11700.htm> (accessed 5 January 2010)).

[123] Parmar (2011); Further examples are provided in Hallsworth (2006: 296–298) about patrol officers' thinking on who to target.

[124] Quoted in Metropolitan Police Authority, Counter-Terrorism: The London Debate (London; MPA, 2007) pp 51–52.

The Metropolitan Police Authority responded: 'This arbitrary and discretionary practice can only leave the door wide open for officers to base their selection of whom to stop on prejudice, unconscious or otherwise.'[125]

While the availability of the powers reviewed in this sub-section depend, in the main, on a prior assessment by a senior officer that *serious* offences are in the offing, in practice it is clear that they can be used in more mundane ways at the point of application. Thus whilst s.60 CJPO was 'sold' politically as a way of tackling serious violence, in reality it has become a useful police resource in responding to low-level disorder where no other power fits the bill. Thus one officer said he used s.60 for: 'Anyone causing trouble really – but people who aren't worth pulling [arresting] "cause they haven't done enough"' (Quinton et al, 2000: 50).[126] And it is telling that it was thought necessary to include in the official police guidance on the use of s.44 (NPIA, 2008: 17) that 'stop and search powers under the Terrorism Act 2000 must never be used as a public order tactic'.

Between 1997 and 2008 the recorded use of the s.60 power grew by over 600% within a decade, with use of the s.44 power showing a similar trajectory, then trebling between 2007 and 2008. The importance of the lack of a reasonable suspicion criterion is demonstrated by very low—and deteriorating—arrest rates. In 2007/08, the arrest rate for s.60 stop-searches was 3.8% (compared with 7.2% in 1996), and for s.44 stop-searches was 1.0% (compared with 1.9% in 2001/02).[127] In line with our discussion of stop-search powers requiring reasonable suspicion (see section 2.2.1.1), we suggest that the deterioration in arrest rates is consistent with ever less discriminating use of the power reflecting the push towards pre-emption of crime and terrorism, and also consistent with greater recording of unproductive searches over time. The explosion of unproductive s.44 stop-searches became so great that even the police themselves acknowledged that they had 'the potential to have a negative impact, particularly on minority communities' and were planning to use s.44 powers only in specific locations and for specific reasons.[128] Following the UK government's defeat in the *Gillan* litigation before the European Court of Human Rights, a shift in policy was in the offing. In brief, the Court decided that s.44 stop-searches constituted interferences with the right to respect for private life under Art 8. Further, it ruled that such an interference was not justifiable because the powers of authorisation and confirmation, as well as the powers of stop-search themselves, were 'neither sufficiently circumscribed nor subject to adequate legal safeguards against abuse'.[129] The lack of any need for suspicion led the court to conclude that there was too much discretion afforded to individual officers, arguably an inevitable consequence of 'all risks policing' whereby the police are empowered to treat anyone and everyone as a risk and when there is insufficient intelligence to foresee who represents a risk.[130] Such broad, imprecise street policing powers are likely to contribute to long-lasting negative perceptions of police legitimacy, especially if some groups have a higher risk of being the target of searches and disproportionate numbers of innocent people in those

---

[125] Ibid, p 52. Much the same could be said of the long-standing power of searching for the purpose of examination at ports of entry into England and Wales, which is now contained in the Terrorism Act 2000, Sch 7. This is yet another power where reasonable suspicion is not required.

[126] This is contrary to the Code of Practice (Note for Guidance 10) which states that the s.60 power should not be 'used to replace or circumvent the normal powers for dealing with routine crime problems'.

[127] Povey D and Smith K (eds), *Police Powers and Procedures, England and Wales 2007/08* (Home Office Statistical Bulletin 7/09) (London: Home Office, 2009).

[128] John Yates, Head of Counter-Terrorism at the Metropolitan Police, writing in a consultation document, reported by *The Guardian*, 7 May 2009.

[129] *Gillan and Quinton v the United Kingdom* (App No 4158/05) Judgment 12 January 2010 [87].

[130] Walker C, 'Know Thine Enemy as Thyself': Discerning Friend from Foe under Anti-terrorism Laws' (2008) 32(1) *Melbourne University Law Review* 275–301.

groups are being searched.[131] Section 44 attrition rates in terms of actual arrests for terrorism were astoundingly low. For example, in 2009/10, less than 1% (429) of the 85,311 s.44 stop and searches recorded resulted in an arrest.[132]

Despite the ECHR ruling that s.44 searches were unlawful, the police continued to use these powers for more than a year.[133] Finally, in March 2011 the Home Secretary replaced s.44 with s.47A Terrorism Act 2000 (TACT) inserted by the Protection of Freedoms Act 2012, s.61.[134] Most notably, s.47A required a senior officer to reasonably expect acts of terrorism to take place. At the time of writing, s.47A has only been authorised a handful of times, recording 149 stop and searches resulting in four arrests.[135] Despite the clear reduction in police use of suspicionless powers, some have argued that s.47A only provides weak protection against arbitrary stop and search and concerns remain about how the power will be applied in practice and whether changes in the political or security climate could reinstate widescale use of no suspicion searches.[136]

2.2.2.3 Allied powers of stop and search

Section 163 of the Road Traffic Act 1988 provides police officers with a general power to stop vehicles, and related powers to require drivers to produce certain documentation, such as a driving licence, certificate of insurance and MOT certificate. If drivers do not have these documents with them, then they can be required to produce them within seven days at a police station (or face prosecution for failing to do so). These 'stop and produce' powers can therefore be useful to the police both for gaining information about those using public space that attract their attention, and to cause inconvenience to those on whom they wish to impose their authority. There is no requirement that any specific offence is suspected, still less reasonably suspected. The only restriction that has been read in by the courts is that the stop would be unlawful if made capriciously, oppressively or exhibited some other form of malpractice. Thus it was held to be a lawful use of the power to stop cars at random with a view to checking whether there was evidence (e.g. smell of alcohol) that would justify a formal breath test.[137] If the police stop a car under this section, they do not have the right per se to search for stolen goods, drugs or prohibited articles. However, if in the course of the stop under s.163 police suspicion relating to, for instance, theft or drugs is aroused, then the police will be able to continue the stop and search for that second purpose. No official statistics are produced on the use of s.163 or its relationship to stop-search and arrests, and citizens stopped under this power do not have the right to a record of the encounter.

This is a very broad power and as many adults experience a non-consensual stop when driving a vehicle (where reasonable suspicion is not required) as experience one when on foot (where it usually is). The power can be used proactively as a means of generating the level of suspicion required to carry out a more extensive search, as when a police officer on motorised patrol decided to follow a hatchback with three occupants in it. The officer noticed that the rear occupant 'was fidgeting around and moving his left arm behind his back'.

---

[131] Lennon G, 'Precautionary Tales: Suspicionless Counter-terrorism Stop and Search' (2015) 15(1) *Criminology and Criminal Justice* 44–62.

[132] *Statistics on Race and the Criminal Justice System 2010* (London: Ministry of Justice, 2011b).

[133] Parmar (2011).

[134] Home Secretary Theresa May told the House of Commons that she would not allow the continued use of s.44 in contravention of the European Court's ruling.

[135] *The Terrorism Acts in 2018 Report* by Jonathan Hall, Independent Reviewer of Terrorism Legislation, March 2020. Available at <https://terrorismlegislationreviewer.independent.gov.uk/wp-content/uploads/2020/03/Terrorism-Acts-in-2018-Report-1.pdf>.

[136] Cape E, 'The Counter-terrorism Provisions of the Protection of Freedoms Act 2012: Preventing Misuse or a Case of Smoke and Mirrors?' (2013) (5) *Criminal Law Review* 385–399.

[137] *Chief Constable of Gwent v Dash* [1986] RTR 41.

He decided to stop the car because (the court assumed) he suspected that this person might be in possession of drugs. On opening the driver's door the officer noticed Rizla cigarette papers on the dashboard and a smell of cannabis. He decided to search the rear occupant for drugs under s.23 of the Misuse of Drugs Act 1971. The rear occupant resisted and was charged with obstructing an officer in the execution of his duty. The question therefore arose of whether the officer had been acting in the execution of his duty when stopping the car. The defence argument was that the officer had stopped this car, which contained three black men, speculatively and that this was a capricious exercise of the s.163 power. The court decided that the police officer's initial suspicion that the rear occupant was in possession of drugs (as evidenced by his 'fidgeting around and moving his left arm behind his back') was sufficient to defeat that argument.[138] So, if you feel tempted to scratch your back when next in a car, check first that you are not being watched by the police. But do not become statue-like either, as that might be construed as just as suspicious; as might checking to see if you are being watched by the police before deciding on your posture.[139]

Section 4 of PACE (as amended) enhances the s.163 power to stop vehicles in that it enables a senior officer to authorise a road check (the mass stopping of either all vehicles, or all vehicles that match a particular criterion) where reasonable grounds exist to believe that someone who is unlawfully at large, or who has committed (or who intends to commit) an indictable offence (or is a witness to such an offence) would be in the locality where the checks are to take place. The number of road checks has reduced in recent years, no doubt because the police now feel that they have more effective ways of stopping vehicles, as by using s.43(1) of the Terrorism Act 2000. Between 2009/10 and 2018/19 there were 7,129 stop and searches in London under s.43 powers and approximately 6% of these resulted in an arrest.[140] Even in previous years, when there were more arrests (but still less than 1% of all stops), the arrests connected with the reason for the road check were smaller in number than unrelated arrests that follow the use of this power.

2.2.2.4 Does the law really require individualised suspicion of a specific offence?

The following two lists divide the main stop and search powers into those that do (list A), and those which do not (list B), require individualised reasonable suspicion at the time of the stop, indicating the type of criminal activity they are aimed at:

A– *powers requiring reasonable suspicion*

s.1 PACE 1984 (prohibited fireworks, 'stolen' goods; articles for use in offences of dishonesty; offensive weapons; bladed objects without lawful excuse; items for use in criminal damage)

s.23 Misuse of Drugs Act 1971 (drugs)

s.43 and s.43A Terrorism Act 2000 (terrorist offences)[141]

B– *powers not requiring reasonable suspicion*

s.163 Road Traffic Act 1988 (stop and produce driving documents)

s.4 PACE (road checks in relation to indictable offences)

s.60 CJPO 1994 (stop-search for offensive weapons/dangerous implements)

ss 47A Terrorism Act 2000 (stop-search for articles connected with terrorism)

Sch 7 Terrorism Act 2000 (terrorist activities: examinations at ports and airports)

---

[138] *R (on the application of Smith) v DPP* (QBD (Admin Ct)) [2002] EWHC 113.

[139] See Pearson and Rowe (2020) esp. ch 5 and 6 for numerous examples.

[140] *Operation of Police powers under the Terrorism Act 2000 and subsequent legislation, year ending March 2019* (London: Home Office).

[141] See Walker C, *Blackstone's Guide to the Anti-Terrorism Legislation* 3rd edn (Oxford: OUP, 2014) pp 192–197.

List B powers are clearly enabling rules par excellence, lacking most of the due process elements one might expect to find when police powers are extended by statute. Although these powers are directed at specific activities (such as the threat of violence), most of the resulting arrests are unconnected with the ostensible reasons for the stop and search. For example, in 2019 only around 4% of arrests were connected with the reason for the stop in relation to s.60 CJPO.[142]

We need to reflect now on the extent to which stop-search powers really are directed at specific offences. Despite the great increases in these powers since PACE was enacted, it remains true that the police have no general powers to stop-search simply because someone is thought to be in some general sense 'suspicious'. Either the individual has to be suspected of something in particular (e.g. PACE, s.1) or something in particular has to be suspected in that vicinity (e.g. PACE, s.4; CJPO, s.60; Terrorism Act 2000, s.47A), or someone has to belong to a category which is deemed 'suspicious' (e.g. Terrorism Act examinations). However, it will often not be possible to know why someone appears 'suspicious'. Only a conversation and/or search will reveal the knife, drugs, stolen credit card, soft-core pornography, medical records, love letters, anarchist literature, banker's bonus, or contraceptives about which the individual may be embarrassed. Is the requirement that suspicion relate to a particular offence simply a presentational rule? In one of McConville et al's cases (McConville M, Sanders A, Leng R, *The Case for the Prosecution* (London: Routledge, 1991) p 28), a youth ran away when he saw the police, so he was chased and searched. A Krugerrand (gold coin) was found, so he was arrested. It turned out that he had this lawfully, but that hardly matters. The police often stop, search and arrest people who run away when they see police officers. This is, by any standards, suspicious behaviour. But of what can one reasonably suspect of such people? In this particular case, was it really reasonable suspicion of theft? Overall, the arrests that resulted from stops in this study were often unrelated to the reasons for the stops. Observational research 30 years later shows that little has changed.[143]

Suspicion of an offence to which PACE, s.1 applies is sometimes used as a pretext when other offences are suspected. For example, police often try to find illegal immigrants by carrying out stops and searches of black and Asian people in vehicles or on foot.[144] Section 42 of the Immigration Act 2016 also brought in new powers to equip authorised officers (including the police and immigration officers) with stop and search and seizure powers to collect evidence to secure civil penalties and removals and to work closely with the police by aligning existing warrant powers. For example, officers now have powers to search people and to enter premises to search for driving licences, payslips and identity documents for anyone they reasonably suspect not to be lawfully resident in the UK. Prior to this, whilst there was no power to detain or search a person in the street on suspicion of immigration offences, some other justification could usually be found for the original stop.[145]

However, in some areas and in some contexts, there are simply numerous mundane crimes (such as possession of cannabis) waiting to be discovered. The fact that there is no specific reason to stop particular individuals or cars in these contexts does not alter

---

[142] *Police powers and procedures, England and Wales, year ending 31 March 2019*, chapter on Best Use of Stop and Search, Table 3.2 (London: Home Office). Available at <https://assets.publishing.service.gov.uk/government/uploads/system/uploads/attachment_data/file/841408/police-powers-procedures-mar19-hosb2519.pdf> (accessed 4 September 2020).   [143] Pearson and Rowe (2020).

[144] Parmar A, 'Arresting (non)citizenship: The Policing Migration Nexus of Nationality, Race and Criminalization' (2019a) 24(1) *Theoretical Criminology* 28–49.

[145] Smith D, 'Origins of Black Hostility to the Police' (1991) 2 *Policing and Society* 6. See also, Gordon P, *Policing Immigration: Britain's Internal Controls* (London: Pluto Press 1985) for a detailed history of how the police have long been involved in the enforcement of immigration control.

the fact that statistically the officer is more likely to notch up a successful 'collar' by stopping them than by stopping people randomly, or by stopping respectable-looking people in affluent suburbs. Most stops are in inner-city areas, largely because they are inner-city areas. These areas are not necessarily more criminogenic than others, but the crimes which predominate in them (drugs, car theft, burglary and street violence) are more amenable than most to discovery by stop and search. Not surprisingly, the attempt of legislators in the early 1980s through PACE, s.1 to require specific suspicion of specific offences as a condition of using stop and search powers is proving unsuccessful.

2.2.3 Stop-search powers, consent and the rise of 'stop and account'

When we talk about 'the power' to stop-search, we are actually referring to a bundle of powers. For example, PACE, s.1(2)(b) states that a police officer 'may detain a person or vehicle for the purpose of ... a search', and s.1(6) provides a power to seize certain property discovered in the course of this search. In addition, the police have an implicit power to question.[146] However, the power of an officer to question is slightly different from the other powers contained in s.1: suspects must submit to search and detention (and indeed 'reasonable force' may be used if the suspect objects),[147] but they need not answer questions. Any answers they do give may be sufficient to dispel the officer's reasonable suspicion, in which case the power to search is lost (Code A, para 10.2). Other stop-search powers discussed earlier, in the CJPO, Terrorism Act 2000 and elsewhere in PACE, also contain these powers to detain, question and seize as well as to stop and to search.

Early versions of the Code of Practice allowed police officers to search persons with their consent. Such consensual searches did not require the exercise of formal powers, and, as a corollary, none of the restrictions outlined earlier—such as suspicion of specific offences—applied. Nor did the other controls to be discussed later in section 2.4. Research conducted soon after PACE was enacted found most stops to be 'consensual' in the sense that 'a lot of people are not quite certain that they have the right to say no and then we sort of bamboozle them into allowing us to search'.[148] After various attempts to restrain the police from evading the PACE safeguards through the use of consensual searches were found to have failed, all versions of Code of Practice A from 2003 onwards have prohibited them completely:

> An officer must not search a person, even with his or her consent, where no power to search is applicable. Even where a person is prepared to submit to a search voluntarily, the person must not be searched unless the necessary legal power exists, and the search must be in accordance with the relevant power and the provisions of this code (para 1.5).[149]

This provision, important as it is, has not resolved all of the problems inherent in the relationship between police power and public consent. First, it is sometimes simply ignored, as in one of the five forces examined in one study (Home Office 2005a: 39). Second, the Code of Practice also makes clear, in relation to searches requiring reasonable suspicion, that while there is no power to *stop or detain* a person against their will in order to find grounds for a search (para 2.11),[150] there is nothing to prevent an officer without such

---

[146] *Daniel v Morrison* (1979) 70 Cr App Rep 142.   [147] Code A, para 3.2.
[148] Police officer, quoted in Dixon et al, 'Consent and the Legal Regulation of Policing' (1990b) 17 *Journal of Law and Society* 345 at p 348.
[149] But note that (a) this para specifically exempts sports grounds and similar venues, where searches are often carried out routinely; (b) community support officers (quasi-police) can carry out certain searches *only* with the consent of suspects: Annex C to Code of Practice A.
[150] But see the discussion in section 2.2 earlier on the Road Traffic Act power to stop vehicles regardless of any individualised suspicion (which falls outside the provisions of Code A).

grounds simply speaking to, or questioning, someone 'in the ordinary course' of their duties, and this is said to be so even if the person is unwilling to reply (Note 1).

In theory this means an officer could try to break down a person's unwillingness to reply by following them down the street while asking an unanswered question repeatedly. In practice, the police often *ask people to stop* and to answer questions in order to gather information on incidents and to assess whether those present should be classified as suspects and searched or arrested accordingly. These kinds of stops became controversial as a result of the Macpherson Report's recommendation that all stops, including 'voluntary' ones, should be recorded.[151] While this recommendation was accepted and a record of encounters was necessary under Code A of PACE 2013, the provision was subsequently updated and, according to the revised Code of Practice (effective from March 2015), there is no requirement for officers who apply stop and account to make any record of these 'voluntary' encounters or to give the person a receipt.[152] One might think that, as far as voluntary stop and accounts are concerned, a member of the public spoken to in this way could simply walk away, given that, by definition, the officer has no power to detain them. Unfortunately the law fails to address this crucial issue. Officers are told by the Code (para 4.12) that there 'is no power to require the person questioned to provide personal details' (such as ethnic background), but is silent on whether persons questioned have to account for themselves. The use of the word 'request' in para 4.12 (quoted above), suggests that they do not. But the Code of Practice neither requires officers to make this clear at the start of the encounter, nor stipulates whether or not a refusal to answer questions or an attempt to walk away could give grounds for the statutory power of stop-search (or even arrest) to be invoked.[153]

Much of the surrounding post-Macpherson literature on stop and account assumed, without argument or analysis, that the police can 'require', or even 'demand' an account.[154] Taken in combination with the law's silence on the ramifications of failing to give an account, there may be a perception that the police acquired a new 'stop and account' power. What was happening was to some extent, merely a legitimation of long-standing police practice. As one Superintendent involved in piloting the Macpherson recommendation told Shiner (2006: 28):

> All this is doing is introducing a form into the equation. Now what officers were doing before in this division, if I stop you and ask you to account for your actions, behaviour or possession, I've asked your name and address, I'm going to check you out on the radio ... *I'm not going to let you walk away without knowing who you are.* So I'll take your details, I'll take your personal details, and I'll probably take a description of what you are wearing ... [and write it down in my notebook]. Now what I always say to people is 'all this is just your medium for recording those details, that's all that's changed ... you just write it down on a different piece of paper.' [emphasis added]

---

[151] Prior to this, only stops that resulted in searches (i.e. 'stop-searches') had to be recorded. See further section 2.4.1.

[152] PACE, Code A 2014 paragraphs 2.11 and Notes 22A and 22B.

[153] If a police officer *detains* somebody without reasonable suspicion then any answers (or refusals to answer) the officer's subsequent questions cannot *retrospectively* provide the reasonable grounds for suspicion necessary to justify the initial detention (Code A, para 2.9). But this provision has no application to the case of a *consensual* stop and account. These supposedly consensual encounters thus provide the police with an opportunity to generate reasonable suspicion sufficient to justify a non-consensual stop and search. Code A (para 2.11) recognises this very point, but is silent on whether 'non-answers' can found reasonable suspicion.

[154] See, for example, Lister et al (2008: 44) who write of 'low-level uses of police powers such as stop and account', and Ministry of Justice, *Statistics on Race and the Criminal Justice System 2006/7* (London: MoJ, 2008d) which uses the term 'required' to account and repeatedly refers to 'stop and account' as a police 'power' (e.g. p 26).

As Dixon et al (1990b) point out, when an officer asks someone on the street whether they would mind answering questions, this is usually perceived (correctly) not to be a genuine request, admitting either 'yes' or 'no' as an answer, but a polite way of insisting. But the drift towards thinking of 'stop and account' as a *power*, (which can turn these encounters into systematic intelligence-gathering opportunities),[155] may also be having an enabling effect.

Consistent with that hypothesis, the number of stop and accounts rose from 1.4 million in 2005/06 (the first year in which records of these encounters were kept) to 2.35 million in 2007/08,[156] although this rise may be as much to do with better recording practices. What proportion of these stops were 'voluntary' as opposed to involuntary is not known. In practice this distinction is unlikely to be prominent in officers' thinking, and it will certainly remain wholly obscure to the people asked to provide accounts.[157] Nor can we be sure that officers are keeping records consistently across the different types of stop and account. Thus we cannot know what proportion of stop and accounts are taking place on a 'voluntary' basis or accurately measure the enabling effects of these recent developments.[158] This is of particular concern given that stop and account interactions are likely to exacerbate racial disproportionalities that already pattern stop and search practices.[159] It is also an issue that is difficult to reveal the extent of, given that forces have discretion to direct officers to record the self-defined ethnicity of persons they request to account for (Code of Practice Notes for guidance para 22A).

There are other difficulties with consensual encounters. What, for instance, of suspects who do not simply refuse to answer questions, but who refuse rudely and aggressively (or start scratching their backs)? Is this 'behaviour of the person' creating reasonable suspicion?[160] And what of people who seek to avoid being spoken to by the police in the first place? Quinton et al (2000: 27) found that a quarter of the 90 police officers they interviewed regarded such elusive behaviour as a prompt for a stop. For example: 'You see someone and you just know he's not right. It's the way people react to you – won't look you in the eye; go in different directions; [they] give indication [they] don't want to speak or be seen.'[161] Moreover, breaking stop and search down into discrete actions takes no account of the social processes involved. In an encounter that begins with a consensual and innocuous conversation, suspicion may develop and the suspect may get impatient. The point in the 'flow of the encounter'[162] at which consent is no longer present and formal powers are, or should be, invoked cannot be identified with precision. Indeed, from the suspect's perspective, it may remain unclear that a non-consensual search has in fact

---

[155] As one officer told Shiner (2006: 24), 'stop and account in its basic form helps us to gain intelligence that we might not previously have got.' See further section 2.5.1 on the intelligence-gathering role of stop-search practices.

[156] Ministry of Justice, *Statistics on Race and the Criminal Justice System, 2007/8* (London: MoJ, 2009b) table 4.9. The requirement to record stop and account was removed as part of the Crime and Security Act 2010, so more recent figures are not available. See also discussion in ch 10.

[157] Pearson and Rowe (2020), ch 6.

[158] At the time of writing, no British Crime Survey figures on police stops for the same period were available, which means we cannot be sure whether 'stop and account' is having an enabling effect.

[159] See Bridges L, Shiner M, Delsol R and Gill K, *StopWatch Statement on Police Stop and Account* (2011) ch 5. Available at <https://www.stop-watch.org/uploads/documents/StopWatch_Statement_on_Police_Stop_and_Account_-_21Dec11-_FINAL_(2).pdf> (accessed 29 August 2020).

[160] See the arrest case of *Ricketts v Cox* (1981) 74 Cr App Rep 298, discussed in ch 3.

[161] See also Fitzgerald (1999: ch 4) who found that the grounds given for searches in police records included references to suspects being 'uncooperative', 'evasive to police questioning' and 'very anti-police'.

[162] See Shiner (2006: 19).

taken place. This is because: 'The cooperation of the person to be searched must be sought in every case, even if the person initially objects to the search' (Code A, para 3.2). While it is understandable and desirable that the law should seek to restrain the use of forcible searches in this way, where suspects have co-operated in a search they are likely to understand that legal power has been exercised over them only if the police tell them (as they are supposed to do—see 2.4) that this is so.

2.2.4 Citizens' powers to stop-search

A citizen's arrest is a familiar notion in England and Wales (see section 3.3.5) but a citizen's stop-search much less so. Most of us have, however, been stop-searched by someone other than a police officer at some point in our lives, most obviously when passing through security checks within an airport. Security personnel carry out routine stop-searches at the entrance to many courts, sporting events and various venues within the night-time economy. And shoppers (some honest, some not) who set off security alarms when leaving stores are likely to find themselves stop-searched by store detectives. All these stop-searches take place on the basis of *contract* or implied *consent*.

As part of the recent trend towards the pluralisation of policing, with many civilian bodies and individuals now seen as part and parcel of the crime control apparatus and 'responsibilised'[163] accordingly, *statutory* stop-search powers have been given to some categories of private citizen and members of the 'extended police family'. Most notably, PCSOs now have the following standard stop and search powers:[164]

- to carry out an authorised road check under s.4 of PACE;
- to stop and search pedestrians and vehicles under s.43 of the Terrorism Act 2000 when in the company, and under the supervision, of a constable;
- following a refusal to surrender alcohol or tobacco when lawfully required to do so, to search for alcohol or containers for alcohol (possessed by children,[165] or by anyone in designated areas[166]), or tobacco (in the case of children)[167] and to seize and dispose of the same.[168]

PCSOs do not (yet) have the standard s.1 PACE power to stop-search with reasonable suspicion, or the power to stop any vehicle (other than as part of a s.4 road check), or the s.60 CJPO power to search for weapons. While there may be good arguments for not providing PCSOs with all the search powers of police officers, the inconsistency in treatment does make it harder for people to know their rights when required to submit to a search by someone who, for most intents and purposes, looks and acts like a police officer.

---

[163] See ch 1.
[164] PCSO powers were first provided for by the Police Reform Act 2002 (Sch 4), and then extended by Sch 8 of the Serious Organised Crime and Police Act 2005. Many of them were available only if the local Chief Constable so designated, but s.7 of the Police and Justice Act 2006 enabled the introduction of SI 2007/3202 which established a set of standard powers and duties applicable to all PCSOs.
[165] See Confiscation of Alcohol (Young Persons) Act 1997.
[166] See s.12 of the Criminal Justice and Police Act 2001, allowing for the designation of what might be termed alcohol exclusion zones.
[167] See s.7 of Children and Young Persons Act 1933.
[168] If they find drugs during such a search they may seize and dispose of these too.

Most notable (and controversial) of other civilian stop-search powers are those provided by ss.45–46 of the Violent Crime Reduction Act 2006. Under s.45, any member of staff of a school who reasonably suspects a pupil on those premises of having a blade or offensive weapon with them or in their possessions (e.g. in a school locker) may search them and their possessions (but only in their presence) if authorised to do so by the head teacher. *Anything* found during the search that is reasonably suspected to be evidence of an offence (e.g. cannabis) may be seized and must then be handed over to the police. Many school teachers were unhappy at having this crime control function foisted on to them and the Act accordingly provides that they (unlike school security personnel) may not be required by the head teacher to carry out such searches. Section 46 provides similar powers for the further education sector.

2.3 Stop and search and racial discrimination

Now that we have introduced a wide range of stop and search powers we need to address a question that has provoked deep concern for decades: is the practice of stop and search characterised by racial discrimination? This question was brought into sharp focus with the murder of George Floyd by Minneapolis police officers in March 2020. Video footage of the brutal force applied to Floyd during his stop and subsequent arrest and the unrelenting attitude of the officers despite his pleas for them to stop were circulated around the world, prompting outrage, widespread protest and despair that racial minorities have come to expect this type of treatment from the police in the US and beyond. But the US is not exceptional in this regard. In the UK numerous deaths and injuries of black and minority ethnic group men and women have emanated from what may have started as a 'police stop' or attempted stop and search, and as discussed here, the use of force is disproportionately applied to BAME groups.[169]

An obvious starting point for analysis is whether people of different ethnic backgrounds are stopped in proportion to their numbers in general population. We know that broadly speaking the proportion of stop and searches for white groups has decreased from 75% in 2014/15 to 59% in 2018/19. In contrast, for the same time periods, the proportion for black and minority ethnic groups has increased from 13% to 22% for black people and from 8% to 13% for Asian people.[170] In Table 2.2 the relevant figures are presented for the stop and search powers where record-keeping on the part of the police is required.

While it is evident from Table 2.2 that more white people are subjected to stop and search than BAME people, as one would expect given that close to 9 out of 10 people in England and Wales are white, in the case of every stop and search power, black and Asian people are greatly *over-represented* in those searched. More specifically, there were four stop and searches for every 1,000 white people, compared with 38 for every 1,000 black people, 11 for every 1,000 Asian people and 11 for every 1,000 mixed-race people. Similar patterns have been found year on year, although the disproportionality has reduced markedly from

---

[169] For example, Jordan Walker Brown was left paralysed in May 2020, following being shot with a taser weapon by the Metropolitan Police. He ran away from the police as he was carrying a small amount of cannabis and was afraid of being detained by the police. Following being shot by the taser gun, Brown was handcuffed and dragged to his feet despite being unable to move his legs: *The Guardian*, 24 June 2020 (accessed 4 September 2020). In 2017, Junah Adumbi was tasered in the face by police officers who tried to stop him in Bristol outside his home. BBC News <https://www.bbc.co.uk/news/uk-england-bristol-38691162> (accessed 4 September 2020). See also *The Independent*, 1 August 2017: 'Metropolitan Police Use Force Disproportionately Against Black People in London, New Statistics Reveal'.

[170] Ministry of Justice, *Race and the Criminal Justice System 2018* (2019).

Table 2.2 Proportion (%) of ethnic groups stopped and searched in England and Wales 2018/19[171]

	White	Black	Asian	Chinese or Other	Mixed	Not Stated	Total[172]
General population[173]	86	3.3	7.5	1	2.2	0.0	100
PACE s.1[174]	51	18	11	2	3	15	100
s.60 CJPO stop-searches	20	37	14	2	5	22	100
All Searches	53	20	10	2	4	11	100

2009/10.[175] Most of the stop and searches for all ethnic groups were carried out under s.1 PACE. Prior to the changes to the Terrorism Act 2000 in February 2011 (discussed earlier), black and Asian people were particularly singled out to be stopped and searched under s.44. Although the rate increased across all ethnic groups in 2009/10 compared to 2006/7, for black people the number of stops and searches increased by 212% and by 202% for Asian people, compared to an increase of 115% for white people.[176]

We are limited by the ethnic categories used by the police and official statistics, which are flawed. For example, the 'Asian' group is presented as homogenous, therefore amalgamating the stop and search rates for Pakistani, Bangladeshi and Indian people, masking differences between intra-ethnic Asian and Muslim and other religious groups.[177] Also, the 'mixed' category conflates a range of varying experiences and misrepresents black mixed-race men's experiences of stop and search in particular as they are more likely to be identified through their monoracial minority identity than are other mixed-race groups.[178]

The huge disparities in stop and search rates discussed above could be a product of direct discrimination, indirect discrimination, legitimate factors, or a combination of all three.[179] These are the main issues that need to be taken into account:

- The overall ethnicity trends for stop and searches tend to be influenced by stop and searches conducted in London. London's ethnic composition is made up of a higher proportion of people from BAME groups compared to the rest of England and Wales and so this may influence levels of ethnic disproportionality.

---

[171] Source: Ministry of Justice (2008d) ch 4.
[172] Individual figures in row may not sum to 100 due to rounding.
[173] 2011 census figures. The census figures tell us what proportion of people are, for example, white, black or Asian. Police records of stop-searches tell us what proportion of stop-searches are of white, black or Asian people and the same people are often targeted for repeated stop-searches.
[174] This row is mainly comprised of stop-searches under s.1 PACE and s.23 of the Misuse of Drugs Act.
[175] *Police Powers and Procedures, England and Wales* (2019) Section 4.
[176] *Statistics on Race and the Criminal Justice System 2010* (London: Home Office 2011b).
[177] Parmar A, 'Race, Ethnicity and Criminal Justice: Refocusing the Criminological Gaze' in Bosworth M, Hoyle C and Zedner L (eds), *Changing Contours of Criminal Justice* (Oxford: OUP, 2016).
[178] Long L and Joseph-Salisbury R, 'Black Mixed-race Men's Perceptions and Experiences of the Police' (2019) 42(2) *Ethnic and Racial Studies* 198–215.
[179] For a range of different perspectives see the *Lammy Review: An independent review into the treatment of, and outcomes for Black, Asian and Minority Ethnic individuals in the Criminal Justice System* (2017); Equality and Human Rights Commission, *Police and Racism: What has been Achieved 10 Years after the Stephen Lawrence Inquiry Report?* (2009) esp. pp 24–25; Bowling B and Phillips C, 'Disproportionate and Discriminatory: Reviewing the Evidence on Police Stop and Search' (2007) 70(6) *Modern Law Review* 936; Stenson K and Waddington P, 'Macpherson, Police Stops and Institutionalised Racism' in Rowe M (ed), *Policing Beyond Macpherson* (London: Routledge, 2007). Also see the small-scale study: Sharp D and Atherton S, 'To Serve and Protect? The Experiences of Policing in the Community of Young People from Black and Other Ethnic Minority Groups' (2007) 47(5) *British Journal of Criminology* 746.

- It may be that black and Asian people appear to behave more suspiciously than other people. However, we have seen that 'suspiciousness' is not an objective criterion, and much of the behaviour that looks suspicious to patrol officers (such as evasiveness) is itself a product of long-standing poor relations between ethnic minorities and the police.
- It may be that black and Asian people are more visible (or 'available') in areas and during time periods in which the police focus stop-search activity. This is likely to be true to some extent, as black and Asian people tend to be less affluent than white people, so they spend more time on the streets and in public places. But treating people who 'hang around' in public, for example, as suspicious, and going for these 'easy options' ('low hanging fruit' as the former Chair of the Youth Justice Board once put it) is again a matter of police choice based on unproven assumptions. Further, there is some evidence that in 'entrepreneurial spaces' (such as shopping malls), where risk-management techniques are used a lot, black males become targets for stop-search.[180]
- A clutch of northern forces, and forces in rural Wales, maintain low disproportionality rates while others, particularly in the south, maintain high rates. Also neighbouring forces often have very different rates. This suggests that the disproportionality figures are a product of police policy and practice rather than a simple reflection of suspicious behaviour.
- Racial discrimination can mean two different things. First, using powers unlawfully against black and Asian people more than against whites. Second, using powers lawfully against black and Asian people in circumstances where they are used less against whites. We simply have no robust evidence that disentangles these points. One suggestive study, but dating back to 1990, divided the reasons for the stops the researchers observed into 'tangible' and 'intangible' reasons, and found that black people were more frequently stopped for 'intangible' reasons than were white people.[181]
- Disproportionality is at its worst in relation to stops under s.60 of CJPO (black people) and s.44 of the Terrorism Act (Asian people) when it was still in force. These are the most important powers where no reasonable suspicion is required. Thus, almost by definition, BAMEs are stopped more often, proportionately, where there is little or no objective evidence—and the very low arrest rates for stops under these powers illustrate this. Yet this will mostly be lawful.

Black and Asian people are, when stopped, far more frequently searched and arrested than are white people. Whether this means that their disproportionately bad treatment is compounded by search and arrest behaviour, or that the stops have more substance to them, is open to debate. But black and Asian people also report more dissatisfaction with police behaviour. This may be due to being stopped more often, but may also be due to the way the police treat them, and their perception (whether justified or not) of being treated disproportionately badly. The question of the way in which police exercise these powers will be examined later. For now, note this critique by a former (black) Met Chief Superintendent of the use of stop-search: 'The answer is to stop stereotyping black people as low status, unintelligent, aggressive, dangerous, self-destructive and subhuman.'[182]

---

[180] Hallsworth (2006: 301–302).
[181] Norris et al, 'Black and Blue: An Analysis of the Influence of Race on Being Stopped by the Police' (1992) 43 *British Journal of Sociology* 207.
[182] *The Guardian*, 15 June 2020.

2.4 Constraints and controls on the exercise of discretion

The Philips Commission was aware that the criterion of reasonable suspicion could become devalued in practice, and that random stops should be guarded against. Its solution was to introduce a battery of secondary controls.

> We consider that the notification of the reason for the search to the person who has been stopped, the recording of searches by officers, and the monitoring of the records by supervising officers would be the most effective and practical ways of reducing the risk.[183]

In recent years, all police forces signed up to the 'Best Use of Stop and Search Scheme', announced in 2014.[184] This aims to improve recording of stop and search, to implement lay observation policies, and create a community complaint policy requiring the police to explain how powers are being used where there is a large volume of complaints. A precursor to the scheme was an HMIC inspection, which found that stop and search was being overused and poorly targeted (between 2012 and 2013, 27% did not have reasonable grounds for suspicion recorded).[185] The use of stop and search then declined significantly, as discussed, until recently. However, levels of disproportionality continue to rise: the benefits of the reduction in stop-search were experienced only by white people.[186]

2.4.1 Giving and recording reasons for stop-searches

A police officer must take reasonable steps to provide certain information to suspects *before* searching them, including the officer's name and police station, the object of the proposed search and the grounds for proposing to make it.[187] Except where it is impracticable, the officer must also make a written record of the search and provide the suspect with either a copy or an electronic receipt stating how the full record can be accessed.[188]

Section 3(6) of PACE provides that the record must state:

(1) the object of the search (i.e. stolen goods or prohibited articles);

(2) the grounds for making it (i.e. what has given rise to the suspicion);

(3) the time and date when it was made;

(4) the place where it was made;

(5) whether anything (and if so what) was found;

(6) whether any (and if so what) injury to a person or damage to property appears to the officer to have resulted from the search;

(7) the identity of the officer making the search.

---

[183] Royal Commission on Criminal Procedure, *Report* (Cmnd 8092) (London: HMSO, 1981) para 3.25.
[184] Available at <https://assets.publishing.service.gov.uk/government/uploads/system/uploads/attachment_data/file/346922/Best_Use_of_Stop_and_Search_Scheme_v3.0_v2.pdf> (accessed 31 August 2020).
[185] HMIC, *Stop and Search Powers: Are the police using them effectively and fairly?* (London: HMIC, 2013) p 30.
[186] Hargreaves J, Linehan C and McKee C, *Police Powers and Procedures, England and Wales, Year ending 31 March 2016* (London: Home Office, 2017).
[187] PACE, s.2. This, and s.3 discussed later, applies to searches under all legislation, not just PACE (see s.2(1)). They therefore apply to the powers discussed in section 2.2. The requirement to give this information was held to be mandatory in *R v Christopher Bristol* [2007] EWCA Crim 3214. See also *B v DPP* [2008] EWHC 1655 (Admin).
[188] Sections 2(3)(d) and 3; PACE Code of Practice A, paras 4.2, 4.2A and 4.10A.

One purpose of providing information before search, committing it to writing afterwards and providing suspects with access to those records is to enable suspects to hold police officers to account if they misuse their powers. This is intended to provide a remedy for those who are wrongly stopped, and the fear of complaints should produce more compliance in the first place. There are a number of reasons to question the realism of this.

First, research has consistently shown a significant level of non-compliance with the obligation to give reasons prior to search. This is sometimes where suspects are deferential and co-operative, and sometimes where the police are willing or even keen to stop-search without first obtaining co-operation (as where they wish to impose discipline or avoid the loss of authority involved in admitting that they are accountable to 'police property'). As one experienced constable put it: ' … you can't lose face in dealing with a member of the public, especially in a confrontational situation'.[189]

Second, there is significant under-recording of searches and inconsistency in recording practices (HMIC 2013). College of Policing guidance indicates that officers *should* turn on their body-worn video during a search (if they have it), but this is a suggestion rather than a requirement.[190] Why do the police fail to make records for some searches? One officer, commenting on under-recording, explained simply: 'Some informal searches not included, checking "scallywags"—what's in their pockets.'[191] It is exactly for oppressive or unnecessary searches that we should expect under-recording to occur since it may then simply be the suspect's word against the officer's word as to whether a search took place at all. It is in such searches too (carried out primarily against 'police property') that the police may feel they have little to fear from not recording (and not giving reasons to suspects) since they know that the oppressed rarely seek to hold officers accountable for their actions and even more rarely succeed (see section 2.4.3).

Where accountability becomes a live issue, as where the search leads to an arrest, or an articulate and rights-conscious suspect is encountered, a record is much more likely to be made. Many officers told Dixon et al (1990b) that they made a record only if they feared that there would be some sort of 'comeback'. If, for example, a middle class person who was aware of the law happened to be stopped 'you would probably revert to the standard opening speech procedure and complete a form' (Dixon et al, 1990b: 349). Recording and non-recording decisions are strongly influenced by whether or not officers believe that record-keeping will further *police* goals.[192] Such beliefs can be influenced by external factors.

Thus the rise of managerialism and target-driven policing has led to some supervising officers encouraging recording on the basis that it provides good evidence of the *amount* of work the police do,[193] while the modern emphasis on intelligence-led policing—e.g. electronic databases and body-worn footage—has turned the stop and search record into an increasingly valued information-gathering tool, notwithstanding that the use of intelligence gathered in this way remains haphazard.[194]

Third, the government has sought to 'reduce the bureaucracy' associated with stop-search by removing the long-standing requirement that the person searched be given a copy of the search record there and then. Thus, following a limited pilot, the 2009 and subsequent versions of Code of Practice A were amended so that the police now need only

---

[189] Quoted by Fitzgerald (1999: ch 4).

[190] College of Policing, *Authorised Professional Practice guidance–Stop and search: transparent* (2020) section 2.2.4. Online at <https://www.app.college.police.uk/app-content/stop-and-search/transparent/#using-body-worn-video-to-record-information> (accessed 16 September 2020) For examples of failure to do this see e.g. Pearson and Rowe (2020: 126).   [191] Quoted by Bland et al (2000: 36).

[192] See further Bland et al (2000: 29–37) and sections 2.5.1 and 2.5.2; Pearson and Rowe (2020).

[193] Home Office, *An Evaluation of the Phased Implementation of the Recording of Police Stops* (London: Home Office, 2004d) p 19.

[194] See, for example, Home Office (2004d: 8 & 19); Shiner (2006: 50–53).

give a 'receipt' so long as this 'explains how they can obtain a copy of the full record or access to an electronic copy of the record' (para 4.2). Where police officers are using the necessary electronic devices, those searched must now take the initiative by requesting a copy of the full record from their local police station, or by accessing it via the Internet. The Equality and Human Rights Commission (2008: 23) expressed 'grave disquiet' at this retrograde shift:

> It seems likely that many of those (predominantly young, male, black and working class) who receive a receipt will be daunted by the prospect of presenting themselves at a police station with their receipt and requesting the full record. They may feel that this will bring them to further police attention, and mark them out as potentially a 'troublemaker'. Also not everyone has access or the skills to use a website to get an electronic version of the report.

The fourth reason to question the usefulness of records as a safeguard for suspects is that historically they only applied to searches. The great majority of stops did not go this far, and therefore remained unrecorded. As we have seen (see section 2.2.3), the Macpherson Report recommended that all stops should be recorded, 'consensual' or not, and regardless of whether they resulted in a search.[195] A pilot project to test the feasibility of this recommendation found that the police failed to complete a record in 79% of recordable instances (Bland et al, 2000: 31).[196] This figure looks even worse once one realises that the project did not require the police to record the 'frequent informal' stops where 'known criminals' or 'informants' were stopped by the police for the purpose of gathering 'criminal intelligence' because officers had objected that such recording might 'impact on their working practices' (Bland et al, 2000: 14–15). Thus members of the public in the pilot sites who reported being stopped and searched repeatedly, sometimes in the course of just one day, were almost never given records of these encounters. The HMIC inspection report in 2013 suggests that little improvement has been made with regards to recording practices as they found that many forces did not record information or intelligence gathered from their use of stop and search powers to contribute to the force's overall intelligence picture. Furthermore, in a case study of Lambeth's gang unit, many of the Metropolitan Police Service officers did not switch on their body-worn video at the start of the event, and so the footage did not always capture the entire encounter. Despite the opportunities for technology to reduce bureaucracy for the officer, and for establishing real-time necessary grounds for reasonable suspicion and increasing accountability the potential merits of body-worn cameras are not being seized.[197]

As noted earlier, the 2003 version of the Code of Practice A introduced a nationwide requirement to record encounters that amounted to a 'stop and account' (implemented in 2005), thus continuing to exclude encounters where the police seek to gather more general criminal intelligence from 'informants'. The police complained that even this restricted definition of stops resulted in too much bureaucracy.[198] Home Office research indicated that three-quarters of stops were recorded in five minutes or less, with no adverse effect evident on either crime or the number of searches carried out.[199] On the other side of the argument, the Flanagan review of policing estimated that in London alone 'Stop and Account consumes over 48,000 hours annually of officers' time', not counting the time

---

[195] Macpherson (1999) recommendation 61.

[196] Observational research conducted once phased implementation of the Macpherson recommendation began in five sites found a recording level of just under 45%: Home Office (2004d: 13).

[197] HMIC (2013).

[198] For an overview of police concerns see Wilding B, 'Tipping the Scales of Justice?' in Cape E and Young R (eds), *Regulating Policing* (Oxford: Hart, 2008) pp 131–138).   [199] Home Office (2004d: 2).

supervisors spent checking each form, and recommended a drastic reduction in recording requirements.[200]

The 2009 version of the Code accordingly removed the requirement to provide the person 'held to account' with a form recording the encounter. This obligation was gradually whittled away. By the last edition of this book, police officers were only obliged to record the ethnicity of the person stopped (with the intention being that this will be transmitted electronically back to the station), and to give that person a 'receipt'. The potential for meaningful supervision had been reduced.[201] From 2011, police forces were no longer obliged to record stop and account at all. By 2019 a Freedom of Information request revealed that only three forces continued to record stop and account.[202] This is another example of the triumph of efficiency over our other 'core values' of justice and democracy. And all these changes, and the proliferation of different powers, mean that many police officers do not know the rules and so often fail to give reasons for, and record, stops and searches when they should.[203]

The most obvious problem with requiring officers to provide reasons for stop-searches to suspects, and to record those reasons in writing, is that police officers will tend to give accounts designed more to fit the statutory criteria than the actual events. In particular, it is unrealistic to expect an officer to record on his stop-search form that his reason for exercising a power was that a 'Rastafarian out at night', was inherently suspicious[204] or that someone was stopped 'because he's a fucking Paki in a Jaguar',[205] yet we know that such racist actions do occur. Only the bravest (or most foolish) officers would complete written records in such ways as to make clear the unlawfulness of a stop. So if there were a challenge to a particular stop, it would be the suspect's word against the officer's, just as if there were no written record. The 'smell of cannabis made up around half of the searches we saw', but that smell was often undetectable to the researchers observing those searches in one recent study.[206] The record therefore may be more of a protection for the officer than it is for the suspect.

Lack of knowledge on the part of suspects further undermines the likelihood of police accountability. It is no use having a right not to be stopped and searched unlawfully if people do not know what that right entails. The difficulties discussed earlier in defining reasonable suspicion mean that it is virtually impossible to know what a right not to be stopped and searched unlawfully means. This problem has been greatly exacerbated by the post-PACE proliferation of stop-search powers, and the different pre-conditions for use that apply to each of these. Matters have only become worse with the advent of quasi-police, such as the Police Community Support Officer (PCSO), who sometimes have stop-search powers and sometimes not.

Similarly, it is no use having a record made if people do not know of its existence. This is why the police are obliged under PACE to inform suspects that they are entitled to a copy of the record. However, if the officer fails to inform the suspect, then the suspect will remain unaware of the entitlement to a copy of the record so will not know that the officer breached the legal duty to explain this. Bland et al (2000): 29) found that only 'a handful' of people had applied in the last year for a copy of their search record. The Code of Practice

---

[200] Flanagan R, *The Review of Policing: Final Report*, (2008) pp 61–64 available at <http://police.homeoffice.gov.uk/publications/police-reform/Review_of_policing_final_report/>(accessed 5 January 2010).

[201] See the critique by the Equality and Human Rights Commission (2008: 23).

[202] See Powell-Smith A, *Stop and account: how is this little-known police practice being used?* (2020) Online at <https://missingnumbers.org/stop-and-account/> (accessed 3 September 2020).

[203] Pearson and Rowe (2020) ch 6.   [204] Officer quoted by Quinton et al (2000: 24).

[205] Reason given for a stop by PC Rob Pulling and PC Andy Hall in 'The Secret Policeman'. PC Pulling accepted that 'I'd obviously have to think of something else', i.e. to give as the ostensible reason for the stop.

[206] Pearson and Rowe (2020: 108).

now obliges the searching officer to provide suspects with a copy of the record (or at least a receipt) there and then but the problem of non-compliance, and the suspect's lack of awareness that non-compliance has occurred, remains.

Dixon et al argued that one major reform which is needed if PACE is to be at all effective in relation to powers on the street is for citizens to be fully educated about their rights and, by implication, not to have to rely on the police for this knowledge.[207] This would certainly help enhance police accountability, but the very complexity and ambiguity of the law means that the goal of full education is probably unattainable.[208] Take, for example, the Association of Police Authorities' (APA) leaflet on 'Stop & Search: Know Your Rights', designed to be carried in a purse or wallet. This makes no reference to reasonable suspicion and lapses into misleadingly broad statements such as 'You can be stopped and searched *anywhere* when an officer believes that you are carrying drugs, weapons or stolen property ... ' (emphasis in original).[209] From this one might infer that the police can forcibly enter your home and search you for drugs on the basis of mere belief, however unreasonable.[210] It is impossible to create a statement of stop-search rights that is both accurate and handy-sized. But carrying around a chapter of this length and referring to it when stopped is hardly a practicable option (and is liable to get you arrested for challenging police authority, so do not put this idea to the test).[211]

2.4.2 Monitoring of search records

What of the Philips Commission's belief that scrutiny of search records by supervising officers would help guard against unlawful stop-searches? There are two major problems here. First, when a supervisory officer scrutinises such records, the scrutiny is not of what the officer did or whether it was within the law but of the officer's account of what was done. A police officer fearing rigorous managerial supervision would be unlikely to portray a stop-search as anything other than lawful.[212]

But it seems that police officers do not fear this. For the second major problem with supervision is that it rarely occurs. Only a quarter of police supervisory officers questioned by Dixon et al mentioned checking paperwork as a form of supervision. Over three-quarters of the constables and sergeants interviewed said that their stops were not generally supervised (Dixon et al, 1989: 200–201). Over 10 years later, in the late 1990s, separate studies by Bland et al (2000) and Fitzgerald (1999) found that nothing had changed.

---

[207] Dixon et al, 'Reality and Rules in the Construction and Regulation of Police Suspicion' (1989) 17 *International Journal of the Sociology of Law* 185 at p 203.

[208] 'I am acutely aware of the confusion between stop and account and stop and search among both the public and police officers': Berry J, *Reducing Bureaucracy in Policing: Interim Report* (2009) p 9 (available from: <http://police.homeoffice.gov.uk/publications/police-reform/reducing-bureaucracy-report.html> – accessed 5 January 2010). Jan Berry was appointed the 'Independent Reducing Bureaucracy in Policing Advocate' by the Home Secretary on 1 October 2008. She was previously chair of the Police Federation (the main police trade union).

[209] Published by the APA in September 2008, and distributed by individual police authorities.

[210] See also the information on stop-search rights on the APA website, which seems to reduce the question of rights to whether one is given a form by the police or not (<http://www.apa.police.uk/APA/> – last accessed 5 January 2010).

[211] Take the following example of a black man, regularly stopped and search throughout his life, who happens to be a church elder, a magistrate and a manager at the Equality and Human Rights Commission: 'In a recent incident he produced a leaflet that outlines the rules for stop and search. In response a police officer remarked: "Oh, we've got a clever one here." ': Equality and Human Rights Commission (2008: 21).

[212] 'A few sergeants interviewed held very strong views on what could be expected from examining forms. They firmly pointed out that they could only check how well the form had been filled out. Because officers were effectively invisible on the streets, they were unhappy about signing off the form to say that the encounter was appropriate': (Home Office, 2004d: 19).

Fitzgerald, for example, stated that the only supervision she discovered was where a probationer reported that his sergeant had put pressure on him to conduct unethical searches.[213] It is thus not surprising that all these studies report that some forms were completed tersely or even tautologically: grounds for search being stated as 'suspicious behaviour' (Dixon et al, 1989), 'drugs search', 'info received' and 'acting furtively' (Bland et al, 2000). Furthermore, as the 2013 HMIC inspection report discussed earlier showed, compliance with the law and guidance with regard to monitoring of records remains contentious. Forces continue to monitor their own records, which the HMIC has repeatedly criticised. In 2020, the inspectorate found that only 10 out of 19 forces reviewed body-worn video footage of stop and search encounters as part of their internal or external scrutiny; and five forces were not monitoring a wide enough range of data to allow a full understanding of how stop and search was being used.[214]

Recent versions of Code of Practice A have taken account of the earlier research findings by stating that supervisors and senior officers with area- or force-wide responsibilities must monitor the use of these powers, considering in particular whether there is any evidence that they are being exercised on the basis of stereotyped images or inappropriate generalisations.[215] In addition such scrutiny must be supported by the compilation of comprehensive statistical records of stops and searches at force, area and local level. Paragraph 5.3 continues: 'Any apparently disproportionate use of the powers by particular officers or groups of officers or in relation to specific sections of the community should be identified and investigated.'[216] Further guidance is also provided in the Code about how to deal with officers suspected of misusing their powers at 5.5 and 5.6, with suggestions to ask individual officers to account for the way in which they conducted and recorded particular searches and supervisors are advised to take both timely and appropriate action to deal with all improper cases that come to their notice.

It is doubtful whether these recommendations have made a significant difference particularly in light of the 2013 HMIC report that showed that 27% of the records they reviewed did not have reasonable grounds for suspicion recorded. Each force used its own stop and search form, obstructing accurate statistical analysis. More worryingly in nine forces the stop and search forms did not allow recording of sufficient information to comply with all the legal requirements of PACE. It seems that little has changed since 2008 when over 8,000 stop-searches were carried out on those protesting against a proposed coal-fired power station at Kingsnorth power station and fewer than 25% of the forms were found by a police review to be legible.[217] Recorded accounts of stop and search continue to bear little relation to the nature and pattern of the interactions that actually take place so how can transparency and fairness be achieved?

Police stop and search is inherently difficult to supervise adequately due to its relatively low visibility. So it is dishonest to pretend that fully effective supervision is possible and

---

[213] Fitzgerald (1999: ch 5). Miller et al (2000: 16–17) provide a similar example. And see Bland et al (2000: 58–60, 44).

[214] HMICFRS, *PEEL spotlight report: Diverging under pressure*, February 2020b.

[215] Paragraph 5.1. This is in line with the Race Relations (Amendment) Act 2000 which imposed a positive duty on the police 'to have due regard to the need – (a) to eliminate unlawful racial discrimination, and (b) to promote equality of opportunity and good relations between persons of different racial groups.' The Equality and Human Rights Commission has been given powers to oversee compliance with the 2000 Act.

[216] Paragraph 5.4 adds that: 'In order to promote public confidence … forces in consultation with police authorities must make arrangements for the records to be scrutinised by representatives of the community, and to explain the use of the powers at a local level' although concerns about preserving the anonymity of those searched means that scrutiny is likely to be confined in practice to statistics generated by the search records (Note 19).

[217] See <http://www.guardian.co.uk/environment/2009/jul/22/kingsnorth-police> (accessed 5 January 2010).

that written records of stop-searches are an adequate check on their legality. Adequate supervision may not be possible, but better supervision certainly is: pressure from 'above' is rare, but has an effect when it is applied;[218] and senior officers can hardly be unaware of photographs of criminals on parade room walls with notes urging stops simply because of their criminal records.[219] One police commander of a town is reported to have responded to complaints of disproportionate stop-searches of ethnic minorities by checking the paperwork. His conclusion was that those searched 'in almost all cases were men known to be involved in street crime, whom sensible, intelligence-led policing suggests I should be keeping under surveillance and the very people I should be telling my men to stop and search'.[220] The problems inherent in attempts to control low visibility and discretionary police work are compounded by laxity in the law and by a pervasive policing and political culture which emphasises 'results' rather than procedural propriety. Thus, day-to-day supervisory and oversight practices remain patchy and ineffective, with racial disparities in stop-search statistics and practices as pronounced as ever. The Equality and Human Rights Commission (2008: 24) quotes an unpublished HMIC report into police compliance with the race equality duty as follows:

> HMIC found that generally, forces could not give a clear account of the reasons for disproportionality. It was apparent that, although a great deal of information is collected, inspected forces lacked the in-house resources to analyse it in any detail, although some have since introduced dedicated analysts ... The inspection team found that forces were inconsistent in implementation and adherence to stop and search policies.[221]

In terms of police response to racial disparities, forces have been criticised for example for not implementing training on unconscious bias.[222] Whilst we recognise that unconscious bias training is not a panacea for years of entrenched racial disproportionality in policing, the unwillingness to ensure consistent training and the lack of immediacy to the issue is perturbing. Police training in general is insufficient to improve understanding of legal powers, to help decide when they have reasonable grounds for suspicion, to assess the impact stop and search has on communities and to know how to effectively use stop and search powers to prevent and detect crime. In 2013 half of all forces did not carry out stop and search training at all or provide opportunities for learning beyond that delivered on recruitment.[223] Arguably, officers should have the discipline to apply learning as part of their professional practice on the streets as well adequate supervision and oversight. However supervisors are given little or no training on how to supervise or to help them understand what is expected of them.[224] The rules, policies and practices on supervision remain in part presentational and enabling. Though good supervision is inhibitory to some extent we do not know how widespread it is.[225]

---

[218] Snapshot observations carried out by academics from the London School of Economics in four forces and one London borough revealed front-line supervision to be of highly variable quality, and working best where monitored and supported by senior line management: Home Office (2005a: 38–39). See also Pearson and Rowe (2020).   [219] See the reference to this in section 2.2.1.
[220] HC Stdg Comm D, 13 April 2000, col 27. Discussed by Lustgarten L, 'The Future of Stop and Search' (2003) *Criminal Law Review* 603 at 612.
[221] Pressure from the police on HMIC to not publish this report seems to have been successful, although an anodyne two page summary can be tracked down at <http://webarchive.nationalarchives.gov.uk/20070708092741/> and <http://inspectorates.homeoffice.gov.uk/hmic/inspections/ptd/diversity/duty-calls-hmic-inspection.pdf> (accessed 5 January 2010).
[222] HMCFRS (2020: 17).   [223] HMIC (2013: 42).   [224] HMIC (2013: 44).
[225] In the most recent research, Pearson and Rowe (2020) consider this to be a significant element with even potential to be of greater value.

2.4.3 **Remedies**

Where a stop is legally questionable, what is the probability and likely consequence of a successful challenge? If a stop is unsuccessful, suspects will usually want to put the matter behind them, and the absence of reasonable suspicion (assuming any is required) will rarely be an issue. If the stop is successful, in the sense of a crime being discovered, it will rarely be questioned because the initial illegality becomes overshadowed by the crime itself. We have seen, however, that some groups are subjected to repeated stops and stop-searches and that they do not have the option of 'putting the matter behind them'. They are in a continuing conflictual relationship with the police and might see a legal challenge as the only way out. But many such groups are socially marginalised and perceive the law as remote and inaccessible. As one youth told Goldsmith (2008: 234):

> we were all actually thinking about doing ... like ... getting a campaign to sue [the police] because we couldn't ... literally it was so bad we'd be getting stopped every five minutes. But we just couldn't do it because we didn't know how and we can't pay.[226]

Thus stop-search practices are rarely challenged, and such challenges tend to come from articulate and organised adults, such as the protester and the journalist in the *Gillan* case. In the unlikely event of challenges being made to stop-searches, what actions or remedies are available?

The ECHR, PACE, the Terrorism Act, the CJPO and so forth are all silent on this point, neither making it a crime nor a tort to stop and search someone unlawfully, to fail to provide information before search, or to make a record of it afterwards.[227] At common law, a failure by an officer to provide information prior to search renders the stop and search unlawful: when a suspect used force to free himself from an unlawful detention and was, in consequence, charged with assaulting an officer in the execution of his duty it was held that the unlawfulness of the detention meant that the officer was not acting in the execution of his duty, and so the assault was not criminal.[228] Similarly, a forcible search under s.60 of CJPO was held unlawful where the officers did not give their names and station.[229]

A stop and search which was unlawful—whether because inadequate reasons were provided or because inadequate reasons existed (such as no reasonable suspicion in the case of a PACE search)—could constitute the tort of assault. However, there have been no reported cases of this, partly because such an action would be speculative, and partly, no doubt, because the loss or damages suffered as a result of an unlawful stop and search tends to be regarded by the domestic courts as insignificant.[230] If charges followed the discovery of stolen or prohibited articles, a motion to exclude from court evidence discovered as a result of the stop and search is possible although unlikely to succeed.[231] If PACE stops

---

[226] See also Flacks (2018).

[227] PACE, s.67(10) provides that a failure on the part of a police officer to comply with the provisions of Code of Practice A 'shall not of itself render him liable to any criminal or civil proceedings'.

[228] *Pedro v Diss* [1981] 2 All ER 59. See, similarly, *Christopher Bristol* [2007] EWCA Crim 3214; *B v DPP* [2008] EWHC 1655 (Admin).

[229] *Osman (Mustapha) v Southwark Crown Court* (1999) 163 JP 725. But also see *DPP v Avery* [2002] 1 Cr App R 31.

[230] See *Gillan* [2006] UKHL 12 [25] where Lord Bingham characterised a stop-search as akin to being 'kept from proceeding or kept waiting'. For critique see Ashworth A, 'Case Comment: Police Powers-Whether Authorisation Given under Terrorism Legislation Lawful' [2006] Crim LR 751, 755.

[231] In *McCarthy* [1996] Crim LR 818 the Court of Appeal approved of a judge's decision not to exclude evidence obtained as a result of a stop-search where the police had lied about the true basis for the search. As ch 11 will show, *McCarthy* is consistent with the courts' normal interpretation of the exclusionary provisions of PACE.

are challenged in court (in either of these ways), and the officers' accounts differ from those of the suspect what would or could the court do? If defining the absence of reasonable suspicion is difficult, proving it is all the more so: these are low visibility decisions where there are seldom other civilian witnesses and where—because those stopped are so often people with previous convictions—suspects are easily 'discredited'.[232]

The main problem with all of the remedies discussed so far is that they are individualistic in nature. The most troubling aspect of stop-search, however, is the way in which the power is deployed disproportionately against certain social groups. In other words, remedies are needed that can take into account overall patterns of discretionary decision-making rather than focusing on the much narrower question of whether a particular constable had reasonable suspicion in a particular case. This is something the ECtHR sometimes takes into account, as it did in *Gillan* when deciding that s.44 Terrorism Act 2000 stop-search powers unjustifiably breached Art 8. It stated that ' ... there is a clear risk of arbitrariness in the grant of such a broad discretion to the police officer. While the present cases do not concern black applicants or those of Asian origin, the risks of the discriminatory use of the powers against such persons is a very real consideration ... '[233] But it took more than six years from the date of the stop-searches in question to secure this judgment.

Are there any more accessible domestic remedies? Following a recommendation of the Macpherson Report, the Race Relations (Amendment) Act 2000 makes it unlawful for any public authority to do any act that constitutes racial discrimination. This extension of the race discrimination legislation, combined with the impact of the European Council 'Race Directive' (2000/43), means that acts of direct discrimination (overt racist behaviour) as well as practices that amount to indirect discrimination (because they unjustifiably disadvantage people of a particular ethnic group) are all actionable in the domestic courts.[234]

Another non-individualistic approach is to seek a judicial review. In 2008 Kent police used s.1 of PACE to stop-search everyone entering and leaving a peaceful climate camp demonstration against a proposed new power station. This included two children aged 11. The children, along with another man, argued that such a blanket practice was unlawful. Shortly before the case was due to be heard the police finally disclosed a briefing document in which senior officers had asserted that all demonstrators should be searched because

---

[232] See the discussion of discrediting in the context of complaints against the police in ch 11.

[233] *Gillan and Quinton v the United Kingdom* (Application no. 4158/05) Judgment 12 January 2010 [85].

[234] The Equality and Human Rights Commission has the power to assist individual complainants and launch proactive investigations of its own. As to possible human rights arguments and remedies see further Feldman D, *Civil Liberties and Human Rights in England and Wales* (Oxford: OUP, 2002) pp 302–307 and 318–19, Moeckli (2007), and De Schutter O and Ringelheim J, 'Ethnic Profiling: A Rising Challenge for European Human Rights Law' (2008) 71(3) *Modern Law Review* 358. The ECHR does not mention stop-search, but Art 5(1) states that: 'No one shall be deprived of his liberty save in the following cases and in accordance with a procedure prescribed by law'. The relevant following case is contained in Art 5(1)(b) which allows detention 'in order to secure the fulfilment of any obligation prescribed by law'. The European Commission has held that examinations under the terrorist legislation comply with this provision (see discussion of *McVeigh, O'Neill and Evans v UK* (1981) 25 DR 15 in 3.3.3), which means that it seemed arguable that all the other stop and search powers would also comply. Indeed, the English courts have said that stop-search will rarely amount to a deprivation of liberty within the meaning of Art 5: *Gillan* [2006] UKHL 12. This case also indicates that the domestic courts are most unlikely to uphold the argument that stop-search threatens Art 11 (freedom of assembly) or Art 10 (freedom of expression) rights, or has a chilling effect upon their exercise, unless the powers were used wrongly (as *seems* to have happened in that case—and as certainly happened in the *Kingsnorth* case; see next footnote and accompanying text) in order to control or deter attendance at demonstrations. However, when *Gillan* reached the ECtHR the court dropped a heavy hint (without having needed to do so) that the degree of coercion involved in a stop-search was 'indicative of a deprivation of liberty within the meaning of Article 5 ... ': *Gillan and Quinton v the United Kingdom* (Application no. 4158/05) Judgment 12 January 2010 [57]. As noted in the text, the ECtHR also found a breach of Art 8 in this case. It declined to comment on the arguments relating to Arts 10 and 11.

there were reasonable grounds to do so. In 2010 the police admitted 'total surrender' accepting an order that the searches of the claimants had been 'unlawful', and constituted a violation of their human rights to privacy (breach of Art 8 of the ECHR), to freedom of expression (breach of Art 10) and freedom of association (breach of Art 11).[235]

One other possible remedy is the making of a complaint against the police officer concerned. PACE, s.67(8) originally made it a disciplinary offence to breach any of the provisions in the Codes of Practice, but this was repealed in the 1990s. Repeal sent a crime control signal to the police, although complaints can still lead to disciplinary action on some other footing such as 'incivility'. In practice, relatively few of the many people aggrieved by police actions ever make an official complaint. One factor behind the low complaint rate is the correct perception that the chances of having a complaint upheld are low. Of 100 cases involving formal complaints of stop-search practices, in just eight was the complaint substantiated. Thirty-one of the 100 cases were sent to the CPS for consideration of criminal culpability, but charges were brought in only one case (indecent assault) and the officer concerned was acquitted at Crown court.[236] The low rates of substantiation and prosecution are partly because of the difficulty of establishing that an officer lacked reasonable suspicion or failed to give information prior to search or conducted the encounter in a disrespectful or abusive way,[237] and partly because of the failings or inadequacies of the police complaints machinery (see chapter 11). Factors such as self-confidence, determination and confidence in the system affect the willingness and likelihood of making a complaint against the police and these are likely to be lower amongst racial minorities and socially marginalized groups.[238] This is unfortunate as the fear of a complaint or disciplinary action may nonetheless deter some officers from breaching the stop-search rules, particularly when the use of the power becomes a matter of public controversy and officers sense that 'management' would not support their actions.[239]

In a few rare instances, the police have overstepped the boundaries of legality so blatantly and ineptly that the courts have felt obliged to take meaningful remedial action. In *Somers*, for example, the appellant had been driving a hire-car when he was stopped by police officers, supposedly acting under Road Traffic Act powers. They claimed they wished to check whether the car was stolen since a similar vehicle had been stolen in the same area shortly before. The appellant was placed in the police car and was not permitted, despite his request, to witness the police officers entering the hire-car. The officers made a check with the licensing authority which revealed that the car appeared to be genuine in the sense that it was owned by a hire-car company. Moreover, the appellant produced the hire agreement. The officers claimed, however, that they wanted to go further by checking the chassis number or the engine number and so entered the car to find the bonnet release switch. They claimed that while looking for this switch they found a bag of crack cocaine in a small compartment immediately below the radio and above the ventilation control. As Lord Justice Pill put it: 'It is not a place where, in the experience of anyone in court, a bonnet release would be found.'[240]

---

[235] See <http://www.indymedia.org.uk/en/2010/01/445509.html> (last accessed 18 February 2010).
[236] Havis and Best (2004: 36, 40).
[237] This is particularly true where there are no independent witnesses (relatives or friends of the complainant do not count as sufficiently independent). If the person stop-searched is an off duty police officer, the chances of success are evidently greater: see Havis and Best (2004: 19, 31, 38).
[238] Smith G, 'Why Don't More People Complain against the Police?' (2009b) 6(3) *European Journal of Criminology* 249–266.
[239] As seems to have happened in the aftermath of the Macpherson Inquiry: Fitzgerald (1999: ch 5); Fitzgerald et al (2002: 101).   [240] *R v Somers* [2003] EWCA Crim 1356 [5].

Other curious features of the case noted by the court included: (i) the persistence of the police investigation into the ownership of the car given that it was quite obvious that it was a hire-car legitimately in the possession of the appellant (the signs of the car-hire company were displayed prominently on the passenger door!); (ii) the failure of the police to find the bonnet release handle (and the fact that they gave up looking for it after 'finding' the drugs); (iii) two other police cars were summoned to the scene, arriving within six minutes, despite the fact that the suspect was perfectly co-operative; (iv) no record was kept of the search; (v) the co-operation of the suspect had not been sought in carrying out the search; (vi) several officers had failed to note the incident in their pocket books; (vii) a copy of one of the relevant police documents appeared to have been doctored prior to it being sent to the defence.

The appellant's fingerprints were not found on the bag of drugs. Although he had previous convictions for 'serious offences', and had in 2002 been convicted of obstructing a police officer, he had no convictions for drug offences. By his own admission, he did not like or trust the police. The clear implication was that the police had planted the drugs in the car of a 'usual suspect' thought to merit severe social disciplining. He was convicted at first instance but the conviction was quashed as unsafe because the trial judge had not drawn the jury's attention sufficiently to the unsatisfactory nature of, and inconsistencies in, the police evidence. The prosecution had the cheek to ask for a retrial as this, they said, 'would give the opportunity for the Crown to iron out any curiosities within the case ... '[241] This application was refused. Nonetheless, Mr Somers had served nine months in prison prior to his appeal being heard so it is difficult to argue that the quashing of the conviction amounted to a complete remedy. It is sometimes said that the innocent have nothing to fear from increases in police powers. Do you think Mr Somers would agree?

A rare legal challenge to s.60 CJPO concerned a police officer questioning a middle-aged woman about offensive weapons.[242] Although the challenge was unsuccessful, the case raised questions about the violation of human rights by police officers during suspicionless stop and searches and also prompted an immediate operational response from the Metropolitan Police Deputy Commissioner informing officers of the challenge and requiring s.60 authorisations to be 'necessary' rather than merely 'expedient'.[243]

2.5 The impact of stop-search powers

The question for us in this section is whether the freedom gained for 'society' by catching criminals through stop-search exceeds, or is less than, the freedom lost by those who are stop-searched.

2.5.1 Success rates and crime control

How valuable are stop-search powers for the police? Under both PACE and the CJPOA, in 73% of stop and searches the outcome was 'no further action' and in around 16% of cases the initial outcome was an arrest.[244] However, at best the targeted use of stop and search seems to have only marginal reductions in local crime, having relatively little

---

[241] *R v Somers* [51].

[242] *R (on the application of Roberts) v Commissioner of the Police of the Metropolis* [2015] UKSC 79, [2016] 1 WLR 210. Discussed in section 2.2.2.2.

[243] Mackey C, 'S 60 Criminal Justice and Public Order Act 1994' *The Guardian*, 12 January 2012, at <https://www.theguardian.com/law/2012/jan/12/craig-mackey-letter-chief-constables> (accessed 3 September 2020). See Bowling and Marks E (2017: 62–88).

[244] *Police Powers and Procedures, England and Wales*, March 2019.

deterrent effect.[245] In recent years, knife crime has increased and figures are particularly high in London.[246] An evaluation of a Metropolitan Police Service knife initiative to tackle knife crime between 2008 and 2011 (Operation BLUNT 2) found no statistically significant crime-reducing effect from the large increase in weapons searches during the course of the operation. Furthermore, ambulance call outs for weapons-related injuries did not fall more in London boroughs where searches were carried out up to three times more than the previous year.[247] This is consistent with earlier research: 'there are forces that have high levels of search-arrests that achieve only low primary clear-up rates, as well as forces with lower levels of arrests from searches that achieve good clear-up rates' (Miller et al, 2000: 22). At first sight this is surprising, as every successful search-arrest counts as a cleared-up crime, whereas unsuccessful searches do not add to the stock of crimes to be cleared-up. But use of the power involves opportunity costs: while police officers are busy proactively stop-searching they cannot do anything about the other crimes that are clamouring for attention. Also, only about half of arrests following a search result in caution or conviction (Miller et al, 2000: 24–26).

That the crime uncovered by 'reasonable suspicion' stop-search is often mundane is indicated by the fact that around 60% of all searches are for drugs, around 11% are on suspicion of stolen property and around 16% for suspected offensive weapons. Furthermore, in the year ending 2019, little over one in five stop and searches resulted in an outcome that was related to the reason for the search. This varied by the reason for the search from 28% for 'drugs' to 21% for 'stolen property' and just over 12% for searches relating to 'offensive weapons' and 'going equipped'. The link between the reason for the search and it being related to the reason for arrest varied across ethnic groups. For example, 8% of BAME people stopped under suspicion of firearms by the police were arrested for a firearms offence compared to 16% of white people stopped under suspicion of firearms. Most other offence categories were similar across ethnic groups, however the finding related to firearms suggests that the police may be making a higher proportion of spurious stops of BAME groups under suspicion of firearms offences than they do of white groups.[248]

While searches for uncovering the more serious crime of carrying offensive weapons may seem justified, warnings about the cost in terms of groundless stops and consequent community resentment go back years.[249] Overall, then, the opportunity costs involved in extensive stop-searching, the infringement of civil liberties involved, and the low haul of productive arrests secured, all suggest that stop-search as currently practised is not a freedom-enhancing way of tackling crime. That, however, is not the end of the matter, for the widespread use of stop-search powers may be effective in deterring potential offenders. As one officer put it: 'If active criminals know that they can't go out without being searched that tends to put a damper on their activities.'[250] The effectiveness of such a policy is extremely doubtful. The problem was highlighted by Swamp 81.[251] This massive

---

[245] Tiratelli M, Quinton P and Bradford B, 'Does Stop and Search Deter Crime? Evidence From Ten Years of London-wide Data' (2018) 58(5) *British Journal of Criminology* 1212–1231.

[246] Allen G, Audickas L, Loft P and Bellis A, *Knife Crime in England and Wales*, House of Commons Briefing Paper SN4304 (London: House of Commons Library, 2019).

[247] Home Office (2016) *Do initiatives involving substantial increases in stop and search reduce crime? Assessing the impact of Operation BLUNT 2* (London: Home Office, 2016).

[248] *Police Power and Procedures, England and Wales*, March 2019.

[249] e.g. Fitzgerald (1999: ch 2).

[250] Quoted by Fitzgerald (1999: ch 2). See also (Chief Constable) Wilding (2008: 135) who writes: 'Is the power to stop account/stop and search a deterrent? I have no doubt that it is…' His claim that reduced stop-search in London following the MacPherson report resulted in street-crime 'shooting up' is highly debatable. For more measured analysis see Hallsworth S, *Street Crime* (Cullompton: Willan, 2005) esp. ch 9.

[251] Scarman (1981: para 3.27), discussed in section 2.2.

operation, in which the police made 943 stops, saturated the streets of Brixton for several days and triggered a riot. Even taking the riot out of the equation:

> the evidence is not clear that a street saturation operation does diminish street crime: it may well only drive it elsewhere. And, after the operation has ended, street crime returns.[252]

So extensive stop and search may impact upon crime at one time and in one place, but otherwise allows crime to flourish. This 'displacement' phenomenon can be overstated, but the resources needed to protect against it, and to sustain aggressive crackdowns in the long term, would be enormous, as indeed would be the damage done to police-community and intra-community relations by such a policy. That is all the more so now that the 'crime' being targeted includes low-level 'anti-social behaviour'. Thus intense surveillance and stop-searching in one deprived area of social housing led to bitter resentment amongst the targeted youths, who retreated to 'hidden' spaces, such as stairwells of flats and isolated park areas in order to avoid further contact with the police.[253] That outcome is hardly likely to be reassuring for local adults, and the potential for an escalation of tension within the community is obvious.[254] We should not be surprised then, to find that any crime-reductive effects of intensive stop-search are cancelled out by displacement and crime-fuelling effects.

Another way in which stop and search may contribute to crime control is in augmenting 'criminal intelligence'. Police collators, for instance, build up computer databases of information about suspects and witnesses based on information derived from stop-searches.[255] Some police services used to use the amount of information submitted by uniformed officers as a criterion for promotion to CID, thus encouraging enthusiastic use of stop-search powers.[256] The Home Office and the Association of Chief Police Officers (now known as the National Police Chiefs Council) have in the past given the following advice to front line officers:

> Remember that when a stop-search does not lead to an arrest this in no way means that the stop and search was unlawful, inappropriate or of no value. Although the reason for conducting a stop and search is detection, any search can yield valuable intelligence, which must be captured. Do not underestimate the potential value of small pieces of information (Home Office 2005a: 28).

This still rings true in the 2020s. Written records in particular—ostensibly introduced as protections *for* suspects—provide the basis for systematic collation of information *about* suspects.[257] In some areas, more stops lead to fewer arrests, precisely because the criminal intelligence normally gathered after arrest is collected on the street instead. Complex systems of data storage are thereby created, allowing certain target populations to be monitored.[258] This happened on a large scale in relation to the use of anti-terrorism

---

[252] Scarman (1981: para 4.78). For evidence of displacement, see the study by Hallsworth (2005: 114): 'Gains made in one place by community safety effort were offset by increases in other areas as the street robbers moved on.' See also Lister et al (2008: 48–49) who found that drug users were not deterred by street policing from either drug using or the acquisitive crime which funded their habit.

[253] Goldsmith (2008: 235).

[254] See the account by Blincoe N, 'Me v the Kids' *The Guardian* ('Weekend' magazine), 7 February 2009.

[255] Dixon et al (1989: 189); Fitzgerald (1999: ch 5); Home Office (2005e).

[256] Barton A and Evans R, *Proactive Policing on Merseyside* (Police Research Series Paper 105) (London: Home Office, 1999).

[257] Willis (1983: 15); Bridges L and Bunyan T, 'Britain's New Urban Policing Strategy' (1983) 10 *Journal of Law and Society* 85; Home Office (2005e).

[258] See Meehan A, 'Internal Police Records and the Control of Juveniles' (1993) 33 *British Journal of Criminology* 504; Ericson R and Haggerty K, *Policing the Risk Society* (Oxford: Clarendon Press, 1997); Home Office (2005e).

legislation to monitor the Irish population in Britain and Northern Ireland[259] and many Muslims (especially young men) are now getting similar treatment.[260] Tilley also notes that stop and search is often used proactively for a wide range of offences to disrupt the activities of organised crime groups and to gather intelligence on them.[261] We noted in section 2.4.1 that in recent years the government scaled back the requirement to give copies of written stop-search records to suspects, and keeping detailed records of 'stop and account' for accountability purposes is now discretionary. But this does not mean that the police will desist from their long-standing practice of recording intelligence gleaned from stop-searches and 'stop and accounts' that *they* find useful. Indeed, intelligence gathering is becoming increasingly easy through such technological developments as digital cameras with facial recognition software, on-the-street fingerprinting devices[262] and the widespread use of hand-held computers that can exchange information with centralised databases.[263] Whilst the joining up of information through technology may make police work easier, allowing the police to access immigration databases whilst using mobile fingerprint scanners has racially uneven consequences.[264]

Is intelligence gathering through stop-search desirable? It could help in solving grave crimes, helping to place suspects in particular locations at particular times. On the other hand such intelligence can usually be obtained in less intrusive ways, such as through CCTV, or a less intrusive stop without a search. More fundamentally, from a freedom perspective one might question whether the cost to society of using stop-search for the systemic gathering, storage, dissemination, sharing and use of information concerning 'risky populations' justifies the crime-control benefits: 'A society fearful of being pried upon, a society in which personal data may be collected for uncontrolled speculative use, is not a free society.'[265]

This argument is unlikely to persuade policy-makers, given their preoccupation with crime control and the logic of risk management.[266] When the risks run as high as major terrorist incidents, such as those that occurred in the United States on September 11 2001, this is understandable.[267] But all of those who committed those outrages were subjected

---

[259] Hillyard P, *Suspect Community* (London: Pluto Press, 1993) esp. ch 12, and Walker C, 'Miscarriages of Justice' in McConville M and Wilson G, *Handbook of the Criminal Justice Process* (Oxford: OUP, 2002) p 156.

[260] Pantazis C and Pemberton S, 'From the "Old" to the "New" Suspect Community: Examining the Impacts of Recent UK Counter-Terrorist Legislation' (2009) 49(5) *British Journal of Criminology* 646. The notion that Muslims have become en masse a 'suspect community'. See also Hargreaves J, 'Police Stop and Search Within British Muslim Communities: Evidence From the Crime Survey 2006–11', (2018) 58(6) *British Journal of Criminology* 1281–1302, in which he found that being Muslim increased the likelihood of being subjected to a foot stop and once stopped, increased the likelihood of being searched. This suggests that searches of Muslims are discriminatory but the processes involved are complex and not yet understood.

[261] Tilley N, 'Intelligence-led policing and the disruption of organized crime: motifs, methods and morals' in Delpeuch T and Ross J (eds), *Comparing the Democratic Governance of Police Intelligence* (Northampton, MA: Edward Elgar, 2016).

[262] The Metropolitan Police Service and other forces have been using mobile fingerprint devices since 2012 and recently reported the development of a new and faster mobile device <http://news.met.police.uk/news/met-develops-mobile-fingerprint-device-to-save-time-and-public-money-317200> (accessed 31 August 2020).

[263] See Home Office (2005a: 50).

[264] Parmar A, 'Policing Migration and Racial Technologies' (2019b) 59(4) *British Journal of Criminology*. See also Liberty's report on mobile fingerprint scanners and the hostile environment. Available at <https://www.libertyhumanrights.org.uk/issue/mobile-fingerprint-scanners-bring-a-dangerous-new-front-to-the-hostile-environment/> (accessed 31 August 2020).

[265] Sharpe S, *Search and Surveillance: The Movement from Evidence to Information* (Aldershot: Ashgate, 2000) p 223.

[266] On the self-fuelling nature of this logic see Ericson and Haggerty (1997: 449–452).

[267] On the use of risk-management in this field see Walker C and McGuinness M, 'Commercial Risk, Political Violence and Policing the City of London' in Crawford A (ed), *Crime and Insecurity: The Governance of Safety in Europe* (Cullompton: Willan, 2002).

to the information-gathering and stop-search procedures routinely applied to air travellers as a condition of flying. Also, if particular objects or places are subjected to saturation stop-search practices terrorists will simply choose other means or places to attack; they can more easily engage in displacement than can 'normal' criminals. Broadening stop-search powers is therefore unlikely to help prevent terrorism, as the (then) Assistant Commissioner Andy Hayman (in charge of anti-terrorist operations in London) himself recognised in 2006.[268]

How are we to explain the continuing attachment to ever more extensive stop-search in the light of its limited effectiveness? Brogden argues that stop-search is actually part of a wider social control function: that historically the police have been more concerned with social control of the streets than with detecting crime.[269] From medieval times, such laws 'to keep in order the unruly' or to apprehend 'rogues, vagabonds and other disorderly persons' were common. The Head Constable of Liverpool instructed his men in 1878, for instance, to watch 'vigilantly the movements of all suspected persons … For the purposes of seeing whether his suspicions are well founded, he may stop any person …' (Brogden, 1985: 106–7). Reasonable suspicion, as found in the legislation of the 1970s and 1980s, was in many instances an afterthought—one which, we have seen, was increasingly dispensed with in the 1990s. Thus s.60 of the CJPO and s.44 of the Terrorism Act, far from providing a different kind of power for the police armoury, represent historical continuity and ultimately their introduction and implementation are influenced by the law, politics and police culture.[270] It is the attempt to impose due process on street policing which is the novelty. Stop-search, and the street policing which stop-search facilitates, is as much about monitoring, controlling and disciplining groups of 'suspicious' people, as about detecting specific crimes and specific criminals.[271] The new millennium emphasis on 'reassurance policing' (that is to say, providing highly visible policing to reassure 'the public' that order is being maintained) feeds into this long-standing phenomenon.[272]

This is where we see the importance of stop-search being limited to public places. For it is those at the bottom of the socio-economic heap who tend to gather in such places and are thus, as a group, subjected to stop-search most frequently (see also chapter 10, esp. sections 10.2.3 and 10.4). As Lord Scarman observed in his report on the Brixton disorders of 1981, young unemployed black people had little alternative but to make their lives on the streets:

> And living much of their lives on the streets, they are brought into contact with the police who appear to them as the visible symbols of the authority of a society which has failed to bring them its benefits or do them justice.[273]

In the twenty-first century much the same could be said of other groups of street-users including youths living in deprived areas, political protesters, the homeless, beggars, asylum seekers, those with drug addictions or mental health conditions. At the same time, there are growing tensions evident between different groups who use the streets.

---

[268] 'It's a power that's well intended: it's there to try and prevent, deter and disrupt terrorist activity. So the test is: to what extent does it achieve that aim? And I have to say, it doesn't … There's a big price to pay for probably a very small benefit': Quoted in Metropolitan Police Authority (2007: 52).

[269] Brogden M, 'Stopping the People' in Baxter J and Koffman L (eds), *The Police: The Constitution and the Community* (Abingdon: Professional Books, 1985).

[270] See Bowling and Marks (2017).

[271] See Choongh S, *Policing as Social Discipline* (Oxford: Clarendon Press, 1997) esp. chs 2–3, and the analysis by Lister et al (2008) of the 'communicative surveillance' practised by the police on street drug users.

[272] 'In a number of forces stop and search was used as a tool for public reassurance and to prevent people who were seen as creating a public nuisance from gathering in certain places, although there was no reasonable suspicion of a crime' (Home Office 2005a: 38).

[273] Scarman (1981: para 2.23).

Town centre managers and business leaders want protesters, drug users, the homeless and those begging to be swept out of sight to avoid harm to tourism or sales figures; fearful adults (and zero-tolerance minded policy-makers) put pressure on the police to disperse groups of youths 'hanging around'; the media (with able support from some senior police leaders)[274] fuel growing fears and prejudices about ethnic minorities, youths, asylum seekers and those with mental health conditions; and the potential for inter-group tensions multiplies as society becomes ever more ethnically, culturally and socially diverse. In this volatile situation, it is easy to see how stop-search could become employed by the police as much to 'reassure the public' and reassert their own authority on the streets as to detect specific crimes.

2.5.2 **The experience of being stopped and searched**

If being stopped and searched by the police was a one-off event in someone's life, the effect on their freedom would be slight. But not for those who typically attract police suspicions. Hundreds of thousands of people a year are stopped or stop-searched. Levels of racial disproportionality have continued to widen, and Asian males are more likely to be stopped and searched than at the time PACE was enacted.[275] Those who are stop-searched repeatedly are often well aware, and resentful, of the working assumptions and rules that underpin this pattern of police discretion. Choongh (1997: 45), for instance, found many members of ethnic minorities and people with criminal records saying the same things: 'Once you got a record or anything they're always trying to catch you on something.' Young people, who are subject to more stop and search in Scotland than those in England, perceive the police not to be procedurally fair and have negative attitudes towards the police (Murray et al 2020).

Freedom is undermined not only by the frequency of stop-search, or its duration, but also by its nature.[276] How invasive can it be? PACE Code of Practice A, which applies to all stop-search powers, states that: 'All stops and searches must be carried out with courtesy, consideration and respect for the person concerned … Every reasonable effort must be made to reduce to the minimum the embarrassment that a person being searched may experience' (para 3.1).[277] Further, according to paras 3.5–3.7:

- a search in public should consist only of a superficial examination of outer clothing, although this can extend to feeling inside pockets, collars, socks and shoes (and within a person's hair) if this is reasonably necessary to look for the object of the search;
- when a search is in public the only clothes that can be compulsorily removed are coats/jackets and gloves;
- a police officer cannot order the removal of a head or face covering, except where there is reason to believe that the item is being worn by the individual wholly or mainly for the purpose of disguising identity, not simply because it disguises identity;

---

[274] See, for example, Waddington D, *Policing Public Disorder* (Cullompton: Willan, 2007) pp 99 and 107–108.

[275] *Statistics on Race and the Criminal Justice System 2018* (London: Ministry of Justice, 2019h).

[276] A large body of research has examined the question of the nature of the encounter and how much it shapes people's perceptions, confidence, trust and legitimacy in the police. See for example Bradford B, Jackson J and Stanko E, 'Contact and Confidence: Revisiting the Impact of Public Encounters with the Police' (2009) 19(1) *Policing and Society* 20–46.

[277] Authorised Professional Practice guidance by the College of Policing reinforces this, noting the importance of treating people with dignity and respect. See <https://www.app.college.police.uk/app-content/stop-and-search/professional/#treat-people-with-dignity-and-respect> (last accessed 17 September 2020).

- a search 'out of public view' such as in a police van may be made if a more thorough search (for example requiring removal of a shirt or hat) is sought on reasonable grounds;
- if there are grounds to conduct a search which would expose intimate parts of the suspect's body such a search may take place in a police station or other nearby location, but not in a police vehicle;
- in any search going beyond the removal of headgear, footwear, coats/jackets and gloves the officer conducting the search must be of the same sex as the suspect, and no one of a different sex may be present unless requested by the suspect.

The guidance does not stop some stop-searches being humiliating, however. The very act of being forced to submit to police authority in this way is often embarrassing, as where people are searched outside their place of work or worship, or in view of their friends or family. Such feelings were reported to be even more acute when people are stopped under s.44 of the Terrorism Act, as Londoners explained to the Metropolitan Police Authority:

> We heard of embarrassment and humiliation. We heard of stigmatisation, worse than that associated with being stopped under normal police powers, because the signal given out to onlookers under Section 44 Terrorism Act 2000 is not 'this person is a robber' but 'this person is a terrorist'.[278]

At the extremes, stop-search is experienced as a public humiliation, particularly when the search appears arbitrary or discriminatory. In section 2.2.1.2 we discussed how the Bishop of Stepney was stopped by the police. He said that he felt 'demeaned' even though it was 'only' his car, and not himself, that was the object of the officer's intended search: 'When you ask and somebody doesn't give a reason and they seem to be hiding behind a uniform … that creates a feeling that they are more powerful than you and can act in any way they want over you. I just felt as if I was being treated like a little boy.'[279] At the time of writing this chapter there have been a number of other similar cases in the UK where black members of parliament, athletes and key workers (including police officers) have been stopped and searched arbitrarily and have reported the incidents as evidence of police racism.[280]

In an anti-terrorism example, a woman, seven months pregnant, had travelled from England to Dublin where she had been researching for a book she was writing. She was stopped and questioned on her way back.[281] She was treated lawfully and politely. But she was questioned closely about her work, her luggage was searched twice, she was confined to a small room, her personal correspondence was read, and she was anxious about her husband and child who were waiting for her without knowing what was going on. She feared that, if they were so suspicious of her, she might be excluded from England (she was originally from Belfast) and thus permanently separated from her husband and child.[282]

---

[278] Metropolitan Police Authority (2008: 52).   [279] *The Guardian*, 24 January 2000.

[280] *The Guardian*, 18 June 2020 <https://www.theguardian.com/world/2020/jun/18/nurse-claims-met-police-wrongfully-arrested-her-because-she-black-neomi-bennett> (accessed 1 September 2020); *The Guardian*, 5 July 2020 <https://www.theguardian.com/uk-news/2020/jul/05/met-police-deny-misconduct-after-linford-christie-athletes-stopped> (accessed 1 September 2020); *The Guardian*, 9 July 2020 <https://www.theguardian.com/uk-news/2020/jul/09/cases-that-highlight-claims-of-police-racial-profiling-in-england> (accessed 1 September 2020); *The Guardian*, 9 August 2020 <https://www.theguardian.com/uk-news/2020/aug/09/labour-mp-dawn-butler-stopped-by-police-in-london> (accessed 1 September 2020); *The Guardian*, 18 August 2020 <https://www.theguardian.com/uk-news/2020/aug/18/black-met-police-inspector-stopped-by-officers-while-driving-home-from-work> (accessed 1 September 2020).

[281] Under powers now contained in the Terrorism Act 2000, Sch 7.

[282] All the terrorist legislation examples are from Hillyard (1993: ch 3). See ch 1 for other examples. The specific anti-terrorist power to exclude was repealed by the Terrorism Act 2000.

Although well within the guidance given in the relevant Code of Practice, this examination was highly intrusive and upsetting.

Hillyard recounts a number of instances where women, in particular, were humiliated by examining officers. One said that: 'It felt like rape' when her diaries and letters were read in front of her, another was both distressed and outraged when two officers read her diary (including her noting of her periods) aloud to each other. Sometimes it appears the police intend to humiliate those they search as part of a policy of intimidating those they see as 'undesirables' or 'police property'. The stop-search power becomes just one among an array of coercive devices such as the power to 'move on' those deemed to be obstructing the highway, the right to question people regardless of the level of suspicion (so long as the person questioned is not actually detained), the discretion to enforce the law harshly and the ability to make it known to someone that they are under police surveillance.[283]

The invasion of liberty is felt more deeply still if it is, or is perceived to be, a product of prejudice or racism, which, in the light of the discussion in section 2.3 and chapter 10, is an understandable perception. The post-Macpherson research by Bland et al (2000): 87) confirmed that the manner in which the police exercise their powers is a crucial determinant of whether their actions were regarded as legitimate: 'It's not what they say, it's how they say it'. Later research by Bradford confirmed this, suggesting a 'double penalty' that affects minority ethnic groups because not only are they more likely to be stopped by the police but when they are, they are treated negatively (2017: 177). Police stops contribute to people's social identity and their sense of belonging to the extent that they come to 'expect' racist treatment by the police and by extension, the state (Parmar 2019a). The result of all this is that BAME people are significantly more likely than white people to report feeling upset, embarrassed or angry about being stopped (Allen et al, 2006: table 2.07). Asked what improvements they would like to see, young people who had been stop-searched asked that the police: 'Be more polite, less hostile, give reason … '; 'Stop being racist', and 'If they were less aggressive and listened to what I say … ' (NACRO, 1997: 45–46). One Pakistani young adult described his interaction with the police as follows:

> their exact words were, yeah (and I've got witnesses because I was with two other people, yeah) was: 'Don't fuck me about right, and I won't fuck you about, where have you got your drugs?' (Bland et al 2000: 82).

Bland et al (2000: 82) found that black people were far less likely than Asian or white people to report any positive experiences of respectful treatment by the police. Dissatisfaction is higher than average for the young and unemployed too.[284] Vulnerable people are also likely to be badly affected by stop-search. An 11-year-old boy stop-searched at the climate camp discussed in section 2.4.3 was 'crying and shaking' because he had a sticker, and heard that the police were confiscating them; he feared he would 'go to prison' for this.[285]

In other words, dissatisfaction among those who are stopped is directly related to membership of those groups which are disproportionately stopped. Either, stop for stop, the police treat members of these groups worse than they do others, or being in a group which believes itself to be targeted creates sensitivity—which is another way of saying that the stop is, or is perceived to be, a greater invasion of their freedom. In reality both of these

---

[283] See, for example, the case of the 30-year-old black social worker who appears to have been harassed in a variety of ways by officers from one police station in seven separate, but clearly related, incidents variously involving stop-search, mockery, arrest and overnight detention (case dismissed by the court the following morning), threats of arrest, handcuffing in public and a strip-search: Havis and Best (2004: 26–27).

[284] Bucke T, *Ethnicity and Contacts with the Police: Latest Findings from the British Crime Survey* (Home Office Research Findings No 59) (London: Home Office, 1997). Similar findings are reported by Sharp and Atherton (2007).   [285] *The Guardian*, 7 May 2009.

explanatory factors are at work here. Thus, increased use of the power has an exponential effect on the resentment it causes. In many of the examples given here, PACE and the Code of Practice were adhered to, but the encounters were nonetheless humiliating or aggravating. In evaluating the impact and value of stop-search much more needs to be examined than how far the police follow the rules. European Court of Human Rights adopted a similar form of analysis to that presented here, holding that:

> the use of the coercive powers conferred by the legislation to require an individual to submit to a detailed search of his person, his clothing and his personal belongings amounts to a clear interference with the right to respect for private life. Although the search is undertaken in a public place, this does not mean that Article 8 is inapplicable. Indeed, in the Court's view, the public nature of the search may, in certain cases, compound the seriousness of the interference because of an element of humiliation and embarrassment.[286]

2.5.3 Stop-search and police-community relations

The notions of 'policing by consent' and 'community policing' are not as straightforward as they sound, and the assumptions on which they are based are questionable.[287] However, in so far as these notions are tenable and desirable, the negative impact on them of the way stop and search operates needs to be considered.[288] Community is itself a loaded term, of course, and the reality is that society is made up of overlapping networks of relationships based on work, age, blood, friendships, interests, geography, religion and so forth. Each 'community' will have its own set of unique relations with the police that vary over time. Space precludes fine-grained analysis of all these permutations so here we will focus on race, because, as we have seen, stop-search is experienced as particularly demeaning by large sections of ethnic minority communities.[289]

The examples of racist stop and searches discussed in this chapter are examples of the types of police encounters that are widely disseminated and long remembered. They form part of the collective memory of those who come frequently into contact with the police, whether as suspects, volunteers, witnesses or victims,[290] spreading out even into the ranks of 'respectable', white, middle-class society.[291] The sharing of experience is more likely now as stop and search encounters are captured immediately as video footage on mobile phones and circulated to peers and the wider public within moments of the incident occurring. Recorded stop and search encounters—such as the killing of George Floyd and shooting

---

[286] *Gillan and Quinton v the United Kingdom* (Application no. 4158/05) Judgment 12 January 2010 [63].

[287] There is a contradiction between the aspiration to foster community solidarity and the encouragement of an informant culture, which is increasingly the direction of 'proactive policing'. See McConville M and Shepherd D, *Watching Police, Watching Communities* (London: Routledge, 1992) and Gordon P, 'Community Policing: Towards the Local Police State' in Scraton P (ed), *Law Order and the Authoritarian State* (Milton Keynes: Open UP, 1987).

[288] Even those sections of the community who experience high levels of stop-search do not generally question the need for the *existence* of this police power: Fitzgerald (1999: ch 2); Stone V and Pettigrew N, *The Views of the Public on Stops and Searches* (London: Home Office, 2000) p 29; Fitzgerald et al (2002: 45). Rather the public favours more restrained, discriminating and respectful use of stop-search.

[289] Whereas the age and gender profile of those using the formal police complaints system in relation to stop-search practices is little different from the total population using that system, black complainants are responsible for 40% of all stop-search complaints compared with just 10% of all complaints (Havis and Best 2004: 47).

[290] Fitzgerald et al (2002: 49, 92–93); Bland et al (2000: 82); Britton N, 'Examining Police/Black Relations' (2000b) 23(4) *Ethic and Racial Studies* 696. The fact that stop-search usually takes place in public increases its collective impact: Stone and Pettigrew (2000: 11).

[291] See Loader and Mulcahy (2003: esp. 156–161).

of Jacob Blake in the US—can therefore 'go viral' in moments.[292] In other words, a minority of racist or aggressive officers can do immense damage to police-community relations, as more enlightened officers are only too aware.[293] When the issue of racist policing becomes a matter of high public profile, the sense of collective injustice is reinforced still further.

But simply rooting out overtly racist police officers will not restore confidence in the fairness of policing, given the continuing undercurrent of more subtle forms of direct and indirect racial discrimination through implicit bias or institutional policies and processes. A senior black former police officer points, for example, to the 'growing practice of officers handcuffing young black boys who have not been arrested and are not resisting or showing any signs of aggression, before they start searching them … The misuse of stop and search exemplifies the notion of police "property" … Black boys are treated as police "property" whilst their white friends that are with them are treated very differently, with courtesy and respect.'[294] The perception of police practices as discriminatory provoke enormous resentment amongst ethnic minority communities.[295] This was belatedly recognised, in relation to s.44 powers at any rate, by the Metropolitan Police anti-terrorism chief and by Lord Carlisle (the government-appointed independent reviewer of anti-terrorism legislation). The latter, prior to its repeal in 2011 said: 'S 44 is over-used … and that is causing alienation to some communities.'[296] And it has not gone away: as a Chief Constable said in 2020: 'The slower rate of progress in recruiting black police officers is likely to reflect the fact that confidence in police has historically been lower among black people than white or Asian—although the latest statistics show an improving picture.'[297]

If people believe the police to be against them—whether or not this belief is justified—then they are far less likely to participate in community policing. This is important because of the huge overlap between the suspect population and the victim/witness population. The nature of personal contact is argued to be central to understanding how people perceive the police.[298] A recent US study for example found that respondents who had experienced more stops by the police and who felt as though they were handled in a disrespectful manner were less willing to report victimisation to the police.[299] Interactions between young people and the London Metropolitan Police Service were found to be formative in terms of the young people developing positive or negative perceptions of the police. Stop and search was a common process through which perceptions of the police were formed and those young people who were wary of the police were subsequently reluctant to initiate contact with the police to report incidents relating to their own safety or the victimisation of others for fear of coming under scrutiny themselves.[300]

---

[292] Jacob Blake a black man was shot seven times by the police in his car which had his three children inside in Kenosha, Wisconsin in the US on 23 August 2020. The incident sparked widespread civil unrest and became the latest flashpoint in a summer which has vividly exposed the brutal force used on black people in particular: *The Guardian*, 25 August 2020 (see <https://www.theguardian.com/us-news/2020/aug/25/wisconsin-police-fire-teargas-during-second-night-of-protest-over-shooting-of-black-man> – accessed 1 September 2020).

[293] 'I've seen behaviour in the past that was absolutely atrocious … it only takes a couple of people to destroy all the good work': sergeant quoted by Fitzgerald (1999: ch 4).

[294] *The Guardian*, 15 June 2020.   [295] See, for example, Clancy et al (2001: 73–78).

[296] *The Guardian*, 7 May 2009. This report also quotes the Metropolitan anti-terrorism chief, who argues for reduced use of s.44 (see section 2.2.2.2).

[297] *The Guardian*, 15 June 2020. See, further, Newburn et al (2016).

[298] See Bradford et al (2009).

[299] Renfigo et al, 'From Impressions to Intentions: Direct and Indirect Effects of Police Contact on Willingness to Report Crimes to Law Enforcement' (2019) 56(3) *Journal of Research in Crime and Delinquency* 412–450.

[300] Norman J, 'Seen and Not Heard: Young People's Perceptions of the Police' (2009) 3(4) *Policing: A Journal of Policy and Practice* 364–372.

2.6 Conclusion

We have seen that ss.1–3 of PACE are not of great inhibitory effect. Why? First, the main legal constraint—reasonable suspicion—is too vague to act as a standard by which most police actions can be judged. Second, the provisions for providing information and recording of searches are difficult to enforce. Third, many pedestrian stops—probably most—are in legal terms achieved without the exercise of a power, and this provides the police with the opportunity to generate grounds for a subsequent search. Fourth, Road Traffic Act powers give the police the same opportunity in relation to vehicle stops. Fifth, these due process provisions envisage a model of policing which does not accord with 'cop culture', the modern reality of street policing, or its history. When the police comply with PACE safeguards they do so primarily because these serve policing goals (such as securing co-operation, or building up intelligence) rather than actually protecting suspects. Sixth, even when the police do exercise discretion in accordance with the rules, the attitudes and values which underlie their suspicions influence the *manner* in which stop-search is conducted. This exacerbates the invasion of privacy that is inherent to stop-search. Seventh, the remedies for unlawful stop and search are uncertain in scope, inadequate in operation and insufficiently stringent in effect. Finally, there are powers outside ss.1–3 of PACE that allow stop-search without even the nominal requirement that there be reasonable suspicion. One of the most controversial, s.44 of the Terrorism Act, was repealed in 2011, but its lasting legacy has been to reduce confidence and trust in the police among Asian communities. Also, when s.44 was implemented the proportion of stop-searches of Asian people rocketed and searches under PACE have remained disproportionate to the Asian population since.[301]

The result is that the police still primarily act according to working assumptions based on 'suspiciousness', i.e. hunch, incongruity and stereotyping on the basis of types of people, previous records and so forth. These are all crime control norms, rooted as they are in the world of professional experience and police culture. The police sometimes discover crime when acting upon their instincts, but such suspicion as they have is seldom in relation to any particular offence, and therefore rarely is it 'reasonable' in terms of the due process norms of s.1 of PACE. Stop and search in operation corresponds far more closely to the crime control model than the due process model to which the law is purportedly oriented, which means that s.1 of PACE is primarily presentational, legitimising and enabling. One important consequence of this is the over-representation of ethnic minority people in the stop-searched population, which in turn contributes to their over-representation in the arrested, prosecuted and imprisoned populations.[302] This does not mean that the police do literally just as they wish: recent research found that 'while officers did not always follow law, policy, or accepted practice, deliberate or malicious abuses of power such as unlawful arrests, unnecessary use of force, or racial bias were, from our observations, exceptionally rare.'[303] This is a fair summary. But it begs the question of the extent to which, when the police follow the law, they are prevented from achieving whatever objective they have in mind.

Perhaps requiring the police to claim that they have 'reasonable suspicion' in relation to a particular offence when in fact they are simply generally suspicious encourages them to treat the law with contempt (while pretending otherwise to suspects and courts). This cannot be healthy either for the law in general or for the regard in which the police are held.

---

[301] See Parmar (2011).
[302] As documented in summary form by Bowling and Phillips (2007).
[303] Pearson and Rowe (2020: 4).

Would it be better either to allow stops on grounds of general suspicion or not to allow stops at all? The former option is unattractive from a due process perspective. Laws such as these could be seen, like speed limits, as broadly inhibitory, whereby no-one expects precise compliance, but blatant transgression is rare. Relaxing the limits might only encourage the police to overstep the mark once again. Policing on the streets might then be based on random stops rather than, as now, on general suspicion. Or, more likely, 'general suspicion' could become the basis for non-random stops that are even more discriminatory than is usual now. The shift already evident in the post-PACE law away from a requirement of individualised suspicion in favour of rules enabling risk-based, actuarial policing of entire social groups (the young, ethnic minorities, the homeless, protesters etc) would then be complete.

On the other hand, attempting to 'firm up' the law and make it more inhibitory might be both undesirable and impossible. Police behaviour on the street is inherently fact-finding—i.e. inquisitorial—and the skilful finding of facts requires streetwise knowledge, technique, and experience. Talking to people with their consent—the starting point for many stops and often the ending point too—can and should never be prevented. Imposing an adversarial due process structure onto this craft is an attempt to deny one of the key elements of what policing is about. If policing is more about general social control than detection of specific crimes, then this is all the more true. And if the managerialist ethos identified in chapter 1 continues to reward officers for their 'productivity' (including arrests arising from stops) this will be more true still.

In chapter 1 we argued that the purpose of criminal justice is, or should be, to promote freedom. This chapter has shown that the freedom of actual and potential victims is protected to some extent through the arrest, deterrent and information-gathering effects of stop-search. But the freedom of suspects is hugely violated on three levels: at the community level, certain groups in society disproportionately suffer from both the actual exercise of the power and the fear that it will be exercised when in public places; at the quantitative level, the chances of being repeatedly stop-searched are very high if one is a member of one or more of those groups; and at the qualitative level, the exercise of the power, especially when it is repeated, represents suffering for the suspect which, in its different way, is as real as the suffering of many a victim. Indeed in some ways the loss of freedom of suspects and victims is similar. In many cases both groups fear that the invasion will recur. Feelings of persecution and loss of control over one's life sometimes arise. Behaviour changes, in an effort to avoid recurrence. Further, when stop-search triggers offences as a reaction to it (as in the examples given in section 2.5.3) and leads to the alienation of the community (and hence less assistance with crime-solving) freedom that is gained by stop-search is lost in the crimes which are not solved and which are even created. In terms of the 'core values' derived from the 'freedom perspective', we have seen that stop-search is fundamentally unjust, offends democracy by alienating whole communities, and is not even a good use of resources. It fails every test.

Who is to weigh up the competing demands of crime control versus liberty? Those in positions of power in this debate (Royal Commissions, Members of Parliament and the government, Home Office and Ministry of Justice officials, senior police officers, and, at the local level, councillors and residents who turn up to neighbourhood policing team meetings, etc) are not a representative cross-section of society. The law is mostly reviewed, made and implemented by the white middle-aged middle classes. Those who are stopped and searched are primarily the marginalised elements of society: the young unemployed, the homeless, those with mental health conditions, the Irish, black people, Asian people, drug users and all the other 'toe rags', 'scum' and 'losers' who attract the attention of the police. One section of society shapes the law (both in books and in action) which bears down on the other. It is easy for the decision-making community to decide that it is in 'society's' interests for suspects to have their liberty compromised and their privacy invaded, when those suspects are overwhelmingly drawn from the non-decision-making community. One fundamental question raised by stop and search in a divided society is how far police powers are used to help perpetuate existing structures of inequality, subordination and social exclusion.

Further reading

Bowling B et al, *The Politics of the Police* 5th edn (Oxford: OUP, 2019).

Bradford B, *Stop and Search and Police Legitimacy* (London: Routledge, 2016).

Charman S, *Police Socialisation, Identity and Culture: Becoming Blue* (London, Palgrave MacMillan, 2017).

Delsol R and Shiner M (eds), *Stop and Search: The Anatomy of a Police Power* (London: Palgrave Macmillan 2015).

Hallsworth S, 'Racial Targeting and Social Control: Looking Behind the Police' (2006) 14 *Critical Criminology* 293.

Jones T et al, 'Policing and the Police' in Liebling A et al (eds), *Oxford Handbook of Criminology* 6th edn (Oxford: OUP, 2020).

Pearson G and Rowe M, *Police Street Powers and Criminal Justice* (London: Bloomsbury, 2020).

Quinton P, 'The formation of suspicions: police stop and search practices in England and Wales' (2011) 21(4) *Policing and Society* 357–368.

3

Arrest

KEY ISSUES

- arrest and its relationship to freedom
- the lawful and unlawful purposes of arrest
- the growth of preventive forms of arrest and quasi-arrest
- the legal basis for arrest, and reasonable suspicion
- the working rules shaping the patterns of arrest
- arrest, terrorism, and the rise of young, male Muslims as the new prime suspects
- race, class, gender and arrest
- the miserable experience of being arrested
- the lack of effective remedies for wrongful arrest

3.1 Introduction: what is an arrest?

In *Lewis v Chief Constable of the South Wales Constabulary*[1] it was stated that:

> Arrest is a matter of fact; it is not a legal concept … Arrest is a situation … Whether a person has been arrested depends not on the legality of his arrest but on whether he has been deprived of his liberty to go where he pleases.[2]

There need be no explicit statement of arrest; arrest occurs if it is made clear that the arrestee would be prevented from leaving.[3] PACE, s.28 and the ECHR, Art 5(2) oblige the police to give the reason for arrest explicitly, and as soon as is reasonably practicable.[4] This is because: 'If the State is taking away your liberty, you are entitled to know why.'[5] But the police may not be subject to the degree of due process rigour that one might think from this.

---

[1] [1991] 1 All ER 206 at 209–210, confirming *Spicer v Holt* [1977] AC 987.

[2] This definition was endorsed in *Dawes v DPP* [1995] 1 Cr App Rep 65. In this case, the offender broke into a car which had been set up by the police to lock automatically when the door was closed, trapping him. This was the point at which he was held to be arrested.

[3] *Shaaban Bin Hussien v Chong Fook Kam* [1970] AC 942 at 949. Confirmed in *Walker v MPC* [2015] 1 Cr App R 22, which also confirmed, as is logical, that a trivial restraint of an individual, by, say, tugging someone's sleeve to attract their attention, is not an arrest.

[4] The reason(s) need not be a precise formulation of the law (see *Abbassy v Metropolitan Police Comr* [1990] 1 All ER 193, where the defendants were arrested for 'unlawful possession' of a car. There is no such offence, but as this encompassed all the criminal possibilities the officers had in mind, the Court of Appeal said that this was satisfactory).

[5] *Taylor v CC of the Thames Valley* [2004] 1 WLR 3155 per Sedley LJ para 58.

INTRODUCTION: WHAT IS AN ARREST?   111

First, the reason for arrest: when a drunk man was apprehended sitting in his car claimed that he went to his car from his house to 'cool off', the police officer asked him to stay where he was while she asked the man's wife if his story was true. She did not tell him at this point that he was under arrest but it was held that this did not matter as the arrest was 'completed' after it became obvious that he had lied.[6] And when a man was aggressive and threatening and told he would be arrested if he did not calm down, it was—the Court of Appeal thought—so obvious why he was being arrested when he did not calm down that not being explicit about the reasons for arrest did not matter.[7]

Second, how soon? In a terrorism case, soldiers went to the defendant (M's) house at 7am, detained everyone and searched the premises. The soldier in charge remained with M. At 7.30am, he informed M of her arrest under summary arrest powers similar to those of the police. On the basis that M had been 'deprived of her liberty' at 7am, she had been under de facto arrest and not informed of this for 30 minutes. But according to Lord Griffiths: 'If words of arrest are spoken as soon as the house is entered … there is a real risk that the alarm may be raised.'[8] It was therefore not practicable in his opinion to inform M of the fact of, and reasons for, her arrest immediately; the arrest was therefore not unlawful. This seems to assume that the alarm was not raised when the group of armed soldiers entered the house, rounded everyone up, gave it a thorough search and did not even tell the occupants what was going to happen to them. The decision in this case does not alter the principle at stake but—unless 'terrorist' cases are being treated as special cases—it shows that drawing the line about when something is reasonably practicable is not easy.

So in reality, there are many circumstances where arrestees need not be told they are being arrested immediately, or given the reasons why. The police can use such force as is reasonable in the circumstances to effect an arrest.[9] The result sometimes is that arrest is resisted by people who do not know they are being arrested, force is used on both sides, and arrestees find themselves charged with obstruction or assault.[10]

While every arrest involves a deprivation of liberty to go where one pleases, not every such deprivation amounts to an arrest. For example, the police may (temporarily) detain or restrain a person or persons for their own safety or in order to prevent an imminent breach of the peace without this amounting to an arrest (or a deprivation of liberty within the meaning of Art 5 of the European Convention on Human Rights (ECHR)).[11] When designated with the power by a Chief Constable, police community support officers (PCSOs) can detain for up to 30 minutes those who they believe have committed one of a broad range of offences or to be acting anti-socially and who refuse to provide their name and address (or provide one reasonably believed to be false). When designated with the power, PCSOs may also use reasonable force to prevent a detained person making off and to keep that person under control.[12] And lawful searches of the person (during which the police may use such force as is reasonable to enable the search to take place, as by forcibly

---

[6] *Fiak* [2005] EWCA Crim 2381.   [7] *Walker v MPC* [2015] 1 Cr App R 22.
[8] *Murray v Minister of Defence* [1988] 2 All ER 521 at p 527. Endorsed by the ECtHR: (1994) 19 EHRR 193.
[9] Criminal Law Act 1967, s.3; Police and Criminal Evidence Act 1984, s.117.
[10] As in *Walker v MPC* [2015] 1 Cr App R 22. For another example see *DPP v L* [1999] Crim LR 752.
[11] *R (on the application of Jane Laporte) v (1) Chief Constable of Gloucestershire Constabulary & Others* [2006] UKHL 55; *Austin and Another v Commissioner of Police for the Metropolis* [2009] UKHL 5 (both cases are discussed in section 3.3.4).
[12] These powers were initially enacted in the Police Reform Act 2002, though are now contained in the Policing and Crime Act 2017. The purpose of the detention is to allow a police officer to attend and formally arrest the suspect. PCSOs can give a detainee the option of going to a police station with them instead of waiting to be arrested.

detaining them) are not arrests.[13] Since the borderline between arrests and other forms of restraint is incapable of precise definition, officers are often confused.[14] If an arrest is unlawful it may negate police actions following the purported arrest and police officers may face civil (and occasionally criminal) proceedings as we will discuss at the end of the chapter and in chapter 11.

Arrest often renders suspects powerless, humiliated or even terrified. The Philips Commission in the 1980s recognised this:

> Arrest represents a major disruption to a suspect's life … police officers are so involved with the process of arrest and detention that they fail at times to understand the sense of alarm and dismay felt by some of those who suffer such treatment.[15]

That arrest can be distressing without the police deliberately abusing their powers is evident from accounts provided by arrestees, such as the following:

> Two of them turned to my husband and said, 'We are arresting you under the Prevention of Terrorism Act.' I'm not kidding you, I was glad I was sitting down because I could feel my stomach going down to my feet. The Birmingham Six flashed through my mind. This is how innocent people are picked up. Up to then I had thought that the police didn't pick up people who are completely innocent. ...[16]

The 'pains of police detention' described here, which are sometimes rooted in the reasons for and circumstances of someone's arrest, were found in recent research too.[17] Distress can give way to humiliation or even terror when the police do abuse their arrest powers. Abuse may take many forms, including arresting for an improper purpose or conducting the arrest in a deliberately disrespectful manner. Both forms of abuse appear in the following exchange between an arrestee named Natt and a police constable:

Natt:	Why am I being arrested?
PC:	You're just a pain in the arse ain't yer?
Natt:	Oh, God.
PC:	Why don't you go and set fire to yourself or something?
Natt:	You carry on arresting me without reason. Why?
PC:	Because you are a shit.
[later] Natt:	Why beat me? Why?
PC:	Because I like it.
Natt:	You like to beat me?
PC:	I got no respect for someone like you.

---

[13] See, for example, *DPP v Meaden* [2004] 4 All ER 75 discussed in Healy P, 'Investigative Detention in Canada' [2005] *Criminal Law Review* 98.

[14] In *Adler v Crown Prosecution Service* [2013] EWHC 1968 (Admin) an off duty police officer detained a person on observing him breaking into a car. Although the plain clothed officer did not say the words 'I am arresting you' there was sufficient evidence for the judge to conclude that a lawful arrest had been made as the police officer explained to the detainee who he was. See commentary on the case by Cape [2014] *Criminal Law Review* 224.

[15] Royal Commission on Criminal Procedure (RCCP), *Report* (Cmnd 8092) (London: HMSO, 1981) para 3.75.

[16] Hillyard P, *Suspect Community* (London: Pluto Press, 1993) pp 111–113.

[17] Skinns L and Wooff A, 'Pain in Police Detention: A Critical Point in the "Penal Painscape"?' (2021) 31(3) *Policing and Society*. 245–262.

We know that this is an accurate report of what happened because Natt tape-recorded it, having been verbally abused when previously stopped by police officers.[18] It is difficult, however, to quantify the extent to which arrest powers are abused and harder still to explain it. What is unquestionable is that the arrest powers provided to the police give them the opportunity to infringe people's freedom in many ways, and that they should therefore be subject to careful scrutiny. At the same time, sensitive and proportionate use of the arrest power is vital to the effective disruption and investigation of crime. As in other areas of criminal justice, the law can be seen as striking a balance with a view to ensuring that the freedom-enhancing aspects of arrest outweigh the threats to freedom inherent in coercive state power. That the law may neither have got this balance right nor be respected by the police in practice are key questions for consideration here.

In this chapter we therefore look at how far the police are, and should be, allowed to infringe the freedom of the individual through arrest. In other words, we will examine the legal rules and how effective they are in controlling the use of this power. We will also look at the actual, as well as lawful, reasons for arrest. As with stop-search, this means we have to understand the informal working rules that help to structure police discretion, so section 2.1 is as applicable to arrest as it is to stop-search. We will also need to explore the racial stereotyping and differential treatment of ethnic minority groups discussed in chapters 2 and 10 that is as prevalent in arrest practices as with stop-search, sometimes with lethal consequences.[19] The growth in members of the public video recording arrests in order to document this interaction and hold the police to account for racial profiling (see chapter 11), demonstrates that levels of trust in the police, especially amongst minority ethnic citizens, continue to wane. We also examine some forms of detention that are not defined as arrest, since it would be artificial to ignore these closely related infringements of liberty.

3.2 Arrest and the purposes of criminal justice

3.2.1 The ostensible purposes of arrest

There are several lawful purposes of arrest, with or without subsequent detention. The *traditional* purposes include securing someone's appearance at court who has breached a court order or failed to answer a summons or requisition (a written command to attend court);[20] as part of transit between court and prison; and holding someone in custody in order to charge them. Arrests for these reasons are all to facilitate an ongoing prosecution. They pose no great problems of principle or practice, and we will not be dealing with them in this chapter.

---

[18] A fuller extract is provided in Holdaway S, *The Racialisation of British Policing* (Houndmills: Macmillan, 1996) pp 72–73.

[19] See for example the case of Olympic Black female Athlete Bianca Williams who was handcuffed alongside her partner in front of her baby son in July 2020. She felt that racial profiling was the only reason for the stop. *The Guardian*, 6 July 2020 at <https://www.theguardian.com/uk-news/2020/jul/06/bianca-williams-athlete-stopped-by-met-police-being-black-is-a-crime> (accessed 14 October 2020). Also see the jury inquest verdict into the death of Kevin Clarke—a black man who was restrained by the Metropolitan Police in 2018. The inappropriate use of restraints by the police was said to contribute to his death: *The Guardian*, 9 October 2020 at <https://www.theguardian.com/uk-news/2020/oct/09/met-police-restraint-contributed-death-mentally-ill-man-kevin-clarke-jury-finds> (accessed 14 October 2020).

[20] Prosecutors used to secure a court summons by 'laying an information' (i.e. setting out the particulars of an alleged offence) before a court. Section 29 of the Criminal Justice Act 2003 now requires *public* prosecutors to proceed instead by way of a written charge and 'requisition' to attend court to answer it. The position regarding *private* prosecutors remains unchanged. For the sake of convenience the traditional term 'summons' will be used in this chapter to cover 'requisitions'.

Another traditional use of arrest is for the arrestee's own protection. For example, someone who appears to be intoxicated or experiencing a mental health crisis and is in immediate need of care or control can be taken to a place of safety for up to 24 hours (extendable by 12 hours) in order that a medical assessment can be undertaken. This power (deriving from s.136 of the Mental Health Act 1983) is not dependent on an offence having been committed but it may be used to arrest only those found anywhere but in a private dwelling where a constable believes removal to a 'place of safety' is necessary in the interests of that person or for the protection of others.[21] In practice, such preventive arrest powers can be used for other purposes, such as maintaining police authority, 'reassuring' the public, or managing people seen as carriers of 'risk'. Unfortunately we have no space to explore this in depth, notwithstanding their importance.[22] However 'risks' can be broadly defined and context-led. The Coronavirus Act 2020 extends police powers, allowing officers to detain potentially infectious persons, to prevent mass gatherings and impose criminal sanctions for disease transmission. This power extends to immigration officers and public health officers to detain anyone they have 'reasonable grounds' to suspect is 'potentially infectious' for up to 14 days (para 15(1)). Many infected individuals are asymptomatic, so the risk of arbitrary or discriminatory use of these powers is obvious and, it seems is already happening.[23]

The other traditional purposes of arrest are to prevent a crime (or a further crime) taking place, and to maintain public order. Arrests for these purposes are not always to facilitate prosecution, and there may not be enough evidence to prosecute at the time of arrest (although the use of investigative powers allied to arrest may result in such evidence emerging). This type of pre-emptive arrest appears to be growing in importance and is increasingly controversial. It is lawful provided that at the time of the arrest there is an intention to take the arrested person before the courts.[24]

Preventive quasi-arrest powers have multiplied in recent years as part of the growing emphasis on risk management. For example, s.16 of the Crime and Disorder Act 1998 gave the police the power to 'remove' school age children in certain circumstances from public places, and take them to their school or other appropriate place. The aim here is not to take police or court action, but to deal with truancy and the crime problems which sometimes accompany it.[25] The ASB and Policing Act 2014 is another example of legislation seeking risk management through restricting freedom of movement through, for example, dispersal powers.[26]

---

[21] Policing and Crime Act 2017. It is now unlawful for police cells to be used as places of safety for those under 18 years, and they are only available for use in 'specific circumstances' for adults.

[22] See for example: Menkes D and Bendelow G, 'Diagnosing Vulnerability and "Dangerousness": Police Use of Section 136 in England and Wales' (2014) 13(2) *Journal of Public Mental Health* 70–82. Note the 2017 Act changed the law after this research was done.

[23] Jones D, 'The Potential Impacts of Pandemic Policing on Police Legitimacy: Planning Past the COVID-19 Crisis,' (2020) 14(3) *Policing: A Journal of Policy and Practice* 579; Dodd V, 'Met police twice as likely to fine black people over lockdown breaches' *The Guardian*, 3 June 2020.

[24] *R (Hicks) v Commissioner of Police of the Metropolis* [2014] EWCA Civ 3.

[25] See Leng et al, *Blackstone's Guide to the Crime and Disorder Act 1998* (London: Blackstone, 1998) pp 37–39.

[26] This builds on earlier legislation including the 1998 Act. Arbitrariness, discrimination and unintended consequences were all revealed by research on those measures. See, e.g., Crawford A and Lister S, *The Use and Impact of Dispersal Orders* (London: Policy Press, 2007); Nixon J and Hunter C, 'Disciplining Women: Anti-social Behaviour and the Governance of Conduct' in Millie A (ed), *Securing Respect* (Bristol: Policy Press, 2009). An illustration is *Bucknell v DPP* [2006] EWCH 1888 where it was held that it was wrong for a constable to seek to disperse two groups of black and Asian schoolchildren who had congregated to chat after school on a summer's afternoon in a designated dispersal area. There was no actual behaviour by the groups indicating harassment, alarm, intimidation or distress, and no member of the public had complained about their mere presence. For comment and research on the 2014 legislation see, for example, Demetriou S, 'From the ASBO to the Injunction: A Qualitative Review of the Anti-social Behaviour Legislation Post 2014' (2019) *Public Law* 343; Demetriou S, 'Crime and Anti-social Behaviour in England and Wales: An Empirical Evaluation of the ASBO's Successor' (2020) 40 *Legal Studies* 458; Brown K, 'Punitive reform and the cultural life of punishment: moving from the ASBO to its successors' (2020) 22 *Punishment & Society* 91.

Finally, many arrests, for a variety of offences, are made, at least ostensibly, with a view to developing a case against someone suspected of having already committed a specific criminal offence. A less traditional purpose of arrest, then, which developed in the late twentieth century, is in order to obtain or secure evidence. This evidence can come from a variety of sources, including interviews with witnesses, searches of property, collection of forensic evidence and questioning of the suspects themselves. As this is now the main form and function of arrest, let us consider how different models of criminal justice view the relationship between arrest powers and the investigation of crime.

3.2.2 Models of criminal justice and arrest

3.2.2.1 Due process

Under this model, no-one should be arrested unless it is clear that they probably committed a specific offence. Normally such a determination should be made by a magistrate who would then issue a warrant authorising the police to arrest. In situations of necessity the model would accept that the police may act without prior authority, but only on hard evidence which would be subject to subsequent judicial scrutiny.

This model accepts that these standards would impair police efficiency, and that this is the price to be paid to protect personal privacy and the dignity and inviolability of the individual. In other words, our core value of 'justice' would be prioritised over 'efficiency'. Moreover, if the police were to be given wider powers to arrest suspects for questioning, it is unlikely that all classes of society would suffer greater interference, since the outcry would be too great. Rather, police powers would 'be applied in a discriminatory fashion to precisely those elements in the population—the poor, the ignorant, the illiterate, the unpopular—who are least able to draw attention to their plight and to whose sufferings the vast majority of the population are the least responsive'.[27]

3.2.2.2 Crime control

The adherent of this model would argue that the police need broad powers of arrest which they can deploy without prior authorisation from a judicial body. They need to be able to round up known offenders from time to time to see if they are responsible for crimes occurring in the locality. They also need the power to act on their instincts by arresting suspicious looking characters. It may be that no crime will be detected by these methods, but the very fact of arresting such persons may prevent a planned crime. Periodic infringements of the liberty of known criminals may be enough to persuade them to leave the area or desist from their illegal activities.

The innocent have nothing to fear from such broad arrest powers. In the rare case where they are arrested by mistake, release will quickly follow. The police should therefore be given powers to arrest citizens irrespective of whether they are reasonably suspected of committing a particular crime. The standard should be no more than that a police officer honestly thinks that an arrest will serve the goal of crime control. Alternatively, the substantive laws must be so broadly defined that the reasonable suspicion hurdle can be easily overcome. A combination of vague laws and lax standards is ideal. The 'freedom approach' would steer a path between these two extremes, taking particular note of the actual way the police use their arrest powers as well as how they are supposed to behave.

---

[27] Packer H, *The Limits of the Criminal Sanction* (Stanford: Stanford UP, 1968) p 180.

3.2.3 **The place of arrest in the criminal process**

If we look back at the development of the main form and function of arrest, a shift from a due process to a crime control model can be seen. Until the early part of the nineteenth century, magistrates determined whether or not someone should be prosecuted, usually on the basis of information provided to them by other enforcement agencies or private citizens. If they were satisfied by this evidence, they could issue a warrant for arrest or a summons to the defendant to appear in court at a later time. Some people were arrested first and then immediately brought before the magistrates, who, again, decided whether or not a prosecution should follow.[28] Arrest used simply to be a mechanism for bringing offenders to court.

Arresting in order to take an offender to court was, therefore, pointless unless evidence had already been gathered sufficient to justify a prosecution. Accordingly, the police or any other law enforcer would investigate and then arrest (or not) at the end of that investigation. This means that the investigation took place (in theory) before the police exercised coercive powers. So in 1969, the police were criticised for making:

> a premature arrest rather than one that was unjustifiable from first to last. The police made the mistake of arresting before questioning; if they had questioned first and arrested afterwards, there would have been no case against them.[29]

In reality, and certainly by the middle of the twentieth century, many people 'helped the police with their inquiries' in the police station: they were not formally arrested but rather were portrayed as attending the police station voluntarily. If, as a result of this 'voluntary help', the police secured enough evidence to prosecute, they would arrest and bring the suspect before the magistrates; if they did not have enough evidence, the suspect was (eventually) released. Gradually, the legal fiction of 'helping the police with their enquiries' broke down, being in detention came to be seen as being under arrest, and so arrest moved nearer to the beginning of the investigative process. Arrest's main form and function became the forcible removal of a person from conditions of freedom to conditions of detention in the police station, in order to facilitate evidence gathering through interrogation. This was formalised by successive Acts of Parliament, each of which gave the police more arrest powers. Now all offences are arrestable without warrant so long as the police have reasonable grounds for believing that it is necessary to arrest the person in question 'to allow the prompt and effective investigation of the offence or of the conduct of the person in question'.[30]

On the whole, the law now makes it difficult for the police to ask detailed questions of suspects prior to arrest, except when such questions are asked of citizens on a 'voluntary' basis either in the course of a 'voluntary' interview on the street or whilst 'voluntarily' attending a police station by appointment.[31] Questioning away from the police station has been restricted in order to protect suspects, but with the ironic result that many arrests are 'premature' in the *Shaaban* (1969) sense. Freedom is accordingly lost through a more extensive use of arrest and detention, but possibly gained through greater protection of suspects when participating in police interviews whilst formally arrested and detained. Whether or not these changes have led to a net gain in freedom is unclear. In the 1960s and 1970s, pre-trial detention was secured unlawfully or quasi-lawfully through the mechanism of 'helping the police with their inquiries', but now it is secured openly and lawfully

---

[28] See Sanders A, 'Arrest, Charge and Prosecution' (1986) 6 *Legal Studies* 257.
[29] *Shaaban Bin Hussien v Chong Fook Kam* [1970] AC 942, 949.
[30] PACE, ss.24 and 25, as amended by the Serious Organised Crime and Police Act 2005, s.110.
[31] See section 5.4.1.

through the mechanism of arrest and detention, but also increasingly through the growing use of voluntary interviews.[32]

In terms of the legal rules discussed in section 2.1.3, the legal rules we shall be discussing in this chapter are therefore legitimising rules (legitimising the 'helping the police with their inquiries' fiction) and enabling rules (enabling the police to act as they wish to do without fear of legal repercussions). The extent to which they are also inhibitory, preventing abuse of power through restrictions on their use, will be a key issue in this chapter and the next two.

3.2.4 The unofficial purposes of arrest

We have seen that arrest and prosecution are now entirely separate in both theory and practice. Anything can follow arrest and detention: no action at all, an official police caution or other kind of out of court disposal (see chapter 7), an 'on the spot' fine,[33] a police charge (a formal allegation forming the starting point for a prosecution), release followed by a summons to appear at court, or release whilst the police continue their inquiries. Studies in the 1990s found that around 50% of all arrests lead to prosecution, although the exact figures varied according to offence type, police force and even police station.[34] The number of prosecutions following arrest for indictable offences has been falling since 2009, with just 19% prosecuted in 2019.[35]

Arrest is now simply an exercise of police power that does not, in itself, determine the next stage. Arrest and detention now often has 'unofficial' purposes, some of which amount to an abuse of power. Some arrests are to secure evidence of offences unrelated to the offences for which arrests are ostensibly carried out, committed either by the arrestees or by others.[36] Another purpose is to put the 'frighteners' on arrestees—to warn them not to take certain action or to punish them for actions they are believed to have carried out. Here, there is no intention to prosecute. Arrest and detention is used as a form of 'social disciplining'[37] or summary justice. Sometimes it appears that the police arrest someone in order to distract attention away from their own malpractice.[38] Another purpose is to control individuals and groups, especially in public order situations, again with no intention of prosecuting (see section 3.4.3). We shall see that the courts often fail to acknowledge these 'unofficial' purposes of arrest, reducing their ability to restrain the police.[39]

For a time, this led to an increase in arrests, rising from 1.27m per annum in 1981 to 1.96m per annum in 1997. But between April 2018 and March 2019 there were only 671,126 arrests. Racial disparities are present here too, as we might expect given that disproportionate stop and searches are likely to trickle down to arrest. In 2019, black people were over three times as likely to be arrested as white people.[40] It is not known precisely

---

[32] As discussed in chapter 5, particularly where these voluntary interviews take place on the street, this may undermine important due process safeguards, making them a 'back-to-the-future' set of police practices.

[33] These are also known as 'penalty notices for disorder' and are discussed in section 7.4.3.

[34] Phillips C and Brown C, *Entry into the criminal justice system: a survey of arrests and their outcomes* (Home Office Research Study 185) (London: Home Office, 1998) pp 81–83.

[35] Ministry of Justice, *Criminal Justice Statistics Quarterly 2019* (2020) see <https://www.gov.uk/government/publications/criminal-justice-system-statistics-quarterly-december-2019/criminal-justice-statistics-quarterly-december-2019-html#overview-of-the-criminal-justice-system> (accessed 12 September 2020).

[36] See, for example, *Chalkley and Jeffries* [1998] 2 Cr App Rep 79, discussed in section 3.4.3.

[37] Choongh S, *Policing as Social Discipline* (Oxford: Clarendon Press, 1997).

[38] See the distressing case of *Paul v Humberside Police* [2004] EWCA Civ 308.

[39] See *Plange v Chief Constable of South Humberside* [1992] 3 WLUK 20.

[40] Home Office, *Arrests, September 2020*, see <https://www.ethnicity-facts-figures.service.gov.uk/crime-justice-and-the-law/policing/number-of-arrests/latest> (accessed 24 September 2020).

how many people are arrested each year: some people are arrested more than once; arrests for 'non-notifiable' (i.e. minor) offences are not included in the official statistics; if the arrestee is released before being taken to a police station it may not be recorded;[41] and not all notifiable arrests are actually notified to those responsible for compiling the statistics.[42]

Readers may begin to be worried by now. Despite the fall in arrest rates over the years there are still nearly 700,000 arrests each year, many of which may be frightening for the arrestee. While it might be thought that these figures suggest that the police arrest whenever they can, this is far from the truth. Chapter 2 showed that the law is permissive. It allows the police to exercise all manner of powers, but does not require them to do so. In reality, the police decide not to arrest far more often than they decide to actually do so. This, and the fall in arrests in recent years, seems in part because of the constraints of the law but also because of 10 years of austerity (see chapter 1): there were many fewer police officers in 2020 than in 2010, and time spent arresting one person means not having time to arrest someone else.[43]

Turning a blind eye, or not investigating suspicious people or circumstances, varies from offence to offence. Officers do not ignore bank robberies and rapes just because they are not obliged to arrest suspects. But in some situations certain types of offence are routinely ignored or dealt with informally. Waddington, for example, comments that in the early 1990s 50,000 supporters of the miners' union and 150,000 trade union demonstrators protested against pit closures without one arrest being made: 'On some occasions the police would have been lawfully entitled to make wholesale arrests, but they consciously chose not to do so.'[44]

Similarly, it appears that the police rarely use the arrest powers provided under the Criminal Justice and Public Order Act 1994 in relation to 'raves' and 'trespass'. In some cases, the threat to use these powers may be effective,[45] but in other cases they may not. During the national Covid-19 lockdown and later when restrictions were relaxed in the summer of 2020 mass gatherings, so-called quarantine raves, were a regular occurrence, being easily promoted by social media, but hard to police. There were few arrests, and even fewer arrests for less blatant breaches of the rules.[46] It follows that much of what the police do is not overtly coercive, although this does vary as mentioned earlier in relation to different crimes and the suspect population that is ostensibly being targeted. Section 60 search powers have been increasingly used in response to knife crime, and tend to be directed towards black, Asian and minority ethnic groups resulting in the disproportionate number of arrests arising from s.60 searches for these groups (see discussion in section 2.2.2.2 in relation to s.60 suspicionless searches). The police frequently use fewer powers than they are entitled to, being influenced by the general considerations examined in section 2.1. Now that arrest has become primarily a policing resource, one question for this chapter is what leads them to arrest one person, in one context, and not another person in a different context.

---

[41] Under s.30(8) of PACE such releases from arrest must be recorded by the constable, but whether this always happens, and such arrests always find their way into the statistics, is not known. The legal basis for de-arresting a suspect was for some time unclear but s.4(4) of the Criminal Justice Act 2003 amends PACE by requiring the police to release without bail someone arrested outside the police station where there are no longer any grounds for keeping that person under arrest or releasing them on bail.

[42] Hillyard P and Gordon D, 'Arresting statistics: the drift to informal justice in England and Wales' (1999) 26 *Journal of Law and Society* 502.

[43] Pearson G and Rowe M, *Police Street Powers and Criminal Justice: Regulation and Discretion in a Time of Change* (Oxford: Hart Publishing, 2020) ch 7.

[44] Waddington PAJ, *Liberty and Order* (London: UCL Press, 1994) p 39.

[45] Bucke T and James Z, *Trespass and Protest: Policing under the Criminal Justice and Public Order Act 1994* (London: Home Office, 1998); Cowan D and Lomax D, 'Policing Unauthorised Camping' (2003) 30 *Journal of Law and Society* 283.

[46] See <https://www.wired.co.uk/article/uk-coronavirus-raves-party-police> (accessed 3 September 2020).

3.3 The legal basis for arrest

3.3.1 With warrant

The move away from arrest warrants, which is part of the general move away from judicial supervision of police powers, means that most arrests are now made by the police acting on their own knowledge and initiative rather than acting under the supervision of magistrates. It mirrors the decline in the use of summonses (issued by magistrates) and search warrants (also issued by magistrates). Nowadays, the police themselves generally decide what powers they will exercise and when. This is a crime control approach.

Warrants are nowadays mainly used when a suspect fails to appear in court to answer a summons or to answer bail. In these circumstances, the police or prosecutor would apply to the magistrates for a warrant,[47] which would usually be granted straight away, authorising the arrest of that suspect.[48] The European Arrest Warrant has been used by EU Member States including the UK since 2004. Its aim was to facilitate cross-border law enforcement within the European Union by, for example, allowing a Member State to make a request when they wanted to prosecute or imprison a person who was in another Member State. Mutual recognition ensured that authorities could arrest and surrender a person to another Member State.[49] The UK's imminent withdrawal from the European Union will require new arrangements that, at the time of writing have not yet been finalised.[50]

3.3.2 Summary arrest: the withering away of the 'non-arrestable' offence

We have already noted that all offences are now arrestable without warrant. In order to appreciate the significance of this, it is crucial to understand how the law has developed. The Royal Commission on Criminal Procedure (Philips Commission) wanted to constrain the use of arrest. It believed that coercive powers like arrest were often used unnecessarily, as variations between police forces in the use of arrest, on the one hand, and summons, on the other were huge.[51] In other words, it seemed that similar offences in similar circumstances were subject to arrest, detention and charge in some areas, where in other areas they would be subject to a summons to appear in court on a specified date. These concerns were reflected in PACE although not in the way the Royal Commission had envisaged. Under s.24 of PACE the police were entitled to arrest anyone for an 'arrestable offence' without a prior warrant. Any offence punishable by a jail term of five years or more was arrestable (PACE, s.24(1)), as were miscellaneous other offences. The use of the concept of arrestable offences meant that arrest powers were different according to which side of the 'more serious' or 'less serious' definitional divide an offence fell. For 'more serious' offences it was simply assumed by those framing the legislation that arrest should be the normal way of processing those suspected of such offences. But the less serious 'non-arrestable'

---

[47] Under the Magistrates' Courts Act 1980, s.125, as amended by PACE, s.33.

[48] Arrests should not also be used in place of applying for warrants as in the case of *Hanningfield v Chief Constable of Essex* [2013] 1 WLR 3632 where someone suspected of fraud was arrested in his home when the police should have rather applied for a search warrant for entry and search of premises for the purposes of arrest under s.17 PACE.

[49] Extradition Act 2003. See Caolan E, 'Reciprocity and Rights under the European Arrest Warrant Regime' (2007) 123 *Law Quarterly Review* 197.

[50] But see <https://services.parliament.uk/Bills/2019%9621/extraditionprovisionalarrest/documents.html> (accessed 24 September 2020).

[51] Royal Commission on Criminal Procedure, Report (Cmnd 8092) (London: HMSO, 1981) paras 3.75–3.79. For details see Gemmill R and Morgan-Giles R, *Arrest, Charge and Summons* (Royal Commission on Criminal Procedure, Research Study no 9) (London: HMSO, 1981).

offences were arrestable under certain circumstances—if, for example, a summons was inappropriate or impractical (PACE, s.24).

A Home Office review of PACE and its Codes and related legislation sought to 'modernise' police powers and simplify the 'complex and often bewildering array of [arrest] powers and procedures'[52] (which post-PACE legislation had created). The PACE distinction between arrestable and non-arrestable offences was swept away by s.110 of the Serious Organised Crime and Police 2005 (SOCPA) Act. Thus the safeguard introduced via a democratic accountability mechanism was swept away by a government review—exemplifying the erosion of criminal justice accountability discussed in chapter 11. Section 110 inserts a new s.24 into PACE, providing that the police may arrest without warrant anyone who is or who is reasonably suspected to be:

- about to commit an offence;
- in the act of committing an offence; or
- guilty of an offence already committed.

This power of summary arrest is exercisable only if the police have reasonable grounds for believing that it is *necessary* to arrest the person(s) in question for any one of these reasons:[53]

- to ascertain their name/address;
- to prevent them:
    - causing physical injury to himself or others;
    - causing loss of, or damage to, property;
    - committing an offence against public decency; or
    - causing an obstruction;
- to protect a child or other vulnerable person;
- to allow the prompt and effective investigation of an offence or their 'conduct';
- to prevent non-appearance in court if there is a prosecution.

These 'enabling' rules are offensive to the 'freedom' approach. To allow arrest for *any* offence (if, for instance, the offender is thought unlikely to answer a summons) fails to balance the certain freedom lost by arrest with the possible loss of freedom involved when it is only feared (not known) that an offender will not answer a summons—for defendants who do not turn up at court can usually be found and arrested, the crime may be trivial (e.g. graffiti on a wall). The 2005 Act prioritises considerations of police efficiency over the interests of suspects. This extreme crime control approach appears to be balanced by two due process/freedom-oriented considerations identified in the Code of Practice:

1.2 The exercise of the power of arrest represents an obvious and significant interference with the Right to Liberty and Security under … the Human Rights Act 1998.

1.3 The use of the power must be fully justified and officers exercising the power should consider if the necessary objectives can be met by other, less intrusive means … When the power of arrest is exercised it is essential that it is exercised in a non-discriminatory and proportionate manner.[54]

---

[52] Home Office, *Modernising Police Powers to Meet Community Needs—A Consultation Paper* (2004b), p 4.
[53] This is a summary of PACE s.24 (5) as amended by SOPCA. See PACE Code G (2012), para 2.9 for a full list of these criteria, with examples.   [54] Home Office, PACE Code of Practice G, 2012.

The police must:

- exercise arrest powers in 'a non-discriminatory and proportionate manner';
- as stated in Serious Organised Crime and Police Act 2005, s.110 (4), have 'reasonable grounds for believing that for any of the reasons mentioned in sub-section (5) [summarised earlier] it is necessary to arrest the person in question'.

It might seem astonishing that any public official needs to be told not to be discriminatory, but we know from the stop-search research, and will see from research on arrest later in this chapter, that the police not only do need to be told this, but they pay too little attention to it.

And the courts' interpretation of 'necessary' is also questionable. Not only need it only be proven that arresting officers 'reasonably believe' an arrest to be necessary, but there is no need for those officers to actively consider alternatives to arrest—as in a case where an arrestee met the arresting officer voluntarily to discuss an allegation against him. He was not asked, for example, to attend a voluntary interview at the police station, but the arrest was held to be justifiable anyway.[55] However, 'voluntary' interviews at police stations are common, and should be considered (PACE Code G Guidance Notes). So arrests made with no good reason for not considering a voluntary interview have been ruled unlawful.[56] But if the police have reason to believe that a suspect would try and leave in the course of a voluntary interview, arrest can be seen as 'necessary' 'to allow the prompt and effective investigation of an offence or their "conduct"' (PACE s.24(5)),[57] which is one of the most frequently stated reasons for arrest.[58]

'Necessity' is not, in reality, part of the routine thinking of police officers. Practical, policy and personal reasons tend to dominate the decision-making processes of officers rather than 'necessity' and the rest of the s.24 conditions. Unlawful and non-human rights compliant arrests continue to be regularly made, where, for example, arrest is used tactically—such as simply to take members of criminal gangs out of circulation. Not surprisingly, in light of the case law, there is confusion amongst officers as to what constitutes a necessary and lawful arrest. Arrest alternatives are rarely considered by officers, particularly in domestic abuse cases where officers are conscious of police and government policies strongly encouraging arrest as the default option.[59] In short, the necessity principle seems to play a largely presentational role—giving the appearance of due process while doing nothing to promote its substance.

3.3.3 Terrorism and arrest

Terrorism-related arrests have long been subject to specific powers that act as a gateway to enhanced investigatory powers such as longer than normal periods of detention for questioning. The 1989 Prevention of Terrorism (Temporary) Provisions Act (PTA) allowed the

---

[55] *Hayes v Chief Constable of Merseyside* [2012] 1 WLR 517. See also discussion by Cape E [2012] Crim LR 35.

[56] *R (on the application of TL) v Chief Constable of Surrey Divisional Court* [2017] EWHC 129 (Admin): arrest had been done simply because it was 'convenient' and 'desirable'. See discussion by Cape E [2017] Crim LR 576. And a doctor who co-operated with a police investigation was held to have been wrongfully arrested because it was unnecessary: *Rashid v CC West Yorkshire* [2020] EWHC 2522 (QB).

[57] *Richardson v CC of the West Midlands* [2011] Cr App R 1; *TL* op cit.

[58] Pearson G, Rowe M and Turner L, 'Policy, Practicalities and PACE S 24: The Subsuming of the Necessity Criteria in Arrest Decision Making by Frontline Police Officers' (2018) 45(2) *Journal of Law and Society* 282–308.

[59] Pearson, Rowe and Turner (2018). These domestic abuse policies, which have developed over the last 20 years, are discussed in ch 10.

police to arrest for various terrorist offences simply on 'suspicion' that a terrorist offence had been, or was about to be, committed, but this was held to violate the ECHR, Art 5(1) requirement of 'reasonable suspicion'.[60] The PTA was replaced by the Terrorism Act 2000 and the Anti-terrorism, Crime and Security Act (ATCSA) 2001. Arrest on mere suspicion is not allowed, except that Part 4 of the ATCSA originally allowed indefinite imprisonment (without trial) of foreign persons denied asylum on grounds of national security or international crimes. This required the government to derogate from the ECHR, on the grounds of the scale and nature of the threat of terrorism,[61] but this was subsequently held to be invalid.[62] The government's response to the judgment was to introduce control orders that were a form of 'house arrest' sometimes for up to 14 hours a day.[63] Though these have been replaced by Terrorism, Prevention and Investigation Measures, these 'control order lite',[64] as some describe them, remain a source of concern due to their effects on citizens (see section 3.4.5).

There remain three other principal concerns. First, there is the main provision in the 2000 Act: s.41(1) 'A constable may arrest without a warrant a person whom he reasonably suspects to be a terrorist.' Being 'a terrorist' is not, as such, an offence. Terrorism can cover a wide range of violence—actual and threatened, to property as well as persons—and includes people who help terrorists, or (in ATCSA 2001, s.21(2)) have 'links with an international terrorist group'. This can include those who 'support' such groups, which could be a major breach of freedom of speech,[65] or who (under s.1 of the Terrorism Act 2006) 'glorify' terrorism. One might 'support' the aims of terrorist groups whilst deploring their methods, so that, for example, animal rights protesters could be arrested under this provision.[66]

Second, what is 'reasonable suspicion' in the terrorism context? In *Fox, Campbell and Hartley v UK*, the Court said that:

> What may be regarded as 'reasonable' will however depend on all the circumstances … in view of all the difficulties inherent in the investigation and prosecution of terrorist-type offences in Northern Ireland, the 'reasonableness' of the suspicion justifying such arrests cannot always be judged according to the same standards as are applied in dealing with conventional crime. Nevertheless, the exigencies of dealing with terrorist crime cannot justify stretching the notion of 'reasonableness' to the point where the essence of the safeguard secured by Art 5 (1) is impaired …[67]

This meant that the government had to furnish some information that could lead the court to accept the reasonableness of the suspicion. In that particular case the only basis for suspicion was the convictions of the suspects for terrorist acts seven years previously, so there was held to be a breach of Art 5 of the ECHR.

---

[60] *Fox, Campbell and Hartley v UK* (1990) 13 EHRR 157.

[61] Despite the international nature of the 'war on terrorism' ushered in by '9/11', to which ATCSA was a response, the UK is the only one of 41 states ratifying the ECHR who derogated from it over this matter: Tomkins A, 'Legislating against Terror: The ATCS Act 2001' [2002] *Public Law* 205. See generally Walker C, 'Terrorism and Criminal Justice – Past, Present and Future' [2004] *Criminal Law Review* 311.

[62] *A & Ors v Secretary of State for the Home Department* [2004] UKHL 56.

[63] Prevention of Terrorism Act 2005.

[64] Liberty online at <https://www.libertyhumanrights.org.uk/human-rights/countering-terrorism/tpims> (accessed 27 August 2019). See the Terrorism, Prevention and Investigation Measures Act 2011 as amended by the Counter-Terrorism and Security Act 2015. Discussed by Fenwick H, 'Terrorism and the Control Orders/TPIMs Saga' (2017) *Public Law* 609.

[65] Tomkins A, 'Legislating against terror: the ACTS Act 2001' (2002) Public Law 205

[66] As was held in relation to similar PTA offences by the ECtHR in *Brogan* (1988) 11 EHRR 117. See Walker C, *Blackstone's Guide to the Anti-Terrorism Legislation* 3rd edn (Oxford: OUP, 2014); Hodgson J and Tadros V, 'The Impossibility of Defining Terrorism' (2013) 16 *New Criminal Law Review* 494; Cornford A, 'Terrorist Precursor Offences: Evaluating the Law in Practice' (2020) *Criminal Law Review* 663.

[67] (1990) 13 EHRR 157.

Third, for what purposes may there be an arrest? Article 5(1)(b) requires that in the absence of reasonable suspicion arrest may be made only pursuant to a 'lawful order of a court or ... any obligation prescribed by law' (excepting some other technical reasons of no relevance here). In *McVeigh, O'Neill and Evans v UK* (1981) 25 DR 15 the applicants were arrested in Liverpool, when they arrived from Ireland, in order to be 'examined' (a procedure akin to extended stop, search and questioning specific to the terrorism legislation, discussed in section 2.2.2). The European Commission on Human Rights (in a preliminary procedure to a Court hearing) decided that:

> the existence of organised terrorism is a feature of modern life whose emergence since the Convention was drafted cannot be ignored any more than the changes in social conditions and moral opinion which have taken place in the same period ... the Convention organs must always be alert to the danger in this sphere adverted to by the Court, of undermining or even destroying democracy on the ground of defending it [However] ... some compromise between the requirements for defending democratic society and individual rights is inherent in the system of the Convention ...

Applying that principle to the specific context of the case, the Commission decided that the requirement to be examined was a lawful obligation for the purposes of Art 5(1)(b), but only because of the limited circumstances (travel across a border), the 'threat from organised terrorism', and the fact that arrest and detention was rarely used to secure examinations.

In these cases the European Court is adopting a 'context-sensitive' approach.[68] However, whether its sensitivity is accurate depends on whether it is justified in its confidence that the UK government and its agencies rarely abuse these provisions. Hillyard estimates that, out of some 2,308 people arrested under the previous legislation between 1974 and 1981, 1,984 (86%) were released without any legal action being taken.[69] He argues that most of these arrests were information-gathering in purpose and that, with such a high no-action rate, it is implausible that there was reasonable suspicion in most of these cases. He points out that after major events there are often mass arrests. After the Woolwich and Guildford bombings of 1974, for example, 76 people were arrested, but only four—the 'Guildford Four'—were charged. Could there really have been 'reasonable suspicion' against the other 72, or even the majority of them? Mass arrests can also be criticised for being applied pre-emptively. On the opening night of the 2012 Olympic Games in London, the police arrested 182 cyclists for causing a public nuisance. The cyclists were detained and released before the 24 hour limit, however their bail conditions prohibited them from entering areas of London, including the Olympic venues. Within this mass arrest it was later revealed that a 13-year-old and a tourist were included, showing how sweeping application of arrest powers can often fail to be proportionate.[70]

Some have argued that, since 9/11 in 2001 and the July 2005 attacks on users of London's transport system Muslims (who make up less than 3% of the population in England and Wales) have increasingly become the new prime suspect community.[71] One high profile

---

[68] Another example of the Court's misplaced sense of context-sensitivity is its view that the Convention obligation to inform someone promptly the reason for their arrest (discussed in section 3.4.5) is discharged if the reason for the arrest becomes apparent in the interview. This is of little value if the reason for the provision is to reduce the initial disorientation of the suspect.   [69] Hillyard (1993: ch 4).

[70] See *The Guardian*, 3 August 2012 at <https://www.theguardian.com/sport/2012/aug/03/olympic-tourist-cycling-protest-arrest> (accessed 12 September 2020); *The Guardian*, 29 July 2012 <https://www.theguardian.com/uk/2012/jul/29/critical-mass-police-arrest-three> (accessed 12 September 2020).

[71] See further Spalek et al, 'Minority Muslim Communities and Criminal Justice: Stigmatized UK Faith Identities Post 9/11 and 7/7' in Bhui H, *Race & Criminal Justice* (London: Sage, 2009); Pantazis C and Pemberton S, 'From the "Old" to the "New" Suspect Community: Examining the Impacts of Recent UK Counter-Terrorist Legislation' (2009) 49(5) *British Journal of Criminology* 646, and section 3.4.4. Choudhury T and Fenwick H, *The Impact of counter-terrorism measures on Muslim communities* (2011) Equality and Human Rights Commission.

case occurred in April 2009 when the then Prime Minister Gordon Brown spoke of the police having foiled 'a very big terrorist plot' following a series of coordinated arrests of (mainly) Pakistani citizens in the north of England who had entered the country on student visas. In fact, all 12 arrestees were subsequently released without charge, even though 11 were held in police custody for a fortnight while they were interrogated and their homes and computers searched.[72] Given the breadth of the offences created under anti-terrorism laws, the objective basis for the initial suspicion against these arrestees must have been very thin indeed.

Between March 2019 and March 2020, there were 261 arrests for terrorism-related activity. Of these, 92 (35%) were released pending further investigation, 82 (31%) resulted in a charge of which 66 were for terrorism-related offences and 58 people (22%) were released without charge. Nineteen of these were given an alternative outcome such as recall to prison, passed on to immigration or cautioned and 10 cases were pending an outcome.[73]

The ethnic appearance of those arrested over the years have disproportionately been Asian. For example, data for the year 2019/20 showed that 38% arrested were of Asian appearance, 41% white and 8% of black appearance. Those of other ethnic appearance accounted for 12% of arrests. Asian people make up only 7.5% of the population of England and Wales whereas white groups make up 86%, according to the 2011 Census. Of those arrested, 74% considered themselves to be British or British dual nationals. The overwhelming majority of the terrorist prison population is made up of Islamic extremists and, up to 31 March 2019, 47% of these prisoners defined themselves as Asian or Asian British, 27% as white and 15% as Black or black British. The majority (79%) stated themselves to be Muslim and 9% were Christian.[74]

Views will naturally differ on what conclusions should be drawn from such statistics. Some of the more obvious points to make are:

- the majority of those arrested for terrorism-related offences since 9/11 are not charged and for those proceeded against, the conviction rate is by no means stable;
- many of the total number of arrests that are initially for terrorist related activities result in convictions under 'ordinary' (non-terrorist) legislation. It is plausible to suppose that such legislation might have served perfectly well for a large proportion of those that are now dealt with under terrorism laws. In other words, terrorism legislation may be less important than it appears to be;
- the non-charge and non-conviction rates mean that a large proportion of arrestees are being unnecessarily subjected to the special terrorism-related investigatory regime to no freedom-enhancing end; and
- the inherent losses of freedom this investigatory regime involves bears down on some communities more than others, thus fuelling concerns about the breadth and improper use of arrest powers.

3.3.4 Common law breach of the peace

The common law has long recognised that all citizens should have a power of arrest to prevent or end breaches of the peace. A breach of the peace is not a stand-alone offence, but a court can bind over someone arrested on this basis to be of good behaviour in future.

---

[72] *The Guardian*, 22 April 2009.

[73] *Operation of police powers under the Terrorism Act 2000 and subsequent legislation*, Bulletin 15/20 (London: Home Office, 2020).

[74] Allen G and Kirk-Wade E, *Terrorism in Great Britain: the statistics*, House of Commons Briefing Paper CBP7613, March 2020.

Police may arrest if a breach of the peace is occurring, is imminent, or has recently happened and is likely to recur.[75] This means that the powers of arrest for breach of the peace are rather more restricted than most other powers of arrest. Judgement is required, not only in relation to whether the breach of the peace is occurring, but also in relation to the question of imminence and recurrence. The police have 'the right to take reasonable steps to make the person who is breaking or threatening to break the peace refrain from doing so; and those reasonable steps in appropriate cases will include detaining him against his will.'[76] Any person detained under this power should be released as soon as there are no longer reasonable grounds for fearing a further breach of the peace but otherwise be taken before a court at the earliest practicable opportunity.[77]

One problem with the concept of 'breach of the peace' is that its legal meaning is narrower than the words themselves might suggest. It must be related to violence: a breach of the peace occurs when harm is done or is likely to be done to any person (or, in their presence, to their property), or if someone fears being so harmed by an assault, unlawful assembly or other disturbance.[78] Thus, despite what some law enforcement agents appear to believe, rowdy, abusive or insulting behaviour does not in itself constitute a breach of the peace, although a preventive arrest will still be lawful if a police officer reasonably perceives a threat of imminent violence.[79] Demonstrations, picketing, disputes between neighbours or intimates, disputes with police officers, street brawls and so forth are the usual context for this type of problem, although this does not mean that most demonstrations—any more than most disputes between neighbours—actually end in breach of the peace in the legal sense. The lack of precision here offends the freedom perspective, for it leaves citizens unclear about what they can and cannot do without risking a 'breach of the peace arrest'.[80] Arguably it should also cause these laws to fall foul of the ECHR's principles of legality and foreseeability,[81] but the ECtHR has upheld the use of this power and the 'bind-over' orders generally used to enforce it.[82]

Belief in the imminence of a breach of the peace is necessarily difficult to pin down. This was particularly evident in the miners' strike of the mid 1980s where there were several violent confrontations at pits where miners refused to strike. In *Moss v McLachlan*,[83] 60 miners were stopped by a police roadblock on the M1 motorway while on their way to picket some pits a few miles away. They carried banners and shouted abuse at a lorry driver

---

[75] *Howell* [1981] 3 All ER 383.   [76] *Albert v Lavin* [1981] 3 All ER 878 at 880.
[77] *Chief Constable of Cleveland Police v Mark Anthony McGrogan* [2002] EWCA Civ 86.
[78] *Howell* [1981] 3 All ER 383.
[79] An example is *Hawkes v DPP* [2005] EWCA 3046 where D swore at officers and refused to get out of a police car in which her arrested son had been placed. Her arrest for having actually committed a breach of the peace was unlawful as no violence had taken place or been threatened. The police could, however, have used force to remove D from the police car on the basis that she was obstructing them in the course of their duty, and left open the possibility that they could have arrested her in order to prevent an *imminent* breach of the peace. Confirmed in *Rawlins v Crown Prosecution Service* [2018] EWHC 2533 (Admin).
[80] Note, however, that in *Bibby v Chief Constable of Essex* [2000] EWCA Civ 113 (where a bailiff seeking to enforce a debt was arrested in order to defuse a volatile situation), the circumstances in which someone *not* acting unlawfully could be arrested to avert a breach of the peace were confirmed as very narrow. The court ruled that there must be: the clearest of circumstances and a sufficiently real and present threat to the peace to justify this extreme step; the threat must be coming from the person who was to be arrested; the conduct must clearly interfere with the rights of others; the natural consequence of the conduct must be violence from a third party (that violence not to be wholly unreasonable); and the conduct of the person arrested must be unreasonable. Thus the bailiff's arrest was unlawful as his conduct did not interfere with the rights of another and any force used by the debtor to resist the bailiff would have been unreasonable.
[81] Nicolson D and Reid K, 'Arrest for Breach of the Peace and the European Convention on Human Rights' [1996] *Criminal Law Review* 764.
[82] *Steel v UK* (1988) EHRR 603.   [83] *Moss v McLachlan* [1985] IRLR 76.

who was passing the road block to break the strike. The men could only be arrested if it was suspected that a breach of the peace was likely to occur. Skinner J stated that, provided the police officers 'honestly and reasonably form the opinion that there is a real risk of a breach of the peace in the sense that it is in close proximity both in place and time then the conditions exist for reasonable preventive action including if necessary the measures taken in this case [that is to say arrest]'.

In this particular case, the miners were abusive and the pits to which they were travelling were nearby, so it may be that the police were justified in the arrest of the men on those grounds.[84] However, in another miners' strike incident, the police established a roadblock at the Dartford Tunnel near London, over 100 miles from the area which some miners intended to picket. The miners were turned back on the same basis as in *Moss v McLachlan*, even though it could hardly be said that a breach of the peace was imminent or proximate in these circumstances.[85]

There were many other incidents where striking miners were stopped by the police and were told when and how they could travel in the vicinity of working mines. Sometimes these miners were on their way to picket, and arguably there was a risk of a breach of the peace. However, police invocation of the breach of the peace law against striking miners spilled over into general restrictions on the liberty of striking miners and other members of mining communities. As one present put it: 'There were no justifications, just the threat of arrest if we failed to comply.'[86] It seems that a lot of police action threatened the use of these arrest powers to prevent picketing, regardless of whether there was an imminent risk of breaches of the peace. At times, such as these, of crises of law and order, legalistic models of policing may simply collapse.[87] Police powers are stretched to enable the police to fulfil wider functions than would be possible if due process principles prevailed. And the way those powers are used are often aggressive, frequently to the point of violence. One result, according to a police officer, is that: 'You enjoy the power it gives to inflict the collective will of the job on to a large crowd of people… . You are part of a vast crowd and if the whole thing is wrong or illegal, it's not you who's going to be picked up for it. That sort of violence becomes addictive.'[88]

By using arrest powers in respect of breach of the peace to protect the working miners, the police and judiciary elevated the freedom of strike-breakers and their employers over that of the striking miners. Nicolson and Reid argue that this could be a breach of Arts 10 and 11 of the ECHR (the protection of freedom of expression, peaceful association and assembly).[89] The excessive force in, and 'stretched' legal justification for, many of these arrests are also antithetical to the freedom model. Finally, as the last chapter showed in a less extreme form in relation to stop-search, this type of policing alienates the communities subject to this policing, as well as causing concern to other communities, groups

---

[84] In *Laporte* [2006] UKHL 55 some of the speeches indicated unease about the decision in *Moss*, with Lord Brown stating that it went 'to the furthermost limits of any acceptable view of imminence, and then only on the basis that those prevented from attending the demonstration were indeed manifestly intent on violence' [118]. See also Lord Mance [150].

[85] East R and Thomas P, 'Freedom of Movement: *Moss v McLachlan*' (1985) 12 *Journal of Law and Society* 77.

[86] Green P, *The Enemy Without: Policing and Class Consciousness in the Miners' Strike* (Milton Keynes: Open UP, 1990) p 63.

[87] See Balbus I, *The Dialectics of Legal Repression* (New York: Russell Sage, 1973); and Vogler R, 'Magistrates and Civil Disorder' (November 1982) LAG Bulletin 12.

[88] Graef R, 'A Spiral of Mutual Mistrust' *The Independent*, 12 May 1989. It is this kind of mentality that we think is likely to have lain behind the death of Ian Tomlinson, caught up in the policing of the G20 protests in April 2009.

[89] Nicolson and Reid (1996: 772–774). However, in the light of *Steel v UK*, it is unlikely that the ECtHR or the English courts will agree with them.

and individuals sympathetic to those being policed in this way. That creates further losses of freedom: the police receive less co-operation from those they have already alienated, become more divided from the rest of society, and become brutalised, increasingly seeing coercion rather than co-operation as the most viable law enforcement strategy. As the officer quoted in the preceding paragraph put it, the use of direct power in these ways 'was slightly awesome but after a while it became easy'. And the chief constable also quoted there feared, as a result, 'that the whole perception of police–public relations has changed in people's minds'.[90]

The miners' strike of the 1980s may seem like a long time ago, but the same types of problem recur periodically in different contexts. Protests against the war in Iraq provided another flashpoint, while also providing a good example of how stop-search, breach of the peace and arrest powers may interact. In *Laporte*[91] the police detained three coachloads of people on their way to join a protest outside a nearby airbase using the stop-search power under s.60 of the Criminal Justice and Public Order Act 1994 (see chapter 2). They found a number of items on board which might have been used offensively in a protest, and one passenger was arrested for incitement to cause criminal damage relating to an earlier incident at the airbase. On the basis that they feared a breach of the peace if the coaches continued to the airbase, the police then deployed motorcycle outriders to escort the coaches on a non-stop two and a half hour journey back to London.

Similarly, in *Austin and Saxby*,[92] the police deployed various powers in the policing of the 2001 May Day protest, when huge numbers of protesters converged on London's Oxford Circus. First, relying on the need to prevent a breach of the peace, they cordoned off the area, preventing thousands from leaving the area for over seven hours (a practice known as 'kettling').[93] Then they sought to segregate some members of the crowd from the others by asking them questions and by using s.60 of the Criminal Justice and Public Order Act 1994 to conduct searches for offensive weapons and dangerous instruments. Finally, they entered the corralled crowd from time to time to arrest those suspected of throwing missiles at the police. By contrast, during the Extinction Rebellion (XR) demonstrations about climate change that grew in scale and frequency in 2019 and 2020, the police seem to rarely rely on breach of the peace to arrest protestors. They opt instead for arrests for obstructing the highway, obstructing the police and breaching public order conditions imposed when such demonstrations are known to be taking place.[94]

These examples show how unrealistic it is to view each police power in isolation. In practice, the police can use, or threaten to use, their powers in an overlapping, fluid manner in order to achieve broader policing objectives. In other words, police powers in a legal sense are constitutive of police power in a broader, sociological sense. In the human rights era, however, there is closer scrutiny of, and more careful reflection about, police tactics. Thus in *Laporte* the courts ruled that what the police had done was unreasonable

---

[90] See generally Townshend C, *Making the Peace: Public Order and Public Security in Modern Britain* (Oxford: OUP, 1993) ch 9.
[91] [2006] UKHL 55; The UK ruling was upheld by the ECtHR: *Austin v United Kingdom* (2012) 55 EHRR 14.
[92] *Austin and Another v Commissioner of Police for the Metropolis* [2009] UKHL 5.
[93] It was accepted that the two claimants (one of whom was not a demonstrator but had simply been caught up in the cordon) had done nothing to give rise to any fear that they would breach the peace, but it was held by the House of Lords that the police were justified in detaining them, along with everyone else in the demonstration, as a breach of the peace from some demonstrators was likely and no preventive alternative to the cordon was available.
[94] There are no official data published on the reasons for arrest during XR demonstrations, but during one of the most recent demonstrations at the time of writing in London in September 2020, these were the reasons for arrest reported in the press at the time. See <https://www.standard.co.uk/news/crime/extinction-rebellion-protests-arrests-breached-restictions-a4538886.html> (accessed 9 September 2020).

and in breach of the common law, not least because they had less restrictive alternatives open to them, such as removing known 'troublemakers' from the coaches and allowing the other passengers to continue to the demonstration (where there were sufficient officers stationed to deal with any breaches of the peace that then occurred). And in *Austin and Another* Lord Neuberger of Abbotsbury observed that if it transpired 'that the police had maintained the cordon, beyond the time necessary for crowd control, in order to punish, or "to teach a lesson" to, the demonstrators within the cordon' then 'there would have been a powerful argument for saying that the maintenance of the cordon did amount to a detention within the meaning of article 5.'[95]

Police services themselves sometimes make strenuous efforts to ensure that protesters' rights to freedom of assembly and expression are not infringed disproportionately.[96] Many senior police officers are well aware of the long-term damage that may be done to police–community relations by heavy-handed tactics, and some pursue more constructive strategies. Thus in the 1990s South Yorkshire Police, under the leadership of a new Chief Constable, sought to repair its tarnished reputation following the miners' strike and the Hillsborough disaster[97] by inculcating a more restrained, professional policing style, and its new approach was reflected in its generally successful regulation of protests when the G8 summit was held in Sheffield in 2005.[98]

But cases like *Laporte* and *Austin and Saxby* demonstrate that police services still sometimes stretch their legal powers.[99] Indeed, pre-emptive arrests and detention to prevent a breach of peace have provided consistent controversy—for example, arrests were carried out to prevent a breach of the peace during the royal wedding of Prince William and Kate Middleton in 2011. These were challenged under Art 5 ECHR. The arrests were held to be lawful as there was reasonable suspicion of an imminent breach of the peace. The fact that the arrestees were released without further action being taken, and that prosecution had never been contemplated, was held not to violate Art 5 (the requirement prohibiting arbitrary arrest) since if the breach of peace had occurred they could have been prosecuted.[100] While requiring prosecution to make an arrest lawful would be irrational, the only other way to challenge what might be arbitrary or discriminatory arrests would be to judicially review them, as in this case—which is far from easy, stressful, very expensive and (as in this case) usually unsuccessful.

Abolition of 'breach of the peace', while long overdue,[101] may not make much difference to the underlying issues and problems discussed here, given the broad powers the police now possess to summarily arrest where they reasonably suspect that an offence is *about* to be committed. Now that breach of the peace is defined in terms of threatened or actual violence it is difficult to conceive of a situation where the police could arrest for breach of the peace but not for some other offence.

---

[95] [2009] UKHL 5 [63].

[96] See Waddington P, 'Controlling Protest in Contemporary Historical and Comparative Perspective' in della Porta D and Reiter H (eds), *Policing Protest: The Control of Mass Demonstrations in Western Democracies* (Minneapolis: University of Minnesota Press, 1998).

[97] In 1989, 96 football fans were crushed to death at the Hillsborough football stadium in Sheffield following disastrously bad decision-making by the police responsible for controlling the crowd. Discussed in ch 11.

[98] See Waddington D, *Policing Public Disorder: Theory and Practice* (Cullompton: Willan, 2007) ch 6.

[99] For another example, see *R (on the application of Kay) v Commissioner of Police of the Metropolis* [2008] UKHL 69. See generally, Glover R, 'Keeping the Peace and Preventive Justice' [2018] *Public Law* 444.

[100] *R (on the application of Hicks) v Commissioner of Police for the Metropolis* [2017] UKSC 9.

[101] The Law Commission recommended in 1994 that the 'bind-over' associated with breach of the peace be abolished: Law Commission, *Binding Over* (Report No 222) (London: HMSO, 1994a).

3.3.5 **Citizen's arrest**

Before 1829, there was no organised professional police force in England and Wales, and it was many years before the police operated across the whole country. Before the establishment of the modern police, all citizens had the power to arrest suspects, and police powers were originally no greater than those of ordinary citizens. Little or no distinction was made, in theory, between the two, and arrestees had to be taken before the magistrates immediately, no matter who arrested them. Thus we find the Royal Commission on Police Powers and Procedure of 1929 saying:

> The principle remains that a police officer, in the view of the common law, is only 'a person paid to perform, as a matter of duty, acts which if he [or she] was so minded he [or she] might have done voluntarily'.[102]

However true this might once have been, the police (including police community support officers)[103] are now in a completely different position from that of a citizen. In recent years in particular, police officers have been given considerably more power than ordinary citizens. The powers of arrest in the Terrorism Acts, for example, are available to police officers only. And a citizen's arrest does not act as a gateway to other powers (such as the power to search, or to take bodily samples) in the way that a police power of arrest now does.

Section 110 of the Serious Organised Crime and Police Act 2005 (inserting s.24A into PACE) now governs citizens' arrest powers. In brief, this Act preserved existing powers, extended them somewhat (broadening their application from 'arrestable offences' to all indictable offences) but subjected them to a necessity principle. Citizens may now arrest without warrant persons who are committing, or are reasonably suspected to be committing, an indictable offence. Where such an offence has actually been committed, citizens may arrest anyone guilty, or reasonably suspected to be guilty, of the offence. This means that citizen's arrests may lawfully take place for past and present but not future offences; and, for past offences, the offence must have been committed. It is not enough that there be reasonable suspicion that an offence occurred. There are two further conditions. First, the citizen must believe that it is not reasonably practicable for a police officer to make the arrest instead. Second, the citizen must have reasonable grounds for thinking that arrest is necessary for most, though not all, of the reasons applicable to police arrest powers (section 3.3.2), and in practice it will usually be possible to argue that arrest was 'necessary' to stop someone 'making off'.

The citizen nonetheless faces procedural complications that do not apply to police officers. For example, in *Self*[104] the defendant was seen taking a box of chocolates out of a shop. After being followed, he was arrested for theft and for 'assault with intent to resist lawful arrest' (he hit the shop assistant who carried out the citizen's arrest). He was acquitted of theft but convicted of assault. On appeal, it was held that if he had not committed theft the arrest was unlawful, even though reasonable suspicion existed, and therefore the conviction for assault must be quashed, since it is not a crime to resist unlawful arrest.

A large number of arrests, especially for shoplifting, are made by citizens. In most of these cases, the initial arrest is carried out by a shop employee; either a security officer or store detective employed for that purpose, or a member of the management. These are

---

[102] Cmd 3297. Quoted in Royal Commission on Criminal Procedure, *The Investigation and Prosecution of Criminal Offences in England and Wales: The Law and Procedure* (Cmnd 8092–1) (London: HMSO, 1981) p 2.

[103] Technically, police community support officers are civilians (employees of the police authority rather than sworn police officers), but they possess a distinctive set of powers deriving from s.38 of the Police Reform Act 2002, as amended by ss.7–9 of the Police and Justice Act 2006.

[104] *Self* [1992] 3 All ER 476.

ordinary citizens for the purposes of the law, so if they detain people until the police arrive, they make citizen's arrests. In practice, security staff commonly *request* suspected thieves to accompany them to a management or security office so that the police can be called, thus relying on consent rather than a legal power to achieve their aims.[105] If they then simply convey the information that led to suspicion to the police, then any subsequent arrest is that of the police, against whom any claim of unlawful arrest would then lie.[106] Increasingly, citizen arrests are used by vigilante groups of so-called 'paedophile hunters'. They deploy crude and controversial proactive policing methods, in which they may pose as children online in order to lure potential sex-offenders to illicit meetings, then make citizens' arrests whilst also filming the encounters and posting the recordings online.[107] These citizen's arrests are controversial, as the 'law, both in books and action, seems to afford more investigatory discretion to paedophile hunters than to state law enforcement agencies. Paedophile-hunting groups can circumvent procedural safeguards and regulations that exist to moderate state power and protect the human rights of those subject to a criminal process.'[108]

The subject of a citizen's arrest must be placed in lawful custody as soon as is practicable. This generally means either the custody of the police or (as used to be usual) a magistrate, but in some circumstances it might be better to take the suspect briefly elsewhere. This is not covered by statute. In *John Lewis & Co Ltd v Tims*,[109] the defendant (D) was arrested by a store detective and brought before the store manager for questioning. Even though D was not brought before the police or magistrates, this was held to be valid on the grounds that the arrestor was acting for someone else. It would be far from helpful to arrestees had the law been decided otherwise; for the consequence of citizen's arrest would usually then be that the police be contacted immediately without the victim (or, more usually, a shop manager) considering whether such drastic action was desirable. Large stores often require their store detectives or employees to bring alleged thieves before the management to decide what should be done, and this can hardly be criticised.[110]

A similar situation arose where a child was arrested by an ordinary person, who brought him before his father. This was held to be an unlawful arrest, since the arrest was not made on behalf of the father and there was no firm intention to take the child to the police.[111] As a Crown court decision, this is not authoritative, but it does illustrate the problem, and helps us understand why security staff have a strong inclination (often inculcated through training)[112] to use consent rather than arrest. Perhaps legislation should authorise the arrestor to bring the arrestee before whoever could most sympathetically and usefully take the next step although there would be too much scope for abuse in such a vaguely worded provision. This is not the most likely future trajectory for the law, anyway. Given the growth of 'private policing' in various forms in recent years,[113] including in relation to paedophile

---

[105] Button M, *Security Officers and Policing* (Aldershot: Ashgate, 2007) pp 88–90.

[106] *Davidson v Chief Constable of North Wales* [1994] 2 All ER 597. If, however, the security staff *encourage* the police to arrest then they may be liable if the arrest turns out to be unlawful: *Shamoon Ahmed v Mohammed Shafique, Kapil Arora* [2009] EWHC 618.

[107] Purshouse J, '"Paedophile Hunters", Criminal Procedure, and Fundamental Human Rights' (2020) 47 *Journal of Law and Society* 384–411.

[108] Purhouse (2020: 409–10). See also Gillespie A, '"Paedophile Hunters": How Should the Law Respond?' [2019] *Criminal Law Review* 1016.

[109] *John Lewis & Co Ltd v Tims* [1952] AC 676.

[110] Adu-Boyake K, 'Private Security and Retail Crime Prevention' (MSc Dissertation, University of Portsmouth, 2002) conducted a covert study as a security officer in a large inner-city supermarket and found that only one of the 29 people arrested for shop-theft by security staff was subsequently handed over to the police by the store managers (cited in Button (2007: 88)).

[111] *Brewin* [1976] Crim LR 742.   [112] Button (2007: 88).

[113] Crawford A, 'Plural Policing in the UK: Policing beyond the Police' in Newburn T (ed), *Handbook of Policing* 2nd edn (Cullompton: Willan, 2008) pp 147–181.

hunting, the importance of citizen's arrest powers is likely to increase rather than diminish and pressure may grow for extending to 'citizens' the sweeping summary powers of arrest now enjoyed by police officers. While this would promote 'efficiency' and remove the procedural complications currently facing those carrying out private policing functions,[114] it would represent a further erosion of due process and jeopardise justice and freedom.

3.4 Arrest discretion and reasonable suspicion

3.4.1 When the ends can justify the means

One of the peculiarities of the law of arrest both as enacted by PACE 1994 and as subsequently amended by the Serious Organised Crime Act 2005 is that reasonable suspicion is not made a pre-condition of a lawful arrest. Thus, so far as PACE is concerned, the police can lawfully arrest even when they have no reasonable suspicion, so long as it turns out that the arrested person had in fact committed an offence, or was in the course of doing so, or was about to do so (see section 3.3.2). This is a classic crime control norm since desirable ends are regarded as justifying undesirable means. It does not matter that the arrest was speculatively made, so long as the suspect turns out to have been engaged in a crime. The police might, for instance, see a well-known burglar walking down the street and simply arrest him on a hunch that he was responsible for a burglary committed earlier that day. If, in the police station, he confessed to that crime, his guilt would be clear and his arrest would be valid.

And in *DPP v L*[115] the suspect was arrested for an alleged public order offence, but not told this. She was taken to the police station where she assaulted an officer. She argued that she was being held unlawfully, therefore her assault was of an officer *not* executing his duty. On appeal the Divisional Court held that her initially unlawful arrest did not prevent the arrest becoming lawful when, in the police station, proper procedures were adopted. Her acquittal was therefore held to be wrong.

3.4.2 Reasonable suspicion

In practice, the police will usually want to generate reasonable suspicion prior to an arrest, as this ensures that they cannot be sued for wrongful arrest should it turn out that the suspect is innocent. Whether 'reasonable suspicion' means the same across the contexts of stop and search and arrest is unclear. Reasonable suspicion is a lower standard than information sufficient to establish a prima facie case:

> Suspicion arises at or near the starting point of an investigation of which the obtaining of prima facie proof is the end ... Prima facie proof consists of admissible evidence. Suspicion can take into account matters that could not be put in evidence at all.[116]

It has been held that 'the amount of material that is known to the arresting officer in order to found "reasonable grounds" for suspicion may be small, even sparse'.[117] This makes it difficult to control police discretion. And the courts have hardly tried. When, for example, the police arrested a middle-aged woman for burgling the firm from which she had

---

[114] These should not be overstated. Button (2007: 84) found that the 49 security officers he studied had a good level of knowledge about their arrest powers, and we have already noted their awareness of how to use consent to avoid some of the potential problems the law poses. Good training is clearly important here—see also Wakefield A, *Selling Security* (Cullompton: Willan, 2003) pp 151–152.

[115] [1999] Crim LR 752. Discussed further in section 4.3.4.

[116] *Shaaban Bin Hussien v Chong Fook Kam* [1970] AC 942 at 948–949. Confirmed in *Parker v CC Essex* [2019] 1 WLR 2238. See section 2.2.1 for a related discussion in the context of stop and search powers.

[117] *Alanov v Chief Constable of Sussex* [2012] EWCA Civ 234 at [25], per Aikens LJ.

previously been dismissed, the grounds of suspicion were that the burglary appeared to be 'an inside job'. She was presumed by the police to have a grudge. Against this, she had no criminal record, and even the victim thought that she was an unlikely culprit. Nonetheless, the evidence was held sufficient to warrant reasonable suspicion. The court ruled that it was not a precondition of a lawful arrest that the police believe a suspect to be guilty. The issue was whether, given the information the police had at the time of the arrest, their suspicion could be regarded as reasonable.[118] The decision gives the police considerable freedom to follow crime control norms, in that it allows them to arrest on little hard evidence:

> If the police are justified in arresting a middle aged woman of good character on such flimsy grounds, without even questioning her as to her alibi or possible motives, then the law provides very scant protection for those suspected of crime.[119]

This approach was used when a man was observed trying door handles, and this should have been captured on CCTV. But it was not, leading the police to believe that the tape had been interfered with by one or more of six CCTV operators, who they arrested for perverting the course of justice. The Court of Appeal noted that those arrested were of good character and accepted that the arrests had caused them distress, fear and humiliation. It nonetheless upheld the legality of the arrests on the basis that where a small number of people could be clearly identified as the only ones capable of having committed the offence, that in itself could afford reasonable grounds for suspecting each of them of having committed that offence, in the absence of any information which could or should enable the police to reduce the number further.[120]

Arrests are frequently made by officers on the basis of briefings from senior officers. A simple order or request to arrest cannot, by itself, found the required reasonable suspicion on the part of the arresting officer: some objective information must be provided, but the arresting officer need not question it: 'For obvious practical reasons police officers must be able to rely on each other in taking decisions as to whom to arrest.'[121] This is in line with the doctrine of constabulary independence (see chapter 11).

It is not just police powers of arrest that give the police discretion, but also many substantive laws. Vague laws give the police considerable latitude in deciding for themselves what behaviour is or is not criminal and, therefore, arrestable. Ashworth singles out the Public Order Act 1986 (POA) for particular criticism. He points out that the essence of a public order offence might be thought to be that it engenders fear of violence and disorder among bystanders. Yet, as he says, the 1986 Act:

> goes so far as to include an express dispensation from proof that any member of the public was even at the scene, let alone put in fear – a dispensation which virtually undermines the rationale of the offence. These dispensations undoubtedly smooth the path of the prosecutor and make it correspondingly more difficult for defendants to obtain an acquittal ... Does it seem right to convict a person of a serious public order offence without the need to hear the evidence from a member of the public?[122]

---

[118] *Castorina v Chief Constable of Surrey* [1988] NLJR 180. Followed in *MPC v MR* [2019] EWHC 888 (QB).
[119] Clayton R and Tomlinson H, 'Arrest and Reasonable Grounds for Suspicion' (1988) 7 September, *Law Society Gazette* 22 at p 26.
[120] *Cumming v CC Northumbria* [2003] EWCA Civ 1844.
[121] *O'Hara v CC of the RUC* [1997] 1 All ER 129 per Lord Hope at 142. This decision, which was confirmed by the ECtHR in *O'Hara v United Kingdom* (2001) 34 EHRR 32, was applied in *Hough v CC Staffordshire Constabulary* [2001] EWCA Civ 39, where a police officer's suspicion was based on information in the Police National Computer about the suspect. See also *Didier Coudrat v Commissioners of Her Majesty's Revenue and Customs* [2005] EWCA Civ 616; *Parker v CC Essex* [2019] 1 WLR 2238.
[122] Ashworth A, 'Defining Criminal Offences without Harm' in Smith P (ed), *Criminal Law: Essays in Honour of J C Smith* (London: Butterworths, 1987) p 17.

Ashworth's point here is that the police are enabled to prove that a public order offence occurred by virtue of what they alone saw and what they infer from what they saw. This gives the police enormous discretion in deciding what is criminal, and therefore in deciding when they should or should not, and can or cannot, arrest. Thus a Home Office study found that some police officers use the most minor offence in the 1986 Act (s.5) to cover 'misbehaviour' that was not previously criminal, while other officers stated that this was unnecessary, as 'in the past, they would always have found a means to arrest if misbehaviour was sufficiently offensive'.[123] In one study of 60 disputes to which the police were called, there were six arrests. There was evidence to justify arrest on the grounds of the victims' complaints, such as criminal damage or assault, but the arrests were actually for breach of the peace, drunkenness or possession of an offensive weapon. This was because these public order charges:

> only required police evidence and, therefore, did not require the production of independent evidence from witnesses or victim statements ... because of the permissiveness of public order legislation, they can figure out precisely how to charge a person after they have made the arrest.[124]

In sum, 'reasonable suspicion' has an uncertain meaning, making police discretion hard to regulate by the courts who thus rarely act. Very little evidence is needed, and even that need not be correct if it was plausible at the time.[125] Vagaries in the law about whether a criminal and therefore arrestable offence has been committed, and reliance on police judgements about this, rather than those of independent witnesses, add to the possibility of an arrest. Lastly, vagaries about the boundaries between when a voluntary interview as opposed to an arrest may permissible and, indeed, more appropriate, have a similar effect.[126] The overall result is that police officers can arrest in such a way as to make conviction much more likely. Their choice reduces the ability of suspects to challenge their actions and minimises the accountability of the police to the judiciary.

3.4.3 Working rules

We have seen that 'reasonable suspicion' is an 'enabling rule' allowing—but not requiring—arrest in a very wide spectrum of circumstances (and that the substantive law itself also often enables this). But if the law does not dictate when and who the police arrest, what does? We saw in chapter 2, regarding stop-search, that in deciding when and how to exercise their powers the police draw on their experience and institutional objectives, as mediated by cop culture. On this basis, McConville et al identified various 'working rules' that structure police decision-making.[127] These apply to arrest just as they do to stop and search. What are these working rules? How far are they consistent with the reasonable suspicion criterion and legality in general?

3.4.3.1 Disorder and police authority

Ever since the modern police was established in the early nineteenth century, the maintenance of public order has been its prime concern.[128] With no national riot squads and with

---

[123] Brown D and Ellis T, *Policing Low Level Disorder: Police Use of section 5 of the Public Order Act 1986* (Home Office Research Study no 135) (London: Home Office, 1994) p 21.
[124] Kemp et al, 'Legal Manoeuvres in Police Handling of Disputes' in Farrington D and Walklate S (eds), *Offenders and Victims: Theory and Policy* (London: British Society of Criminology, 1992) p 73.
[125] *Jarrett v CC of the West Midland Police* [2003] EWCA Civ 397.
[126] See for example *Rashid v Chief Constable of West Yorkshire* [2020] EWHC 2522 (QB).
[127] McConville et al (1991: 27).
[128] Loader I, *Revisiting the Police Mission* (London: Police Foundation, 2020). Online at: <https://www.cgi-group.co.uk/sites/default/files/2020%9604/the-police-foundation-strategic-policing.pdf> (accessed 6 August 2020).

very sparing use of armed forces in situations of disorder, the police have the lead role in these matters. Consequently, the maintenance of order is always a concern of the police, in general policy terms and at the street policing level. The maintenance of police authority is linked to this. Since the police usually do not carry firearms, they rely on numbers and their moral and legal authority (as distinct from fear) to persuade people to do as they are told. This is particularly important when disorder is imminent (e.g. street fights and pub brawls) but also in 'straightforward' criminal situations such as theft and burglary, and even for minor matters such as cycling on a pavement.[129] In order to maintain the authority of the police, people must believe that when police officers make requests or give orders they have a moral right to do so or that they can enforce compliance. Thus, as we saw in relation to 'consent' searches, the police often secure co-operation because people believe that they will have to do as requested anyway.

It follows that when there are challenges to police authority or outbreaks of disorder, the police feel the need to get on top of the situation quickly, preferably by securing voluntary submission. For this reason, threats of arrest are probably a lot more common than arrests themselves.[130] If submission is secured, and if no serious offences have been committed, the police usually take no further action. Thus Shapland and Hobbs found that only 19–25% of 'disturbances' attended by the police led to arrest.[131] Kemp, Norris and Fielding found the police taking 'immediate authoritative action' (which includes arrest, but also removing suspects, reporting the incident and so forth) in just one-third of criminal disputes.[132] However, if submission is not voluntary, the police will enforce it. Now that naked violence is unacceptable,[133] arrest (with any 'reasonably necessary' accompanying force) is all that is left to the police. In one of McConville et al's cases, the police officer explained that it 'would have been all right if he'd just gone away but he had to be Jack the Lad … I grabbed him and arrested him.' In another a police officer explained the arrest by saying 'you come to the point like a parent with a child where if you don't do something the others will all join in'.[134] Similarly Loftus relayed the following conversation between officers in which 'contempt of cop' arising from members of the public swearing at officers, particularly in front of others, resulted in an arrest:

Peter: Most officers challenge it [swearing].

Scott: Yeah, that's a big problem for me. I'm a big one for that. If someone swears at you, then they're coming in—I don't get paid for that. They wouldn't do it to a bus driver …

Gareth: If there's an audience, there's no alternative.

Jake: If there's an audience, you've got to save face. You've got to take them away

Scott: Give them a chance to apologise. If they make the wrong decision, they'll get locked up and if they do, then they have learnt a lesson.[135]

---

[129] See Young R, 'Integrating a Multi-Victim Perspective through Restorative Justice Conferences' in Crawford A and Goodey J (eds), *Integrating a Victim Perspective within Criminal Justice* (Aldershot: Ashgate, 2000) at pp 240–242.

[130] For an example drawn from the policing of football crowds, see Stott et al, 'Policing Football Crowds in England and Wales: A Model of Good Practice?' (2008) 18(3) *Policing and Society* 258 at 268.

[131] Shapland J and Hobbs R, 'Policing Priorities on the Ground' in Morgan R and Smith D (eds), *Coming to Terms with Policing* (London: Routledge, 1989).

[132] Kemp et al (1992). Also see Clarkson et al, 'Assaults: The Relationship between Seriousness, Criminalisation and Punishment' [1994] *Criminal Law Review* 4.

[133] That officers would habitually mete out 'street justice' in times gone by is well documented. See, e.g., Brogden M, *On the Mersey Beat* (Oxford: OUP, 1991) pp 96–100.

[134] McConville et al (1991: 25).

[135] Loftus B, *Police Culture in a Changing World* (Oxford: OUP, 2009) pp 114.

When policing the night-time economy the police will also often seek to neutralise potentially volatile situations by arresting and removing a suspect to a police station rather than attempt to issue an on-the-spot fine, because of what they call 'the "obvious risk" to them and others of attempting to issue a fine on the street when surrounded by the offender's mates and other interested and inebriated parties'.[136]

In the more politically charged atmosphere of major strikes, riots, confrontations with 'alternative' movements and so forth, the police—as upholders of order and the status quo—seek to arrest those who challenge their authority.[137] However, the re-establishment of order frequently requires that the police take a longer view than simply arresting all and sundry: in order to retake control of the streets in the 'riots' of 1981, for example, the police sometimes allowed a remarkably large number of offences to take place without arrest.[138]

Arrests are often avoided during political demonstrations. This is in part because the police acknowledge the importance of the right to protest, in part because arrests could cause trouble to escalate, and in part because they know that the policing of the protest may be filmed, drawing unwelcome attention to dubious riot control tactics.[139] The working rule of 'avoiding in-the-job trouble' means that the police seek in the main to avoid violent confrontations and arrests that would place their own legitimacy in question, at least at the time of the disorder. This was part of the commentary that surrounded the policing of the 2011 riots in London, in which the police were initially seen as not being heavy-handed enough in their attempts to control the rioting, though a wave of arrests and convictions subsequently followed thereby distinguishing it from the riots that had gone before.[140] During the policing of protests and disorder, in some cases, any arrests that do take place may also be strategic in nature. Thus in the policing of the G8 summit in 2005 one group of protesters was corralled in a side street for over two hours, and subjected to occasional incursions by police snatch-squads bent on arresting 'known anarchist ringleaders.' Independent observers, including a BBC reporter, were later to assert that none of those snatched from the crowd was doing anything sufficiently criminal to justify their arrest.[141] This is an example of actuarial policing, with the tactics used aimed at managing and neutralising those deemed particularly 'risky'.

What does all this tell us about how far 'reasonable suspicion' is an inhibitory rule? Clearly, the 'reasonable suspicion' element is often missing from public order arrests. When asked the basis for the arrest of 'Jack the Lad', all the officer could say was 'it's Ways and Means, just to get him away, control the situation … '[142] In most situations, the flexibility of public order-type laws discussed earlier makes it difficult to say that there was insufficient evidence to arrest, for little evidence is required by them. Such laws are therefore favoured by the police precisely because they do not rely on the co-operation of witnesses, and arrests based upon them are very difficult to challenge.

---

[136] Halligan-Davis G and Spicer K, *Piloting 'On the Spot' Penalties for Disorder: Final Results from a One-year Pilot, Findings 257* (London: Home Office, 2004) p 5.

[137] See, on the miners' strike, Green (1990: ch 3) and Fine B and Millar R (eds), *Policing the Miners' Strike* (London: Lawrence and Wishart, 1985).

[138] Vogler R, *Reading the Riot Act* (Milton Keynes, Open UP, 1991) ch 8; Waddington P, *The Strong Arm of the Law* (Oxford: Clarendon Press, 1991) ch 6.

[139] Waddington (1994: 38–39). Overbearing, insensitive or excessively forceful arrests may trigger wider disorder within a community, as happened in Bradford in 1995: Bagguley P and Hussain Y, *Riotous Citizens* (Aldershot: Ashgate, 2008) pp 50–51.

[140] Newburn T, 'The 2011 England Riots in Recent Historical Perspective' (2015) 55(1) *British Journal of Criminology* 39–64.   [141] Waddington (2007: 157–158).

[142] McConville et al (1991: 25–26). The wryly named (and fictitious) 'Ways and Means Act' is frequently invoked in the absence of more helpful legislation.

Where order or authority are jeopardised, especially if this is in front of other members of the public, arrest is a resource for the police. It is not so much a means of getting someone to court as a means of control. Not only is prosecution not the main concern, but sometimes it is not envisaged at all, and persons arrested in this way are frequently released without charge.[143] Thus Waddington discusses a 'gay pride' demonstration which was about to disrupt a royal procession: 'the protesters were arrested and ... not charged, for the police purpose had been to maintain the dignity of the event by removing the protesters ... '[144] An almost exactly identical set of arrests were made at a Royal Wedding in 2011.[145] More generally, Choongh (1997) observed that some sections of the population are subjected to 'social discipline' by the police precisely by arresting on flimsy or no legal grounds, humiliating them while in custody, then releasing them without ever having intended to charge them. The aim is to leave them in no doubt that they are 'police property', to be treated as the police wish. More recent research does not take such an extreme view, but generally found that the police thinking and arrest behaviour documented by research over the last 40-plus years discussed in this section has not changed much.[146]

3.4.3.2 Demeanour

Even where there is reasonable suspicion, whether arrest takes place depends on a combination—all other things being equal—of offence seriousness and offender seriousness. The police judge the latter, in the absence of information about 'previous', by the attitude displayed by the suspect. As noted earlier, arrests for 'contempt of cop' are fairly common. One officer, referring to a police Support Unit, said ' ... these boys, they won't wear it [back-chat from "undesirables"] ... if they get any mouth, they'll drag 'em in'.[147] Another told Choongh that if someone swore at an officer he deserved to be arrested as: 'We shouldn't have to take that kind of shit, and we won't take it.' This is why, he explained to Choongh, there were often arrests for seemingly trivial matters under s.4 and s.5 of the Public Order Act 1986.[148] Brown and Ellis cite many examples throughout their report, concluding that the police view is that if those who abuse the police 'realise that they can get away with it, respect for the police will decline further, and they will be the targets of more abuse in the future ... '[149] Pearson et al say: 'Abusive words or aggressive behaviour ... substantially increased the risk of an arrest ... As one officer explained, having arrested an offender who had sworn at them, "I treat everybody the same, but not when they don't treat me the same" ... "Fronting up" to an officer was the ultimate challenge to her authority and would also most likely result in an arrest.'[150]

However, sometimes the police themselves directly provoke 'mouthiness', knowing that this will provide a justification for arrest. As one drug user complained:

> If there's a load of them and you get pulled by them, they seem to take the piss and that, show off in front of them. But the coppers and stuff like that they try to just take the piss out of you, calling you a fucking divvy and this and that and if you call them owt back and that they'll just arrest you.[151]

---

[143] Kemp et al (1992).   [144] Waddington (1994: 184).
[145] See *Hicks* [2017] UKSC 9, discussed in section 3.3.4.   [146] Pearson and Rowe (2020: ch 7).
[147] Choongh (1997: 68).
[148] Choongh (1997: 75). These legislative provisions are discussed in section 3.4.1.
[149] Brown and Ellis (1994: 42–3 and passim); also see, for one more example out of many, Waddington P, *Policing Citizens* (London: UCL Press, 1999b) p 135.
[150] Pearson and Rowe (2020: 136).
[151] Quoted in Lister S, Seddon T, Wincup E, Barrett S and Traynor P, *Street policing of problem drug users* (York: Joseph Rowntree Foundation, 2008) p 47.

This is not to suggest that the police always arrest those that are abusive or not cooperative. The police have wider goals, as embodied in the working rules, in mind. So where one working rule (order, for example) is more powerful than another (appropriate demeanour), arrest is unlikely. Context is very important. Swearing in the context of a political or environmental protest is something the police are more likely to tolerate than when dealing with 'away' football fans, or 'rough' youths in a city centre or on a problem estate. Thus one of the senior commanders of the South Yorkshire Police responsible for the policing of the Sheffield G8 anti-poverty protests in 2005 briefed his public order units of the need for a subtler approach than they typically deployed when controlling football crowds:

> So that was the tenor of the brief: only respond and react if you have to and that will be dictated to by the … commanders, the sergeants and the inspectors; no unilateral, sort of 'I'm going to arrest him because he's upset me.' In any case, they were the more professional of my public order units; they can stand around and take that sort of stuff all day.[152]

We have given qualitative examples here, but attempts have also been made to quantify the importance of demeanour in particular samples of cases. In a classic American study, Piliavin and Briar observed police decisions whether or not to arrest or warn youths on the street: 25 youths were arrested or given official reprimands and 41 youths were released with no official action at all. These different dispositions had little to do with their alleged offences, but had a lot to do with their demeanour. Most of the co-operative youths were released with no official action, while most of the un-cooperative youths were arrested or given official reprimands. As Piliavin and Briar put it:

> Assessment of character—the distinction between serious delinquents, 'good' boys, misguided youths, and so on—and the dispositions which followed … were based on youths' personal characteristics, and not their offences.[153]

In other words, the police attempted to avoid rigidity by taking action only in 'deserving' cases, but they based that judgement on rather superficial personal characteristics. In Britain, Southgate reported similar findings. Observers noticed cases where officers enforced the law 'by the book' in response to difficult or hostile people, whereas they applied discretion to offenders of a similar kind who were more amenable.[154] The result in Southgate's study was that official action (including arrest) was taken against 45% of 'rude, hostile' suspects, 22% of 'civil' suspects, 11% of 'friendly' suspects, and 5% of those who displayed 'particular deference'.[155] More recently, Pearson and Rowe similarly note the distinction officers draw in their arrest decisions between 'decent folk' and the 'criminal types'. They give an example of 'a driver who had a police-style baton in the doorwell of his van. He was again only "given an advisory" because he did not belong to the criminal type category … For the same offence, a "suspected OCG [organised crime group member]" would have "definitely" been taken into custody.'[156] It is difficult to make sense of the disproportionate amount of police resources devoted to such offenders and offences, and of the tactics used, except by reference to macho police culture and the working rule that suspects should show the police respect by submitting to their authority.

The weak inhibitory quality of 'reasonable suspicion', combined with the overwhelming desire of the police to maintain order and authority has powerful consequences. It means that arrestees tend to be those with an 'attitude problem' and those perceived as

---

[152] Quoted in Waddington (2007: 150).
[153] Piliavin I and Briar S, 'Police Encounters with Juveniles' (1964) 70 *American Journal of Sociology* 206.
[154] Southgate P, *Police-Public Encounters* (Home Office Research Study no 90) (London: HMSO, 1986) p 47.
[155] Southgate (1986: 101).   [156] Pearson and Rowe (2020: 137).

'criminal types'. This falls disproportionately on those who dislike the police—particularly young, socially marginalised males—whose dislike is thus compounded, increasing the probability of 'attitude problems' next time round. Stop-search, which we saw in the previous chapter is disproportionately used against these people, frequently adds another twist to this spiral of mistrust. For example, as we saw in chapter 2, there is a 'double penalty' at work for minority ethnic groups because not only are they more likely to be stopped by the police, but when they are, they are more likely to feel treated negatively due to the connections they are likely to make between the stop and prejudice/racism. This leads to less trust in and satisfaction with the police both during that encounter and in the future.

3.4.3.3 Suspiciousness and previous convictions

There is a line in the classic film 'Casablanca' when, following a serious crime, the police chief instructs his officers to 'round up the usual suspects'. These are, of course, people with 'previous', meaning relevant previous convictions. It does not usually happen quite like this, although it can if the police mount a major investigation.[157] Indeed, such investigations provide a good excuse for arresting local 'villains' to see what else they will 'cough' to. Many people are arrested for serious offences because they are known to favour the modus operandi employed,[158] and many police officers spend time with arrestees in order to get to know their criminal character traits for future reference.[159]

'Previous' triggers arrest in four common ways. It is sometimes the first lead in a reported crime, the police arresting someone known to do this kind of thing or to have previously pestered the victim in question. Thus McConville et al cite examples where this was the totality of evidence; no further police action, not surprisingly, was the frequent result.[160] Second, the police may catch someone committing a trivial offence and then use technology to check whether they have any previous convictions. If they do, arrest is more likely.[161] Third, knowledge of someone's previous convictions leads to that person being followed (either physically or by CCTV), thus allowing the suspect to be watched until he commits a crime.[162] Finally, as we saw in the previous chapter, just being a known criminal can be enough to prompt a stop and search; if this reveals, say, drugs then arrest will follow.[163]

The point in these third and fourth situations is not that arrest is per se wrong (although frequently there will be no reasonable suspicion for the stop, where it occurs, which preceded it), but that if such people had no 'previous', their offences would probably not have been discovered. Again, the pattern created is one which leaves 'respectable' people out of the criminal justice net and repeatedly enmeshes those with low status. McAra and McVie looked at contacts between the police and young people over several years from the late 1990s onwards. They found that every time a youth was arrested or given a formal warning the probability of this happening again increased, regardless of that individual's actual level of crime. Having friends who had been in trouble with the police and generally living life 'on the street' were also factors.[164] In a more recent example, several Asian teenagers

---

[157] McConville et al (1991: 24).

[158] See Smith D and Gray J, *Police and People in London* (Policy Studies Institute) (Aldershot: Gower, 1983) vol 4, p 345 and Sanders A and Bridges L, 'Access to Legal Advice and Police Malpractice' [1990] *Criminal Law Review* 494.

[159] McConville et al (1991: 23).   [160] McConville et al (1991: ch 2).

[161] See Warburton H, May T and Hough M, 'Looking the Other Way: The Impact of Reclassifying Cannabis on Police Warnings, Arrests and Informal Action in England and Wales' (2005) 45 *British Journal of Criminology* 113 at 119–121).

[162] McConville et al (1991: 24); Wakefield (2003: 174–175); Lister et al (2008: 28).

[163] Lister et al (2008: 53).

[164] McAra L and McVie S, 'The Usual Suspects: Street Life, Young People and the Police' (2005) 5 *Criminal Justice* 5.

were described by police officers as generally looking unruly and making gestures at their police van as it passed them—which, the teenagers said, was caused by repeated stops and poor treatment by the police in the past. This prompted the police to stop and search them despite having insufficient grounds for suspicion. The young men were awarded damages for racial abuse, assault, wrongful arrest and false imprisonment. The case underlines the targeting and differential treatment of black and Asian young people (as discussed in chapter 2) and the ways in which stop-searches sometimes quickly escalate into unlawful arrests and strip searches in police custody. The trial took eight years to come to court, and evidence from another police officer proved crucial in the evidence put forward by the teenagers being believed.[165]

Targeting 'known criminals' is encouraged at the highest levels. In the 1990s the Audit Commission called for a greater focus on criminals rather than crimes: 'Target the Criminal', it urges, by developing an 'intelligence strategy based on target criminals … build an element of proactivity into all detective duties … encourage the use of informants.'[166] This approach continues to be endorsed by government—in its 2004 White Paper, for example, where again the call is to move (further) away from reactive to proactive policing and to target 'prolific offenders'.[167] This is part of the managerialist strategy discussed in chapter 1 in which speed and efficiency comes to be prioritised over justice. Rather than being the neutral efficient strategy implied, the result is a skewed suspect population suffering frequent and disproportionate invasions of liberty.

Being 'known to the police' is only a special case of appearing 'suspicious', which we saw was a key working rule in relation to stop-search. Association with other criminals, such as sharing a house where drugs are dealt or being seen in public together, is particularly important. Some associates are arrested even when the police have no evidence at all of their guilt; here, arrest is used to secure witness statements and is entirely without reasonable suspicion.[168] Other 'suspicious' characteristics include appearance and attitude to the police. Attitude is related to the question of authority, discussed earlier. Suspects who are not co-operative when apprehended are often formally arrested without more ado, allowing further investigation to determine whether or not they are likely to be the culprits. In cases like this, it is clear that arrest has moved to the start of the investigative stage—too early in many instances for reasonable suspicion to be formed, and much earlier in any event than used to be common.

3.4.3.4 Taking account of the victim

Subject to other factors, a decision to arrest will in part depend on whether formal police action is desired by the victim (in crimes, such as assault, where there are victims). If the victim's evidence is essential to any consequent prosecution (which is by no means always the case) then there may seem to be little point making an arrest without his or her agreement. Reality is not, however, so straightforward.

First, the police themselves sometimes influence victims. When the police attend the scene of alleged assaults, for example, they are expected to use their judgement to decide

---

[165] *Mohidin v Commissioner of the Police of the Metropolis* [2015] EWHC 2740(QB). Discussed in Flacks S, 'Law, Necropolitics and the Stop and Search of Young People' (2020) 24(2) *Theoretical Criminology* 387–405.

[166] Audit Commission, *Helping with Enquiries—Tackling Crime Effectively* (London: HMSO, 1993) exhibit 20.

[167] Home Office, *Building Communities, Beating Crime—A Better Police Service for the 21st Century*, CM 6360 (London: TSO, 2004a). For a general (if somewhat uncritical) review of the field, see Ratcliffe J, *Intelligence-Led Policing* 2nd edn (London: Routledge, 2016).

[168] These specific examples are taken from several others discussed by Leng R, *The Right to Silence in Police Interrogation: A Study of Some of the Issues Underlying the Debate* (Royal Commission on Criminal Justice Research Study no 10) (London: HMSO, 1993) p 25.

which courses of action (conciliation, informal warning, on-the-spot fine or arrest) would be better for the victims. They will often discuss these alternatives with them, who may have a preference but who will usually be open to advice. Officers who do not wish to arrest can easily make this appear to be an unattractive option, which it may indeed be.[169] For assaults which arise in domestic abuse cases, however, the introduction of positive arrest policies has to some extent curtailed the latitude available to officers when making arrest decisions in such cases: see chapter 10 (section 10.4.1) on domestic abuse.

Second, the police always pursue grave offences. McConville et al report a serious rape case which led to mass arrests of a broad category of suspect, largely for purposes of elimination.[170] Clarkson et al (1994) examined nearly 100 assault cases. The police pursued five of the most serious cases (all meriting charges of inflicting grievous bodily harm) despite the reluctance and unreliability of the victims.

Third, some victims are more influential than others. Ignoring the views of some—local businessmen and politicians, for instance—would cause more trouble for the police than ignoring others.[171] So Kemp et al. comment that in civil disputes, such as trespass,[172] where no criminality is involved:

> the police often take immediate action ... to end the dispute, generally by ensuring the physical removal of the 'offender' from the scene. For instance, all 11 requests made by publicans, security guards, shop/office managers, and private landlords in our 60 disputes were supported by the police.

Kemp et al point out that the police have no power to force individuals to leave, and that they could simply explain to the complainants their civil law rights. The important point for us, apart from demonstrating the willingness of the police to exercise authority even where they have no power to back it up, is that police authority is generally exercised in favour of powerful high status victims, rather than victims of low status.[173] Where the latter are concerned, Kemp et al found that:

> Victims' views were basically ignored and the offence and the offender became police property to be disposed of in the manner which most suited police rather than victim priorities.[174]

The police are perhaps the most influential victims of all. This was explored earlier, in the sense that threats to their authority make them victims. But it goes further than this. Brown and Ellis found that in many of the public order arrests they looked at, the police appeared to be the only victims, even though the Public Order Act is supposed to protect the public: 'what is at issue in many of the cases ... is the enforcement of respect for the police'.[175] And nothing attracts the immediate and disproportionate attention of the police quite like a serious assault on a fellow officer.

---

[169] Edwards S, *Policing Domestic Violence* (London: Sage, 1989); Kemp et al (1992).

[170] McConville et al (1991: ch 2).

[171] Although the police may be reluctant to act on the wishes of high status victims if the alleged offenders are also high status, as the latter are capable of causing the police 'in-the-job trouble' by complaining about the arrest (as illustrated by the furore surrounding the arrest in November 2008 of the Opposition front bench spokesperson on immigration, Damian Green MP: <http://news.bbc.co.uk/1/hi/uk_politics/7754099.stm> (accessed 5 January 2010).   [172] Kemp et al (1992: 65).

[173] Thus the 'victims' in *Steel v UK* were powerful arms dealers, government and grouse shoots, all of whose interests were facilitated by police arrests of the people protesting against their activities. Note, however, that it is unlawful for the police to solicit or accept financial contributions from victims to help fund an investigation, as this would jeopardise impartial and even-handed law enforcement: *R v Hounsham & Ors* [2005] EWCA Crim 1366.

[174] Kemp et al (1992: 73). See further Sanders A, 'Personal Violence and Public Order' (1988a) 16 *International Journal of the Sociology of Law* 359.   [175] Brown and Ellis (1994: 42).

The police are acting entirely within the law in these examples, for there are no laws establishing rights for victims in relation to arrest, and the Code of Practice for Victims[176] only says that victims will be able to explain how the crime has affected them and that this will be 'taken into account' by the police and other agencies. Exactly the same findings have been made in the United States, suggesting that this is not a local or temporary phenomenon.[177] As with many aspects of the operation of police powers, what matters most is not what was done, but who did it or who the victim was.

3.4.3.5 Other factors

The other main working rules give primacy to organisational factors, 'information received' from informants or co-suspects, and workload. We examined the impact of organisational and societal factors on police discretion in general in section 2.1. Arrests are as subject to such influences as any other aspect of policing. Periodic panics over vice, drugs, 'mugging', knife crime and so forth lead to surges in arrests for these offences. In the case of knife crime, the picture is complex and the media, proactive police practices, government strategies and so on have been shown to influence the increase in stop and searches, arrests and custodial sentences.[178]

Sometimes individual communities or police forces adopt particular arrest policies. In an American study, the arrest rate in town A was over three times as high as in town B, giving the impression of a much lower crime rate in the latter. In reality, though, the crime rates were very similar. The true difference was that the affluent middle class residents of town B put enormous pressure on the police not to arrest their offspring.[179] Similar things happen in the UK. One study of drugs enforcement found a considerable number of arrests for possession of cannabis, while another found that the police forces it looked at had reoriented their drugs arrest policies to higher-level trafficking.[180]

The police frequently arrest suspects purely on the strength of an allegation, or 'information received'. If the allegation coincides with 'previous', so much the better, as in a case cited by McConville et al: 'you have to react on what you hear initially ... when we checked his form we thought there might be a chance; the name even rang a bell to the lads ...'[181] Since this arrestee did not fit the description and absolutely nothing connected him with the offence, it would have been difficult for the police to claim that they had 'reasonable suspicion'. Societal pressures often lie behind legally dubious arrests. For example, the Macpherson Inquiry's sharp criticisms of the police for failing to act quickly in arresting the prime suspects in the Stephen Lawrence case[182] resulted in a perception by senior homicide detectives in London that early arrest was now virtually mandatory ('even if knowledge and information was sparse').[183]

---

[176] For discussion of the Code, see ch 12.

[177] See Buzawa E and Buzawa C, 'The Impact of Arrest on Domestic Assault' (1993) 36 *American Behavioural Scientist* 558.

[178] Grimshaw R and Ford M, 'Young people, violence and knives- revisiting the evidence and policy discussion' *UK Justice Policy Review Focus* (Centre for Crime and Justice Studies, 2018): see <https://www.crimeandjustice.org.uk/sites/crimeandjustice.org.uk/files/Knife%20crime.%20November.pdf> (accessed 11 September 2020).

[179] Meehan A, 'Internal Police Records and the Control of Juveniles' (1993) 33 *British Journal of Criminology* 504.

[180] May T et al, *Times They are a Changing: Policing of Cannabis* (York: YPS, 2002); Newburn T and Elliott J, *Policing Anti-drug Strategies: Tackling Drugs Together 3 Years On* (London: Home Office Police Research Group, 1998).

[181] McConville et al (1991: 30).   [182] Macpherson (1999) para 13.41.

[183] Foster J, ' "It Might Have Been Incompetent, But It Wasn't Racist": Murder Detectives' Perceptions of the Lawrence Inquiry and its Impact on Homicide Investigation in London' (2008) 18(2) *Policing and Society* 89.

Workload can have all sorts of effects. Police officers avoid arresting when they have too much to do or when their shift is about to end so that they do not have to spend hours sometimes beyond the end of their shift waiting for the person they arrested to be booked-in to police custody, and they sometimes also look for arrests when they have too little to do.[184] The weather can also be important (when it is cold and wet, almost any excuse to get back to the station will do), as can a host of other factors including the time of day or night when the suspect was arrested.[185]

Young ('Testing the Limits of Restorative Justice: The Case of Corporate Victims' in Hoyle C and Young R (eds), *New Visions of Crime Victims* (Oxford: Hart, 2002) p 2002: 200) notes that the use of arrest to 'solve' problematic situations, for example, involving people with mental health conditions was valued by many of the officers in her in-depth study of two police stations, not least because it was perceived to reduce future workload. This was particularly evident where the police were faced with repeated calls to attend the same address. As one officer recalled: 'On our way back to the address my colleague, of quite a few years in, was such that he said: "right, that's it, we'll just nick her, we'll have her out of there" … I didn't think it was the right thing to do, trying to put her through the system, even though, yes, it's going to save you having to go back there again during the night.' By the same token, at the time of the research, arrests of those with mental health conditions (whether for protective or prosecution purposes) were sometimes avoided because of the 'downstream workload consequences' of taking formal action. Officers felt that it was unfair (on the custody officer) to bring people with mental health conditions to the police station because 'they are more likely to attack police officers because they panic, … are difficult to cope with' and because the custody staff are blamed for any consequent self-harming behaviour. Indeed, this position has more recently been supported by changes to the Mental Health Act 1983 introduced by the Policing and Crime Act 2017 which mean that police cells may only be used as a place of safety in exceptional circumstances for adults and not at all for children and young people. Thus the working norm in favour of upholding order in public has to be weighed against the working rule of avoiding disorder and disproportionate workload in the police station, whilst also working within legal requirements.

Another important factor is the drive for 'figures' and 'quality figures' in particular. As Young says:

> In this [CID] world the detection rate is of vital concern, and a succession of poor returns in the monthly or quarterly detection figures can break the ambitious detective inspector … As a result, those calls for a change of emphasis to such matters as 'crime prevention' have little or no chance of obtaining prominence.[186]

Exactly the same point is made by Maguire and Norris, who observe that arrest and detection rates are still important promotion criteria; by Choongh, who observes that uniformed branches, as well as the CID, are under pressure to arrest;[187] and by officers themselves who sometimes suggest that cannabis possession arrests are easy to 'notch up' for probationers.[188] Since a charge counts as a detection regardless of the outcome (hence regardless

---

[184] Pearson and Rowe (2020: 139); Choongh (1997: 71–72).

[185] Skinns L, 'Stop the Clock? Predictors of Detention Without Charge' (2010) 10(3) *Criminology and Criminal Justice* 303–320.

[186] Young M, *An Inside Job* (Oxford: OUP, 1991) p 255.

[187] Maguire M and Norris C, *The Conduct and Supervision of Criminal Investigations* (Royal Commission on Criminal Justice, Research Study no 5) (London: HMSO, 1992) ch 5; Choongh (1997: 69–72). See also Young (2002: 201) who quotes a patrol officer's explanation of why 'quick fixes' were valued over the kind of complicated proactive problem-solving that might be necessary in the case of those experiencing a mental health crisis.   [188] May et al (2002).

of the evidence) the pressures to treat 'reasonable suspicion' lightly are difficult to resist. Yet even police officers recognise the futility of this. Smith and Gray,[189] for example, report many officers saying that they end up making 'pointless ... unnecessary or unjustified arrests and stops'. That is they recognise the drive for 'figures' as pure window-dressing, and therefore no more about crime control than it is about due process or freedom.

The use of working rules to guide arrest very often leads to more of a crime control than a due process approach. Moreover, the overuse of arrest is more likely to generate fear, resentment and non-co-operation than respect.[190] In other words, it generally has the same counterproductive effect as extensive stop-search practices. This can be illustrated by way of 'easy' arrests for drug possession.[191] Not only are they financially costly in terms of police resources, these resources may be better spent dealing with more serious forms of crime and/or protecting vulnerable victims. The police are aware of such opportunity costs,[192] as can be seen in this officer's comment: 'I would feel dreadful if an urgent assistance came over the radio and I was in custody dealing with a tinpot bit of cannabis whilst one of my shift were getting the shit kicked out of them.'

Hence, since the last edition of this book was published, national guidance, force policies and police practices have increasingly moved away from arresting and detaining citizens for cannabis possession, and towards the use of warning and fines. As Pearson and Rowe say, that 'with the exception of arrests for OCG disruption purposes, officers usually preferred not to take an individual [suspect of cannabis possession] into custody on this basis. Force policies on "cannabis warnings", which followed from ACPO [national] guidance, directed officers away from arrest and towards warnings and penalty notices.'[193] Nonetheless, as this quotation reveals, whether an arrest happens may also still depend on who the suspect is (e.g. OCG member or not), but also on some of the factors that have already been discussed in this chapter, such as the circumstances in which the cannabis came to light, and the person's demeanour, what time it is, resources available etc. In conclusion, we can see that when the police follow working rules (which are subject to interpretation and weighting by individual officers) they do not always follow the legal rules. This is because:

(a) some working rules prescribe for the police unlawful purposes in some circumstances, and
(b) some working rules prescribe unlawful criteria for arrest in some circumstances.

3.4.3.6 Working rules and legality

Arrests made without any intention to prosecute, or made because the police are concerned with order rather than specific offences almost certainly violate the necessity principle for arrest discussed in section 3.3.2, as is evident from the case law on breach of the peace (section 3.3.4). As the European Commission has said, arrest 'must be for the purpose of securing [the] fulfilment [of an obligation prescribed by law] and not, for instance, punitive in character'.[194]

---

[189] Smith and Gray (1983: 60).
[190] See, for example, Brown and Ellis (1994: 43); Bagguley and Hussain (2008: 101–103).
[191] See Lister et al (2008: 48–52).
[192] And this is reflected in their formal policies on cannabis enforcement, although these have shifted in recent years as the government first downgraded and then upgraded the classification of this particular drug. That these policies do not affect the doctrine of constabulary independence can be seen from *R (on the application of Mondelly) v Commissioner of Police of the Metropolis* [2006] EWHC 2370 (Admin).
[193] Pearson and Rowe (2020: 142).   [194] *McVeigh* (1981) 25 DR 15.

This means that many unofficial purposes of arrest—such as to put the 'frighteners' on people, or to secure information about other people's crimes—appear to breach the common law. Commendable from both a due process and freedom viewpoint though this may be, the courts appear unaware of the large number of arrests which would be outlawed by this reasoning. Furthermore, the costs—personal and financial—of wrongful arrests are often palpable as shown in the case of the couple who were wrongfully arrested on suspicion of flying drones over Gatwick airport, resulting in chaos and the cancellation of numerous flights. Despite it being clear from early on in the case that the couple were unlikely to have been responsible as they did not possess any drones and were at work during the time of the drone sightings, they were held incommunicado for 36 hours.[195]

In an earlier case another common police practice was questioned. The defendants were arrested for a credit card fraud for which there was reasonable suspicion. The real reason for the arrest was, however, to give other officers time to install bugging equipment in their house in order to gather evidence of a far more serious conspiracy to rob. At trial, the defendants applied for this evidence to be ruled inadmissible because it was, they said, obtained unfairly. The judge refused to do this. The defendants pleaded guilty because this evidence was so incriminating, but then appealed. The Court of Appeal said that 'holding charges' (that is, arrests for one purpose while gathering evidence of a more serious charge) were entirely proper if those arrests were lawful. Whether they were lawful or not depended on whether a prosecution was possible or not—and prosecution for the fraud was a possibility.[196]

3.4.4 Race, class, gender and arrest

It is clear that police working rules do not impact equally upon all sections of society. 'Cop culture'—but not the research literature—regards some social and racial groups as more criminogenic than others. Some groups probably do commit some types of crime more than do others. For example, young socially marginalised youths are almost certainly involved in more street drug dealing and robbery than are older people in regular work; but those older people commit other drugs offences and fraudulent crimes in large numbers instead. 'Targeting' may therefore be justified, but not when considerations of equity and offence seriousness are disregarded such that the offences which are primarily targeted are those which are, or are thought to be, committed by small, disadvantaged, sections of society.

The result of skewed targeting and the general operation of working rules based on police officers' cultural assumptions is a pattern of unjustified discrimination. For example, Stevens and Willis found that black people in deprived socio-economic conditions were no more likely to commit crimes than were white people in those conditions.[197] Yet this study (pre-PACE) and post-PACE studies[198] have found disproportionate arrest rates among black people. The official statistics for recent years are in line with this research (Table 3.1). They show that each year from 2014 to 2019 black people were three times

---

[195] 'Gatwick airport drone arrest couple to receive £200,000 police payout' *The Independent*, 14 June 2020 <https://www.independent.co.uk/news/uk/home-news/gatwick-airport-drones-couple-arrest-police-compensation-sussex-a9565616.html> (accessed 10 September 2020).

[196] *Chalkley and Jeffries* [1998] 2 Cr App Rep 79.

[197] Stevens P and Willis CF, *Race, Crime and Arrests* (HORS No 58) (London: HMSO, 1979).

[198] Jefferson T and Walker M, 'Ethnic Minorities in the Criminal Justice System' [1992] *Criminal Law Review* 83. Fitzgerald M and Sibbitt R, *Ethnic Monitoring in Police Forces* (Home Office Research Study no 173) (London: Home Office, 1997).

(9–10%) more likely to be arrested than would be expected given their proportion in the population. Asian people's proportion of arrests matched their general population make up (7%), and the mixed group was arrested at twice the proportion (3–4%) that would be expected given their demographic profile.[199] Although the disproportionate arrest rate for black people could be partly due to a higher proportion of black people than white people in the general population being young and socially marginal, some of it is a product of proactive and targeted policing of groups and areas.

Stevens and Willis found that black people were particularly liable to be arrested for offences such as preparatory and public order offences where 'there is considerable scope for selective perception of potential or actual offenders'.[200] Brown and Ellis also found disproportionate arrests of black people for public order offences, perhaps because black people are more likely to perceive s.5 warnings about their behaviour as provocation, leading to an escalation of the situation, and the police are more ready to react adversely where they receive abuse from black people.[201] Racial stereotyping was highlighted in a case, where a mixed-race woman was arrested and handcuffed whereas her two white companions were not.[202] It makes us question how much has changed in the 27 years since Stephen Lawrence was murdered and the (black) friend who called an ambulance for him was treated by the police 'like a liar, like a suspect instead of a victim.'[203]

As with stop and search, the arrest rate for women is much lower than for men; 86% of arrests were of men in 2018/19 though women are slightly more likely to be arrested for fraud offences.[204] Asian women and girls are under-represented in arrest figures overall, but are 26% more likely than other women and girls to be arrested for fraud offences. Black women are more than twice as likely to be arrested as white women but 10% less likely to be prosecuted following an arrest, suggesting that arrest powers are over-used with this population. Children from minority ethnic backgrounds—girls as well as boys—account for two thirds of children's arrests, and the majority of these are black.[205]

Public order-type offences are classic products of proactive policing. They are, in other words, usually discovered as a result of police initiative, like other 'victimless' crimes (e.g. drugs, prostitution). Around 75% of all arrests are for incidents reported to the police by the public.[206] It might be thought that this means that police bias through proactive policing would play only a small part in shaping the ethnic (and class) profile of the population of arrestees. However, just because the public report an incident, it does not follow that the public identifies the suspected offender. Phillips and Brown found that in 40% of arrests the main evidence was police evidence—evidence which is often secured through the operation of working rules.[207]

---

[199] Demographic information about the proportion of different ethnic groups in England and Wales is taken from Census figures from 2011 which showed that black people accounted for 3.3%, white people accounted for 86%, Asian people accounted for 7.5% and mixed background people accounted for 2.2%. Source: Office for National Statistics <https://www.ethnicity-facts-figures.service.gov.uk/uk-population-by-ethnicity/national-and-regional-populations/population-of-england-and-wales/latest> (accessed 11 September 2020).

[200] Stevens and Willis (1979: 41). [201] Brown and Ellis (1994: 33).
[202] *Durrant v Chief Constable of Avon and Somerset* [2014] EWHC 2922 (QB).
[203] *The Guardian*, 25 February 1999. This case, and its aftermath, is discussed later in this section and in chs 10 and 12.
[204] *Police Powers and Procedures, England and Wales, year ending March 2019*. HOSB 25/19 London: Home Office.
[205] *Statistics on Race and the Criminal Justice System 2018* (2019h) London: Ministry of Justice.
[206] Phillips and Brown (1998: ch 2). [207] Phillips and Brown (1998: 41).

Arrest rates are important because they determine which cases are passed on to the CPS. Hence racial disproportionalities go on to shape who enters the criminal justice system. It seems that just being black makes one suspicious and thus more liable to being arrested.[208] Fitzgerald and Sibbitt (1997) show this happening at a more general statistical level. Being young and male, as well as black, is even more risky. This is confirmed by Phillips and Brown who, as Home Office researchers, are understandably cautious in their interpretation of their figures. They show that not only are ethnic minorities over-represented among those who are arrested, but also that the evidence against ethnic minority arrestees is, on average, significantly weaker than against white arrestees. For example, in violent offences there was enough evidence to charge on arrest in 45% of white cases but only 37% and 17% respectively in cases involving black and Asian suspects, while for public order offences the corresponding figures were 84% (whites) 65% (blacks) and 64% (Asians).[209]

As stated earlier, it seems little has changed since the Official Inquiry into the failure to apprehend the murderers of black London teenager Stephen Lawrence, concluded that the Metropolitan Police embodied 'institutional racism'. Not only does simply being young and black increase the probability of attracting police suspicion, in addition ethnic minority victims are less likely than white victims to have their cases 'solved' by arrest.[210] The extent to which this takes place is a matter of debate,[211] but it seems that: 'It is not *either* structural factors *or* police discrimination that lead to high crime rates for black youth but both.'[212] Because, as we shall see in later chapters, police and CPS prosecution decisions largely endorse the wishes of the arresting/investigating officers, one consequence is that many more cases, proportionately, involving ethnic minorities fail in court than do those involving white people.[213]

Unemployed and low-paid people are also massively over-represented in the arrest statistics, even taking into account socio-economic conditions.[214] Only one-quarter of all the arrests in Philips and Brown's random sample were of employed people.[215] Hillyard and Gordon (1999) observe that arrest rates in the poorest areas of the UK are massively higher than in wealthier areas, reinforcing the 'north-south divide'. In addition to community pressures and 'attitude' problems, these people are simply more vulnerable to being arrested, for they spend much of their time in public spaces where police powers can most easily be deployed. In section 3.4.3.3 we discussed research by McAra and McVie showing that youths with 'previous' contact with the criminal justice system were more likely to be arrested or formally warned than those with no 'previous' contact, even after the level of their crime was taken into account. This was especially if their friends had similar

---

[208] The overall disproportionate arrest rates of blacks, as compared to whites, can only partially be explained in this way. The difference appears also to be due to the greater social deprivation of blacks and reporting and recording differences: Jefferson and Walker (1992). Note that all these studies found that Asians were arrested disproportionately infrequently, but see discussion post 9/11 and 7/7.

[208] Phillips and Brown (1998: 45).

[210] Macpherson of Cluny, Sir W, *The Stephen Lawrence Inquiry* (Cm 4262-I) (London: SO, 1999); Bowling B, *Violent Racism* (Oxford: OUP, 1998).

[211] Murder investigations post-Macpherson continue to have a racialised dimension (notwithstanding denials by the police that this is so): Foster (2008).

[212] Holdaway S, *The Racialisation of British Policing* (Houndmills: MacMillan, 1996) p 96. It should be borne in mind that the term 'high crime rates', in common use, relates to the recorded figures, which are a product of arrest practices as well as 'actual' crime. See pp 84–104 of Holdaway's book for a sophisticated discussion of race, crime and arrests; and also Bowling B and Phillips C, *Racism, Crime and Justice* (Harlow: Longman, 2002) ch 6.

[213] HM Crown Prosecution Inspectorate, *Thematic Review of Casework having an Ethnic Minority Dimension* (London: HMCPI, 2002).

[214] Meehan (1993); Sanders A, 'Class Bias in Prosecutions' (1985) 24 *Howard Journal of Criminal Justice* 76.

[215] Phillips and Brown (1998: xii).

experiences and if they spent much time on the streets. These youths were overwhelmingly working class. In other words, police working rules unwittingly pick out the socially marginal.[216]

How can we explain the fact that many people are arrested on little or no evidence, in defiance of 'reasonable suspicion' laws, and that poor, black and Asian people disproportionately suffer from this? We need to ask what the police want, and what they might fear, when they arrest. What they want is: to punish, by arrest and detention, those who fail to display respect; to maintain order and prevent further disorder or crime; or to secure evidence leading to prosecution and conviction. What they fear is adverse comeback if they 'mess up'. Arresting people on 'fishing expeditions' who may provide information, arresting people for the purpose of elimination, or arresting people to enforce order is therefore viable for the police if the arrestee is unlikely to sue, make a plausible complaint, or otherwise challenge their actions.[217] This is true largely of those they consider low status people: those who are young, black/Asian or working class (and especially of those who possess all three characteristics). Hence the pattern observed in relation to stop-search is repeated and amplified at the arrest stage. Patterns of bias are created by following police working rules that influence who to select for arrest out of a much larger group of arrestable suspects. The rule that the police must act only when they have 'reasonable suspicion' is sometimes ignored in this process, but the flexibility of this requirement means that breach is often not necessary. It is therefore in part an enabling rule, allowing the police to use informal norms, and in part a presentational rule with little inhibitory effect.[218]

Having said all that, recent governments have tried to tackle racial discrimination within the criminal justice system (even as anti-terrorist legislation exacerbates the problem, as shown in section 3.3.3), and Table 3.1 shows that in some areas the patterns of apparent bias are not stark. But statistics create crude racial categorisations such as 'blacks' and 'whites', that can obscure as much as they reveal. For example, white people of Irish origin long suffered more at the hands of the police than the 'indigenous white' population,[219] but this was difficult to monitor when all 'white people' were lumped together in the official statistics. Similarly, many Muslims living in England and Wales would be classified by the police as white or black rather than Asian, and those classified as Asians are obviously not all followers of Islam or constitute a single community.[220] The intensity with which the police focus their attention on Asian/Muslims may currently be very different from the policing of other Asian/faith groups such as Sikhs, Hindus or Christians. More nuanced arrest figures based on *self-defined* ethnicity were published for the first time in 2007/08 and appear to indicate exactly this: there were 20 arrests per 1,000 population aged 10 and over for people who self-defined their ethnicity as Indian (most of whom will not be Muslim) while the equivalent rate for those self-defining as Pakistanis or Bangladeshi

---

[216] McAra and McVie (2005). The ethnic minority dimension is not discussed, perhaps because Edinburgh, where the research was carried out, is overwhelmingly white.

[217] Consider, for example, the anxiety and attempted buck-passing evident within the police when a decision had to be made regarding whether or not to arrest the former MP Neil Hamilton, and his wife Christine, in connection with (concocted) sexual assault allegations: *Miller v Associated Newspapers Ltd* [2005] EWHC 557. Arguably a similar situation arose when the police decided not to arrest and prosecute the Prime Minister's chief political advisor, Dominic Cummings for breaching coronavirus laws and perverting the course of justice by claiming he took a 60-mile round trip to test his eyesight (*The Guardian*, 30 October 2020). If he needed to take such a long drive (with his wife and children) to test his eyesight he should have been arrested for dangerous driving at the very least.

[218] See generally Rowe and Pearson (2020: ch 7).   [219] See Hillyard (1993).

[220] The 2001 Census was the first to collect information on religion. See Peach C, 'Islam, Ethnicity and South Asian Religions in the London 2001 Census' (2006) 31 *Transactions of the Institute of British Geographers* 353–370. See further Modood T, 'Muslims and the Politics of Difference' (2003) *Political Quarterly* 100 at 103–104 in particular.

Table 3.1 Percentage of Arrests in England and Wales by Ethnicity 2014/15 to 2018/19[221]

Year	Ethnic appearance of person arrested				
	White	Black	Asian	Mixed	Chinese or Other
2014/15	79	9	7	3	2
2015/16	78	10	7	3	2
2016/17	77	10	7	4	2
2017/18	77	10	7	4	2
2018/19	77	10	7	4	2

Source: Statistics on Race and the Criminal Justice System 2018 available from the Home Office and Ministry of Justice websites. The statistics are generally accurate however have missing data at times (for example these figures do not include those for Lancashire) Thus Table 3.1 should be treated as providing only a reasonable approximation of disproportionality trends.

(who will overwhelmingly be Muslims) was just over double this.[221] Finally, calculating quantitative rates of arrest tells us nothing about the qualitative experience of arrest and it is to this that we now turn.

3.4.5 **The experience of arrest**

So far we have focused on what 'reasonable suspicion' means in the context of arrest, how far arrest discretion actually adheres to this standard, and what the impact is on socially disadvantaged groups of the pattern of arrests. We did this because 'reasonable suspicion' is the key standard set out by law, and adherence to it ought to eliminate, or at least reduce, unfair discrimination. However, it is not just the basis on which police power is exercised that is important, but also the way it is exercised. Tyler, for example, has found that most people can accept unjust results if they think the process by which those results were reached is fair.[222] If people are treated with dignity and respect, and feel that they have a voice in what is happening to them, then they are more likely to see the police as legitimate and to co-operate with them both at that time and in the future, for example, when considering whether to report crime to the police.[223] If we accept, as the Philips Commission did,[224] that arrest is intrinsically coercive, it follows that even a little overbearing behaviour on the part of the police encroaches significantly on the suspect, their autonomy and their liberty. The manner in which arrests are made is therefore of fundamental importance to the criminal justice system. And, as we saw in the previous chapter, the manner in which police powers are exerted is crucially important for police–citizen relations, which impact upon citizens' willingness to help clear up crime, which in turn impacts on everyone in society.

In section 3.1, and in chapter 1, we gave some examples of the way in which arrest can be humiliating or even terrifying. In another example, Choongh was told by a suspect that when he told police officers who stopped him on the street to 'leave me alone', they told him he was under arrest. When he objected 'he [an officer] punched me in the balls'.[225] Some readers might doubt the credibility of such a story, but in the Internet age it

---

[221] Ministry of Justice (2009b) table 5.2b, p 79. Interestingly, this table shows that white Irish people (25 arrests per thousand) now have a slightly lower arrest rate than white British people (26 arrests per thousand)—which is consistent with our argument (see section 3.3.3) that young, male Muslims have replaced 'the Irish' as the prime suspects so far as terrorism is concerned.
[222] Tyler T, *Why People Obey the Law* (New Haven: Yale University Press, 1990).
[223] See the discussion of legitimacy in ch 1.   [224] See section 3.1.   [225] Choongh (1997: 65).

is easy to observe violent arrests for oneself.[226] Examples like these often involve minority groups, such as black people and—increasingly since 9/11—Asians. In a prevention of terrorism example, 'out of nowhere, various plain clothes detectives pounced on us from behind and threw us up against the wall ... they spread-eagled our legs. They told us not to turn around ... One of them grabbed me by the throat and dragged me into one of the Black Marias that had appeared from nowhere'.[227] The Campaign Against Criminalising Communities (CAMPACC) (2003) gives examples of terrorism arrests (that proved groundless) which terrorised the arrestees.

CAMPACC also documents other serious, although probably unintended, effects of arrest for highly stigmatic 'crimes' such as terrorism. Whole Asian communities (including those studying at university)[228] have come to fear police action after a series of apparently groundless mass arrests, including that in April 2009 discussed in section 3.3.3. One arrestee was ostracised by neighbours who either feared him or feared being 'tarred with the same brush' (perhaps wisely in the sense that being associated with terrorists is a ground for arrest!). Another was afraid of accepting support from an Asian charity, fearing that this would make him guilty of something by association. This was all regardless of the lack of prosecutions in these cases.

There is a growing body of evidence that shows that socially marginal groups are treated disproportionately badly when arrested, that a minority of these arrests are unnecessarily violent and abusive and that many are humiliating. Unsurprisingly, there are many complaints against the police to the Independent Office of Police Complaints—over 61,000 in 2017/18—and whilst the figures do not specify exactly how many were in relation to arrest, 2,282 were categorised as breach of Code C PACE on detention, treatment and questioning (i.e. including arrest).[229] But most such complaints meet with little success, which in large part comes down to the powerless position of the complainant relative to the police. These and other remedies for wrongful arrests and other forms of police malpractice are discussed more fully in chapter 11.

Occasionally, however, 'respectable' arrestees do challenge the manner of their arrest successfully. For example, a bailiff in dispute with a debtor was arrested to prevent a breach of the peace, put in handcuffs and taken to the police station where he was released an hour later. The bailiff argued that even if the arrest was lawful the use of handcuffs was unreasonable given that he had made no attempt to resist the arrest. The court agreed:

> placing the bailiff in handcuffs and taking him in handcuffs through a public place and on the journey to the police station in a police car was in my view wholly unjustified. Even if the arrest had been justified, which it was not, the situation did not require that further indignity.[230]

Domestic courts must also take into account Art 2 of the ECHR, under which: 'No-one shall be subjected to torture or to inhuman or degrading treatment or punishment.' The examples we have referred to in this section of the chapter seem to us to amount to

---

[226] For example, at <http://news.bbc.co.uk/1/hi/england/nottinghamshire/8103707.stm> (accessed 5 January 2010).

[227] Hillyard (1993: 129).

[228] A particularly notorious example being the arrest in May 2008 of a University of Nottingham PhD student who had downloaded from the US justice department website an 'al-Qaida Training Manual' (a declassified document which anyone can buy from Amazon!) on to his computer in connection with his doctoral research. See Hicham Y, 'Britain's Terror Laws have Left Me and My Family Shattered', *The Guardian*, 18 August 2008.

[229] *Police Complaints: Statistics for England and Wales 2017/18* (London: Independent Office for Police Conduct) <https://policeconduct.gov.uk/sites/default/files/Documents/statistics/complaints_statistics_2017_18.pdf> (accessed 12 September 2020).

[230] *Bibby v Chief Constable of Essex* [2000] EWCA Civ 113 per Pill LJ. Discussed briefly in section 3.3.4.

'degrading treatment', and the courts seem to agree. The best possibility of *effective* control, however, would be if police officers monitored and checked each other's behaviour. While this might seem somewhat idealistic in the light of our discussion of 'cop culture' especially its emphasis on solidarity between police officers, and institutional racism in chapter 2, we also noted there that there is reason to believe that attitudes within the police are slowly changing. With that in mind it is both heartening and depressing to find in a national newspaper in 2005 that: 'Recently a constable was suspended for making monkey noises at a [black] youth he was arresting. Two officers reported the incident. A third who did not was disciplined.'[231] And in the policing of protests, police officers have on occasion been observed to intervene when their colleagues use excessive force.[232] But the deadly assault on Ian Tomlinson at the G20 protest in April 2009 indicates that numerous supervising officers are still prone to doing nothing when they observe a fellow officer resorting to unprovoked violence. The capture of the assault on video, and the media's response in setting the agenda for public debate, were key to how the case proceeded. This created a new 'politics of visibility' towards policing practices that impacted significantly on police accountability and legitimacy (see chapter 11 for further discussion).[233]

None of this is intended to suggest that all or even most arrests are unnecessarily degrading. Sometimes the police make special efforts to arrest as clinically as possible. Waddington shows how when protests are arranged in advance, the policing strategy is also planned, usually with a view to minimising trouble for the police and disruption for the public. In an anti-poll tax riot, 'several people were arrested ... the suspect was whisked away ... what senior officers feared was the sight of officers struggling on the ground ...'.[234] In this kind of situation, behaving badly to the suspect (in public at any rate) would conflict with police working rules. But sometimes behaving badly accords with such 'rules'. We need to question the idea that 'degrading' treatment on arrest is always 'unnecessary' in the sense that it is accidental or merely an expression of prejudice. We have seen that many arrests are made largely to effect control or assert authority. Sometimes the manner of arrest is intrinsic to this.[235] Holdaway discusses how police officers often exercise powers intending 'education and punishment'. One example is where officers arrested some demonstrators who were sitting in the road. An officer told him: 'There was a bloody great puddle by the side of the road, and when they were nicked they were swept right through this puddle.'[236] A less clear-cut example is where arrests are made at people's homes in the middle of the night. No doubt the police would argue that this method minimises the chance of violent resistance or escape but this has to be balanced against the greater infringement of liberty involved, and the risk that some officers will use this method simply in order to intimidate. As one Muslim arrested under the counter-terrorism legislation has recently put it: 'I am

---

[231] *The Guardian*, 18 August 2005. Another example is where an officer who was asked in a police canteen if someone he had arrested had been black replied: 'We are sending him back to the jungle' and made a spear-throwing action. A colleague made an official complaint and the officer was required to resign by a disciplinary tribunal: reported in the *Sun*, and the *Evening Standard*, on 12 November 2008.

[232] Waddington (2007: 154–155).

[233] See Goldsmith A, 'Policing's New Visibility' (2010) 50(5) *British Journal of Criminology*, 914–934; Greer C and McLaughlin E, '"This is not Justice": Ian Tomlinson, Institutional Failure and the Press Politics of Outrage' (2012) 52(2) *British Journal of Criminology* 274–293.

[234] Waddington (1994: 56).

[235] Similarly, it may be intrinsic to a police goal of provoking resistance by the arrestee, such resistance amounting to 'revelatory knowledge'—as only the guilty would resist the police. For a sustained analysis to this effect (taken to apply equally to interrogation and other methods of evidence construction) see Green A, *Power, Resistance, Knowledge: The Epistemology of Policing* (Sheffield: Midwinter & Oliphant, 2008).

[236] Holdaway S, *Inside the British Police* (Oxford: Blackwell, 1983) p 10. See also Choongh (1997) for the argument that many arrests are made solely for these purposes, and that humiliation is central to this process.

not saying these arrests are a bad thing, they're not, they are a good thing, but why do they have to be accompanied by middle of the night raids terrifying our children and wives?'[237]

We might therefore classify arrest-manner as follows:

(a) normal, by which we mean they are in accordance with legal rules and officers treat arrestees with dignity and respect, recognising them as fellow human beings;

(b) rude/aggressive (to further working rules); and

(c) rude/aggressive (due to spite or lack of sensitivity).

We do not know the size of one group relative to another. Reducing the incidence of the third is realistic if police training and monitoring took these concerns seriously, but reducing the size of the second will be almost impossible whilst the police seek to 'discipline' large sections of society.

With that in mind, the use of 'kettling' tactics, where the police immobilise large numbers of protesters or football fans, often with a view to stop-searching or arresting 'ringleaders' or 'troublemakers', raises particular concerns about degrading treatment. This approach was deployed in the policing of the May Day protests in 2001 when several thousand people were caught within a police cordon, on a wet and chilly afternoon, for over seven hours. Conditions became increasingly squalid, as people, in the absence of toilets, were forced to relieve themselves in public: 'This and other problems bore particularly hard on some of the women.'[238]

Moreover, there is a worrying trend towards using ever more violent methods of effecting an arrest (in the name of reducing the risk of harm to police officers) which increases still further the potential for severe discipline to be inflicted on the socially marginal who challenge police authority. Thus, police officers now often resort to the use of disabling devices when arresting suspects, such as incapacitant spray (PAVA) designed to temporarily blind, and increasingly tasers (devices that incapacitate suspects through the delivery of an electric shock).[239] We suspect that the use of such levels of force is frequently objectively unreasonable, but if police officers write up the arrest 'in the right way', as by claiming that the arrestee violently resisted the arrest, challenging their actions successfully is extremely difficult, although less so when film exists of the encounter.

3.5 Conclusion

The law of arrest has evolved to accommodate changes in police practice, although it has not legitimated all of these changes. The police can now use arrest to facilitate investigation, rather than conducting their investigations in advance and just using arrest as a mechanism to bring alleged offenders before the courts. The courts and Parliament have allowed policing considerations instead of due process considerations to shape the law.

Crime control values underlie the law of arrest in several respects. First, although the Philips Commission rightly saw arrest as intrinsically coercive and wanted to restrict it to

---

[237] Forum Against Islamophobia and Racism, *Counter-terrorism Powers, Reconciling Security and Liberty in an Open Society: Discussion Paper. A Muslim Response*, para 70. Available at <http://www.fairuk.org/policy.htm> (accessed 12 September 2020).

[238] Per Sir Anthony Clarke MR, *Austin and Saxby v Comr of Police for the Metropolis* [2007] EWCA Civ 989 at para 7. See also *Laporte* [2006] UKHL 55 per Lord Bingham at para 12, describing the forced (and unlawful) return of protesters' coaches from Gloucestershire to London. No toilet breaks were permitted, which caused 'acute physical discomfort and embarrassment'.

[239] See generally Waddington P and Wright M, 'Police Use of Force, Firearms and Riot Control' in Newburn T (ed), *Handbook of Policing* 2nd edn (Cullompton: Willan, 2008) 465–496.

serious offences, 20 years after PACE partially enacted its recommendations the police were given a power of summary arrest in respect of all offences, however trivial. Second, while that power might appear to be subject to the inhibitory 'necessity' rule, PACE s.24 (5) (as amended by SOPCA) specifies arrests that 'allow the prompt and effective investigation of an offence or their "conduct"' are 'necessary'. This makes the 'necessity' rule primarily presentational, and has been found to have little effect on officers' practical decision-making. Third, much that is a product of unlawful police action is held to be lawful, thus allowing the end to justify the means—e.g. where PACE, s.24 allows arrest without reasonable suspicion of 'anyone who is guilty', and where the courts allow an unlawful arrest to be turned into a lawful arrest. Fourth, the substantive law in most public order offences and in common law breach of the peace is so vague that the police have even more freedom to arrest according to their own priorities than they would otherwise have.

The final problem is how to make the police accountable. Exclusion of evidence obtained unlawfully is possible; but this only arises in a trial, and most wrongful arrests do not lead to prosecutions. There is a complaints mechanism, but unless the latest one is dramatically better than all the previous ones this is of little use. Civil actions for wrongful arrest are possible, but difficult (in section 2.1 we saw, for example that the common law requirement that suspects be told of their arrest and the reasons for it, has been watered down by the courts). This is all discussed further in chapter 11. And while most executive agencies are increasingly subject to searching review based on the '*Wednesbury*' principles, this remains exceptional in respect of arrest. When using arrest powers, police officers—like any other executive officers exercising power—must act in good faith, use the powers for the purposes they were given, take into account relevant matters and disregard the irrelevant, and not act in ways so unreasonable that no reasonable officers could have so acted.[240] In a due process system concerned to protect justice and freedom, failing, or refusing, to look into a suspect's explanation for what the police think could be criminal would be considered '*Wednesbury*' unreasonable. But:

> There is ample authority for the proposition that courses of inquiry which may or may not be taken by an investigating police officer before arrest are not relevant to the consideration whether, on the information available to him at the time of the arrest, he had reasonable cause for suspicion. Of course, failure to follow an obvious course in exceptional circumstances may well be grounds for attacking the executive exercise of that power under *Wednesbury* principles (at 181).[241]

Failure to follow up exculpatory lines of enquiry is not, it seems, wrong in the eyes of the judges, and so only exceptionally will judicial reviews or civil actions be successful for this reason.

The main due process element in arrest law is the 'reasonable suspicion' requirement, but this is such a low threshold that the majority of arrests are probably based on weak evidence, and many are based on virtually no evidence. More investigation would be possible prior to most arrests, but this is not required by the law except in exceptional cases. The law offers little due process protection and, instead, gives the police wide boundaries within which to operate according to their own working rules. Offence seriousness, the probability that the suspect has committed an offence and the views of the victim (although some victims more than others) all influence police decisions whether or not to arrest, but other police working rules are equally important. These are based on criteria of 'suspiciousness' and 'disorder' that—like stop and search—bear most heavily on disadvantaged sections of society. Patterns of bias result that are a product only in part of police rule

---

[240] *Associated Provincial Picture Houses Ltd v Wednesbury Corpn* [1948] 1 KB 223.
[241] *Castorina v Chief Constable of Surrey* [1988] NLJR 180 at 181.

breaking. Disadvantaged sections of the population are constantly singled out when others are also likely to be guilty of many crimes. A skewed suspect population is constructed, which distorts the whole criminal process thereafter. As for 'crimes of the powerful': to the small extent that they are enforced at all, arrest is hardly ever available, so skewing the suspect population even further (see chapter 7).

As with stop-search, police–suspect interactions leading to arrest are fluid and unpredictable. As with stop-search, arrest is sometimes used in order to gather information (including DNA, fingerprint and photographic evidence) or to discipline, rather than as a prelude to court processes (thus limiting the accountability of the police to the law). Different arrest (and stop-search) patterns may not reflect different crime rates so much as different ways of securing criminal intelligence information and engaging in communicative surveillance.[242] Consequently, the police often arrest in ways that are abusive and humiliating,[243] they do so in large numbers, and get poor results—'poor' in the sense that detections are relatively few in number, generally for relatively minor offences, and discriminatory in the patterns they produce. For those of us who instinctively lean towards due process the response should not necessarily be to demand tighter definitions of 'reasonable suspicion', for this strategy is unlikely to work. Instead, we might require the police to arrest less and use summons more, as the Philips Commission recommended back in the 1970s. This would produce less coercion and less loss of freedom. But twenty-first century legislative developments are moving in the opposite direction.

If we are to accept the necessity of crime control techniques, we might nonetheless seek a greater say in the crimes to be controlled. We might, for example, seek more public control over the types of situation for which arrest is and is not to be regarded as appropriate. These are matters of accountability and regulation discussed in chapter 11. The core value of 'democracy', as well as justice, is therefore generally trumped by 'efficiency'. To its credit, the government has demanded a stronger response to domestic abuse over the years in response to mounting public concern, although chapter 10 will show that the police are adept at avoiding arresting when they want to. The use of brief periods of arrest in such situations often protects victims while impacting only marginally on arrestees. Using arrest as a punishment, such as Choongh discusses, is, however, another matter entirely. And the rapid growth in the use by the police of 'on-the-spot' fines is arguably fuelling and intensifying this function of arrest.

Overall, it is plain that the ECHR only protects people against the most egregious arrests, and arrest will never conform to 'due process'. Nor should it. If we adopted the 'freedom' approach we would accept that sometimes only the police can judge when arrest is necessary to avoid serious risk. But what is and is not 'serious' and how great those risks should be, should be a matter of public debate, and the police should be held to the standards then set. Finally, if we do accept the necessity of some methods of crime control in the interests of protecting the public (e.g. victims of domestic abuse), it does not follow that we should accept that model's assumptions about the reliability of administrative fact-finding. Instead, we should treat with scepticism police claims that, as professionals, they can be trusted not to make mistakes. No one with the amount of power the police possess should ever be trusted to that extent. The tragic killing of an innocent man, Jean Charles de Menezes, at Stockwell tube station by armed police in the aftermath of the murderous

---

[242] See Meehan (1993) and section 2.5.

[243] At the time of writing, South Wales had sought to defend their actions in using a taser during an arrest on a pregnant woman, who subsequently lost her baby. See <https://www.theguardian.com/uk-news/2020/oct/21/south-wales-police-defend-use-of-taser-on-pregnant-woman> (accessed 24 October 2020).

attacks on London's transport system in July 2005 underpins that conclusion, as do more recent cases in which arrests have been accompanied by the use of lethal or near lethal force or other harmful consequences for the arrestee.[244]

Further reading

CHOUDHURY T and FENWICK H, *The Impact of Counter-terrorism Measures on Muslim Communities* (2011) Equality and Human Rights Commission.

CORNFORD A, 'Terrorist Precursor Offences: Evaluating the Law in Practice' (2020) *Criminal Law Review* 663.

GLOVER R, 'Keeping the peace and preventive justice' [2018] *Public Law* 444.

PEARSON G and ROWE M, *Police Street Powers and Criminal Justice: Regulation and Discretion in a Time of Change* (Oxford: Hart Publishing: 2020). See especially ch 7.

PEARSON G, ROWE M and TURNER L, 'Policy, Practicalities, and PACE s. 24: The Subsuming of the Necessity Criteria in Arrest Decision Making by Frontline Police Officers' (2018) 45 *Journal of Law and Society* 282–308.

ROWE M, 'Rendering Visible the Invisible: Police Discretion, Professionalism and Decision-making' (2007) 17(3) *Policing and Society* 279.

---

[244] See Neyland D, 'Surveillance, Accountability and Organisational Failure: The Story of Jean Charles de Menezes' in Goold B and Neyland D (eds), *New Directions in Surveillance and Privacy* (Cullompton: Willan, 2009) pp 107–132 and ch 11.

4

Detention in the police station

KEY ISSUES

- The limited effectiveness of suspects' rights
- Who is considered 'vulnerable' in police custody and how their needs are addressed
- Why do people die in police custody?
- Defence lawyers—why aren't they more adversarial?

4.1 Introduction

When the police arrest suspects they usually take them to a police station, especially if they plan to subject those suspects to an investigation or to prosecute.[1] However, alternative courses of action include: releasing suspects immediately, though this is rare; reporting them for summons; releasing them on 'street bail'; requesting that the suspect attend a police station for a voluntary interview, often by appointment (see later in this chapter); or subjecting them to a voluntary interview at the scene of an alleged offence using body-worn videoing technology, though this is a relatively new police practice, about which a limited amount is currently known.

The Police and Criminal Evidence Act 1984 (PACE) regulates the rights of suspects and powers of the police in the police station.[2] In this chapter we assess the key provisions of PACE, the associated Code of Practice (Code C),[3] and subsequent developments. In the next two chapters we look at police questioning and at other forms of evidence-gathering. First we need to understand how the different models outlined in chapter 1 approach the treatment of suspects in the police station.

In a crime control system, the police would have discretion to deal with arrested suspects as they thought fit in order to ascertain the truth. Suspects are most likely to co-operate with the police and reveal the truth if denied the opportunity to consult with friends, family or, in particular, a lawyer. The length of detention should be governed by considerations of efficiency alone. Suspects should be held for as long as it is thought that further questioning and custody-based evidence-gathering may provide useful information, but no longer.

---

[1] Skinns L, Sprawson A, Sorsby A, Smith R and Wooff A, 'Police Custody Delivery in the Twenty-first Century in England and Wales: Current Arrangements and their Implications for Patterns of Policing' (2017) 4(3) *European Journal of Policing Studies* 325, note the shift towards police forces having a smaller number of larger out-of-town designated police custody facilities, meaning lengthier journey times for suspects, the police and for other criminal justice practitioners who may need to attend.

[2] See Bryan I, *Interrogation and Confession* (Aldershot: Dartmouth, 1997) chs 7–9 for discussion of the pre-PACE situation.

[3] Code of Practice C: The Detention, Treatment and Questioning of Persons by Police Officers. Available online at: <https://www.gov.uk/government/publications/pace-code-c-2018> (accessed 27 April 2019).

In a due process system, the detention of suspects in police custody would be very tightly controlled, if it was allowed at all. Since the police should not arrest unless they first have sufficient information to prove guilt, it follows that there is no necessity to secure a confession from the suspect. Arrest should be followed by charge and judicial proceedings, not by administrative investigation. There will always be some time between arresting suspects and bringing them before the courts, however. It may be in the suspect's interests to talk to the police during this period since this may dispel suspicion and lead to earlier release. But this opportunity for dialogue may be abused, so safeguards must be provided. Suspects must be told that they are under no obligation to answer questions, that it will not be held against them at court if they maintain silence, that anything said may be used in evidence, and that they are free to consult with a lawyer before answering questions.

We will see that the law steers something of a middle course between crime control and due process, although frequently this is not how it works out in reality. PACE allows detention for the purpose of questioning, but seeks to regulate this. Police officers do not have complete discretion, but direct and more immediate control or supervision is exercised by other (more senior) police officers, and less direct control occurs through accountability bodies such as Independent Custody Visitors, the IOPC and HMICFRS (see chapter 11). In short, PACE gave the police more powers but also provided checks and controls on the use of those powers including more safeguards and rights for suspects.

This approach is consistent with the European Convention on Human Rights (ECHR). Article 5 allows arrest and detention on various grounds. The ones that concern us in this chapter and the next are:

1.(b) … to secure the fulfilment of any obligation prescribed by law;

1.(c) … for the purpose of bringing him before the competent legal authority on reasonable suspicion …

One of the aims of this chapter and the next two is to see how real the checks, controls and safeguards provided in PACE are. Another is to evaluate the effect of the ECHR and Human Rights Act (HRA).

4.2 The powers and duties of the custody officer

We saw in chapter 3 that the police station has become the primary site of criminal investigation through changes in police practice. The 'Confait' scandal illustrated the importance of the power of the police over detained suspects.[4] This led to the acceptance that clear legal regulation of what goes on in the police station was necessary.

4.2.1 The custody officer

Police stations that hold suspects for significant lengths of time must have a 'custody officer' available at all times.[5] Custody officers must be at least of the rank of sergeant,[6] but any other officer may carry out their functions when they are not available.[7] Custody officers now routinely work alongside civilian detention officers, who are non-warranted staff,

---

[4] Fisher H, *Report of an Inquiry into the Circumstances leading to the Trial of Three Persons on Charges arising out of the Death of Maxwell Confait and the Fire at 27 Doggett Road, London SE6* (HCP 90) (London: HMSO, 1977). See Baxter J and Koffman L, 'The Confait Inheritance – Forgotten Lessons?' [1983] *Cambrian Law Review* 14.   [5] PACE, s.36.
[6] PACE, s.36(3).   [7] PACE, s.36(4).

with more limited powers than police officers, who are employed either by the police or by the private security sector.[8] Civilian detention officers (CDOs) were originally appointed to carry out a small number of tasks, such as drug-testing detainees or taking fingerprints or photographs, with chief officers being able to designate them with powers to do so under the Police Reform Act 2002, but their role has since expanded. In a recent survey of custody managers in 40 of the 43 police forces in England and Wales, Skinns et al found that custody officers were responsible for issues related to the legitimacy of detention and adherence to PACE codes, whilst CDOs were responsible for the well-being of detainees and the administering of police procedures, though this also sometimes extended to initial booking-in procedures, including risk assessments and the reading of suspects' rights, with custody officers only providing a cursory check on the authorisation of detention.[9] The post of the custody officer is important, however, as it is on this officer that the main responsibility rests for the maintenance of the rights of suspects.[10]

Custody officers should be independent of any investigation in which a detained suspect is involved, so anyone acting as a custody officer must not be involved in the process of securing evidence from or about suspects (PACE s.36(5)). By and large, custody officers do that job and no other for lengthy periods, sometimes for years at a time and sometimes as a route to promotion,[11] though sometimes sergeants who usually perform other roles may be drafted in to work in custody to cover staff shortages and to earn some over-time pay. At root, custody officers are still police officers with all the typical attitudes associated with 'cop culture' (see section 2.1.4).

Once arrested, suspects are taken to a police station and immediately brought before the custody officer. The principle is that nothing may happen to that suspect prior to being 'booked in' by the custody officer. The custody officer fills in a 'custody record' for each suspect. After some personal details (name, address and so forth) are taken down and a risk assessment carried out, the custody officer has to decide whether or not to detain the suspect, that is, whether to authorise their detention, and, if so, on what grounds, and whether or not to charge the suspect (and, again, on what grounds). This is all written on the custody record.

PACE also introduced a new regime for questioning aimed at eliminating the abuses which used, sometimes, to occur. The police may interrogate several times in any period of detention, subject to the rights of the suspect discussed later. But they may normally only do so in a room equipped for this purpose with recording facilities, in the presence of an appropriate adult (AA) (if the suspect is considered 'vulnerable') and in the presence of a legal advisor (if requested by the suspect). It is the responsibility of the custody officer to ensure that all these conditions are met. Details of any visits to suspects in their cells have to be recorded on the custody record in case unfair inducements or threats are made or alleged.

The custody officer also has to decide whether to seek authorisation for further periods of detention (discussed later) and whether to allow other powers to be exercised. These may include strip searches, intimate and non-intimate searches of suspects, and, as we shall see in chapter 6, house searches, and the holding of identification parades. The custody officer decides whether or not to ask the CPS to charge and prosecute suspects

---

[8] Skinns et al (2017).   [9] Skinns et al (2017); Skinns (2011).
[10] Sections 120–121 of the Serious Organised Crime and Police Act 2005 enable, but do not require, police services to designate civilians in their employ as 'staff custody officers'. The police resisted the civilianisation of the custody officer role and the government has indicated that it will repeal these provisions: Home Affairs Select Committee, *Policing in the 21st Century* HC 364-I, Seventh Report (2007–2008), para 227. Many of the detention staff working under custody officers are now civilians, however.   [11] Skinns (2011).

(discussed in chapter 7) and, if so, whether they should be held in custody or released on bail (discussed later in this chapter). Again this is all noted on the custody record.

Code C (which sets out the rights of suspects in the police station and the powers of the police) also requires custody officers to ensure that suspects are treated properly in terms of food, sleep, warmth, sanitary and safe conditions, medical treatment and so on. These provisions comply with Art 3 of the ECHR whereby no-one should be subject to torture or inhuman or degrading treatment. No research has suggested that, since PACE was enacted, these provisions are frequently or systematically breached, but regular government inspections routinely pick up on lapses in these material conditions, such as in regards to access to showers and exercise yards, appropriate clothing, sanitary products for women or the presence of ligature points in cells. Later we reveal many breaches of more serious rules (e.g. regarding covert surveillance—see chapter 6; completion of the custody record—see Marlon Downes' case, in section 4.4) and abuses leading to deaths in police custody.

Clearly the custody officer's role is of central importance. But s/he is a relatively junior police officer. Moreover, in 2008, the Police Federation spokesperson on custody issues noted that 'training … is a postcode lottery', with this picture being confirmed by recent scoping research by a working group on police custody training, as part of the police custody portfolio of the National Police Chiefs' Council.

Throughout this and the next chapter we will see that, for these and other reasons, custody officers do not always carry out their protective role as one would expect from the wording of PACE and Code C.

4.2.2 **The rights of suspects**

Custody officers should immediately inform those suspects who are to be detained of their most important rights,[12] both orally and by giving them a notice in writing. These include the right to consult a lawyer privately, which we will discuss in section 4.5. Other rights include having someone informed of one's arrest, consulting a copy of Code C and making a telephone call to anyone of their choice. The right to have someone informed when arrested—otherwise known as 'intimation'—is described in Code C as the 'right not to be held incommunicado' (para 5). Under s.56(1) of PACE, a suspect may have:

> One friend or relative or a person who is known to him or is likely to take an interest in his welfare told, as soon as is practicable except to the extent that delay is permitted by this section, that he has been arrested and is being detained …

The police are not allowed to stop suspects exercising this right. They may delay its exercise, but only under very strict conditions[13] and in practice rarely do so.[14] However, Note D to para 5 of Code C provides that: 'In some circumstances it may not be appropriate to use the telephone' in compliance with s.56. This means that the custody officer can require that intimation be made in a written form only.

The exercise by suspects of the *separate* right to a telephone call or to contact someone by letter[15] may be delayed on a similar basis to the right of intimation. Suspects may

---

[12] The outline provided here will not attempt to discuss comprehensively these rights. A good reference text is Ozin P and Norton H, *PACE—A Practical Guide* (Oxford: OUP, 2019).
[13] The conditions are similar to those which apply to the delaying of a suspect's access to legal advice, discussed in section 4.5.
[14] Brown D, Ellis T and Larcombe K, *Changing the Code: Police Detention under the Revised PACE Codes of Practice* (Home Office Research Study no 129) (London: HMSO, 1992) pp 54–56.
[15] Code C, para 5.6.

also receive visits 'at the custody officer's discretion'.[16] Discretion is to be exercised in the light of the availability of sufficient personnel to supervise visits 'and any possible hindrance to the investigation'.[17] These last two 'rights' (to a phone call/letter and to receive visits) need not be communicated orally to suspects by custody officers on reception, or indeed at any other time. The only way in which suspects who do not already know of these rights can find them out is by consulting Code C or the written notice. Not surprisingly, few people ask for visits, though a higher proportion request intimation, ranging from 10% to 33% of suspects.[18] Although intimation is formally delayed rarely, informal delay is more common. According to Dixon et al,[19] informal delay in intimation 'may be deliberate, for example, when officers who wish to search premises wait to inform a suspect's family of arrest until they arrive to search his/her house'. Informal delay can also be an unintentional product of the pressures of work, particularly in light of cuts to police budgets and a decade of austerity. The result is that the provisions on intimation, while embodying due process values, are not always fully adhered to. However, since s.56(1) merely provides that intimation should be done 'as soon as is practicable', it is difficult for suspects to demonstrate that the law has been broken. Thus there are very few cases where delay of intimation or refusal to intimate was an issue.[20] Requests for phone calls also frequently appear to be informally delayed or ignored. Brown et al[21] found that custody records noted requests in 7–8% of cases, but they observed requests being made in 10–12% of cases.[22] Further, it is no use telling suspects what rights they have if they do not understand what they are being told. The police often made little or no effort to help suspects understand their rights when PACE was first enacted, and it appears that little had changed 30-plus years later.[23]

Suspects detained under the anti-terrorism legislation[24] have the same rights as other suspects, but the police are allowed to delay the granting of these rights on broader grounds than usual.[25] Nearly half of all suspects held under the Prevention of Terrorism Act 1989 (the previous legislation) requested that someone be informed, and delay was imposed (often for more than 24 hours) in around three quarters of these cases.[26]

At first glance it might seem that whether these rights are granted or not, or whether they are delayed, is peripheral to the big issues—whether suspects are intimidated or not, whether suspects are legally detained or not, and so on. However, they can make a great difference to the *experience* of being in custody. And who knows how many deaths in custody (see section 4.4) would be prevented if suspects were less isolated?

---

[16] Code C, para 5.4.   [17] Code C, Note 5B.   [18] Skinns (2011: 109); Brown et al (1992: 55).

[19] Dixon et al, 'Safeguarding the Rights of Suspects in Police Custody' (1990a) 1 *Policing and Society* 118.

[20] See Mirfield P, *Silence, Confessions and Improperly Obtained Evidence* (Oxford: Clarendon, 1997) p 185 for a discussion of some of these cases.   [21] Brown et al (1992: 55).

[22] Similar findings are reported by Choongh S, *Policing as Social Discipline* (Oxford: Clarendon, 1997) ch 6.

[23] Sanders et al, *Advice and Assistance at Police Stations and the 24 Hour Duty Solicitor Scheme* (London: Lord Chancellor's Department, 1989) ch 4; Choongh (1997: ch 6); and Britton N, 'Race and Policing: A Study of Police Custody' (2000a) 40(4) *British Journal of Criminology* 639 (reporting research showing that some custody officers did not inform black detainees of a scheme established to provide extra advice and support). Unfortunately there has been little recent research.

[24] Terrorism Act 2000; Anti-Terrorism, Crime and Security Act 2001; Prevention of Terrorism Act 2005. See Walker C, *Blackstone's Guide to the Anti-Terrorism Legislation* 3rd edn (Oxford: OUP, 2014) and other references in section 4.3.3.   [25] Walker (2014).

[26] Brown et al (1992). More recent research on terrorist suspects who are held incommunicado could not be found during the updating of this edition.

4.2.3 Vulnerable suspects

Though a capacious, confusing and thus problematic concept,[27] the notion of vulnerable suspects is an important one in PACE Code C, which was significantly revised in July 2018. Children and young people under the age of 18 years are considered vulnerable. So too are those who a police officer has any reason to suspect:

(i) may have difficulty understanding or communicating effectively about the full implications for them of any procedures and processes connected with:
- their arrest and detention; or (as the case may be)
- their voluntary attendance at a police station or their presence elsewhere (see paragraph 3.21), for the purpose of a voluntary interview; and
- the exercise of their rights and entitlements.

(ii) does not appear to understand the significance of what they are told, of questions they are asked or of their replies:

(iii) appears to be particularly prone to:
- becoming confused and unclear about their position;
- providing unreliable, misleading or incriminating information without knowing or wishing to do so;
- accepting or acting on suggestions from others without consciously knowing or wishing to do so; or
- readily agreeing to suggestions or proposals without any protest or question.[28]

Suspects who are identified as vulnerable have special protections, in recognition of their greater welfare needs and susceptibility to coercion or suggestion.[29] The police must inform an AA of their detention and ask that person—usually a parent, relative, guardian, social worker or volunteer—to attend the station.[30] Where there are concerns about mental ill-health, learning disabilities, substance misuse or other vulnerabilities liaison and diversion teams, who are located in police custody, may be contacted to help identify, support and divert vulnerable suspects from the criminal justice process.[31] The police may also contact healthcare practitioners, mostly nurses and paramedics, who are also located in police custody, who can assess the physical and mental well-being of a suspect and can help inform a custody officer's decision about whether someone is fit for detention and/or interview. Custody officers are warned that people who are, or appear, intoxicated or dependent on alcohol or drugs may need clinical attention either because of their intoxication or dependency or because there might be a serious underlying condition.[32] The importance of this is evident when we look at deaths in custody in section 4.4.

Broadly speaking the role of the AA is to safeguard the interests of the detainee and they are expected to take an active role in various parts of the police custody process. More specifically, they have several responsibilities: to see or speak to the detainee in private, though

---

[27] Dehaghani R, *Vulnerability in Police Custody* (Abingdon: Routledge 2019) ch 4; Skinns L, *Police Powers and Citizens' Rights* (Abingdon: Routledge, 2019) ch 7.   [28] Code C, para 1.13d.

[29] It is no accident that in the 'Confait Affair' two of the wrongly convicted youths were under 18 years of age, while the 18-year-old had a mental age of 13: Baxter and Koffman (1983). In more recent years, a large number of 'miscarriage' cases have concerned those with mental health conditions or learning disabilities. The Cardiff 3 is one notorious post-PACE case in which the coerced confession of a mentally vulnerable suspect resulted in three co-defendants serving a total of over 30 years in prison: O'Brien M, *The Death of Justice* (Talybont: Y Lolfa Cyf, 2008). See also section 1.4.   [30] Code C, paras 3.13–3.20.

[31] As of 2016, liaison and diversion teams covered 68% of the population, with plans to reach 75% of the population by April 2018 (NHS England, <https://www.england.nhs.uk/commissioning/health-just/liaison-and-diversion/about/>).   [32] Code C, Note 9C.

unlike legal advisors they do not have legal privilege, meaning that AAs could be required to speak to the police about what a suspect told them; they are to advise, support and assist a suspect for example in understanding and using their rights; to observe and inform senior officers if suspects' rights are breached; assist the vulnerable suspect with communication so that they understand and are understood; protect the rights of vulnerable suspects such as by checking if they understand their rights and providing further information.[33] Interviews with vulnerable suspects cannot take place without an AA except in the most extreme circumstances.[34] Although there is some overlap with the role of a legal advisor (and in the early days of PACE, lawyers were frequently asked to fulfil the dual role) having an AA does not diminish the suspect's separate right to legal advice. However, in practice the police are reluctant to call a lawyer until the AA arrives,[35] even though such a delay is a clear breach of Code C.[36] If an AA's arrival is delayed for an hour or more, for example, to coincide with the police interview, not only does this inhibit their ability to fully support a vulnerable suspect, it also acts as a disincentive to put up with further delay whilst waiting for a lawyer. The police know this, and sometimes exaggerate the likely delay in order to discourage requests for legal advice,[37] although this is, again, prohibited by Code C.[38]

Vulnerable suspects are by no means rare (see also chapter 10). It seems that around one-tenth of all suspects are children, and in some stations the percentage may be higher.[39] Suspects also experience other forms of vulnerability at a higher rate than the general population. In a systematic review of the evidence, it was found that 20% of the suspect population in the sample had psychiatric conditions, 50% had problems with alcohol and drugs and up to 74% had physical health conditions requiring regular medication.[40] These vulnerabilities may also be hard to identify. People with learning disabilities or other educational disadvantages often try to hide these problems, and thus learn to appear confident and capable.[41] Gudjonsson et al found that, in a sample of 156 adult detainees, the police only called AAs in 4% of cases.[42] Yet clinical psychologists in the research team identified

---

[33] Code C, para 1.7A; see also the guidance produced by the National Appropriate Adult Network online at: <https://www.appropriateadult.org.uk/index.php/information/guidance-aa> (accessed 10 July 2019).

[34] However, procedures such as breathalyser tests, where time is of the essence, need not be delayed: *DPP v Evans* [2003] Crim LR 338. See related discussion in relation to legal advice in breathalyser cases, section 4.5.1.

[35] Bevan M, *Children and young people in police custody* (PhD thesis, LSE, 2019) 191–192; Skinns (2011: 175–178); Brown et al (1992: 62).

[36] Para 6.5A states that the appropriate adult may seek legal advice for the young suspect, but since para 6.1 states that 'all detainees' have the right to legal advice, the power of the appropriate adult to seek advice should be interpreted as additional to that of the young suspect, not as an alternative. Delay is only allowed if Annex B applies—in the rare circumstances when this would hinder the investigation.

[37] Sanders A and Bridges L, 'Access to Legal Advice and Police Malpractice' [1990] *Criminal Law Review* 494; Brown et al (1992) pp 31–34; Skinns L, '"Let's Get it Over With": Early Findings on the Factors Affecting Detainees' Access to Custodial Legal Advice' (2009a) 19 *Policing and Society* 58; Skinns L, '"I'm a Detainee; Get Me Out of Here" Predictors of Access to Custodial Legal Advice in Public and Privatized Police Custody Areas in England and Wales' (2009b) 49 *British Journal of Criminology* 399.   [38] Code C, para 6.4.

[39] In the year ending March 2018, there were 65,800 arrests of 10–17 year olds, which represents approximately 10% of the total 700,000 or so arrests in the same time period. Research in the 1990s found this proportion to be higher at around 20%. The absolute numbers of young arrestees has also declined by 78% in the last 10 years. See: YJB, *Youth Justice Statistics 2017/18 England and Wales* (London: HMSO, 2019: 6); Bucke T and Brown D, *In Police Custody: Police Powers and Suspects' Rights Under the Revised Pace Codes of Practice* (Home Office Research Study no 174) (London: Home Office, 1997) p 6.

[40] Rekrut-Lapa T and Lapa A, 'Health Needs of Detainees in Police Custody in England and Wales: Literature Review' (2014) 27 *Journal of Forensic and Legal Medicine* 69–75.

[41] Examples include the 'Tottenham Three' and 'Cardiff Three' cases: see ch 5 for discussion of these cases.

[42] Indeed, the percentage of suspects treated by the police as disordered or handicapped is generally far lower than this: only 2% in the large sample examined by Bucke and Brown (1997) p 7, and even less in the sample examined by Nemitz T and Bean P, 'The Use of the Appropriate Adult Scheme' (1994) 34 *Medicine Science and the Law* 161.

15% of the detainees as vulnerable after an interview of 10–15 minutes, and a further 5% after more extensive tests. This shows that vulnerability can sometimes be confirmed only after fairly extensive professional examination. There is also sometimes an expectation that a vulnerable suspect must 'display the symptoms of his or her condition and must perform his or her vulnerability' before it is recognised and acted on by the police, such as by requesting an AA.[43]

Failures to identify suspects with learning disabilities or mental ill-health not only leads to breaches of Code C and PACE, for example, because of failures to provide an AA, but can also lead to tragedy. Mental ill-health, and the failures to identify it, along with the use of drugs and alcohol and the use of restraint by the police, is a key contributing factor to a death in police custody or following police contact (see later in this chapter).[44] This was tragically illuminated by the case of Mr Sean Rigg, a young black man, whose death in the holding area of Brixton police station in 2008 was pivotal to the first *Independent review of deaths and serious incidents in police custody* by Dame Elish Angiolini in 2017. At the time of death, Mr Rigg was experiencing a mental health crisis connected to his diagnosis of schizophrenia, which went unaddressed by arresting officers, who instead arrested him for various alleged criminal matters, which involved handcuffing him and placing him in a prone position. On arrival at Brixton police station, he was kept in the back of the van for 10 minutes before being brought in a collapsed state to the holding area known as 'the cage'. Though medical attention was sought, he died within an hour of arrival at the police station. His case has prompted significant and ongoing public concern about the intersection of policing, race and mental health (see further section 4.4 and chapter 10).

Limited resources and the pressures of the PACE clock (see section 4.3.2) mean that staff are under pressure to process cases as quickly as possible. For these and other reasons they may decide not to seek an AA for suspects who are perceived to have relatively mild disorders or disabilities. Dehaghani notes for example that, as a result of concerns about potential delays and the additional resources required, an AA was not always sought for suspects seen as having mild depression.[45] This was further enabled by the discretionary powers of the police, so she argues. In the past, custody officers were also found not to routinely request a medical opinion when suspects acted strangely.[46] For example, Palmer reported a custody officer speaking of a suspect who the police put in a paper suit without zips (for fear he would self-harm) yet for whom they did not call a healthcare practitioner or AA because they did not consider him to have a mental health condition.[47] These are clear breaches of the Code. Since then, however, access to healthcare practitioners has become more widespread, with nurses and paramedics being based in most custody facilities for significant periods of the day. Hence, Dehaghani found more recently that, in practice, decisions about whether to seek AAs were sometimes being de facto delegated to healthcare practitioners, even if this went against custody officer's initial intentions. Suspects' wishes about whether to have an AA were also found by Dehaghani to be taken into account by custody officers. Nonetheless, there remains a significant under-identification of need for an AA amongst vulnerable adults, especially when compared to young

---

[43] Dehaghani (2019: 80).
[44] Hannan et al, *Deaths in or following police custody: examination of the cases 1998/09–2008/09* (London: HM Inspectorate of Constabulary, 2011); Lindon G and Roe S, *Deaths in police custody: A review of the international evidence* (London: Home Office, 2017).   [45] Dehaghani (2019: 121–122).
[46] Phillips C and Brown D, *Entry into the Criminal Justice System* (Home Office Research Study no 185) (London: Home Office, 1998) pp 55–56; Nemitz and Bean (1994); Jacobson J, *No One Knows: Police Responses to Suspects with Learning Disabilities and Learning Difficulties* (London: Prison Reform Trust, 2008).
[47] Palmer C, 'Still Vulnerable After All These Years' [1996] *Criminal Law Review* 633.

suspects, most of whom do have one. Bath et al found that though up to 39% of the adult suspect population has either a learning disability or mental health condition, in 2017/18, only 6% of adults were recorded as needing an AA (up from 3% in 2013/14).[48] This under-identification of need can have grave consequences. The *Aspinall* case, where the suspect was a schizophrenic, illustrates this. Doctors considered him fit to be interviewed, whilst confirming his mental illness. He was interviewed without an AA, and gave answers which undermined his credibility at his trial. He was convicted of drugs offences, but won his appeal because the absence of an AA invalidated his interview.[49]

Aside from the aforementioned inadequacies in the identification of suspects' vulnerabilities and their need for AAs, there are also further difficulties with insufficient availability, particularly at night (between 22.00 and 9.00),[50] meaning potentially lengthy delays before an AA arrives. On average, it is reported that a vulnerable adult spends over 4.5 hours in custody prior to the AA's arrival, with some waiting more than 20 hours.[51] As we shall see (see section 4.3.5), a few hours' detention can be highly stressful for even the most 'normal' people, so for vulnerable people this can be very serious indeed. During the Covid-19 pandemic, which is ongoing at the time of writing, it is highly likely that these difficulties with accessing an AA will be further accentuated. Though the Law Society in conjunction with other bodies have recommended that AAs be present for interviews,[52] some AAs refused to enter police custody where social distancing measures were not in place, for example.[53] Also, all visitors to police custody in some forces have been made to wear personal protective equipment (PPE), which, although essential, may hamper communication between AAs and vulnerable suspects.[54]

Under normal circumstances, the quality of AA provision has also been found to be variable raising further questions about how useful their presence is during a police interrogation and at other points in the police custody process (when rights and entitlements are read, during strip searches, when charged etc), if they are present at all. Many AAs misunderstand what is happening, fail to realise how an apparently innocent series of questions and answers can be incriminating, and are just as intimidated as the suspects whilst on 'police territory' and in the face of the powerful role played by the custody officer who also informs them of what they may or may not do.[55] Bucke and Brown[56] report many family members acting as AAs who clearly either did not understand or pay attention to what was happening. This is true also of many professional social workers and nominees from local victim support volunteer groups who the police select precisely because, according to one officer, they are 'on our side—on the side of the victim.'[57] Social workers have dual

---

[48] Bath et al, *There to help: Ensuring provision of appropriate adults for mentally vulnerable adults detained or interviewed by police* (London: NAAN, 2015); Bath C, *There to Help 2: Ensuring provision of appropriate adults for vulnerable adults detained or interviewed by police—An update on progress 2013/14 to 2017/18* (London: NAAN, 2019).

[49] [1999] Crim LR 741. On exclusion of evidence obtained in breach of PACE or the Codes, see ch 12.

[50] Bath et al (2019: 94).

[51] Medford et al, *The Identification of Persons at Risk in Police Custody. The Use of Appropriate Adults by the Metropolitan Police* (London: Jointly published by the Institute of Psychiatry and New Scotland Yard, 2000).

[52] Law Society (2020a) Coronavirus (Covid-19) interview protocol. Online at: <https://www.lawsociety.org.uk/support-services/advice/articles/coronavirus-covid-19-interview-protocol/> (accessed 10 July 2019).

[53] Kempen, K (2020) ICVA update 1/5/20.

[54] See also Essex Police online at: <https://www.essex.police.uk/police-forces/essex-police/areas/essex-police/au/about-us/visitors-to-essex-police-custody-facilities---covid-19/> (accessed 1 May 2020).

[55] Brown et al (1992: 72); Bevan (2019: 200).

[56] Bucke and Brown (1997: 14–15).   [57] Quoted in Nemitz and Bean (1994).

'welfare' and 'control' roles, and since they have to work closely with the police it is difficult for them to act as advocates for suspects when acting as AAs. There is therefore often more of an illusion of protection than the reality. Thus Dixon et al say that some parents:

> are notoriously keen to help the police in obtaining confessions from their children. In one incident a mother promised to 'get my fist round his lug' (which she later did ... much to the approval of the investigating officers).[58]

Bucke and Brown and, more recently, Bevan, report similar findings about the unduly compliant nature of familial AAs, such as the parents who asked the custody officer to give their 'lad the fright of his life'.[59] This partly reflects the contradictory and compendious nature of the role of the AA, which is, inter alia, 'to advise and support suspects', 'to encourage the police to act fairly and respect the rights of the detainee' and 'to facilitate communication'.[60] It may be proper to advise a suspect to remain silent (especially if no lawyer is present) but this cannot be said to facilitate communication. As Bevan also observes, the main aspects of the role—support and advice, respect for detainee rights and the facilitation of communication—require a set of skills unlikely to be found in one person e.g. a parent can reassure a young suspect, but may not be able to advise on due process rights.[61] Hence not only parents, but also professional social workers, are left not understanding their proper role. Many professional social workers were horrified, after taking a training course for AAs, to find that they had previously been failing to intervene in coercive interviews when they were entitled to do so.[62] The police do not help here, often failing to explain to AAs the rudiments of what is *legally* expected of them,[63] despite Code C (para 11.17) saying that they should.[64] A survey of volunteers who act as AAs (who do have some training) found that they intervene in interviews more than professionals and parents, but that they are still insufficiently interventionist.[65]

Clearly at present only a minority of vulnerable (adult) suspects secure the help they need from AAs. However, given the growing routine presence of not only healthcare practitioners but also liaison and diversion teams in police custody, if the latter are given greater involvement in helping to identify vulnerability and determine whether an AA is required, as recommended by Bath,[66] this may help reduce some of the existing difficulties in relation to AA provision for vulnerable adults. Even then, to dichotomise 'vulnerable'

---

[58] Dixon et al (1992: 119).

[59] Bucke and Brown (1997: 14). See also Quinn K and Jackson J, 'Of Rights and Roles: Police Interviews with Young Suspects in Northern Ireland' (2007) 47(2) *British Journal of Criminology* 234 at 245.

[60] Code C, para 11.17. Role conflict is exacerbated by the imposition of a crime prevention role on appropriate adults by the Crime and Disorder Act 1998 (CDA), s.37. See Williams J, 'The CDA: Conflicting Roles for the Appropriate Adult' [2000] *Criminal Law Review* 911. See also Bevan (2019: 204).

[61] Bevan (2019: 205)

[62] Hodgson J, 'Vulnerable Suspects and the Appropriate Adult' [1997] *Criminal Law Review* 785 at 791.

[63] Bucke and Brown (1997: ch 2); Nemitz and Bean (1994). The police 'promote a very passive role for appropriate adults in interview': Quinn and Jackson (2007: 244).

[64] See Brown et al (1992: 72). Also see Palmer (1996); and Littlechild B, 'Reassessing the Role of the "Appropriate Adult" ' [1995] *Criminal Law Review* 540.

[65] Pierpoint H, 'The Performance of Volunteer Appropriate Adults' (2001) 40 *Howard Journal of Crime and Justice* 255. Also see Pierpoint H, 'Reconstructing the Role of the Appropriate Adult in England and Wales' [2006] *Criminology and Criminal Justice* 6, 219; Medford S, Gudjonsson G, and Pearse J, 'The Efficacy of the Appropriate Adult Safeguard during Police Interviewing' 8 *Legal and Criminological Psychology* (2003) 253; Leggett J, Goodman W and Dinani S, 'People with Learning Disabilities' Experiences of being Interviewed by the Police' (2007) 135 *British Journal of Learning Disabilities* 168. The legal pitfalls, and the complex and often contradictory roles, are discussed by Parry L, 'Protecting the Juvenile Suspect: What is the Appropriate Adult Supposed to Do?' [2006] *Child and Family Law Quarterly* 18: 373.

[66] Bath (2019: 8).

and 'normal' people in this way is unrealistic. For when in police detention, most of us would be vulnerable to some extent, but often in unpredictable ways. Moreover, this would not address some of the difficulties with the availability and quality of AAs and the need for better resourcing of most AA schemes.

4.2.4 Police bail

Suspects who have no further action taken against them or who are immediately cautioned (i.e. officially warned) or given a 'penalty notice for disorder' (see chapter 7) are generally released unconditionally from detention. In most other cases, custody officers have to decide whether or not to grant bail, which can either be pre- or post-charge. The bail options available to police officers are discussed in chapter 7, but it is worth also saying here that following the introduction of the Policing and Crime Act 2017 *pre-charge* bail practices have changed significantly. On the one hand, a suspect may be released under investigation (RUI) for an indefinite period and without any conditions placed upon them. On the other hand, the now much lesser used pre-charge police bail involves tighter controls on the police and on suspects subject to it.[67] Suspects can only be placed on pre-charge police bail for 28 days, though this may be extended in complex cases by three months by a superintendent or above and by a further period by magistrates. Suspects may also be subject to certain requirements whilst on pre-charge police bail such as to live at a certain address, avoid contact with certain people or surrender their passport. As such, pre-charge bail processes can be a powerful police tool, where more time is required by the police, especially in the context of austerity and limited investigative resources, and one which can also protect the public, especially victims and witnesses. However, they can also have serious impacts on suspects, particularly where they are not subsequently charged with anything. Concerns about pre-charge bail arrangements have continued since 2017, for example, about the still lengthy time that suspects may spend whilst RUI'd and the sense of uncertainty and stress this creates for them, but also about the harmful effects on victims of the growing number of suspects who are RUI'd without bail conditions.[68] Furthermore, at the time of writing in May 2020, HMICFRS and HMICPSI are due to publish a long-awaited thematic inspection into the practice of RUI. It is hoped that, like the Law Society,[69] they will be recommending the introduction of clearer time limits for the use of RUI and greater guidance on the circumstances in which the use of RUI is appropriate.

Most suspects are more concerned about securing bail (i.e. being released) than they are about being charged.[70] This makes bail and RUI important bargaining counters, particularly in relation to confessions, as we shall see in chapter 5. Legal advisors can make representations about bail to the police, but lawyers rarely remain until this decision is made, particularly under the current climate of austerity and fixed fees as described in chapter 1.[71] Giving the police the power to make bail conditions provides them with a new stack of bargaining chips during the detention period.

---

[67] Law Society (2019c) *Release under investigation: September 2019*. Online at: <https://www.lawsociety.org.uk/policy-campaigns/campaigns/criminal-justice/release-under-investigation/#> (accessed 1 October 2019).
[68] Based on a FOI data requested by a law firm, The Law Society (2019) note that RUIs have massively expanded in use, with more people being RUI'd than bailed, meaning that it is being used as an alternative to police bail. Also, on average suspects spent a greater number of days RUI'd than on police bail in 2017–18. See further section 7.3.2
[69] Law Society (2019).
[70] Sanders et al (1989: 72–73).   [71] See section 4.5.

4.3 Detention without charge

4.3.1 'Helping the police with their inquiries' or 'voluntary attendance'

According to s.29 of PACE, anyone who is at a police station voluntarily (i.e. not there under arrest):

(a) shall be entitled to leave at will unless he is placed under arrest;
(b) shall be informed at once that he is under arrest if a decision is taken by a constable to prevent him leaving at will.

This is at first sight an odd provision for all it is saying is that if someone is not under arrest—that is, not deprived of their liberty—then they are not to be deprived of their liberty. This tautology can only be understood in its historical context.

Before 1964, a suspect normally could not be questioned following arrest. Arrest marked the end of the investigation, and its purpose was to enable the suspect to be brought to court (see section 3.2). The solution for the police who needed extra evidence through questioning was to put people in a situation where they could be interviewed without formally arresting them. Even then, the fiction that the police did not interrogate was still maintained, through the mechanism of the 'voluntary statement' of confession. This might mean detaining someone at their home or another place, or in the police station. The limbo in which such people were placed was known as 'helping the police with their inquiries', generally understood to mean people who were involuntarily detained but not formally arrested. A revision to the Judges Rules in 1964 made it easier for the police to interrogate following arrest but it was still common for suspects to 'help the police with their inquiries'.[72] Section 29 is designed to make it absolutely clear that this limbo is no longer allowed. Taken on its own, s.29 appears to be an inhibitory rule providing more due process for suspects than had existed hitherto. Initially, however, it did little to affect police practices.[73] Now that PACE is long established it seems that the flouting of s.29 is rare.[74] It is likely that this is because the police have come to realise that the 24-hour (or sometimes 36-hour) detention time-limit which applies for most offences is usually more than adequate for their purposes. It is to these time-limits that we turn shortly.

However, it is also worth noting at this juncture that 'helping the police with their inquiries' or 'voluntary attendance' at the police station or 'voluntary police interviews' as they are now known are becoming normalised once again. Though little is known about these practices, suggesting a further area that is ripe for research, the growing use of voluntary attendance/interviews is thought to be one of the reasons why the number of citizens arrested and detained by the police have decreased since a peak in 2008.[75] On the one hand, such a decrease is welcomed, particularly if it means that fewer vulnerable suspects are being held in police cells. On the other hand, though voluntary attenders are permitted access to the same rights and entitlements as those formally arrested and detained in police custody (i.e. to an AA, legal advice etc), there is less oversight of the provision of

---

[72] The historical background is discussed by Dixon D, *Law in Policing* (Oxford: Clarendon, 1997) pp 126–47; Bryan (1997: chs 6–8).

[73] McKenzie et al, 'Helping the Police with their Enquiries' [1990] *Criminal Law Review* 22.

[74] Brown D, *PACE Ten Years On* (Home Office Research Study no 155) (London: Home Office, 1997) pp 68–70.

[75] Home Office statistics show that in the year ending March 2018 there were 698,737 arrests carried out by police in England and Wales, a fall of 8% on the previous year. This is a continuation of the downward trend in the number of arrests in the year ending March 2008, when there were 1,475,266 arrests. *Home Office, Police powers and procedures, England and Wales, year ending 31 March 2018* (London: Home Office, 2018d).

these rights and entitlements, for example, by the custody officer. This is particularly so if 'voluntary' police interviews are not held at the police station and are instead held in citizens' homes, in the back of police cars or at the scene of an alleged offence, as is the case in some police force areas given the growing use of body-worn cameras to interview suspects outside the police station.[76] Lawyers are highly critical of these practices, regarding them as a return to a 'dark age' and a threat to suspects' access to free and independent legal advice.[77] It remains unclear, though, how extensive 'voluntary' at scene interviews using body-worn video are, and how many and which forces are engaging in these practices.

4.3.2 Time limits for detention: non-terrorism cases

PACE originally stated that, for *serious* arrestable offences, involuntary detention could be for up to 36 hours initially, but for 'normal' offences the limit was 24 hours.[78] In an unashamedly crime control measure, the Criminal Justice Act 2003 amended PACE, s.41 to allow involuntary detention for up to 36 hours for *all* arrestable offences of a senior police officer considers it necessary. The concept of an 'arrestable offence' was subsequently eliminated by the Serious Organised Crime and Police Act 2005 (see section 3.3), so the potential 36-hour detention limit now applies to all indictable offences instead.[79] Thus any either way offence (i.e. that can be tried either in the magistrates' court or the Crown court) is now subject to the 36-hour detention provision.

Detention has to be reviewed periodically by a senior officer independent of the investigation. This 'review officer' will be the custody officer if the suspect has been charged but an inspector or more senior officer if not.[80] Detention must be reviewed 'not later than six hours after the detention was first authorised'.[81] The second review must be 'not later than nine hours after the first' and subsequent reviews must be at intervals of not more than 12 hours.[82] To extend detention beyond 24 hours (in the case of indictable offences) the review must be conducted by an officer of superintendent rank or above. Reviews may be postponed but only under exceptional circumstances and for as short a time as is practicable. The reviewing officer may only authorise continued detention if the original purpose of detention still holds good and if the investigation is being conducted 'diligently and expeditiously'.[83] The reviewing officer must seek and take note of any representations against continued detention which the suspect may make.[84] In reality, though:

> the review procedure tends to be routinised and insubstantial, at least in its early stages; the opportunity to make representations can often consist merely of an inspector asking the suspect, 'All right mate?' through the hatch in the cell door (Dixon et al 1990: 130–1).

Indeed, reviews may even take place over the telephone or via a video link known as a 'live link'.[85] Rather than this being exceptional, as was originally doubtless intended, Dixon et al

---

[76] Ng W and Skinns L (2021) 'A Formal Interview Tool in an Informal Setting? An Exploratory Study of the Use of Body-Worn Video at the Scene of an Alleged Crime', *Criminal Law Review,* June.

[77] Murray R, 'Police Body Camera Interviews are Taking us Back to a Dark Age' (online at: <https://mintedlaw.wordpress.com/2018/03/23/police-body-camera-Interviews-are-Taking-us-Back-to-a-Dark-Age/> (accessed 1 October 2019)).

[78] PACE, ss.41(1) and 42(1).   [79] Schedule 7, para 43(7).   [80] PACE, s.40(1).
[81] PACE, s.40(3)(a).   [82] PACE, s.40(3)(b)–(c); Code C, para 15.2.   [83] PACE, s.42(1)(c).
[84] PACE, s.40(12)–(14). It is not clear how wide are the purposes of reviews. See Cape E, 'Detention Without Charge: What Does "Sufficient Evidence To Charge" Mean?' [1999] *Criminal Law Review* 874.
[85] PACE, s.40 (as amended by CJA 2003) and Code C, paras 15.3C and 15.9–15.11. However, if video-conferencing facilities are both available and a practical option at the relevant time, they must be used instead: Code C, para 5.9B and Note 15G. We present here a simplified account of the rules on time limits and reviews, which are extremely complicated. See Ozin and Norton (2019) ch 4.

(1992: 131) found use of the telephone to be common. Moreover, custody record entries often failed to note this use of the telephone, giving the impression that the review was carried out in person. Frequently, Dixon et al say, 'the inspector's role is purely presentational'. Though decisions to extend detention beyond 24 hours used to have to be made *in person* by a superintendent (Code C, Note 15F), since the Policing and Crime Act 2017, these are permitted via live link.[86] In previous editions of this book concern was expressed about such changes which were seen as watering down suspects' rights. These changes also undermine the possibility of suspects, particularly vulnerable ones, fully participating in decisions taken about them and increase the chances of suspects' rights being subordinated to the convenience of senior officers and the drive for operational efficiency. This 2017 change represents yet another step away from the due process approach.

If the police wish to continue the detention beyond 36 hours (in the case of indictable offences) this is possible, up to a maximum of a further 60 hours.[87] The same criteria apply as above, but authorisation must be by an officer of the rank of superintendent or above, and the police must apply to a magistrates' court for a 'warrant of further detention'.[88] As with extension of detention from 24 to up to 36 hours, this decision may be taken via a video link.[89] This application must generally be made before the 36-hour period has expired but, in exceptional circumstances, there is some leeway. The criteria on which magistrates decide whether or not to grant such a warrant are broadly similar to the criteria which the superintendent must apply under s.42 in deciding whether to authorise continued detention in the first place. If the police still wish to detain a suspect without charge after the period of further detention has expired, they may apply to a magistrate again for an extension of the warrant for further detention. Such an extension may be granted by a magistrate under s.44 as long as that extension neither exceeds 36 hours nor ends later than 96 hours after the initial 'relevant time'.[90] This means that the police may apply for, and secure, two warrants of further detention following the initial 36-hour detention. But 96 hours is the overall maximum permissible length of detention without charge.

We do not know the total number of detentions beyond 24 hours. However, data is available on those detained beyond 24 hours who are subsequently *released without charge*. Table 4.1 shows that over 2,800 detainees were detained for 24–36 hours in 2017/18 and then released without charge. Warrants of further detention are now sought in over 300 cases each year, and are almost always granted. This is to be expected, since the magistrates apply the same criteria as the police and on the basis of information which the police provide. While the suspect will usually be legally represented, there are few grounds on which defence arguments can be made for release. For instance, if there is little evidence against a

Table 4.1 Number of detainees held for more than 24 hours

	Released with no charge		Warrants of further detention (over 36 hours)		
	24–36 hours	Over 36 hours	Applications	Refused	% charged
2003-4	527	94	304	0	69%
2005-6	2350	113	525	10	73%
2007-8	4079	165	630	26	73%
2017-18	2,831	217	354	6	63%

Source: Povey and Smith, Police Powers and Procedures, England and Wales 2007–8 and 2017-18 (Home Office Statistical Bulletin, London: Home Office)

[86] Code C, paras 15.11A and 15.11B [87] PACE, ss.42–43. [88] PACE, s.43.
[89] PACE, Code C, para 15.11C. [90] PACE, s.44(3).

suspect, this would scarcely ever justify release since the point of the extended detention is precisely to secure more evidence. Just under two thirds to three quarters of these suspects are eventually charged.

The fact that detention beyond 24 hours is relatively infrequent, making up a small proportion of the 671,126 people who were detained in England and Wales in 2018/19, does not necessarily mean that the safeguards are adequate. The police usually have no reason to detain once they consider that they have obtained full information from the suspect concerning the alleged offence. To detain any further would be inefficient. Occasionally, though, the police may wish to prolong detention, regardless of evidential or other legal considerations (as where they are seeking information on other suspects). The detention provisions, and the way in which legal duties are carried out by senior police officers, gives them the scope to do almost as they see fit in those few cases of such importance to them. Nonetheless, although Art 5(3) of the ECHR provides that suspects in detention must be brought before a court 'promptly', detention for further investigation has been held not to violate the ECHR when the grounds for arrest are reasonable and when there is recourse after a reasonable period (as under PACE) to judicial oversight.[91]

Suspects must be released when either the period of detention expires or when detention is no longer necessary because the original reason for detention no longer applies. Release is either unconditional, on bail or under investigation to return to the police station pending further inquiries, or (having been charged) on bail to appear in court. The only circumstances in which the suspect would not be released would be if he or she was charged and kept in custody (i.e. denied bail) pending the earliest available court hearing.[92] The existence of virtual courts—i.e. video links between police custody blocks and magistrates' courts—in a number of police force areas mean that increasingly these hearings take place at the police station, with those remanded into prison custody by magistrates being held sometimes for long periods in the police station awaiting transport to prison, particularly at weekends. Recent research has also shown that such video-enabled court appearances mean that defendants are less likely to have a legal advisor present, the importance of which is discussed in section 4.5, and the quality of the hearings can also sometimes be poor due to problems with the IT, Internet and positioning of the cameras etc.[93] These issues were likely to have been more acute during the Covid-19 pandemic, when virtual courts became the only available option for these initial magistrates' court hearings.[94] Suspects who are released because the time limit has been reached cannot be rearrested without warrant for the same offence unless new evidence is uncovered.[95]

When suspects are released on bail or under investigation to return to the police station pending further inquiries the police are entitled to detain again, 're-starting the clock' where it had previously been 'stopped', but only if those inquiries produced more evidence (PACE, s.34(2)). One of the purposes of this part of PACE was to shorten the length of detention, in the interests both of suspects and police efficiency. Because there were no proper records prior to PACE it is difficult to know whether PACE has succeeded in this objective or not. Phillips and Brown (1998: 109–11) found, in the 1990s that, on average, suspects were held for 6 hours and 40 minutes, but that increased to nearly 9 hours and

---

[91] *Brogan v UK* (1988) 11 EHRR 117.

[92] Or whilst advice is being sought on charging: see sections 4.3.4 and 7.3.2. Police bail is discussed in section 4.2.4.

[93] Fielding N, Braun S and Hieke G, *Video Enabled Justice Evaluation* (2020) online at: <http://spccweb.thco.co.uk/our-priorities/access-to-justice/video-enabled-justice-vej/video-enabled-justice-programme-university-of-surrey-independent-evaluation/> (accessed 5 May 2020).

[94] Transform Justice *Can we access video enabled justice?* (2020) online at: <http://www.transformjustice.org.uk/can-we-access-video-enabled-justice/> (accessed 5 May 2020).

[95] PACE, s.41(9).

18 minutes on average in 2009 and to over 12 hours and 50 minutes in 2017.[96] Detention is, on average, increased when an AA or lawyer is sought, for example. This may be due to delays with these practitioners being identified and with them arriving at the police station, though lawyers are obliged by their legal aid contracts to make first contact within 45 minutes of being notified that the person has requested legal advice. However, there can also be delays with the police investigation, with the police then seeking to coordinate the arrival of other practitioners to suit when they are ready to interview the suspect.[97] Indeed, these difficulties may have been accentuated as a result of the reorganisation of police investigation processes which have meant that police interviews are no longer carried out by the arresting officers, rather by officers from specialist investigative teams who do not work round the clock.[98]

4.3.3 Time limits for detention: terrorist cases

Under the Prevention of Terrorism Act 1989 (PTA) the police used to be able to detain suspected terrorists for up to 48 hours on their own authority (with periodic reviews by senior officers); and, with the permission of the Secretary of State, for a further five days. The Terrorism Act 2000, which replaced the PTA, extended the period to 14 days, but only after judicial (not mere Ministerial) approval.[99] In the wake of bombings and attempted bombings in London on 7 and 21 July 2005, the government brought forward in October 2005 proposals for the law to be amended again to allow a detention period of three months. The government was defeated on these proposals but was still able to effect (through s.23 of the Terrorism Act 2006) a doubling of the detention period permissible to 28 days.

The Anti-Terrorism, Crime and Security Act 2001 (ATCSA), Part 4 which allowed indefinite detention of foreign persons denied asylum who were suspected international terrorists, was even more controversial. With limited judicial oversight, and no time limit on detention, these provisions, like those of the preceding less draconian PTA, required derogation from the European Convention on Human Rights. Derogation was, however, held to be disproportionate to the threat of terrorism and discriminatory, primarily because there is no good reason to treat foreign nationals and citizens of the UK so differently.[100] The irrelevance of nationality was evident from the July bombings and attempts,

---

[96] In a study of 24,992 custody records in 44 police stations Kemp et al (2012) found the average length of detention in 2009 to be 9 hours and 18 minutes, whilst in a smaller study of 871 custody records in 2 police stations Skinns (2010) found the average length of detention in 2007 to be 9 hours and 55 minutes. More recently, Kemp (2020) found the average length of detention to be 12 hours and 50 minutes, though this was as high as an average of 17 hours and 46 minutes in one police force area (Kemp V, 'Authorising and Reviewing Detention: PACE Safeguards in a Digital Age' (2020) *Criminal Law Review* 569–584; Kemp et al, 'Whose Time is it Anyway? Factors Associated with Duration in Police Custody' (2012) 10 *Criminal Law Review* 736–752; Skinns L, '"Stop the Clock": Predictors of Detention without Charge in Police Custody Areas' (2010) 10(3) *Criminology and Criminal Justice* 303–320.

[97] Skinns (2010).   [98] Kemp (2020).

[99] Terrorism Act 2000, s.41 and Sch 8 originally allowed a 7 day period only. It was doubled to 14 days by the Criminal Justice Act 2003, s.306. The judicial review provision, after 48 hours of police detention, is similar to PACE provisions for further detention, complying with the ECHR—by contrast with the need to derogate from the ECHR (which was held to be lawful in *Brannigan and McBride v UK* (1993) 17 EHRR 539) when the PTA was in force.

[100] *A (FC) v Home Secretary* [2004] UKHL 56. See Hickman T, 'Between Human Rights and the Rule of Law: Indefinite Detention and the Derogation Model of Constitutionalism' (2005) 68(4) *Modern Law Review* 655 and the other articles in this special issue. See also Fenwick H, 'The Anti-Terrorism, Crime and Security Act 2001: A Proportionate Response to September 11?' (2002) 65(5) *Modern Law Review* 724.

at least some of which were carried out by British citizens.[101] The Prevention of Terrorism Act (PTA) 2005 (as amended and extended by the Counter-Terrorism Act 2008) has now replaced this part of ATCSA, but is arguably even more crime control-oriented.

ATCSA established 'special advocates' to represent the interests of detainees but who were prevented from communicating to 'their clients' much of the evidence against them (evidence which, in the opinion of the Secretary of State would endanger national security). Two of these advocates resigned in 2005. They felt that effective representation was impossible, as their clients could not challenge the evidence against them as they were not able to tell them what it was. The PTA 2005 retained special advocates, replaced indefinite detention in custody with 'control orders', and made these measures applicable to UK citizens as well as foreign nationals. 'Control orders' were a form of semi-house arrest: individuals were subject to curfews; they had to report regularly (e.g. twice a day) to the police; and their movements away from their homes, who they saw or spoke to, and their other communications, were restricted and subject to electronic monitoring. The specific conditions were tailored to each individual. Breach of these orders was a criminal offence, punishable by up to five years imprisonment. Orders could be made except by, or with the permission of, the courts, but the standard of proof required of the state was low. The legislation recognised that some of these orders would be so draconian that they would be incompatible with ECHR, Art 5, and so provision was made for 'derogating' as well as 'non-derogating' control orders. The former could last only six months, while the latter could be for 12 months, but both types were renewable on application to the courts. Prior to the making of a control order, suspects were detained by the police for up to 48 hours (renewable, on application to the courts, for another 48 hours). Whilst in use control orders rarely led to prosecutions and they meant that those subject to them sometimes spent two or three years under semi-house arrest.[102] As we shall see, the experience of long periods of detention, including house arrest, can be traumatic, and the small numbers involved should not blind us to the cruelty of this legislation.

At the time, there were two human rights objections: (1) They were seen as a deprivation of liberty (Art 5). In 2007 the House of Lords ruled that control orders do not, in general, infringe Art 5,[103] but the particular conditions in one case, where the detainee was made to live in a flat that was not his home, did do so as he suffered virtual solitary confinement for the greater part of the day;[104] (2) That withholding the evidence on which the state's case is based, despite the special advocate system, violated the Art 6 right to fair trial. In 2009 the House of Lords ruled that Art 6 was not necessarily violated if some evidence was withheld, but only if the detainee was given insufficient information to be able to challenge it.[105] Accordingly, all the cases in question were sent back to the lower courts to be dealt with on a case-by-case basis. The first result of this was the revocation of AN's control order.[106] Thus while this judgment did not sweep away the special advocate system, much

---

[101] See, e.g., *The Guardian*, 25 August 2005.
[102] See further Campbell D, 'The Threat of Terror and the Plausibility of Positivism' [2009] *Public Law* 501; Bates E, 'Anti-terrorism Control Orders: Liberty and Security Still in the Balance' (2009) 29 *Legal Studies* 99 at 123.   [103] *Secretary of State for the Home Department v JJ* [2007] UKHL 45.
[104] *Secretary of State for the Home Department v MB and AF* [2007] UKHL 46; E [2007] UKHL 47. Discussed by Bates (2009) and Ewing K and Tham J-C 'The Continuing Futility of the Human Rights Act' [2008] *Public Law* 668.
[105] *Secretary of State for the Home Department v N and others* [2009] UKHL 28. The House regarded itself as bound by a decision of the Grand Chamber of the ECtHR in *A v United Kingdom* [2009] ECHR 301. It was clear that several of the judges would rather have found in the government's favour. By contrast, Sedley's dissenting judgment in the Court of Appeal ([2009] 2 WLR 423 paras 107–121) makes a strong case in principle against the use of secret evidence.
[106] *Secretary of State for the Home Department v AN* [2009] EWCC 1966 (Admin).

less control orders themselves, the continued existence started to be in doubt.[107] As the independent reviewer of the operation of the legislation acknowledged, while all the control orders sought appeared justified from the written evidence, in some cases substantial doubts were raised in court hearings.[108]

But the battle against control orders was still far from won at this point in time. The 'reasonable suspicion' threshold required to secure such an order was far lower than that needed to prosecute, and so it remained difficult to challenge: indeed, on 31 July 2009 the government issued a new control order against AN, making a mockery of the court revocation of his original one.[109] Counter-terrorism measures like this were termed 'laws against law' because 'they are the antithesis of criminal justice due process'.[110] They were not proportionate responses to crime but rather devices which focused on 'pre-crime', a term that captures the key problematic of the counter-terrorism legal regime. Pre-crime suggests a crime may be committed, while *simultaneously* evoking 'the crime that hasn't happened.'[111] A time limit that required the end of the order or a prosecution would offer some hope of resolution.[112]

When the Coalition government came to power in 2010 they ordered a review of terrorism laws and policies put in place by the previous Labour government. As a result, control orders were scrapped and replaced with 'Terrorism, prevention and investigation measures' (TPIMs) under the Terrorism Prevention and Investigation Measures Act 2011, with these measures being enhanced by the Counter Terrorism and Security Act in 2015. Compared to control orders, TPIMs allow for briefer periods of house arrest (it is set at a maximum of two years though this can be extended if another TPIM is successful applied for). Originally, they did not allow for forced relocation, but this changed in 2015. The lengthier house detention requirements under control orders were relaxed, becoming an overnight residence requirement. TPIMs also include fewer restrictions on a suspect's movement including electronic tagging, and also on their communication and property. Travel abroad is prevented without permission of the Secretary of State.[113] However, scholars and campaigners have been 'unimpressed' with these new measures, describing them as a 'control order lite'.[114] Therefore, many of the concerns raised above about control orders still apply, even though, like control orders, these new measures have been little used.

The numbers detained under the anti-terrorism legislation has varied from year to year, from 34 to over 200. These variations reflect frequent political changes, originally concerning Northern Ireland and, since the '9/11' attacks on the Pentagon and World Trade Center

---

[107] In the first control order challenge following this judgment, the government revoked the order as it was unwilling to disclose the intelligence evidence that had hitherto been withheld (*The Guardian*, 8 September 2009).

[108] Carlisle A, *Fourth Report of the Independent reviewer pursuant to Section 14 of the PTA 2005* (London: SO, 2009).   [109] *Liberty* Press Release 31 July 2009.

[110] McCulloch J and Pickering S (2009) 'Pre-Crime and Counter-Terrorism: Imagining Future Crime in the 'War on Terror' 49 *British Journal of Criminology* 628 at 640. Also see Walker C, 'The treatment of foreign terror suspects' (2007) 70 *Modern Law Review* 427.   [111] McCulloch and Pickering (2009: 641).

[112] For other examples of the government imposing 'measures that operate on the edge of human rights guarantees', see Forster S, 'Control Orders: Borders to the Freedom of Movement or Moving the Borders of Freedom?' in Wade M and Maljevic A (eds), *A War on Terror? The European Stance on a New Threat, Changing Laws and Human Rights Implications* (New York: Springer, 2009).

[113] Information about the features are available online at: <https://www.gov.uk/government/collections/terrorism-prevention-and-investigation-measures-act> (accessed 27 August 2019).

[114] Walker C and Horne A, 'The Terrorism Prevention and Investigations Measures Act 2011: One Thing But Not Much the Other?' (2012) 6 *Criminal Law Review* 421–438; Liberty online at: <https://www.libertyhumanrights.org.uk/human-rights/countering-terrorism/tpims> (accessed 27 August 2019).

in 2001, terrorist activity carried out by al-Qaeda and similar groups. The trend is for the numbers to rise over time. In 1996, for example, there were 84 detentions (not including 'examinations' of people entering or leaving Great Britain or Northern Ireland). Only two of these people were charged under the PTA, and 15 were charged with offences under other legislation. Twenty-three of the 84 had their detention extended beyond 48 hours, of whom 10 were released without charge.[115] Since 2002/3 on average there have been 227 terrorism arrests per year, with a similar proportion charged. One-third are detained for two days or more, but several have been detained for the maximum of 28 days, not all of whom were charged.[116]

There is a striking parallel between detention under anti-terrorism legislation and stop-search: both provisions allow such a wide 'sweep' that only a minority of people subjected to these powers are ever charged (let alone convicted) with offences connected with the reason for initial suspicion. A further small minority are charged with unrelated offences. But most are released unconditionally, on classic crime control lines. In one case a man was held for a week, yet was questioned for a total of just 4 hours, on matters not apparently related to terrorism.[117] When the risk to be averted is as great as a terrorist atrocity many believe that this curtailment of freedom is necessary in terms of the core value of justice (particularly when the 'many' cannot conceive of themselves as ever being subjected to terrorism-related powers). A question that might, however, give 'the many' pause to think is whether the draconian use of arrest and detention powers against certain prime suspects (previously the Irish, now young, male Muslims) increases the sense of alienation and bitterness amongst the communities to which they belong, thereby undermining the core value of democracy. While this may or may not create new terrorists, it certainly makes it less likely that these communities will identify with British security policy and actively co-operate with the police in terrorism investigations.[118]

4.3.4 The purpose of detention

Now that we have examined the *mechanisms* for authorising and reviewing detention, we need to examine the *criteria* used to decide whether or not detention should be authorised or continued. Under s.37 of PACE:

(1) The custody officer ... shall determine whether he has before him sufficient evidence to charge that person with the offence for which he was arrested and may detain him at the police station for such period as is necessary to enable him to do so.

(2) If the custody officer determines that he does not have such evidence before him, the person arrested shall be released:

   (a) without bail unless the pre-conditions for bail are satisfied, or

   (b) on bail if those pre-conditions are satisfied,

(3) If the custody officer has reasonable grounds for believing that the person's detention without being charged is necessary to secure or preserve evidence relating to an offence for which the person is under arrest or to obtain such evidence by questioning the person, he may authorise the person arrested to be kept in police detention.

---

[115] Home Office, *Statistics on the Operation of Prevention of Terrorism Legislation* (Statistical Bulletin, 4/97) (London: Home Office, 1997b).

[116] Home Office, *Statistics on Terrorism Arrests and Outcomes, 2001–8* (Statistical Bulletin 04/09) (London: Home Office, 2009a). See also section 3.3.3 above.   [117] *The Guardian*, February 8 2007.

[118] See further Mythen et al, '"I'm a Muslim, but I'm not a Terrorist": Victimization, Risky Identities and the Performance of Safety' (2009) 49 *British Journal of Criminology* 736. See also ch 10.

These provisions broadly follow the Philips Commission's recommendations and embody its 'necessity principle'. We saw in the chapter on arrest that the Philips Commission believed that many suspects who were arrested and charged could be reported and summonsed instead. It wished to ensure that arrests which led to detention would only be made when necessary. At least half of all formally arrested suspects are detained under s.37 for questioning.[119] In these cases, if the arrests were on reasonable grounds and there existed sufficient evidence to prosecute, arrest will be lawful but pre-charge detention following the arrest would be unlawful. This is because s.37 requires the custody officer to charge and then either release or detain (pending a court appearance) any suspect brought into the station against whom there is already sufficient evidence to prosecute. But custody officers are rarely in a position to determine whether there is such evidence unless an arresting officer wishes them to know it, and it is not clear what duties custody officers have to seek to discover it.[120]

In practice, custody officers seem to act on the assumption that a determination of whether there is sufficient evidence to charge cannot be made until after questioning has taken place. The law envisages, however, that custody officers must make their determination as soon as the arrestee comes to the head of the queue in front of the custody desk. The obvious solution to this dilemma is to couple a determination that there is insufficient evidence to charge with a decision under s.37(2) that there are reasonable grounds for believing that detention without charge is 'necessary' in order to obtain evidence by questioning. But what does 'necessary' in this statutory context mean?

The then Home Secretary, Douglas Hurd, said in Parliament in 1984, that the question is whether 'this detention was necessary—not desirable, convenient or a good idea but necessary.'[121] A reasonable interpretation of a convenient or desirable detention would be one that was convenient in the sense that it increased the probability of confession and/or was the most cost-effective way of carrying out enquiries. A reasonable interpretation of a necessary detention would be one where there was no other practicable way of gathering, securing or preserving evidence in relation to the offence in question. If the latter interpretation was adopted by custody officers then there should be proportionately few authorisations of detention. A determination that there was insufficient evidence to charge would ordinarily be coupled with a decision that such evidence could be obtained in ways that did not require the detention of the arrestee. The presumption in s.37(2) would then apply, and the custody officer would then be obliged to release the arrestee either on bail or unconditionally.

The scenario envisaged here—of large numbers of perfectly lawful arrests being rejected by custody officers refusing to authorise detention—is not a likely scenario, nor does it correspond with reality. Research has established that virtually all arrested suspects are detained. For example, Phillips and Brown (1998: 49) found that there was only one case (out of 4,246) where a custody officer did not authorise a suspect's detention.[122]

---

[119] Brown et al (1992: 90). Skinns (2011: 120–5) also found that 66% of suspects in her study of two police custody areas were interviewed at least once. Moreover, at the first and second detention review, the main reason given for continuing someone's detention was to interview them. However, as noted in section 4.3.1, 'voluntary' interviews are becoming increasingly commonplace including at the scenes of alleged offences.

[120] Cape (1999). Officers may withhold knowledge that there is sufficient evidence to charge because they may have a variety of reasons for wanting to question suspects (see section 5.1). Although the CJA 2003 transfers the decision to prosecute from the police to the CPS (discussed in ch 7), this does not significantly change this process or the decision-making criteria. However, custody officers are now entitled to detain suspects after determining that they have sufficient evidence if they have good reason to seek charging advice from the CPS: PACE, s.37 (7) as amended by Police and Justice Act 2006, s.11.

[121] HC Official Report, SC E, 16 February 1984, col 1229.

[122] Dehaghani R, 'Automatic authorisation: An Exploration of the Decision to Detain in Police Custody' (2017) 3 *Criminal Law Review* 187–202.

One custody officer interviewed by McConville et al, when pressed on whether he would ever refuse to authorise detention, replied: 'Probably not in practice, no'.[123] Another said:

> Often the bloke's remonstrating saying 'Not me, it wasn't me. I haven't done it, you've got the wrong man', but of course I have to take the policeman's word, so I accept him on what the policeman tells me.

In the past, most custody officers simply wrote out the words of s.37—some even asked for a rubber stamp with these words already on it[124]—and so 'reception into custody was an essentially routinised process'.[125] More recent research has painted a broadly similar picture. Kemp found that, in 2017, 32 police forces authorised detention in over 99 per cent of cases. Dehaghani observed that, sometimes due to the pressures of large volumes of detainees or too limited numbers of staff, and, other times, due to the loyalty of custody staff to arresting officers or the pressures placed on them by managers, custody officers in two sites routinely authorised suspects' detention on arrival into custody. These officers, however, were more circumspect in interview in her research and did note factors that would theoretically cause them *not* to authorise someone's detention, such as youthfulness linked to campaigning work about the overnight detention of children, as well as related changes to police policies. Other research has also shown that though the legal authority for authorising someone's detention rests with the custody officer, this has been eroded by the growing role played by civilian detention officers, which has expanded to include the 'booking-in' of suspects, with custody officers sometimes only cursorily checking the decision to authorise detention.[126] Thus the overall picture is that, as was the case in the 1990s, the decision to detain someone is not subject to a robust and independent check and, contrary to s.37, custody staff tend to routinely authorise detention.

In *DPP v L* the Divisional Court accepted this to the extent of saying that custody officers need not inquire into the lawfulness of an arrest.[127] Here the arrest was unlawful because the suspect had not been informed of the reason for the arrest. The Divisional Court said that this did not invalidate her detention, because, *it assumed*, in the absence of evidence to the contrary, that the custody officer gave her the reason when he 'booked her in'. Obviously the Divisional Court is unaware of the research which shows that custody officers so routinise the detention process that this is not a reasonable assumption to make. Also, in *Al-Fayed v Commissioner of the Police of the Metropolis*,[128] which endorsed the decision in *DPP v L*, suspects who attended the police station voluntarily to undergo questioning were immediately arrested and detained under s.37. The Court of Appeal held that there was no reason to think that the custody officer did not have reasonable grounds for believing that detention was necessary. Similarly in *Richardson v Chief Constable of West Midlands Police*,[129] even though the claimant's arrest following a voluntary interview was considered unlawful, the courts seemed unwilling to interfere with the custody officer's decision to authorise the claimant's detention. They saw the custody officer's decision as separate from that of the arresting officer, stating that it is the custody officer's role to decide whether detention is necessary and not whether the arrest was necessary. As such, it was concluded that when authorising detention, the custody officer is not there to 'cure' any defect in the arrest. The decision in *Richardson* was also endorsed in *Hanningfield v Chief Constable of Essex* where it was held that 'the lawfulness of the custody officer's acts

---

[123] McConville et al (1991: 44).   [124] McKenzie et al (1990: 24).
[125] Dixon et al (1990a: 130). See also Phillips and Brown (1998: 49).   [126] Skinns (2011: 140).
[127] [1999] Crim LR 752, discussed in section 3.5. The same position was adopted by the Court of Appeal in *Clarke v Chief Constable of North Wales Police* (Lawtel 5 April 2000; *The Independent*, 22 May 2000).
[128] *Al-Fayed v Commissioner of the Police of the Metropolis* [2004] EWCA Civ 1579.
[129] *Richardson v Chief Constable of West Midlands Police* [2011] EWHC 733 (QB).

must be judged in the light of his knowledge at the time. He may or may not know the same facts as his colleague(s) who carried out the earlier arrest.'[130] Together these cases show the reluctance of the courts to challenge the decision not to authorise someone's detention. The authorisation of detention by custody officers is permitted, even when the reasons for someone's arrest are unlawful and irrespective of whether custody officers have enquired into these reasons for arrest. Moreover, the courts have encouraged the view that the decision to authorise detention should not be seen as a cure for improper decisions about the necessity of arrest, in large part due to the supposed independence of the custody officer role. Yet, paradoxically, the courts are also content for custody officers to base their decisions about the authorisation of detention on the material facts in front of them on booking-in, even though these will invariably have been provided to them by the arresting officers.

We have seen that the function and place of arrest in relation to investigation has changed over time: whereas at one time arrests came at the end of an investigation and were the inevitable prelude to prosecution, arrest has gradually moved nearer to the beginning of the investigation. Arrest can be made on the basis of a bare reasonable suspicion, and it often is. Since that will not suffice to prosecute, the law now envisages that the police will frequently need to get more evidence in order to prosecute.[131] This development occurred gradually and along with this, of course, came the limbo of 'helping the police with their inquiries'. Section 37 of PACE formalises the process by recognising that suspects will be detained without charge following arrest when there is insufficient evidence to prosecute and that the main purpose of this detention is to secure that evidence.

This endorses the decision in *Holgate-Mohammed v Duke*[132] where the House of Lords ruled that the greater likelihood of confession if a suspect was held at a police station was a legitimate reason for detention. This decision is entirely consistent with the crime control model. It is, however, entirely inconsistent with the supposed due process presumption in s.37 against detention. This is a bad bargain as the police could clear up crime in ways less costly to citizens and their freedom. Securing evidence through custodial questioning is rarely necessary, but it is considerably more convenient for the police than securing evidence in most other ways. As investigation by questioning is envisaged in PACE and its Codes as usually taking place during detention (see chapter 5), the authorisation of detention must be the norm.

Moreover, there is little to prevent pre-charge detention for questioning taking place even in cases where there is already sufficient evidence to charge (as there was in 61% of cases in one study: Phillips and Brown 1998). Arresting officers usually want to strengthen their cases against suspects regardless of whether there already exists sufficient evidence to charge or not. In practice, they know that a recorded confession from the arrestee will make the case watertight and that to get such evidence they have to question the arrestee in custody prior to charge. As we will see in chapter 5, they may also have other reasons for wanting to detain suspects for questioning, such as general intelligence-gathering or the imposition of authority.[133] By not telling custody officers the full extent of the evidence already obtained against the suspect, it is easy for arresting officers to secure pre-charge detention in all cases.

---

[130] *Hanningfield* [2013] EWHC 243 (QB); [2013] 1 WLR 3632 at [32].
[131] This is in fact the reality: McConville M, *Corroboration and Confessions* (Royal Commission on Criminal Justice Research Study no 13) (London: HMSO, 1993).
[132] *Holgate-Mohammed v Duke* [1984] AC 437.
[133] Note also that other types of evidence are often secured from suspects as a result of their detention: see ch 6.

The presumption against detention in s.37 is thus entirely presentational since it goes against the crime control grain of the rest of the law and practice in this area. It seems then that—rather than the police carrying out the law as made by Parliament—Parliament makes laws aimed at legitimising existing police practice. What was once part of a judicial process (arrest followed by the prosecution decision) is now part of an Executive process. Not only does this mean that the police make initial decisions relating to detention (as we have seen, up to 36 hours without judicial authority) but in nearly half of all cases this detention is not followed by any judicial proceedings (see chapter 7). TPIMs take matters one stage further, as this is detention without charge primarily as a means of incapacitating people against whom there is insufficient evidence to prosecute. This is the slippery slope towards an authoritarian state which prioritises risk management over all other considerations.

4.3.5 The experience of detention

The average (non-terrorist) detention period of around 12–13 hours appears not to be excessive. But what do those hours feel like? We all know the difference between three hours in a darkened cinema and only one in a tedious lecture. Imagine a period 13 times as long as the latter, with fear, uncertainty and anticipation thrown in, and the worry that one might be in the cells overnight. The fact that the length of detention is in the hands of the police leads suspects to believe that the police 'can do anything they want. They can keep you in overnight if they want'.[134]

Police control is asserted from the moment staff begin the 'booking in' procedure. Suspects are immediately deprived of autonomy, and the police demand deference and compliance with police processes such as risk assessments. Those who do not provide it may be laughed at,[135] or in some instances, forcibly removed to the cells, where they may have their clothes removed by force and be made to wear 'rip-proof' police issue paper suits. For example, in police custody inspections conducted by Her Majesty's Inspectorate of Constabularies, Fire and Rescue (HMICFRS) in 2016 and 2017, concern was expressed about the over-use of paper suits, particularly when force was also used to remove suspects' clothing and when these suspects were also left naked or partially clothed in their cells. In the report on Lancashire Constabulary, for example, they say:

> We found a small number of very concerning cases of a lack of regard for detainees' dignity. For example, … a male detainee was verbally insulted by a sergeant and left naked in his cell with no replacement clothing, and male officers were involved in the forcible removal of clothing from a female detainee who was left naked in her cell for almost three hours.[136]

This highlights some of the indignities that may arise in police custody, rooted in the 'total power' of the police and in the lack of autonomy afforded to detainees as a result. As one of Choongh's detainee interviewees says:

> The bottom line is that they've got the power, yea? Like one of them said to me out there, 'You keep your mouth shut in here, because we can do whatever we want to you in here.' And that's all it boils down to.[137]

---

[134] Sanders et al (1989: 77).   [135] Choongh (1997: 89); Skinns (2011: 73).

[136] HMICFRS Report on an unannounced inspection visit to police custody suites in Lancashire 31 May–10 June 2016 by HM Inspectorate of Prisons and HM Inspectorate of Constabulary (HMICFRS, 2016a: para 5.2). Available online at: <https://www.justiceinspectorates.gov.uk/hmicfrs/our-work/article/criminal-justice-joint-inspection/joint-inspection-of-police-custody-facilities/#reports> (accessed 20 September 2019).

[137] Choongh (1997: 87).

In more recent research, police custody staff confirmed this sense that all detainees would comply with the police in the end, as the police saw themselves in charge, saying: if [detainees] dick around then we will win … We have tools at our disposal, we have leg straps, we have handcuffs, we can get officers off the street to restrain them and hold them down. It's not ideal, it's not the best but if we need to then we can do it.[138]

After being booked-in, which includes enduring a lengthy risk assessment process,[139] suspects are usually searched, fingerprinted, photographed and/or may be asked to participate in a drug test. Almost everything that happens next is in the hands of the police too. For substance abusers, the police control when the next 'fix' or drink becomes possible. They control food, drinks, lighting, heating and what one might share one's cell with. It may smell of the previous or co-occupant's urine or vomit, but it is up to the police to decide whether to move someone to a different cell. Though most police custody blocks now have in-cell toilets, in the past, the police even controlled when and if suspects were allowed to use the toilet—no joke if, as in one of the cases described by Hillyard,[140] you are a woman arrested after an evening in the pub and the male custody officer makes you wait four hours.[141]

Crime control adherents argue that innocent people have nothing to worry about if they are arrested. Maybe it has never happened to them. Listen to someone to whom it did happen:

> There I was banged up in a jail and I hadn't done anything, and I was being taken away from my place of work, I'd been separated from my family … Here was a policeman telling me that I had nothing to fear from him and he couldn't see the stupidity of his statement.[142]

Many suspects also have to endure much of what other suspects are going through in neighbouring cells. Irving reports an almost constant din of 'rhythmic banging and hammering, shouting and cursing, groaning, screaming and crying.'[143] As one custody officer acknowledged to Britton,[144] custody areas are 'like submarines … they're pretty grim aren't they?' Detention is boring, scary, unpleasant, uncertain, isolating, disorienting and humiliating. As we saw earlier, the police control visits, phone calls, and messages to the outside world. Also, personal effects, including wedding bands, spectacles, mobile phones, are taken away. At one and the same time one is isolated yet without privacy. Detainees are usually alone in their cells, often with no idea of the passing of time (watches are usually removed and clocks are not available in the cells), yet they are also able to be viewed by the police, by the now ubiquitous in-cell CCTV cameras. Intimate bodily functions have to be announced to the world—the world shrinks to the police station—as one has to ask for toilet paper or for menstrual products, for example.[145] Hence, Skinns and Wooff point to the varied pains of police detention that detainees experience, some of which are similar to the pains of imprisonment, which is remarkable given that those in police custody are only suspected of wrongdoing, rather than convicted and sentenced prisoners.[146]

---

[138] Skinns L and Wooff A, 'Pain in Police Detention: A Critical Point in the "Penal Painscape"?' (2020) 31(3) *Policing and Society* (245–262). See also Britton (2000a: 653).

[139] As Stoneman et al (2019) show, this risk assessment varies considerably between police forces. Stoneman et al, 'Variation in detainee risk assessment within police custody across England and Wales' (2019) 29(8) *Policing and Society* 951–967. Bevan (2019) also notes how difficult young suspects find the often lengthy booking-in and risk assessment process. For them it is something to be endured.   [140] Hillyard (1993: 151).

[141] On the importance of police control, see Leo R, 'Police Interrogation and Social Control' (1994) 3 *Social & Legal Studies* 93.   [142] Hillyard (1993: 186–7).

[143] Irving B, *Police Interrogation: A Study of Current Practice* (Royal Commission Research Paper No 2) (London: HMSO, 1980) p 122.   [144] Britton (2000a: 652).

[145] Newburn T and Hayman S, *Policing, Surveillance and Social Control* (Cullompton: Willan, 2001) pp 96–7.

[146] Skinns and Wooff (2020).

All suspects are fingerprinted.[147] Custody officers also have to identify all property that suspects have, and remove anything that is dangerous, illegal or evidence of crime; they can, but need not, authorise a search of the suspect for this purpose.[148] The Philips Commission recognised how invasive even a 'normal' search (involving removal of outer clothing only) is, and said that searches should not be carried out routinely,[149] but as it can be argued that only a search can demonstrate that suspects have no such articles, this recommendation has been ignored.[150] The police may, if they are still concerned, authorise strip-searches and/or intimate searches of body orifices; the latter requires authorisation by an inspector and should be carried out by a doctor where practical.[151]

There are relatively few intimate searches each year. In the year ending March 2018, there were 105 intimate searches carried out by the police in England and Wales and an object was found in 11% of cases.[152] In 90% of cases, they were used to search for Class A drugs.[153] There are many more strip-searches: about 12% of detainees in a study in a London police station in 1999–2000, with a similar figure of 16% being recently reported for 15 police stations inspected by HMICFRS in the North and North-East of London in 2017.[154] Grossed up that would amount to about 84,000–112,000 strip-searches nationally every year, based on the 700,000 people that are currently detained by the police each year (no official records are collected on strip searching). The factors most often associated with strip-searches are: reason for arrest, age, gender and ethnic identity (drugs offences and young black men featured most often). In 1999/2000, there was evidence of minority ethnic citizens being over-represented in strip searching data, even when other factors were taken to account, such as the reasons for arrest (see also chapter 10).[155] This concern remains a current one, as highlighted by the recent inspection of police custody facilities in North and North-East London. HMICFRS reported that their figures included a high proportion of children and a disproportionately higher number of detainees from minority ethnic backgrounds when compared against the overall throughput for custody during that time (these minority ethnic detainees accounted for 25% of the throughput and 51% of those strip-searched). Not all the strip searches during the inspection were warranted or properly justified (2019: para 4.14).

In addition, 'intimate' and 'non-intimate' samples may be taken. Intimate samples include semen and blood. 'Non-intimate' sample taking includes having hairs plucked, fingernails scraped and your saliva examined. If someone put a gloved finger in your mouth in order to scrape out some saliva, would you see that as a 'non-intimate' act? That is how PACE sees it. At one time, the consent of suspects was needed before samples could be taken for all but the most serious offences, but as in many other instances, the Criminal Justice Act 2003

---

[147] PACE, s.61 routinised this although the provisions were complex. The CJA 2003, s.9 amended s.61 to provide simply that everyone arrested for a recordable offence may be fingerprinted.

[148] PACE, s.54 as amended by CJA 2003. Also see Code C, para 4.1.

[149] RCCP (1981: para 3.117).

[150] Zander M, *The Police and Criminal Evidence Act 1984* (London: Sweet and Maxwell, 2005) p 194.

[151] PACE, s.55 and Code C, Annex A.

[152] Home Office, *Police powers and procedures, England and Wales, year ending 31 March 2018* (London: Home Office, 2018d). Interestingly, some forces perform intimate searches more than others. Of the 40 forces supplying data, only 23 performed intimate searches with Suffolk, Surrey and Norfolk using these searches the most.

[153] Home Office (2018).

[154] HMICFR, *Report on an unannounced inspection visit to police custody suites in the Metropolitan Police Service, 8–20 July 2018* (2019) online at: <https://www.justiceinspectorates.gov.uk/hmicfrs/our-work/article/criminal-justice-joint-inspection/joint-inspection-of-police-custody-facilities/#reports> (accessed 1 October 2019).

[155] Newburn et al, 'Race, Crime and Injustice? Strip-search and the Treatment of Suspects in Custody' (2004) 44(5) *British Journal of Criminology* 677 at p 689.

has given the police almost carte blanche in relation to non-intimate samples.[156] Hillyard comments that:

> These processes are common to the initiation into many 'total institutions' and Goffman has described them as 'mortification processes' because the self is systematically, if often unintentionally, mortified through a series of debasements, degradations, and humiliations.[157]

The insistence of human rights and due process theorists on 'rights' makes little sense in these conditions:

> Yea, I understood me rights, but do you get rights in here? The loo don't flush, it stinks. You get breakfast in a cardboard box and it's freezing cold … it's not the law, it's just the fucking conditions … no fags, nowhere to wash, you've no idea what time it is … [158]

Choongh asked the suspects he interviewed how they felt when locked up.[159] He classified the 72 replies as 'intolerable', 'distressing' or 'indifferent'. One quarter were indifferent to the experience, but one fifth found the experience 'intolerable'. A little over half found it 'distressing', using phrases like feeling 'trapped', 'powerless' and 'angry'. No wonder then that the pains of imprisonment, or more aptly, the pains of police detention, linked in particular to the loss of liberty, autonomy and basic goods and services, resonate with detainees.[160]

Detention is not awful for everyone. Occasionally the police have to detain people who they see as allies, not as threats, such as the well-dressed and well-spoken driver in the study by Choongh[161] who had a little too much wine at lunchtime. Unlike most detainees, he did not have to 'buy' good treatment by being deferential and showing the police that they know who is in charge.[162] Choongh also found that large numbers of suspects had such low expectations of their treatment that they were indifferent to things that most people would find outrageous. Nonetheless, it is not surprising that time in detention feels stretched, and that therefore the most important factor affecting suspects' decisions whether to ask for legal advice is the likely length of detention.[163] As one detainee in Choongh's research told him, when asked why he had not requested a solicitor, 'I'm happy I'm out, yea? That's the only thing I care about, I don't care what happens to me in court.'[164] Moreover, the significance of detention lengths is not only the actual detention length but also the threat created by the 36 hour limit. Suspects do not know that the average detention lasts 'only' thirteen hours or so, and rightly fear that the way they behave could lead to their being confined for longer—or could affect whether they get out at all before being hauled off to court. The subjective experience of 'only' thirteen hours detention, and of the threat of longer detention, is something which few legislators, judges, academics or university students are likely to have endured. This sense of uncertainty and liminality—that is, of being betwixt and between—which is most evident in relation to when someone will be released or not from police custody is a further pain of police detention.[165]

For detainees under the anti-terrorism legislation detention can be a very long time in both objective and subjective terms. Apart from anything else, police station cells may provide virtually no natural light or opportunity to walk, let alone exercise. At its most extreme, indefinite detention can lead to traumatic psychological disturbance: some of the

---

[156] PACE, ss.62 and 63, as amended by CJA 2003, s 10.   [157] Hillyard (1993: 151).
[158] Choongh (1997: 178).   [159] Choongh (1997: 97–8).   [160] Skinns and Wooff (2020).
[161] Choongh (1997: 206–7).
[162] This is a further example of class/socio-economic differentials at work that are discussed in ch 10.
[163] Sanders et al (1989: ch 4).
[164] Choongh (1997: 149). *Aspinall* [1999] Crim LR 741 (section 4.2.3) concerned a particularly vulnerable suspect who was prepared to say anything to get out after being isolated for over 13 hours.
[165] Skinns and Wooff (2020).

ATCSA detainees who successfully challenged their detention in 2004[166] suffered so much that by the time of the court challenge they were already in a psychiatric hospital.

Looking at the experience of detention in the light of its purposes and time limits, we can see that crime control considerations clearly outweigh those of due process, particularly in relation to serious suspected offences. But it may be that the detention of suspects in some circumstances where evidence is thin and detention not strictly necessary is justified—especially if the detention is for a short period and the offence serious. Britain used to (crudely) adopt this approach by providing great detention powers for suspected terrorism, less for 'serious arrestable offences' and less still for 'arrestable offences', but the CJA 2003 gave the police the same power for 'arrestable' as for 'serious arrestable' offences. Human rights perspectives are of little use here, for only the most extreme behaviours documented in this section (beating and gross abuse) contravene the ECHR or Code C.[167] Intimate body searches, for example, have been held compatible with the Art 3 right not to be subjected to degrading treatment.[168] The same is true when detainees have all or some clothes removed, perhaps because they are seen as a suicide risk, but this is also sometimes done in a humiliating way.[169] From a police legitimacy perspective, however, police custody can be seen as 'the ultimate teachable moment', in which detainees, separated from their family, friends, lives outside, are primed to learn a great deal about how the police and indeed wider society views them, through their interactions with the police. Being treated in a way that detainees see as humiliating or lacking in respect is likely to undermine police legitimacy and the likelihood that suspects will co-operate with the police. Most of this police behaviour is not illegal or even deliberately degrading—it is simply an inevitable product of involuntary detention and of the prioritisation of crime control over due process and over considerations of police legitimacy. Deaths in custody are another matter, however.

4.4 Deaths in custody

Following a death in custody the area has to be secured, the Independent Office of Police Conduct (IOPC) informed, and an investigation begun. There is then an inquest by a coroner and, depending on the findings of the investigation and inquest, consideration is given to possible prosecution and/or disciplinary proceedings against the officers involved (see chapter 11). In the past, the force in which the death occurred used to carry out that investigation—in other words, whether the police involved were held to be responsible for a death in custody was determined in large part by an investigation carried out by those officers' colleagues. Even though these investigations are now carried out independently of the police by the IOPC, they remain a grave source of concern for lawyers, bereaved families, for charities such as Inquest and for the wider public. A key recent concern has been around the limited amount of legal aid available to bereaved families during inquests (see chapter 11). Were automatic non-means tested funding available for legal representation following state related deaths, including in police custody, families, like that of Sean Rigg (whose death in police custody is considered in more detail shortly) would not have to suffer further in the aftermath of a death. Automatic legal aid would also enable bereaved families to have a similar level of legal representation as the police force implicated in their family member's death.

---

[166] *A (FC) v Home Secretary* [2004] UKHL 56.
[167] On beating and psychologically damaging interrogation techniques, see *Ireland v UK* (1978) 2 EHRR 25.
[168] *McFeeley v UK* (Application no 8317/78, (1980) 20 DR 44).
[169] See, for example, the Cambridgeshire inspection: (HMIP and HMIC, 2009).

Here we focus on deaths in or following police custody. These are defined as:

> Deaths that happen while a person is being arrested or taken into detention. It includes deaths of people who have been arrested or have been detained by police under the Mental Health Act 1983. The death may have taken place on police, private, or medical premises, in a public place or in a police or other vehicle.[170]

They include any deaths that follow police custody for up to two days after someone's release, which may for example be as a result of injuries or medical problems identified whilst in police custody. Apparent suicides which occur within two days of someone being held in police custody or where the time in police custody may be relevant, are not included in the 'deaths in or following police custody' category, but in a separate category of 'apparent suicides', a large proportion of which arise following someone's arrest for sexual offences, particularly where children are involved.[171]

In a review of the international evidence on deaths in custody Lindon and Roe note that figures for England and Wales only began to be reliably recorded from 1998/99.[172] They say:

> Trend data show a sharp fall in deaths in or following police custody from 1998/99 (49 deaths) to 1999/2000 (31 deaths), followed by a period of relative stability. There is then another more gradual fall between 2004/05 (36) and 2008/09 (15), followed by another period of relative stability … On average there have been 16 deaths each year in police custody between 2008/09 and 2015/16.[173]

More recent figures show that in 2016/17 deaths in or following police custody remained stable at 14, but then rose to a 10 year high in 2017/18 of 23 fatalities, before dropping back to 16 in 2018/19, which is in-line with average figures.[174] However, whilst the overall trend since 1998/99 seems to be downwards this may be, in part, explained by the dramatically decreasing police custody populations. Bucke and Brown (1997), for example, noted that in the late 1990s there were approximately 1.5 million detainees entering police custody each year compared to the approximately 700,000 per year at the time of writing.[175] There has also be intensifying public concern, especially among ethnic minority communities, and growing political pressure in relation to deaths in or following police custody, which may have encouraged police forces and those who hold them to account, such as the IOPC, to do more to prevent deaths from occurring in the first place. These concerns culminated in the government establishing an 'Independent Review of Deaths and Serious Incidents in Police Custody' in 2015, which published its findings in 2017. This was led by Dame Eilish Angiolini, becoming known therefore as the 'Angiolini Review'.

Though the numbers of deaths in or following police custody may be declining in the long-term, each one is a tragedy. They may also be seen as symbolic of relationships between citizens, the police and the state more generally. Baker, for example, regards them as the 'touchstone for legitimate, transparent and consensual policing in England and Wales'.[176] With this in mind, here are a few examples of some of the worst cases see in recent years. In 1997 two inquest juries found that Oluwashhijibomi Lapite and Richard O'Brien had been 'unlawfully killed' while in police custody. Lapite had 45 injuries.

---

[170] IOPC, 'Deaths during of following police contact' (IOPC, 2019). [171] Ibid. p 22.
[172] Lindon and Roe (2017). [173] Lindon and Roe (2017: 14). [174] IOPC (2019: 20).
[175] Home Office, *Police powers and procedures, England and Wales, year ending 31 March 2018* (London: Home Office, 2018d) available online at: <https://www.gov.uk/government/statistics/police-powers-and-procedures-england-and-wales-year-ending-31-march-2018> (accessed 1 October 2019).
[176] Baker D, *Deaths After Police Contact: Constructing Accountability in the 21st Century* (London: Palgrave, 2016).

An officer admitted kicking him in the head as hard as he could, claiming that he was the most violent prisoner he had ever encountered, but the officers involved had only superficial injuries. O'Brien had 31 injuries. The last words his wife heard him say were: 'I can't breathe, let me up, you win.'[177] Christopher Alder—another black man—was arrested and dumped half-naked and handcuffed onto a police station floor in 1998. As he lay dying, gasping for breath as blood blocked his air passages, he was accused by an officer of 'faking it'. Four other officers also watched, and only took action—too late—to save his life after he stopped breathing. For once we know the truth, because all this was caught on a 12-minute police video.[178] And in 2003 Mikey Powell—yet another black man—was deliberately hit by a moving police car, sprayed with CS gas, struck with a baton, put on the floor of a police van face down and carried into a police cell still face down. Only then did the police realise he had stopped breathing. In December 2009 the jury at the inquest concluded that this man who experienced mental ill-health (but had no criminal record) had died from positional asphyxia following police restraint.[179]

We do not know how many cases there are like this. What we do know is that even some of the most suspicious circumstances do not lead to unlawful killing verdicts or prosecutions. For example, of the eight prosecutions of police officers following a death in police custody in the last 15 years, all have ended in acquittals, even when coroners have given a verdict of unlawful killing.[180] Take the case of Marlon Downes, a young black man found hanging in his cell in 1997. The police argued that he must have committed suicide, even though the grille from which he was hanging was so high that, they said, he must have stood on two rolled-up mattresses. However:

- Police photos of the cell showed only one mattress.
- The shoelace with which he allegedly hanged himself could not have supported his weight.
- The custody record stated that he was still alive at least one hour after he actually died.
- Attempts had been made to erase an even later entry claiming he was still alive.
- His solicitor gave evidence that he had seen Marlon in a different cell, but the police denied moving him.
- The station cleaner cleaned the cell in which he was found before the investigation began.

The inquest recorded an open verdict, and Marlon's family will never know what really happened to their son.[181] This was not an isolated case. In a number of high profile cases in the last 30 years or so, where witnesses agreed that suspects had been subjected to more force (beaten and kicked) than was necessary to restrain them, inquest verdicts of 'justifiable homicide' and 'death by misadventure' resulted, this being one of many reasons for the inquest system coming under critical scrutiny.[182] And the suspicion of a 'cover-up' occurs

---

[177] *Statewatch*, July–Oct 1997, p 19; Smith G, 'The DPP and prosecutions of police officers' (1997) 147 *New Law Journal* 6804.

[178] *The Guardian*, 25 August 2000. See *The Guardian*, 18 August 2005 for a discussion of these and several other cases. (Type 'Christopher Alder' into YouTube for excerpts from the police video).

[179] See <http://www.guardian.co.uk/commentisfree/libertycentral/2009/dec/27/mikey-powell-inquest-death-in-custody> (accessed 5 January 2010).

[180] Angiolini E, 'Report of the Independent Review of Deaths and Serious Incidents in Police Custody' (2017: 201) available online at: <https://www.gov.uk/government/publications/deaths-and-serious-incidents-in-police-custody> (accessed 1 October 2019). [181] Newburn and Hayman (2001: ch 2).

[182] Scraton P and Chadwick K, *In the Arms of the Law: Coroners' Inquests and Deaths in Custody* (London: Pluto, 1987); Vogt G and Wadham J, *Deaths in Police Custody: Redress and Remedies* (London: Civil Liberties Trust, 2003).

in case after case (such as Rigg's, discussed next). Faisal Al-Ani died in hospital in 2005 of injuries sustained while being restrained by police initially in the street, then on the journey to the police station, then in the station; and Sean Rigg, died after being arrested and dumped in a metal cage in a police station yard in 2008, whilst Mr Rigg was in the midst of a mental health crisis. The then IPCC criticised the police in Al-Ani's case for using techniques 'in contravention to all guidance'. However, although officers admitted striking him several times 'in self defence' while he was handcuffed, and the police initially claimed that their first contact with him was when he walked into the police station (a claim withdrawn later only because of CCTV evidence contradicting it), both the IPCC and inquest jury concluded that the police actions were 'reasonable'.[183] In the case of Sean Rigg, the tragic circumstances of his death have been the subject of much dispute after a coroner's inquest reached different conclusions to those of the original IPCC investigations, for example, about basic facts such as the time of his death and whether it was in the so-called 'cage' at the back of Brixton police station or in fact in hospital. The inquest concluded that the way that Mr Rigg was restrained 'more than minimally' contributed to his death. These discrepancies arose in part because the IPCC relied predominantly on accounts provided by police officers, whilst the inquest into his death relied to a greater extent on painstaking examination by Sean Rigg's family of CCTV footage.[184] The officers involved were not charged with any criminal offence around the time of his death or following a subsequent review of the case in 2017, due to a lack of evidence, and in 2019 five officers were acquitted of gross misconduct charges. His case was a catalyst for the Angiolini Review, with Theresa May, the then Home Secretary, meeting with his family prior to announcements being made that it would take place.

As well as deaths in custody raising questions about police policy and practice—and, indeed, the principle established in PACE that the police should be able to use custody to facilitate their work—there is a legal dimension. The ECHR Art 2 'right to life' not only prohibits the state from taking life except where absolutely necessary, but also imposes on it a duty to protect life and to effectively investigate deaths.[185] The procedures leading to unsatisfactory verdicts such as in Marlon Downes' case undoubtedly were in breach of Art 2[186] and so the IPCC, which was supposed to be independent of the police, now takes the lead. The IPCC has since been replaced by the IOPC (chapters 1 and 11). The IPCC's endorsement of police behaviour in the Al-Ani case, and investigative failures in Rigg's case, suggest that the police view of events continues to dominate responses to deaths in custody.[187]

In terms of the causes of deaths in or following custody, there are a range of complex factors at play. A report published in 2011 by the IPCC, provides the most up-to-date and comprehensive assessment of these factors, though it is important to bear in mind that the research was founded on official versions of events. In this report, researchers collected data from IPCC investigations between 1998/99 and 2008/9, as well as from other sources,

---

[183] *The Guardian*, 2 June 2009 (Al-Ani); *The Guardian*, 22 August 2009 (Rigg).
[184] Baker (2016).
[185] *Osman v UK* [1998] 29 [EHRR] 245; *McCann v UK* [1995] 21 ECHR 97.
[186] This is true of inquests as well as the pre-2004 investigations. See Vogt and Wadham (2003).
[187] IPCC investigators waited eight months before interviewing the officers in Rigg's case because they thought 'there was nothing to suggest wrong-doing.' Their suspicions were not alerted by the (disputed) failure of CCTV cameras covering the metal cage in which Rigg was dumped. (*The Guardian*, 22 August 2009). For a good discussion of the dominance of the police view see Pemberton S, 'Demystifying Deaths in Police Custody: Challenging State Talk' (2008) 17 *Social and Legal Studies* 237. The IPCC and decisions about prosecution and discipline of police officers are discussed in ch 12.

such as coroners' inquest verdicts. In total, they collected data from 333 cases over an 11-year period. They found a number of factors explained why people died in or following police custody:

1. Drugs and alcohol—By far the biggest set of factors in the cases in their sample were drugs and alcohol. 72% of their sample were either intoxicated or arrested for drug or alcohol related offences (e.g. drunk and disorderly or drunk and incapable) or both. In such cases, drugs/alcohol were seen as key cause of their death. Therefore, the authors in their report argue that police custody, as per police guidelines, is not an appropriate place for someone who is intoxicated. Intoxication was also sometimes linked to other factor such as head injuries. Cell checks on the intoxicated were sometimes poor and/or they were not risk assessed in the first place. Heide and Chan reiterate this finding about the importance of drugs/alcohol. They note that across Europe the use of drugs (both licit and illicit) and alcohol were the leading causes of death in police custody.[188]

2. The use of restraint—26% (n=87) of their sample were physically restrained on arrest, during transportation, in custody or in hospital. This restraint mostly involved being held down by police officers and for 5% of those who were restrained (n=16) restraint was either the primary or secondary cause of death. Restraint was also significantly used to a greater extent with 25–34 year olds and members of racialised groups. But how many detainees abuse, struggle and assault officers through fear of custody or because of what custody has done to them, especially if they are drunk, drugged or in the midst of a mental health crisis? This may therefore lead to a lethal escalation of the use of force.

3. Mental health conditions—Of their sample, 19 died after being taken to police custody as a place of safety under s.136 of the MHA or under other provisions of the Act. Thirty-nine were identified on arrest as having mental health needs and a further 11 had markers on their record relating to self-harm/suicide. In total, 21% (n=69) cases involved those with mental health conditions. Cell checks on those with warning markers on their record for self-harm and suicide were also found to be lacking.

4. Inadequate or non-existent risk assessments, as well as inadequate cell checks— Of the 247 who should have been risk assessed in police custody, just under half actually were. These risk assessments were not completed, largely because detainees were intoxicated. Part of the purpose of the risk assessment is for staff to determine how often they need to check on detainees when they are placed in the cells. This study showed that several people did not receive checks as often as they should have done (as indicated in the risk assessment). Furthermore, when checks were performed at appropriate intervals they were not always performed in ways that alleviated risks to detainees, e.g. they observed them through the hatch rather than asking them a question or going into the cell to physically rouse them.

5. Failures to abide by police policies and procedures—There was a failure to abide by police force policies or procedures in 27% of cases (though they do not say what these breaches were), albeit that such breaches did not necessarily impact on someone's death.

A further factor present in deaths in or following police custody is that of race and ethnicity. For example, in the case of Christopher Alder, an IPCC review of the original Police Complaints Authority investigation of his death concluded that his death was

---

[188] Heide S and Chan T, 'Deaths in Police Custody' (2018) 57 *Journal of Forensic and Legal Medicine* 109–114.

'unnecessary, undignified and unnoticed' and that the neglect of duty in particular by the sergeant responsible for the custody area denied Mr Alder the chance of life.[189] Moreover, the Review concluded that there was evidence that the behaviour of the officers amounted to unwitting racism, as defined by Macpherson as 'processes, attitudes and behaviour which amount to discrimination through unwitting discrimination, ignorance, thoughtlessness and racist stereotyping'. This included:

- A belief that Mr Alder's behaviour was due to alcohol, amphetamines or steroids, rather than a head injury;
- A belief that he was unhurt despite having been assaulted, struck over the head and rendered unconscious;
- A belief that his behaviour was due to a bad attitude, rather than a head injury;
- A reluctance to touch or rouse him at the police station;
- The use of racist language including 'coloured' and 'of negroid appearance'.
- The use of monkey imitations directed at a white detainee, as well as references to hoods with slits and banana boots. None of these comments were directed at Mr Alder, but they occurred whilst Mr Alder's body lay on floor, demonstrating gross insensitivity.

Together, these attitudes and behaviours were seen as showing stereotypical assumptions and attitudes based on Mr Alder's race. This racism resulted in a failure to provide a professional service to Mr Alder.

However, whether race/ethnicity is a factor when looking at the number of deaths in or following police custody as whole, is a contested matter. In some years, citizens from ethnic minority backgrounds do appear to be over-represented in the statistics for deaths in or following police custody. For example, in the last edition of this book, it was noted that in 2008/9 around a third of the 15 people who died in police custody, were black or Asian, when these groups made up only 13% of the general population. However, data cited by Lindon and Roe over a longer period show that between 2004/5 and 2014/15, 12% of deaths in or following police custody were of minority ethnic citizens, which is more in-keeping with proportions of such citizens in the general population. Furthermore, the Institute for Race Relations found that, between 2002 and 2012, 18% of people who died in police custody were from an ethnic minority background,[190] so there is some disparity in the figures. The circumstances in which racialised citizens die in or following police custody have also been found to vary by race/ethnicity. There is evidence to suggest that drug/alcohol overdose is more likely for minority ethnic citizens, as is airway obstruction following the swallowing of drug packages.[191] Hannan et al also found that detainees from minority ethnic backgrounds who died were statistically significantly more likely to have had restraint used on them whilst in the custody of the police.[192] Interviews and focus groups with detainees from racialised groups also point to the importance of racist stereotyping (as illustrated by the Christopher Alder case), which informs how detainees are treated and also whether force is over-used.[193] What is also important to consider is how deaths of minority citizens in or following police custody are perceived by families, local

---

[189] IPCC, Report, dated 27th February 2006, of the Review into the events leading up to and following the death of Christopher Alder on 1st April 1998 (England and Wales: IPCC, 2006).

[190] Athwal H and Bourne J, *Dying for Justice* (Institute of Race Relations, 2015).

[191] Lindon and Roe (2017).

[192] Hannan M, Hearnden I, Grace K and Bucke T, *Deaths in or following police custody: examination of the cases 1998/09–2008/09* (England and Wales: HM Inspectorate of Constabulary, 2011).

[193] HMIC, *The welfare of vulnerable people in police custody* (England and Wales: HM Inspectorate of Constabulary, 2015).

communities and the wider public. Some of the deaths involving racialised citizens have been the most controversial, in part because they involve very serious allegations of wrongdoing on the part of the police. For example, Hannan et al found that in their sample of 333 cases, 13 cases resulted in prosecutions of staff, of which nearly half (n=7) involved minority ethnic citizens (compared to the 7% of minority ethnic citizens in their overall sample).

Clearly many deaths in custody are preventable. In some cases all that is needed is a speedy response to a call for help. In one study, researchers interviewing suspects in their cells were locked in on more than one occasion for half an hour or more before the police came to 'rescue' them, despite the cells having a call button (immobilised by the custody officer) and shouting and beating on the cell doors.[194] An official inspection found custody suite staff turned cell bells down rather than attending to the calls.[195] CCTV cameras that work would also be helpful, to say the least. Then we would really know what happened to people like Downes, Rigg and Al-Ani. The Home Office study found that there were warning signs or explicit warnings (such as 'suicide markers' on the Police National Computer (PNC)) in over 30% of all deaths by deliberate self-harm. Some had actually tried to commit suicide while already in police custody or shortly before. Some people who died from their medical conditions also displayed signs of major illnesses that were often mistaken for simple drunkenness.[196] On the other hand it has to be acknowledged that many attempts at self-harm and other life-threatening conditions are identified by police who prevent very large numbers of deaths and serious injuries. The number of actual deaths are dwarfed by nearly 40 times as many 'near-misses', some of which would have been fatal had it not been for police vigilance.[197]

From the perspective of ECHR, Art 2 and citizens' right to life, one sets this death toll against the reasons for custodial detention. Astonishingly, nearly half of detainees who died in or following police custody between 2004/5 and 2014/15 had been arrested for non-notifiable offences, i.e. more minor offences such as breach of peace, drunk and disorderly and driving offences.[198] There can surely be no justification for a criminal justice system that allows people to be put in a situation where *we know that some will die* when their alleged crimes are this trivial. Without denying that some police officers are culpable for deaths in custody, the main concern should be a double system-failure: that too many people are detained by the police when they should not be; and that the police are not trained or resourced to deal with circumstances that lead to deaths. As Best and Kefas (2004) concluded, ' … drunken detainees should not be taken to police stations in other than the most extreme circumstances.'[199]

---

[194] Newburn and Hayman (2001: 123). See also Skinns (2011: 82–84); Skinns and Wooff (2020).

[195] HMIP and HMIC (2009).

[196] Leigh A, Johnson G and Ingram A, *Deaths in Police Custody: Learning the Lessons*, Home Office Police Research Series, Paper 26 (London: HMSO, 1998) pp 8–39 and, again, Al-Ani. Code C, paras 3.6–3.10 now require custody officers to make risk assessments that include, inter alia, PNC checks.

[197] It is estimated that there are around 1,000 'near misses' per year. While many would have been fatal without police vigilance, in others only good fortune prevented a lack of vigilance leading to fatal consequences: IPCC, *Near Misses in Police Custody: A Collaborative Study with Forensic Medical Examiners in London* (London: IPCC, 2008b). [198] Lindon and Roe (2017: 29).

[199] Best D and Kefas A, *The role of alcohol in police-related deaths: analysis of deaths in custody (category 3) between 2000 and 2001* (London: Police Complaints Authority, 2004). A similar point, in relation to prison custody as well as police custody, is made by the Parliamentary Joint Committee on Human Rights, *Deaths in Custody* (2004). A Forum for Preventing Deaths in Custody was established by the government in 2006 to advise the government. It does not seem to have been effective, and was wound up in 2009. It was replaced in 2009 by a Ministerial Council on Deaths in Custody, in which an Independent Advisory Panel on Deaths in Custody (IAPDC) provides independent advice and expertise to the Ministerial Board on Deaths in Custody, with the central aim of preventing deaths in custody. The work of the IAPDC was given renewed momentum following the publication of Angiolini review of deaths and serious incidents in police custody in 2017. See also section 11.3.7.

Historically, part of the problem was that s.136 Mental Health Act 1983 (MHA) designated police stations (as well as hospitals) as 'places of safety' to which police officers could take those experiencing a mental health crisis in immediate need of care and control, where they could be detained for up to 72 hours whilst a mental health assessment was undertaken and whilst a bed in an appropriate mental health hospital was found, if this was required. For a variety of reasons, including the overuse of police custody as a 'place of safety' and growing recognition that 'the police are not health care providers',[200] noted in the previous edition, the law has now changed. Following changes to the Mental Health Act in 2017, in theory, it is more difficult for those in crisis to be taken to police custody as a place of safety. This provision may only be used for adults in 'exceptional circumstances' and only for up to 24 hours, and children and young people in crisis may not be taken there at all. This is not to say that people with mental health conditions will not end up in police custody, as the police may arrest someone in crisis for a criminal offence instead, and then later decide to section them under mental health legislation. Indeed, this was identified as an issue in a recent HMICFRS inspection of Sussex Police.[201] However, it does provide greater impetus on the police and mental health providers not to place vulnerable detainees at greater risk of police use of force and of self-harming in a police cell as a 'place of safety'.[202] The impacts of these changes to the law and how they are put into practice in relation to police custody represents a further area where more research is required.

4.5 The right to legal advice

Prior to PACE, access to legal advice was governed by the Judges' Rules. The Rules stated that a suspected person should be able to consult privately with a solicitor provided that it caused the police no unreasonable 'hindrance'. But what was or was not reasonable was never clearly established, and the Judges' Rules were not 'law' in the sense of being common law or statute. All that a suspect who was denied access to legal advice could do was to ask for the evidence obtained as a result to be excluded from trial, if there was one. Further, the Fisher inquiry into the 'Confait Affair' found that many suspects (including the wrongly convicted youths in that case) did not know they had such a right, even though the police were supposed to inform them of it. Fisher (1977) quotes a deputy assistant commissioner of the Metropolitan Police saying that 'it has never been recognised by the police … as a duty to tell a prisoner … that he has the right to consult a solicitor'.

Thus, few suspects were informed by officers of this right, fewer tried to exercise it and fewer still had their requests granted. Softley's study of four police stations, found that around 9% sought advice and around 7% actually secured it.[203] Even these figures are artificially high, for in one of these police stations the police were told (for the purposes

---

[200] Coppen (2008). His concern about s.136 is endorsed by a Chief Constable in Wilding (2008) and by IPCC research (Docking et al 2008). See: Coppen J, 'PACE: A View from the Custody Suite', in Cape E and Young R (eds), *Regulating Policing* (Oxford: Hart, 2008); Wilding B (2008) 'Tipping the Scales of Justice?: A Review of the Impact of PACE on the Police, Due Process and the Search for the Truth 1984-2006' in Cape and Young (2008); Docking M, Grace K and Bucke T, *Police Custody as a 'Place of Safety': Examining the use of s 136 of the MHA 1983* (London: IPCC, 2008).

[201] HMICFRS (2020) *Sussex Police—Joint Inspection Report—February 2020*. Online at: <https://www.justiceinspectorates.gov.uk/hmicfrs/our-work/article/criminal-justice-joint-inspection/joint-inspection-of-police-custody-facilities/> (accessed 1 October 2020).

[202] Baker D and Pillinger C (2019) '"These People are Vulnerable, They aren't Criminals": Mental Health, the use of Force and Deaths after Police Contact in England' (2019) *The Police Journal* 65–81.

[203] Softley P, *Police Interrogation: An Observational Study in Four Police Stations* (Royal Commission on Criminal Procedure Research Study no 4) (London: HMSO, 1980).

of the research) that they had to inform all suspects of their right to a solicitor, whereas in the other three stations they were not so directed. In the station in which suspects were routinely informed of their rights, the numbers requesting and securing access were considerably higher than in the others. As one would expect, being told one's rights is vital. The Philips Commission recognised this, and its recommendations, which aimed to make the right to advice truly available to all, were implemented by the government in PACE.

4.5.1 The right to advice under PACE and the HRA

Section 58 of PACE states the right of access in the clearest possible terms:

(1) A person arrested … shall be entitled, if he so requests, to consult a solicitor privately at any time …

(4) If a person makes such a request, he must be permitted to consult a solicitor as soon as is practicable except to the extent that delay is permitted by this section … .

Delay in compliance with a request is only permitted if an officer of at least the rank of superintendent authorises it.[204]

This differs from the old Judges' Rules. It is an unequivocal statutory provision although there is still no clear remedy available to suspects who are denied this right. Second, advice cannot be refused but merely delayed. All suspects must be permitted, if they wish, to consult a solicitor within 36 hours (the period beyond which suspects cannot be held without the authorisation of a magistrate).[205]

The 'right to consult a solicitor privately at any time' is a powerful one. As we shall see, legal advice to detainees is always available free of charge. Suspects who initially decline a solicitor can demand one later, even in the middle of an interview. And they can require that the solicitor be present in the interview and may consult with that solicitor (publicly or privately) during it.[206] As part of the ECHR 'right to a fair trial', everyone 'charged with a criminal offence' has the right to legal assistance. Suspects are 'to be given it free when the interests of justice so require.'[207] Although this only seems to apply to people being prosecuted (i.e. charged), the European Court held in *Murray* that it applies to suspects under arrest too if what happens when under arrest could affect the fairness of a subsequent trial: 'The concept of fairness enshrined in Art 6 requires that the accused had the benefit of the assistance of a lawyer already at the initial stages of police interrogation.'[208] The Court held that a defendant could not have a fair trial if he had been interviewed while access to advice was being withheld, especially as adverse inferences could be made had he remained silent.[209] Further weight has since been given to suspects' right to a lawyer prior to their first interrogation as a result of the *Salduz* ruling. This required suspects arrested by the police to be given access to a lawyer prior to their first interrogation, unless there are

---

[204] Code C, Annexe B, para 1.
[205] PACE, s.58(5). Delay is only possible if the offence is indictable: PACE, s.58(6)(a) as amended by the Serious Organised Crime and Police Act 2005, Sch 7 (watering down the previous rule that delay was only permitted for serious arrestable offences).
[206] Code C, para 6.8 and notes 6B and 6D, and PACE, s.58(1).
[207] Article 6, para 3(c). See *S v Switzerland* (1991) 14 EHRR 670; *Brennan v UK* (2001) 34 EHRR 507. On the meaning of 'the interests of justice', see Ashworth A, 'Legal Aid, Human Rights and Criminal Justice' in Young R and Wall D (eds), *Access to Criminal Justice* (London: Blackstone, 1996a) at pp 61–3, and section 9.2.
[208] *Murray v UK* (1996) 22 EHRR 29. Quoted by Cape E, 'Sidelining Defence Lawyers: Police Station Advice after *Condron*' (1997) 1 *International Journal of Evidence and Policy* 386 at p 398. In this case, access to a lawyer was delayed in accordance with the PTA 1989, s.14. This allowed delay on similar, but less stringent grounds, to those of PACE, and for up to 48 hours. The current terrorist legislation is similar.
[209] See section 5.3, for discussion of the right of silence.

compelling reasons to restrict this. This doctrine applies even if a suspect exercises their right to silence.[210]

There are obvious potential difficulties with the right of access. One is that the interview might be delayed while waiting for a solicitor. If the consequences would be truly serious an officer of the rank of superintendent or above may authorise the interview in the solicitor's absence.[211] If a lawyer's advice and assistance in the interview is such that the police are 'unable properly to put questions to the suspect', the lawyer can be required to leave, but only if authorised by a superintendent (or an inspector if a superintendent is not 'readily available'), and an opportunity must be given to the suspect to be represented by a replacement lawyer.[212]

Another problem is where the police need to carry out procedures such as breath tests on suspected drunken drivers. Decisions that the 'as soon as is practicable' provision in s.58(4) mean that such procedures need not wait on a legal consultation, and that this is not inconsistent with Art 6, seem sensible to us.[213] However, we do not understand why the police routinely delay even seeking a solicitor until after a sample is taken (preventing even the possibility of speedy advice), nor why the courts largely accept this.[214]

Yet another problem is the right of privacy. This is difficult to guarantee in a busy police station, though it should not be impossible if sufficient resources were allocated. As it is, the English courts make a distinction between conditions under which consultations could be overheard (which are not seen as violating the principle),[215] and deliberate attempts by police to overhear, regardless of whether or not this helps the police case (which does violate the principle).[216]

4.5.1.1 Delaying access

Section 58(8) of PACE provides that (in cases of indictable offences only):

> ... an officer may only authorise delay where he has reasonable grounds for believing that the exercise of the right ...
>
> (a) will lead to interference with or harm to evidence ... or interference with or physical injury to other persons; or
>
> (b) will lead to the alerting of other persons suspected of having committed such an offence ... ; or
>
> (c) will hinder the recovery of any property obtained as a result of such an offence.

In *Samuel*[217] and thereafter, the courts made it clear that access could only be delayed in exceptional circumstances, such as some reason to believe that, in the particular case, access could lead to one of these consequences. The Court of Appeal went on to note that if, as in this case, the solicitor was a duty solicitor (i.e. not known to the suspect) this would

---

[210] *Salduz v Turkey* [2008] ECHR 1542; Blackstock J, Cape E, Hodgson J, Ogorodova A and Spronken A, *Inside Police Custody: An Empirical Account of Suspects' Rights in Four Jurisdictions* (Cambridge: Intersentia, 2014).
[211] Code C, para 6.6.   [212] Code C, paras 6.9–6.10.
[213] *Campbell v DPP* [2003] Crim LR 118; *Whitley v DPP* [2004] Crim LR 585.
[214] See Commentary on *Kennedy v DPP* [2003] Crim LR 120 (which applied *Campbell*) at 121. Because breath tests provide objective evidence, courts and commentators alike see denial of advice as largely unproblematic. The value of legal advisors (and AAs, where there is a similar issue—see section 4.2.3) as emotional and practical supporters is routinely ignored.
[215] *La Rose* [2002] Crim LR 215, [2001] EWHC Admin 553. The ECtHR was less sympathetic to the police in *Brennan v UK* (2001) 34 EHRR 507.
[216] *Grant* [2006] QB 20. See also Pattenden R and Skinns L 'Choice, Privacy and Publicly Funded Legal Advice at the Police Station' (2010) 73(3) *Modern Law Review* 349–70.
[217] *Samuel* [1988] 2 All ER 135.

be virtually impossible for the police to prove, since neither the police nor the suspect would know who that individual was until such time as he or she arrived at the police station.[218]

In 1987, delay was authorised in around 1% of all cases,[219] but in research covering 12,500 cases conducted in the mid-1990s, no delays were authorised at all.[220] We shall see later on that the problem now is not formal delay of access but the informal delay which results from the police bending or breaking the rules, and legal changes that reduce the value of legal advice for suspects. Delay under the terrorism legislation is still doubtless contemplated from time to time, but as we saw earlier, this is now very difficult to justify, given the way that Art 6 of the ECHR is interpreted.[221]

4.5.1.2 Notification of the right to advice and provision of advice

Not all suspects know their rights and few know them in detail. Code C is intended to deal with this:

> 3.1 When a person is brought to a police station under arrest or arrested at the station having gone there voluntarily, the custody officer must make sure the person is told clearly about:
>
> (a) the following continuing rights, which may be exercised at any stage during the period in custody:
>
> (i) their right to consult privately with a solicitor and that free independent legal advice is available … ;
>
> (ii) their right to have someone informed of their arrest … ;
>
> (iii) their right to consult the Codes of Practice … ; and
>
> (iv) if applicable, their right to interpretation and translation … and their right to communicate with their High Commission, Embassy or Consulate

This should ensure that arrested suspects are told their main rights orally, and para 3.2 provides that detainees must be given a written notice too, which sets out these and their other rights. But there are two loopholes here. First, as noted in section 4.2, the duty to tell suspects their rights orally does not apply to the right to a telephone call or the right to receive visits (at the custody officer's discretion). Second, the obligation begins only when the suspect is brought to the police station, if they are under arrest.[222] Suspects who are arrested some distance from the place of the alleged crime are therefore in police custody for a long time (whilst being transported to the relevant police station) before they are informed of their rights other than the right to silence. This provides scope for illegal interviewing to occur en route to the police station, and there is no prohibition on letting suspects incriminate themselves voluntarily—if that is an appropriate way of describing the actions of suspects in police custody.

---

[218] A similar view was taken by the ECtHR in *Brennan v UK* (2001). In *Alladice* (1988) 87 Cr App Rep 380 the (differently constituted) Court of Appeal regarded itself as bound by *Samuel* but was rather more sympathetic to the police. This led them to a different view of the consequences following on from unlawful delay of access: see section 11.3.1.2.

[219] Brown D, *Detention at the Police Station under the Police and Criminal Evidence Act 1984* (Home Office Research Study no 104) (London: HMSO, 1989) p 68.

[220] Bucke and Brown (1997: 23). [221] See earlier discussion of *Murray v UK* (1996) 22 EHRR 29.

[222] If suspects are participating in 'voluntary interviews', meaning that they are not under arrest but will have received the police caution, this means they have similar rights, entitlements and safeguards as those arrested and/or detained in police custody, i.e. to be informed of their rights including in writing, to legal advice, an AA, interpreter etc. See PACE, Code C, para 3.21.

The procedure to be adopted on arrival at the station is as follows. After authorising detention, custody officers must tell suspects of their main rights. They will be asked specifically whether they want to consult a solicitor. If so, this should be facilitated (as described shortly) as soon as possible. Every step in this process must be recorded on the custody record. For this set of protections to work it is essential that the police operate the system in good faith, and that a solicitor be readily available.

Obviously not all solicitors are available around the clock and many suspects are arrested at night, weekends or other awkward times. Before PACE this was a major problem. Softley (1980) found that around one-quarter of all suspects who requested advice did not get any. This was sometimes because the police refused to let them see a solicitor, but often a solicitor simply could not be found. There was a clear need to provide some form of scheme which secured access within a reasonable amount of time for the sake of both the suspect and the police so that unreasonable delay was not caused. This was bound to cost a lot of money. While the government in the 1980s provided such money as was required, we shall see that this is no longer true.

Suspects requesting legal advice now have two choices. They may speak to their 'own' lawyer if they have one. Alternatively, they are put in contact with a national Defence Solicitor Call Centre (DSCC) which decides whether to route the request to a nationwide service, CDS Direct (this provides advice over the phone for relatively minor offences), or to an individual solicitor, if the offence is sufficiently serious, who will decide whether to attend the station. This may be a duty solicitor but requests by a suspect for their own solicitor are also processed via the DSCC.[223] The country is divided into a number of legal aid regions, within each of which are several areas. Each area has a duty solicitor scheme.[224] There is no obligation on solicitors to participate, but in reality most defence firms do because the duty scheme provides access to clients, and therefore income. But, some schemes are over-stretched, and research by Kemp indicated that small firms suffer particular problems providing out-of-hours police station legal advice, and that this situation has worsened due to legal aid cuts that have led firms to employ fewer legal advisors.[225]

4.5.2 The take-up of advice by suspects

Despite large increases in the request rate since 1988, less than half of all suspects receive advice.

Within these general figures, there are considerable variations. For instance, advice is sought more often for serious than for minor offences (advice is sought and received in over half of all cases involving offences tried in the Crown court)[226] and is sought more often by adults than by young offenders even though the latter are vulnerable.[227] Great variations exist between different police stations, perhaps due to the different cultures and attitudes of staff who work there or the quality and availability of legal advisors, all of which may feed into detainee decisions about whether to take up this right.[228]

---

[223] Pressure to reduce the amount of advice given face-to-face has increased over the years (discussed further later). The latest changes are made in the 2008 version of Code C, para 6.1 and Note 6B. Art 6 imposes no obligations concerning the way in which advice is provided as long as it fulfils the 'fair trial' requirement: *Salduz v Turkey* [2008] ECHR 1542.

[224] These were originally established under s.59 of PACE. See now the Access to Justice Act 1999, s.3 and Criminal Defence Service *Duty Solicitor Arrangements* 2001.

[225] Kemp, V (2018) *Effective Police Station Legal Advice Country Report 2: England and Wales* University of Nottingham, online at <http://eprints.nottingham.ac.uk/51145/1/Country%20Report%20England%20and%20Wales%20Final%20.pdf> (accessed 1 October 2019). [226] RCCJ (1993: 35).

[227] Although trained volunteers acting as AAs generally advise suspects to request advice in strong terms: Brookman F and Pierpoint H, 'Access to Legal Advice for Young Suspects and Remand Prisoners' (2003) 42(5) *Howard Journal of Crime and Justice* 452.

[228] Brown et al (1992); Bucke and Brown (1997: ch 3); Skinns (2009b).

Table 4.2 Request and consultation rates, 1988–1996

	Request rate (%)	Consultation rate (%)
1988	25	19
1991	32	25
1995–6	40	34
2007	60	45
2009	48	35

All figures derived from Bucke and Brown (1997: ch 3) except 2007, derived from Skinns (2009b) and 2009 derived from Pleasence et al (2011), with the latter being the most reliable recent estimate as it draws on a large sample of 30,921 custody records, across 44 police stations in 4 police force areas.

Despite the general increase, only around half of suspects exercise their right to advice, and just over a third actually secure it. This seems difficult to understand at first sight. Nearly all are in the police station involuntarily. Most will be frightened or apprehensive, unsure of their rights and worried about how long they will be detained. Many perceive the police to be 'against' them—as of course they are in an adversarial system. Against this intimidating backcloth they are being offered something for nothing: a lawyer, whose sole job whilst in the station will be to help that suspect, at precisely nil cost. Yet the response of around half is to say 'no thanks' (44%), and many that do request legal advice later change their mind.[229]

In the earliest study of PACE, Maguire (1988) observed that some suspects have a predisposition to seek advice while others do not, and some are very much easier to influence than are others. Suspects arrested for trivial offences like drunkenness are entitled to advice but they correctly perceive that it would usually be of little use to them. There is a low elasticity of demand among these suspects. Other suspects who reject the idea of legal advice include those who are confident that they can handle the situation and, at the opposite end of the spectrum, fatalistic suspects who believe that nothing can help them at all. Needless to say, neither the confidence nor the fatalism are always justified (Bucke and Brown 1997: 22). Some suspects simply trust the police to deal with them so fairly that they see no need for advice or help from anyone else,[230] which will again be true only some of the time and, of course, begs the question of what is 'fair' in an adversary system.[231]

As we saw earlier, the main goal of many suspects is to get out of the station as soon as possible. These suspects refuse advice only because it might delay their departure.[232] Most suspects who refuse advice do so because of the actual or likely wait.[233] These suspects make strategic decisions based on their past experience with police and solicitors. Sometimes their bad experiences with solicitors make them reluctant to request them. Others have a low opinion of duty solicitors in particular, mistakenly believing them not

---

[229] Kemp V, 'Digital Legal Rights: Exploring Detainees' Understanding of their Right to have a Lawyer and Potential Barriers to Accessing Legal Advice' (2020) *Criminal Law Review* 129–147.

[230] That this attitude can contribute to major miscarriages of justice is evidenced by the post-PACE case of Sheila Bowler: Devlin A and Devlin T, *Anybody's Nightmare* (East Harling: Taverner Publications, 1998) at p 87.

[231] Discussed more fully in Sanders A and Bridges L, 'The Right to Legal Advice', in Walker C and Starmer K (eds), *Miscarriages of Justice* (London: Blackstone, 1999); and in Sanders A, 'Access to Justice in the Police Station: An Elusive Dream?' in Young and Wall (1996a). [232] Kemp (2020).

[233] Kemp V and Balmer N, *Criminal Defence Services: Users' perspectives* Research Paper No. 21 (London: Legal Services Research Centre, 2008); Brown et al 1992: 53.

to be independent of the police: 'Duty solicitors are crap anyway, they work for the fucking police and the courts.'[234] Most suspects have no opportunity to plan ahead. The defendant in *Aspinall*[235] requested a solicitor but, because of a mix-up, he did not see one. After 13 hours in custody he signed the custody record to say that he no longer wished to see a solicitor, 'the reason being I want to get home to my missus and kid.'

Some suspects have an inflexible elasticity of demand because they always want a solicitor. Many of these are likely to be charged with serious offences, have long records or believe that a solicitor can do them no harm and may well do them some good. These suspects demand solicitors in almost any circumstances, and would do so even if the police did not have to inform them of their rights and to arrange advice for them.

Between these two groups, Maguire (1988) argued, there is a large group of suspects, accused of moderately serious crimes such as shoplifting, car theft, handling stolen goods, burglary and deception, who have a very high elasticity of demand. Many of these suspects, when they do not seek advice, say that this is because it is 'not worth it', or that they will wait to see what happens (very few later deciding to seek advice).[236] Decisions about whether or not to seek advice are influenced by a large number of factors. These include the attitudes and practices of the police and the availability and likely quality of the advice.

4.5.3 The attitudes and practices of the police

Many suspects learn about their rights for the first time when told them by the custody officer. Others may know some of their rights but not crucial details (such as advice being free and independent). Others may be afraid to ask for a lawyer. It follows that the way the police inform suspects of their rights—whether the choice is put as a 'question expecting the answer yes or the answer no'—could be an important influence upon them.[237] Sanders et al in the late 1980s observed the reception of suspects into custody in 10 police stations and concluded that the police utilise 'ploys' to dissuade suspects from seeking advice in over 40% of all cases. Kemp very recently found that the police continue to use ploys to dissuade suspects from seeking legal advice.[238] Table 4.3 shows the great range of ploys used.

It is likely that ploys are (or were) even more extensively used than this study detected, since, in this context, the presence of an observer inevitably affects the process being observed. In one example given by Sanders et al,[239] two children suspected of shoplifting from Mothercare were being processed by a custody officer. When the researcher walked into the custody area, he heard and saw the custody officer reading out the suspects' rights in an incomprehensible manner. The custody officer looked up, saw the researcher and said, 'Are you the chap from Mothercare?' The researcher replied, 'No, I am the chap from Birmingham University', whereupon the custody officer went bright red, stopped, and started reading out the suspects rights very slowly and clearly from the beginning.

Comments such as 'you'll have to wait in the cells until a solicitor gets here' are a dire threat to those suspects for whom length of detention is a greater concern than whether or not they are charged. One suspect told Kemp that, having been brought to the police station at 2am, his case would be dealt with by 8am and that having a solicitor might delay things, so he didn't bother. Twelve hours later, he had not yet been interviewed.[240] So, whilst

---

[234] Suspect quoted in Choongh (1997: 149). Sanders et al (1989) and Kemp and Balmer (2008) also found suspects who believed this. This belief is understandable in view of the way many duty solicitors used to, and sometimes still do, behave. [235] *Aspinall* [1999] Crim LR 741.

[236] See Bucke and Brown (1997: 22) and Skinns (2009a and b) who also found that the prospect of spending longer in the cells dissuaded many from seeking advice. [237] Maguire (1988: 31).

[238] Kemp V, 'Digital Legal Rights: Exploring Detainees' Understanding of their Right to have a Lawyer and Potential Barriers to Accessing Legal Advice' (2020) *Criminal Law Review* 129–147.

[239] Sanders et al (1989: 63). [240] Kemp (2020).

Table 4.3 Police ploys

Ploy	Amount used (principal ploy only)
1. Rights told too quickly/incomprehensibly/incompletely	142 (42.9%)
2. Suspect's query answered unhelpfully/incorrectly	5 (1.5%)
3. Suspect told that inability to name own solicitor may affect right to have one contacted	2 (0.6%)
4. 'It's not a very serious charge'	1 (0.3%)
5. 'You'll have to wait in the cells until the solicitor gets here'	13 (3.9%)
6. 'You don't have to make your mind up now. You can have one later if you want to'	27 (8.2%)
7. 'You're only going to be here a short time'	25 (7.6%)
8. 'You're only here to be charged/interviewed'	14 (4.2%)
9. [To juvenile] 'You'll have to [or "do you want to"] wait until an adult gets here' [before decision can be made]	18 (5.4%)
10. [To adult] '[Juvenile] has said he doesn't want one'	8 (2.4%)
11. Combination of 9 and 10	4 (1.2%)
12. 'We won't be able to get a solicitor at this time/none of them will come out/he won't be in his office'	6 (1.8%)
13. 'You don't need one for this type of offence'	2 (0.6%)
14. 'Sign here, here and here' [no information given]	7 (2.1%)
15. 'You don't have to have one'	4 (1.2%)
16. 'You're being transferred to another station—wait until you get there'	6 (1.8%)
17. CO interprets indecision/silence as refusal	9 (2.7%)
18. 'You're not going to be interviewed/charged'	1 (0.3%)
19. 'You can go to see a solicitor when you get out/at court'	9 (2.7%)
20. 'You're (probably) going to get bail'	6 (1.8%)
21. Gives suspect *Solicitor's Directory* or list of solicitors without explanation/assistance	3 (0.9%)
22. Other	19 (5.7%)
Total	331 (100.0%)

Source: Sanders A and Bridges L, 'Access to legal advice and police malpractice' [1990] *Criminal Law Review* 494.

the warning is true it is also incomplete: it ignores the fact that most suspects are put in the cells until they are interrogated anyway. It also means that many suspects, often incorrectly, think that if they refuse advice they will get out sooner.[241] Solicitors interviewed by Kemp

---

[241] Skinns (2009a) found that suspects who received advice were in custody on average for 4.6 hours longer than those who did not, but this may reflect the types of case in which advice is sought as much as delay caused by waiting for advice.

in another study report that the police continue to suggest that requesting legal advice will delay release, with one saying:

> For the past 20 years I've been told the same thing by clients that they didn't have legal advice because they were told by the police that we'd keep them waiting a long time. They want to get out quickly, either because they have a job to go to, they have their kids to sort out, or they need a fix. We're blamed for the delay, but we'll be ready for the interview as soon as the police are ready to go.[242]

It is difficult to establish a causal link between the use of police ploys and actual requests for advice by suspects. Sanders et al found that there was little correlation between the two but this may have been because the police use these ploys primarily against those suspects whom they thought would ask for a solicitor anyway, or for whom they particularly did not want a solicitor involved. Brown et al considers the lack of correlation to be evidence that custody officers are not deliberately trying to obstruct suspects. They argue that:

> … over-speedy and unclear expositions of rights may have occurred simply because custody officers were all too familiar with what they were saying and failed to appreciate that to some suspects the information was new and unfamiliar … (1992: 29)

Similarly, Morgan et al found 'active discouragement, leading questions, or incomplete statement of rights' in 'only' about 14% of cases. In the rest, they say, rights were presented 'reasonably', but that 'few suspects are in a "reasonable" frame of mind at the time. There is usually no attempt to make sure the statement has been understood.'[243] Bucke and Brown (1997: ch 3) found that few suspects (almost none at all in two stations) were asked by the police why they had refused legal advice, a clear breach of Code C (para 6.5). The failure to test for understanding, or to seek reasons for decisions, is important because research carried out in the 1990s and more recently has found that many suspects think they have grasped what the police tell them, even though often unaware of important details, while many others are unsure about what is going on.[244]

How far the police engage in 'ploys' remains a matter of debate, but the fact that they inadvertently and sometimes purposefully break the rules is indisputable. The notification provisions of Code C were breached, in the opinion of Brown's observers, in 16% of the cases observed prior to the revision of the PACE Codes of Practice in 1991, and in 26% of the cases observed after that revision, which required the police to give more information to suspects. Occasionally, suspects were simply asked if they wanted a solicitor. About 7–8% of suspects were warned about the likely delay if they requested a lawyer, though Brown et al (at p 42) do not interpret this as a 'ploy'. It seems, then, that the police go through the motions of providing due process-based rights to advice, but insufficient attention is paid to ensuring that the message gets through to the vulnerable, and the anxious, who need them most.

Whether or not advice was originally requested, the police are supposed to remind suspects of their right to legal advice at the time of each review of detention and at the start

---

[242] Kemp V, *Effective Police Station Legal Advice Country Report 2: England and Wales* (Nottingham: University of Nottingham, 2018) p 6 online at <http://eprints.nottingham.ac.uk/51145/1/Country%20Report%20England%20and%20Wales%20Final%20.pdf> (accessed 1 October 2019).

[243] Morgan et al, *Police Powers and Policy: A Study of the Work of Custody Officers* (report to ESRC) (unpublished).

[244] Brown et al (1992); Choongh (1997); Kemp and Balmer (2008) (who found that 16% had 'no idea' what was going on, and as many more were not sure what was going on). Though now rather dated, Clare and Gudjonsson, for example, found that only 40% of suspects could fully understand the written notice of rights provided to them (Clare I and Gudjonsson G, *Devising and Piloting an Experimental Version of the Notice to Detained Persons* (Royal Commission on Criminal Justice, Research Study no 7) (London: HMSO, 1993).).

of the interview.[245] That the police often fail to do so is evident from the following extract from the transcript of a trial:[246]

> Q: [Defence Counsel]: At the end of that interview you offered the opportunity to have a lawyer?
>
> A: [Officer]: That is correct.
>
> Q: Why did you not do that at the beginning?
>
> A: Because he had already been offered the opportunity to have a solicitor. If he wanted a solicitor he was welcome to have one but I am not going to encourage it.
>
> Q: You did not offer him one for that reason?
>
> A: No, not at the beginning of the interview.
>
> Q: You suspected that if he did get a solicitor he would be advised to say nothing?
>
> A: Yes.
>
> Q: Which is why he was not offered one?
>
> A: Yes.

Another complaint sometimes made is that the police try to rush people into accepting cautions without the benefit of prior legal advice, and try to avoid giving lawyers, when suspects persist with their requests, sufficient information to advise properly. In *DPP v Ara*[247] this was held to be unlawful, but this ruling seems to be ignored: in 2008 a Crown prosecutor told a group of visitors to a police station that: 'We disclose the best evidence to elicit a guilty plea.'[248]

It is clear that, whether by accident or design, many officers discourage recourse to legal advice much of the time. But it is equally clear that many suspects—those with relatively inelastic demand—increasingly persevere with their requests. The police usually accept this, and the request rate is consequently rising. However in some cases—presumably where the police are particularly keen to interrogate the suspect without a lawyer present—the police go to great lengths to block access by, for example, using multiple ploys.[249] Sometimes the police do not call the lawyer at all, which is clearly unlawful. Sometimes the call is delayed, allowing time to persuade suspects to withdraw their requests for advice, to be interrogated before the lawyer arrives, or to be informally interviewed.[250] Dixon et al (1990: 128) comment that solicitors frequently complain that on arrival at the station they are 'informed by officers that the suspect has changed his mind, agreed to talk to them, and confessed.' The suspicion is that the police play a large part in this volte face. Unfortunately, custody records give no reason for failure to secure advice in one quarter of all such cases, thus making it difficult to account for the gap between the numbers requesting advice and those actually securing it.[251]

It would appear that giving the police the job of 'triggering' legal advice is a major obstacle to the success of the scheme. If the scheme were modified to allow solicitors to be in the

---

[245] Code C, paras 15.4 and 11.2.
[246] Letter from the trial judge published at [1989] *Criminal Law Review* 763.
[247] [2002] 1 Cr App R 159. See Azzopardi J, 'Disclosure at the Police Station, the Right of Silence, and *DPP v Ara*' [2002] *Criminal Law Review* 295.
[248] Thanks to Ed Cape—who will now probably never be invited to a police station again—for this snippet. On disclosure, see ch 5.
[249] Sanders et al (1989: 57) found that in these cases the request rate is noticeably lower than average.
[250] Sanders and Bridges (1990). All these abuses were also observed in the small-scale observational study by Choongh (1997: ch 6).
[251] Brown et al (1992: 61). The most recent research also found that a significant minority of requests were not met, and that police ploys were still widespread: Skinns (2009a and b).

police station round the clock it would almost certainly increase the advice rate, although it would be difficult and expensive to organise. Alternatively, s.58 might be amended so that advice would be provided unless actively refused. This would at least ensure that all the confused suspects who currently do not secure advice would do so. The Runciman Commission recommended none of these solutions.[252] Apart from some minor changes, it recommended that suspects who refuse advice 'should then be given the opportunity of speaking to a duty solicitor on the telephone.' Suspects are already entitled to do this, but the Code now requires the custody officer to tell suspects who refuse advice that they can speak on the phone if they are concerned about having to wait (paras 6.4–6.5). This could have been taken further, by putting all suspects automatically into telephone contact with a duty solicitor (or, now, CDS Direct) in order to discuss the question of legal advice. The only losers, apart from crime control adherents, would be the Treasury. However, this makes assumptions about the value of telephone advice which we shall see are unwarranted.

4.5.4 The attitudes and practices of the legal profession

It would be misleading to give the impression that all, or even most, of the problems of securing legal advice in police stations are the fault of the police. Many suspects do not want legal advice because of their experiences with duty solicitors or even with lawyers in general. Delivering legal services to suspects in police custody has many difficulties.

4.5.4.1 Unavailability and contact time

We have seen that not all suspects who request advice get any. This is sometimes due to cancellation of requests because suspects do not want to wait any longer for advice to be provided. In some cases an able and willing solicitor simply cannot be located. This is bound to happen when suspects want to speak to their own solicitors, and this is what most suspects want.[253] Duty solicitor schemes are supposed to provide a safety net.

On average, nearly four hours elapses between a request for advice and getting it.[254] This is a greater delay than used to be normal,[255] probably because of the arrangements introduced in 2008 (see later). Delay is sometimes unavoidable, especially at night or if a solicitor is already dealing with a client. However, solicitors are reluctant to attend a police station simply 'to hold a suspect's hand'—especially since any time spent waiting for the police to be ready for interview is no longer a bill-able activity—so they usually delay attendance until the police are ready to interview. During the Covid-19 pandemic these issues were accentuated, with legal advisors refusing to attend police stations where social distancing was not in place and with the Law Society agreeing guidance with various other bodies permitting legal advisors to 'attend' police interviews via audio-link.[256] Although understandable that solicitors may not always be available to attend the police station and that initial phone contact may be seen by solicitors as providing all the reassurance suspects need, this ignores the frightening isolation of detention discussed earlier. As one more sensitive solicitor put it: ' … I think the terror of being alone in the police station is such, it [contact with a solicitor] may have no legal value whatsoever, but the psychological value of speaking to a solicitor early is not inconsiderable.'[257]

---

[252] RCCJ (1993: 36).
[253] Phillips and Brown (1998: ch 4) found that about 65% of suspects seeking advice wanted their own solicitor. Kemp and Balmer's findings (2008: 35, 48) were similar.
[254] Skinns (2009a: 63).
[255] Brown et al (1992: 62).
[256] Law Society (2020).
[257] Bridges et al, 'Quality in Criminal Defence Services' (London: Legal Services Commission, 2000) pp 67–8.

4.5.4.2 Solicitor or non-solicitor

Of those suspects who do secure advice, a large number do not see a solicitor at all, but a trainee solicitor, para-legal or police station representative, some of whom are former police officers. This was so in around 30% of cases observed by Sanders et al in the 1980s, the proportion being rather higher for 'own' solicitors (50%) than for duty solicitors (16%). Although the numbers fluctuate, a large minority of suspects continue to see non-solicitors.[258] This proportion is likely to rise again in the future now that all 'franchised' duty solicitors are allowed to use non-solicitors who are trained or in training, although a solicitor must first speak on the phone to the suspect before a non-solicitor is allowed to advise.[259]

There is nothing wrong with the use of trained paralegals or well-supervised trainees, but in the 1980s and early 1990s many were not trained or supervised properly and there were terrible abuses.[260] Now, however, all solicitors and non-solicitors wishing to do duty solicitor work have to be trained and to pass tests, or be in training. The aim of this 'accreditation' scheme is to ensure that suspects are not disadvantaged by being advised by non-solicitors, and it appears to be successful. It seems to have led to better advice, more time spent with suspects, and a more adversarial approach in police interviews.[261] However, the level from which quality has been raised, and which was set by many qualified solicitors, was not very high, as we shall see.[262]

If junior staff are to be used extensively it is important that they, and the quality of their work, be supervised. Traditionally this is done in an ad hoc way, if at all, in solicitors' firms. The Legal Aid Agency (LAA) (which oversees publicly-funded criminal defence work) now insists on supervision, usually in the form of reviews of completed cases, but ensuring firms do this is almost impossible. Research carried out in the late 1990s indicated that some firms do not take it seriously. As a senior member of a firm which had reviewed only one case in 10 months wrote to his colleagues: 'We must complete the periodic reviews ... We cannot afford to leave it any longer. It will not take a minute to do it'.[263] Even firms that do appear to take it seriously identify very few of the flaws in case handling that the researchers identified, and remedial action where flaws are identified appear very rare.[264] In light of some of these concerns, the LAA now requires all firms that hold contracts to provide duty solicitor services to undergo periodic assessment of file reviews, training and appraisal schemes. Failure to comply with the standards that are set will result in disciplinary sanctions, accreditation being withdrawn and ultimately the contract being cancelled.[265] Firms must also bear the costs of accreditation, so there is significant incentive to comply. However, reviews are conducted between one and three years apart (depending on the chosen scheme) so the potential for firms to fall into bad habits between review remains.

---

[258] McConville M and Hodgson J, *Custodial Legal Advice and the Right to Silence* (Royal Commission on Criminal Justice Research Study no 16) (London: HMSO, 1993) p 17. Also see McConville et al, *Standing Accused* (Oxford: Clarendon, 1994); Phillips and Brown (1998: ch 4).

[259] For details see Cape E, *Defending Suspects at Police Stations* 5th edn (London: Legal Action Group, 2006c) ch 1.

[260] See, for example, discussion in the 1st edn of this book. Also see Sanders (1996) and McConville et al (1994).

[261] Bridges L and Choongh S, *Improving Police Station Legal Advice* (London: Law Society, 1998) ch 4. But note that solicitors may advise their own clients without being accredited, so long as they hold a general criminal contract with the Legal Aid Agency. [262] Bridges and Choongh (1998); Bridges et al (2000).

[263] Bridges et al (2000: 99). [264] Bridges et al (2000: ch 6).

[265] See *Legal Aid Agency Quality Standards* at <https://www.gov.uk/guidance/legal-aid-agency-quality-standards> (accessed 15 October 2019).

4.5.4.3 Advice in person or over the telephone

About a fifth of all advice is over the phone alone.[266] Telephone advice is not necessarily inappropriate. The offence may be trivial and guilt not in doubt; the suspect may want advice on one specific thing only; the police may want to know something discrete and straightforward before, for instance, releasing on bail. Telephone advice will, however, be inappropriate where:

(a) the suspect is disputing, or unclear about, the allegations;

(b) the offence is serious;

(c) the suspect is vulnerable;

(d) detention is likely to be lengthy;

(e) the police are planning to question the suspect;

(f) the police plan to subject the suspect to an ID parade or similar; or,

(g) there may have been police malpractice.

Solicitors are professionals who ought to be able to judge these matters. Official guidance to assist them was devised, including the principle that, when in doubt, they should go to the station (and, once at the station they should stay, in all but exceptional cases, for any interview that might take place).[267] However, amendments to Code C (Note 6B), and the rules by which DSCC operate, now prevent advice being given in person in many cases (see later).

In reality, solicitors are often guided by considerations other than the needs of the suspect, and much telephone advice is unsatisfactory. Advice is sometimes given to remain silent, for instance. Although this tells suspects their rights, it does not actually help them to remain silent in the face of vigorous questioning. Sanders et al found that solicitors were wanted for many things other than the simple provision of legal advice—to witness what went on, to act as emotional supports, to secure bail, and to take action over alleged malpractice. As the legislation acknowledges, access to a solicitor is to provide not just advice but also assistance. Little assistance can be provided over the telephone.

Just as the police fail to adhere, in many cases, to their code of practice, so some solicitors fail to adhere to theirs. This was particularly evident shortly after PACE came into operation. Around 14% of all suspects in 1988 saw a legal advisor in person. Of all interrogated suspects, about 22% saw a legal advisor in person, but only about 14% had a legal advisor with them in the interrogation, because many solicitors who attended the station did not attend the interrogation.[268] The result was that many suspects might as well not have received any advice for all the use their lawyer was to them. Many suspects will not be frank with an often unknown voice on the phone: they may not trust the person, and in any case the police sometimes listen to the conversation. As one suspect told Sanders et al: 'If you met him face to face you could talk'.[269] Another, asked if she would have the same solicitor again, replied: 'We've not really had him have we? For all I know it might not have been a solicitor!' Cases were seen where suspects who told the solicitor that they had been assaulted were left to languish in the cells for half the weekend, and where suspects were told on the phone 'not to say anything' in the interview when it must have been known that for most suspects this advice would be impossible to follow.[270] As we have seen, many suspects are vulnerable (but not recognised as such) and many more are less than fully

---

[266] Phillips and Brown (1998: ch 4); Pattenden and Skinns (2010). Telephone advice used to be used even more. See Brown et al (1992) and Sanders et al (1989).

[267] For details of the guidance, see Cape (2006c: paras 3.52–3.70).

[268] Sanders et al (1989: ch 6).   [269] Sanders et al (1989: 119–20).

[270] Sanders et al (1989: 117–26).

rational as a result of their predicament. Most of these people need the support of someone whose duty is to look after their interests.

As a result of these abuses the official guidance for solicitors on when to attend stations was tightened up in the 1990s, creating much clearer obligations for duty solicitors. In 1995/6 a large research study found that only 37% of suspects had an advisor with them in all their interviews.[271] It seems that the type of service given depends as much on the status of the client and the 'culture' of the law firm in question as the nature of the case, although solicitors deny this.[272] Many solicitors argue that, even if telephone advice is sometimes given inappropriately, this is all that can be expected of an under-remunerated profession under pressure. Attendance at the police station in person is, however, incentivised—lawyers receive a much reduced payment for giving advice over the telephone only. This will be all the more so now that solicitors are paid a fixed fee for police station visits that may be lengthy, demanding and at unsocial hours.[273] To compound the problem, in most police stations phone conversations may be held in the main custody room, as are many face-to-face consultations.[274] Police officers are therefore able to listen to these conversations, sometimes on purpose but sometimes because they have to continue with their work within earshot. This has been held to breach s.58 and ECHR Art 6, but only if the absence of privacy is deliberate, rather than for logistical reasons.[275] In some new police stations there are in-cell intercom systems, but these work badly and the sound of suspect-solicitor telephone consultations often carries beyond the cell (Skinns 2009b).

4.5.4.4 The quality of advice and assistance

In an adversarial system, solicitors would be expected to advise and assist suspects in the police station to the best of their abilities, regardless of how difficult this might make it for the police to secure evidence sufficient to prosecute. Under due process, we would expect to find protections for suspects detained against their will, and would expect legal advisors to help suspects to use these protections. Thus in Britain there are rules which aim to prevent oppressive questioning and allow suspects to stay silent (albeit with a possible penalty—see chapter 5), which solicitors should use to their clients' advantage. As Code C itself states: 'The solicitor's only role in the police station is to protect and advance the legal rights of his client.' (Note 6D).

What should legal advisors do? According to Cape, a leading practitioner/academic on this topic, they should:

- advise suspects as to their best interests;
- keep an accurate record of their consultations with their clients and of the police interview;
- ensure their clients act according to their best interests (subject to not knowingly lying or actively misleading);
- ensure the police act fairly and lawfully; and
- protect clients from unnecessary pressure and distress.[276]

---

[271] Bucke and Brown (1997: ch 4). Most suspects are interviewed only once. Bucke and Brown found that in the minority of cases where there is more than one interview an advisor is normally, but not always, present for them all. [272] Sanders et al (1989: ch 6); Bridges et al (2000).
[273] The 'pressure' argument is supported by Brown et al (1992: 88), but rejected by McConville et al (1994) who point out that some firms, albeit a minority, provide a very good service without noticeable financial hardship. Also see Hodgson J, 'Adding Injury to Injustice: the Suspect at the Police Station' (1994) 21 *Journal of Law and Society* 85. On the new remuneration structure, see later in this chapter.
[274] Phillips and Brown (1998: ch 4); Pattenden and Skinns (2010); HMIP and HMIC (2009).
[275] The case law is contradictory. See Pattenden and Skinns (2010) and also *Roques*.
[276] Cape (2006c: chs 3, 5, 7).

What all this means in concrete terms will vary from case to case. If suspects who indicated they would remain silent start to answer they can be reminded of their right to silence and, if necessary, a private consultation can be demanded. If suspects' answers are unclear, or points that could help them are not brought out, the advisor can ask clarificatory questions or suggest that the suspect may want to add something. If questioning becomes hectoring or abusive, or threatening looks or gestures are used, the advisor should intervene by, for example, objecting, asking for re-phrasing, asking for a break or advising silence. Advisors have to be careful not to contravene Code C for if they do the police may require them to leave the interview.[277]

Early research into the work of legal advisors found that legal advisors did very little when they attended interrogations, frequently seeing their task as facilitating the process, rather than protecting the rights of their clients.[278] Baldwin, for example, described most legal advisors as 'essentially passive',[279] while Quirk reports that there is a lack of adversarialism among many legal advisors who attend the police station.[280] Similarly, Pivaty also notes of the lawyers encountered in her study that some were reluctant to challenge police behaviour in interviews and were also found to co-operate with 'police efforts to nudge admissions from suspects in exchange for out-of-court settlements or bail'.[281] However, Roberts points out that a lack of adversarialism does not mean that lawyers fail to do their job in most cases ' … if the police interviewer was behaving professionally and the suspect did not need assistance, intervention on the part of the solicitor would be quite unnecessary.'[282]

Without matching the behaviour of the police and of the solicitor against Code C and the official guidance, we cannot know whether non-intervention was justified or not. Bridges and Choongh did this, finding that in around one quarter of interviews no intervention is called for. Advisors do intervene in most of those in which it is called for, but in over half of all such cases they do so less often than they should.[283] This level of performance, while not brilliant, is better than it used to be. Failure to adequately challenge police behaviour, such as objectionable police questioning can be crucial, as the 'Cardiff Three' case shows.[284] In this case, three men were convicted of killing a woman after one 'confessed'. He challenged the confession in court, but the trial judge ruled it admissible. The tapes of questioning were played to the Court of Appeal, which condemned them as contrary to Code C, quashed the convictions and criticised the defendant's lawyer for sitting through these interrogations without objecting.

The problem is that adversarialism is not a natural stance for most defence lawyers, particularly those who spend a lot of time advising suspects. To such lawyers, the police station is the workplace and maintaining good relations with work colleagues (i.e. the police) is important:

---

[277] Paras 6.1–6.15 with accompanying notes (discussed earlier).

[278] See Brown et al (1992: 89), and McConville and Hodgson (1993). See also, for further examples, Sanders and Bridges (1999: 51) and Dixon D, 'Common Sense, Legal Advice, and the Right of Silence' [1991] *Public Law* 233 at p 242.

[279] Baldwin J, *The Role of Legal Representatives at the Police Station* (Royal Commission on Criminal Justice Research Study no 3) (London: HMSO, 1993b) Table 1.

[280] Quirk H, *The Rise and Fall of the Right to Silence* (Abingdon: Routledge, 2016).

[281] Pivaty A, *Criminal Defence at Police Stations: A Comparative and Empirical Study* (Abingdon: Routledge, 2020) p 91.

[282] Roberts D, 'Questioning the Suspect: the Solicitor's Role' [1993] *Criminal Law Review* 369.

[283] Bridges and Choongh (1998: ch 8). This research, done in the mid-1990s, shows that, despite limitations in quality, there has been a big improvement since McConville and Hodgson (1993) carried out their research in the late 1980s.   [284] *Paris, Abdullahi and Miller* (1993) 97 Cr App R 99.

You've got to do the best for your client, but you've still got to live with the system many years on. So ... most solicitors do their best for their clients, but they also ... won't generally upset the police.[285]

Nearly 30 years later, recent research has reached a similar conclusion, with Pivaty noting that part of the reason why lawyers did not intervene in police interviews was due to a concern with maintaining a 'good' working relationship with the police.[286] Even Roberts, the author of the original Law Society guidance for police station advisors, is not sure what the role of the advisor should be: 'Interviews run better if the solicitor is able to establish a working relationship with the interviewer based on mutual respect.'[287] Better for whom? And at what cost are those working relationships purchased? Advisors are in a position of role conflict on potentially hostile territory. Given the nature of most custodial legal advice, it is not surprising that the police are less hostile to the provision of advice than they used to be, even though advice rates have risen. The police know that advice rarely gets in the way of them carrying out their adversarial role. Yet the response of the Runciman Commission to all this evidence—which it did not challenge—was simply to call for more and better training of solicitors and paralegals, and for more monitoring.[288] As Baldwin, author of some of the research on which this recommendation was based, comments, this 'looks at best superficial'.[289]

Since PACE was passed in 1984 the numbers of suspects securing advice and assistance, and having an advisor with them in interviews, has risen dramatically. Training for advisors has improved, and they have been made increasingly aware of their adversarial role in defending their clients. This should have led to greatly improved protection for suspects, but the improvements are limited, for various reasons.

First, it is difficult to give good advice without knowing the police case against the suspect. But the police need tell suspects and their advisors little or nothing,[290] and solicitors report that the quality of disclosure received varies considerably.[291] Accordingly, in order to get information from the police the defence usually needs to offer something in return. That 'something' is usually information, as distinct from silence. The police are well aware of the hold they have over solicitors: 'One of the solicitors from Gutts and Co asked me why some CID officers were walking towards the cell blocks. Cheeky bastard! ... He's getting no co-operation from me from now on – not until I get an apology' (Custody officer).[292]

Second, remaining silent can, as a result of the CJPO 1994, lead to great disadvantages at trial, as we shall see in chapter 5. Advisors have to make very difficult judgements. Silence alone is not enough to convict a defendant. So, if the police have no admissible evidence, a client would be well advised to remain silent; but since the police need not tell suspects and their advisors what evidence they have, it is often not possible to know whether such

---

[285] Solicitor, quoted in Dixon (1991: 239). Also see Baldwin (1993c: Table 1).
[286] Pivaty (2020: 91). [287] Roberts (1993: 370).
[288] RCCJ (1993: 35–39). The recommendations have been largely implemented. See Cape E, 'The Rise (and Fall?) of a Criminal Defence Profession' [2004] *Criminal Law Review* 401.
[289] Baldwin J, 'Power and Police Interviews' (1993b) 143 *New Law Journal* 1194 at 1195.
[290] This is a perennial problem. A 2018 review of disclosure practices by the Attorney General's office noted that disclosure obligations were not being given sufficient attention from the outset of a criminal investigation and not necessarily due to incompetence or ignorance on the part of the police (p 22). See 'Review of the efficiency and effectiveness of disclosure in the criminal justice system' (2018, Attorney General's Office). See also *Imran and Hussain* [1997] Crim LR 754; *Thirlwell* [2002] EWCA Crim 2703.   [291] Kemp (2018).
[292] Choongh (1997: 85). This is a good example of both the control that custody officers have in the station, and their lack of independence, both discussed earlier in this chapter.

advice is good advice.[293] Thus, paradoxically, in many cases advisors can best help their clients by encouraging co-operation with the police, even though co-operation is the antithesis of adversarialism.[294]

4.5.5 The erosion of the legal advice safeguard

The Access to Justice Act (AJA) 1999 established the Criminal Defence Service (CDS), which administered criminal legal aid for the Legal Services Commission (LSC). In 2001 the CDS introduced the General Criminal Contract, which was then extended in 2004 and again in 2008. In 2013, the LSC (a non-departmental government body) was replaced with the LAA, a department that sits squarely within the Ministry of Justice. The contracting regime continues, now with the Standard Crime Contract, which places the lawyer in a difficult position between the demands and expectations of the Ministry of Justice and of their clients.[295] Solicitors who wish to do publicly funded criminal defence work have to accept the conditions of this contract. If they wish to do duty solicitor work they additionally have to 'bid' for police station 'slots' according to the number of duty qualified solicitors that are employed at the firm. Anecdotally, it seems that this system may be open to abuse with some less reputable firms employing 'ghost' solicitors who were employed in name only in order to secure more slots. That practice has been clamped down on, with firms now required to demonstrate to the LAA that their duty solicitors are actively employed.[296] The major driver in these changes is to reduce the cost of legal aid, a pressure that is of increased urgency since the financial crisis of 2008 (see chapters 1 and 8). The CDS created the DSCC through which all requests for publicly funded advice must go. The DSCC now decides whether the case can be handled by telephone by CDS Direct or by a solicitor. The major changes are, in brief:[297]

> (a) Publicly funded face-to-face advice is now, as previously explained, restricted. This is not, in principle, wrong, as telephone advice is sometimes adequate. But whereas in the past this was a matter of professional judgement (not always, as we have seen, professionally carried out) now decisions are for a state agency (the DSCC) that has to meet financial targets. Further, we have already seen that vulnerable people, who especially need face-to-face advice and assistance often miss out currently. This will be worse when DSCC has to make a judgement based on what an officer says. And as we discussed earlier, in most police stations there is limited privacy when telephone advice is given.

---

[293] In a series of cases following *Condron v UK* (2001) 31 EHRR 1, the Court of Appeal has been increasingly unsympathetic, in applying s.34 CJPO, towards defendants who followed their lawyers' advice to remain silent. See Cooper S, 'Legal Advice and Pre-trial Silence - Unreasonable Developments' (2006) *International Journal of Evidence and Proof* 10, 60. For a good practical discussion see Cape (2006c: esp chs 4–5). See further Quirk (2016).

[294] For further discussion of these and other ways in which advisors need to negotiate with the police, albeit from a position of inequality, in order to serve their clients' interests, see Sanders (1996). It seems that the police now disclose more to advisors than they used to: Bridges and Choongh (1998). On the problems posed by the changes to the right of silence, see Jackson J, 'Silence and Proof: extending the boundaries of criminal proceedings in the UK' (2001) 5 *International Journal of Evidence and Proof* 145; Leng R, 'Silence Pre-trial, Reasonable Expectation and the Normative Distortion of Fact-finding' (2001) 5 *International Journal of Evidence and Proof* 240.

[295] Welsh L, 'The Effects of Changes to Legal Aid on Lawyers' Professional Identity and Behaviour in Summary Criminal Cases: A Case Study' (2017) 44(4) *Journal of Law and Society* 559–585.

[296] See, for example, Fouzder M, 'LAA relaxes "ghost" solicitor rule' *Law Society Gazette*, 2 July 2018.

[297] This sub-section is largely based on Bridges L and Cape E, *CDS Direct: Flying in the Face of the Evidence* (London: CCJS, Kings College London, 2008).

(b) If, as happens in many cases, CDS Direct decides that the case is not suitable for telephone advice, the case is then re-referred to DSCC who then contacts a solicitor. This causes huge delays—hence the longer contact times noted earlier reported by Skinns (2009a and b and 2010).

(c) Even if CDS Direct does deal with the case it has to phone the station to give the telephone advice. An evaluation carried out for the CDS found that in nearly a quarter of all cases the phone was not answered and, equally frequently, the police said that they were 'not ready' to allow the suspect to receive the advice at that time.

(d) Much more advice than ever before is now given by duty solicitors (including CDS Direct), which is generally contrary to the wishes of suspects.

(e) Police station work is now governed by fixed fees. This reduces the incentive for lawyers to spend time on cases, attend interviews, engage in lengthy consultations, argue for bail, and so forth.

The LAA argues that as it sets standards for law firms who could lose their contracts if they fail to meet them, this system will not lead to reduced standards. However, as observed earlier, the supervision requirements are of limited effectiveness. Bridges et al (2000a: ch 5 and 6) set a threshold whereby essential work should be carried out in at least 70% of all cases. A total of 44% of firms in their research failed this test. Sixty per cent failed a more rigorous test of quality. Very few of these flaws in case handling are either identified or acted upon. Thus most firms had a long way to go in delivering legal advice of adequate quality even before the new financial arrangements were established. Standards are now likely to deteriorate further. Solicitors' firms are businesses. They act according to the profit motive. The less they get paid for, the less they tend to do.[298] Moreover, this scheme increases the ability of the police to discourage suspects from seeking, or waiting, for advice. They can say, with even more justification than ever, that suspects will probably have to wait a long time, and that the advice when (if) it arrives may be of little value.[299]

It seems that suspects are at as much risk from the legal profession, legal changes (particularly to the right of silence) and the cost-cutting CDS (at the behest of government) as from the police. We have seen that the police station is police territory. When the whole purpose of due process rights is to protect suspects from the police, to make the police the main gatekeepers to these rights and to information and other needs of suspects is plainly illogical. The counter-argument would be that the purpose of the custody officer as an independent officer is precisely to stand between suspects, on the one hand, and investigating officers, on the other. Since custody officers have no specific interest in any one case, the custody officer will protect suspects by full enforcement of the rights in Code C, even if investigating officers object. This, however, relies on the rather formalistic distinction between a custody officer's duty and an investigating officer's duty. It does not take into account the shared outlook of different police officers. It also does not take into account the fact that an officer who wishes to secure the co-operation of fellow officers one day will not wish to 'get in their way' by acting out the custody officer role to perfection another day. Both custody officers and solicitors have to get on with other police officers in the latter's territory. 'Independent' operation under these conditions is hardly conceivable.

---

[298] For evidence from a Scottish experiment see Tata et al, 'Does Mode of Delivery Make a Difference to Criminal Case Outcomes and Clients' Satisfaction? The Public Defence Solicitor Experiment' [2004] *Criminal Law Review* 120; Tata C and Stephen F, 'The Impact of Fixed Payments: The Effect on Case Management, Case Trajectories, and "Quality" in Criminal Defence Work' online at <http://strathprints.strath.ac.uk/5420/2/impact_of_fixed_payments_Tata_and_Stephen.pdf> (accessed 10 April 2012) Fazio S and Tata C, 'Incentives, Criminal Defence Lawyers and Plea Bargaining' (2008) 28(3) *International Review of Law and Economics* 212.

[299] See, for example, Kemp (2018).

Suspects also need protecting from themselves. Voluntarism (consent) is completely misplaced when dealing with an intrinsically coercive situation.[300] Just as it is nonsense to argue that most confessions are voluntary, the same is true of decisions about advice. The rules at present are operated contrary to the interests of suspects because their interests and the interests of the gatekeepers diverge.

To make the rules work it would be necessary to install gatekeepers with the same interests as suspects, perhaps by paying solicitors or trained paralegals for effective police station work, and locating them in police stations so that they can see suspects with no delay. This might appear to be a ludicrous and expensive idea. But in 1997 a government committee argued that police-CPS working methods could be improved by installing prosecutors in police stations.[301] This recommendation was speedily implemented without regard to cost or other factors (see chapter 7). The Runciman Commission could have made recommendations on these lines for police station defence but did not do so. Clearly helping the police and CPS takes far higher priority than helping suspects.

Yet the future looks set to get worse, not better. For example, the CDS has since 2001 created a salaried 'public defender service' (PDS), in some areas of the UK (though only three of the original five offices remain), with the MOJ recently going on a 'hiring spree' to raise staffing levels.[302] This service suggests that some defence solicitors have become part of the machinery of the criminal justice system and committed to fulfilling its objectives. These include speedy justice, which sometimes conflicts with full justice. This may lead to further role confusion for defence lawyers. At the same time one of the objectives set for the PDS is to provide examples of excellence in criminal defence work and to provide 'benchmarking' information with a view to driving up standards in private firms.[303] An interim report from a team of independent researchers found relatively few examples of excellence in the areas piloting the new service. 'Public defenders' were, however, more likely than their private practitioner counterparts to advise their clients to give a 'no comment' interview and they also compared well in an assessment of the quality of the advice given. Yet in many ways public defender offices operated similarly to private firms. For example, they were more likely to give just telephone advice if they were acting as duty solicitor rather than own solicitor, and they relied heavily on accredited representatives (in at least 45% of the cases studied) to attend police stations. And both public defenders and private practitioners did a generally poor job of recording advice they had given to suspects on their legal position and the strategy they should adopt in interview. Given the discontinuous nature of legal representation, in which a case may be dealt with by several different defence advisors during the lifetime of a case, this suggests that much criminal defence work is still poor.[304] If 'public defenders' can develop a distinctly adversarial ethos in their work we might hope that the lessons learnt will indeed be used by their paymasters to drive up standards in private practice.

---

[300] See Young R and Wall D, 'Criminal Justice, Legal Aid and the Defence of Liberty' in Young and Wall (1996a).

[301] Home Office, *Review of Delay in the Criminal Justice System* (Narey Report) (London: Home Office, 1997a).

[302] Fouzder M, 'MoJ goes on hiring spree to strengthen Public Defender Service' (2018, online at: <https://www.lawgazette.co.uk/practice/moj-goes-on-hiring-spree-to-strengthen-public-defender-service/5067311.article> (accessed 10 July 2019)).

[303] *Public Defender Service: first year of operation* (London: Legal Services Commission, 2002) para 6.1.

[304] The report was available on the Legal Services Commission website at <www.legalservices.gov.uk/criminal/pds/evaluation.asp> (accessed 5 January 2010). See further Newman D, *Lawyers, Legal Aid and the Quest for Justice* (Oxford: Hart, 2013).

As it is, most solicitors tend to discourage suspects from pleading not guilty or failing to co-operate with the police. This is not just because, as noted earlier, of the pressure for reciprocal co-operation. It also stems from the non-adversarial character of the profession, the dim view some lawyers take of suspects and (especially when acting as duty solicitors)[305] the limited effort lawyers will provide for a limited reward. Compounding all of this are the institutional incentives (primarily a substantially reduced sentence) designed to encourage suspects to confess at the earliest opportunity (see further chapter 7). An example of how these factors interact is the case of a lorry driver arrested for importing cannabis and ecstasy in his lorry. He declined a solicitor, and, when questioned, denied knowing anything about the drugs. He was then advised by the police to secure legal advice. The duty solicitor, without asking to hear his story, advised him that he would get six years if he pleaded guilty to knowingly importing cannabis but 12 years if he contested this and was convicted after a trial of importing both types of drug. Eventually he pleaded guilty to knowingly importing cannabis but changed his plea, citing the pressure put on him to plead guilty by the solicitor. When asked about this, the solicitor admitted not seeking the lorry driver's side of the case, saying that as a solicitor practising in Dover who had been a duty solicitor in many cases like this, he was 'only' giving his standard advice based on his experience that 99% of cases like this end in conviction.[306]

In summary, police station legal advice and assistance often provides the most bare protection because: the police are gatekeepers, allowing them to manipulate the rules and the situation to dissuade suspects from seeking advice; the law gives the police a dominant bargaining position vis-à-vis both suspect and lawyer; the financial incentives for solicitors to do a minimalist job are greater than for them to do a fully adversarial job; and the professional ideology of the majority of solicitors, similar to that of the police, holds most suspects to be guilty and unworthy of a 'Rolls Royce' service.

4.6 Conclusion

The treatment of suspects in the police station is central to criminal justice. This is agreed by adherents of due process and crime control alike. For the latter, important evidence can be secured in the police station. This is precisely what worries due process adherents. Few would argue with the Runciman Commission that:

> The protection of suspects from unfair or unreasonable pressure is just as important to the criminal justice system as the thoroughness with which the police carry out their investigations.[307]

Yet the police are allowed to detain for a considerable period of time in order to let them investigate even though for many people this detention is coercive in itself. We have seen that especially vulnerable people are given special protection but that vulnerability is not always recognised by the police. Further, to allocate everyone into either a 'vulnerable' or 'normal' category is unrealistic. And the rights which apply to all suspects in detention, while an advance on what existed prior to PACE, have a limited protective effect. This is partly because of the way those rights work in practice, but also partly because of the legal rules themselves. These rules allow lawyers and police officers to behave in

---

[305] Choongh (1997: ch 6).
[306] Thanks to Ed Cape for details of this case. Examples of many other cases of incompetent and/or poor advice and negligent and dismissive attitudes towards clients are given in his 'Incompetent Police Station Advice and the Exclusion of Evidence' [2002] *Criminal Law Review* 471.   [307] RCCJ (1993: 25).

ways that dissuade many suspects from exercising their rights; allow police detention to be so unpleasant that many suspects are prepared to do almost anything, including waiving their rights, to get out as quickly as possible; and, especially since the changes to the right of silence in 1994, and to legal aid provisions in the last few years, make it difficult for lawyers to give useful advice and assistance to suspects.

Perhaps suspects in police custody should be *told* that they will see a lawyer, not *asked* if they want one. It is true that, in normal circumstances, people do not have things foisted on them against their will simply because someone else thinks it will be good for them. But suspects are not in normal circumstances. If they can be held in coercive conditions against their will, their mouths and hair invaded against their will, and questioned against their will why shouldn't they be given something that does them some good against their will? Vulnerable suspects are given AAs whether they like it or not. This is because they are vulnerable. But in police custody, many 'normal' people are also vulnerable, by virtue of their circumstances.

The detention regime is offensive to due process. Yet the floor of rights provided by the ECHR is so minimal that suspects are given more protection than our human rights obligations require. For example, the ECHR says nothing about vulnerable suspects, many specific rights to assistance (such as intimation and visitors) or police bail. Nor is the length of detention regulated except at the most extreme end.

The traditional way of protecting people's rights is by providing them with remedies when their rights are breached. But we have seen that the rights which we examined in this chapter are hardly protected in this way at all. The ostensible reason for this is that custody officers are supposed to safeguard the interests of suspects. Without police rule breaking, there would be no need to have custody officers. But custody officers are police officers. If suspects need protection from the police, then by what logic can custody officers be expected to provide that protection? The Runciman Commission recognised, to some extent, the failures of custody officers such as allowing cell visits by officers, rubber stamping detention, failing to provide clear information about rights and adopting ploys to avoid suspects receiving legal advice. Their performance, they say: ' … still leaves something to be desired … it may also be unrealistic to expect a police officer to take an independent view of a case investigated by colleagues.'[308]

After considering the poor performance of custody officers, the Runciman Commission then discussed (very briefly) whether another body could do the job of the custody officer. They decided that all the pressures on them would also be on a replacement body without that body even having the authority, vis-à-vis the police, of a custody officer. This was a due process/crime control crossroads. The Runciman Commission could either allow things to go on, more or less as now and accept the coercive nature of police station detention; or it could take police investigation out of the police station. It chose the former.[309] It is true that it recommended some enhancement to the custody officer role, and CCTV in custody areas and corridors leading to cells to deter malpractice.[310] Belatedly, in the late 1990s, CCTV was gradually introduced into custody areas in some police stations in most police force areas, with it now becoming ubiquitous including in cells. There is some evidence that CCTV has reduced police malpractice or—that, at least, is what many experienced detainees say.[311] But it did not recommend CCTV in cells because this eliminates the last vestige of privacy remaining to detainees, even though it provides added protection for them. Where CCTV has been introduced in cells this is a concern among detainees, who are understandably not keen on the possibility of being watched using the toilet and while

---

[308] RCCJ (1993: 31). Also see Choongh (1997: 172–177) for a catalogue of abuses allowed or perpetrated by custody officers. [309] RCCJ (1993: 31–34).
[310] RCCJ (1993: ch 3, paras 35–38). [311] Newburn and Hayman (2001: chs 1, 5, 6).

being strip-searched. Indeed, concerns about the lack of privacy afforded to detainees has recently and repeatedly been flagged in police custody inspection reports for infringing detainee dignity.[312]

The privacy versus protection dilemma, which entails setting Art 2 and 3 protections against those of Art 8, only arises once it is decided, as the Runciman Commission did, that the police station should be the focus of investigation, and that the police should be free to detain suspects for 24 hours or more in order to interrogate them. This is acceptance of the crime control framework.[313] The room for due process is thereby fundamentally circumscribed. To fully appreciate the real power this puts into the hands of the police, we need to examine questioning in detail. That is the subject of chapter 5.

Further reading

BLACKSTOCK J, CAPE E, HODGSON J, OGORODOVA A and SPRONKEN A, *Inside Police Custody: An Empirical Account of Suspects' Rights in Four Jurisdictions* (Cambridge: Intersentia, 2014).

DEHAGHANI R, *Vulnerability in Police Custody: Police Decision-making and the Appropriate Adult Safeguard* (Abingdon: Routledge, 2019).

LINDON G and ROE S, *Deaths in Police Custody: A review of the international evidence*. Research Report 95 (London: Home Office, 2017).

PIVATY A, *Criminal Defence at Police Stations: A Comparative and Empirical Study* (Abingdon: Routledge, 2020).

SKINNS L, *Police Powers and Citizens' Rights: Discretionary Decision Making in Police Custody* (Abingdon: Routledge, 2019).

---

[312] For example, in the HMICFRS inspection report on Lancashire Police in 2016, they note that 'detainees in cells with CCTV could still be observed when using the toilet, which showed a continued lack of respect for their dignity, and it was unacceptable that to date there had been insufficient action to address this' (para 5.2).

[313] For further discussion see Sanders A and Young R, 'The Rule of Law, Due Process, and Pre-Trial Criminal Justice' (1994b) 47 *Current Legal Problems* 125.

5

Police questioning of suspects

KEY ISSUES

- The expanding powers of the police to question suspects
- The multiple aims of police questioning
- The dwindling away of the right to silence
- The (inadequate) regulation of police questioning
- Traditional, accusatory police interrogation tactics
- Investigative interviewing: theory and (mal)practice
- Why do the innocent confess?
- The need for a corroboration rule

5.1 Questioning: the drift from due process to crime control

In chapter 4 we saw that the Police and Criminal Evidence Act 1984 (PACE) allows the police to detain suspects in order to question them. It is not self-evident that the police should have this power. The presumption of innocence is a basic human right: 'Everyone charged with a criminal offence shall be presumed innocent until proved guilty by law.'[1] The due process perspective insists that it is for the prosecution to rebut this presumption by proving guilt; it is not the suspect's duty to establish innocence. The presumption of innocence is connected with the right to remain silent and not incriminate oneself.[2] This right was recognised as an implicit element of Art 6 of the European Convention on Human Rights (ECHR) by the European Court of Human Rights (ECtHR) in *Funke v France*.[3] Building on this, in *Saunders v United Kingdom*[4] the ECtHR held that if methods of coercion or oppression are used to procure self-incriminating statements that are subsequently used in a prosecution, the suspect's right to a fair trial under Art 6 will have been breached. But neither the due process model nor the ECHR rule out all police questioning. The due process model acknowledges that suspects may wish to co-operate with the police, including by confessing. But since a confession is usually not in a suspect's self-interest, police accounts of how 'voluntary' confessions were made should be viewed sceptically, and strict limits should be placed on their powers to put questions to those whom

---

[1] Art 6(2) ECHR. The term 'charged' is interpreted to include arrested even if not charged in the English sense of prosecution being initiated.
[2] The scope of, and relationship between, these two rights has produced an enormous literature which we cannot cover here but see, e.g., Quirk H, *The Rise and Fall of the Right of Silence* (Abingdon: Routledge, 2016).
[3] (1993) 16 EHRR 297 [44–45].   [4] (1997) 23 EHRR 313 [68–69].

they suspect of crime.[5] The ECtHR takes a less stringent view of these matters, as we shall see later in this chapter. For its part, the crime control model assumes that largely unfettered police interrogation of suspects is the most efficient way of distinguishing between the guilty and the innocent. Here the models tussle between the 'core values' of 'justice' and 'efficiency'.

The law used to be based on due process principles, and police questioning in custody was all but ruled out, at least in theory. This position was reflected in the original version of the Judges Rules in 1912, although this did allow the police to invite suspects to make voluntary statements. Persons making voluntary statements were not to be 'cross-examined' and only questions aimed at 'removing ambiguity' were to be asked. As the Judges Rules were transformed over the years, however, police interrogation became more acceptable. The final formulation of the Judges Rules (in force from 1964 until their replacement by PACE in 1984) no longer purported to discourage questioning but merely to regulate its methods. PACE and its Code of Practice, most notably Code C (para 12.5) maintained the general rule that no one need talk to the police, but made clear that the police may nonetheless persist in interrogating non-cooperative suspects in order to persuade them to talk. Changes to the right of silence in 1994 took the system even further down the crime control path. Just how far down that path we have moved is the subject of this chapter.

5.2 Why do the police value suspect interviews?

The police are judged—for instance by politicians—primarily on how successful they are in 'catching criminals' and bringing them to justice,[6] so they naturally favour the crime control position on interviewing. It will be recalled that in *Holgate-Mohammed v Duke*[7] (see chapter 4) the police acknowledged that they arrested the suspect and took her to the police station, rather than interviewing her at home, because people are more likely to confess when interrogated while involuntarily detained. Indeed, during police questioning, the majority of suspects speak to the police, thereby increasing the likelihood of them confessing or making incriminating statements.[8] A clear and credible confession often eliminates the need to secure extra evidence, enabling more cases to be cleared up more quickly than would otherwise be possible. Confessions make it difficult to plead not guilty: Phillips and Brown (1998:158) looked at defendants prosecuted in the magistrates' courts and found that 92% of those who had self-incriminated in police interview pleaded guilty compared with 76% of those who had made no admission.[9]

In legal terms, one key aim of interviewing is to establish evidence of the suspect's thought processes at the relevant time. The most often prosecuted (non-Road Traffic Act)

---

[5] Packer H, *The Limits of the Criminal Sanction* (Stanford: Stanford University Press, 1969) pp 190–192.

[6] After becoming Home Secretary in 2019, Priti Patel espoused a clear connection between growing police numbers and reductions in crime, for example, through the investigative function of the police. See Dodd V, 'Extra officers must lead to less crime, Priti Patel tells police chiefs' *The Guardian*, 26 February 2020.

[7] [1984] 1 All ER 1054.

[8] It is hard to find up-to-date evidence about the proportion of suspects who confess during police questioning as it is not routinely collected by governmental bodies. Drawing on Bucke et al (2000), Quirk (2016: 78) notes that in 2000 only 16% of suspects gave a selective or full no comment interview during police questioning. See also: Moston S and Engelberg T, 'The Effects of Evidence on the Outcome of Interviews with Criminal Suspects' (2011) 12 *Police and Practice Research* 518–526.

[9] This is also influenced by the availability of the sentencing discount—the earlier the confession the greater the reduction in sentence. See further ch 7, and Redlich A, Yan S, Norris R and Bushway S, 'The Influence of Confessions on Guilty Pleas and Plea Discounts' (2018) 24(2) *Psychology, Public Policy, and Law* 147–157.

criminal offences in England require evidence of mens rea (intent or recklessness) in order to convict defendants. Assault is only a crime if a person is hurt intentionally or recklessly as distinct from someone stumbling or being careless and hurting the victim accidentally. Taking another's goods accidentally is not theft. But how are the police to prove that an item was taken, or a person injured, deliberately rather than accidentally? Sometimes there will be objective evidence of intent, such as a written plan, but this is rare. Sometimes intent can be inferred from the purposive nature of the act in question (as where somebody stabs another person repeatedly). But best of all is a statement by the person who committed the crime. Much police interrogation is geared not to establishing the objective facts—who took the articles or injured the victim, about which there is often no dispute—but what the person intended by his or her actions.[10]

There are many other functions of interviewing. First, it enables the police to seek valuable information unrelated to the offence in question, such as suspects' other possible crimes. In the largest-scale academic study conducted to date, Phillips and Brown found that 11% of suspects admitted to offences additional to those for which they were arrested.[11] In the year ending 2019, 5,371 (0.1%) of the offences recorded by the police resulted in a 'taken into consideration' outcome, meaning that suspects will have admitted to additional offence(s) whilst being primarily questioned about something else.

Second, policing is increasingly proactive. That is, the police target certain suspects or locations, often acting on tip-offs or surveillance-based information. Over time, the police secure sightings, film and so forth which may point to the involvement of certain suspects in particular crimes. When based on this kind of intelligence, interviewing then is not so much to secure confessions, as to either catch offenders out in lies (such as denying being in a location where a crime was committed) or to secure silence about suspicious activities.[12] Coupled with the adverse inferences that can be drawn against both silence and failure to account for being somewhere suspicious (see section 5.3), silence or lies can be equally useful to the police. Similar tactics are also often used when the police are operating in reactive mode since routine recorded surveillance of much public, private and now cyber space is now the norm thanks to the widespread use of CCTV and body-worn cameras in this country, and the digital tracking of citizens such as through their mobile phones, use of social media and the Internet more generally.[13] All may be used as evidence to shape the police investigation, providing the police with a potential trap to spring on suspects in interview.

Third, information about past or planned crimes in which the suspect is not involved, or general 'criminal intelligence', is also often provided. This is sometimes part of a 'deal', the information being exchanged for bail, lesser charges, or no prosecution at all. All suspects (including children and young people)[14] are treated by the police as potential informants.[15] Gathering

---

[10] McConville et al, *The Case for the Prosecution* (London: Routledge, 1991) pp 66–75; Innes M, *Investigating Murder: Detective Work and the Police Response to Criminal Homicide* (Oxford: OUP, 2003) at pp 150–151. Questions about intention are encouraged to be included in the police written interview plan. See College of Policing, *Investigative interviewing* (2013) online at <https://www.app.college.police.uk/app-content/investigations/investigative-interviewing/> (accessed 1 July 2020).

[11] Phillips and Brown (1998: 73); see also Bucke and Brown (1997: 34).

[12] The provisions on bad character introduced by the Criminal Justice Act 2003 (discussed in ch 9) entail that interrogation can now also be useful in prompting statements that amount to attacks on the character of another (such as a claim of self-defence). This can result in a suspect's previous convictions being admitted in evidence at any subsequent trial, as confirmed by *R v Lamaletie and Royce* [2008] EWCA Crim 314.

[13] See: Button M, 'The "New" Private Security Industry, the Private Policing of Cyberspace and the Regulatory Questions' (2020) 36(1) *Journal of Contemporary Criminal Justice* 39–55. In 2010, the British Security Industry Association estimated that there are 4.25 million CCTV cameras in operation in the United Kingdom (<http://www.bsia.co.uk/LY8VMY74118> (accessed 5 January 2010)).

[14] Ballardie C and Iganski P, 'Juvenile Informers' in Billingsley et al (eds), *Informers: Policing, Policy, Practice* (Cullompton: Willan, 2001) at p 120.

[15] Informants are discussed in ch 6.

information about possible planned crimes is particularly important in the context of terrorism; sometimes there is no intention to bring legal proceedings against the interrogatee,[16] at other times there is no 'deal' on offer other than an end to what is sometimes close to torture.[17]

Finally, interrogation by, and confession to, the police is part of a wider exercise of social and political power. Foucault identified new forms of power in modern societies which had been added to the traditional armoury of overt coercion and control. These include the allocation of space (for example, where certain categories of people are, and are not, allowed to go without permission), the regulation of time (through, for example, work and school) and surveillance (through street policing and its partial replacement, CCTV cameras). He also identified specialist knowledge, in the professions and the police, as a form of power.[18] To simplify, power provides the means to gain knowledge over a subject that in turn increases the power over the now better-known subject. A central element here is confessional statements.[19] Confession, usually as a result of questioning, intrudes on the most intimate aspects of personal and social life.

The more the police are given powers to question, the more suspects are in their power. As we see in chapter 10, the social distribution of suspects and defendants is skewed towards the most socially marginal. Nor are these suspects merely interrogated because they are believed to have committed a specific crime. As Choongh demonstrates, the police sometimes arrest and interrogate those belonging to social groups which are regarded as 'police property' precisely because this exercise of power is a form of discipline:

> Interrogation is something which the police can do to a suspect whether the suspect likes it or not ... the police use the interview room as a forum to inform 'policed' communities that they can be asked any question, and in any manner, regardless of whether it relates to the original suspicion.[20]

This discussion of discipline and confessions is not entirely in line with Foucault's governmentality thesis that power is increasingly dispersed through society. For we are arguing that the traditional criminal justice system is developing in such a way as to concentrate power in the hands of the police, power which is mostly used against the socially marginalised.[21] Foucault's insights nonetheless alert us to the value to the powerful of being able to make those with less power account to them through questioning. In the next section we consider the extent to which suspects can resist this form of 'accountability' by remaining silent.

---

[16] Gelles et al, 'Al-Qaeda-related Subjects: A Law Enforcement Perspective' in Williamson T (ed), *Investigative Interviewing: Rights, Research Regulation* (Cullompton: Willan, 2005).

[17] See *The Guardian*, 8 July 2009 and section 5.5.1.3 for an example.

[18] Foucault M, *Discipline and Punish* (London: Allen Lane, 1977). See Watson S, 'Foucault and Social Policy', in Lewis G et al (eds), *Rethinking Social Policy* (Milton Keynes, Open UP, 2000) for an accessible summary of Foucault's work. See also, in the context of neoliberal governance, Johnson A, 'Foucault. Critical Theory of the Police in a Neoliberal Age' (2014) 61(141) *Theoria* 5–29 and Lippert R, 'Neo-Liberalism, Police, and the Governance of Little Urban Things' (2014) 18 *Foucault Studies* 49–65.

[19] Foucault M, *The History of Sexuality* vol 1 (London: Allen Lane, 1979).

[20] Choongh (1997: 135–136). Also see Hillyard (1993: ch 8); Waddington P, *Policing Citizens* (London: UCL Press, 1999) especially ch 5; Leo R, 'Police Interrogation and Social Control' (1994) 3 *Social and Legal Studies* 93.

[21] We contend this is so notwithstanding the growing importance of such forms of dispersed power as private policing and the novel forms of regulatory activity which are shaping the global economy. Braithwaite J, 'The New Regulatory State and the Transformation of Criminology' (2000) 40 *British Journal of Criminology* 222 at p 299 argues that criminology, 'with its focus on the old state institutions of police-courts-prisons' is of 'limited relevance' given 'the crimes which pose the greatest risks to all of us'. This ignores that these 'old' state institutions are a) thriving and expanding, and, b) not just posing a 'risk' of intrusive interference with citizens' freedom, but severely (and ever more intensively) limiting that freedom for some, but certainly not 'all of us'. We think that documenting this is of more than 'limited relevance', at least to the interests of the most marginal groups in society. See further Crawford A, 'Networked Governance and the Post-regulatory State? Steering, Rowing and Anchoring the Provision of Policing and Security' (2006) 10(4) *Theoretical Criminology* 449–479.

5.3 The right of silence

The right of silence occurs at three stages in the criminal process: on the streets when grounds for suspicion arise, in the police station and at court. On the streets, people need not speak to police officers if they are stopped and questioned, whether or not PACE, s.1 stop-search powers are being exercised.[22] Further, para 10.1 of Code of Practice C provides:

> A person whom there are [reasonable][23] grounds to suspect of an offence ... must be cautioned before any questions about an offence, or further questions if the answers provide the [reasonable] grounds for suspicion, are put to them if either the suspect's answers or silence (i.e. failure or refusal to answer or answer satisfactorily) may be given in evidence to a court in a prosecution.
>
> The caution begins: 'You do not have to say anything . . .'.

On arrest, suspects must be cautioned unless this is impracticable because of the condition or behaviour of the suspect or unless the suspect had been cautioned immediately before arrest.[24] The second stage where the right of silence may be exercised is in the police station, which we shall focus on in this chapter. Thus suspects must be cautioned again at the start of any and every interview.[25] Finally there is the right to silence in court, looked at in chapter 9. The practical value of the right of silence depends on the balance of the advantages and disadvantages which accrues to those who stand upon it. As we shall now see, the disadvantages have become acute in recent years while the advantages have been diminished.

5.3.1 Eroding the suspect's right of silence through adverse inferences

The ECtHR has ruled that the right of silence 'lies at the heart' of Art 6 but that it is not an absolute right: *Condron v UK*.[26] This leaves governments and courts room for manoeuvre over the extent to which this right—and the related 'privilege against self-incrimination'— should be preserved. For the due process adherent, it is up to the prosecution to find its own evidence; anything else negates the presumption of innocence. For the adherent to crime control, only the guilty have something to hide; innocent people can only gain by assisting the prosecution. As Bentham infamously expressed this point: 'Innocence claims the right of speaking, as guilt invokes the privilege of silence.'[27]

As we have seen, there was a drift away from the due process position over the course of the twentieth century.[28] Indeed some modern statutes have adopted an extreme crime control position in order to deal with certain crimes where suspects have particular advantages. The best example is the investigation, by such bodies as HM Revenue & Customs, of shady financial dealings. These agencies have the power to compel answers on pain of fines for silence. As a result of *Saunders v UK*[29] the Youth Justice and Criminal Evidence

---

[22] But note that a refusal to answer questions might have legal consequences (such as providing grounds for a stop-search or even an arrest), as discussed in ch 2.

[23] Paragraph 10.1 does not use the word 'reasonable', but Note 10A does, and the latter (despite not being formally part of the Code—para 1.3) undoubtedly represents the law: *R v James* [1996] Crim LR 650; *Sneyd v DPP* [2006] EWHC 560.   [24] Code C, para 10.4

[25] Code C, paras 10.1, 11.1A and 11.4 (but if there is merely a break during an interview, then the suspect need only be made aware that they remain under caution—para 10.8).   [26] (2001) 31 EHRR 1.

[27] Quoted by Greer S, 'The Right to Silence: A Review of the Current Debate' (1990) 53 *Modern Law Review* 719.

[28] See section 5.1. Detailed accounts are provided in Bryan I, *Interrogation and Confession* (Aldershot: Avebury, 1997) chs 1–7 and Easton S, *The Case for the Right to Silence* (Aldershot: Ashgate, 1998) ch 1.

[29] (1996) 23 EHRR 313.

Act 1999 (s.59 and Sch 3) amended the bulk of such legislation in order to prevent the admissibility in criminal proceedings of answers which are extracted in this way.[30]

It has been claimed by some that suspects retain a right of silence as long as it is no crime to remain silent.[31] Even if one accepts this approach, the right is nonetheless eroded if suspects and defendants suffer as a result of silence. Such erosion has been taking place for many years, and the process was accelerated as a result of the Criminal Justice and Public Order Act 1994 (CJPO).[32] Under the CJPO, courts may draw adverse inferences when defendants:

- rely upon facts in their defence which they did not mention to the police when questioned under caution prior to being charged (s.34);
- fail to testify at court in their own defence (s.35);
- failed (following arrest) to provide explanations for incriminating objects, substances or marks (s.36);
- failed (following arrest) to provide explanations for their presence near to the scene of crimes (s.37).

Thus the caution now says:

> You do not have to say anything. But it may harm your defence if you do not mention when questioned something which you later rely on in court. Anything you do say may be given in evidence.[33]

Typically, the adverse inference which will be drawn is that the 'fact' later relied upon in court is a post-interrogation fabrication, which may therefore be read as indicator of guilt.[34] Previously, courts were not supposed to take into account a suspect or defendant's refusal to speak, nor the fact that the first mention of a particular defence might be in court.[35] The CJPO changes all that by eroding the right of silence in general in the police station (s.34) and in court (s.35) and in relation to certain types of circumstantial evidence (ss.36, 37).

It may seem that the CJPO allows courts to convict people merely because they are silent, or because they answer some questions but not all. While this could sometimes be the effect of the CJPO in practice, this is not what the letter of the law says. First, the CJPO itself states that no-one should have a case to answer or be convicted on the basis of adverse inferences alone (s.38(3)). This restriction has been tightened up as a result of the ECHR. In *Murray*[36] it was held by the ECtHR that a conviction must not be based

---

[30] Not all of the potentially objectionable legislation was amended, however. For example, the Road Traffic Act 1988 requires the owner of a vehicle to declare who was driving it at a particular time; refusal is a criminal offence but there is no bar on using the information obtained in criminal proceedings. This was found to be compatible with Art 6 both by the Privy Council in *Brown v Stott* [2003] 1 AC 681, and by the European Court of Human Rights in *O'Halloran and Francis v UK* [2007] ECHR 544.

[31] This was the view of the Lord Chief Justice in *Cowan* [1996] QB 373.

[32] Mirfield P, *Silence, Confessions and Improperly Obtained Evidence* (Oxford: Clarendon, 1997) p 246.

[33] PACE Code C, para 10.5.

[34] Though s.34(2) states that the jury can draw whatever inferences from silence as appear proper, including none at all. The judicial direction does, however, suggest that the jury may wish to draw an inference that the defendant has not got an answer to the case against them. See further, Judicial College, *Crown Court Compendium, Part 1. Jury and Trial Management and Summing Up* (2018) (<https://www.judiciary.uk/wp-content/uploads/2018/06/crown-court-compendium-pt1-jury-and-trial-management-and-summing-up-june-2018-1.pdf> (accessed 1 July 2020).

[35] There were many statutory and common law incursions into this principle: see later and ch 9.

[36] (1996) 22 EHRR 29 at para 47.

'solely or mainly' on the fact of silence. The logic of this was questioned in *O'Donnell v UK*,[37] with one judge remarking that the provisions of the CJPO on the one hand require the suspect to provide an explanation because the circumstances call for one, but on the other hand the suspect's account is unnecessary if there is already strong evidence upon which a conviction could be based. The ECtHR has made clear, however, that adverse inferences could properly be drawn from silence 'in situations which clearly call for an explanation', and that those inferences may then be taken into account 'in assessing the persuasiveness of the evidence adduced by the prosecution.' The question whether failure to answer questions during interrogation is a situation which 'clearly called for an explanation' was considered in *Condron*. The ECtHR ruled that adverse inferences could properly be drawn (under s.34, CJPO) from a suspect's silence in the face of police questioning, but that a jury must be told that they should not do this unless that silence could 'sensibly' be attributed *only* to the accused having no answer to the questions, or none that would stand up to scrutiny. In other words, the Court decided that silence in the face of police questions can, but does not necessarily, amount to a situation which so clearly called for an explanation that adverse inferences may be drawn.[38]

Second, inferences can only be drawn in relation to ss.36 (objects) and 37 (presence at crime scene) if the police have first told the suspect what offence is being investigated, what facts they believe are incriminating and that adverse inferences could be drawn from failure to account for them.[39] Similarly, inferences can only be drawn under s.34 if the police through their questioning made it reasonable to expect suspects to volunteer the facts which they later rely on at trial. If, for example, the police simply read out a complainant's statement without asking the suspect to correct anything he or she disagrees with then no adverse inference should be drawn: *Hillard*.[40]

Third, it will amount to a breach of the right to a fair trial under Art 6 ECHR if inferences are drawn from silence in the police station at a point when the suspect has not had the opportunity to take legal advice. In *Murray* the ECtHR noted that, where adverse inferences could be drawn from silence, access to legal advice was of paramount importance 'at the initial stages of police interrogation'.[41] The police had denied Murray access to a solicitor for the first 48 hours of his detention and the ECtHR said that, in the circumstances, this amounted to a breach of Art 6. In response domestic legislation was changed to provide that adverse inferences cannot be drawn under ss.34, 36 or 37 in respect of a person who is at an authorised place of detention and who has not been allowed the chance to consult a solicitor prior to interview.[42]

Fourth, it is not proper under s.34 to draw an adverse inference from silence in the face of questioning if the defendant does not rely on a fact at the trial that might reasonably have been mentioned to the police. This has led to a series of cases on what counts as relying on a fact at trial and, in particular, whether a defendant who neither gives, nor calls, evidence can be said to be relying on any fact in his defence.[43] The House of

---

[37] [2015] ECHR 16667/10. See further discussion in Owusu-Bempah Abenaa, *Defendant Participation in the Criminal Process* (Abingdon: Routledge, 2017).
[38] (2001) 31 EHRR 1. See the comments made by Rix LJ in *Pektar* [2004] 1 Cr App R 22.
[39] Code C, para 10.11.   [40] [2004] EWCA Crim 837.   [41] *Murray v UK* (1996) 22 EHRR 29, at 66.
[42] The Youth Justice and Criminal Evidence Act 1999, s.58 created s.34(2A) CJPO. Both this legislation and *Murray* itself leave unclear whether silence in the face of an 'adverse inferences caution' administered by a police officer at the point of an arrest could damage a defendant's case at court. In practice, it may be doubted whether arresting officers will comply with all the pre-conditions necessary for an adverse inference to be drawn in relation to silence on arrest. If they did, then it would be arguable that they were in substance starting to interview the arrestee prior to their arrival at the police station, which is *generally* unlawful in any event (Code C).
[43] The relevant authorities were reviewed by the House of Lords in *Webber* [2004] UKHL 1.

Lords in *Webber* answered this question in the affirmative, ruling that a fact is relied upon 'when counsel, acting on his instructions, puts a specific and positive case to prosecution witnesses ... whether or not the prosecution witness accepts the suggestion put.'[44] Thus if the defence simply probes the prosecution case (e.g. 'are you sure he threw the first punch?'), without 'putting to' prosecution witnesses specific suggestions concerning 'the facts' of the case (e.g. 'I put it to you that he threw the first punch') no adverse inference should be drawn.

Fifth, no adverse inference should be drawn if the fact subsequently relied upon at trial is agreed to be true.[45] There is no scope here for the inference that the explanation for silence in interview is that the fact is a post-interrogation fabrication.

Sixth, where a defendant hands a prepared statement to the police in interview of *all* the facts that he or she subsequently relies on at trial, no adverse inference should be drawn simply from the fact that a defendant responded 'no comment' to every police question.[46] It is not a refusal to answer questions that engages s.34 but rather a failure at this stage of the investigation to disclose facts which are subsequently relied upon. Legal advisors preparing statements at this stage need to be careful, as omitting something important that is later raised at trial could result in the adverse inference being drawn.[47]

The question of when and how adverse inferences can be drawn is evidently complex. However, one should not be blinded by the blizzard of technical detail to the fact that, sociologically speaking, fact-finders have always been able to hold silence against suspects and defendants. Prior to the introduction of the CJPO, in 80% of all Crown court trials where defendants were silent under police questioning, this became known to the jury.[48] Juries and magistrates probably took silence into account even when they were not supposed to. As one police officer put it,

> ... in the past you may have actually been happy for him to give a 'no comment' interview, go to court, offer an explanation and let the jury sit and think: 'This man has already been interviewed by the police, why didn't he answer the questions then?' (Bucke et al 2000: 35)

Certainly this is how many suspects think silence will be interpreted.[49] The House of Lords in *Webber* depicted the effect of s.34 as bringing the law back into line with 'common sense' (that 'common sense' being that innocent suspects would answer police questions).[50] This stance is indicative of long-standing judicial hostility to the right of silence.[51] In light of all this it is not surprising that the changes in the law brought about by the CJPO made little difference to rates of confession or conviction at the time, and there has been little subsequent academic research further scrutinising these links (see section 5.3.4).

5.3.2 Eroding the suspect's right of silence through custodial interrogation

As chapter 4 showed, s.37 of PACE allows detention in a police station to be authorised in order to obtain evidence by questioning. There is nothing a suspect can gain by saying to a custody officer: 'There is no point in you holding me for questioning, because I intend to

---

[44] Ibid, para 34.
[45] *Wisdom and Sinclair* (Court of Appeal, 10 December 1999, Lawtel 6/1/2000, unreported elsewhere); approved by *Webber*.   [46] *McGarry* [1998] 3 All ER 805; *T v DPP* [2007] EWHC 1793 (Admin).
[47] *Turner* [2004] 1 All ER 1025.
[48] Zander M and Henderson P, *Crown Court Study* (Royal Commission on Criminal Justice Research Study no 19) (London: HMSO, 1993).   [49] Choongh (1997: ch 6).
[50] *Webber* [16–18 & 33]. See also *Hoare and Pierce* [2004] EWCA Crim 784 [53].
[51] Before 1994, trial and appellate judges often used or advised the equivalent of a 'nod and a wink' as a way of inviting juries to draw adverse inferences (e.g. *Gilbert* (1977) 66 Cr App R 237). For a relatively recent review see Quirk (2016).

remain silent.' Suspects who refuse to speak can be held until they do so, subject to the time limits. Lengthy and uncertain periods of detention, particularly overnight, are the most feared consequences of arrest for most suspects.[52] Not only can silence lengthen detention, but in the words of PACE Code C:

> If a suspect takes steps to prevent themselves being questioned or further questioned, e.g., by refusing to leave their cell to go to a suitable interview room or by trying to leave the interview room, they shall be advised their consent or agreement to interview is not required. The suspect shall be cautioned ... and informed if they fail or refuse to co-operate, the interview may take place in the cell and that their failure or refusal to co-operate may be given in evidence. The suspect shall then be invited to co-operate and go into the interview room. If they refuse and the custody officer considers, on reasonable grounds, that the interview should not be delayed, the custody officer has discretion to direct that the interview be conducted in a cell.[53]

In the 'Cardiff Three' case the suspect asserted from time to time that he had nothing further to say. Examples of police responses included:

- 'I'm never gonna leave it at that... you know that. Cause I am still gonna keep going and I'm gonna put things into you everytime because I know the truth.'
- 'Now we're going to have the truth out of you one way or ... you know.'
- 'I'll keep digging and I'll keep digging because I believe you were there. I will keep digging.'[54]

In the event the interviews lasted for 12 hours and 42 minutes, spread over five days. Suspects still possess the remnants of a right to their own silence but they manifestly do not have a right to police silence.

5.3.3 Eroding the defendant's right of silence through disclosure rules

It might be thought that one advantage of standing on the right to silence is that a defendant would be able to reserve his or her defence until after the prosecution had made out a prima facie case in court. In that way the presumption of innocence would be respected, as would the dignity and privacy of the individual.[55] Suspects who remain silent in the police station may, however, be effectively compelled to provide relevant information if subsequently prosecuted. There were for many years various statutory exceptions to the principle that defendants could withhold the nature of their defence until trial.[56] The principle itself was swept away by the Criminal Procedure and Investigations Act 1996. The defence was placed under a duty by s.5 to disclose an outline of its case or risk an adverse inference being drawn at Crown court trial (chapter 9). In practice the sketchy information provided

---

[52] Sanders A and Bridges L, 'Access to Legal Advice and Police Malpractice' [1990] *Criminal Law Review* 494; Choongh (1997: ch 6); Skinns L, '" Let's Get it Over With": Early Findings on Factors Affecting Detainees' Access to Custodial Legal Advice' (2009) 19(1) *Policing & Society* 58, 63–64; Skinns and Wooff (2020).

[53] Paragraph 12.5. See also Code A, Note 1. Thus refusing to go into the interview room does not circumvent the adverse inferences provisions of s.34 CJPO (as happened in *R v Johnson; R v Hind* [2005] EWCA Crim 971) so long as the police conduct a cell interview instead.

[54] Quoted in Gudjonsson G, *The Psychology of Interrogations and Confessions: A Handbook* (Chichester: Wiley, 2003) at p 108.

[55] For the counter-arguments to this position see Redmayne M, 'Disclosure and its Discontents' [2004] *Criminal Law Review* 441.

[56] For example, since 1967 defendants have been obliged to give advance warning if they wished to provide evidence of an alibi: Criminal Justice Act 1967, s.11. And under PACE, s.81 and Crown Court Rules 1987, SI 1087/716 they are obliged to disclose the contents of any expert reports on which they intend to rely.

was found to be of little help to prosecutors.[57] Section 33 of the Criminal Justice Act 2003 accordingly imposed a much more stringent duty of disclosure. The defence *must*[58] now, in advance of trial, provide a statement which (i) sets out the nature of the accused's defence; (ii) indicates any point of law on which reliance will be placed (including any point as to the admissibility of evidence); and, (iii) provides details of any alibi witnesses. Section 34 of the same Act requires the accused to give the court and prosecutor a notice setting out the details of any other witnesses he or she plans to call to give evidence at trial; and s.39 allows for adverse inferences to be drawn where any of the duties of disclosure are breached or a defence is presented at court which is inconsistent with, or goes beyond, the initially disclosed information.

These duties of disclosure have been imposed with a view to enabling the police and prosecution to investigate the claims of the defence. There is an obvious danger here of the police 'tampering' with, or intimidating, defence witnesses or adapting the prosecution case with a view to making the defence evidence irrelevant. In the 'Confait Affair', a pathologist was persuaded to change the estimated time of the victim's death in order to neutralise the suspect's alibi.[59] In the case of the Taylor sisters, an alibi witness was arrested at dawn and told that she would face a charge of conspiracy to murder if she did not change her story.[60] Thus police power is not necessarily neutralised where suspects remain silent when interrogated. Where prosecutions take place, the police can secure much valuable information through defence disclosure instead.

5.3.4 The extent of use of the 'right' in the police station

Around one-third of all suspects deny, with some sort of explanation, the offence(s) of which they are suspected. It appears that few suspects exercise the right of silence in totality, but though the information is contained in police records it is not collated nor made publicly available and estimates from somewhat dated academic research vary, hence the need for more empirical research in this area. In one academic study on this, Brown estimated that, between 1985 and 1994, between 5% and 9% of all interviewed suspects exercised total silence, and a similar number refused to answer some questions.[61] The rights provided to suspects in PACE as such do not appear to have led to more use of silence, although there was some increase in both the total and selective use of silence, especially in London, just before the introduction of the CJPO (Phillips and Brown 1998).

In research carried out after the introduction of the CJPO, refusal to answer all or some questions was back down to the 1985–1994 levels. This appears to be mostly because lawyers advise silence less readily than previously.[62] Table 5.1 presents figures on the use of the right of silence in eight police stations studied by Phillips and Brown (1998) just over

---

[57] Taylor et al, *Blackstone's Guide to the Criminal Justice Act 2003* (Oxford: OUP, 2004) p 40.
[58] *R v Essa* [2009] EWCA Crim 43 [18]. This obligation can also be found in the Criminal Procedure Rules 2015, pt 15.
[59] See *Report of an Inquiry into the Circumstances leading to the Trial of Three Persons on Charges arising out of the Death of Maxwell Confait and the Fire at 27 Doggett Road, London SE6* (HCP 90) (London: HMSO, 1977).
[60] *The Observer*, 13 June 1993. *Higgins* [2003] EWCA 2943 (discussed in section 5.5.1.2) is another example.
[61] Brown D, *PACE Ten Years on—A Review of The Research* (Home Office Research Study no 155) (London: HMSO; 1997).
[62] Phillips and Brown (1998: 32–33) found that, following the CJPO, the use of silence fell from 39 to 22% among legally advised suspects and from 12 to 8% among those not advised. This suggests both that lawyers are now advising co-operation more frequently *and* that suspects are being cowed by the adverse inference warnings.

Table 5.1 The use of the right of silence

	Refused all questions	Refused some questions	Answered all questions
Pre-CJPO	10%	13%	77%
Post-CJPO	6%	10%	84%

a year before the introduction of the CJPO and in the same eight stations five months after the CJPO came into force (Bucke et al, 2000: 31). They show a fall in the proportion of suspects using the right to silence of about a third (down from 23% to 16%).

In another post-CJPO study Quirk found the rate at which suspects made no comment in interviews varied between 1.2 and 15.1% between police Operational Command Units, with an overall rate of 6.1%.[63] Silence has historically been higher in London than elsewhere, higher among black suspects than white and Asian suspects, and higher among those who had legal advice than those who did not (Quirk, for example, found that 82% of those suspects that made no comment were legally advised). The steepest falls in the use of silence following the CJPO occurred among black suspects (Bucke et al 2000: 31–33).

Silence seems to be more frequently exercised in serious than in trivial cases.[64] This does not necessarily mean, however, that silence helps serious criminals escape charge and conviction, as the police often claim. Leng found that in only a tiny percentage of non-prosecuted cases and acquittals was silence exercised, and that these outcomes rarely seemed to be a product of silence.[65] Few 'ambush' defences (i.e. defences based on 'facts' not known to the police and not disclosed in interview) were mounted in court, and none successfully. Quirk (2016) also noted a lack of empirical evidence suggesting that the right of silence and ambush cases have in fact caused real problems in the administration of justice. In some cases, successful defences were based on points suspects attempted to raise in interviews but to which the police refused to listen. Leng concluded that there were as many cases where the police could have acted on what suspects told them, or attempted to tell them, as where suspects refused to tell them material things. The spectre of the professional criminal avoiding justice by remaining silent in interrogation appears, therefore, to be largely a myth.

The most striking finding of the post-CJPO research is that whereas the use of the right of silence has declined, the rates at which admissions are made and convictions secured have not been affected (Bucke et al 2000: 34, 66–67). We indicated at the end of section 5.3.1 why this finding should not have come as a great surprise. The notion that the right of silence prior to the CJPO 1994 was a major obstacle to convicting the guilty was seriously misconceived. The pressures and incentives to make incriminating statements in the police station were already enormous prior to the CJPO. It is therefore tempting to regard that Act as having greater symbolic-electoral value than instrumental use. But we should not forget the broader purposes of interrogation, discussed in section 5.2, such as gaining general criminal intelligence, and exercising disciplinary power over suspects. The conviction rate may not have increased, but the rate at which the privacy of the citizen is invaded certainly has.

---

[63] Quirk (2016). Data for this study were collected in 1999.
[64] Moston S and Williamson T, 'The Extent of Silence in Police Interviews' in Greer S and Morgan R (eds), *The Right to Silence Debate* (Bristol: University of Bristol, 1990) p 38; Phillips and Brown (1998: 78).
[65] Leng R, *The right to silence in police interrogation* (RCCJ Research study no 10) (London; HMSO, 1993).

5.3.5 'Sidelining' legal advice

One of the most important pieces of advice which legal advisors can give to suspects is that they need not answer questions and, in some circumstances, that it is not in their interests to do so. If, for example, the police have no objective basis for suspicion, silence should lead to release without charge, while answering questions could lead to enough evidence for a charge even if the suspect is innocent. Another situation in which it may not be wise to answer police questions is when the legal advisor and suspect know too little about the police case to answer it effectively. Consistent with this, McConville and Hodgson found that when silence was advised it was most often because advisors felt that they had insufficient information about the case and when they felt that suspects might wrongly incriminate themselves.[66]

We saw in chapter 4 that the police need not disclose anything about the case.[67] Legal advisors sometimes seek to secure the disclosure of the police case by advising that the client remain silent until this information is provided.[68] Bucke et al (2000: 23) found that the erosion of the right of silence brought about by the CJPO 1994 was causing legal advisors to more frequently seek disclosure of the police case on the basis that without that disclosure it was not reasonable to expect their clients to answer questions in interview. This stance flowed from s.34 which limits the drawing of adverse inferences to cases in which suspects failed to mention facts which they later relied on when it would have been *reasonable* to expect them to have mentioned them in interview. Equally, they found that the police were disclosing at least some of their case more readily now, knowing that this made the drawing of adverse inferences more probable (Bucke et al 2020: 22–24). Paragraph 11.1A of Code C states that the police should disclose sufficient information to allow the defence to understand the case and exercise its rights.[69] However, the police retain control. The same paragraph goes on to confirm that the officer need not disclose information where it would prejudice the investigation, and that the decision about what to disclose remains with the investigating officer. That is, they decide whether to disclose anything, what to disclose, and when to do so.[70] Officers vary in their practices,[71] with many categorically unwilling to disclose evidence prior to a first interview, while some 'never disclose or allude to "golden nugget" or "trump card" evidence, particularly fingerprints, DNA, and CCTV'.[72] Quirk's (2016) research suggests that the police might be more willing to disclose, and disclose more, to legal advisors that they know and trust. But, of course, it is the client's trust that lawyers should seek and not that of the police.

Sometimes police disclosure of part of a case can give a misleading impression.[73] Although no adverse inferences should be drawn if the police actively mislead the suspect,

---

[66] McConville M and Hodgson J, *Custodial Legal Advice and the Right to Silence* (Royal Commission on Criminal Justice Research Study no 16) (London: HMSO, 1993).

[67] They must disclose some relevant details, however, if they want adverse inferences to be drawn from silence (see section 5.3.1). See also Toney R, 'Disclosure of Evidence and Legal Assistance at Custodial Interrogation: What Does the ECHR Require?' (2001) 5 *International Journal of Evidence and Proof* 39.

[68] See, for example, Quinn K and Jackson J, 'Of Rights and Roles: Police Interviews with Young Suspects in Northern Ireland' (2007) 47 *British Journal of Criminology* 234 at 241.

[69] This is also the stance taken by the ECtHR. See comments made in 2009 regarding disclosure in *A and Others v the United Kingdom* (Application no 3455/05).

[70] Sukumar D, Hodgson J and Wade K, 'How the Timing of Police Evidence Disclosure Impacts Custodial Legal Advice' (2016a) 20(3) *The International Journal of Evidence & Proof* 200–216.

[71] Quinn and Jackson (2007: 241); Quirk (2016); Sukumar D, Hodgson J and Wade K, 'Behind Closed Doors: Live Observations of Current Police Station Disclosure Practices and Lawyer-Client Consultations' (2016b) 12 *Criminal Law Review* 900.

[72] Shepherd E, *Investigative Interviewing: The Conversation Management Approach* (Oxford: OUP, 2007) p 331.

[73] Sukumar, Hodgson, and Wade (2016b).

partial disclosure which has this effect is not necessarily construed as active deception.[74] Moreover, case law has made clear that neither limited disclosure of the police case, nor legal advice to remain silent, necessarily insulates the suspect from adverse inferences. In *Argent*[75] silence was advised because, it seems, the solicitor felt the police were being unusually non-cooperative and were refusing to disclose important evidence in their possession. In court it was argued that there should be no adverse inference from silence both because it was as a result of legal advice, and because the police had failed to make full disclosure of their evidence at that stage. The Court of Appeal, while accepting that the police had disclosed less evidence than normal, rejected both arguments, saying that the test in the CJPO is whether it was reasonable to have mentioned the fact subsequently relied on when initially questioned. Whether legal advice to stay silent made silence reasonable depended on what passed between lawyer and suspect. And police non-disclosure of certain evidence was relevant only if fuller disclosure was necessary in order for the suspect's silence to be regarded as unreasonable. Other appellate cases decided soon after adopted the same line.[76]

This makes it difficult for lawyers to advise silence and for suspects to know whether to follow that advice.[77] Some suspects doubtless rely on legal advice because they lack confidence in their own judgement in unfamiliar circumstances, but to convince a court of this they might have to reveal what passed between them and their lawyers.[78] This amounts to a waiver of legal professional privilege, allowing the prosecution to expose all that passed between them, which might be against the wishes or interests of the suspects[79] and which certainly undermines the potential for openness and trust on which an effective client-lawyer relationship depends (Bucke et al 2000: 51).

The ECtHR position does not remove the problems facing lawyers and their clients. In *Condron v UK*[80] suspects had been advised by their solicitor not to answer police questions because they were suffering from the symptoms of heroin withdrawal. The ECtHR said that if a defendant refuses to answer questions on the advice of a solicitor it would be wrong to allow a jury to draw an adverse inference from that silence unless they were first told that they must not do so unless they believed that silence could only sensibly be attributed to the suspect having no good answer to the questions. The ECtHR reiterated this position in *Beckles v UK*[81] when it noted that a jury should be directed to consider whether the reason for silence was a genuine one or whether, on the contrary, reliance on legal advice to remain silent was merely a convenient self-serving excuse.

It seems that the ECtHR is concerned that some (factually guilty) suspects may claim that they remained silent on legal advice in situations where they were determined to remain silent in any event in order to avoid incriminating themselves. Moreover, the court in *Condron* found nothing wrong with the fact that defendants may, because of the *Argent* decision, experience 'indirect compulsion' to reveal the content of the advice received from

---

[74] See, for example, *Imran and Hussain* [1997] Crim LR 754, discussed in section 5.5.2.6; see also *Rosenberg* [2006] EWCA Crim 6.   [75] [1997] 2 Cr App Rep 27.
[76] See *Roble* [1997] Crim LR 449; *Moshaid* [1998] Crim LR 420 and *Condron* [1997] 1 WLR 827. More recently, in *Lee* [2015] EWCA Crim 971, it was appropriate to draw inference from silence where the police did not have full details of the allegation but the direction of questioning was clear.
[77] See Cape E, 'Sidelining Defence Lawyers: Police Station Advice After *Condron*' (1997) 1 *International Journal of Evidence and Proof* 386 at p 398 and Cape E, *Defending Suspects at Police Stations* 5th edn (London: LAG, 2006c) ch 5.   [78] See also *T v DPP* [2007] EWHC 1793 (Admin).
[79] See *Roble* [1997] Crim LR 449 and *Lisa Loizu* [2006] EWCA Crim 1719.
[80] (2001) 31 EHRR 1.
[81] (2003) 36 EHRR 13 [62]. See also *Averill v UK* (2000) 31 EHRR 36, where the ECtHR did not regard the suspect as having genuinely relied on legal advice to remain silent (so did not see the drawing of adverse inferences as unfair).

a lawyer. Thus, the effect of *Argent* was, at least in theory, ameliorated, rather than neutralised, by *Condron* and *Beckles*. In practice, the English courts have arguably turned something of a blind eye to these decisions, for the Court of Appeal has continued to affirm that where a defendant claims to have remained silent on legal advice, adverse inferences can be drawn, unless the jury believes that the defendant genuinely *and reasonably* relied on that advice.[82] At root the English courts are simply hostile to suspects remaining silent. In *Howell*,[83] for example, the Court of Appeal said that:

> There must always be soundly based objective reasons for silence, sufficiently cogent and telling to weigh in the balance against the clear public interest in an account being given by the suspect to the police.

The Court went on to say that 'merely because a solicitor has so advised' it did not follow that there was a sufficiently cogent reason for remaining silent.[84]

One effect of all this is that legal advisors have to second guess what the courts would judge to be a 'good enough' reason to remain silent. Some hints have been provided that good reasons might include that the interviewing officer has disclosed little or nothing of the case against the suspect, or where the nature of the offence or of the material in the hands of the police is so complex, or relates to matters so long ago, that no sensible immediate response is feasible.[85] Additionally, making a line of defence clear, even though some details are missing might be enough to avoid an inference.[86] In *Argent* itself it was said that a jury might conclude that silence was reasonable for a 'host of reasons, such as that he was tired, ill, frightened, drunk, drugged, unable to understand what was going on, suspicious of the police, afraid that his answer would not be fairly recorded . . .'.[87] The problem is that all these reasons involve matters of judgement on which trial judges and juries may take different views.[88] As Cape notes, given that the courts have not taken a consistent line on such matters, the defence lawyer is placed in difficulty in formulating advice whether or not to remain silent, and must now warn the client that advice to remain silent will not necessarily prevent inferences from being drawn.[89] This damages the lawyer-client relationship, and undermines the effectiveness of legal representation.[90] The judiciary clearly supports the rationale of s.34 in 'flushing out innocence at an early stage or supporting other evidence of guilt at a later stage'.[91] This is the classic crime control position. The courts seem oblivious to the due process argument that there is also a 'clear public interest' in protecting (i) the privacy and dignity interests of the individual suspect (ii) the confidentiality of what passes between lawyers and their clients and (iii) the presumption of innocence. Instead, they have 'absorbed the crime-control assumptions underlying the CJPOA.'[92] As Cooper says: 'The vulnerable suspect, in unfamiliar surroundings and

---

[82] See *Beckles* [2004] EWCA Crim 2766 (the case was referred back to the Court of Appeal by the Criminal Cases Review Commission). This is incompatible with the ECtHR approach—if reliance on legal advice is the genuine reason for remaining silent then there is no room for a belief that silence is attributable only to the fact that the suspect has no good answer to the questions. The question of 'reasonableness' should not arise.

[83] [2003] Crim LR 405.

[84] *Howell* was clarified and confirmed in *Knight* [2004] 1 Cr App R 9 and followed in *Hoare and Pierce* [2004] EWCA Crim 784, and *Bresa* [2005] EWCA 1414. For discussion, see Quirk H, 'The Case for Restoring the Right of Silence' in Child J and Duff R (eds), *Criminal Law Reform Now. Proposals and Critique* (Oxford: Hart, 2019) 253–279, and Pivaty A, *Criminal Defence at Police Stations: A Comparative and Empirical Study* (Abingdon: Routledge, 2020).

[85] *Roble* [1997] Crim LRW 449.   [86] *Johnson* [2016] EWCA Crim 191

[87] *Argent* [1997] 2 Cr App Rep 27 [33E–F]. See also *Howell*, and *R v Essa* [2009] EWCA Crim 43 [15].

[88] In *Howell* itself the defence solicitor judged the police had not made sufficient disclosure but the Court of Appeal disagreed.   [89] Cape (2006c: 199–200).

[90] Quirk H, 'Twenty Years On, the Right of Silence and Legal Advice: The Spiralling Costs of an Unfair Exchange' (2013) 64(4) *Northern Ireland Legal Quarterly* 465–83.

[91] *Hoare and Pierce* [54].   [92] Quirk (2013: 483).

emotionally weakened, accepts the professional advice he is given rather than answering the questions put, only to discover later that by taking and acting upon that advice, the case against him has been strengthened. . . . Was it ever envisaged that legal advice honestly given and genuinely received might culminate in a stronger case against a defendant?'[93]

5.3.6 Conflating silence with guilt

A major concern is that courts might convict defendants on the assumption that silence or lies are tantamount to an admission of guilt. As we saw earlier, under the ECHR silence should not form the main or sole basis for a conviction.[94] A model direction for juries now states that jurors may take silence into account as 'some additional support' for the prosecution case.[95] But the model direction does not specifically warn juries not to view silence as direct evidence of guilt.

Precisely what silence can be evidence *of* is a practical, as well as a theoretical, problem. In *Hart*,[96] for example, the main evidence of drug smuggling by the defendant, which he did not explain, was possession of an incriminating phone number. There was a bare prima facie case, and Hart was convicted. This is an example of speculation (about the defendant's motives in remaining silent) masquerading as 'common sense'.[97] As Pattenden puts it, silence becomes 'evidential poly-filler for cracks in the wall of incriminating evidence which the prosecution has built around the accused'.[98] Much depends on whether the courts interpret the CJPO in ways that assist the defence or the prosecution. Pattenden, in line with most other commentators, states that the Court of Appeal is 'so committed to crime control that at almost every turn—even when an interpretation favourable to the defence is plausible—the legislation has been construed in the prosecution's favour',[99] and the same is true of the former House of Lords.[100] This undermining of adversarialism and due process has continued in the second decade of the twenty-first century.[101]

5.3.7 Debating the right to silence

The right of silence has long aroused fierce debate. The Royal Commission on Criminal Procedure (Philips Commission) recommended retention.[102] Then, in 1987, the matter was raised again by the Home Secretary following complaints by the police that 'their' conviction rate was being halved. In *Alladice*[103] the Lord Chief Justice joined in on the side of the police. The Home Secretary announced in 1988 that he intended to modify the right of silence. This led to a change in the law in Northern Ireland in 1989, but proposals for

---

[93] S Cooper, 'Legal Advice and Pre-trial Silence –Unreasonable Developments' (2006) 10 *International Journal of Evidence and Proof* 60 at 68–69.

[94] *Murray v UK* (1996) 22 EHRR 29.

[95] Approved by the Court of Appeal in *Cowan* [1996] QB 373. See discussion in Owusu-Bempah, Abenaa (2017: ch 6).

[96] Unreported, 23 April 1998 (CA). Discussed by Birch D, 'Suffering in Silence' [1999] *Criminal Law Review* 769.

[97] Cape (1997); Easton S, 'Legal Advice, Common Sense and the Right of Silence' (1998) 2 *International Journal of Evidence and Proof* 109. Hart was lucky because his conviction was quashed on appeal; as explained in ch 11 it is very difficult to win appeals.

[98] Pattenden R, 'Inferences from Silence' [1995] *Criminal Law Review* 602 at p 607.

[99] Pattenden R, 'Silence: Lord Taylor's Legacy' (1998) 2 *International Journal of Evidence and Proof* 141 at p 164.

[100] In *Webber* it not only gave a very broad interpretation of a 'fact' that the defendant relies upon at trial which was not mentioned in police questioning (see section 5.3.1), but explicitly cast doubt on two Court of Appeal decisions that had adopted a pro-defence interpretation of s.34 concerning whether adverse inferences should be drawn if initial silence concerned the key fact in the case.

[101] Johnston E, 'The Adversarial Defence Lawyer: Myths, Disclosure and Efficiency—A Contemporary Analysis of the Role in the Era of the Criminal Procedure Rules' (2020) 24 *International Journal of Evidence and Proof* 35–58.

[102] RCCP (1981: 80–91).   [103] (1988) 87 Cr App Rep 380.

England were deferred pending the report of the Royal Commission on Criminal Justice (Runciman Commission).

The Runciman Commission was split on whether to recommend that adverse inferences be drawn from silence. But the majority agreed with the Philips Commission that:

> It might put strong (and additional) psychological pressure upon some suspects ... This in our view might well increase the risk of innocent people ... making damaging statements.[104]

They also thought that erosion of the right of silence would have little effect on experienced criminals, whose conviction rate would therefore not be substantially increased. Despite the views of Runciman, for which the government had deliberately waited before deciding what to do about the right of silence, the CJPO was nonetheless enacted.

There are good practical reasons for reverting to the pre-CJPO position. First, the changes have caused more trouble for courts than they have resolved,[105] creating what Owusu-Bempah describes as 'an extensive and complex body of case law'.[106] In particular, the Court of Appeal has spoken of s.34 as a 'minefield' and cautioned trial judges not to give adverse inference directions to juries without first discussing the matter with counsel.[107] What can be read into a suspects' silence is also hard for juries to understand and apply.[108] Second, these complexities also mean that suspects, particularly those who are vulnerable, struggle to grasp the meaning of adverse inferences and the police caution, not helped by the fact that police officers and sometimes legal advisors struggle to explain them.[109] This raises serious questions therefore about whether or not suspects are making a fully informed choice when exercising this important due process right to silence. Third, they have swung the balance too far to the police by sidelining custodial legal advice, for example, because it makes it more difficult for legal advisors to know how best to advise their client and because by advising a suspect to remain silent, a legal advisor may inadvertently help build the case against them.[110] Fourth, they pressure vulnerable suspects into speaking against their will, but probably have little effect on professional criminals.[111] Fifth, they have not increased the rate at which suspects make incriminating statements or the rate at which conviction is achieved at court. Sixth, they undermine attempts to make the criminal process more inclusive, because black suspects are more likely to rely on the right to silence than suspects from other groups (see further chapter 10). There is no doubt that the erosion of the right of silence by the CJPO has produced minimal gains to off-set significant losses.

5.4 Regulating police questioning

5.4.1 Questioning outside of the police station

The police question citizens in many types of situation and for many reasons. We saw in chapter 2 that 'stop-search' often enables the police to gather intelligence through questioning. The police may also 'stop and question' citizens to enquire about their name, address and where they are going, though citizens may choose not to answer these questions. These powers have taken on a new significance during the Covid-19 pandemic when the police were encouraged to seek voluntarily compliance with police questions and

---

[104] Royal Commission on Criminal Justice (RCCJ) Report (Cm 2263) (London: HMSO, 1993) p 55, quoting RCCP (1981: para 4.50). [105] Birch (1999).
[106] Owusu-Bempah, Abenaa (2017: 114). [107] See, for example, *Hillard* [2004] EWCA Crim 837.
[108] Quirk (2016: 155).
[109] Quirk (2016: 62–67); Blackstock et al, *Inside Police Custody* (Cambridge: Intersentia, 2014) pp 378–380.
[110] Johnston (2020). [111] Bucke et al (2000); see generally, Easton (1998).

also with directions to go home.[112] Officers and particularly Police Community Support Officers working in Neighbourhood Policing Teams may also routinely and informally gather information and intelligence through the day-to-day interactions that they have with citizens sometimes over a cup of tea, who may be seen as suspects, but also victims or witnesses.[113]

Thus the police only sometimes have suspicions about those they question. Once they have suspicions one might expect that the law would require the standard caution 'You do not have to say anything...' to be given, as this reminds suspects of an important due process protection (the right to silence). But the courts decided[114] that this is required only if the police have *reasonable* suspicion that they committed the offence (see section 5.3). This means that the police can ask some probing questions, such as about name, address and where someone is going, of those against whom they have 'mere' suspicion without having to give the caution. There are a number of risks here, as can be seen from accounts of spectacular miscarriages of justice: first, that the police will avoid the cautioning requirement (and the associated risk that the suspect will seek legal advice) by acting as if they do not have reasonable suspicion when they plainly do;[115] second, that suspects will give less than considered answers or fail to grasp how their behaviour might be (mis-)interpreted when not appreciating that they are under suspicion,[116] and, third, that the police will record any answers given or behaviour observed on a selective (inculpatory) basis.[117] To take the example of police questioning of citizens during Covid-19 restrictions again, by either answering or not answering questions asked by police officers citizens may give the police cause to believe that they did not have a reasonable excuse for being outside their home.[118] At the time, this could also result in them being taken home (by force) or being arrested, charged and/or issued with a fixed penalty notice. This illustrates how police questioning of citizens, even where there is no immediate reasonable suspicion, can result in serious consequences.

Moreover, even where they do have reasonable suspicion that someone has committed an offence they are not obliged to give the caution if the questions put 'are for other necessary purposes' (Code C, para 10.1). Examples of such necessary purposes given by the Code include 'in furtherance of the proper and effective conduct of a search' or 'solely to establish their identity or ownership of any vehicle' (ibid). Thus, it appears that much of the questioning that accompanies a stop-search based on reasonable suspicion (such as

---

[112] College of Policing, Briefing on the Health Protection (Coronavirus, Restrictions) (England) Regulations 2020 (2020) Online at: <https://www.college.police.uk/News/College-news/Pages/Health-Protection-Guidelines.aspx> (accessed 20 May 2020).

[113] This role as a conduit for information has dwindled in recent times, however, due to austerity-related cuts to PCSO numbers. See: O'Neill M, *Police Community Support Officers: Cultures and Identities within Pluralised Policing* (Oxford: OUP, 2019). Greig-Midlane J, 'An Institutional Perspective of Neighbourhood Policing Reform in Austerity Era England and Wales' (2019) 21(4) *International Journal of Police Science & Management* 230–243.

[114] E.g. *Sneyd v DPP* [2006] EWHC 560.

[115] Devlin A and Devlin T, *Anybody's Nightmare: The Sheila Bowler Story* (East Harling: Taverner Publications, 1998) pp 52–64 & 158. In *Alford v Chief Constable of Cambridgeshire* [2009] EWCA Civ 100, the level at which reasonable suspicion is formed was considered to be a low one, meaning that officers should not require much information before the threshold is crossed.

[116] Devlin and Devlin (1998: 63–64); Cannings A, with Lloyd Davies M, *Against All Odds: A Mother's Fight to Prove Her Innocence* (London: Time Warner Books, 2006) pp 42–43.

[117] Devlin and Devlin (1998: 62–70); Callan K, *Kevin Callan's Story* (London: Little, Brown and Company, 1997) pp 26–27.

[118] See here for a list of reasonable circumstances in which people could leave their homes as of 13 May 2020: <https://www.libertyhumanrights.org.uk/advice_information/coronavirus-when-can-i-leave-my-home/> (accessed 20 May 2020).

'do you have a knife in your pocket'?) does not have to be preceded by the administering of a caution. If the police search results in finding evidence of a crime (e.g. a knife), however, then at this point a caution must be given before further questions are put.[119]

If there is 'reasonable suspicion' in relation to a particular suspect, the police can arrest. If they decide to arrest, questioning must usually cease temporarily, as we shall see. If there is no 'reasonable suspicion', the police cannot arrest, but questioning may continue wherever it began until the suspicions are either allayed or increased. In the latter case the suspect would usually be arrested. But even if the police develop very strong suspicions, there is no obligation to arrest and so nothing to prevent further questioning.[120] Much police questioning, both of suspects and non-suspects, therefore takes place outside the police station without (or prior to) arrest. This is a form of 'informal questioning' to be discussed in detail in section 5.5.

Once the police decide to arrest, para 11.1 of Code C states that the suspect 'must not be interviewed about the relevant offence except at a police station... unless the consequent delay would be likely to lead to...' a number of specified possibilities such as serious damage to property or interference with evidence. In other words, where there is an urgent need to interview (sometimes referred to as a 'safety interview'), the police may do so. For example, where people are arrested on suspicion that they have just committed arson, the police can ask questions there and then about the location of the fire.

PACE, s.30(1A) states that the suspect 'must be taken to a police station by a constable as soon as practicable after the arrest'. As so often with criminal justice, the phrase 'as soon as practicable' is of prime importance. Under s.30(10) and s.30(10A) the police can delay taking an arrestee to a police station 'if the presence of that person elsewhere is necessary in order to carry out such investigations as it is reasonable to carry out immediately.' So the police can take the arrested person somewhere other than a police station to conduct a safety interview. The police can also simply release an arrestee instead of taking him/her to the station if 'there are no grounds for keeping him under arrest.'[121] Finally, s.4(7) of the Criminal Justice Act 2003, inserted s.30A into PACE which allows an arrested person to be released on bail at any time before reaching the police station. This enables the police to require the suspect to attend the police station at a time that suits the interviewing officer.

Thus, generally speaking, if people who are arrested are to be questioned, this must be only in a 'formal interview'. That is, they must be taken to a police station at once, booked in by the custody officer, offered their rights as set out in chapter 4, and questioned (with recording equipment switched on) only after that. But situations are envisaged where police officers can justifiably delay taking suspects to a police station after arrest and interrogate them elsewhere. Why does this matter? There are dilemmas here which do not involve the clash of due process and crime control principles, but which create problems for due process itself. Taking arrested persons to a station immediately can be seen as desirable for two main reasons. First, it enables custody officers to decide whether or not arrests are justified and whether suspects are particularly vulnerable. Second, it allows as little time to elapse as possible after arrest before suspects have the opportunity to exercise their rights under ss.56 and 58 to consult a lawyer and to have their arrest made known to a relative or friend, thus preventing police officers from interrogating suspects

---

[119] *R v Cheb Miller* [2007] EWCA Crim 1891.
[120] See, for example, *R v Moore* [2004] EWCA Crim 1624, where the Court of Appeal accepted the evidence of customs officers that the interview of a suspect in her mother's home took place prior to a decision to arrest—and was thus lawful.
[121] PACE, s.30 (7) and s.30(7A).

incommunicado in unregulated conditions.[122] On the other hand, we saw in section 3.5 that it is undesirable to encourage peremptory arrest on bare reasonable suspicion if the suspect has an exonerating story. If the story can be checked by, for instance, going to a shop where the suspect says he bought allegedly stolen goods or to a place of work where an alibi could be confirmed, this must be better for the suspect than being held in custody while these investigations are made. Then there are suspects who feel, and often are, under less pressure if interrogated somewhere they feel comfortable, such as at home or in the office of their solicitor. Indeed, some of these countervailing factors may explain the growing use of 'voluntary' police interviews (relative to formal arrest and detention),[123] which can take place by appointment at a police station or at the scene of an alleged offence. They may be used where police officers consider that necessity of arrest criteria have not been met. However, these voluntary interviews are still under police caution and are far from a cosy or indeed 'voluntary' chat, given the possibility of subsequent arrest depending on what is said.[124]

Section 30 of PACE is thus a messy compromise. Its imprecision provides an opportunity for the operation of crime control working rules in relation to interrogation. So, despite the fact that it might have due process potential, it is primarily a crime control enabling rule. It enables the police to insist on immediate police station interrogation except when they determine that some other course of action is preferable. The suspect has no say in the matter. This enables the police to lengthen the time between arrest and police station detention, exacerbating another problem. Incriminating statements made to the police prior to arrest, or en route to a police station or some other place envisaged in s.30(10) (such as the suspect's home or place of work), are not invalidated simply because the information was not given in the police station. This gives the police an incentive to seek a confession prior to arrival at the police station, the Code of Practice gives the police permission to do this both before and (when the safety conditions are met) after arrest, and the courts will not necessarily exclude any evidence obtained even when these already broad enabling rules are overstepped.[125]

5.4.2 What is a police interview?[126]

Drawing a clear line between formal post-arrest interviews, a voluntary interview and a discussion or conversation is difficult. Yet it is vital to do so because Code C, para 11.1, which sets out the general (not total) prohibition against post-arrest questioning away

---

[122] In *Kerawalla* [1991] Crim LR 451 the defendant was arrested in a hotel room and questioned there without being allowed to exercise his ss.56 and 58 rights. The Court of Appeal held that, while the suspect should have been taken to a police station straight away (as required by s.30 of PACE), ss.56 and 58 rights were not applicable to persons detained at premises other than a police station. This precedent was applied in *DPP v Kirkup* [2003] EWHC 2354 (where the court ruled that the right to legal advice arose in the police station only after the custody officer authorised detention). In *R v Moore* [2004] EWCA Crim 1624 [17], however, the Court of Appeal said that each case depended on its own facts, and opined that a suspect about to be questioned under caution at her mother's home should have first been advised that she could seek legal advice before giving answers (although it accepted the trial judge's view that no unfairness resulted as a result of this omission).

[123] Between 2013/14 and 2017/18, the estimated number of detentions reduced by around 30% and voluntary interviews by around 20%, suggesting a growing role for voluntary interviews relative to police detention. See Bath C, *There to help 2*, (NAAN, 2019) p 6.

[124] See: PACE Code C, paras 3.21 to 3.22B.

[125] See *Kerawalla*. See further discussion in Cosigan R and Stone R, *Civil Liberties and Human Rights* 11th edn (Oxford: OUP, 2017) ch 3.

[126] In this section, the main focus is on formal interviews that take place post-arrest as opposed to voluntary interviews.

from the police station.[127] It therefore offers some protection to the post-arrest suspect. These post-arrest provisions only apply to those taking part in a formal 'interviews'. According to para 11.1A of Code C:

> An interview is the questioning of a person regarding their involvement or suspected involvement in a criminal offence or offences which, under paragraph 10.1, must be carried out under caution.

It is obvious that all post-arrest questioning about suspected offences should be regarded as falling within the definition of an interview because an arrested person is, by definition, a suspect against whom reasonable suspicion exists (and is thus covered by the para 10.1 obligation to caution).[128] This much is (usually) accepted by the courts. In *Absolam*[129] the defendant was arrested for suspected drugs offences. He was questioned in the charge room and allegedly gave incriminating answers. Only then was he read his rights and cautioned. If this was an 'interview', then the questioning was unlawful because it took place before the suspect was read his rights and before he had had the opportunity to seek legal advice. If it was not an interview, then it was not unlawful and those protections were not applicable. The Court of Appeal held that this was an interview.[130]

Interactions between the police and arrestees are often fluid, however, as are conversations between officers and mere suspects, and the less any oral exchanges 'look' like an interview, the more likely a judicial conclusion that no interview took place. Thus for some time it looked as though interviews were being defined as conversations which took place in police stations; anything which took place outside a police station was not an interview.[131] But allowing the place of the discussion to determine its legal status made little sense. If the place of the conversation was to determine whether the protection of PACE and the Code of Practice is provided, the police would simply do more interviews outside.

Another approach is to examine the intention of the officers in question. But as Field points out, it is easy for officers to claim that it was their intention merely to seek information when in fact it was not.[132] The courts have seemed gullible in this respect. In *Maguire*[133] two youths, seen pushing open the door of a flat, were told on the way to the police car, 'You've both been caught. Now tell us the truth . . . It's for your own good.' This was held not to be an interview. Similarly, in *Pullen*[134] the court believed that officers visited the defendant's cell 'with the object of relaxing him and . . . restoring some of his dignity', thus holding that only a conversation took place.[135] Whilst in *Shepherd*[136] the appellants appeal against his manslaughter conviction was rejected after the court upheld that his recorded interview with the police as a significant witness to a boat crash on the Thames resulting in the death of the woman with whom he had been on a date, could not be seen as a criminal investigative interview. This was because the investigating officers did not intend the

---

[127] A formal post-arrest interview should generally take place at a police station or other authorised place of detention except in some circumstances, such as where a delay might increase the risk of interference with or harm to evidence relevant to the offence being investigated. See PACE Code C, 2019: 11.1 (a).

[128] But note that para 11.1A of Code C expressly excludes procedures for testing breath, blood or urine in connection with driving whilst intoxicated offences.

[129] (1988) 88 Cr App Rep 332.

[130] Interviews were also held to have taken place in *Miller* [1998] Crim LR 209 (one question asked in the charge room) *Oransaye* [1993] Crim LR 772 (questioning at the custody officer's desk) and *Goddard* [1994] Crim LR 46 (questioning prior to being taken to the police station). Code C warns police-station based officers not to invite comments from suspects outside the context of a formal interview (paras 3.4 and 15.6).

[131] See, e.g., *Maguire* (1989) 90 Cr App Rep 115; *Younis* [1990] Crim LR 425; *R v Bhambra* [2008] EWCA Crim 2317. [132] Field S, 'Defining Interviews under PACE' (1993) 13 *Legal Studies* 254.

[133] (1989) 90 Cr App Rep 115.   [134] [1991] Crim LR 457.

[135] Note, however, *Hunt* [1992] Crim LR 582, where the court was more sceptical.

[136] [2019] EWCA Crim 1062.

interview to be as such, as they did not realise that some of the matters discussed (e.g. the appellants' intoxication and the high speed of travel of the boat he and his date were in) were criminal offences under byelaws. Hence, he was not cautioned or offered legal advice. The court said that the officers were 'not . . . acting in bad faith . . . [nor] suspected the appellant of having committed a criminal offence' and had been merely trying ascertain what had happened from the person who was most likely to be able to help.

Some cases, such as *Younis*[137] where the conversation took place in a police car, have been decided on the basis that an exchange is not an interview if it is initiated by the suspect. This could only be relevant if the whole discussion was on the lines initiated by the suspect, which was not so in *Younis*. In any event, whether someone needs protection depends on the nature of the discussion, rather than on where it takes place, who initiated it or on the intention of the police.[138] This seems to have been recognised in *Weekes*.[139] Here the Court of Appeal said that an 'understandable enquiry' became an 'interview' when the suspect started making admissions. But what good is this if the purpose of defining a conversation as an 'interview' is to prevent admissions being made without due process protections? This would be a helpful ruling only if it meant that whatever was said as a result of 'understandable enquiries' became unusable as a result of the exchange's transformation into an 'interview'.[140] This was not the line taken subsequently, however. In *James*,[141] for example, a man disappeared. His business partner was questioned without suspicion initially existing, but suspicion that he murdered the missing man grew in the course of discussions during which no caution was given. The Court of Appeal held that these were not interviews (even when they asked 'Have you killed David Martin?'), that the police were not wrong to have given no caution, and that the evidence of the discussions could be used against James. Other more recent cases point to a similar direction of travel with regards the admissibility of evidence obtained through conversations. In *Skrzypiec*,[142] conversations between the claimant and the arresting officer about a drink-driving matter, initially, on her doorstep (following a police caution, though not following information that she was participating in a voluntary interview and was free to leave) and in the custody suite whilst being booked-in were deemed inappropriate but still admissible, once her formal police interview was also deemed admissible. This was also in part because these first two informal interviews were seen as due to inexperience rather than bad faith or a disregard for PACE on the part of the arresting officer.

Police-citizen encounters away from the police station are usually characterised by their low visibility. To some extent this may be changing owing to the 'new visibility' of police work afforded by citizens' use of camera phone technology.[143] Nonetheless, generally speaking what went on (who initiated the conversation, what was being sought by it, what the intentions of the officers were and so forth) is only the officers' word against the suspect's. The whole point of PACE and Code C promoting and regulating formal 'interviews' was to eradicate this problem by being able to verify what was said and done objectively. It is precisely this objective verification which the police seek to avoid by so often trying to ensure that their discussions are not classified as interviews. Recent cases show that the

---

[137] [1990] Crim LR 425. Similar cases are discussed by Field (1993: 261–263).
[138] See *Sparks* [1991] Crim LR 128.   [139] (1993) 97 Cr App Rep 222.
[140] See Fenwick H, 'Confessions, Recording Rules, and Miscarriages of Justice: A Mistaken Emphasis?' [1993] *Criminal Law Review* 174.   [141] [1996] Crim LR 650.
[142] [2010] EWHC 1418 (Admin). Other cases where evidence has been admitted from conversations prior to formal questioning include *R v Van Gelderen* [2008] EWCA Crim 422; *R v Neill* [1994] Crim LR 441.
[143] Goldsmith A, 'Policing's New Visibility' (2010) 50(5) *British Journal of Criminology* 914–934. See further ch 11.

problem of the pre-interview question and (incriminating) answer session has not gone away.[144] The incentive to secure, through informal questioning, confession evidence which can be used in court will still be there for as long as the rules of evidence allow it.[145]

5.4.3 Recording of interviews

Accurate recording of interviews is essential. Without knowing what was said and done, by both police officers and suspects, it is impossible to know what pressure was placed on suspects to confess or even whether they confessed at all. Prior to PACE, questions and answers were rarely tape recorded. Confessions and denials came in one of two forms. First, 'verbals'; these were police officers' accounts of suspects' (supposedly) voluntary verbal statements, usually written down some time after they were made. Second, 'voluntary' written statements, written either by the suspect or, at the suspect's dictation, by a police officer. Both came to be challenged increasingly frequently. 'Verbals' were often said not to reflect accurately what suspects really said, and were sometimes alleged to be complete fabrications.[146] Similarly, voluntary written statements were often said to have been the work of the officers themselves.[147]

Inaccuracy, commonly known as 'gilding the lily', took three forms. First, there was alteration of the words used to create a different impression, either deliberately or inadvertently. Police officers, like everyone else, have imperfect recall, and mistakes are made when conversations are reconstructed at a later time, especially when the purpose of the reconstruction is to prove a point.[148] Second, there was the incomplete recording of what was said. It was common to only write down what suspects said 'when they start telling the truth', that is, when they agreed with the allegations being put to them.[149] We shall see that police tactics can lead suspects to 'confess' against their will, and this is difficult to challenge if previous denials are not recorded. Third, there is fabrication. In *Blackburn*,[150] for example, a 15-year-old boy was convicted of attempted murder following his alleged voluntary confession written, so the police claimed, entirely in his own words. Blackburn spent 24 years in prison as a result. After his release, expert evidence showed that the wording of the confession had been heavily prompted by the police and his conviction was quashed as unsafe.

The Philips Commission realised the dangers of all these forms of inaccuracy. It did not believe that all, or even most, alleged statements were false. But some were, as even police officers will admit.[151] The problem was in distinguishing the false from the true. The Philips Commission recommended that all exchanges be accurately written down so

---

[144] See, e.g., *Ridehalgh v Director of Public Prosecutions* [2005] EWHC 1100; *Senior* [2004] Crim LR 749; *Sneyd v DPP* [2006] EWHC 560. See also *Van Gelderen, Neill and Skrzypiec op cit*.

[145] See Maguire M and Norris C, *The Conduct and Supervision of Criminal Investigations* (Royal Commission on Criminal Justice, Research Study no 5) (London: HMSO, 1992) p 46. Ch 11 discusses the exclusion of unlawfully obtained evidence.

[146] The Royal Commissions of 1929 and 1962, as well as the Philips Commission, were concerned about 'verbals'. See Cox B, *Civil Liberties in Britain* (Harmondsworth: Penguin, 1975) ch 4.

[147] In a scandal of the 1960s, Sergeant Challenor and several colleagues were eventually successfully prosecuted for these practices (and many instances of corruption and brutality) when it was found that statements made by suspects he had arrested all used the same improbable phrases such as 'travelling in a northerly direction' (Cox 1975).

[148] Stephenson G, 'Should Collaborative Testimony be Permitted in Courts of Law?' [1990] *Criminal Law Review* 302.

[149] Sanders A, 'Constructing the Case for the Prosecution' (1987) 14 *Journal of Law and Society* 229.

[150] [2005] EWCA Crim 1349. [151] See McConville et al (1991: 84–87).

that the question of fabricated confessions did not arise. So, Code of Practice C (para 11.7) requires 'an accurate record' of interview (regardless of whether the interview occurs at the police station or elsewhere) to be made either 'during the course of the interview' (and to be a 'verbatim record') or, if this was not practicable, 'an account of the interview which adequately and accurately summarises it'.

When these provisions were first introduced, there were several problems with them. For the police, the laborious writing down of everything said slowed the interview, gave suspects time to think, and inhibited the establishment of rapport.[152] Also, just as before, what was written down might not be accurate or complete. The only difference was that the police would have to claim that it was written contemporaneously instead of afterwards, which is only a small safeguard.[153] Finally, there was the problem of informal interviewing outside the interrogation room for here it was easy for the police to claim that it had not been 'practicable' to record contemporaneously.

The glaring nature of these problems led to many eminent figures asking, well before the Philips Commission reported, for the routine audio recording of interrogations.[154] This was initially resisted by the police, but following the introduction of a new Code of Practice on Tape Recording in 1988 (Code E), and later on audio-visual recording in 2013 (Code F) the police adapted rapidly, and audio recording is mandatory in all indictable and either-way cases except in exceptional circumstances (including certain terrorism provisions). A more recent change to PACE has broadened the possibilities for audio-visual recording of interviews even further. Since 2018, interviews may take place on 'authorised recording devices', though PACE does not refer specifically to body-worn cameras, their use for police interviews, particularly voluntary interviews, would comply with this part of the PACE Code of Practice,[155] including potentially in locations outside the police station. There is no requirement that interviews be visually recorded (except in certain investigations into suspected terrorism), and para 2.2, Code F gives examples of when an officer might consider visual recording to be appropriate, including where the officer simply believes it will 'assist in the conduct of the investigation'. Haworth suggests that 'the vast majority of day-to-day interviewing is still only audio-recorded'[156] but one author's experience suggests that most interviews are both audio and visually recorded, and most police stations are now equipped with audio-visual recording equipment.[157] As with many discretionary procedures—especially ones that allow broad application of discretion—use is likely to vary according to geography. As Haworth says, this topic would benefit from further research. Either way, it is more difficult for the police to record proceedings selectively, and virtually impossible for them to fabricate recordings, but the third problem, interrogation outside

---

[152] Maguire M, 'Effects of the PACE Provisions on Detention and Questioning' (1988) 28 *British Journal of Criminology* 19.

[153] Although it was enough (eventually) in the 'Birmingham Six', 'Guildford Four' and 'Tottenham Three' cases. The convictions in all these cases were largely based on allegedly contemporaneously written confessions which later scientific evidence proved not to have been written at the time. See Rozenberg J, 'Miscarriages of Justice' in Stockdale E and Casale S (eds), *Criminal Justice Under Stress* (London: Blackstone, 1992), and Walker C, 'Miscarriages of Justice in Principle and Practice' in Walker and Starmer (1999a).

[154] See especially Williams G, 'The Authentication of Statements to the Police' [1979] *Criminal Law Review* 6.

[155] An authorised recording device is determined by Chief Officers and could therefore include body-worn cameras (PACE Code C: para 1.6(a)(i)).

[156] Haworth K, 'Tapes, Transcripts and Trials: The Routine Contamination of Police Interview Evidence' (2018) 22(4) *The International Journal of Evidence & Proof* 428–450.

[157] Home Office, *Interviewing Suspects* (2020b) <https://assets.publishing.service.gov.uk/government/uploads/system/uploads/attachment_data/file/864940/interviewing-suspects-v7.0.pdf> (accessed 1 October 2020).

the interview room, remains.[158] General conversation rarely appears on recorded interviews, even though conversation between suspect and interviewer at some point is usual. This confirms the inadequacy of the audio recording 'inside the police station as a wholly adequate record of all relevant verbal exchanges between suspect and interviewer.'[159]

Under Code C paras 11.8–11.10, if no recording is made, a verbatim record or adequate summary must be written down (during the interview, if practicable, or as soon as practicable thereafter). Further, 'unless it is impracticable the person interviewed shall be given the opportunity to read the interview record and to sign it as correct or to indicate how they consider it inaccurate' (para 11.11). This is to ensure that what actually was said is written down and that nothing that was not said is not written down. It is also to ensure that suspects who agree that everything has been written down fairly and accurately indicate that this is their view.

There are three problems with records of interview. First, even though suspects may sign what is written down, this does not mean that what was written down was accurate, for people frequently fail to read documents which they sign. In theory, accuracy should not be a problem in the majority of formal interviews now that they are audio recorded. In practice, however, few defence or prosecution lawyers listen to these recordings and they are only very rarely played in court.[160] Instead reliance is placed on summaries prepared by the police or, in serious cases, full transcripts. These summaries[161] and transcripts have been found to contain many inaccuracies. For example, Gudjonsson (2003) and Pearse (a senior detective) examined 20 transcripts of interviews in serious cases and concluded 'in all cases discrepancies [were identified] between the official transcripts and the audio recordings. In some of the cases the inaccuracies were seriously misleading' (p 114).[162] An example is given of a typed transcript in which the suspect is said to have replied 'yes' to the question: 'Did you ever touch their private parts?'. The audio recording showed the suspect had actually responded 'no'.[163] Similarly, in a recent Criminal Justice Joint Inspectorate report, it was found that in 25% of the 436 case files examined in the inspection, interview summaries varied in their style, quality and detail. 'Some were too long and others did not contain any details of the questions that were put to the defendant in a "no comment" interview'.[164] Summarising interviews in this way has become more popular as demands for efficiency increased, especially through the streamlined processes in magistrates' courts (see chapter 8). Furthermore, Haworth has demonstrated that the people who prepare the transcripts tend to assume that the allegations put by the police are being confirmed, and are thus influenced by the prosecution perspective and that this bias can be built into the transcript; and that lawyers still sometimes unquestioningly accept the accuracy of transcripts, even in serious cases.[165]

---

[158] Thus video recording is not necessarily helpful, and may even be harmful to suspects (particularly when the camera focuses only on the suspect) both because video evidence seems so compelling, and because it can lead to amateurish assessments of demeanour by prosecutors and judges who overestimate their ability to detect deception. See Dixon D, '"A Window into the Interviewing Process?" The Audio-visual Recording of Police Interrogation in New South Wales, Australia' (2006) 16(4) *Policing & Society* 323; Lassiter et al, 'Evidence of the Camera Perspective Bias in Authentic Videotaped Interrogations' (2009) 14(1) *Legal and Criminological Psychology* 157.

[159] Moston S and Stephenson G, *The Questioning and Interviewing of Suspects Outside the Police Station* (Royal Commission on Criminal Justice Research Study no 22) (HMSO, 1993) p 36.

[160] Gudjonsson (2003:112); Taylor C, *Criminal Investigation and Pre-Trial Disclosure in the United Kingdom: How Detectives Put Together a Case* (Lampeter: Edwin Mellen Press, 2006) at p 154 (n 51).

[161] Baldwin J and Bedward J, 'Summarising Tape Recordings of Police Interviews' [1991] *Criminal Law Review* 671 (almost half of the summaries were adjudged unfair, misleading, distorted or of poor quality).

[162] See further Haworth (2018).   [163] See also Taylor (2006: 148, n 37).

[164] HMIC, *Witness for the prosecution: Identifying victim and witness vulnerability in criminal case files* (London: HMIC, 2015) p 6.   [165] Haworth (2018).

The second problem with the record of interview is that although what is written down (or audio recorded) may be accurate (in the sense of reflecting what was said), it may none the less be unreliable when suspects are induced to confess, are subjected to oppressive pressure or have words put into their mouths. Not only do these things sometimes happen during the audio recording and with a lawyer present, but they also happen before or between interviews. It is true that Code C demands that: 'A written record shall be made of any comments made by a suspect, including unsolicited comments, which are outside the context of an interview but which might be relevant to the offence' (Code C, para 11.13). But it need not be written at the time, and it need only be provided to the suspect for verification and signing 'where practicable'.[166] If these comments were made as a result of unlawful pressure, the full exchange is not likely to be fully recorded by the police and, as with pre-PACE 'verbals', what was said (and why) often becomes simply a matter of who is believed.

In spite of these potential difficulties with audio-recordings and summaries of them, the situation is far worse when there is no formal record at all. When alleged confessions are not contemporaneously recorded, the opportunities for dispute about what was really said are many. In *Khan*,[167] for instance, one interview took place in the police car from Wales back to Birmingham, and one took place later in the police station. The defendant was alleged to have confessed to robbery during the journey, but he denied the offence in the police station and also denied making the earlier alleged confession. The police claimed that they took contemporaneous notes of the interview in the car (which were not shown to Khan at the time). This was accepted at his trial, and he was convicted. It later became clear that the police officers did not write the notes in the car, casting doubt on whether he really did confess, and so his conviction was quashed on appeal. In a sensationalised example of the courts upholding the police's duty to comply with the interview requirements of PACE, the trial judge in the case of Christopher Halliwell ruled confessions allegedly made (that included leading the police to two bodies) were inadmissible because the alleged confession was made before the suspect had been cautioned or taken to the police station, and he later made no comment during interview, meaning that the police had insufficient evidence to proceed with prosecution in one alleged murder.[168] Mrs Justice Cox, was, in this case, prepared to acknowledge—at para 118—that the breaches of provisions requiring the police to take the suspect to the police station, give them their rights and to record interviews 'were indeed significant and substantial breaches of the Codes, in circumstances deliberately designed to persuade the Defendant to speak.' The courts are prepared (and PACE requires them) to exclude valuable evidence where the police have significantly and substantially breached PACE and its related codes in relation to interviews. However, that depends on the issue coming to light in the first place, on the evidence available about the breach and on the efficiency of the defence team (where there is one).[169]

---

[166] Moreover, para 11.13 does not apply to anything said which itself constitutes the crime in question (e.g. when swearing at a police officer is labelled as a s.5 Public Order Act 1986 offence) but only to statements of a self-incriminatory nature made on or after arrest in relation to that crime: *DPP v Lawrence* [2007] EWHC 2154 (Admin).

[167] (1990) unreported, CA. Discussed by Kaye T, 'Unsafe and Unsatisfactory?' Report of the Independent Inquiry into the Working Practices of the West Midlands Police Serious Crime Squad (London: Civil Liberties Trust, 1991).

[168] *R v Halliwell* (unreported) Bristol Crown Court T2011/7126. The ruling can be found here: <https://www.judiciary.uk/wp-content/uploads/JCO/Documents/Judgments/halliwell-ruling.pdf> (accessed 1 October 2020). Police were able to uncover other evidence which led to Halliwell's conviction for the second murder in 2016. The 'significant and substantial' breach provisions which allowed the trial judge to make this ruling can be found in *Keenan* [1990] 2 QB 54 and s.78 PACE. This case was the subject of an ITV drama entitled *A Confession* in 2019.

[169] On the last point, see ch 8 in particular.

A contra example is *Dunn*.[170] The defendant was interviewed with his legal advisor present and denied criminal activity. At the end, while reading through the interview notes, the police claimed that he confessed. The police said that they wrote down this alleged confession, but they did not show this record to the suspect or to his legal advisor, in clear breach of Code C. The court nonetheless allowed it to be used as evidence, as did the Court of Appeal, even though both the suspect and the legal advisor denied that the alleged confession had been made.

These examples show that even when the police are proved to have broken these provisions of Code C for no good reason, the Court's approach to the evidence secured as a result varies, sometimes with disastrous results for the suspect. They also illustrate the wide scope the police have for breaking them, and the opportunities thus provided simply to fabricate confessions and/or impose unlawful pressure on suspects to confess. For every instance where fabrication is proved there must be a dozen where it is alleged. As *Dunn* and *Khan* show, it is often impossible to establish who is telling the truth. Sometimes, and we will never know how often, the courts get it wrong. These problems, and these mistakes, will continue for as long as confession evidence secured in the absence of an independent party remains admissible in court.

5.4.4 The protection offered by legal advice and appropriate adults: safety first?

All suspects in custody are entitled to legal advice, and all vulnerable suspects must normally be accompanied in formal interviews by an appropriate adult.[171] Because the right to legal advice is a continuing one, suspects are able to request a solicitor when an interview is about to take place, or even during one, as the Code of Practice C (para 11.2) acknowledges:

> Immediately prior to the commencement or re-commencement of any interview at a police station or other authorised place of detention, the interviewer should remind the suspect of their entitlement to free legal advice, and that the interview can be delayed for legal advice to be obtained . . .

The normal rule is that suspects may not be interviewed if they ask for solicitors who have yet to arrive, and questioning must stop if a request for legal advice is made during any interview.[172] But the police are allowed to interview even if legal advice has been requested but not yet received if a senior officer (superintendent or above) has reasonable grounds for believing that delay will involve a serious risk of harm (to evidence, persons or property) or 'unreasonable' delay.[173] Similarly, such 'safety interviews' can take place with children and the mentally vulnerable without the presence of an appropriate adult.[174]

---

[170] (1990) 91 Cr App Rep 237. Discussed in Hodgson J, 'Tipping the Scales of Justice' [1992] *Criminal Law Review* 854. There are many other examples, such as *Gillard and Barrett* (1991) 92 Cr App R 61. For a case that went in the defendant's favour see *Canale* [1990] 2 All ER 187 or *Weerdesteyn* [1995] 1 Cr App Rep 405. See also discussion in Doak and McGourlay (2012: ch 8) and Keane A and McKeown P (2020) *The Modern Law of Evidence* (Oxford: OUP, 2020) ch 15.

[171] These topics are discussed fully in ch 4.   [172] Code C, paras 6.1 and 6.6.

[173] PACE, s.58 and Code C, para 6.6—discussed in ch 4. Broader exceptions apply to those detained under the Terrorism Act 2000: see Code C, Annex B. These safety provisions were invoked by DS Fulcher as his explanation for breaching PACE in relation to Christopher Halliwell's case (earlier).

[174] Code C, paras 11.15 and 11.18. The superintendent must be satisfied that the interview would not 'significantly' harm the suspect's physical or mental state. Amazingly, para 11.18 countenances that safety interviews may take place with those who appear 'unable to appreciate the significance of questions and their answers' or 'understand what is happening because of the effects of drink, drugs, or any illness, ailment or condition.'

In previous editions of this work we have mentioned the 'safety interview' provisions only in passing, but the recent marked shift towards pre-emption and public protection in criminal justice, and rising concern about terrorism, means that such interviews are of increasing importance, although no proper statistics are published.

In a 'safety interview' the police are meant to give the old-style pre-CJPO caution: 'You do not have to say anything, but anything you do say may be given in evidence', as no adverse inferences may be drawn from silence in a situation where the suspect has been denied the right to consult with a solicitor.[175] We saw in chapter 3, however, that in situations that represent crises of law and order, legalistic models of policing tend to break down.

In *R v Ibrahim, Omar, Osman and Mohamed*[176] the appellants were arrested in respect of the attempted bombings in London on 21 July 2005 (two weeks after the murderous bomb attacks on London's transport system). They were interviewed under the 'emergency' provisions of the Terrorism Act 2000, Sch 8, paras 7–9 which, like PACE, allows safety interviews, albeit in a wider range of circumstances. The relevant police station was holding 18 people suspected in relation to the 21 July attack. The police, who were under intense pressure to find out whether further bomb attacks were imminent, accordingly denied legal advice to Omar, Ibrahim and Mohamed for 8, 7.5 and 4 hours respectively so that safety interviews could take place without delay.[177] In a number of these interviews the police gave the wrong ('adverse consequences') caution. The suspects then told demonstrable lies whilst, at the same time, not indicating the defences later advanced at trial. The trial judge held that it was not unfair to admit as evidence what had been said in the safety interviews. While acknowledging that using the wrong caution unfairly pressured them, the trial judge ruled that the suspects were not induced to incriminate themselves but rather told deliberate, exculpatory lies.[178]

While it is difficult to feel any sympathy for these particular defendants, it is worth recalling that most of those arrested in relation to terrorism are later released without charge (chapter 3), and that telling lies in interview can be extremely damaging to any later *truthful* defence one might have. The suspects in this case incriminated themselves in the long run by the lies they told in interview, and the police, by giving the wrong caution, contributed to this. It goes against the grain of police culture for officers to remind suspects *accurately* of rights designed to protect the latter against those very officers—a point we wish judges would bear in mind.

Interviews may also take place following an unmet request for legal advice if suspects change their minds about wanting to see a solicitor. In these circumstances, suspects must give their agreement, in writing or in an audio-recording, to being interviewed without legal advice and an officer of the rank of inspector or above must inquire about the reasons for the change of mind and give authority for the interview to proceed.[179]

---

[175] Code C, Annex C.   [176] [2008] EWCA Crim 880.

[177] The trial judge found that Ibrahim had been wrongfully (if unintentionally) denied access to a solicitor who was available to speak to him prior to his safety interview (i.e. without causing the police any delay). He nonetheless allowed Ibrahim's statements to be used as evidence, and this was upheld by the Court of Appeal.

[178] See *Ibrahim & Ors* [56]. The Court of Appeal agreed with the judge. It also rejected an argument that it would be good public policy to encourage suspects to speak freely in safety interviews by banning the admissibility of any self-incriminating evidence thus obtained. Furthermore, the ECtHR decided that, as a result of the exceptionally serious and imminent threat to public safety, there had been no breach of Art 6 in relation to three of these defendants (*Ibrahim v UK* [2016] ECHR 750) This case does nothing to encourage the police to take their due process responsibilities seriously. See further the UK case report and commentary by Andrew Roberts at [2009] Crim LR 110.   [179] Code C, para 6.6(d).

Given the rights of suspects to be accompanied by legal advisors[180] (and, where applicable, appropriate adults) why is police questioning still a problem? First, questioning in the absence of a legal advisor (or an appropriate adult) is not invalid if the above provisions are complied with. And even scrupulous compliance with all due process safeguards (including telling the suspect of their right to free legal advice) does not usually result in a lawyer attending for interview. Only a relatively small proportion of suspects who are interviewed by the police will receive legal advice in the police station and are thus likely to have a legal advisor present to support them,[181] with this situation no doubt worsening as a result of the diminishing resources available to legal advisors who may therefore have less capacity to attend the police station to accompany their client into interview.[182] Even though some more suspects secure advice or support of some kind (e.g. over the telephone, or from an 'appropriate adult') this does not wrest control of questioning from the police. In the mass of mundane criminal cases, the police can rarely delay access lawfully, and rarely try, but many suspects do not secure legal advice.[183]

Second, many legal advisors and appropriate adults are supine in the face of oppressive or unfair interrogation, as in the 'Cardiff Three' case and the more general research discussed in section 4.5.4.4. We saw there that standards have improved in recent years, particularly amongst accredited legal representatives and volunteer appropriate adults,[184] but we also know that changes to legal aid payments have negatively affected legal representatives' ability and/or willingness to engage properly with their clients and that suspects need for an appropriate adult can go unidentified and access to them can be variable.[185] It also has to be recognised that, even if legal advisors or appropriate adults are minded to intervene, the police interview, like many other parts of police detention is police territory.[186] It is therefore controlled by the police, as in the following example:

Solicitor:	'. . . the second clarification is the wallet.'
Detective Constable:	'We're not on trial here; we're asking the questions, not you; we don't have to clarify anything.'
Solicitor:	'I am entitled as any defence solicitor would be to ask for clarification—you don't need to give it, officer.'
Detective Constable:	'We're not clarifying things here, we're not on trial. You can ask these things later when it comes to court.'[187]

---

[180] Note that no such right exists under Art 6 of the ECHR. Denying a solicitor access to an interrogation is merely a factor to consider when assessing whether a defendant had a fair trial: *Brennan v UK* [2001] ECHR 596. In nearly all respects English law regulating interviews is more generous to suspects than ECHR law, which is why we say little about the latter in this chapter.

[181] See section 4.5.4. The position is likely to be even worse where other law enforcement bodies are concerned. In one study only 4% of the interviews conducted by Department of Work and Pension benefit fraud investigators were attended by a legal representative: Walsh D and Milne R, 'Keeping the Peace? A Study of Investigative Practice in the Public Sector' (2008) 13 *Legal and Criminological Psychology* 39 at 52.

[182] See Pivaty (2020: ch 6).

[183] See section 4.5 for discussion of how the right to legal advice operates in practice.

[184] See, for example, Pierpoint H, 'Reconstructing the Role of the Appropriate Adult in England and Wales' (2006) 6(2) *Criminology & Criminal Justice* at 225–226. But also see Leggett et al, 'People with Learning Disabilities' Experiences of Being Interviewed by the Police' (2007) 135 *British Journal of Learning Disabilities* 168.

[185] Bath et al (2019) *There to help 2*, online at: <https://www.appropriateadult.org.uk/policy/policy-publications/there-to-help-2> (accessed 1 July 2020); Dehaghani R and Newman D, 'Can – and Should – Lawyers be Considered 'Appropriate' Appropriate Adults?' (2019) 58(1) *Howard Journal of Crime and Justice* 3–24; Dehaghani R, 'Exploring the Implementation of the Appropriate Adult Safeguard in Police Custody' (2016) 55(4) *The Howard Journal of Crime and Justice* 396–413.

[186] See for example Hodgson J, *The Metamorphosis of Criminal Justice* (Oxford: OUP, 2020) pp 205; Skinns L, *Police Powers and Citizens' Rights* (Abingdon: Routledge, 2019) pp 151–153.

[187] McConville and Hodgson (1993: 127). The authors note that the solicitor made no further attempt to interrupt the interrogation.

Legal advisors (and appropriate adults) can only intervene to prevent interrogation methods which fail to conform to the standards discussed later. But we will see that many of the key standards are unclear. Not only does this give the police considerable leeway, but it would produce uncertainty in the mind of the most assertive solicitor, let alone an inexperienced police station legal representative, or appropriate adult who may either be a volunteer (who will have had limited training) or a parent and who therefore tend to play a passive role.[188]

Third, we should note that the police sometimes seek to maintain control over lawyer-attended interrogations by various subtle and not-so-subtle ways of undermining the legal advisor. They may try to assert control over a legal advisor not just a suspect, for example, by fitting the arrival time of legal advisors at the custody suite around police timescales and then by keeping them waiting for a lengthy period outside the custody suite until the police are ready to interview a suspect.[189] Once inside the custody suite, the legal advisor is, like the suspect, on police territory and may therefore be ejected if they are seen as 'misbehaving' and not following police directions,[190] though this may amount to an unlawful denial of legal advice if alternative legal advisor is not sought, as was the case in *McDonagh*.[191] The role of the legal advisor is therefore shaped as much by police attitudes towards them, as by their own understandings of it and the relationship they are able to build with their client.[192] In the police interview itself, Shepherd (2007: 311) notes that some police interviewers 'put down' legal advisors who were not solicitors by pointing out their status to suspects as a way of implying that their advice is incompetent. A less subtle tactic is to dispute directly the content of legal advice given to a suspect. A legal advisor complained to Bucke et al (2000: 29) that in one interview the 'police turned round and said that "the advice you've been receiving is incorrect and an inference [from silence] can be drawn."' In these ways the police can seek both to make interventions from legal advisors less likely, and, if made, less likely to be influential.

Finally, legal advisors and appropriate adults will inevitably be absent during informal 'conversations' between the police and suspects (see section 5.4.2 and 5.5.3), many of which will result in admissible self-incriminating statements.[193] This is particularly so given the tendency for solicitors to be largely only present for the police interview or shortly before it, if they turn up at all. Dwindling resources and a decade of austerity have meant that solicitors do not have the capacity to provide much by way of support outside of the formal police interview and may also provide telephone legal advice only where a suspect is likely to plead guilty.[194]

5.4.5 When interviews must end

When PACE was first enacted it adopted the common law position that it would be unfair to continue an interrogation once the police were satisfied that they had obtained sufficient evidence for a prosecution to succeed. The only latitude given to the police in this

---

[188] See Medford et al, 'The Efficacy of the Appropriate Adult Safeguard During Police Interviewing' (2003) 8 *Legal and Criminological Psychology* 253; Pierpoint (2006: 221 & 230); Farrugia L and Gabbert F, 'The "Appropriate Adult": What They Do and What They Should Do in Police Interviews with Mentally Disordered Suspects' (2019) 29(3) *Criminal Behaviour Mental Health* 134–141.

[189] Skinns L, *Police Custody* (Cullompton: Willan, 2011) p 176.

[190] Skinns (2001: 180).

[191] [2013] EWHC 4690.

[192] Welsh L, 'The Effects of Changes to Legal Aid on Lawyers' Professional Identity' (2017) 44(4) *Journal of Law and Society* 559–585; Blackstock et al (2014: 336).

[193] For further discussion of these issues, see Dehaghani and Newman (2019: 3–24).

[194] Smith T and Cape E, 'The Rise and Decline of Criminal Legal Aid in England and Wales' in Flynn A and Hodgson J (eds), *Access to Justice and Legal Aid* (London: Bloomsbury, 2017); Kemp V, '"No Time for a Solicitor": Implications for Delays on the Take-up of Legal Advice' (2013) 3 *Criminal Law Review* 184–202.

situation was that they were allowed to ask the suspect if they had anything further to say. But where interviewers took this opportunity to press their questions further, the courts held that this was permissible. In *McGuiness*,[195] the Court of Appeal said that, without giving the suspect a full opportunity to explain himself, including questions and answers, the police would not know whether they should prosecute.[196] A subsequent revision to Code of Practice C incorporated this greater degree of latitude. Paragraph 11.6 now provides that the interview or further interview of a person about an offence with which that person has not been charged must cease when the officer in charge of the investigation:

(a) is satisfied all the questions they consider relevant to obtaining accurate and reliable information about the offence have been put to the suspect, this includes allowing the suspect an opportunity to give an innocent explanation and asking questions to test if the explanation is accurate and reliable, e.g. to clear up ambiguities or clarify what the suspect said;

(b) has taken account of any other available evidence; and

(c) the custody officer. . . reasonably believes there is sufficient evidence to provide a realistic prospect of conviction. . .

This wording makes clear that a police interview may continue even though the police believe they already have sufficient evidence to make conviction a realistic prospect.[197] Indeed, it is difficult to think of situations in which the police would not be able to claim that there was an outstanding need to 'clear up ambiguities' or obtain clarifications of what the suspect has already said. And if the suspect is silent in interview this provision enables the police (regardless of the strength of the case they have already assembled) to ask all relevant questions in order to lay the groundwork for adverse inferences to be drawn at trial. Even after a suspect has been charged there is provision made (Code C, para 16.5) for further interviewing but only if an interview is necessary:

(i) to prevent or minimise harm or loss to some other person, or the public

(ii) to clear up an ambiguity in a previous answer or statement, or

(iii) in the interests of justice for the detainee to have put to them, and have an opportunity to comment on, information concerning the offence which has come light since they were charged or informed they might be prosecuted.

In post-charge interviews the old-style caution is given, which means that adverse inferences may not be drawn from silence.[198] The suspect is also reminded of their right to legal advice.

The law continues to develop in favour of greater police powers in this area. Thus, the Counter-Terrorism Act 2008 Part 2 (in force since 2012) permits post-charge police questioning of a person about a terrorism-related offence, including after they have been sent for trial.[199] However, by 2016 there had been no documented cases of post-charge

---

[195] Crim LR [1999] 318. *Odeyemi* [1999] Crim LR 828 was decided similarly.

[196] See also *Elliot* [2002] EWCA Crim 931 and *Howell* [2002] EWCA Crim 1.

[197] This appears to conflict with the language of s.37 of PACE and other provisions within Code C (see Cape E, 'PACE Then and Now: 21 Years of "Re-balancing"' in Cape E and Young R (eds), *Regulating Policing* (Oxford: Hart, 2008) pp 205–208) although there seems little doubt in the light of *McGuiness*, that the courts will give full effect to the wording of para 11.6.

[198] Code C, para 16.5(a).

[199] But only if authorised by a Crown court judge, who must be satisfied that further questioning is necessary in the interests of justice, that the investigation is being conducted diligently and expeditiously, and that questioning 'will not interfere unduly' with preparation of the defence. The judge must specify the period for which questioning is authorised (up to a maximum of 48 hours, although nothing prevents further authorisations being given) and may impose other conditions.

questioning in terrorist cases, perhaps because 'the misgivings of police and especially prosecutors remain strong'.[200]

Does any of this matter? It is, at least arguably, generally wrong to allow the police to continue to question suspects once they have sufficient evidence to prosecute. For without a cut-off point until the permissible period of detention has ended they will always be able to claim that further information (or useful silences) might be forthcoming, but only under conditions of involuntary detention. Moreover, since this questioning is allowed, it follows logically that voluntary incriminating statements in these circumstances are allowed to be used as evidence, as in a Scottish case.[201] But the courts do not acknowledge that it is impossible to be confident that statements made post-interview, without the protections provided in official interviews, are truly voluntary. On the other hand, suspects who are innocent or whose mitigating circumstances point towards diversion from prosecution might benefit from the police probing further. Whether the police, as currently constituted, can be relied upon to operate in the latter manner is doubtful. For while the increased capacity of the police to interview suspects makes them powerful inquisitors, their objective is not a neutral 'search for the truth' but rather to obtain evidence which the prosecution can use for adversarial purposes.[202] This brings us to the subject of police interrogation tactics and strategy.

5.5 'We have ways of making you talk'

Interviewing may take place over the 24 (or 36, where authorised by at least a superintendent) hour period (or up to four days, for indictable offences, or 28 days for terrorist offences) of compulsory detention.[203] PACE Code of Practice C provides for this interrogation to take place under reasonable conditions, specifying adequate breaks for rest and refreshment (paras 12.2 and 12.8), adequate heating, lighting and ventilation in the interview room (para 12.4) and allowing the presence of a legal advisor (if requested). Code C also requires the custody officer to assess whether the detainee is fit to be interviewed: 'This means determining and considering the risks to the detainee's physical and mental state if the interview took place and determining what safeguards are needed to allow the interview to take place' (para 12.3). The purpose of all this is in part humanitarian but it is also to ensure that confessions or other information is secured by fair means, is reliable, and thus usable in court.[204] However, acceptable methods of questioning and the number of interviews are not specified. Code C (para 11.5) merely indicates in broad terms what may not be done.

> No interviewer may try to obtain answers or elicit a statement by the use of oppression . . . [or] . . . shall indicate, except to answer a direct question, what action will be taken by the police if the person being questioned answers questions, makes a statement or refuses to do either.

---

[200] Walker C, 'Post-charge Questioning in UK Terrorism Cases: Straining the Adversarial process' (2016) 20(5) *The International Journal of Human Rights*, 649–665 at 659.
[201] *Birnie v HM Advocate* [2012] SLT 935.
[202] Cape E, 'The Revised PACE Codes of Practice: A Further Step Towards Inquisitorialism' [2003] *Criminal Law Review* 355 at 369. See also Walker C, 'Post-charge Questioning of Suspects' [2008] *Criminal Law Review* 509, who discusses the dangers of allowing 'a process of wearing away the will of suspects until they are exhausted into a state of complicity' (p 521) and the strong due process safeguards needed to counterbalance the shift towards enabling post-charge questioning.
[203] Detention periods were discussed in section 4.3.
[204] As the Code's Annex G on fitness to be interviewed puts it, a detainee should be regarded as 'at risk' if either the interview could harm their physical or mental state *or* if anything they said in the interview might be considered unreliable in subsequent court proceedings because of their physical or mental state.

Some suspects are happy to tell the police everything they know. They may be confident of their ability to establish their innocence or be anxious to clear their conscience by confessing. For many suspects, however, telling the police what they know gains them nothing and can lose them a lot. In the main, then, the interview is about negotiating release of information (in exchange for something worth gaining) and/or attempting to persuade suspects to provide information which they do not want to provide. Whatever the situation, police strategy is first directed to establishing control. Subject to the provisions outlined, the police control where, when and how interrogations take place, what is asked, what information is given to suspects and their legal advisor if they have one, and what is said to suspects or solicitors outside the interrogation. This keeps suspects on the defensive, nervous, less able to exercise their normal powers of judgement, and unsure of the applicability of any rights of which they may have knowledge.

Police interrogation has to be coercive if it is to produce results in most cases, because the police have to try to induce suspects to talk about things that most do not want to talk about. At one time, before the forms of regulation discussed in the previous section were established, coercion quite frequently took the form of actual violence. Examples include the 'Sheffield Rhino whip' scandal (in the 1960s), the notorious West Midlands Police 'Serious Crime Squad'[205] (in the 1970s), and even incidents following the enactment of PACE.[206] We do not know how common this was, in part because there was even less control and monitoring of interrogations then than there is now. Probably the best evidence we have comes from an unpublished Masters dissertation by Walkley reporting 1980s interviews with fellow police officers. It seemed the threat of violence was as important as the actual use of violence, if suspects knew or feared that the police were prepared to use it. Thus Walkley reported that half the police officers he interviewed agreed that: 'Some suspects expect rough treatment in police stations, and, if it suits the circumstances, I don't do anything to allay their fears'.[207] The fact that arrests are often violent or accompanied by rough treatment (see section 3.4.4) must create a fear of repetition in some suspects' minds. Moreover, the level of deaths in custody (see section 4.4 and chapter 10) indicates that violence in the police station has not disappeared. There is little doubt, however, that violence, and the explicit threat thereof, is now infrequent within the context of a formal police interview. The police have had to develop non-violent 'tactics' which aim at the same results through legal means.

5.5.1 Police interrogation tactics: legal standards

Nowhere does PACE or Code C specify in detail what tactics are, and are not, lawful. 'Torture' is a crime.[208] But torture still happens when UK law enforcement personnel work overseas in legal twilight zones. For example, secret documents revealed in 2009 showed that the British government condoned the use of torture in Pakistan, arranging for a terrorist suspect to be detained in that country for this purpose.[209] Similarly, a 2018 review

---

[205] Aptly named in view of the serious crimes it committed. See further Kaye (1991).

[206] One suspect interviewed in 1987 was forced to sign a confession after having been butted and punched by a detective and threatened with injection by a syringe: *Daily Telegraph*, 20 January 1998. See also Newburn T and Hayman S, *Policing, Surveillance and Social Control* (Cullompton: Willan, 2002) at pp 115 and 126.

[207] Cited in Milne R and Bull R, *Investigative Interviewing: Psychology and Practice* (Chichester: Wiley, 1999) at pp 73–74.

[208] Criminal Justice Act 1988, s.134. Evidence obtained by torture is inadmissible in English judicial proceedings: *A (FC) and Others (FC) v Secretary of State for the Home Department* [2005] UKHL 71, confirmed in *A and Others v United Kingdom* (Application no 3455/05); *Jalloh v Germany* (2007) 44 EHRR 32.

[209] *The Guardian*, 8 July 2009. For analysis, see Gaskarth, J, 'Entangling Alliances? The UK's Complicity in Torture in the Global War on Terrorism' (2011) 87(4) *International Affairs* 945–64.

of rendition practices and the mistreatment of detainees in the wake of 9/11 found evidence of two cases where UK intelligence personnel were directly involved in the mistreatment of detainees by others whilst they were held in locations in Afghanistan, Iraq and Guantanamo Bay. This included practices such as hooding during interrogations, sleep deprivation, being placed in stress positions (e.g. kneeling for prolonged periods with their hands behind their back) and the deliberate irregular spacing of meals.[210] There were 166 incidents where such personnel were aware of mistreatment taking place, but they turned a 'blind eye' so as not to disrupt the flow of intelligence or relationships with their overseas counterparts.[211]

In police interrogation in England and Wales, the standards imposed on such practices arise solely from laws that regulate the acceptability or exclusion, at trial, of evidence (see chapter 11). This means that breaches of these legal standards only affect the police adversely if they prosecute the suspect(s) in question, and seek to use the evidence obtained from them. If, for example, the police interrogate largely to discipline (not prosecute) someone, they have nothing to fear by breaching any or all of these standards. But since the police cannot usually be certain in advance that they will not wish to use the fruits of such an interview in support of a prosecution they will generally seek to remain broadly within the legal standards. As we shall now see, however, the relevant standards are unclear and do not preclude officers from using interviews to 'put the frighteners' on suspects.

5.5.1.1 The police must not offer 'inducements'

Paragraph 11.5 of Code C (quoted earlier) implicitly prohibits the offering of 'inducements', such as bail, non-prosecution or a lighter sentence if prosecuted.[212] The ban on inducements reflects a fear that people offered inducements may say whatever they think the police want to hear, regardless of whether or not it is true. The fear is entirely justified, but it cannot be simply legislated away. The only way substantially to inhibit inducements to confess would be to reduce or eliminate the value of confessions to the police. As matters stand, 'deals' and 'bargains' in which information is exchanged for 'favours' are central to many police–suspect relationships,[213] and what is a deal other than an agreement that each side will accept the inducements offered by the other? According to one CID officer, suspects are often keen to open negotiations: 'They [suspects] always want to deal. When they're arrested they're immediately in the game of damage limitation.'[214] Suspects are in a relatively weak position in these negotiations—'they want to deal' because of the coercive setting in which they find themselves, and the police use this to their advantage. Thus Dunninghan and Norris found that 84% of informers were either in custody or had proceedings against them when they were recruited, and in 85% of cases it was the 'handler' who initiated the discussion about becoming an informer.[215]

---

[210] Intelligence and Security Committee of Parliament, *Detainee Mistreatment and Rendition: 2001–2010* (2018) pp 25-28, see online at <http://isc.independent.gov.uk/committee-reports/special-reports> (accessed 9 June 2020).   [211] Intelligence and Security Committee of Parliament (2018: 4).

[212] See Baldwin J, 'Police Interview Techniques: Establishing Truth or Proof?' (1993a) 33(3) *British Journal of Criminology* 325–352; *Northam* (1967) 52 Cr App Rep 97 and *Howden-Simpson* [1991] Crim LR 49.

[213] See, for example, Lister et al, *Street policing of problem drug users* (York: Joseph Rowntree Foundation, 2008) p 25. Patrick R, '"A Nod and a Wink": Do "Gaming Practices" Provide an Insight into the Organisational Nature of Police Corruption?' (2011) 84(3) *The Police Journal* 199–221 See also Billingsley R, 'Informers' Careers: Motivations and Change' in Billingsley et al (2001: 86). When 120 informers were asked why they had started informing, 16 said 'reduced sentence', nine 'looking for a favour', four 'police pressure' and two 'part of a deal'.

[214] Quoted by Maguire and Norris (1992: 47).

[215] Dunninghan C and Norris C, 'A Risky Business: The Recruitment and running of Informers by English Police Officers' (1996) 19(2) *Police Studies* 1.

The rule against inducements is thus largely presentational, and rendered still more so by the courts seeking a causal connection between the inducement and the confession. In *Weeks*,[216] for example, the police implied that the suspect would be held in custody until he told them what they wanted to hear. His partial confession was not excluded because the court did not believe that he was influenced by this. The gap between the law and reality could hardly be greater than it is here. However, what remains less clear is the extent to which inducement remains a part of day-to-day police investigative interviewing and the role it plays in securing (false) confessions. In theory, the Planning and Preparation, Engage and Explain, Account, Closure and Evaluation (PEACE) investigative interviewing model should have enabled a move away from such practices, but there has been limited empirical examination of police interrogation practices in the real world in England and Wales.[217] Once again, more research, easily enabled by the growing use of audio-visual recording by the police, is needed.

5.5.1.2 Interrogation must not be 'unfair'

This is not mentioned in Code C, but it arises because PACE, s.78 allows any evidence to be excluded at trial (at the discretion of the judge) if the circumstances in which the evidence was obtained have an unduly adverse effect on the fairness of the case. Examples arising out of the conduct of the interrogation include lies and deception, failure to record suspects' statements contemporaneously, questioning children and young people or vulnerable adults without an appropriate adult, unnecessary/excessive delay in allowing access to legal advice and failing to caution a suspect against whom there is reasonable suspicion.[218] But what a judge may regard as 'unfair' is something of a lottery, and the courts have shied away from issuing guidance about what is and is not considered to be fair. The courts have instead taken the view that the judge must weigh all the factors in any give case to come to an overall decision about fairness.[219] The Court of Appeal, while unpredictable,[220] rarely interferes with this discretionary power of the trial judge, and if a legal representative is in the interrogation this is usually regarded as sufficient protection to blunt any unfairness.[221]

A good example of the meaning of 'fairness' can be seen in *Higgins*.[222] The Court of Appeal noted that the police questioning in this case was 'assertive and confrontational, but not untypical of rigorous testing in cross-examination by police of suspects in interview'. The suspects had been arrested on suspicion of conspiracy to pervert the course of justice—the police alleging that the evidence for the defence that they proposed to give at the trial of X was false. The Court acknowledged that the interviews were lengthy and repetitive (focusing in minute detail on alleged inconsistencies between the suspects' initial statements and their answers to questions in interview), that they had culminated in suggestions that the suspects were lying, and that the police had warned the suspects that they would risk perjury charges if they gave evidence at the trial of X. In addition, one of the interviewing officers misled one of the suspects by claiming (untruthfully) that another of the suspects had cast doubt on his story. One of the suspects subsequently refused to give evidence at X's trial and another was so reluctant to give evidence that defence counsel

---

[216] [1995] Crim LR 52.
[217] Walsh et al, 'One Way or Another? Criminal Investigators' Beliefs Regarding the Disclosure of Evidence in Interviews with Suspects in England and Wales' (2016) 31 *Journal of Police Criminal Psychology* 127–140.
[218] See, respectively, *Mason* [1988] 1 WLR 139; *Canale* [1990] 2 All ER 187; *Fogah* [1989] Crim LR 141; *R v Cheb Miller* [2007] EWCA Crim 1891; *R v W* [2010] EWCA Crim 2799; *Beuze v Belgium* (2018) ECHR 382.
[219] *Misick v The Queen* [2015] 1 WLR 3215 PC. See also discussion in Dickson B, *Human Rights and the United Kingdom Supreme Court* (Oxford: OUP, 2013) ch 7 and ch 11 of this volume.
[220] Compare its reasoning in *R v Cheb Miller* [2007] EWCA Crim 1891 with that provided in *R v Rehman* [2007] Crim LR 101 and *R v Maya Devani* [2007] EWCA Crim 1926.
[221] See *R v Maya Devani* [2007] EWCA Crim 1926.   [222] [2003] EWCA Crim 2943.

decided not to put him on the witness stand. Nonetheless, the Court judged that 'viewed as a whole', the police behaviour was neither oppressive nor unfair, and that it did not believe the police had acted in 'bad faith', that is, with a view to denying X a fair trial. It is evident that the fairness standard, as interpreted by the courts, covers relatively little of what might ordinarily be regarded as 'unfair'.

5.5.1.3 Interrogation must not be 'oppressive'

Section 76(8) states that oppression 'includes torture, inhuman or degrading treatment, and the use or threat of violence (whether or not amounting to torture).' Confession evidence obtained in this way must be excluded under s.76(2). However, as mentioned at the start of this section, this does not mean that torture is unknown to the UK. A man later convicted of serious terrorism offences was effectively placed in the hands of Pakistan's secret service, who ripped out his fingernails and deprived him of sleep, and whipped, beat and sexually humiliated him over several days. British authorities effectively subcontracted this to Pakistan, feeding agents questions to be asked about his suspected co-conspirators.[223] That this evidence could not be used in court proceedings was irrelevant, as it could be used to track down people who could then be put under surveillance. As noted in a subsequent 2018 review of similar cases, what is important is that the flow of information and intelligence is maintained.[224]

Many practices short of torture are considered oppressive and are banned by Code C. Thus, suspects cannot be made to stand during interview (para 12.6) and individual interview sessions should not normally last more than two hours (para 12.8). On the other hand, nothing is said in the Code concerning what might constitute an oppressive style of questioning and the case of *Higgins* (see preceding sub-section) illustrates that the courts do not necessarily regard interrogation that is lengthy, repetitive, confrontational, and deceitful as oppressive. In *Emmerson*[225] rude, discourteous questioning in a raised voice, peppered with swearing, was held not to be oppressive.

A relentless refusal to entertain the possibility that a suspect's answers may be truthful has, however, been regarded by the courts as amounting to oppression.[226] Gudjonsson gives the example of an arson case in which the officer repeatedly interrupted the suspect and dismissed his replies. The 22 minute interview contained 52 such tactics, as well as the manipulation and distortion of evidence, and culminated in a confession. As Gudjonsson puts it this 'brings into sharp focus the speed with which a person's resolve may crumble' (2003: 91). In another of his examples (2003: 91–94) a police 'question' (actually a series of abusive accusations) lasted more than five minutes, and many other forms of intimidation and persuasion were used. In both these cases the courts ruled the resultant confessions inadmissible on the grounds of oppression.

Quite when a confrontational interview becomes oppressive thus remains a matter of judgement; there are no 'bright lines' in law to guide police officers, defence lawyers or trial judges. In the 'Cardiff Three' case the police were (eventually) adjudged to have gone too far (see section 5.5.2.9). The Chief Constable of South Wales responded by saying that, although he did not support oppressive interviewing, two High Court judges had allowed the 'Cardiff Three' confession evidence and 'a full debate on what constituted oppressive questioning was now needed'.[227] The leading case remains *Fulling*[228] in which the defendant made incriminating statements after being told that her lover had been having an

---

[223] *The Guardian*, 8 July 2009.   [224] Intelligence and Security Committee of Parliament (2018).
[225] (1990) 92 Cr App Rep 284.
[226] Gudjonsson (2003:82), citing *Heron* (1993, unreported) and the 'Cardiff Three' case (*Paris, Abdullahi, Miller* (1992) 97 Cr App Rep 99).
[227] *The Guardian*, 17 December 1992.   [228] [1987] QB 426.

affair with the occupant of the next cell. The Court of Appeal adopted the dictionary definition of oppression, which is:

> Exercise of authority or power in a burdensome, harsh, or wrongful manner, unjust or cruel treatment of subjects, inferiors etc.; the imposition of unreasonable or unjust burdens.

This extremely wide definition was qualified with the view that this would normally have to include an 'impropriety' by the police. The courts do not view all 'improprieties' as oppressive.[229] Presumably this is why the police were held not to have acted 'oppressively' in this case, for the trick played on *Fulling* was undoubtedly 'cruel', although perhaps not what one would normally think of as oppressive. The recourse to the dictionary definition by Lord Lane CJ in *Fulling* was essentially rhetorical, and the courts have yet to clarify what is meant in law by oppression. In the case of *Hussein*, the court said that an assessment of oppression will depend on an assessment of what might amount to inhumane treatment, and that Art 3 of the ECHR (prohibition on torture, inhumane and degrading treatment) would provide useful guidance,[230] but much discretion is still left in the hands of the court and is circumstance-dependent (meaning that cases can easily be distinguished from each other on a factual basis). This uncertainty can be useful for the police because it gives them latitude and enables them to shrug off responsibility if their tactics subsequently attract criticism. By the same token, it means that, even if the police want to behave ethically, they cannot know how far they can go. For example, in a murder case where the trial judge refused to accept alleged confessions secured after the police wrongly told the defendant that they had identification evidence and 'pounded him with sexual allegations' the head of CID for the force concerned said: 'It is a matter of interpretation as to what is oppressive . . . It is rather difficult to establish the truth by pussyfooting about.'[231]

5.5.1.4 'Unreliable' answers and statements

Under PACE, s.76(2)(b) confession evidence must be excluded if 'anything said or done' was likely to render it 'unreliable'. This overlaps substantially with 'oppression' and 'inducements' as the fruit of these would often be regarded as unreliable. The wording of s.76 makes clear that confessions which may have been obtained as a result of circumstances conducive to unreliability (or which may have been obtained through oppression) *must* be excluded even if extrinsic evidence shows that the confession was in fact true.[232] This is an example of a strong due process rule since the crime control end of true confession evidence is not regarded as justifying the means used to secure it. However, as with all rules, much depends on how it is interpreted by the courts and it is plain that the exercise of standard police powers and procedures as provided for by Parliament will not be allowed to trigger s.76.[233] Thus, although repeated and lengthy interviewing is 'something done' to a suspect which might be thought likely to render a resultant confession unreliable within the terms of s.76, the courts can hardly exclude such a confession without undermining the entire practice of custodial interrogation.[234]

---

[229] In *Davison* [1988] Crim LR 442, for instance, unlawful denial of access to a solicitor was held not to be oppressive. See also *Parker* [1995] Crim LR 233.

[230] *Hussein v Secretary of State for Defence* [2013] EWHC 95 (Admin).

[231] *The Guardian*, 22 November 1993. This was *Heron*. See Dixon (1997: 169–177) for discussion of this and other cases illustrating the judicial approach to interrogation standards.

[232] A rule re-affirmed in *Blackburn* [2005] EWCA Crim 1349.

[233] For illustration, see *Kirk* [1999] 4 All ER 698, in which a 'confession' obtained after a series of interviews was not regarded as engaging s.76(2)(b), even though the police had not told the suspect the nature of the offence they suspected him of, and even though the confession contained many erroneous details.

[234] At least so far as non-cooperative suspects in serious criminal cases are concerned (see section 5.6). In any case, evidence discovered as a result of a confession ruled inadmissible under s.76 is not itself inadmissible (s.76(4)(a)), which rather undermines the due process pretensions of this section.

5.5.2 **Traditional police questioning tactics**

Legal standards exist ostensibly to prevent questioning falling below minimal human rights standards and to attempt to ensure that confessions and other information provided is reliable. Yet we have seen that police questioning is inherently coercive. As one suspect put it:

> You see, like, they tell you you don't have to talk, then they pressure you to talk. You say 'no comment, no comment', and they keep asking you questions . . . It's nonsense innit?[235]

It is to the nature of that pressure, steering a course between illegality and ineffectiveness, that we now turn.

5.5.2.1 **Use of custodial conditions**

Custodial conditions can be manipulated by the police as one of several tactics used to secure confessions. This was first identified by Irving,[236] and subsequently by others,[237] though this is not something that has been empirically researched for some time. Much of the more recent literature on police interviews is psychological in orientation and tends to focus on the language and inter-personal dynamics of the interview, rather than on the material conditions in which suspects are held prior to this interview and their impact on how they respond to police questioning. Nonetheless, it is likely that these material conditions amount either purposefully or inadvertently to a coercive environment, which may frighten suspects and serve to encourage them to comply with police directions, including in police interviews. This may be particularly the case for vulnerable suspects. As one of the authors notes:

> [T]o an extent all the detention facilities in the research exercised some degree of coercive control over detainee. This was evident in the routine use of the term 'prisoner' to refer to those who were merely suspected of having committed an offence, in the routinely poor quality and physically oppressive conditions in which suspects were detained, as well as in how these physical spaces were used . . . What was also found to be coercive was the routinised and ritualised nature of the processes and procedures that detainees faced on arrival into police detention facilities . . . police detention was the point at which detainees joined the endlessly churning criminal justice conveyor belt over which they had limited control as to when and at what point they could get off.[238]

These conditions mean that it is readily apparent to suspects that they must depend on the police for everything whilst they wait in the cells and they feel helpless as a result.[239] Detainees must depend on the police for example for clothing (if their own clothing has been taken away as evidence), food, drinks, blankets, and even toilet paper, as well as access to key rights and entitlements such as legal advice or intimation.[240] Whilst in the cells, many of these requests are now mediated through cell intercoms, which can further reinforce detainees' sense of isolation if they are muted because the police come to regard a detainee as being too demanding and 'trigger happy' on the buzzer.[241]

---

[235] Adams C, *Balance in Pre-Trial Criminal Justice* (unpublished PhD thesis, LSE, 1995) p 247.

[236] Irving B, *Police Interrogation: A Study of Current Practice* (Royal Commission on Criminal Procedure Research Paper No 2) (London: HMSO, 1980).

[237] Choongh (1997: 109–110); Evans R, *The Conduct of Police Interviews with Juveniles* (Royal Commission on Criminal Justice Research Study no 8) (London: HMSO, 1993) p 25; Sanders et al 1989.

[238] Skinns (2019: 112).   [239] Skinns and Wooff (2020).

[240] Skinns L, '"Seeing the light": material conditions and detainee dignity inside police detention', All Souls Seminar Series, Centre for Criminology, University of Oxford, 23 January 2020.

[241] Skinns (2011: 96).

Some of these material goods furthermore become 'bargaining tools', which are used to induce compliance in detainees. In the past, these were cigarettes,[242] but in the smoke free world of twenty-first century custody suites, hot drinks have become the new currency. One of the authors found that 'if detainees were respectful towards staff and complied with their orders, then they were rewarded, such as with additional hot drinks'.[243] For example, staff sometimes said to detainees that if they came calmly to have their fingerprints taken then they would reward them with a hot chocolate. Similarly the due process requirement that there should be breaks in the interviewing process can present another way of encouraging detainee compliance with the interview process, whilst also contributing to the crime control mandate of the police. They: (i) allow interrogators (not just suspects) the chance to rest and recuperate; (ii) give the police a chance to compare the suspect's story with other evidence with a view to exploiting any inconsistencies in the next interview; and (iii) provide time for suspects to forget precisely what they have already said to the police (particularly likely where the break takes the form of a night's sleep) or to become worked up and anxious about the next interview.[244]

In the interrogation itself police authority is crucial, for example, 'I'll decide when the interview finishes', and '... don't think we'll just let it go just because in one interview you make no replies—we're just starting.'[245] Recalcitrant suspects are returned to or threatened with being returned to the cells.[246] This serves as a warning of how they will have to spend the rest of their 36-hour detention; a severe threat in view of the feelings of most suspects about detention and their desire to depart from police custody as soon as possible. Thus Softley found that occasionally a confession was produced almost immediately on return to the cells.[247]

5.5.2.2 Police discretion

Sometimes the police allude to their discretion in relation to bail, the level and number of charges to be preferred, other suspects to be investigated and so forth. Examples include the police saying threateningly to a legal representative, in the presence of the suspect, 'We'll have to see about bail if he's not talking', and the police telling a legal representative that they would not charge his client if he confessed.[248] The interviews from one police station looked at by Baldwin contained a spate of inducements to confess on the promise that the offences would merely be 'taken into consideration' (TIC).[249] Skinns also found evidence of police bail conditions being used in a punitive fashion when a suspect acted in a contemptuous fashion towards the police. They were set in a way that could not be met by the suspect and whilst, in this case, this was not necessarily about securing an admission, it is clear how bail conditions can be used in this way.[250] These are all examples of inducements and, as such, contrary to Code C. Estimates vary regarding how frequently unlawful inducements are used. Irving and McKenzie found none,[251] whereas McConville

---

[242] Skinns (2011: 98–99); Dunninghan and Norris (1996: 8).   [243] Skinns et al (2017: 603).
[244] Skinns (2019: 131); Innes (2004: 149).
[245] Both examples taken from McConville and Hodgson (1993: 126). Also see Hillyard (1993: ch 8).
[246] Skinns (2011: 96).
[247] Softley P, *Police Interrogation: An Observational Study in Four Police Stations* (Royal Commission on Criminal Procedure Research Study no 4) (London: HMSO, 1980).
[248] McConville and Hodgson (1993: 121–122). See also Lister et al (2008: 25) and the extract from an informal interview quoted in section 5.5.3.
[249] Baldwin (1993a: 348–349). Offences taken into consideration are put before the court in abbreviated form at a normal hearing for some other offence, allowing 'the slate to be wiped clean'. See also section 5.5.3 and Gudjonsson (2003: 93). Similar issues were noted by Patrick (2011: 199–221).
[250] See Skinns (2019: 149–150). This example comes from research in an Australian jurisdiction.
[251] Irving B and McKenzie I, *Police Interrogation: The Effects of the Police and Criminal Evidence Act 1984* (London: Police Foundation, 1989).

and Hodgson (1993) found some, but not many.[252] How frequently unlawful inducements are offered outside the formal interview setting cannot be known (but see section 5.5.1.1).

An entirely lawful use of discretion is the withholding, or drip-feeding, of selected items of information, for example, about external sources of knowledge, such as victim or witness statements, which can serve to elicit admissions.[253] As we saw in section 5.3.5 the police need not tell suspects what they know or suspect, and so they often use 'phased disclosure', as a bargaining chip.[254] While this is encouraged by psychologists as a way of preventing guilty suspects from fitting their false exculpatory stories to the 'known facts',[255] it also has the effect of disorienting innocent suspects and undermines the efficacy of any legal advice they may have received.[256] Choongh (1997: 112–115) reports several suspects saying that they answered police questions in the hope that then they could discover of what they were suspected. By withholding or drip-feeding information the police can engage in active or passive deception, of which the latter is entirely lawful (see section 5.5.2.6).

5.5.2.3 Provision of expert knowledge

This is where the police play on their specialist knowledge of the legal system to suggest what the effect will be of co-operation on the attitude of the court, likely sentence, the chance of receiving expert help, and so forth.[257] In the 'Cardiff Three' case, one of the suspects attempted to retract earlier incriminating statements he had made, and was immediately told that 'you're looking at a life sentence if this goes wrong'. He thereupon continued to 'confess' (to something he did not actually do).[258] Paragraph 11 of Code C prohibits the police from telling suspects what action they will take if they do or do not answer questions except in response to a direct question (and then only if the action is proper). This is designed to guard against the police initiating a deal (e.g. non-prosecution in return for a confession) with the suspect. But the police are now obliged to point out that adverse consequences may flow where suspects stand on their right to silence. Many suspects do not understand what is meant by this caution,[259] and even the police acknowledge that some

---

[252] Note, though, that they only observed cases in which there was a legal advisor present. See also Choongh (1997: 110–111).

[253] See Carter E, *Analysing Police Interviews: Laughter, Confessions and the Tape* (London: Bloomsbury, 2013) pp 127–128.

[254] Cape (2006c: 287–288) notes that this strategy is particularly used in more serious cases and that a 'disclosure officer' may be given the job of observing interrogations and advising the interviewers on disclosure strategy. See further Walsh D, Milne B and Bull R, 'One Way or Another? Criminal Investigators' Beliefs Regarding the Disclosure of Evidence in Interviews with Suspects in England and Wales' (2015) 31(2) *Journal of Police and Criminal Psychology* 127, in which over 2/3 of police respondents preferred phased (or what they referred to as 'gradual') disclosure.

[255] See Shepherd (2007: 334 & 338–339); Hartwig et al, 'Police Interrogation from a Social Psychology Perspective' (2005) 15(4) *Policing & Society* 379 at 395.

[256] For discussion of the impact on suspects, see Sukumar D, Wade, K and Hodgson J, 'Strategic Disclosure of Evidence: Perspectives from Psychology and Law' (2016) 22(3) *Psychology, Public Policy, and Law* 306–313, which also suggests that phased disclosure might be inefficient in terms of both time and resources.

[257] See, for example, Skinns (2009a: 66–67). The sentence discount offered to those who co-operate in their own conviction is discussed in ch 7. [258] *Paris, Abdullahi, Miller* (1992) 97 Cr App Rep 99.

[259] None of the 30 suspects in one study could provide an accurate explanation of the caution: Fenner et al, 'Understanding of the police caution' (England and Wales) Among Suspects in Police Detention' (2002) 12 *Journal of Community & Applied Social Psychology* 83. See also Shepherd (2007: 341). See also Quirk (2016: 62–67), for the difficulties that (vulnerable) suspects have in understanding the police caution and adverse inferences, which are compounded by the difficulties that police officers and lawyers have in explaining it. Even though the police may present themselves as experts who can explain the police caution to the suspect, they may not be.

suspects think that the caution requires them to answer questions. The investigators only checked suspect understanding of the caution in 23% of cases studied by Walsh and Bull, and no suspects in the same study were able to provide an accurate explanation of the caution when asked to do so.[260] Some officers play on this by repeating the caution throughout the interview, even when asking questions that have nothing to do with the offence in question. Other officers find explaining the caution a useful way of building 'rapport' with the suspect or even try to present themselves as a more reliable advisor than the defence solicitor.[261] Since only about just over a third of suspects receive legal advice (see section 4.5.2) the police are the only source of advice most suspects have.

5.5.2.4 Consequences of confession

Persuasive interviewers can lead suspects to believe that confession will make them appear to be more worthy people and that non-co-operation is socially, emotionally and practically undesirable. For example, 'What's your girlfriend to think about you?', and 'sometime you'll have to stand up like a man ...' (McConville and Hodgson 1993: 123–4). The suspected 21 July 2005 terrorist Ibrahim was reminded at the start of his safety interview of his (alleged) comment on arrest that a 'good Muslim' would tell the truth.[262] Even Shepherd, who is acutely aware of the danger that suggestible people will make false confessions (2007: 16), advises interviewers to say to suspects: 'It will help all concerned if you can tell me what happened then' (ibid: 366).

5.5.2.5 No decision to be made

While the other tactics attempt to force suspects to make a decision, this tactic suggests that there is no decision to make. The suspect is led to understand that the police have sufficient evidence anyway, so that there is no point in non-co-operation, as when an officer said: 'We've had a complaint saying you were there ... There are five people to say you were there' (McConville and Hodgson 1993: 125). Whether such persuading suspects of the futility of their situation continues to be used in present-day police interviews remains an open question. A study of 80 randomly selected police interviews in one police force area in the 2000s found that this tactic was not used at all.[263] Nonetheless, this tactic is lawful if the police are telling the truth, but not (in the sense that it is 'unfair' in terms of s.78 PACE) if it is untrue.[264] Where, as often happens, the strength of such evidence is misrepresented, the legality of this depends on how great was the misrepresentation, whether the police were acting in a bona fide way and so forth. Since the police do not have to disclose any of their evidence to suspects or their lawyers at the interrogation (see section 5.2) it will often not be known at that time whether such claims are true, untrue or exaggerated.

---

[260] Walsh D and Bull R, 'Interviewing Suspects of Fraud: An In-Depth Analysis of Interviewing Skills.' (2010) 38(1–2) *The Journal of Psychiatry & Law* 99–135.

[261] Bucke et al (2000: 27–30); see also Tully B and Morgan D, 'Fair Warning?' (1997) (29 September) *Police Review* 24. Interviewers are not required by Code C to test whether suspects have understood the caution, and most do not do so (see section 5.5.4).

[262] *R v Ibrahim, Omar, Osman and Mohamed* [2008] EWCA Crim 880 [96]. Traditional interrogation techniques are particularly likely to be deployed in safety interviews (discussed in section 5.4.4), because they take place as a matter of urgency in relatively unregulated conditions and concern emotionally-laden crimes: Roberts K, 'Investigative Interviewing and Islamic Extremism: The Case of Public Safety Interviews' (undated) 2(1) iIIRG Bulletin 30 (available from <http://www.tees.ac.uk/schools/SSSL/iiirg.cfm> (accessed 29 July 2009)).

[263] See Soukara et al, 'What Really Happens in Police Interviews of Suspects? Tactics and Confessions' (2009) 15(6) *Psychology, Crime & Law* 493–506.   [264] *Mason* [1987] 3 All ER 481.

5.5.2.6 Deception

As we have seen, lying to suspects is generally regarded as 'unfair' in England and Wales,[265] though it may depend who exactly is being lied to and in what way.[266] But there are other forms of deception, both active and passive, which the police often use, which are generally lawful.[267] For example, one of the writers once asked a detective how he got a suspect to admit to a factory break-in. The officer replied that he had asked the works manager if anyone had a grudge against the factory. The suspect was named as being aggrieved about being sacked shortly before. When interviewed he denied the break-in. So the detective told him that he might as well confess, since his fingerprints were all over the place: a classic example of the 'no decision to be made' tactic. He did confess, the writer commented that this was not surprising given the evidence against him, and the detective fell about laughing, for the writer had fallen for the same deception as the suspect: since the suspect had worked there, of course his fingerprints were all over the place, but this was not evidence that he had broken in.

An example of 'passive' deception occurred in *Imran and Hussain*.[268] The suspects had been videotaped, without their knowledge, going into a shop where there had been an attempted robbery. The police did not tell them this, and they did not admit going into the shop. At trial this left them vulnerable under the CJPO (discussed in section 5.2), and they contended that adverse inferences should not be drawn since the police had passively deceived them. They were convicted, and the Court of Appeal held that what the police had, and had not, said was entirely lawful.

Arrestees must be cautioned and given a valid reason for arrest,[269] but the police may give the impression that the arrest and interview is largely for one offence when in reality they have something else in mind.[270] The courts did not object to this in *Chalkley and Jeffries*[271] (see discussion in section 3.4.3.6) where the arrest and interview were engineered simply to get the defendant out of his house while bugging equipment was installed. But the situation is different if the police use the interview to obtain incriminating evidence in relation to a matter on which they have deliberately left the suspect in the dark. In *Kirk*[272] the accused was initially arrested for burglary but re-arrested at the police station for assault and interviewed on that basis. The police deliberately chose not to disclose the

---

[265] By contrast, deception through minimisation and maximisation techniques, which communicate implicit promises and threats of more lenient or harsher punishment, and ploys about false and non-existent nature of evidence against a suspect are seen as integral to American police interrogations and, indeed to the adversarial nature of criminal justice and are also legally permitted there, even though they have been found to increase the risk of false confessions. Leo R, 'Structural Police Deception in American Police Interrogation: A Closer Look at Minimization and Maximization' (2020) *Interrogation Confession and Truth: Comparative Studies in Criminal Procedure* 183–207. Soukara et al (2009) found in England, by contrast, that minimisation was not used at all in the sample of 80 police interviews in their research and maximisation was used in only 1% of these.

[266] In *Mason* [1988] 1 WLR 139, the police deceived the legal advisor about the extent of the available evidence, which led to exclusion of a confession. The court was most concerned that the lawyer, and not only the suspect, had been tricked, and that stopped the solicitor from being able to perform his role as an officer of the court.

[267] Their morality is another matter of course: see Ashworth A, 'Should the Police be Allowed to Use Deceptive Practices?' (1998) 114 *Law Quarterly Review* 108.

[268] [1997] Crim LR 754. Another example is *Daly* [2001] EWCA Crim 2643.

[269] Although where an offence is vaguely defined, this reason may not be particularly illuminating.

[270] The scope for passive deception is even greater for non-arrestees. Since those who attend at the police station 'voluntarily' (see section 4.3.1) are not under arrest, the police do not need to provide accurate reasons prior to interview for wanting to speak with them. Innes (2003: 181–184) gives the example of how the police secured damaging admissions from a suspect by pretending that 'they just needed to eliminate him from enquiries'. This 'volunteer' was arrested for murder at the end of his interview.

[271] [1998] 2 Cr App Rep 79.   [272] [1999] 4 All ER 698.

crucial detail that the alleged victim had died, and that the charges they actually had in mind were robbery and manslaughter.[273] The Court of Appeal held that the trial judge had been wrong not to exclude the confession thus obtained under s.78.[274]

A tactic may be unlawful but it may still be employed if the police think they can get away with it. Waddington (1999: 136–137) gives an example of a man suspected of a series of thefts from work. The last in the series was of money that had been treated with a chemical which was supposed to show up, under UV light, on the hands of anyone who touched it. The man's hands were passed under the light, the detectives commented on the clear chemical reflection, told the suspect they had enough evidence to charge him, and then turned to the other thefts, to which the suspect confessed. In fact, unknown to the suspect, the machine was faulty and had not picked out the chemical. Since the suspect was charged only with the crimes to which he confessed (and not to the one about which he had been deceived) the police may have got away with this even if they had been challenged.[275] As a detective told an American researcher: 'Interrogation is essentially a cross between a chess game and poker: you have to carefully strategise and outsmart the suspect with each move you make, but a lot of it really comes down to how well you can bluff and deceive' (Leo 1994: 107).[276]

5.5.2.7 Now is the time to explain

This implies to suspects who divulge only a little information that failure to explain fully will lead to unspecified harmful consequences. For example: 'It's only fair to tell you that it's in your own interests and to your benefit to give your version of events.'[277] The changes to the right of silence discussed earlier mean that sometimes this will be true,[278] but at other times the suspect (whether innocent or not) may suffer more by speaking than by keeping silent.[279] A similar tactic has been used by the police giving suspects leaflets on these lines: 'My position is one of impartiality. I am here to seek the truth . . . . Have you any information you can now furnish me with which would ultimately assist the CPS in making a decision not to prosecute in this matter?'[280]

5.5.2.8 Softly softly

Developing rapport with suspects is often regarded by police officers as key to a successful interview. If suspects can be misled into believing that the police 'are on their side' or have sympathy for what the suspect is alleged to have done, the suspect's defences may be lowered and useful information obtained. The police were found to show a similar kind of concern or empathy of suspects in 19% of a sample of 80 interviews in Soukara et al (2009).

---

[273] This phased arrest policy was evidently designed to cohere with a phased disclosure strategy as discussed in section 5.2.2.2.

[274] Code C now provides (para 11.1A) that: 'Whenever a person is interviewed they must be informed of the nature of the offence, or further offence.' Whether this opaquely worded provision will lead to a change in police behaviour remains to be seen.

[275] Any challenge would most likely be under s.78 PACE, whereby exclusion is a discretionary matter for the judge: ch 12.

[276] For the situation in the USA see Leo R, *Police Interrogation and American Justice* (Cambridge MA:, Harvard University Press, 2008).

[277] McConville and Hodgson (1993: 129); Leo (1994).

[278] Similarly, those suspects who do not co-operate fully with the police deny themselves the enhanced sentencing discount on offer to those who do (see further ch 7).

[279] Shepherd (2007: 354–358) discusses 13 different reasons why the safest defence may be to exercise the right to silence, many of which apply to the innocent as well as the guilty.

[280] Extracted from a pro-forma used at one time by officers in Avon and Somerset: Cape (2006c: 289).

The following exchange between detectives and someone suspected of murdering his wife illustrates the use of this tactic:

Detective: 'Why is your marriage breaking up?'

Suspect: 'She doesn't love me... I'm just one of those wasters at the bar.'

Detective: 'Having been through a broken marriage myself I know how difficult it can be' (quoted in Innes 2004: 151).

Empathetic stances are rarely spontaneous responses to expressions of distress by suspects, but rather are deliberately adopted in an attempt to maximise co-operation, and there is evidence that this technique works.[281] David et al describe rapport building as 'part of a larger deception—creating the impression of a relationship that only exists for the purposes of gaining the suspect's trust.'[282] Thus, when Innes asked a pair of detectives why they had not been more confrontational in their interview with a murder suspect, they revealed the level of planning that underlay their choice of tactic:

Detective 1: 'Well we did talk about that didn't we, before we started.'

Detective 2: 'Yeah, we thought about it quite hard.'

Detective 1: 'Mmm. But after talking to the boss we came to the conclusion that if we just walked in and started banging the table and shouting and pushing him, he might just close off from us. So we decided to see if we couldn't play it a bit more "softly, softly".'

Detective 2: 'The thing is, what you're looking for is how can I get this person talking to me. You've got to think, "what is it that I've got that I can use to my advantage over this person?" Sometimes you might decide to go in and hit 'em with it straight off and try to simply confront them with it. On other occasions, like in this case, we went in there with a "Yeah, look we understand, we know it must be difficult for you" approach because that's what we thought would work' (quoted in Innes 2004: 149)

The detectives here make no reference to the legal standards governing interrogation, but rather focus on the perceived psychological vulnerabilities of the suspect.

5.5.2.9 Accusation or abuse

At the other end of the spectrum from the softly-softly approach is aggressive confrontation. The former is broadly said to involve humane treatment, while the latter is overtly a tactic of domination,[283] though we suggest both are tactics where dominance is sought to be achieved through different means. In *Higgins*[284] (discussed at 5.5.1.2) the Court of Appeal acknowledged that assertive and confrontational questioning was 'not untypical'

---

[281] Goodman-Delahunty J, Dhami M and Martschuk N, 'Interviewing High Value Detainees: Securing Cooperation and Disclosures' (2014) 28 *Applied Cognitive Psychology* 883–897; Bull R, 'PEACE-ful Interviewing/Interrogation' in Shigemasu K, Kuwano S, Sato T and Matsuzawa T (eds), *Diversity in Harmony – Insights from Psychology* (Hoboken, NJ: Wiley, 2020) pp 189–210

[282] David G, Rawls A and Trainum J, 'Playing the Interrogation Game: Rapport, Coercion, and Confessions in Police Interrogations' (2018) 41(3) *Symbolic Interaction* 3–24 at 6. See further Walsh D and Bull R, 'Examining Rapport in Investigative Interviews with Suspects: Does its Building and Maintenance Work?' (2012) 27 *Journal of Police Criminal Psychology* 73–84 and Vallano J, Evans J, Schreiber Compo N and Kieckhaefer J, 'Rapport-Building During Witness and Suspect Interviews: A Survey of Law Enforcement' (2015) 29 *Applied Cognitive Psychology* 369–380.

[283] Oxburgh G, Ost J, Morris P and Cherryman J, 'The Impact of Question Type and Empathy on Police Interviews with Suspects of Homicide, Filicide and Child Sexual Abuse' (2014) 21(6) *Psychiatry, Psychology and Law* 903–917.   [284] [2003] EWCA Crim 2943.

of police practice, which is also confirmed by Soukara et al (2009) who found evidence of direct accusations of a suspect about their involvement in an alleged crime in 74% of their sample of 80 police interviews and repetitive questioning in 84% of these interviews. However, confrontation may sometimes go beyond this, in which interviewing officers hector, shout at, threaten and belittle suspects over prolonged periods. Examples include: 'Why are they [witnesses] lying? . . . I asked for a reason – there isn't one – why?', 'You, young man, are a liar basically . . .'[285] and the infamous 'Bad cop, Good cop' routine.

In the 'Cardiff Three'[286] case, Miller—a young man with learning difficulties—was subjected to no less than 19 separate interrogations, held over a five-day period.[287] According to the Lord Chief Justice:

> Miller was bullied and hectored. The officers . . . were not so much questioning him as shouting at him what they wanted him to say. . . . It is impossible to convey on the printed page the pace, force, and menace of the officer's delivery.

After 300 denials Miller eventually 'confessed'. As the Court of Appeal put it: 'The officers made it clear to Mr Miller that they would go on interviewing him until he agreed with the version of events they required.' He, and two associates, were convicted of murder. They appealed. When the Court of Appeal judges began hearing the interrogation recordings, they stopped the case and allowed the appeal of all three men on the grounds of oppression before they reached the end, so shocked were they at the behaviour of the police. We have seen that in less extreme cases, however, as in *Higgins*, accusation and abuse is not regarded as either oppressive or unfair. For vulnerable people, though, even mild abuse—which is sometimes used—can be highly intimidating (Leggett et al 2007).

Baldwin (1993a: 347) also provides examples. At one point in a series of very aggressive interviews of a youth for murder, the officer said:

> You can sit here, looking at the floor, crying and crying, but I am not going to walk out of that door; you are not going to leave here until I hear it from your own lips. Do you understand? Did you murder that boy? (Baldwin 1993a: 347).

These were not idle threats. Custodial interrogation lasted three days. For indictable offences, the police do not only have ways of making you talk. They have days to make you talk too.

Many of these examples in this section are drawn from research and cases from several years ago. We shall see that the PEACE model of 'investigative interviewing' discourages accusation and abuse but not all officers who interview suspects are PEACE trained and, even those who are, sometimes deviate from this model.[288] Once again, more research is needed to understand the realities of police interviewing, how far the law is adhered to, and how far the law allows suspects to be manipulated in ways that distort the truth and/or brutalise them.

5.5.3 Informal questioning

Some of the interviewing tactics we have just discussed, such as 'doing deals', lying about evidence, and oppressive questioning, may lead to a defence lawyer intervening or to any evidence obtained thereby being ruled inadmissible by the courts. One way for the police to avoid these possibilities is to use these tactics only in informal settings. Questioning is

---

[285] McConville and Hodgson (1993: 128). Also see JUSTICE, *Unreliable Evidence? Confessions and the Safety of Convictions* (London: JUSTICE, 1994); Hillyard (1993: ch 8).
[286] *Paris, Abdullahi, Miller* (1992) 97 Cr App Rep 99.
[287] For an extensive analysis of the interrogation tactics used in this case (and extracts from the transcript) see Gudjonsson (2003: 106–112). [288] Quirk (2016: 70); Blackstock et al (2014: 374).

'informal' if, instead of taking place in a police station interview room, it is done in the street, in the car, at the custody officer's desk or in the cells and is not part of a formal post-arrest or voluntary interview; or if proper cautions and rights are not provided and if the proceedings are not recorded.

There are many reasons why the police question suspects informally. Some of these reasons are lawful. Sometimes the police suspect an individual of a crime but cannot, or choose not to, arrest. The police therefore can continue to question, so long as they caution the individual once their suspicions cross the 'reasonable' threshold (see section 5.4.1). The suspect need not answer, but usually does. Also, informal interviews are sometimes initiated by suspects who wish to 'deal' confidentially. This makes it hard to disprove police claims that informal discussions began at the behest of the suspect as said in, for instance, *Younis*, *Khan* (discussed in sections 5.4.2 and 5.4.3) and *Menard*.[289] And we have seen that the police are entitled to undertake informal safety interviews in situations of urgency, as where suspected terrorists are questioned by arresting officers about the possibility of explosive materials thought to still be at large.[290] Much informal questioning is, however, clearly unlawful: where the police have reasonable suspicion in relation to individuals but do not caution them. Informal conversations may also be used to minimise or maximise the seriousness of offences, thereby persuading suspects to talk to the police. These conversations may be used to 'put the frighteners on' suspects due to the gravity of the alleged offence or persuade them that the offence they have been arrested for is not that serious and that they need not be worried.[291] We saw in section 5.4.1 that if suspects are arrested, the police cannot question them until 'booked in' and their detention authorised at the police station, unless the provisions for safety interviews apply. Informal questioning is attractive to the police because it is uncontrolled and unsupervised, there is no time clock running, no legal advisor will be present and there are no independent witnesses or checks on the tactics used to elicit incriminating material. In short, it subverts the PACE framework of rules designed to protect the suspect.

In cases where someone has been arrested, the most obvious place to question informally is in the car on the way to or from the police station.[292] As a CID officer said to Maguire and Norris: 'You can't just sit in the car in silence' (1992: 46). Talking is not, in itself, unlawful and it need not amount to an interview but, even without the ever-present prospect of a deal, it would be unnatural for conversation not to turn to the reason for the arrest. Maguire and Norris (1992: 46) quote another officer who said that he 'would not be doing his job' if he did not talk to prisoners.[293] Sometimes the police (unlawfully)[294] opt for the 'scenic route' in the knowledge that the longer the journey the more likely it is that useful information will be forthcoming.[295] Where someone is participating in a voluntary interview outside the police station and at the scene of alleged offence, these informal conversations are potentially more possible and are most likely to happen before or after a recording device (e.g. body-worn camera) is switched on. Attempts to estimate the frequency with which informal interviewing takes place outside the police station are

---

[289] [1995] 1 Cr App Rep 306.

[290] As happened in *R v Ibrahim, Omar, Osman and Mohamed* [2008] EWCA Crim 880 [59 & 83] (informal interviews conducted with arrestees in the car on the way to the police station).

[291] Skinns (2011: 123–124).

[292] For a recent example see Skinns L, '"I'm a Detainee; Get me Out of Here"' (2009b) 49(3) *British Journal of Criminology* 399 at 409.

[293] This echoes the officer who told McConville et al (1991: 58) that 'no policeman who did his job is going to say "no" if a suspect wanted to talk "off the record"'.

[294] PACE, s.30(1), requires transfer to a police station as soon as reasonably practicable.

[295] McConville M and Morrell P, 'Recording the Interrogation: Have the Police got it Taped?' [1983] *Criminal Law Review* 158; Maguire and Norris (1992: 46).

bedevilled by methodological problems, although it seems that around in one in five suspects are questioned unlawfully in this way.[296]

Historically, informal interviewing in the police station was been found to be prevalent, though once again more up-to-date research is needed. Dixon et al, for instance, found 53% of officers admitting always or often 'clarifying' suspects' accounts before beginning the 'proper' interview.[297] Many officers say that pre-interview questioning is important to establish a rapport, as might be expected given the importance of relationships and dealing. This is particularly important for the police if the suspect wants a solicitor. Some custody officers, one investigating officer told McConville et al, 'will just bend a little bit, if you want a quick word with [suspects] to see . . . if somebody wants a solicitor and you haven't had a chance to chat and don't want him to have a solicitor yet.'[298] The co-operation of the custody officer in allowing 'off the record' access to suspects is not essential, however, since informal interviews can take place immediately prior to the audio-recorded session. As an officer told Evans and Ferguson: 'I like to have a little chat to get things straight before I switch on the tape.'[299] This is unlawful, yet apparently frequent if we can judge by the number of times interviews appear to be 'little more than an attempt to validate what has already been rehearsed' (Baldwin 1993a: 347). One danger of using an informal interview to 'rehearse' the suspect's story is that the police may deliberately or inadvertently disclose facts that 'only the criminal would know' which are then incorporated by the suspect in any subsequent false confession (see further section 5.7). This type of false confession can be very difficult to retract successfully since the initial police disclosure will usually remain hidden.

Informal conversations have been found to happen during cigarette breaks, when police procedures such as fingerprinting and photographing are being carried out, as well as during cell visits and when interview recordings are switched off. When smoking was still permitted on police station premises, cigarettes were used in the past to secure detainee compliance, sometimes being provided immediately after someone's interview as a reward for their co-operation with this and before being taken back to the cells.[300] These accompanied trips to a police station's exercise yard for a cigarette provide ample opportunity for informal conversations between officers and detainees to take place. The disarming demeanour and greater rapport that suspects have with civilian detention officers means that informal conversations between them offer further fertile ground for information and intelligence gathering whilst they carry out police procedures such as fingerprinting and photographing.[301] The content of these conversations may be formally recorded, though, on the suspect's custody record or other police records. As for cell visits, in *McPhee*, the custody record showed that the suspect had been absent from his cell for prolonged periods without explanation (and without legal advice), and the court decided that these irregularities were such as to render the confession obtained unreliable so the conviction was quashed.[302] But, at other times, the courts have turned a blind eye to such practices. In *Williams*[303] a suspect had been interviewed with a lawyer present and made

---

[296] See Moston and Stephenson (1993); Brown et al, *Changing the Code* (Home Office Research Study no 129) (London: HMSO, 1992); Choongh (1997: 169). More up-to-date evidence on this does not exist.
[297] Dixon et al, 'Safeguarding the Rights of Suspects in Police Custody' (1990a) 1 *Policing and Society* 115.
[298] McConville et al (1991: 58–59). Examples are also given by Sanders and Bridges (1990) and Choongh (1997: 175).
[299] Evans R and Ferguson T, *Comparing Different Juvenile Cautioning Systems in One Police Force Area* (Report to the Home Office Research and Planning Unit) (1991).
[300] Skinns (2011: 99).   [301] Skinns (2011: 150–152).
[302] [2016] UKPC 29. This did, however, take place in the Bahamas.
[303] *The Times*, 6 February 1992, cited by Cape (2006c: 314).

no admissions. After the lawyer had left the police station, the interviewing officers paid an hour-long 'social visit' to the suspect in the cells. As a result, he agreed to be interviewed again in the absence of a lawyer and confessed. The Court of Appeal upheld the conviction, finding no breach of PACE had occurred. In the police area researched by Dixon et al (1990), these visits were systematically recorded as 'welfare visits', showing that custody officers allow custody records to be doctored to hide the truth. As well as cell visits, informal interviews also occur at the end of the 'official' questioning, as when a detective inspector joined other officers and proceeded to threaten the suspect in an 'unpleasant, hectoring and abusive tone'.[304] In this case, microphones installed for the purpose of a TV documentary recorded the informal interview, providing us with an insight into the behaviour of police officers when they believe themselves to be 'off the record'. The defendant had been arrested on suspicion of several burglaries but denied involvement in any of them. Once the police tape recorder was switched off, the detective inspector slipped into 'informal' mode:

DI:	'... I ain't bullshitting you, I'm gonna charge you with six [offences]. If you want six fucking charges, you can have six charges—your barrister ain't got much of a fucking argument at the end of the day. I don't really want to charge you with six fucking charges: I'd rather charge you with a couple and you can have four TICs. You can rip the fucking TICs up once you get to court—I don't really give a shit. Do you understand what I am saying?'
Suspect:	'Mmm.'
DI:	'Now bullshit aside now, that's the deal I can offer. Quite simply you fucking take it or leave it. You know what's going to happen if you fucking leave it. I mean you ain't going to fucking lose nothing, you don't lose anything by saying "OK, I'll fucking take that." '
Another detective:	'Plus the fact that you've got a couple of charges, court in the morning, def the breach of curfew, "he's got two charges of burglary, he's helped us out." We won't oppose bail. Otherwise we get six charges, "he didn't wanna fucking know" and remand in custody.'
DI:	'As I say, we'd lay it on heavy or we come off fucking light, it's a matter for you. The most important thing is you've got a fucking decision to make. You're either going to have six fucking charges or you're going to have two and the only fucking way you're having two is you start fucking talking to us.'[305]

None of this exchange was discoverable from the official audio recording of the formal questioning, and the custody officer noted in the custody record that: 'PACE codes of practice complied with' (McConville 1992: 544–545). Informal questioning is usually officially acknowledged only when a confession is made or alleged by the police, as for example, in *Dunn*,[306] discussed at section 5.4.3. The fact that informal interviewing is an under-recorded phenomenon does not mean, however, that its products are always unrecorded. Cape (2006c: 12) counsels legal advisors that suspects may need to be warned that their 'informal' conversations may be bugged since it has become clear that the police do sometimes (no-one knows how often) covertly place listening devices in cells and

---

[304] McConville (1992: 542). [305] For the full exchange see McConville (1992: 542–543).
[306] (1990) 91 Cr App Rep 237.

elsewhere in the police station.[307] Electronic surveillance recording of audio-visual material throughout all areas of custody facilities (charge room, cells, corridors etc) is now ubiquitous across England and Wales. When installed openly, it can deter some forms of informal interviewing. For example, when CCTV was introduced into one police station, custody officers commented that this had made it harder for investigators to do deals, and have 'quick words' with detainees (Newburn and Hayman 2002: 81).

Informal interviewing inside the station is usually a blatant breach of PACE and Code C, for it can rarely be impractical to turn an informal chat into a formal interview if one is already inside a police station. It often occurs between interviews precisely because the suspect in question does not want to talk. Since the aim of the informal chat is to change the minds of suspects, the dangers of coercion or unlawful inducements—precisely the dangers which the formal interviewing regime of PACE is ostensibly designed to combat—are obvious. Despite this, the products of these interviews are usable as evidence in court as long as the judge determines that the defendant will not suffer unfairness (in the judge's own view).[308]

The wrongful conviction and jailing of *Khan* (see section 5.4.3) is an example of what can happen not only when crime control practices are followed, but also when legal rules—in this case, the rule that information freely volunteered may be written down and used—contain crime control values. This is not an isolated example. Many of the infamous miscarriages of the 1990–93 period involved fabricated confessions. And in *Miller*,[309] in which the defendant was alleged to have dropped a bag of Ecstasy tablets as he was being escorted to the custody room, the police officer claimed she said to him, 'I have just seen you drop this . . . Are these Ecstasy tablets?', to which he is alleged to have said 'Yes'. He denied dropping the tablets, having ever had them, and having the conversation. The Court of Appeal held that the judge had wrongly allowed this conversation to be used as evidence. This was an interview held in breach of the Code and, one suspects from the Law Report, the Court was dubious about the veracity of the police.

Despite the growing use of electronic surveillance of police–suspect interactions throughout all parts of the custody suite, informal interviewing will never be eradicated. All that can be done is to refuse to accept its products as evidence in court. The Runciman Commission, however, simply accepted that there was a considerable amount of questioning outside the station, and did not discuss informal interviewing inside the station. It commented that 'many witnesses suggested to us that spontaneous remarks uttered on arrest are often the most truthful. We agree' (RCCJ 1993: 28, 61). No evidence or reasoning was given for their agreement with this suggestion.[310] This attitude is likely to encourage police officers to provoke 'spontaneity' on the part of arrestees or, at least, to claim that remarks were spontaneously made.[311] The conclusion flowing from Runciman's approach

---

[307] *Stephen Roberts* [1997] Crim LR 222 is an instructive example. Here the police persuaded X (in informal discussions, themselves held in breach of the Codes of Practice) to effect the 'informal interview' of X's co-suspect in a bugged cell. The resultant confession was held to be admissible. In *Allan v United Kingdom* (2003) 36 EHRR 12, the domestic trial court had ruled admissions made in similar circumstances admissible, but the ECtHR found that the practices obtained had violated Art 6.

[308] The case of *Kuruma v R* [1955] 2 WLR 223 indicated that the test for admissibility of evidence is whether it is relevant to the matters in issue. If the evidence is relevant, it is prima facie admissible and the court will not necessarily concern itself about the way in which the evidence was obtained. See also *Skrzypiec* discussed in section 5.4.2.   [309] [1998] Crim LR 209.

[310] Vrij A, *Detecting Lies and Deceit* 2nd edn (Chichester: Wiley, 2008a) pp 378–379 notes that many guilty suspects will prepare plausible stories in anticipation of an arrest.

[311] Again, as happened in *R v Ibrahim, Omar, Osman and Mohamed* [2008] EWCA Crim 880 [106].

is that courts should continue to accept evidence provided in such exchanges otherwise 'some reliable confessions might be lost' (RCCJ 1993: 60–61). The absence of concern that some unreliable confessions might also be lost betrays the crime control thinking of Runciman and its reluctance to impose inhibitory rules on the police.

5.5.4 Investigative interviewing

In the early 1990s criticism of traditional police interrogation techniques spread from the 'usual suspects' (that is, academics like us, along with a few pressure groups and defence-oriented lawyers) to the courts, Home Office officials and even the police themselves.[312] The Runciman Commission complained that there is:

> ... an over-ready assumption on the part of some interviewing officers of the suspect's guilt and on occasion the exertion of undue pressure amounting to bullying or harassment ... They entered the interview room with their minds made up and treated the suspect's explanation with unjustified scepticism.

This behaviour was predominantly a product, as one would expect in a crime control system, of a belief in the suspect's guilt and of resource and legal constraints which put a premium on confession evidence. As an officer told Choongh (1997: 124), '... we certainly question on the basis that the person sitting in front of us is guilty—that's what we're paid to do, I mean we can't assume they're innocent, we'd never get the job done.' Research conducted at this time found that in over 70% of cases studied police interviewers declared themselves sure of the suspect's guilt before the interview began, and in 80% of the cases the interviewers stated that the aim of the interview was to obtain a confession.[313] Miscarriages of justice have been found to burgeon when the primary aim of an interview is regarded as being that of securing a confession[314]

In 1992 the Home Office issued a circular to the police setting out 'Principles of Investigative Interviewing'. In its current format, this guidance is published by the College of Policing and is as follows:[315]

1. The role of investigative interviewing is to obtain accurate and reliable information from suspects, witnesses or victims about matters under police investigation.

2. Investigators must not approach any interview with prejudice, and must ensure that they comply with the Equality Act 2010 and the Human Rights Act 1998 ... The interviewer should be prepared to accept the account they are being given, using common sense and judgment to assess accuracy.

3. Investigative interviewing should be approached with an investigative mind-set. Interviewee accounts should be tested against what the interviewer knows or can reasonably establish.

---

[312] See, for example, Williamson T, 'Reflections on Current Police Practice', in Morgan D and Stephenson G, *Suspicion and Silence* (London: Blackstone, 1994). The availability of tape-recordings of interviews for academic and court scrutiny was undoubtedly a major factor in building the momentum necessary for reform (Shepherd, 2007: 17).

[313] Moston et al, 'The Effects of Case Characteristics on Suspect Behaviour During Police Questioning' (1992) 92 *British Journal of Criminology* 23.

[314] Bearchell J, 'UK police interviews with suspects: a short modern history' in Adler J and Gray J (eds), *Forensic Psychology. Concepts, Debates and Practice* (Cullompton: Willan Publishing, 2010) pp 58–71.

[315] Home Office Circular 22/1992. Most recent guidance comes from the College of Policing *Authorised Professional Practice. Investigative Interviewing*. <https://www.app.college.police.uk/app-content/investigations/investigative-interviewing/#principle-1> (accessed 1 July 2020). This was last updated in March 2019.

4. Investigators can ask a wide range of questions to obtain material that might assist an investigation, and are not bound by the same rules of evidence that lawyers must abide by, as conducting an investigation is not the same as proving an argument at court. Interview style must not be unfair or oppressive
5. Investigators should recognise the positive impact of an early admission.
6. Questioning is not unfair merely because it is persistent, and investigators are not bound to accept the first answer given.
7. Even when the right of silence is exercised by a suspect, the police still have a right to put questions.

A 'Guide to Interviewing' expanded these principles of investigative interviewing,[316] based around the acronym PEACE, which stands for: (i) Planning and preparation; (ii) Engage and explain; (iii) Account; (iv) Closure; (v) Evaluate. The PEACE model, as it has become known, was seen by many as heralding a revolution in police interview methods. Davies, for example, argues that:

> The issue in 1992 to all detectives of a new guide to investigative interviewing, based on the results of applied psychological research, marked a major turning point in police culture and attitudes.[317]

That remarkable claim requires scrutiny. The 1992 Guide set out two approaches to interviewing. The first, 'cognitive interviewing', encourages the interviewee to re-live the event in question and provide an account with minimal interference. However, although cognitive interviewing has been found to be valuable with willing participants (especially prosecution witnesses) it has not worked well with unwilling participants.[318] For this reason, no doubt, the Guide advocated the 'Management of Conversation' approach for most suspects. The interviewee is asked to provide an account of what happened. The interviewer then divides this account up, homing in on each element in turn, particularly with a view to the 'points to prove'. It is at this point that principles 6 (persistent questioning) and 7 (continued questioning notwithstanding the silence of a suspect) come into play. Effective management of the interview is seen as requiring interviewers to be aware of and manage the verbal and non-verbal behaviour of themselves, interviewees and third parties such as appropriate adults and legal advisors.[319] The Guide and related training package have been revised a number of times since 1992 (e.g. to take account of the changes to the right of silence brought in by the CJPO 1994), but the basic approach has remained broadly the same. Recently, however, the principles seem to reflect something of an official shift back towards supporting the use of interviews to gain confessions in that investigators are told to '... recognise the positive impact of an early admission in the context of the criminal justice system', alongside encouraging 'testing'—in a persistent way, if necessary— the first account provided.

Whichever version of investigative interviewing is studied, it is evident that the main focus is on obtaining as much information as possible from the suspect while minimising the risk of it being ruled inadmissible by a court. Thus closed or leading questions and constant interruptions are discouraged not because these practices are unfair, but rather because they can lead to the suspect 'clamming up' or to any evidence obtained being

---

[316] Home Office, Central Planning and Training Unit, *Guide to Interviewing* (London: HMSO, 1992a).
[317] See preface to Milne and Bull (1999: xi).
[318] Cherryman J and Bull R, 'Investigative Interviewing' in Leishman F, Loveday B and Savage S (eds), *Core Issues in Policing* (Harlow: Longman, 1996).
[319] Milne and Bull (1999: 56); Shepherd (2007: 20); Oxburgh G and Dando C, 'Psychology and Interviewing: What Direction Now in our Quest for Reliable Information?' (2011) 13 *British Journal of Forensic Practice* 135–147.

judged unreliable. Consistently with this, Bucke et al (2000: 28) found that some officers had been told during their investigative interviewing training not to probe whether a suspect had actually understood the new caution concerning adverse inferences, in part because this might reveal a lack of understanding of that caution which would put the admissibility of anything said (or not said) in doubt.[320] It is this emphasis on the admissibility of evidence rather than fairness that leads Newton to comment: 'I have difficulty in recognising this package as an ethical framework for interviewing.'[321] Moreover, investigative interviewing shares many similarities with the traditional approach to interrogation as can be seen in its support for persistent questioning of those who remain silent.[322]

One might still argue, however, that investigative interviewing represents a welcome shift away from the assumption that a good interviewer is one that assumes guilt and accuses the suspects from the outset, and browbeats or tricks a suspect into confession. Official support for this key aspect of the 'investigative interviewing' approach is now reflected in Code C, which states that:

> 'In conducting an investigation, the investigator should pursue all reasonable lines of enquiry, whether these point towards or away from the suspect . . .' Interviewers should keep this in mind when deciding what questions to ask in an interview.[323]

This support has not merely been at the level of policy pronouncements. A massive programme to train police officers in investigative interviewing was instituted in the 1990s and, by the end of that decade, over two-thirds of police officers had received this training.[324] The key question, however, is whether the training resulted in changes in practice.

Clarke and Milne[325] conducted a major evaluation of its effectiveness after a number of smaller-scale studies had indicated that investigative interviewing was not having the impact that some had anticipated. Their evaluation involved skilled police officers reviewing and rating the audio-recordings of interviews with suspects without knowing whether the interviewing officer had been trained in investigative interviewing or not. Compared to earlier studies, the research indicated a decline in the use of leading questions and the more frequent provision of information required by law, such as the right to legal advice. These are welcome changes but it is doubtful whether they can be attributed to the training, since trained and untrained officers were found to interview in much the same way as each other.[326] In any event, standards of interviewing indicated that the training had failed

---

[320] This is completely contrary to the advice of key academics in this applied field of psychology (e.g. Shepherd, 2007: 341–345). The problem is that most training courses will be delivered by police officers who are likely to share in, and reinforce, the predominant cop culture. In practice, testing for understanding by the suspect of the caution remains rare: Walsh and Milne (2008: 42 & 52).

[321] Newton T, 'The Place of Ethics in Investigative Interviewing by Police Officers' (1998) *Howard Journal of Crime and Justice* 52 at p 66.

[322] Suspects can find such tactics very distressing: Pierpoint (2006: 226).

[323] PACE Code C, para 11B. The wording within the quote marks is taken from the Criminal Procedure and Investigations Act 1996, Code of Practice para 3.4.

[324] Since this time, police have been trained to use a PEACE model in investigative interviews, of which cognitive interviewing (referred to earlier) forms part. For discussion, see e.g. Clarke C and Milne R, 'England and Wales' in Walsh D, Oxburgh G, Redlich A and Myklebust T (eds), *International Developments and Practices in Investigative Interviewing and Interrogation: Volume 2: Suspects* (Abingdon: Routledge, 2016) pp 101–118 and Howes L, 'Interpreted Investigative Interviews under the PEACE Interview Model: Police Interviewers' Perceptions of Challenges and Suggested Solutions' (2020) 21(4) *Police Practice and Research* 333–350.

[325] Clarke C and Milne R, *National Evaluation of the PEACE Investigative Interviewing Scheme*, Police Research Award Scheme Report No: PRAS/149 (London: Home Office, 2001).

[326] It is possible that the untrained had picked up better habits by watching the trained in action, but it is more plausible to suggest that the recording of formal interviews (opening them up to external scrutiny) has led to an across the board reluctance to use tactics that might render evidence obtained in that setting unreliable in judicial eyes.

to bring about any immediate radical change in police behaviour. For example, listening skills were rated as poor, interviews were found to be dominated by the use of closed questions,[327] and 10% of the interviews were considered to involve possible breaches of PACE. Subsequent research on benefit fraud investigators reached broadly similar conclusions, with three-quarters of those trained in investigative interviewing performing no better than those without such training.[328]

Why do interviewers not put their training more fully into practice? First, the new techniques are difficult to use. Second, many police officers argue that they simply do not have the time to interview witnesses in this way given the mass of routine crimes they deal with.[329] In response, evidence-based attempts are now underway to develop easier and more efficient interviewing techniques while still retaining core cognitive interviewing principles.[330] But there are deeper problems. Thus Clarke and Milne (2001: 110) reported that their research into interviews with victims and witnesses found 'damning' evidence of interviewers apparently looking to interviewees to confirm police suspicions rather than provide their own accounts. The research also found that there was little effective supervision of interviewing and that scant interest had been shown by police leaders in ensuring that their officers actually used the skills taught in training.[331] These research findings undermine the notion that the introduction of investigative interviewing marked a major turning point in police culture. In a more realistic vein, Maguire notes that 'changing what is still a strongly ingrained element of police culture—the view that the overriding aim of an interview is to obtain a confession—is an ambitious task, and there is little doubt that poor interviewing practices still persist to a considerable extent.'[332] In short, before any ethical or cognitive approach can fully supplant the traditional approach, officers need to be adequately trained and supervised, training needs to be related to practical policing problems, this approach needs to become part of the whole ethos of policing, and officers need to be rewarded for changing the way they do things. There is little evidence of substantial progress on any of these points as yet.[333]

---

[327] A closed question is one that invites a brief confirmatory answer, such as, 'Did you kick the victim in the groin?'. Use of such questions enables the police to speed up the interview, reduces the possibility that the suspect will introduce exculpatory evidence into the interview, increases the risk that suggestible suspects (whether innocent or not) will compliantly incriminate themselves, and takes the pressure off skilful liars (Shepherd: 2007, 191–192).

[328] Walsh and Milne (2008) 39–57 at 51; Walsh and Bull (2010: 99–135). The same researchers stated elsewhere that '[i]t is generally accepted that the implementation of the PEACE framework has enhanced interviewing skills' (Walsh D and Bull R, 'Interviewing Suspects: Examining the Association between Skills, Questioning, Evidence Disclosure, and Interview Outcomes' (2015) 21(7) *Psychology, Crime & Law* 661–680 at 661).

[329] Dando et al, 'The Cognitive Interview: Inexperienced Police Officers' Perceptions of their Witness Interviewing Behaviour' (2008) 13 *Legal and Criminological Psychology* 59 at 65.

[330] See, for example, Dando et al, 'A Modified Cognitive Interview Procedure for Frontline Police Investigators' (2009) 23 *Applied Cognitive Psychology* 698.

[331] See also Dando et al (2009: 65). For a (characteristically) more positive reading of the research evidence see Dixon (2005: 336–338).

[332] Maguire M, 'Regulating the Police Station: The Case of the Police and Criminal Evidence Act 1984' in McConville M and Wilson G (eds), *The Handbook of the Criminal Justice Process* (Oxford: OUP, 2002). See also Gudjonsson G, 'Investigative Interviewing' in Newburn et al (eds), *Handbook of Criminal Investigation* (Cullompton: Willan, 2007) who accepts that investigative interviews with suspects remain, in general, 'inherently guilt presumptive' (p 475). Presumptions that interviewees are guilty are just as evident amongst benefit fraud investigators and their supervisors: Walsh D and Milne R, 'Giving P.E.A.C.E. a Chance: A Study of DWP's Investigators' Perceptions of their Interviewing Practices' (2007) 85 *Public Administration* 525 at 535.

[333] See, for example, Choongh (1997: 128–130); Milne and Bull (1999: ch 9), Quinn and Jackson (2007: 251). A relatively recent empirical study of CID confirms that many police remain committed to (and adept at) avoiding exculpatory lines of enquiry (Taylor: 2006, e.g., at pp 116, 129 & 147). Walsh and Bull (2015) call for more research to be conducted in this area.

Nonetheless, the fact that there are aspirational policy statements, guides, training packages and so forth is significant. First, aspiration is the first stage in any effective reform; it is a necessary if insufficient condition of change. If nothing else, the official policy provides a yardstick by which to judge and criticise (or reward) practice and, over time, this has undoubtedly brought about some improvement. Second, the principles of investigative interviewing form a kind of 'soft law' which may have some regulatory impact. For example, Cape (2006c: 308) recommends that legal practitioners who attend interrogations should remind interviewing officers of these principles in appropriate cases, and it is possible that the courts will take account of the investigative interviewing norms when determining the admissibility of evidence. Third, the fact that Britain is seen as leading the way in ethical interviewing, with police forces from other countries such as Australia,[334] and New Zealand[335] adopting many of the same techniques, means that this approach has considerable cultural prestige (at least amongst the converts) and this may help entrench better practices.[336] Fourth, the approach is evidence-based, initially drawing heavily on the work of academic psychologists,[337] many of whom now play an active part in developing, evaluating and refining best practice,[338] training packages, and so forth. Thus considerable momentum has now built up behind investigative interviewing. As we have seen, however, even if such interviewing were to become second-nature to the police, which is far still not fully from being the case at present, the continuities with old-style interrogation would be almost as important as the discontinuities.

5.6 The effectiveness of interrogation tactics

When assessing the effectiveness of tactics in formal interviews, it is important to bear in mind that they are nowadays deployed primarily against non-cooperative suspects in serious cases. Many suspects readily confessed in their first and only interview. Evans (1993), for example found that 92% of children and young people in the 164 interviews he studied were interviewed only once and that 77% of them confessed quickly.[339] In the remainder, persuasive tactics were more likely to be used, particularly for serious offences (see also Baldwin 1993a). Pearse and Gudjonsson found that interviews for non-serious crimes tend to be short with little attempt made to challenge the suspect's story.[340] Following his review of the literature, Gudjonsson (2003: 55) concludes that PACE brought about a marked reduction in the use of manipulative tactics in interrogations. But when the police are under pressure 'to get a result' in a high profile case they will typically deploy their full arsenal of tactics (Gudjonsson 2003: ch 4) notwithstanding any training in investigative interviewing.

---

[334] Dixon (2006: 328).

[335] Grantham, R, 'Investigative Interviewing in New Zealand' iIIRG Bulletin, vol 1(1) p 10. In 2016, the United Nations Special Rapporteur on Torture and Other Cruel, Inhuman or Degrading Treatment or Punishment even referred to PEACE as capable of providing positive guidance in interrogation practices (Bull in Shigemasu et al (2020: 189–210).

[336] The introduction of advanced training courses for specialist interviewers (e.g. of vulnerable witnesses, or murder suspects), and the positioning of these within the broader 'professionalising investigation programme' further enhances this prestige. See NPIA (2009).

[337] See, in particular, the account by Shepherd (2007: 17–33).

[338] Shepherd (2007) devotes over 500 pages to helping police officers understand the 'conversation management approach'. In the USA, Dr. Mary Schollum, a British consultant trains police officers using the PEACE model (Schollum M, 'Bringing PEACE to the United States' (Nov 2017) *The Police Chief* 3.

[339] Evans R, *The Conduct of Police Interviews with Juveniles* (Royal Commission on Criminal Justice Research Study no 8) (London: HMSO, 1993b).

[340] Pearse J and Gudjonsson G, 'Police Interviewing Techniques at Two South London Police Stations' (1996) 3 *Psychology, Crime and Law* 763.

One reason why this training has been only partially effective may relate to the confidence of the police in their own ability to detect lies and to reliably distinguish the innocent from the guilty.[341] If this confidence were justified police use of persuasive or deceptive tactics in interview would be less troubling. Tactics would be used only against the actually guilty, false confessions would be treated sceptically, and miscarriages based on unreliable confession evidence would be rare. Vrij (2008a) has shown in a literature review, however, that the crime control belief in the accuracy of police judgements on these matters is contrary to the best available scientific evidence.[342] This evidence is based primarily on tests of ability to make accurate yes/no judgements as to whether someone is lying or telling the truth. In other words, a 50% accuracy rate should be achievable simply by guessing. The salient points can be summarised as follows:

(i) The mean average accuracy rate for professional lie-catchers (a category made up predominantly of police officers) was 55.91% compared with 54.27% found in studies with laypersons (a category predominantly comprised of undergraduates) as observers;

(ii) When laypersons and police officers have participated in the same experimental studies, only one study found any difference in accuracy rates between the two groups (with laypersons outperforming police investigators);

(iii) Police officers were more confident than students in their decision-making, suggesting that confidence is not related to accuracy. In fact confidence may impair accuracy because it tends to result in quick judgements and inadequate heuristics such as 'liars won't look you in the eye' or 'liars fidget';

(iv) Black suspects make a more suspicious impression on white police officers than do white suspects, regardless of whether they speak the truth or not. This is because black people more often exhibit behaviour (such as gaze aversion) that white police officers find suspicious;

(v) When evidence-based psychological training was provided in advance of a lie-detection exercise, accuracy rates went up in the case of students, but down in the case of police officers.[343]

Vrij speculates that a possible reason for this last finding is that police officers refused to use the information provided in the training because they did not believe it—'the observers were told that liars typically show a decrease in hand and finger movements. This contradicts police officers' beliefs, as they typically assume that an increase in hand and finger movements indicates deception'.[344] Poor police judgement of deception increases

---

[341] Vrij (2008a: 164). See further on how police belief in guilt influences interview technique: Adams-Quackenbush N, Vrij A, Horselenberg R, Satchell L and van Koppen P, 'Articulating Guilt? The Influence of Guilt Presumption on Interviewer and Interviewee Behaviour' (2020) *Current Psychology*; Roulin M and Ternes M, 'Is it Time to Kill the Detection Wizard? Emotional Intelligence Does Not Facilitate Deception Detection' (2019) 137 *Personality and Individual Differences* 131–138.

[342] The bulk of deception studies are rather artificial in nature (e.g. based on 'laboratory experiments' involving students), and doubts can be raised about how far such findings can be generalised to real-life police interview settings. Vrij (2008a: 166–167) summarises the few studies that have examined more realistic 'high stakes' situations (as where officers are shown extracts from real-life interviews with suspects) and suggests that the results here are somewhat more positive while nonetheless concluding that 'in high-stakes situations police officers will still frequently make errors in truth/lie detection'.

[343] Vrij (2008a) p 162 (points i, & ii), pp 164–167 & 173 (point iii) pp 179–180 (point iv) and p 400 (point v). Benefit fraud investigators working within the civil service are similarly prone to the (erroneous) belief that they can detect lies from physical behaviour: Walsh and Milne (2007: 535).

[344] Ibid, pp 400–401. But why did they get *worse* at detecting lies after the training? Perhaps the training sensitised them to hand and finger movements which they then interpreted according to ingrained police lore.

the likelihood that tactics will be deployed against the innocent as well as the guilty. Tactics should thus be thought of as effective in terms of producing incriminating evidence (much of which will be false or unreliable) rather than 'getting at the truth'.

With any one suspect it may be difficult to guess what tactic will be effective. If one tactic does not work, the police move on to another.[345] Only rarely (usually when there is an immediate confession) is no tactic used (McConville and Hodgson 1993: 129). But tactics are thought to fail to elicit confessions as often as they succeed (Evans 1993: 44–46), or even most of the time (Baldwin 1993a). Police interrogation in general is described in most research reports as often ineffective, clumsy, rambling, repetitious and hit and miss.[346] Effectiveness may also be affected by the presence or absence of lawyers and appropriate adults, and so forth.

The vulnerability of the suspect is crucial. Some police officers may regard the essence of interrogation tactics is to locate a particular vulnerability and exploit it.[347] In a sense all suspects are vulnerable as a result of the circumstances of their detention (e.g. due to the length of time in detention, the material conditions, feelings of dependence on the police and of helplessness), with imported vulnerabilities (mental health conditions, learning disabilities, etc) also being under identified and thus not formally responded to through the provision of an appropriate adult.[348] Tactics will tend to be used more when the police are convinced that a suspect is lying, a working rule which, as we have seen, will bear down most heavily on black suspects. This presents another set of vulnerabilities, therefore, as do circumstances in which there is no ready confession and where the other evidence is weak or lacking in a crucial respect, such as intention.[349] Suspects may also be vulnerable to interrogation tactics where the police think the case important enough to merit the additional time and effort involved. To act on these working rules carries with it an obvious risk of grave miscarriages of justice. As Gudjonsson (2003: 624) observes:

> The higher the base rate of innocent suspects interrogated, which is not uncommonly seen in terrorist cases and some notorious murder cases where the police trawl in a large number of people for interrogation, the greater the proportion of false confessions that are likely to occur. In such cases there is often a great deal of pressure on the police to solve the case and this often influences their methods of extracting confessions from suspects.

Though there is some research on the kind of tactics likely to yield confessions (e.g. open questions and disclosure of evidence),[350] there is little evidence on the circumstances in which these tactics may be used, although some recent exploratory studies have indicated that murderers and sex offenders may be *more* likely to confess when treated humanely (rather than subjected to insult and confrontation).[351] Ironically, it seems that vulnerable

---

[345] Hillyard P (1993) *Suspect Community* (London: Pluto Press), ch 8.

[346] See Baldwin (1993a); Pearse and Gudjonsson (1996); Moston S and Engelberg T, 'Police Questioning Techniques in Tape Recorded Interviews with Criminal Suspects' (1993) 3 *Policing and Society* 223; Walsh and Milne (2008: 52–53). But note that academic assessments based on transcripts or tapes that interviewing is incompetent may simply reveal a misunderstanding about the interrogator's goals: Green A, *Power, Resistance, Knowledge: The Epistemology of Policing* (Sheffield: Midwinter & Oliphant, 2008) pp 14 and 172.

[347] See the comments of the homicide detectives quoted in section 5.5.2.8.

[348] Skinns (2019: 178–181); Dehaghani (2019: 130–131); Bath (2019: 6); Evans (1993).

[349] Evans (1993: 31); Hakkanen et al, 'Police Officers' Views of Effective Interview Tactics with Suspects: The Effects of Weight of Case Evidence and Discomfort with Ambiguity' (2009) 23 *Applied Cognitive Psychology* 468.

[350] Soukara et al (2009).

[351] For a good summary of earlier research, as well as the presentation of new findings, see Kebbell et al, 'Sex Offenders' Perceptions of the Effectiveness and Fairness of Humanity, Dominance, and Displaying an Understanding of Cognitive Distortions in Police Interviews: A Vignette Study' (2008) 14(5) *Psychology, Crime and Law* 435. See further Westera N and Kebbell M, 'Investigative Interviewing in Suspected Sex Offences' in Bull R (ed), *Investigative Interviewing* (New York: Springer, 2014) pp 1–18.

suspects are particularly suggestible in PEACE interviews, especially when minimisation tactics methods are used.[352] If the innocent are *less* likely to confess when treated humanely (as one might expect), and the police come to accept this, there might be a way of *reducing the proportion* of confessions made by innocent people. But improved questioning techniques are unlikely to *eradicate* false confessions, for reasons we will now explore.

5.7 Confessions

5.7.1 False confessions

False confessions were one of the motors driving the Philips Commission and PACE. Although the Confait Affair was the cause celebre of the 1970s, other cases included that of Errol Madden, who was accused of stealing a model car, and a man who 'confessed' to stealing money from his employer (Cox 1975: 177). The claims in both cases that the confessions were false and made because of pressure from the police were verified by the fact that both the model car and the money turned out not to be stolen at all. The PACE framework of contemporaneous recording and interviewing in the station, together with the outlawing of oppressive treatment, was developed in order to prevent such cases.

Contrary to the expectations of some commentators, and widespread beliefs amongst police officers,[353] the overall confession rate has not been affected by the regime for custodial interrogation ushered in by PACE.[354] What is difficult to assess is whether false confessions have also declined. Usually, it is unclear whether confessions made under pressure are false or not, but the problem of false confessions remains. One estimate is that in the USA about 25% of convictions are based on false confessions.[355] In the UK, in the 'Cardiff Three' case, for example, DNA evidence resulted in a new suspect being identified and convicted in 2003, 11 years after the convictions of the original suspects had been quashed due to the oppressive nature of the police interrogation.[356] And Sean Hodgson was released in 2009 after serving 27 years in prison following his (false) confession to a crime subsequently shown by DNA evidence to have been convicted by another man (David Lace). When the police re-opened the investigation they found that they had records of seven men (including Hodgson and Lace) separately confessing to this crime.[357] Most recently, the convictions of the 'Oval Four'—originally based on false confession evidence—were quashed, it having been found that the officer in charge of the case had himself been involved in crimes of dishonesty and had expressed racial bias. They had been convicted nearly 50 years previously.[358]

Occasionally it is possible both to ascertain that a convincing confession is false and to establish that it was made due to manipulative police tactics. Gudjonsson (2003: 227–230)

---

[352] Farrugia L and Gabbert F, 'Vulnerable Suspects in Police Interviews: Exploring Current Practice in England and Wales' (2020) 17 *Journal of Investigative Psychology and Offender Profiling* 17–30.

[353] See Gudjonsson (2003: 138).

[354] Vrij A, 'Editorial: Interrogation Techniques, Information-gathering and (False) Confessions' (2011) 16(2) *Legal and Criminological Psychology*.

[355] See <https://www.innocenceproject.org/dna-exonerations-in-the-united-states/> (accessed 27 June 2020). For detailed discussion see Woody W and Forrest K, *Understanding Police Interrogation: Confessions and Consequences* (New York: NYUP, 2020).

[356] See section 5.5.2.9. For a fuller account of this case go to <http://www.innocent.org.uk> (accessed 5 January 2010) where details of a number of other post-PACE cases can be found. For another example, in the Republic of Ireland, see O'Connell M, 'Confessions in Police Custody' *Counsel* (2005) September p 12.

[357] *The Guardian*, 18 September 2009.

[358] Campbell D, '"Oval Four" men jailed in 1972 cleared by court of appeal in London' *The Guardian*, 5 December 2019.

gives another example: Mr Z made a detailed confession in 1991 to a double murder and related sexual assault of a child. This was prompted partly through lengthy custodial interrogation (five interviews over two days) and partly through a promise/threat made 'off the record' that he would get medical help if he confessed but would otherwise be sent to prison. In addition, the police blurred the line between witness interviews (which do not need to be recorded) and suspect interviews in order to accuse Mr Z (again 'off the record') of the crime at a point when he was formally being treated as a witness. The police are also alleged to have persuaded Mr Z (who had a mild learning disability) to be interviewed without an appropriate adult or solicitor present so that confession would then be less embarrassing for him. The audio-recorded confessions seemed compelling as they appeared to contain facts or 'special knowledge' that 'only the murderer could have known'. After Mr Z had spent almost 10 weeks on remand in prison, DNA evidence established that he could not have sexually assaulted the murdered child. Soon afterwards the real murderer was apprehended. The apparently damning 'special knowledge' turned out to have been gleaned by Mr Z from the media and through his 'informal' interactions with the police.[359]

In discussing false confessions we need to distinguish between innocent people who confess 'voluntarily'; innocent people who confess as a result of the pressure inherent in custodial interrogation and/or police tactics; and people whose innocence is unknown, who allegedly confess but who in fact do not. The last category concerns fabricated confessions, and was discussed earlier (sections 5.4.3 and 5.5.3). There are a number of reasons why people who are, or may be, innocent confess[360] but here we will concentrate on the relationship between police tactics and false confessions.

5.7.1.1 'Coerced-compliant' confessions

Here the suspect knows that the confession is false, but is prepared to confess to escape pressure. This pressure will sometimes be the result of oppressive questioning tactics, or sometimes of the 'mere' experience of custody and questioning.[361] Coerced-compliant confessions were a feature of several of the infamous miscarriage cases, including the 'Cardiff Three'. Many of these cases involved vulnerable suspects, but people with average IQ and normal personality characteristics are also vulnerable to tactics of this type, as in a false murder confession discussed by Gudjonsson and Mackeith.[362] These confessions can also arise from strong inducements as the case of Mr Z illustrates.[363]

---

[359] While a court is yet to be persuaded of this, experts discussing the Brendan Dassey case (made famous by the series *Making a Murderer*) rely on similar circumstances to argue that Dassey's confession is unreliable and his conviction should be further reviewed. See Kassin S, 'Why SCOTUS Should Examine the Case of "Making a Murderer's" Brendan Dassey' (2018) see <https://www.apa.org/news/press/op-eds/scotus-brendan-dassey> (accessed 1 July 2020).   [360] For a full discussion see Gudjonsson (2003: ch 8).

[361] See, for example, Quinn and Jackson (2007: 243). For further discussion see Watson C, Weiss and Pouncey C, 'False Confessions, Expert Testimony, and Admissibility' (2010) 38 *Journal of the American Academy of Psychiatry and the Law* 174–86.

[362] Gudjonsson G and Mackeith J, 'A Proven Case of False Confession: Psychological Aspects of the Coerced-compliant Type' (1990) 30 *Medicine, Science and the Law* 187.

[363] In a fourth, but relatively under-researched type of coerced-compliant confession, the pressure might come from outside the police and custodial setting. One example of this occurred in the Swedish case of Thomas Quick, which Stridbeck uses as an example of a coerced-reactive confession (Stridbeck U, 'Coerced-Reactive Confessions: The Case of Thomas Quick' (2020) 20 *Journal of Forensic Psychology Research and Practice* 305–322). Arguably this is simply a voluntary false confession (such as occurred in the Judith Ward case), and the boundaries appear somewhat blurred. See further, Gudjonsson G, 'Memory Distrust Syndrome, Confabulation and False Confession' (2017) 87 *Cortex* 156–165.

5.7.1.2 'Coerced false belief' confessions

Here, suspects begin to doubt their own memory. They temporarily believe in their own guilt because of disorientation.[364] Carol Richardson, one of the 'Guildford Four' (imprisoned for terrorist offences for 14 years before having their convictions quashed), reported this experience after being told of the alleged confession of a fellow suspect.[365] Similarly, in the remarkable 'Kerry Babies' case, a whole family falsely confessed to murdering a baby as a result of the pressure to which they were subjected. One said, 'I didn't think my mind was my own. . . in the end I was convinced I had done it.'[366] In a post-PACE example from the early 1990s the police used an 'informal interview' to persuade Mr J that he had set fire to six caravans but had blocked out his memory of doing so. They said they had witnesses to the arson attacks (none were in fact ever identified),[367] that he must have 'done it in drink' and that they were there to help him. Mr J, who had great faith in the police, came to believe that he must have committed the offence and accordingly tried his best to please his interviewers by constructing plausible-sounding confessions during the formal audio-recorded interviews. The case was dropped by the CPS once psychological assessments had revealed how suggestible and compliant Mr J was and how vague his 'spontaneous confessions' actually were. There was no other evidence against Mr J (Gudjonsson 2003: 239–241).

5.7.1.3 'Coerced-passive' confession

Here questioning leads suspects to 'admit' to committing an offence without necessarily adopting or even understanding the substance of this admission. In one case discussed by McConville et al, it was accepted that the suspect broke a car windscreen in the course of an argument. The question was, why? The following exchange took place:

Police: 'Did you intend to smash the windscreen?'

Suspect: 'No.'

Police: 'So you just swung your hand out in a reckless manner?'

Suspect: 'Yes, that's it, just arguing . . . Just arguing, reckless, it wasn't intentional to break it.' (McConville et al 1991: 70)

Although the suspect probably did not understand this, here the interviewer was not offering a way 'out' of guilt but a way 'in' to an acceptance that the act was done with the mens rea required for criminal damage.[368] Sometimes the police will be confident that, if they can establish that a suspect committed the actus reus of the crime, no claim of lack of mens rea or justification will stand up in court. In such cases they may induce the suspect to admit to committing the act in question by suggesting that the suspect was justified in carrying it out (and thus would have a defence). A journalist who carried out an observational

---

[364] Such cases can be distinguished from 'coerced false memory' confessions, which is where suspects not only come to believe that they must have committed the crime, but actually remember (erroneously) doing so. These are probably much rarer than 'coerced false belief' confessions: Leo (2008: 220–225).

[365] Stephenson G, *The Psychology of Criminal Justice* (Oxford: Blackwell, 1992) p 127.

[366] This was an Irish case which happened in 1984 when there were no PACE-type protections. For an analysis of this fascinating case, see O'Mahony P, 'The Kerry Babies Case: Towards a Social Psychological Analysis' [1992] 13 *Irish Journal of Psychology* 223.

[367] Experimental research confirms that a false confession is the likely result when suspects are misled into thinking that there is strong incriminating evidence against them: Nash R and Wade K, 'Innocent but Proven Guilty: Eliciting Internalised False Confessions Using Doctored Video Evidence' (2009) 23 *Applied Cognitive Psychology* 624.

[368] See Criminal Damage Act, s 1, which provides that criminal damage can be committed either intentionally *or* recklessly.

study of American homicide detectives saw many examples of suspects being offered such ways 'out' that were actually ways 'in'.[369] As he puts it:

> The majority of those who acknowledge their complicity in a killing must be baited by detectives with something more tempting than penitence. They must be made to believe that their crime is not really murder, that their excuse is both accepted and unique, that they will, with the help of the detective, be judged less evil than they really are . . . the detective must let the suspect know that his guilt is certain and easily established by the existing evidence. He must then offer the Out . . . 'Look, bunk, I'm giving you a chance. He came at you right? You were scared. It was self-defense . . . He came at you right?' 'Yeah, he came at me.' The Out leads in.

5.7.1.4 Interrogative suggestibility

This involves suspects receiving messages from interviewers in ways which affect their subsequent response. This can occur in all three of the confession types discussed so far. 'Vulnerable' suspects are particularly susceptible,[370] as are those with 'adverse life experiences' (such as unemployment or being a victim of crime).[371] Stefan Kiszko had a mental age of 12, and was jailed for life in 1976 for murdering a schoolgirl. He had been interrogated repeatedly, and eventually 'confessed' after his sixth interrogation. In 1992, his conviction was quashed after it was found that the semen on the victim's body could not have been his. This evidence was available at the time of the trial but was not revealed.[372]

Vulnerable people now have the additional protection during questioning of an 'appropriate adult'. But the police often fail to identify vulnerable suspects. This was so in the 'Tottenham Three case,[373] and lower profile examples include *Brine*[374] and *Miller*.[375] In the first two of these cases, confessions were rejected by the Court of Appeal because of the vulnerability of the defendants, but this was not the result in *Miller*. There is also the problem that the police sometimes seek to undermine the protection supposedly offered by legal advisors and appropriate adults, as seen in the case of Mr Z discussed earlier in this section. Further, neither appropriate adults nor legal advice prevent the police from placing on suspects the kinds of pressures faced by the 'Cardiff Three'.

The dangers of interrogative suggestibility are enhanced by the types of question commonly asked. If questioning was primarily fact-finding, as the PEACE model encourages, questions would generally be of an open kind ('what did you see?', 'what did you do?') where there would be fewer dangers of false confessions, if only because the criminal alone would be able to provide the correct details. It may be true, as Soukara et al (2009) and Evans (1993) found, that most questioning is like this.[376] In Evans' study, most suspects readily confessed. The important question is what happens in questioning where suspects do not readily confess? McConville and Hodgson (1993: 137) argue that the questions then turn to admission seeking. The most important question forms of this type which they

---

[369] Simon D, *Homicide: A Year on the Killing Streets* (London: Hodder & Stoughton, 1992) at pp 194–207.

[370] Gudjonsson (2017); Gudjonsson G, Sigurdsson J, Sigurdardottir A, Steinthorsson H and Sigurdardottir V, 'The Role of Memory Distrust in Cases of Internalised False Confession' (2014) 28 *Applied Cognitive Psychology* 336–348. See also Farrugia and Gabbert (2020).

[371] Drake K, Bull R and Boon J, 'Interrogative Suggestibility, Self-esteem, and the Influence of Negative Life Events' (2008) 13 *Legal and Criminological Psychology* 299.

[372] Kiszko died, aged 41, less than two years after his release. A family friend commented: 'After being released, Stefan could not rouse himself and never recovered from what happened . . . He could not face the world': *The Guardian*, 24 December 1993.

[373] *Raghip, Silcott and Braithwaite* (1991) *The Times*, 9 December.

[374] [1992] Crim LR 122.   [375] [1986] 1 WLR 1191.

[376] Note, however, that Evans' study was of juveniles only and, as he recognises, many formal interrogations were preceded by informal questioning, the content of which he was unaware.

identify are, first, leading questions. These seek particular answers by foreclosing others (for example, 'You went down there to get the stuff and you assaulted her, didn't you?'). Second, there are statement questions (such as, 'You did it. You went there. There is no sign of entry, no force; whoever did it, did it by key.'); third, there are legal closure questions ('So you stole the goods?'); fourth, there are questions seeking the adoption of police opinions ('You are not innocent, you know what goes on.'). Finally, there are accusatory questions.[377] Soukara et al (2009) similarly noted that leading questions were used in 73 out of the 80 interviews they studied (which is not in line with the PEACE model), though these closed questions were uncorrelated with confessions.

In the process of 'asking' admission-seeking questions, the police sometimes let information slip which suspects may incorporate into their answers.[378] Whether such 'slips' are advertent or not is difficult to tell, although it seems reasonable to infer deliberate manipulation when the police disclosure takes place in an informal exchange just prior to a formal interview, as in the case of Mr Z discussed at the beginning of this section. Sometimes as the police ask for detail to confirm what they already know, and the innocent suspect gets it wrong, the suspect is contradicted until, by chance, the correct answer is produced. Gudjonsson analysed one notorious post-PACE miscarriage of justice case and observed that:

> From the transcript it would appear that Heron was prompted and led in connection with almost every conceivable corroborative point. These included the point of entry to the disused building, the victim's clothing, the weapon or weapons, wounds (number and type), the position of the body and the route used inside the premises. . . . the weapons suggested by Heron. . . included brick, hands, metal, metal pipe, sharp metal and base metal. Eventually he was asked, was it a knife?[379]

We noted at the end of section 5.5 that there is now research to suggest that a strategy of treating suspects more humanely (i.e. not bullying or, denigrating them) might lead to an increase in confessions amongst the guilty. We also posited that such a strategy should also reduce the confession rate amongst the innocent.[380] But whatever questioning style is adopted, custodial interrogation will remain inherently coercive, and some innocent people will continue to confess their guilt under these conditions. The radical solution to this problem is not to have custodial questioning, or at least not to rely on it so heavily. This raises the question of corroboration.

5.7.2 **Corroboration**

At present it is possible to convict on confession evidence alone in a contested case, though the courts are warned to be especially careful to ensure fairness and to carefully check reliability in such cases.[381] There is no need for independent evidence of guilt (corroboration).[382]

---

[377] For an illustration, see the extract from the 'Cardiff Three' interviews, quoted in section 5.3.2.

[378] In the 'Cardiff Three' the police 'fed' Miller with the idea that the reason he could not 'remember' being present at the murder was that he was under the influence of drugs at the time. Also see O'Connell (2005) and Leggett et al (2007). [379] Gudjonsson (2003: 103–105), (*Heron* (1993, unreported)).

[380] See also Sigurdsson J and Gudjonsson G, 'Psychological Characteristics of "False Confessors": A Study Among Icelandic Prison Inmate and Juvenile Offenders' (1996) 20 *Personality and Individual Differences* 321 and Gudjonsson (2003: 627). This is probably because the innocent (lacking a guilty conscience or need to talk about the offence) are, on the whole, more reluctant to confess than the guilty, and are also faced with weaker police cases. See further Gudjonsson (2003: ch 6).

[381] *Beeres v CPS West Midlands* [2014] EWHC 283, at para 10

[382] Code C, Note for Guidance 11C, suggests that because juveniles and the mentally vulnerable are particularly prone to providing unreliable self-incriminating evidence, it is important to obtain corroboration of any facts admitted. This falls far short of a *general duty* to at least *seek* corroboration, not least because the Notes for Guidance are not even regarded as formally part of the Code.

The police frequently fail to interview witnesses to crimes, to secure identification evidence and to do scientific tests on fingerprints, blood, hair samples and so forth. In one study, reasonable steps (not including scientific tests) were taken to secure additional evidence in around 80% of the cases, but available sources were, for no apparent reason, not checked in over 10%. In most of the rest, investigation stopped after a confession was obtained because a guilty plea was anticipated.[383] It is not that further investigation was impossible in most of these cases, but that it was simply thought unnecessary to go through these costly and time-consuming processes when the law allows conviction on confession evidence alone and a decade of austerity has reduced the police workforce. Even when the law does not allow conviction solely on the basis of confession evidence, such as in American jurisdictions, it has been shown that the assumptions that lead police officers to accept false confessions also affect the way that corroboration evidence is sought, rendering that process unreliable too.[384] This attitude increases the risk of a miscarriage of justice in cases where innocent suspects make false confessions. Sometimes the simplest of post-interrogation steps (such as the holding of an identification parade) has not been taken and it has only been by chance that a prosecution witness has subsequently (at the trial, or even post-conviction, stage) learned of the defendant's identity and told the police that they have definitely got the wrong person.[385]

Many different types of corroboration rule are conceivable, all of which would have different effects.[386] However, McConville found that, in most prosecution cases, where there is a confession there is also admissible independent evidence.[387] A Home Office study carried out for the Runciman Commission found even fewer cases dependent on confession evidence alone.[388] Quirk's study suggests that the police and CPS are aware that it could be dangerous to rely solely on confession evidence (though this does not always stop them from doing so). One officer interviewed by Quirk said 'a cough [confession] is always nice but you need to nail the coffin shut', while another recognised that confessions alone are a 'dangerous method of deciding guilt'.[389] What of the remainder, which would have fallen foul of a corroboration rule? McConville found that in many of them independent evidence existed which could have been produced at court, and in many others it may have been possible to collect such evidence. About one third of the confession-only cases (about 3% of all prosecuted cases in which the police had interrogated) could not have satisfied a corroboration requirement. In some of these cases, this was because the confessions were so uncertain that they were incapable of being substantiated by reliable evidence. They ended in acquittal anyway. The others, which did end in conviction, would probably not have survived a corroboration rule (sometimes deservedly, given the dubious circumstances of the confessions) but were not particularly serious offences.

As McConville concludes, even the most stringent corroboration rule would affect relatively few cases and lead to few extra acquittals. However, the majority of the Runciman Commission (which was split on the issue) was concerned that the small percentage of cases which would be affected would amount to a large number in absolute terms, and that such a rule 'would not by itself prevent miscarriages of justice resulting from fabricated confessions and the production of supporting evidence obtained by improper means.'[390]

---

[383] McConville M, *Corroboration and Confessions* (Royal Commission on Criminal Justice Research Study no 13) (London: HMSO, 1993) Table 5.1.

[384] Woody W and Forrest K, *Understanding Police Interrogation: Confessions and Consequences* (New York: NYU Press, 2020).

[385] For examples, see *Brady* [2004] EWCA Crim 2230 and Gudjonsson (2003: 230–231).

[386] See McConville (1993: 50–58); Pattenden R, 'Should Confessions be Corroborated?' (1991) 107 *Law Quarterly Review* 319. For a general discussion which includes a review of the law in Scotland and Australia, see Mirfield (1997: 345–352).

[387] This was true of 86.6% of the cases in his study: McConville (1993: 61).

[388] RCCJ (1993: 65).   [389] Quirk (2016: 68).   [390] RCCJ (1993: 65).

It was worried that a corroboration rule would lead to too many guilty defendants walking free, whilst offering negligible protection to the innocent; and that the benefits to be derived from such a rule would not justify the cost of more thorough investigations.

Runciman's reasoning is flawed. First, it amounts to saying that a valid reason for not having a safeguard is that it might be abused by the police. In that case, we might as well do away with all safeguards for suspects, for, as we have seen, they are all abused to a lesser or greater degree. But how much abuse is likely? It is one thing for police officers to pressurise or trick suspects into confessing or to 'gild the lily' and another deliberately to frame suspects (e.g. by planting incriminating evidence on them). Only rarely, in the latter case, will the risk of discipline or dismissal be seen as worthwhile.[391] It follows that a corroboration rule probably would offer significant protection.

Second, it is irrational to assert that, under a corroboration rule, the police would frame the innocent *and* let the guilty walk free. If anything, one would imagine that it would be easier to 'frame' the guilty, since there are likely to be more raw materials to work with in constructing a prosecution case if a person is actually guilty. If the police did set out to frame any suspects in such a crude fashion, the innocent would suffer no more than the guilty, and probably less so. The other side of the coin is that the innocent would stand to gain more from a corroboration rule than would the guilty, since it would be easier to corroborate a true confession than a false one. It is in this light that one must place Runciman's anxiety over the resource implications of corroboration. The main purpose of a corroboration rule would be to protect the victims of false and fabricated confessions. We know that there are such cases, we know that currently some such cases end in conviction and lengthy prison sentences, and that only a mixture of luck and hard work by those who re-investigate cases leads to the eventual release of some of the defendants involved. There may be only a few, perhaps a few dozen, such cases each year. But if a corroboration rule led to the non-prosecution or the acquittal of at least some of these few then, to the adherent of due process or freedom, that rule would be worth its weight in gold.

5.8 Conclusion

The due process/crime control debate about police questioning usually revolves around the problem of false confessions and wrongful convictions. But viewing the topic through the lens of the three 'core values' shows that abuse of powers, regardless of the outcome, is equally important as this is also a matter of 'justice'. Civil libertarians advocating a due process approach have had some success in controlling the crime control tendencies of the police and government. This has led to the establishment of a set of standards, set out in PACE, its Codes, the ECHR and in the cases on all these provisions; and the protections analysed in chapter 4, especially the right to legal advice and assistance. But this success is limited:

- these standards are vague;
- the value of advice and assistance (especially intervention during questioning) is blunted by the practical problems of legal practice and by the effect of the CJPO;
- suspects who suffer from breaches of these standards usually have no remedy apart from the capricious possibility of the exclusion of evidence.

---

[391] Undoubtedly, however, the police do sometimes break the rules to this extent. For post-PACE examples see the *Darvell* case (1992 unreported) discussed in Gudjonsson (2003: 530–533).

PACE and its associated codes of practice created a legal framework which deliberately shifted suspect-focused police investigation into the police station. In this respect, and in the detailed rules provided, the change followed an established trend rather than producing a radical break with the past. As McConville and Baldwin said in 1982, before PACE was even drafted:

> ... the really crucial exchanges in the criminal process have shifted from courts into police interrogation rooms. It is these exchanges that, in a majority of cases, colour what happens at later stages in the criminal process. Indeed they often determine the outcome of cases at trial.[392]

Restricting the location of formal post-arrest interviewing to the police station and nowhere else could only be regarded as a due process protection if the context of detention was governed by due process standards. The reality is that, despite the growing number of criminal justice actors in custody suites and the ubiquity of CCTV cameras therein,[393] it remains 'police territory' and cannot be easily wrested from police control. Hence due process safeguards for suspects in the police station are much weaker than they appear, and largely fail to 'balance' the powers of the police. Investigators are increasingly trained and expected to employ the fact-finding approach set out in the PEACE model, but crime control laws tolerate barely restricted questioning, the use in court of police evidence of what was said, and convictions based on that evidence even when it is contested and uncorroborated.

The crime control reality is hidden by the sanitised language of 'interviews' and 'questioning' but the police know very well what they are doing and the imbalance of power that exists between them and suspects:

> It's not an interview, let's face it. I mean most people don't want to be in there, it's not pleasant for them. We know what we want out of it. It's an interrogation, that's what it is, we just don't use the word because it doesn't sound nice (Police sergeant, quoted by Choongh 1997: 117).

What about the shift in questioning techniques over the years from violence to manipulation and the more gradual shift away from psychological tactics towards official support for 'investigative interviewing' and the PEACE model? While there is some consensus that police interview techniques have generally improved, problems remain. This is not surprising given that guidance and training may go against the grain of police culture (e.g. suspiciousness and thus the tendency to presume those in police custody are guilty), and the continuing and profoundly mistaken belief of the police that they can reliably distinguish the guilty from the innocent, based on non-verbal cues or through their use of their emotional intelligence to 'read' the suspect. Then there is that great mass of cases which the police anticipate ending in no further action, a police caution, or some other pre-trial disposal (see chapter 7), thus leaving any illegalities hidden, the perpetrators unaccountable, and exclusionary remedies unavailable. As Jackson argues, the police station is now the site of formal accusation and disposition as much as investigation, yet court-like safeguards, controls and remedies are badly lacking.[394]

Once it is decided that the police station should be the focus of investigation, and that confession evidence alone can form the sole basis for conviction (or other punitive

---

[392] McConville M and Baldwin J, 'The Role of Interrogation in Crime Discovery and Conviction' (1982) 22 *British Journal of Criminology* 165 at p 174.

[393] Kendall J, *Regulating Police Detention* (Bristol: Police Press, 2019) p 122; Skinns (2011: 188–189).

[394] Jackson J, 'Police and Prosecutors after PACE: The Road from Case Construction to Case Disposal' in Cape and Young (2008).

disposition), the crime control framework is accepted, and the room for due process is fundamentally circumscribed. An alternative approach would try to counter-balance police power effectively, as would be expected in a fully adversarial system. This means *not* making the rights of suspects, particularly for more vulnerable suspects (e.g. children and young people) dependent on police officers, but making them either automatic, with the possibility of opting out rather than in, if a suspect so wished, or guaranteed by a genuine third party. Independent lawyers working in police stations might be a solution. Unlike most legal aid lawyers at present, however, they would need to attend all interrogations and possess an adversarial ethos. If they were based in law centres rotating with other law centre lawyers, they might not get 'captured' by the police ethos.[395]

To support this shift towards genuine adversarialism, the law could provide that no evidence obtained through questioning would be admissible in evidence unless a defence lawyer was present. If that is too much for managerialists and crime control adherents to stomach, could we not at least have a rule that rendered confessions to the police inadmissible in evidence unless audio-recorded or possibly even audio-visually recorded, and the recording is made available in full to the court? Where a suspect wishes to impart confidential information to the police, this could be done informally but without the evidence being directly usable in court.

Such reforms are inconceivable at present and the trend is in fact towards increasing police power in such a way that they no longer need to engage in practices that the courts find objectionable. Blatant police oppression and trickery is being replaced by latent police power and control. The attenuation of the right to silence brought about by the CJPO is one clear example of that, and the increase in the length of police-authorised custody for all offences from 24 hours to 36 hours (and, with limited judicial oversight, from seven to 28 days for terrorist offences) in the present decade (see chapter 4) is another. More recent examples include the growth of 'voluntary' interviews on the street, which on the one hand may prevent vulnerable suspects from sitting unnecessarily in police cells, but also potentially pose grave threats to hard-won due process safeguards and mean that a suspect may have made an admission without even needing to be taken to the police station at all. Release under investigation provisions (see chapter 4) are another example of latent police power in that those suspected of an offence can languish for up to 228 days in a state of uncertainty, not knowing what is happening with their case or even whether the police are actively investigating it.[396] This situation and the uncertainties it induces in the suspect can largely only be brought to an end by the police as and when the investigation reaches a conclusion. No-one should mistake the overall trend towards increasing latent police power. The core value of 'efficiency' is prioritised over 'justice' as is especially evident from the resistance to funding legal assistance properly, allowing cases to be built on the products of interviews alone, and the resistance to corroboration rules that other jurisdictions, including Scotland, have. Against this background, ethical custodial interrogation looks increasingly like a contradiction in terms.

---

[395] See the related discussion in O'Brien D and Epp J, 'Salaried Defenders and the Access to Justice Act 1999' (2000) 63 *Modern Law Review* 394, building on McConville et al, *Standing Accused* (Oxford: Clarendon Press, 1994) pp 296–297.

[396] The Law Society, *Release under investigation* (2019) available at <https://www.lawsociety.org.uk/policy-campaigns/campaigns/criminal-justice/release-under-investigation/> (accessed 1 July 2020).

Further reading

COLLEGE OF POLICING (2019) *Investigative Interviewing. Authorised Professional Practice*. Online at: https://www.app.college.police.uk/app-content/investigations/investigative-interviewing/.

FARRUGIA L and GABBERT F, 'The "Appropriate Adult": What They Do and What They Should Do in Police Interviews with Mentally Disordered Suspects' (2019) 29(3) *Criminal Behaviour and Mental Health* 134–141.

KASSIN S, 'Confession Evidence: Commonsense Myths and Misconceptions' (2008) 35(10) *Criminal Justice and Behavior* 1309.

KEBBELL M, ALISON L and HURREN E, 'Sex Offenders' Perceptions of the Effectiveness and Fairness of Humanity, Dominance, and Displaying an Understanding of Cognitive Distortions in Police Interviews: A Vignette Study' (2008) 14(5) *Psychology, Crime and Law* 435.

PIVATY A, *Criminal Defence at Police Stations: A Comparative and Empirical Study* (Abingdon: Routledge, 2020).

QUIRK H, *The Rise and Fall of the Right of Silence* (Abingdon: Routledge, 2016).

SOUKARA S, BULL R, VRIJ A, TURNER M and CHERRYMAN J, 'What Really Happens in Police Interviews of Suspects? Tactics and Confessions' (2009) 15(6) *Psychology, Crime & Law* 493–506.

SUKUMAR D, HODGSON J and WADE K, 'Behind Closed Doors: Live Observations of Current Police Station Disclosure Practices and Lawyer-Client Consultations' (2016) 12 *Criminal Law Review*.

VRIJ A, 'Nonverbal Dominance Versus Verbal Accuracy in Lie Detection: A Plea To Change Police Practice' (2008b) 35(10) *Criminal Justice and Behavior* 1323.

WOODY W and FORREST K, *Understanding Police Interrogation: Confessions and Consequences* (New York: NYUP, 2020).

6

Non-interrogatory evidence and covert policing

KEY ISSUES

- Witness and identification evidence
- Entry, search and seizure
- Covert policing—including interception of communication, data surveillance, police informants, undercover policing, covert surveillance
- Scientific evidence
- Privacy, transparency and accountability

6.1 Introduction

Arrest, detention and interrogation are the key strategies that the police use to investigate suspects.[1] However, other methods include interviewing witnesses and seeking identification evidence from witnesses, searching people and property and seizing potential evidence, scientific examination of materials such as fingerprints and DNA samples, and various forms of covert policing. Covert policing includes the interception of communications, data surveillance, CCTV, the use of informants and undercover police agents, and covert surveillance. These investigative measures are both extensive and complex. So, whilst this chapter explains how they are regulated, and how they work in practice, it is an introduction to these topics rather than a definitive account.

Whilst these activities and methods are described here as 'investigative', some of them are often deployed for other purposes—crime-detection, intelligence-gathering, disruption of criminal activity—rather than to gather evidence for use in a criminal prosecution. An obvious example is CCTV surveillance. CCTV cameras have become ubiquitous in the UK, deployed not only in public spaces such as streets and parks, but also outside and inside shops, offices and other buildings, and also outside (and sometimes even inside) private dwellings. Some are publicly owned, but many are privately owned and/or managed. Clearly, images captured by CCTV cameras can be used for the purposes of crime investigation, and ultimately used as evidence in court. However, this is not their sole, or even primary, purpose.[2]

---

[1] For arrest and detention, see chs 3 and 4, and for interrogation (or questioning) see ch 5.
[2] Piza E, Welsh B, Farrington D and Thomas A, 'CCTV Surveillance for Crime Prevention: A 40-year Systematic Review with Meta-analysis' (2019) 18 *Criminology and Public Policy* 1, 135–159.

Some of the methods covered in this chapter—interception of communications, data surveillance, covert surveillance and covert human intelligence sources—are particularly utilised by policing agencies other than 'the police' as traditionally conceived. Security services, in particular, play a significant role in relation to the prevention and detection of terrorist activity. Much of what is true of, and for, the police is also true of those agencies. Generally, however, both regulation and oversight of such agencies differs from that governing the police, and the focus in this chapter is on the police.

The covert policing methods described in this chapter were largely prompted, in the UK, almost three decades ago by a report by the Audit Commission which encouraged the development of 'proactive' and 'intelligence-led' policing.[3] This was, perhaps, a shift towards a 'surveillance society'. Ericson even argued that 'crime control [had been] displaced by surveillance' allowing him to define criminal justice as 'a system co-ordinated by knowledge, communication and surveillance mechanisms.'[4] The *system* was developing rights to as much knowledge as it could accrue, at the expense of everyone else's rights to privacy—described memorably as 'surveillance creep'.[5] Whilst the terrorist attacks in the USA in September 2001 (known as '9/11') intensified surveillance creep in Western societies the phenomenon was already well established before that event.[6] Since then, the introduction of the 'smart phone', burgeoning social media, and other technological developments, have led to massively more surveillance and information-gathering, both by private companies (especially those delivering social media services) and policing agencies. Not only do the police now have more powers than ever to acquire information—both covertly and from other organisations such as tax, social security and local government authorities[7]—but they can increasingly keep it for later, unspecified, use and share it with other national, European and global agencies.[8]

The development of covert policing methods does not only have implications for the privacy of individuals—it is a matter, in the language of our 'core values', of 'justice'. By definition, proactive policing is a police initiative. The police cannot target all suspected crime, so they must inevitably prioritise particular types of crime and types of suspected criminal. Increasing pressures to use resources efficiently—another of our 'core values'—risks this being done to pick off 'low hanging fruit' or use easy stereotypes. With the exception of a few 'Mr Bigs',[9] this means the targeting not simply of individuals but of specific groups and sections of society.[10] In the context of the kinds of police working rules described in chapter 2, this results in a skewed 'suspect population' (see further chapter 10). Some types of crime and some types of people become not only more heavily policed, but also more known about, than others.[11] This is a matter of democracy—our third 'core value'—both in terms of unequal treatment and the effect on community trust in the police. In an era of

---

[3] Audit Commission, *Helping with enquiries: tackling crime effectively* (London: Audit Commission, 1993).

[4] Ericson R, 'The Royal Commission on Criminal Justice System Surveillance' in McConville M and Bridges L (eds), *Criminal Justice in Crisis* (Aldershot: Edward Elgar, 1994) p 139.

[5] Marx G, *Undercover: Police Surveillance in America* (Berkeley: UCLA Press, 1988).

[6] Ball K and Webster F (eds), *The Intensification of Surveillance* (London: Pluto Press, 2003).

[7] Ericson R and Haggerty K, *Policing the Risk Society* (Oxford: Clarendon, 1997). For statistics on the use of surveillance powers, see the *Annual Report of the Investigatory Powers Commissioner 2018* (HC 67).

[8] See generally Lyon D, *The Culture of Surveillance: Watching as a Way of Life* (Cambridge: Polity Press, 2018).

[9] For an example involving international police co-operation in cracking an encrypted communications system, see Dodd V, 'Hundreds arrested as UK organised crime network is cracked', *The Guardian*, 2 July 2020.

[10] O'Neill and Loftus, for example, note the growth of intrusion into the lives of marginalised groups through everyday policing practices. See O'Neill M and Loftus B, 'Policing and the Surveillance of the Marginal: Everyday Contexts of Social Control' (2013) 17(4) *Theoretical Criminology* 437–454.

[11] For a classic examination of some of the issues involved see Maguire M, 'Policing by Risks and Targets: Some Dimensions and Implications of Intelligence-led Crime Control' (2000) 9 *Policing and Society* 4, pp 315–336. See also Ratcliffe J, *Intelligence-led Policing* (London: Routledge, 2016).

6.2 Witness and identification evidence

We saw in chapter 2 that a huge number of crimes and possible crimes come to police notice through reports from members of the public. Some members of the public, encouraged by neighbourhood watch schemes, make a habit of looking for crimes and criminals and reporting anything vaguely suspicious to the police. The police and local authorities support 'Crimestoppers', a charitable organisation that facilitates the provision of information about crime to the police, anonymously if that is the wish of the informant.[12] And there are the mass of one-off reports of possible crimes experienced by victims or witnessed by members of the public, ranging from careless driving, drunkenness and dog fouling through to domestic violence, burglary, armed robbery and worse.

This brings into relief the classic problem of policing: how do, and how should, the police sift information sufficiently thoroughly so as not to miss anything important whilst not pursuing cases unnecessarily, but sufficiently speedily to investigate efficiently whilst not overstretching their resources? As we saw in chapters 2 and 3, one answer is for the police to stereotype—to judge what they see, or are told, by reference to what they know, or think they know, of the source. Not only do the police have to decide who and what to take notice of, they then have to decide *how* to take notice of it. In this section we are concerned with only one aspect of this; the method and regulation of securing evidence from witnesses who are not victims. In chapter 12 we examine victims (and, to some extent, non-victim witnesses) from the point of view of their involvement in the criminal justice system in general, and, in chapters 9 and 12, in giving evidence in court in particular. Here, we deal with two issues: interviewing and taking statements from witnesses, and identification by witnesses.

6.2.1 Interviewing witnesses

We saw in chapter 5 that police questioning of suspects is not a simple matter of eliciting objective facts from people. Some 'facts' may be matters of opinion or interpretation, such as a mental state or a response to perceived aggression. Some people will not be sure of the 'facts'. Some people may be highly suggestible and/or easily intimidated or eager to please. The police will often be objectively seeking the truth but, unaware of these problems, will inadvertently put words or ideas into the minds and mouths of interviewees. Sometimes they are so eager to secure evidence of what they think is the truth that they do this deliberately. And sometimes they simply 'gild the lily' for a variety of thoroughly bad reasons. This is all as true of the interviewing of non-suspects as it is of suspects though coercion and ill-treatment of non-suspects is rare. Such issues sometimes arise, however, where the police believe a witness is hiding the truth, as some undoubtedly do. Most police officers, in common with many lay people, believe that they can 'spot a liar', but rely on techniques, such as focusing on non-verbal cues like gaze aversion and fidgeting,[13] that are now discredited by modern research.[14] Thus both truthful and untruthful witnesses can come under pressure to change their stories.

---

[12] For a rosy picture written by police officers involved with Crimestoppers, see Griffiths B and Murphy A, 'Managing Anonymous Informants Through Crimestoppers' in Billingsley et al (eds), *Informers: Policing, Policy, Practice* (Cullompton: Willan, 2001).

[13] Vrij A, Granhag P and Porter S, 'Pitfalls and Opportunities in Nonverbal and Verbal Lie Detection' (2010) 11(3) *Psychological Science in the Public Interest* 89–121.

[14] See section 5.5 for discussion in relation to interviewing of suspects. And see Costigan R, 'Identification from CCTV: The Risk of Injustice' (2007) *Criminal Law Review* 591, and Heaton-Armstrong A et al (eds), *Witness Testimony* (Oxford: OUP, 2006) for reviews of the psychological evidence and its reception by the courts.

When these problems came to light in relation to suspects the pre-PACE practice of suspects 'writing a statement' was largely abandoned, because such statements were to a greater or lesser extent written by the police themselves. Contemporaneous notes of interviews and, subsequently, electronic recordings and transcripts of the interviews (governed by codes of practice)[15] replaced the unreliable statements. Whilst the same problems potentially apply to non-suspect witness interview statements, they are not regulated by a code of practice or otherwise, unless they are deemed vulnerable.[16] The College of Policing states that police officers are required to produce a statement from an interview conducted with a witness, and encourages them to ensure that the witness statement accurately reflects what the witness has said. However, electronic recording is not advised unless the witness is a key or significant witness in the investigation of a serious offence.[17] As a result, few witnesses write their own statements; instead, the interviewer usually writes a 'good' statement. For many officers a 'warts and all' statement is a waste of time or even counter-productive. For them, a statement should be consistent with, or at least not damage, the police case and the prosecution evidence.[18] In the past, research on witnesses with learning disabilities has revealed that, where the police regarded the witness as credible, they would sometimes write the statement in language that the witness could not possibly have used. This has the potential to distort what the witness is trying to say, and creates opportunities for defence lawyers to discredit the testimony of the witness at trial.[19] There are powerful arguments for recording all key witness statements in at least the most serious cases so their value can be properly evaluated in court[20] but while this is encouraged in relevant guidance,[21] it is neither legally required nor the norm.

For these reasons, the developments in 'cognitive interviewing' discussed in chapter 5 are as applicable to non-suspect interviewees as to suspects. As Milne and Bull say, '. . . suggestibility is not a property of children but is a property of their interviewing'. This is equally applicable to adults, for as they also say, 'All interviewees are vulnerable.'[22] Eliciting what the interviewee really saw/heard/knows is best done through open-ended non-leading questions, but the police also have to challenge and test what is said as any purported witness may lie or exaggerate for any number of reasons. This approach was recommended around a decade ago by the National Strategic Steering Group on Investigative Interviewing (NSSGII), and incorporated into the College of Policing's Authorised

---

[15] Interviews with suspects must normally be contemporaneously recorded (PACE Code C para 11.7) in accordance with the procedures set out in PACE Code E (audio-recording) or Code F (audio-visual recording). See further ch 5. For the circumstances in which the electronic record may be played at trial, see the Criminal Practice Directions V Evidence 16C: Evidence of audio and video recorded interviews.

[16] Ministry of Justice, *Achieving Best Evidence in Criminal Proceedings: Guidance on interviewing victims and witnesses, and guidance on using special measures* (2011a) available at: <https://www.cps.gov.uk/sites/default/files/documents/legal_guidance/best_evidence_in_criminal_proceedings.pdf> (accessed 9 October 2020).

[17] College of Policing, *Authorised Professional Practice: Investigation: Working with victims and witnesses* (2020), available at: <https://www.app.college.police.uk/app-content/investigations/victims-and-witnesses/#video-of-witness-interview> (accessed at 9 October 2020).

[18] Shepherd E and Milne R, 'Full and Faithful: Ensuring Quality Practice and Integrity of Outcome in Witness Interviews' in Heaton-Armstrong et al (eds), *Analysing Witness Testimony* (London: Blackstone, 1999) pp 132–133.

[19] Sanders et al, *Victims with Learning Difficulties* (Oxford: CCR, 1997). For two more recent studies see Vanderhallen M, Vervaeke G and Holmber V, 'Witness and Suspect Perception of Working Alliance and Interviewing Style' (2011) 8 *Journal of Investigative Psychology and Offender Profiling* 2, and Sagana A, Saverland M and Merckelbach H (2017) 'Witnesses' Failure to Detect Covert Manipulations in their Written Statements' 14 *Journal of Investigative Psychology and Offender Profiling* 3.

[20] Heaton-Armstrong A and Wolchover D, 'Woeful Neglect' (2007) 157 *New Law Journal* 624.

[21] Ministry of Justice (2011) para 1.26.

[22] Milne R and Bull R, *Investigative Interviewing: Psychology and Practice* (Chichester: Wiley, 1999) at pp 150 and 189.

Professional Practice.[23] Research pre-dating the NSSGII recommendations indicated that, just as with the questioning of suspects, that approach was not being internalised effectively by the police. Clarke and Milne evaluated the effectiveness of 'cognitive interviewing' training and found 'damning' evidence of police interviewers apparently looking to interviewees to confirm police suspicions, rather than to provide their own accounts.[24] However, there has been little recent research on the impact of investigative interviewing training programmes on policing practice.[25]

If witnesses are lying, as distinct from mistaken or confused, then cognitive interviewing using open-ended non-leading questions will probably not persuade them to tell the truth. This is why the police may instead adopt hostile interviewing techniques when they believe that witnesses are lying. A good example is Dwayne Brooks, who witnessed the murder of his friend, Stephen Lawrence, but who was treated, in a hostile manner, as a suspect by the police. In another example, a defendant charged with assault told the police that there were four witnesses who would support his claim of self-defence. They were all associates of the defendant and the police believed that they had perjured themselves for him before. They therefore interviewed them in an 'assertive and confrontational' way, and one of the interviewing officers misled, or lied to, one witness in an attempt to get him to 'tell the truth'.[26] The police clearly tried to get the witnesses to change their stories in order to support their own case theory. Unusually, this was all documented on tape because the police treated the witnesses as perjury suspects; but as we have seen, the police are (still) not required to electronically record interviews with witnesses.

We have focused on the way the police sometimes manipulate witnesses to make statements that fit police preconceptions to the detriment of the suspect. But sometimes the problem is the reverse. Vulnerable witnesses, such as youth and people who are learning disabled were, in the past, often perceived by the police to be incapable of being 'good' witnesses so little attempt was made to take statements from them and those who victimised them frequently remained unpunished.[27] This began to be officially recognised around the turn of the century, and in 2002 the government published *Achieving Best Evidence*, which was updated and re-published in 2011.[28] This provides information and guidance on identifying witnesses as vulnerable, and interviewing and supporting them, and also on the special measures that were introduced for the giving of evidence in court by vulnerable witnesses that were introduced by the Youth Justice and Criminal Evidence Act 1999 (see chapters 9 and 12). Much of this has been incorporated into guidance for the police provided by the College of Policing's Approved Professional Practice.[29] What is less clear is how this has translated into practice, particularly, policing practice.[30]

---

[23] College of Policing, *Authorised Professional Practice: Investigation: Investigative interviewing*, available at <https://www.app.college.police.uk/app-content/investigations/investigative-interviewing/> (accessed 9 October 2020). See, generally, Shepherd E and Griffiths A, *Investigative Interviewing: The Conversation Management Approach* (Oxford: OUP, 2013).

[24] Clarke C and Milne R, *National evaluation of the PEACE investigative interviewing scheme* (PRAS Paper 149) (London: Home Office, 2001).

[25] For a round-up of international research on investigative interviewing, see Walsh D, Oxburgh G, Redlich A and Myklebust T, *International Developments and Practices in Investigative Interviewing and Interrogation Vol. 1: Victims and Witnesses* (London: Routledge, 2016).   [26] *Higgins* [2003] EWCA Crim 2943.

[27] Sanders et al (1997).   [28] Ministry of Justice (2011).   [29] College of Policing (2020).

[30] See, for example, Burton et al, 'Implementing Special Measures for Vulnerable and Intimidated Witnesses: The Problem of Identification' [2006] *Criminal Law Review* 229, and see generally Ratcliffe P, Gudjonsson G, Heaton-Armstrong A and Wolchover D, *Witness Testimony in Sexual Cases: Evidential, Investigative and Scientific Perspectives* (Oxford: OUP, 2016).

6.2.2 Identification evidence

Eyewitness identification is a particular aspect of witness evidence that deserves separate treatment. It has been estimated to be of some importance in around 25% of all Crown court cases,[31] yet it is a major source of miscarriages of justice.[32] The combination of witnesses having unreasonably strong beliefs in themselves, combined with the tendency, discussed earlier, of the police to lead witnesses to support their cases is a recipe for error and injustice.[33] So are the classic courtroom drama scenarios where victims are asked if they can identify their attackers, whereupon the accusing finger is pointed at the dock, accompanied by a sharp intake of breath from the public gallery and a bewildered look from the suspect.[34]

Where victim and defendant are not otherwise known to each other, an advance on dock identification, where there is only one candidate for the dubious honour of being pointed out, was needed. And so the ID parade was born and the regulation of which was, in particular, refined following the Devlin Report in 1976.[35] Occasionally, in the past, police officers would 'fix' ID parades: packing them with people who looked nothing like their prime suspect, finding a way to make the person they believed to be guilty stand out, or showing the witness a photograph of the suspect in advance. These abuses led to official inquiries, judicial guidelines, Home Office guidelines and then successive editions of PACE Code D that regulates ID procedures in some detail.[36] Whilst ID parades are still occasionally held, technological developments have meant that the 'go to' form of identification procedure is now the video identification.

All the concerns raised about witness evidence in general are equally applicable to identification evidence. Memory decays over time, more than the individual witnesses often realise, and so people can be very suggestible.[37] Moreover, witnesses are error-prone, as what is seen may have taken place in a split-second without prior warning and yet, whilst mistaken, may be convinced that their identification is correct. Psychological research shows that even when the police are trying not to influence witnesses they may inadvertently do so by, for example, their glance lingering on the suspect in the course of an ID procedure.[38] Recognition and identification from images circulating on social media has caused significant problems in terms of the value and reliability of the evidence thus produced and, therefore, for how it should be regulated. Other forms of identification, such as voice identification have, so far, defeated attempts to regulate them in order to safeguard reliability.[39]

---

[31] Zander M and Henderson P, *Crown Court Study* (RCCJ Research Report, London: HMSO, 1993).

[32] For historical accounts, see Criminal Law Revision Committee, Eleventh Report (General), Cmnd 4991 (London: HMSO, 1972).

[33] See, for example, Hain P, *Mistaken Identity* (London: Quartet, 1976).

[34] This manifestly unsatisfactory form of identification evidence is frowned upon by the courts (e.g. *Reid* [1994] Crim LR 442) but is admissible at the discretion of the trial judge.

[35] *Report of the Committee on Evidence of Identification Evidence in Criminal Proceedings* (the Devlin Report), Cmnd 338 (London: HMSO, 1976).

[36] Although as late as 2000, this did not stop the police from putting a suspect in prison stripes in an ID parade (*Kamara* [2000] WL 664383). See also *R v Pecco* [2010] EWCA Crim 972, in which the suspect had a tattoo on her neck which was not concealed in the image used for the video identification, but the police used comparators who did not have such a tattoo.

[37] See, e.g., extensive work conducted by Elizabeth Loftus; Loftus E , 'Eyewitness Testimony' (2019) 33 *Applied Cognitive Psychology* 498–503.

[38] Phillips et al, 'Double-Blind Photoarray Administration as a Safeguard Against Investigator Bias' (1999) 84 *Journal of Applied Psychology* 940. For recommendations about this see Wells G, Kovera M, Douglass A, Brewer N, Meissner C and Wixted J, 'Policy and Procedure Recommendations for the Collection and Preservation of Eyewitness Identification Evidence' (2020) 44(1) *Law and Human Behavior* 3–36.

[39] In 2003 the Home Office announced that it was working on guidelines for conducting voice identification, but it was never forthcoming. For discussions of the issues concerning voice identification see Robson J, 'A Fair Hearing? The Use of Voice Identification Parades in Criminal Investigations in England and Wales' [2017] Crim LR 36, and Morrison G, 'Admissibility of Forensic Voice Comparison Testimony in England and Wales' [2018] Crim LR 20.

6.2.2.1 The requirements of Code of Practice D

Code of Practice D, the Code of Practice for the Identification of Persons by Police Officers, para 3.1, requires a detailed note to be made of the first description of the suspect in every case where identification is likely to be an issue.[40] This is so that any concrete identification made later can be compared to the witness' first statement; an attempt, amongst other things, to guard against 'contamination' by police manipulation. However, in the light of the earlier discussion about manipulation of witness statements this, whilst important, is a relatively weak safeguard.[41]

Code D distinguishes between three types of identification or recognition: identification of a suspect by an eye-witness (Part 3(A)); recognition by a controlled showing of films, photographs and images (Part 3(B)); and recognition by uncontrolled viewing of films, photographs and images (Part 3(C)). We will focus here on the first of these scenarios, but it is worth noting that Part 3(C) was developed to try to deal with some of the problems caused by identification or recognition resulting from images released on social or other media. In respect of identification by an eye-witness (i.e. Part 3(A)), Code D distinguishes between three situations, depending on whether a suspect is known and available. A suspect is 'known' if there is sufficient information available to the police to establish that there are reasonable grounds to suspect a particular person of involvement in the suspected offence (Code D, para 3.1A(a)). A suspect is 'available' where they are immediately available or will shortly be available, for example, because they have been or are about to be arrested. The three situations are:

- *Where the suspect is not known:* The police may take a witness to the area where the offence allegedly occurred or show them photographs or other visual images. Should the suspect be identified in either of these ways, there may be no point holding a further ID procedure for that witness, as s/he will have already picked out the suspect.[42] There is a clear danger of the police 'leading' witnesses in these procedures; this is discussed further later, but it is difficult to see what else can be done. If there are other witnesses, an identification procedure for these other witnesses should be held, providing some safeguard.

- *Where the suspect is known to the police and is available:* In this situation, a formal identification procedure must normally be conducted, unless it would serve 'no useful purpose in proving or disproving whether the suspect was involved in committing the [suspected] offence' (Code D, para 3.12). Normally, this will be a video identification conducted in accordance with Code D, Annex A. A group identification (where the witness views an informal group of people, for example at a cafe/tube station), or an identification parade, or a confrontation, can be held as an alternative, but only if a video identification is not practicable or suitable.

- *Where the suspect is known but not available:* Here a video identification may be conducted if the police have, or are able to obtain, suitable visual images of the suspect. Alternatively, they could hold a group identification or show the witness photographs or other visual images (Code D, para 3.21).

---

[40] Note that the PACE Codes of Practice are regularly revised. The current versions can be accessed at <https://www.gov.uk/guidance/police-and-criminal-evidence-act-1984-pace-codes-of-practice>. For a lawyers' guide to the identification provisions see Cape E, Hardcastle M and Paul S, *Defending Suspects at Police Stations* (London: LAG, 2020) ch 8.

[41] Identification evidence will not necessarily be excluded even though the police breached the obligation to take a record of the original description (*Marsh v DPP* [2006] EWHC 1525 (Admin); [2007] Crim LR 162).

[42] As in *Marsh v DPP* [2007] Crim LR 162.

6.2.2.2 Problems with identification evidence

Allowing the police to judge whether it is practical to hold an ID procedure, albeit with court oversight at trial, is not ideal as is obvious from earlier discussions in this chapter and chapters 3–5 about the way the police exercise discretion.[43] Identification parades present particular problems. Volunteers on parades are inevitably more relaxed than suspects, and witnesses may detect this.[44] They are particularly unfair for any type of suspect who is unusual in a particular area, particularly members of ethnic minorities, since they rely on police officers being able to recruit sufficient similar comparators for the parade at short notice: people are often unaware of significant differences between individuals of different ethnic groups, and black and ethnic minorities are over-represented among the suspect population and under-represented in the police.

Some of these problems have been eased now that video identification is the default identification procedure. The police have available a large database of images, so that it is easier to use comparators who are sufficiently similar to the suspect, and Code D provides that the suspect or their lawyer must be given the opportunity to see the complete set of images before they are shown to an eye-witness (Code D, Annex A, para 7). Whilst the suspect is not permitted to be at the video-identification (think about it!), they can have their lawyer there, and the procedure must itself be audio-visually recorded so that it may be subsequently scrutinised (Code D, Annex A, para 9). So, there is some evidence that video identification is more reliable than an identification parade.[45] However, whilst some improvements are possible, this does not make video identification entirely reliable.[46]

Ensuring that the images are fairly selected can still be problematic with video identification—for example, in one case, the police used an image of the suspect, who habitually wore glasses, without those glasses. The complainant had described her attacker as not wearing glasses, and none of the comparator images were shown wearing glasses. The court found that the fact that the suspect had been asked to remove glasses did not render the procedure unfair.[47] Another problematic issue is whether a witness is an identification witness (in which case an ID procedure must normally be held) or a recognition witness (in which case an ID procedure does not have to be held).[48] Then there is the viewing of images on social media prior to formal identification procedures. Code D, Part 3(C) attempts to regulate the police release of visual images (e.g. CCTV footage) to the public in order to see whether anyone can be recognised. However, it does not regulate the situation where images circulate on social media and, as a result, someone purports to recognise a person shown on those images. Clearly the circumstances in which people recognise images on social media are not regulated (for example, a friend might suggest who the person is), and it may have an adverse impact

---

[43] For discussion, see Roberts A, 'The Problems of Mistaken Identification: Some Observations on Process' (2004) 8 *International Journal of Evidence and Proof* 100.

[44] See examples given by Tinsley Y, 'Even Better Than the Real Thing? The Case for Reform of Identification Procedures' (2001) 5 *International Journal of Evidence and Proof* 235.

[45] Valentine T and Heaton P, 'An Evaluation of the Fairness of Police Line-ups and Video Identifications' (1999) 13 *Applied Cognitive Psychology* 59.

[46] It has been argued that the use of sequential presentation of images (where the witness is required to make a decision before being shown the next image) may reduce the number of false positive identifications, but Code D requires all images to be shown at least twice before an identification is made. See Roberts A, 'Eyewitness Identification Evidence: Procedural Developments and the Ends of Adjudicative Advocacy'(2009) 6(2) *International Commentary on Evidence* 3. See also Memon H, 'Video Identification of Suspects' (2013) 7 *Policing* 3.

[47] *Day* [2019] EWCA Crim 935.

[48] See the cases referred to in Cape E, Hardcastle M and Paul S, *Defending Suspects at Police Stations* (London: LAG, 2020), at para 8.6.

on any subsequent formal identification procedure. The police and prosecution must obtain detailed evidence in relation to the initial identification.[49]

This brings us to the question of how identification evidence, and disputes over such evidence, are dealt with at court. There are two aspects to this—first, how the courts deal with cases where the Code D procedures were not properly followed and, second, how judges should guide juries on dealing with identification evidence. With regard to the first, breach of the PACE Codes is not, in itself, a ground for excluding evidence. Generally, defendants who want to argue that identification evidence should not be used at court because the police breached Code D have to persuade the court that permitting the prosecution to rely upon it would have an adverse effect on the fairness of the trial.[50] It was settled in 1998 that the critical question is not whether the police breached the code, but whether the overall purpose of the code—securing fair identification practices leading to reliable identification evidence—has been respected.[51] For example, in one case, whilst it was accepted that the failure of the police to disclose the first description given by an eye-witness to the suspect was a clear breach of Code D, para 3.1, this did not render the conviction unsafe given the strength of circumstantial evidence supporting the identification.[52]

How much weight should be given to identification evidence at trial is addressed by case law, including the requirement that trial judges warn juries about the dangers of convicting on identification evidence, especially if it is weak.[53] What does 'weak' mean? Weak in the sense of a witness not being certain, or in the sense that the witness is certain but on the basis of a fleeting glimpse? Davies, on the basis of the psychological research literature and his own experience as an expert witness, has argued that consideration be given to requiring corroboration for all identification evidence. He pointed to the large number of convictions wholly or largely on this basis that were overturned on appeal—where the convicted person may have spent months or years in prison[54]—and the large number that were not overturned, where there are at least some grounds for thinking they should be.[55] It is true that in some of the most serious cases, such as rape, there are often no witnesses other than the victim, but advances in DNA technology makes identification through scientific methods both practical and difficult for rapists to avoid if they are identified (see section 6.5).

6.3 Entry, search and seizure

It has long been recognised in English law that the tort of trespass stops everyone—including the police—entering a person's private property or searching a person without good reason prescribed by law. It does not matter if the trespass is slight, does no tangible harm, or is done without the occupier knowing of it. This is also reflected in the ECHR,

---

[49] *Alexander and McGill* [2012] EWCA Crim 2768. See the subsequent College of Policing guidance: *Internet Social Media and Identification Procedures*, available at: <http://library.college.police.uk/docs/APPREF/NVVIS-Guidance-on-Internet-Social-Media-and-Identification-Procedures.pdf> (accessed 9 October 2020).

[50] This is the ground for exclusion of evidence under PACE 1984, s.78(1).

[51] *Popat* [1998] Crim LR 825.

[52] *Cole* [2013] EWCA Crim 1149. See also *Williams* [2003] EWCA Crim 3200, discussed by Roberts (2009). He convincingly argues that where no significant adverse consequences follow the use of unreliable processes there is little incentive for the police to change their ways. The process in *Williams* could hardly have been more suggestive (showing the suspect in handcuffs).

[53] *Turnbull* [1977] 2 QB 224.   [54] See, for example, *Ali* [2009] Crim LR 40.

[55] Davies G, 'Mistaken Identification: Where Law Meets Psychology Head On' (1996) 35 *Howard Journal* 232.

Art 8, which protects privacy, including the privacy of a person's home.[56] The significance of the right to privacy is recognised in the PACE Code of Practice for search and seizure (Code B), which states that these powers 'should be fully and clearly justified before use because they may significantly interfere with the occupier's privacy. Officers should consider if the necessary objectives can be met by less intrusive means' (para 1.3). Nevertheless, police powers to search persons, and to enter and search property, and to seize potential evidence, are extensive.

The questions that arise for us are: for what reasons do the police seek to enter property and/or make searches, what counts in law as a 'good reason', and what does the law and practice tell us about criminal justice in general? In this section we will look at searches of property, but not at searches of people.[57] Street searches of people are covered in chapter 2, and searches of people arrested and detained at police stations in chapter 4. There are two types of powers to search property: those that can be carried out without a warrant issued by a court, and those that can only be carried out on the authority of a court warrant.[58] The former are mostly confined to circumstances where the police want to enter premises in order to arrest a person or that are occupied or controlled by a person who has been arrested. In general, powers of entry (whether by warrant or not) allow search of premises but not of people on those premises unless *either* the premises are those to which the public has access (in which case stop-search powers can be exercised) *or* the relevant people are or have been arrested. However, some legislation granting a power of entry does permit search of people (e.g. search of school premises under the Criminal Justice Act 1988, s.139B, which can be conducted without a warrant), although sometimes only if the warrant specifically authorises this (e.g. search warrants issued under the Misuse of Drugs Act 1971, s.23(3)).

There is a range of reasons why the police may want to enter property; for example, to prevent a breach of the peace (not dealt with here), to 'bug' it (see section 6.4), to search it for evidence of crime, or to arrest a person they suspect is on the property. For many years, entry, search and arrest were regarded, from a legal point of view, as similar since all three can amount to trespass (to the person or to property), and so a warrant was needed in all but exceptional circumstances. As with arrest warrants, search warrants have become increasingly rare since—in accordance with criminal justice policy in general and crime control ideology—the police have been given ever more power to make decisions free of judicial oversight. Even before PACE was enacted in 1984, warrants were used in only about 17% of searches. Now, it appears, warranted searches are used even less often, although statistics on search of property are not routinely collected or published.[59] Nevertheless, search warrants are still significant, not just because they are used a lot by comparison with arrest warrants, but also because they tell us something about the value placed on the sanctity of private property as opposed to the value placed on personal integrity, and about the limited potential for judicial oversight of investigative powers.

---

[56] For a discussion of the history and constitutional background of the law, see Sharpe (2000: ch 1).

[57] For a detailed and up-to-date account of the law, see Ormerod D and Perry D (eds), *Blackstone's Criminal Practice 2021* (Oxford: OUP, 2020) paras D1.96 and D1.147–D1.185, and for more extended treatment (although a little out of date), Stone R, *The Law of Entry, Search and Seizure* (Oxford: OUP, 2013). Note that there are many powers of entry, search and seizure in addition to those described in this section, and that many central and local government departments, and some private institutions, have powers to seek search warrants.

[58] A recent report by the Law Commission provides an extensive account of search warrant powers, and makes extensive recommendations for reform: Law Commission, *Search Warrants* HC 852, October 2020.

[59] Brown (1997: 34); Clark D, *Bevan and Lidstone's The Investigation of Crime* (London: LexisNexis, 2004) p 122.

6.3.1 **Entry and search without consent**

6.3.1.1 **To make an arrest (without a search warrant)**

PACE, s.17 empowers the police to enter any premises to arrest a person for an indictable offence. This may be where the police have seen a person suspected of committing an offence enter the building, or where they have received information to that effect.[60] The section also provides for a power to enter and search premises to execute a search warrant, to 'save life and limb' or prevent serious damage to property,[61] to recapture someone 'unlawfully at large' (e.g. a prison escapee), and for certain other purposes specified in the section. No search warrant is needed, and it would often be impractical to require one—when, for example, the police are in hot pursuit of someone they or a witness thought they saw committing an offence. Sometimes they will have an arrest warrant when seeking someone for an indictable offence or who is unlawfully at large, or for other reasons (e.g. because of unpaid fines, breach of injunction, or failure to answer a court summons), so s.17 also allows them to enter premises to execute that warrant. Generally, a police officer must have reasonable grounds for believing that the person they are seeking is on the premises (s.17(2)), and the test for reasonableness is similar to that which applies in respect of stop-search and arrest (dealt with in chapters 2 and 3); although there is case law suggesting that 'reasonable grounds for believing' is a higher threshold than 'reasonable grounds for suspecting'.[62] However, the threshold is low,[63] and there is no need for the evidence on which it is based to be admissible in court, nor for it to be corroborated. A tip-off from an informer, for example, may in some circumstances be adequate, and—according to a sergeant in charge of a local drugs squad in conversation with one of the authors and also confirmed by recent research—frequently this is the sole basis for a raid, 'especially if this tip-off needed to be acted upon immediately and indicated that the target and evidence linking them to a drug offence would be present at the time of execution'.[64] However, in many cases, this tip-off may also be combined with police intelligence—either police or citizen-generated—not because of concerns for suspects' privacy and the disruption that a 'police raid' may cause, but because the police do not wish to go away 'empty handed'.[65]

6.3.1.2 **After arrest (without a search warrant) (PACE, s.32 and s.18)**

People who are arrested other than at a police station may be searched at once.[66] Also the premises in which they were arrested, or left immediately before they were arrested (whoever happens to own or occupy it), may be entered and searched if the suspected offence is indictable.[67] This power enables the police to search for evidence relating to the suspected offence in question but only if there are reasonable grounds for believing that there is such evidence there.[68] Whilst a 's.32 search' need not be done immediately following an arrest, it must be carried out promptly. The police are not allowed to return to the premises to

---

[60] Note that a police officer would normally have to have reasonable grounds for suspecting the person has committed an offence, and reasonable grounds for believing that arrest is necessary. See ch 3.
[61] Which covers saving someone from themselves as well as saving from a third party: *Baker v CPS* [2008] EWHC 299 (Admin).
[62] *Eastenders Cash & Carry PLC v South Western Magistrates' Court* [2011] EWHC 937 (Admin); *Rashid v Chief Constable of West Yorkshire Police* [2020] EWHC 2522.
[63] See, in respect of reasonable suspicion for arrest, *Armstrong v Chief Constable of West Yorkshire Police* [2008] EWCA Civ 1582, and *Alford v Chief Constable of Cambridgeshire Police* [2009] EWCA Civ 100.
[64] Bacon M, *Taking Care of Business: Police Detectives, Drug Law Enforcement and Proactive Investigation* (Oxford: OUP, 2016) pp 200. [65] Ibid.
[66] PACE, s.32(1) and (2)(a). [67] PACE, s.32(2)(b). [68] PACE, s.32(6).

search it hours later.[69] A s.32 search does not require judicial approval, and neither does it require authorisation by a senior police officer.

However, the requirement for promptness under s.32 may not inhibit the police much because under PACE, s.18, they have power to search *any* premises occupied or controlled by someone arrested for an indictable offence for evidence relating to the suspected offence in question or an offence connected with, or similar to, it. The power is subject to the usual 'reasonable grounds' provision and, like s.32, it can be exercised immediately after arrest, but more usually while the suspect is detained in the police station. In the latter case it must be authorised in writing by an officer of at least the rank of inspector. In the late 1990s most searches were apparently conducted under PACE s.18, and this is probably still true (Brown, 1997: 34).

Since searches under PACE s.32 or s.18 do not involve any judicial supervision and, in the former case, can be carried out without even authorisation by a senior officer, it is evident that use of these powers is likely to be more attractive to police officers than applying for a search warrant. In 2017 the High Court held that the safeguards involved in a warranted search should not be circumvented by the police arresting a person with the principle purpose of carrying out a search under either of those two sections.[70] However, within a year, in another case the High Court, in effect, back-tracked and held that provided arrest was legally justified, the police have a choice as to whether to apply for a warrant or use a non-warrant search power.[71] It is easy to guess which may be more attractive to the police.

6.3.1.3 In other circumstances (with a warrant)

The police may seek warrants when they are looking for evidence to assist in the detection of a suspected crime, or the construction of a prosecution case, but have not yet made an arrest. They also sometimes need to seek a warrant because a substantial amount of time has elapsed since an arrest or because they want to search premises not occupied, controlled or recently vacated by an arrestee (see earlier). Warrants can be obtained, in other words, to search premises occupied by people who are not suspected of any crime at all.

There are around 176 different statutory provisions regarding search warrants, but the most commonly used power is under PACE, s.8, which is available where the suspected offence is 'indictable'.[72] The statutory provisions are supplemented by PACE Code of Practice B. Applications for search warrants under s.8 are made to a justice of the peace (magistrate). Applications must specify the grounds for the application, the enactment under which the warrant would be granted, the premises to be searched, and the articles and persons sought (as far as practical).

If the application is for a warrant authorising entry and search on more than one occasion, the grounds for applying for such a warrant must be set out. If the application is for a warrant covering more than one set of premises, each set of premises must be specified; but it is possible for an application to be for an 'all premises' warrant, that is, all premises occupied or controlled by a specified person.[73] There have been many cases where magistrates have issued warrants without these requirements being fully satisfied. When challenged, the High Court has often been very critical of both the police and the magistrates—for example, where a warrant to search a pub specified 'search for drugs and

---

[69] *Badham* [1987] Crim LR 202. In *R (Hewitson) v Chief Constable of Dorset Police* [2003] EWHC 3296 (Admin) a gap of 2 hours and 10 minutes was held to be too long.

[70] *R (TL) v Chief Constable of Surrey Police* [2017] EWHC 129 (Admin).

[71] *R (Virdee) v NCA* [2018] EWHC 1119 (Admin).

[72] For a full account of search warrant powers see Law Commission, *Search Warrants* HC 852 October 2020.

[73] PACE, s.15.

associated paraphernalia' but did not mention search of anyone working or drinking there. A customer who was injured while being restrained prior to search was held to have been unlawfully assaulted by the police because holding him to search him was not authorised by the warrant.[74]

Applications should normally be authorised by an officer of at least the rank of an inspector.[75] Code B provides that before making an application, the officer making the application must take reasonable steps to check that information on which the application is based is accurate, recent, and not provided maliciously or irresponsibly. An application should not be based on anonymous information unless corroboration has been sought. Furthermore, the officer must make reasonable enquiries to establish whether anything is known about the likely occupier of the premises, the nature of the premises, and whether they have been searched before.[76] Despite these protective provisions, searches can still be conducted in such a way as to leave people feeling harassed. PACE, s.16(4) provides that searches must be conducted at a reasonable hour.[77] The 'reasonable hour' provision was an attempt to curb the police habit of raiding homes in the middle of the night, as this can be terrifying for the occupants, who may include young children. But since it has been decided that a 6 a.m. raid was not 'unreasonable' because the early hour made it likely the householder(s) would be at home,[78] the police are not likely to be overly restrained by this provision. In any case, s.16(4) goes on to provide that the 'reasonable hour' requirement may be circumvented if 'it appears to the constable executing it that the purpose of a search may be frustrated on an entry at a reasonable hour'. The spectre thus arises of repeated midnight raids on the homes of suspects, some of whom will be completely innocent of any crime. According to the drugs squad sergeant cited earlier, raids for drugs, at any rate, were always made in the early hours when the occupants were likely to be asleep and thus unable to flush drugs down the toilet, which again has been confirmed in recent research.[79]

The provisions described are applicable to all requests for search warrants except where certain categories of material are sought. Before issuing a warrant under PACE, s.8, a justice of the peace must have reasonable grounds for believing:

(a) the material sought will be of substantial value and admissible as evidence;

(b) the material sought is not one of various special categories of material (see later); and

(c) it is not practical to secure entry by consent without the purpose of the search being frustrated or prejudiced (e.g. through the concealment or destruction of the evidence).

The police need not show that other methods of obtaining the material were unsuccessfully tried, nor that such methods had been considered and rejected because they were bound to fail.[80] In other words, if the police say that they reasonably believe that they will need the power to enter without consent there is little magistrates can do to probe further—this virtual police self-certification is a classic crime control provision. Hence, research shows that the police tend to regard the warrant application process as little more than a 'rubber stamping' exercise in which they cut and paste information between applications that have been used previously and in which they are on first-name terms with the

---

[74] *Chief Constable of Thames Valley v Hepburn* [2002] EWCA Civ 1841. See also *R (Lees) v Solihull Magistrates' Court* [2013] EWHC 3779 (Admin) and *R (Cheema) v Nottingham and Newark Magistrates' Court* [2013] EWHC 3790 (Admin). [75] Code B, para 3.4.
[76] Code B, paras 3.1 and 3.3. [77] PACE, s.16(4).
[78] *Kent Pharmaceuticals Ltd v Director of the SFO* [2002] EWHC 3023. [79] Bacon (2016: 203).
[80] *Billericay Justices ex parte Frank Harris (Coaches) Ltd* [1991] Crim LR 559.

magistrates authorising the applications who are thus easily amenable to police persuasion (e.g. about the supposed infallibility of the intelligence), should the magistrate initially look to turn the application down.[81] In addition to these s.8 powers, many other statutes allow magistrates to issue search warrants for specific offences. Many of these are not particularly serious—they include theft, controlled drugs, obscene publications, forgery and counterfeiting, criminal damage, offensive weapons, and numerous others that are fairly minor.[82]

There is little, if any, recent research on search warrants. Research in the past has, not surprisingly, found that virtually all applications for warrants—over 99%—were granted.[83] Thus Lidstone (1984) found that in only four out of 32 applications that were observed did the magistrates ask any questions of the police, a finding that has been recently confirmed in relation to warrants for drug related offences by Bacon.[84] Magistrates and judges are hampered in their ability to genuinely check on the police as all the information they receive is from the police. Hearings are *ex parte* (i.e. with the other party excluded). The property sought is often described vaguely (e.g. 'electrical goods'). Moreover, as noted earlier, the majority of applications state, in a formulaic manner, that they are based on 'information received'. This, as will be seen in section 6.4, means information from one or more informants, and magistrates and judges are reluctant to risk blowing informants' cover, which the police would refuse to divulge anyway.[85] The nature of information from informants is such that the police also frequently do not know how reliable the information is, such as when the police were given information about a person suspected of armed robbery allegedly connected with two addresses. The police obtained search warrants, broke in to one of them with a battering ram at 7am, and found a completely innocent family lived there. Had the police made the most basic enquiries—e.g. of the electoral roll—they would have discovered this. The magistrates who granted the warrant asked if the officers were confident the information was accurate and they assured them that their grounds were reasonable. The Court of Appeal held that the negligence of the officers neither invalidated the warrant nor gave cause for any other action.[86]

Forty years ago, the Royal Commission on Criminal Procedure (RCCP) said, 'too often they [magistrates] merely rubber stamp police requests [for warrants].'[87] In order to rectify this, the Commission recommended that responsibility for issuing most warrants should be given to judges, but this was not implemented by the government. The lack of due process control over the police in this area of work was clearly of little concern to the government then, and so it has remained ever since. Some attempt to regulate search warrants more effectively has been made by revisions to the Criminal Procedure Rules. For example, they require that the courts allocate sufficient time to dealing with warrant applications, and that the 'gist' of questions and replies at warrant hearings are recorded.[88] However, neither PACE nor the Criminal Procedure Rules require that the courts provide and record reasons why the conditions for issuing a warrant are satisfied. We saw earlier that both the police and magistrates often fail to comply with the legal requirements regarding the issuing of warrants. In one case, in 2014, the Lord Chief Justice said that it was 'time that the message was brought home clearly' to the police that they must comply

---

[81] Bacon (2016: 202–203).
[82] For a list of such powers, see Law Commission, *Search Warrants: Consultation Paper* Consultation Paper 235, 5 June 2018, Sch 1.   [83] Clark (2004: 123).
[84] Bacon (2016: 202–203).   [85] Lidstone (1984). See Brown (1997: 33) for similar findings.
[86] *Keegan v Chief Constable of Merseyside Police* [2003] 1 WLR 2187. The ECtHR subsequently found that Art 8 was violated because, although the police were not acting maliciously, their actions were not necessary in a democratic society because their misconception could have been avoided with proper precautions (*Keegan v UK* (2007) 44 EHRR 33).
[87] RCCP, *Report* (1981) para 3.37.   [88] Rule 47.25.

with the duty of full disclosure, and to the court service that it must make the necessary resources available so that applications can be dealt with properly.[89] In another case in the same year, the High Court quashed warrants because of a 'lamentable failure to observe the guidance given by the courts',[90] and in yet another case that year the court set aside a warrant on the grounds that there had been a manifest failure by the applicants to provide full and frank information.[91] Despite this, the remedies for those who are the subject of search warrants, especially those who do not have significant financial resources, are limited. Most of the cases referred to here are judicial review cases, which are expensive to conduct.[92] Furthermore, it has been held that the test for setting aside a warrant on the grounds that the police failed to disclose relevant information to the magistrate 'is whether the information it is alleged should have been given to the magistrate might reasonably have led him to refuse to issue the warrant'.[93] In any event, in a criminal trial, the mere fact that evidence has been obtained unlawfully does not mean that it will necessarily be excluded (see further chapter 11).

In 2018, the Law Commission, at the request of the Home Office, issued a consultation paper on search warrants. The terms of reference were to rationalise and streamline the law, identify and address pressing problems, and make the legislation more transparent in order to reduce the scope for errors.[94] The Commission's final report, published in October 2020, is almost 600 pages long and makes 64 recommendations.[95] It identifies procedural inefficiency, frequent errors, and inadequate safeguards as major problems with the current regime, but also suggests that law enforcement agencies lack sufficient powers, particularly in respect of electronic material. It remains to be seen what, if any, action the government takes to implement the Commission's recommendations, and whether it will respect, in the Commission's words, 'the proper balance between the powers of the state and the rights and freedoms of individuals'.[96]

6.3.2 **Seizure without consent**

The police have wide powers to seize *almost* anything that they have reasonable grounds for believing has been obtained as a result of crime or which may be evidence of crime. We saw earlier that searches may be made only for evidence of crimes related to those for which arrest has been made, or for which warrants were issued. However, provided the police are lawfully on any premises, they can seize anything that they have reasonable grounds for believing has been obtained in consequence of the commission of an offence, or that is evidence in relation to an offence.[97] The common law went some way towards this extreme crime control position,[98] and PACE and other legislation, and case law, has continued on that path.[99] All that Code B states, by way of limitation, is that if PACE and the Code are not adhered to, evidence gained may be 'open to question'.[100] It has been held that property that has been unlawfully seized cannot be lawfully re-seized when it is

---

[89] *R (Golfrate) v Crown Court at Southwark* [2014] EWHC 840 (Admin).
[90] *Sweeney v Westminster Magistrates' Court* [2014] EWHC 2168 (Admin).
[91] *R (Mills) v Sussex Police* [2014] EWHC 2523 (Admin).
[92] According to the Law Commission, between 2010 and 2018 there were 50 judicial review cases concerning search powers. See Law Commission, *Search Warrants: Consultation Paper* Consultation Paper 235, 5 June 2018, para 1.2.   [93] *R (Mills) v Sussex Police* [2014] EWHC 2523 (Admin).
[94] Law Commission, *Search Warrants: Consultation Paper* Consultation Paper 235, 5 June 2018.
[95] Law Commission, *Search Warrants* HC 852, October 2020.   [96] Ibid, p 4.
[97] PACE, s.19.   [98] *Jeffrey v Black* [1978] QB 490.
[99] E.g. *HM Customs & Excise v Michael Atkinson and others* [2003] EWHC 421. See generally, Sharpe (2000: chs 2, 3).   [100] Code B, para 1.5.

taken to a police station on the basis that the officer is then lawfully on those premises.[101] However, from the police perspective there may be a work-around by applying to a judge to authorise retention under the Criminal Justice and Police Act 2001, s.59(5)(b).[102] To cater for circumstances where the police are not sure whether material comes within their power of seizure, the law permits them to seize the whole or part of a suspect item so that they can subsequently determine whether or not it falls within the power.[103] These 'seize and sift' powers are further enhanced where seizable property cannot reasonably practicably be separated from something else which is not seizable (for example, a computer hard disk containing some seizable information and some which is non-seizable); in this case, the police can seize the whole thing, and work out later what they can keep and what should be returned.[104]

The word 'almost' was emphasised at the beginning of the previous paragraph because there are three categories of material in respect of which seizure is closely controlled and for which the police cannot obtain ordinary search warrants.[105]

6.3.2.1 Items subject to legal privilege

These are communications between a legal advisor and a client or anything relating to actual or planned legal proceedings.[106] This material cannot be lawfully seized. However, if the police doubt claims that material falls into this category they may seize it for detailed inspection and return that which is not seizable, although inspection should be carried out by someone independent of the police.[107]

6.3.2.2 Excluded material

This consists of material that is held in confidence, and which consist of personal records held in the course of a legitimate business or trade (e.g. records held by members of the clergy, banks or doctors), human tissue or tissue fluid taken for medical reasons, and journalistic material consisting of documents or records.[108]

6.3.2.3 Special procedure material

This includes journalistic material not covered above and other material held in confidence.

Seizure of, and applications to search for, 'excluded material' and 'special procedure material' must be authorised by a judge. This must normally be done on an *inter partes* basis. In other words, the person or institution in possession of the material (as opposed to the owner of the material) must be notified of the application, and all of the information on which the applicant intends to rely must be made available to them.[109] The person or institution in possession must not conceal, destroy, alter or dispose of the material without leave of the judge or written permission from the police. There is a complex set of conditions, governed by PACE, Sch 1, that must be satisfied in order for a judge to make an order for access to 'excluded' or 'special procedure material', and the judge must be satisfied that it is in the public interest to make to order.

Generally, then, the *owners* (as opposed to those who are in possession of it) of 'excluded' and 'special procedure' material are little or no better able to contest seizure of material they may wish to keep from public gaze than owners of 'normal' material for which search

---

[101] *R (Cook) v SOCA* [2010] EWHC 2119 (Admin).
[102] *R (El-Kurd) v Winchester Crown Court* [2011] EWHC 1853 (Admin).
[103] Criminal Justice and Police Act 2001, s.50.
[104] Criminal Justice and Police Act 2001, ss.50–70 and Code B, paras 7.7–7.13.
[105] PACE, s.9 and Sch 1.   [106] PACE, s.10.
[107] Criminal Justice and Police Act 2001, s.53, and see *R (McKenzie) v Director of the SFO* [2016] EWHC 102 (Admin).   [108] PACE, ss.11–13.
[109] *R (British Sky Broadcasting Ltd) v Central Criminal Court* [2011] EWHC 3451 (Admin).

warrants are sought. Arguably such people are less well off, as at least people whose premises are searched for 'normal' material know when that has happened and can challenge it after the event. Owners of 'excluded' and 'special procedure' material may not know that their material has been seized at all. On the other hand, more stringent conditions apply than with 'normal' material, particularly in the case of 'excluded material'. In relation to both types of material, only in exceptional circumstances (similar to those applicable to a s.8 warrant) can a warrant be sought and granted *ex parte*.[110]

It is worth considering why such complex procedures are in place for these relatively obscure categories of material. Most searches for, and seizure of, material in these categories relate to financial crime. Access to such material was very difficult prior to PACE, making enforcement of the law in respect of fraud very difficult. These provisions have, therefore, made the enforcement of fraud law easier than before, but still difficult, when fraud is difficult enough to enforce as it is. Perpetrators of fraud are generally wealthy individuals and companies, while perpetrators of assault, theft and other crimes are generally relatively poor and socially marginalised members of society. Bearing in mind the themes of chapters 2, 3, and 10, the pattern that emerges is so obvious we will not labour the point.[111]

6.3.3 Entry, search and seizure with 'consent'

It was stated earlier that the police should seek to search property by consent if this is practical. Even when the police have a search warrant, they should seek entry from the occupier, declaring their identity and authority, unless there are reasonable grounds to believe that this would obstruct the purpose of the search or endanger anyone.[112] There is historical evidence that the police often rely on the latter,[113] and according to the drugs squad sergeant cited earlier, he never sought entry by consent, but always smashed the door in, to prevent drugs being flushed away. When asked about the presence of children who might be terrified or injured by this, he said they always carry out a 'risk assessment': 'looking through the letter box—and then smashing the door in!' Officers in Bacon's research also talked about doing 'a recce', though this was not because of concerns about children at the address; rather they sought to find the best approach routes and methods of entry and also any escape routes, so that they could protect themselves and ensure that they did not leave empty-handed.[114]

Research evidence from the 1980s and 1990s found that around one-third of all searches were by consent. Unfortunately, statistics on search powers are not routinely collected and there is no recent research available. As with stop-search, the nature of 'consent' when sought 'in the shadow of the law' is often questionable. Many people doubtless allow the police to search their homes, believing that the police have the power to do so, or to get a warrant to do so, when this may not be so.

---

[110] For a detailed discussion of this complex area of law, see Stone R, *The Law of Entry, Search and Seizure* (Oxford: OUP, 2013). For critical comment see Zuckerman A, 'The Weakness of the PACE Special Procedure for Protecting Confidential Material' [1990] *Criminal Law Review* 472. The law has changed little since this was written.

[111] As for the restrictions on seizing journalistic material, the explanation here lies in the lobbying that newspapers engaged in during the run up to PACE to maximise the degree of protection for their own interests. Whilst protection of journalistic sources may well be regarded as, and is, important nevertheless one can see that criminal justice reflects the interests of those who are powerful enough to make their voices heard in political debates.

[112] Code B, paras 6.4–6.8.   [113] Brown (1997: 36–38).   [114] Bacon (2016: 202).

The problem here is not simply deception of suspects (who may, in some cases, have been arrested primarily to facilitate a search), but also the circumvention of the legal safeguards described earlier. Whereas the current version of Code A (for stop-search) prevents searches with consent where there is no power to search (see discussion in chapter 2), Code B (for entry and search of premises) has no equivalent provision. Consent should, if practicable, be given in writing, and the person asked for consent should be told that they do not have to consent.[115]

However, as we know from chapters 2 and 3, police working rules, rather than formal legal rules such as 'reasonable suspicion', frequently form the basis of police decision-making. So, to the extent that entry and search rules are inhibitory, the police may seek to circumvent them. In *Sanghera*,[116] for example, a postmaster reported an alleged robbery. Acting on what seems to have been a hunch, the police conducted a thorough 'consensual' search of the premises and found that the allegedly stolen money had been hidden by the 'victim'. This case also illustrates the need to obtain an explicit consent (if no warrant has been obtained or if there is no statutory power to search without warrant) rather than an implied consent, for the police completed an authorisation for the search and ticked the 'consent' box but omitted to obtain the alleged victim's actual consent. The Court of Appeal held that even though the victim would doubtless have consented to a search, the search was illegal without it. This finding was of little use to the appellant, however, as the Court took the view that since there was no question as to the reliability of the evidence seized, the conviction should be upheld. This approach to the admissibility of illegally obtained evidence does little to deter the police from abusing their powers. A further problem with 'consent' searches is that since the police are 'lawfully on property', they can seize property without the occupier's consent.[117]

6.3.4 Case studies and conclusions

In 2002 about 20 police officers entered and searched the Stormont (NI Assembly) offices of Sinn Fein. Official sources claimed that the aim was to break an Irish Republican spy ring, and that Sinn Fein had collected confidential information that would be used to target police and prison officers. Four people were charged with various offences, but all charges were dropped in December 2005. It then emerged that one of those charged, Denis Donaldson, a senior Sinn Fein official, was an undercover member of the security services. Rather than Sinn Fein spying on the government, it seems, the government had been spying on democratically elected members of a regional legislature. We have here entry, search and seizure based on faulty information from an undercover agent and informer. And, according to an official inquiry, no one was to blame and no official agencies did anything illegal.[118] The murky morality and dangers inherent in this area of 'policing' could scarcely be better illustrated. In another example, from 2009, the police searched the House of Commons offices of Damian Green MP. The police did not obtain a warrant but instead put the Sergeant-at-Arms under 'considerable pressure' to consent to the search—the police having left her with the impression that otherwise she would be obstructing a serious criminal investigation. The police seem not to have made it clear to her that there was no obligation to consent to a search without a warrant which, as we have seen, is required where a person has not been arrested. As the Sergeant-at-Arms put it: 'At no time was I informed that I did not have to give my consent or that I could insist on

---

[115] Code, B paras 5.1 and 5.2. [116] *Sanghera* [2001] 1 Cr App R 299.
[117] PACE, s.19(2) and (3), and see section 6.3.2. [118] *The Guardian*, 20 December 2005.

a warrant or that I could withdraw my consent at any time.'[119] The police were searching for evidence relating to leaks of confidential government information, but the CPS subsequently decided that there was insufficient evidence to prosecute Mr Green and the Home Office official allegedly involved. The police were, nevertheless, exonerated by an internal Metropolitan police inquiry.[120]

The experience of having one's house broken into in the early hours by people in plain clothes not immediately identifiable as police officers (as sometimes happens) is often distressing and sometimes terrifying. *Murray v Minister of Defence*[121] is just one example. This is particularly important as the people at the receiving end are often not merely thought guilty but actually innocent (as with many stopped and searched, arrested and detained people), but also sometimes not even believed to be guilty: as we have seen, the police are entitled to seek warrants to search the premises of entirely innocent people if they believe that evidence of criminal offences will be found there. The same applies when they pursue people who they seek to arrest. And even if the person(s) they seek are guilty, the premises where they live that are searched often have friends and family living there who are innocent.[122]

As we have seen, the police have extensive powers to search property and to seize material that they find, both with warrants obtained from a court and without warrants. In relation to the latter there is no judicial supervision of the decision to conduct a search or to seize material unless or until the search is subsequently challenged by way of judicial review or in criminal proceedings. With regard to warranted searches, we have seen that whilst they appear to be closely regulated, both by legislation and by PACE, Code B, the regulation is often ineffective in that (judging by the number of judicial review cases) warrants appear to be frequently granted on the basis of inadequate information from the police, and without the magistrates and judges concerned keeping adequate records of the information on which their decisions are based or of the reasons for their decisions. Enforcement of the legislative protections is difficult and patchy. Given the general principle that evidence is not inadmissible simply because it has been obtained illegally, whether evidence obtained in consequence of an unlawful search, or unlawfully seized, is excluded at trial depends upon whether the court determines, under PACE, s.78, that it is so unfair to allow the prosecution to use it that it ought not to be admitted. In the case of 'real' evidence, the temptation for the court is to take the view that, whilst unlawfully obtained, you cannot argue with the fact that such evidence was found.[123] The alternative method of challenge, by way of judicial review proceedings, is also problematic (see chapter 11). The availability of this remedy depends, to a large extent, on the financial resources of the applicant and, as we have seen, even if the search or seizure is found to be unlawful this will not necessarily result in the court ordering the return of the material to the person to whom it belongs.

6.4 Covert policing

In this section we will deal with a number of forms of covert policing. The use of the term 'covert' indicates that it is policing that is carried out in a manner that is calculated to ensure that the person or persons who are the subject of the policing are not aware that

---

[119] House of Commons, Minutes of Evidence taken before the Committee on Issue of Privilege (Police Searches on the Parliamentary Estate), 7 December 2009, Q.701.

[120] *The Telegraph*, 16 April 2009.   [121] [1988] 2 All ER 521, discussed in ch 3.

[122] For an example, where the police obtained a search warrant to search the house of criminal defence lawyers who were related to the person the police were seeking, and where the police had not disclosed this to the magistrates, see *R (AB and CD) v Huddersfield Magistrates' Court* [2014] EWHC 1089 (Admin).

[123] For examples of the general approach to PACE, s.78, see *R v Walsh* (1989) 91 Cr App R 161 and *R v Keenan* [1989] 3 All ER 598.

it is taking place. This definition is taken from the definition of covert surveillance in the Regulation of Investigatory Powers Act (RIPA) 2000, s.26(9).[124] However, it can also be used to describe other forms of covert policing and investigation such as the interception of communication, and the use of police informants and other covert human intelligence sources (CHIS) which, together with covert surveillance, will be covered in this section. It is important to recognise that whilst such methods may be used in order to investigate particular crimes, they are often used to gather intelligence which may, or may not, be used to investigate and prosecute individuals. This means that a person may never know that they have been the subject of covert policing, and thus this form of policing raises questions of transparency, accountability and privacy in particularly acute ways. There has also been growing recognition of the ways in which covert policing and investigation have become normalised, in the face of greater scrutiny of visible forms of policing. It has slowly come to assume the status of 'police operational orthodoxy'. Though it has not surpassed uniformed, visible policing, it has 'come to occupy and absorb important spheres of the police organization and the cultural domain. Covert investigation is a key feature of late modern policing, empowered by the creation of a bureaucratic infrastructure initially designed for exceptional requirements and demands'.[125]

The forms of covert policing we will cover in this section are primarily regulated by RIPA 2000. This legislation was largely prompted by two factors. The first was the significant technological developments that had taken place since the Interception of Communications Act 1985 that, as the name suggests, was limited in scope. The second factor was the Human Rights Act 1998, which made the European Convention on Human Rights domestically 'enforceable'.[126] In *Halford v UK*[127] the ECtHR found the UK to be in breach of the ECHR, Art 8 in respect of interception of a telephone communication in the course of its transmission by a private system, since it was not regulated by law. It was also (correctly) anticipated that the ECtHR would find against the UK in respect of the use of a secret listening device placed on the wall of a private house, which was also not regulated by law.[128] As well as regulating the interception of telecommunications, covert surveillance and CHIS, RIPA 2000 provided for the creation of a number of codes of practice dealing with these in more detail, and for the creation of a number of commissioners with oversight functions. In the intervening years there have been a number of changes. In particular, the Investigatory Powers Act 2016 replaced the interception of communications regime formerly governed by RIPA 2000, and the various commissioners established by RIPA 2000 were replaced by one, Investigatory Powers Commissioner. Nevertheless, overall the regulatory structure remains very similar to that established in 2000.

We will not be dealing with CCTV in any depth, partly because it is not subject to the same regulatory regime as other forms of covert policing dealt with here—in fact, it is hardly regulated at all—and also because it raises many issues and we cannot afford for the book to be any longer! However, it has become an increasingly important form of public surveillance, particularly in city centres and on major roads. CCTV has become a major element of the 'information' and 'security' society,[129] and the UK is the 'world capital' of

---

[124] For a critical discussion of RIPA 2000 following its introduction, see Akdeniz Y, 'Regulation of Investigatory Powers Act 2000: Part 1: bigbrother.gov.uk: State Surveillance in the Age of Information and Rights' [2001] *Criminal Law Review* 73.

[125] Loftus B, 'Normalizing Covert Surveillance: The Subterranean World of Policing' (2019) 70 *British Journal of Sociology* 2070–2091, 2085.

[126] Also relevant was the Telecoms Data Protection Directive (97/66/EC), which was adopted by the European Community in December 1997, and which required Member States to ensure the confidentiality of communications made by means of public telecommunications networks and services.

[127] (1997) 24 EHRR 523.   [128] *Khan v UK* Application no 35394/97 ECtHR 12 May 2000.

[129] Lyon D, *Surveillance Society: Monitoring Everyday Life* (Buckingham: Open University Press, 2001); Coleman R, *Reclaiming the Streets: Surveillance, Social Control and the City* (Cullompton: Willan, 2004).

CCTV, with pretty much everyone being recorded repeatedly whilst going about their daily business.[130] Whilst CCTV cameras are usually both owned and managed by non-police agencies, and often by private companies and individuals, CCTV is used in conjunction with 'regular' policing by facilitating 'targeting'—of offenders, types of situation and events (such as football matches) and areas—by, for example, 'flagging up' particular people who are programmed into the CCTV system.[131] Of particular concern in recent years has been the use by the police of facial recognition technology, even though there is evidence that it often leads to false identification.[132] CCTV can give early warning to the police of gatherings that could turn violent, and when crimes are reported as having been committed in the vicinity of CCTV cameras one of the first things the police do is to look through the recordings for evidence. This is often with some success, but there are also dangers from the false confidence it gives some people—police officers and civilians—that they have made an accurate identification.[133] CCTV images are often very poor yet, as noted, this form of public surveillance is hardly regulated by law, although evidence produced as a result can be used in trials.[134]

6.4.1 Interception of communications

The Investigatory Powers Act (IPA)[135] 2016, s.3 makes it an offence to intentionally intercept communications in the course of their transmission unless this is lawfully authorised. In addition, s 11 creates an offence of unauthorised obtaining of communications data. The main circumstances in which an interception is lawful are:

- consent—where both the sender and the intended recipient consent to its interception (s.44);[136]

- participant monitoring—where the communication is sent by, or intended for, a person who has consented to the interception and it is authorised under RIPA 2000 Part II or its Scottish equivalent (s.44);

---

[130] Lyon D, *Surveillance Studies: An Overview* (Cambridge: Polity Press, 2007) p 39. See 'Surveillance fears for the UK', BBC News, 4 May 2009, for comment on the coupling of CCTV with face-recognition algorithms and other surveillance technology.

[131] Norris et al (eds), *Surveillance, CCTV and Social Control* (Aldershot: Ashgate, 1999); Goold B, *CCTV and Policing* (Oxford: OUP, 2004).

[132] 'Met police deploy live facial recognition technology' *The Guardian*, 11 February 2020, and see Fussey P and Murray D, *Independent Report on the London Metropolitan Police Service's Trial of Live Facial Recognition Technology*, July 2019, available at: <https://48ba3m4eh2bf2sksp43rq8kk-wpengine.netdna-ssl.com/wp-content/uploads/2019/07/London-Met-Police-Trial-of-Facial-Recognition-Tech-Report.pdf> (accessed 9 October 2020).

[133] Levesley T and Martin A, *Police Attitudes to and use of CCTV* (Home Office On-Line Report 09/05); Costigan R, 'Identification from CCTV: The Risk of Injustice' [2007] *Criminal Law Review* 591. See further section 6.2.2. Note other negative findings, including the displacement effects of CCTV, that are often ignored: Lyon (2007: 39).

[134] For an example of some of the consequent problems see *Chaney* [2009] Crim LR 437 and commentary at 438.

[135] For a full account of the IPA, see McKay S, *Blackstone's Guide to the Investigatory Powers Act 2016* (Oxford: OUP, 2018).

[136] Note, in relation to data, that the Information Commissioner has criticised the police regarding the extent of mobile phone data extraction in the course of criminal investigations. The police sometimes tell complainants, especially those complaining of sexual offences, that they will not investigate unless the complainant gives their consent to this. See Information Commissioner's Office, *Mobile phone data extraction by police forces in England and Wales: Investigation Report*, June 2020, available at <https://ico.org.uk/media/about-the-ico/documents/2617838/ico-report-on-mpe-in-england-and-wales-v1_1.pdf> (accessed 10 October 2020). Indeed, many such cases are dropped: *The Guardian*, 17 June 2020.

- warrant—neither party consents, but it is authorised by a warrant from the Secretary of State and approved by a Judicial Commissioner (the 'double-lock' procedure) (IPA 2016 Part 2).

A primary concern regarding the warrant procedure under RIPA 2000 was that warrants were issued by a government minister (the Secretary of State). Under the IPA 2016 this is still the case, but in order for it to be valid, a warrant must also be approved by a Judicial Commissioner. For the Secretary of State to issue a warrant he or she must be satisfied that it is necessary in the interests of national security, for the purpose of preventing or detecting serious crime, or in the interests of the economic well-being of the UK. A Judicial Commissioner can only approve a warrant if satisfied that the Secretary of State has applied the criteria for issuing a warrant in accordance with the standards that would apply when considering judicial review,[137] and that the conduct that is authorised by the warrant is proportionate to what is sought to be achieved by that conduct (s.23).

A warrant cannot be considered necessary if it is only requested for the purpose of gathering evidence for use in legal proceedings (s.20(5)). The reason for this is that, generally, intercept evidence is not admissible in court because this would reveal the product and fact of interception, thus limiting its effectiveness in future. In fact, the prohibition extends to any indication that any 'interception-related conduct' has, or may have occurred, or may occur in the future (s.56(1)). Some years before enactment of the IPA 2016 the government set up a review of the use of intercept as evidence which concluded that it should be possible to use some material provided key conditions were met[138]—such as ensuring that the disclosure of material could not be required against the wishes of the agency originating the material; and not allowing the defence to conduct 'fishing expeditions' for intercept allegedly held by any agency.[139] Some trials of the use of intercept evidence apparently highlighted 'real legal and operational difficulties' which led the Interception of Communications Commissioner to urge caution in ending the ban on the use of intercept as evidence.[140] The government was clearly more persuaded by these calls for caution, which were echoed by the security services, than they were by the difficulties that the ban creates for the prosecution.

The change in the law regarding the approval of interception warrants are an improvement on the previous procedure (although see later regarding the rate of approval by Judicial Commissioners). However, the changes in the IPA 2016 regarding access to, and retention of, communications data (Parts 3 and 4), were more controversial. The Investigatory Powers Commissioner can authorise a public authority to obtain communications data if satisfied that it is necessary for one or more of a range of purposes, including national security and for preventing or investigating crime or preventing disorder (s.60A). The Secretary of State can issue 'bulk interception' warrants (s.138), and can also require a telecommunications operator to retain communications data for a variety of purposes (s.87). These provisions were challenged by Liberty on the grounds that they breached both EU law and the ECHR. Part of their challenge was successful, and resulted in amendments to the IPA 2016. However, the argument that the powers to gather 'bulk data' breached the privacy and freedom of expression rights guaranteed by the ECHR failed.[141]

---

[137] Broadly, that the Secretary of State has taken into account only those factors that are relevant to the decision, and that the decision is '*Wednesbury* reasonable'.

[138] Sir John Chilcot *Privy Council Review of Intercept as Evidence* (Cm 7324, 2008).

[139] See Ryder M, 'RIPA Reviewed' (2008) Archbold News 4, 6.

[140] Report of the Interception of Communications Commissioner for 2008 (HC 901, 2009) p 4.

[141] The arguments put forward by Liberty and the judgments are available at: <https://www.libertyhumanrights.org.uk/issue/legal-challenge-investigatory-powers-act/> (accessed 10 October 2020).

Under the RIPA 2000 there were serious concerns about whether the oversight provided by the Interception of Communications Commissioner was sufficient to address the power to issue warrants.[142] In 2008, for example, 1,503 warrants were authorised by the Secretary of State.[143] Given the volume of authorisations, could it credibly be maintained that the Secretary of State discharged effective and proper review? The Commissioner did not adjudicate on whether particular warrants were justified, but he did report on errors and breaches of the law where they were apparent. His report for 2008 observed that 50 errors or breaches were reported to him during the year, but whilst this was 'too high' none except one were deliberate, and commonly included incorrect telephone numbers.[144] The Commissioner's overall conclusion echoed that of previous years, that interception is 'vital in the battle against terrorism and serious crime' and carried out 'diligently and in accordance with the law' (para 7.1).

As noted earlier, the Interception of Communications Commissioner has been replaced by the Investigatory Powers Commissioner, who has responsibility for overseeing a wide range of covert policing activities, not only those conducted by the police but also by other agencies including the security services. In 2018 there had been 3,765 targeted interception warrants[145]—more than double the number granted 10 years earlier. There were also more than 200,000 communications data authorisations. This gives some indication of the scale of communications interceptions and data collecting in the current era. The Commissioner believed that the new 'double-lock' arrangements were working well: 'We have been increasingly impressed by the advantage of IOPC's dual role: first, undertaking the review of warrants and, second, having retrospective oversight of the use of investigatory powers. This combination of responsibilities provides IPCO with a detailed level of insight into the factors relevant to applications for warrants and the use of covert powers which otherwise would not exist'.[146] However, this is a judgement on whether the law governing interception of communications and access to communications data is being complied with, not on whether this level of surveillance is justified. Furthermore, the statistics revealed in the IPCO report may not disclose the full extent of such surveillance. For example, Liberty and Privacy International have been seeking to challenge police use of 'International Mobile Subscriber Identity catchers' which can mimic mobile telephone towers and trick mobile phones into connection with them and disclosing personal information. So far, the police have refused to confirm or deny that they are using such devices.[147]

6.4.2 Covert human intelligence sources

Covert human intelligence source (CHIS) is the expression used in the RIPA 2000 to cover people involved in two very distinct types of policing strategies. One is the use of non-police informers who, as we will see, are likely to be people who are themselves involved in crime. The second involves the use of police officers as undercover operatives who are tasked to infiltrate criminal and other organisations. In spite of the rise of technology-based forms of surveillance considered earlier in section 6.4.1, 'informing by humans

---

[142] Liberty argued for judicial involvement, noting that most comparable common law jurisdictions require judicial authority and judicial oversight would strengthen the case for intercept as evidence (Liberty, 2009: 10); and this was, to an extent, recognised by the introduction by the IPA 2016 of the role of judicial commissioners.
[143] HC 901 (2009: 9). A further 844 were reported as being in force. [144] HC 901(2009: 6–8).
[145] IPCO, Annual Report 2018, HC 67 (2020). [146] IPCO (2020: 10).
[147] See Liberty, 'Privacy International and Liberty in court to uncover police phone spying technology', available at: <https://www.libertyhumanrights.org.uk/issue/privacy-international-and-liberty-in-court-to-uncover-police-phone-spying-technology/> (accessed 10 October 2020).

remains a crucial type of intelligence-gathering for modern state security agencies'.[148] To an extent these two types of CHIS raise different issues under RIPA 2000, but are subject to the same regulatory regime. We will first examine that regulation, and then go on to examine some of the issues raised by the use of these policing strategies.

6.4.2.1 The legal regulation of CHIS

Traditionally, CID officers had their own 'snouts' and they resisted any attempts to control or share them with others. We will examine the dangers of informers later, but having been largely unregulated for many years, attempts were made to regulate the use of informers, concentrating on increasing the visibility of the police–informer relationship to police managers (but, initially, not to the courts or the rest of the outside world). According to Innes, these attempts had four aims: improving the quality of information and making it more widely available within the police organisation; reducing opportunities for police corruption; protecting officers from spurious accusations of corruption; and controlling the activities of informants.[149]

RIPA 2000 and its associated code of practice relating to CHIS[150] represented the first systematic attempt to legally regulate the use of informants and police officers acting undercover. Section 26 defines as a CHIS a person who establishes or maintains a personal relationship with a person for the purpose of covertly obtaining or providing access to information, or to covertly disclose information obtained by such a relationship. This definition clearly covers not only civilians who engage in such activities, but also police officers. CHIS have special status and protection, and in return they have to be registered and authorised.[151] Authorisation has to be in writing, with reasons, made by designated senior officers. Authorisation must only be granted if it is believed to be 'necessary' in the pursuit of one of a number of general objectives (including crime control and preserving national security) that the CHIS be used (s.29), and that it is proportionate to what is sought to be achieved (CHIS Code, para 3.3). What the CHIS is authorised to do ('tasked') has to be specified in writing, and substantial changes to the 'task' must also be registered. However, the 'task' can be in general terms, so specific activities need not be identified. This all has to be reviewed regularly. Separate 'handlers' and 'controllers' must be identified. There is no direct oversight by the courts over any of this,[152] so the effectiveness of RIPA relies primarily on the honesty of the police and their willingness to comply with its regulations.

General oversight over the use of CHIS was initially provided by the Surveillance Commissioners, but as with the other commissioners, the IPA 2016 replaced them with the Investigatory Powers Commissioner. There is also the Investigatory Powers Tribunal (IPT), now also governed by the IPA 2016, to hear complaints and provide redress. Between them these bodies are supposed to address privacy concerns, but this is self-evidently difficult if not impossible. How can someone object that their Art 8 ECHR right to privacy, for example, was infringed by the placing of a CHIS in their midst when the very definition of a CHIS indicates that they act covertly and keep those on whom they inform in the dark about their activity? The IPT states that in recognition of this, a complainant is not required to provide evidence for their claim, but is merely asked to specify what activity they know or believe to have taken place. However, there were only 250

---

[148] Hewitt S, *Snitch! A History of the Modern Intelligence Informer* (London: Continuum Books, 2010) p 147.
[149] Innes M, '"Professionalising" the Role of the Police Informant' (2000) 9 *Policing and Society* 357.
[150] Home Office, *Covert Human Intelligence Sources: Revised Code of Practice (CHIS Code)*, August 2018.
[151] See generally Harfield C and Harfield K, *Covert Investigation* (Oxford: OUP, 2018a).
[152] In its response to a consultation on revision to the RIPA Codes a decade ago, Liberty criticised the fact that authorisation was still within the organisation and did not rule out officers authorising their own activities Liberty (2009: 12).

complaints in 2015, only 15 hearings held in open court, and only 4% of complaints were upheld.[153] We must remember that it is not only offenders who have their Art 8 rights breached in this way: many people informed on will be innocent, for if the police knew they were guilty of anything substantial they would usually have sufficient evidence to prosecute without needing an informer. One safeguard would be to require disclosure in all cases where suspects who are prosecuted on the basis of information discovered by a CHIS are not found guilty, but RIPA does not do this and it is highly unlikely that the government would adopt this approach in the foreseeable future.

One problem is that informers plausibly claiming to provide information as a result of a relationship that is not established or maintained for the purposes set out in the RIPA 2000, s.26 are not defined as CHIS and are therefore not subject to regulation. Even if there was a good reason for drawing this fine line, which is hard to discern, the potential for abuse is obvious. Whether or not an informer is officially authorised, their use in a particular case is often hidden by the officers involved for a number of different reasons. Norris and Dunnighan, in the 1990s, found that in not one of the 114 cases involving informers that they looked at (including 31 prosecution files) was there any indication that an informer had been used.[154] In 2004, the Chief Surveillance Commissioner complained that 'there is still a tendency not to recognise as CHIS, sources who should be so recognised.'[155] The basis for this judgement was not revealed. Bacon also notes the use of some 'off the books' unregulated informers by the drug detectives in his research, as well as the use of 'off the record' conversations to seek as much information from potential informers before they were formally passed to the source unit to manage, as required by the RIPA.[156] In any event, the number of authorisations for CHIS has been declining for over a decade. In 1998—before RIPA and any rigorous oversight—there were estimated to be around 50,000 informers.[157] However, there were only 3,722 CHIS authorisations in place by the end of March 2009,[158] and in 2018 there were only 1,958 CHIS authorisations.[159] It is difficult to believe that the informer network (leaving aside the numbers of police officers acting undercover) has shrunk so dramatically since the RIPA regime was introduced, particularly when the police have been urged to use this type of method more, not less. It would seem that most informers are simply hidden, and if that is the case, most are unregulated.

6.4.2.2 The use of informers

> Informants are, and always have been, an essential source of police knowledge . . . every person you deal with, and in particular offenders, should be viewed as a potential informant.[160]

The police secure information about possible crimes and suspects from a range of sources. Apart from suspects themselves, sources include witnesses, informers and surveillance. When the police say that they acted on 'information received' this often means informers were involved. We mentioned at the beginning of this chapter that in the early 1990s

---

[153] Figures taken from the IPT website, which can be accessed at: <https://www.ipt-uk.com/content.asp?id=30> (accessed 10 October 2020).
[154] Norris C and Dunnighan C, 'Subterranean Blues: Conflict as an Unintended Consequence of the Police Use of Informers' (2000) 9 *Policing and Society* 385.
[155] Chief Surveillance Commissioner, *Annual Report 2004–5* (HC 444) (London: 2005) para 2.3, confirming the continued relevance of the findings of Innes (2000) and Norris and Dunnighan (2000) and others prior to the Act. [156] Bacon (2016: 188–189).
[157] This is 'a surprisingly high figure revealed for the first time by a senior police officer': *The Guardian*, 12 October 1998.
[158] Chief Surveillance Commissioner (2009: para 4.9). [159] IPCO (2020: 68).
[160] Source: Anonymised UK police force policy documents, quoted by Innes (2000: 362 and 367).

the Audit Commission encouraged pro-active policing, especially the use of informers (which were already widely used anyway) because this is an (economically) efficient and effective strategy.[161] It has been estimated that about one third of detections involve the use of informants in the widest possible sense of the term.[162] Further impetus came with the creation of the Serious and Organised Crime Agency and the provisions in the Serious Organised Crime and Police Act (SOCPA) 2005, encouraging prosecutors to make written deals with professional criminals, offering the prospect of lighter sentences or even immunity in return for 'grassing' on associates and 'bosses'.[163]

Informers are motivated by many factors including: money;[164] promises of immunity, leniency or other 'favours' if they have themselves committed crimes; competitive advantage; revenge (common among ex-criminal associates and ex-wives/partners); dislike of a particular type of crime or person, and police pressure.[165] Gill categorised informants as follows:[166]

- *Sources*: Witnesses who give information philanthropically or as a 'one-off', with no expectations of reward.
- *Non-participating informers*: People who are cultivated on a medium- or long-term basis for general intelligence purposes or to infiltrate specific criminal conspiracies (e.g. drugs rings, armed robbery gangs, fraudsters). They are 'criminal insiders',[167] usually with a history of criminal activity.
- *Participating informers*: People who actually participate in the crimes about which they are giving information to the police.
- *'Supergrasses'*: People who give evidence in court about the many criminals of whom they have knowledge in exchange for immunity or substantial leniency.

In this section we are only concerned with participating and non-participating informers.[168] Sometimes the police seek to recruit specific people as informers, or informers for specific suspected criminal conspiracies. Some drugs dealers appear to be given a 'licence to deal' by the police in exchange for information on other dealers, giving the informers a competitive advantage.[169] If not a licence to deal, the police may simply turn a 'blind eye' 'to offending by CHIS as long as it stayed 'under the radar' and did not cross lines imposed by police officers.[170] For example, in Bacon's research, being present at a drugs transaction was deemed permissible as long as the informer did not participate in the transaction.[171] An alternative strategy is for the police to make themselves disruptively visible near certain people engaged in 'shady' activities, leading those people to tell the police what they want to know in order to get them off their backs.[172] But much of the time, police officers

---

[161] Audit Commission, *Helping with Enquiries: Tackling Crime Effectively* (London: Audit Commission, 1993).
[162] Billingsley et al (2001: 5).
[163] SOCPA 2005, ss.71–75. The sentence discount provisions are discussed in ch 7.
[164] 'Police pay out at least £22m to informants in five years', *The Guardian*, 8 February 2017.
[165] See Collison M, *Police, Drugs and Community* (London: Free Association Books, 1995) for a typology of motivations. Also see Billingsley et al (2001: ch 5).
[166] Gill P, *Rounding Up the Usual Suspects? Developments in Contemporary Law Enforcement Intelligence* (Aldershot: Ashgate, 2000) ch 8.
[167] The phrase is that of Greer S, 'Towards a Sociological Model of the Police Informant' (1995) 46 *British Journal of Sociology* 509.
[168] Supergrasses raise different issues as they are recruited as informers after arrest and are not put back into the underworld: Greer S, *Supergrasses* (Oxford: OUP, 1995).
[169] Bean P and Billingsley R, 'Drugs, Crime and Informers' in Billingsley et al (2001). Bean P, *Drugs and Crime* 3rd edn (Cullompton: Willan, 2008) ch 8.
[170] Bacon (2016: 185).   [171] Bacon (2016: 185).
[172] Hobbs D, *Doing the Business* (Oxford: OUP, 1988).

are simply alert to the possibilities. Thus, Innes gives an example of a man arrested for possession of drugs who after two hours in the cells told the arresting officer that he could not face going to prison: 'So I said to him "Well you've got to give me something and I'll see what I can do". As it happens, for procedural reasons a prosecution would have failed, but the suspect was not told that. Instead he was told that all the charges would be dropped if he did 'some work for me. Sure enough he was good as gold and for a long time after he would pass me little bits about what was going down and where'.[173]

6.4.2.3 The dangers of informers

Any relationship between police officers and 'criminal insiders', other than an adversarial one aimed at ending the informer's criminality, is inevitably dangerous.[174] First, there is the encouragement and condoning of crime. If informers are themselves criminals (as is most common), immunity can put the public at risk. Delroy Denton, for example, committed rape and murder while acting as a police informer.[175] Stephen McColl committed at least one murder while acting as an informer for Greater Manchester Police (GMP) and was so dangerous that Glasgow Police warned GMP about him.[176] Eaton Green committed armed robbery while infiltrating Jamaican gangs in London; the Metropolitan police were initially so keen to keep Green on the streets, and then to obscure their relationship with him, that they deliberately misled another police force, the CPS and a trial judge.[177] Sometimes the 'deal' is bail, a lesser charge, or a letter to the judge asking for leniency, but whenever these stratagems keep informers out of jail, they are as potentially dangerous as immunity. In seeking to minimise this danger, police integrity can suffer. Thus, the police sometimes 'trump up the charges',[178] so that what appears to be a concession is not really one, and most officers who handle informers believe that to 'run informers you have to be as devious as they are.'[179]

Even an informant who was not previously involved in crime might still be drawn into the criminal activity in question in order to gather the information sought by the police. How far the police should permit informants to become, or continue to be, involved in crime, and the extent of their immunity, has never been resolved. Police officers themselves have expressed concern about 'the tail wagging the dog' in many different ways.[180] Then there are the informers who expect members of their families to benefit from the same protection that they get, and informers who cross the line to become *agents provocateurs* (which, as we shall see later in this section, is legally problematic).

A second danger when police officers deal covertly with criminals without apprehending and prosecuting them is the risk of police corruption. It is easy to see how this relationship could be continued through payments from the immune criminal to the police officer. And if an officer is already corrupt, or is seeking an opportunity to make money illegally, what could be better than officially encouraged non-adversarial relationships with criminals? Historically a common factor in corruption scandals has been involvement with informers.[181] According to Clark, a high-ranking officer who led the Metropolitan

---

[173] Innes (2000: 368).

[174] For consideration of the ethical issues involved, see Harfield C, 'Police Informers and Professional Ethics' (2012) 31 *Criminal Justice Ethics* 2, 73–95. For a compelling account from a USA perspective of problems with informers and other forms of covert policing, see Ross J, 'Betrayal by Bosses: Undercover Policing and the Problem of "Upstream Defection" by Rogue Principals', in Brown D, Turner J and Weisser B (eds), *The Oxford Handbook of Criminal Process* (Oxford: OUP, 2019).

[175] *The Guardian*, 16 July 1999.   [176] *The Guardian*, 1 September 2006.

[177] *The Guardian*, 6 November 1995. The Denton and Green cases are discussed in Gill (2000: 190–191).

[178] Innes (2000).

[179] Dunnighan C and Norris C, 'A Risky Business: The Recruitment and Running of Informers by English Police Officers' (1996) 19 *Police Studies* 1 at p 7.

[180] See, for example, Norris and Dunnighan (2000: 395).

[181] Maguire M, 'Policing by Risks and Targets' (2000) 9 *Policing and Society* 315.

police anti-corruption drive in the late 1990s, some criminals regard every arrest as an opportunity to corrupt officers, or to make contact with officers who are already corrupt. One of the many examples he gave is that of a drug dealer named Cressey who, in the early 1990s, persuaded DC Donald, in exchange for a large sum of money, to secure him bail (allowing him to continue criminal activity) and to try to destroy documents that were vital in securing his conviction. Cressey also agreed to pay Donald to supply him with information about planned police raids—information from which he presumably made even more money from the intended targets of the raids. This all required the two men to meet regularly, and the only way that could be facilitated was by registering Cressey as an informer. Ironically, a role reversal took place—as is common with this kind of corruption—by which the officer became the informer in exchange for the criminal's money. Both men were eventually given long prison sentences.[182] In *Davies, Rowe and Johnson* the corruption consisted of some police officers conspiring with their informers to give perjured evidence in court.[183]

Third, informers risk injury or worse if they are discovered. especially given the growing pressure on communities to 'stop snitching', which is no longer just a US a phenomenon, but also a feature of police–citizen relations in the UK.[184] Whether or not people who voluntarily become informers for money or immunity deserve sympathy is debatable since, in some circumstances, they bring this danger on themselves. But not everyone is a genuine volunteer. Just as some people are deceived into believing they are guilty of a crime and thus confessing, some are similarly tricked into becoming informers. Threats are sometimes made by officers against them and/or their family and friends, who are themselves sometimes persuaded to become informers. All the techniques discussed in chapter 5 to produce confessions can be used to pressure people into becoming informers, with one difference. Formal interrogations are reasonably well controlled. Discussions with potential informers are not controlled at all. The potential for abuse is virtually unlimited. Thus, in many cases, money is less a motivator for informers than, as one officer put it, 'legal blackmail'.[185] It is frequently observed that officially recorded payments for informers are generally very small. As noted earlier, it was reported in 2017, on the basis of Freedom of Information requests, that the police paid out at least £22 million to informers over five years. However, it is not known how accurate this information is, or how many informers were in receipt of payment.[186]

Fourth, the motivations that drive informers raise more doubts about the veracity of their evidence than that of other witnesses. In the 'murky world of informers' it may be difficult to 'know where the truth starts and ends'.[187] For example in *G and B* the Court of Appeal concluded that the evidence of an informer was not reliable because he gave information to secure a reduction in his sentence, and commented on the 'cynical and manipulative' nature of the witness: it was difficult to know if he was truthful because he

---

[182] Clark R, 'Informers and Corruption' in Billingsley et al (2001). This account is from the police officer's viewpoint. It is equally likely that PC Donald was the instigator and that some officers regard all encounters with well-connected criminals as opportunities to make money corruptly.

[183] (2001) 1 Cr App R 115.

[184] Westmarland L, '"Snitches get Stitches": US Homicide Detectives' Ethics and Morals in Action' (2013) 23(3) *Policing and Society* 311–327; Clayman S and Skinns L 'To Snitch or Not to Snitch? An Exploratory Study of the Factors Affecting Active Youth Co-operation with the Police' (2012) 22(2) *Policing and Society* 1–21.

[185] Dunnighan and Norris (1996: 6); Cooper P and Murphy J, 'Ethical Approaches for Police Officers When Working With Informants in the Development of Criminal Intelligence in the UK' (1997) 26 *Journal of Social Policy* 1.

[186] 'Police pay out at least £22m to informants in five years', *The Guardian*, 8 February 2017.

[187] Bean (2008: 207).

had demonstrated that he was prepared to say anything to serve his own purposes.[188] At least if information is to be used as evidence in court its veracity is normally tested openly. However, this is often impossible where informers are involved. If informers are involved in the crimes in question they can refuse to answer questions that would incriminate them.[189] Even when informers do give evidence, their identities will be protected if their lives are in danger, thus preventing the defence investigating whether motivations such as money or immunity might have distorted the evidence. An example is the 'Essex Range Rover Murders', where an informer named Nicholls could have been implicated in the murder of three drug dealers in 1995. As the trial judge told the jury, 'I need hardly stress the importance of Nicholls' evidence. So much hinges on what he said.' The two accused men, friends of Nicholls, were convicted of murder, almost wholly on his evidence. The case was returned to the Court of Appeal because it later transpired that he had sold his story, in advance, to a journalist who wrote a lurid best-seller. It is alleged that Nicholls may have been tempted to 'spice up' his evidence to enhance the appeal of the book.[190] It has also been known for 'informers' to stage crimes so that they can then provide related information to secure a benefit for themselves.[191]

Even if informers are not at risk of being incriminated, the police and prosecution may claim public interest immunity (PII). This protects the identity of informants, preventing their questioning in court. For many years PII was granted without question as it was thought that the identity of people who give information leading to detection of crimes should be protected in the interests of their safety and, often, so they could continue to be used as informers by the police. It has now been held that ECHR Art 6 prevents PII unless the public interest in withholding identity outweighs that of the defendant's right to a fair trial.[192] This is a very vague principle capable of a range of interpretations. The domestic courts have held that despite evidence being withheld to protect police informers, the equality of arms principle is not offended if adequate safeguards are in place to enable the defendant to argue his case effectively.[193] Defendants do not need to be given specific information; provided they know the essence of the allegations against them, information to protect an informant can be withheld.[194] Nevertheless the disclosure provisions may result in the police trying to hide their informants from superiors or the CPS,[195] avoiding using them to give evidence in court or dropping cases half way through if required to reveal information that would identify them.[196]

---

[188] [2009] EWCA Crim 1207. See also *B(J)* [2009] EWCA Crim 1036, and Adam's case: *The Observer*, 14 January 2007.

[189] This is part of the right of silence guaranteed by the ECHR Art 6, discussed in ch 5.

[190] *The Observer*, 1 January 2006. The book is Thompson T, *Bloggs 19* (London: Time Warner, 2000). 'Bloggs 19' was Nicholls' code-name under the police witness protection programme.

[191] See the example of Haase and Bennett, convicted prisoners who recruited others to 'fake' crimes for which they posed as informers to obtain early release. See *The Observer*, 23 November 2003.

[192] See, in particular, *Rowe and Davies v UK* (2000) 30 EHRR 441, *Fitt v UK* (2000) 30 EHRR 480, *Jasper v UK* (2000) 30 EHRR 1; *Edwards and Lewis v UK* [2003] Crim LR 891. For a comparative discussion see Mares H, 'Balancing Public Interest and a Fair Trial In Police Informer Privilege: A Critical Australian Perspective' (2002) 6 *International Journal of Evidence and Proof* 94. For other concerns about the abuse of PII, see *The Guardian*, 2 December 2003.

[193] *C and H* [2004] 2 AC 134. There is no blanket rule requiring the appointment of special counsel. Despite statutory provisions for Witness Anonymity Orders following the House of Lords decision in *Davis* [2008] UKHL 36, the common law principles of PII are preserved. Anonymity orders will probably be used to protect undercover police officers rather than civilian informers, for whom the prosecuting authorities will no doubt continue to rely on PII.

[194] *R (on the application of Ajaib) v Birmingham Magistrates Court* [2009] EWHC 2127 (Admin).

[195] Norris and Dunnighan (2000).

[196] Billingsley et al (2001: 8–10). For a good example of the dilemmas involved see *R (on the application of WV) V CPS* [2012] Crim LR 456.

Many of the problems relating to the use of informers generally are heightened in the case of children and young people who inform. This is even more so in light of the growing involvement of vulnerable young people in 'county lines' drug dealing in recent years,[197] which places them at even greater risk of being pressured into being an informant or of being harmed if they do, the risks of which they may not be fully able to assess for themselves.[198] Historically, the police made considerable use of young people; one research study published at the turn of the century found that 62 out of 75 informer handlers used them.[199] However, the majority kept them hidden from their supervisory officers, some wrongly believing that the regulations for 'normal' informers did not apply to young people, when in fact stricter regulations applied.[200] The potential usefulness of youth informers cannot be denied.[201] However children and young people are particularly at risk of being drawn into criminal circles, and of being threatened, harmed and blackmailed by police and criminals alike. Threats and blackmail breed lies and unreliability, among other things. The police acknowledge many of these problems and some say that they keep them hidden because they fear they would, in the light of all this, not be allowed to use them. The desire to excel in detecting crime overrides both bureaucratic procedural rules and ethical considerations.

One consequence of the unreliability of informer information and much of it not being tested in court is false accusations and miscarriages of justice. According to Greer, several 'supergrasses' not only re-offended, but then admitted that the evidence they had previously given at trial had been false.[202] In an attempt to counter this, the Court of Appeal issued guidelines stating that prosecutions should never be based on uncorroborated informer evidence,[203] but this does not prevent convictions being based *mainly* on informer evidence which, as in the 'Essex Range Rover Murders', might not look dodgy until years after the trial.

6.4.2.4 Police officers acting undercover

We saw at the beginning of this sub-section that police officers acting undercover also come within the definition of a CHIS. They should therefore be authorised and regulated in accordance with RIPA 2000 if they establish or maintain a relationship of some kind for a purpose specified in s.26 (see Windle et al (2020)). We will look at this further later, but we must recognise that the police act covertly in many other ways too. One way is by keeping people under covert surveillance (see section 6.4.3). Another is using deception to secure evidence of offending. This sometimes strays into encouraging people to commit offences that they otherwise would not have committed. The term 'entrapment' is often used, but there has been a lack of clarity and consistency about whether it applies only to entrapping people into committing offences or whether it also applies to obtaining evidence by deception.

The use of deception to obtain evidence has never, in itself, been regarded as problematic by English and Welsh courts. Such evidence is, on the face of it, admissible.[204]

---

[197] Windle et al, '"Vulnerable" Kids Going Country: Children and Young People's Involvement in County Lines Drug Dealing' (2020) 20 *Youth Justice* 64.

[198] Gillespie A, 'Juvenile Informers: Is it Appropriate to Use Children as Covert Human Intelligence Sources?' (2020) 79 *Cambridge Law Journal* 459.

[199] Ballardie C and Iganski P, 'Juvenile Informers' in Billingsley et al (2001).

[200] Now see the Regulation of Investigatory Powers (Juveniles) Order 2000, SI No 2793, and the CHIS Code, section 4.

[201] Gillespie A, 'Juvenile Informers' in Billingsley R (ed), *Covert Human Intelligence Sources; The 'Unlovely Face of Police Work'* (Hampshire: Waterside Press, 2009).

[202] Greer S, 'Where the Grass is Greener? Supergrasses in Comparative Perspective' in Billingsley et al (2001).

[203] *Turner* [1975] Cr App R 67.

[204] See, for example, *Smurthwaite* [1994] 1 All ER 898, in which the court set out five factors as being relevant to the question of whether such evidence should be excluded.

However, entrapment in the sense of encouraging the commission of offences that otherwise would not have been committed, and the line between that and mere deception, has been more difficult. The ECHR Art 6 right to a fair trial prevents people being convicted of offences committed only because they were lured into it.[205] This is categorised as abuse of process.[206] However, subtle and unworkable distinctions are made by the courts between 'entrapment' in the sense described, which they condemn, and the provision of an 'unexceptional opportunity' to commit crime, which they endorse (as long as there is reasonable suspicion and properly authorisation of the activity). Two cases illustrate the kind of conduct that the police have engaged in, and the distinctions made by the courts. In *Christou and Wright*[207] the police set up a bogus jeweller's shop in order to recover stolen property and to collect evidence against thieves and handlers of stolen property. Admissions made in the course of conversations between officers masquerading as the shopkeepers and people who went into the shop to sell stolen property were held to be admissible. In *Bryce*[208] a police officer contacted a man to ask if he could supply a stolen car, and the court held that the admissions made by the defendant in the course of this transaction should not be admitted. The main factor to be considered is, therefore, the degree of incitement offered to the defendant.[209] This is not a line between 'entrapment' and 'acceptable' behaviour, but between entrapment (which is allowed) and being an *agent provocateur* (which is not).[210] It is worth noting that most of the cases referred to here pre-dated the RIPA 2000, and whether the undercover officers would now be regulated by the CHIS provisions of the 2000 Act would depend upon whether the officers were treated as having 'established or maintained a personal or other relationship' for a specified covert purpose.

In the last decade the nature and extent of undercover policing has begun to be exposed and, understandably, this has generated a lot of controversy. It has been revealed that since the late 1960s the police have spied on more than 1,000 political groups, although there is no official list.[211] Police officers acting undercover infiltrated environmental and social justice groups over decades, and in a number of cases not only formed intimate relationships with women involved in those groups, but in some cases also had children with them; without ever revealing their true identity.[212] The police even used an undercover officer to spy on the grieving family of Stephen Lawrence, the teenager murdered by racist thugs in 1993; and this meant that the police were also spying on other grieving families.[213] It was

---

[205] *Teixeira de Castro v Portugal* (1999) 28 EHRR 101.
[206] *Looseley* [2001] UKHL 53. An example of a failed entrapment defence is *Shannon* [2000] Crim LR 1001. See generally ch 11.
[207] [1992] 4 All ER 559.   [208] [1992] 4 All ER 567.
[209] For critical comment see Ashworth A, 'Re-drawing the Boundaries of Entrapment' [2002] *Criminal Law Review* 161; Ormerod D and Roberts A, 'The Trouble with *Teixeira*: Developing a Principled Approach to Entrapment' (2002) 6 *International Journal of Evidence and Proof* 38.
[210] See further Squires D, 'The Problem of Entrapment' (2006) *Oxford Journal of Legal Studies* 26(2) 351; Hofmeyr K, 'The Problem of Private Entrapment' [2006] *Criminal Law Review* 319; and *Ramanauskas v Lithuania* [2008] Crim LR 639. For a largely American discussion see Lippke R, 'A Limited Defence of What Some Will Regard as Entrapment' (2017) 23 *Legal Theory* 283.
[211] See the list compiled by the Undercover Research Group, available at: <http://undercoverresearch.net/2018/09/18/a-who-is-who-of-spycop-targets/> (accessed 10 October 2020).
[212] See, for example, the many articles concerning such relationships published in *The Guardian* newspaper, available at: <https://www.theguardian.com/uk/undercover-police-and-policing> (accessed 10 October 2020). The use of sex by undercover officers is nothing new. See, for example, Marx G, 'Under-the-covers Undercover Investigation: Some Reflections on the States' Use of Sex and Deception in Law Enforcement' (1992) 11 *Criminal Justice Ethics* 1.
[213] See Blowe K, 'British police spied on grieving black families for decades', *The Guardian*, 25 October 2019. For context, see Woodman C, *Spycops in context: A brief history of political policing in Britain* (London: Centre for Crime and Justice Studies, 2018); and Bonino S et al, 'Preventing Political Violence in Britain: An Evaluation of over Forty Years of Undercover Policing of Political Groups Involved in Protest' (2015) 38 *Studies in Conflict and Terrorism* 10. Also see Hyland K and Walker C, 'Undercover Policing and Underwhelming Laws' [2014] *Criminal Law Review* 555.

also revealed that some undercover officers had stolen the identity of dead people in order to cover their tracks. In 2014 Theresa May, then Home Secretary, set up an inquiry, the Undercover Policing Inquiry (UPI), to investigate what she described as the 'very real and substantial failings' of undercover policing. The UPI was initially headed by Lord Justice Pitchford, but he was replaced because of ill-health by Sir John Mitting, a judge and former vice-president of the Investigatory Powers Tribunal. Mitting, a controversial appointment, published the fake identities of over 50 undercover officers, but granted anonymity to many more. In March 2020 the Independent Office for Police Conduct (IOPC) announced that it had discovered that a large number of documents wanted by the inquiry had been shredded.[214] The first evidence hearings of the UPI were due to take place in June 2020, some six years after the inquiry was established, but they were postponed because of the Covid-19 pandemic.[215]

Some of the undercover operations under investigation pre-dated the RIPA 2000, but many were conducted after the CHIS regulatory regime came in, for example, the activities of the National Public Intelligence Unit which operated between 1999 and 2010, and the fake identities of whose members have been concealed by the UPI.[216] The lack of progress of the UPI, the fact that it is chaired by a judge with a background at the top of the Tribunal which has upheld very few complaints, and the destruction of many key documents, does not inspire confidence that the government is serious about exposing the undercover activities of the police. Whether the regulation of undercover policing through the CHIS mechanism ensures that this form of policing is only deployed where absolutely necessary, and that the management of undercover officers ensures that their conduct is both lawful and appropriate is, because of a lack of transparency, unknowable.[217] The IOPC reports that the number of CHIS authorisations involving undercover officers has declined to less than 1,000 a year,[218] but whether this is an accurate reflection of the number of cases in which undercover officers are deployed in circumstances in which they should be authorised as a CHIS is open to question.

6.4.3 Covert surveillance

Covert surveillance is regulated by the RIPA 2000 Part II and the Covert Surveillance and Property Interference Code of Practice (Covert Surveillance Code). For the purposes of regulation under the Act, surveillance is covert if, and only if, it is carried out in a manner that is calculated to ensure that persons who are subject to the surveillance are unaware that it is or may be taking place (s.26(9)(a)). It is not only the police who are covered by these provisions; they also apply to some other public authorities, and there are similar provisions applicable to the security services. Broadly, authorisation for covert surveillance may only be granted if it is proportionate and necessary, and collateral intrusion must be minimised. However, evidence and intelligence obtained through surveillance for one purpose can be used in other investigations. Authorisation for surveillance is required from a senior official within the relevant organisation, and may only be given for

---

[214] See the press release of the IOPC, available at: <https://policeconduct.gov.uk/news/materials-may-have-been-relevant-undercover-policing-inquiry-were-shredded-metropolitan-police> (accessed 11 October 2020).

[215] See the statement issued by the chairman of the Undercover Policing Inquiry, issued on 7 April 2020, available at: <https://www.ucpi.org.uk/2020/04/07/chairman-statement-special-measures/> (accessed 11 October 2020).

[216] See Evans R, 'Undercover police to have fake identities hidden at inquiry', *The Guardian*, 29 April 2019.

[217] The College of Policing issues brief guidance on the management of undercover officers. See Authorised Professional Practice, *Covert Policing: Undercover policing*, available at: <https://www.app.college.police.uk/app-content/covert-policing/undercover-policing/> (accessed 11 October 2020).

[218] IPCO (2020: 116). The number given by the IPCO would also include officers of non-police agencies.

purposes specified in the RIPA 2000 (which includes preventing or detecting crime and preventing disorder). Generally, authorisation must be given in writing and, other than in urgent cases, authorisation for intrusive surveillance will not take effect until approved by a Judicial Commissioner.

This kind of work typically involves electronic information gathering, as well as video and audio surveillance, including through mobile and local surveillance teams, who respectively track subjects travelling in vehicles and on foot or who watch the movements of subjects from various observational posts, such as surveillance vans.[219] Another common example of covert surveillance is the bugging of police station visiting rooms, cells and exercise yards. There is no restriction on recording conversations between suspects or between suspects and others, such as family members, friends or informers 'planted' by the police. But since this is covert surveillance, it must be authorised (as directed surveillance) under RIPA 2000—such as when police station waiting rooms[220] and police vans[221] are bugged. The covert surveillance of conversations between detainees and their legal advisors used to be thought to be subject to legal privilege. But detainees have been denied assurances that their consultations with solicitors would not be subject to covert surveillance: RIPA establishes exceptions to legal privilege, allowing the monitoring of legal consultations, if authorisation is through the enhanced process which applies to 'intrusive' surveillance (rather than the internal authorisation procedure that 'directed' surveillance ordinarily requires).[222] There are three forms of covert surveillance.

6.4.3.1 Property interference

This concerns actions that would otherwise amount to trespass or criminal damage, such as entering property to bug it or download information from a computer, or putting a tracking device into a car (but not to intercept telecommunications or secure access to communications data which, as we have seen, is regulated under the IPA 2016). Applications by the police can usually be authorised by an assistant chief constable (or equivalent), but if the application relates to interference with a dwelling, hotel bedroom or office, or is likely to involve acquisition of information covered by legal professional privilege (and certain other information), it must be approved by a Judicial Commissioner. Authorisation can only be given if the proposed interference is proportionate and necessary to prevent or detect serious crime, and as long as the object could not reasonably be achieved by other means.[223] Details must be given of the targets, the property and the nature of the interference with it, the offences in question, and so forth. Authorisations, renewals and cancellations must be notified to a Judicial Commissioner. There were 1,735 property interference authorisations in 2018,[224] compared with 2,681 in 2008/9.[225]

6.4.3.2 Intrusive surveillance

This means surveillance of residential premises or a private vehicle by a person in that property or vehicle, or by a bugging device that gives information of the quality and detail that would be provided by a person in that property or vehicle.[226] Whilst such forms of

---

[219] Loftus (2019).   [220] *Button* [2005] Crim LR 572.
[221] *Plunkett* [2013] EWCA Crim 261. The principle is the same as when a suspect talks to a 'plant' without a bugging device (*Allan* [2005] Crim LR 716).
[222] See *Re M, Re McE* [2009] UKHL 15. The Covert Surveillance Code was introduced following this case. Section 9 requires authorisation and approval by a Judicial Commissioner.
[223] Police Act 1997, Part III. The procedures are explained in the Covert Surveillance Code, section 7.
[224] IPCO, Annual Report 2018, HC 67, p 115. In addition, there were 594 authorisations granted under the Intelligence Services Act 1994.   [225] Chief Surveillance Commissioner (2009).
[226] RIPA 2000, s.26.

surveillance might not amount to crimes or torts (unless they involved unlawful entry onto the property), without proper authorisation they would breach the right to privacy under Art 8 ECHR. Subject-unaware CCTV surveillance of residential premises is included in this category. However, if, someone else directs CCTV cameras at a suspect (or installs a bugging device or similar), and the police use the evidence thus obtained, no authorisation is needed as it is not 'police' surveillance.[227] This pedantic and irrational distinction illustrates the limitations of the regulatory regime.

The procedures and criteria for 'intrusive surveillance' are similar to those for property interference, but an authorisation does not take effect until it has been approved by a Judicial Commissioner, except in an emergency when it does take effect provided that a Judicial Commissioner is notified.[228] There were 536 authorisations granted for intrusive surveillance in 2018,[229] compared with 384 in 2008/9.[230] Oddly, the 2018 report of the IPCO gave no breakdown of suspected crimes that were the subject of authorisations.

6.4.3.3 Directed surveillance

This is covert surveillance that is not 'intrusive' (as defined earlier) but which is likely to result in private information about a person being obtained.[231] It includes surveillance of non-residential premises, such as business premises. It is generally case-specific, as distinct from 'intrusive' surveillance (that need not be). There is no requirement that the crime under investigation be serious, but the procedures and criteria are otherwise similar to those for intrusive surveillance except that authorisation can be made by a middle-ranking officer (similar to those authorising the use of informers), and authorisation by a Judicial Commissioner is not required. There were 7,774 authorisations for directed surveillance in 2018,[232] less than half of the 16,118 authorisations in 2008/9.[233]

6.4.4 The problems with, and potential gains from, covert policing

We have already identified some of the problems with the use of informers in terms of the potential for corruption, not just of police officers and informers themselves, but also of the criminal justice process. Some of these problems also apply to undercover policing. For not only have the police kept under surveillance many people who are law-abiding citizens but, in some cases, have actually encouraged crime. In addition, in the past decade or so, technological developments have massively increased the capacity to keep people under surveillance and to collect their data without them ever knowing that this is happening, or being able to do anything about it even if they do.

Running through all of this is a lack of transparency and accountability. It is true that the IPA 2016 appeared to increase the safeguards against inappropriate or unlawful use of covert policing powers, particularly through the so called 'double-lock' procedures that apply to some of the powers considered in this section. However, it is almost impossible to know whether they have been effective in this respect. In his introduction to the 2018 IPCO report the outgoing Investigatory Powers Commissioner said that 'the fact that Judicial Commissioners had refused very few applications for the use of covert policing authorisations should not be interpreted as a failure by the JCs to provide rigorous scrutiny of the applications. Nothing could be further from the truth'.[234] He went on to explain that applications only appeared before Commissioners at the end of a 'critical filtering process', and therefore there had been detailed scrutiny by multiple people before

---

[227] *Rosenburg* [2006] EWCA Crim 6.　[228] See the Covert Surveillance Code, section 6.
[229] IPCO, Annual Report 2018, HC 67, p 115.　[230] Chief Surveillance Commissioner (2009).
[231] RIPA 2000, s.26.　[232] IPCO (2020: 115).　[233] Chief Surveillance Commissioner (2009).
[234] IPCO, Annual Report 2018, HC 67, p 7.

the applications were received by the ICPO. What is not disclosed, however, is how many potential applications were filtered out and, of course, it says nothing about whether the criteria for granting warrants and authorisations are, themselves, appropriate.

Defenders of covert policing argue that the safeguards discussed in this section guard against the various dangers identified. However:

- Whilst warrants and authorisations for some forms of covert policing require prior approval of Judicial Commissioners, others do not.
- Even in those cases that do require approval by a Judicial Commissioner, the only information on which they can base their decision is provided by the individuals and agencies that seek the authorisations or warrants.
- The agency itself may have neither the ability nor the will to probe its officers about why the intercept or surveillance is sought or why and how the particular targets were chosen. Even if they could, those engaged in covert policing are likely to be capable of concealing their working practices, given the low visibility of their work and the normalised necessity of lying that has been found to be a distinct part of the working culture of undercover police officers.[235] Moreover, increasingly those engaged in covert policing are trained and indeed even take pride in being knowledgeable about its regulation,[236] which on the one hand is important, but on the other may also enable them to avoid scrutiny should they wish to.
- The 'necessity' requirement is potentially as devoid of meaning as the 'necessity' requirement for police station detention, discussed in chapter 4.
- The proportionality requirement may deter the police from seeking surveillance hammers to crack petty crime nuts (in the unlikely event that the police were that bothered about petty crime), but proportionality is a very flexible notion. This partly explains research findings which show that covert policing is no longer the exception but is the rule, becoming normalised and incorporated into everyday policing practices, even for minor offences, such as drug taking, bicycle theft, handling stolen goods and theft from vehicles.[237] In the police forces in one study, this was evident, for example, in the large volume of requests for covert work made by frontline officers to specialist surveillance teams, which were also routinely authorised and carried out.[238]
- There is little effective control over the use to which information obtained by these means is put.
- If the police do not use the information (particularly intercept information, which cannot be used) as evidence in court, if there is abuse of these powers the victims of abuse are unlikely ever to know about the interception or surveillance and will, therefore, not be in a position to seek redress.
- Courts have a tendency to be overly trusting of the police, particularly in accepting PII applications.

We have noted in respect of all of the covert policing powers covered in this section that whilst the official numbers of interception warrants and intrusive surveillance authorisations have gone up, the numbers for directed surveillance and CHIS have significantly declined since RIPA 2000 came into effect, particularly in the past decade. Are the police deploying the latter covert methods less frequently than in the past, or are they by-passing

---

[235] Loftus et al, 'From a Visible Spectacle to an Invisible Presence: The Working Culture of Covert Policing' (2016) 56(4) *British Journal of Criminology* 629–645.
[236] Bacon (2016: 213).   [237] O'Neill and Loftus (2013).   [238] Loftus (2019).

the regulatory regimes? We do not have the evidence needed to answer this question satisfactorily. One possibility is that interception of communications and intrusive surveillance have supplanted other forms of covert policing. Another is that the cuts to police budgets since 2008 under the government's austerity programme resulted in a reduction in this form of police activity. However, this probably does not explain much of the apparent fall in, in particular, the use of informants and undercover policing operations.

There is a crucial difference between the regulation of telecommunications and data collection, and the regulation of other forms of covert policing. It is a crime to intercept telecommunications or collect data without proper authorisation; but not, generally, to engage in unauthorised covert policing. A police force that routinely ignores the approval requirements for the use of informers, and surveillance, is likely to be heavily criticised, and any evidence obtained by unauthorised investigative methods might well be excluded at trial. However, it must be remembered that covert policing is often deployed to secure intelligence rather than evidence, and that factor together with the low visibility of covert policing activity means that if individual officers ignore the authorisation requirements this may never come to light. The victims of the undercover policing that is the subject of the UPI, for example, had to fight for years to expose the practice, and most of them have still not seen justice done. There may be a parallel here with what happened following the introduction of the regime regulating police bail without charge. The Policing and Crime Act 2017 introduced a requirement that a person who had not been charged with a criminal offence could only be bailed (rather than released unconditionally) if bail was necessary and proportionate, and the decision to keep a person on bail was subject to a regime of internal and external scrutiny, including by the courts. Having previously argued that bail was an essential tool, the police responded by dramatically reducing their use of bail, and releasing many suspects, including those suspected of serious offences, unconditionally (known as release under investigation, or RUI. See further chapter 7). Where the police could avoid scrutiny and transparency, they did.[239]

6.5 Scientific evidence

'Scientific' evidence takes many forms, including analysis and matching of bodily fluids, fibres, and other materials; analysis of voice, visual and electronic evidence; medical, psychological and psychiatric evidence and so forth. Innovations such as DNA testing and the computerised matching of fingerprint records have increased the importance of scientific evidence over the past three decades. Particular confidence has been placed in the National DNA Database (NDNAD) and the increased use of DNA for both investigatory and evidence purposes, sometimes portrayed as having unrivalled ability to solve crime.[240] Scientific evidence can lead the police to suspect one or more individuals, or provide particular lines of investigation that may not produce evidence as such, but which may be valuable or even essential in the detection of the crime.

Since the first use of mass DNA screening in the 1980s, which eventually led to the identification of Colin Pitchfork as a double rapist and murderer, there have been some

---

[239] See Cape E, 'The Police Bail Provisions of the Policing and Crime Act 2017' [2017] *Criminal Law Review* 587–600; and his blog-piece 'Police bail without charge – leaving suspects in limbo' available at: <https://www.crimeandjustice.org.uk/resources/police-bail-without-charge-leaving-suspects-limbo> (accessed 11 October 2020).

[240] This view is critiqued in McCartney C, 'The DNA Expansion Programme and Criminal Investigation' (2006a) 46(2) *British Journal of Criminology* 175 and her *Forensic Identification and Criminal Justice* (Cullompton: Willan, 2006b). Also see Williams R and Johnson P, *Genetic Policing: The Use of DNA in Criminal Investigations* (Cullompton: Willan, 2008).

notable successes in using DNA analysis to identify potential suspects and contribute to convictions. One gripping example is provided by the case involving the eventual conviction, in 2003, of Jeffrey Gafoor for the murder of Lynette White in 1988. Three men, Yusef Abdullahi, Stephen Miller and Tony Paris ('The Cardiff Three'), were initially convicted of her murder in 1990, largely on the basis of the 'confession' of Miller. In 1992 they successfully appealed against their conviction on the grounds that the police had used oppression to secure that confession (see chapter 5).[241] Around the turn of the century, as part of a cold-case review, the police returned to the scene of the crime. By scraping off paint in the flat where the murder had taken place (which had been re-decorated), they found DNA samples that were sufficient for analysis. By this time, the national DNA database had developed significantly, and a close match was found with the DNA of a 14-year-old boy who had been arrested and had, therefore, had a DNA sample taken. He would have been too young to have been involved in the murder, but the police took DNA samples from his male relatives, one of whom was Gafoor. He was arrested just after taking a large number of sleeping tablets with the intention of killing himself. The police rushed him to hospital, and as he was being wheeled in he said, 'Just for the record, I did kill Lynette White. I have been waiting for 15 years for this. Whatever happens to me, I deserve'.[242] Both DNA analysis, and the DNA database, were critical in securing Gafoor's arrest and conviction.

However, it is important not to overestimate the significance of the role of science in investigating crime. To take a dramatic example, in November 2000 a 10-year-old boy, Damilola Taylor, was murdered. Four teenagers were prosecuted but acquitted. Years later, blood and fibres that could be linked with Damilola Taylor were found on the clothes of two teenagers unconnected with the original defendants but who had been arrested and then released in the original investigation. These teenagers were subsequently tried and acquitted for murder, but convicted of manslaughter at a retrial.[243] The prosecution was not helped by the fact that the Forensic Science Service (FSS) (see section 6.5.2) was unable to explain how it had missed this scientific evidence on its initial examination (thus leaving open the possibility of innocent or corrupt contamination of the clothing prior to the re-examination), and the defence were able to cast doubt on whether the defendants had been wearing the clothes at the time of Damilola's death. An independent review was set up to examine how the FSS had missed such important forensic evidence. The review concluded that the errors were due to 'human fallibility . . . no scientist however experienced or skilled can ever be guaranteed to find the evidence sought'.[244]

Forensic evidence has the ability to exonerate the wrongly convicted as well as incriminate. In another case the FSS wrongly indicated that they had not retained samples which showed that Sean Hodson was not guilty of the murder for which he served 27 years in prison. The samples could have been examined 11 years earlier but for the FSS error.[245]

---

[241] *R v Paris, Abdullahi and Miller* (1993) 97 Cr App R 99. The judgment is well worth reading because of the comments that the Court of Appeal made about the conduct of the police, and the conduct of the solicitor who was acting for Miller when he was being interviewed by the police. Yet no police officer was ever disciplined in relation to the investigation.

[242] For a full account, see Sekar S, *The Cardiff Five: Innocent Beyond Any Doubt* (Hook: Waterside Press, 2012). A 13-part podcast series, *Shreds: Murder in the dock*, which covers the whole case and provides important background including on the underlying racism in the original investigation, is available at: <https://www.bbc.co.uk/programmes/p071cll5> (accessed 11 October 2020).

[243] *The Times*, 9 August 2006.

[244] Rawley A and Caddy B, *Damilola Taylor: An independent review of forensic examination of evidence by the Forensic Science Service* (London: Home Office, 2007). Other cases where the FSS had allegedly failed to find blood and bodily fluids were examined. It was concluded that the risk of similar failings was 'low' and that there was no need to make changes to the examination procedures or the recruitment, training or management of forensic scientists by the FSS.

[245] *The Guardian*, 23 March 2009.

We will look at a number of limitations of scientific evidence later, but first it is worth spelling out the role it plays more generally in crime detection:

- In large numbers of 'volume' crimes such as theft, burglary, criminal damage and assault scientific evidence is not sought.
- When it is sought, useable scientific evidence is often not found (fingerprint evidence, for example, is found in less than 5% of all burglaries).
- When it is found it is often—probably in about one-third of cases—not of use in detection.
- When it is of use in detection it is often not determinative of guilt. For example, in around 11% of cases prosecuted where there is forensic evidence there is no conviction.
- In many cases the prosecution decision and, where applicable, the verdict would have been the same without the evidence.[246]

Even apparently 'hard' scientifically determined facts about times of death, the matching of materials at the scene of a crime, fingerprints, DNA and so forth often add little strength to cases. For example, even when there is a DNA match there is still frequently no formal action. In half such cases it is because there was no supporting evidence (frequently because the suspect claimed legitimate access).[247] McCartney has pointed out the dilemmas of introducing DNA into criminal investigations, including the suspect interview: police guidance warns against premature disclosure that may provide an opportunity to fabricate an explanation to support legitimate access.[248] At the same time there is a danger that lawyers may overestimate the significance of DNA matches and advise their clients to plead guilty without querying its strength or reliability.[249] Contrary to popular belief, DNA matches are not always wholly conclusive.[250]

The number of cases in which scientific evidence is obtained but discarded as useless is not known, but it seems to play a relatively small role in the prosecution process. A study published in 2005 found that in 'volume crime', for example, forensic evidence was estimated to be the primary source of evidence in around 25% of detections. A more recent study, published in 2014, found that whilst there had been an increase in the use of forensic science in the investigation of crime, the impact has been limited.[251] Some studies have found that cases with scientific evidence are more likely to end in guilty pleas or guilty verdicts, and less likely to be discontinued, than those without it.[252] But, looking at a range of studies, the difference seems not to be huge and it varies by crime type.[253] It is clear that, despite advances in scientific knowledge and, therefore, the success of forensic scientists, the capacity of science to assist criminal justice processes will always be limited. As Bradbury and Feist (2005: 70) concluded: 'The proportion of offences in general (and volume crime in particular) that are detected by the use of forensic techniques is relatively small; most crimes are actually detected by other means.' In the rest of this section, further major limitations will become apparent.

---

[246] These points and data are taken from Bradbury S and Feist A, *The Use of Forensic Science in Volume Crime Investigation: A Review of the Research Literature* (Home Office Online Report 43/05) (London: Home Office, 2005). [247] Bradbury and Feist (2005: 56).
[248] McCartney C *Forensic Identification and Criminal Justice* (Cullompton: Willan, 2006b).
[249] See ch 7 for a fuller discussion of the role of defence lawyers in securing guilty pleas.
[250] Dror I and Charlton D, 'Why Experts Make Errors' (2006) 56 *Journal of Forensic Identification* 600.
[251] Ludwig A and Fraser J, 'Effective Use of Forensic Science in Volume Crime Investigation: Identifying Recurring Themes in the Literature' (2014) 54 *Science and Justice* 1 at pp 81–88.
[252] See especially, Burrows et al, *Understanding the attrition process in volume crime investigations*, Home Office Research Study 295 (London: Home Office, 2005). [253] Bradbury and Feist (2005: ch 8).

6.5.1 Scientific evidence: value-free or constructed?

We think of scientific evidence as objective, but it, and its use, is not trouble-free. Even fingerprint evidence, which has been used in courts for well over a century, has been questioned in terms of both its scientific basis and its analysis and presentation at trial.[254] First, unlike most scientists, forensic scientists have little or no control over the material that they are testing, and the conditions in which it was collected and stored. Usually they test material collected by police officers. They have to rely on those officers not to contaminate the evidence, either deliberately or accidentally, and to report all the relevant conditions in which it was collected. Or, in the case of medical evidence, injuries may be too old to allow definite conclusions to be drawn, or medical problems may be muddied by alcohol or drugs. The material itself may be only partially adequate for testing—for example, blood may have been contaminated by other substances before the police arrived at the crime scene. There is some evidence that the police sometimes forward for forensic examination evidence that might help their case but not that which might undermine it.[255] In a complex investigation there may be hundreds of actual or potential items for examination, and so there often has to be some selectivity anyway. Even in 'volume' crime investigations selectivity is needed because the time the police can give to any one routine incident is very limited. Thus, most focus on fingerprint evidence, and one or more of, for example, shoe marks, organic matter, and physical matter (such as glass, plastic, fibres) or markings (from tools etc).[256]

Second, unlike 'pure' science, forensic examination does not take place in a (literal or metaphorical) vacuum: scientists are asked whether particular substances can be identified, or whether a sexual assault could have occurred. This is often unavoidable, for any one substance might contain an infinite number of constituents. Without knowing what to test for, some analyses might never end. The police always have to decide how much it is worth spending on such tests in any given case, especially in light of austerity and budget cuts discussed in chapter 1. But pointing scientists in a particular direction and restricting them from doing what scientists classically do—i.e. follow their own, rather than someone else's priorities—has many dangers. For example, in *Ward*, forensic scientists deliberately withheld information from the defence because they identified with the police and the desire of the police to convict Ward. As the Court of Appeal acknowledged, 'a forensic scientist conjures up the image of a man in a white coat working in a laboratory, approaching his task with cold neutrality, and dedicated only to the pursuit of the truth. It is a sombre thought that the reality is somewhat different... Forensic scientists may become partisan.'[257] Cases like this and *Maguire* (discussed later, in which similar processes were at work) are not as unusual as one might think.[258]

---

[254] See *Smith* [2011] EWCA Crim 1296, in which the Court of Appeal was very critical of the police monopoly of fingerprint analysis training and presentation of expert opinion as fact, and also the Scottish *Fingerprint Inquiry Report* (Edinburgh: APS Group Scotland, 2011) which was established following the misidentification, by fingerprint evidence, of a former police officer.

[255] Roberts P and Willmore C, *The Role of Forensic Science Evidence in Criminal Proceedings*, Royal Commission on Criminal Justice Research Study no 11 (London: HMSO, 1993). Also see, for good general discussions: Roberts P, 'Science in the Criminal Process' (1994) 14 *Oxford Journal of Legal Studies* 469; Walker C and Stockdale E, 'Forensic Science and Miscarriages of Justice' (1995) 54 *Cambridge Law Journal* 69; Jones C, *Expert Witnesses* (Oxford: OUP, 1994); Redmayne M, *Expert Evidence and Criminal Justice* (Oxford: OUP, 2001). [256] Bradbury and Feist (2005: ch 4).

[257] Glidewell LJ in *Ward* (1992) 96 Cr App Rep 1 at 51. Judicial notice might also be taken of the fact that some forensic scientists are female. See ch 10 for further discussion about the impact of gendered judicial assumptions.

[258] Many examples are given by Redmayne (2001: ch 2). Consider also the murder convictions involving evidence given by Dr Heath, that took multiple contradictory pathologist reports to overturn: *The Guardian*, 25 November 2005, and Sekar S, 'The Failure of the Review of the Possible Wrongful Convictions Caused by Michael Heath' in Naughton (ed) *The Criminal Cases Review Commission* (London: Palgrave Macmillan, 2009). Also see the *Cannings* and *Clark* cases discussed later.

Third, scientists sometimes disagree on the interpretation of their findings: scientists prefer to make clear the limits of their ability to reach black and white conclusions, but the criminal process discourages shades of grey. Scientists have to report on their findings, but cannot report on everything seen and found. They report on what appears relevant, and relevance is frequently a creation of the initial premises on which an investigation is based. In the *Maguire* case there was no doubt that the defendants had a substance on their hands that *could* have derived from nitro-glycerine (an explosive). Only after the Maguires had spent several years in prison did it become clear that the forensic tests had not been sufficiently specific to justify accepting the scientists' opinion that this was a more likely source than many others, such as playing cards or plastic gloves.[259] Or take Danny McNamee, the 'Hyde Park bomber', jailed for life in 1987. His conviction was largely based on fingerprint evidence given by the police's own experts. But at his successful appeal, over 10 years later, 14 fingerprint experts gave evidence. According to the Court of Appeal: 'Remarkably, and worryingly, save for those who said the print was unreadable, there was no unanimity between them, and very substantial areas of disagreement.'[260]

Fourth, much 'science' is highly speculative. DNA evidence was wrongly used at first, leading to many erroneous convictions, because the science (including that of probability) was not properly understood.[261] Thus, as Roberts points out, the newer the theory or technique, the more cautious we should be. This caution clashes with the understandable desire of investigators and scientists to make especial use of new theories and techniques, for many are developed in response to problems that had not been hitherto solvable.

Two notorious miscarriages of justice in the first few years of the new millennium came about because medical scientists came to believe in such theories as 'shaken baby' syndrome so rigidly that their judgement became seriously impaired. Coupled with failures to disclose evidence to the defence, and the over-eagerness of judges and juries to defer to 'experts', this led to too little scrutiny of their evidence until some years had passed with the wrongly convicted mothers in prison.[262] These two cases led to the Attorney-General's review of infant death cases, which resulted in some cases being referred back to the Court of Appeal and a small number of convictions being quashed.[263] More important, in the long run, the courts now acknowledge that what had been thought to be medical 'fact' was informed speculation and that evidence would usually be needed from more than one source.[264]

Another problem lies in the weight to be attributed to the evidence of the prosecution scientist. In the 'Confait Affair' the inability to fix the time of death of Confait accurately allowed the obfuscation of the facts by the prosecution which led to the wrongful conviction of the three defendants.[265] As Glidewell LJ warned in *Ward*, it is vital to recognise the

---

[259] See May, Sir J, *Report of the inquiry into the circumstances surrounding the convictions arising out of the bomb attacks in Guildford and Woolwich in 1974*, Second Report (1992–3 HC 296).

[260] Quoted in Woffinden B, 'Thumbs Down' *The Guardian*, 12 January 1999.

[261] Roberts P, 'Science, Experts and Criminal Justice' in McConville M and Wilson G (eds), *Handbook of the criminal justice process* (Oxford: OUP, 2002). See also the Nuffield Council on Bioethics report, *The forensic use of bioinformation: ethical issues*, September 2007, available at: <https://www.nuffieldbioethics.org/wp-content/uploads/The-forensic-use-of-bioinformation-ethical-issues.pdf> (accessed 11 October 2020).

[262] *Clark* [2003] EWCA Crim 1020; *Cannings* [2004] 1 All ER 725, Crim LR [2005] 126. See discussion by Wells C, 'The impact of feminist thinking on criminal law and justice' [2004] Crim LR 503; Nobles R and Schiff D 'A story of miscarriage: law in the media' (2004) 31 *Journal of Law and Society* 221; and, more generally, Redmayne (2001: ch 7).   [263] *The Guardian*, 21 July 2005.

[264] In fact, most of these cases did have corroborative evidence, which is why there were substantial doubts in so few. The CPS is rightly reluctant to prosecute unless there is corroborative evidence in 'shaken baby' cases: Copley C, 'Prosecuting Cases of Suspected "Shaken Baby Syndrome" – A Review of Current Issues' [2003] *Criminal Law Review* 93.

[265] Rozenberg J, *The Case for the Crown* (Wellingborough: Equation, 1987). The quote from Glidewell LJ earlier in *Ward*, some 20 years after *Confait*, indicates that the problems in the latter case were neither unique nor of only historical interest.

lack of objectivity of much forensic science. This includes DNA evidence, which suffers from the same problems of selection and interpretation as all other scientific evidence.[266] Scientific results have to be interpreted accordingly. If scientists remain detached and relatively non-partisan they have such little control over the information they handle that their dependence upon the police becomes near-total. Alternatively, if they seek to reduce their dependence on the police by getting involved in the investigation (directing the samples to be examined for example), their partisanship will increase. In the search to blame individuals for the errors inherent in systems, scientists have frequently been blamed for taking one stance and then, only a short time later, for taking the other.[267] In order to deal with some of these problems, the Law Commission proposed:

- a new admissibility test, whereby expert evidence should not be admitted unless it is adjudged to be sufficiently reliable; in the case of doubt, expert evidence presented as evidence of fact should be treated as evidence of expert opinion;
- a proper framework for screening expert evidence at the admissibility stage of criminal proceedings;
- guidance for judges for applying the admissibility test.[268]

The government of the day indicated that it would not implement the majority of the Commissions' recommendations—governments have consistently shied away from regulating this area—although amendments were made to the Criminal Procedure Rules designed to give effect to some of them.[269]

6.5.2 Regulating scientific evidence

Traditionally, the police generally used scientific evidence to corroborate existing evidence against existing suspects.[270] However, over the past few decades the powers of the police to collect, store and analyse material with the potential to provide scientific evidence—fingerprints, photographs, footprints, DNA samples, etc—has massively increased,[271] and they have increasingly used its potential to create suspects as part of the shift in emphasis towards proactive policing.[272] Either way, the need for a regulatory structure, such as govern the police in relation to the other topics in this chapter, is obvious.

Until 2012 most forensic analysis was conducted for the police by the Forensic Science Service (chapter 1), although some police forces had their own department for conducting some forensic analysis, especially of fingerprints. The Forensic Science Service (FSS) was a government agency with seven main laboratories across England and Wales. There were concerns that the FSS was too aligned with the police. Indeed, the now defunct Association of Chief Police Officers and the FSS saw their close association as an asset: 'the forensic scientist should be treated as a member of the investigative team.

---

[266] See, for example, Redmayne M, 'Doubts and Burdens: DNA Evidence, Probability and the Courts' [1995] *Criminal Law Review* 464; Redmayne M, 'The DNA Database: Civil Liberty and Evidentiary Issues' [1998] *Criminal Law Review* 437; McCartney (2006b).

[267] See Jones (1994: ch 10), which includes discussion of *Confait* and several of the 'Irish' miscarriages of justice.

[268] Law Commission *Expert Evidence in Criminal Proceedings in England and Wales* HC 829 (London: Stationery Office, 2011).

[269] See Criminal Procedure Rules 2015 (as amended), Part 19 Expert Evidence, available at: <https://www.justice.gov.uk/courts/procedure-rules/criminal/docs/2015/crim-proc-rules-2015-part-19.pdf> (accessed 11 October 2020). [270] Redmayne (2001: ch 2).

[271] For a brief account, see Cape E, 'The Protection of Freedoms Act 2012: The Retention and Use of Biometric Data Provisions' (2013) *Criminal Law Review* 23–37.

[272] Burrows et al (2005). This applies particularly to DNA evidence: Bradbury and Feist (2005: 50).

His/her professionalism ensures that the independence and integrity of findings are in no way compromised by actual involvement in the process.'[273] Since, as we shall see in chapter 7, a prosecution service (the CPS), independent of the police, was created precisely because it was not thought that investigators could be impartial prosecutors, that was mere piety. The idea that scientists were on a par with the police was also unrealistic. Tilley and Ford concluded that the police treat scientists 'as technicians contracted to answer questions at the lowest possible price, rather than as partners in an integrated investigative process.'[274]

The danger of partiality, and of low standards, increased from the mid-1990s as successive governments attempted to cut costs by subjecting the FSS to free market pressures.[275] This culminated in the abolition of the FSS in 2012, the government asserting that forensic science services would be better provided by private providers. Standards were to be assured by the establishment of a Forensic Science Regulator who would issue codes of practice and conduct. The result has been disastrous. The Regulator herself reported in 2019 that 'forensic science has been operating on a knife-edge for years, with particular skills shortages in digital forensics and toxicology', and that '[s]tandards need to be implemented across the board if the sector is to learn from the past and improve for the future.'[276] A House of Lords report is even more damning: defendants are denied access to forensic science experts because the Legal Aid Agency refuses to pay. The report went on to say that '[t]he UK was once regarded as world-leading in forensic science but an absence of high-level leadership, a lack of funding and an insufficient level of research and development now means the UK is lagging behind others. The forensic science market is not properly regulated creating a state of crisis and a threat to the criminal justice system.'[277] The government's responses to the crisis in forensic science services does not inspire confidence that the situation will improve any time soon.[278] However, the privatisation of most of the probation service by Justice Secretary 'Failing Grayling' in a similar 'free market' experiment led to a similar disaster, and probation will now be back in (slightly safer) public hands;[279] we can only hope that forensic science comes to be saved in a similar way.

The other main problem of regulation is what to do with scientific evidence once a case is over—particularly when there is no prosecution or there is an acquittal. Given that fingerprints and DNA samples are routinely taken, with or without consent, from everyone detained for a recordable offence,[280] that so many arrests are based on little or no objective

---

[273] FSS, *Using Forensic Science effectively: A joint project by ACPO and the FSS* (Birmingham: FSS, 1996), p 42.

[274] Tilley N and Ford A, *Forensic Science and Crime Investigation* (Crime Prevention and Detection Series Paper 73) (London: Home Office, 1996) p 22.

[275] Roberts P, 'What Price a Free Market in Forensic Science?' (1996) 36 *British Journal of Criminology* 37.

[276] Forensic Science Regulator, *Annual Report 17 November 2018–19 November 2019*, 25 February 2020, available at: <https://assets.publishing.service.gov.uk/government/uploads/system/uploads/attachment_data/file/877607/20200225_FSR_Annual_Report_2019_Final.pdf> (accessed 11 October 2020).

[277] House of Lords Science and Technology Committee, *Forensic science and the criminal justice system: A blueprint for change*, HL Paper 333, 1 May 2019, available at: <https://publications.parliament.uk/pa/ld201719/ldselect/ldsctech/333/33302.htm> (11 October 2020).

[278] See Home Office, APCC, and NPCC, *Forensics Review: Review of the provision of forensic science to the criminal justice system in England and Wales, April 2019*, available at: <https://assets.publishing.service.gov.uk/government/uploads/system/uploads/attachment_data/file/911660/Joint_review_of_forensics_and_implementation_plan__accessible_.pdf> (accessed 11 October 2020); and *Government Response to the Lords Science and Technology Select Committee Report: Forensic science and the criminal justice system: A blueprint for change*, July 2019, available at <https://www.parliament.uk/documents/lords-committees/science-technology/forensic-science/Govt-response-forensic-science.pdf> (accessed 11 October 2020).

[279] See <https://www.parliament.uk/business/news/2020/june/statement-probation-services/> (accessed 11 October 2020).

[280] The Criminal Justice Act 2003, ss.9 and 10, amended PACE, ss.61–63 to allow 'non-intimate' samples, on which DNA tests can be conducted, to be taken from most arrested suspects.

evidence, and the inescapable fact that some sections of the population are at more risk of arrest than others, it seems wrong that this information should be kept and perhaps used in the future in unrelated investigations. It increases the chances of the crimes of some sections of the population being detected, as compared with those of other sections, and is an invasion of privacy. Also, the information could be misused, to track people associated with out-of-favour political groups, for example. On the other hand, it is argued that innocent people have nothing to fear, and that DNA and fingerprint evidence, in particular, is, in itself, objective even though the use to which it is put and the weight given to it can be contested.[281]

On the basis of the latter argument, following amendment in 2001,[282] PACE s.64 allowed fingerprint evidence and samples (e.g. DNA) to be kept after they had fulfilled their original purpose. By 2012 the national fingerprint database contained at least 8.3 million 'ten-print' records (i.e. records of all 10 digits), and the national DNA database had grown to over 6.5 million profiles relating to an estimated 5.5 million individuals. Even at a time when the databases were smaller, concerns were raised that the 'racially skewed DNA database will exacerbate the racial bias already present in the criminal process'.[283] The extent (but not the fact) of racial disproportionality in this context was disputed by the Home Office, but in 2009 one estimate was that almost 1 in 4 black children over the age of 10 were on the database compared with 'only' 1 in 10 of their white counterparts.[284] In addition, the database contained the profiles of many people who have never been charged with a crime. PACE, s.64 was challenged on the grounds that it was incompatible with ECHR Art 8 (right to privacy).[285] The House of Lords held (with one dissent) that Art 8(1) was not infringed, since keeping the evidence did not affect the individuals' private life, and safeguards were in place to prevent their misuse. The majority judges went on to consider whether, if Art 8(1) had been infringed, this could have been justified on the grounds of necessity for the prevention of crime (the 'proportionality' principle in Art 8(2)). They considered that it could, as the police could not be expected to review the circumstances of each case. The ECtHR took quite a different approach, holding that the indefinite retention of fingerprint and DNA samples following acquittal or discontinuance of criminal proceedings did breach Art 8.[286] It was argued that the ECtHR decision sent a clear message to national authorities that they must tread carefully when handling personal information for the purposes of crime prevention'.[287] However the effect of the judgment 'should not be overstated': it did not rule out the retention of samples after acquittal or discontinuance, only blanket and indiscriminate retention.[288]

The government's response to the ECtHR decision was to amend PACE, s.64, creating a complex regulatory regime governing the retention and use of biometric data.[289] The starting point under the amended legislation is that biometric material (defined as fingerprints or a DNA profile derived from a sample) must be destroyed unless its retention is permitted under the legislation. Retention is initially permitted for the purposes of a criminal investigation or prosecution and, beyond that, if the person concerned is convicted of an offence. Where the person is not charged, or is charged but not convicted, the biometric material must be destroyed, although there are a number of modifications and exceptions

---

[281] For discussion, see Redmayne M, 'Appeals to Reason' (2002a) 65 *Modern Law Review* 19.

[282] By the Criminal Justice and Police Act 2001: before this, samples of non-convicted suspects and defendants had to be destroyed.

[283] McCartney (2006b: 154). See further on databases skewed by racial bias in ch 10.

[284] *The Observer*, 20 July 2009.

[285] *R (on the application of S) v CC South Yorkshire, R (on the application of Marper) v CC South Yorkshire* [2004] UKHL 39.   [286] *S v UK; Marper v UK* [2009] 48 EHHR 50.

[287] Heffernan L, 'DNA and Fingerprint Retention; *S and Marper v UK*' (2009) *European Law Review* 34(3) 491.

[288] Heffernan (2009).   [289] Explained in Cape (2013).

to this rule where the material was taken in connection with certain serious offences, or where the person from whom it was taken has a previous conviction for a recordable offence. Thus, the caution expressed at the end of the previous paragraph was fully justified. Whilst the new regime represents a considerable improvement on the previous regulatory regime, elements of it still breach the Art 8 right to private life.[290]

6.5.3 Summary

There is no easy solution to the dilemmas discussed here, other than to recognise that since—like eyewitness evidence—science rarely provides *conclusive* proof, the *degree* of proof required should be high in order to minimise wrongful convictions. In summary, science is, like almost all other evidence:

- based, to a greater or lesser extent depending on the specific context, on speculation and theory and is therefore generally 'grey' in nature rather than 'black and white';
- subject to the biases of police and scientist;
- in need of interpretation and weighing against other evidence by juries and courts;
- in need of regulation with regard to its collection (e.g. how far privacy should be invaded or deception used to secure it), analysis (e.g. who should examine it, under what conditions), and use (e.g. how it is to be presented in court, and whether it should be put to use for purposes other than it was collected).

In a statement that still resonates today, Roberts cautioned us against placing, in the criminal justice context, our usual faith in the power of science.[291] Instead, '[t]he uses of science in the criminal process should be approached with a healthy scepticism and subjected to on-going critical scrutiny.' Should this 'healthy' scepticism go as far as regarding scientific evidence as 'negotiated constructs' like witness and confession evidence?[292] Or should it lead us to agree that: 'The already uneasy relationship between law and science has now reached breaking point'?[293] In its report on the use of expert evidence, the Law Commission offered solutions to some of the problems associated with scientific evidence. Unfortunately, the government took no action, and has also ignored the problems associated with the analysis of scientific evidence, including the decline in standards. There is simply no sign that the government is willing to engage with these challenges.

6.6 Conclusion

Misuse of many of the police powers discussed in this chapter involve the tort of trespass and breaches of ECHR Art 8. But without any tangible or provable damage, there is little point taking the police to court. As with most misuse of powers, the potentially most powerful remedy, if evidence is discovered as a result of the misuse and if there is a prosecution, is exclusion of that evidence. But few abuses of the powers discussed in this chapter

---

[290] Purshouse J, 'Article 8 and the Retention of Non-conviction DNA and Fingerprint Data in England and Wales' [2017] *Criminal Law Review* 253. Indefinite retention of biometric data (as opposed to retention during the person's lifetime) is definitely a breach of Art 8 right to private life: *Gaughran v UK* (ECtHR, 2020) No 45245/15.
[291] Roberts P, 'Science, Experts and Criminal Justice' in McConville, M and Wilson, G (eds), *Handbook of the Criminal Justice Process* (Oxford: OUP, 2002) p 252.   [292] Jones (1994: 273).
[293] Commentary to *Cannings* [2005] *Criminal Law Review* 126 at p 127. For even greater scepticism about how far law and science can ever speak the same language, see Nobles and Schiff (2004).

give rise to this, and breach of Art 8 in itself does not result in exclusion.[294] As so often in this book this causes us to question the value of declaring that something—in this case, privacy—is a 'human right', at least from the standpoint of the defendant whose privacy rights were invaded.[295]

Thus, while PACE, s.16(8) provides that the police may only search 'for the purpose for which the warrant was issued', any evidence discovered as a result of an illegal general search can still be used. There is, therefore, implicit encouragement for the police to use search warrants as licences to ransack homes and places of work. The same applies, for example, to telephone intercepts, bugging, fingerprints or DNA samples authorised for one thing but which lead to, or constitute, evidence of something else. And *Sanghera* (discussed earlier)[296] illustrates the way the courts on the one hand declare the need for searches, for example, to be based on explicit consent or legal grounds, yet on the other hand allow the evidence obtained illegally to be the basis for a conviction. Again, as seen in earlier chapters, many of these powers are not exercised, for 'consent' is obtained from people who doubtless believe that if they do not consent they will be given no choice anyway. Records are supposed to be kept. But with regard to the special categories of material that cannot be sought and seized except in exceptional circumstances, research has found that consent seizures were generally not recorded.[297]

There are many other common threads linking the topics in this chapter. First, information from informers, undercover policing, surveillance, and witnesses have in common that—by contrast with information from suspects themselves—the suspects usually do not know that information is being gathered about them. Thus, however inadequate the due process protections for, say, suspects in police custody, and whatever the scope for abuse, there are many procedural standards that the police rarely now ignore. And if they do overstep the mark, suspects may become aware of this (particularly likely if—though we saw in chapter 4 that it is a big 'if'—they have the assistance of a good legal advisor) and at least have the chance of redressing their grievances. But if you do not know that your cell, home or place of work is being bugged, or that there is an informer in your midst, or that a witness is being 'prepared' for an identity parade, or even that your partner is an undercover officer, you cannot be on your guard against abuse or know that abuse has occurred. The ability to act like this with little fear of detection increases the incentive to resort to such covert methods—which, when undercover officers deceptively form intimate relationships, are arguably criminal offences.[298] Indeed, this limited visibility and scrutiny of covert policing has led some academics to see it as having been normalized and integrated into everyday policing practices. For example, covert operations are routinely requested by uniformed officers and they are used for minor matters, not just for exceptional serious and organised crimes, with these operations having a significant impact on the most powerless sections of society.[299]

---

[294] *Khan* [1996] 3 WLR 162, and see Ormerod D, 'ECHR and the Exclusion of Evidence: Trial Remedies for Article 8 Breaches' [2003] *Criminal Law Review* 61.

[295] The main value of a successful challenge in the European Court of Human Rights is to prompt changes in the law so as to benefit (some) future suspects and defendants, as happened in the wake of the *Marper* judgment on DNA retention. However, UK governments often set their face against complying with ECtHR judgements. See, in particular, the scandalous failure to comply with the judgment on a blanket ban on prisoner voting in ECtHR 6 October 2005 *Hirst (No 2) v UK* No 74025/01, although the UK government has now reached a compromise with the Council of Europe on the issue.

[296] *Sanghera* [2001] 1 Cr App R 299.   [297] Clark (2004: 122–123).

[298] McCartney C and Wortley N, 'Under the Covers: Covert Policing and Intimate Relationships' [2018] *Criminal Law Review* 137.   [299] Loftus (2019), Bacon (2016), O'Neill and Loftus (2013).

A second common thread is the lack of solidity to apparently 'hard' evidence. We have seen that most scientific evidence requires interpretation and, like witness testimony, the answers it gives often depend on the questions asked. ID and fingerprint evidence is often flawed and imprecise. Even mobile phone data is sometimes problematic,[300] even leaving aside the way demands for access can re-victimise victims and overwhelm prosecutors.

Third, we have the importance of property rights. Whether, and under what circumstances, your property can be searched or your conversations recorded, for example, depends in large part on whether you are on your own property or not and whether the police have been invited there or not. The fact that Art 8 ECHR gives a right to privacy is seen as secondary to the traditional capitalistic focus of English law makers and judges on property rights. The police can deceive but they cannot trespass. What kind of moral values are those to instil in our society?

Finally, authorisation of use of these powers. Most authorisation has to be by a senior officer although we have seen that search warrants, for example, are a matter for magistrates and, in some cases, judges. Although police self-authorisation is a classic crime control and managerial approach, the level of seniority of the officer varies according to, for example, the level of intrusion. This is a partial incorporation of the 'freedom' approach, although the way the police are allowed to run their own ID procedures, when impartial civilians could do it on a double-blind basis, is difficult to justify on any basis. Police self-authorisation is much criticised by academics and the ECtHR, all urging judicial authorisation.[301] However, judicial authorisation is no panacea. As we saw in section 6.3, judges and magistrates exercise little control over the police or, in some cases, may even have close working relationships with them. Judicial authorisation may act as a safety net against the worst policing abuses, but its main function appears rather to be one of adding a veneer of legitimacy to the underlying crime control reality of evidence gathering. Much the same is true of human rights discourses. Certainly, the Human Rights Act 1998 has had limited effect.[302]

The 'war on terror' and allied moves toward pre-empting crimes ranging from the very serious to 'anti-social behaviour', as discussed in chapter 1, means that there is little prospect of reversing the continuing drift towards 'crime control' at the expense of due process norms. But it is not only that the 'justice' core value is gradually being suffocated on the altar of short-term 'efficiency'. Medium and long-term effectiveness also suffers from ideologically-driven policies such as privatisation of forensic science services. And the use of deception, political targeting and assumptions about who, where and what present the most pressing criminal problems revealed by successive 'undercover cop' scandals erode faith and trust in the police, Worse, this shows how relatively marginalised and oppositional sections of society are targeted by the forces of the state. Democracy itself is being undermined.

---

[300] O'Floinn M and Ormerod D, 'Social Networking Material as Criminal Evidence' [2012] *Criminal Law Review* 486.

[301] See, for example, Hyland K and Walker C, 'Undercover Policing and Underwhelming Laws' [2014] *Criminal Law Review* 555.

[302] Although ECtHR decisions, especially on the right of access to a lawyer at the investigative stage of the criminal process, did have a major impact in other jurisdictions, including Scotland.

Further reading

Bacon M, *Taking Care of Business Police Detectives, Drug Law Enforcement and Proactive Investigation* (Oxford: OUP, 2016) chs 7 and 8.

Campbell L, Ashworth A and Redmayne M, *The Criminal Process* 5th edn (Oxford: OUP, 2019), chs 3, 4 and 5.

Evans R and Lewis P, *Undercover: The True Story of Britain's Secret Police* (London: Faber and Faber, 2013).

Heaton-Armstrong A et al (eds), *Witness Testimony* (Oxford: OUP, 2006).

Hyland K and Walker C, 'Undercover Policing and Underwhelming Laws' [2014] *Criminal Law Review* 555.

Jackson J, 'Justice, Security and the Right to a Fair Trial: Is the Use of Secret Evidence Ever Fair?' [2013] *Public Law* 720–736

Law Commission, *Search Warrants: Consultation Paper*, Consultation Paper 235, 5 June 2018.

Law Commission, *Search Warrants*, HC 852, October 2020.

Loftus B, 'Normalizing Covert Surveillance: The Subterranean World of Policing' (2019) 70(5) *British Journal of Sociology* 2070–2091.

Lyon D, *The Culture of Surveillance: Watching as a Way of Life* (Cambridge: Polity Press, 2018).

McCartney C and Wortley N, 'Under the Covers: Covert Policing and Intimate Relationships' [2018] *Criminal Law Review* 137.

McCartney C, *Forensic Identification and Criminal Justice: Forensic Science, Justice and Risk* (Cullompton: Willan, 2006).

Ratcliffe J, *Intelligence-led Policing* (London: Routledge, 2016).

7

Prosecutions and constructing guilt

KEY ISSUES

- The respective roles of the police and CPS in prosecution decision-making
- How cases are constructed *for* prosecution (rarely *against*)
- The criteria for prosecution decision-making
- Diversion from prosecution
- Types of incentives/pressures to plead guilty
- The roles of defence lawyers, prosecutors and judges in the pleading process
- Defendants and victims' rights in relation to plea bargaining

7.1 Introduction

Before police forces were established in 1829 and for some years thereafter, prosecutions could be initiated by anyone. Suspects were generally prosecuted, if at all, by the victim. Even by the mid-nineteenth century, if the police or anyone else wished to prosecute, they had to 'lay an information' before the local magistrates. If the latter were satisfied that there was sufficient evidence they would issue a warrant for the suspect's arrest or a summons to appear in court. Prosecution decisions were judicially controlled.

As police forces and police powers grew throughout the nineteenth and twentieth centuries, victims came to expect the police to initiate and conduct prosecutions for them. Extra arrest powers were provided to the police and they developed the practice of 'charging' suspects, whereby they took suspects before the magistrates without laying an information in advance. Magistrates lost control of prosecution decisions, but no specific prosecution powers or responsibilities were conferred on the police. Private prosecution remained the model on which police prosecutions were based, and the right of private prosecution has remained to this day.[1] In the nineteenth and twentieth centuries various agencies were created to investigate and prosecute crime in their specialist areas, such as health and safety. The statutes creating them were ad hoc and so too were the prosecution powers granted.

In the absence of specific laws to regulate prosecutions, the police and other agencies evolved their own systems. The police prosecuted most of their own cases in the magistrates' courts, but instructed lawyers in Crown court cases. Gradually the larger police

---

[1] On the history, see Sanders A, 'Arrest, Charge and Prosecution' (1986) 6 *Legal Studies* 257. On private prosecutions, see section 7.2.3.

forces began to employ their own prosecuting solicitors, who had to carry out the instructions of the police.[2] If the police insisted on prosecuting a weak case to further their crime control goals, or bring more serious charges than were warranted by the evidence ('overcharging'), there was little or nothing the prosecutor could do about it.[3] These arrangements came under fire in the 'Confait Affair': three youths were wrongfully convicted of murder, partly because the prosecutor was unable, or unwilling, to act independently.[4] The Royal Commission on Criminal Procedure (Philips Commission) proposed an independent prosecution service to take over cases that the police had decided to prosecute. If the prosecutor did not agree with the police, the case could be dropped, the charges changed, or more evidence sought.[5] In the Prosecution of Offences Act 1985, the government accepted the main thrust of the Commission's proposals by establishing the Crown Prosecution Service (CPS). Then the Criminal Justice Act 2003 transferred the power to charge (i.e. to decide to prosecute) suspects from the police to the CPS in all but very minor cases. However, the power to make charging decisions in the majority of cases was returned to the police in 2012, giving the police wide discretion to prosecute or not in most cases. This move was designed to 'strip out bureaucracy and reduce delays'.[6] Whether it had this effect will be discussed later in this chapter.

The head of the CPS is the Director of Public Prosecutions (DPP).[7] Most prosecutors are based locally, in areas that broadly match police force areas, each headed by a Chief Crown Prosecutor. The area structure has been altered several times since 1986, reflecting conflicting and changing views about what the CPS is for and to whom or what it should be accountable (see section 7.6 and chapter 11). This chapter will examine whether the combination of laws, policies and procedures of different prosecuting and enforcement agencies is fair and effective. First we examine prosecution decisions. Then, in the second half of the chapter, guilty pleas.

7.2 Discretion

Prosecution is discretionary, like stop-search and arrest. When the police do not seek to prosecute they may:

- delay the decision. They can either release the suspect under investigation or on police bail, or report the suspect to the magistrates' court (known as a summons);[8] or

---

[2] See Sigler J, 'Public Prosecution in England and Wales' [1974] *Criminal Law Review* 642 for a general account of the system up to the 1970s; Weatheritt M, *The Prosecution System* (Royal Commission on Criminal Procedure, Research Study no 11) (London: HMSO, 1980); Royal Commission on Criminal Procedure (RCCP), *The Investigation of Criminal Offences in England and Wales: The Law and Procedure* (Cmnd 8092–1) (London: HMSO, 1981) pp 49–52.

[3] RCCP, Report (Cmnd 8092) (London: HMSO, 1981) para 6.27.

[4] See *Report of an Inquiry into the Circumstances leading to the Trial of Three Persons on Charges arising out of the Death of Maxwell Confait and the Fire at 27 Doggett Road, London SE6* (HCP 90) (London: HMSO, 1977).

[5] RCCP Report (1981: ch 7).

[6] Home Office, 'Police Powers to Prosecute Strengthened' (2012) <https://www.gov.uk/government/news/police-powers-to-prosecute-strengthened> (accessed 2 July 2018).

[7] The DPP was established in 1879 to advise the police on criminal matters and to handle particularly important cases.

[8] In the past, the police had to put evidence before the court to obtain a summons, but it is also now possible for the police to use postal charging instead where, in appropriate cases, they may post details that someone has been charged directly to them. See <https://www.app.college.police.uk/app-content/prosecution-and-case-management/charging-and-case-preparation/#postal-requisitions-and-postal-charging> (accessed 17 August 2019).

- release the suspect after giving them an out of court disposal such as a penalty notice for disorder (PND) if out on the streets or a simple or conditional caution on admission of an offence in police custody;[9] or
- take no further action (NFA) at all.

This is all broadly true of prosecution agencies in general, all of which have many different reasons for deciding not to prosecute in particular circumstances. These include insufficient evidence, triviality and extenuating circumstances. Sometimes immunity from prosecution is given, in exchange for information about other offences and other offenders. In this section we examine how these discretionary decisions are regulated.

7.2.1 'Legality' and 'opportunity'

It is usual to describe prosecution systems as falling into one of two types. In 'legality' systems (Germany and Spain, for example), the police must report all offences to the prosecutor, who must prosecute. In principle, there is no discretion, although the police screen out cases where there is no evidence. Common law countries, on the other hand, such as Britain and the United States, tend to have 'opportunity systems' in which there is complete discretion. As a former Attorney-General, Lord Shawcross, put it: 'It has never been the rule in this country—I hope it never will be—that suspected criminal offences must automatically be the subject of prosecution.'[10] Recently, for example, under the new coronavirus laws restricting movement in mid-2020,[11] police chiefs have told officers that enforcement actions such as arrest or the issuing of a fine should be used as a last resort: 'We should reserve enforcement only for individuals who have not responded to engage, explain, and encourage, where public health is at risk.' In many forces no formal action had been taken against anyone in the first couple of months, despite widespread flouting of the rules.[12]

Legal systems do not, in reality, divide neatly into the two systems. Many, like France, combine elements of both.[13] And while police and CPS discretion in England and Wales is usually exercised in favour of prosecuting, this is not true of all law enforcement bodies. Thus discretion is usually exercised by *non*-police agencies (such as HM Revenue and Customs) *against* prosecution (see section 7.5). On the other hand, even in the most rigid legality-based systems discretion is exercised more and more frequently. This is usually a product of specific provisions, especially for children and young people, in the laws of those countries. As in Britain, children and young people, old people and motoring offences tend to be given special consideration.

So 'legality' and 'opportunity' systems sometimes produce similar practical outcomes. But because diversion in legality systems is an exception to a general rule, non-prosecution decisions are relatively strictly controlled. The relatively small number of

---

[9] The possible out of court disposals available to the police have grown in number and the circumstances in which they may be used for children, adults and foreign nationals, either out on the streets or inside police custody. Their consequences can be far-reaching. For example, the primary condition attached to conditional cautions for foreign nationals is that they must leave the UK and not return for five years. See the College of Policing for a full list of available out of court disposals: <https://www.app.college.police.uk/app-content/prosecution-and-case-management/justice-outcomes/> (accessed 14 May 2020), and further discussion later in this chapter.

[10] Quoted approvingly in the Attorney-General's guidelines for prosecution.

[11] See Coronavirus Act 2020 and the Health Protection (Coronavirus, Restrictions) (England) Regulations 2020.

[12] *The Guardian,* 1 April 2020.

[13] For comprehensive comparative surveys see Tak P (ed), *Tasks and Powers of the Prosecution Services in the EU Member States* (2 vols) (Nijmegen: Wolf, 2005). Also see Hodgson J, *The Metamorphosis of Criminal Justice* (Oxford: OUP, 2020).

senior decision-makers fosters consistency and adherence to official policy.[14] In England and Wales, by contrast, discretion is not closely controlled. Neither the basis for the exercise of discretion nor the level of decision-maker is consistent throughout the system. Further, in Britain the prosecution system is the same no matter how serious the offence.[15]

7.2.2 'Constabulary independence'

One consequence of the 'opportunity principle' in the United Kingdom is the doctrine of 'constabulary independence' which holds that, in general, no one has the authority to tell law enforcement agencies that they must, or must not, arrest and prosecute in particular circumstances. This is exemplified by *Arrowsmith v Jenkins*.[16] The defendant (D) spoke for 30 minutes at a public meeting that obstructed a highway. She was arrested for this offence and was convicted. She appealed on the basis that many meetings had been held in that place previously and that in the past the police had not prosecuted anyone for a criminal offence. D in effect asked: 'Why pick on me?' The court's answer on appeal was: 'That, of course, has nothing to do with this court. The sole question here is whether the defendant had contravened s.121(1) of the Highways Act 1959' (per Lord Parker CJ).

What of a policy not to prosecute certain offences at all? In *Metropolitan Police Comr, ex p Blackburn*[17] the policy of the Metropolitan Police at that time not to prosecute certain establishments for illegal gambling was challenged. The police altered their policy in the course of the case thus removing the need for a judicial decision. Lord Denning, however, made an obiter statement (i.e. not binding on future courts):

> There are some policy decisions with which, I think, the court in a case can if necessary interfere. Suppose a Chief Constable were to issue a directive to his men that no person should be prosecuted for stealing any goods less than £100 in value. I should have thought that the court could countermand it. He would be failing in his duty to enforce the law [at 136].

This is powerful rhetoric, but to date, there has been no successful challenge to the application of a prosecution policy, such as the need to balance offence seriousness against use of resources.[18] This autonomy in enforcement and prosecution decisions in theory protects enforcement bodies from interference from individuals and from local and central government, including from the party political interests of Policing and Crime Commissioners, who were elected for the first time in 2012.[19] But should these enforcement agencies be virtually the sole judges of when arrest and prosecution is, and is not, appropriate? We are not advocating political decisions about individual cases, but greater accountability for prosecution policies would be entirely compatible with the rule of law.[20] The Home Office formulates policy for the police in relation to case disposals and the CPS has a Code for

---

[14] Jehle J and Wade M, *Coping with Overloaded Criminal Justice Systems: The Rise of Prosecutorial Power Across Europe* (Berlin: Springer, 2006); Wade M and Jehle J (eds), 'Prosecution and Diversion within Criminal Justice Systems within Europe' (2008) 14 (2, 3) *European Journal of Criminal Policy and Research*, Special Issue.

[15] Although the DPP's consent is needed before prosecutions of particularly sensitive or serious offences (e.g. riot) can be launched.

[16] *Arrowsmith v Jenkins* [1963] 2 QB 561.

[17] *Metropolitan Police Comr, ex p Blackburn* [1968] 2 QB 118.

[18] *Chief Constable of Sussex, ex p ITF* [1999] 1 All ER 129.

[19] Whether this is true in practice remains to be seen, particularly given the fine line between the strategic focus of Policing and Crime Commissioners and the operational remit of Chief Constables. See Lister S, 'The New Politics of the Police: Police and Crime Commissioners and the "Operational Independence" of the Police' (2013) 7(2) *Policing: A Journal of Policy and Practice* 239–247. See, further, ch 11.

[20] Jefferson T and Grimshaw R, *Controlling the Constable: Police Accountability in England and Wales* (London: Muller, 1984).

Crown Prosecutors. But these policies are vague, though we shall see later in the chapter that there are more detailed guidelines on specific topics.

The courts have developed three broad legal principles to limit the discretion of prosecution agencies. First, a prosecution must not be pursued in bad faith, i.e. for personal, corrupt or other improper reasons. If it is, the court may hold it to be an abuse of process and dismiss the case. In *DPP v Ara*[21] the police offered a caution to a youth but refused to let his solicitor hear the tape of the interview so he could be advised. The police prosecution was stayed because this obstruction of effective legal advice was seen as an abuse of process. Though the Divisional Court did not explicitly say that the police were acting in bad faith, this was the impression given.[22] Courts will stop cases where it is impossible to have a fair trial, or where what happened grossly offends the courts' sense of justice and propriety.[23] However, this is a remedy of last resort,[24] as the courts are reluctant to use their powers to discipline the police for poor practice or bad faith.[25]

Decisions taken in bad faith not to prosecute are not reviewable in these ways. There is no such thing as an action for malicious non-prosecution or abuse of no-process. A second principle, though, which applies to all prosecution decisions, positive or negative, is that they must not be *Wednesbury* unreasonable.[26] This means that courts will not interfere with the decision of the enforcement body in question unless the exercise of discretion was so offensive or incompetent that it was completely unreasonable.[27] An example would be a prosecution decision (positive or negative) based on an error about the sufficiency of evidence.[28] However, following a series of court decisions, the Code for Crown Prosecutors now provides a 'right to review'.[29]

Third, prosecution decisions must be taken only after consideration and application of a consistent policy. Thus cautions have been successfully challenged because official guidelines on cautioning were not followed. An example is when the High Court took the exceptional step of ordering the CPS to review its decision not to prosecute for rape when the complainant challenged the way the Code for Crown Prosecutors had been applied.[30] Generally, however, the courts exercise a light touch in controlling prosecution policy and practice (see further chapter 12, section 12.3.4).[31] The judges are right not to do the legislature's job of establishing prosecution policy, but it leaves a vacuum that agencies have to fill with their own policies and practices within the broad limits set by the courts.

---

[21] [2002] 1 WLR 815.
[22] See Hilson C, 'Discretion to Prosecute and Judicial Review' [1993] *Criminal Law Review* 739 for discussion of earlier cases. [23] *Maxwell* [2011] 1 WLR 1837
[24] *Crawley* [2014] EWCA Crim 1028. See Wells C, *Abuse of Process* 3rd edn (Oxford: OUP, 2017).
[25] See, for example, *Warren v Att General for Jersey* [2012] 1 AC 22, and ch 11.
[26] This concept derives from *Associated Provincial Picture Houses Ltd v Wednesbury Corpn* [1948] 1 KB 223.
[27] Thus the decision not to prosecute police officers in the *Treadaway* case was quashed as a result of a successful judicial review action. See Burton M, 'Reviewing CPS Decisions Not to Prosecute' [2001] *Criminal Law Review* 374 for discussion.
[28] See, for example, *DPP, ex parte Jones* [2000] Crim LR 858, and *R (on the application of Joseph) v DPP* [2001] Crim LR 489, where the CPS were held to be wrong to discontinue a case on grounds of insufficient evidence when, on the face of it, there did appear to be substantial evidence.
[29] Discussed later and in ch 12. See especially *Killick* [2011] EWCA Crim 1608; *R (FNM) v DPP* [2020] EWHC 870 (Admin).
[30] *R (on the application of F) v The Director of Public Prosecutions and 'A'* [2013] EWHC 945 (Admin). For other examples, see *Chaudhary* [1995] 1 Cr App R 136; *Metropolitan Police Comr, i.e. ex p P* (1996) 8 Admin LR 6; *R (on the application of Guest) v DPP* [2009] Crim LR 730.
[31] For a statement of principles from the House of Lords illustrating judicial reluctance to interfere with prosecution decisions see *DPP ex parte Kebilene* [2000]. See generally, Burton (2001). For cases illustrating this, and contrary to *Metropolitan Police Comr, ex p P*, see *R v Commissioner of Police of the Metropolis* [2007] Crim LR 298; *R (Mondelly) v Commissioner of Police of the Metropolis* [2006] EWHC 2370 (and comment by Leigh L, 'The Seamless Web?' (2007) 70 *Modern Law Review* 654).

It is therefore vital to examine prosecution policies, and to see how they are implemented. All agencies work within the broad framework established by the 'Attorney-General's Guidelines on Prosecution', whereby prosecution can be pursued only if there is sufficient evidence *and* it is in the 'public interest'.[32] According to the Code for Crown Prosecutors, a case must not be prosecuted if it does not pass the evidential stage, 'no matter how serious or sensitive it may be'.[33] In sections 7.3 and 7.4 we look at how the police and CPS operate these two tests, and then we look at the markedly different response of non-police agencies to the same tests. However, first we briefly look at private prosecutions.

7.2.3 **Private prosecutions**

This is not just an abstract right, but a reality: there are probably thousands each year.[34] Most are carried out by organisations such as the Federation Against Copyright Theft; shops probably account for less than 10%, and private individuals even fewer, examples of the latter.[35] The main argument in favour of retaining private prosecutions is that it holds the police and CPS to account in, for example, cases with a political edge or where the police are accused of misconduct.[36] Or even where law enforcement resources are simply over-stretched, 'given the budget and resource constraints faced by the police, prosecution and enforcement agencies'.[37] The argument is weaker, though not eliminated, now that victims have 'the right to review' (see later). But some crimes are very specialist, which is why the 'official' non-police agencies considered later have a role; but the CPS could still take prosecutions over, and be advised by such organisations, as it is advised in 'normal' cases by the police.

Against this is the lack of constraints on private prosecutors: they do not need to have the 'public interest' in mind (though many do), but can instead pursue their private interests; and the evidential threshold is lower ('prima facie' evidence, as against conviction being more likely than not). The CPS can take over prosecutions that fail to meet these tests, and then halt them.[38] However, most cases do not get seen by the CPS.[39] The Post Office 'false accounting' cases are a particularly scandalous set of examples. Hundreds of sub-postmasters were successfully prosecuted for theft and fraud-related offences on the basis of what turned out to be inaccurate IT records—faults in the software were known by the Post Office but were kept secret from their own investigators and lawyers as well as the defendants.[40] Many were jailed. Following investigation by the CCRC (discussed in chapter 11) 47 convictions were referred to the Court of Appeal, of which 44 were

---

[32] See Sanders A, 'Prosecution Decisions and the Attorney-General's Guidelines' [1985b] *Criminal Law Review* 4. For a critique of the 'public interest' test see Rogers J 'Restructuring the Exercise of Prosecutorial Discretion in England and Wales' (2006) 26 *Oxford Journal of Legal Studies* 775.

[33] Code for Crown Prosecutors (London: CPS, 2013b) para 4.4.

[34] An estimate given by Lord Thomas CJ in *R (on the application of Virgin Media Ltd) v Zinga (Munaf Ahmed)* [2014] 1 WLR 2228 at [10].

[35] De Than C and Elvin J, 'Private Prosecution: A Useful Constitutional Safeguard or Potentially Dangerous Historical Anomaly?' [2019] *Criminal Law Review* 656.

[36] On the former, see the attempt to prosecute Prime Minister Johnson: <https://thesecretbarrister.com/2019/07/03/boris-johnson-and-misconduct-in-public-office-8-things-you-should-probably-know/> (accessed 29 August 2019). On the latter see, e.g., *Daily Telegraph*, 15 August 2012.

[37] See <https://private-prosecutions.com/> (accessed 6 November 2020). This private prosecutors' association is an indication of how this 'trade' is flourishing. Also see Lewis C et al, 'Evaluating the Case for Greater Use of Private Prosecutions in England and Wales for Fraud Offences' [2014] 42 *International Journal of Law, Crime and Justice* 3.

[38] *R (on the application of Gujra) v CPS* [2013] AC 484. See commentary at Crim LR [2013] 337.

[39] De Than and Elvin (2019).

[40] Rogers J, 'Private Prosecutions and Safeguards' [2020] *Criminal Law Review* 769.

unopposed by the Post Office.[41] We do not think of the Post Office as a 'private' organisation, but it was privatised in 2013. This shows the danger of allowing criminal justice powers to be exercised in the private interests of individuals or organisations. The appearance of democracy is greater than the reality here, with 'justice' undoubtedly suffering.

7.3 Evidential sufficiency: police and CPS

7.3.1 Deciding that there is insufficient evidence

The police frequently decide that they have insufficient evidence to prosecute. Many arrests are of the 'wrong' suspect as one would expect when the police trawl large suspect populations in major crime enquiries, or in more minor cases, people are arrested indiscriminately or on unreliable 'information received'. Sometimes the police believe that they have the right suspect, but still consider that they have insufficient evidence to take the matter further.[42] Influential factors here are whether the victim supports the prosecution and, if they do, whether the police then believe them. The latter has been highlighted by recent criminal investigations into rape, including that of the serial rapist John Worboys, who was not initially charged by the Metropolitan Police, in part because they did not accept two of the victims' accounts of what happened to them in Worboys' Black Cab taxi. He subsequently went on to commit further sexual offences.[43] Historically, the police sometimes dropped cases to conceal their malpractice. As a police inspector in the 1980s put it, prosecution 'might prove embarrassing to the police' because of racist language used during the arrest.[44] Together this helps us to understand why only a minority of crimes recorded by the police result in a charge or summons to court. In 2018/19, this figure was 7.8%, which was down on the 9.1% in 2017/18. Of these recorded crimes in 2018/19, 32.5% were discontinued due to evidential difficulties (of which 22.6% were attributed to victims' wishes to drop the prosecution). By far the biggest category in police recorded data, however, is when an investigation is completed but no suspect is identified (44.4% in 2018/19).[45]

As a result of the Philips Commission finding that large numbers of weak cases were being prosecuted by the police, the Attorney-General's guidelines for prosecution set out a 'realistic prospect of conviction' test, under which conviction has to be more likely than acquittal. This does not require a belief in the innocence of a defendant in order for a case to be dropped, nor a belief in guilt for a case to be proceeded with. Rather it requires a prediction of what will happen in court, which is likely to be influenced by prosecutorial views of jury decision-making. Williams argues that the test should not be whether a jury is likely to convict, but whether it ought to convict, given the admissible evidence available

---

[41] *The Guardian*, 2 October 2020.

[42] Sometimes the evidence cannot be secured, but in other cases the police decide that it is not worth investing the time and trouble to pursue the matter further. This was their traditional attitude to 'domestics', which were in the past seen as a private not a police matter, although the situation is now changing, at least as far as domestic abuse against women is concerned, for example, as result of positive arrest policies and risk-based decision-making, notwithstanding the challenges this presents. See Robinson et al, 'A Small Constellation: Risk Factors Informing Police Perceptions of Domestic Abuse' (2018) 28(2) *Policing and Society* 189–204.

[43] Such were the failures of this rape investigation, in 2018, two of the victims received financial compensation from the Metropolitan Police because of the violation of their rights under Art 3 of the ECHR (*Commissioner of Police of the Metropolis v DSD* [2018] UKSC 11).

[44] McConville et al, *The Case for the Prosecution* (London: Routledge, 1991) p 111.

[45] For a full breakdown of crime outcomes in 2018/19, see Home Office, *Crime Outcomes in England and Wales: year ending March 2019: Statistical bulletin HOSB 12/19* (London: HMSO, 2019a) pp 10.

to the prosecutor. It is bad enough, he says, that someone believed to be guilty gets acquitted, but to spare them the anguish of the trial too is over-generous.[46]

The 'realistic prospect' test creates a tougher threshold for the police and CPS to surmount than did the old prima facie test. One might have hoped for fewer weak arrests, but instead over the last 40 years there appear on the whole to be more arrests without prosecution. This has been facilitated by the provisions of Police and Criminal Evidence Act 1984 (PACE) that allow the police to arrest, collect evidence and weed out cases which they decide do not warrant judicial proceedings. This is a classic crime control strategy. The degree of interest shown by the police in any particular case or category of case is crucially affected by their own working rules. So, for example, the public prosecution collapsed in the Stephen Lawrence murder investigation because the police had insufficient interest or competence to investigate thoroughly, which combined with working practices regarded as 'institutionally racist', a matter we return to in chapter 10.[47]

The statutory charging scheme retains the central characteristics of the 'opportunity' system—that is, constabulary independence generally allows the police to not prosecute as they wish, and the police have no duty to report non-prosecuted cases to the CPS. Even when cases are referred to the CPS, one must remember that it is the police themselves who control how much admissible evidence is collected and made available to the CPS. This will undoubtedly affect charging decisions, particularly as resources are stretched in such a way that the time spent analysing cases is likely to diminish.

7.3.2 Police working rules, the custody officer and the statutory charging scheme

Since arresting officers will sometimes have strong personal reasons for prosecuting, it was obvious that the imposition of objective standards would be impossible without the decision to prosecute being made independently. The Philips Commission therefore proposed the 'arrest only when necessary' principle, the 'realistic prospect of conviction' test, the introduction of the custody officer role and the creation of the CPS.

The defect in this part of the Philips Commission's strategy was that the custody officers who were to be responsible for charging decisions were in exactly the same social, occupational structural and situational position as the old charge sergeants. Research subsequently showed that it was rare for custody officers to caution or NFA when arresting officers wanted to charge, or vice versa. As one custody officer said: 'I would go along with what the arresting officers have to say.'[48] Giving the CPS the power to drop ('discontinue') prosecutions initiated by the police was supposed to improve police decision-making. The CPS, like the custody officer, had to ensure that prosecution cases passed the test of evidential sufficiency but the threat of the CPS dropping cases did not seem to have this effect. For Crown prosecutors were in a similar position to that of the custody officer in having to rely on what they were told by police officers and this made it difficult for them to take a truly independent view of the case.

The CPS position was not, however, quite so dependent as that of the custody officer on the arresting or investigating officers' version of events. Particularly in cases where suspects were not sitting in the cells awaiting a decision, there was less time pressure on the CPS. On the other hand, the CPS was not a decision-taker but a decision-confirmer or

---

[46] Williams G, 'Letting off the Guilty and Prosecuting the Innocent' [1985] *Criminal Law Review* 115.

[47] Macpherson of Cluny, *The Stephen Lawrence Inquiry* (Cm 4262-I) (London: SO, 1999). See section 7.6, and ch 3.

[48] McConville et al (1991: 119). For recent research showing some change in attitudes of custody officers, but not a lot, see Pearson G and Rowe M, *Police Street Powers and Criminal Justice* (Oxford: Hart, 2020) ch 7.

sometimes a decision-reverser. It is more difficult to reverse a decision of which one disapproves than it is to refuse to take it in the first place. The result was 'prosecution momentum': the continued prosecution of cases which perhaps should never have begun. We say 'perhaps' because the CPS will often, through no fault of its own, not know how weak or strong a case is when it first sees the file if, for example, identification or scientific evidence is still being processed.[49] Suppose the scientific evidence, when it arrives, is inconclusive. The problem is that it is even more difficult to reverse a decision to prosecute a case that has been ongoing for weeks or months than it is to reverse it when it is first received from the police. Consequently, as we shall see later, discontinuance rates are low even though acquittals remain reasonably high.

Auld's recommendation that charging become the responsibility of the CPS was an acknowledgement of these problems.[50] However, as we shall see in section 7.4, the police retained significant prosecution powers to divert cases from courts, and police powers to make charging decisions were expanded again in 2012. For a time, Crown prosecutors would be present at the police station to assist with charging decisions at speed, though more recently this pre-charge advice has become provided almost entirely over the telephone through CPS Daytime Direct and CPS Direct for out-of-hours enquiries or via a secure digital service.[51] In light of budgetary and resource constraints, CPS Direct was expanded to enable the police to discuss charging decisions with prosecutors at any time of day, and every day of the year. The return of charging powers to the police is likely to have relieved the CPS of some of that burden. With the stated aim to reduce bureaucracy, and therefore save time (and money), charging decisions were given back to the police in approximately 80% of cases. In particular, the police may charge nearly all summary offences irrespective of plea and any either way offences anticipated as a guilty plea and suitable for sentence in a magistrates' court, except for cases involving a death, terrorist acts, hate crime, sexual offences and certain violent offences.[52] This is the assertion of the 'efficiency' core value over 'justice'.

The return of greater powers to prosecute to the police is likely to exacerbate problematic aspects of police culture, particularly racial discrimination, whether through conscious or unconscious bias. This is evident in the US,[53] and there should be further research here too.[54]

When making charging decisions, the following options exist:

(i) *Release without charge*: Custody officers remain gate-keepers, putting to (duty) prosecutors cases that they think should be considered for prosecution, or making those decisions themselves in most cases, and sometimes releasing suspects to return at a later date when the evidence has been collated and evaluated.

---

[49] Ashworth A and Fionda J, 'The New Code for Crown Prosecutors: Prosecution, Accountability and the Public Interest' [1994] *Criminal Law Review* 894; and reply by Daw R, 'A Response' [1994] *Criminal Law Review* 904.

[50] Auld R, 'Review of the Criminal Courts of England and Wales' (2001) <http://www.criminal-courts-review.org.uk/auldconts.htm> (accessed 5 October 2008).

[51] In more serious or complex cases, the police make arrange a face-to-face appointment with the CPS. See here: <https://www.app.college.police.uk/app-content/prosecution-and-case-management/charging-and-case-preparation/> (accessed 15 May 2020).

[52] Baksi C, 'Charging powers passed from CPS to police' *Law Society Gazette*, 9 May 2011 <https://www.lawgazette.co.uk/news/charging-powers-passed-from-cps-to-police/60359.article> (accessed 15 February 2020).

[53] Sommers S and Marotta S, 'Racial Disparities in Legal Outcomes: On Policing, Charging Decisions, and Criminal Trial Proceedings' (2014) 1(1) *Policy Insights from the Behavioral and Brain Sciences* 103–111. See also ch 10.

[54] Phillips S and Varano S, 'Police Criminal Charging Decisions: An Examination of Post-arrest Decision-making' (2008) 36(4) *Journal of Criminal Justice* 307–315.

The choices facing prosecutors then are to: take no further action (NFA) or order that one of various types of warning be given; prosecute (see (ii) in this list) or delay the decision (see (iii) and (iv) in this list).

(ii) *Immediate charge*: This can be done only if the usual two-stage test is satisfied—that there is sufficient evidence (a 'realistic prospect of conviction') and that prosecution is 'in the public interest'.

(iii) *Release (with or without bail) pending a future decision*: When presented with evidence, prosecutors will sometimes need more evidence in order to make a definite decision. Prior to April 2017, it was common for suspects to be released on bail (with or without specific conditions)[55] while the police conducted further investigations and/or waited for a charging decision to be made.[56] Amid criticism that suspects were being released on bail for months, and sometimes years, before decisions were made,[57] in 2017 a presumption was introduced that suspects should simply be 'released under investigation' unless the imposition of bail is necessary, proportionate and authorised by an officer of at least inspector level.[58] There are now fewer people formally 'on bail' following the introduction of these provisions, but many more are instead 'released under investigation', which arguably reduces the urgency with which the police will conduct their investigation.[59] As noted in chapter 4 (section 4.2.4), suspects released under investigation will feel no less restricted (mentally at least), and complainants will not be relieved of uncertainty, by the provisions. This is actuarial justice in action; the new rules will have a positive impact on the statistics relating to the amount of time people spend on pre-charge bail (though not on those released under investigation), but only a marginal, if any, impact on the effects of being arrested and subject to police investigation on victims and suspects (and their families, employers etc). In cases where bail is appropriate, statute suggests that there is a presumption in favour of granting bail,[60] but this may vary depending

---

[55] Criminal Justice and Public Order Act 1994, s.27. This amends PACE, s.47 and the Bail Act 1976, ss.3 and 5. See ch 8 for discussion of the principles regarding bail, which are the same for courts and the police. this gives the police considerable power to control the movements of released suspects or to operate conditions as informal punishments. The dangers, as well as the benefits, of giving police this discretion are discussed by Raine J and Willson M, 'Just Bail at the Police Station?' (1995) 22(4) *Journal of Law and Society* 571. See also ch 3, section 3.4.

[56] McGuiness T, *Pre-charge Bail* (House of Commons Library Number 7469, 15 January 2016) p 3.

[57] Hucklesby A, 'Pre-charge bail: an investigation of its use in two police forces' (2013) available at: <https://essl.leeds.ac.uk/dir-record/research-projects/771/pre-charge-bail> (accessed 18 April 2020); College of Policing, 'Pre-charge bail: the possible implications of research' (2016) available at: <http://www.college.police.uk/News/College-news/Documents/College_of_Policing_Pre-charge_Bail_Briefing.pdf> (accessed 18 April 2020).

[58] See s.50A Police and Criminal Evidence Act 1984, as amended by Policing and Crime Act 2017.

[59] Law Society (2019c) *Release under investigation: September 2019*. Online at: <https://www.lawsociety.org.uk/policy-campaigns/campaigns/criminal-justice/release-under-investigation/#> (accessed 15 May 2020) Anecdotal evidence from practitioners also suggests that an extremely high proportion of suspects are RUI'd, and those that are bailed are then RUI'd when bail can no longer be justified. One Crown court judge expressed concern that one effect of the RUI procedure is that cases are not being prepared at an early stage, so the judges do not really know what is coming, and magistrates too readily bail people who were RUI'd for serious allegations. A review of RUI was announced in 2019, and a consultation was launched on 5 February 2020 (which remained open at the time of writing). See Brown J, *Why is police bail being reviewed again?* House of Commons Library (2020) available at: <https://commonslibrary.parliament.uk/insights/why-is-police-bail-being-reviewed-again/> (accessed 15 May 2020) and Home Office, *Police Powers: Pre-charge Bail Government consultation* (2020d) available at: <https://assets.publishing.service.gov.uk/government/uploads/system/uploads/attachment_data/file/863726/20191127_ConDoc_PCB.pdf> (accessed 15 May 2020).

[60] PACE, s.38; Magistrates' Court Act 1980, s.43, as amended by PACE, s.47.

on the category of offence for which someone has been charged.[61] There has been a wide disparity in bail rates from one police station to another,[62] and disparity according to race is highlighted in chapter 10, section 10.4. Subjectivism and discretion allow the police to make decisions which are wholly unrelated to the nature of the individual offence or suspect. Thus at times of riot (or disorder characterised as such) '. . . police bail was denied *en masse* as a matter of policy.'[63]

(iv) *Remanded into (prison) custody pending a future decision*: In situations such as (iii) above, but where suspects are considered unsuitable for release, they may be held in custody and charged if a 'threshold test' is satisfied. In this circumstance, the suspect must be brought before the magistrates at their next sitting. The threshold test requires 'reasonable suspicion' that the suspect committed an offence and a belief that, on the face of it, it is in the public interest to prosecute. This can also be seen as another lurch in the direction of crime control, allowing charges to be laid on the basis of nothing more concrete than 'reasonable suspicion'. As noted in chapter 4, increasingly these hearings are held via video links between police custody and magistrates' courts, particularly following Covid-19, in spite of concerns raised about this, e.g. about suspects' access to legal advisors during their virtual court hearing.[64]

(v) *Out of court disposals* of either the formal (e.g. cautions and PNDs) or informal kind (e.g. Cannabis/Khat warnings) or are also an option available to the police inside and outside of police custody (see section 7.4.1).

7.3.3 Case construction, evidential sufficiency and the CPS

The CPS is under a duty to continuously review cases until their completion, but the 'prosecution momentum' referred to earlier is an obstacle to that. The statutory charging scheme aimed to help the CPS to screen cases effectively for evidential strength by eliminating prosecution momentum, but HMCPSI found that initial case reviews are still given precedence over further reviews.[65] Early legal advice should help the police to secure the evidence needed for successful prosecutions in more cases. It enables prosecutors to discuss possible charges with investigating officers at a point when the police, but not the CPS, may think there is sufficient evidence, again giving the police the opportunity to secure that evidence whilst, for example, the suspect is still in custody. Seeking and taking advice, and engaging constructively with prosecutors, requires a cultural change on the part of the police. And, as a senior prosecutor warned,[66] the CPS also requires a cultural change: to assert its independence at the same time as working closer with the police is not straightforward. Thus HMCPSI/HMIC found that in a large number of face-to-face interactions between prosecutors and police, there was little or no discussion, and that 'action agreements' were frequently inadequately followed up and carried out.[67]

---

[61] CPS, 'Bail – legal guidance' (CPS, 2019, online at: <https://www.cps.gov.uk/legal-guidance/bail> (accessed 15 July 2019).
[62] Phillips and Brown (1998: 115–118). Different offence and offender mixes will also affect bail rates.
[63] Vogler R, *Reading the Riot Act* (Milton Keynes: Open UP, 1991) p 118.
[64] Fielding N, Braun S and Hieke G, *Video Enabled Justice Evaluation* (2020) online at: <http://spccweb.thco.co.uk/our-priorities/access-to-justice/video-enabled-justice-vej/video-enabled-justice-programme-university-of-surrey-independent-evaluation/> (accessed 15 May 2020).
[65] HMCPSI, *Business as usual? A follow-up review of the effectiveness of the Crown Prosecution Service contribution to the Transforming Summary Justice Initiative* (London: HMCPSI, 2017).
[66] Brownlee I, 'The Statutory Charging Scheme in England and Wales: Towards a Unified Prosecution System?' (2004) *Criminal Law Review* 896.   [67] HMCPSI/HMIC (2008) paras 11.26–31 and 13.8–13.22.

But the problem is also structural. One reason why charge sergeants and custody officers were 'bounced' into making poor decisions by investigating officers was because all their information came—orally—from investigating officers. They could listen to suspects, but rarely did. Indeed, the 'threshold test' invites prosecutors to initiate prosecutions on the basis of a low level of evidence. The full evidential test should be applied when the file is complete but this is done in less than half of all such cases.[68] Prosecutors, like custody officers, now have to be speedy decision-makers—not just for 'efficiency' in the crime control sense, nor just to satisfy the custody time limits in a bureaucratic sense, but also because many suspects about whom decisions have to be made are waiting in the cells, often in ghastly conditions. But to be speedy, prosecutors will sometimes have little or nothing more on which to base decisions than custody officers have. Whilst prosecutors will later review cases on the basis of a written file, when they do this they will again be decision-reversers.

Role-conflict is another structural problem. The government's 'Narrowing the Justice Gap' initiative requires the CPS to increase the numbers of offenders 'brought to justice'. This means more guilty pleas, more convictions in general, and fewer discontinuances (i.e. dropped cases).[69] The 2016/17 CPS Annual Review report proudly proclaims 'we are encouraging early guilty pleas'.[70] But the Crown prosecutor is also supposed to act as a neutral truth-seeking 'minister of justice'.[71] This requires the discontinuance of weak (and cautionable) cases. Whilst the statutory charging scheme aims to identify and eliminate weak cases before prosecution is initiated, thus reducing the numbers of cases that should be discontinued, CPS guidance on the use of the threshold and then the full two-stage test recognises that in many cases initial decisions will be taken on inadequate information and will need to be reversed eventually. Discontinuances, then, are double-sided. The government sees them as indicators of poor CPS decision-making because of poor case preparation, for example; but they can also be seen as indicators of CPS fairness to defendants, wishing to prosecute only those against whom the evidence is strong. For example, discontinuances in cases with racialised defendants are higher than in cases with white defendants, and this is because there are more of the former cases that should not be prosecuted.[72] We need to know *why* cases are discontinued before judgement can be passed on whether discontinuance rates should rise or fall.

The proportion of cases discontinued by the CPS declined from 12.5% for most of the 1990s to 8.7% in 2008/9 (with a spike at around 15% in 2002/3).[73] However, discontinuances spiked again in 2014/15 when 12.5% of Crown court cases were dropped,[74] dropping

---

[68] HMCPSI/HMIC (2008) paras 12.8–10.

[69] Home Office, *Justice for All* Cm 5563 (London: TSO, 2002a), ch 1.

[70] CPS, *Annual Review and Accounts 2016–2017* online at: <https://www.cps.gov.uk/sites/default/files/documents/publications/annual_report_2016_17.pdf> (accessed 10 May 2020). This was notably omitted from the 2018/19 report, which instead talked about securing efficiency and value for taxpayers (CPS, *Annual Report and Accounts 2018–19* HC 2286 online at <https://www.cps.gov.uk/sites/default/files/documents/publications/CPS-Annual-Report-and-Accounts-2018-19.pdf> (accessed 10 May 2020)).

[71] See *Holloway, R (On the application of) v Bhui and Ors* [2019] EWHC 1731 (Admin) at 19 per Males LJ: '. . . in their role as "ministers of justice" prosecutors have a duty to undertake an independent and objective analysis of the evidence before commencing proceedings to determine whether there is a realistic prospect of a conviction. This requires an assessment not only of what evidence exists, but also of whether it is reliable and credible, and whether there is other evidence which might affect the position. . .'. This ethical dimension is discussed in Young R and Sanders A, 'The ethics of prosecution lawyers' (2004) 7 *Legal Ethics* 190.

[72] HMCPSI, *A follow-up review of cases with an ethnic minority dimension* (London: CPSI, 2004b) paras 11.21–3. See ch 10 for a discussion on unequal treatment across criminal justice.

[73] Barclay and Tavares (1999) ch 4; CPS, *Annual Report, 2008–9* (London: SO, 2009).

[74] 'Number of dropped Crown court prosecutions at highest level in five years' 11 April 2016 available at https://www.bbc.co.uk/news/uk-36010691 (accessed 4 May 2021).

back to 11.8% in 2018/19[75] (still higher that in the late 2000s). In 2018/19, 9.9% of magistrates' court cases concluded by way of discontinuance, up 0.5% from 2017/18.[76] Over two thirds of these are cases dropped for evidential insufficiency or because the prosecution is unable to proceed (e.g. material witnesses went missing or refused to give evidence).[77] In 2017, 916 cases were dropped as a result of failures to disclose evidence, compared to 537 cases being dropped for the same reason in 2014/15.[78] This might suggest that the CPS was doing the job which Philips set out for it, and that the decision to grant the police more charging powers has led to a return to high discontinuance rates. The problem for the CPS is that, in any group of cases with a realistic prospect of conviction, we would expect some cases to end in acquittal, and some to end in conviction. It is impossible for the CPS to be sure which will fall into which category and so it is not surprising that there is a significant acquittal rate. To drop all cases predicted as possible acquittals would lead to convictions as well as acquittals being reduced. However, the number of judge-ordered and directed acquittals has remained reasonably high in actual number (399 of 69,713 cases in 2018/19),[79] albeit on a slow downward trend, and (admittedly dated) research shows the weakness of many cases is often obvious from the start.[80] There therefore seem to be too few, not too many, discontinuances.[81]

Then there are the cases which appear weak, which the police do not wish to drop and which the CPS do prosecute. Sometimes this is because the police working rules which led to the initial charges embody values shared by the CPS. As one prosecutor told McConville et al (1992), when one suspect gets 'away with it . . . it gets back to the others. You've got to get to know your territory—it's a bit of a policy decision.' Despite the statutory charging scheme, some defence solicitors say the police continue 'to be influential in prosecution decision-making, by exaggerating the strength of the evidence and pushing through weak cases.'[82] Shared working rules need not always involve weakness or cynical calculation. A commitment to do whatever is reasonably possible for distressed victims has also been found to lead to prosecutions continuing despite evidential weakness.[83] At other times there is a good chance of a guilty plea or the chance of a freak conviction (see chapters 8 and 9). This can be made more likely by the police and prosecutors working together, manipulating their power over suspects in custody. When a colleague of ours visited a police station in 2008 he asked about the disclosure of evidence to suspects before interview and was told by the prosecutor: 'We disclose the best evidence to elicit a guilty plea . . . that is what we want'. The prosecutor also said they had a target of increasing the number of guilty pleas by

---

[75] CPS, *Annual Report and Accounts 2018–2019*.   [76] Ibid.

[77] HMCPSI, *Discontinuance (Thematic Review)* (London: HMCPSI, 2007). Similar patterns were found in HMCPSI, *Thematic review of attrition in the prosecution process (the Justice gap)* (2003).

[78] BBC News, 'Hundreds of cases dropped over evidence disclosure failings' 24 January 2018 online at: <https://www.bbc.co.uk/news/uk-42795058> (accessed 15 August 2019).

[79] CPS, *Annual Report and Accounts 2018–2019*.

[80] Block et al, *Ordered and Directed Acquittals in the Crown Court* (Royal Commission on Criminal Justice Research Study no 15) (London: HMSO, 1993); HMCPSI, *Review of adverse cases* (London, HMCPSI, 1999b); Zander M and Henderson P, *Crown Court Study* (Royal Commission on Criminal Justice Research Study no 19) (London: HMSO, 1993) pp 184–185.

[81] McConville M and Sanders A, 'Weak Cases and the CPS' (1992) *Law Society Gazette*, 12 February, p 24

[82] Kemp V, *A scoping study adopting a 'whole-systems' approach to the processing of cases in the Youth Courts* (London: Legal Services Research Centre, 2008) p 32.

[83] On vulnerable victims, see Sanders et al, *Victims with Learning Disabilities* (Oxford: Centre for Criminological Research, 1997) summarised in Home Office Research Findings no 44 (London: HMSO, 1996) which the CPS actually sought to publicise to deflect criticism that it was not doing enough in such cases. On road deaths see Cunningham S, 'The Unique Nature of Prosecutions in Cases of Fatal Road Traffic Collisions' [2005] *Criminal Law Review* 834 at 842.

30% (although he did not say over what period) and made a point of the fact that the police and prosecutor form a 'prosecuting team'. This anecdotal evidence is supported by a recent inspectorate report that discovered many cases would have been discontinued had a proper review of them taken place.[84] But why look for problems in cases that are likely to end in a guilty plea? And if problems are found, why give up the possibility of a conviction for the certainty of a 'failure'? All this is not only consistent with the government's 'narrowing the justice gap' policy—it is demanded by it.

In addition, the police and CPS—like all prosecution-minded law enforcement agencies[85]—'construct' cases to be strong. This is a natural part of the adversarial system, and would be unobjectionable if the defence had similar resources and a similar approach, but they have neither.[86] Police constructions therefore tend to dominate prosecution and court processes, giving them enormous power in the process of determining guilt and innocence. Let us examine some of the ways this is done.

7.3.3.1 Fabrication of evidence

One way of constructing cases is by creating the facts. Occasionally this may be pure fabrication. There was fabrication in many miscarriages of justice in the 1980s and 1990s, for example, the 'Guildford Four' case.[87] Another way in which the police can create prosecution evidence is by holding rigged witness identification parades. For example, in *Kamara* the defendant was placed in a 'line-up' wearing prison clothes![88] Scandalous police behaviour persisted in the aftermath of PACE 1984 and the creation of the CPS two years later. Police officers have admitted planting evidence on drug offence suspects,[89] as almost certainly happened in *Somers*.[90] In July 2000 three men sentenced to 10 years each for armed robbery in 1995 were released by the Court of Appeal. The crucial evidence against them was a witness identification of one of them, and a palm print of one of the others at the scene of the crime together with the discovery in his flat of a stun gun allegedly used in the robbery; strong evidence indeed. Eventually it was discovered, because the officers involved had been subsequently convicted of a series of corruption offences that the ID parade had been rigged, and that other evidence had probably been planted by officers.[91] Every time scandals like these erupt the police say that they have rooted out the corruption and law-breaking and tightened up procedures, or that the law has changed to prevent them happening again. But in 2016, a Metropolitan Police Officer working for the specialist rape unit was sentenced to two years in prison for misconduct in a public office after he falsified witness statements and forensic evidence reports in a rape case investigated

---

[84] HMIC and HMCPSI, *Making it Fair. A Joint Inspection of the Disclosure of Unused Material in Volume Crown court Cases* (2017) online at: <https://www.justiceinspectorates.gov.uk/cjji/wp-content/uploads/sites/2/2017/07/CJJI_DSC_thm_July17_rpt.pdf> (accessed 17 July 2019).

[85] See Nelken D, *The Limits of the Legal Process* (London: Academic Press, 1983) for a study of case construction by housing officials in relation to harassment cases.

[86] McConville et al, *Standing Accused* (Oxford: Clarendon, 1994). More recently, see Newman D, *Lawyers Legal Aid and the Quest for Justice* (Oxford: Hart Publishing, 2013); Welsh L, 'The effects of changes to legal aid on lawyers' professional identity and behaviour in summary criminal cases: a case study' (2017) 44(4) *Journal of Law and Society* 559–585 and Thornton J, 'The Way in Which Fee Reductions Influence Legal Aid Criminal Defence Lawyer Work: Insights from a Qualitative Study' (2019) 46(4) *Journal of Law and Society*.

[87] Documentary analysis showed a note of interview the police claimed was contemporaneous was not. See Rozenberg J, 'Miscarriages of Justice' in Stockdale E and Casale S (eds), *Criminal Justice Under Stress* (London: Blackstone, 1992) p 94.

[88] *Kamara* [2000] EWCA Crim 37. He was picked out despite not matching the description the witness had previously given of the suspect. The murder conviction was quashed after 19 years.

[89] Keith M, *Race Riots and Policing* (London: UCL Press, 1993) p 138.

[90] *Somers* [2003] EWCA Crim 1356. [91] *Martin, Taylor and Brown* [2000] EWCA Crim 104.

between 2010 and 2012.[92] We could detail many other instances, recent and more distant, of improper police practices that are often termed 'noble cause corruption'.[93]

7.3.3.2 Interrogation and witness evidence

The process of construction is more subtle when evidence is obtained through 'interviews'. Confessions, and other self-incriminating statements, are usually the product of interrogation (chapter 5). Thus even 'non-fabricated' confessions are created by the police (in conjunction with the suspect). The police construct cases both in the questions asked and in those not asked. The police do not seek all the evidence which might bear on the guilt or innocence of suspects, but only the evidence which will strengthen the case against them. The same processes are at work when interviewing other witnesses and in the construction of identification evidence. Taylor quotes an officer as follows: 'Police officers tend to look at prosecuting somebody and all they look towards is getting the evidence to secure the conviction . . . For example, the defendant had two mates who witnessed the assault, shall we interview them? Well, they're going to back the defendant aren't they? So the investigators don't bother going to see them. . .'[94]

7.3.3.3 Summaries of interviews

It is standard for the police to prepare a summary of any audio-recorded interview with a suspect. In practice, both defence and prosecution lawyers tend to rely on these summaries in order to save time and money,[95] all the more so in a system running on efficiency and austerity. For many years these particular police constructions have been known to be inaccurate.[96] Their inaccuracy is, however, unidirectional; they nearly always overstate the extent to which a full confession or an incriminating statement was made. Prosecution files are therefore constructed to appear to be stronger than they 'really' are. Sometimes it is only when cases are contested that different versions of the facts emerge. Thus in one case a youth was prosecuted instead of being cautioned because, according to the police summary, he denied the offence. Only when the defence solicitor showed the prosecutor the interview transcript was this shown not to be true (Kemp 2008: 38). The pressures on defendants to plead guilty early in the life of a case, often before a recording of it can be heard or transcribed, are, however, intense. Prosecutors are, and will continue to be, under pressure to make concrete decisions as often as possible, particularly as charging many

---

[92] Barton S, 'Rare jail term for former officer who falsified evidence in sexual assault case' (2016) online at: <https://www.hja.net/rare-jail-term-for-former-officer-who-falsified-evidence-in-sexual-assault-cases/> (accessed 15 May 2020).

[93] DS Stephen Fulcher's role in taking murder suspect Christopher Haliwell to the police station via the 'scenic route' in the hope of finding the victim, Sian O'Callaghan, alive is a recent example of such 'noble cause' corruption in action. See <https://www.theguardian.com/global/2017/jun/25/catching-a-serial-killer-stephen-fulcher-police> (accessed 15 May 2020). See also, for example, Elks L, *Righting Miscarriages of Justice? Ten Years of the Criminal Cases Review Commission* (London: Justice, 2008) ch 10; Waddington (1999: 147–149), Robins J, *Guilty Until Proven Innocent* (London: Biteback Publishing, 2018), and the quashing in July 2000 of the convictions in 1990 of the 'M25 Three' (police found to have conspired with an informant to give perjured evidence in court): *Davis, Rowe and Johnson* [2001] 1 Cr App R 115.

[94] Taylor C, *Criminal Investigation and Pre-Trial Disclosure in the UK—How Detectives Put together a Case* (Lampeter: Edwin Mellen Press, 2006), p 119.

[95] See Baldwin J and Bedward J, 'Summarising Tape Recordings of Police Interviews' [1991] *Criminal Law Review* 671 at 672.

[96] See ibid; van Charldorp T, 'Reconstructing Suspects' Stories in Various Police Record Styles' in Mason M and Rock F (eds), *The Discourse of Police Interviews* (Chicago: Chicago University Press, (2020); Johnson A, '"From Where We're Sat . . .": Negotiating Narrative Transformation Through Interaction in Police Interviews with Suspects' (2008) 28(3) *Text & Talk* 327–349; McConville et al (1991).

cases on the basis of the threshold test is allowed. Reduced staff numbers and access to resources is likely to increase pressure to make decisions at speed with little interrogation of issues that arise.

7.3.3.4 Scientific evidence

Scientific evidence is not as solid and objective as it may seem. Forensic scientists have little or no control over the material which they are testing, and the conditions in which it was collected and stored. The material will often be incomplete or contaminated, sometimes selected to prove a point, and occasionally tampered with. Take the relatively simple matter of fingerprints: 'You might have 3 or 4 sets of fingerprints at the crime scene, one of which matches the defendant. Someone should be saying "but what about the other 3 sets? Who do they belong to?" but they never do and we never tell them.'[97] Scientists also often have to be 'led' by the police because to be asked to simply 'test' a substance will often be pointless. But the process of leading is a construction process. Much science is 'cutting edge', which is another way of saying 'unproven'. The prosecution will seek experts with the theories to back their cases. Overall: 'At each stage of the pre-trial process, forensic science is utilised by prosecution agencies as a tool for case construction.'[98] Or, as Taylor puts it, in relation to evidence in general, including witness evidence: '. . . the instinctive reaction is still to seek the evidence that supports the charge.'[99] Thus, balance is needed by providing the defence with appropriate resources, so that they can engage in counter case-construction by seeking their own scientific evidence, but restrictions on legal aid funding prevent this in most cases.[100] This problem is particularly worrying in light of the Forensic Science Regulator's report conclusion that outsourcing forensic science services (after the closure of the government's Forensic Science Service in 2012) resulted in greater inconsistency and more quality failures.[101] In 2009, and later in 2011, the Law Commission made comprehensive recommendations designed to bolster the reliability of expert evidence,[102] and guidance was introduced via Criminal Practice Direction V, paras 19A.4–19A.6. This was said to reflect a 'new and more rigorous' approach to how expert evidence is to be handled.[103] However, expert witness fees were cut in 2013, creating concern about the number of suitably qualified experts who would actually be prepared to provide reliable evidence in criminal cases.[104] At the twentieth anniversary conference of the Criminal Cases Review Commission (November 2017) difficulties in obtaining reliable expert evidence in an era of austerity emerged as a key area of concern.

---

[97] Detective, quoted by Taylor (2006: 146). Taylor observes that the existence of the other fingerprints is frequently not disclosed to CPS or defence lawyers.

[98] Roberts P and Willmore C, *The Role of Forensic Science Evidence in Criminal Proceedings* (Royal Commission on Criminal Justice Research Study no 11) (London: HMSO, 1993) at p 26.

[99] (2006: 12).

[100] Expert's fees were further reduced under the Criminal Legal Aid (Remuneration) Regulations 2013. This lack of funding may violate the principle of 'equality of arms' (Art 6 of the ECHR). See Ashworth A, 'Legal Aid, Human Rights and Criminal Justice' in Young R and Wall D (eds), *Access to Criminal Justice* (London: Blackstone, 1996); Welsh L, 'Transforming Legal Aid in the UK' *Human Rights in Ireland* online at: <http://humanrights.ie/civil-liberties/transforming-legal-aid-in-the-uk/> (accessed 20 July 2019); Justice Committee, *Transforming Legal Aid: evidence taken by the Committee* HC91 (London, The Stationery Office, 2013)

[101] Forensic Science Regulator, *Annual Report 2016*, online at: <https://www.gov.uk/government/publications/forensic-science-regulator-annual-report-2016> (accessed 15 August 2019).

[102] See Law Commission (2009, Consultation Paper No. 190) and Law Commission (2011, Report No. 325).

[103] *R v H* [2014] EWCA Crim 1555.

[104] Bowcott O, 'Criminal case faces collapse following legal aid cuts for medical experts' *The Guardian*, 1 May 2014. The authors are aware of ongoing, but yet to be published, research in this field.

7.3.3.5 Non-disclosure of evidence

Many of the cases discussed earlier illustrate another form of case construction; non-disclosure. The failure of the police to disclose relevant information can not only make cases appear strong to prosecutors, but actually to be strong in court—often leading to wrongful convictions.[105] The type of evidence in question is almost infinite. It includes scientific tests and identification evidence that point to suspects other than the defendant or initial failures to match fingerprint or identification evidence with the accused; witness statements or fingerprint evidence (see the example in section 7.3.3.4) that contradicts or undermines prosecution evidence (e.g. that suggest the defendant was somewhere else when the crime occurred or acted in self-defence); and acknowledgement that some prosecution witnesses are informers or have other characteristics that raise doubts about their reliability.[106] In *Ward*[107] the police hid certain evidence from the prosecution and the defence, and the prosecution hid other evidence from the defence. Government scientists had also deliberately suppressed material unhelpful to the Crown's case, and had created a distorted picture of the forensic evidence. The Court of Appeal responded by laying down strict rules for disclosure which reduced the right of the prosecution to suppress evidence. *Ward* represented the high-water mark of a trend towards due process in the law of disclosure. Subsequent cases began a judicial retreat back towards crime control, supported by the Runciman Commission on the ground that *Ward* 'created burdens for the prosecution that go beyond what is reasonable'.[108] A new scheme was enacted in the Criminal Procedure and Investigations Act 1996 (CPIA). It was so crime control-oriented that the DPP himself accepted that it could lead to miscarriages of justice.[109] Although the scheme was presented in terms of 'efficiency'[110] it was actually very inefficient, so it was amended by the Criminal Justice Act (CJA) 2003.[111]

The statutory disclosure scheme applies to all Crown court cases and contested magistrates' court cases. The prosecution must now, at the earliest possible stage, disclose all material (unless it is 'sensitive')[112] which 'might reasonably be considered capable of undermining the case for the prosecution or of assisting the case for the accused' (CJA 2003, s.32, amending CPIA, s.3(1) (a)). One gap was created by the English courts deciding that, if 'unused material' relates to informants or the work of undercover police officers, the prosecution can make an ex parte application to the court for permission not to disclose such material and the defence need not be told of this application.[113] It follows that defendants may decide to plead guilty in ignorance of evidence withheld (quite lawfully) by the prosecution that would have helped to establish innocence.

---

[105] See generally Jones C, *Expert Witnesses* (Oxford: OUP, 1994) ch 10.
[106] See, e.g., *Blackwell* [2006] EWCA Crim 2185 (12 September 2006).
[107] *Ward* [1993] 1 WLR 619.   [108] RCCJ (1993: 95).   [109] *The Guardian*, 15 July 1999.
[110] Redmayne M, 'Process Gains and Process Values: the CPIA 1996' (1997) 60 *Modern Law Review* 79.
[111] We will only give the broadest outline of the law and its problems. For detailed discussions see Redmayne M, 'Disclosure and its Discontents' [2004] *Criminal Law Review* 441; Quirk H, 'The Significance of Culture in Criminal Procedure Reform: Why the Revised Disclosure Scheme Cannot Work' (2006) 10 *International Journal of Evidence and Proof* 42.
[112] The test for sensitive material is whether disclosure would create 'a real risk of serious prejudice to an important public interest' (*H & C* [2004] Cr App R 179), such as from informers and from bugging and phone tapping. Police officers told Quirk (2006) and Taylor (2006: 172) that awkward information that could undermine the case is sometimes classified as 'sensitive', in the hope the CPS would not notice or care. In *Rowe and Davis v UK* (2000) Application no. 28901/95, the prosecution withheld evidence on the grounds of 'public interest immunity' without informing either the trial judge or the defence. This was found to be in breach of the Convention duty on the prosecution to disclose 'all material evidence in their possession for or against the accused'. The solution is to ask the trial judge to rule that the information can be withheld on the grounds of public interest immunity (PII)
[113] *Davis, Johnson and Rowe* [1993] 1 WLR 613. For subsequent developments including the views of the ECtHR see Redmayne (2004: 454–459).

In Crown court cases the defence provide a statement setting out its main points, if a not guilty plea is anticipated (CPIA, s.5); as with the right of silence provisions,[114] adverse inferences may be drawn in relation to major issues raised at trial that are not covered in this statement. Following this, and throughout the pre-trial and trial stages, prosecutors must keep this test under review—in other words, if they become aware subsequently of material that should, but has not been, disclosed they must disclose it (CJA 2003, s.37, creating CPIA, s.7A).

There are several problems. Prosecutors can only disclose material of which they are aware. It is up to police 'disclosure officers' to fully inform the CPS. They send the CPS 'schedules' (i.e. lists) of all non-used items that they think meet the test in CPIA, s.3(1)(a). These should describe the items sufficiently clearly for the CPS to decide what should be disclosed to the defence—or, at least, to decide what the CPS should examine so that informed decisions can be made. The scheme therefore depends on the competence and honesty of the police. However, most disclosure officers are inadequately trained, which they acknowledge themselves.[115] And, except in the most serious or complex cases, the disclosure officer is the main officer in the case (over 90% of the time in the HMCPSI (2008a) research), who therefore has a stake in securing a conviction. The position does not appear to have improved in 10 years, with a joint inspectorate report in 2017 describing the way that police officers complete disclosure records as 'routinely poor' (see section 1.4).

The way the police describe unused material much of the time makes it impossible for prosecutors to assess its likely importance (e.g. 'contents of a drawer').[116] And relevant material is frequently missing (e.g. the omission of significant negative forensic findings in a child abuse case).[117] Some non-disclosure is due to laziness, antipathy to 'paperwork', error and lack of understanding. Some arises from reluctance to disclose information, because: 'If I mention something on a schedule I might get asked questions about it but if I don't mention it on the schedule...'[118] An example would be where informers are involved: 'I am sure that there are a lot of cases where there are informants involved and we are never ever told about it.'[119] Then there is what Taylor calls the 'ideological resistance which many officers feel towards the legislation'. As an officer quoted by Quirk (2006) commented, 'this thing where you've got to give them all your, all the weaknesses in your case. Well, if they can't find them, why should we give them?' Finally, there is the nature of police work itself. Taylor observes that the police can 'exclude material such as witness statements, not by refusing to disclose it, but by choosing not to record it at all'—for example where a witness description is, said one officer '... not what I'm trying to prove here ... It should be going down that the woman in number 33 has given a contradictory description but it just won't happen' (2006: 102–103). As another put it, as in most cases officers work alone: 'If you wanted to hide something you could—easily' (2006: 147). And so recent research on murder cases found that 'breaches of procedure range from police misconduct, to piecemeal disclosure, to disclosable items simply not being listed on schedules'. [120]

---

[114] See Quirk H, *The Rise and Fall of the Right to Silence* (Oxford: Routledge, 2016).

[115] HMCPSI, *Disclosure—Thematic Review* (London: HMCPCI, 2008a) para 4.13. This has been a consistent research finding for years: Quirk 2006; Taylor (2006: 53–56).

[116] This was a problem in around half the cases in the HMCPCI (2008a) research (paras 5.7 and 7.17).

[117] HMCPSI (2008a: para 7.17). For similar findings from pre-2003 research see Crown Prosecution Service Inspectorate, *Thematic Review of the Disclosure of Unused Material*, (London: Crown Prosecution Service Inspectorate, 2000) Plotnikoff J and Woolfson R, *'A Fair Balance'? Evaluation of the Operation of Disclosure Law* (London: Home Office, 2001), Quirk (2006), Taylor (2006). On the other hand, many disclosure officers err so far on the side of caution that they disclose almost everything, having given little or no thought to its relevance: HMCPSI (2008a: para 5.9).   [118] Quoted by Taylor (2006: 153).

[119] Prosecutor, quoted by Taylor (2006: 108). On 'paperwork' see pp 108–121; 132–173.

[120] Dargue P, 'An Analysis of Disclosure Failings in Murder Appeals Against Conviction 2006–2018' [2020] *Criminal Law Review* 707 at 726.

And so there is a fundamental contradiction: the police job is to construct as strong a case as is possible without being overtly dishonest; the CPIA is designed to recognise and remedy the problem that what is left out of that construction might be more revealing of the truth than what is put in it, and so the defence should be provided with that material. However, the people given the job of identifying what the defence should be provided with are the very people who the CPIA is designed to protect the defence against! Moreover, there is little evidence that—when prosecutors are aware of omissions—the CPS do much to remedy the situation (other than to make late disclosure when they are aware of relevant material).

A second problem with the disclosure regime is that the CPS, like the police, have conviction-oriented goals that conflict with whatever due process philosophy underlies the CPIA. Moreover, while prosecutors are better trained than are the police, much of this preparatory work is done by paralegal CPS officers with little legal training, court experience or cultural affinity for neutral justice. One paralegal said of the way the CPIA reduced the disclosure obligation on the prosecution: 'Now we are entitled to say "on your bike, why should we do it all?" Sometimes you were ending up doing their defence work for them because you were giving them their defence' (Quirk: 2006). These views are not universally held in the CPS, and—as in all areas of criminal justice where there is discretion—practice varies between individuals and offices. The law is too imprecise to restrict discretion and judgement, as is probably inevitable when dealing with material that might assist a case (the defence) about which one knows little. Thus some officers and prosecutors disclose on the basis of interpretations of the law that are ungenerous to the defence, while others give the defence the benefit of the doubt.[121] In light of disclosure failures contributing to a rise in case discontinuance (see section 7.3.3), a new National Disclosure Improvement Plan was implemented in 2018 to increase the quality of disclosure decision-making between the police and CPS. The CPS reported that 97% of phase 2 had been successfully implemented during 2018/19.[122] The impact of this on conviction, acquittal and discontinuance rates remains to be seen.

The use of barristers, particularly in the Crown court, is a further complicating factor. Barristers tend to provide the defence with far more material than necessary, often on the day of trial (HMCPSI, 2008a, para 2.23). Quirk (2006) found barristers to be very opposed to the restrictive CPIA regime. This could reflect their lack of 'belonging' to any organisation or 'side', raising questions about how impartial state-salaried prosecutors can ever be. Quirk (2006) found that relevant material is often revealed by chance during trials, exactly as happened in the case against Liam Allen.[123] Doubtless it would come to light more often if prosecutors had the time and inclination to search for it. In the current austerity climate very few, if any, prosecutors will have the former even if they have the latter. Frequently disclosure is done to a low standard. In 2017, the joint inspectorate report found that 'the police do not understand what constitutes sensitive material and are routinely not scheduling sensitive material correctly' and that 'Neither party is managing sensitive material effectively and prosecutors are failing to manage ongoing disclosure.'[124]

A fourth problem with the regime is that the defence disclosure obligation, which has been expanded by the CJA 2003, could infringe the presumption of innocence enshrined in Art 6.2 because it requires the defence to assist the prosecution.[125] However, given the tendency of common law judges to interpret domestic law as already compatible with

---

[121] HMCPSI (2000); Taylor (2006: 98–101). [122] CPS, *Annual Report and Accounts 2018–19*.
[123] *R v Allan* [2017] Croydon Crown Court. See Smith T, 'The "Near Miss" of Liam Allan: Critical Problems in Police Disclosure, Investigation Culture, and the Resourcing of Criminal Justice' [2018] *Criminal Law Review* 711.
[124] HMCPSI and HMIC (2017).
[125] See *DPP, ex p Lee* [1999] on the original CPIA. For an analysis of the obligations, see Redmayne (2004).

European norms, and the 'margin of appreciation' doctrine of the European Court of Human Rights, commentators think it unlikely that a successful challenge to this aspect of the CPIA could be mounted under either the Human Rights Act 1998 or by taking a case to Strasbourg.[126] In fact, the duty of the defence to co-operate and thereby assist the prosecution has expanded in the last few years.[127] Quirk (2006) comments: 'The statutory regime requires the culturally adversarial police to fulfil an effectively inquisitorial function; prosecutors to view material from a defence perspective; the defence to act in the interests of the administration of the justice system rather than of their clients; and defendants to cooperate with proceedings against themselves.'

The CCRC identified non-disclosure as the third most common reason for referring convictions to the Court of Appeal in 1999/2000. In its 2015/16 Annual Report and Accounts, the CCRC said: 'The single most frequent cause [of miscarriages of justice] continues to be failure to disclose to the defence information which could have assisted the accused.'[128] This is hardly surprising in light of the damning findings of the joint HMIC and HMCPSI report on disclosure which called for urgent review of procedures[129] and the findings of a huge CPS review of cases following the collapse of Liam Allen's trial on the basis of non-disclosure.[130] In their responses to the latest report, both the DPP and the leader of the National Police Chiefs' Council admitted that there are significant problems with disclosure procedures, following which a new protocol and the National Disclosure Improvement Plan were introduced.[131] Just as well, as the number of cases discontinued by the CPS due to disclosure failures rose from 583 in 2013/14 to 833 in 2017/18.[132] But according to HMCPSI research in 2018/19 there are still poor levels of compliance despite some improvements. There are significant police errors in 22% of cases, with omission of items that should have been disclosed being the most common. Prosecutors also gave bad advice to the police in over half of all cases, and failed in their disclosure duties to the defence in around one-quarter of cases.[133]

The problem is not confined to the police and CPS.[134] Indeed, the Court of Appeal has noted 'substantial evidence' suggesting an HMRC *policy* of non-disclosure of crucial

---

[126] See Sharpe S, 'HRA 1998: Article 6 and the Disclosure of Evidence in Criminal Trials' [1999] *Criminal Law Review* 273.

[127] Criminal Procedure Rules (2015 as amended) <http://www.legislation.gov.uk/uksi/2015/1490/contents> (accessed 15 May 2020). See Sprack J and Sprack M, *A Practical Approach to Criminal Procedure* 16th edn (Oxford: OUP, 2019).

[128] CCRC, *Annual Report and Accounts 2015/2016* (2016) online at: <https://s3-eu-west-2.amazonaws.com/ccrc-prod-storage-1jdn5d1f6iq1l/uploads/2017/01/CCRC-Annual-Report-and-Account2015-16-HC244-Web-Accessible-v0.2-2.pdf> (accessed 7 April 2020).

[129] HMCPSI and HMIC (2017). Smith T, 'The "Near Miss" of Liam Allan: Critical Problems in Police Disclosure, Investigation Culture and the Resourcing of Criminal Justice' [2018] Crim LR 711.

[130] CPS, *Rape and serious sexual offence prosecutions—Assessment of disclosure of unused material ahead of trial* (2018d) online at: <https://www.cps.gov.uk/publication/rape-and-serious-sexual-offence-prosecutions-assessment-disclosure-unused-material> (accessed 6 April 2020). For more scandals where cases were discontinued and convictions were overturned, see *Ratcliffe-on-Soar Power Station Protest Inquiry into Disclosure* (available at <http://www.statewatch.org/news/2011/dec/uk-mark-kennedy-inquiry-report.pdf> (accessed 6 April 2020)); and Ellison M and Morgan A, *Review of Possible Miscarriages of justice—Impact of Undisclosed Undercover Police Activity on the Safety of Convictions Report to the Attorney General* (HC 291, 2015).

[131] CPS, *CPS publishes outcome of sexual offences review* (2018a) online at: <https://www.cps.gov.uk/cps/news/cps-publishes-outcome-sexual-offences-review> (online accessed 6 April 2020).

[132] CPS (2018). See Dargue P, 'An Analysis of Disclosure Failings in Murder Appeals Against Conviction 2006–2018' [2020] *Criminal Law Review* 707, Table 1.

[133] HMCPSI, *Disclosure of Unused Material in the Crown Court* (2020) (online at <https://www.justiceinspectorates.gov.uk/hmcpsi/inspections/> (accessed 6 April 2020)).

[134] *The Guardian*, 24 June 2005. For discussion see Taylor C, 'Advance Disclosure and the Culture of the Investigator' (2005) 33 *International Journal of Sociology of Law* 118.

details in drug importation cases 'not only to the defence but also to members of HMRC's legal department, prosecuting counsel and of course trial judges.'[135] And the 44-plus wrongful convictions in the recent Post Office scandal discussed in section 7.2.3 were also because of non-disclosure.

The disclosure system as actually operated leads to delays, adjournments, inappropriate discontinuances and a waste of public money. Worse, it is a continuing recipe for miscarriages of justice. The changes brought in by the CJA 2003 were made in full knowledge of this. They are ECHR-compliant, and go some way to remedying the most unjust aspects of the CPIA regime. Why not go the whole way, and simply open the police file to the defence (excepting sensitive material that could be dealt with via PII applications as now)? Or why not require certain types of information (e.g. previous convictions of prosecution witnesses) to always be disclosed? One answer is that in some cases there is a vast amount of material, such as CCTV footage. The force of this point weakens in a digitalised system (although the joint inspectorate report also had concerns about that process), but, in any event, who is going to pay for what, in most cases, would be lengthy and unproductive trawls? Another is that, if the police are determined to keep evidence from the defence, they might simply remove the most damaging parts anyway.

In conclusion, it is clear that non-disclosure, along with the other issues discussed here, allows the police to construct cases to their advantage that increase the prospects of conviction. Prosecutors are to some extent unaware of these constructions, to some extent aware but supportive of them, and to some extent mediators between police and defence. But the extent to which the last point is true is insufficient to justify their characterisation as 'neutral' ministers of justice.[136]

7.4 The public interest, the police and the CPS

If, and only if, a case passes the 'evidential' test, the police and CPS have then to consider whether prosecution is in the 'public interest'. This is a flexible concept, and the most recent version of the Code for Crown Prosecutors specifically asks prosecutors to consider whether out of court disposals (see section 7.4.1) are more appropriate. Para 4.10 of the Code states:

> It has never been the rule that a prosecution will automatically take place once the evidential stage is met. A prosecution will usually take place unless the prosecutor is satisfied that there are public interest factors tending against prosecution which outweigh those tending in favour.[137]

While prosecutors are guided about what to consider when applying the test by a series of questions contained in the Code, what is perceived as in the public interest will vary according to one's experiences and political views. In some types of case evidential and 'public interest' matters get blurred. For example, prosecutors are reluctant to prosecute doctors for gross negligence manslaughter so they set their evidential requirements higher than necessary.[138]

---

[135] Quoted in Elks (2008: 257). See further *R v Choudhery and others* [2005] EWCA Crim 2598.

[136] See further Young and Sanders (2004); Dennis I, 'Prosecution Disclosure: Are the Problems Insoluble?' [2018] *Criminal Law Review* 829.

[137] CPS, *The Code for Crown Prosecutors*, online at: <https://www.cps.gov.uk/publication/code-crown-prosecutors> (accessed 2 April 2020).

[138] Griffiths D and Sanders A, 'The Road to the Dock: Prosecution Decision-making in Medical Manslaughter Cases' in Sanders A and Griffiths D (eds), *Bioethics, Medicine and the Criminal Law: Medicine, Crime and Society vol. 2* (Cambridge: CUP, 2013) 117–158.

Assisted suicide is a particularly difficult issue. It is a crime (contrary to the Suicide Act 1961) but is it in the public interest to prosecute someone who is only helping 'victims' to do as they (lawfully) wish? Should prosecutors condone homicide in the absence of a change in the law by Parliament? Should people be forced to live against their will simply because Parliament lacks the will to enter this controversy, or are there legitimate fears that some terminally ill or incapacitated victims may feel under pressure to terminate their lives? Until 2009 the CPS dealt with these cases on an ad hoc basis, though it seems it rarely prosecuted. But everyone who helped loved ones to die feared they might be prosecuted. Debbie Purdy did not want to place her partner in legal jeopardy when the time came for her to want his help in dying. She persuaded the courts to order the DPP to publish a policy on such cases so that people would know where they stand.[139] The result (a policy initially published in 2010, updated in 2014) does not rule out prosecutions where there is a cause for concern, but cases like Purdy's are not prosecuted. So there have, in the 10 years to the time of writing, been only three 'successful' prosecutions for assisted suicide out of 100-plus referred to the CPS by the police.[140]

The majority of cases involving the 'public interest' are dealt with by warnings as alternatives to prosecution. Also known as 'diversion' (that is, diversion from the courts), warnings are part of the armoury of all law enforcement agencies.[141] Police warnings (often referred to as 'cautioning') attracted little public controversy for many years until their use became so frequent that government and police spokespeople in the early 1990s began to blame them for rising crime rates. In this section we will look behind the generous facade of cautioning and other forms of diversion that have expanded at a particularly rapid rate over the last decade or so.

7.4.1 Cautions and other out of court disposals

Prosecution is potentially harmful, largely because of its stigmatising effects. It is equally plausible that cautioning erodes the deterrent effect of the law and thus tacitly encourages crime. There is no reliable evidence on this issue one way or the other. It is almost impossible to know the best strategy for any one person, and the best aggregate strategy for society as a whole will always be contestable. The Labour government of the late 1990s decided that cautioning should be restricted, more on the basis of the electoral appeal of 'tough' policies than their basis in research.[142] The number of cautions administered for both summary and indictable offences then fell, and has continued to fall, with some ups and downs, ever since.[143] This fall has been accompanied by a rise in the use of some other types of out of court disposal (OOCD), particularly 'community resolution' (see section 7.4.2). Ministry of Justice guidelines indicate that police officers

---

[139] *R (on the application of Purdy) v Director of Public Prosecutions* [2009] UKHL 45.

[140] CPS, *Assisted Suicide* (2020) online at: <https://www.cps.gov.uk/publication/assisted-suicide> (accessed 2 April 2020). For general discussion see Sanders A, 'The CPS, Policy-making and Assisted Dying: Towards a "Freedom" Approach' in Child J and Duff A (eds), *Criminal Law Reform Now: Proposals and Critique* (Oxford: Hart, 2018).

[141] For extended discussions, see Smith R, *Diversion in Youth Justice* (Abingdon: Routledge, 2017); Dingwall G and Harding C, *Diversion in the Criminal Process* (London: Sweet & Maxwell, 1998).

[142] Evans R, 'Cautioning: Counting the Cost of Retrenchment' [1994] *Criminal Law Review* 566; Sanders A, 'What Principles Underlie Criminal Justice Policy in the 1990s?' (1998) 18 *Oxford Journal of Legal Studies* 533.

[143] Ministry of Justice, *Criminal Justice Statistics quarterly, England and Wales, October 2018 to September 2019* (2020) online at: <https://assets.publishing.service.gov.uk/government/uploads/system/uploads/attachment_data/file/867102/criminal-justice-statistics-quarterly-september-2019.pdf> (accessed 10 April 2020).

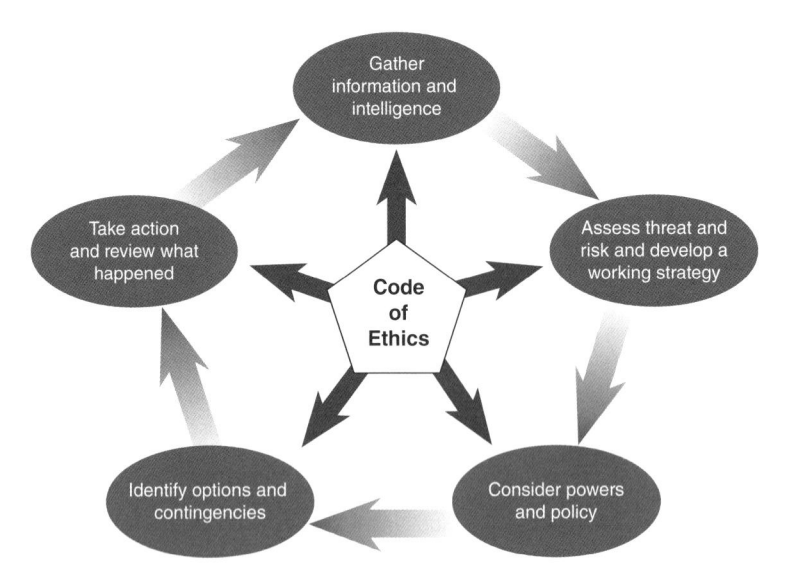

Figure 7.1 Police National Decision Model
Source: College of Policing <https://www.app.college.police.uk/app-content/national-decision-model/the-national-decision-model/>

now have to consider whether administering a caution is appropriate in the context of all available OOCDs.[144]

The process begins with the investigating officer's opinion regarding what action should be taken in a case. That decision should be made in line with the National Decision Model, prepared by the College of Policing. The existence of a national model is, presumably, also designed to encourage consistent (and perhaps easily measurable) administration of OOCDs. Officers are often, throughout their careers, required to act quickly and rely heavily on intuition and/or emotional reaction.[145] Such skills encourage officers to act first and reflect later, and the extent to which asking them to change tack and apply a particular model will in fact influence decision-making is questionable. The model (see Figure 7.1) asks police officers to consider six key things when deciding how cases should proceed.

Adult cautions are available for offenders aged 18 or over. A Youth Caution, which operates in a similar way, was introduced under the terms of the Legal Aid, Sentencing and Punishment of Offenders Act 2012 (LASPO). Whether a suspect is eligible for a simple caution is an operational decision for the police, but they cannot be given to a person who has not admitted commission of an offence. Nor can they be issued without the agreement of the recipient. Cautions should not be given simply because there is not enough evidence to instigate formal prosecution, or if the officer believes that the public interest would be better served by prosecution.[146] Furthermore, the Criminal Justice and Courts Act 2015 imposes a number of restrictions about when cautions may be administered for indictable offences and upon people with an offending history, although the police decision-maker is still left with considerable discretion on the issue of whether 'exceptional circumstances' exist such that would allow a caution to be administered.

---

[144] Ministry of Justice, *Simple Cautions for Adult Offenders* (2015b) online at: <https://assets.publishing.service.gov.uk/government/uploads/system/uploads/attachment_data/file/708595/cautions-guidance-2015.pdf> (accessed 20 August 2019).

[145] Brown D and Daus C, 'The Influence of Police Officers' Decision-making Style and Anger Control on Responses to Work Scenarios' (2015) 4(3) *Journal of Applied Research in Memory and Cognition* 294–302.

[146] Ministry of Justice, *Simple Cautions for Adult Offenders* (2015b).

As a mechanism for protecting innocent suspects from administrative determinations of guilt, the pre-conditions have been found wanting. Some cautions are administered precisely because there is insufficient evidence, and sometimes in the absence of consent or an admission.[147] Nor is consent or an admission a safeguard in reality. Some children and young people will admit and consent to almost anything to escape from the 'coercive jaws' of the criminal process.[148] In *Metropolitan Police Comr, ex p Thompson*[149] the cautioning inspector admitted that he often offered a caution and then asked the alleged offender if he understood that this amounted to an admission of the offence, with the implicit threat that if the suspect did not agree to this, he or she would be prosecuted instead of cautioned. Although the Divisional Court held that cautions offered as an inducement to confess, such as happened here, are invalid, having to 'bargain in the shadow of the law'[150] clearly had been a common practice and—having come to light again in 2002[151]—probably still is. Another caution was quashed by the Divisional Court after a youth was incorrectly told that what he did (watch his cousin shoplift) amounted to theft. It was on this basis that he admitted his 'guilt' and consented to be cautioned. But as there was insufficient evidence to prosecute, there was no informed consent.[152] Relatedly, so-called diversion schemes result in new populations of minor offenders being drawn into the criminal justice net or experiencing more intervention than is justified given the seriousness of their offence. This is driven in part by a deliberate attempt by government to bring more offenders into the net of formal social control through requiring the police to achieve 'measurable targets' while at the same time providing them with administratively efficient methods of 'closing cases'.[153] There are many dangers here, including that innocent people get caught up in the net and that serious offenders are not put before the courts. Given the type of people most likely to be vulnerable to the effects of net widening, those trends are in line with the neoliberal punitive turn and increased othering of marginalised populations. Concerns about inconsistent application of the provisions, and disproportionate use against particular groups of suspects continue to be uncovered.[154]

Moreover, we have seen that investigating officers who favour prosecution over caution can have the individual charged with little chance of resistance from other officers. Some safeguards do exist under PACE in the form of the right to disclosure and legal advice before a caution is administered. However, with less than half of suspects taking up their right to legal advice at the police station,[155] it is likely that many people are

---

[147] Evans R, *The Conduct of Police Interviews with Juveniles* (Royal Commission on Criminal Justice Research Study no 8) (London: HMSO, 1993b) p 41; Sanders (1998); Evans R and Puech K, 'Reprimands and Warnings: Populist Punitiveness or Restorative Justice?' [2001] *Criminal Law Review* 794; Holdaway S 'Final Warning: Appearance and Reality' [2003] 4 *Criminal Justice* 355; and other research cited in Field S, 'Early Intervention and the "New" Youth Justice' [2008] *Criminal Law Review* 177 at 178–179.

[148] Young R, 'The Sandwell Mediation and Reparation Scheme' (Birmingham: West Midlands Probation Service, 1987).   [149] *Metropolitan Police Comr, ex p Thompson* [1997] 1 WLR 1519.

[150] Dignan J, 'Repairing the Damage: Can Reparation Be Made to Work in the Service of Diversion?' (1992) 32(4) *British Journal of Criminology* 453.

[151] *R (U) v Metropolitan Police Commissioner* [2003], endorsing the decision in *Thompson*.

[152] *Metropolitan Police Comr, ex p P* (1995) 160 JP 367 discussed by Evans (1996).

[153] See, for example, the comments of the Home Secretary on 14 December 2009 reported at: <http://www.justice.gov.uk/news/newsrelease141209b.htm> (accessed 5 January 2010).

[154] See McGlynn C, Westmarland N and Johnson K, 'Under the Radar: The Widespread Use of "Out of Court Resolutions" in Policing Domestic Violence and Abuse in the United Kingdom' (2018) 58(1) *British Journal of Criminology* 1–16 and, for a useful overview of the issues, Neyroud P, *Out of Court Disposals managed by the Police: a review of the evidence* (2018) online at: <https://www.npcc.police.uk/Publication/NPCC%20Out%20of%20Court%20Disposals%20Evidence%20assessment%20FINAL%20June%202018.pdf> (accessed 14 March 2020).

[155] Kemp V, '"No Time for a Solicitor": Implications for Delays on the Take Up of Legal Advice' (2013) 3 *Criminal Law Review* 184–202.

cautioned without the benefit of legal advice and therefore placing great reliance on the police 'advice' about whether or not there is sufficient evidence upon which a case could be prosecuted.[156]

One way of addressing such problems would be to take away the power of the police to determine who gets cautioned and in what way. This is not on the agenda as far as ordinary cautions and warnings are concerned, but there is some CPS involvement where 'conditional cautions' are concerned. 'Conditional cautions' were introduced for adults by the CJA 2003 (ss.22–27) and for youths under LASPO, and should be used when there is sufficient evidence to prosecute but the public interest is best served by the offender complying with suitable conditions aimed at rehabilitation or reparation, and/or a penalty.[157] Conditions must be proportionate, achievable and appropriate. The most recent guidance issued is intended for use by both Crown prosecutors and the police. When first introduced, conditional cautions could only be authorised by Crown prosecutors. However, the police are now, also as a result of LASPO, authorised to administer conditional cautions except in indictable or sexual offences, or in cases involving hate crimes. If any condition is breached, prosecution is not automatic—it is for the CPS to decide.[158] Prior to the extension of police powers, prosecution would have been the expected outcome, but the police have been given greater discretion to look into the 'reasonableness' of a breach or deem a condition fulfilled. Conditional cautions are not to be the 'next step' for someone who has been previously given a 'simple' caution, as someone previously cautioned for a similar offence should only exceptionally be conditionally cautioned. Conditional cautions were fairly slow to take off: despite being introduced as a part of the Criminal Justice Act 2003, in 2009 only around 15,000 were wielded (5% of all cautions) (CPS 2009). The data has now been combined with that for simple cautions, making caution and conditional caution rates difficult to examine.[159]

7.4.2 Community resolution and restorative Justice

Community resolution is a non-statutory OOCD available for adults and for youths. Despite being available since 2008,[160] data on community resolution has only been collected centrally since 2015. In the year to end March 2019, 100,542 community resolutions were dispensed by the police—the only form of OOCD not to decrease in use.[161] A number of factors are likely to feed into this: a desire to encourage offenders to confront the consequences of their actions and therefore take responsibility (and be rehabilitated), seeking to involve victims more actively in the criminal process, to reduce the number of offences being prosecuted and therefore reduce cost and increase efficiency in the courts. Community resolution is intended to be used for minor crime and anti-social behaviour, when the offender accepts responsibility for the behaviour, agrees to participate and has no relevant offending history. It is important that the views of the victim are taken

---

[156] See further, Cushing K, 'Diversion from Prosecution for Young People in England and Wales – Reconsidering the Mandatory Admission Criteria' (2014) 14 *Youth Justice* 140.

[157] CPS, *Adult Conditional Cautions (Director's Guidance)* (2013a) online at: <https://www.cps.gov.uk/legal-guidance/adult-conditional-cautions-directors-guidance> (accessed 14 March 2020).

[158] Criminal Justice Act 2003, s.24. See further Ministry of Justice, *Code of Practice for Adult Conditional Cautions* (London, The Stationery Office, 2013).

[159] See Home Office (2019). In 2018/19, 54,207 (1%) recorded crimes resulted in an adult caution, compared to 63,608 (1.3%) in the previous year.

[160] Flanagan R, *The Review of Policing* (2008) online at: <https://www.justiceinspectorates.gov.uk/hmicfrs/media/flanagan-review-of-policing-20080201.pdf> (accessed 14 August 2019).

[161] Home Office (2019: 10).

into consideration before an agreement about how to proceed is reached. Resolution can include paying compensation or apologising to the victim as part of a restorative justice procedure. Restorative Justice (RJ) can be conducted via a third party or via a community conference. As long as they consent, victims are invited to take an active role in the process, and RJ features in the Victims' Code.[162] Many current 'restorative justice' initiatives attempt to be both rehabilitative and directly victim-oriented.[163] These objectives are laudable but not always mutually compatible. This goes to the root of the problem of multiple objectives discussed in chapter 1. RJ projects need to calibrate the degrees of freedom given to and taken away from both offenders and victims (both current and in future) by these projects, taking into account the importance of securing the human rights of all concerned, in order to assess the way in which the greatest overall amount of balance can be secured.

RJ is, generally speaking, a process through which those involved in a particular offence collectively resolve how to deal with it. Definitions of RJ are contested,[164] although Daly persuasively argues that we cannot have a fully innovative and integrated approach to RJ as part of the criminal process unless we clearly define what it is.[165] Although it can occur at any stage of a case, RJ is most commonly used as part of an OOCD. There is evidence that RJ can directly improve the emotional wellbeing of victims,[166] and that it may help offenders to reintegrate in the 'moral' society.[167] There is also evidence that RJ processes reduce reoffending[168] by encouraging empathy through shaming as a form of social control.[169] Shapland argues it could be used in a more innovative and integrated way,[170] but it seems unlikely that there would be much appetite for agencies of the criminal justice system to move away from conventional practices.

RJ has gained increasing traction in recent years, and it works well with recent government and public concerns that victims should (rightly) not be minimised in the criminal justice process. However, questions arise about who is being 'encouraged' to undergo RJ processes and why. We have seen throughout this book that marginalised populations are more likely to be criminalised. It is likely to be similar populations who are 'encouraged' to undertake RJ. This fits with a neoliberal government agenda which seeks to responsibilise, or re-moralise, citizens into 'appropriate' ways of behaving. The extent to which marginalised and minority groups are being persuaded to conform to a particular capitalist agenda is questionable, particularly when the resources to 'conform' (such as access to education, healthcare, etc) may not be readily available as a result of other austerity measures. It is therefore vitally important that appropriate standards are set for procedures to

---

[162] Ministry of Justice (2015a) *Code of Practice for Victims of Crime* online at: <https://www.cps.gov.uk/sites/default/files/documents/legal_guidance/OD_000049.pdf> (accessed 10 October 2019).

[163] For good discussions of many of the problems see Gray P, 'The Politics of Risk and Young Offenders' Experiences of Social Exclusion and Restorative Justice' (2005) 45 *British Journal of Criminology* 938; Fox et al, 'Restorative Final Warnings: Policy and Practice' (2006) 45 *Howard Journal* 129.

[164] Mika H and Zehr H, 'Fundamental Concepts of Restorative Justice' (2017) *Restorative Justice* 73–81.

[165] Daly K, 'What is Restorative Justice? Fresh Answers to a Vexed Question' (2015) 11(1) *Victims & Offenders* 1–21.

[166] Walters M, *Hate Crime and Restorative Justice: Exploring Causes, Repairing Harms* (Oxford: OUP, 2014).

[167] Shapland J, 'Forgiveness and Restorative Justice: Is It Necessary? Is It Helpful?' (2016) 5(1) *Oxford Journal of Law and Religion* 94–112.

[168] See, for example, Strang H and Braithwaite J (eds), *Restorative Justice: Philosophy to Practice* (Dartmouth: Ashgate, 2000)

[169] Maxwell G and Morris A, 'The Role of Shame, Guilt, and Remorse in Restorative Justice Processes for Young People' in Weitekamp E and Kerner H-J (eds) *Restorative Justice: Theoretical Foundations* (Devon: WIllan Publishing, 2002) 267–284; Kyd S, Elliot T and Walters M, *Clarkson and Keating: Criminal Law* 9th edn (London: Sweet and Maxwell, 2017).

[170] Shapland (2016).

be both balanced and effective.[171] Indeed, RJ is, like other criminal justice disposals, more likely to be effective if it is seen as fair.[172]

As with other OOCDs, community resolution, and therefore Restorative Justice, is likely to be affected by the way that police exercise discretion, which is likely to be influenced by operational agendas within police areas. In 2012, community resolution was used in 10,160 cases of 'serious violence', including offences of causing grievous bodily harm,[173] likely to be the result of target chasing. The then Shadow Home Secretary linked this misuse of community resolution to police budget cuts and falling numbers of police officers, leading to increased pressure on services. This makes clear that, at times of austerity, it is even more important that appropriate standards are set.

7.4.3 Penalty notices for disorder (PNDs)

These police-administered fines were introduced by the Criminal Justice and Police Act 2001 for a small number of specified offences for adults, and subsequently extended.[174] The offences include causing harassment, alarm or distress (Public Order Act 1986, s.5), drunk and disorderly, minor theft and criminal damage. In 2009, the reach of PNDs was extended to include a second offence of cannabis possession (a warning should normally be given for a first offence, and a third should be prosecuted).[175] Most recently, PNDs can be issued for breach of the Covid-19 laws.[176] The annual number of PNDs rose sharply in the late 2000s (over 207,000 were issued in 2007—representing over 10% of all detected crime), but has declined significantly in recent years. In the year to September 2019, 20,400 PNDs were issued,[177] falling (in line with a steady year on year decrease) from 25,900 in 2017.[178] Use of PNDs varies across police forces,[179] but most are issued for drunk and disorderly behaviour, possession of cannabis, retail theft valued at less than £100 and threatening or abusive words/behaviour. Provisions inserted by LASPO allow the police to issue a PND-E which 'allow' an individual to discharge liability to be convicted of an offence by paying for and completing an educational course relevant to the offence. This can again be situated in the political trend to encourage citizens to take responsibility for

---

[171] Braithwaite J, 'Setting Standards for Restorative Justice' (2002) 42(3) *British Journal of Criminology* 563–577.

[172] See, for example, Tyler T, 'Procedural Justice, Legitimacy, and the Effective Rule of Law' (2003) 30 *Crime and Justice* 283–357.

[173] BBC News (2013) '"Community resolutions" used in 10,000 serious violence cases' <https://www.bbc.co.uk/news/uk-22346971> (accessed 2 July 2018). See also Westmarland N, Johnson K and McGlynn C, 'Under the Radar: The Widespread Use of 'Out of Court Resolutions' in Policing Domestic Violence and Abuse in the United Kingdom' (2018) 58(1) *British Journal of Criminology* 1–16 in relation to use for serious domestic offences.

[174] For details see Young R, 'Street Policing After PACE: The Drift to Summary Justice' in Cape and Young (eds) *Regulating Policing: The PACE Act, Past, Present and Future* (Oxford: Hart, 2008).

[175] Ministry of Justice Circular 2009/05, under the authority of the CJPO 2001, ss.1–11.

[176] The Health Protection (Coronavirus, Restrictions) (England) Regulations 2020, reg 10. For a discussion about the importance of the perceived fairness of such encounters, see Grace S, 'Policing the coronavirus lockdown: The limits of on-the-spot fines' (2020) online at: <https://bscpolicingnetwork.com/2020/04/02/policing-the-coronavirus-lockdown-the-limits-of-on-the-spot-fines/> (accessed 5 May 2020).

[177] Ministry of Justice, *Criminal Justice Statistics quarterly, England and Wales, October 2018 to September 2019* online at: <https://assets.publishing.service.gov.uk/government/uploads/system/uploads/attachment_data/file/867102/criminal-justice-statistics-quarterly-september-2019.pdf> (accessed 5 March 2020).

[178] Ministry of Justice, *Criminal Justice Statistics quarterly, England and Wales, April 2016 to March 2017 (provisional)* (2017a) online at: <https://assets.publishing.service.gov.uk/government/uploads/system/uploads/attachment_data/file/638225/cjs-statistics-march-2017.pdf> (accessed 20 June 2018).

[179] Sosa K, 'Proceed with Caution: Use of Out-of-Court Disposals in England & Wales' (2012) *Policy Exchange* online at: <https://policyexchange.org.uk/wp-content/uploads/2016/09/proceed-with-caution-2.pdf> (accessed 20 July 2019).

their behaviour and adapt it to prescribed norms. It is, however, likely to disproportionately affect poor and marginalised groups, who may be less able to undertake a course and therefore remain open to prosecution if they also cannot pay the course fee or fine that is attached to the PND. Fines are fixed according to the seriousness of the offence, but the payment rate is low even though failure to pay then triggers court enforcement procedure. Between 2007 and 2011, 47% of PNDs issued in England and Wales went unpaid.[180] Recent data on the number of PNDs that are challenged in court is not available, but early data suggested that the rate of challenge is negligible at 1% in 2008.[181]

The lack of challenge should not be taken to mean that this summary justice is necessarily fair. Fines are low (currently £80 at most) so many people pay them whether or not they feel the PND was justified, but they may not appreciate the consequences of this: a record on the Police National Computer (though not a conviction), likelihood of prosecution for subsequent offences, and so forth. They also, in the same way as PND-Es, mean that poor and marginalised groups are more likely to face formal prosecution or enforcement measures as a result of inability to pay the financial penalty, if it is offered in the first place. The net widening, and drawing into court of those who 'fail' these 'alternatives', that we saw happening in relation to cautioning, is almost certainly equally true of PNDs. Net widening was acute in the pilot studies—around half of all PNDs were issued to juveniles who would not even have been reprimanded, and many of the others replaced reprimands and warnings.[182] Thus the 'punitive turn' is made yet more acute, as reflected in 45% of the youths in the pilot study saying the police had been unfair.

As always, police officers driven to achieve arrest targets find the 'low-hanging fruit' all too easy to pluck.[183] If PNDs are only for trivial offences, why take up so much police (and court fine enforcement) time with them? The answer is, in part, because PNDs are not so much about prosecution of individual cases as about controlling suspect populations, and should be seen as part of the wider movement to increase surveillance and control 'anti-social' behaviour.[184] Now the police have an additional weapon to back up the order to 'move on', which was also deployed to control movement in the Covid-19 outbreak.[185] And the victims who the government claims to be putting 'at the heart' of the criminal justice system? The PND scheme completely sidelines them, as it does not allow for the payment of compensation. But the victim perspective on PNDs has not been evaluated, nor the danger that ethnic minorities are likely to be overrepresented (especially as ethnicity is very often not recorded) (Amadi, 2008), nor the way poorer people are disproportionately affected by fixed penalties.

To sum up, taken together with the various forms of police and CPS caution, around one-third of crime is now prosecuted without reference to a court. The police can therefore 'get a result' with little or no scrutiny from any other agency. Yet PNDs are effectively

---

[180] Sosa (2012).   [181] Ministry of Justice, *Criminal Statistics England and Wales 2007* (2008).

[182] Grace S, '"Swift, Simple, Effective Justice?" Identifying the Aims of Penalty Notices for Disorder and Whether these have been Realised in Practice' (2014) 53(1) *Howard Journal* 69–82; Amadi J, *Piloting PNDs on 10–15 Year Olds* (MoJ Research Series 19/08, 2008); Young R, 'Ethnic Profiling and Summary Justice – An Ominous Silence' in: Sveinsson K (ed), *Ethnic Profiling: The Use of 'Race' in UK Law Enforcement* (London: Runnymede Trust, 2010) pp 43–49.

[183] See Young (2008) for discussion of the research on which this is based.

[184] See, e.g., Wacquant L, *Punishing the Poor: The Neoliberal Government of Social Insecurity.* (Durham NC: Duke University Press, 2009). Another manifestation of these practices is via the use of Public Spaces Protection Orders, on which see Brown K, 'The Hyper-Regulation of Public Space: The Use and Abuse of Public Spaces Protection Orders in England and Wales' (2017) 37(3) *Legal Studies* 543–568.

[185] See Health Protection (Coronavirus, Restrictions) (England) Regulations 2020, subject to review by the Secretary of State.

prosecutions, and so embody all the problems of case construction, use of prosecution for policing purposes, vagueness in the case of public order offences and a cavalier attitude to evidence (Young, 2008). The growing power of the police to finalise cases leads Jackson to argue that safeguards for suspects in police stations are more important than ever—at a time when they are being eroded.[186]

7.4.4 Police working rules and OOCDs

Policing considerations such as order and authority, and the 'bad attitude' of the suspect, influences many officers (Field 2008: 185)[187]. Field quotes an officer saying that suspects with criminal associates would be unlikely to be cautioned as 'they've not changed their ways have they?' (2008: 185). Warburton et al found that officers admitted that cannabis users who they informally warned on the street would have been arrested had they been 'mouthy' (2005: 120). The same patterns of race bias which can be observed in street policing also seem to operate here. In typically guarded Home Office-speak they say: 'The possibility must be considered that, where the defendant was from an ethnic minority group, the police were more likely to submit for prosecution cases in which the evidence was weaker than average or where the public interest was against prosecution.'[188] More recent research showing the same patterns is also 'consistent with discriminatory treatment'.[189] The long history of discriminatory treatment causes (an understandable) lack of trust between members of the non-white community and the police, which means that non-white suspects are less likely to make an admission, meaning that the same suspects are more likely to be prosecuted (and consequently overrepresented throughout the criminal justice process) rather than offered an OOCD (see further chapter 10).[190] It may well be that the relatively low cautioning rates of Afro-Caribbean (as compared to white), and poor (as compared to middle class), suspects are contrary to the Art 14 ECHR principle of equality of treatment. But the chances of any one member of a marginalised social group proving discrimination *in his or her case*, given the ability of the police to construct cases, would be vanishingly small except in particularly blatant cases. A further problem is that Art 14 is not a standalone provision; it only comes into play once some other Convention right is engaged. As in other areas of the criminal process, the practical value of the ECHR is not as great as might first appear.

The custody officer is supposed to be a protection. But as with evidential issues, the custody officer either acts as a rubber stamp or empathises with the arresting officer. Most custody officers, like police officers in general, are against extensive cautioning for adults in particular[191] and rely on the arresting officer alone for their information about the suspect: 'I'm dependent completely on what the officer says happened.'[192] What the arresting

---

[186] Jackson J, 'Police and Prosecutors after PACE: The Road from Case Construction to Case Disposal' in Cape and Young (2008). Not that this would help in the case of many PNDs and cannabis warnings, which are administered on the street.

[187] Field S, 'Early Intervention and the "New" Youth Justice' (2008) *Criminal Law Review* 177.

[188] Phillips and Brown (1998) p 148. See also Mhlanga (1999) summarised in: s 95 Findings no 1 (London: Home Office, 2000).

[189] Feilzer M and Hood R, *Differences or Discrimination?* (London: Youth Justice Board, 2004).

[190] Lammy D, *The Lammy Review: An independent review into the treatment of, and outcomes for, Black, Asian and Minority Ethnic individuals in the Criminal Justice System* (2017) online at: <https://www.gov.uk/government/uploads/system/uploads/attachment_data/file/643001/lammy-review-final-report.pdf> (accessed 18 August 2019).

[191] Evans R, 'Comparing Young Adult and Juvenile Cautioning in the Metropolitan Police District' (1993a) *Criminal Law Review* 572 at 577. They are certainly against taking personal circumstances into account: Field (2008). [192] Quoted by McConville et al (1991: 122).

officer does and does not say determines the construction of the case as serious or trivial, and the construction of the suspect either as a public enemy or as a temporarily lapsed paragon. All this was found by Young in relation to the processing of mentally ill suspects. Diversion decisions were often taken when, because of mental illness, mens rea was thought to be hard to prove (that is, in cases which should not be prosecuted anyway), but less often when the mental illness was simply a mitigating factor. The wishes of influential victims and offence seriousness tended to 'trump' mental illness in determining what happened.[193]

The CPS can, in principle, ensure that cautionable cases are not prosecuted by discontinuing them or, since 2003, by directing that they be cautioned.[194] But not in the case of—in a not-isolated example—Sacha Hall, prosecuted for 'handling stolen goods' (food thrown away by a supermarket).[195] The most important problem for the CPS, however, is that police construction makes it often difficult and sometimes impossible to identify cautionable cases. Factors which could point towards caution or other forms of diversion are downplayed in the file, or such facts are not brought out by the police because of failure to ask appropriate questions. One of the functions of the CPS is to exercise control over the 'public interest' dimension of prosecutions. But it cannot do anything about cases which were cautioned when they should have been NFA'd or prosecuted. Indeed, the police can even tie the hands of the CPS by promising that a case will be dropped. Although discontinuance is the prerogative of the CPS alone, it was held in *R v Croydon Justices, ex p Dean*[196] to be an abuse of process for prosecution to be continued after a promise, even from the police, that it would be dropped. In this case the 'deal' was discontinuance in exchange for the suspect giving evidence for the prosecution in a murder trial. This illustrates both the structurally weak position of the CPS as compared to the police, and the way the police use prosecution and non-prosecution in the 'public interest' as part of broader policing strategies.

7.5 Non police-prosecution agencies

As noted in chapter 1, substantial numbers of crimes are enforced by non-police agencies, such as those concerning financial crime, pollution, health and safety, benefit fraud and drug importation. These are commonly regarded as 'regulatory offences' rather than as 'real crimes'. They are not, however, always less serious than police-enforced laws. Tax frauds involve at least as much money as dishonesty offences enforced by the police. More people die through the negligence of employers in breach of health and safety laws than die as a result of pub brawls, muggings and street fights, and pollution is more of a threat to the public's safety than is drunkenness, prostitution and criminal damage.[197]

The decision-making structure of non-police agencies facilitates a propensity not to prosecute. Decisions to prosecute are always taken in the cold light of day, on the basis of a full written file, by senior officials, while decisions not to take formal action, even when there is clear evidence of crime, need not be—and frequently are not[198]—transmitted to senior officials. In principle, the approach of non-police agencies is the same as that of the

---

[193] Young H, 'Securing Fair Treatment: An Examination of the Diversion of Mentally Disordered Offenders from Police Custody', Unpublished PhD, (Birmingham University, 2002) ch 6.
[194] CJA 2003, s.37B(3)(b).
[195] <https://www.bbc.co.uk/news/magazine-13037808> (accessed 10 May 2020).
[196] [1993] QB 769.
[197] See generally, Barak G (ed), *Routledge International Handbook of Crimes of the Powerful* (Abingdon: Routledge, 2015). [198] Hawkins K, *Law as Last Resort* (Oxford: OUP, 2002).

police but the emphasis is usually completely different. It has to be: these agencies have few, if any, powers of arrest, and therefore stop-search, detention and coercive interviews are unavailable to the enforcement bodies. Investigation is either reactive, in response to major incidents, or routine, in which case appointments are made with the potential criminals—a bit like making appointments with known bank robbers to see if they have safe-cracking equipment at home. The result is that these offences have a low profile in the criminal justice system and society at large; this creates a vicious circle, whereby because they are little known there is little concern about them, meaning there is little pressure to enforce them more vigorously.

Take the Environment Agency: 'our first response is usually to give advice and guidance',[199] rather than issue an OOCD or prosecute. The enforcement pattern adopted by non-police agencies has been characterised as comprising a 'pyramid' of sanctions, the frequency of use of each sanction decreasing as one ascends the pyramid. This strategy, some argue, will usually be as effective a deterrent as a 'first-resort' prosecution strategy, but without its disadvantages, particularly if failure to comply at one level means that the next-level sanction is the automatic result.[200] The result is 'compliance' modes of working. Rather than treating their suspects as criminals, regulatory agencies seek to maintain continuing relationships with companies, to create 'a friendly working atmosphere',[201] to try to persuade them to comply with the law, and to avoid prosecution wherever possible.

The aim of the compliance strategy is prevention rather than deterrence and punishment. This recognises, among other things, that different companies respond differently depending on a range of factors including their size and market position.[202] Whether it works or not will depend, in part, on the speed at which the pyramid is ascended, whether failure to comply automatically moves the sanction up a level and the size of its prosecution apex. But there are several questions of principle: Is the compliance approach an effective method of crime prevention? Are political and financial resources adequate to enable movement up the pyramid? Is it justifiable for this strategy to be adopted by non-police agencies but not by the police?

Regarding effectiveness, this is a relative matter. How effective would these agencies be if their energies were dissipated by court cases? The answer is dependent on their resources, which are minimal and declining. The Environment Agency (EA), which is supposed to inspect sites, said: 'We haven't got the resources to do it.'[203] This might be why, in 2006 there were only 744 prosecutions by the EA, of which only 29 were against directors/senior managers: 'The majority of EA prosecutions are brought against ... micro businesses'[204] who are least able to defend themselves and so are less expensive to prosecute. As Hawkins says: 'Regulatory agencies could, as a matter of policy, double or treble the number of cases prosecuted, but to

---

[199] Environment Agency, *Environment Agency enforcement and sanctions policy* (2018) online at: <https://www.gov.uk/government/publications/environment-agency-enforcement-and-sanctions-policy/environment-agency-enforcement-and-sanctions-policy> (accessed 15 July 2019). The HSE's official policy is similarly revealing: <http://www.hse.gov.uk/pubns/hse41.pdf> (accessed 15 July 2019).

[200] Ayres I and Braithwaite J, *Responsive Regulation: Transcending the Deregulation Debate* (New York: OUP, 1992), Braithwaite J, *Restorative Justice and Responsive Regulation* (Oxford: OUP, 2002). For further discussion see Baldwin R and Black J, 'Really Responsive Regulation' (2008) 71 *Modern Law Review* 59. The approach was endorsed by Hampton P, *Reducing Administrative Burdens: Effective Inspection and Enforcement* (HM Treasury, London: SO, 2005) discussed later.

[201] Hutter B, *The Reasonable Arm of the Law?* (Oxford: Clarendon, 1988) p 189.

[202] Lynch-Wood G and Williamson D, 'Regulatory compliance: organisational capacities & regulatory strategies for environmental protection' in Quirk et al (eds) *Regulation and Criminal Justice* (Cambridge: CUP, 2010).

[203] *The Guardian*, 5 April 2000.

[204] Abbot C, *Enforcing Pollution Control Regulation* (Oxford: Hart, 2009), p 115, 150, 127. Also see Macrory R, *Regulatory Justice: Making Sanctions Effective* (London: Cabinet Office, 2006b) para E3.

do so would be at the cost of other regulatory activities deemed essential.'[205] Lack of resources also means that, according to the Chair of HMRC: 'We cannot prosecute everybody.' This is why 36 barristers repaid £605,000 to HMRC instead of being prosecuted.[206]

The government's 'austerity' policy from 2010–19 made things even worse. For example, in the environmental sphere, at a time when government policy supposedly viewed climate change as the world's biggest challenge, real terms funding of environmental agencies fell by an average of 50% between 2009/10 and 2015/16; in line with this, prosecutions of businesses by the Environment Agency fell by 80% in the same period.[207] Water firms discharged raw sewage into English rivers 200,000 times in 2019, and just 3.6% of fly-tipping and pollution complaints lead to penalties.[208] Similarly, health and safety prosecutions in the south-west halved between 2014 and 2019, which has also been blamed on huge cuts to local authorities and the Health and Safety Executive (HSE).[209] The office of the director of labour market enforcement said in its 2018 strategy paper that the average employer could expect to be inspected by the HMRC's minimum wage team once every 500 years. This is despite widespread evasion of minimum wage and health and safety laws—such as the 'shocking' situation in Leicester's clothing workshops in 2020.[210] The enforcement of 'regulatory' offences is not, it seems, a 'law and order' matter (police and CPS budgets have also been cut, as we saw in chapter 1, but by a smaller percentage).

Questions about the methods of these agencies thus cannot be divorced from political choices about the allocation of resources. The 'pyramid' idea can only work if agencies have the resources and political backing to use all its layers effectively. The 'compliance' strategy of non-police agencies produce enforcement patterns that are the mirror image of those of the police, who usually use a deterrent and punitive strategy. Why do such differences arise and how are they maintained in practice?[211]

The reality of these approaches, as might be expected, is that some people, and some organisations, behave more morally than others. Thus Haines, for example, examining work-place deaths in Australia, found that some companies responded to deaths by trying to eliminate future risk, while others confined themselves to changes aimed at limiting their legal liability.[212] However, this is not just a matter of individual or randomly-appearing morality. Haines found that 'virtuous' organisational cultures were made less virtuous by adverse economic and financial factors. Even the most moral business-people behave less morally when economic competition creates pressure to cut costs. Thus Thames Trains rejected plans to introduce an £8.2m safety system because it estimated that this would save only one life. Its valuation of a life at only £2.5m meant that the investment was thought uneconomic. In the event, 31 people died two years later when one of its trains went through a red light in an accident that the safety system would have prevented. In those two years £7.5 m was paid to shareholders.[213]

---

[205] Hawkins (2002: 441). See also Middleton D, 'The Legal and Regulatory Response to Solicitors Involved in Serious Fraud' (2005) 45 *British Journal of Criminology* 810.

[206] *The Guardian*, 9 December 2008. Tax avoidance schemes by large companies—including the newly part-government owned banks that started paying huge bonuses to senior traders again in 2010—that may not be criminal are arguably even more of a problem. See *The Guardian*, 2 February 2009.

[207] <https://www.desmog.co.uk/2019/08/23/environmental-enforcement-agencies-crippled-austerity-report> (accessed 1 May 2020). [208] *The Guardian*, 1 July 2020 and 21 July 2020.

[209] <https://www.business-live.co.uk/professional-services/hs-prosecutions-sw-halve-five-17684406> (accessed 1 May 2020). [210] *The Guardian*, 12 July 2020 and 30 August 2020.

[211] There is a sharp debate here. See Pearce F and Tombs S, 'Ideology, Hegemony and Empiricism: Compliance Theories of Regulation' (1990) 30 *British Journal of Criminology* 423 and the reply by Hawkins K, 'Compliance Strategy, Prosecution Policy, and Aunt Sally: A Comment on Pearce and Tombs' (1990) 30 *British Journal of Criminology* 444.

[212] Haines F, *Corporate Regulation: Beyond 'Punish or Persuade'* (Oxford: Clarendon, 1997).

[213] *The Times*, 12 May 2000. This was the Paddington rail crash of 1999.

It is often said that these (white collar) crimes and criminals are 'different' from those the police and CPS deal with.[214] Braithwaite is one of the few influential figures to challenge this. He argues that the regulatory pyramid should be applied to all types of crime, defined in the broadest sense, with sanctions moving up in all cases from informal mild sanctions through restorative sanctions to 'traditional' criminal sanctions. 'Regulation' and 'law enforcement' should be available, though used sparingly, for all offences, regardless of how we classify them.[215] So far, these arguments have fallen on deaf ears. One result is that neither the public at large nor traditional text books treat 'regulatory offences' as 'real' crimes (*mala in se*). They are seen, instead, as *mala prohibita*—not things wrong in themselves, but merely things that society requires to be better regulated. Divisions such as these tell us more about the sources of power in society than about the acceptability or harm of the behaviour in question. We have seen that much crime, of the conventional as well as corporate kind, imposes greater burdens on socially disadvantaged people, as does law enforcement. Class bias—like race bias—can arise indirectly through the application of criteria which bear more heavily on one section of society than another.[216] Thus Hawkins argues that, in the enforcement of 'regulatory' criminal laws, there is a 'need to preserve a fragile balance between the interests of economic activity on the one hand and the public welfare on the other.'[217] It is the unfortunate lot of the poor, the main target group for the police, that their economic activity has increasingly become non-existent through unemployment or easily replaceable through de-skilling. Thus, major economic loss and injury caused by the criminal acts of companies are routinely treated 'administratively', any companies accused of fraud, for example, are now frequently offered 'deferred prosecution agreements', which are basically ways of buying themselves out of prosecution.[218] Meanwhile, astonishingly trivial cases are still being prosecuted when committed by the poor or the politically motivated.[219]

Credence is given to this explanation by the fact that the only non-police agencies 'out of line' are those that deal with the poor and/or street criminals. First, there is the Department of Work and Pensions fraud inspectorate which deals with social security claimants. Cook (1989) found that in 1986/87, for instance, 8,000 supplementary benefit fraudsters were prosecuted, as compared to 459 tax cheats. The Social Security Administration (Fraud) Act 1997 made prosecution of possibly fraudulent claimants even easier despite the increasing complexity of regulations that produce as many accidental errors as dishonesty; yet most of this fraud is committed by organised criminals (landlords, for example, persuading tenants to make claims) on whom few resources are expended.[220] This strategy makes sense only in ideological—rather than practical—terms. The ideologies relate to 'deserving' and 'undeserving' groups, to those who work and those who do not, and so forth. Thus corporations act according to capitalist laws of economic behaviour rather than laws of due process or social justice.

---

[214] For further reading, see Van Slyke S, Benson M and Cullen F (eds), *The Oxford Handbook of White Collar Crime* (Oxford: OUP, 2016) and Benson M and Simpson S, *Understanding White Collar Crime: An Opportunity Perspective* 2nd edn (London: Routledge, 2015).

[215] Braithwaite (2002). Braithwaite has successfully promoted the growth of restorative justice for 'normal' crime, and has also had some influence in relation to 'regulation'. But he has not yet persuaded governments to see the varying forms of crime as part of the *same* problem meriting the same solution.

[216] Sanders A, 'Class Bias in Prosecutions' (1985a) 24 *Howard Journal of Crime and Justice* 76, Slapper G and Tombs S, *Corporate Crime* (Harlow: Longman, 1999). See ch 10.

[217] Hawkins K, *Environment and Enforcement* (Oxford: OUP, 1984) p 9.

[218] Bisgrove M and Weekes M, 'Deferred Prosecution Agreements' [2014] *Criminal Law Review* 416.

[219] For examples, see Sanders A, 'The CPS 30 Years On' (2016) *Criminal Law Review* 82 at 87.

[220] McKeever G, 'Detecting, Prosecuting and Punishing Benefit Fraud: The Social Security Administration (Fraud) Act 1997' (1999) 62 *Modern Law Review* 261; Larkin P, 'The Criminalisation of Social Security Law; Towards a Punitive Welfare State?' (2007) 34 *Journal of Legal Studies* 295.

Ultimately, it is not possible to accurately assess the effectiveness of either compliance or deterrent strategies. First, deterrent strategies are hardly ever used in this context so no direct comparison is possible. Second, the investigative resources necessary for a deterrent strategy are generally not provided. Third, since we do not know how much of this type of crime there is (partly because of inadequate investigative resources), we cannot assess the effect of enforcement. The view of Gobert and Punch[221] that self-regulation by socially-responsible corporations would be preferable to either deterrent or compliance approaches is equally simplistic. For there is no evidence that companies are (or, as they argue, could be made to be) socially responsible unless it is profitable to be so. One of the principles of 'smart' regulation is the creation of opportunities for 'win-win' situations, 'so that, for instance, corporations can behave more responsibly and maximise profits at the same time'.[222] What might help achieve that is a context-sensitive use of the regulatory pyramid, allowing the use of whichever strategy is most appropriate in the circumstances, and encouraging compliance by applying criminal sanctions when voluntary or non-criminal methods fail.

In general, economic competitiveness is enhanced by taking a relaxed view of health and safety and environmental crime, but a harsh view of property crime. So the patterns we have explored in this section should not surprise anyone who understands that the rule of law plays second fiddle to the rule of profit. Even the relatively vigorous approach to financial crime can be explained in this way, as Britain's pre-eminence in the financial world relies on confidence in the financial markets and a 'level playing field'. Despite this, it seems that the UK is even softer on corporate financial crime than is the USA: between 2008 and 2018 there were no prosecutions of any banks in the UK (but fines of £2.5 billion were imposed), while the USA prosecuted 'nearly 20' banks, and fines of £25 billion were imposed.[223] The implication of the 'smart' principle that corporate compliance should be made profitable is that where it is not profitable it will be absent unless it is imposed by law enforcement. Whether through austerity or blatant cronyism, there is little deterrent against non-compliance in the UK.

7.6 Organisation of the Crown Prosecution Service

The CPS was established to be independent from both the police and government because it was agreed that suspects and defendants needed an extra layer of protection. It was to be accountable, not to defendants, but to the law in a neutral fashion. The natural affinity of CPS thinking with police thinking makes this aspiration unrealistic, as we have seen. But an effort was nonetheless made to establish organisational independence. The Philips Commission recommended that for each police force area there be a Chief Crown Prosecutor, each with his/her own staff, and accountable to a local Police and Prosecutions Authority and responsive to a local democratic voice. This would have been consistent with the 'justice' and 'democracy' core values. But the government instead established the CPS as a national agency under the DPP. The CPS asserted its independence from the police by creating large areas, many of which covered several police forces; siting its offices away from police stations; and discouraging direct contact with the police. As a former DPP put it: 'Suddenly a steel curtain came down between the two services and this went

---

[221] Gobert and Punch (2003: 314, ch 10).
[222] Baldwin R, 'Is Better Regulation Smarter Regulation?' (2005) *Public Law* 485 at p 507. Baldwin discusses self-regulation, and the formidable obstacles to success that are in its path, as part of a broader 'better regulation' movement. Also see Lynch-Wood G and Williamson D 'The Social Licence as a Form of Regulation for Small and Medium Enterprises' (2007) 34 *Journal of Legal Studies* 321, who argue that small/medium firms very often fail to self-regulate and thus need a regulator to enforce environmental laws.
[223] See <https://www.ft.com/content/52101b3e-3f51-11e9-b896-fe36ec32aece> (accessed 15 August 2019).

a bit too far. People in both services, both the police force and ourselves, felt that we must keep our distance, we must not talk to each other, we must not communicate, the CPS is independent of the police and must be seen to be so.'[224]

The CPS therefore became increasingly bureaucratic, developing its own priorities, procedures and criteria for decision-making. Victims and the police expressed unhappiness at the remoteness of 'Fortress CPS', yet, as we have seen, there is no evidence that defendants were greatly protected by this inglorious isolation. So the CPS was reorganised into 42 areas—one for each police force, and one for London as a whole. At the same time, the government-appointed Narey (1997) and Glidewell (1998) reports recommended, among other things, that some CPS staff be stationed in police stations in order to process simple cases more speedily.[225] This 'co-location' of prosecuting lawyers was practised in some areas prior to the establishment of the CPS and was an example of the chumminess which the CPS was supposed to have eradicated. Thus a drop in discontinuances in one co-located area is cited by government as a positive result of prosecutors and police working together,[226] but it could equally be seen as a worrying sign of 'capture' of the CPS by the police. In 2014, the CPS was again restructured into 14 areas, each covering several policing areas. HMCPSI found a 'striking difference' in the performance of different CPS areas when examining the impact of efficiency drives.[227] This is likely to have caused greater levels of fragmentation between agencies and increased distance between the CPS and police but in the context of increased stress and less time, which in themselves will discourage challenge of police decisions and practices.

Glidewell set out five objectives for the CPS. Four were concerned with efficiency and quality of decision-making (including fairness to the defendant) and the fifth with 'meeting the needs of victims and witnesses. . .'[228] While there is nothing wrong with these objectives the omission of any democratic element is striking. Glidewell did recommend some 'local answerability', but explicitly rejected any involvement with local police authorities or police consultative committees.[229] The CPS makes a huge amount of policy on the basis of unstated principles and virtually no accountability.[230] The arrangements leave a gap that only the Home Office, the police and, to a limited extent, the victim, can fill. Other enforcement agencies similarly lack accountability. But there is an important difference. While the CPS keeps its distance from defendants (and would see this as an integral part of its 'independence'), most other agencies pride themselves on their links with offenders. In contrast to the CPS, then, where the main influence is a crime control agency (the police), the main influence on these other agencies is due process or the freedom of the offender. The consequences pervade the post charge process, through which efficient processing of early guilty pleas is encouraged in numerous ways.

7.7 Post charge: producing guilty pleas

If a case is prosecuted, it takes place either in the magistrates' courts (the lower courts) or the Crown court. The features of these courts and the allocation of cases between them are looked at in detail in chapters 8 and 9, but this half of the chapter discusses a phenomenon that is common to both levels of court: the mass production of guilty pleas.

---

[224] Sir Allan Green, speaking in 1989 – quoted by Glidewell I, *Review of the Crown Prosecution Service: A Report* (Cm 3960) (London: HMSO, 1998) p 37.
[225] Home Office, *Review of Delay in the Criminal Justice System* (London: Home Office, 1997) – the Narey Report. For an evaluation, see Baldwin J and Hunt A, 'Prosecutors Advising in Police Stations' (1998) *Criminal Law Review* 521.
[226] Criminal Justice System, *Narrowing the justice gap, 2002* available at http://www.cps.gov.uk/publications/docs/justicegap.pdf (accessed 23 December 2009), p 12.
[227] HMCPSI (2017).   [228] (1998: ch 7).   [229] (1998: 206–207).   [230] Sanders (2016: 93–95).

One of the most remarkable features of criminal justice in England and Wales—like the USA—is the tiny proportion of prosecutions that are contested. Most defendants give up their right to trial by pleading guilty. In the last quarter of 2019 the guilty plea rate in the Crown court was 68%—just a slight drop since 2015.[231] 77.7% of magistrates' court cases in 2018/19 were guilty pleas.[232] Many people who initially plead not guilty change their mind at the last moment: why does the resolve of so many defendants to plead not guilty 'crack'? In the Crown court 33% of trials cracked in 2019.[233] One key question for us to consider is why is it that the majority of those defendants who are presented directly with the chance to put the prosecution to proof choose not to do so?

A high rate of guilty pleas ensures that many of the most important due process protections which might apply in an adversarial system do not come into play. Crucially, the prosecution is not obliged to prove its case beyond reasonable doubt before an impartial tribunal. Its evidence is not scrutinised, witnesses are not cross-examined, and no question as to the exclusion of evidence (on the grounds that it was obtained oppressively, unfairly, or in circumstances that might render it unreliable) can arise. The defendant stands condemned merely by uttering the single word 'guilty' in open court. But is this absence of due process attributable to a free and informed decision by the defendant? Or does the criminal process itself encourage defendants to waive their due process rights by pleading guilty?

Guilty pleas are likely to be motivated by a variety of factors but two important variables are the perceived likelihood of conviction, and the perceived differential between the penalty likely to be imposed on a plea of guilty and what would follow one of not guilty. On the basis of interviewing 282 defendants convicted in the Crown court Hedderman and Moxon concluded that: '. . . decisions to plead guilty were largely based on a realistic assessment of the chances of acquittal, and the potential benefits in terms of sentence severity.'[234] The researchers do not explain how they formed the view that the assessments made by defendants were 'realistic' although they do point to the crucial influence of legal advice in decisions regarding pleas. Thus, of those who changed their pleas, only one respondent said that this decision had been entirely his own; the rest said that they had been advised by their solicitor or barrister to plead guilty. It follows that we need to look both at the systemic pressures on defendants to plead guilty, and the way that these are mediated in practice by lawyers, court officials, magistrates and judges. We need, in particular, to consider whether assessments of the chances of acquittal, and likely sentence if convicted, are 'realistic' or not.

---

[231] Ministry of Justice *Criminal court statistics quarterly, England and Wales, October to December 2019* online at: <https://assets.publishing.service.gov.uk/government/uploads/system/uploads/attachment_data/file/875838/ccsq-bulletin-oct-dec.pdf>. Note that the CPS reports a slightly higher guilty plea rate of 70% (CPS, *Annual Report and Accounts 2018–19*).

[232] CPS, *Annual Report and Accounts 2018–19*.

[233] Ministry of Justice *Criminal court statistics quarterly, England and Wales, October to December 2019*. Judicial and Court Statistics in 2007 indicated that 62.5% entered a late guilty plea, approximately 17% entered a plea to a lesser charge and a similar proportion were acquitted once the prosecution offered no evidence, with the remaining 2.1% being dealt with by way of a bind over (*Judicial and Court Statistics* 2007, table 6.11). In 2016/17, around 22% of trials cracked in the magistrates' courts for prosecution reasons (such as witness non-attendance) (*CPS Annual Report 2016–7* (London: HMSO, 2017)).

[234] Hedderman C and Moxon D, *Magistrates' Court or Crown Court? Mode of Trial Decisions and Sentencing* (Home Office Research Study no 125) (London: HMSO, 1992).

There are four ways of securing a lighter sentence by pleading guilty: the sentence discount principle, the restrictions on the sentencing powers of magistrates, charge bargaining and 'fact bargaining'. We will examine each of these in turn.[235]

7.8 The sentence discount principle

The most naked attempt to persuade defendants to plead guilty lies in the sentencing principle established by the courts that defendants pleading guilty (in either the magistrates' or Crown court) should receive a lighter sentence than those convicted after a contested trial. As McConville and Marsh put it, 'under the current regime, the defendant is expected to capitulate at the earliest possible moment so as to relieve the state of the expense and trouble of proving guilt. . .'[236] This principle was first put on a statutory basis by s.48 of the Criminal Justice and Public Order Act 1994, now replaced by the Criminal Justice Act 2003, s.144(1) (and due to be amended again following passage of the Sentencing Bill 2020). This provides as follows:

> In determining what sentence to pass on an offender who has pleaded guilty to an offence in proceedings before that or another court a court must take into account:
> (a) the stage in the proceedings for the offence at which the offender indicated his intention to plead guilty, and
> (b) the circumstances in which this indication was given.

Section 174(2)(d) of the same Act adds that 'where as a result of taking into account any matter mentioned in s.144(1), the court imposes a punishment on the offender which is less severe than the punishment it would otherwise have imposed, [it must] state that fact' in open court. In other words a guilty plea can make a difference to the *type* of penalty imposed. Before we turn to look at how particular types of courts use (or abuse) the sentence discount principle, it is important to stress that, notwithstanding legal constraints and guidelines, all sentencers have ample room for exercising individual judgement and discretion. The Criminal Justice Act does not demand explicitly that any discount in fact be given. Similarly the Act does not require sentencers to refer to the discount principle in all circumstances, but only when discounts have in fact been given as a result of a guilty plea. Thus sentencers must turn to the common law for an understanding of how the discount principle is meant to work in practice.

Sentencers are bound to follow sentencing guidelines prepared by the Sentencing Council (SC, formerly the Sentencing Guidelines Council). In mid-2017, the SC introduced new guidelines to courts about the way the sentencing discount should be applied. A maximum discount of one third will be given only if a guilty plea is indicated at the first hearing (in the magistrates' court), even when a formal plea cannot be entered at that stage. The full discount should be given even when the evidence is overwhelming

---

[235] While we focus here on the most immediate pressures to plead guilty, it should not be overlooked that these are experienced differently depending on other systemic factors such as whether or not a defendant has been remanded in custody pending trial (Kellough G and Wortley S, 'Remand for Plea: Bail Decisions and Plea Bargaining as Commensurate Decisions' (2002) 42 *British Journal of Criminology* 186 at p 199) as well as on the individual characteristics and situation of the defendant such as degree of trust in lawyers and the courts, ability to resist pressure, desire to bring proceedings to an end, willingness to take the blame so as to protect a co-defendant from conviction (Jones S, 'Partners in Crime: A Study of the Relationship Between Female Offenders and their Co-defendants' (2008) 8(2) *Criminology & Criminal Justice* 147 at 156–157) and so forth.

[236] McConville M and Marsh L, *The Myth of Judicial Independence* (Oxford: OUP, 2020).

(meaning that the defendant had little realistic choice but to plead guilty). Remorse for commission of the offence is to be treated as an additional mitigating factor. After the first stage in the proceedings, the maximum level of reduction is one quarter, which decreases to a maximum discount of 10% on the day the trial is due to begin.[237]

Guidance issued by the original Sentencing Guidelines Council, required courts only to 'have regard' to the definitive guideline issued for each offence. Now, all courts *must* follow sentencing guidelines that are relevant to the offender's case and the exercise of the sentencing function, unless the court is satisfied that it would be contrary to the interests of justice to do so.[238] Lord Justice Leveson stated that the aims of the more robust approach included increasing consistency and confidence in sentencing.[239] Further, in the context of rising prison populations, it was hoped that a more rigid approach to the use of guidelines would help control the prison population.[240] However, we can see that judges still retain a considerable amount of discretion when deciding how the guidelines should (not) apply. They appear to only be bound by those that are, in their view, 'relevant', and even then only if it would not, in their opinion, be contrary to the interests of justice.

The SC included another 'get out clause' in allowing the sentencing court to reduce sentence by one third if it is satisfied that it would have been unreasonable for the defendant to enter a guilty plea at an earlier stage because the circumstances meant that he or she was unable to understand what was alleged (such as the unavailability of legal advice and/or evidence). This is a welcome caveat in light of difficulties obtaining case papers[241] and legal aid funding,[242] and seems to be in line with earlier case law.[243] Perhaps the retention of such discretion is why, as Allen notes, use of the guidelines is 'widely accepted' by judges.[244] One analysis by Hough et al concluded that judicial emphasis upon personal mitigation, including the elusive concept of 'remorse', rendered the sentencing exercise a 'highly subjective one',[245] while another study in Tel Aviv found that the more judges' discretion was restricted, the harsher sentencing tended to be.[246] As Tata argues, sentencing practices retain elements of performativity based on what is expected from the professional role and characteristics in spite of the existence of rules designed to limit discretion.[247] It is

---

[237] Sentencing Council (2017) *Reduction in Sentence for a Guilty Plea* available at <https://www.sentencingcouncil.org.uk/wp-content/uploads/Reduction-in-Sentence-for-Guilty-plea-Definitive-Guide_FINAL_WEB.pdf> (accessed 1 June 2017).

[238] Coroners and Justice Act 2009, s.125.

[239] Leveson B, 'Consistency and Confidence' *Counsel* available at <https://www.counselmagazine.co.uk/print/14371> (accessed 24 July 2018).

[240] Allen R, *The Sentencing Council for England and Wales: brake or accelerator on the use of prison?* (London: Transform Justice, 2016) online at: <http://www.transformjustice.org.uk/wp-content/uploads/2016/12/TJ-DEC-8.12.16-1.pdf> (accessed 12 July 2019). Although there was a slight drop in the prison population around 2010, numbers have generally continued to rise (Sturge G, *UK Prison Population Statistics* House of Commons Briefing Paper Number CBP-04334 (2018) online at: <http://researchbriefings.files.parliament.uk/documents/SN04334/SN04334.pdf> (accessed 15 July 2019)).

[241] See, for example, The Secret Barrister, *Stories of the Law and How It's Broken* (Basingstoke: Macmillan, 2018).

[242] Newman (2013); Welsh (2017: 559–585).

[243] *Last* [2005] EWCA Crim 106; applied by *McDonald* [2007] EWCA Crim 1081; See also *Peters & Ors* [2005] EWCA Crim 605.   [244] Allen (2016).

[245] Hough et al, *The Decision to Imprison: Sentencing and the Prison Population* (London: Prison Reform Trust, 2003) p 3. The multiple and sometimes conflicting aims of sentencing outlined in s.143 of the Criminal Justice Act 2003 have enlarged the judicial room for manoeuvre (Von Hirsch A and Roberts J, 'Legislating Sentencing Principles' [2004] *Criminal Law Review* 639).

[246] Pulver H, 'Less Discretion for Judges Means Harsher Sentences for Convicts, Study Finds' *Haaretz* (2016) online at: <https://www.haaretz.com/israel-news/.premium-study-less-discretion-for-judges-means-harsher-sentences-for-convicts-1.5428905> (accessed 10 May 2019).

[247] Tata C, *Sentencing: A Social Process* (London: Palgrave Macmillan, 2020). As Tata goes on to say, 'It is in the attempt to operationalise these rules that their indeterminacy becomes apparent', especially once we start to examine the construction of case facts in greater depth. (Tata (2020: 53)).

therefore important to examine judicial practice as well as the more structured approach envisaged by the SC guideline.

The fact that Crown court judges are trained lawyers does not mean that their decisions will be free of bias. Indeed, Hood found evidence consistent with *direct* racial discrimination in one of the four Crown court centres he studied, and Feilzer and Hood found that the odds of a young black male's custodial sentence at a Crown court being 12 months or longer (once other relevant factors such as previous record, type of offence and plea were held constant) was 6.7 times the odds of a young white male receiving a sentence of a similar length.[248] Recent research indicates that this problem persists: in 2015 defendants from black, Asian, Chinese or other backgrounds were at least 53% more likely to be imprisoned for an offence than self-reported white defendants.[249]

In further unpublished work they generously conducted to help inform the analysis in this book, Feilzer and Hood report:

(a) that plea appeared to have no effect on whether or not custody was imposed for those cases close to the custody threshold; and

(b) that a guilty plea was associated with shorter custodial sentences.

In investigating the second finding, logistic regression revealed that once other known factors that might influence sentence length were taken into account, defendants pleading not guilty were 1.8 times more likely to receive a sentence of two years or longer, compared with similarly situated defendants pleading guilty.[250] These findings are the mirror image of those for the youth court where Feilzer and Hood found no impact of plea on sentence length but evidence consistent with an impact on the custody/non-custody decision. More recent research which draws on data from sentencing judges suggests that there is in fact a significant degree of judicial compliance with sentencing guidelines, and that the discount 'awarded' for a guilty plea is perhaps more modest than indicated by earlier studies.[251]

7.8.1 The sentence discount principle in legal theory

The obvious rationale for encouraging an accused to plead guilty lies in the time and expense that is saved.[252] The average hearing time for a not guilty plea sent to trial is 18 hours compared with 1.5 hours for a guilty plea,[253] amounting to a significant cost difference. This 'efficiency' core value is recognised in the SC guideline's 'key principles', along with 'sparing' witnesses from having to attend court and from what may be the distressing experience of giving evidence.[254] If, for example, a defendant contests a charge of rape or assault, the complainant will nearly always face lengthy cross-examination in an attempt to

---

[248] Hood R, *Race and Sentencing* (Oxford: OUP, 1992); Feilzer and Hood (2004: 112).

[249] Hopkins K, Uhrig N and Colahan M, 'Associations between ethnic background and being sentenced to prison in the Crown court in England and Wales in 2015' (2016) online at: <https://www.gov.uk/government/statistics/asssociations-between-ethnic-background-and-being-sentenced-to-prison-in-the-crown-court-in-england-and-wales-in-2015> (accessed 10 May 2019). Although The Secret Barrister urges some caution in the way that 'similar offences' were categorised (The Secret Barrister (2018)). See further ch 10

[250] Private communication dated 29 November 2005. Note that this finding was not statistically significant, probably due to the relatively small numbers of not guilty cases in this analysis (31).

[251] Roberts J and Bradford B, 'Sentence Reductions for a Guilty Plea in England and Wales: Exploring New Empirical Trends' (2015) 12(2) *Journal of Empirical Legal Studies* 187–210.

[252] Cases in which this was explicitly recognised include *Boyd* (1980) 2 Cr App Rep (S) 234, *Hollington and Emmens* (1985) 7 Cr App Rep (S) 364, and *Buffrey* (1992) 14 Cr App Rep (S) 511.

[253] Ministry of Justice (2008a: 115, Table 6.21).   [254] Sentencing Council (2017).

destroy his or her credibility as a witness.[255] The sentence discount principle thus operates as an inducement to the defendant to make life 'easier' for others. The SC guideline also identifies the time benefits of an early guilty plea, reflecting the contemporary concern with 'bringing offenders to justice' as speedily as possible. There is some acknowledgement in the latest SC guideline that the existence of the discount might place pressure on defendants to plead guilty, which was not a feature of earlier guidelines.[256]

In addition to the 'routine' discounts available for guilty pleas there are 'further' and 'enhanced' discounts available for defendants who provide assistance to the prosecuting authorities. The common law has long recognised that defendants could expect large discounts for helping the police and prosecution to investigate and prosecute cases against their criminal associates, for example by providing information or testifying against them.[257] The 'enhanced' discount, which is in the range of one half to two thirds of the sentence deducted before any reduction for guilty plea, is said to operate as a pragmatic convention to incentivise defendants to help convict serious criminals who might otherwise escape justice.[258] To sum up, the effect of a guilty plea on sentencing is variable, uncertain and often at odds with the law's requirements. To put this more bluntly, in the context of sentence discount 'bargains', large numbers of defendants are getting ripped off.

7.8.2 Communicating the discount to defendants

7.8.2.1 Sentencing remarks

One way in which defendants, particularly the courts' repeat clientele, can learn about the sentence discount is if courts regularly articulate the fact that they are giving a discount and specify its size.[259] Judicial practice in relation to this was inconsistent, and case law demonstrated that it was be difficult to disentangle the impact of a guilty plea from other mitigating factors.[260] However, even when the discount and amount are articulated there is no way of being certain of the veracity of a sentencer's claim. In order to try and combat this problem, part two of the Crown Court Compendium guides judges through the statutory principles of sentencing, including when and how the discount must be applied, and how it should be expressed to defendants.[261] No doubt this is intended to further harmonise sentencing practices, particularly as the type and complexity of sentence provisions has increased dramatically since 1997.[262]

---

[255] Brereton D, 'How Different are Rape Trials?: A Comparison of the Cross-Examination of Complaints in Rape and Assault Trials' (1997) 37 *British Journal of Criminology* 242; Birch D, 'Rethinking Sexual History Evidence: Proposals for Fairer Trials' [2002] *Criminal Law Review* 53; Brewis B, 'The Interpretation of s. 41 of the Youth Justice and Criminal Evidence Act 1999 and the Impact of R v A (No 2) ([2002] 1 AC 45) Armando Andrade v R [2015] EWCA Crim 1722' (2016) 3 *Journal of Criminal Law* 169.

[256] This issue was judicially acknowledged, for example in *Clark and Ors* where it was observed 'some pressure cannot be avoided. Pressure is inherent in the giving of credit for plea' [2008] EWCA Crim 3221 at para 48.

[257] *A and B* [1998] Crim LR 757.

[258] See also Serious Organised Crime and Police Act 2005, ss.73–75 formalise 'enhanced' discounts for such assistance.

[259] CJPOA, s.48(2) provides for the sentencer to indicate a discount has been given, but says nothing about indicating the amount.

[260] *Peters* [2005] EWCA Crim 606; *Kluk* [2005] EWCA Crim 1331.

[261] Courts and Tribunals Judiciary, *Crown Court Compendium Part 2: Sentencing* (2018) online at: <https://www.judiciary.uk/publications/crown-court-bench-book-directing-the-jury-2/> (accessed 10 August 2019).

[262] The complexity caused by the introduction of numerous, and overlapping, types of available sentence, designed to variously deal with public concerns about serious offenders and prison overcrowding, increased calls for a harmonised sentencing code. See further, O'Sullivan H and Ormerod D, 'Time for a Code: Reform of Sentencing Law in England and Wales' (2017) 19 *European Journal of Law Reform* 285. A Sentencing Bill was undergoing reading in parliament at the time of writing, which affects all sentencing related statutory references in this text.

7.8.2.2 The role of defence lawyers

The defence lawyer has an ethical duty to the client to 'promote fearlessly and by all proper and lawful means the client's best interests' without regard to their own interests.[263] Like solicitors, barristers are sensitive to the economic incentives represented by the fee structure made available by the state, and it had been suggested that it can be to the financial advantage of barristers to crack cases at the last moment rather than engineer a plea of guilty at an earlier stage or take the case to trial.[264] The counterpoint to such claims is that the fee system also encourages working to volume and a high early guilty plea rate allows lawyers to take on more cases. However, the suggestion that lawyers favoured late guilty pleas for financial reasons took hold in government circles, and the legal aid fee structure was changed so that early guilty pleas were incentivised, sometimes by up to 75%. The London Criminal Courts Solicitors' Association described the plans as an 'affront to justice',[265] recognising that they appear to be driven more by ideological reasons than by actual financial need. The Ministry of Justice did resile from its original position in relation to Crown court fees, but the issue remains in magistrates' courts,[266] which is significant because it is where all criminal cases begin and the initial plea indication is requested (see chapter 8).

In a system that operates a sentence discount principle, a defence lawyer is obliged to point out the pros and cons to the defendant of pleading guilty.[267] As Lord Parker CJ put it in *Turner*:[268]

> Counsel must be completely free to do what is his duty, namely to give the accused the best advice he can and, if need be, advice in strong terms. This will often include advice that a plea of guilty, showing an element of remorse, is a mitigating factor which may well enable the court to give a lesser sentence than would otherwise be the case.

Although Lord Parker went on to say that the defendant 'having considered counsel's advice, must have a complete freedom of choice whether to plead guilty or not guilty', one may question whether such freedom can co-exist with strong advice from counsel to plead guilty.[269] This is compounded by the fact that, in the magistrates' and Crown courts, there are procedures designed to ensure the routine application of pressure on defendants to plead guilty as soon as possible to reduce delays and late guilty pleas (cracked trials).[270]

---

[263] *The Bar Standards Board Handbook* 3rd edn (effective from May 2018), (available from <https://www.barstandardsboard.org.uk/media/1933294/bsb_handbook_version_3.3.pdf>). The code laying down equivalent professional standards for solicitors is available <https://www.sra.org.uk/solicitors/handbook/code/content.page> (both accessed 24 July 2018).

[264] For the argument that barristers' incentives in counselling clients, financial or otherwise, do not always point towards cracking trials, and that in some situations barristers may encourage or recommend guilty pleas when it is not in their own interests, see Tague P, 'Barristers' Selfish Incentives in Counselling Clients' [2008] *Criminal Law Review* 3 and Alge D, 'The Effectiveness of Incentives to Reduce the Risk of Moral Hazard in the Defence Barrister's Role in Plea Bargaining' (2013b) 16(1) *Legal Ethics* 162–181.

[265] Bowcott O, 'Lawyers to earn higher legal aid fees for early guilty pleas' *The Guardian*, 1 November 2013; Wright O, 'Legal aid reforms could undermine fundamental principles of justice, warns CPS' *The Independent*, 6 July 2013.

[266] McGuinness T, *Changes to Criminal Legal Aid* House of Commons Briefing Paper No 6628 (2016).

[267] See Blake M and Ashworth A, 'Ethics and the Criminal Defence Lawyer' (2004) 7(2) *Legal Ethics* 167 at pp 179–182.   [268] [1970] 2 WLR 1093 at 1097.

[269] See the critique by McConville M, 'Plea Bargaining' in McConville M and Wilson G (eds), *The Handbook of the Criminal Justice Process* (Oxford: OUP, 2002) at pp 357–360. This is especially the case when the passivity of most defendants is factored in (see, e.g., Tata C and Gormley J, *Sentencing and Plea Bargaining: Guilty Pleas Versus Trial Verdicts* in *Oxford Handbooks Online* Oxford: OUP, 2016).

[270] Criminal Procedure Rules; Sprack and Sprack (2019). For discussion of these factors, see Helm R, 'Conviction by Consent? Vulnerability, Autonomy, and Conviction by Guilty Plea' (2019a) 83(2) *Journal of Criminal Law* 161–172.

Counsel for the defence must in every case assist in the completion of a standard form, and the judge must record on the form that the defendant is aware of credit for an early guilty plea.[271] In the magistrates' court, advocates are required to complete a standard case management form which also asks the defence to confirm that the defendant is aware about the issue of credit.[272] Lawyers must, therefore, demonstrate to the court that they have advised clients about the advantages of pleading guilty, which is likely to influence how lawyer/client relationships develop.

There can be little doubt that many defence solicitors in the magistrates' courts do communicate the fact of the discount 'in strong terms'. In their observational study, McConville et al (1994) found that most defence lawyers generally seek to persuade their clients to plead guilty. More recently, Newman (2013) reinforced these findings. Both studies indicate that the main factors behind an unethical preference for trial-avoidance are a presumption that the client is guilty, and a belief that the client is unworthy and undeserving of a contested trial.[273] Where a client wishes to maintain innocence, the solicitor will emphasise (and usually exaggerate) the perils of pleading not guilty, such as increased costs, reduced scope for mitigation, and so forth.[274] The sentence discount principle provides a useful additional pressure solicitors can bring to bear on defendants. It dovetails with their practice of seeking to mitigate on the basis that the defendant had co-operated with the needs of crime control, as in this often used example: 'I ask you to give my client credit for his plea. He was also co-operative with the police'.[275]

Many of the examples of pressure observed by McConville et al (1994) occurred on the day of the trial itself. The role of the defence solicitor in engineering changes of plea at the last moment is valuable from a crime control perspective, but more valuable still would be the communication of advice to plead guilty at an earlier stage. Amendments to the legal aid rules in recent years have been designed to ensure that it is in the financial self-interest of lawyers to drive cases forward to an early conclusion.[276] Conflicts of interest may arise not only with the solicitors' own interests vis á vis the client but also with the duties the solicitor owes to the court, not least in terms of co-operating with policies designed to ensure efficient case management.[277] Over the years, policy-makers have established various pre-trial initiatives designed to promote earlier case settlement. Plea before venue,[278] and the 'Narey reforms' were early examples of these initiatives, in the 1990s,[279] and they continued relentlessly over the following two decades. McConville and Marsh argue that the defence lawyers are being co-opted more and more into encouraging clients to plead guilty because the Criminal Procedure Rules require them to assist the court in actively managing cases.[280] The government continued to believe that the criminal justice system

---

[271] An example Plea and Trial Preparation Form is available at <https://www.justice.gov.uk/courts/procedure-rules/criminal/forms> (accessed 24 July 2018).

[272] Welsh L and Howard M, 'Standardisation and the Production of Justice in Summary Criminal Courts: A Post Human Analysis' (2018) 28(6) *Social and Legal Studies* 774–793.

[273] McConville et al (1994: ch 8). This argument finds further support in Mulcahy A, 'The Justifications of Justice: Legal Practitioners' Accounts of Negotiated Case Settlements in Magistrates' Courts' (1994) 34 *British Journal of Criminology* 411, and in Newman (2013).

[274] See the case studies they present at McConville et al (1994) pp 193 and 195–196 in particular.

[275] McConville et al (1994: 205). [276] Welsh (2017: 559–585); Newman (2013).

[277] Smith T, 'The 'Quiet Revolution' in Criminal Defence: How the Zealous Advocate Slipped into the Shadow' (2013) 20(1) *International Journal of the Legal Profession* 111–137. See also Tata C, '"Ritual Individualisation": Creative Genius at Sentencing, Mitigation and Conviction' (2019) 46(1) *Journal of Law and Society* 112–140.

[278] Introduced by s.49 of the Criminal Procedure and Investigations Act 1996.

[279] Home Office, *Review of Delay in the Criminal Justice System: a Report* (London: Home Office, 1997a).

[280] McConville M and Marsh L, *Criminal Judges: Legitimacy, Courts and State-Induced Guilty Pleas in Britain* (London, Edward Elgar, 2014).

routinely allows delay, and therefore sought to increase 'efficiency', even though it accepted that 'target chasing has replaced professional discretion and diverted practitioners' focus from delivering the best outcomes using their skill and experience',[281] thus marginalising defendants' (and, by implication, victims') needs. A further incarnation of efficiency drives appeared through the *Better Case Management* policy, which supports *Transforming Summary Justice*.[282] Like its predecessors, the policy seeks to encourage robust case management, reducing the number of hearings per case and encouraging co-operation among the parties.[283] There has long been disquiet about the impact of policy led efficiency drives on defence lawyers, particularly concerning how they can reconcile their duty to assist the court in managing the case expeditiously with their duty to act in their client's best interests.[284] The concept of a 'virtual' court, where the client may be compelled to appear without his consent via live link from the police station, also raises dilemmas for defence lawyers in fulfilling their formal commitment to act in the best interest of their client (see chapter 1). Not all defence solicitors will succumb to these pressures to expedite cases in the magistrates' court, but few need persuading that the appropriate advice for most clients is to enter a guilty plea at the earliest opportunity.

Is the position any different in the Crown court? Baldwin and McConville's study in the 1970s of late plea changers revealed that 40% of defendants had changed their plea as a result of pressure exerted by their barristers, in over half of which 'the advice counsel gave was of such a nature that no reasonable person could say that it was fair or proper or that the final decision to plead guilty was made voluntarily'.[285] The policy of offering large sentence discounts for guilty pleas provided barristers who wished to settle cases with powerful ammunition to fire at defendants. As one explained:

> The barrister then said, 'If you're found guilty you will get about 10 or 15 years but if you plead guilty you will get 4 or 5 years.' I was really shocked. I was so scared, sweating and nervous and he frightened me with this 10–15 years stuff and saying I had no chance.... I agreed to plead guilty but it wasn't my decision; I had no choice about it.[286]

The study by McConville et al, conducted some 15 years later, showed that little had changed and their findings were again further supported by Newman (2013), although not all barristers are the same.[287] McConville et al observed pre-trial conferences between counsel and client, held at court in order to settle the plea, and found that half the defendants involved were persuaded to enter guilty pleas immediately by their barristers but the pressure tended to be subtle, and designed to sap the defendant's determination to go to trial rather than undermine it completely there and then, so many pleaded guilty later. Even when the instructing solicitor told a barrister to give the client 'a talking to' the barrister chose not to give the client an ear-wigging, justifying this afterwards by saying: 'If you get too tough at the start, they sack you!'[288] A more recent study by Alge confirmed that the legal profession as whole tends to 'view guilty pleas as a standard outcome and

---

[281] Ministry of Justice, *Swift and Sure Justice: The Government's Plans for Reform of the Criminal Justice System* (Ministry of Justice Command Paper CM 8388, 2012) 5.
[282] CPS (2015) online at: <https://www.cps.gov.uk/sites/default/files/documents/publications/transforming_summary_justice_introduction_may_2015.pdf> (accessed 6 April 2020).
[283] See <https://www.judiciary.uk/publications/better-case-management/> (accessed 24 July 2018).
[284] Mountford L and Hannibal M, 'Simpler, Speedier Justice for All?' (2007) 158 *Solicitors' Journal* 1294. Rayner notes, 'the defence's role is to evaluate each case as lawyers...whereas the court's priority is to dispose of cases quickly – and the two approaches are incompatible' (Rayner J, 'Duty Calls' (2009)(1 October) *Law Society Gazette*; 11). See further Tata (2019).
[285] Baldwin J and McConville M, *Negotiated Justice* (London: Martin Robertson, 1977) p 45.
[286] Baldwin and McConville (1977: 49–50).   [287] Alge (2013a).
[288] McConville et al (1994: 253–254).

continue[s] to engage in informal plea bargaining as a routine means of case disposition, regardless of defendants' interests',[289] often not because of a desire to coercively persuade defendants to plead guilty, but because of a need to balance a range of competing interests (including financial incentives) which weaken counsels' resolve to keep the defendant's interests in sharp focus.

7.8.3 Sentence indications and sentence bargaining

Should the law permit sentencers to indicate to defendants (or their lawyers) in advance what view they take of the alleged offence and what discount they would be prepared to give if a guilty plea was entered? The advantage of this would be that defendants would know exactly where they stood (although this assumes fair dealing on the part of the sentencer). The disadvantage would be that the impartiality of the court would be brought into question by such communications. It might seem as if the court had already made up its mind about the defendant's guilt and were seeking to assist the prosecution in obtaining a conviction, thus placing even more pressure on the defendant to plead guilty.

For several decades, following the key decision in *Turner*,[290] appellate judges insisted that the only acceptable advance indication of sentence was one to the effect that, regardless of how the defendant pleaded, a particular type of sentence (such as a fine) would be imposed. Anything more (such as declaring that a non-custodial penalty would follow a guilty plea but saying nothing about what would happen if the defendant was convicted following a full trial) was seen as restricting the defendant's choice as to plea. Over this same period, however, trial judges continually flouted the *Turner* rules, although the problem was very largely a Crown court phenomenon.[291] Here, barristers and judges (who are mostly ex-barristers) formed a close-knit workgroup with shared values. Judges and counsel frequently met privately before or during the trial, and this allowed illegal forms of sentence bargaining to flourish. In the multitude of reported cases, defence counsel and Crown court judges seemed to be equally implicated in sentence bargaining. Sometimes defence counsel took the initiative by going to see the judge in private, but often the judge summoned counsel to initiate discussions over sentence.[292] Trial judges, no less than barristers, are allocated more trial cases than they can handle on the assumption that some will 'go guilty' and this expectation then becomes self-fulfilling. Thus in *Nazham and Nazham*[293] in a private discussion with counsel the trial judge expressed his interest in cracking the case (scheduled for trial in Birmingham) given that he had yet to finish hearing another case and might also have to sit at Lincoln the following Friday. He said, 'this has got plea written all over it and bags of credit' and expressed his view that the defendants 'have got an eye for a deal'. The gist of this was conveyed to the defendants who pleaded guilty, thus rendering the trial judge's workload more manageable. The Court of Appeal's attempt to inhibit sentence bargaining met with only limited success.[294]

---

[289] Alge (2013b: 181). Also see Thornton J, 'Is Publicly Funded Criminal Defence Sustainable?' (2020) 40 *Legal Studies* 230.

[290] [1970] 2 WLR 1093.

[291] There are fewer incentives and opportunities for the defence and the sentencer to conduct back-stage sentencing negotiations in the magistrates' court than in the Crown court, particularly as there is little opportunity for informal relations to build up between part-time lay magistrates and lawyers (McConville et al 1994: 186). That the position is probably different with professional magistrates is exemplified by the facts in *In re McFarland* [2004] UKHL 17.

[292] For a full list of citations to the case law from the 1970s up to the early 1990s see the 2nd edition of this book at p 424.

[293] [2004] EWCA Crim 491.

[294] McConville et al (1994: 253); Morison J and Leith P, *The Barrister's World* (Milton Keynes: Open UP, 1992) p 135; Plotnikoff J and Woolfson R, *From Committal to Trial: Delay at the Crown Court* (London: Law Society, 1993a) pp 67–68.

This suggests that lawyers and judges in the Crown court, just like the police in their milieu, habitually followed their own working rules rather than adhering to the law. Many barristers and trial judges appeared to disagree with the *Turner* rules, believing they should be reformed to permit full and realistic discussion between counsel and the judge about plea and sentence.[295]

In 2005 a five-strong Court of Appeal in *Goodyear*[296] decided to abandon the *Turner* rules and legitimise a form of sentence bargaining as follows:

(1) The essential principle remains that the defendant's plea must always be made voluntarily and free from any improper pressure.

(2) Allowing judges to respond to a request by the defendant to indicate the maximum sentence that would follow an immediate guilty plea would not constitute such improper pressure.

(3) Judges must not go further in their sentence indication by also stating what the maximum possible level of sentence would be following a contested trial.

(4) Judges remained free, however, to indicate that the sentence, or (more likely) the type of sentence, would be the same regardless of how the defendant pleaded.

(5) While judges should not give an advance indication unless one was sought, they were entitled to remind counsel in open court, in the presence of the defendant, of the defendant's entitlement to seek an advance indication of sentence.[297]

(6) If, notwithstanding such a reminder from the judge, the defendant did not seek an indication of sentence, 'then, at any rate for the time being, it would not be appropriate for the judge to give or insist on giving an indication of sentence' (para 51).

(7) Judges retained an unfettered discretion to decline to give a sentence indication. They might so decline in a variety of circumstances including where they believed defendants were already under pressure, or were vulnerable, or had not appreciated that they should not plead guilty unless they were in fact guilty.

(8) Judges might also decline to give an indication where they considered 'that the application is no less than a "try on" by a defendant who intends or would be likely to plead guilty in any event, seeking to take a tactical advantage of the changed process envisaged in this judgment' (para 57).

(9) Any indication given by a judge binds both that judge and any other judge who becomes responsible for that case, although the indication will cease to have effect if the defendant fails to plead guilty after a reasonable opportunity to consider his or her position. In straightforward cases it would be reasonable to expect the guilty plea to be entered on the same day the indication was given. One point which is clear is that a *Goodyear* indication will only bind the court if the defendant pleads guilty more or less there and then.[298]

(10) The defendant's advocate should not seek a sentence indication unless they had first obtained a written signed request from the defendant.

---

[295] Zander and Henderson (1993: 145).

[296] [2005] EWCA Crim 888. See the Attorney-General's Guidelines (2012) based on this: <https://www.gov.uk/guidance/the-acceptance-of-pleas-and-the-prosecutors-role-in-the-sentencing-exercise> (accessed 15 July 2019). This reflects the trend towards involving judges in case management, and followed considerable pressure from government-appointed Inquiries: Runciman Commission (1993: 112–113); Auld LJ (2001: 434–444).

[297] This should be done with caution in order to avoid creating (i) pressure on the defendant to plead; and (ii) the perception that the judge had pre-judged the issue of guilt or for some reason did not want to try the case.

[298] *Patel and Ors* [2009] EWCA Crim 67. Following the decision in *Newman* [2010] EWCA Crim 1566 an indication once given is, save in exceptional circumstances, binding on that and any subsequent judge in the case.

(11) Defence advocates were to be personally responsible for ensuring that defendants fully appreciate that (i) they should not plead guilty unless they are guilty; (ii) any sentence indication remains subject to the entitlement of the Attorney-General to refer an unduly lenient sentence to the Court of Appeal; (iii) the indication ceases to have effect if not acted upon (by entering a guilty plea) at the first reasonable opportunity by the defendant; (iv) the indication has no bearing on ancillary matters such as confiscation proceedings.[299]

(12) Sentence indications should normally be sought at the Plea and Trial Preparation Hearing but later requests, including during the trial itself, should not be ruled out.

(13) The request should normally take place in open court (with the public present), with a full recording of the entire proceedings, and both sides represented, in the defendant's presence.

This guidance attempts to bring sentence bargaining into the open, regulate it, and encourage more guilty pleas.[300] This increases the likelihood that, as Helm states, guilty pleas are 'not always or even typically consensual admissions of guilt, but are rather tactical decisions based on forecasting the probability of conviction at trial and the likely outcomes of trial, and evaluating potential discounts in exchange for pleading guilty.'[301] Nevertheless, the Court of Appeal took the opportunity to reinforce the approach in *Goodyear* in *Kunle Omole*.[302] It is arguable, however, that the guidelines are too open-ended and self-contradictory to provide a stable legal framework. For example, the use of the word 'normally' in point 13 means that private discussions about sentencing have not been banned. The self-contradictory nature of the guidelines is evident in the use of the concepts of pressure and improper pressure. Thus, while spelling out, in response to a request from the defendant, the potential difference in sentence depending on plea is regarded as improper pressure (point 3) it is regarded as proper pressure for the judge actively to prompt the defendant to request a sentence indication (point 5) and even to tell the defendant (unprompted) that the sentence would be of the same type (e.g. a fine) whatever the plea (point 6). Quite how such an active judge is supposed to preserve the appearance of not having pre-judged the case (as required by point 5) is unclear. Finally, the operation of the guidelines remains heavily dependent on judicial judgment and discretion. Thus judges are said to have an 'unfettered discretion' to refuse to give a sentencing indication (point 7). The scope for unfair discrimination is evident.[303]

A case decided just a few months after *Goodyear* illustrates some of these concerns. In *Attorney General's Reference (No. 80 of 2005)*[304] the defendant was charged with wounding with intent to cause grievous bodily harm, an offence that carries a maximum penalty of life imprisonment. He had attacked the new partner of his former wife with a large torch and knife after laying in wait for him. The attack was prolonged, and the victim suffered sufficiently severe lacerations to require surgery and suffered permanent injury affecting his ability to work. The defendant had four previous convictions including one for wounding. The trial judge initiated a discussion about sentencing without any request from the defence (breach of *Goodyear* point 5), out of public view in his chambers (breaching the spirit of point 13), and said that a guilty plea would result in a non-custodial outcome whereas conviction after trial would attract a long-term prison sentence (breach of point 3).

---

[299] For examples of how confiscation proceedings can get tangled up in (and unsettle) sentence bargains, see *Mahmood and Shahin* [2005] EWCA Crim 1268 and *Karim* [2005] EWCA Crim 533.
[300] This is all now formalised in the Criminal Procedure Rules.
[301] Helm (2019a: 162).   [302] [2011] EWCA Crim 1428.
[303] See further Peay J and Player E, 'Pleading Guilty: Why Vulnerability Matters' (2018) 81 *Modern Law Review* 929.   [304] [2005] All ER (D) 214 (Nov).

The judge also said in his sentencing remarks that he was aware of the Sentencing Guideline Council's view that an appropriate reduction for a late guilty plea was one tenth but that he was going to knock a third off. In fact he imposed a two year suspended sentence. There could scarcely be a better illustration of the disregard of guidelines that seems to occur with some regularity in the Crown court. In this case, however, the Court of Appeal became involved. It said that the appropriate sentence following the late guilty plea would have been four years' imprisonment and the trial judge was castigated for misapplying *Goodyear* and disregarding the SGC's views.[305]

The Crown also invokes the supervision of the Court of Appeal for a dodgy plea and sentence bargain in less extreme cases. Closed discussion between counsel and the judge about the strength of evidence, leading to the acceptance of lesser pleas, led to the successful appeal by the prosecution in *Attorney General's Reference (No. 3 of 2010)*.[306] However, whether it will do so in all cases seems unlikely given that prosecuting counsel is often party to such bargains in the first place.[307] Without a proper study of Crown court decision-making the impact of *Goodyear* will remain unknown. Although the government is unlikely to fund research on the way that courts deal with requests for *Goodyear* directions, Darbyshire's research indicates that judges' views on the usefulness of *Goodyear* differs.[308] This is likely to result in inconsistent use, and uncertainty for all parties. The fact that such cases reach the appellate courts shows that defendants may be being subject to 'improper pressure' by judicial indications of maximum sentences for alternative pleas.

The Supreme Court seems to have a very high tolerance threshold for what constitutes acceptable levels of pressure to plead guilty. This is demonstrated by the case of *McKinnon v US* in which the defendant was fighting against extradition to the US where he faced charges relating to alleged damage caused by his hacking into US government computers.[309] He was offered a plea bargain by a US prosecutor to the effect that if he did not contest extradition and pleaded guilty he would face a 3–4 year prison sentence, most of which would be served in the UK. However if he decided to contest he was told he would face a sentence of 8–10 years without repatriation. McKinnon argued that the disparity in the outcomes subjected him to too much pressure to plead guilty and was inconsistent with *Goodyear* principles. Strictly *Goodyear* does not apply to the US plea bargaining system. However the then House of Lords was of the opinion that the differences between the US and England and Wales in respect of plea bargaining were not 'so stark' as some would contend, noting the trend towards greater formalisation of the process in England and Wales. On the issue of pressure the court said: 'In one sense all discounts for pleas of guilty could be said to subject the defendant to pressure, and the greater the discount, the greater the pressure. But the discount would have to be very substantially more than anything promised here . . . before it constituted unlawful pressure such as to vitiate the process'.[310] It continued that only in extreme cases, for example where the prosecutor effectively threatened rape during incarceration, would the 'encouragement' to plead guilty be unconscionable. Little, or nothing, short of threat of unlawful action would be enough. That the then House of Lords was willing to countenance the level of pressure exhibited in the *McKinnon* case shows that judicial restraint of the process is weak. If the defendant does not get a strong lawyer then it seems unlikely that the *Goodyear* rules will be sufficient to safeguard him against considerable pressure to plead guilty.

---

[305] *Attorney General's Reference (No. 80 of 2005)* [2005] EWCA Crim 3367.
[306] [2010] EWCA Crim 2055.
[307] See, for example, *Attorney General's Reference No 44 of 2000 (Peverett)* [2001] 1 Cr App R 416.
[308] Darbyshire P, 'Judicial Case Management in Ten Crown Courts' (2014) *Criminal Law Review* 30–50.
[309] [2008] UKHL 59.   [310] Para 38.

7.8.4 Accepting guilt in order to avoid the Crown court

The two-tier nature of criminal courts in England and Wales puts pressure on defendants to plead guilty. The advantage to the defence of having the trial heard in the magistrates' court is that the sentencing powers of the magistrates are limited. Regardless of the statutory maxima prescribed for offences, the maximum penalty which magistrates can impose is 12 months' imprisonment for two or more 'either way' offences.[311]

But even leaving aside the fact that magistrates' sentencing powers are limited, research shows that a de facto sentence discount can be achieved by having a case disposed of at the lower level. This is because magistrates on average sentence more leniently than do Crown court judges, although the extent of the difference is disputed.[312] Some practitioners are sceptical of these research results,[313] but as most practitioners have experience of only a few courts this may simply reflect variation in sentencing practice across courts.

One way of boosting the number of summary trials was created by the 'plea before venue', or 'allocation' procedure. For 'either way' offences, magistrates must now enquire what the defendant's plea is likely to be before deciding on whether the venue for trial should be the magistrates' court or the Crown court. If defendants indicate an intention to plead guilty then the magistrates record a conviction and determine if their sentencing powers are sufficient or the case needs to be transferred (or 'allocated') to the Crown court. If defendants indicate a not guilty plea or decline to enter a plea then the magistrates move on to the mode of trial hearing and hear representations from the prosecution and the defence, then decide whether to allocate the case to the magistrates' court or the Crown court for trial (see further chapter 8, section 8.5.3). A defendant is, at this stage, entitled to ask for an indication of whether or not a custodial sentence would be imposed if a guilty plea is entered in the magistrates' court. Though magistrates are not bound to provide such an indication, it can operate as an incentive for a defendant to remain in the magistrates' court and enter an early guilty plea. A substantial disincentive to a defendant who might otherwise have been willing to plead guilty in order to avoid a Crown court sentence is the power of the magistrates to commit defendants to the Crown court for sentencing following conviction for an either way offence if they feel that their own sentencing powers are inadequate.[314] This innovation resulted in about 15,000 fewer committals to the Crown court for trial but about 15,000 more committals for sentence.[315]

Another time-honoured way of keeping a case in the magistrates' courts is for the defence to achieve a re-labelling of the charge as something less serious. Summary sentencing is guaranteed if the prosecution can be persuaded to drop an either way charge in return for a plea of guilty to a summary charge. Where the defendant is facing a charge triable only on indictment then a charge bargain which involves pleading guilty to a lesser either way offence makes summary sentencing possible. The lower the either way charge achieved through the bargaining process, the more likely it is that that magistrates will regard the matter as within their sentencing powers, thus reducing the risk of committal to the Crown court for sentence. The two-tier nature of the criminal courts thus fuels the practice of charge bargaining, which we discuss in the next section.

---

[311] Sentencing guidelines for magistrates can be found at: <https://www.sentencingcouncil.org.uk/the-magistrates-court-sentencing-guidelines/> (accessed 24 July 2018).

[312] Hedderman and Moxon (1992: 37); Bridges L, 'False Starts and Unrealistic Expectations' (1999) *Legal Action*, October 6; Flood-Page C and Mackie A, *Sentencing Practice: an examination of decisions in magistrates' courts and the Crown Court in the mid-1990s* (Home Office Research Study no 180) (London: Home Office, 1998).

[313] Herbert A, 'Mode of Trial and Magistrates' Sentencing Powers' [2003] *Criminal Law Review* 314 at 323.

[314] The main relevant legislative provision is the Magistrates' Courts Act 1980, s.38.

[315] Department for Constitutional Affairs (2005a: Table 6.1).

7.9 Charge bargaining

Charge bargaining typically involves the defendant agreeing to plead guilty in exchange for the prosecution proceeding on a less serious charge. For example, theft may be substituted for the original charge of burglary, or rape replaced by sexual assault. Alternatively, where the defendant is facing multiple charges, an agreement to plead guilty to at least one may result in the dropping of others. Unlike the sentence discount principle, where it is the law itself which exerts pressure to plead guilty, charge bargaining relies on advocates on each side of the adversarial divide reaching an agreement. In the magistrates' court charge bargaining takes place mainly between Crown prosecutors and solicitors, whereas in the Crown court prosecution and defence barristers take centre stage.[316]

The government denies that this form of settlement amounts to plea bargaining to try to rid it of the negative connotations it perceives as attaching to it, in its associations with the United States system: 'This is absolutely not plea bargaining, it is plea negotiation' the Attorney-General has said.[317] However, plea bargaining by any other name smells just as sour to us.

7.9.1 Charge bargaining in the magistrates' courts

7.9.1.1 The role of the prosecutor

The law places little constraint on the ability of prosecutors to charge bargain. Under the Prosecution of Offences Act 1985, Crown prosecutors have the power to make additions, deletions or alterations to the charges, and can terminate proceedings altogether. Even on the day of the trial itself the prosecutor can secure the dismissal of the case by offering no evidence. In the past there were strong incentives for the police to 'over-charge' suspects[318] and this provided the CPS with the means and a motive to bargain with the defence, as shown in research from the 1980s by Baldwin.[319] The 1992 version of the Code for Crown prosecutors which stressed 'the resource advantages both to the Service and the courts generally' of charge bargaining, made it clear that such deals were not merely tolerated but encouraged. Subsequent versions of the Code were more coy but charge bargaining remained rife in the magistrates' courts through the 1990s and beyond,[320] particularly as demands to reduce cost increased. Soubise found that a modern culture of efficient and cheap case progression has created an environment in which Associate Prosecutors (AP)[321] frequently breach rules which limit their ability to accept charge bargains without the approval of Crown prosecutors. APs lack the time and resources to seek such approval and so they often make decisions to accept guilty pleas to lesser charges when they are not authorised to do so.[322]

---

[316] However, in certain cases of serious and complex fraud a new phenomenon of pre-charge bargaining has emerged. This stems from a review of fraud in 2006 which recommended a system of more open discussions of plea bargains (<www.attorneygeneral.gov.uk/FraudReview/FraudReviewFinalReportJuly2006.pdf> (accessed 5 January 2010)). There are some safeguards built into the process for the suspect. Notably, the Criminal Justice and Immigration Act 2008 made provision for legal aid to be available before charge where this scheme is used.

[317] 'Plea bargaining fraudsters may find that truth pays', *The Times*, April 4 2008.

[318] See Genders E, 'Reform of the Offences Against the Person Act: Lessons from the Law in Action' [1999] *Criminal Law Review* 689 at pp 692–693.

[319] Baldwin J, *Pre-Trial Justice* (Oxford: Basil Blackwell, 1985).

[320] For evidence that this remained so, see HMCPSI, *Thematic Review of Attrition in the Prosecution Process (The Justice Gap)* (2003) ch 5 (London: HMCPSI) available at <http://hmcpsi.gov.uk/> (accessed 5 January 2010).

[321] Associate Prosecutors are legal executives (rather than fully qualified lawyers) who have undertaken specialist training to conduct litigation and are employed by the CPS.

[322] Soubise L, 'Prosecuting in the Magistrates' Courts in a Time of Austerity' (2017) 11 *Criminal Law Review* 847–859.

Charge bargains not only enable the prosecution to secure convictions in weak cases that would not have succeeded in court but may also lead to an increase in the number of such weak cases being prosecuted. Where a high guilty plea rate is achieved through such inducements there is little need for the prosecuting authorities to ensure that only properly prepared cases are brought to trial. When one United States jurisdiction 'banned' various forms of plea bargaining one effect was that prosecutors refused to proceed with weak cases and this, in turn, forced the police to investigate crimes more carefully and thoroughly from the outset.[323] Crown prosecutors have always been directed by their Code to discontinue cases in which the evidence is weak, and this provides a theoretical safeguard against improper charge bargains. However, the due process model warns us that prosecutors cannot be trusted to screen out weak cases any more than the police can.[324] Research by McConville et al in the late 1980s found that Crown prosecutors, for a variety of reasons, rarely took the initiative in dropping cases.[325]

McConville et al's research was conducted shortly after the CPS was created. Are their findings still valid in the light of subsequent changes? First, the CPS has taken over responsibility for determining the initial charge in non-minor cases.[326] This was meant, amongst other things, to deal with the problem of over-charging by the police. Second, the CPS has been increasingly subject to managerialist target-setting and performance monitoring, which include reducing 'unsuccessful' outcomes (discontinuances and acquittals) and increasing the guilty plea rate. This looks like a recipe for unethical over-charging and charge bargaining.[327] The call of the CPS Inspectorate for a changed ethos in which the CPS selects the right charges from the outset and then sticks to them,[328] looks pious and unrealistic. The latest edition of the Code for Crown Prosecutors states that prosecutors should not proceed with multiple charges, or more serious charges, simply in order to encourage the defendant to enter into a charge bargain (para 6.3).[329] Rather, prosecutors should select charges that reflect the seriousness and extent of the offending. But the Code acknowledges that defendants may be willing to plead guilty to fewer, or less serious, charges than those brought. In this situation it stipulates that:

> Prosecutors should only accept the defendant's plea if (a) the court is able to pass a sentence that matches the seriousness of the offending, particularly where there are aggravating features ... Prosecutors must never accept a guilty plea just because it is convenient.[330]

The courts recognise that charge bargains are commonplace and that the integrity of criminal proceedings require that they be adhered to, so a magistrates' court decision that the reinstatement of a charge by the CPS which had been dropped as part of a charge bargain was an abuse of process was upheld.[331] But while there are elements within legal culture that remain decisively in favour of charge bargaining and other methods of cost-cutting achieved by 'defining deviance down'[332] the rise of concern for victims and witnesses has caused a rethink in some quarters.[333] Adherence to the Code for Crown Prosecutors, in

---

[323] Carns T and Kruse J, 'A Re-Evaluation of Alaska's Plea Bargaining Ban' (1981) 8 *Alaska Law Review* 27.
[324] Packer H, *The Limits of the Criminal Sanction* (Stanford: Stanford UP, 1969) p 207.
[325] McConville et al (1991: 146, 158, 159, 166).
[326] Criminal Justice Act 2003, s.28. See section 7.3 for discussion.
[327] See generally Young R and Sanders A, 'The Ethics of Prosecution Lawyers' (2004) 7 *Legal Ethics* 190.
[328] HMCPSI (2003: paras 5.24, 9.19–9.24).   [329] The code is available at <https://www.cps.gov.uk>.
[330] CPS, *Code for Crown prosecutors* (2020: paras 9.2–9.4).   [331] *CPS v Edgar* (2000) 164 JP 471.
[332] See Garland D, 'The Limits of the Sovereign State: Strategies of Crime Control in Contemporary Society' (1996) 36 *British Journal of Criminology* 445.
[333] See, for example, Alge D, 'Negotiated Plea Agreements in Cases of Serious and Complex Fraud in England and Wales: A New Conceptualisation of Plea Bargaining?' (2013a) 19(1) *European Journal of Current Legal Issues*.

which victims' interests must be considered, may, however, be easier said than done in an era of stretched resources and performance management. For example, in unpublished research, one prosecutor said that victims' needs tend to go on the 'backburner' in relation to plea negotiations because they are 'a great way of carving a case up, getting it finalised at the first hearing, which is all anyone wants because that's what the statistics say we have to do'.[334]

7.9.1.2 Defence lawyers and case management hearings

It might be thought that, given professional codes and ethical standards, defence lawyers could be relied upon to ensure that innocent persons do not accept the offer from the prosecution of a charge bargain.[335] On the other hand, we have already seen that many defence lawyers presume their clients to be guilty and unworthy of a contested trial and accordingly put pressure on them to plead guilty, and that financial self-interest often trumps selfless promotion of the client's interests. Although the prosecution have been directed to provide advance disclosure in at least summary form for cases triable either way that were to be heard in the magistrates' courts since 1985,[336] in practice the extent of disclosure made by the CPS is often perceived to be inadequate by the defence.[337] HMCPSI note that the ability of the CPS to progress cases at an early stage is still hampered by the way the police compile case files. Less than 40% of cases they examined in 2017 complied with national guidance on the construction of case files, and only 60.1% of papers were served by the CPS on the defence in accordance with the timescales specified by policy.[338] This leads some, but not necessarily all, solicitors to advise their clients to plead not guilty in order to obtain 'adequate information on which to base advice or conduct meaningful negotiations'.[339]

So charge bargaining at case management hearings is flawed because the material on which the parties base their negotiations is at best partial and at worst thoroughly misleading. For example, the lawyers usually rely on summaries of tape-recordings prepared by the police.[340] As one would expect in an adversarial system, these summaries tend to exaggerate the strength of the prosecution case.[341] There may also have been failures by the police, by forensic experts and Crown prosecutors to comply with the statutory obligation of disclosure in respect of 'unused material' to the defence, as alluded to earlier.[342] These circumstances, far from allowing defendants to make a realistic assessment of their prospects of acquittal, paint a systematically distorted portrait of 'the facts' which mislead some defendants into believing that there is no option but to plead guilty. One obvious due process objection to pre-trial bargaining is thus that the lawyers are not negotiating

---

[334] This data was obtained during the course of PhD research (Welsh L, *Magistrates, Managerialism and Marginalisation: Neoliberalism and Access to Justice*. Doctoral thesis (PhD), University of Kent (2016)) but is previously unpublished.

[335] For a discussion of the relevant ethical standards, see Blake and Ashworth (2004).

[336] Magistrates' Courts (Advance Information) Rules 1985, SI 1985/601. In summary only cases the prosecution was under no obligation to disclose its case until the issue of guidelines by the Attorney-General in November 2000.

[337] The Secret Barrister (2018).   [338] HMCPSI (2017).

[339] Herbert (2003: 321). This is supported by more recent PhD research (Welsh (2016)).

[340] Defence solicitors cannot be sure that they will be reimbursed for the costs of listening to tape-recorded interviews. See, for example, Moorhead R, 'Legal Aid and the Decline of Private Practice: Blue Murder or Toxic Job?' (2004) 11(3) *International Journal of the Legal Profession* 160 at 182–184.

[341] Baldwin J, *Preparing the Record of Taped Interview* (Royal Commission on Criminal Justice Research Study no 2) (London: HMSO, 1992). And see section 7.3.3.3.

[342] This is what happened in the narrowly avoided miscarriage of justice in relation to the case of Liam Allen, discussed in section 7.3.3.5.

on the basis of 'evidence' at all since the summaries and statements in the prosecution file are merely indications (or, at worst, one-sided versions) of what witnesses will say in court.

Another immediate difficulty is that much pre-trial manoeuvring and negotiation is not subject to public scrutiny. Lawyers freely admit, however, that wheeling and dealing is an integral part of their trade, and last-minute negotiations can be observed taking place on a daily basis in court buildings. Prosecutors accordingly tended to see defence solicitors as their allies rather than as their opponents.[343] In Crown courts, the close-knit social world of a local Bar means that the negotiating parties will, in all likelihood, have concluded many similar agreements in the past and that a relationship of trust will have built up between them. Agreement is further facilitated by the fact that both sides are bound by the same code of professional ethics and owe a duty to the court to pursue the efficient (as well as the proper) administration of justice. McConville et al adopted a research method which allowed them to observe key interactions between defence solicitors and clients. They concluded that most bargains:

> ... are not struck under pressure from, or even at the suggestion of, the prosecution. It is usually the defence solicitor who decides to press the matter. Trials are overbooked and under-prepared in the expectation that clients will plead guilty on the day – an expectation that solicitors ensure is fulfilled. Clients rarely put up any resistance to suggestions to plead guilty, and accept the advice of their lawyer – the expert – even where there is no clear admission of guilt.[344]

Bargains sealed in such a manner do not strike us as proper. Moreover, case management hearings do not just *legitimise* a pre-existing practice of furtive negotiation as standard practice, but rather *enable* it to take place on a wider basis by *institutionalising* improper bargaining.[345] In much the same way as lawyers are asked to confirm that clients are aware of credit for an early guilty plea, the standardised case management forms specifically invite the parties to enter into plea negotiations.[346]

We have seen that the Criminal Procedure Rules now require courts actively to manage cases and promote pre-trial settlement wherever possible. For pre-trial negotiation to give greater priority to due process values would seem to require, at the very least, the transformation of the ideology and culture of defence lawyers. One strategy was pursued over the last decade or so by the Law Society and former Legal Services Commission (now the Legal Aid Agency, an arm of the Ministry of Justice) sought to encourage an 'active defender' role for the defence solicitor.[347] Whether such a transformation in values is possible without wider cultural and structural changes in the legal system and in society itself seems doubtful. Such changes are simply not on the agenda. Indeed, the government and the judiciary seem, if anything, to be bent on undercutting the scope for adversarial behaviour, co-opting defence lawyers still further into the pursuit of system efficiency,[348] which is further encouraged by funding cuts touted as 'necessary' austerity measures.

7.9.2 Charge bargaining in the Crown court

In the Crown court, just as in the magistrates' court, charge bargaining is rife, as numerous studies show. For example, 29% of the Hedderman and Moxon sample of defendants claimed to have pleaded guilty as a result of a charge bargain and the authors found plenty

---

[343] e.g. Carlen P, *Magistrates' Justice* (London: Martin Robertson, 1976); Baldwin (1985: 81–82); Young (2013); Newman (2013); Welsh (2017: 559–585).
[344] McConville et al (1994: 198).
[345] For an illustration of the normative pressure to deal exerted by the pre-trial review see Baldwin (1985: 42–44).
[346] Welsh and Howard (2019).
[347] Cape (2004); Edwards T, 'The Role of Defence Lawyers in a Re-Balanced System' in Cape E and Young R (eds), *Regulating Policing* (Oxford: Hart, 2008). [348] Cape (2004: 413–416); Welsh (2017); Tata (2019).

of evidence consistent with these claims.[349] Henham's study of six Crown court centres found that 61.7% of defendants originally indicted for the offence of causing grievous bodily harm with intent subsequently pleaded guilty to a lesser offence.[350] And of those proportionately few alleged rapists who are convicted of something, many are convicted of a lesser charge than rape following a charge bargain.[351]

Early studies of charge bargaining emphasised the crucial role of barristers in particular and painted a highly critical picture of rushed, last-minute negotiation which appeared to pay scant regard to defendants' rights or expressed wishes.[352] That the cracked trial remains a barrister-centred phenomenon is well captured in Bredar's description:

> This is a drama that usually unfolds in the corridors outside of court, in the barristers' robing rooms, and in the court cells. What generally happens is that prosecuting and defending counsel compare views on the strengths and weaknesses of their respective cases, and, in an indirect way, discuss what it would take from each side to get the case to 'crack.' Counsel come to a unified view about what would be an appropriate settlement of the matter, and generally that involves dismissal of one or more charges outstanding against the defendant, and guilty pleas to all the remaining charges, or to amended charges. . . . Defending counsel discusses the option with his client and instructing solicitors, with an eye towards gaining acceptance.[353]

7.9.2.1 The role of the defence barrister

In many cases a solicitor representing a defendant hands over the conduct of the case in the Crown court to a barrister who, on reading the brief prepared by the solicitor, may take a different view of the prospect of winning a case. A solicitor may have been over optimistic about the prospects for the defence either due to lack of experience or a desire to keep his client happy with false expectations of success. Indeed, one of the advantages claimed for the split profession is that a barrister, with no direct relationship with the client, can be more objective about the prospects of winning a case in court. The introduction of a barrister into the case may thus lead to a change of plea being advised.[354] Few defence solicitors dissent from counsels' opinion. Barristers, after all, are acknowledged experts in the Crown court arena, although they will try to maintain good reputations with instructing solicitors, which highlights the importance of local practices.[355] Furthermore, as we have seen, most defence solicitors operating in the magistrates' courts seem more interested in settling than contesting cases. It is true that it is because of their advice that many defendants decide to elect trial by jury and plead not guilty. This may not, in every case, reflect any genuine commitment to adversarial due process values. Solicitors may have made tactical use of a not guilty plea to strengthen a defendant's bargaining position vis-à-vis the prosecution, to increase the chances of legal aid being granted and so on. In many instances, particularly where conferences are held on the day of the trial, the solicitor will

---

[349] Hedderman and Moxon (1992: 10).

[350] Henham R, 'Further Evidence on the Significance of Plea in the Crown Court' (2002) 41 *Howard Journal of Crime and Justice* 151 at 153; Jeremy D, 'The Prosecutor's Rock and Hard Place' [2008] *Criminal Law Review* 925.

[351] Harris J and Grace S, *A question of evidence? Investigating and prosecuting rape in the 1990s* Research Study 196 (London: Home Office, 1999) at pp 31–32; Lea et al, 'Attrition in Rape Cases' (2003) 43 *British Journal of Criminology* 583 at p 592: Kelly et al, *A Gap or a Chasm? Attrition in reported rape cases* (HORS 293) (London: Home Office, 2005).

[352] McCabe S and Purves R, *By-passing the Jury* (Oxford: Basil Blackwell, 1972a) pp 9–10; Bottoms A and McLean J, *Defendants in the Criminal Process* (London: Routledge and Kegan Paul, 1976) p 130; Baldwin and McConville (1977a).

[353] Bredar J, 'Moving Up the Day of Reckoning: Strategies for Attacking the "Cracked Trials" Problem' [1992] *Criminal Law Review* 153 at p 155.

[354] See further, Morison and Leith (1992: 67–69).   [355] Alge (2013a).

not be present when counsel advises a client to plead guilty.[356] The high rate of guilty pleas and late plea changing by defendants indicates that many[357] defence solicitors are happy to allow barristers to fulfil their hired gun role of settling cases.[358]

Barristers are self-employed but group together in chambers, sharing office overheads. Barristers, like all criminal lawyers, tend to accept 'too much' work in the expectation that many cases will be settled out of court.[359] This, in itself, provides them with an incentive to try to settle cases through negotiation. If barristers find that they cannot conduct a case at all due to pressure of work then briefs have to be returned to solicitors and another barrister found to handle the case. This happens in nearly half of all contested cases.[360] As barristers are self-employed, a returned brief represents lost income. Barristers who are double-booked commonly wait until the last possible moment before returning a brief. As one barrister has put it: 'You say to yourself, "Well, if something happens to the other case I'll be able to do this one, whereas if I pass it now and something happens to the other case next week I'll be unemployed".'[361] Add the fact that the Crown court issues a definitive list of the day's business it intends to transact as late as 4pm the previous day,[362] and it is not surprising that in contested cases a third of defence barristers say that they receive the brief on the day before the hearing or on the day itself.[363] In consequence, barristers commonly arrive at court following late preparation, and their conferences with defendants are often hurried affairs.[364] Economic incentives such as this clearly influence the operation of labour markets and there is no evidence to suggest that lawyers are different in this regard.[365]

Most Crown court work is poorly funded by the state. As in the magistrates' courts, practitioners say that the only way to make criminal work pay is to turn over a high volume of cases in a relatively standardised fashion.[366] This is not to imply that all barristers in all cases are unethical seekers after settlement. Some have a genuine commitment to defence work, others will fight if briefed by solicitors who expect them to fight, and others are no doubt keen to contest 'good' cases in order to develop their reputations as effective advocates worthy of elevation to the ranks of Queen's Counsel or the judiciary.[367]

Equally important is the role allotted to defence counsel. Barristers are not expected to use every resource at their disposal to secure an acquittal for persons accused of crime.

---

[356] See generally McConville et al (1994) for a dissection of the discontinuous nature of legal representation provided for defendants and the extensive use of unqualified staff at all stages of case processing. That study has been updated by Newman (2013), who recorded similar findings.

[357] But not all—Tague (2008) argues that some barristers may be fearful of settling cases due to sanctions that might be applied by upset solicitors who have to deal with disgruntled clients, and that the barrister's reputation with solicitors for adversarial adroitness is more important than a reputation for adept plea negotiation.

[358] Morison and Leith (1992: 67–69). [359] Morison and Leith (1992: 64).

[360] Zander and Henderson (1993: 32).

[361] Morison and Leith (1992: 64). See further The Secret Barrister (2018).

[362] Rock P, *The Social World of an English Crown Court* (Oxford: Clarendon, 1993) pp 271–273.

[363] Zander and Henderson (1993: 30). The barrister's clerk also plays a role here in trying to keep cases in his/her own Chambers: Rock (1993: 272).

[364] Defence barristers commonly claim that despite the late receipt of instructions they have sufficient time to prepare the case: Zander and Henderson (1993). This raises the question of what defence barristers regard as 'adequate' preparation, and for what purpose. See also The Secret Barrister (2018).

[365] See the discussion in Gray et al, 'Controlling Lawyers' Costs through Standard Fees: An Economic Analysis' in Young R and Wall D (eds), *Access to Criminal Justice* (London: Blackstone, 1996).

[366] Morison and Leith (1992: 43–44). Supported by Newman (2013), Welsh (2017), Smith T and Cape Ed, 'The Rise and Decline of Criminal Legal Aid in England and Wales' in Flynn A and Hodgson J (eds), *Access to Justice and Legal Aid: Comparative Perspectives on Unmet Legal Need* (Oxford: Hart Publishing, 2017).

[367] Tague (2008). Note that Tague's work was based in London where there seems to be a more adversarial culture than on many other circuits, hence his data is often inconsistent with that of other research.

The barrister owes a duty first and foremost to the court.[368] In understanding what assisting the court in the administration of justice now encompasses it is necessary to turn to the Criminal Procedure Rules which require barristers, no less than solicitors, to assist the court in avoiding delay and 'unnecessary hearings'.[369] While the overriding objective set by these Rules is that cases should be dealt with justly, the notion of justice at work here includes dealing with the case efficiently and expeditiously. In comparison with a contested case a charge bargain represents an efficient and expeditious disposal of a case, and although this might conflict with the barrister's job to promote a client's best interests, it has been judicially acknowledged that this does not always mean contesting a case.[370] Barristers are obliged by law to make plain to defendants the considerable advantages to be gained through pleading guilty as part of a charge bargain. To ensure that this obligation is discharged, the standard form used as part of the pre-trial Plea and Trial Preparation Hearing (PTPH) asks 'might the case against a defendant be resolved by a plea of guilty to some counts on the indictment or to a lesser offence? If so, how?'[371] These pre-trial hearings, attended by the judge as well as by prosecuting and defending barristers, are clearly intended to further charge bargaining. For example, in *Hall* the appellant claimed that he had been pressurised into pleading guilty by his counsel. In dismissing the appeal Lord Parker stated that:

> What the Court is looking to see is whether a prisoner in these circumstances has a free choice; the election must be his, the responsibility his, to plead Guilty or Not Guilty. At the same time, it is the clear duty of any counsel representing a client to assist the client to make up his mind by putting forward the pros and cons, if need be in strong language, to impress upon the client what the likely results are of certain courses of conduct.[372]

Both solicitors and barristers adopt unduly pessimistic views of the likelihood of acquittal in order to increase the pressure on defendants to plead guilty. In most cases the client is simply presumed guilty and there is little attempt made to scrutinise the evidence or its relationship to legal categories of offence.[373] Research by McConville et al[374]—more recently supported by Newman (2013)—confirmed that many solicitors and barristers (and the unqualified staff they commonly use throughout the life of a case) continue to treat prosecution evidence uncritically, ignore protestations of innocence, and advise defendants that they have 'no choice' but to plead guilty. This advice is clearly contrary to the *Turner* rules under which barristers were supposed to tell clients that they must only plead guilty if they accept that they are guilty.

7.9.2.2 The role of prosecuting counsel

The CPS gained full rights of audience in the higher criminal courts through s.36 of the Access to Justice Act 1999. In 2004 the CPS began to increase the proportion of cases prosecuted by its own staff, enabling greater control over costs as budgets are cut.[375] Nevertheless, barristers in private practice still handle a lot of CPS Crown court work. They have always

---

[368] The duty to the court is 'Core Duty 1' in *The Bar Standards Board Handbook* 3rd edn (effective from May 2018).   [369] Criminal Procedure Rules; Sprack and Sprack (2019).
[370] For a general discussion of how ethical duties may conflict see Blake and Ashworth (2004).
[371] The Consolidated Criminal Practice Direction, Annex E.
[372] (1968) 52 Cr App Rep 528 at 534–535.
[373] See, in particular, McConville et al (1994: 188, 267–269). This appears to be less true of the London Bar: Tague P, 'Tactical Reasons for Recommending Trials Rather than Guilty Pleas in Crown Court' (2006) *Criminal Law Review* 23.   [374] McConville et al (1994: chs 7–10).
[375] HMCPSI, *Report of the thematic review of the quality of prosecution advocacy and case presentation* (London: HMCPSI, 2009).

maintained that they have an advantage over CPS advocates in not being psychologically committed to either side of the process; they may be defending one day and prosecuting the next. This suggests that in the higher courts defendants may be better protected from 'unfair' charge bargaining than in the magistrates' courts because prosecuting counsel external to the CPS are not so concerned as in-house advocates with achieving 'a result'.

The claim to objectivity needs to be seen in the light of how prosecuting and defence work is allocated and conducted in practice. Many barristers become type-cast as either defenders or prosecutors. The CPS, for example, maintains a panel of barristers in 'designated chambers' to whom as a matter of course briefs will be sent.[376] These barristers may well become 'prosecution-minded' and in any event would be anxious not to jeopardise an important source of business by ignoring the wishes of their institutional client. Baldwin's interviews with barristers, for example, revealed a self-interested reluctance to suggest to the CPS that weak cases should be discontinued. One barrister said that he would be 'too terrified of the demi-gods at the CPS, particularly in these days of preferred chambers' while another revealed that 'there are some cases—the ones that are borderline—where, for my own position (as someone who is acceptable to the CPS), I would run it because I don't want to make enemies out of these people.'[377] This desire not to upset the CPS has perhaps become more important as the amount of advocacy work the CPS keeps in house has increased reducing the flow of work to chambers.[378] This scarcely accords with the official image of the fearless independent barrister projected by the Bar.

Prosecuting counsel have much the same financial and practical interest in driving charge bargains as do their defence counterparts. Also some in-house advocates seem to be prone to crack trials due to pressure from defence counsel or fear of the judge:

> The perception of several stakeholders was that some crown advocates had little appetite for contested trials which could be compounded by a listing in front of a judge who was known to be intolerant of in-house advocates.[379]

In-house CPS advocates are not necessarily less competent overall than counsel, but they are less able when it comes to contested cases.[380] Lack of confidence at trial and inexperience, particularly in cross-examination of witnesses, may add to the pressure on CPS advocates to settle cases pre-trial if possible. When cases cannot be settled pre-trial, counsel may find themselves instructed at very late notice and in receipt of a poorly prepared file.[381] When poor preparation leads to cases being dismissed, counsel may find themselves the public face of systemic CPS failures.

All advocates, whether external or internal to the CPS, are expected to consider charge bargaining as part of the PTPH.[382] As with defence barristers, it would be misleading to portray a prosecuting barrister engaging in charge bargaining as having deviated from a legal duty to fight cases. The Court of Appeal views charge bargaining as a proper part of a prosecuting barrister's duty, not a deviation from it.[383]

---

[376] Temkin J, 'Prosecuting and Defending Rape: Perspectives from the Bar' (2000) 27 *Journal of Law and Society* 219 at 228.

[377] Baldwin J, 'Understanding Judge Ordered and Directed Acquittals in the Crown Court' [1997] *Criminal Law Review* 536 at 552–553.

[378] See HMCPSI (2009: 92).   [379] HMCPSI (2009: 29).

[380] In so far as the quality of advocacy was concerned the CPS Inspectorate found it was variable across both in-house and external advocates. The majority of all advocates were judged to be competent or better but a quarter of both external and in-house advocates were said to be 'lacklustre'. Of the 7.9% judged less than competent or poor most (25/29) were in-house advocates: HMCPSI (2009: 25).

[381] The Secret Barrister (2018).

[382] See <https://www.justice.gov.uk/courts/procedure-rules/criminal> (accessed 26 July 2018).

[383] *Herbert* (1991) 94 Cr App Rep 230.

7.9.2.3 Keeping the customer satisfied

Most defence barristers are skilled advocates and it is no real surprise to find that defendants are persuaded into believing that their interests have been well served. It is in this context that one must place findings that the great majority of defendants express satisfaction with the service provided by their legal representatives.[384] The stark conclusion reached by Moody and Tombs[385] suggests that the defendants' perceptions are often mistaken:

> There are constant factors which must be present if prosecution and defence are to agree. These centre round the notion of trust resulting in a co-alignment of interests and co-operation between traditional adversaries, while the accused, in the vast majority of cases where pleas are negotiated, stands to gain very little in material terms.

A decade later McConville et al observed case conferences between defence counsel and clients held at court on the date fixed for settling plea.[386] They report that the 'common denominator of court conferences is the determination of counsel to secure a guilty plea to some or all of the charges... To secure this result, barristers deploy a range of techniques some of which are designed to stress the advantages of a prosecution offer and the bleakness of any alternative, and others of which are designed to encourage the client to hand the decision over to the barrister as an expert.' Thus client satisfaction was sought by describing offers of a charge-bargain as 'excellent', 'the best that can be achieved' and 'better than we could have hoped for', and as something to be accepted rapidly whilst it was still on the table.[387] Most defence counsel pressed this kind of advice without having first tested whether the evidence would justify either the original charge or that now on offer. Trials may also not be anywhere as risky for defendants as their barristers may suggest given the high rate of acquittal in the Crown court.[388] The potential for injustice is obvious.

7.9.2.4 Judicial supervision of charge bargaining in the Crown court

If anyone could be expected to monitor the propriety of charge bargains it would surely be the judge. In an early study every one of the charge bargains identified had been expressly endorsed by the judge.[389] Zander too argues that judicial supervision provides a safeguard in this area, citing in support the 'Yorkshire Ripper' case in 1981.[390] Here, the trial judge refused to endorse the prosecution's acceptance of Peter Sutcliffe's plea of guilty to manslaughter, insisting that the original murder charge be proceeded with. However this case was exceptional in terms of the public and media pressure to proceed with a murder charge.[391]

This attitude has since been replaced by a recognition of the advantages of charge bargaining. The Court of Appeal decided in *Herbert*[392] that it was proper for prosecuting counsel to take into account the savings in public expenditure that a charge bargain could achieve. The Court of Appeal in *Grafton*[393] subsequently decided that the trial judge is powerless to prevent counsel dropping or reducing any charges except where the latter seeks the seal of judicial approval for a proposed deal. Thus, if a case similar to that of Peter

---

[384] Zander and Henderson (1993: 67).
[385] Moody S and Tombs J, 'Plea Negotiations in Scotland' [1983] *Criminal Law Review* 297 at p 307.
[386] McConville et al (1994: 256–257).   [387] McConville et al (1994: 257).
[388] Tague (2006). This is particularly true for rape where the conviction rate is very low (Kelly et al, 2005).
[389] McCabe and Purves (1972a: 29). See also Bredar (1992: 155).
[390] Zander M, *Cases and Materials on the English Legal System* 9th edn (London: LexisNexis, 2003) p 310.
[391] The prosecution were left in the unfortunate position of arguing that what Sutcliffe did (brutally mutilate and kill 13 women) was rational; a response to the way he had been treated by various women, rather than a product of diminished responsibility. See Bland L, 'The Case of the Yorkshire Ripper: Mad, Bad, Beast or Male?' in Radford J and Russell D (eds), *Femicide: The Politics of Woman Killing* (New York, Twayne Publishing, 1992).
[392] (1991) 94 Cr App Rep 2.   [393] [1993] QB 101.

Sutcliffe were to go before the courts today, prosecuting counsel would be free to accept a plea of guilty to manslaughter so long as no express approval was sought from the judge. Because the great majority of Crown court judges are recruited from the ranks of the practising Bar, prosecution and defence counsel have little to fear in seeking the approval of a judge for a charge bargain because all of the parties involved share a common outlook, all stand to gain from short-circuiting the formal trial process, and all are encouraged to enter into negotiations by the Court of Appeal. The PTPH standard form, which invites Crown court judges to prompt pre-trial charge bargaining, in the same way as the magistrates' court case management form, should be seen as legitimising (and further enabling) a long-standing judicial practice.

Linked to this is the idea that nothing is more likely to cause a defendant to abandon a not guilty plea than the official(s) conducting the trial expressing a view that the defendant is guilty, will be found guilty, and is wasting the court's time by pleading not guilty. The defendant can hardly expect a fair trial in such circumstances. With the dice so heavily loaded, all the defendant then has to decide is whether to opt for a more lenient sentence by pleading guilty. In other words, there is no longer a meaningful decision to be made. Thus, some of Baldwin and McConville's respondents claimed that they had been compelled to plead guilty by the judge, as in the following example:

> The barrister came back from seeing the judge and said, 'Well, the judge says we can argue as long as you like but you'll be found guilty anyway.' . . . I think I was more forced into it [pleading guilty] than anything, personally. I was flogging a dead horse. I mean the judge had made up his mind before I even walked through the door.[394]

The Court of Appeal made it clear that judges should not comment on the strength of the prosecution case as a way of persuading the defendant to enter a guilty plea.[395] But for years afterwards, reported cases revealed an astonishing level of judicial interference into the conduct of trials supposed to be conducted on adversarial principles of due process.[396]

But perhaps this is not so astonishing. So long as trial judges continue to engage in sentence bargaining the likelihood is that they will either volunteer (or become drawn into giving) their views on the likely outcome of the case. In the world of judicial make-believe, trial judges can initiate sentence bargaining without giving the impression to defendants that their case is perceived to be a weak one.

7.9.3 Fact bargains and multiple discounts

Fact bargains are a form of deal under which the prosecution and defence agree a factual basis upon which a guilty plea is acceptable to both sides. When the factual basis is not agreed, the court must follow a special procedure which originates from the case of *Newton*.[397] In *Beswick*[398] the Court of Appeal attempted to regulate such agreements, stipulating that the prosecution should not agree to a fact bargain which would result in sentencing on an unreal or untrue set of facts. Further guidance was issued in *Underwood*,[399] which stated that the defence must take the initiative in such cases, and the prosecution must take time to consider its position and the interests of justice. The extent to which fact bargains result in just such distortions is not known, but prosecutors are encouraged not to gainsay the defendant's account.[400] What *is* known is that fact bargains can combine

---

[394] Baldwin and McConville (1977a: 33).   [395] See, for example, *Barnes* (1970) 55 Cr App Rep 100.
[396] See, for example, *Llewellyn* [1978] 67 Cr App R 149; *James* [1990] Crim LR 815; *Pitman* [1991] 1 All ER 468; *Pitts* [2001] EWCA Crim 846; and *Nazham and Nazham* [2004] EWCA Crim 491.
[397] (1983) 77 Cr App R 13, CA.   [398] [1996] 1 Cr App Rep (S) 343.
[399] [2005] 1 Cr App R (S) 90.   [400] *Attorney General's Reference (No 89 and 90 of 2007)*.

with charge bargains and the sentence discount principle to produce an enormous discount for defendants. In *Attorney General's Reference No 44 of 2000 (Peverett)*,[401] for example, a former headmaster was faced with 16 charges of indecent assault involving 11 of his pupils committed over a period of eight years when the victims were aged between 11 and 13. Counsel reached a charge bargain (in the presence of the trial judge) under which seven of these counts were not proceeded with, which meant that four of the complainants dropped out of the picture altogether. In addition, a fact bargain was reached under which the nature of the conduct was transformed from spanking to fondling and 'tapping', and the motivation was agreed to be the desire to express his position of power over the children rather than sexual gratification. The final element in the bargain was that the judge promised, following a request from counsel, that a suspended sentence of imprisonment would be imposed if the defendant pleaded guilty in accordance with the terms of the charge-fact-sentence bargain. The defendant, described by the trial judge in his sentencing remarks as guilty of an 'appalling abuse of a position of immense trust', accordingly walked 'free' from court. The victims, understandably, were left feeling that they had been denied justice.[402]

7.10 Do the innocent plead guilty?

Many people would perhaps be prepared to tolerate sentence discounts and bargains concerning facts, charges and sentence if the net result was more convictions of the guilty and no corresponding increase in convictions of the innocent. The fact that the convictions in question may be for less serious offences than those actually committed might cause them pause for thought but the ends might nonetheless be seen to justify the means. The problem is that in practice no guarantee can be given that the innocent will not be made to suffer as a result of bargain justice despite the ostensible concern of the appellate courts to ensure that the innocent are not induced to plead guilty. Thus in *Turner* Lord Parker CJ was at pains to stress that counsel 'of course will emphasize that the accused must not plead guilty unless he has committed the acts constituting the offence charged'[403] and *Goodyear*[404] similarly makes defence barristers personally responsible for ensuring that defendants fully appreciate that they should not plead guilty unless they are guilty. The difficulty here is that a defence lawyer will not know if a particular client is innocent or not and indeed may be anxious not to find out. Lawyers to whom confessions of guilt are made are subject to strict restrictions in how they may conduct a defence. Certain things they may still do, such as challenge the admissibility of prosecution evidence, but, according to their professional rules, lawyers must not mislead the court, particularly about guilt. Thus, in a somewhat contradictory account to others recorded by McConville et al that are discussed earlier, counsel, on being told by a client that he had committed the offence of stealing a television as charged, feigned deafness, saying 'I don't hear so good when people make admissions.'[405]

Many innocent persons will thus inevitably receive advice from their barristers about the advantages of pleading guilty. The court in *Goodyear* implicitly recognises this in insisting that barristers must ensure that their clients appreciate that they should not plead guilty unless they are guilty. There would be no need for such an exhortation if only the

---

[401] [2001] 1 Cr App R 416.   [402] 'So why didn't he go to prison?' *The Guardian*, June 22 2000.
[403] [1970] 2 WLR 1093 at 1097.   [404] [2005] EWCA Crim 888 [65].
[405] McConville et al (1994: 251). Contradictory in that their other findings suggest that defence lawyers assume, and seek to confirm through plea, guilt.

guilty were to receive advice on the advantages of pleading guilty. The final choice of plea is, however, the accused's alone: 'The defendant is personally and exclusively responsible for his plea.'[406] Nothing prevents accused persons from proclaiming innocence to their lawyers yet pleading guilty in court. The defence lawyer is not deceiving the court, because the lawyer need not reveal the accused's true state of mind. Both barristers and solicitors are permitted to represent people who plead guilty while believing them to be innocent, as long as they do not advance innocence as part of mitigation. Older editions of the barristers' code of conduct indicated that no claim of remorse can be made (as such a claim would be inconsistent with the defendant's private assertion of innocence and thus amount to the barrister deceiving the court),[407] but the particular provisions are omitted from the latest version of the code of conduct.[408] This creates an incentive for the client to abandon the claim of innocence so that the guilty plea can be advanced on a remorseful basis and thus attract a lower sentence than might otherwise be imposed. Whichever course a truly innocent client chooses, the court is being deceived.

Just as innocent people sometimes 'confess' to the police under interrogation, so too, it seems, (and often in consequence of having 'confessed' at an earlier stage) do innocent people plead guilty. Baldwin and McConville (1977a) found that nearly half of the late plea changers in their study made substantial and credible claims of innocence. They acknowledged that they had no way of telling whether defendants were in fact innocent or not. But in a substantial number of these guilty plea cases independent assessors judged the evidence against the defendant to be weak. The more recent studies by McConville et al (1994) and Newman (2013) detail numerous examples of legal advisors ignoring clients' protestations of innocence[409] and failing in their legal duty to emphasise to clients that they should not plead guilty unless they were guilty. They also went on to assert in court things that they knew to be false in order to maximise the mitigating effects of the plea of guilty, such as counsel telling the court that the offence occurred in the 'spur of the moment' (p 262) for which the client should be given credit because he had 'the courage to plead guilty today.' Anecdotally, the Criminal Cases Review Commission has, in the last few years, seen a rise in the number of people seeking to appeal despite entering a guilty plea.

In a recent survey '[n]inety per cent of the [90] legal professionals said that they do think that some defendants plead guilty just because it is quicker and easier than going to trial', and 61% per cent of those respondents believed that this included innocent defendants.[410] A horrifying example is the Post Office 'false accounting' scandal discussed in section 7.2.3. Many of the defendants eventually proved innocent in 2020 pleaded guilty because of technicalities in the 'false accounting' offence that made innocence hard to prove, fear of going to prison (many did anyway) and the sheer power of the vast resources of the Post Office ranged against them. As in other areas of criminal justice, the innocent who belong to marginalised populations (and there are plenty more marginalised than postmasters!) tend to suffer more from plea-bargaining than privileged defendants.[411] The presumption of guilt will tend to be stronger in respect of those who are stereotyped as criminogenic or prone to lying.

---

[406] *Goodyear* [2005] EWCA Crim 888 [30].

[407] Code of Conduct (2004: para 11.5.1) available at the Bar Standards Board website. This is not the only dilemma facing a defendant. If a claim of remorse is made then this will prejudice any future argument (on appeal) that the guilty plea was entered as a result of improper pressure and should thus be treated as a nullity: *Karim* [2005] EWCA 533 at paras 27–31. See also *Hayes* [2004] All ER(D) 315.

[408] *The Bar Standards Board Handbook* 3rd edn (effective from May 2018).

[409] E.g. at McConville et al (1994: 167).

[410] Helm R, 'Constrained Waiver of Trial Rights? Incentives to Plead Guilty and the Right to a Fair Trial' (2019b) 46(3) *Journal of Law and Society* 423–447; 443 See further Nobles R and Schiff D, 'Criminal Justice Unhinged: The Challenge of Guilty Pleas' (2018) 39 *Oxford Journal of Legal Studies* 100.

[411] Peay and Player (2018).

7.11 Should plea bargaining be abolished?

The possibility of regulating or even eradicating charge bargaining has been much discussed,[412] and has been attempted (with some success) in one American jurisdiction.[413] Why?

7.11.1 Plea bargaining and models of justice

7.11.1.1 Due process objections

Encouraging defendants to convict themselves through a guilty plea undermines the principle that the burden of proof rests on the prosecution. It may seem that little harm is done to that principle by denying a discount or dropped/reduced charges, for example, to guilty defendants who stand on their right to put the prosecution to proof.[414] But there is a systemic value in requiring the prosecution to prove guilt which plea bargaining overlooks. Under a system in which guilty pleas are mass produced the prosecution of cases involving no more than vague allegations and other potential misuses of state prosecutorial power may be left unchecked. The number of weak cases prosecuted increases, as does the number of innocent persons wrongly convicted. The risk of miscarriages of justice is exacerbated by the enhanced inducements offered to suspects to testify against their co-accused or to help the police suppress serious crime. This is because of the temptation to provide perjured testimony and to make unfounded allegations in order to further their own interests.[415]

A related problem is the intensification of the pressure to plead guilty at a stage when the defendant may not have received adequate disclosure of the prosecution case. The defendant may thus either feel pressurised into pleading guilty to something the prosecution could not have proved, or be penalised for refusing to indicate a guilty plea until more was known about the prosecution case. The courts are meant to take into account inadequate disclosure of the evidence when judging whether the failure to signal a willingness to plead guilty at a particular stage of the proceedings was unreasonable.[416] But the defence cannot predict with any certainty what a court will view as 'reasonable' in this regard, so the pressure to throw in the towel prematurely remains.

Sentencing discounts, in particular, *penalise* those who stand on their right to put the prosecution to proof. This is an elementary point and yet many in the past have disputed it, claiming that discounts operate to reward those who plead guilty rather than punishing those who contest their case.[417] Lord Justice Auld recognised the double-talk at work here and argued that courts should openly accept that 'once guilt has been established, there is no logical reason why a dishonest plea of not guilty should not be openly treated as an aggravating factor just as an honest plea of guilty is treated and rewarded as a mitigating factor'.[418] But, since we know that the innocent sometimes are convicted following a not guilty plea, 'logic' also tells us that the sentence discount principle results in innocent people who enter an honest plea of not guilty receiving more punishment than they would have done had they entered a 'dishonest plea' of guilty (since 'dishonest pleas of guilty' will justify sentencing discounting no less than an 'honest plea of guilty').

---

[412] See Galligan (1987) and Bottomley A, 'Sentencing Reform and the Structuring of Pre-trial Discretion' in Wasik M and Pease K (eds), *Sentencing Reform* (Manchester: MUP, 1987).
[413] Carns and Kruse (1981).
[414] An approach taken by Auld (2001: 439, para 104).
[415] See Walker C, 'The Agenda of Miscarriages of Justice' in Walker C and Starmer K (eds), *Miscarriages of Justice* (London: Blackstone, 1999b) at p 6 and references cited there.
[416] *Rafferty* [1998] Crim LR 433 at 434; see guidance issued by SC at section F (Sentencing Council (2017)).
[417] See, for example, *Harper* [1968] 2 QB 108 at 110.   [418] Auld (2001: 439).

This chapter has also highlighted the potential of the principle to work racial injustice. Is it acceptable that those from ethnic minorities receive longer custodial sentences than white people simply because they exercise the right to put the prosecution to proof? To the crime control adherent this pattern of sentencing would be regarded as the product of the need for efficiency, it being mere coincidence that it happens to impinge more on black people. From the due process perspective, however, it is predictable that black people would plead not guilty more often, as one would expect them more often to be at the receiving end of abuses of police and prosecutorial power. Faced, as they are on average, with cases based on weaker evidence or evidence so tainted by unfairness that a reasonable argument can be made for excluding it, it is no surprise that black people have a higher rate of pleading not guilty (see further chapter 10).[419] Plea bargaining penalises those who insist on trial, and thus works indirect racial discrimination. Auld's answer to this objection was that the root causes of any unfair discrimination (e.g. proportionately more black people being prosecuted on weak evidence) should be tackled and that abolishing the sentence discount principle was neither necessary nor sufficient in achieving that end.[420] To which one might reply, 'yes, but it would help.' Tackling racial discrimination is never easy and is almost bound to require that all available levers of influence are brought to bear. The real question is whether saving the system money is more important than tackling the problem of the current vast over-representation of black people in prison.[421]

7.11.1.2 The human rights perspective

Article 6(2) of the European Convention on Human Rights (ECHR) states that 'everyone charged with a criminal offence shall be presumed innocent until proved guilty according to law'. It is not contrary to that presumption for a defendant to make a free and informed decision to waive their right to a trial; a guilty plea can clearly be one way of proving guilt according to law. But it does appear contrary to that presumption for the state to seek to *induce* defendants to enter guilty pleas on the assumption that they are guilty. If the state were to offer a defendant £10,000 to induce them to plead guilty to a theft we would rightly be appalled at this attempt to negate someone's rights. But this is exactly how plea bargaining can work in practice, particularly since the reintroduction of means testing for legal aid,[422] meaning that it can literally cost defendants thousands of pounds to defend themselves. This alone increases the likelihood of someone entering into and accepting a plea bargain.[423]

Further, the inducements discussed earlier could be seen as a breach of the 'right of anyone charged with a criminal offence to remain silent and not to incriminate himself.'[424] The indirect form of racial discrimination discussed earlier undermines Art 14 of the ECHR, which requires that the rights in the Convention 'shall be secured without discrimination on any ground such as sex, race, colour . . .' Arguably the right to be presumed innocent is currently one that is more fully enjoyed by white people than black people. And, to the extent that bargaining continues in private, it may contravene Art 6(1) (the right to a fair and public hearing).

When the last edition of this book was written, it was unclear whether the European Court of Human Rights (ECtHR) would accept that plea bargaining is contrary to the ECHR. However, the ECtHR has since ruled in favour of plea bargaining, noting that it

---

[419] Lammy Review (2017).   [420] Auld (2001: 440–441).   [421] Lammy Review (2017).
[422] Welsh (2017).
[423] For the potential impact on plea, see further discussion in Helm (2019b). A briefly introduced criminal courts charge exacerbated this issue in 2015. The charge was scrapped a few months after its introduction in recognition of just such criticisms.   [424] *Funke v France* (1993) 16 EHRR 297.

is a feature of many European jurisdictions—but only if the bargain is voluntary, done in the defendant's full knowledge of the facts and legal consequences, and with the judge reviewing the content of the bargain and the fairness of the circumstances in which it was reached.[425] However, it remains unclear what the appropriate level of judicial supervision of the bargain should be, which represents a dilution rather than a reversal of the triumph of the crime control model in this sphere. We have already seen that English law only wants voluntary and informed pleas in name. In practice, voluntariness is undermined by incentives that seek to encourage the entry of an early guilty plea, and 'informed' is undermined by problems with the quality of both disclosure and of legal advice.[426]

7.11.1.3 Crime control and managerialism

From the crime control perspective, the only problem with plea bargaining is that it does not always operate as efficiently as it should—for example, as we saw in section 7.1, each year thousands of people do not plead guilty until the date set for trial. This is why early pleas of guilty merit the largest discounts. But even the Runciman Commission accepted that it would be 'naive to suppose that innocent persons never plead guilty because of the prospect of the sentence discount', choosing to put greater value on people pleading guilty.[427] The Auld Report similarly argued that:

> no system can guarantee that individual defendants, however innocent, will not regard the likelihood of a lesser sentence as an incentive to trade it for the risk of conviction and a more serious sentence, or that lawyers will not sometimes advise their clients badly. But these are not reasons for rejecting a sentence practice if in general it serves a proper sentencing purpose, operates justly and assists the efficient administration of justice.[428]

A sentencing practice which results in the conviction of the innocent can be described as 'in general' operating 'justly' only once one accepts that no special weight should be placed on avoiding such miscarriages of justice. Runciman and Auld went on to reject the possibility that the clearer articulation of the discount principle they advocated would increase the risk that defendants may plead guilty to offences which they did not commit.[429] Nor did these review bodies take seriously the racial injustice caused by the discount principle, pretending that 'more research was needed'.[430] Overall, they adopted the self-serving assumption that one can increase the pressure on the guilty to plead guilty without increasing the pressure on the innocent to do the same—maybe because that pressure is already unbearable for many? Anyway, the research has been done by Lammy, and we now know for sure that plea bargaining is a form of structural racism.

7.11.2 Sparing victims the ordeal of bargain justice?

The case of *Peverett* discussed in section 7.9.3 is a good example of how bargain justice can result in a conviction that bears little relation to the underlying 'facts' of a case. In another example the CPS indicated that they would not proceed on an affray charge if the defendant pleaded guilty to the less serious charge of using threatening behaviour. The defendant was only willing to do this if assured of a non-custodial penalty. The judge

---

[425] *Natsvlishvili and Togonidze v Georgia* – 9043/05 Judgment 29 April 2014 [Section III]. See discussion in Bachmaier L, 'The European Court of Human Rights on negotiated justice and coercion' (2018) 26 *European Journal of Crime, Criminal Law and Criminal Justice* 236 and Helm (2019b).
[426] See generally, Thornton (2020).
[427] Royal Commission on Criminal Justice (RCCJ), Report (Cm 2263) (London: HMSO, 1993), pp 110. Section 48 of the CJPO implemented its recommendation.   [428] Auld (2001: 440 para 105).
[429] RCCJ (1993: 112); Auld (2001: 441 para 109).   [430] RCCJ (1993: 114); Auld (2001: 441 para 108).

sealed the deal by giving that assurance to counsel in a private meeting, adding that if the defendant was convicted following a trial of the affray charge a prison sentence was a virtual certainty. The charge concerned the kicking and beating of two victims while on the ground. So the term 'threatening behaviour' seems little better than a judicially approved lie, while the punishment 'on offer' bears scant relation to the harm the offenders caused. As defence counsel put it in his record of this case: 'Given the gravity of the offence alleged and the injuries to the victims, I found this offer to be unexpected and surprising.'[431]

The clash between expediency and just deserts has been brought into sharper relief by the rise of concern for the interests of victims.[432] On the one hand devices designed to secure guilty pleas are often justified on the grounds that they spare victims the 'ordeal' of giving evidence. On the other, last minute bargains that result in offenders getting less than their just deserts often appal victims. In *Peverett*, the five victims who had attended court ready to give evidence were said to be stunned by the non-custodial outcome,[433] as was this rape victim following a cracked trial:

> The judge praised [the offender for pleading guilty]. I was angry. He only did it because all my witnesses turned up. Men who leave the victim till the last minute before going into court should not be congratulated . . . They played down the violence. The violence was worse than the rape.[434]

There is also the point that many victims *want* a full-blown trial to take place, partly because this will lead to them learning more about the offence and the offender but also because they value their day in court. As one of the *Peverett* victims put it: 'The trial was going to be our chance to say "Hello. I'm back. I'm going to tell those 12 good men and women of the jury exactly what you did to me."' Instead, the victims felt that their voices had not been heard and that they had been cheated.[435] *Peverett* caused such an outcry that the Attorney-General immediately responded with new guidelines discouraging plea bargaining and requiring prosecutors minded to accept a plea to liaise with victims.[436] These guidelines are reflected in the most recent version of the Code for Crown Prosecutors, para 9.5 of which states:

> In considering whether the pleas offered are acceptable, prosecutors should ensure that the interests and, where possible, the views of the victim, or in appropriate cases the views of the victim's family, are taken into account when deciding whether it is in the public interest to accept the plea. However, the decision rests with the prosecutor.

This provision can be read as an implicit acknowledgement that charge bargains will be struck that involve the application of legal labels that victims may find offensive, as when rape is downgraded to sexual assault, or racially aggravated assault is downgraded to simple assault.[437]

---

[431] *Bargery* [2004] EWCA Crim 816. As this sentence indication breached the *Turner* rules and was held to have brought improper pressure to bear on the defendant resulting in a plea of guilty, the conviction was quashed by the Court of Appeal.

[432] See generally Fenwick H, 'Charge Bargaining and Sentence Discount: the Victim's Perspective' (1997) 5 *International Review of Victimology* 23, and ch 12.   [433] *The Guardian*, 30 October 2000.

[434] Quoted in Kelly et al (2005: 75). The public similarly regards guilty plea discounts as highly problematic: Clarke et al, *Attitudes to Date Rape and Relationship Rape: A Qualitative Study* (London: Sentencing Advisory Panel, 2002) pp 49–50, para 4.8.   [435] *The Guardian*, 22 June 2000.

[436] *Attorney-General's Guidelines on the Acceptance of Pleas* [2001] 1 Cr App R 28.

[437] See Burney E, 'Using the Law on Racially Aggravated Offences' [2003] *Criminal Law Review* 28; Burney E and Rose G, *Racist Offences – How is the Law Working?* Home Office Research Study 244 (London: Home Office, 2002); HMCPSI, *Report on the Thematic Review of Casework Having a Minority Ethnic Dimension* (London: HMCPSI, 2002b) para 8.26.

Victims are not always opposed to bargains. In domestic violence cases it is not unknown for victims to be keen to downplay the impact of the offence against them, thereby supporting charge reduction, particularly where the prosecution continues without their support.[438] However, the fact that a victim approves of a charge bargain does not make it right. There are other interests in play, including those of potential future victims, and ensuring equality of treatment as between similarly situated defendants.

7.12 Conclusion

Discretion permeates the processes through which cases eventually, if ever, reach trial. The police minimise the impact of external scrutiny of their prosecution decisions by choosing different dispositions (e.g. case construction, use of PNDs, or cautioning) according to their purposes in specific cases. The courts largely opt out of scrutiny, and neither they nor government care that different agencies adopt radically different approaches. The net result is a pattern of prosecution decisions that harmonise with economic imperatives but which, as a by-product, penalise the unfortunate and reward the powerful. The class and race differences created by stop-search and arrest practices are magnified by prosecution processes within the police and by separating police and non-police enforcement and prosecution.

This remains true despite major changes in prosecution practices since 1985. The CPS drops more weak and cautionable cases than the police used to. Some of the direct or indirect discrimination exercised by the police against ethnic minorities is blunted by CPS decision-making. Government guidelines do have some effect. But these rules, guidelines and controls are all only partially inhibitory. When the police want to, they often secure cautions or prosecutions in breach of the rules. Little can be done about it. Inhibitory rules need to be backed up by effective sanctions, otherwise they are largely 'presentational'. Alternatively, we need to achieve a change in police culture so that adherence to the rules is regarded by officers as good policing, but that will not be easy given the structural position of the police within the adversarial system. And it will be impossible for so long as the government (and others) sets priorities in such crude terms as 'catching criminals', 'narrowing the justice gap' and 'improving public confidence'.

Is prosecution policy about fairness and keeping criminalisation as well as crime within bounds (due process) or about balancing expediency with police working rules (crime control)? Our discussion of cautioning suggests that we may be moving back towards the latter. For although cautioning is used for humanitarian reasons, it also: increases social control through net widening; saves money where there is little to be lost by not prosecuting; punishes those against whom there is insufficient evidence of guilt to justify this; and avoids prosecuting those people who could embarrass authority. When government itself uses both prosecution and prosecution immunity to further its own narrow political causes, why should the police behave less cynically?

Not content with apprehending suspected offenders, the police have, with the increased use and range of available OOCDs, become triers of fact, deciders of guilt and innocence and dispensers of penalties. Just as the police cannot be expected to protect the rights of suspects, nor can we expect the CPS to do so. It is the job of defence lawyers to protect suspects' rights. But while expenditure on the CPS is now rising (partially reversing the

---

[438] Although the charges selected in domestic violence cases may be low to start with leaving less room for reduction. This seemed to be the case in the first specialist domestic violence courts evaluated. See Cook et al, *Evaluation of Specialist Domestic Violence Courts and Fast Track Systems* (London: CPS, 2004) p 106. For further discussion see ch 10.

austerity cuts of 2010/19), the legal aid budget is ever more tightly controlled (see further chapter 8). So, the police and CPS are no longer castigated for producing and accepting summaries of audio-recorded interrogations, but encouraged to do so under the statutory charging scheme; defence lawyers should check the accuracy of summaries, but without a remuneration structure that rewards this work, they will rarely do this, and 'fast-tracking' of cases will not give them the opportunity. Similarly, the retreat from full disclosure and restrictions on legal aid for defence forensic science also prevent defence lawyers matching the power of the prosecution.

Pre-trial processes in the criminal courts, with their emphasis on case settlement, also exhibit many of the hallmarks of the crime control model. But this is not just, or even primarily, a matter of lawyers seeking to make their lives easier. Rather, the system itself is geared towards the routine production of guilty pleas, as can be seen in the organisation of the legal profession and the sentence discount principle.

At one time the legal system pretended that plea bargaining did not take place. There was a gap, in other words, between due process rhetoric and crime control reality. Developments such as the Sentencing Council's guidelines on sentence discounts, and the provisions allowing magistrates and judges to give advance indications of sentence, have been accompanied by increasingly shrill crime control rhetoric. The system is now formally, and nakedly, based on crime control norms. These developments have been sponsored by governments who have tied their political fortunes to achieving increases in the number of 'offenders brought to justice', especially through increases in guilty plea rates but while also reducing budgets and demanding greater efficiency. The concern is with aggregate outcomes that contribute to the impression that the government has crime under control. The political context thus produces a decline in concern for miscarriages of justice and for achieving individualised justice in which sentences match offence seriousness. The adoption of crime control ideology by many solicitors, barristers and judges further oils the conveyor belt moving most defendants towards conviction.[439] That some defendants insist on trial by jury is in some ways the most remarkable feature of the criminal justice process. But few do so. This rare example of democracy in the criminal justice system is therefore in decline—along with justice (one of the other core values)—all because of populist politics and neo-liberal demands for efficiency (the other core value).

So what is to be done? Eliminating bargain justice would represent progress, but it leaves in place so many incentives to plead guilty that one might argue that the presumption of innocence would still effectively be undermined. A more radical proposal would be to do away with the concept of a guilty plea altogether. Inquisitorial jurisdictions have traditionally functioned without it.[440] Under this proposal there would be, in every case that fell within the no-plea regime, a degree of judicial scrutiny of the prosecution case, to ensure that convictions are always based on relevant, sufficient, reliable and fairly obtained evidence. Defendants could be given a choice of trial by jury and judge, or trial by judge alone. Those not actively contesting guilt would be funnelled towards the latter option, whilst others could be given a more open choice.[441] Schulhofer has estimated that abolishing all systemic incentives to plead guilty in this way and replacing the guilty plea system with bench trials by judges sitting alone would increase the trial rate by some 650% but with only a 20% increase needed in judicial resources at the adjudication stage.[442] That seems a small price to pay for a more victim-centred system that better protects human

---

[439] Newman (2013).
[440] Less so in recent times. See Hodgson J, *The Metamorphosis of Criminal Justice* (Oxford: OUP, 2020).
[441] See Doran S and Jackson J, 'The Case for Jury Waiver' [1997] *Criminal Law Review* 155.
[442] Schulhofer S, 'Plea Bargaining as Disaster' (1992) 101 *Yale Law Journal* 1979.

rights and innocent defendants.[443] But it would mean some re-ordering of the priorities given to the three different 'core values'.

It seems unlikely that the CPS would have prevented the infamous miscarriages of justice that gave rise to the Runciman Commission, and the fact that miscarriages of justice have continued since its inception shows it is an inadequate safeguard for suspects. Expecting it to perform a 'ministry of justice' role is unrealistic.[444] Strong and committed defence advocacy is needed to counter-balance the weighty forces lined up on the other side of the adversarial divide, but it is difficult to inspire this in a system that encourages co-operation and efficient working practices. The mass production of guilty pleas has become a systemic imperative in the criminal courts. Government rhetoric constructs defendants as 'undeserving' of due process, presuming them guilty, and portraying them as cynical manipulators of the system who warrant swifter punishment. Yet, in reality, defendants do not commonly play the system; the system plays with them, their rights, and their freedom.

Further reading

ALGE D, 'The Effectiveness of Incentives to Reduce the Risk of Moral Hazard in the Defence Barrister's Role in Plea Bargaining' (2013b) 16(1) *Legal Ethics* 162–181.

DENNIS I, 'Prosecution Disclosure: Are the Problems Insoluble?' [2018] *Criminal Law Review* 829.

FOX D, DHAMI M and MANTLE G, 'Restorative Final Warnings: Policy and Practice' (2006) 45 *Howard Journal Of Crime and Justice* 129.

R v Goodyear [2005] EWCA Crim 888; [2005] 1 WLR 2532.

HELM R, 'Constrained Waiver of Trial Rights? Incentives to Plead Guilty and the Right to a Fair Trial' (2019b) 46(3) *Journal of Law and Society* 423–447.

HODGSON J, *The Metamorphosis of Criminal Justice* (Oxford: OUP, 2020).

LUNA E and WADE M (eds), *The Prosecutor in Transnational Perspective* (Oxford: OUP, 2012).

NEWMAN D, *Legal Aid Lawyers and the Quest for Justice* (Oxford: Hart, 2013).

SANDERS A, 'The CPS 30 Years On' (2016) *Criminal Law Review* 82.

SANDERS A, 'The CPS, Policy-making and Assisted Dying: Towards a "Freedom" Approach' in CHILD J and DUFF A (eds), *Criminal Law Reform Now: Proposals & Critique* (Oxford: Hart, 2018).

TAGUE P, 'Barristers' Selfish Incentives in Counselling Clients' [2008] *Criminal Law Review* 3.

THORNTON J, 'Is Publicly Funded Criminal Defence Sustainable?' (2020) 40 *Legal Studies* 230.

---

[443] The extent to which innocent defendants are better protected under a non-bargain system is, we should acknowledge, a matter of controversy: see Scott R and Stuntz W, 'A Reply: Imperfect Bargains, Imperfect Trials and Innocent Defendants' (1992) 101 *Yale Law Journal* 2011.   [444] Sanders (2016).

8

Summary justice in the magistrates' court

KEY ISSUES

- The importance of the magistracy
- The involvement (and funding) of lawyers in summary justice
- Significant pre-trial decisions (including bail and mode of trial)
- Where is summary justice on the crime control/due process spectrum, and to what extent does it adhere to the core values of criminal justice

8.1 Introduction

In England and Wales, trials are held either in the magistrates' courts or the Crown court. There used to be a magistrates' court in most large towns and cities. No longer. Driven by austerity, between 2010 and 2020 164 magistrates' courts closed, out of 320 (51%).[1] Court service funding was reduced by 37.8% between 2012 and 2016.[2] The impact of court closures has been under-researched, but one regional study identified many adverse impacts on magistrates, defendants and defence lawyers, reducing access to the courts and diversity among magistrates.[3] Many magistrates have resigned in protest.[4] Magistrates interviewed by Ward (2016) felt that local justice outcomes—one element of judgement by peers—are undermined by court closures, especially as many defendants cannot afford to travel long distances to attend court.

All adult prosecutions begin in a magistrates' court, but the ultimate disposal of a case depends on the age of the defendant and the offence classification. There are special youth courts for persons aged 10–17, although exceptionally youths can be proceeded against in the adults' magistrates' courts, or in certain cases committed to the Crown court for trial.[5]

---

[1] <https://commonslibrary.parliament.uk/home-affairs/justice/courts/constituency-data-magistrates-court-closures/> (accessed 11 May 2020).
[2] Ward J, *Transforming Summary Justice: Modernisation in the Lower Criminal Courts* (London: Routledge, 2016).
[3] Adisa O, *Access to Justice: Assessing the Impact of the Magistrates' Court Closures in Suffolk* (Institute for Social and Economic Research, 2018).
[4] Halliday J, 'Magistrates quitting in "considerable" numbers over court closures' *The Guardian*, 29 November 2016. See Day A, 'Magistrates' Courts Are Closing In Communities Across The UK. Is Austerity Harming Our Access To Justice?' *Huffington Post*, 20 April 2019.
[5] Youth courts are presided over by specially trained magistrates and are not open to the public. If cases are transferred to the Crown court special procedures to help them cope apply. See further Aubrey-Johnson et al, *Youth Justice Law and Practice* (London: Legal Action Group, 2019). For a critical analysis of youth justice, see Case S, *Youth Justice: A Critical Introduction* (London: Routledge, 2018).

Adult defendants charged with motoring offences or other summary offences such as common assault and drunk and disorderly behaviour have their cases heard in the magistrates' courts. The essence of summary justice is a speedy procedure, uncluttered with elaborate judicial rituals. To try a case summarily in the magistrates' courts is to try it without many of the formalities required by the common law, though this does not necessarily mean that the cases it deals with and penalties handed down are trivial.[6] As we shall see, the 'formalities' absent from magistrates' courts include juries and (in many cases) professional judges, for most magistrates are unpaid, part-time amateurs.

Defendants charged with offences triable only on indictment, such as murder, wounding with intent to cause grievous bodily harm and rape, are tried in the Crown court. In between there is a large band of offences—e.g. theft, burglary and assaults causing actual or grievous bodily harm—which are triable either way; that is, they may be tried either summarily in the magistrates' courts or on indictment in the Crown court. At one time, if an indictable or either way case was to go to the Crown court the magistrates had to decide whether there was a case to answer before 'committing' it to the Crown court. This is now usually a formality, and indictable-only cases are now sent to the Crown court immediately after the defendant's first appearance without any scrutiny at all.[7]

The magistrates' court is the workhorse of the system, dealing with around 95% of all criminal cases. Table 8.1 shows the numbers of defendants prosecuted in the magistrates' courts in recent years has been declining from a peak of around 2m 15 years ago.[8] The decline is at least partially due to an increase in the number of defendants subject to out of court disposals such as cautions and penalty notices. Around a quarter of proceedings in the magistrates' court are in respect of indictable and either way offences, and the rest concern motoring offences and other types of summary offence. Around 65% of those facing either way charges have their case heard in the magistrates' courts. In 2018, 36% of the 103,000 cases received by Crown courts were either way offences.[9]

The question of who may represent the prosecution and the defence also depends on the level of court. Barristers in private practice (lawyers who specialise in court-based negotiation and advocacy, and the drafting of legal advice) may appear in all levels of court to prosecute or defend. Defence solicitors in private practice (sometimes regarded as the junior branch of the legal profession) historically lacked rights of audience in the Crown court and therefore appear as advocates mainly in the magistrates' courts.[10] Now that employed lawyers can appear in the Crown, as well as magistrates', courts, the CPS is increasingly using its own lawyers for Crown court advocacy work (see chapter 7). It is 'backfilling' by increasingly deploying semi-qualified staff, known as Associate Prosecutors (APs) in the magistrates' court. The use of non-lawyers for magistrates' court work reflects the belief that the skills of a lawyer are not required for the simplest cases. So the types of work that APs are allowed to undertake are expanding. APs can now be used for most types of non-trial hearing. In 2015, the Prosecution of Offences Act 1985 was amended to allow APs to conduct summary only trials, even though an inspectorate report of the same year indicated that all Crown advocacy could be better prepared and would benefit

---

[6] See Ward (2016).
[7] Crime and Disorder Act 1998, s.51, as amended by Criminal Justice and Courts Act 2015.
[8] Ministry of Justice, *Criminal Statistics 2007* (London: MoJ, 2008b) Table 2.1.
[9] Sturge G, *Court statistics for England and Wales* Briefing Paper Number CBP 8372, 16 December 2019, House of Commons Library.
[10] Solicitors are able to obtain a 'Higher Courts Qualification' certificate (under a procedure and criteria established by the Courts and Legal Services Act 1990 amended by Access to Justice Act 1999, Part III), enabling these 'solicitor-advocates' to appear in the Crown court.

Table 8.1 Proceedings in magistrates' courts in selected years

2016	2017	2018	2019
1.52m	1.51m	1.46m	1.48m

from improved presentation skills.[11] Budget cuts appeared to have a negative impact on initiatives designed to improve the quality of advocacy. The use of less qualified staff is indicative of the lesser importance attached to magistrates' court work and the 'ideology of triviality' that permeates the magistrates' court.[12]

It should not be assumed that magistrates deal only with simple factual matters or guilty pleas and are never confronted with complicated matters of law, although discussion of legal issues may be resisted. A colleague of one of the authors was also a practising barrister in Yorkshire. In a rural court one day she sought to argue a point of law by reference to a leading House of Lords (now Supreme Court) judgment. She was stopped before she had finished and informed that, as she was appearing before the Bogsworth magistrates, not the House of Lords, could she please get to the point?[13] This example illustrates how magistrates sometimes like to give the impression that they only deal with simple matters, and is supported, to an extent, by Darbyshire's research on the attitude of District Judges (who also sit in magistrates' courts and are qualified lawyers themselves). As well as indicating that they give credit for guilty pleas to free up magistrates' court time (see section 7.8), one District Judge appeared to be especially unenthusiastic about legal argument in magistrates' courts, describing them as 'law free zones'.[14] He did, however, maintain an up-to-date knowledge of the law, and other research suggests that the law is, as one would expect, a key feature of magistrates' court proceedings albeit that it is used in a more subtle way than in the Crown court.[15]

The summary nature of magistrates' courts justice is reflected, as one might expect from the above description, in lower running costs. Crown court cases cost, on average, over three times that of equivalent cases in the magistrates' courts.[16] But is there an adequate justification for the difference in treatment meted out to defendants according to the offence with which they are charged? One argument would be that since the sentencing powers of magistrates are generally limited to six months' imprisonment for a single offence (12 months for two separate, either way, offences) there is less of a need for due process safeguards to apply than in the Crown court, where (depending on the offence) a defendant may face life imprisonment.[17] Another would be that summary offences involve straightforward issues, the determination of which do not require anything other than a straightforward procedure. This is certainly true, for example, of many motoring offences. As nearly half of the magistrates' workload is made up of such offences, and given the very

---

[11] HMCPSI, *Thematic review of the CPS advocacy strategy and progress against the recommendations of the follow-up report of the quality of prosecution advocacy and case presentation* (2015) online at: <https://www.justiceinspectorates.gov.uk/hmcpsi/wp-content/uploads/sites/3/2015/03/ADVST_thm_Mar15_rpt.pdf> (accessed 8 June 2018).

[12] McBarnet D, 'Magistrates' Courts and the Ideology of Justice' (1981) 8(2) *British Journal of Law and Society* 181–197.

[13] See McConville et al (1994: 225): '... magistrates' court cases are not argued on legal issues, which are usually assumed to be inappropriate in such a forum.'

[14] Darbyshire P, *Sitting in Judgment: The Working Lives of Judges* (Oxford: Hart, 2011).

[15] Welsh L, *Are magistrates' courts really a 'law free zone'? Participant observation and specialist use of language. Papers from the British Criminology Conference* (2013) 13, pp 3–16.

[16] *Mail Online*, 16 January 2012.

[17] For the complex legal provisions regulating magistrates' sentencing powers see Sprack and Sprack (2019).

high guilty plea rate across all types of offence (see chapter 7), observers in these courts might be forgiven for thinking that 'real crime' and courtroom drama were to be found elsewhere. Often, there are no observers. Journalists and curious members of the public tend to prefer the 'juicier' cases in the Crown court.[18] The lack of public scrutiny of these magistrates' courts is particularly helpful for white collar offenders anxious to avoid any damaging publicity.[19] To summarise, the signals given off by magistrates' courts are that they deal with trivial matters in which the issues are straightforward, defendants willingly accept their guilt and the consequences for defendants of conviction are slight.

In truth, however, magistrates are responsible for decisions of far-reaching importance. They decide whether defendants should be released on bail or should lose their liberty pending trial. So, in 2017 magistrates remanded 57,000 defendants in prison.[20] Magistrates can direct that either way contested cases should be heard in the Crown court, notwithstanding any objections from the defendant. They also help supervise the work of other agencies, such as the police in relation to pre-charge detention of suspects and warrants allowing entry, search and seizure. Finally, magistrates have the ultimate power of depriving convicted defendants of their liberty. Ninety-three per cent of all offenders were sentenced in magistrates' courts in 2014.[21] In 2017, magistrates sent 42,000 offenders to prison.[22] If they feel their sentencing powers are inadequate, they can commit defendants convicted of either way offences to the Crown court for sentence. This is the fate of around 35,000 people each year.[23] One way or another, between a quarter and a third of the prison population is there as a result of the decisions of magistrates.

The operation of the magistrates' courts appears to be consistent with the crime control model of criminal justice. If so, the two 'core values' (justice and democracy) are being subordinated to a third (efficiency).[24] We saw in chapter 7 that the high rate of guilty pleas ensures that many of the most important due process protections central to an adversarial system do not come into play. This chapter will show that the antipathy towards due process values in the lower courts is deep-rooted. This is demonstrated in part at least by the approach to the provision of legal aid for criminal defence services.

8.2 Legal aid and legal representation

Legal representation is central to the functioning of the due process and human rights models, since it should guarantee that defendants are made aware of their rights and that the remedies available for any abuses of those rights are secured. The principle of equality requires that wherever the criminal process affords a theoretical right to legal representation the means should be made available to enable defendants to exercise that right. To do otherwise would place the poor and those of modest means in an unequal position with the rich. These principles appear at first sight to be enshrined in the ECHR (and, therefore,

---

[18] For recent confirmation that this is the case, see Chamberlain P, Keppel-Palmer M, Reardon S and Smith T ,'It's Criminal: The State of Magistrates' Court Reporting in England and Wales' (2019) *Journalism* 1–17.

[19] White collar 'regulatory' crimes are rarely prosecuted (see ch 7), but when they are, they are mainly kept in the magistrates and dealt with in separate sittings, reducing their visibility and helping offenders to play down the seriousness of their crimes. See the discussion by Croall H, 'Mistakes, Accidents and Someone Else's Fault: The Trading Offender in Court' (1988) 15 *Journal of Law and Society* 293.

[20] Ministry of Justice, *Criminal Court Statistics Quarterly*, December 2018b (London, MoJ).

[21] Roberts J and Ashworth A, 'The Evolution of Sentencing Policy and Practice in England and Wales, 2003–2015' (2016) 45 *Crime and Justice* 307–358.

[22] Ministry of Justice, *Criminal Court Statistics Quarterly*, December 2018b (London, MoJ).

[23] Ministry of Justice, *Criminal Court Statistics Quarterly*, December 2019.

[24] See ch 1 for discussion of 'core values'.

the Human Rights Act 1998). Article 6(1) guarantees the right to a fair trial, and Art 6(3) guarantees every defendant the right '. . . to defend himself in person or through legal assistance of his own choosing or, if he has not sufficient means to pay for legal assistance, to be given it free when the interests of justice so require'. For suspects detained for questioning in the police station, these due process principles are broadly accepted.[25] But in the magistrates' courts legal representation is, for many, more of a privilege than a right. This is compatible with the letter (but perhaps not the spirit) of the ECHR because of the proviso in Art 6.3 concerning 'the interests of justice'.

During the last two decades there have been several suggested and implemented reforms aimed at transforming the provision of criminal defence services. These reforms have been driven by the rising costs of legal aid and a desire to control expenditure on criminal legal aid in particular.[26] In this section we provide a brief overview of the services available and examine the impact of reforms on the availability and quality of defence service provision in the magistrates' court. Notable developments include the introduction of a public defender service in some areas (from 2001) and controversial proposals for price competitive tendering, which many lawyers feared would put firms out of business and result in a reduction in the quality of defence services available. Currently three 'levels' of criminal defence service are available, two without means testing.[27] First, 'advice and assistance,' which largely covers police station work and potentially some follow up work. Second, those who arrive at court unrepresented may receive 'advocacy assistance' from a duty solicitor, but must satisfy a merits test. A defendant can only use the services of the duty solicitor once per case. These cases are frequently dealt with at that one hearing. Non-imprisonable cases are not covered, and for most cases that are adjourned, the defendant will be expected to apply for full legal representation. To obtain full legal representation, the third level of service, a defendant must make an application to the Legal Aid Agency (LAA) and satisfy both means and merits testing.

8.2.1 **The means test**

In 2001 the government abolished the means test for magistrates' courts work but reintroduced it in 2006. We would have no objection to a test which excluded the wealthiest households, but this was clearly not the intended effect. The Bach Commission showed that means testing is so tightly restricted that people of modest incomes are often denied legal aid,[28] while Kemp found that the provisions are particularly onerous on self-employed defendants.[29] Between 2005 and 2009 £80 million was saved,[30] the government then using this to justify its extension into Crown court proceedings in 2010. The government exceeded its legal aid savings predictions more than twice over.[31] The government believes that savings can be made by targeting those who can afford to contribute towards all or part of their legal costs. But many defendants on average or middle incomes are suffering and the number of unrepresented defendants is increasing in both Crown and

---

[25] See ch 4.
[26] Lord Carter's Review of Legal Aid Procurement, *Legal Aid: a market-based approach to Reform* (2006) (<www.legalaidprocurementreview.gov.uk/publications.htm> (accessed 5 January 2010)). Ministry of Justice, *Legal Aid: Funding Reforms*, Consultation Paper 18/09 (MoJ, 2009c).
[27] See generally Legal Aid, Sentencing and Punishment of Offenders Act 2012 (LASPO).
[28] Bach Commission, *The Right to Justice* (2017). Available at <http://www.fabians.org.uk/wp-content/uploads/2017/09/Bach-Commission_Right-to-Justice-Report-WEB.pdf> (accessed 10 October 2019).
[29] Kemp V, *Transforming Legal Aid: Access to Criminal Defence Services* (London: Legal Services Commission, 2010).
[30] Ministry of Justice, *Crown court means testing: Response to consultation CP(R) 06/09* (London: MoJ, 2009d).
[31] Bach Commission (2017).

magistrates' courts.[32] This potentially breaches the obligations of Art 6(3) ECHR, but, to date, there has been no such challenge. One potential hindrance to any appeal on a human rights basis may be the ability to make a financial hardship application to the LAA, but this procedure is also very onerous on both defendants and their lawyers and is—in one author's experience—seldom used.

8.2.2 **The merits test**

Schedule 3 of the Access to Justice Act 1999 (AJA) provides that representation may be granted where it appears desirable 'in the interests of justice' to do so, and specifies a number of factors which must be taken into account in determining this matter. Those same criteria have now been enshrined in LASPO, s.17. Some of these 'Widgery' criteria[33] concern the seriousness of the consequences to the defendant of a conviction. If a defendant is facing the likelihood of loss of liberty, livelihood or reputation, more favourable consideration should be given to granting legal aid. The remaining criteria concern the inability of the defendant adequately to conduct a case in person. Thus a grant of legal aid is more likely (at least in theory) if the case requires the tracing and interviewing of witnesses, consideration of a substantial question of law or expert cross-examination, or if the defendant has inadequate knowledge of English or suffers from some learning disability, mental health condition or physical disability. One final factor to be taken into account is whether it is in the interests of another that the accused be represented. This covers situations where it might lead to difficulties if the accused had to cross-examine witnesses in person, such as in child abuse cases. This is an area in which more due process for the accused can lead to better protection for victims.

There seems little doubt that the Widgery criteria are ECHR-compliant since Art 6(3) itself uses the phrase 'interests of justice' to indicate when legal aid should be granted. And judicial interpretation of this phrase seems fully in accordance with the English position (which, if anything, is more generous). Thus, the European Court of Human Rights has repeatedly held that when assessing the interests of justice test within Art 6 regard must be had to the seriousness of the offence and the severity of the penalty at stake, and the complexity of the case.[34] The European Court has also upheld a French claim where a man who faced a very large fine was denied free legal aid,[35] showing that loss of liberty is not the only important criterion.

The criteria are not exclusive—other factors may be taken into account.[36] For some time it seemed that it could be refused even if a case fell squarely within one or more of the statutory criteria.[37] But the Divisional Court has become increasingly willing to substitute its own view for those of decision-makers by quashing refusals to grant legal

---

[32] 'Unrepresented defendants crowd criminal courts', *Law Society Gazette*, 2 May 2016; *The Guardian*, 24 November 2019.

[33] They derive from the Report of the Departmental Committee on Legal Aid in Criminal Proceedings (Cmnd 2934) (London: HMSO, 1966) para 56 (chaired by Mr Justice Widgery).

[34] See, in particular, *Quaranta v Switzerland* (1991) Eur Court HR Series A 205; *Benham v United Kingdom* (1996) 22 EHRR 293.

[35] *Pham Hoang v France* (1992) 16 EHRR 53, discussed by Ashworth A, 'Legal Aid, Human Rights, and Criminal Justice', in Young R and Wall D (eds), *Access to Criminal Justice* (London: Blackstone, 1996).

[36] *Liverpool City Magistrates, ex p McGhee* [1993] Crim LR 609.

[37] See, in particular, *Macclesfield Justices, ex p Greenhalgh* (1979) 144 JP 142; *Crown court at Cambridge, ex p Hagi* (1979) 144 JP 145 and *Havering Juvenile Court, ex p Buckley* (LEXIS 554 1983).

aid.[38] Much, then, relies on the correct identification of cases where the criteria apply. How much care is exercised in legal aid decision-making? Applications for state-aided representation (referred to from now, for simplicity, by the old term 'legal aid') used to be made in writing to clerks and could be appealed orally. This enabled the defence to have the application put before a different decision-maker, although, since the magistrates are used to relying on the advice of their clerk (who will be present in court when the application is renewed) the value of this 'second bite of the cherry' was not as great as it might be.[39]

Research by Young et al on the pre-1999 system found that grant rates were high, at 90% (although substantially less than 90% of cases were represented, as solicitors only applied in cases that had a good chance of success). Application forms were frequently completed by unqualified staff employed by the defendant's solicitor using standard wording which often exaggerated the case for granting legal aid.[40] In turn, court clerks were found to give little weight to the statutory criteria but applied a crude rule of thumb in determining an application. Defendants perceived to be charged with a 'serious' offence would almost automatically be granted legal aid, whereas those charged with a 'trivial' offence would similarly be refused. In the middle lay a grey area, which differed from court to court, wherein the chances of obtaining legal aid would depend on how well the legal aid application was argued.[41]

Young, with Wilcox, replicated his study in 2004, by which time grant rates had risen to nearly 95% of all applications (again, not of all cases). As before, some courts granted virtually all applications, whereas others refused one in five (previously, some refused as many as one in four). The authors judged that courts had not generally become more generous, apart perhaps from the least generous ones, but as sentencing had become tougher, and legal proceedings more complex, more cases had become deserving of assistance. Some inconsistency of decision-making was found, but less than before. They proposed moderate reforms (such as re-designing the application form) in an attempt to address this and improve the consistency of decision-making.[42] However, the government seemingly thought that those proposals did not go far enough, and instead gave the power to make decisions about legal aid to non-legally qualified employees of the LAA. The LAA—created under the provisions of LASPO in 2013—is a department of the Ministry of Justice, which raises obvious doubts about the independence of decision-makers (unlike its predecessor, the Legal Services Commission, which was a step removed from government). Informal

---

[38] See for example *R on the Application of Luke Matara v Brent Magistrates' Court* [2005] EWHC 1829 where the defendant had applied for legal aid partly on the basis of 'inadequate English'. The magistrates' court had discounted this criterion on the basis that an interpreter would be provided, but the Divisional Court noted that the requirement that the proceedings be in a language that the defendant understood was 'merely one aspect' of the requirements of Art 6.

[39] For many years, applicants had the right to appeal to an area committee of the Legal Aid Board. When the Board was abolished by the 1999 Act, so was the right of appeal. This illustrates how defendants charged with 'minor' offences are increasingly afforded fewer due process safeguards.

[40] Young et al, *In the Interests of Justice?* (Birmingham: Birmingham University, 1992) at pp 62–86. See also Wall D, 'Keyholders to Criminal Justice' in Young and Wall (eds) (1996).

[41] Young et al (1992: 25–39). For summaries of some of the main findings of this report see Young R, 'The Merits of Legal Aid in the Magistrates' Courts' [1993] *Criminal Law Review* 336 and Young R 'Will Widgery Do?' in Young and Wall (eds) (1996).

[42] Wilcox and Young (2006: ch 10). See also Young R and Wilcox A 'The Merits of Legal Aid in the Magistrates' Courts Revisited' [2007] *Criminal Law Review* 109. A redesigned application form along the lines advocated by Young and Wilcox was put into use for a short period but then was itself replaced due to the re-introduction of means testing and a re-design of the form to achieve this. In other words, the lessons of the research were almost immediately forgotten.

conversations with defence lawyer colleagues of one author in 2018 revealed continuing concerns about inconsistent, flawed decision-making by the LAA.[43] If an applicant does not pass the merits test, he or she can appeal to the LAA by completing a standard form. If legal aid is again refused, it is possible to make an application in open court. But given that courts are reluctant to adjourn cases for legal aid issues to be resolved (because efficiency and court statistics are key),[44] irreparable damage may have already occurred to a case by the time legal aid is granted, if at all.

The main problem with the discretion left to officials of the executive in deciding which defendants should receive legal aid is the potential it creates for subverting adversarial procedures, although the same can also be said for decisions made by court clerks—each group has their own vested interests in the decision. An adversarial system cannot work properly if there is an inequality of resources available to the prosecution and the defence. The prosecution is always represented, even if not always by a qualified lawyer,[45] however 'trivial' or 'straightforward' the case might be, so why should the defence not be treated in the same way? And, because cases are constructed by the prosecution to appear strong on paper,[46] it cannot safely be predicted in advance which cases might lead to injustice if representation was not provided. Good legal representation can: lead to the emergence of previously hidden aspects of the case; render problematic the prosecution version of events; and raise questions about the integrity of the procedures followed. Magistrates' court cases can be complex, but the 'ideology of triviality' usually hides this successfully. It is impossible to estimate the proportion of cases in which legal aid is currently refused (or not applied for) that would benefit from legal representation. The proportion may be small, but if the system is to give priority to acquitting the innocent and other due process values, legal aid should surely be more widely available. But, as we have seen, the ECHR does not require this, and it is unlikely that the LAA will be allowed to foster more generous decision-making in future even despite a review of legal aid in criminal cases that is ongoing at the time of writing.[47]

8.2.3 The cost of legal aid

For many years, expenditure on criminal legal aid rose significantly, but had stabilised at around £1.2 bn, just over half the £2 bn total legal aid budget by 2010.[48] As seen in section 8.2.2, the government has made significant savings to legal aid expenditure since that time. Overall spending in 2016 had reduced to £1.6bn, and between June 2016 and June 2017,

---

[43] Lawyers surveyed as part of ongoing research recently described LAA decision-making as flawed, perverse and inconsistent. See <https://legalaidandrepresentatives.wordpress.com/news/> and <https://ccrc.gov.uk/ongoing-research-legal-aid-project/> (both accessed 20 April 2020).

[44] Welsh L, 'The Effects of Changes to Legal Aid on Lawyers' Professional Identity and Behaviour in Summary Criminal Cases: A Case Study' (2017) 44(4) *Journal of Law and Society* 559–585.

[45] We have noted an increase in non-legally qualified CPS advocates (section 8.1). The fact the prosecution is legally represented does not mean that magistrates' are bound to grant legal aid (*Havering Juvenile Court ex p Buckley*, Lexis CO/554/83, 12 July 12 1983).

[46] See McConville et al, *The Case for the Prosecution* (London: Routledge, 1991). Discussed in ch 7.

[47] See <https://www.gov.uk/guidance/criminal-legal-aid-review> (accessed 8 April). Some proposals were put forward as part of an accelerated review package, but were met with criticism from the profession. See The Law Society *Criminal legal aid review: latest proposals are insufficient*, 28 February 2020, online at <https://www.lawsociety.org.uk/news/stories/criminal-legal-aid-review-latest-proposals-are-insufficient/> (accessed 8 April 2020).

[48] For an overview of the history of legal aid and levels of expenditure see Hynes S and Robins J, *The Justice Gap-Whatever Happened to Legal Aid?* (London: LAG, 2009). See also Hynes S, 'Fixed Fees, best value tendering and the CDS' *Legal Action*, March 2008, 6; Cape E, 'Legal Aid Spending: Looking the other way', *Legal Action*, July 2008, 8.

criminal legal aid expenditure declined by 9%.[49] Other data indicates that expenditure on legal aid has fallen by one third in real terms since 2011.[50] Despite those reductions, the government continued to pursue proposals to further reduce criminal legal aid costs. In 2006, Lord Carter proposed a controversial market based reform called 'Best Value Tendering' (BVT); a process whereby every supplier who wanted to take part in publically funded criminal defence work would bid in an auction to do the work at the lowest price.[51] That proposal was eventually shelved due to its widespread unpopularity, but the suggestion that firms would bid for the 'privilege' of being contracted to provide legally aided services was resurrected under the new name, 'Price Competitive Tendering', in the Ministry of Justice's 2013 consultation, *Transforming Legal Aid*. The same consultation also proposed a total of 17.5% fee cuts (to be introduced in two tranches) and a complicated contracting system depending on whether a firm would represent only those people who specifically requested their services or would also be able to act as duty (on call) lawyers.

The proposals were again extremely controversial and attracted in the region of 16,000 responses from lawyers, NGOs, academics and other interested parties. Eventually, after two legal challenges, most of the more controversial proposals were abandoned but a fee cut of 8.75% was introduced in 2014. A second proposed fee cut of a further 8.75% has been suspended since 2016, but could be resurrected if the government makes another u-turn. Such an approach would not be surprising because the government has attempted to introduce cuts to other areas of legal aid since 2016, such as reducing fees for Crown court preparatory work. Lawyers have, however, successfully challenged Ministry of Justice procedures in relation to cuts several times since 2013,[52] and there was some increase in funding for advocacy (Crown court) work in 2018.[53] The legal challenges have largely been successful because correct consultation procedures had not been followed, rather than because the proposals themselves were unacceptable to the courts.

8.2.4 The quality of defence work under legal aid

At around the same time as fixed fees were being introduced in England and Wales (in the late 1990s), they were also introduced in Scotland. The rates were low and the income of specialist criminal defence firms initially fell sharply but then rose to the previous levels because firms increased their caseloads.[54] However, the introduction of fixed fees resulted in firms reporting a decline in client contact, although they were more willing to say this had been the effect on their rivals' working practices than their own.[55] This matters,

---

[49] Pepin S, Lipscome S and Zayed Y, *Provision of Legal Aid. House of Commons Debate Pack* (2017) CDP 207–0239.
[50] Croft J, 'UK court overturns government cuts to legal aid fees for solicitors' *Financial Times*, 3 August 2018.
[51] *Best Value Tendering of Criminal Defence Services* (LSC, December 2007); *Best Value Tendering for CDS Contracts: A Consultation paper* (LSC, March 2009). For further details see <http://www.legalservices.gov.uk/criminal/a_market_based_approach.asp> (accessed 22 October 2009).
[52] See *R (the Law Society & Criminal Courts Solicitors' Association & Others) v Lord Chancellor* [2015] EWCA Civ 230; *Fair Crime Contract Alliance v Legal Aid Agency (Legal Aid Procurement Challenge); R (Law Society) v The Lord Chancellor* [2018] EWHC 2094 (Admin); *R (Howard League and the Prisoners' Advice Service) v The Lord Chancellor* [2017] EWCA Civ 244.
[53] Thornton J, 'The Way in Which Fee Reductions Influence Legal Aid Criminal Defence Lawyer Work: Insights from a Qualitative Study' (2019) 46(4) *Journal of Law and Society* 559–585.
[54] A similar phenomena has probably occurred in England and Wales. See Makepeace A, 'Pumping up the volume to make legal aid profitable' *Law Society Gazette*, 25 January 2008, 24; Welsh (2017) and Thornton (2019).
[55] Stephen et al, *Impact of the Introduction of Fixed Fee Payments into Summary Criminal Legal Aid: Report of an independent study* (Scottish Executive, 2007) available at <http://www.scotland.gov.uk/Publications/2007/06/22104314/0> (accessed 22 October 2009).

because without the informal unproductive parts of client interviews, less valuable information is secured from the formal productive parts, as a good rapport increases the information that defendants give their lawyers.[56] Lawyers in England also admitted that, while a fixed fee payment scheme is acceptable in principle, it does disincentivise provision of a good quality service.[57] It does not seem to be that the fixed fee system itself disincentivises a good level of service, but that the level at which fees are set is too low, thus requiring lawyers to work to volume and reduce time spent on any given case.[58] If it is important to take into account the way that criminal justice is experienced—as we argue throughout this book—giving time to building the solicitor–client relationship is not money down the drain. As well as asking whether resources suffice to enable a basic minimum of work to be done, the question is whether the level of fees and structure of remuneration puts prosecution and defence on a level playing field. The evidence is that it does not.

Has criminal defence work, in the light of the income levels produced by such devices as low-rate standard fees, become a second-rate service? It leads to experienced criminal practitioners seeking to achieve greater financial security and status by switching to more lucrative types of legal activity such as corporate and commercial work.[59] One author's experience and research suggests this to be the case. For example, in research, one defence lawyer said:

> The people with options, the brightest will have plan Bs and will take those plan Bs and as soon as they walk out of the criminal legal aid system they will be lost to the system forever because frankly once you have gone through this process you are not going to want to come back to it and you will have an exodus of talent and those that are left behind will provide a far worse service than as is presently the case.[60]

Moreover, the profession is an ageing one because young lawyers cannot afford, and are not attracted to, what is seen as low status and less well-paid criminal defence work.[61] The organisation of specialist criminal practices is a key determinant of the quality of defence work.[62] The essential point here is that solicitors are business people. Either they make a profit or they go out of business. Many solicitors argue that the only way to make legal aid pay is to handle large numbers of cases in a streamlined and bureaucratic fashion. One lawyer interviewed by Thornton said: 'What's happening now is that you're getting what I would describe as bare minimum preparation'; that being seen as a distasteful but necessary practice in order to prevent firms from going bust.[63]

---

[56] Unsurprisingly, no-one in government seems to object to the police using 'unproductive' rapport at the start of an interrogation as a way of getting suspects to lower their guards and reveal more information during the 'productive' part of the interaction: see further ch 5.

[57] Welsh (2017).   [58] Welsh (2017); Newman (2013).

[59] See Smith R, 'Resolving the Legal Aid Crisis' *Law Society Gazette*, 27 February 1991, p 17. Moorhead R, 'Legal Aid and the Decline of Private Practice: Blue Murder or Toxic Job?' (2004) 11(3) *International Journal of the Legal Profession* 160 at p 179 noted that a newly qualified solicitor in 2003 in London might expect to earn around £15,000 in a legal aid firm compared with £50,000 in one of the top London commercial firms.

[60] The research was conducted as part of doctoral research. See Welsh L, *Magistrates, Managerialism and Marginalisation: Neoliberalism and Access to Justice*, unpublished PhD thesis, University of Kent (2016).

[61] 'Criminal defence solicitors may be extinct in five years, says Law Society' *The Guardian*, 17 April 2018. For discussion, see Newman D and Welsh L, 'The Practices of Modern Criminal Defence Lawyers: Alienation and its Implications for Access to Justice' (2019) (48) *Common Law World Review* 64–89 and Thornton J, 'Is Publicly Funded Criminal Defence Sustainable? Legal Aid Cuts, Morale, Recruitment and Retention in the English Criminal Law Professions' (2020) 40(2) *Legal Studies* 230.

[62] See the insightful analysis of legal aid practices by King M, *The Framework of Criminal Justice* (London: Croom Helm, 1981) pp 68–75, and the empirical study by McConville et al (1994).

[63] Thornton (2019: 580).

Profits can be maximised by the routine allocation of legally aided work to non-solicitors. Non-solicitors often attend at police stations. They are also employed in carrying out initial interviews with defendants and applying for legal aid, although the use of staff without *any* legal training seems to have declined since the early 1990s.[64] This all affects the quality of service unless training and supervision is stringent. Criminal legal aid representation can therefore be characterised by *routinisation, delegation* and *discontinuous representation*.[65] Fixed fees make this more inevitable in order that criminal legal aid be efficient and cost-effective. But whether it can at the same time be 'justice-effective' is another matter. The ideal of a close client–lawyer relationship in which the lawyer conducts the case in person from the police station right through to the courts is only rarely realised in practice. We are not suggesting that solicitors are completely unprofessional and mercenary. Few would generally act unethically. But fee structures and other structural aspects of the system are likely to alter behaviour substantially in areas of 'ethical uncertainty'[66]— in other words, where doing a less thorough job may be an ethically defensible but less-preferred course of action—such as giving unqualified staff responsibilities that need not be done by a professional, but which would be better so done, or eliminating time spent with clients aimed at building rapport and trust. One area of 'ethical indeterminacy'— where lawyers face a choice between two courses of action but are unsure which is better for their client—might be whether to advise a guilty plea (section 7.7).

A further problem is that a legal aid order may not cover all the work that the solicitor thinks is necessary in preparing the defence. In assessing claims for payment for legal services not covered by a fixed fee or contract price, the LAA is supposed to allow a reasonable amount in respect of all work actually and reasonably done. In practice this means that solicitors often find themselves wrangling with LAA officials over the correct level of payment to be made, or, indeed, over whether any payment at all should be forthcoming. Some solicitors have simply stopped carrying out certain preparatory steps in their cases, such as tracing and interviewing witnesses, or through review of unused material,[67] for fear that they will not receive payment for such work.[68] Furthermore the government was keen to cut the costs of using experts in the same way as it aims to control criminal legal aid expenditure in general,[69] which raises concerns about whether a suitably qualified pool of experts will remain available to the defence if rates are set too low (see section 7.3.3.4). Scientific and other forms of expert evidence are not uncontroversial and continue to contribute to miscarriages of justice.[70] It is therefore important that defence firms have access to levels of funding which enable them to instruct experts to scrutinise and challenge prosecution expert evidence. The government claims that efforts to control criminal legal aid expenditure can succeed without any reduction in the quality of services available, because quality measures are in place which solicitors will have to meet if they want their relationship with the LAA to continue. It is a prerequisite to a contract award that a firm is able to show compliance with quality mark standards (at the firm's own expense). This is so up to a point, but many firms struggle to provide the level of service they might otherwise have offered and some have been driven out of business. Over four years to 2018, the number of practising criminal defence solicitors fell by 9.4%, and by July 2018, the House of Commons Justice Committee reported that the criminal legal aid sector is now so fragile that human rights are being put at risk.[71]

---

[64] Compare McConville et al (1994) and Young et al (1992: 81–86), with Wilcox and Young (2006: 136–138).
[65] McConville at al (1994); Newman (2013).
[66] Tata C and Stephen F, 'Do Changes to the Structure of Legal Aid Remuneration Make a Real Difference to Criminal Case Outcomes?' (2006) *Criminal Law Review* 722; Stephen et al (2007).
[67] Thornton (2019).   [68] See Young et al (1992: 75–76) for instance.
[69] Criminal Legal Aid (Remuneration) Regulations 2013.   [70] See the discussion in ch 6.
[71] Fouzder M, 'Criminal legal aid fragility putting rights at risk – MPs' *Law Society Gazette*, 26 July 2018.

The creation of a salaried public defender service (PDS) creates further competition for private firms offering criminal defence services. It might seem that such a system, by removing the profit motive from defence work, would lead to improved standards. However, this depends upon the aims and funding of the service. PDS systems in the United States are generally poor,[72] although jurisdictions such as Canada have introduced such systems with greater success.[73]

Public defender offices were opened in six sites in England and Wales in 2001/2 and July 2002. The objective of the PDS was to provide a service that was as good as or better than that provided by private practice. An early evaluation measured its performance by comparing the quality-of-service provision at three stages of the criminal process including representation at the magistrates' courts. Quality and practices varied across sites but in some respects the PDS seemed to be doing better than private practice. For example, in relation to police station work PDS clients were more likely to make a 'no comment' interview which suggests that the PDS adopts a 'more adversarial approach' than private firms.[74] There were no significant differences in bail outcomes and although the PDS had more guilty pleas they also had more discontinued cases and the levels of conviction rates for PDS and private firms were similar, as were sentencing outcomes. The researchers conclude the picture is 'broadly positive about the performance of the PDS offices relative to private practice'.[75] Outside the PDS there were generally positive perceptions about the quality of advocacy and independence of public defenders, believing them to be as willing as private firms to challenge the police and prosecution and stand up for clients (although perhaps not surprisingly solicitors in private practice were less complimentary). But this level of service came at substantially higher costs per case than private practice.[76] It would probably not be able to maintain a similar level of service on the more constrained funding available to private firms. In fact the LAA closed down the least cost-effective branches of the PDS (at Birmingham, Chester and Liverpool), and the only branches currently operating are at Darlington, Pontypridd, Swansea and Cheltenham. They operate as a department of the LAA.[77]

The poor will always be dependent on the state to fund their defence regardless of whether legal services are based on private sector provision or salaried defenders. Either way, the state tends to draw the purse strings much tighter in relation to defence work than it does in sponsoring prosecutions. On both sides of the Atlantic, the state is more interested in cut-price efficient crime control than in expensive adversarial due process. So, in 2019 the government boosted CPS funding by £85m, but additional funding offered to defence services in early 2020 amounted to between £32m and £50m.[78] There is a political

---

[72] For a critical overview, see McConville M and Mirsky C, 'The State, the Legal Profession, and the Defence of the Poor' (1988) 15 *Journal of Legal Studies* 342. For a report showing the differences within the US, see JUSTICE, *Public Defenders: Learning from the US Experience* (London: JUSTICE, 2001).

[73] See O'Brien D and Epp J, 'Salaried Defenders and the Access to Justice Act 1999' (2000) 63 *Modern Law Review* 394. On the dangers of making cross-jurisdictional comparisons see Tata C, 'Comparing Legal Aid Spending' in Regan et al (eds), *The Transformation of Legal Aid* (Oxford: OUP, 1999). A pilot scheme ran in Scotland with mixed results: Goriely et al, *The Public Defence Solicitors' Office in Edinburgh: An Independent Evaluation* (Edinburgh, Scottish Executive Central Research Unit, 2001); Goriely T, 'Evaluating the Scottish Public Defence Solicitors' Office' (2003) 30 *Journal of Law and Society* 84; Tata C et al 'Does Mode of Delivery Make a Difference to Criminal Case Outcomes and Clients' Satisfaction?' (2004) *Criminal Law Review* 120.

[74] Bridges et al, *Evaluation of the Public Defender Service in England and Wales* (2007) at p 91—available from <http://orca.cf.ac.uk/44472/1/1622.pdf> (accessed 18 March 2015).

[75] Bridges et al (2007:110). [76] Bridges et al (2007: 231).

[77] See <https://publicdefenderservice.org.uk/> (accessed 20 July 2019).

[78] See BBC News, 'Law and order: Extra £85m for CPS to tackle violent crime', 12 August 2019 and Ministry of Justice (2020c) Criminal Legal Aid Review. An accelerated package of measures amending the criminal legal aid fee schemes, online at: <https://consult.justice.gov.uk/criminal-legal-aid/criminal-legal-aid-review/supporting_documents/criminallegalaidconsultationdocument.pdf> (accessed 10 April 2020).

dimension to this preference. Whereas cuts in spending on the police and prosecution services might be perceived as the government going 'soft' on crime, the due process rights of suspects present an easier target for cuts. Put crudely, there are currently more votes in crime control than in due process. The implications for the quality of defence services in particular, and adversarial justice in the magistrates' courts in general, seem (to us at least) obvious. Overall, the legal aid scheme provides a basic due process protection for many defendants but also nudges defence lawyers into a crime control mode of operation.

This has become even more true since defence lawyers, in their criminal legal aid work, have become obliged to subscribe to the goals of the LAA as a government agency. They have become further tied into the 'efficiency agenda' by rules of criminal procedure.[79] In chapter 7 we examined how this translates into pressure to deal with cases more quickly and to advise clients to plead guilty earlier. This is not what adversarialism—or, more important, justice—is supposed to be about.

The due process argument for near-universal high quality criminal legal aid has to be balanced against competing demands on financial resources from other sectors of society (such as education and health). So it is right to ask whether the money is being spent properly. It is often said that much of the increase in the criminal legal aid bill is down to solicitors and defendants incurring unnecessary expenditure. But as a government Green Paper accepted, 'demand is determined by the state' in the sense that if people were not arrested and prosecuted they would not seek criminal legal aid.[80] The accelerated part of the Criminal Legal Aid Review further acknowledged that criminal proceedings have become increasingly complex[81] (as a result of changes to procedural and evidential rules). In other words, if the state is concerned about rising legal aid expenditure (as it should be) then the state should take responsibility for at least a part of the problem and alter its behaviour accordingly.

8.3 Justices' clerks and legal advisors: liberal bureaucrats?

The primary function of justices' clerks in England and Wales is to give accurate and consistent legal advice to lay magistrates (i.e. people who are not legally qualified). Justices' clerks are qualified lawyers who exercise judicial functions themselves. They also delegate judicial and advisory functions to other lawyers employed by HM Court Service, known as assistant Justices' Clerks or 'legal advisors'. In addition to advising magistrates on law, procedure and sentencing they are responsible for training magistrates, assisting unrepresented defendants, and shaping the conduct of proceedings in court through their role in managing the court's business.[82] Thus, they handle many pre-trial proceedings aimed at reducing delays in processing cases and they determine listing policies which might, for example, aim to dispose of as many cases in a single sitting of the court as possible. In carrying out these tasks, are clerks influenced by, and do they seek to advance, due process or crime control values?

The role of the clerk in assisting unrepresented defendants has been examined in a few separate (but mostly ancient) studies. Darbyshire found that some clerks were helpful and

---

[79] Criminal Procedure Rules (2015 as amended). See Sprack and Sprack (2019). For discussion, see Johnston E, 'The Adversarial Defence Lawyer: Myths, Disclosure and Efficiency—A Contemporary Analysis of the Role in the Era of the Criminal Procedure Rules' (2020) 24(1) *International Journal of Evidence and Proof* 35–58.
[80] Lord Chancellor's Department, Legal Aid: Targeting Need (Cm 2854, 1995: 30).
[81] Ministry of Justice (2020) Criminal Legal Aid Review.
[82] See generally, Darbyshire P, *Darbyshire on the English Legal System* 12th edn (London: Sweet and Maxwell, 2017).

patient whilst others were brusque and intimidating.[83] Mulcahy found that clerks often presumed defendants were guilty,[84] which shapes the way they process cases. Astor also noted varying standards of help on offer from clerks but made the important point that the 'allegiance of the clerks was ultimately not to the defendants, but to the rules—their insistence was that the court be run "properly", not necessarily that the defendant understood what was going on.'[85] She argues that court clerks have a genuine interest in due process, since as the magistrates' courts' legal advisors they must ensure that the legitimacy of the court is not called into question. At the same time, she acknowledges, they have a strong bureaucratic interest in efficiency and saving court time. Astor's understanding appeared to be borne out in more recent research, in which one defence lawyer said of magistrates' clerks: 'some magistrates simply do what the clerk tells them and too many clerks simply say "we're following the rules, you can't have an adjournment, there should be no adjournments simply because of legal aid problems."'[86] Astor accordingly follows Bottoms and McClean in arguing that the model of the criminal justice process which most accurately described the values 'typically held by humane and enlightened clerks'[87] was neither crime control nor due process, but the liberal bureaucratic model.[88]

The liberal bureaucratic model differs from crime control in that the need for justice to be done and seen to be done is accepted as ultimately overriding the importance of repressing criminal conduct. Priority must be given to protecting the innocent and the importance of formal adjudicative procedures is recognised. Thus far, this sounds like a fair account of the due process model. Bottoms and McClean argue, however, that the liberal bureaucrat's strong interest in the efficient throughput of cases limits commitment to due process protections. As they put it:

> If it were not so, then the whole system of criminal justice, with its ultimate value to the community in the form of liberal and humane crime control, would collapse. Moreover, it is right to build in sanctions to deter those who might otherwise use their 'Due Process' rights frivolously, or to 'try it on'; an administrative system at State expense should not exist for this kind of time-wasting.[89]

They go on to note how the pressures on defendants to elect summary trial—in particular, the fear of a heavier sentence at the Crown court—and the pressures on defendants to plead guilty all help to smooth the administrative operation of the system. They conclude that:

> Despite the superficially apparent similarity of the value-systems underlying the Liberal Bureaucratic and Due Process Models, in practice the Liberal Bureaucratic Model offers much stronger support to the aims of the Crime Control Model than the Due Process Model.[90]

Bottoms and McClean contradict themselves here by claiming that 'humane and enlightened' court clerks are genuinely concerned about protecting the innocent and upholding formal adjudicative procedures, at the same time as suggesting that they support rules and sanctions designed to deter defendants from exercising their due process rights. Such rules and sanctions are, after all, quintessential to the crime control model. The essential point to

---

[83] See Darbyshire P, *The Magistrates' Clerk* (Chichester: Barry Rose, 1984). See also Darbyshire P, 'For the New Lord Chancellor-Some Causes for Concern about Magistrates' (1997) *Criminal Law Review* 86.

[84] Mulcahy A, 'The Justifications of "Justice": Legal Practitioners' Accounts of Negotiated Case Settlements in Magistrates' Courts' (1994) 34(4) *British Journal of Criminology* 411.

[85] Astor H, 'The Unrepresented Defendant Revisited: A Consideration of the Role of the Clerk in Magistrates' Courts' (1986) 13(2) *Journal of Law and Society* 225–239 at 232. [86] Welsh (2016: 186).

[87] Bottoms A and McClean J, *Defendants in the Criminal Process* (London: Routledge & Kegan Paul, 1976) p 228.

[88] For a full appraisal of the due process and crime control models see sections 1.5–1.5.4.

[89] Bottoms and McClean (1976: 229). [90] Bottoms and McClean (1976: 232).

grasp here is that the crime control model represents one end of a spectrum of possible criminal justice systems, at the other end of which lies the due process model. By setting up these two opposing models, Packer hoped to illuminate the competing claims and tensions within criminal justice.[91] By contrast, the so-called liberal bureaucratic model is simply a factual description of the operation of the courts. This description reveals that court procedures display elements of the due process model in that contested trials do occur (albeit rarely), legal aid is available in some cases, court clerks will (on occasion) assist unrepresented defendants and so forth. However, the predominance of guilty plea cases, and the pressures on defendants to refrain from pushing the available due process levers, means that the magistrates' courts correspond much more closely to the crime control model than its polar opposite.

To return to Astor's work, while she is undoubtedly correct in suggesting that court clerks are anxious to see the rules followed, what is overlooked is that these rules themselves often incorporate crime control values. In a system that demands efficiency, those rules become ingrained in standardised processes with little consideration given to what they mean for 'justice'.[92] This means that the needs of vulnerable defendants, for example, are sometimes swept aside or lost in the system even when clerks and legal advisors want to assist.[93] A denial of due process can accordingly be achieved without breaking the rules and without any undermining of the court's legitimacy.

An illustration of this is provided by the court clerk's role at the pre-trial stage. Clerks played a leading role in developing pre-trial reviews in the form of 'early administrative hearings' (EAHs) introduced by the Crime and Disorder Act 1998. The Act granted to clerks powers previously reserved to magistrates and arguably blurred the advisory and judicial line between justices' clerks and magistrates. EAHs were part of a package of measures attempting to reduce delays in the magistrates' court.[94] Clerks were granted further case management powers pursuant to the Criminal Procedure (Amendment) Rules 2020. Providing clerks with extra powers of this kind is also an example of the managerialism discussed in chapter 1. Court clerks are expected actively to encourage defence disclosure and case settlement.[95] These demands have increased since EAHs were introduced, as detailed in section 8.5.2, and we need new research on the lines of Darbyshire's or Astor's to see whether this shrine of independence is merely presentational.

8.4 Bail or jail

Should defendants awaiting trial (or sentencing) be imprisoned? Imprisonment without trial has three obvious attractions for adherents to the crime control model: first, it secures the attendance of defendants at court; second, it impairs the ability of defendants to interfere with prosecution witnesses; and, third, it prevents defendants from committing further offences whilst awaiting trial. That imprisoned defendants might not have committed any offence in the first place hardly arises due to the factual presumption of guilt at work in this model. Contrast this with the due process model. The normative presumption of innocence is antithetical to pre-trial custody.[96] Preserving the freedom of the innocent

---

[91] Packer H, *The Limits of the Criminal Sanction* (Stanford: Stanford UP, 1968). See our discussion in ch 1.
[92] Welsh and Howard (2019).
[93] Chadwick D and Wesson C, '"Blocked at Every Level": Criminal Justice System Professionals' Experiences of Including People With Intellectual Disabilities Within a Targeted Magistrates' Court' (2020) (forthcoming) *Journal of Intellectual Disabilities and Offending Behaviour*.
[94] Home Office (Narey Report), Review of Delay in the Criminal Justice System: A Report (London: Home Office, 1997a). [95] See, e.g., Baldwin J, *Pre-Trial Justice* (Oxford: Basil Blackwell, 1985) p 43.
[96] Especially as custodial remands can be for months: see later. Also see Raifeartaigh U, 'Reconciling Bail Law with the Presumption of Innocence' (1997) 17 *Oxford Journal of Legal Studies* 1.

and guarding against abuses of state power should be priorities. Pre-trial imprisonment may undermine the defendant's ability or willingness to contest the case. Punishment is unwarranted for innocent persons, regardless of whether they are ultimately acquitted or convicted on a guilty plea entered under pressure. It will also be excessive for those who are guilty but who face charges which would normally attract a non-custodial or short custodial penalty.

To this the crime control adherent can retort that it is all to the good that defendants' willingness and ability to contest cases is undermined by pre-trial detention. The vast majority of defendants are factually guilty and it would put an intolerable strain on the system if they all contested that fact. Moreover, the obvious conclusion to draw from the argument that pre-trial detention may involve punishment which exceeds that likely to be imposed by a court on conviction is that sentencers are too lenient. As Packer puts it: 'For many such persons, a short period spent in jail awaiting trial is not only a useful reminder that crime does not pay but also the only reminder they are likely to get.'[97] The model nevertheless accepts that it would be counter-productive to crime control to overload police cells and the prison system with minor offenders. It maintains, however, that any limits to pre-trial detention should be governed by this consideration of crime control efficiency, rather than by any abstract notion of a right to pre-trial liberty.

People charged with minor offences usually receive a summons to appear on a particular date and no further restriction on their liberty is imposed.[98] With more serious charges, the courts typically proceed by way of a series of remand hearings. The purpose of these hearings is to determine what degree of liberty defendants should be permitted to retain pending trial. Defendants may either be remanded in custody or remanded on bail. Since 1991 magistrates have been empowered to remand defendants for extended periods in custody of up to 28 days in duration.[99]

The *proportion* of defendants who are remanded in custody is small, but the numbers involved are large. Numbers peaked at the turn of the century and have declined since that time apart from a 4% rise in numbers again during 2017 (albeit still at lower levels than at the beginning of this century). In 2017, 13,000 (58%) of people who were remanded into custody pending trial or sentence in the magistrates' court did not go on to receive prison sentences. In 2018, untried prisoners on remand made up around 10% of the prison population (peaking at 17% a few years earlier), and therefore contribute to prison overcrowding.[100] Remand prisoners have played an active role in the sporadic outbreaks of rioting that left some establishments (most notably Strangeways in April 1990) in smouldering ruins.[101] Keeping unconvicted defendants in stinking conditions might not conflict with the letter of the law, but if the concept of human rights is to mean more than a mere sign-up to an international treaty the least we could do is to treat remand prisoners more favourably than convicted offenders.[102] HM Chief Inspector of Prisons found that remand prisoners lacked effective access to legal reference books, had their legal correspondence

---

[97] Packer (1968: 212).

[98] Police and prosecutors also have powers to issue a written charge and requisition. Now see Criminal Procedure Rules; Sprack and Sprack (2019).

[99] Magistrates' Courts (Remand in Custody) Order 1991, SI 1991/2667. Magistrates' Court Act 1980, s.128A

[100] Transform Justice *Presumed Innocent but Behind Bars—is Remand overused in England and Wales?* (2018). Available at: <http://www.transformjustice.org.uk/wp-content/uploads/2018/03/TJ_March_13.03-1.pdf> (accessed 15 July 2019).

[101] See Morgan R and Jones S, 'Bail or Jail?' in Stockdale E and Casale S (eds), *Criminal Justice Under Stress* (London: Blackstone, 1992).

[102] See Woolf, Prison Disturbances, April 1990: Report of an Inquiry (Cm 1456) (London: HMSO, 1991), discussed by Morgan and Jones (1992).

opened and examined far more often than appeared justified, and experienced great difficulties in speaking to their solicitors by phone. He concluded that: '...the barriers to effective communication with legal advisers constitute an obstacle to the fair and just treatment of unsentenced prisoners which may well not stand up to legal challenge under the Human Rights Act, Article 6, which guarantees rights consistent with the proper preparation and conduct of a defence, including the right to consult with a lawyer prior to and during the trial.'[103] Despite this warning, in 2018 the chief inspector of prisons warned that conditions were the 'most disturbing ever seen',[104] and living conditions in 2019 were described as 'appalling'.[105] Some prisoners have received compensation for breach of their human rights due to the lack of integral sanitation in cells of more than single occupation.[106]

8.4.1 The principles of bail law

Art 6(2) ECHR affirms the presumption of innocence. Although the provision that allows arrest and detention in order to bring a suspect before a court (discussed in chapter 4) clearly also allows pre-trial remands in custody, this may be done only 'when it is reasonably considered necessary to prevent his committing an offence or fleeing after having done so' (Art 5(1)(c)). This is qualified by Art 5(3):

> Everyone arrested or detained... shall be brought promptly before a judge... and shall be entitled to trial within a reasonable time or to release pending trial. Release may be conditioned by guarantees to appear for trial.

To comply with the ECHR (and thus the HRA 1998), then, it seems that the law:

(a) must allow remands in custody only when reasonably considered necessary;

(b) can allow conditions to be set for bail;

(c) must minimise delay for defendants remanded in custody.

English law is largely governed by the Bail Act 1976, along with some important later additions. Section 4(1) provides that a defendant 'shall be granted bail except as provided in Sch 1 to this Act'. This creates a due process presumption in favour of bail (a right to bail)[107] although the strength of that presumption depends on the nature of the exceptions set out in Sch 1. On the face of it, this complies with the ECHR,[108] but we shall see that English law does not, or may not do so (depending on how the courts apply it) in some important respects. In addition, there is the right to legal representation.[109] As we shall see later, whether this is of much value depends on the information the police and CPS disclose to the defence and court, and on how adversarial the lawyer is. Another important due process protection is the right of appeal against adverse bail decisions. In the rest of

---

[103] This was a decade after the Woolf report: *Unjust deserts: A thematic review of the Chief Inspector of Prisons of the treatment and conditions for unsentenced prisoners in England and Wales* (London: Home Office, 2000) p 52. A more recent inspection found little had changed: HM Inspectorate of Prisons, *Remand prisoners: A thematic review* (HM Prison Inspectorate, London 2012).

[104] Bulam M, 'Prison conditions "most disturbing ever seen" with staff now accustomed to jails not fit for 21st century, watchdog says' *The Independent*, 11 July 2018.

[105] HM Chief Inspector of Prisons *Annual Report for 2018–19* HC 2469.

[106] <http://news.bbc.co.uk/1/hi/scotland/7060991.stm> (accessed 5 January 2010).

[107] Confirmed in *Michalko v Slovakia* (ECtHR 2010, No. 35377/05), para 145.

[108] See, in particular, *Caballero v UK* (2000) 30 EHRR 643.

[109] Directive 2013/48/EU of the European Parliament and of the Council of 22 October 2013. This is given effect in England by the Criminal Procedure Rules. See Cape E and Smith T, *The practice of pre-trial detention in England and Wales: Research report* (2016) (<https://uwe-repository.worktribe.com/output/917566> (accessed 15 July 2018)) pp 11 and 30–31. But representation is not mandatory, and unrepresented defendants must be assisted by the magistrates' legal advisors.

this section we will examine each of these issues in turn, seeing how far the law corresponds with the reality, and how valuable the human rights approach is in protecting the freedom of defendants.

8.4.2 Criteria for withholding bail: the law

Defendants charged with imprisonable offences need not be granted bail if the court is satisfied that there are 'substantial grounds' for believing that the defendant, if released on bail, would either fail to appear, commit an offence or interfere with witnesses or otherwise obstruct the course of justice.[110] Nor need bail be granted if a court is satisfied that the defendant has previously failed to answer bail for the offence or ought to be kept in custody for his or her own 'protection' or 'welfare'. In determining whether there are substantial grounds for believing that a defendant would fail to appear, commit an offence or obstruct the course of justice, Sch 1 to the Bail Act 1976 provides that the court is to have regard to, first, the nature and seriousness of the offence; second, the character, previous convictions, associations and community ties of the person; third, the person's record in regard to any previous grant of bail; and finally, the strength of the evidence against the person.[111]

In the context of contemporary concerns about prison overcrowding, Sch 11 of LASPO introduced an important precondition to considering whether or not bail should be granted: is there a realistic prospect of a custodial sentence being imposed on conviction? Prosecutors should not seek a remand into custody for an unconvicted defendant who has no real prospect of receiving a custodial sentence.[112] This should mean that no one is ever remanded into custody if charged with a non-imprisonable offence. Schedule 11 was clearly designed to limit the disproportionate use of remands. But, several years on, little has changed: over around half of people remanded into custody were not convicted or not imprisoned if they were convicted.[113]

The due process model would object to most of the grounds for detention laid down in the 1976 Act. We will examine here the three main grounds for refusing bail.

8.4.2.1 Obstructing the course of justice

To detain someone because they might interfere with a prosecution witness is manifestly unsatisfactory, since it penalises the defendant for what the police think the defendant might do. Undoubtedly some witnesses do get intimidated by defendants. But sometimes this is by family members and friends, so detaining in custody does not help. Other ways of reducing interference include offering police protection to particularly vulnerable witnesses, making bail conditional on the defendant keeping well away from such persons, and enforcing crimes against intimidation.

8.4.2.2 Committing an offence

A similar objection lies against the ground that the defendant will commit an offence if released. Again, defendants are penalised for what the police think they might do.

---

[110] Bail Act 1976, Sch 1, Pt 1 paras 2–6, although s.52 of the Criminal Justice and Immigration Act 2008 amended the Bail Act so that the grounds on which bail can be refused for imprisonable summary only offences (and criminal damage below £5,000) are more in line with non-imprisonable offences. Essentially the distinction between non-imprisonable and imprisonable summary offences was removed, but some new grounds for refusing bail in imprisonable summary cases were granted including where the court has insufficient information and where it believes the defendant may commit an offence of violence or put a person in fear of violence.

[111] Bail Act 1976, Sch 1, Pt 1 para 9.

[112] CPS, Bail (2019), online at: <https://www.cps.gov.uk/legal-guidance/bail> (accessed 10 July 2019)

[113] Cape and Smith (2006); Transform Justice (2018).

The objection is stronger here, however, since a prediction that someone will commit an offence if released rests on the assumption that the defendant committed the offence with which he or she is currently charged. The law thus allows a factual presumption of guilt to override the normative presumption of innocence. Nor should we forget that putting someone behind bars pending trial does not stop them committing offences as violence and other crime is rife in prison.[114]

The issue of 'dangerousness' as a ground for detaining persons not yet convicted of crime, or for extending (perhaps indefinitely) the period of detention for those who have been convicted, has been much debated in the context of sentencing and parole, and a similar dilemma applies to the bail decision.[115] The due process model would argue that the defendants' interests should in every case be given special weight. But it would be an affront to common sense to say that a suspected serial killer or pathological rapist should automatically be released on bail. There is also the particular problem of people charged with offences committed while already on bail.[116] Bail for those accused of murder became controversial as a result of high profile cases where murders have been committed by offenders already on bail for murder or serious violent offences.[117] Consequently, ss.114 and 115(1) Coroners and Justice Act 2009 significantly restrict when bail may be granted to those who are accused of murder or who have previous convictions for very serious offences.

8.4.2.3 Failure to answer bail

To detain defendants because of a fear that they might not attend voluntarily to answer the charges against them has greater merit, since the presumption of pre-trial liberty would quickly fall into disrepute if defendants absconded in large numbers. This fear should be properly grounded, however, and much depends on how magistrates make their predictions as to who is likely to abscond if granted bail and what level of risk they are prepared to tolerate. The factors that they are required to take into account, such as the seriousness of the offence and previous bail record, while clearly bearing on the risk of a defendant absconding, are open to wide interpretation.

Three things are necessary to ensure that fair decisions are made. First, the offence needs to be sufficiently serious for the loss of freedom of the detained defendant to be outweighed by the interests of the state in securing a conviction (if guilt is proved) and imposing immediate punishment. Second, mechanisms to achieve attendance short of detention should be used wherever possible. Section 6 of the 1976 Act makes it an offence punishable by imprisonment and/or a fine to fail to answer to bail without reasonable cause. This threat should be enough to guarantee the attendance of most people facing less serious charges, while most of the rest can eventually be tracked down and punished accordingly. In addition, s.3(6) allows for persons to be released on bail subject to conditions (examined next). Finally, decision-making needs to be consistent, principled and based on high quality information (examined thereafter).

---

[114] See, for example, <https://www.gov.uk/guidance/violence-reduction-in-prison> (accessed 8 May 2020).

[115] For general discussions see Brown D, Turner J, and Weisser B (eds), *The Oxford Handbook of Criminal Process* (Oxford: OUP, 2019) ch 23, 24, 39; and Eijk G, 'Exclusion through Risk-Based Justice: Analysing Combinations of Risk Assessment from Pretrial Detention to Release' (2020) *British Journal of Criminology*.

[116] See ss.25 and 26 CJPO 1994, as amended by CJA 2003, discussed later.

[117] See Coroners and Justice Act 2009, discussed later. A major catalyst was the case of Gary Weddell, who had been on bail for murder when he appeared to kill his mother-in-law before also killing himself. See <https://www.theguardian.com/uk/2008/jan/14/ukcrime1> (accessed 15 May 2019).

8.4.3 Conditional bail

Section 3(6) of the 1976 Act allows for persons to be released on bail subject to such conditions as appear to the court to be necessary to secure that the defendant surrenders to the court at the appropriate time, does not commit an offence on bail or obstruct the course of justice and is available for the purpose of enabling a court report to be prepared to assist in sentencing. Section 13(1) of the CJA 2003 made it possible to add conditions for an adult defendant's own protection, or for a youth's welfare. Defendants released on conditional bail typically have to report to the police at periodic intervals, or must reside at a specified address (such as a bail hostel) or must keep away from certain places or people. Since 2007 the government has funded a Bail Accommodation and Support Service (BASS), providing housing and support services for people in, or at risk of entering, the criminal justice process. The aim is to encourage a greater use of conditional bail for defendants thought to pose too great a risk if released unconditionally. Bail hostels provide more intensive supervision. Despite very few BASS or hostel places being available, neither are used as much as they could be.[118]

There are many difficulties with bail conditions. The breadth and vagueness of many criminal laws entails that highly restrictive conditions may lawfully be imposed. Thus in *Mansfield Justices, ex p Sharkey*[119] the Divisional Court upheld the legality of a condition that defendants facing charges arising out of picketing did not take part in any further demonstration connected with the trade dispute between striking miners and the National Coal Board. The court's reasoning was that those attempting to prevent miners going to work by force of numbers and threats of violence would have been guilty of at least the public order offence of threatening behaviour. Anyone attending such a demonstration must be regarded as knowingly taking part in that threatening behaviour. To guard against the risk of the defendants committing offences on bail, it was, the court argued, necessary to prevent them from picketing. However, Percy-Smith and Hillyard argue that the widespread policy of imposing this form of conditional bail on striking miners was motivated by a desire not to control crime, but to hamper legitimate protest.[120] When laws are drawn in broad crime control terms there is the clear potential for them to be used in a repressive manner for political reasons.[121] More recently, a number of Extinction Rebellion protesters have been arrested across the globe, with some being given bail conditions that prevented them from engaging with other members of the movement, arguably in breach of their rights in relation to political assembly.[122] The scope for variability is shown by Dhami, who also found significant reliance on extra-legal factors, as well as on factors specified in the legislation.[123] Of course, the committed political protester may simply ignore bail conditions, and hope to escape detection for breach of bail by merging with the crowd. But this

---

[118] Transform Justice (2018). See <https://www.gov.uk/government/publications/bail-accommodation-and-support-service-bass> (accessed 8 April 2020). Also see Strickland P, Bail Accommodation and Support Service (House of Commons Briefing Paper, 2015). [119] [1985] 1 All ER 193.

[120] Percy-Smith J and Hillyard P, 'Miners in the Arms of the Law: A Statistical Analysis' (1985) 12 *Journal of Law and Society* 345. See to like effect Blake N, 'Picketing, Justice and the Law' in Fine B and Millar R (eds), *Policing the Miners' Strike* (London: Lawrence and Wishart, 1985); On the 1981 'riots' see Vogler R, *Reading the Riot Act* (Milton Keynes: Open UP, 1991) p 153.

[121] See our earlier discussion of this in the context of stop-search powers in ch 2.

[122] Lewis P, 'Lawyers to fight bail conditions that 'stifle' climate protests' *The Guardian*, 9 May 2009; Zhou N, '"Absurd" bail conditions prevent Extinction Rebellion protesters "going near" other members', *The Guardian*, 9 October 2019. In the UK, Extinction Rebellion protesters actually sought to be arrested to provoke disruption in police custody. In response, the Met Police imposed a blanket ban on the protest, which was ruled to be an illegitimate use of power in November 2019. See Gayle D and Dodd V, 'Extinction Rebellion protesters may sue Met as ban ruled unlawful', *The Guardian*, 6 November 2019.

[123] Dhami M, 'Conditional Bail Decision Making in the Magistrates' Court' (2004) 43 *Howard Journal of Crime and Justice* 27.

is not so easy now that the Criminal Justice and Immigration Act 2008 has amended the Bail Act to make clear that electronic monitoring can be imposed as a condition of bail.[124]

The second difficulty with bail conditions is that they are sometimes unrelated to the objection to bail voiced by the CPS. This sometimes happens when solicitors offer any conditions to bolster their application for bail, or when courts simply attach conditions indiscriminately.[125] It also happens when conditions are imposed as a form of 'summary punishment'—for example, imposing a condition of residence to stop a defendant going on holiday or visiting friends.[126]

Third, conditions are imposed on some defendants who would otherwise have received unconditional bail, rather than those who were genuinely at risk of a custodial remand. The evidence on this point is equivocal although it seems that some 'net widening' has taken place.[127] Many defence solicitors routinely offer bail conditions to the court in cases where they might have secured unconditional bail, and sometimes a defence solicitor and a prosecutor will strike a 'deal' that the latter will not oppose bail if the former does not oppose conditions.[128]

Although breach of a condition of bail is not an offence, it may lead to defendants being brought back before the court for reconsideration of their remand status. Indeed, defendants can be arrested if the police have 'reasonable grounds' to believe that they have broken, or '*are likely to break*', any of their conditions.[129] Under any of these circumstances 'the defendant need not be granted bail'.[130] Conditions often operate in arbitrary and discriminatory ways. Financial conditions weigh far more heavily on poor people than on others, and sometimes lead to remands in custody.[131] Residence conditions similarly operate unfairly on the homeless and rootless. Most other conditions are largely unenforceable. When curfews, for example, are breached, the only defendants at any risk at all of being caught (leaving aside those who are electronically tagged) are those who the police recognise. These will usually be defendants who are 'known to the police' or who stand out—such as members of ethnic minorities (BAME) in largely-white areas.[132] The opportunity for the discriminatory use of discretion is obvious.

8.4.4 Criteria for withholding bail: the decision-making process

The custody remand rate varies considerably between different courts. Hucklesby, for example, found custody rates of 9% in two of the courts she studied, but 25% in the other court, even though the case mix was substantially the same in all three. Even in the two

---

[124] Section 3AB Bail Act 1976 (as amended by s.51 and Sch 11 CJIA 2008). The courts may only impose such a condition if the defendant would otherwise not be granted bail.

[125] Hucklesby A, 'The Use and Abuse of Conditional Bail' (1994) 33 *Howard Journal of Crime and Justice* 258.

[126] Raine J and Willson M, 'The Imposition of Conditions in Bail Decisions' (1996) 35 *Howard Journal of Crime and Justice* 256.

[127] Consider e.g. the debate concerning whether bail hostels are being used to accommodate persons who would otherwise have been remanded in custody: Pratt J and Bray K, 'Bail Hostels – Alternatives to Custody?' (1985) 25 *British Journal of Criminology* 160; Morgan P and Henderson P, Remand Decisions and Offending on Bail (Home Office Research Study no 184) (London: Home Office, 1998). Also see Hucklesby (1994).

[128] Hucklesby A, 'Remand Decision Makers' [1997b] *Criminal Law Review* 269.

[129] Bail Act 1976, s.7.

[130] Bail Act 1976, s.4. In an attempt to ensure ECHR compliance, the CJA 2003 amended provisions of the Bail Act 1976 so that courts are now required to focus on whether there are substantial grounds for fearing that a defendant charged with a non-imprisonable offence who has already failed to appear at court or breached a bail condition (etc.) would *in future* fail to surrender, commit an offence, or obstruct the course of justice. For details see Taylor et al, *Blackstone's Guide to the Criminal Justice Act 2003* (Oxford: OUP, 2004) p 18.

[131] Cavadino P and Gibson B, *Bail: The Law, Best Practice and the Debate* (Winchester: Waterside Press, 1993) p 170.   [132] Hucklesby (1994); Raine and Willson (1996).

apparently similar courts, similar cases were treated dissimilarly. Variations between courts in the way criteria are evaluated therefore produce a 'justice by geography' effect:[133] what happens to a defendant in a borderline case depends as much on the court as on the case, just as with other aspects of magistrates' decision-making such as sentencing. This is due largely to different 'court cultures'. One element in a court's culture is whether or not it includes a stipendiary (who, Hucklesby found, granted bail less often).[134] Nonetheless, despite the *differences* between courts, the features which are *common* to all courts are more important.

8.4.4.1 The absence of adversarialism

The ECHR and the Bail Act 1976 appear to require bail to be granted, in normal circumstances, unless there is clear evidence to substantiate a belief that one of the evils envisaged by Sch 1 will occur if the defendant is released. Most remand hearings are uncontested. Hucklesby's pre-LASPO study of 1,524 remand hearings found that in around 85% of cases the CPS did not request a remand in custody. And in only just over a halfof all cases where the CPS requested a remand in custody was this opposed by the defence. It is very rare for magistrates to question these agreed proposals.[135] Hucklesby therefore argues that the real decision-makers are the police (who make recommendations to the CPS), the CPS and defence lawyers. She found that in virtually every case where unconditional bail was recommended by Crown prosecutors, this was granted; in virtually every case where conditional bail was recommended by Crown prosecutors, this was also granted; and in 86% of cases where custody was requested by Crown prosecutors, this was granted too. And although police or prosecution objections to bail are not invariably upheld by magistrates, *un*conditional bail is hardly ever granted when bail is opposed.[136] In one respect the analysis by Hucklesby is thin. When she argues that the lack of adversarialism indicates that magistrates are less active in decision-making than are police, CPS and lawyers, she does not refer to her own findings elsewhere that these professionals know their local courts and tailor their applications accordingly. In other words, Crown prosecutors will apply for remands in custody in certain types of borderline case in some courts but not others, and defence solicitors will oppose this more in some courts than others.[137] However, all these findings are broadly confirmed in the much more recent—and post-LASPO—research by Cape and Smith. They found that part of the problem was the lack of time defence (and prosecution) lawyers had to prepare applications: less than two hours in over one-third of cases, which is usually the short time before court starts when most lawyers would have several applications to prepare at the same time.[138] Inadequate information was the other problem (see next section).

In only a small proportion of remand hearings, then, is bail contested—less than 10%. The low percentage of cases in which the defence challenges CPS recommendations for custody has to be seen in the context of s.154 of the Criminal Justice Act 1988. This provides that, once a defendant has been refused bail, any argument may be used to support an application at the next remand hearing whether or not it has been used previously but thereafter 'the court need not hear arguments as to fact or law which it has heard

---

[133] Similar to the effect of local police decision-making leading to cautioning variations—see section 7.4.1.
[134] Hucklesby A, 'Court Culture: An Explanation of Variations in the Use of Bail by Magistrates Courts' (1997a) 36 *Howard Journal of Crime and Justice* 129. The differences between lay and stipendiary magistrates are discussed in section 8.5.1. For another example showing differences between courts, see Paterson F and Whittaker C, *Operating Bail* (Edinburgh: Scottish Office, 1994).
[135] Hucklesby (1997b: 271).   [136] Hucklesby (1997b: Table 1).
[137] Hucklesby (1997a). This happens in Scotland too: Paterson and Whittaker (1994).
[138] Cape and Smith (2016: ch 4).

previously'. Courts often interpret this as a licence to hear a maximum of two applications.[139] Thus Hucklesby found that where bail was opposed by Crown prosecutors, defence lawyers usually applied for bail at the first appearance (in 85% of these cases) but did so in less than half of subsequent appearances. This may be because they wish to appeal to the Crown court or it may be reflective of the evaluation that many defence lawyers make—rightly or wrongly—of their clients' cases. Put bluntly, they do not want to lose credibility with the court.[140] Both Hucklesby and McConville et al found that when lawyers are instructed, contrary to their professional advice, to apply for bail, they let the court know that they do not have their heart in it by using coded language such as 'I am instructed to say that . . .'. Sometimes the code is not difficult to crack, as with the following lawyer's culinary comments to the bench:

> He tells me—and I know you will take this with a pinch of salt, but I am instructed to say it so I shall say it—that he intended to surrender to the warrant. As I say, you may take that with a pinch of salt but I have said what I was instructed to say by my client.[141]

8.4.4.2 The information on which bail decisions are made

The Bail Act's presumption in favour of bail fits with the ECHR's stipulation that bail decisions be based on *evidence* (not 'speculation') and that the burden of proof be on the prosecution.[142] But Hucklesby found that bail was granted in less than one in three contested bail applications, partly because defence solicitors are seen by magistrates as less objective than the CPS. Consequently, challenging the police version of events, as put forward by the CPS, is usually unsuccessful, despite the fact that strength of evidence is supposed to be a consideration under the Bail Act.[143] Clearly defendants have an uphill struggle to overcome CPS objections to the 'right to bail'.

But how, in reality, could it be otherwise? Terms like 'prediction' and 'risk' are virtual synonyms for 'speculation', so how could it ever be *proved* that someone will abscond or commit 'further' offences? Moreover, how could it be proved *beyond reasonable doubt* as some ECHR cases seem to suggest?[144] The rhetoric is here at odds with the law, as well as the practice. As Hayes, a magistrate and academic points out:

> the bail decision is a matter of guesswork, of hunches, not capable of precise explanation. Will he turn up, will he do it again? Each magistrate will apply his own criteria and his own values to his decision.[145]

The complexity of the Bail Act's provisions and the importance of what is at stake might lead one to think that bail hearings are painstaking affairs. Go and visit your local magistrates' court and you will see for yourself the whirlwind reality. In Zander's study of London courts, the amount of time spent discussing whether defendants should retain their liberty was five

---

[139] See also *Blyth Juvenile Court, ex p G* [1991] Crim LR 693 and *Dover and East Kent Justices, ex p Dean* (1991) 156 JP 357. [140] Hucklesby (1997b); McConville et al (1994).
[141] McConville et al (1994: 181). See also Brink B and Stone C, 'Defendants who do not ask for Bail' [1988] *Criminal Law Review* 152
[142] *W v Switzerland* (1993) 17 EHRR 60.
[143] Hucklesby A, 'Bail or Jail? The Practical Operation of the Bail Act 1976' (1996) 23 *Journal of Law and Society* 213. And see Cape and Smith (2016).
[144] See cases cited in Burrow J, 'Bail and the Human Rights Act 1998' (2000) 150 *New Law Journal* 677. The same problem arises concerning defendants 'likely' to breach bail conditions.
[145] Hayes M, 'Where Now the Right to Bail?' [1981] *Criminal Law Review* 20 at p 22. The 'values' of magistrates, and of the legal framework they operate within, may result in some women getting a raw deal: Eaton M, 'The Question of Bail' in Carlen P and Worrall A (eds), *Gender, Crime and Justice* (Milton Keynes: Open UP, 1987).

minutes or less in 86% of the 261 remand cases observed.[146] Even where a remand in custody is sought, proceedings are rapid. As many as 60% of such decisions in Zander's study were reached within five minutes.[147] These findings were recently borne out by those of Transform Justice, which found that prosecution submissions in relation to bail took an average of 3.5 minutes, with the defence taking 5.5 minutes for the same.[148] Doherty and East identify the main reason for the speed with which bail decisions are taken as being the heavy workload of the magistrates' courts. The participants in the proceedings are all well known to each other and are aware that they are expected to assist in the speedy disposal of business:

> In these circumstances it is probably inevitable that a camaraderie develops between the participants, and this no doubt partially explains why so few of the hearings attended were markedly adversarial in character... In a situation where there is an expectation that cases are dealt with quickly, often in a non-adversarial fashion, it is perhaps not surprising that only limited information of a low quality is made available to the courts.[149]

In addition to the limited information given to the courts, most information comes from the police. Just as the police 'construct' cases for prosecution, making cases appear stronger (or weaker) than they might otherwise appear,[150] so they can do this with remand applications and, as we have seen, the CPS generally do as the police ask, and the magistrates generally follow suit.[151] The police decision to either bail a suspect from the police station or remand to next court appearance is an important factor in determining whether the CPS and the court will favour bail or remand.[152] This is something akin to prosecution momentum (see chapter 7). Magistrates, with their concern for upholding authority, are naturally disinclined to 'overturn' a police decision to hold someone in custody pending trial. The police thus exert a strong influence over bail processes.

Bail information schemes could go some way towards remedying these problems. They are meant to operate in all prisons holding remand prisoners as well as in magistrates' courts. 'It is HMPPS [the Prison and Probation Service] responsibility to provide information to the courts under the Offender Management Act 2007.'[153] These schemes involve HMPPS providing verified information to the CPS in cases where the police indicate an objection to bail. It is argued that such schemes are successful in persuading prosecutors and magistrates to adopt a more liberal attitude to the grant of bail without leading to more offending on bail or absconding.[154] Since some courts (albeit the smaller ones) currently operate without bail information schemes, and since many of those remanded in custody find it difficult to access prison-based schemes,[155] many magistrates have little on

---

[146] Zander M, 'Operation of the Bail Act in London Magistrates' Courts' (1979) 129 *New Law Journal* 108.
[147] Zander (1979). [148] Transform Justice (2018).
[149] Doherty M and East R, 'Bail Decisions in Magistrates' Courts' (1985) 25 *British Journal of Criminology* 251 at p 263. [150] McConville et al (1991); case construction is discussed in ch 7.
[151] Also see Phillips C and Brown D, Entry into the Criminal Justice System (Home Office Research Study no 185) (London: Home Office, 1998); Mhlanga B, Race and the CPS (London, SO, 1999) pp 134–135.
[152] Burrows et al, Improving Bail Decisions: the bail process project, phase 1 (Research and Planning Unit Paper 90) (London: Home Office, 1994).
[153] See <https://yjlc.uk/wp-content/uploads/2020/05/Bail-information-service-.pdf> (accessed 15 May 2020). And see HM Prison Service Order 6101 Bail Information Scheme (2013) <https://www.justice.gov.uk/downloads/offenders/psipso/pso/pso-6101-bail-info-scheme.pdf> (accessed 15 May 2020). See generally Mair G and Lloyd C, 'Policy and Progress in the Development of Bail Schemes in England and Wales' in Paterson F (ed), *Understanding Bail in Britain* (Edinburgh: Scottish Office, 1996).
[154] Mair and Lloyd (1996). The same is true of Scotland where similar schemes have been established: McIvor G, 'The Impact of Bail Services in Scotland' in Paterson (1996).
[155] HM Inspectorate of Prisons for England and Wales, Unjust Deserts (December 2000) pp 47–48 (available from <http://www.justice.gov.uk/inspectorates/hmi-prisons/docs/unjust-rps.pdf> (accessed 5 January 2010)). Cape and Smith (2016).

which to base their decisions. The effect of bail information schemes is limited. Indeed, Dhami, argues that the only thing that these schemes increase is the confidence that magistrates have in their decisions.[156] Frequently the information provided is that the only problem with granting bail is the absence of suitable accommodation. But this is often not acted on due to insufficient knowledge and availability of BASS accommodation and bail hostels.[157] This, together with the inadequate information and time that many defendants and their solicitors are provided with, means that in many cases both domestic law and the ECHR are routinely breached.

8.4.4.3 Breach of bail

The police and press often complain that too many defendants are released on bail and, in particular, that many offend while on bail.[158] But relatively few offences are committed by offenders on police or court bail: just 13,456 in 2018.[159] Many regard any level of offending on bail as unacceptable, but it is exceptionally difficult to identify who will, and who will not, offend while on bail. The greater the number of defendants remanded in custody because of fears of offending, the more remands in custody there will be of defendants who would *not* offend while on bail. Indeed, a Scottish study found that offending on bail was hardly higher in the court with the highest bail rate than in the court with the lowest rate.[160]

Despite these objections, the government gave the prosecution the right to appeal against a grant of bail (see section 8.4.5). Another initiative was contained in s.26 of the Criminal Justice and Public Order Act 1994 (CJPO) aimed at reducing the likelihood of 'bail bandits' getting further bail.[161] This was taken further by s.14 of the CJA 2003 which states that adults charged with an indictable or either way offence committed whilst already on bail, 'may not be granted bail unless the court is satisfied that there is no significant risk of his committing an offence on bail', thus introducing another exception to the ever-diminishing 'right to bail.' However, the practical impact of these provisions has probably been limited since alleged offending on bail could always have been used as a reason for refusing bail (constituting, as it does, compelling evidence of a risk of the offender committing an offence if released on bail).[162]

In addition to the problem of some defendants offending on bail, some defendants fail to appear at court (or abscond). Magistrates' courts issue arrest warrants for people who fail to appear without offering good reason, and issued 71,000 such warrants in the year to end September 2019.[163] Remember that the same courts deal with about 1.48m cases per year. The rate at which failing to attend warrants are issued has tended to fall gradually

---

[156] Dhami M, 'Do Bail Information Schemes Really Affect Bail Decisions?' (2002) 41 *Howard Journal of Crime and Justice* 245.

[157] See Cape and Smith (2016: ch 6, (4)) and discussion in section 8.4.3.

[158] See, e.g. <https://www.telegraph.co.uk/news/uknews/crime/11266188/Crimes-committed-on-bail-Key-facts-on-worst-offenders.html> (accessed 15 July 2019).

[159] According to a FOI request. See Davis M, 'Crime Britain: 60 rapes and killings last year carried out by offenders on bail' *The Express*, 22 September 2019. This is a huge drop since 2013 (see FOI number 92280) that might result from a decrease in the formal use of bail as suspects are 'released under investigation' (see section 7.3.2). Also see Cape and Smith (2016: 32–33) and Hucklesby A and Marshall E, 'Tackling Offending on Bail' (2000) 39 *Howard Journal of Crime and Justice* 15. [160] Paterson and Whittaker (1994).

[161] The 1994 provision made little difference to bail rates: Hucklesby and Marshall (2000).

[162] Hucklesby and Marshall (2000). Section 14 also changes the test for youths, but here again little change in practice is likely. For details see Taylor et al (2004: 19).

[163] HM Courts and Tribunal Service and Ministry of Justice, *Experimental statistics on Failure to Appear warrants in the magistrates' courts*, online at: <https://assets.publishing.service.gov.uk/government/uploads/system/uploads/attachment_data/file/851924/experimental-statistics-failure-to-appear-september-2019.pdf> (accessed 10 April 2020).

since 2010, to 6.2% in 2014.[164] All such bare numbers must be treated with caution. For example, statistics on absconding may overstate the problem in that there may be good reasons why defendants fail to appear at court (e.g. illness or death). Statistics of offending on bail may understate the problem, in that much offending on bail no doubt remains undetected, or may overstate it in that they take no account of the possible triviality of the offences in question or the fact that the longer the delay in prosecuting cases the more offending on bail there will be. That people 'abscond' or offend on bail is not necessarily a sign that the remand decision was wrong.

8.4.4.4 Wrongful denial of bail

It is similarly impossible to estimate the number of defendants who are wrongly denied bail. There are three broad categories. First, in the year to end March 2018, 5,453 of the 56,727 (9.6%) of defendants remanded in custody were acquitted or not proceeded against. Second, 33% of those convicted were given non-custodial sentences.[165] This is, on the face of it, a gross denial of due process and human rights standards. However, the fact that many persons denied bail are not subsequently convicted may be testimony to the fairness of the courts. In other words, adjudicators seem able in at least some cases to overcome the prejudicial effect created by the sight of an accused being brought up from the cells under the courtroom. Similarly, the high proportionate use of non-custodial sentences for those denied bail and subsequently convicted does not prove that the remand decision was incorrect. Defendants may, for example, have been remanded for their own protection or because it was feared that they would not answer to bail.[166] Some defendants will have been judged to have suffered enough and not be given the custodial sentences that they might otherwise have got.

A third category of defendants wrongly denied bail is those who would not have breached their bail. This is even more difficult to quantify. The enormous disparities in the rates at which different courts refuse bail discussed earlier shows that some, without good reason, remand more than others.[167] Moreover, bail information schemes seem to indicate that many remands in custody where such schemes do not operate are unwarranted and that the standard of decision-making can be improved.[168] As is so often the case in the criminal process, certain groups suffer more than others as a result of the law allowing a large element of discretion to those taking decisions. Hood, for example, found that black defendants had a greater likelihood of being remanded in custody than white defendants, even when all factors legally relevant to the bail decision were taken into account.[169] Ten years later, the same pattern of race discrimination was still observable, among adults and youths. Moreover, the proportions of black defendants remanded in custody who were not convicted is much higher than that of white people.[170] Another 15 years on, patterns

---

[164] Cape and Smith (2016: 90).

[165] Ministry of Justice (2018c) *Criminal Justice Statistics: Overview tables*. Available at <https://www.gov.uk/government/collections/criminal-justice-statistics> (accessed 15 July 2019).

[166] On this, see the letters from two judges: [1993] Crim LR 324.

[167] See Hucklesby (1997a); Paterson and Whittaker (1994).

[168] The original experiment from which these schemes developed showed that the increase in granting bail resulting from the provision of better information on defendants did not result in an increase in the failure rate, whether measured as offending on bail, breach of bail conditions or non-attendance at court. See Stone C, *Bail Information for the Crown Prosecution Service* (New York: VERA Institute of Justice, 1988). But note the concerns raised by Dhami (2002).

[169] Hood R, *Race and Sentencing* (Oxford: Clarendon Press, 1992) pp 146–149. The treatment of women is discussed in Player E, 'Remanding Women in Custody: Concerns for Human Rights' (2007) 70(3) *Modern Law Review* 402.

[170] Gus John Partnership, *Race for Justice* (London: CPS, 2003); Feilzer M and Hood R, *Differences or Discrimination?* (London: YJB, 2004).

of race discrimination were again observable (see further chapter 10). Data in relation to remands is somewhat lacking, but black people continue to be overrepresented in custody and non-white children are more likely to be remanded to youth detention than equivalent white children.[171] Parliamentary research briefings confirm that, in 2018, 26% of the prison population was BAME compared to 13% of the general population.[172] Court clerks are obliged to record a court's reasons for refusing bail, or imposing or varying conditions.[173] In addition, the defendant must be informed as to the reasons for any refusal of bail. These requirements are supposed to ensure that magistrates keep within the terms of the Act. But as White has observed:

> it would be a poor clerk who could not formulate a reason falling within the terms of the Act and it would be a foolish magistrate who insisted on recording a personal prejudice as the reason for the decision.[174]

Further, reasons are often given by way of a pro forma which fails to explain why defence arguments were rejected, a breach of the ECHR.[175] The framework created by the Bail Act clearly does little to prevent bad, arbitrary or even racist decision-making.[176] As Cape and Smith say, in general decisions are made by the courts without full knowledge of the relevant facts.[177]

8.4.5 Appeals against bail decisions

An appeal against a refusal of bail may be made to the Crown court.[178] Section 16 of the CJA 2003 further provided the Crown court with the power also to hear appeals against the conditions attached to a grant of bail. But appeal is difficult when, in so many cases, the reasons given for refusing bail are formulaic (not referring to the specific facts of the case) and judges regard the onus of proof as on defendants.[179]

The converse of defendants appealing against the refusal of bail is the prosecution appealing against its grant. The Bail (Amendment) Act 1993, gave the prosecution for the first time the right to appeal against a grant of bail, and s.19 of the CJA 2003 considerably widened that right. Now, an appeal lies to a judge in chambers where the defendant stands charged with any imprisonable crime. A defendant must be remanded in custody pending the outcome of the appeal which must take place within 48 hours. This gives the prosecution the power, in effect, to override (albeit temporarily) a judicial decision to release on bail. The CPS has as yet no right to challenge a refusal to impose the conditions it requested in a grant of bail.

8.4.6 Time spent on remand

There are legislative time limits where defendants are in custody awaiting trial, but courts can, and usually do, grant extensions.[180] In 1990 the usual wait in custody for a Crown court trial was 17 weeks, but only three weeks for a magistrates' court trial. By 2019 the average wait

---

[171] The Lammy Review (2017).
[172] Sturge G, *UK Prison Population Statistics* Commons Library Briefing CBP 04334 (2018).
[173] Bail Act 1976, s.5.
[174] White R, *The Administration of Justice* (Oxford: Basil Blackwell, 1985) p 84.
[175] Law Commission, Bail and the Human Rights Act 1998, Report 269 (London: Law Commission, 1999) para 4.21. Confirmed by the ECtHR in *Buzadj v Moldova* (2014) and in the UK in *Snaresbrook Crown Court* [2011] EWHC 3569.
[176] Compare this with the situation applying in countries which have fundamental rights enshrined in constitutional charters. See, e.g., Padfield N, 'The Right to Bail: a Canadian Perspective' [1993] *Criminal Law Review* 510.
[177] (2016: 7). [178] Criminal Justice Act 1982, s.60.
[179] Cape and Smith (2016: ch 5 and 7).
[180] Prosecution of Offences Act 1985 as amended. For details, see Cape and Smith (2016: ch 4).

in custody for those committed to the Crown court was down to 7.9 weeks.[181] Two months may seem a long time to wait in prison for a trial at the conclusion of which there is an even chance of an acquittal or non-custodial sentence, but this pales into insignificance by comparison with some other countries and indeed Britain in the past. It seems doubtful that when delay is measured in months rather than years that any rights in the ECHR will be regarded as breached.[182] So unconvicted prisoners in the UK can expect little help from the HRA.[183]

8.4.7 A right to bail?

For most defendants the presumption in favour of bail is uncontested. But most defendants are charged with minor offences and given non-custodial sentences anyway. The situation is different when the police and CPS consider that a defendant should be remanded in custody. In these cases the crime control presumption of guilt, which operates not only on the courts but also on defence solicitors much of the time, is more powerful than legal rules and human rights principles. At times of stress, such as 'riots' and industrial strife courts get overloaded with defendants. The 1981 Liverpool 'riot' led to:

> an almost complete surrender of the magistrates to policing rather than judicial priorities.... In these circumstances, the presumption regarding bail became reversed, and the major, most severe single punishment inflicted by the court became the custodial remand rather than the post-conviction sentence.[184]

A similar pattern was observed during the riots which broke out across several British cities in 2011. When the police sought curfew conditions, the magistrates complied. Remands in custody were 'rubber stamped' and used as a blanket form of punishment.[185]

At a more obviously political level, the governments of the last 25 years have responded similarly to populist panics. Most notably, the Criminal Justice and Public Order Act 1994 (CJPO) and CJA 2003 altered bail law for high profile defendants.[186] Initially under s.26 of the CJPO defendants charged with offences allegedly committed while on bail 'need not' be presumed to be entitled to bail. And s.25 banned bail for anyone charged with rape or homicide offences (or attempts) who had a previous conviction for such an offence. The fact that courts hardly needed reminding that such defendants (especially in the s.25 category) would need a particularly persuasive argument if they were to secure bail was irrelevant: appearing 'tough' was more important than human rights or matters of principle. Sections 25 and 26 were amended by s.56 of the Crime and Disorder Act 1998 and then again by ss.14 and 15 of the CJA 2003, so that in such cases there is a rebuttable presumption against bail when an offence has been committed while on bail (and when a defendant has failed to answer bail without a reasonable excuse).[187] The provisions arguably violate

---

[181] Ministry of Justice, *Criminal court statistics quarterly, England and Wales, April to June 2019* <https://assets.publishing.service.gov.uk/government/uploads/system/uploads/attachment_data/file/834217/ccsq-bulletin-q2-2019.pdf> (accessed 10 April 2020).

[182] See the cases reviewed by Emmerson et al, *Human Rights and Criminal Justice* 2nd edn (London: Sweet & Maxwell, 2007) pp 498–501.   [183] Law Commission (1999: para 12.19).

[184] Vogler (1991: 143–144).

[185] Lightowlers C and Quirk H, 'The 2011 English "Riots": Prosecutorial Zeal and Judicial Abandon' (2015) 55(1) *British Journal of Criminology* 65–85.

[186] In addition to the categories discussed in the text, s.19 of the CJA 2003 places tough restrictions on granting bail to class A drug users who decline to take part in a programme designed to curb their drug use. For details see Taylor et al (2004: 23–24), and for the particular dilemmas this creates for female remand prisoners see Player (2007: 411–412).

[187] Note that whether or not the reason for failing to attend court is reasonable is irrelevant in deciding whether a condition is breached, but 'reasonableness' is always relevant in determining whether or not this makes a further breach likely if the defendant is released on bail again: *R (on the application of Vickers) v West London Magistrates' Court* [2004] Crim LR 63.

the presumption of innocence because they place the burden of proof onto the defendant. The Law Commission stated s.25 was: 'liable to be... applied in a way which would violate the Convention.'[188] However the amended s.25 has been interpreted to make it compatible with Art of the ECHR. It should not be interpreted as placing the burden of proof on the defendant to make out 'exceptional circumstances' for allowing bail. Instead, it would be enough for the defendant to point to material which might support the existence of such a circumstance.[189]

Another example is s.114 Coroners and Justice Act 2009, which greatly restricts the defendant's right to bail in murder cases (see earlier). It is unlikely that such provisions would be held to violate the ECHR, even though similar Australian provisions were found to be in violation of the right to liberty in 2010.[190] By analogy with s.25 the courts would probably say that the provision should be 'read down' to ensure compatibility with Art 5. The government argues that the provision has been drafted in such a way as to make clear that it is not for the defendant to show that there is no 'significant risk', but for the prosecution to show that there is such a risk. It is therefore, in its opinion, ECHR compliant. But some aspects of bail processes—such as the failure in many cases to provide proper information to defendants to enable them to argue properly for bail, and the frequent failure to give proper reasons for denying it—are not ECHR compliant. So the ECHR appears to have had little impact on bail decision-making either in principle or in practice—speedy and 'efficient' (but actually slipshod) decision-making has remained the order of the day at the cost of the 'justice' core value. This brings us to a more general evaluation of procedural fairness in the magistrates' courts.

8.5 The quality and fairness of summary justice

When most people think of criminal prosecutions they think of jury trials. But only the Crown court has jury trials. The most serious cases have what is assumed to be the best system, and the one that commands the most public support, especially among BAME communities.[191] Leaving aside the issue of cost, the reason for magistrates' courts not having juries can therefore be only because *either* the nature of magistrates' court cases makes jury trial unsuitable; *or* the relative triviality of magistrates' court cases makes jury trial unnecessary. The former is untenable. As far as triviality is concerned we know that this is the *ideology* surrounding magistrates' work, but that it is not the reality. Consequently, we should strive to bring as many elements of judge-and-jury trial as is reasonably possible to the magistrates' courts. Crown court trials embody the three 'core values', albeit imperfectly.[192] First, the jury embodies 'justice' because it is made up of ordinary people without an institutional stake in 'either side' of the criminal justice system, makes decisions after group discussions and cannot find anyone guilty unless an overwhelming majority are in favour. The judge embodies 'justice' in the sense of the dispassionate application of the rule of law, explaining the relevant law to juries, who then adjudicate between competing factual claims. Second, 'democracy': the jury commands public confidence and, by its existence, makes (a small part of) the criminal justice system accountable to the community.

---

[188] Law Commission (1999: para 9.30). Note a similar warning regarding s.26: para 6.14.
[189] *O v Crown Court at Harrow* [2006] UKHL 42. Arguably the defendant should not bear even this limited evidential burden: Ashworth A, 'Bail; Human Rights' [2007] *Criminal Law Review* 63.
[190] *In the Matter of an Application for Bail by Isa Islam* [2010] ACTSC 147.
[191] Sanders A, *Community Justice: Modernising the Magistracy in England and Wales* (London: IPPR, 2001).
[192] See generally ch 9, where various exceptions and caveats to the points we make here are discussed.

Finally, the judge's professionalism and knowledge assists efficiency.[193] In this section we assess the extent to which magistrates and magistrates' courts give effect to these principles by being adequate substitutes for judge-and-jury trial. This is important, as there are many more magistrates' court trials than there are Crown court trials.

8.5.1 The magistrates

For the last two to three hundred years, magistrates' courts have been largely presided over by lay magistrates, who rely upon the court clerk for legal advice. The exception has been Inner London, where stipendiary magistrates have traditionally heard a high proportion of cases. These full-time judges, who have been practising lawyers or qualified court clerks, are now called 'District Judges (Magistrates Courts)'. We shall use both terms in the following analysis.

The complex separation of function and mixture of professional expertise and lay involvement in the Crown court is in contrast with magistrates' courts proceedings. Questions of both law and fact are there decided upon by a bench of three[194] lay magistrates, or by a stipendiary magistrate sitting alone. In 2020 there were just 14,000 lay magistrates.[195] So stipendiary magistrates are increasingly being used both within and outside London. Numbers of lay magistrates have halved in 20 years, and diversity is being reduced.[196] There is little differentiation between the work done by stipendiaries and that done by lay justices, except that the occasional lengthy or more legally complex trial is generally given to stipendiaries. Government policy has been to resist calls to allocate lay justices one type of work and stipendiaries another because of a belief that lay justices would resent being deprived of the whole range of work.[197] So, whether decisions on bail, guilt and sentencing are taken by a professional or by a group of amateurs is a matter of chance.

Many common law based jurisdictions have lay justices. But there are few, if any, which give lay justices sentencing powers as extensive as exist in England and Wales.[198] On the other hand, professional judges sitting alone are also rarely given the power that stipendiaries have here. Stipendiaries are now even allowed to sit alone in the youth court.[199] This is surprising because, even in jurisdictions where lay magistrates are little used, it is generally thought valuable to involve lay people and/or experts in child development as well as lawyers when dealing with young people.[200] At least, under 'referral orders', youth offender panels (which have a varied membership) do much of the sentencing work of the youth court, going some way towards ameliorating this development.[201]

---

[193] Sanders A, 'Core Values, the Magistracy, and the Auld Report' (2002) 29(2) *Journal of Law and Society* 324; 341.

[194] In some circumstances two lay magistrates suffice, and for certain types of simple decision only one lay magistrate is needed.

[195] See <https://www.judiciary.uk/about-the-judiciary/who-are-the-judiciary/judicial-roles/magistrates/#whoarethey> (accessed 1 May 2020).

[196] Bowcott O, 'Fall in number of magistrates will mean less diversity' *The Guardian*, 22 June 2016.

[197] Seago et al, 'The Development of the Professional Magistracy in England and Wales' [2000] *Criminal Law Review* 631; Donoghue J, 'Reforming the Role of Magistrates: Implications for Summary Justice in England and Wales' (2014) 77 *Modern Law Review* 928.

[198] See, for a range of jurisdictions, Skyrme T, *History of the Justices of the Peace* (Chichester: Barry Rose, 1994).

[199] Crime and Disorder Act 1998, s.48; AJA 1999, Sch 11.

[200] On Northern Ireland, see Doran S and Glenn R, Lay Involvement in Adjudication: Review of the Criminal Justice System in Northern Ireland (Criminal Justice Review Research Report no 11) (Belfast: SO, 2000); in Scotland most youth justice is diverted to 'Children's Hearings' which are quasi-judicial and include non-lawyers.

[201] Youth Justice and Criminal Evidence Act 1999, s.1. For an evaluation see Crawford A and Newburn T, *Youth Offending and Restorative Justice* (Cullompton: Willan, 2003). Further powers to allow youths to undertake referral orders were granted by the Crime and Courts Act 2015.

How well do magistrates embody the three core values of justice, democracy and efficiency? Anyone may apply to become a lay magistrate, but most people do not know that, and even the Magistrates' Association described the committee system as 'a self-perpetuating oligarchy'.[202] Although the lay magistracy is now more representative of the community than it used to be, successive surveys of its membership shows that it remains predominantly middle aged and middle class.[203] Statistics from 2018 reveal that only around 13% of magistrates are BAME (compared with around 20% of defendants) and 85% are aged 50 or over.[204] A typical magistrate's response to this type of point was that: 'If a person's still on the shop floor when they're of an age to be appointed then they probably haven't got what it takes to be a magistrate'.[205] Brown found that youth court magistrates in the late 1980s judged the families of the children and young people appearing before them by standards that were 'deeply gender and class biased'.[206] In a striking echo of what we know of the world-view of the police, she concluded that magistrates 'perceived themselves as representatives of the upright conscience. . . . The "threat" of disorder posed by the judged to the judges, is a threat of all the other undisciplined young "out there".'[207] This may explain why some defence lawyers give clients advice or criticism about their attire; admonishing them for appearing too scruffy or 'flashy'.[208] They are attempting to create an appearance of orderliness which, although it will never equate to that of uniformed police officer witnesses, might at least offer less of a stark contrast.

Magistrates have an undue respect for, and trust in, authority. The typical view, expressed to Hucklesby regarding bail, was: 'I think for the protection of the public you've got to come down on the side of the CPS or the police who say "we want this person in custody".'[209] We saw earlier that in politically charged situations, in particular, magistrates effectively put themselves at the disposal of police and government. They value authority, and identify with other institutions (such as the police and CPS) which wield it. There may be a lack of understanding on the bench as to why a defendant might resist arrest, or refuse to answer police questions, dissemble or make a false confession. Magistrates may have standards of behaviour which are unrepresentative of the wider community and this may be of importance in applying the law. There is some evidence that magistrates have become more sceptical towards defendants since more crime control oriented provisions were introduced (Quirk, 2017). For example, what is 'reasonable' depends on an interpretation of a number of personal circumstances. If charged with a crime of violence you can escape liability if you acted in reasonable self-defence. Views on what would be reasonable resistance if wrongfully arrested in the presence of one's family, friends or workmates might depend on whether one has ever experienced something similar. But magistrates have seldom had adversarial contacts with the police. Juries are less susceptible to these forms of unconscious class bias.

Not only are lay magistrates less representative than juries, they are also 'insiders'. Although lay justices are unpaid part-time volunteers, they are quite different from

---

[202] Darbyshire P, 'For the New Lord Chancellor: Some Causes for Concern About Magistrates' [1997b] *Criminal Law Review* 861.

[203] For example, Burney E, *Magistrate, Court and Community* (London: Hutchinson, 1979); King M and May C, *Black Magistrates* (London: Cobden Trust, 1985); Gibbs P and Kirby A, 'Judged by peers? The diversity of lay magistrates in England and Wales' (2014) Working Paper, Institute for Criminal Policy Research, Birkbeck, University of London, London, UK.

[204] HM Courts and Tribunals Judiciary, *Judicial Diversity Statistics 2018*. Available at: <https://www.judiciary.uk/publications/judicial-diversity-statistics-2018/> (accessed 10 April 2020). Also see Vennard et al, 'Ethnic minority magistrates' experience of the role and of the court environment' DCA Research Report 3/2004 (London: DCA, 2004). [205] Darbyshire (1997b).

[206] Brown S, *Magistrates at Work* (Milton Keynes: Open UP:1991) pp 112–113. [207] Ibid.

[208] McConville et al, *Standing Accused* (Oxford: Clarendon Press, 1994) p 228.

[209] Hucklesby (1997b: 276).

unprepared and predominantly once-in-a-lifetime jurors. Magistrates may be only lightly trained compared to professional judges, but they serve substantial apprenticeships. Most of them sit in court once-a-week, some sit twice a week, and all sit at least once a fortnight. These magistrates may be lay in the sense that they not legally qualified, but they are not untutored amateurs. By contrast, juries come fresh to the criminal courts, hear one or more cases, then leave again to return to their normal occupations. It must be difficult for magistrates to treat each case on its individual merits when they have heard the same stories countless times before. Moreover, every magistrates' court seems to have its fair share of 'regulars', defendants well known to the bench. When asked if magistrates' familiarity with the regulars was a problem, the Chief Executive of Nottingham magistrates' court replied:

> If your name is Bane or Pain in Nottingham, then you're notorious. Some of them have changed their name by deed poll. The Banes and the Pains provide a lot of work for this court and everybody knows them. If it's a problem at this court, the biggest Bench in the country, with over 450 justices, then it could be a problem anywhere.[210]

So not only do magistrates (and their clerks) hear the same stories all the time, they hear them in relation to the same people. As one magistrate acknowledged to Darbyshire: 'Oh, yes. Whenever we see a certain solicitor we always know we've got Doris Day up before us and she always pleads not guilty.'[211] This level of familiarity must sometimes induce in defendants (or their solicitors) feelings of the 'que sera, sera' variety, as appears to have been the case in the following fatalistic exchange observed by McConville et al:

> Solicitor: I'll suggest conditional bail, I'll see. The Chairman's not bad but the clerk's a cow—you had her last time...
>
> Client: If I get bail, I'll be surprised![212]

Particular problems may be faced by unrepresented defendants. The work of Carlen suggests that magistrates (and their clerks) have a greater interest in maintaining social control in their courtrooms than in giving free rein to defendants to challenge authority by contesting the prosecution version of events or by, for example, raising awkward questions about behind the scenes negotiations regarding bail or plea.[213] Further, since juries are 'outsiders', lawyers have to explain things in everyday language in Crown court trials, ensuring that justice is public in substance as well as in form, and giving defendants, victims and others a fair chance of understanding what is going on. Because magistrates are 'insiders', none of this is true. Defendants are often bewildered by magistrates' courts hearings.[214]

On the criterion of 'democracy', lay magistrates are clearly a poor substitute for the jury. But stipendiaries are even less satisfactory. If we need juries to bring a holistic perspective into the Crown court because judges are professionally and socially elite then the same applies when a District Judge (magistrates' court) presides. At least a bench of lay magistrates is more likely to have one person under 40 and/or one person with an average income; and, in areas with large ethnic minority populations, BAME communities are

---

[210] Quoted by Darbyshire P, 'Previous Misconduct and Magistrates' Courts: Some Tales from the Real World' [1997c] *Criminal Law Review* 105 at p 107.

[211] Darbyshire (1997c: 107).   [212] McConville et al (1994: 174).

[213] Carlen P, 'Remedial Routines for the Maintenance of Control in Magistrates' Courts' (1974) 1 *British Journal of Law and Society* 101 and Carlen P, *Magistrates' Justice* (London: Martin Robertson, 1976).

[214] Carlen (1976); McBarnet (1983). While those findings are of some age, they are supported by more recent work, such as Young R, 'Exploring the Boundaries of the Criminal Courtroom Workgroup' (2013) 42(3) *Common Law World Review* 203–239 and Welsh (2016).

also likely to be represented. None of this is true of stipendiaries, as judges are even less representative than are magistrates.[215] Further, lay justices make most of their decisions in panels of three after group discussion, unlike lone stipendiaries.

Nor do magistrates serve to make the criminal justice system accountable to the community in the way that juries do. They are insufficiently representative of the communities they supposedly serve to be able to fulfil this function. It is true that lay magistrates stress their 'local' character, but it is not clear why 'localness' should be a virtue of justice.[216] In any case, few magistrates live in the same locales as prosecuted offenders. What is true of lay justices regarding accountability is even more true of stipendiaries, who often do not even have the dubious virtue of being 'local'.

On the 'justice' and efficiency criteria, stipendiaries are doubtless a good substitute for Crown court judges, but lay magistrates are, by definition, not legally qualified. Their clerks are supposed to make up for their deficit, in the same way that judges advise juries on the relevant law. But stipendiaries are, as one would expect, much more efficient than are lay justices if we define 'efficient' as 'quick'.[217] They are also thought to adjourn cases less readily, to stand up more robustly to prosecution and defence lawyers alike, and to be better at case management.[218] Darbyshire found that District Judges' 'working style was characterised by speed, command and readiness to challenge CPS representatives and lawyers (compared to lay justices)'.[219] Perhaps as a result, defence lawyers tend to prepare more thoroughly when appearing in a case before a District Judge.[220]

In conclusion, it seems undeniable that magistrates are a poor substitute for judge-and-jury.[221] Magistrates' court trials embody two (fairness and accountability) of the three basic principles far less well than do Crown court trials. However, lay justices embody these principles better than do stipendiaries. Yet we are seeing more work being done by stipendiaries, rather than less. The 'efficiency' principle is implicitly being prioritised over the principles of fairness and accountability.[222]

Efficiency was also prioritised amid suggestions that there is little need for the involvement of most magistrates in many guilty plea cases. The Criminal Justice and Courts Act 2015 introduced the Single Justice Procedure (SJP). Adults who are charged with non-imprisonable summary only offences will be able to enter pleas online (via gov.uk) or in writing, and the case will then be dealt with by a single magistrate and legal advisor without lawyers attending court for either party. Cases suitable for this procedure should be identified by the police, investigators at other agencies (such as TV Licensing) and prosecutors, and a notice should be sent to defendants advising them about the procedure and their options. This leaves decisions about appropriate court procedures and venue squarely in the hands of investigators and prosecutors. The defendant is able to request that the case be dealt with by way of a 'traditional' hearing in open court,[223] but time, cost, disenfranchisement from the court process, lack of understanding and bureaucracy all

---

[215] Lammy Review (2017: ch 4).   [216] Seago et al (2000).
[217] Seago et al (2000: table 4). Court personnel certainly seem to regard District Judges as more efficient than lay magistrates (Welsh (2016)).
[218] See Home Office (1997a).   [219] Darbyshire (2011: 160).
[220] Morgan R, 'Magistrates: The Future According to Auld' (2002) 29(2) *Journal of Law and Society* 308.
[221] See Bankowski et al, *Lay Justice?* (Edinburgh: Clark, 1987) ch 9 for a discussion of the analogy between juries and lay magistrates. Note that we are talking in terms of judge-and-*jury*, and *trials*, rather than the whole range of court proceedings, because juries are not involved in Crown court sentencing. It is not obvious that they should be left out. If the 'community' element embodied in lay justices is thought valuable for sentencing in magistrates' courts, why not similarly involve juries in the Crown court? See Sanders (2001).
[222] Fitzpatrick et al, 'New Courts Management and the Professionalization of Summary Justice in England and Wales' (2000) 11 *Criminal Law Forum* 1.
[223] Criminal Procedure Rules; Sprack and Sprack (2019).

disincentivise both asking for the matter to be dealt with in a traditional court and act as disincentive to plead not guilty. Furthermore, the procedure assumes that defendants both receive and understand the procedural notice. Transform Justice found that over 80% of people who are sent an SJP notice enter no plea at all[224] and are fined administratively, as their lack of engagement means that guilt is proved in absence.[225]

The SJP seems to amount to another form of justice on the cheap, or efficiency by another name. 784,325 cases (57% of magistrates' courts cases) were disposed of using the SJP in 2019. 87% were dealt with in a single day.[226] Recall that in many of those cases no plea whatsoever was entered. The lay Bench, despite its problems, perhaps represents a symbolically democratic form of community justice dating back hundreds of years, and offers a form of open justice by public tribunal. Conducting even more cases administratively behind closed doors further removes the public from processes of criminal justice and is unlikely to increase confidence in magistrates' courts. This issue has been recognised by the Magistrates' Association, whose chair commented: '. . . it is essential that openness and transparency are not compromised. How the Single Justice Procedure can be opened to public scrutiny must be addressed.'[227]

8.5.2 Acquittals and convictions

Many defendants do not expect justice to be done in the magistrates' court. Typically, they regard the Crown court as fairer and more thorough in its approach and offering a better chance of acquittal. By contrast, magistrates' courts are seen as amateurish and pro-police, but speedier and offering the prospect of a more lenient sentence.[228] Vennard's study of contested cases in the magistrates' courts found that there was a tendency for magistrates to accept the accuracy of police eye witness evidence and their interpretation of events as against the defendant's denial of the alleged conduct or a claim that the act did not occur. We saw in section 8.4 that magistrates generally prefer to believe the police and CPS rather than the defence, turning the burden of proof on its head. Vennard found that, even where defendants' credibility was not directly impugned and there was no confession the majority of cases ended in conviction.[229] A further study by Vennard concluded that for

---

[224] Transform Justice, *The right to know you are accused of a crime*, 19 August 2019 <http://www.transform-justice.org.uk/the-right-to-know-you-are-accused-of-a-crime/> (accessed 1 May 2020).

[225] The Criminal Procedure Rules allows magistrates' courts to proceed with cases in the absence of the defendant, which in practice means that the defendant will be taken to have entered a not guilty plea, and the prosecutor is allowed to present the evidence (in these cases, on the papers alone) and invite the court to find that the defendant is guilty in a streamlined hearing.

[226] Ministry of Justice, *Criminal Court statistics quarterly: October to December 2019 (tables)* (2020) <https://www.gov.uk/government/statistics/criminal-court-statistics-quarterly-october-to-december-2019; Ministry of Justice, *Criminal court statistics quarterly, England and Wales, January to March 2019* (2019b) <https://assets.publishing.service.gov.uk/government/uploads/system/uploads/attachment_data/file/812556/ccsq-bulletin-q1-2019.pdf> (both accessed 10 April 2020).

[227] Bache, J *Magistrates Association comment on the Single Justice Procedure*, 20 August 2019 <https://www.magistrates-association.org.uk/News/magistrates-association-comment-on-the-single-justice-procedure> (accessed 1 May 2020). Other magistrates have raised a range of concerns, such as the SJP becoming a rubber stamp exercise. See House of Commons Role of the magistracy within the criminal justice system (2016) <https://publications.parliament.uk/pa/cm201617/cmselect/cmjust/165/16505.htm> (accessed 1 May 2020).

[228] See Bottoms and McClean (1976: 87–100); *Gregory J, Crown court or Magistrates' Court?* (Office of Population Censuses and Surveys) (London: HMSO, 1976) and Riley D and Vennard J, *Triable-Either-Way Cases: Crown court or Magistrates' Court?* (Home Office Research Study, no 98) (London: HMSO, 1988) pp 16–18.

[229] Vennard J, *Contested Trials in Magistrates' Courts* (Home Office Research Study no 71) (London: HMSO, 1981) p 21.

contested either way cases, the chances of acquittal were substantially higher in the Crown court (57%) than in the magistrates' courts (30%).[230] More recent research, by Bridges et al (discussed later) lends support to the belief that, case-for-case, acquittal is far less likely in the magistrates' courts than in the Crown court. In 2016, 36% of defendants in the Crown court were acquitted by jury verdict,[231] with magistrates' court conviction rates sitting about 15% higher than Crown court conviction rates.[232]

There are a number of possible explanations for the higher acquittal rate in the Crown court. The first is that the magistracy and juries are, as we have seen, very different. We might expect case hardened 'insiders' with little experience of the conditions to which many defendants are subjected to be sceptical of what defendants say and to be over-ready to believe the police. A defence solicitor made this telling remark:

> We sometimes wonder [at the magistrates' court] who has to prove guilt or innocence. Certainly, sometimes I've felt that I'm the one who's having to do all the work—whereas really it should be the prosecution who are proving all the elements, rather than the defence having to disprove the elements of the offence.[233]

The second is simply numerical. At the Crown court, the prosecution has to convince at least 10 out of the 12 jurors that the defendant is guilty.[234] In the magistrates' court, it is enough to convince two out of the three lay magistrates, or even just one stipendiary magistrate. As one defendant has put it:

> ... when you go to a magistrates' court, there is only one thing—you are guilty ... at the Crown court, you've got a better chance because you've got 12 people and at the magistrates' court, you've got either one or three people to decide.[235]

Finally, the procedures in the lower courts place defendants at a distinct disadvantage. The prosecution need not disclose its case in advance to defendants charged with summary offences[236] and legal aid is less freely available than in the Crown court. Furthermore, magistrates, unlike jurors, are privy to much inadmissible evidence. This is because the admissibility of evidence is a question of law which is decided by the judge in the absence of the jury in the Crown court. Magistrates, by contrast, determine both questions of fact and law. Even if they decide, for example, that a disputed confession is inadmissible, they may still be prejudiced by the knowledge that an alleged confession exists.[237] For this reason this procedure could fall foul of Art 6 ECHR. A 'mixed panel' system could ameliorate this problem, as the professional chair could hear the legal arguments in the absence of the lay 'wingers'. There is also some evidence that justices' clerks may occasionally, whether in private or in whispers, transmit opinions, prejudices and hearsay information

---

[230] Vennard J, 'The Outcome of Contested Trials' in D Moxon (ed), *Managing Criminal Justice* (London: HMSO, 1985). Ashworth A, 'Plea, Venue and Discontinuance' [1993] *Criminal Law Review* 830, who does not cite the Vennard (1981) study, argues for caution in interpreting this finding.

[231] Ministry of Justice (2018) *Criminal Courts Statistics*, online at: <https://www.gov.uk/government/collections/criminal-court-statistics> (accessed 10 July 2019).

[232] CPS, *Key Measures 2017–2018*. Available at <https://www.cps.gov.uk/key-measures> (accessed 10 July 2019).

[233] Bucke et al, *The right of silence: the impact of the Criminal Justice and Public Order Act 1994* (Home Office Research Study no 199) (London: Home Office, 2000) p 47.

[234] Until 1967 the jury's decision had to be unanimous. Now, under the Criminal Justice Act 1967, s.13(3), the court is not supposed to consider the possibility of a majority verdict until at least two hours have elapsed since the jury retired.

[235] Quoted by Bridges L, 'Taking Liberties' *Legal Action*, 6 July 2000 at p 8.

[236] Only once a defendant has pleaded not guilty does the Criminal Procedure and Investigations Act 1996 require the prosecutor to make 'primary disclosure'. On disclosure generally, see discussion in ch 7.

[237] See further Wasik M, 'Magistrates: Knowledge of Previous Convictions' [1996] *Criminal Law Review* 851.

to magistrates.[238] Magistrates' courts are also less accountable in that their proceedings are not recorded in full. If the defence wish to appeal on a point of law to the Divisional Court, the magistrates draw up a statement of the facts, the cases cited and their decision. This gives justices' clerks ample opportunity to cover their tracks.[239]

In drives to increase 'efficiency', successive governments introduced several reforms aimed at reducing delay. These include 'early administrative hearings' (EAHs) (see section 8.3) and 'early first hearings' (EFH) introduced in the 1990s.[240] Then, under the *Criminal Justice Simple Speedy Summary* (CJSSS) regime[241] the aim is to dispose of guilty pleas in just one hearing (which might be by video link from the police station) or, in contested cases, have two hearings at most. It follows that applications to adjourn are viewed negatively, even though many defendants may appear without having had legal advice, and advance information (disclosure) from the prosecution will not have occurred. Court duty solicitors are available, but have little time to take instructions. The Coalition government of 2010 continued to believe that the criminal justice system habitually tolerated delay, and that defence lawyers benefitted from such delay, even though the Ministry of Justice accepted that 'target chasing has replaced professional discretion and diverted practitioners' focus from delivering the best outcomes using their skill and experience.'[242] So *Transforming Summary Justice* was introduced,[243] with the same aims as *CJSSS*: reducing delay, conducting fewer hearings per case and increasing the number of effective trial listings. But all these aims require appropriate levels of disclosure at an early stage in cases—and we saw in chapter 7 that this remains a major problem. HM CPS Inspectorate raised concerns about the effect of inadequate disclosure on the effectiveness of *Transforming Summary Justice* in 2017.[244] Inadequate resources and 'unjoined up' working between the various agencies of criminal justice remain hindrances to effective case progression in the criminal justice system, which no policy alone can improve. This managerialism gone mad is completely incompatible with the freedoms owed to both defendants and complainants.

8.5.3 **Trial venue allocation**

In 'either way' cases adult defendants have the 'right' to elect a jury trial in the Crown court. Youths (those aged 17 or under) have no such right; they are prosecuted in the youth court, which is essentially the magistrates' court in (supposedly) more paternalistic guise, unless charged with a grave crime, or if they are to be co-tried with adult defendants. Although little remarked upon in the literature, this is actually a major restriction on trial by jury. Vast numbers of citizens enter 'adulthood' with convictions for such

---

[238] See McLaughlin H, 'Court Clerks: Advisers or Decision-Makers' (1990) 30 *British Journal of Criminology* 358 at 364.

[239] For fuller discussion see Heaton-Armstrong I, 'The Verdict of the Court... and its Clerk?' (1986) 150 *JP* 340, 342, 357–359.

[240] Under the EFH 'fast-track' procedure for anticipated guilty pleas in 'simple' cases, hearings are intended to be within 24 hours of charge where possible (s.46 of the Crime and Disorder Act 1998).

[241] Department for Constitutional Affairs, *Delivering Simple, Speedy, Summary Justice* (London, 2006).

[242] Ministry of Justice, *Swift and Sure Justice: The Government's Plans for Reform of the Criminal Justice System* (Ministry of Justice Command Paper CM 8388, 2012) 5.

[243] Crown Prosecution Service (2015a) *Transforming Summary Justice*. Available at: <https://www.cps.gov.uk/publication/transforming-summary-justice-criminal-justice-system-wide-initiative-improve-how-cases> (accessed 10 July 2019). For a critical analysis of the system, see Ward J, *Transforming Summary Justice: Modernisation in the Lower Criminal Courts* (London: Routledge, 2016).

[244] HMCPSI (2017) *Business as usual? Transforming Summary Justice Follow Up Report*. Available at: <https://www.justiceinspectorates.gov.uk/hmcpsi/inspections/business-as-usual-transforming-summary-justice-follow-up-report/> (accessed 10 July 2019).

serious offences as theft or fairly serious violence, without ever having had the chance to contest their guilt before the 'community' as embodied by the jury.[245] One can legally have sex and get married at 16, drive a car at 17, yet not be entitled to what is generally regarded as a superior form of justice until 18. Youth court is often thought of as a liberal measure, deigned to spare 'kids' the trauma of a judicial setting designed for adults. But it also results in young adults being funnelled into the conviction sausage-machine that is the magistrates' court. This puts the supposed liberality of the youth court mechanism in a rather different light.

Not surprisingly, in view of our earlier discussion, many adults exercise their right to trial by jury if they intend pleading not guilty. Adults intending to plead guilty usually prefer to stay in the magistrates' court as its sentencing powers are restricted to six months' imprisonment for any one offence. This is not such a restriction as it might seem as magistrates can, as with youths, send the case to the Crown court for sentencing following a conviction regardless of the defendant's wishes. So the majority of either way cases are dealt with in the magistrates' courts. For several decades policy-makers have been concerned about the proportion committed to the Crown court and sought to reduce this, primarily for reasons of economy.[246] Committal of either way cases involves increased costs for the courts, the CPS, the probation service, the legal aid fund and the prison system. It is also a factor in fuelling prison overcrowding, both because defendants remanded in custody have longer to wait if committed to the Crown court,[247] and because Crown court judges make much more use of custodial sentences than do magistrates.[248]

On the face of it, there appear to be two types of Crown court adult defendant in either way cases. There are the defendants who plead guilty in the Crown court and who could have been dealt with identically (but more quickly and cheaply) in the magistrates' courts. And there are the defendants who opt for the Crown court because they think they are more likely to be acquitted. For the crime control adherent, defendants who are acquitted in the Crown court are seen to have cheated the system, whereas either way defendants who are convicted (whether following a contested trial or not) are perceived to have wasted the time and money that would have been saved had they stayed in the lower courts. Various attempts underpinned by these crime control assumptions have been made to restrict the flow of cases committed from the magistrates' courts. Unfortunately these attempts have not separated out the different reasons for opting for the Crown court and so have ended up penalising those who wish to plead not guilty before a jury as well as the committed guilty pleaders.

One way to keep more cases in the magistrates' courts would be to increase their sentencing powers, but policy makers appear to be wary of this option on the ground that it is likely to fuel prison overcrowding.[249] Another way of reducing the numbers of Crown court cases of all kinds is simply to reclassify either way offences as summary only.

---

[245] Aubrey-Johnson et al (2019); Case (2018).

[246] Cammiss S and Stride C, 'Modelling Mode of Trial' (2008) 48(4) *British Journal of Criminology* 482.

[247] Morgan and Jones (1992: 38). In 2007 the average wait was around 13 weeks for those in custody (MOJ, 2008; table 2.2)

[248] Hedderman C and Moxon D, *Magistrates' court or Crown Court? Mode of trial decisions and sentencing* (Home Office Research Study no 125) (London: HMSO, 1992). Although Cammiss and Stride (2008) notes that this was queried by Halliday J, *Making Punishments Work: Report of a Review of the Sentencing Framework for England and Wales* (London: Home Office, 2001).

[249] The CJA 2003, s.154 increased the maximum sentence magistrates could impose for a single offence to twelve months imprisonment, but the provision has yet to be implemented. See further <http://business.timesonline.co.uk/tol/business/law/article5941754.ece> (accessed 5 January 2010).

Thus, s.15 of the Criminal Law Act 1977 made a number of public order offences and drink-driving offences purely summary. Similarly, the Criminal Justice Act 1988 (ss.37 and 39) reclassified the offences of taking a motor vehicle, driving whilst disqualified and common assault as summary offences. A more subtle approach has been to encourage magistrates to accept jurisdiction in a higher proportion of cases, and to exhort CPS lawyers to suggest this to them, most notably through 'allocation guidelines'.[250] The allocation hearing affords both the prosecution and defence an opportunity to make representations on the appropriate venue. As with bail decision-making, there is usually a high degree of agreement between prosecutors' representations and magistrates' decisions. The reasons for this are unclear.

It has been suggested that the CPS strategy has been to encourage the charging of offences which are summary only in preference to those that are triable either way. The CPS now has a range of 'Charging standards'. While such standards have been welcomed as a step towards achieving consistency, they also have effectively broadened the band of criminal behaviour that can fall within the summary only offences. The CPS is frequently accused of charging summary offences instead of either way offences (e.g. minor assaults instead of s.47 assaults), or even altering the charges to this effect once the case is under way, to keep the case in the magistrates' courts, thus depriving defendants of a Crown court trial.[251] In 2013, one sample of prosecutors did indicate that CPS charging policy encouraged them to keep borderline cases in the magistrates' courts, and to charge a summary only offence where possible so that the defendant did not have the opportunity to elect Crown court trial.[252] While measures to encourage magistrates to deal with more cases have led to a drop in the numbers of cases sent to the Crown court for trial by magistrates, this is more than compensated for by a sharp rise in the numbers sent to the Crown court for sentence.[253] Sixty-three per cent of defendants remanded into custody by magistrates in 2019 were committed to the Crown court for sentencing.[254] Nonetheless, there are likely to have been some cost savings as Crown court contested trials are far more expensive than Crown court sentencing proceedings. On the other hand, the allocation procedure, by advancing the moment at which defendants are asked to indicate their plea, has increased the pressure to plead guilty. This is because the sentence discount principle (discussed in chapter 7) works by offering the greatest discounts to those who plead guilty at the earliest opportunity. These crime control approaches are frequently at odds with the wishes, and sometimes the interests, of victims. Crown prosecutors interviewed by Porter complained that the role of statistics often takes away from the needs and wishes of the victim.[255] Many victims, especially of sexual offences, seek charges, procedures and sentences that fit what they believe to be the seriousness of the crime.[256]

The allocation guidelines also encouraged magistrates to accept jurisdiction in more cases, and the number of cases received by Crown courts has declined in recent years, though the statistics do not make clear the impact of the allocation guidelines, and that decline could be a result of a general decline in the number of case received by all courts.[257]

---

[250] See Sentencing Council, *Allocation guideline* (2016) and CPS *Allocation of cases and Sending to the Crown Court* (2019a).

[251] Genders (1999); Jeremy D, 'The Prosecutor's Rock and Hard Place' [2008] *Criminal Law Review* 925.

[252] Welsh (2016).   [253] Bridges (1999).

[254] Ministry of Justice, *Criminal Justice Statistics quarterly, England and Wales, October 2018 to September 2019* (2020).

[255] Porter A, 'Prosecuting Domestic Abuse in England and Wales: Crown Prosecution Service "Working Practice" and New Public Managerialism', (2019) 28(4) *Social & Legal Studies* 493–516.

[256] See Fenwick H, 'Charge Bargaining and Sentence Discount: the Victim's Perspective' (1997) 5 *International Review of Victimology* 23. The issue is discussed more fully in chs 7 and 12.

[257] Ministry of Justice, *Criminal court statistics quarterly, England and Wales, January to March 2019* (2019b).

A more radical initiative would be to remove the power of magistrates to send cases to the Crown court for sentence so that many more defendants might voluntarily elect for trial in the lower courts, especially if the fairness of those trials was enhanced. Removing the right of magistrates to decline jurisdiction in either way cases would also reduce pressure on the Crown court. The suspicion must be that government attempts to reduce jury trial are motivated by wanting to increase guilty pleas and convictions, regardless of whether this is justified by the strength of the prosecution evidence.

Why do so many defendants want to be heard in the Crown court but then plead guilty? Over a quarter of defendants in Hedderman and Moxon's study who elected Crown court trial did so intending to plead guilty.[258] Most of the defendants who they interviewed who elected Crown court trial (including some of those who intended to plead guilty), together with over a third of the solicitors interviewed, believed that Crown court judges imposed lighter sentences than magistrates.[259] In other words they thought magistrates' courts are less just than the Crown court. More recently, Dhami and Mandel found that hypothetically guilty defendants were more likely to choose to have their case dealt with in a magistrates' court—seemingly as a result of sentencing powers—while both hypothetically innocent and guilty defendants perceived the chances of acquittal to be greater in the Crown court.[260] Further, Bridges et al looked at why defendants elected jury trial, and found that they fell into two main groups. First, there were those that denied the charges, pleaded not guilty and were either tried by a jury or had the case dropped. Second, were defendants who contested one or more of the (often several) charges against them or the seriousness of the charge(s). Most of this group pleaded guilty to lesser charges when these were offered by the prosecution, or contested the charges they disagreed with. In most cases in the second group the 'deals' could have been done without going to the Crown court, but it was the unwillingness of the CPS, not the defence, to alter its position that led to the unnecessary Crown court appearances. Often, it was only moving 'up' to a court with a 'proper' judge (and, perhaps, having to instruct an independent barrister to prosecute) that prompted the CPS to scrutinise its case sufficiently to let itself 'deal'.[261] In many of these cases, pressure to drop or reduce charges comes from the judge who has read the committal papers, so this is not simply a matter of the CPS having no stomach for a fight. So the defendant's right to a Crown court trial gives defendants bargaining power. Who knows what would have happened if the cases in which the CPS dropped or reduced charges had gone to trial before less independently minded magistrates? When Bridges et al looked at the cases in their sample which were tried in the magistrates' court they found that only one (out of 14) ended in acquittal. More recently, the Lammy Review found the same for women BAME defendants.[262]

The loss of jury trial would not impact evenly across all types of adult defendant. Cases with BAME defendants are disproportionately discontinued, dismissed and acquitted (chapter 10). So the right to choose Crown court trial is especially important for them. It makes up, to some extent, for their disproportionate presence in the stop-search, arrest

---

[258] Hedderman and Moxon (1992).

[259] Hedderman and Moxon (1992: 20). This finding departs from the pattern found by other studies. See further Bridges L, 'The Right to Jury Trial: How the Royal Commission Got it Wrong' (1993) 143 *New Law Journal* 1542 and Bridges (2000).

[260] Dhami M and Mandel R, 'How Do Defendants Choose Their Trial Court? Evidence for a Heuristic Processing Account' (September 2013) 8(5) *Judgment and Decision Making* 552–560.

[261] This practice remains the case according to The Secret Barrister (2018).

[262] Lammy Review (2017: ch 4); Bridges et al, *Ethnic Minority Defendants and the Right to Elect Jury Trial* (London: Commission for Racial Equality, 2000b) summarised in Bridges (2000). For further discussion, see Dhami and Mandel (2013).

and charge statistics. It seems that when the CPS, juries and (to a lesser extent) magistrates are put to the test, they see the flaws in many weak cases and act accordingly. Perhaps surprisingly, in one study, BAME Crown court defendants were less happy, and perceived more racism, than did BAME defendants in the magistrates' courts. However, though their perceptions of justice were more favourable than the researchers expected, a significant minority perceived some decision-making in both types of court to be unfair, and particularly so due to perceived racism.[263] This has been confirmed more recently in work suggesting that many BAME defendants chose Crown court trial rather than magistrates' because of their perception of the greater fairness of juries (hence those opting for magistrates' justice might be those who do not share that perception).[264] The appearance of justice is important. Bridges et al show that, much of the time, it is election for Crown court trial that puts the rest of the criminal justice system to the test. The more that cases are kept in the magistrates' courts, the less will be the ability of the defence to put pressure on the CPS, and this will have a disproportionately adverse impact on BAME defendants. It is not defendants who are abusing the system, but the system that is abusing defendants.[265]

8.6 Specialist magistrates

In recent years a new phenomenon has emerged of specialist courts of summary jurisdiction. This is based on policy makers looking over the Atlantic at a range of American 'problem solving' courts, particularly to deal with issues such as drugs related offending and domestic abuse.[266] As a result there has been a programme for introducing drugs courts,[267] community justice courts[268] and domestic abuse courts into England and Wales. Despite evidence that problem solving courts may lead to greater compliance with orders,[269] plans to expand them were abandoned in 2016 amid speculation that the rehabilitative approach was seen as 'too soft' on defendants.[270] That decision is consistent with the more punitive approach taken by government towards defendants in recent years.

Domestic abuse courts are the most significant numerically. These now exist in over 100 magistrates' courts in England and Wales.[271] The magistrates are specially trained on domestic abuse and are thus supposed to be alert to the power dynamics that exist in abusive relationships and to appropriate attitudes and responses to display in court.[272] In specialist domestic violence courts (SDVCs) the magistrates work in partnership with other agencies, both from within and outside the criminal justice system, with the dual aims of improving victim satisfaction and safety and increasing offender accountability. Thus, unlike in traditional non-specialist courts, victims have 'advocates' who may speak

---

[263] Shute et al, *A Fair Hearing? Ethnic Minorities in the Criminal Courts* (Cullompton: Willan, 2005).
[264] Lammy Review (2017: ch 3).   [265] See ch 7 and Bridges (2000).
[266] Plotnikoff J and Woolfson R, *Review of the effectiveness of specialist courts in other jurisdictions* (Department for Constitutional Affairs, 2005).
[267] Matrix Knowledge Group, Dedicated Drug Court Pilots; A process report (London: Ministry of Justice, 2008).
[268] Brown R and Payne S, Process Evaluation of Salford Community Justice Initiative (London: Ministry of Justice, 2007).
[269] Centre for Justice Innovation (2015) *Problem-solving courts: An evidence review*. Available at <http://justiceinnovation.org/wp-content/uploads/2016/08/Problem-solving-courts-An-evidence-review.pdf> (accessed 8 July 2019).
[270] Doward J, 'Liz Truss abandons Gove's plan for problem-solving courts' *The Guardian*, 21 August 2016.
[271] Centre for Justice Innovation (2014) *The case for dedicated domestic violence courts*. Available at <http://justiceinnovation.org/portfolio/the-case-for-dedicated-domestic-violence-courts/> (accessed 10 April 2020).
[272] For research on the first domestic violence courts in England and Wales, which provided the basis for the programme for national roll out, see Cook et al, *Evaluation of Specialist Domestic Violence Courts/Fast Track Systems* (Crown Prosecution Service and Department for Constitutional Affairs, 2004).

to the prosecution on their behalf and thereby communicate information to the magistrates.[273] It is debatable whether having SDVCs has any significant effect on the outcomes of domestic abuse cases in the magistrates' courts. Victim retraction rates are still high.[274] Little progress has been made in continuing prosecutions without the victim's support (for example through use of other evidence), and in some SDVCs contested cases are transferred to 'regular' magistrates' courts.[275] Between 2010 and 2013, the number of convictions for domestic abuse fell by 11% despite the continued rise in the number of incidents reported to police.[276] However, some SDVCs have increased their conviction rate through increased guilty pleas and convictions following trial.[277] Specialist courts can be seen as part of a phenomenon, observed in the Canadian context by Roach (1999),[278] of harnessing victims' rights in pursuit of crime control, paying scant attention to either the victim's interests or the defendant's due process rights. Less cynically, at best they are an underfunded gesture towards one of the most pernicious forms of crime where victims are doubly or even triply victimised.

8.7 Conclusion

It is no exaggeration to say that magistrates' courts are crime control courts overlaid with a thin layer of due process icing, or in the case of specialist courts, victim orientated icing. At every twist and turn in the process, defendants are faced with obstacles that undermine their willingness or ability to stand on their rights in court. Some are denied legal aid, some are denied bail, and some do not receive proper assistance and advice from their legal advisors. Some will not receive advance disclosure of the prosecution case and many more will receive inadequate or misleading disclosure. Some defendants will be offered tempting oven-ready deals prepared by prosecutors and served up by legal advisors. Many adult defendants will be told that longer delays and a higher sentence can be expected if they elect trial by jury but that the prospects of acquittal before the magistrates are bleak. Many will already know this from previous experience. Youths who would like to contest their guilt before a jury have no choice but to lump magistrates' court trial.

For defendants, the process must seem like an obstacle course with formidable impediments to them continuing to maintain their innocence. Meanwhile managerialist reforms hurry and harry the defendant on to the ever-more smooth path of least resistance, the guilty plea. Some will end up pleading guilty to, or being found guilty of, crimes they did not commit. These miscarriages of justice are not the stuff of headline news. The fact that some innocent people plead guilty is even now little recognised and excites little concern. Appreciation of the role that more due process could play in protecting us against the abuse of police and prosecutorial power is very limited, but this is to be expected. For, as made clear in chapter 10, it tends to be marginalised groups (black people, the unemployed and the poor) who suffer most from whatever abuse of power takes place. It is easy

---

[273] These 'advocates' are from a range of voluntary sector support agencies such as Women's Aid (see Cook et al, 2004).

[274] Hoyle C, 'Feminism, Victimology and Domestic Violence' in Walklate S (ed), *Handbook of Victims and Victimology* (London: Routledge, 2012).

[275] For example, in Northumbria: Baird V et al, *Special Domestic Violence Courts – How Special are they?* (2017), see <http://www.northumbria-pcc.gov.uk/v2/wp-content/uploads/2018/07/OPCC_037_Specialist-domestic-violence-courts-Court-Observers-Panel-A4-booklet-2018-V2.pdf> (accessed 10 April 2020).

[276] Centre for Justice Innovation (2014).

[277] See Burton M, *Legal Responses to Domestic Violence* (Abingdon: Routledge-Cavendish, 2008) ch 7.

[278] See discussion in ch 1.

for the rest of us to turn a blind eye to this as we gratefully focus instead on the high conviction rate that our courts achieve in seeking to repress crime on our behalf.

This is usually done in the name of 'efficiency', and occasionally in the name of victims' rights. The cost of these approaches appears small because these low-profile courts appear to deal with trivia. But in reality they deal with a vast amount of serious issues. The processes and sentencing outcomes in many cases are enormously intrusive, yet most adjudication is done by either a bench of case-hardened lay magistrates or a similarly case-hardened lone professional judge—chosen, in any one case, at random. Doris Day, and other 'regular' defendants, will continue to be caught between an all too familiar rock and a hard place, with diminishing prospects of being allowed to take their case before a jury. Despite the HRA, the ECHR has failed to bolster the fairness of trial by magistrates: human rights do not cover most of these issues, and even where they do, ECHR safeguards are not always observed. Programmes of managerial reforms have reduced the jury-like qualities of the magistracy. Reform ideas on the lines of German courts, with a mix of lay and professional judges that would cost less than Crown court but be more democratic and just than current magistrates' courts, are dismissed.[279] The government seems to be less interested in the rights of victims and defendants to a fair trial than it is in the responsibility of defendants to plead guilty and the responsibility of magistrates' courts to convict to save time and money. The result is an exclusionary system that piles further disadvantage onto the already-disadvantaged. The core value of 'efficiency' trumps those of justice and democracy. The monetary cost may be low but the cost in terms of justice and fairness is priceless. This may not even be cost-effective, given the numbers who end up in jail through wrongful denial of bail, coerced guilty pleas and wrongful convictions. The cost in freedom is immeasurable.

Further reading

DARBYSHIRE P, 'An Essay on the Importance and Neglect of the Magistracy' (1997) *Criminal Law Review* 627.

CAMMISS S and STRIDE C, 'Modelling Mode of Trial' (2008) 48(4) *British Journal of Criminology* 482.

MCCONVILLE M et al, *Standing Accused* (Oxford: Clarendon, 1994).

MARSH L, 'Leveson's Narrow Pursuit of Justice: Efficiency and Outcomes in the Criminal Process' (2016) 45 *Common Law World Review*.

NEWMAN D, *Legal Aid Lawyers and the Quest for Justice* (Oxford: Hart Publishing, (2013).

NEWMAN D and WELSH L, 'The Practices of Modern Criminal Defence Lawyers: Alienation and its Implications for Access to Justice' (2019) *Common Law World Review*

SANDERS A, 'Core Values, the Magistracy, and the Auld Report' (2002) 29(2) *Journal of Law and Society* 324; 341.

THORNTON J, 'Is Publicly Funded Criminal Defence Sustainable? Legal Aid Cuts, Morale, Recruitment and Retention in the English Criminal Law Professions' (2020) *Legal Studies*.

WARD J, *Transforming Summary Justice: Modernisation in the Lower Criminal Courts.* (London: Routledge, 2016).

WELSH L and HOWARD M, 'Standardization and the Production of Justice in Summary Criminal Courts: A Post-Human Analysis' (2019) 28(6) *Social & Legal Studies* 774–793.

YOUNG R and WILCOX A, 'The Merits of Legal Aid in the Magistrates' Courts Revisited' [2007] *Criminal Law Review* 109.

HOUSE OF COMMONS JUSTICE COMMITTEE, *Criminal Legal Aid* HC 1069 (2018).

---

[279] Sanders (2002).

9

Trial by judge and jury

KEY ISSUES

- The influence of the judge on the trial process and outcome
- How jury composition affects perceptions of the fairness and legitimacy of jury trial
- The impact of jury composition and juror attitudes on verdicts
- Whether key evidential rules unduly favour the defence or prosecution
- Attempts to further erode the practical significance of jury trial

9.1 Introduction

Jury trial is the public face of the criminal justice system, the image with which we are all familiar from countless news reports and fictionalised accounts. The jury trial is a key battleground for the due process and crime control models, because it is used in the most serious cases such as murder and rape. A high rate of guilty verdicts is thus essential to the strategy of effective crime control. The deterrent aim of the system would be undermined if in 'too high' a proportion of these widely publicised cases the defendants were allowed to walk free from the court. Similarly, the very authority of the state might be called into question if juries acquitted too readily, especially in overtly political cases concerning official secrets, terrorist activities and so forth.

Trials by jury can be sharply contested affairs in which the case construction techniques used at earlier stages of the criminal process (see chapters 2–7) are exposed to 12 members of the public. These dozen jurors have to choose who to believe, and their choice may depend to a large extent on their backgrounds and prior experiences, as well as the mores, prejudices and panics of the wider society in which they live. Sometimes it may come down to little more than whether people have faith in the police or not; people who have experienced negative encounters with the police may perhaps be more willing than others to believe that the police might, for example, sometimes fabricate evidence.

Although jury trial offers a measure of external scrutiny to the case constructions of criminal justice professionals, it is statistically speaking largely an irrelevance. The Crown court determines fewer than 10% of criminal cases in England and Wales (most criminal proceedings being concluded in the magistrates' courts: see chapter 8), and of all defendants proceeded against in the criminal courts, about 1.5% have their fate determined by a jury. The majority of those appearing at the Crown court do so only to be sentenced, and are not therefore afforded the due process protections that might ordinarily be associated with the public image of jury trial.[1] In 2019, 1.48m cases were prosecuted, of which around

---

[1] Jacobson J, Hunter G and Kirby A, *Inside Crown Court* (Bristol: Policy Press, 2015).

60,000 were intended for trial at the Crown court, but only 19,395 of those defendants pleaded not guilty.[2] Just over half of people pleading not guilty in the Crown court in 2019 were acquitted,[3] either by jury or by judge ordered or directed acquittals. So, even where it is left to the jury to decide whether the prosecution has proved guilt beyond reasonable doubt, judges often exert a strong influence on the outcome and are far from being the passive impartial referee as depicted in adversarial theory.

Judicial influence has been increasing in recent years as judges have been called upon to play an ever more active part in managing cases.[4] In 2015, the Criminal Procedure Rules were updated to expand the duty of the court to actively manage cases by early identification of the issues, abolishing preliminary and pre-trial review hearings in favour of a single Plea and Trial Preparation Hearing (PTPH) and restricting the instances in which a further pre-trial case management hearing will be held. Informal conversations with one Crown court judge in 2018 raised the possibility of PTPHs being conducted online in future in the name of saving cost by reducing the court estate, and this process might have been accelerated after the move to online courts during the Covid-19 pandemic. Such measures would remove the human element of case progression even further, particularly when face to face discussion about cases can often resolve issues far more easily than proceedings conducted at arm's length.

This is all part of a trend to use judicial duty as a means to implement technological change and pull lawyers in to make justice even swifter, all in the name of efficiency. This is described by McConville and Marsh as 'unchastened by empirical findings' and reflecting 'an impoverished conception of judicial reasoning'.[5] Further evidence of that impoverished view of judicial reasoning is found in the Better Case Management initiative, which was adopted in 2016 to further encourage robust case management by Crown court judges.[6] These measures contributed to reconfiguring the role of judges further into case management, rather than the traditional understanding of a judge as the impartial 'umpire' in an adversarial setting. Trial by jury is widely thought of as 'a cornerstone of our system of criminal justice',[7] commanding considerable support from the public[8] and members of the judiciary.[9] This supports the core values of 'justice' and 'democracy' but it is important to remember the significant role of the judge in 'trial by judge and jury'. We will see that, undoubtedly, these values are strengthened by judge and jury carrying out the roles of law-finder and fact-finder respectively; the question is whether, in making judges case managers, and reducing defence input into that management, the core value

---

[2] Ministry of Justice, *Crown Court Plea Tool. Criminal court statistics quarterly: October to December 2019* (2019f) online at <https://www.gov.uk/government/statistics/criminal-court-statistics-quarterly-october-to-december-2019> (accessed 20 April 2020).

[3] Ministry of Justice, *Criminal Court Statistics. Overview Tables September 2019* (2019e) online at <https://www.gov.uk/government/statistics/criminal-justice-system-statistics-quarterly-september-2019> (accessed 20 April 2020).

[4] See Rule 3.2 of the Criminal Procedure Rules (<http://www.justice.gov.uk/criminal/procrules_fin/rules-menu.htm> (accessed 5 January 2010); see further *K & Ors* [2006] EWCA Crim 724.

[5] McConville M and Marsh L, *The Myth of Judicial Independence: Criminal Justice and the Separation of Powers* (Oxford: OUP, 2020).

[6] Hungerford-Welch P, 'Better Case Management' *Counsel Magazine*, October 2017. This was a product of Lord Justice Leveson's *Review of Efficiency in Criminal Proceedings* (2015), which McConville and Marsh (2020) describe as an exercise in locating 'areas of the criminal process where further compression could occur.'

[7] Home Office, *Juries in Serious Fraud Trials* (London: Home Office Communication Directorate, 1998a) para 2.2.

[8] Roberts J and Hough M, *Public Opinion and the Jury: An International Literature Review* (Ministry of Justice Research Series 1/09) (London: Ministry of Justice, 2009).

[9] Lord Phillips, 'Trusting the Jury', Kalisher Lecture 23 October 2007 (<http://www.judiciary.gov.uk/docs/speeches/lcj_trusting_juries_231007.pdf> (accessed 5 January 2010)).

of 'efficiency' is being given undue prominence. Hodgson points out that '. . .invocation of system efficiency in purely positive terms masks the more ideologically driven desire to remove due process safeguards that protect fundamental rights and which ensure some degree of equality of arms.'[10]

9.2 Directed and ordered acquittals—weak cases?

The formal distinction between directed and ordered acquittals is not difficult to grasp. If the prosecution indicates that it will not be offering evidence at trial, the judge orders the jury to acquit. A directed acquittal, by contrast, occurs on the instigation of the prosecutor, the defence or the judge, after the trial has begun and '[w]here the judge comes to the conclusion that the prosecution evidence, taken at the highest, is such that a jury properly directed could not properly convict upon it, it is his duty, upon a submission being made, to stop the case.'[11]

In 2017 there were 8,107 judge ordered and 1,009 judge directed acquittals. There has been a reduction in the percentage of judge ordered and directed acquittals in recent years, but acquittals by jury following trial still only amount to 36% of all acquittals.[12] The level of directed and ordered acquittals raises the question of whether the prosecution is adequately discharging its duty in the Code for Crown Prosecutors to continue only with those cases where a court is more likely than not to convict. That it is not so doing is suggested by research showing many acquittals are foreseeable.[13] Bureaucratic pressures or professional misjudgement may explain the failure to discontinue some foreseeably weak cases, or the prosecution may simply be hoping the defendant will plead guilty.[14] If a defendant calls the prosecution's bluff by insisting on trial by jury, one natural response is to drop the case by offering no evidence.

In a now rather old study Block et al (1993) noted that around half of the directed acquittals occurred before the end of the prosecution case at the intervention of the judge. There were also cases in which the judge pressured the prosecution into offering no evidence by revealing that the result of the case would be a bind over whether or not the prosecution went ahead.[15] In the researchers' view, the seriousness of the offence and the strength of the evidence in many such instances was such that the case should have been left to the jury to decide. From a due process perspective it could be said that by directing or ordering acquittals judges are giving priority to ensuring innocent defendants are not convicted. But it can also be argued that crime control concerns may explain why, at a relatively late stage in the process, judges and prosecutors might abandon weak cases; they may take the view that less serious cases, such as minor assault or theft, do not merit the resources of jury trial in circumstances where the defendant maintains a not guilty plea.

---

[10] Hodgson J, *The Metamorphosis of Criminal Justice: A Comparative Account* (Oxford: OUP, 2020) p 61.

[11] *Galbraith* [1981] 1 WLR 1039 at 1042. Submissions made that there is no case to answer are often referred to as 'half time submissions', due to the fact they occur after the close of the prosecution case, which is nominally half way through the trial process.

[12] In 2007, 29% of acquittals were by jury verdict, rising steadily to 36% in 2017 (Ministry of Justice, *Criminal Court Statistics (annual)* (2018a) <https://www.gov.uk/government/statistics/criminal-court-statistics-annual-january-to-march-2018> (accessed 30 August 2019)).

[13] Block et al, *Ordered and Directed Acquittals in the Crown Court* (Royal Commission on Criminal Justice, Research Study no 15) (London: HMSO, 1993a). The results are summarised by the authors in 'Ordered and Directed Acquittals in the Crown Court: A Time of Change?' [1993b] *Criminal Law Review* 95.

[14] See McConville et al, *The Case for the Prosecution* (London: Routledge, 1991) ch 8.

[15] The bind over is best described as a 'suspended fine' and may be imposed on anyone involved in court proceedings, whether found guilty of an offence or not.

It is perhaps more difficult to explain why judges would acquit in strong cases of serious crime, but seriousness and strength of evidence are both factors that are open to interpretation. Some trial judges may simply be taking a different view from prosecutors, police or researchers as to what counts as an important enough case to justify the resources involved in a Crown court contest, perhaps because they feel less susceptible to the pressure that the police and CPS have come under in recent years to pursue cases involving vulnerable victims.[16]

The study by Block et al (1993) raises further questions about the propriety of defence solicitors or counsel advising defendants that, given the 'strength' of the prosecution case, they should plead guilty (see chapters 7 and 8). The strength of the case on paper will often not be reflected in court should the defence decide to fight. But the Block et al study was not one of weak cases per se, but of cases that ended in an ordered or directed acquittal (some of which were in fact considered to be strong). It would be wrong to assume that all weak cases end in acquittal. Some end in conviction. In another now rather dated study judges, defence barristers, and prosecution barristers agreed that around one-fifth of all contested cases were a weak. Although the great majority of these cases ended in acquittal, between 4–8% ended in conviction. Conversely, strong cases do not always end in conviction—the acquittal rate in such cases was between 21 and 27% according to barristers and judges.[17]

Clearly, the outcome of contested cases is often uncertain. This helps explain why the CPS prosecutes so many weak cases. Where the CPS drop a case, a conviction is lost, whereas one which is continued may result in conviction, notwithstanding its apparent weakness. The police know this, and also know that most cases will, in any event, terminate with a guilty plea. To attempt to secure more evidence in order to 'firm up' a prosecution case, or to clarify ambiguous statements made by witnesses, 'would often be, from the police point of view, wasted effort'.[18]

The outcome of cases is also dependant on the level of preparatory work carried out by the prosecution and the defence. In reality the defence rarely does more than respond to the prosecution case, so the level of care and effort that the police commit to a case is the crucial factor determining outcome. As earlier chapters have shown, police commitment is more a product of their own informal working rules and assumptions than officially sanctioned criteria such as the seriousness of the case. As a corollary, the minority of Crown court cases that go before a jury for determination range from the fairly trivial to the very serious, from the evidentially weak to those in which the prosecution appears to hold all the aces. It is important to keep this in mind when we consider (later) the various attempts that have been made to evaluate the performance of the jury and whether the acquittal rate by the jury is 'too high'.

We have suggested that practice in this area has been influenced by both due process and crime control values. These models do not help us determine how these tensions should be resolved and they leave out of consideration the interests of victims. It is not acceptable

---

[16] The influence on the police of changing public attitudes to offences involving vulnerable victims is discussed in Gregory J and Lees S, 'Attrition in Rape and Sexual Assault Cases' (1996) 36 *British Journal of Criminology* 1 at pp 2–8. And see the scandal involving Carl Beech (ch 1). For a discussion of whether the CPS has been effective in this endeavour, see ch 12.

[17] Zander M and Henderson P, *Crown Court Study* (Royal Commission on Criminal Justice, Research Study no 19) (London: HMSO, 1993) pp 184–185.

[18] McConville et al (1991: 171). Later research found the same attitude among some CPS lawyers: Baldwin J, 'Understanding Judge Ordered and Directed Acquittals in the Crown Court' [1997] *Criminal Law Review* 536.

to have defendants run the risk of conviction, particularly in a serious case, where the evidence is weak. But because resources are limited, the victim perspective contends that strengthening would be the better option in cases of seriousness, and discontinuing the better option in relatively trivial matters. In the 1990s, Crown prosecutors considered that, even if they were inclined to do so, they did not have the time or resources (legal, financial and organisational) to review cases thoroughly or to arrange for their strengthening.[19] As managerialism and actuarial approaches to prosecutions permeated the CPS,[20] time pressures placed on prosecutorial decision-making have increased, impacting upon the degree to which information and evidence can be analysed. Better Case Management was designed to encourage better case ownership among Crown prosecutors, and be supported by digital case management systems, but levels of case analysis and strategic planning remain problematic.[21] A majority of Crown court judges in the Judicial Attitudes Survey rated the quality of IT equipment as poor, while also raising concerns in the survey about decreased staff levels and increased stress.[22] Digitalisation in fact appears to have increased time pressures,[23] reducing the ability of prosecutors to identify and pursue evidential issues and lines of enquiry. Only 56.5% of cases analysed are properly and proportionately reviewed after the first court hearing.[24] Unfortunately, the government's interest is not so much to enhance CPS decision-making as to ensure that more offenders are brought (efficiently, effectively and economically) to justice, so the temptations to prosecute weak cases (given the realistic expectation that many of these will be disposed through guilty pleas) remain.[25]

Since Packer devised his models, the need for vulnerable victims to be empowered so that, for example, they feel able to attend court and give evidence if that is what they wish to do, has been recognised. It is too easy to assume that the retraction of a witness statement or the failure of a prosecution witness to appear at court is 'unforeseeable' and thus nobody's fault. Decisions by witnesses are not taken in a vacuum but are crucially affected by socio-economic factors and the shadow of the law and legal processes.[26] For example, one of us worked on the Baldwin study of non-jury acquittals (cited earlier) and saw from a reading of CPS files how vulnerable witnesses sometimes braved a court appearance only to find that the case was adjourned by the trial judge at the last minute. One can imagine the anxiety, inconvenience and frustration this may have caused. Not surprisingly some of these witnesses failed to appear subsequently. The time and convenience of civilian witnesses has historically ranked low in the priorities of those operating the Crown court.[27] The government belatedly recognised that inadequate 'witness care' leads to adjourned hearings, discontinuances and acquittals, and responded by setting up a *No Witness, No Justice* initiative. This requires the police and the CPS to support witnesses more closely through the prosecution process, including arranging pre-trial familiarisation visits to

---

[19] See Baldwin (1997: 547). Managerialism is discussed in ch 1.

[20] Porter A, 'Prosecuting Domestic Abuse in England and Wales: Crown Prosecution Service "Working Practice" and New Public Managerialism' (2019) 28(4) *Social & Legal Studies* 493–516.

[21] HMCPSI, *Better Case Management. A Snapshot* (2016a) online at: <https://www.justiceinspectorates.gov.uk/hmcpsi/wp-content/uploads/sites/3/2016/09/BCM_thm_Nov16_rpt.pdf> (accessed 10 March 2020).

[22] Thomas C, *2016 UK Judicial Attitude Survey* (London: UCL Judicial Institute, 2017).

[23] Porter (2019).   [24] HMCPSI (2016).   [25] This is more fully discussed in ch 7.

[26] Smith E, 'Victims in the Witness Stand: Socio-Cultural and Psychological Challenges in Eliciting Victim Testimony' in Tibori-Szabó K and Hirst M (eds), *Victim Participation in International Criminal Justice* (The Hague: T.M.C. Asser Press, 2017).

[27] See Rock P, *The Social World of an English Crown Court* (Oxford: Clarendon Press, 1993) ch 7.

the courts, and helping with travel and childcare.[28] There is some evidence that witnesses remain intimidated by the court process, as in this example:

> It just seems very scary when you go in because of the way the set up is and everything. But it has to be that way I know . . . you see all these people with their wigs on and the gowns. It's just very very frightening (Julia, Witness).[29]

9.3 The composition of the jury

In legal theory, jurors are selected at random so that juries will be reasonably socially representative (the 'democracy' core value). In practice, however, this principle has always been subject to exceptions and modifications. For centuries eligibility to serve on a jury was tied to a property qualification, making selection processes undemocratic.[30] Following the Juries Act 1974 (as amended by the Criminal Justice Act (CJA) 2003), a person is eligible for jury service if aged between 18 and 75 (extended from 70 in 2016), included on the electoral register and resident in the UK for at least five years since the age of 13. Whether the electoral register should be used as the only juror source list has been debated as certain groups, such as racialised minorities, the 20–24 age group, and renters, are likely to be under-represented on the register. However, Thomas has argued that there is no need to alter the juror source list to increase the proportion of racialised minorities summoned as they are summoned in proportion to their representation in the juror catchment area in almost every Crown court.[31] Thomas claims to have busted a long-standing myth that racialised minorities are under-represented on juries but, as we discuss, her findings still provide grounds for unease about the racial composition of juries.

Prior to the CJA 2003, many of those falling within the basic eligibility criteria were nonetheless ineligible, disqualified or excusable from jury service. The ineligible included those who might have an undue influence on a jury's deliberations, such as lawyers, judges and the police, and those who are seen as unsuited for a judgmental role, such as nuns, monks and the clergy. The disqualified included people convicted of serious crimes. Members of Parliament, the armed services and the medical profession had the right to be excused if summoned, while any person could be excused service if they could show good cause. Many people, particularly professionals, took advantage of this, so Lord Justice Auld, in his Review of the Criminal Courts, recommended that everyone should be eligible for jury service, save for those who are disqualified by reason of mental disorder or a serious criminal record (as before).[32] This was accepted; the CJA 2003 eliminated most excusals as of right and the categories of ineligibility.[33] The result was that low income, retired and

---

[28] See PA Consulting, *No Witness, No Justice—National Victim and Witness Care Project: Interim Evaluation Report* (December 2004). These services have since largely been outsourced to a specialist witness support service run by the Citizens' Advice Bureau: <https://www.citizensadvice.org.uk/about-us/citizens-advice-witness-service/> (accessed 15 July 2019). [29] Jacobson et al (2015: 66).

[30] For a detailed treatise on the problems with the jury system, see Blom-Cooper L, *Unreasoned Verdict* (Oxford: Hart Publishing, 2018).

[31] Thomas C, *Diversity and Fairness in the Jury System* (Ministry of Justice Research Series 2/07) (London: Ministry of Justice, 2007). See also Thomas C, 'Exposing the Myths of Jury Service' [2008] *Criminal Law Review* 415.

[32] Auld LJ, *Review of the Criminal Courts of England and Wales: Report* (London: TSO, 2001) para 5.13. For discussion of these proposals see McEwan et al, 'Evidence, Jury Trials and Witness Protection – The Auld Review of the English Criminal Courts' (2002) 6 *International Journal of Evidence and Proof* 163.

[33] Anyone sentenced in the past 10 years to a community order, drug order, or prison cannot serve as a juror and those who have at any time been sentenced to prison for five years or more are disqualified for life. For all the changes see CJA 2003, s.321 and Sch 33, amending the Juries Act 1974, s.1.

unemployed people became the least likely to serve.[34] Jury composition is still distorted in certain complex cases, where the anticipated length of the trial means that those with professional commitments may be unable or unwilling to take time off to serve.[35]

Since the disqualification for various criminal justice professionals sitting on juries was removed there have been several appeals against convictions alleging the appearance of jury bias.[36] In *Abdroikov*[37] the House of Lords stated that the test to be applied was whether a fair minded and informed observer would conclude there was a real possibility of unfairness beyond the reach of standard judicial warnings. Lord Bingham observed 'most adult human beings, as a result of their background, education, experience, harbour certain prejudices and predilections of which they may be conscious or unconscious... the safeguards established to protect the impartiality of the jury, when properly operated, do all that can reasonably be done to neutralise the ordinary prejudices and predilections to which we are all prone'.[38] Nevertheless he acknowledged that the allegations against police and prosecutors were not that they were subject to 'ordinary prejudices' but those which might stem from being professionally committed to one side of the adversarial conflict. This led the court to conclude that a CPS prosecutor should never sit as a juror in a CPS prosecution but could sit in a case where the prosecution was being brought by another prosecuting authority. Baroness Hale observed that junior CPS employees might also be allowed to sit as jurors for CPS prosecutions brought by areas other than where they were employed. The court concluded that since Parliament had made police officers eligible to serve there was no basis for disqualifying them simply because of their occupation; they should only be excluded if a challenge to police evidence comprised an important part of the case or if there was some connection between the police juror and a police witness beyond the fact they were from the same police area. Baroness Hale argued there was more distance between the police and the 'prosecution process' than is the case with a CPS lawyer, as police officers are only identified with the 'fight against crime generally rather than the prosecution process in particular'.[39] Those defendants who are unlucky enough to have random selection throw up a police officer on their jury, may not be much comforted by Baroness Hale's questionable distinction.

The courts seems to have taken a wide approach to interpreting *Abdroikov* that leans towards allowing criminal justice professionals to serve. In *Khan*,[40] the Court of Appeal considered the convictions of several defendants whose juries variously comprised serving police officers, prison officers and a CPS employee. The police officer juror in one trial knew a police witness in the case but the conviction was upheld as the court concluded an objective observer would not suspect bias. Another conviction was upheld in the case of a police officer juror called upon to assess a conflict between the evidence of the defendant and police witness, as the court said that the issue in conflict was of 'little significance'.[41] The CPS employee in one case was a former case worker employed as a press officer for the CPS at the time of the trial. The court said this did not create an appearance of bias because the prosecution was being brought by a non-CPS authority. In relation to prison officers

---

[34] Thomas (2007).
[35] Julian R, 'Judicial Perspectives on the Conduct of Serious Fraud Trials' [2007] *Criminal Law Review* 751. Senior judges interviewed supported the principle of random selection but acknowledged that professionals may get excused from long trials. See also section 9.7.
[36] In the first of these, *Pintori* [2007] EWCA Crim 1700, the Court of Appeal quashed the conviction because a juror in the case knew three police witnesses and had worked closely with one of them.
[37] [2007] UKHL 37.   [38] At [23].   [39] At [52].   [40] [2008] 2 Cr App R 13.
[41] To similar effect see *Burdett* [2009] EWCA Crim 543 in which there was an issue between the defendant and a police witness (the sole prosecution witness) but the court upheld the conviction despite a police officer sitting as a juror (and becoming the jury foreman) in the case.

it was stated that there was unlikely to be any (appearance of) bias against the defendant because this could only stem from suspicion that the prison officer juror might recognise the defendant as a former prisoner. The jurors in this case had not encountered the prisoners whilst they had been in prison on remand and in any event it was said knowledge of bad character would not automatically result in the juror ceasing to be independent and impartial. The court concluded by stating that trial judges should be made aware of any connection, past or present, potential jurors have with the administration of justice so that they can address the question of bias. The defendants in the case of the police officer who knew the police witness appealed to the ECtHR, which found that there had been a breach of the Art 6 right to a fair trial.[42] The case was returned to the UK courts, which ordered a re-trial for one defendant, where the evidence of the police witness was important, but not for the other.[43]

Judges are clearly reluctant to interfere with the principle of random selection to remove jurors who may be biased, or appear to be biased, against the defendant because of their professional occupation. This is despite, as the ECtHR noted in the above case, police officers not being allowed to serve on juries in many of the other jurisdictions that have jury trial, However, the principle of random selection has never been sacrosanct. There is a long history of attempts to rig the composition of the jury.[44] In certain cases the prosecution can carry out preliminary investigations into potential jurors, known as jury vetting, and use the information to 'stand by' (i.e. exclude) jurors before the trial begins. This came to light in the 1978 'ABC trial' of a soldier and two journalists for offences under the Official Secrets Act and was admitted in Parliament.[45] The Attorney-General's guidelines for the vetting of jury panels, which had existed as a 'restricted document' for three years previously, were then published.[46]

A 2012 redraft of the Attorney-General guidelines confirms that additional checks may be made with the security services and the police special branch in security and terrorism cases, and in cases of national security where part of the evidence is likely to be heard in a closed court. This is to counter the perceived 'danger that a juror's political beliefs are so biased as to go beyond normally reflecting the broad spectrum of views and interests in the community to reflect the extreme views of sectarian interest or pressure groups to a degree which might interfere with his fair assessment of the facts of the case or lead him to exert improper pressure on his fellow jurors'.[47] Since 'extreme views' is a term capable of wide interpretation there is clearly scope for abuse here.[48] A safeguard is that the Attorney-General must authorise each request for such additional checks, but this clearly does not constitute an independent check on state malpractice. It was said of the 2002 trial of David Shayler (a former MI5 officer charged with disclosing secret information) that the request to the Attorney-General to authorise security checks into the jury panel was the first since Labour came to power in 1997.[49] There may have been more checks since

---

[42] *Hanif and Khan v UK* (2011) (Application nos. 52999/08 and 61779/08).

[43] *Hanif & Anor, R v (No 2)* [2014] EWCA Crim 1678.

[44] See Freeman M, 'The Jury on Trial' (1981) *Current Legal Problems* 65 at pp 75–76 for examples drawn from the eighteenth and nineteenth centuries. For further examples from an even earlier period see Masschaele J, *Jury, State, and Society in Medieval England* (New York: Palgrave Macmillan, 2008) ch 3.

[45] HC Deb 5th Series, vol 958, col 28, 13 November 1978.

[46] *The Times* on 11 October 1978. On the right to stand by up to that time see McEldowney J, 'Stand By for the Crown – An Historical Analysis' [1979] *Criminal Law Review* 272.

[47] Attorney-General's jury vetting guidelines on when to use of right of stand by and what procedure to follow (2012) online at: <https://www.gov.uk/guidance/jury-vetting-right-of-stand-by-guidelines--2#guidelines> (accessed 15 July 2019).

[48] See, for example, East R, 'Jury Packing: A Thing of the Past?' (1985) 48 *Modern Law Review* 518 at 527–528.

[49] *The Guardian*, 29 July 2002.

then, particularly given the number of recent trials for terrorism offences. But the focus of any critical scrutiny should not merely be on the frequency with which authorisation is given, but also on the nature of the cases that trigger the procedure, the reliability of the information held or gathered by the security services, and the impact on jury selection.

The extent, nature and consequences of jury vetting are not known. The secrecy surrounding the practice is itself anti-democratic and a denial of due process values. Also, the prosecution is placed under no duty to 'stand by' (i.e. exclude) jurors when checks suggest that they might be biased against the defendant. Instead, the guidelines provide that:

> Information revealed in the course of an authorised check must be considered in line with the normal rules on disclosure.[50]

This falls short of mandating full disclosure to the defence. The defence may request a jury check via the DPP, and the National Police Chiefs Council indicates that checks will be made if requested by the DPP. All results will be sent to the DPP, who will decide what will be disclosed. There is no law that stops the defence from vetting a jury panel itself, although it might have difficulty in securing the names sufficiently in advance. The problem is most defendants do not have abundant resources and the Legal Aid Agency (LAA)[51] is unlikely to pay for a vetting exercise. The state authorities seem more concerned with ensuring a 'fair' hearing for the prosecution than for the defendant.

Other restrictions on the ability of the defence to influence the composition of the jury support this conclusion. The defence were traditionally allowed to exclude prospective jurors without the need to give any reason. The number of such 'peremptory challenges' allowed was reduced from 20 to seven in 1948 and to three (per defendant) in 1977 before being abolished by s.118 of the CJA 1987. In the White Paper that preceded the 1987 Act the government accepted that peremptory challenge might be used for proper reasons such as to adjust the age, sex or race balance on the jury, but contended that the defence sometimes abused the right so as to remove jurors thought to have too much respect for the law.[52] If the system was serious about prioritising the acquittal of the innocent, one might think that the occasional 'abuse' of the right of peremptory challenge would be regarded as a price worth paying for more representative juries. At the very least one would expect that the right of peremptory challenge in proper circumstances (as described in the White Paper) would be preserved in any reform of the law. Yet despite the timely publication of research showing that peremptory challenges had no discernible impact on the likelihood of acquittal,[53] the government successfully pressed through its plan to abolish this defence right in its entirety.[54] By contrast, the government resisted the powerful argument that fairness demanded that the prosecution should simultaneously lose its equivalent right to 'stand by' jurors without cause. Instead, the Attorney-General issued the guidelines exhorting, but not requiring, prosecutors to exercise this right more sparingly in future.

The defence continues to share with the prosecution the right to challenge any juror 'for cause', but this is of little practical use since jurors may not be questioned about their beliefs

---

[50] Attorney-General's jury vetting guidelines (2012) para 12.
[51] The LAA is responsible for managing publicly funded legal services. Its predecessor (the Legal Services Commission) was semi-independent from government, but the LAA was brought under the direct control of the Ministry of Justice in the Legal Aid, Sentencing and Punishment of Offenders Act 2012. See further ch 8.
[52] *Criminal Justice, Plans for Legislation* (Cmnd 9658) (London: Home Office, 1986) para 33.
[53] See Vennard J and Riley D, 'The Use of Peremptory Challenge and Stand By of Jurors and their Relationship to Final Outcome' [1988] *Criminal Law Review* 731.
[54] Critiqued by Gobert J, 'The Peremptory Challenge – An Obituary' [1989] *Criminal Law Review* 528.

or background unless counsel knows of facts to justify such questioning.[55] Where the fruits of a prosecution vetting are passed on to the defence, the generality of the information supplied may not be enough to support a challenge for cause. Usually defence counsel know no more than a juror's name. But in 2019 a senior police officer was tried for manslaughter as a result of his mishandling of a football crowd in Sheffield in 1989—there were 96 deaths, and hundreds of injuries (see discussion of 'Hillsborough' in chapter 11). A jury pool was given a questionnaire that sought to discover their football allegiances and connections with the police and other criminal justice agencies, as well as their capacity to serve on a lengthy trial. Sixty-eight of the 100 were excused.[56] You cannot help thinking this was not so much because the case was high profile as because the defendant was a police officer.

Jury vetting presents a dilemma for the state. It cannot be seen to interfere with the composition of the jury too readily as this will undermine the useful legitimising effect of jury trial on the criminal process as a whole.[57] Interference on security grounds also makes its refusal to countenance non-random selection to address the problem of racial bias look perverse. On the other hand, the desire to influence the outcome of a particular trial is sometimes overwhelming. The law both reflects this tension and provides for its resolution by enabling interference to take place on a covert basis. The prosecution may simply stand by a juror without giving any reason and the defence need not be told that jury vetting has taken place.[58] The prosecution's duties and powers are governed by broadly-drawn administrative directions and guidelines that provide no sanctions for breach. In stark contrast, the defence has to state reasons for challenging jurors and its more limited powers are governed by restrictive case law. The different treatment of prosecution and defence by the state authorities (including Parliament, the government and the courts) is revealing as to the dominant values in our political and legal culture and the subordination of 'justice' and 'democracy' to political control.

In most cases, the defence can form a visual impression as to the racial, class and age balance on the jury, and this raises the question of whether challenges can be made for cause to achieve a more mixed jury. A Practice Note issued in 1973 stressed that it would be wrong to allow the exclusion of jurors on such 'general' grounds as race, religion, political beliefs or occupation.[59] The Court of Appeal subsequently followed this up by declaring in *Ford*[60] that a judge had no discretion to discharge a juror in order to secure a racially-mixed jury nor otherwise to influence the overall composition of the jury. For the Court, '"fairness" is achieved by the principle of random selection'.[61] Whereas the government had suggested in its 1987 White Paper that it would be proper to peremptorily challenge so as to achieve a socially mixed jury, the courts subsequently denied the defence the ability to

---

[55] See *Chandler (No 2)* [1964] 1 All ER 761. See further Buxton R, 'Challenging and Discharging Jurors' [1990] *Criminal Law Review* 225. If there is prejudicial publicity in advance of the trial, the judge may direct that the jury should answer a questionnaire to test for bias, but this will only be done in fairly extreme cases: see *Andrews (Tracey)* [1999] Crim LR 156 and accompanying commentary. Compare this with the position in the United States where questioning of prospective jurors is standard practice: May R, 'Jury Selection in the United States: Are There Lessons to be Learned?' [1998] *Criminal Law Review* 270.

[56] See <https://www.itv.com/news/2019-01-14/jury-set-to-be-selected-ahead-of-hillsborough-manslaughter-trial/> (accessed 4 June 2020).

[57] Duff P and Findlay M, 'Jury Vetting – The Jury under Attack' (1983) 3 *Legal Studies* 159 at pp 171–173.

[58] If the CPS vetting guidelines are followed, however, the defence can work this out, as prosecutors are only supposed to stand-by jurors if *either* the juror is manifestly unsuitable 'but only if the defence agree', *or* in a terrorist or security case where the Attorney-General has authorised this course following a security check.

[59] [1973] 1 All ER 240.

[60] [1989] 3 All ER 445; followed in *Tarrant* [1998] Crim LR 342 where a conviction was quashed on the basis that the judge was wrong to discharge a jury on the basis that 11 out of 12 of them came from the same postal district, and wrong to direct that the new jury should be drawn from a panel brought in from outside the court's normal catchment area.

[61] [1989] 3 All ER 445 at 449.

challenge for cause on just this basis. Again, the fear seems to be that the defence will seek to 'rig' the jury in its favour. Yet little concern is evident that *random* selection from the available pool of jurors can never guarantee a *representative* jury.

The 2007 research by Thomas, which we discussed earlier, looked at the racial composition of juries and the influence of race on jury decision-making. It found that there was no under-representation of black and minority racialised groups sitting on juries in most of the Crown court centres studied. However, this research revealed that racially mixed juries are only likely to exist where non-white people make up at least 10% of the juror catchment area. Only just over one-fifth of Crown court centres fit this description, so in most centres there is little likelihood of non-white representation on the jury. Thomas concluded that this was a problem for courts where there were significant pockets of minority racialised populations in the catchment area, as in such places a high proportion of non-white defendants and victims faced all white juries.[62]

The importance of the racial composition of juries needs to be considered in the context of the influence that race may have on jury deliberations and verdicts. It has been argued that where the defendant is from an racialised group and there is no non-white representation on the jury there is 'the distinct possibility that the different life style, mentality and experience arising from membership of an racialised minority will not be taken sufficiently into account'.[63] John Kamara, whose conviction was overturned after he spent 19 years in prison for a murder that someone else confessed to committing, is a mixed race man who was convicted by an all-white jury in the context of race related riots that were occurring in the area at the relevant time. His request for the trial to be moved out of area was refused, and this was not an issue that troubled the Court of Appeal.[64] But more worrying still is the likelihood that all juries will be influenced by (at worst) conscious and (at best) unconscious racial biases when interpreting evidence and assessing witness credibility, and that these will remain unexamined and unchallenged if juries are drawn from too homogenous a racial background.[65] As Daly and Pattenden put it:

> To dismiss self-defence because those with dark skins are believed to incline to aggression is unacceptable. Other dangerous – but unfortunately all too common – stereotypes include: black people look much the same, do not respect the law and are sexually promiscuous; Muslims are terrorists or terrorist sympathizers; Jews are greedy; Asians are devious liars.[66]

Thomas attempted to explore the impact of racial composition of juries on outcome by using case simulations with 29 juries made up of real discharged jurors. The jurors saw a version of a filmed trial for assault in which a number of variables such as the defendant's race and the nature of the charge (racially aggravated/non-aggravated) were altered. All the juries were racially mixed. The study found that there was some evidence of same race leniency influencing the votes of individual jurors; non-white jurors were more likely to show

---

[62] Thomas (2007: 193–196). See also Thomas (2008).

[63] Bohlander M, ' "... By a Jury of his Peers" – The Issue of Multi-racial Juries in a Poly-ethnic Society' [1992] XIV(1) Liverpool LR 67.

[64] John Kamara was eventually released from prison in 2000 after the Court of Appeal quashed his conviction. But their decision was not based on any issue to do with the jury or their fact finding (there was also issues with the identification evidence which did not form part of the appeal—see ch 6), but was on the basis of the non-disclosure of more than 233 statements which could have been capable of assisting the defence case. This case provides an example of the appeal court's reluctance to interfere with jury decision-making as opposed to technical legal issues.

[65] We invite readers in doubt about this point to take the Race IAT test at <https://implicit.harvard.edu/implicit/uk/selectatest.jsp> (accessed 22 March 2019).

[66] Daly G and Pattenden R, 'Racial Bias and the English Criminal Trial Jury' (2005) 64(3) *Cambridge Law Journal* 678 at p 681 (internal citations omitted).

this leniency, which Thomas suggests was possibly because they felt the criminal justice system is racially biased. However, she concludes: 'The main finding of the decision-making study is that, while race can have a significant effect on the votes of some jurors in some cases, the verdicts of racially mixed juries on which these jurors sat did not discriminate against defendants based on the defendant's race.'[67] This finding of lack of racial bias in the verdicts of mixed juries is however likely to be of little comfort to non-white defendants who face all white juries. Thomas concedes that the crucial question is whether all white juries, which make up the vast majority of juries in the Crown court, discriminate against non-white defendants. In her updated study, Thomas analysed nearly 400,000 jury verdicts, noting that non-white defendants were disproportionately charged with some types of offence, and more likely to plead not guilty (see further chapter 10). She found that:

> Black, Asian and Other ethnicity defendants had a jury conviction rate of 66% compared to 64% for Mixed ethnicity and White defendants. These results are very similar to the 2010 findings in Are Juries Fair?, and these small differences in jury conviction rate by defendant ethnicity are a strong indication that factors other than ethnicity are likely to be more relevant to jury verdicts.[68]

Essentially, this study suggests that—unlike in the rest of the criminal justice system (chapter 10)—non-white defendants are not disproportionately convicted by juries. The study does report that black defendants have a higher conviction rate for drugs offences than white counterparts, but—perhaps significantly—no data on the composition of juries appears to have been analysed. Without knowing jury composition, it is not possible to determine how an all-white jury will decide a non-white defendant's case compared to mixed race jury deliberations.

Juries themselves believe that diversity is important in reaching a sound verdict free of bias,[69] and despite Thomas's research there is evidence from around the world that the racial composition of a jury does make a difference to verdicts.[70] There is also the point that justice should be seen to be done. In one study of perceptions of fairness, 10 out of 30 black interviewees who had been tried in the Crown court thought that the jury was racially biased or prejudiced against them.[71] An unknown number of defendants in Jacobson et el's (2015) study expressed mistrust of juries resulting from concerns about race, class and associated prejudices. So, even if prejudices do not affect outcomes, defendants perceive a problem, meaning that their trust in the system is likely to flounder.

In high-profile cases heard by all white juries it is not just non-white defendants (or victims) who may feel a sense of injustice, but also the community from which they are drawn. While noting that there is little English research on public attitudes to the racial composition of juries, Roberts and Hough (2009) cite one survey in which one-quarter of white respondents, but almost twice as many non-white respondents, said that they

---

[67] Thomas (2007: 201).

[68] Thomas C, 'Ethnicity and the Fairness of Jury Trials in England and Wales 2006–2014' (2017) 11 *Criminal Law Review* 860–876 at p 872.

[69] Matthew et al, *Jurors' Perceptions, Understanding, Confidence and Satisfaction in the Jury System: A Study in Six Courts*, Online Report 05/04 (London: Home Office, 2004) available at <https://webarchive.nationalarchives.gov.uk/20110218141448/http://rds.homeoffice.gov.uk/rds/pdfs2/rdsolr0504.pdf> (accessed 15 May 2020).

[70] Darbyshire et al (2001: 16–20). For a contrary view see McEwan et al (2002). See also Sommers S and Ellsworth P, 'How Much Do We Really Know about Race and Juries? A Review of the Social Science Theory and Research' (2003) *Chicago-Kent Law Review* 997; and Mueller-Johnson K, Dhami M and Lundrigan S, 'Effects of Judicial Instructions and Juror Characteristics on Interpretations of Beyond Reasonable Doubt' (2018) 24 *Psychology, Crime and Law* 117–133.

[71] Hood et al, *Ethnic Minorities in the Criminal Courts: Perceptions of Fairness and Equality of Treatment* (Research Series No 2/03) (London: DCA, 2003) pp 39–40.

would be concerned about the racial composition of the jury if they were on trial.[72] An extreme example from the USA was the Rodney King case in which a jury with no African-American jurors failed to convict white Los Angeles police officers of misconduct even though they had been videotaped kicking and beating an African-American suspect as he lay on the ground. This 'triggered the worst race riot in American history, two days of violence that cost 58 lives and nearly one billion pounds in property damage'.[73] Whilst the fraught history of unjust race relations in the United States provided the tinder box for this conflagration, it would be naive to think that England and Wales could never experience such problems.[74] As we have seen in earlier chapters, and discuss further in chapter 10, racialised groups often suffer disproportionately from the exercise of police powers and pre-trial discretion, and police–community relations are consequently poor. Anger at racial injustice in some communities in this country could be dangerously exacerbated by convictions (or acquittals, where the defendant is white but the victim is not) delivered by all white juries.

The incorporation through the Human Rights Act of the European Convention on Human Rights (ECHR) has not resulted in any great change in English law and practice concerning jury selection or jury composition. Whilst Art 6 gives defendants the right to a fair trial by an independent and impartial tribunal, the European Court of Human Rights (ECtHR) presumes that members of a tribunal are impartial unless there is evidence of subjective bias.[75] The argument that it is nigh impossible to produce such evidence in the British context, where juries do not give reasons for their decision, and that therefore the subjective presumption should not apply, was rejected by the ECtHR.[76] The Court accepts, however, that if an objective observer would have any ground for a legitimate doubt about a tribunal's impartiality that this is sufficient for a violation (objective bias).[77] Would an all-white jury trying a black defendant give rise to such a doubt? It seems not. In *Gregory v UK*,[78] the black defendant was convicted of robbery on a majority verdict and sentenced to six years' imprisonment. One hour after the jury had retired to consider its verdict, one juror sent a note to the judge reading 'jury showing racial overtones, one member to be excused'. The judge recalled the jury and told them that 'any thoughts of prejudice of one form or another, for or against anybody, must be put out of your minds' and that they must decide the case on the evidence alone. The ECtHR held that this redirection was sufficiently forceful to dispel any objectively held misgivings about the impartiality of the jury. Do you think Mr Gregory will have seen it that way? If you were one of his friends would you not have wanted the judge to identify the jurors showing 'racial overtones' and to have discharged them?[79] In answering these questions it is important to bear in mind the body of psychological research which shows that warnings are often ineffective in preventing or remedying prejudicial reasoning.[80] Given the judgment that a violation of the Convention did not occur in this case, it is simply inconceivable that a violation would be found on the sole ground that an all-white jury had determined the fate of an racialised defendant.

---

[72] BBC race survey cited in Roberts and Hough (2009: 27).
[73] Alschuler A, 'The All-white American Jury' (1995) 145 *New Law Journal* 1005.
[74] See further Herbert P, 'Racism, Impartiality and Juries' (1995) 145 *New Law Journal* 1138.
[75] See, for example, *Sigurdsson v Iceland* (2003) 40 EHRR 15 [37].
[76] *Pullar v UK* (1996) 22 EHRR 391.
[77] *Hanif and Khan v UK* (2011) (Application nos. 52999/08 and 61779/08).
[78] *Gregory v UK* (1997) 25 EHRR 577.
[79] The Juries Act, s.16 allows a jury to continue to hear a case with as few as nine members. Under s.17, a nine-member jury must be unanimous, whereas juries with 10 or 11 members can bring in verdicts so long as there is not more than one dissentient.
[80] See Daly and Pattenden (2005: 690–691) and the many studies cited there.

In a later case the ECtHR found a breach of Art 6 in fairly similar circumstances. Here a juror in the trial of two Asian defendants sent a note to the judge alleging that at least two other jurors were making racist remarks and jokes and that there was a danger that a racist conviction would follow. The judge informed the jury of the complaint and asked them to consider whether they felt able to try the case free of prejudice, solely on the evidence. The next day the judge received two inconsistent letters, one from the whole jury which denied the allegation and affirming their commitment to reach an unprejudiced decision, and one from an individual juror admitting to making racist jokes but denying he was racially biased. The judge decided not to discharge the jury, or any juror, and one of the defendants was convicted. Here the ECtHR decided that there were legitimate grounds for fearing that the tribunal was not impartial (objective bias) even if it could not be sure that the jury was actually prejudiced (subjective bias). It justified its decision in part on the basis that 'generally speaking, an admonition or direction by a judge, however clear, detailed and forceful, would not change racist views overnight' (para 30). That is consistent with the psychological research referred to earlier, but seemingly inconsistent with the ECtHR's stance in *Gregory*. That case was distinguished, however, on the basis that the complaint of racism was vague and not admitted by any juror.[81]

So it seems that if a precise and substantiated allegation of racism is made, the only course available to a trial judge may be to discharge the jury, or at least those jurors believed to be biased. This is a fairly minor inroad into the problem of jury bias, and more radical proposals, such as tape-recording jury deliberations,[82] have not found favour with government. Also, the courts are generally unwilling to investigate allegations of racism, or indeed other kinds of alleged juror bias, once a verdict has been given,[83] though allegations of jury bias are one area in which the Court of Appeal is known to ask for the assistance of the Criminal Cases Review Commission in conducting a review of the allegations.[84] The ECtHR has gone further than the domestic courts, stating that the secrecy of jury deliberations is a legitimate, crucial feature of English trials.[85]

9.4 The verdict of the jury

9.4.1 Majority verdicts

For centuries jury verdicts had to be unanimous but the CJA 1967 permitted a majority of not less than 10 out of 12, so long as the jury has been deliberating for at least two hours. This change has been seen by some critics as undermining the requirement that the prosecution proves guilt beyond reasonable doubt. As Freeman puts it: 'If one or two jurymen conscientiously feel strong enough to dissent from the majority view that demonstrates to my satisfaction that there is reasonable doubt as to the guilt of the accused.'[86] Others have seen majority verdicts as merely a means to prevent rogue jurors blocking convictions or acquittals.[87] The rationale for the 1967 reform was ostensibly to prevent

---

[81] *Sander v UK* (2001) 31 EHRR 44.   [82] Daly and Pattenden (2005).
[83] *Mirza* [2004] 1 AC 1118, discussed by Quinn K, 'Jury Bias and the European Convention on Human Rights: A Well-kept Secret?' [2004] *Criminal Law Review* 998. This makes it all the more important that trial judges deal with racial bias prior to verdict. A practice direction issued in the wake of *Mirza* now requires trial judges to warn jurors that they should bring any concerns about the behaviour of other jurors to their attention.
[84] For a review of this evidence, see Hoyle C and Sato M, *Reasons to Doubt. Wrongful Convictions and the Criminal Cases Review Commission* (Oxford: OUP, 2019). The Criminal Cases Review Commission is discussed in ch 11.   [85] *Seckerson and Times Newspapers Ltd v UK* [2012] ECHR 241.
[86] Freeman (1981: 69).   [87] Auld (2001: para 5.75).

professional criminals escaping conviction by the expedient of bribing or intimidating individual jurors. That this occasionally happens is undeniable. But the question remains of whether the majority verdict is the correct response to that problem.

In answering, one must consider the effect of the change. The introduction of majority verdicts led to a trebling of the rate at which juries fail to reach unanimity and nearly one in five (19%) of guilty verdicts are by majority.[88] As Freeman explains:

> juries when told by judges that they may consider a non-unanimous verdict simply stop deliberating when they reach the requisite majority. This may save time and money and it may be 'convenient' but how relevant should these considerations be? When managerial efficiency becomes the dominant consideration, justice can soon take a back seat.[89]

Researchers who have investigated the dynamics of jury decision-making have concluded that allowing juries to reach verdicts by a majority has resulted in them undertaking a less thorough investigation of the evidence and law,[90] and that juries required to reach unanimity were more inclined to find a defendant not guilty.[91] This is probably because those inclined to one view have less of a need to demonstrate convincing reasons why their opponents are wrong. Instead of allowing their deliberations to be 'evidence-driven' the majority reaches for the verdict it thinks right and then constructs a narrative story of the case that fits that verdict. Unsurprisingly, heterogeneous juries (where differing interpretations of the facts are to be expected) are more likely to engage in lengthy evidence-led deliberations than homogeneous ones.[92] This increases the case against all white juries that we set out earlier.

Majority verdicts have thus prodded jury trial in the direction of crime control. The argument that this was necessary in order to guard against 'jury nobbling' is similar to that used to deny bail to defendants on the ground that they might otherwise interfere with prosecution witnesses.[93] In both cases the argument appears to give greater weight to the conviction of the guilty at the expense of the acquittal of the innocent. In both cases there is a more appropriate response, which is to safeguard the administration of justice by other means, such as more effective protection for witnesses and jurors. The judge can, for example, make a jury protection order, under which the police will provide protection for members of the jury during the course of the trial.[94] Also allegations of 'nobbling' need to be investigated with urgency. In 2016 the Court of Appeal was very critical of the poor police investigation in a rape case.[95] The vast majority of trials do not involve professional criminals and so there is usually no risk of 'jury nobbling'. The solution adopted, allowing (in all cases) the views of one-sixth of the jury to be dismissed as 'unreasonable',

---

[88] Freeman (1981: 70). In 1992 the figure was nearer one in eight: Judicial Statistics 1992 (Cm 2268) (London: HMSO, 1993) p 62, table 6.10, but has sat steadily at around 20% since 2007 (Ministry of Justice (2018) *Criminal Court Statistics (annual)*.

[89] Freeman (1981: 70). See also Darbyshire P, 'Notes of a Lawyer Juror' (1990) 140 *New Law Journal* 1264 at p 1266.

[90] See, in particular, Hastie et al, *Inside the Jury* (Cambridge, MA: Harvard UP, 1983). An accessible summary to the research in this area is provided by Darbyshire et al (2001: 29–32).

[91] Ormston R, Chalmers J, Leverick F, Munro V and Murray L, *Scottish Jury Research: Findings from a Large Scale Mock Jury Study* (2019) online at: <http://nen.press/wp-content/uploads/2019/10/scottish-jury-research-findings-large-scale-mock-jury-study.pdf> (accessed 20 April 2020).

[92] Arce R, 'Evidence Evaluation in Jury Decision-Making' in Bull R and Carson D (eds), *Handbook of Psychology in Legal Contexts* (Chichester: Wiley, 1995).   [93] On bail, see ch 8.

[94] The potential prejudice or fear this might cause in the minds of the jury should be addressed by some explanatory remarks by the trial judge: *Comerford* [1998] 1 Cr App Rep 235. The same case decides that a trial judge may take the precautionary step of having the members of the jury referred to by numbers instead of the more usual procedure of stating their names in open court as they are sworn in.

[95] *McManaman* [2016] EWCA Crim 3.

appears grossly disproportionate to the supposed problem. Moreover, determined 'nobblers' can evade the supposed safeguard by the simple expedient of intimidating three or more jurors. In August 2002, for example, the trial of six defendants in Liverpool for serious drug offences collapsed after two jurors were threatened and a third offered £10,000 to return a verdict of not guilty.[96] In June 2020 a builder and his wife were convicted of perverting the course of justice after handing £20 notes to jurors.[97]

While there has long been a common law offence of perverting the course of justice, Parliament created a new offence of intimidating witnesses and jurors by s.51(1) of the Criminal Justice and Public Order Act 1994. Two years later it went further by enacting a new procedure for re-opening acquittals allegedly tainted by interference with the administration of justice.[98] Seven years on came s.44 of the CJA 2003, which allows the prosecution to apply to a Crown court judge to make an order for non-jury trial. The judge must make this order if there is evidence of a 'real and present danger that jury tampering would take place' and that notwithstanding any steps (including the provision of police protection) which might reasonably be taken to prevent tampering, the likelihood that it would take place would be so substantial as to make it necessary in the interests of justice for the trial to be heard without a jury. Section 46 CJA 2003 allows the judge to discharge the jury and continue alone if he is satisfied that jury tampering has occurred. The provisions of s.44 CJA 2003 were first used in *Twomey*,[99] despite his lawyer's arguments that the information upon which the fear of jury tampering was based had never been disclosed. A previous trial had collapsed amidst an allegation of jury tampering, and information about that was provided only to the judge. Twomey's subsequent complaint to the ECtHR was not upheld, and the ECtHR stated that the right to a fair trial did not necessarily mean that there had to be a trial by jury—both trial by judge alone and trial by jury are equally acceptable under the ECHR.[100] The decision was followed in *McManaman*,[101] though the Court of Appeal did offer further guidance on that occasion. The guidance was to the effect that:

- The judge must be satisfied beyond a reasonable doubt that jury tampering had occurred.
- Where the benefits of further evidence outweighed the need for a rapid decision, the judge should wait for the results of any police investigation.
- The judge does not need to be sure that the defendant was involved in tampering, just that tampering has occurred.
- While case law in relation to s.44 indicates it should only be used a last resort, the same is not said of s.46. In relation to s.46, the judge must only consider whether it is fair to the defendant to continue without a jury, and whether it is in the interests of justice to terminate the trial.

These provisions are all aimed at removing any possible advantage to those tempted to nobble a jury, so the balance is in favour of continuing a trial without a jury. Implicit in this is the assumption that defendants want to delay their cases, even when the nobbling need have nothing to do with a defendant. The creation of these new 'safeguards' against jury

---

[96] For this and other examples see Hansard HL col 1963 (19 November 2003).
[97] *Mail On-Line*, 5 June 2020. And see *The Guardian*, 19 April 2018 for a Scottish example of a juror taking a bribe.
[98] Criminal Procedure and Investigations Act 1996, ss.54–57. That inroad into the rule against double jeopardy was subsequently extended by Part 10 of the CJA 2003. [99] [2009] EWCA Crim 1035.
[100] *Twomey and Cameron v the United Kingdom* (Application no 67318/09). This was a joined appeal involving another jury-less trial; *Guthrie v the United Kingdom* (Application no 22226/12). Both appeals were dismissed. [101] [2016] EWCA Crim 3.

nobbling did not lead to any reassessment by the government of the 'need' for majority verdicts. As in other areas of the criminal process, once a due process safeguard is dismantled or weakened, the chances of it being resurrected are slim.

In so far as the 'extremist' argument is used to justify majority verdicts, there is a double standard at work. By definition, people of extreme views are in a minority in the populace at large. Most juries will have no such jurors and so the problem will rarely arise. The danger of an extremist very occasionally blocking a justifiable conviction (or acquittal) has to be weighed against the overall due process cost of allowing a majority verdict to be returned in any and every criminal case. Like the argument for jury vetting, the extremist argument claims that the random selection principle cannot be trusted in cases where fierce racialised or political conflicts are involved. There is some truth in this and that is precisely why racialised groups demand some black people on juries when the defendant is black. Yet this has been rejected by the government and the courts. In short, the argument that random selection is defective is accepted when this serves prosecution interests, but not otherwise.

Majority verdicts also apply to acquittals in the sense that a defendant is acquitted if at least 10 out of 12 jurors vote for a verdict of not guilty. If a jury cannot reach at least a majority verdict, it is said to be 'hung' and the prosecution may opt for a retrial, or may choose to review and discontinue the case. This symmetry with the requirement for a guilty verdict is impossible to reconcile with the presumption of innocence. For whenever between three and nine jurors vote for acquittal, the prosecution has failed to prove guilt and the presumption of innocence would demand that the defendant be acquitted. Instead, the English system allows guilt or innocence to remain an open question pending a retrial.[102]

9.4.2 The conduct of the trial by the judge

Judges can influence jury verdicts. Historically juries were commonly told by judges what verdicts to return and, although juries had the right in legal theory to rebel, they seldom did so. The advent of defence lawyers in the eighteenth century broke up this cosy relationship between judge and jury, moving the criminal trial much closer to the adversarial ideal with a passive and impartial judge.[103] The judgment by Lord Denning in *Jones v National Coal Board*[104] is generally regarded as the classic statement of the modern position:

> The judge's part in [an adversarial trial] is to hearken to the evidence, only himself asking questions of witnesses when it is necessary to clear up any point that has been overlooked or left obscure; to see that the advocates behave themselves seemly and keep to the rules laid down by law; to exclude irrelevancies and discourage repetition; to make sure by wise intervention that he follows the points the advocates are making and can assess their worth; . . . If he goes beyond this, he drops the mantle of a judge and assumes the robe of an advocate . . .

Only in this century was it made clear law that a judge may not direct a jury to convict in any circumstances.[105] Since judges may direct an acquittal but not a conviction the law on this point reflects the due process stance that wrongful convictions are a greater evil than wrongful acquittals. The same position underlies the duty of the judge to put before the jury any defence which arises from the evidence even if not explicitly raised by defence

---

[102] Statistics on this issue are not published as a matter of course although a Freedom of Information request revealed that there were 157 hung juries between January and September 2017, and 42 of those defendants were convicted after a re-trial. See Ministry of Justice, FOI request 171220007.

[103] Langbein J, 'The Criminal Trial Before Lawyers' (1978) 45 *University of Chicago Law Review* 263 at p 314.

[104] *Jones v National Coal Board* [1957] 2 QB 55 at 64.   [105] *Wang* [2005] UKHL 9.

counsel.[106] But other aspects of the legal framework governing trials give conviction-minded judges ample scope to influence the jury.

The judgment in *Jones v National Coal Board* accepts that judges may properly ask some questions and make some interventions, but its tone suggests that these should be limited in number and scope. In reality, judges have considerable freedom.[107] In *Webb; Simpson*,[108] for example, the Court noted that:

> The judge asked 175 questions, and it is clear that at times he was assuming the role of a prosecutor and was not displaying appropriate judicial impartiality. Even when he was factually in error defence counsel was not permitted to intervene to correct him.

The conviction was nonetheless upheld as safe. Part of the problem here is the Court of Appeal's tendency to focus on whether the conviction is reliable rather than on whether it was fairly obtained (chapter 11). What should matter is whether the degree of intervention from the Bench compromised the appearance or substance of judicial impartiality.[109] The appellate courts seem unable or unwilling to grasp this point. In *Hircock*,[110] the trial judge had muttered 'Oh God', and groaned and sighed throughout defending counsel's closing speech. Surely such gross discourtesy undermined the fairness of the trial. The Court of Appeal decided, however, that the judge's behaviour did not reflect any view of the defendant's case, but was simply implicit criticism of the conduct of the case by defence counsel. One cannot help wondering whether the jury appreciated this subtle distinction. In more extreme cases, interventions may be so frequent and hostile as to amount to a denial of the defendant's right to have his evidence considered by the jury. Where this is so, the appellate courts have little choice but to declare the trial unfair. An example is *Perren*[111] in which the trial judge frequently interfered in the examination in chief in a manner that was hostile and suggested incredulity. The Court of Appeal held that the defendant's story might have been highly improbable but he was entitled to have it heard without being subjected to 'sniper fire'. It appeared to be of particular significance that the judge had effectively subjected the defendant to cross-examination before the prosecution got the opportunity to perform what is, in the adversarial system, their designated role.

Much judicial behaviour is relatively immune from subsequent challenge as it will not appear on the transcript of court proceedings. In *Bryant*,[112] however, a defence barrister and a solicitor's representative both made witness statements to the effect that a trial judge had shown bias during the development of the defence case by sighing, rolling his eyes, and throwing down his pen or papers in exasperation. And Counsel for the Crown conceded that this judge was well known for making such gestures when impatient with the conduct of those appearing before him. The Court of Appeal said it was wholly impermissible for a judge to indicate to a jury in this way that he or she favoured one side or the other, so the conviction was quashed (and a retrial ordered). We can only guess how often this trial judge, and others like him, get away with such behaviour. Note also that the appellate judiciary are unable to criticise or remedy excessive interventions in cases that result in acquittals. This is because there is generally no appeal from an acquittal.[113] Thus

---

[106] See Doran S, 'Alternative Defences: The "Invisible" Burden on the Trial Judge' [1991] *Criminal Law Review* 878.

[107] For reviews of the case law, see Doran S, 'Descent to Avernus' (1989) 139 *New Law Journal* 1147, and Jackson J and Doran S, *Judge Without Jury* (Oxford: Clarendon Press, 1995) pp 104–110.

[108] *Webb; Simpson* [2000] EWCA Crim 56.

[109] ECtHR case law on the ECHR, Art 6 requirement for an *impartial* tribunal would seem to support this position.   [110] [1969] 1 All ER 47.

[111] [2009] EWCA Crim 348.   [112] [2005] EWCA Crim 2079.

[113] Part 9 of the CJA 2003 does give the prosecution the ability to appeal against adverse judicial rulings during trials on indictment. Since the abolition of the double jeopardy rule by the CJA, an acquittal can, exceptionally, be reopened with the permission of the Court of Appeal where there is compelling new evidence.

trial judges can harangue or undermine prosecution lawyers and witnesses with little fear that the case will result in an appeal.

The appellate cases just discussed give an indication of the scope for judicial intervention and provide extreme examples of behaviour by trial judges. By their nature they cannot, however, tell us the frequency with which trial judges *typically* question witnesses or interrupt counsel, the nature of those interventions, or whether such interventions are welcomed by other participants. What little research evidence there is shows considerable variation between judges.[114] Jackson and Doran studied 17 jury trials in Northern Ireland presided over by nine different judges. They found that of the 77 judicial objections to counsel's questioning, two-thirds (54) were made by just two judges in three of the trials. By contrast, four of the judges made no more than one objection per trial they heard. This study also found that one judicial question was asked every 5.5 minutes during the taking of oral evidence from witnesses. Much of this questioning was legitimate in that it was designed to clarify evidence, but 14% of defence witnesses (compared with 6% of prosecution witnesses) were subjected to inquisitorial questioning designed to elicit new information.[115] In other words, the judges often did take on the robe of an advocate. The authors were unable to settle upon an explanation for this greater tendency to probe defence witnesses but note that it may have been that the judges observed were simply more disposed to believe the prosecution evidence. Not surprisingly, they found that 'prosecution counsel were generally happier about judicial questioning than defence counsel'.[116] In England and Wales, the Crown court survey carried out for the Runciman Commission found no support from either prosecuting or defence counsel for more 'robust interventions' from the judge. Where judges had intervened in trials, the interruptions favoured the prosecution much more frequently than they did the defence.[117]

The Runciman Commission[118] advocated that judges should be more interventionist in conducting trials in order to save time and money and because shorter trials would make it easier for jurors to recall the essential facts. It also wanted judges to prevent witnesses being 'subjected to bullying and intimidatory tactics by counsel or to deliberately and unnecessarily prolonged cross-examination'. It brushed aside the suggestion that such interventions might give the 'impression of bias' and failed to acknowledge the impact its proposals would have on the adversarial theory of justice which asserts that the production and presentation of evidence must be left to the parties in dispute.[119] Moreover, its proposals evidence a degree of trust in judicial impartiality that scarcely seems justified on the track record of the courts.

A number of developments since Runciman have required trial judges to take a more interventionist stance.[120] In particular, we saw earlier how judges are now expected actively to manage cases (e.g. by ensuring that evidence, whether disputed or not, is presented in the clearest and shortest way)[121] and also to encourage plea bargaining (chapter 8). The latest additions to the Criminal Procedure Rules make clear that judges are expected to ever more intervene in cases to ensure efficient case progression, reflecting an alignment of judicial and executive aims to ensure cost efficiency instead of principled engagement with the ideals of adversarial justice,[122] and a move away further away from the impartial passive judge described by Lord Denning in 1957. We saw that in *Bryant*,[123] the trial judge

---

[114] See Fielding N, *Courting Violence: Offences against the Person Cases in Court* (Oxford: OUP, 2006) pp 145–158).   [115] Jackson and Doran (1995).
[116] Ibid: 160–162.   [117] Zander and Henderson (1993: 137–138).   [118] RCCJ (1993: 122).
[119] See ch 1 for discussion.
[120] See Doran S, 'The Necessarily Expanding Role of the Criminal Trial Judge' in Doran S and Jackson J (eds), *The Judicial Role in Criminal Proceedings* (Oxford: Hart, 2000).
[121] Rule 3.2(e), Criminal Procedure Rules.   [122] See McConville and Marsh (2020).
[123] [2005] EWCA Crim 2079.

went too far in demonstrating his impatience with those conducting the defence. But the Court of Appeal said that it would support trial judges who helped cases to proceed at a reasonable speed, and who, with that end in mind, robustly rebuked counsel who developed their cases too sluggishly. This illustrates the tightrope that trial judges must now walk. There is an inevitable clash here between the core values of justice and efficiency. This is not just a simple clash between due process and crime control principles, however, as neither model adequately caters for victims and other witnesses. When the conduct of the case is left to defence and prosecution lawyers, victims often suffer. And as we discuss in chapter 10, victims in sexual assault cases in particular not only sometimes deserve to be protected against aggressive defence counsel, but relatively new legislation requires judges to use their discretion whether to allow certain types of questioning by defence counsel; there are many who believe judges are not sufficiently interventionist enough in this respect.[124]

Following the 'freedom' approach (chapter 1), arguments and policy decisions about judicial intervention should be grounded in clear principles and empirical evidence that takes into account the various interests at stake. The ECtHR has provided an important lead here in suggesting that victims' interests, not just defendants' rights, are part of the Art 6 right to a fair trial.[125] In a similar vein the Court of Appeal ruled in *Brown (Milton Anthony)*[126] that: 'It is the clear duty of the trial judge to do everything he can, consistently with giving the defendant a fair trial, to minimise the trauma suffered by other participants'. Parliament, through the Youth Justice and Criminal Evidence Act 1999 (YJCEA), has provided trial judges with various 'special measures' and devices, such as video-recorded examination in chief and giving evidence by live link, to encourage them to safeguard the interests of fearful or vulnerable witnesses in court. Following guidance issued in *Lubemba*,[127] Criminal Procedure Rule 3.9 incorporated provisions that allow judges to order the parties to reduce proposed questions of witnesses to writing in advance of the trial and submit them to the court (and an intermediary, if relevant) for consideration at a Ground Rules hearing. The judge is then entitled to place restrictions on questioning. This approach was very quickly approved in *Sandor Jonas*.[128] However, *R v SG*[129] indicates that trial judges must also be mindful of the need for counsel to develop lines of cross examination. In that case, involving a witness who was intimidated but mature and articulate, the judge should not have asked for a list of questions to be submitted, even though the court concluded that there had been no unfairness to the defendant. We suspect the defendant did not see things that way.

Another measure that has recently been piloted in Crown courts in England and Wales is found in the provisions of s.28 YJCEA, which allows for the cross examination of vulnerable witnesses to be conducted in advance of the actual trial, to be recorded and then played to the jury. This is designed to modernise the court system (for which we could read save time and money), as well as to spare vulnerable complainants the potential revictimisation caused by attending court to give evidence. Research has been conducted on the potential influence this could have on juror deliberations, in light of concerns that defendants' right to fair trials could be compromised by being unable to confront their accusers in the traditional adversarial way. Assessments about body language and non-verbal cues could be missed by the jury to the detriment of the defendant. The research concluded

---

[124] See ch 10; and, for example, Brereton D, 'How Different are Rape Trials? A Comparison of the Cross-Examination of Complainants in Rape and Assault Trials' (1997) 37 *British Journal of Criminology* 242; Smith O and Skinner T, 'How Rape Myths Are Used and Challenged in Rape and Sexual Assault Trials' (2017) 26(4) *Social & Legal Studies* 441–466.
[125] See *Doorson v Netherlands* (1996) 23 EHRR 330 and the discussions in chs 1 and 12.
[126] [1998] 2 Cr App Rep 364 at 391.   [127] [2014] EWCA Crim 2064.
[128] [2015] EWCA Crim 209.   [129] [2017] EWCA Crim 617.

that vulnerable witnesses benefit from being able to give entirely pre-recorded evidence, while the:

> evidence does not establish a significant risk of negative juror influence associated with the use per se of pre-recorded testimony by either child or adult witnesses. Some—but by no means all—studies suggest a preference on the part of jurors for evidence that is presented live in court, but in simulations with a group deliberative component, mimicking actual jury decision-making, the broad consensus of researchers to date has been that this preference does not impact significantly upon verdict outcomes.[130]

This finding must, however, be set in the context of two needs. First, for further research into this issue.[131] Second, for better equipment and training. In a case where faulty equipment meant the witness was not visible and that the jury were consequently unable to assess demeanour, the conviction was nonetheless considered safe.[132] This is a clear indication that the senior judiciary wants cases to be able to proceed regardless of technical difficulties, and is reluctant to interfere with trial judges' decisions.

Whilst this concern for victims and witnesses is welcome, the YJCEA overlooks the fact that trial judges are sometimes directly responsible through their own questioning for the 'trauma' suffered by witnesses in court. There is no recognition by criminal justice policy-makers that some trial judges can and do exhibit bias, more often than not against the defence, through their interventions during a trial. As we have seen, such behaviour is inadequately regulated by the senior judiciary. Also, defendants, who were originally specifically excluded from the 'special measures' introduced by the YJCEA, are still treated less favourably than prosecution witnesses. The fact is that defendants can be vulnerable or fearful in the same way as victims. Cross-examination by the prosecution can be just as humiliating or offensive as cross-examination by the defence,[133] and research suggests that defendants who are accompanied by an intermediary are viewed more favourably by jurors.[134] Defendants and victims are not distinct groups of people, and government concern for 'justice' remains distinctly one-sided,[135] as we discuss further in chapter 12.

9.4.3 Summing up by the judge

The last word in a contested trial before the jury retires to consider its verdict is always that of the judge. The judge explains the law to the jury and provides them with a summary of the evidence.[136] In that summary, the jury are told to draw on their life experiences and use their common sense, but to avoid sympathy and speculation, which appears to be

---

[130] Munro V, *The impact of the use of pre-recorded evidence on juror decision-making: an evidence review* (Edinburgh: Scottish Government, 2018) p iii.

[131] Further research is indeed being conducted by Cheryl Thomas at the time of writing, with a report due imminently. See <https://www.nuffieldfoundation.org/juries-digital-courtroom-and-special-measures> (accessed 20 April 2020).   [132] *PMH* [2018] EWCA Crim 2452.

[133] As where racial stereotypes are invoked against black defendants: Kalunta-Krumpton A, 'The Prosecution and Defence of Black Defendants in Drug Trials' (1998) 38 *British Journal of Criminology* 561.

[134] Smethurst A and Collins K, 'Mock Jury Perceptions of Vulnerable Defendants Assisted in Court by Intermediaries—Are Juror's Expectations Violated?' (2019) 15(1) *Applied Psychology in Criminal Justice* 23–40.

[135] See Fairclough S, '"It Doesn't Happen . . . and I've Never Thought it was Necessary for it to Happen": Barriers to Vulnerable Defendants Giving Evidence by Live Link in Crown Court Trials' (2017) 21(3) *International Journal of Evidence and Proof* 209; Fairclough S, 'Speaking up for Injustice: Reconsidering the provision of special measures through the lens of equality' [2018] *Criminal Law Review* 4–19.

[136] On the extent of this judicial obligation see *Amado-Taylor* [2000] Crim LR 618 and accompanying commentary.

somewhat inconsistent.[137] This gives judges another opportunity to influence the outcome of the trial, and some famous miscarriages of justice have resulted. Thus in the case of Derek Bentley (hanged in 1953) the eminent trial judge (Lord Goddard CJ) suggested in his summary of the evidence that, as witnesses, the police were likely to be accurate and reliable, and defendants inaccurate and unreliable. When the case was referred back to it in 1998, the Court of Appeal concluded that: 'The language used was not that of a judge but of an advocate . . . Such a direction by such a judge must in our view have driven the jury to conclude that they had little choice but to convict'.[138] The most notorious modern example of a biased summing up was in the trial of the 'Birmingham Six', where Bridge J over a three-day summing up skilfully led the jury by the nose to a verdict of guilty.[139] He began by telling the jury that 'however hard a judge tries to be impartial, inevitably his presentation of the evidence is bound to be coloured by his own view'. He then left them in no doubt as to what that view might be.[140] For example, he sought to depict the defence contention that the police had fabricated evidence and lied in court as far-fetched:

> If the defendants are giving you honest and substantially accurate evidence, there is no escape from the fact that the police are involved in a conspiracy to commit a variety of crimes which must be unprecedented in the annals of British criminal history.

Mr Justice Bridge made this performance virtually appeal-proof, however, by continually reminding the jurors that it was for them, not him, to decide where the truth lay. Where this formalistic incantation is omitted, the Court of Appeal has sometimes intervened. Thus in *Berrada*,[141] the judge observed that the defendant's allegations of police misconduct were 'really monstrous and wicked'. The Court of Appeal rebuked the judge, declaring that her duty was to sum up impartially without seeking to inflate evidence by 'sarcastic and extravagant comment'.[142] And in *Wood*,[143] the Court of Appeal accepted that the degree of permissible adverse comment was substantially less than 50 years earlier. More temperate language from the judge is all that the law requires, however. In *DPP v Stonehouse*, for example, Lord Salmon opined that it would be in order for a judge in an appropriate case to sum up to the jury 'in such a way as to make it plain that he considers the accused is guilty and should be convicted'.[144] And in *Kelleher* the Court of Appeal said trial judges, when they think a not guilty verdict would be perverse, may say to the jury 'you may think that there can only be one verdict in this case and that is one of guilty. . .'[145]

It does depend on the strength of the evidence. In the third (and successful) appeal by the Birmingham Six the Court of Appeal acknowledged the forceful nature of the summing up by Bridge J, but did not accept that this had vitiated the proceedings. As Lloyd LJ put it, 'the judge also made it clear throughout the summing-up that it was for the jury, and not for him, to determine where the truth lay'.[146] However, if a summing up is seen

---

[137] Jacobson et al (2015).   [138] *Bentley (Deceased)* [1998] EWCA Crim 2516; [1999] Crim LR 330.
[139] Excerpts from the transcript of the trial are reproduced (with critical commentary) by Wood J in Walker C and Starmer K (eds), *Miscarriages of Justice* (London: Blackstone, 1999) p 226. See also in the same book the discussion by Jackson J, 'Trial Procedures' (at p 199) on the summing up in the Carl Bridgewater case.
[140] After the jury convicted, the judge commented that the evidence in the case was the clearest and most overwhelming he had ever heard.   [141] (1989) 91 Cr App Rep 131.
[142] See also *Osborne-Odelli* [1998] Crim LR 902 and *Gibbons and Winterburn* (22 June 1993) in which convictions were quashed because of an unfair summing up by the trial judge. Amongst many other prejudicial comments the trial judge in the latter case had referred to the defendant as an 'an old lag trying to go straight'. See the discussion by Robertshaw P, *Summary Justice* (London: Cassell, 1998) pp 26–28.
[143] [1996] 1 Cr App R 207.   [144] [1978] AC 55 at 80. See also the speech by Lord Edmund-Davies.
[145] [2003] EWCA Crim 3525, per Mantell LJ, whose judgment was described by the House of Lords in *Wang* [2005] UKHL 9 to be 'a very lucid and accurate exposition of the law'. See also *Bryant* [2005] EWCA Crim 2079.
[146] *McIlkenny* (1991) 93 Cr App Rep 287 at 293.

as fundamentally unbalanced, it cannot be saved by the constant repetition of the phrase 'these are matters for you, the jury, to decide'.[147] Although the Court of Appeal recently endorsed this position in *Reynolds*, at the same time it upheld the conviction because it thought the summing up 'on balance' was fair.[148]

One danger in giving judges such freedom of manoeuvre is that they are privy to evidence that the jury may not be (see section 9.5), and may therefore be biased against the defendant. On the other hand, judges sometimes make clear in their summary of the evidence that they think an acquittal the right result, as in the Stephen Waldorf case in which the two police officers on trial had shot and pistol-whipped an innocent man by mistake.[149] In general, judges simply get case-hardened and sceptical about defendants, particularly when they are not seen as respectable characters. This issue is compounded by Griffiths's argument that judges tend to be politically conservative and seek to uphold the social status quo.[150] McConville and Marsh (2020) argue against the assumption that class structure necessarily results in bias, and point to research that demonstrates a much more nuanced and context dependent relationship between politics, class and judicial decision-making. They do also, however, go on to argue that political influence (in terms of aligned state and public interest views) is strong at the senior levels of judiciary and in the Court of Appeal,[151] by which decisions Crown court judges are bound. Case hardening is one of the central arguments for employing a jury to decide questions of fact. Extensive judicial intervention introduces into trials the very problem that the use of juries is meant to avoid—prejudice.

How frequent are biased summings up? In research that would benefit from updating, Zander and Henderson (1993) report that, according to prosecutors, in over 1,000 cases in 1992 the judge summed up against the weight of the evidence, while the figure was more than 2,000 (nearly 10% of all cases tried by jury) according to defence barristers. Prosecuting barristers tended to think that most summings up against the weight of the evidence favoured acquittals. According to defence barristers, however, in 92% of the cases where the summing up was identified as biased in this sense, the bias was towards conviction.[152] In half of these cases the jury convicted.[153]

The Court of Appeal sometimes defends trial judges making comments 'one way or the other' on the basis that juries 'are more robust than people often give them credit for'.[154] How can we know that juries ignore biased comments in the absence of research evidence? Theoretically, one would expect there to be at least some influence. First, the summaries are clearly intended to influence the jury else there would be no point in making them, and can become exploited to take the form of judicial advocacy.[155] Members of the jury are

---

[147] *Mears* [1993] 1 WLR 818 at 822.

[148] [2020] 4 WLR 16: if the judges comments 'constitute the appearance of advocacy on behalf of the prosecution, they will not necessarily be regarded as appropriate simply because the jury had been told that they are not bound to accept the judge's views or by the use of the timeless refrain, it is entirely a matter for you.'

[149] See *The Times*, 19 October 1983.

[150] Griffith J, *The Politics of the Judiciary* 5th edn (London: Fontana Press, 1997). See issues related to gender bias and the judiciary in ch 10.

[151] It is also worth noting, however, that only 2% of salaried judges reportedly feel valued by the government (*2016 UK Judicial Attitudes Survey* (2017)).

[152] Note that this does not mean that prosecution and defence counsel were disagreeing about where the bias lay in particular cases, since they may well have been talking about different cases. Prosecutors will tend to be alive to bias against their interests but not notice when the bias runs in their favour, and the same is true of defence lawyers.   [153] Zander and Henderson (1993: 135–136).

[154] See, for example, *Spencer (John)*, *The Times*, 13 July 1994, discussed in Robertshaw (1998: 32–33).

[155] Winter J, 'The Truth Will Out? The Role of Judicial Advocacy and Gender in Verdict Construction' (2002) 11(3) *Social & Legal Studies* 343–367.

symbolically and physically constructed as passive and silent observers from the sidelines during the trial. Mulcahy notes how, as advocates came to take centre stage in the adversarial process, juries became much more formally organised into a particular area at the side of the courtroom.[156] By contrast, the judge is raised up on high, centre stage, and given the 'superior status indicators of wig and robes. . . All procedural moves and sequences pass through the judge, to whom deferential behaviour and speech forms are routine. . . The role-expectation for the jury throughout the trial is one of dependence on the judge.'[157]

In the United States, a historical distrust of officialdom is reflected in the rule in most state jurisdictions that the judge in a criminal trial must express no opinion on the weight or credibility of the testimony of a witness, or on the merits of either side of the case.[158] In some continental jurisdictions, such as France, the other extreme of the argument may be seen, in that judges are allowed to retire with juries in order to determine the verdict. The evidence suggests that this co-decision model produces a much lower acquittal rate than when matters are left in the hands of the jury alone.[159] A model nearer to hand is that of Scotland which limits trial judges to directing on the law and explaining how the evidence is relevant to the legal ingredients of each charge. This seems to ensure greater respect for the jury's role as fact-finder and ultimate determiner of guilt.[160] If we think it important that our long-term freedom should not be taken away by a process effectively dominated by state-paid professionals then there is much to be said for the Scottish approach. Even some judicial commentators believe that judges have been too ready in the past to make overtly biased comments about the evidence and questioned whether any judicial comment on the evidence is 'necessary, appropriate or fair'.[161] Rather than ignoring judicial activism, it would be better to 'forge out a theory of judicial truth finding which does not lead to unfairness'.[162] One solution might be to try to build more checks and balances into the trial process itself; for example allowing counsel to comment on judicial summaries of evidence before they are presented to the jury.[163] This could well have saved the defendant in *Abdulkadir Mohamed* (see section 9.5.1.4) from having to ask the Court of Appeal to quash the conviction that the Court believed could have been the result of a misleading summing up in the prosecution's favour.

9.5 Trial: procedure, evidence and law

9.5.1 Procedure and evidence

In an adversarial system the decision-makers are meant to be passive. It is not part of the jury's role to investigate matters for itself away from the courtroom.[164] There have been examples of jurors using the Internet to carry out their own research, but where

---

[156] Mulcahy L, *Legal Architecture: Justice, Due Process and the Place of Law* (London: Routledge, 2010). See further on courtroom layout, Mulcahy L, 'Putting the Defendant in their Place: Why Do We Still Use the Dock in Criminal Proceedings?' (2013) 53(6) *British Journal of Criminology* 1139–1156, and Robertshaw (1998: 15, 192–193); Mulcahy L and Rowden E, *The Democratic Courthouse: A Modern History of Design, Due Process and Dignity* (London: Routledge, 2019). [157] Robertshaw (1998: 32–33).
[158] See Wolchover D, 'Should Judges Sum up on the Facts?' [1989] *Criminal Law Review* 781.
[159] See Munday R, 'Jury Trial, Continental Style' (1993) 13 *Legal Studies* 204 at p 216 in particular.
[160] Robertshaw (1998: 23–25, 179–193).
[161] Madge N 'Summing Up – A Judge's Perspective' [2006] *Criminal Law Review* 817.
[162] Jackson J, 'Judicial Responsibility in Criminal Proceedings' (1996) 49 *Current Legal Problems* 59 at p 92.
[163] Doran (2000: 15–17).
[164] To do so may amount to a serious irregularity vitiating any subsequent conviction. See *Davis, Rowe and Johnson* [2001] 1 Cr App R 115.

this has come to light trials have been abandoned, convictions overturned,[165] and jurors prosecuted. Thomas found that between five and 12% of jurors actively search for online information about their trial, while 13–26% come across it while browsing news websites.[166] Thomas further found that jurors are less likely to report instances of media misuse than other forms of inappropriate juror behaviour such as bias or bullying.[167] Kirk has suggested, based on anecdotal evidence, that jurors ignore judges' directions not to conduct their own research, and that such behaviour is at endemic levels.[168] Courts take a very dim view of any juror behaviour online that impedes the administration of justice, usually imposing prison sentences on jurors who are prosecuted and convicted to punish and deter other jurors from doing the same.[169] As a result of increased concerns about such juror activity, the Criminal Justice and Courts Act (CJC) 2015 introduced a range of criminal offences designed to deter jurors from conducting (and sharing results of) their own research on cases.[170] There is little publicly available information about prosecutions under these sections, but they are unlikely to amount to the 26% of the juror population that Thomas refers to (earlier).

Jurors can ask questions of witnesses in court but rarely do so.[171] Any question is meant to be passed in writing to the judge who will then relay it to a witness if appropriate. The mediated nature and artificiality of this procedure undoubtedly deters jurors from a more proactive role in the trial and they receive little encouragement to assert themselves.[172] It follows that juries should reach their verdicts on the material that is placed before them by counsel for the prosecution and defence. This material is itself shaped by the rules of criminal procedure and evidence, which the Secret Barrister describes as 'horrendously complex'.[173] This body of law accordingly forms yet another battleground for Packer's two models of the criminal process.

The clarion call for the crime control model was sounded by the then Commissioner of the Metropolitan Police, Sir Robert Mark, in 1973.[174] Arguing that the jury acquits an unacceptably high proportion of those whom the police believe to be guilty, Mark pinned the blame on procedural rules and crooked lawyers, asserting 'technical rules' such as those relating to disclosure, the right to silence and evidence of bad character gave 'every

---

[165] *KaraKaya* [2005] EWCA 346. Berlins M, 'Jury's Out on the Net Generation' *The Guardian*, 10 November 2008. See also *Hambleton* [2009] EWCA Crim 13 where a conviction had to be quashed after it was discovered that a discharged juror had made a prejudicial comment about a defendant to one of the jurors hearing the case that was then repeated within the jury retiring room.

[166] Thomas C, *Are Juries Fair?* Ministry of Justice Research Series 1/10 (2010) p 43.

[167] Thomas C, 'Avoiding the Perfect Storm of Juror Contempt' (2013) *Criminal Law Review* 6.

[168] Kirk D, 'Editorial: The Jury's Out' (2013) *Journal of Criminal Law*,173. Also see Harvey D, 'The Googling Juror: The Fate of the Jury Trial in the Digital Paradigm' (2014) *New Zealand Law Review* 203.

[169] *Attorney General v Dallas* [2012], *Attorney General v Davey; Attorney General v Beard* [2013]. For a more recent example see <https://www.thetelegraphandargus.co.uk/news/18216064.former-juror-back-court-web-research-case/> (a juror who did her own research and talked about it to a fellow juror) (accessed 15 May 2020).

[170] Crosby K, 'Juror Punishment, Juror Guidance and the CJC Act 2015' [2015] *Criminal Law Review* 578.

[171] In the Crown court study, under half of jurors had wanted to ask a question and less than a fifth of this number had actually done so: Zander and Henderson (1993: 213).

[172] Nearly a third of jurors in the Crown court study had not been informed at any stage that they could ask questions: Zander and Henderson (1993: 213).   [173] The Secret Barrister (2018).

[174] Mark was the first high-profile police officer to seek openly to influence criminal justice policy-making, although many have subsequently followed his lead. Loader I and Mulcahy A, 'The Power of Legitimate Naming: Part I – Chief Constables as Social Commentators in Post-war England' (2001a) 41(1) *British Journal of Criminology* 41; Loader I and Mulcahy A, 'The Power of Legitimate Naming: Part II – Making Sense of the Elite Police Voice' (2001b) 41(3) *British Journal of Criminology* 252; Wilcox A and Young R, 'How Green was Thames Valley?: Policing the Image of Restorative Justice Cautions' (2007) 17(2) *Policing and Society* 141.

advantage to the defence'.[175] Mark's claims were contested by academics, who argued that there was little evidence that the jury acquittal rate was too high, bent lawyers were helping criminals escape justice,[176] or that professional criminals were exploiting the rules.[177]

In the decades since Mark's comments many of the 'technical' rules of procedure and evidence have been significantly altered, encouraged by Auld's views that defendants have unfair advantages in the criminal process as a result of lenient rules of evidence that their legal representatives seek to exploit. However, such assertions are not grounded in solid empirical evidence. They are anchored in the (pseudo-empirical) premise that people believe that defendants enter late guilty pleas for tactical reasons, undermining attempts to modernise the system and encourage more efficient ways of using evidence. To put it another way, under austerity, the steady development of the Criminal Procedure Rules and rules of evidence have synchronised executive thinking with the senior judiciary to undermine traditional approaches to adversarial justice.[178] To illustrate this, we now examine the rules on disclosure, the right to silence and bad character, showing significant moves in a crime control direction, eroding defendants' rights whilst doing little or nothing to enlarge due process overall.

9.5.1.1 Disclosure of prosecution and defence evidence

The requirement that the prosecution should give disclosure of its evidence to the defence is intended to redress an imbalance between the parties to the case. As was noted by Lloyd LJ in the successful Birmingham Six appeal, that a:

> disadvantage of the adversarial system may be that the parties are not evenly matched in resources . . . But the inequality of resources is ameliorated by the obligation on the part of the prosecution to make available all material which may prove helpful to the defence.[179]

The resources of the police and prosecution far outweigh those available to the defence.[180] Moreover, the police are involved in the case from the outset, whereas the defence will not begin to operate until a suspect is arrested. In these circumstances, it is not possible for the defence to carry out an adequate independent investigation of an offence. Prosecution disclosure should not be seen as advantaging the defence, but as a means of attempting to redress a structural disadvantage. Indeed, unless accused persons are told what the details of allegations against them are, they cannot prepare a defence (for discussion of this in the police station, see chapter 5).

The duty to disclose was by no means as absolute in 1973 as Mark implied. The common law imposed increasingly strict duties on the prosecution over the next two decades. But the police, the CPS and other prosecution agencies often failed to comply,[181] claiming that these duties were too onerous.[182] So the common law was replaced by the Criminal Procedure and Investigations Act 1996. The prosecution duty to disclose was cut back at

---

[175] Mark R, *Minority Verdict* (The 1973 Dimbleby Lecture) (London: BBC, 1973).
[176] See Baldwin and McConville (1979: 118), and, by the same authors, 'Allegations Against Lawyers' [1978] *Criminal Law Review* 744.
[177] Contrast Mack J, 'Full-time Major Criminals and the Courts' (1976) 39 *Modern Law Review* 241 with Sanders A, 'Does Professional Crime Pay? – A Critical Comment on Mack' (1977) 40 *Modern Law Review* 553. See also Baldwin J and McConville M (1979: 110–112). [178] McConville and Marsh (2020).
[179] *McIlkenny* (1991) 93 Cr App Rep 287 at 312.
[180] See Barclay G and Tavares C, *Information on the Criminal Justice System in England and Wales: Digest 4* (London: Home Office, 1999) ch 9.
[181] See O'Connor P, 'Prosecution Disclosure: Principle, Practice and Justice' in Walker C and Starmer K (eds), *Justice in Error* (London: Blackstone, 1993) and our discussion of disclosure at section 7.3 in particular.
[182] See, for example, the views expressed by the then Chief Constable of Thames Valley Police, Pollard C, 'A Case for Disclosure' [1994] *Criminal Law Review* 42.

the same time as a new defence duty to disclose its 'case' was introduced. Research into the operation of the 1996 Act uncovered evidence of significant levels of wrongful non-disclosure (see section 7.3.3.5). Partly in consequence, Part 5 of the CJA 2003 somewhat widened the prosecution duty to disclose, but at the same time widened very substantially the defence duties of disclosure. The defence must now, in advance of trial, provide a statement which sets out the nature of the accused's defence, indicates any point of law on which reliance will be placed (including any point as to the admissibility of evidence), and provides details of any witnesses he or she plans to call to give evidence at trial. Adverse inferences may be drawn where any of the duties of disclosure are breached or a defence is presented at court that is inconsistent with, or goes beyond, the initially disclosed information.

The police have got their way. Disclosure rules are no longer binding only on the prosecution, so no longer do they fulfil their old function of helping to redress the structural imbalance within the adversarial system. Indeed, one could reasonably argue that they now unduly favour the prosecution. And where disclosure is perhaps most needed, by the police in advance of their interrogation of the suspect, no duty to disclose exists (chapter 5). This was true at the time Mark made his claims and it remains true today. What has changed since Mark's time is that, if suspects remain silent when questioned by the police, the odds of adverse inferences being drawn against them at trial have shot up. The 'rules' on disclosure are now indeed somewhat one-sided—in favour of the police.

9.5.1.2 The right of silence

Mark acknowledged the inroad made into the right of silence by s.11 of the CJA 1967. This requires alibi defences to be notified to the police in advance of the trial, so that they may be 'checked'. What he failed to mention was the limited extent to which the right of silence was respected by the courts.[183] The Court of Appeal in *Gerard*[184] declined to intervene when a trial judge commented that an accused's silence before charge might appear 'perhaps a little curious' and 'a little odd'. In *Chandler*[185] the Court of Appeal ruled that where an accused and an accuser were on equal terms it would be in order to invite the jury to consider whether silence in the face of an accusation or question amounted to an acceptance of what had been said. This equal terms doctrine was in accordance with earlier cases such as *Parkes*[186] but the new departure was to assert that suspects might be adjudged as on level or even superior terms vis-à-vis police officers. Thus in *Chandler*, a police officer was held to be on equal terms with a suspect because the latter had his solicitor present during questioning.[187] None of this seems consistent with the view of Mark that procedural rules developed so as to give every advantage to the defence.

Since Mark wrote there have been several major statutory developments. As we have just seen, the Criminal Procedure and Investigations Act 1996 placed a positive duty on the defence to disclose its 'case' prior to trial, and that duty has been greatly increased by Part 5 of the CJA 2003. This is a clear departure from the right to silence. That right had already been weakened by the Criminal Justice and Public Order Act 1994 (chapter 5). Here we look briefly at the sections which allow the jury to draw adverse inferences against accused persons who decline to give evidence *in court* (rather than at the investigatory stage), and which allow the prosecutor to make adverse comment if a defendant remains silent.

---

[183] For a full review of the relevant case law, see the four-part article by Wolchover D (1989) 139 *New Law Journal* at 396, 428, 484 and 501, and also Quirk (2017). [184] *Gerard* (1948) 32 Cr App Rep 132.
[185] [1976] 1 WLR 585. See also *Osborne* [2005] EWCA Crim 3082. [186] (1976) 64 Cr App Rep 25.
[187] See also the case of *Horne* [1990] Crim LR 188 where the equal terms doctrine was applied to silence in response to a victim's accusation made in the presence of police officers.

Section 35(2) imposes a duty on the court, at the end of the prosecution case, to make accused persons aware of the possibility of the drawing of adverse inferences if they choose not to give evidence or refuse to answer any question when giving evidence. Section 38 sets out some restrictions on this new crime control power by stipulating that a person shall not have a case to answer or be convicted of an offence 'solely' through an adverse inference. This section must now be read in the light of subsequent judicial interpretation. In the leading case of *Cowan*[188] the Court of Appeal set out five points which a trial judge must convey to the jury before an adverse inference can be drawn under s.35:

(a) the burden of proof remains on the prosecution at all times;

(b) the defendant is entitled to remain silent;

(c) an inference from failure to give evidence cannot on its own prove guilt;

(d) the jury must be satisfied that the prosecution established a case to answer before drawing any adverse inferences from the defendant's silence;

(e) the jury may draw an adverse inference if it concludes that the silence can only sensibly be attributed to the accused having no good answer to the prosecution case.[189]

In *Murray v UK*[190] the ECtHR accepted that there was no absolute right to not have adverse inferences drawn from silence. But it also held that it was incompatible with the immunity from self-incrimination to base a conviction 'solely or mainly' on a refusal to give evidence at trial. This is a more stringent requirement than s.35 which only expressly prevents a conviction which is based 'solely' on such a refusal.[191] But the fourth *Cowan* requirement requires a jury to believe that there is a case for the defendant to answer before they consider whether to *add* to that prosecution case by drawing an adverse inference from the defendant's silence in court. It is arguable that this requirement of an independent prima facie case means that a conviction will not be based either solely *or mainly* on silence. Not surprisingly, in *Birchall*[192] the Court of Appeal ruled that it was essential that the fourth condition in *Cowan* formed part of the direction to juries in s.35 cases, and that a failure to include it rendered a conviction unsafe. It thus seems that the Convention has softened the crime control impact of the 1994 Act. Nonetheless, whereas at one time, as Mark put it, the police had to keep reminding suspects that they need not say anything, nowadays police, prosecutors and trial judges must remind suspects that they need to say something if they want to avoid seriously damaging the chances of acquittal. This is only one of a number of ways evidential rules pressurise defendants to participate in the process of prosecution that undermines the presumption of innocence and privilege against self-incrimination,[193] reflecting a move towards greater crime control measures that are designed to increase the rate of guilty pleas.

9.5.1.3 The jury's ignorance of the defendant's criminal record

The historical rationale for the principle that juries should not ordinarily be told of a defendant's previous convictions (or otherwise be informed that the defendant is of 'bad character') is that the prejudicial impact of this information outweighs its probative value.[194] Some empirical support for such a prejudicial effect was provided by research done for

---

[188] [1996] QB 373. Approved by the House of Lords in *Becouarn* [2005] UKHL 55.
[189] The Court of Appeal indicated that there might be other circumstances in which a trial judge might think it right to direct or advise against drawing an adverse inference. [190] (1996) 22 EHRR 29.
[191] As confirmed by *Cowan*: see point (c) in the listed paragraph. [192] [1999] Crim LR 311.
[193] See, for example, Owusu-Bempah, Abenaa, *Defendant Participation in the Criminal Process* (London: Routledge, 2017). [194] See *Selvey v DPP* [1968] 2 All ER 497.

the Law Commission by Lloyd-Bostock.[195] Using mock juries she found that knowledge of previous convictions similar to the offence charged increased the perceived probability of guilt. To the extent that previous behaviour is a good predictor of future behaviour (which it sometimes is) this is arguably an example of probative value outweighing prejudicial effect.[196] But Lloyd-Bostock's research also found that convictions for offences which provoke an all-round negative evaluation of the perpetrator, such as indecent assault on a child, are likely to be particularly prejudicial to a defendant whatever the current offence charged.

Whether one sees the principle of not admitting previous convictions into evidence as unduly favouring the defendant depends, in part, on a judgement as to how reliable the police are at identifying the probably guilty in the first place. As we have shown in earlier chapters, the police tend to focus their attention upon 'known criminals'. Statistically, this strategy may be effective in increasing the number of guilty persons detected, but, by giving insufficient attention to independent evidence of guilt, it also increases the risk that innocent people will be drawn into the criminal process, especially where the system is skewed by bias (chapters 6 and 10). From a due process perspective, this insight would strengthen the argument for keeping the defendant's past record from the jury. Denied this knowledge, the jury is forced to focus on the essential issue—is there sufficient evidence that the defendant committed the offence as charged?

As Mark recognised, the bad character rule has never been applied rigidly, and there were long-standing exceptions to it; for example, evidence of the defendant's bad character could be admitted under the 'similar facts' rule,[197] or where the defendant gave evidence suggesting he was of good character, or where he gave evidence against a co-accused. A fourth exception allowed bad character evidence to be admitted if the defence attacked the character of a prosecution witness, sometimes known as the 'tit for tat' rule. Research showed that defendants were often deterred from attacking the character of police witnesses, for example by alleging they had fabricated evidence, because their lawyers advised them it would be counterproductive.[198] Interestingly this advice was sometimes given even when the defendant was of good character so at no risk of convictions being disclosed under the bad character rules.

The CJA 2003 made it easier to introduce evidence of the defendant's bad character.[199] Its provisions are complex and we refer readers to specialist works for more detailed analysis,[200] confining ourselves here to providing some examples of the crime control thrust

---

[195] Law Commission, *Evidence in Criminal Proceedings: Previous Misconduct of a Defendant* (Consultation Paper No 141) (London: HMSO, 1996a) Appendix D. Also reported in Lloyd-Bostock S, 'The Effects of Hearing About the Defendant's Previous Criminal Record: A Simulation Study' [2000] *Criminal Law Review* 734.

[196] Redmayne M, 'The Relevance of Bad Character' (2002b) 61 *Cambridge Law Journal* 684.

[197] If the facts alleged were similar to the facts of previous incidents involving the defendant then the jury could be told of the latter, even if those incidents were the subject of acquittals.

[198] In one study of late plea changers (discussed in ch 7), two-fifths of sampled defendants alleged in interview that the police had falsely attributed to them verbal admissions, and a third of those claiming to be innocent made such allegations. However their counsel almost invariably advised no challenge to the police evidence since the police would be believed and the judge might be sufficiently annoyed to impose a heavier sentence (Baldwin J and McConville M, *Negotiated Justice* (London: Martin Robertson, 1977) pp 68–9).

[199] The government mischaracterised the pre-legislation framework as one where previous convictions were generally inadmissible, when the truth was that 'any evidence of bad character which was more probative than prejudicial was admissible'. See Tapper C, 'Evidence of Bad Character' [2004] *Criminal Law Review* 533 at 538.

[200] Spencer J, *Evidence of Bad Character* 3rd edn (Oxford: Hart Publishing, 2016); Mirfield P, 'Character and Credibility' [2009] *Criminal Law Review* 135; Honess T and Matthews G, 'Admitting Evidence of a Defendant's Previous Convictions (PCE) and its Impact on Juror Deliberations in Relation to Juror Processing Style and Juror Concerns Over the Fairness of Introducing PCE' (2012) 17(2) *Legal and Criminological Psychology* 360–379.

of the legislation. The Act introduces a series of 'gateways' through which bad character evidence can be admitted. The gateways make it easier to admit evidence of the defendant's bad character than that of other witnesses. Under s.100, evidence of the bad character of witnesses other than the defendant is only admissible with the leave of the court if it has 'substantial probative value' and is of 'substantial importance in the context of the case as a whole'. By contrast, evidence of the defendant's bad character does not need to be of 'substantial' value—it may be admitted through the gateway in s.101(1)(d) if it is merely 'relevant to an important matter in issue between the prosecution and defence'. It is evidently regarded as more important to protect prosecution witnesses from the upset that might be caused by attacks on their character than to protect defendants from similar upset *and* the risk of wrongful conviction.

Although the gateway under s.101(1)(d) overlaps with the similar facts rule that previously existed at common law it has much broader scope.[201] Section 103 spells out that matters in issue between the prosecution and defence include 'propensity to be untruthful' and the 'propensity to commit offences of the kind' with which the defendant is charged. This may be established, 'without prejudice to any other way of doing so', by evidence that the defendant has committed an offence of the 'same description' or 'same category' as the one charged. The government subsequently used its power under s.103(4) to prescribe categories of offences in wide terms.

Given the breadth of the legislation the role of the judiciary in interpreting its application is clearly crucial. In *Hanson*[202] the Court of Appeal upheld the conviction of a defendant who entered a guilty plea to stealing money from a bag in a bedroom to which he had access when the judge ruled he would allow the admission of evidence of his previous convictions for dishonesty. However, Rose LJ asserted that where evidence of bad character is admitted to show propensity, either to commit offences or be untruthful, the judge should warn the jury against placing undue reliance on previous convictions: 'Evidence of bad character cannot be used simply to bolster a weak case, or to prejudice the minds of the jury against the defendant' (at para 18).

It has been found that the propensity gateway is the most commonly used provision for admitting bad character evidence, and that the prosecution seeks to rely on it even where the defendant's previous convictions were not similar to the alleged offence. The success rate for applications, in full or part, is high (78% in one study) and defence lawyers are not particularly robust in contesting applications.[203] Although prosecutors claimed in this study that the decision in *Hanson* had made them more selective in their approach, one also admitted that the defence might be put on notice of an application to admit evidence of bad character to try to force the defendant to plead guilty. This is a reminder of the impact of evidential rules on not just the trial itself but the pre-trial processes. The CJA 2003 gave the prosecution greater freedom to use bad character rules to their advantage than previously, although the decision in *Hanson* may have had some limited inhibitory effect. Since *Hanson*, the courts have continued to try to discourage spurious prosecution applications to admit bad character evidence. For example, guidance that it would likely be unjust to admit character evidence where the prosecution case is weak was followed in *Darnley*,[204] while *Samuel*[205] reiterated the need for the prosecution to demonstrate the relevance of character evidence before it will be admitted.

---

[201] Spencer (2016). [202] [2005] EWCA Crim 824.
[203] Morgan Harris Burrows LLP, *Research into the Impact of Bad Character Provisions on the Courts* (Ministry of Justice Research Series 5/09)(London: MoJ, 2009). In this study of six courts, which included three Crown courts, most applications related to similar offences but 13% were applications for previous convictions for dissimilar crimes to be admitted.
[204] [2012] EWCA Crim 1148. [205] [2014] EWCA Crim 2349.

It should be noted that the meaning of 'bad character' is broader than simply previous convictions and includes 'reprehensible behaviour'. What amounts to 'reprehensible behaviour' is unclear,[206] and very few applications appear to be made to admit evidence of this type of behaviour.[207] It is clear that there must be a sufficient nexus between the alleged reprehensible behaviour and alleged offence before the evidence will be admitted.[208] Such applications might be useful in cases of domestic abuse where there may be a history of violence which is not reflected in previous convictions.[209] However, in recent years, 'reprehensible behaviour' has been held to include behaviours as broad as 'excessive' drinking and drug taking[210] or membership of a gang.[211] Lord Phillips argued extrajudicially that juries can be trusted to give bad character evidence no more weight than it deserves.[212] The old common law rules, in his view, 'were part of a criminal system that seemed to weight the scales in favour of the defence' and demonstrated 'a lack of trust of the jury'. The new rules put greater trust in juries to common-sensically assess the weight of relevant evidence. It has been suggested, however, that it may be 'premature' to abandon juries to their common sense understanding of bad character: 'It might be argued that the greater the volume of (prejudicial) evidence which legislation makes potentially admissible, the greater the obligation on the trial judge to guide the jury on how to approach it.'[213]

Whilst many opposed the bad character provisions of the CJA 2003 and argued that they would erode the safeguards against wrongful conviction of the innocent, they have their supporters. Spencer argues that admission of bad character evidence is not inherently unfair provided that there is other solid evidence that links the defendant to the offence.[214] However, as Redmayne observes, this appears to be precisely what the jury at the retrial of Barry George for the murder of Jill Dando were invited by the prosecution to do; convict on the basis of his 'bad character' with weak supporting evidence from eyewitnesses.[215] The prosecution presented the jury with extensive information about George's behaviour, suggesting that he was, to quote the media coverage, a 'celebrity and gun obsessed stalker with a grudge against the BBC'.[216] Although he was acquitted, if the coverage is accurate it does not present a picture of prosecutorial restraint in the face of rules which seem now to be stacked in their favour. Redmayne comments that it is difficult 'to see what sort of rule can be used to prevent weak cases being propped up by unimpressive character evidence, without going back to the unnecessarily strict standards of the old law'.[217] Were they really so strict and unnecessarily so? In our view reasoned and careful law reform that represents a principled balancing of the interests at stake has been abandoned in the government's illiberal pursuit of 'bringing more offenders to justice' more quickly and more cheaply.

---

[206] Munday R, 'What Constitutes "Other Reprehensible Behaviour" under the Bad Character Provisions of the Criminal Justice Act 2003?' [2005] *Criminal Law Review* 24.

[207] Morgan Harris Burrows LLP (2009: 18). It is clear that decisions will be fact and context dependent (*R v AJC* [2006] EWCA Crim 284). [208] *R v Sullivan* [2015] EWCA Crim 1565.

[209] The Morgan Harris Burrows LLP study (2009) found a 'widespread view' amongst practitioners that the new rules were a 'backward step' in domestic abuse cases, where it was said to be previously possible to introduce background evidence, such as an incident log, without giving advance notice (p 19).

[210] *R v Murphy* [2014] EWCA Crim 1457.

[211] *R v Lewis* [2014] EWCA Crim 48. An exchange of social media messages which could be construed as threats were considered to amount to reprehensible behaviour in *Palmer* [2016] EWCA Crim 2237.

[212] Phillips (2007). [213] Ormerod D, 'Editorial' [2008] *Criminal Law Review* 337.

[214] Spencer (2006a).

[215] Redmayne M, 'Book Review of *Evidence of Bad Character* and *Hearsay Evidence in Criminal Proceedings* by J Spencer' (2009) *Howard Journal of Crime and Justice* 108–110.

[216] 'George Not Guilty of Dando Murder', BBC News, 1 August 2008. [217] Redmayne (2009: 109).

9.5.1.4 Other rules of evidence

We have shown that Mark's three examples of rules that favour the defence were neither so absolute nor so one-sided as he contended, and that they have subsequently been remoulded so as to make it still easier to secure convictions. There are many other important procedural and evidential rules that favour the prosecution rather than the defence. For instance, there is no requirement that the prosecution produce evidence to corroborate the confession of an accused yet extreme caution in this area is vital.[218]

Where the evidence against the accused rests substantially on identification evidence judges should direct an acquittal if the quality of the evidence is poor (unless there is other evidence which goes to support the correctness of the identification),[219] but otherwise should warn the jury of the need for caution before convicting on such evidence.[220] Arguably these guidelines do not go far enough in protecting accused persons from wrongful conviction given the inherently unreliable nature of identification evidence, and the role such evidence is known to have played in miscarriages of justice.[221] Furthermore, the senior judiciary are not consistent in their stipulations concerning when this due process safeguard is needed. Jackson noted in 1999 that earlier cases like *Curry*[222] confined the impact of *Turnbull* to 'fleeting glimpse' sightings, but that 'it is now clear that the cases in which the warning can be dispensed with are "wholly exceptional"'.[223] Since then the Court of Appeal has reheated *Curry* by observing[224] that *Turnbull* was intended primarily to deal with cases of fleeting encounters. Trying to derive clarity from this case law is liable to give you indigestion.[225]

A key rule of evidence is that a statement made out of court is inadmissible as evidence of any fact stated. The rules prohibiting the admission of such hearsay evidence (already subject to many exceptions) are weakened considerably by s.114 of the CJA 2003, which introduces a general inclusionary discretion where 'the court is satisfied that it is in the interests of justice for it to be admissible'. The hearsay provisions in the 2003 Act run from ss.114–136 and there is little to be gained by attempting to summarise them here. We instead refer readers to specialist literature on the subject.[226] But three general observations are worth making. First, the old hearsay rules sometimes worked as much against defendants as in their favour (as when a confession made by some other person could

---

[218] See, for example, Pattenden R, 'Should Confessions be Corroborated?' (1991) 107 *Legal Quarterly Review* 317, and Kassin S, 'Why Confessions Trump Innocence' (2012) 67(6) *American Psychologist* 431–445. See also ch 5.

[219] *Turnbull* [1977] QB 224. Confirmed by *Davies* [2004] EWCA Crim 2521.

[220] Voice identification is also subject to the *Turnbull* principles but requires even greater caution according to *Davies* [2004] EWCA Crim 2521. See also the two articles by Ormerod D: 'Sounds Familiar: Voice Identification Evidence' [2001] *Criminal Law Review* 595; 'Sounding Out Expert Voice Identification' [2002] *Criminal Law Review* 771.

[221] See section 6.2.2.2, and Roberts and Zuckerman (2004: 490–496) for fuller discussion. For a review of the conditions under which eyewitnesses tend to make mistakes see Memon et al, *Psychology and Law: Truthfulness, Accuracy and Credibility of Victims, Witnesses and Suspects* 2nd edn (Chichester: John Wiley, 2003).

[222] [1983] Crim LR 737.   [223] Jackson (1999: 195), citing *Shand v R* [1996] 1 All ER 511.

[224] *Beckles and Montague* [1998] EWCA Crim 1494; [1999] Crim LR 148, relying on the view expressed by Lord Widgery CJ (who gave the judgment in *Turnbull*) in *Oakwell* [1978] 66 Cr App R 174.

[225] This is another sphere in which judicial bias may become evident. In *Shervington* [2008] EWCA Crim 648 the judge prefaced his comments on identification evidence by saying that the jury should not allow an over-sophisticated approach to become 'a muggers' charter'; the conviction was nonetheless upheld. In *Abdulkadir Mohamed* [2020] EWCA (Crim) 525 the judge correctly gave a *Turnbull* warning but then implied that the evidence was actually quite strong. The conviction was overturned on appeal.

[226] Spencer J, *Hearsay Evidence in Criminal Proceedings* 2nd Edn (Oxford: Hart Publishing, 2014); Worthern T, 'The Hearsay Provisions of the Criminal Justice Act 2003: So Far, Not So Good?' [2008] *Criminal Law Review* 431; Brodin S, 'The British Experience with Hearsay Reform: A Cautionary Tale' (2016) 84(4) *Fordham Law Review* 1417–1427.

not be admitted in evidence to show that the defendant was unlikely to have committed the offence).[227] Second, the new hearsay rules are not as tilted against the defence[228] as the bad character provisions of the CJA 2003 (see preceding sub-section). Third, the new rules 'enhance the value of material acquired during what might (loosely) be termed the investigative phase of a criminal prosecution' thus reducing one of the distinctions between inquisitorial and adversarial systems 'though without putting in place the former's regulatory safeguards'.[229] To put this more bluntly, it is now easier for the prosecution to adduce evidence that was fabricated or constructed by the police at the pre-trial stage. For example, under s.120(6) of the CJA 2003, statements made by witnesses can be adduced if they were made when matters were fresh in their memory and they cannot reasonably be expected to remember them well enough to give oral evidence of them in court. There has thus been created a new incentive for the police to 'gild the lily' to the detriment of suspects when taking witness statements.

To illustrate the human rights implications of admitting hearsay, it is helpful to examine the issue of 'absent witnesses'. Section 23 of the CJA 1988 allowed first-hand documentary evidence to be admitted if the maker was dead, ill, could not be located and brought to court, or if the statement was made to a police officer and the maker did not give oral evidence through fear or because the authorities deemed it important to keep the witness out of the public arena. Leave was required to introduce such evidence, and the courts had to consider whether it was in the interests of justice to admit the statement, bearing in mind the difficulty of challenging the statement if the maker did not give oral evidence. As the Court of Appeal pointed out 'you cannot conduct an argument with, nor ask questions of, a piece of paper'.[230] That court policed the boundaries of s.23, for example by discouraging judges from allowing juries to speculate that the reason a person did not give oral evidence was fear of the defendant.[231] Nonetheless, as Jackson notes, s.23 'increased the ability of the prosecution to submit dubious documentary evidence against the accused'.[232] Section 116 of the CJA 2003 replaces s.23 of the 1988 Act and extends the admissibility of evidence by absent witnesses to all first-hand hearsay evidence. The leave requirement was abolished for absent witnesses other than the fearful. This will result in the automatic admission of a greater amount of hearsay evidence than previously, unless judges accede to applications to exclude the evidence on the grounds of fairness under s.78 of PACE.[233] By contrast, in the case of 'fearful witnesses' the leave requirement was tightened, by directing the court to consider whether a 'special measures' direction under the Youth Justice and Criminal Evidence Act 1999 (such as the use of live-link video or screens—see section 9.4.2 and chapter 12) might be a fairer way of proceeding. This is a welcome development although much will now depend on how trial judges exercise their discretion.

This is one area in which the ECHR safety net has had some effect, albeit not as much as one might have expected given its wording. Article 6(3)(d) of the European Convention sets out the minimum right of everyone charged with a criminal offence 'to examine or have examined witnesses against him'. At first sight, admitting the evidence of absent witnesses

---

[227] See *Beckford and Daley* [1991] Crim LR 833; *Lawless* [2003] EWCA Crim 271.
[228] See the analysis by Birch D, 'Hearsay: Same Old Story, Same Old Song' [2004] *Criminal Law Review* 556.
[229] Durston G, 'Previous (In)Consistent Statements after the Criminal Justice Act 2003' [2005] *Criminal Law Review* 206 at 214.   [230] *Radak, Adjei, Butler-Rees and Meghjee* [1999] Crim LR 223.
[231] See *Wood and Fitzsimmons* [1998] Crim LR 213. Trial judges are also meant to warn the jury of the dangers of accepting witness evidence not subject to cross-examination, but the warning need not take any specific form: *Batt and Batt* [1995] Crim LR 240.   [232] Jackson (1993: 139).
[233] Section 78 Police and Criminal Evidence Act 1984 enables a judge to exclude evidence when all the circumstances, including those in which the evidence was obtained, mean that admission of the evidence would have such an unfair effect on the proceedings that the court ought not admit it. See ch 11.

would seem to breach this right, but the Court of Appeal has held that statutory provisions which allow this are not in themselves contrary to Art 6 so long as the more general right to a fair trial is not breached.[234] From the ECtHR's perspective, the question of whether the admission of evidence from absent witnesses produces breaches of the Convention is likely to turn on the strength of the rest of the prosecution case, and the provision of compensating safeguards for defendants, such as the warning provided to juries about the danger of relying on statements not subjected to cross-examination.[235] The domestic courts have engaged in battle with the ECtHR about the propriety of the rules in relation to hearsay evidence in several cases, culminating the joint appeal of *Al-Khawaja and Tahery v UK*.[236] It is now clear that the domestic court has a wide margin of appreciation in relation to the admission of evidence. Even where hearsay evidence is the sole or decisive evidence against a defendant, its admission in evidence will not automatically result in a breach of Art 6, 'dissolving the minimum guarantees in Art 6(3) . . .[and] settling for the right to a "fair-ish" trial.'[237]

We conclude by recalling that Sir Robert Mark argued that jury trials were lopsided affairs in which the prosecution was bound by rules whilst the defence could play dirty. In the interests of even-handed analysis let us record that the prosecution authorities are not above foul play themselves. We saw in earlier chapters how these authorities seek to construct cases so as to ensure the outcome they seek, and that this can involve such unethical practices as fabricating and tampering with evidence. Two cases which came to light in the 1990s show that it would be wrong to assume that they would not dare 'tamper' with the jury itself. In *Kaul*[238] the police improperly took away from the court a rucksack already admitted into evidence and even more improperly placed items in it which were prejudicial to the defendant, returning it to court the following day. This only came to light because the jury, having taken the rucksack with them when retiring to consider their verdict, sent a note to the judge querying why the contents of the rucksack had not been mentioned during the trial. The Court of Appeal in quashing the conviction referred to its earlier unreported decision in *Ellis* (10 June 1991) in which 'documents which should not have been shown to the jury were "accidentally" given to them, allegedly by a police witness'.[239] In one sense it is understandable that the police stoop to such tactics. As we saw in section 9.1, despite all the supposed safeguards, weak cases do end up in front of the jury. The police are naturally sometimes tempted to strengthen them through a last minute piece of case construction.

9.5.2 Substantive law and the definition of offences

In understanding how juries come to be convinced of guilt beyond reasonable doubt it is also necessary to look at the structure of substantive criminal law. We can do no more than scratch the surface of this issue here, and discuss it a little further in chapter 10, but the links between criminal law and criminal justice are too important to ignore.[240]

---

[234] Thomas, Flannagan, Thomas and Smith [1998] Crim LR 887; *D* [2002] 2 Cr App R 361.

[235] See Ashworth A, 'Article 6 and the Fairness of Trials' [1999] *Criminal Law Review* 261 at 268–269. The contrasting decisions in the cases of *PS v Germany* (2000) 30 EHRR CD301, [2002] Crim LR 312 and *SN v Sweden* [2002] Crim LR 831 highlighted the importance of the ability of the defence to challenge the evidence.

[236] Application no 26766/05 and 22228/06. The decision was confirmed in *Riat* [2012] EWCA Crim 1509, and in a later appeal of the case which had started the battle; *Horncastle and Others v UK*, ECHR 16 December 2014.

[237] Hoyano L, 'What is Balanced on the Scales of Justice? In Search of the Essence of the Right to a Fair Trial' [2014] *Criminal Law Review* 4 at pp 28–29.   [238] [1998] Crim LR 135.

[239] Commentary to *Kaul* [1998] Crim LR 135 at p 137.

[240] See further Lacey N, 'Legal Constructions of Crime' in Maguire et al (eds), *Oxford Handbook of Criminology* 4th edn (Oxford: OUP, 2007).

We commented in earlier chapters on how the breadth of the criminal law has implications for police powers of arrest and stop and search, and the implications are no less important at the trial stage. The essential point is that the fewer the elements that have to be proved by the prosecution, and the easier the law makes it to prove those elements, the more likely it is that juries will convict. To be presumed innocent is of little significance if the prosecution need do little to prove guilt. This is precisely what makes such definitions attractive to crime control adherents, since they assist in curtailing inefficient and pointless adversarial trials. Moreover, they may deter defendants from opting for trial in the first place and thus contribute to maintaining a high guilty plea rate.

Many examples of broadly drawn offences could be given. McBarnet[241] pointed out in the early 1980s that crimes such as theft and assault cover a much wider range of behaviour than the lay person generally realises. The reach of the criminal law has grown still further since then. There are the obvious examples of 'preventive' offences, particularly in relation to terrorism.[242] And under the Theft Act 1968, the act of theft is the appropriation of property belonging to another, and any assumption of any one right of the owner amounts to an appropriation: *Morris*.[243] Moreover, the House of Lords held in *Gomez*[244] that it is an appropriation notwithstanding that the owner authorises the taking or moving of property. Thus simply taking down a bottle of whisky from a supermarket shelf amounts to an appropriation and if there is, in addition, evidence of dishonesty and an intention to permanently deprive the supermarket of the whisky, then a conviction for theft could follow. As the only evidence of a defendant's state of mind in this situation is likely to be a confession, it is dangerous to reduce the conduct element of the crime of theft to this minimum, and could motivate the police to employ underhand (though not necessarily illegal) tactics to adduce a confession. Furthermore, the bar that the prosecution has to surpass to prove dishonesty has recently been lowered from a subjective to a more objective test.[245] Objective tests are easier for the prosecution to prove as they pay less attention to the actual defendant's state of mind than subjective tests.

General principles of liability further extend the prodigious reach of the criminal law. For example, s.1(1) Criminal Attempts Act 1981 makes it an ('inchoate') offence to do an act which is more than merely preparatory to the commission of an indictable offence if done with intent to commit such offence. To take our earlier example, merely reaching to pick up the bottle of whisky from the shelf may be classified as a criminal attempt. Principles of secondary liability (covering those who assist the principal offender), and of mens rea, are similarly broad in scope, rendering a vast range of behaviour subject to criminalisation. Another crime control tendency—lowering the prosecution burden—has been the general trend to lower the thresholds to prove the defendant's state of mind in relation to criminal conduct. As well as in the example of dishonesty given, the standard to prove an offence of encouraging and assisting a crime has moved from 'intention' to the lower standard of 'belief'.[246] Thus it has been noted that: 'The further cumulation with inchoate offences makes possible applications of criminal law which are of staggering breadth.'[247]

We may also note that the criminal law generally ignores the defendant's motive in defining what counts as a guilty state of mind. Defendants charged with theft of food will not be heard to say in their defence that they were hungry, nor will those who enter

---

[241] McBarnet D, Conviction (London: Macmillan, 1983a) pp 13–14.

[242] Hodgson J and Tadros V, 'The Impossibility of Defining Terrorism' (2013) 16(3) *New Criminal Law Review* 494–526; Ashworth A and Zedner L, *Preventive Justice* (Oxford: OUP, 2014).

[243] [1984] AC 320.   [244] [1993] 1 All ER 1.

[245] *Ivey v Genting Casinos* [2017] UKSC 67—confirmed in *Booth & Anor v R* [2020] EWCA Crim 575—though there is still some debate about the exact scope of the test.   [246] Serious Crime Act 2007, s.45.

[247] Lacey et al, *Reconstructing Criminal Law* 3rd edn (London: LexisNexis, 2003) p 215.

a boarded-up building as trespassers, intending to chop up floorboards for firewood, be allowed to defend a charge of burglary by arguing that they were cold and homeless.[248] Juries are enjoined to do justice according to law, but the law incorporates a particular kind of justice which skates over awkward problems arising from gross inequalities in society (see chapter 10). In this way too, the issues to be debated at trial are narrowed and the potential for adversarial challenge is reduced.

Finally, we should not forget the discussion in chapter 1, regarding the burden of proof. In 1996 it was calculated that 219 out of the 540 indictable (i.e. triable in the Crown court) offences then in common use involved a reversal of the burden of proof. In other words, in relation to some elements of offence definitions the defendant was effectively placed under a duty to prove his or her innocence.[249] This further undermines Sir Robert Mark's implicit claim, set out at the start of this section, that the burden of proof lay only on the prosecution and that the rules 'were designed to give every advantage to the defence'.

9.6 Evaluating the jury's performance

It was argued in chapter 8 that magistrates are more likely than jurors to embrace crime control ideology. This is largely because jurors are outsiders, free of the administrative concerns of dealing speedily with a large caseload. Moreover, unlike magistrates, and unlike in some other jurisdictions, jurors bear no direct responsibility for sentencing,[250] and are accordingly less likely to see themselves as instruments for upholding law and order. As jury service is statistically a less than once in a lifetime opportunity, it seems unlikely that in such circumstances jurors will in general subscribe to the crime control view that their task is to trust the prosecution evidence and convict without more ado. On the other hand, one must not simply assume that the jury operates according to due process principles, particularly in the light of the pro-prosecution bias in the law and practice of jury selection. Rather, we must examine whether juries in practice set aside their prejudices, seek hard evidence of guilt, and apply the appropriate standard of proof.

An immediate problem is that juries are not required to articulate reasons for the conclusions they reach at the end of a case.[251] They deliberate in private and, on their return to the court, merely give a general verdict of 'guilty' or 'not guilty'.[252] Yet the Court of Appeal displays great reluctance to interfere with jury decision-making.[253] Moreover, a stifling and all-embracing concern to protect the secrecy of the jury has prevented any systematic study based on direct observation or recording of its deliberations, which could cause

---

[248] Although when Dominic Cummings, the Chief Advisor to the Prime Minister, was accused of breaking coronavirus laws in May 2020, the Prime Minister defended his almost-certainly criminal acts on the grounds that he was protecting his family and acted on 'instinct'. That 'instinct' included a 50 mile round trip to test his eyesight. *Mail On-Line*, 5 June 2020.

[249] Ashworth A and Blake M, 'The Presumption of Innocence in English Criminal Law' [1996] *Criminal Law Review* 306. Owusu-Bempah Abenaa (2017) and Quirk (2017) have demonstrated how relatively recent changes to rules of evidence have also increased the de facto burden on defendants to prove their innocence.

[250] Munday R, 'What Do the French Think of Their Jury?' (1995) 15 *Legal Studies* 65.

[251] This is Blom-Cooper's primary objection to the jury system. See Blom-Cooper (2018). This would be overcome if jury verdicts were accompanied by explanations: Coen M and Doak J, 'Embedding Explained Jury Verdicts in the English Criminal Trial' (2017) 37 *Legal Studies* 786.

[252] In the case of a 'guilty' verdict the jury foreman will be asked to state the number of jurors voting for and against conviction. To avoid 'second-rate acquittals', this question is not put if a 'not guilty' verdict is returned.

[253] See, for example, *Pendleton* [2001] UKHL 66 and Roberts S, 'Fresh Evidence and Factual Innocence in the Criminal Division of the Court of Appeal' (2017a) 81(4) *Journal of Criminal Law* 303–327. See also ch 11.

perceptions of bias and thereby compromise defendants' right to a fair trial.[254] For many years the exact legal position was unclear on this point, although a convention of jury secrecy was maintained. But s.8 of the Contempt of Court Act 1981 made it a contempt to 'obtain, disclose or solicit any particulars of statements made, opinions expressed, arguments advanced or votes cast by members of a jury in the course of their deliberation.' It is sometimes said that such a rule is necessary to protect individual jurors from reprisals or to preserve the finality of jury verdicts, although closer analysis suggests that the purpose of s.8 was to 'preserve public confidence in regard to the adjudication of issues of fact'.[255]

Do juries deserve public confidence? The answer to this can only be equivocal since the existing studies in England and Wales are either based on individual jurors' accounts, or general surveys, or based on the impressions of judges, lawyers and police officers, or on simulations with 'shadow' or 'mock' juries.[256] To this motley collection can be added surveys of views on the jury. We will look at each type of evidence in turn.

9.6.1 **General impressions**

Individual jurors have published their recollections of their period of service both before and after the Contempt of Court Act 1981. Some have been disillusioned or even dismayed by their experiences while others have reported broad satisfaction.[257] A full review of the 33 (then) available accounts is given in Darbyshire et al.[258] The people who choose to write about their experiences give fascinating insights into jury dynamics but are self-selecting and probably unrepresentative of jurors in general. Moreover, they may have felt moved to write because their experiences were in some sense extraordinary. Some defence lawyers are reportedly concerned about the effects of the publication of the views and experiences of jurors in individual cases.[259]

One way in which such accounts can undoubtedly be valuable is to alert researchers to questions requiring more systematic study. For example, individual jurors have revealed that the standard of proof applied in practice ranges from the balance of probabilities to 100% certainty (neither of which accords with the legal standard of beyond reasonable doubt).[260] The problem seems to stem, at least in part, from the standard direction to the jury which tells them that they must feel sure of guilt before convicting. Zander tested this direction on 1,763 members of the public and found that 51% equated 'sure' with 100% proof (as did almost a third of magistrates and other legal professionals).[261] It is

---

[254] Taylor, N and Denyer, R 'Judicial Management of Juror Impropriety' [2014] 78(1) *Journal of Criminal Law* 43–64.

[255] Jaconelli J, *Open Justice: A Critique of the Public Trial* (Oxford: OUP, 2002) p 244. Thus if a foreman wrongly declares the verdict of guilty to be 'unanimous' the Court of Appeal will refuse to inquire into the matter: *Hart* [1998] Crim LR 417; *Millward* [1999] Crim LR 164. See also Quinn (2004).

[256] Another approach, which is ruled out by s.8 in England and Wales, is to interview jurors immediately after verdict. This produced illuminating results in New Zealand: Tinsley Y, 'Juror Decision-Making: A Look Inside the Jury Room' Selected Papers from the British Criminology Conference, vol 4 (2001), available on <http://www.britsoccrim.org/volume4/004.pdf> (accessed 5 January 2010).

[257] See, for example, the five accounts published in (1990) 140 *New Law Journal* 1264–1276.

[258] Darbyshire et al (2001). Since then several more accounts have emerged, such as by the jurors in the case of a childminder convicted of murdering a child in her care. See 'Juror Speaks Out; "The Court Saw Us as Idiots"', *The Times*, 29 January 2008.

[259] 'Why Juries Just Can't Keep Quiet', *The Times*, 18 March 2008.   [260] Darbyshire et al (2001: 55).

[261] Zander M, 'The Criminal Standard of Proof – How Sure is Sure?' (2000) 150 *New Law Journal* 1517, building on the earlier findings of Montgomery J, 'The Criminal Standard of Proof' (1998) 148 *New Law Journal* 582. But as McEwan et al (2002) point out, given the high conviction rate which obtains in the criminal courts, these results are most likely artefacts of the research.

not possible here, however, to explore all the qualitative points that arise from individual jurors' accounts and we remain sceptical as to the value of doing so given their unrepresentative nature. For the same reason we do not dwell upon the oddities revealed by case law.[262]

The large-scale Crown court survey carried out for the Runciman Commission[263] found that 80% of jurors rated trial by jury as a good or very good system and only 5% rated it as poor or worse. Jurors typically claimed that they had little difficulty in understanding or remembering the evidence, in coping with legalistic language or in following directions on the law from the judge.[264] The judges surveyed thought the jury system was good or very good in terms of 'generally getting a sensible result' in 79% of cases, the prosecution barristers in 82% and defence barristers in 91%. The survey found that 8% of judges rated the system as poor or very poor, compared with 4% of prosecuting barristers and 2% of defence barristers.[265] While such ratings of trial by jury as 'good' or 'bad' are somewhat crude and subjective, the findings of this survey nonetheless reveal a high level of support for this institution. Even more positive support was found by Matthews et al (2004). They interviewed 361 jurors who had recently completed jury service at six Crown court centres in 2001/02. Out of those interviewed, 95% regarded juries as either quite (33%) or very (62%) important to the justice system and just under two-thirds had a more positive view of the jury system after completing their service than they did before. What made jurors so positive about their experience? The most important factor was the perceived benefits of having a diverse jury drawn from different social and economic backgrounds with different viewpoints and experiences. Jurors were also impressed by the fairness of the trial process, praising the performance, commitment and competence of judges, and the way in which the rights of defendants were respected.

Large-scale surveys evidently produce a more rosy picture than individual jurors' accounts. This discrepancy might be accounted for by the greater representativeness of survey data, but it is equally plausible to argue that survey-type questioning conducted within the constraints of s.8 of the Contempt of Court Act is liable to produce general and superficial claims that tell us little about the actual functioning of trial by judge and jury. Jurors may believe that they are doing a great job, but what do other people think?

9.6.2 Professional disagreement with juries

A number of studies have examined the extent of disagreement with jury verdicts. In the USA, Kalven and Zeisel examined 3,576 trials and found that judges agreed with the decision reached by the jury in 75% of cases.[266] This is not a particularly high level of agreement. Stephenson observes that the most striking finding of this study is that judges, as well as agreeing with nearly all jury decisions to convict, would also have convicted 57% of the 1,083 persons whom the jury acquitted.[267] Judges attributed the disagreement between themselves and the juries they instructed to a range of factors. In nearly a third of cases they thought juries had been swayed by their dislike for the law and had exercised 'jury

---

[262] Such as: the foreman who, after the jury retired, produced his own list of the defendant's previous convictions (*Thompson* (1961) 46 Cr App Rep 72); the profoundly deaf jury member who missed half of the evidence and all of the summing up (*Chapman and Lauday* (1976) 63 Cr App Rep 75); and the members of a jury who consulted a 'ouija board' for help in reaching their verdict (*Young* [1995] 2 Cr App Rep 379). For discussion and reform proposals see Kean A and McKeown P, 'Time to Abandon "Beyond Reasonable Doubt" and "Sure": The Case for a New Direction on the Criminal Standard and How it Should Be Used' *Criminal Law Review* [2019] 505.
[263] Zander and Henderson (1993). [264] Zander and Henderson (1993: 232, 206, 208, 212, 216).
[265] Zander and Henderson (1993: 172–173).
[266] Kalven H and Zeisel H, *The American Jury* (Boston: Little, Brown, 1966).
[267] Stephenson G, *The Psychology of Criminal Justice* (Oxford: Basil Blackwell, 1992) pp 180–181.

equity'. (i.e. a broad sense of fairness not bound to the letter of the law). In 15% of cases they acquitted, in the judge's view, because either the defendant or defence counsel had made a favourable impression upon them. In 54% of cases the judge thought that the jury had taken a different approach to the evidence.[268]

The early English studies that measured the extent of agreement amongst lawyers and police officers with jury verdicts concluded that these groups for the most part had no quarrel with the jury's decision.[269] The most substantial study of this type, conducted by Baldwin and McConville in the mid-1970s, painted a more critical picture. Of 370 randomly selected cases heard in one Crown court centre, 114 ended in acquittal. Of the latter, serious doubts were expressed about the jury's verdict by the judge in 32% of cases, by the police in 44%, by prosecuting solicitors in 26% and by defence solicitors in 10% of cases.[270] Baldwin and McConville defined a 'questionable acquittal' as one where the judge and at least one other respondent thought the acquittal was not justified. They considered whether jury equity explained the high incidence of questionable acquittals (36% of all acquittals), but concluded that it did not. The proportion of convictions that were questioned was much smaller, but in 15 cases (6% of all convictions) two or more of the parties to the case had serious doubts about the jury's verdict. Whereas the judge had reservations in eight of these cases, it is striking that the police doubted the verdict in all but two instances. The researchers considered that the most likely explanation for these doubtful convictions was that the jury had failed to appreciate the high standard of proof required in criminal cases and that it had lacked comprehension of the issues involved.[271] There was also evidence to suggest that in some of these cases the jury might have been swayed by racial prejudice.[272] This, from a due process point of view, is the flip side of 'jury equity' and it must be taken into account by those who find attractive the idea of a jury following 'its conscience' rather than the law.[273] Cases like that of Clive Ponting, acquitted by the jury when he was prosecuted under the Official Secrets Act for revealing details of government duplicity during the Falklands War,[274] perhaps show merit in allowing the jury to take a broader view of the justice of the case.[275] However, the power to return verdicts in the face of the law and evidence may result in greater susceptibility to emotional biases.[276]

Two points need to be made concerning Baldwin and McConville's work. The first is that their method for assessing questionable jury acquittals is itself highly questionable. Of the four parties to the case whose views they sought, two (prosecuting solicitor and police) are clearly conviction minded, one (the judge) is, as this chapter has argued, very often pro-conviction, and only one is likely to be pro-acquittal (defence solicitor). Whereas defence

---

[268] Kalven and Zeisel (1966: 115).

[269] See McCabe S and Purves R, *The Jury at Work*, (Oxford: Basil Blackwell, 1972b) and Zander M, 'Are Too Many Professional Criminals Avoiding Conviction?' (1974) 37 *Modern Law Review* 28. For a critique of such research, see Freeman (1981) pp 85–97.

[270] Baldwin and McConville (1979: 45–47). See also Zander and Henderson (1993: 162–72), for the reactions of lawyers, police officers and judges to particular jury verdicts. As with Baldwin and McConville, 'problematic' acquittals were found to be more prevalent than problematic convictions.

[271] Baldwin and McConville (1979: 76).

[272] Baldwin and McConville (1979: 80–81). This could be addressed by ensuring a more representative racial mix on the jury: see earlier.

[273] See also Gordon J, 'Juries as Judges of the Law' (1992) 108 *Law Quarterly Review* 272 at 278; Matravers M, '"More Than Just Illogical": Truth and Jury Nullification' in Duff et al (eds), *The Trial on Trial: Truth and Due Process* (Oxford: Hart, 2004).

[274] Ponting C, *The Right to Know, The Inside Story of the Belgrano Affair* (London: Sphere, 1985).

[275] As has occurred in a number of celebrated cases throughout legal history: Cornish W, *The Jury* (London: Penguin, 1968) ch 5 and Freeman (1991: 90–93).

[276] Horowitz et al, 'Chaos in the Courtroom Reconsidered: Emotional Bias and Juror Nullification' (2006) 30 *Law and Human Behaviour* 163.

solicitors had serious doubts about acquittals in 10% of all acquittal cases, the other three groups had such doubts in much larger proportions ranging from 26% to 44%. By defining a questionable acquittal as one in which the judge and one other party to the case thought the jury's verdict to be wrong, Baldwin and McConville built into their measurements an inherent prosecution bias. That juries were found to be acquittal-prone by the standards of state officials and representatives is not surprising given the state's commitment to crime control values. This methodological flaw was avoided in a New Zealand study, where the researchers scrutinised the evidence given at trial for themselves, and interviewed jurors about their decision-making once the verdict had been given. They counted a verdict as questionable only if:

(a) the judge disagreed with the jury;
(b) the researchers agreed that the verdict was questionable on the basis of the data they had collected; and
(c) an independent barrister experienced in both defence and prosecution work agreed with the researchers.

Whereas the judge disagreed with the jury in 24 out of 48 trials, only three of these were categorised as questionable by the researchers and independent counsel, and there was little evidence of jury equity or of verdicts being influenced by sympathy for the defendant.[277] As Tinsley (2001) puts it, 'overall juries were conscientious in approaching their task and were not usually swayed, as a unit, from making a decision based on the evidence and the law'.

The second point to ask in relation to Baldwin and McConville's work is what meaning to attribute to evidence of disagreement between professionals and lay jurors. If juries always reached verdicts of which judges approved what would be the point of having a jury? One of the strongest arguments for retaining trial by jury is to avoid leaving the fate of defendants to be determined by professionals, applying professional standards. Thus, Mungham and Bankowski contend that since there is no consensus about what constitutes a 'good' jury decision, and because the lawyer's view of a case is not the only sensible or rational interpretation, professional disagreement with jury verdicts tells us nothing meaningful about jury competence.[278]

If one accepts that law is not an absolute but must always be interpreted and applied in specific contexts and circumstances it follows that jurors may take a different view of what the law requires in a particular case from that adopted by lawyers. The institution of the jury represents a policy preference for the process by which this judgment is to be reached to be left ultimately in the hands of lay people rather than professionals. This injection of a lay element into the administering of justice does not have to be justified on the ground that the jury is more reliable or efficient as a finder of fact than a professional judge. Rather, one can argue that lay involvement is necessary in order to allow jury equity to be exercised (if we think this to be desirable) and also to ensure that law and justice do not become monopolised by professionals.[279] This seems consistent with governmental narratives about 'active citizenship' and the oft-repeated view that 'with rights come responsibilities'. There is evidence that serving on a jury can lead to a sense of pride in the accomplishment of an important civic duty and a more general interest in, and

---

[277] Young et al, *Juries in Criminal Trials: A Summary of the Research Findings* (Preliminary Paper 37, Vol 2) (Wellington, New Zealand: Law Commission, 1999), available from <http://www.lawcom.govt.nz> (accessed 5 January 2010).
[278] Mungham G and Bankowski Z, 'The Jury in the Legal System' in Carlen P (ed), *The Sociology of Law* (Keele: University of Keele, 1976) p 209. See also Freeman (1981: 85–88, 95–97).
[279] See Mungham and Bankowski (1976) and Freeman (1981) for extended treatment of this theme.

understanding of, the administration of justice.[280] Lay participation in criminal justice, whether in the form of lay magistrates or the jury, is fundamental to the 'core value' of democracy.[281] Jury service, by furthering transparency and accountability within criminal justice, is a safeguard of a free society.

9.6.3 Shadow and 'mock' juries

An obvious difficulty with all studies that simply measure professional disagreement with verdicts is that they are based on indirect measurements of the jury's work. It is possible that observation of the jury's deliberations would have indicated to Baldwin and McConville a satisfactory explanation (whether of an evidential or equitable nature) for many of the verdicts they classified as questionable. The New Zealand study discussed in the previous section suggests exactly that, although it in turn suffered from the drawback that it relied for its understanding of what took place in the deliberation room on interview material rather than direct observation.

Direct observation of 'shadow' juries—where a panel of people observe or listen to trials in tandem with the real jury, and then retire to consider their 'verdict'—have provided some insight into the dynamics of the jury room. All such studies show a fairly high level of correspondence between the verdicts of the real and the shadow juries, suggesting that the latter approach their simulated task in a reasonably realistic manner. In a study of 30 cases, McCabe and Purves concluded that:

> The 'shadow' juries showed considerable determination in looking for evidence upon which convictions could be based; when it seemed inadequate, they were not prepared to allow their own 'hunch' that the defendant was involved in some way in the offence that was charged to stand in the way of an acquittal ... There was little evidence of perversity in the final decisions of these thirty groups. One acquittal only showed that sympathy and impatience with the triviality of the case so influenced the 'shadow' jurors' view of the evidence that they refused to convict.[282]

Similarly, McConville reported on a televised study of five real cases heard by a shadow jury:

> Although not dealing with the fate of actual defendants, the shadow jury's deliberations have an authentic ring, marked by fierce debate, acute analysis, common sense, personal experience, stubbornness and occasional whiffs of prejudice ... Overall, the quality and power of the argument within the shadow jury room, and the high level of correspondence between the verdicts of the real and shadow juries, suggests that confidence in the jury is well-placed.[283]

Another kind of research, even more artificial than shadow jury studies, involves 'mock juries' in which panels of people observe and then deliberate on mock trials.[284] For example, a study of decision-making in sexual assault cases shows that jurors are influenced by a previous consensual sexual relationship between the victim and defendant and are less likely to find the victim credible when such a relationship exists (see further chapter 10).

---

[280] Munday (1995: 68–71); Matthews et al (2004).
[281] Gobert J, *Justice, Democracy and the Jury* (Aldershot: Dartmouth, 1997); Bankowski et al, *Lay Justice?* (Edinburgh: T & T Clark, 1987) chs 1, 9; Gastil J, Deess P, Weiser P and Simmons C, *The Jury and Democracy: How Jury Deliberation Promotes Civic Engagement and Political Participation* (Oxford: OUP, 2010).
[282] McCabe S and Purves R, *The Shadow Jury at Work* (Oxford: Basil Blackwell, 1974).
[283] McConville M, 'Shadowing the Jury' (1991) 141 *New Law Journal* 1588 at pp 1588 and 1595.
[284] The Lloyd-Bostock research (2000) was of this type. See also the study by Honess et al, 'Juror Competence in Processing Complex Information: Implications from a Simulation of the Maxwell Trial' [1998] *Criminal Law Review* 763. Thomas' research, discussed earlier, involved real discharged jurors observing mock trials.

This may perhaps explain the low prosecution and conviction rate in cases of 'domestic' or marital rape. A variety of extra-legal factors, including stereotypes about behaviour, may enter into jury decision-making: 'the conceptualisation of jurors as rational decision-makers embarking on a fact-finding mission based on the rules of logic and the principles of law is not a valid representation of what happens in jury trials'.[285]

Finch and Munro's study of the impact of complainant intoxication in rape trials used mock juries to investigate how knowledge of intoxication influenced jurors' attribution of blame.[286] They recognise the problems of this method[287] such as ensuring adequate sampling[288] and that mock jurors are given realistic stimuli.[289] Their mock jury sample relied on self-selecting members of the public who responded to advertisements for the research. They were exposed to 75 minute 'mini' trials using actors performing in a university classroom rather than courtroom. Despite these limitations, the researchers argue that their study involved more adequate sampling and realistic stimuli than many. In line with the shadow jury research described earlier they found that mock jurors undertook their task seriously even though no-one's fate really hung in the balance. The ability to observe the group deliberation process was an important advantage of the method.[290]

Finch and Munro's findings have been explored further by Ellison and Munro in a separate study of rape trials again using the mock jury approach.[291] Their research suggests that jurors cannot leave their personal prejudices and stereotypes behind at the door of the courtroom. Jurors make assumptions about the presence or absence of resistance and injury, delay in reporting and the calm demeanour of complainants. For example, many believed that injury was required to corroborate a complaint of real rape, to the extent that jurors expected unrealistically high levels of injury, some even doubting whether non-consensual penetration was possible without vaginal injury. Treatment of delayed reporting was not uniform across mock juries but some saw a three-day delay in reporting as a serious obstacle to conviction whereas victims who called the police immediately were often evaluated positively. Jurors were perplexed when complainants presented as emotionally flat and held calmness against them, although (in a classic double-bind) a 'distressed' complainant was not always seen positively with some jurors suspecting a managed performance. The same issues regarding nature and extent of injury, resistance and complainant reaction were evident in other recent studies,[292] and these findings provide

---

[285] Temkin J and Krahe B, *Sexual Assault and the Justice Gap* (Oxford: Hart Publishing, 2008) p 71.

[286] Finch E and Munro V, 'Breaking Boundaries?: Sexual Consent in the Jury Room' (2006) *Legal Studies* 303; Finch E and Munro V, 'The Demon Drink and the Demonised Woman: Socio-Sexual Stereotypes and Responsibility Attribution in Rape Trials Involving Intoxicants' (2007) *Social and Legal Studies* 591.

[287] Finch E and Munro V, 'Lifting the Veil: The Use of Focus Groups and Trial Simulations in Legal Research' (2008) *Journal of Legal Studies* 30.

[288] One problem with mock juries has been the tendency to rely on students because these are the easiest group for academic researchers to recruit but are obviously not representative of the wider community from which real jurors are drawn.

[289] Often mock jurors are given written vignettes as stimuli, depriving them of the opportunity to assess non-verbal behaviour in the courtroom. Also the vignettes might be deliberately limited in order to enable the researchers to try to isolate the impact of particular variables more clearly, inviting the criticism that they produce the effect they are intended to observe.

[290] Whilst this is also possible with shadow juries, mock jury simulations allow the researcher to try to isolate particular variables more effectively (as by varying the 'story' for some juries).

[291] Ellison L and Munro V, 'Reacting to Rape' (2009a) 49(2) *British Journal of Criminology* 202. See also Ellison L and Munro V 'Of "Normal Sex" and "Real Rape": Exploring the Use of Socio-Sexual Scripts in (Mock) Jury Deliberation' (2009b) 18(3) *Social and Legal Studies* 291.

[292] Lundrigan S, Dhami M and Mueller-Johnson K, 'Predicting Verdicts Using Pre-trial Attitudes and Standard of Proof' (2016) 21 *Legal and Criminological Psychology* 95–110; Ormston et al (2019). Findings regarding the prevalence of rape myths have recently been somewhat contested by Thomas C, 'The 21st Century Jury: Contempt, Bias and the Impact of Jury Service' [2020] *Crim Law Review* 987–1011.

useful insights into the influence of stereotypes on jury decision-making in rape and other cases. This research should inform the policy debate as to what type of instructions or evidence, if any, jurors should be given to counter prejudices they might have which are not supported by psychological and sociological evidence.[293]

When Channel 4 created a televised mock trial that involved practising lawyers, actors as defendants and witnesses and a mock jury, the screening of jury deliberations revealed some interesting points.[294] One juror expressed the view that the 'no comment' police interview was evidence of guilt, while another was concerned that a witness, simply because she was female, would have particular views on domestic abuse. The show did also demonstrate those views being challenged by other jurors, but they provide an indication of how bias and preconceptions could influence deliberations. Thus, research is also valuable for the insights it offers into the nature of jury deliberations.

Past research has shown two broad approaches to deliberation; 'verdict driven' (where the jurors take an early vote and deliberations are driven by their voting positions) and 'evidence driven' (where voting is postponed and the deliberations are guided by a discussion of the evidence). Ellison and Munro found that some of the mock juries in their study tended to be more verdict driven than others, but the approaches are not polar opposites and most juries fell on a continuum between the two.[295] Those juries who were verdict driven tended to be more competitive and confrontational in their deliberations whilst the evidence driven juries tended to be more collaborative. Their research also suggests that the foreperson may influence deliberations, which could be significant in the context of their finding that there was a tendency where such a person was elected, for the person to be an older male.[296] It might be expected from previous research that this would compound a male gender bias against rape victims in jury decision-making but in fact Ellison and Munro found that victim blaming was not limited to male jurors and in some cases male jurors were the most vocal in challenging stereotypes. Their research also confirmed that jurors are confused about the standard of evidence required for conviction, with some jurors expressing the view that this required 100% certainty. They suggest that this may simply have been a strategy to persuade other jurors away from conviction. But Thomas found that 60% of jurors do not understand judges' directions,[297] which would indicate that they are indeed confused about the burden and standard of proof. Further, even when they do understand the directions, juries may dislike being told what to do by judges,[298] and therefore rebel by exercising jury equity.

---

[293] In *R v D* [2008] EWCA Crim 2557 the judge gave a warning to the jury regarding the effect of the delay on the credibility of a complainant in a rape case. The government has been considering whether juries should be given expert evidence to counteract so called 'rape myths'. See Ellison L, 'Credibility in Context: Jury Education and Intimate Partner Rape' (2019) *International Journal of Evidence &Proof* 263; Ellison L and Munro V, 'Turning Mirrors into Windows? Assessing the Impact of (Mock) Juror Education in Rape Trials' (2009c) 49(3) *British Journal of Criminology* 363. This should be read in the context of issues involving sexual history evidence in ch 10.

[294] Channel 4, *The Trial: A Murder in the Family* First aired 21 May 2017.

[295] See Ellison L and Munro V, 'Getting to (Not) Guilty: Examining Jurors' Deliberative Processes In, and Beyond, the Context of a Mock Rape Trial' (2010) 30(1) *Legal Studies* 74–97.

[296] See further Tait D and Goodman-Delahunty J, 'The Effect of Deliberation on Jury Verdicts' in Tait D and Goodman-Delahunty J (eds), *Juries, Science and Popular Culture in the Age of Terror* (London: Palgrave Macmillan, 2017); Salerno J, Peter-Hagene L and Sanchez J, 'Expressing Anger Increases Male Jurors' Influence, but Decreases Female Jurors' Influence, during Mock Jury Deliberations' (2016) 28 *Jury Expert* 29.

[297] Thomas C, *Are Juries Fair?* (2010) Ministry of Justice Research Series 1/10.

[298] Crosby K, 'Controlling Devlin's Jury: What the Jury Thinks, and What the Jury Sees Online' [2012] *Criminal Law Review* 15.

9.6.4 Jury research in context

Criminal justice has undergone a series of fundamental changes since the late twentieth century. Notable amongst these are the Police and Criminal Evidence Act 1984, the inception of the Crown Prosecution Service, the attenuation of the right to silence, and changes to the admissibility of hearsay and character evidence. The impact of all this on the workings of jury trials has yet to be charted properly. The weight of the evidence to date suggests, however, that juries conform more closely to due process values than to crime control ideology. But since, as demonstrated earlier, it is not the jury, but the judge, who is the central directing figure in a trial, and since judges lean towards crime control positions, juries are in reality unlikely to base decisions on anything close to a pure due process approach.

Juries do not act in a vacuum, nor do they act as finders of the truth.[299] They simply decide 'a case'. The case that is presented to the jury is shaped by rules of evidence, procedure and substantive law, the presentation skills of opposing counsel, the preparatory work by the police, the influence of the judge and a host of other factors. We have argued throughout this book that all pre-trial and trial processes are imbued, to a greater or lesser degree, with crime control values and we discuss the influence of inequality throughout and in detail in chapter 10. No matter how due process oriented juries might be, they cannot be relied upon to spot the crime control workmanship that went into building the case put before them. To expect the jury to deconstruct the case and re-examine it under a due process microscope is simply unrealistic. The fact that every major miscarriage of justice case was preceded by a guilty verdict from a jury is evidence of this. But judges are no different from juries in this respect. They too can only deal with the case as presented. And that will have been shaped by the processes covered in earlier chapters of this book. This is a point worth bearing in mind when we consider, in the next section, the value of 'Diplock courts'.

9.7 Narrowing the jury's domain

The prevailing attitude of the state seems to be that juries are costly and too prone to acquit, so it has repeatedly attempted to restrict juries from hearing certain categories of case altogether. In a further move to suggest defendants have 'too many' rights in the criminal justice system, Leveson, in his 2015 Review asserted that 'many people' felt that the court, rather than the defendant, should be able to decide trial venue. As McConville and Marsh (2020) point out, this assertion is not grounded in empirical support. It also further undermines the view that someone who the state, with its greater access to various resources, has chosen to prosecute, is entitled to trial by peers in recognition of the power imbalance between the parties. Although there may be some doubt about the representative nature of juries, they are certainly more representative than judges. Here we review briefly the trend *away* from trial by jury and consider some of the broader implications of the move *towards* other modes of trial.

In 1973 'Diplock courts' were introduced in Northern Ireland for defendants charged with offences deemed to be terrorist-related to be tried by a single judge sitting without a jury.[300] This was justified on the grounds that first, the circumstances of that province

---

[299] See Mungham and Bankowski (1976: 206, 212–213).

[300] See the Northern Ireland (Emergency Provisions) Act 1973. The criteria and methods for directing cases to single judge courts are rough-and-ready and resulted in the diversion of many cases lacking a terrorist connection away from juries: see Jackson J and Doran S, 'Diplock and the Presumption Against Jury Trial: A Critique' [1992] *Criminal Law Review* 755.

left jurors exposed to intimidation and, second, that jurors were likely to return perverse verdicts borne of partisanship.[301] However, the thrust of the report that proposed these courts was to dismantle a series of procedural rights and safeguards for suspects so as to ease the path towards a conviction.[302] As no empirical evidence existed to justify the supposed concerns about jury trials, the suspicion must be that the change was in reality part of the strategy to secure more guilty verdicts.

There were never many cases heard in Diplock courts, falling from less than 400 per annum in the mid 1980s to around 60 per annum 20 years later[303] but this is an area of criminal activity in which, for obvious reasons, the state is particularly keen to secure a high conviction rate. The IRA 'ceasefire' left Diplock courts dealing with a dwindling number of cases, and the Justice and Security (Northern Ireland) Act 2007 began the process of replacing Diplock courts with jury trial. But the Act still allows the DPP for Northern Ireland to certify judge-only trial if he believes that there is a risk of jury intimidation or interference with the administration of justice. The breadth of discretion this gives the DPP is illustrated by a case where a soldier who shot an unarmed man in the 1970s was prosecuted many years later. The DPP asked for judge-only trial as he feared that political allegiances would sway jurors. The defendant challenged this, but the DPP's view was upheld by the Supreme Court.[304]

Research examining Diplock courts gives us some insights into the impact of judge-only trial. It seems that Diplock judges became increasingly prone to accepting police and prosecution evidence in preference to that of the defence and that this 'case-hardening' led to a decline in the acquittal rate, Also, Diplock judges confine their consideration of the case to the strict legal issue of guilt or innocence. In other words, these judges eschew the broader jury role of considering the merits (or morality) of prosecuting and punishing a particular defendant.[305] That role tends to work in the defendant's favour, but does not invariably do so as juries may wish to punish certain individuals even though the legal elements of the offence may not be made out.

In England and Wales jury trial has come under attack in a number of ways, which in recent years includes persistent attempts to introduce judge-only trials in serious and complex fraud cases. The government cajoled Parliament into passing s.43 of the CJA 2003, which, subject to conditions, allowed a judge to order non-jury trial in complex or lengthy fraud cases. There is a long history of debate about the wisdom of asking lay juries to act as fact-finders in complex fraud trials. In 1986 the Roskill Committee recommended that such trials might better be heard by a special tribunal.[306] But the Runciman Commission[307] concluded that, in the absence of research evidence on the workings of jury trials, there was no basis on which to recommend dispensing with juries for complex frauds or other lengthy cases, and in 1998 the government noted that there continued to be a lack of empirical evidence on whether and to what degree juries failed to grasp the evidence and issues in complex fraud trials.[308]

The difficulty of achieving or sustaining convictions in these cases kept this issue alive. However, research in fact found that 'with some screening and more focused help for

---

[301] *Report of the Commission to Consider Legal Procedures to Deal with Terrorist Activities in Northern Ireland* (Cmnd 5185) (London: HMSO, 1972). The Commission was chaired by Lord Diplock.

[302] See Hillyard P, 'The Normalization of Special Powers: from Northern Ireland to Britain' in Scraton P (ed), *Law, Order and the Authoritarian State* (Milton Keynes: Open UP, 1987) pp 285–286.

[303] NI Office, Replacement Arrangements for the Diplock Court System (2006).

[304] *In the matter of an application by Dennis Hutchings for Judicial Review (Northern Ireland)* [2019] UKSC 26. The 2007 Act is extended periodically and was last extended in 2019 (Order no 1097).

[305] Jackson and Doran (1995: 33–36 and 291–294).

[306] *Report of the Departmental Committee on Fraud Trials* (London: HMSO, 1986).

[307] RCCJ (1993: 136).   [308] Home Office (1998a).

the jury, non-specialist jurors are sufficiently competent to understand and deal with the information relevant to their verdicts'.[309] This view is also supported by research examining the experience of jurors in the Jubilee Line case.[310] The trial notoriously collapsed 21 months after it was begun at a cost of several million pounds to the taxpayer. Interviews with the discharged jurors found that they had a good understanding of the evidence and, although they had different levels of specialist knowledge and immediate understanding, they worked co-operatively and took their task seriously. The controversial nature of the provision for non-jury trials was such that further parliamentary action was required to bring it into force and the government was unsuccessful in successive attempts to do this. The provision was eventually repealed by the Protections of Freedoms Act 2012.

According to Matthews et al[311] jurors in complex cases feel frustrated that evidence is 'not always presented in the clearest ways', visual aids are underutilised and jurors are unsure whether they can take notes and ask questions. The Jubilee Line jurors echoed some of these concerns and some felt the pace of evidence was too slow resulting in boredom.[312] Darbyshire et al (2001) identify many ways in which jurors could be helped in their work including judges giving written copies of their directions to juries.[313] Lord Judge has also commented that the Internet generation may be better suited to information presented in a written or visual format.[314]

The problem of jury comprehension needs to be seen within the context of an adversarial system in which each side may be more concerned with 'winning' than 'truth-finding'. This can result in barristers invoking social stereotypes of 'good' and 'bad' behaviour,[315] and in their use of questions designed merely to trap, confuse or mislead witnesses (such as those which include double-negatives, or multiple clauses, or statements dressed up as questions).[316] Tighter judicial regulation of the kind of cross-examination referred to earlier is designed to promote fairness to witnesses, save time, and make the jury's job of assessing the credibility of evidence more straightforward. If this were pursued more thoroughly, the case for judge-only trials in rape cases (particularly 'acquaintance rape' where juries are especially prone to believe rape myths)[317] would be weaker.

Most recently, the idea of Crown court trial without a jury has been suggested as a way to deal with the backlog of cases resulting from the closure of trial courts during the Covid-19 pandemic. In June 2020, this backlog stood at 40,500, and the time it would take for the system to recover was an understandable cause for concern.[318] Unnecessary delay is harmful for victims, witnesses, defendants and their lawyers, but the key word here is *unnecessary*. Opinions about whether delay is necessary or not are likely to vary according to your role in the process. The suggestion that cases could be tried by a judge sitting with two magistrates was widely criticised by the legal profession, and by the Shadow Lord Chancellor, who suggested that other venues, such as sports halls could be made into makeshift courts to assist with the backlog.[319] Several temporary 'Nightingale Courts'

---

[309] Honess et al (1998: 773).

[310] Lloyd-Bostock S, 'The Jubilee Line Jurors: Does their Experience Strengthen the Argument for Judge-only Trial in Long and Complex Fraud Cases?' [2007] *Criminal Law Review* 255.   [311] Matthews et al (2004: 3).

[312] Jacobson et al (2015) also discovered concern among defendants about inattentive jurors.

[313] See also Madge (2006).

[314] Lord Judge 'The Criminal Justice System in England and Wales: Time for Change?', Speech to the University of Hertfordshire, 4 November 2008.

[315] See, for example, Temkin J, 'Prosecuting and Defending Rape: Perspectives from the Bar' (2000) 27(2) *Journal of Law and Society* 219; Willmott et al, 'The English Jury on Trial' (2017) 82 *Custodial Review* 12–14.

[316] A good summary of the research evidence of the effects of such questioning techniques is provided by Kebbell M and Gilchrist E, 'Eliciting Evidence from Eyewitnesses in Court' in Adler J (ed), *Forensic Psychology: Concepts, Debates and Practice* (Cullompton: Willan, 2004).   [317] Willmott et al (2017).

[318] Grey J, 'Lawyers Slam Scheme To Scrap Juries Under Plan To Tackle Backlog Of 500,000 Cases' *Huffington Post*, 23 June 2020.   [319] Grey (2020).

courts were established.[320] Two core values—democracy and efficiency—are brought into direct conflict as a result of Covid-19, and it remains to be seen which value will prevail. But it is worth adding that, despite the pandemic, the Crown court trial backlog is less than it was in 2014 (when it stood at 55,116) yet the suggestion of jury-less trials was not an openly considered remedy at that time.[321]

9.8 Conclusion

The one recommendation of the Runciman Commission[322] that received unequivocal support from the academic community is that s.8 of the Contempt of Court Act 1981 should be amended so as to permit proper (direct) research into real jury decision-making. The government did not support this proposal and so currently we must rely on other, less satisfactory, approaches to evaluating trial by jury. The available research tends to suggest that juries conform more to due process principles than other components of the criminal justice system, but that evidence is not conclusive. Jury trial could probably be improved: cases of non-white defendants facing all white juries, and juries in sexual assault cases relying on outmoded stereotypes, being two examples. There should be further research into jury decision-making but it should not just examine the workings of the jury. Rather, a comparison should be attempted between different possible modes of trial, including: trial by lay magistrates; by a District Judge sitting with or without lay colleagues; by a Crown court judge sitting with lay magistrates and by a Crown court judge alone. For while jury trial undoubtedly has its faults, the real question is whether other modes of trial are, or could be made to be, any better. Where comparisons have been attempted they have tended to flatter jury trial.[323] The empirical evidence concerning the gathering and presentation of evidence by the police and the CPS shows that a degree of wariness is justified. This may convince some of the force of due process arguments in favour of the jury, but the committed crime control adherent may still prefer to see priority given to maintaining a high conviction rate at low cost. Arguments about the future development of the criminal justice system should be informed by facts, but can rarely be resolved by them.

Finally, one should bear in mind that for the vast majority of defendants, arguments about modes of trial are essentially meaningless given the high rate of guilty pleas. Whilst the public think that the right of a defendant charged with a serious offence to be tried by a jury is very important,[324] many defendants waive their right to a trial by judge and jury. Thus, perhaps the single most important reform of the system would be to require that judges should not accept a plea of guilty without first examining closely the adequacy of the prosecution case.[325] This would give more emphasis to the core values of 'justice' and 'democracy', albeit perhaps at the expense of some 'efficiency'. Such a reform could scarcely be effective, however, without a strong cultural commitment to due process amongst trial judges and appeal courts. The research and case law examined in this chapter, for example relating to judicial interventions and summing up, suggest that commitment is sometimes sadly lacking. Evidential rules, once lamented as being overgenerous to the defence, are now openly commended for favouring the prosecution. Relying on the judiciary to

---

[320] See BBC News, Coronavirus: Ten 'Nightingale Courts' in England and Wales to open, 19 July 2020.
[321] Institute for Government, Criminal courts – 10 Key Facts (2019) online at: <https://www.instituteforgovernment.org.uk/explainers/criminal-courts-10-key-facts> (accessed 24 June 2020).
[322] RCCJ (1993: 2).
[323] This is our reading of Jackson and Doran (1995), the best such comparative study within a domestic setting.
[324] Julian and Hough (2009).   [325] Jackson and Doran (1995: 301).

restrain the use of potentially prejudicial evidence seems like an overly optimistic strategy. From this perspective, the jury's injection of due process into a predominantly crime control system might appear to be little more than a placebo. Nevertheless, that 'little more' is well worth preserving both for symbolic and practical reasons.

Further reading

DARBYSHIRE P, with research by MAUGHAN A and STEWART A, 'What Can We Learn from Published Jury Research? Findings for the Criminal Courts Review' [2001] *Criminal Law Review* 970.

DARBYSHIRE P, *Sitting in Judgment: The Working Lives of Judges* (London: Bloomsbury Professional, 2011).

ELLISON L, 'Credibility in Context: Jury Education and Intimate Partner Rape' (2019) 23(3) *International Journal of Evidence and Proof* 263–281.

ELLISON L and MUNRO V, 'Better the Devil You Know? "Real Rape" Stereotypes and the Relevance of a Previous Relationship in (Mock) Juror Deliberations' (2013) 17 *International Journal of Evidence and Proof* 433.

JACOBSON J, HUNTER G and KIRBY A, *Inside Crown Court* (Bristol: Policy Press, 2015).

McCONVILLE M and MARSH L, *The Myth of Judicial Independence: Criminal Justice and the Separation of Powers* (Oxford: OUP, 2020).

OWUSU-BEMPAH ABENAA, *Defendant Participation in the Criminal Process* (London: Routledge, 2017).

QUIRK H, *The Rise and Fall of the Right of Silence* (London: Routledge, 2016).

THOMAS C, 'Ethnicity and the Fairness of Jury Trials in England and Wales 2006–2014' (2017) *Criminal Law Review* 860–876.

10

Inequalities and criminal justice

KEY ISSUES

- How inequalities manifest in the criminal process
- Constructions of dangerousness and the risk society
- Inequality in the construction of law
- Inequality in pre- and post-arrest decision-making
- Sentencing and incarceration
- Inequality and victimisation
- The role(s) of human rights

10.1 Introduction

In mid-2019, a top economist warned that the UK was (is) on route to becoming one of the most unequal countries in the world.[1] The share of income that goes to the richest households in the UK has almost tripled since the 1970s.[2] Recovery from the global financial crisis of 2008 was incomplete when the Covid-19 pandemic hit and damaged economies further. The Brexit referendum and political chaos that ensued after the vote highlighted divisions across urban and rural areas of the country,[3] and among different classes,[4] age groups[5] and races.[6] Globally, children from less wealthy backgrounds now grow up in ever more chaotic, insecure environments.[7]

In 2019, a large-scale review of inequalities in the twenty-first century was announced (the IFS Deaton Review).[8] It will focus on inequality related to wealth, health, family environments, life chances and political influence. There is a growing problem of poor mental health in relation to disadvantaged and socially isolated groups, and people living in disadvantaged communities are disproportionately likely to come into contact with the

---

[1] Partington R, 'Britain risks heading to US levels of inequality, warns top economist' *The Guardian*, 14 May 2019.

[2] Joyce R and Xu X, *Inequalities in the twenty-first century. Introducing the IFS Deaton Review* (London: The Institute for Fiscal Studies, 2019).

[3] Jennings W, Stoker G and Warren I, 'Brexit and Public Opinion: Cities and Towns- The Geography of Discontent' (2019) *Brexit and Public Opinion*. Kings College London.

[4] Jeory T, 'Austerity and class divide likely factors behind Brexit vote, major survey suggests' *The Independent*, 29 June 2016.

[5] Kelly J, 'Brexit: How much of a generation gap is there?' *BBC News Magazine*, 24 June 2016.

[6] Virdee A and McGeever B, 'Racism, Crisis, Brexit' (2018) 41(10) *Ethnic and Racial Studies* 1802–1819.

[7] Putnam R, *Our Kids* (New York: Simon and Schuster, 2015).   [8] Joyce and Xu (2019).

agencies of criminal justice.[9] Approximately 20% of criminal behaviour is strongly connected to poor mental health[10] and contact with the institutions of criminal justice among disadvantaged populations further impairs mental health.[11] There is a complex relationship between social disadvantage and criminal justice, not least because 'criminal justice systems are focused primarily on the crimes of the disadvantaged rather than the "crimes" of the socially privileged'.[12]

This chapter will unpack various manifestations of inequality at different stages of the criminal process, bearing in mind that we must not pathologise disadvantaged groups—many people from those groups will not come into any contact with the criminal justice system—and that '[i]nequality cannot be reduced to any one dimension: it is the culmination of myriad forms of privilege and disadvantage'.[13] We then take a holistic overview of inequality in the criminal process, and consider the potential for change. Inequalities intersect at various points, which we have highlighted where possible. This makes the debate about inequality in the criminal process both theoretically complex and difficult to resolve. We can really do no more than scratch the surface of these issues. Consequently, we focus on three key areas in which the manifestation of social inequality in the criminal process is clear: class, race and gender. We could have focused on, for example, disability, age, neurodiversity or LGBTQI+ issues, but there is comparatively little research on how inequality in these areas[14] affects the criminal process. We will consider issues relating to populations that are disabled and/or LGBTQI+ briefly in our discussion of hate crime (section 10.7.2) and in chapter 12, but there should be more research on how a broader range of inequalities intersect and manifest themselves in the criminal process.

We can return here to the three core values that we discuss elsewhere in this book: justice, democracy and efficiency. From a justice perspective, the criminal process can be used to assert the legitimacy of state authority; state punishment can only legitimately be inflicted on those who have been convicted of a crime. A sense of legitimacy in policing is likely to affect the extent to which people feel obliged to co-operate with, and respect, the police. People are more likely to comply with criminal processes that they regard as fair.[15] So, the authority of the criminal process (and at least one branch of the state) relies heavily on citizens regarding the process as fair. A system that perpetuates inequality is unlikely to be regarded as fair, because it is not a system that takes into account unequal access to justice due to inequality of money and power. The more unfair the process is, the less legitimacy it will have, and democracy is undermined.

---

[9] See, for example, Newburn T, 'Social Disadvantage, Crime, and Punishment' in Dean H and Platt L (eds), *Social Advantage and Disadvantage* (Oxford: OUP, 2016) pp 322–340.

[10] Peterson J, Skeem J, Kennealy P, Bray B and Zvonkovic A, 'How Often and How Consistently Do Symptoms Directly Precede Criminal Behaviour Among Offenders with Mental Illness?' (2014) 38 *Law and Human Behavior* 439–449.

[11] Gottfried E and Christopher S, 'Mental Disorders Among Criminal Offenders: A Review of the Literature' (2017), 23(3) *Journal of Correctional Health Care* 336–346.

[12] Newburn (2016: 322). And see the discussion of non-police enforcement in ch 7.

[13] Joyce and Xu (2019: 14).

[14] One exception to this is the issue of how people with learning disabilities and accused of crimes are treated in the criminal process. See, for example, Jones J, 'Persons with Intellectual Disabilities in the Criminal Justice System: Review of Issues' (2007) 51(6) *International Journal of Offender Therapy and Comparative Criminology* 723–733; Talbot J, 'Prisoners' Voices: Experiences of the Criminal Justice System by Prisoners with Learning Disabilities' (2010) 15(3) *Tizard Learning Disability Review* 33–41; Ali A, Ghosh S, Strydom A and Hassiotis A, 'Prisoners with Intellectual Disabilities and Detention Status. Findings From a UK Cross Sectional Study of Prisons' (2016) 53–54 *Research in Developmental Disabilities* 189–197.

[15] See ch 1 and, for example, Tyler T (ed), *Legitimacy and Criminal Justice: An International Perspective* (New York: Russel Sage Foundation, 2007).

Lower levels of trust in the police among communities that experience socio-economic inequality may lead to higher levels of violent crime (and some types of acquisitive offending), and low social capital contributes to that pattern.[16] As Ward (2016: 115) notes:

> The relationship between social and economic deprivation, poverty and exclusion in criminal offending is not a causal one, yet there is evidence to support the fact that living with certain conditions correlates closely with some crime pathways.[17]

These patterns can contribute to a cycle of distrust as crime both occurs and is processed differently for members of disadvantaged communities than for members of privileged communities. Crime, enforcement and disadvantage all mutually reinforce and exacerbate each other. As law and order has become more politicised since the 1980s alongside the rise of neoliberal political ideology (chapter 1), and as governments became more fixated with achieving quick results, short-term economic and managerialist logic both became more prominent in contemporary crime control polices.[18] Wacquant (2009) persuasively argues that the institutions of criminal justice now collectively represent the power relations that are reproduced through socio-economic capital. But to simply reproduce those power relations fails to take into account the experiences of those subject to, as well as those responsible for, law and policy. Efficiency, which is also an important value, should not trump justice and democracy. The argument that efficiency is prioritised above the values of justice and democracy leads scholars to describe the criminal justice process as a 'sausage factory'.[19] Moreover, if it is true, as we suggested earlier, that crime, enforcement and disadvantage are mutually reinforcing, the short-term efficiency gains from crime control policies (e.g. depriving the process of legitimacy, undermining experience and therefore democracy, increasing the use of prison) are cancelled out by the increased anti-authority attitudes, crime and disadvantage that those policies produce.

Fairness is neither a rigid nor a universal concept, and processes of responsibilisation (chapter 1) appear to have shifted ideas about fairness. Peoples' opinions about inequality are inextricably connected to what they believe to be fair, and people are more likely to accept inequality when they feel it results from merit rather than luck.[20] That is, in turn, dependent on how people determine merit. As the criminal process has shifted further towards crime control, thereby penalising defendants who are considered undeserving of state leniency or assistance, questions of inequality become masked in neoliberal discourse about deserving and undeserving citizens, risk society management and austerity. And those discourses about who is deserving and who is undeserving are infused with ideas about a whole range of socio-economic disadvantages. So, 'people suffer inequalities and discrimination because the groups of which they are members are marginalised, impoverished, repressed or discriminated against. Justice and regulation need to be able to respond to group as well as individual circumstances and experiences'.[21]

---

[16] Newburn (2016).

[17] See also, for example, Reiner R, 'Beyond Risk: A Lament for Social Democratic Criminology' in Newburn T and Rock P (eds), *The Politics of Crime Control: Essays in Honour of David Downes* (Oxford: Clarendon Press, 2006) pp 8–50.

[18] Hughes G, *The Politics of Crime and Community* (London: Palgrave Macmillan, 2007).

[19] See, e.g., Ward (2016) and Newman (2013).

[20] Almås I, Cappelen A and Tungodden B, *Cutthroat Capitalism Versus Cuddly Socialism: Are Americans More Meritocratic and Efficiency-Seeking than Scandinavians?* (2019) NHH Dept. of Economics, Discussion Paper No. 4/2019.

[21] Hudson B, 'Regulating Democracy: Justice, Citizenship and Inequality in Brazil' in Quirk H, Seddon T and Smith G (eds), *Regulation and Criminal Justice* (Cambridge: CUP, 2010) p 285.

10.2 Creating 'dangerous classes' and 'suitable enemies'

Since the industrial revolution, unemployed populations have been viewed as problematic because they create risk[22]—a risk of civil unrest[23] and a risk of coming to enjoy the status of unemployment and thus avoid paid employment in favour of claiming state aid. Concerns about these 'dangerous classes'—a term adopted into mainstream use since the mid-1800s[24]—led to the establishment of workhouses where the population could be controlled, and communities could be relieved of some tax burdens associated with poor relief. The Poor Law Amendment Act 1834 meant that relief could only be given in workhouses, and the conditions in workhouses were designed to be deter people from seeking them as 'soft options'. But they were also designed to clearly segregate paupers from workers.[25] This is all part of Britain's 'historical tradition of managing marginalised populations and the use of the welfare state and welfare sanctions to reform the behaviour of problematised populations.'[26]

This history of viewing poorer people as dangerous to (economic) social order, and therefore in need of segregation, has influenced the development of criminal policy. Those who are seen as undeserving of assistance are further outcast from mainstream society. By segregating certain sections of the population, many are actually pushed further towards criminality, thereby contributing to a cycle of deprivation, criminality and contact with the criminal process. Unemployed and low-paid people tend to be significantly overrepresented in arrest statistics.[27] Only one-quarter of all the arrests in Phillips and Brown's random sample were of employed people.[28] Hillyard and Gordon (1999) observe that arrest rates in the poorest areas of the UK are much higher than in wealthier areas. In addition to community pressures, these people are simply more vulnerable to being arrested, for they spend more of their time in public spaces where police powers can most easily be deployed (see section 2.1). This all gets worse as inequality increases.

10.2.1 Processes of exclusion and colonialism

The British history of colonisation shaped patterns of criminalisation and criminal justice that persist today. Drawing comparison with the way that unemployed populations were viewed as dangerous and in need of discipline and control in Victorian England, native populations and indigenous peoples in colonised countries were viewed with distrust and as a threat to the imposed and enforced social order. They 'needed'—in the eyes of their colonisers—to be controlled and regulated.[29] This process included criminal stereotyping and the use of public, symbolic punishments to maintain order.[30] Such stereotyping was

---

[22] Christie N, *Crime Control as Industry* (Abingdon: Routledge, 1994).
[23] See, e.g., Thompson F, 'Social Control in Victorian Britain' (1981) 34(2) *The Economic History Review* 189–208 and literature on the 'Swing Riots' of the 1830s.
[24] Bell E, *Criminal Justice and Neoliberalism* (London: Palgrave Macmillan, 2011).
[25] A system of punishing able bodied beggars pre-existed the Poor Laws of the Victorian era, and so Britain has a long history of punitive treatment of the unemployed. See, e.g., Spicker P, *How Social Security Works: An introduction to benefits in Britain* (Bristol: Policy Press, 2011).
[26] Flint J and Hunter C, 'Governing by Civil Order: Towards New Frameworks of Support, Coercion and Sanction?' in Quirk, Seddon and Smith (2010: 192).
[27] Meehan (1993); Sanders A, 'Class Bias in Prosecutions' (1985) 24 *Howard Journal of Crime and Justice* 76.
[28] Phillips and Brown (1998: xii).
[29] Nijhar P, *Law and Imperialism. Criminality and Constitution in Colonial India and Victorian England.* (Abingdon: Routledge, 2009).
[30] Jones C and Vagg J, *Criminal Justice in Hong Kong* (Abingdon: Routledge, 2007).

made easier by contemporary interest in the science of difference, which suggested that physical and mental capacity could be ranked by race, and thus the races at the top of the scale felt justified in imposing techniques of control on what they perceived to be lower ranking races.[31] Many white British people in the nineteenth century 'took for granted that the British race stood at the pinnacle of civilisation and led the world in the development of civilized ideas.'[32] Contact with institutions of criminal justice can be used to socialise subservient populations about how racialised populations are viewed as risky or dangerous (see later). The criminal process therefore became a key site for control of colonised (especially non-white) populations through racialised stereotypes about dangerous or risky groups. There are fairly obvious connections with the view taken about lower class populations (as risky and in need of management) in Britain: 'Several anthropologists of colonialism note a comparable stance toward the "dangerous classes" in the metropolitan societies from which the colonists hailed.'[33]

This is also connected to the British role in the slave trade, through which many British families became wealthy. Traders in Britain benefitted from the slave trade long after Britain officially abolished slavery by becoming involved in business connected to slavery (the sugar trade is an obvious example), investment in overseas trade where slavery had not been abolished and the continued use of indentured service.[34] As a result, many former slaves found themselves cast from being regarded in law as property into the lower (lowest) class ranks of society, and thus became members of the so-called 'dangerous classes' in 'need' of surveillance and management through state apparatus. Historically viewing enslaved people and women as property are stark examples of the power of the law to (de) humanise.[35] Slavery and colonialism have legacies in the twentieth and twenty-first centuries that help shape the way class, race and gender can intersect. For example, austerity measures have disproportionately impacted on poor black and Asian women,[36] and racialised urban spaces have come to be associated with poverty and working class communities.[37] White working classes have tended to be pitted against racialised groups, but relationships between class, race and gender are much more complex than a simple binary account.[38]

This colonial and slave-trade backdrop set the stage in the post-WW2 period for further criminalisation of migrant groups and inequalities in the way they were treated, whether as victims or suspects. In theory, everyone born in the British Empire in the Caribbean, Africa and Asia had the right to settle in the UK.[39] Hence, the 1950s and 1960s saw a growth in the number of migrants from the West Indies, many of whom famously came aboard the Empire Windrush (the 'Windrush generation'). Increased immigration from India, Pakistan and Africa followed. These pioneers from the Commonwealth answered

[31] Nijhar (2009).
[32] Brown M, 'Race, Science and the Construction of Native Criminality in Colonial India' (2001) 5(3) *Theoretical Criminology* 345–368 at 346.
[33] Schneider J and Schneider P, 'The Anthropology of Crime and Criminalization' (2008) 37 *Annual Review of Anthropology* 351–373.   [34] See Sherwood M, *After Abolition* (London: I.B. Tauris, 2007).
[35] Dayan C, (2011) *The Law is a White Dog: How Legal Rituals Make and Unmake Persons* (Princeton University Press)
[36] See Khan O and Shaheen F (eds), *Minority Report. Race and Class in post-Brexit Britain* (London: Runnymede Trust, 2017).
[37] Danewid I, 'The Fire This Time: Grenfell, Racial Capitalism and the Urbanisation of Empire' (2019) 26(1) *European Journal of International Relations* 289.
[38] See, for example, Snoussi D and Mompelat L, *'We Are Ghosts' Race, Class and Institutional Prejudice* (London: Runnymede Trust, 2019); Malik K, 'Working class versus minorities? That's looking at it the wrong way' *The Guardian*, 14 July 2019; Sandhu K, 'Working class in Britain? You must be white' *New Internationalist*, 16 March 2018.
[39] Phillips C and Bowling B, 'Ethnicities, Racism, Crime and Criminal Justice' in McAra et al (eds), *Oxford Handbook of Criminology* (Oxford: OUP, 2017).

Britain's call for workers for difficult-to-fill jobs, often taking jobs for which they were over-qualified.[40] Yet, from the perspective of an ill-informed public living in austere post-war conditions in the UK, these workers were generally unwelcome and hence they found it difficult to find work and housing, as well as being excluded from public places such as pubs and hotels.[41] And in 1968 Enoch Powell (the then Shadow Defence Secretary for the Conservative Party) gave his infamous 'Rivers of Blood' speech in which he claimed that mass migration from the Commonwealth would lead to violence. Racial prejudice was common place in this early post-war period; dark skin was viewed as a sign of inferiority. This prejudice—also evident in the police, and no doubt other criminal justice agencies, and still continuing[42]—was accompanied by wilful ignorance about the cultures and customs of migrants. So, the police were reluctant to recognise the racial motivations behind crimes such as the murder of Kelso Cochrane who was stabbed to death in 1959.[43] Similarly, the case of David Oluwale, who was hounded to death by Leeds Police, shows that immigrant communities were persecuted as much as they were protected by the police.[44]

More recently, continuing immigration has added another level of tension to black/brown/white/class intersections in criminal justice.[45] As police and border authorities have been drawn to work together to delineate whether someone 'belongs' in a community (see sections 10.4 and 10.8), 'all racialized groups are treated as automatically suspect; both citizens and those lacking citizenship are thought to be offenders and foreign', which undermines any possibility of equal citizenship.[46] Migration and its racialised aspects have been increasingly criminalised:[47] asylum seekers have been constructed as violent criminals who are a serious threat to national security,[48] particularly fuelled by concerns about terrorism, leading border enforcement agencies to become complicit (whether knowingly or not) in some processes of white supremacy.[49] Terrorism fears mean that young South Asian men in particular have been classed as a risky population, and many people in the Muslim community have experienced prejudice from the police at both individual and community levels through intrusive, frequently encountered surveillance—or worse.[50] Policing of such populations needs to be situated in our history of colonialism, involvement in the slave trade and subsequent patterns of migration, and seen as a continuation of ideas about 'dangerous' populations.

---

[40] Ibid.

[41] Exemplified by the infamous post-war 'No Irish, no blacks, no dogs' signs. See *Irish Post*, 26 January 2018. Irish and, before them, Jewish immigrants were for several generations in a similar position. But the longer period of assimilation and less obvious visual differences have greatly reduced the structural disadvantages of these ethnic groups.

[42] 'British policing is still "institutionally racist" . . . [said] Chief Constable Gareth Wilson, the national lead for diversity, equality and inclusion' *The Independent*, 12 October 2018; In May 2020 a senior Met officer received an undisclosed sum to settle her claim of discrimination against the force: see <https://www.ndtv.com/indians-abroad/top-indian-origin-cop-parm-sandhu-settles-racism-case-with-police-in-uk-2234118> (accessed 25 October 2020).

[43] Whitfield J, 'The Historical Context: Policing and Black People in Post-war Britain' in Rowe M (ed), *Policing Beyond Macpherson* (Cullompton: Willan, 2007).

[44] Aspden K, *Nationality: Wog: The Hounding of David Oluwale* (London: Vintage Books, 2007).

[45] Stenson K, 'The State, Sovereignty and Advanced Marginality in the City' in Squires P and Lea J (eds), *Criminalisation and Advanced Marginality: Critically Exploring the Work of Loic Wacquant* (Bristol: The Policy Press, 2012) p 45.

[46] Parmar A, 'Arresting (Non)citizenship: The Policing Migration Nexus of Nationality, Race and Criminalization' (2019a) *Theoretical Criminology* 1–22, p 2.

[47] Ibid   [48] Hughes (2007).

[49] Davis A and Ernst R, 'Racial Gaslighting' (2019) 7(4) *Politics, Groups and Identities* 761–774.

[50] Mythen, G and Kamruzzaman P, 'Counter-terrorism and Community Relations: Anticipatory Risk, Regulation and Justice' in Quirk, Seddon and Smith (2010). For a distressing example see the case of Girma Belay in the conclusion to ch 11.

10.2.2 **The rise of risk society**

During the late twentieth century, a new discourse in criminal justice emerged. This was less about punishing criminal behaviour than about further identifying and managing aggregate populations.[51] The 1997–2010 Labour government attempted to improve general social conditions and reduce social exclusion (e.g. through the creation of action zones for special attention in health, education and employment), but its contrasting desire for rapid and easily measurable gains meant that sustainable change was hard to achieve.[52] And those who did not, or who were unable to, perform in line with such initiatives were deemed responsible for their disadvantaged state, and therefore undeserving of further assistance. This 'underclass' was seen as having lost mainstream values, and therefore needed to be disciplined: 'Given that criminality was often cited as one of the distinguishing characteristics of the underclass, the responsibilisation of the poor was closely linked to the responsibilisation of offenders'[53]—contrary to powerful groups, whose crimes are more likely to be ignored (see chapter 7).

Modern society's obsession with 'risk' created a criminology of the 'other'—a bad citizen for whom punishment and exclusion is justified. This ignored the way that '[e]xclusion reinforces exclusion when we no longer make any effort to understand difference but rather to eliminate the risk that it represents'.[54] Criminal justice narratives about security, dangerousness and the 'other' intensified concern about risk linked to terrorism since 2001[55] and to social insecurity following Brexit, even though '[r]esearch shows that risk is inherently difficult to predict, which means that many of those classed as dangerous', and incarcerated on this basis, would not offend if at liberty.[56] The rise of concern about, and decreased tolerance for, risk has created what Hudson calls an insatiable demand for security, which creates more fear, more suspicion and undermines solidarity which is essential for social well-being.[57] As economic inequality increases, richer sections of society are able to buy their way out of crime by investing in privatised security measures such as CCTV and gated communities,[58] (further) eroding a sense of community,[59] and increasing divisions among different communities. And of course this means that poorer communities are less protected from crime, reinforcing disadvantage and stereotypes about criminality. The privatisation of security, alongside discourses of responsibilisation, resulted in 'inequalities in security, not merely in rich and poor but also between young and old, male and female' populations.[60]

Although it is rose-tinted to suggest that society was cohesive before modern concentrations on risk intensified, decreased tolerance for 'risk' does shape responses to crime. Increased levels of crime consciousness as a result of greater concerns about risk, alongside progressively weakened access to state supported welfare, lead to more repressive powers to 'manage' the poor. It is easier—and (in the short term) cheaper—for states to cast criminals as rational actors who have chosen to commit offences than it is to accept that social circumstances are the most powerful drivers of crime, or that prisons

---

[51] Christie (1994).
[52] Faulkner D and Burnett R, *Where Next for Criminal Justice?* (Bristol: The Policy Press, 2011).
[53] Bell (2011: 95).
[54] Dingwall G and Hillier T, *Blamestorming, Blamemongers and Scapegoats* (Bristol: The Policy Press, 2016) p 97.
[55] Hodgson J, *The Metamorphosis of Criminal Justice* (Oxford: OUP, 2020) p 88.
[56] Dingwall and Hiller (2016: 44).
[57] Hudson B, *Justice in the Risk Society* (London: Sage, 2003) p 70.   [58] Christie (1994).
[59] Hughes (2007). See discussion in section 10.8   [60] Hudson (2003: 77).

are failing. The by-product of that approach is that members of marginalised groups are further demonised as the agencies of criminal justice act in an increasingly exclusionary manner, resulting in 'more punitive attitudes among significant sections of the public.'[61] Anti-social behaviour policy, through civil preventative measures in particular (discussed in section 1.1.2), provide one example of how modern criminal justice policies focus on so-called 'risky' populations—in that case, youths and underprivileged adults.

10.2.3 Advanced marginality

As neoliberal principles increasingly shaped economic policy at the end of the twentieth and beginning of the twenty-first century, the criminal justice system, particularly through policing, 'began to play an increasing part in the lives of the most disadvantaged, the least well-educated and the most economically marginal.'[62] As such, the social exclusion experienced by groups vulnerable to inequality took an advanced turn through the use of penal state apparatus. While those labelled criminal have a long history of segregation from society through imprisonment (or, historically, transportation to colonies) the neoliberal state has become increasingly interventionist so that (potential) offenders are excluded from mainstream society. The politics of advanced marginality combines a complex web of social and penal policies to present a new understanding of poverty policies.[63] Rather than risk, the theory of advanced marginality regards the punitive turn as about social, not criminal, insecurity. That insecurity is associated with casualised labour and disrupted ethno-racial hierarchies; 'a punitive revamping of public policy that weds the "invisible hand" of the market to the "iron fist" of the penal state.'[64] Through the penal turn, people who are economically poor have been categorised as 'undeserving', while the market appreciates that there is big money in privatised security measures, private prisons and prison equipment.[65] But prisons not only warehouse people, they theoretically attempt to reform behaviour through rehabilitative programmes that orient towards dominant social models.[66] The punitive turn in the United Kingdom reinforced the process that had already 'seen to it that the most disadvantaged, the least well-educated and the most economically marginal always had been the groups of greatest interest to the police and local authorities'.[67] People from non-white populations are disproportionately represented in lower social classes, and are almost twice as likely to be unemployed compared to their white counterparts in the UK.[68] This was further reinforced by the government's 'hostile environment' for illegal immigrants that caught in its net many legal immigrants—including, infamously, many of the 'Windrush generation'.[69] Many black people end up excluded from official economies.[70] Unsurprisingly, 46% (900,000 people) of all people living in families where the household head is black/African/Caribbean/black British are

---

[61] Hughes (2007: 116).
[62] Squires, P 'Neoliberal, Brutish and Short? Cities, Inequalities and Violence's' in Squires and Lea (2012: 220).
[63] Ibid.
[64] Wacquant, L 'The Wedding of Workfare and Prisonfare in the 21st Century: Responses to Critics and Commentators' in Squires and Lea (2012: 247); Wacquant (2009).
[65] Christie (1994).
[66] Bell (2011). Part of the issue with this is that the concept of rehabilitation is not well defined (Moore R, 'The Enigmas of Rehabilitation and Resettlement: Forms of Capital, Desistance and the Contextualisation of Carceral-Community Offender Transitions' (2019) 58(2) The Howard Journal of Crime and Justice 202–219).
[67] Squires in Squires and Lea (2012: 220).
[68] Powell A, Unemployment by Ethnic Background. Briefing Paper, HC 6385 (2019).
[69] Williams W, Windrush Lessons Learned Review HC 93 (2020) online at: <www.gov.uk/official-documents> (accessed 25 October 2020). And see, e.g., Malik K, The Guardian, 28 June 2020.
[70] Stenson in Squires and Lea (2012: 44).

in poverty, compared to 19% (10.7 million people) of those living in families where the head of household is white.[71] Through these processes the criminal justice system delivers 'social order' primarily for privileged populations; and, pushed to meet targets in the neoliberal drive for efficiency, the institutions of criminal justice tend to target the low hanging fruit, i.e. those populations that are easiest to police (due to high visibility (see also section 2.4)), and easiest to punish (as a result of power imbalance and in the name of promoting social responsibility).

10.3 The construction of criminal law

All criminal law is socially constructed because it is dependent on what behaviour society regards as acceptable at any given time, but the general inflexibility of legal definitions makes the law unable to adapt to the reality of socio-economic disadvantage.[72] As such, criminal law itself is infused with social inequality. For example, if D is forced to steal for X because of threats of serious violence, D will in many circumstances have a complete defence; but if D is forced to steal for his or her children because of poverty, D will not even have a partial defence: as with those deported in 2019 whose crimes resulted from the 'hostile environment' policy, according to campaigners.[73]

The legal and political professions have always been male dominated, and the criminal law and criminal process reflects this gender bias. While ever more women are entering both professions, they remain underrepresented at the highest levels of those careers.[74] As with race and class, women are underrepresented on the judicial benches, meaning that cases involving women tend to be viewed from dominant male perspectives, which can skew decisions. This is particularly the case in relation to sexual offences and child welfare offences, both of which are discussed in this chapter. Most criminal laws, and many precedents that remain powerful today, were created when women were even less well represented in law and in politics than now. Even those that have been revised in recent years tend to carry forward ideas of reasonableness and rationality that remain partial despite purporting to be neutral: 'The subject of criminal law on whom constructions of criminality, responsibility, culpability, defences and mitigations are predicated is the "reasonable man",[75] who is not only male but is also white, heterosexual, able-bodied, cis-gender and middle class.

We will take the example of sexual offences.[76] Women have historically been considered the manager of male sexual desire,[77] which led Smart to argue that sexual offence laws

---

[71] Stroud P, *Measuring Poverty 2020* (London: Social Metrics Commission, 2020).

[72] Hudson B, 'Punishing the Poor: Dilemmas of Justice and Difference' in Heffernan W and Kleinig J (eds), *From Social Justice to Criminal Justice: Poverty and the Administration of Criminal Law* (Oxford: OUP, 2000) pp 189–216.

[73] <https://www.bbc.co.uk/news/uk-47123841> (accessed 25 October 2020).

[74] See The Law Society, *Influencing For Impact: The Need For Gender Equality In The Legal Profession* (2019b) available at <https://www.lawsociety.org.uk/support-services/research-trends/gender-equality-in-the-legal-profession/> (accessed 25 October 2020); Bearne S, Bowcott O and Perkins A, 'Lady Hale: courts and judiciary should reflect diversity of UK' *The Guardian*, 15 February 2018; Browning S, *Women in Parliament and Government*. Briefing Paper HC 01250 (2019). [75] Hudson (2003: 138).

[76] Other examples could include defences of loss of control and self-defence. Both have been modified with the aim of being more inclusive (by being more sensitive to difference), but remain predicated in male concepts of aggression and reasonableness. Attempts to avoid men being more easily able to argue loss of control as a result of discovering infidelity by its specific exclusion from the defence in the Coroners and Justice Act 2009, have been undermined by *Clinton* [2012] 2 All ER 947: infidelity was allowed to form part of the circumstances leading to a man's argument that he had lost control when he killed his wife. [77] Hudson (2003).

sustain and celebrate the oppression of women.[78] That ideology can still be seen in the updated offence of rape contained in the Sexual Offences Act 2003. One key element of the offence of rape is that the defendant did not reasonably believe that the victim was consenting to penetration. Prior to enactment of the Sexual Offences Act 2003, a defendant could be acquitted if he honestly believed there was consent no matter how unreasonable that belief might be.[79] This highly subjective test favoured the acquittal of defendants, which is arguably appropriate in situations where someone is at risk of being imprisoned for the rest of his life. But systemic problems meant that victims of sexual offences were unlikely to achieve formal justice. The 2003 Act attempted to address one of these problems by adding a requirement that the defendant's belief in consent must be objectively reasonable, and by adding a set of circumstances in which there is no doubt that consent is absent, or in which it is presumed to be absent and the defendant must prove otherwise.[80] This has undoubtedly made it easier for the prosecution to obtain a conviction in rape cases, but the provisions are diluted by section 1(2) of the 2003 Act: whether a belief is reasonable is to be determined having regard to all the circumstances. This allows defendants to rely on their own understanding of the circumstances to argue that the belief was in fact reasonable. It is still possible that guilt or innocence in a rape case will turn on the male's understanding of the circumstances at the time. If the male defendant can persuade a jury that he had, or might have had, a 'reasonable belief' that consent was present (no matter what the victim says), then he is entitled to be acquitted.[81] Thus, men are still afforded a basis upon which they can assert that their understanding of the situation should trump the victim's account.

We discussed the prevalence of rape myths among jurors, and how they can impact outcomes, in sections 1.7 and 9.6.3. The problem is not, however, just a matter of juror assumption, but is also reflected in the construction of the criminal law and law of evidence in this area. In *R v A*,[82] the House of Lords decided that previous sexual activity could be relevant to the issue of the defendant's belief in consent. This judgment restated the importance of judicial discretion in allowing such evidence to be adduced where the defendants' right to a fair trial depends upon it. This ruling raises at least four questions: whether sexual history evidence is ever essential to a fair trial, as it was ruled to be in *Ched Evans*;[83] if it sometimes can be, under what circumstances; whether those circumstances should be spelled out in statute or left to judicial discretion;[84] and how is judicial discretion exercised? While we would say that the right to a fair trial is paramount to the core values of both justice and democracy, decisions about what is admissible to ensure a fair trial are ultimately made through judicial discretion. This is not the same as saying that sexual history evidence is never relevant, but that there should be greater clarity about when it might be relevant and how, and judges should be guided by more structured principles than the

---

[78] Smart C, *Feminism and the Power of Law* (London: Routledge, 1989).
[79] See *DPP v Morgan* [1975] UKHL 3.   [80] See s.1, s.75 and s.76 Sexual Offences Act 2003.
[81] Appellate case law in this area has thus far focused on circumstances where a male argued that his belief in consent was reasonable, see *R v B* [2013] EWCA Crim 3 and *A* [2012] EWCA Crim 1646. In both cases the courts were not persuaded by the defendant's argument that his belief was reasonable, but the very fact that these cases made it past the stringent tests for appeal (ch 11) illustrate that the focus remains on male understanding of belief in consent. For research which illustrates that jurys might acquit in such circumstances (which we can never know—see ch 9) and that the focus on 'reasonable belief' continues to undermine attempts at victim empowerment, see Gray J, 'What Constitutes a "Reasonable Belief" in Consent to Sex? A Thematic Analysis' (2015) 21(3) *Journal of Sexual Aggression* 337–353.
[82] (No 2) [2001] UKHL 25.
[83] [2016] EWCA Crim 452. *Gjoni* [2014] EWCA Crim 691 illustrates that the defendant's right to a fair trial is paramount, and that a ruling to exclude sexual history evidence will not be interfered with unless the defendant's right to a fair trial is not prejudiced.
[84] Legislative reform is advocated for in McGlynn C, 'Rape Trials and Sexual History Evidence: Reforming the Law on Third-Party Evidence' (2017) 81(5) *The Journal of Criminal Law* 367–392.

rather nebulous concept of a 'fair trial'. While the admission of sexual history evidence is 'tightly circumscribed' by the provisions of s.41 Youth Justice and Criminal Evidence Act,[85] the concept of a fair trial is not, and has the potential to be tainted by systemic bias. In one sample of applications to adduce sexual history evidence, prosecutors resisted the entirety of 35% of applications, and the final arbiter in all such applications is the judge.[86] Recall that most judges are white, older men. McGlynn wrote an alternative feminist judgment to the decision in *R v A*, highlighting that:

> while the assumption is made that once a complainant has agreed to sexual activity with the accused on one occasion, she is more likely to agree on subsequent occasions, the contrary could also be the case. We know that a large proportion of rapes are perpetrated by partners or former partners and not by strangers as is often assumed. In this light, we can see that the problem with this assumption is that it assumes that women are less likely to be raped by their partners or ex-partners which demonstrably is not the case.[87]

The work of feminist judgment projects to encourage judges to see how rape myths are reinforced through the application of criminal law and rules of evidence does not appear to have resulted in the shift that might have been hoped for. In *Ched Evans*, evidence of language and sexual preferences with two other partners was ruled admissible and resulted in a successful appeal against conviction and later acquittal.[88] The decision provoked widespread outrage, with campaigners arguing that previous sexual evidence is still being used in up to 37% of cases, procedures for the admissibility of such evidence are often ignored, and the way the law is being applied continues to deter victims from reporting rape and sexual assault.[89] Some research suggests that victims' prior sexual behaviour is still being questioned in many cases.[90] That research is seemingly contradicted by more recent research.[91] This rightly casts doubt on the robustness of the earlier data, but since the more recent work is based on the views of lawyers—whose failure to change their practices and culture is blamed for the alleged failure of the legislation—this is no more reliable than the other research. So we might say that it is not clear how well the laws restricting the use of sexual history evidence are working. However, that would miss the point. The fact is that in many sexual assault cases there is little objective evidence either way. Sexual history evidence can sometimes shed light on what happened and why. Using it can be prejudicial and traumatic for the victim; and restricting its use can lead to unsafe convictions. There is no ideal solution, but the situation is not helped by judicial interpretation of legal provisions that fails, as McGlynn argues,[92] to properly address gendered rape myths, and therefore perpetuates gender inequality in the construction of criminal law. This situation worsens for black women, who are even less successful than their white counterparts in

---

[85] Ministry of Justice and Attorney-General's Office, *Limiting the use of complainants' sexual history in sex cases* CM 8547 (London: TSO, 2017) p 6. [86] Ibid.
[87] McGlynn C, 'R v A (No 2)' in Hunter R, McGlynn C and Rackley E (eds), *Feminist Judgments. From Theory to Practice* (Oxford: Hart, 2010) p 221. There are feminist judgment projects in Canada, the USA, Australia, Scotland, Northern Ireland and in international law. [88] [2016] EWCA Crim 452.
[89] Bowcott O 'UK rape complainants face unfair questions about sexual history' *The Guardian*, 29 January 2018.
[90] McGlynn C and Munro V (eds), *Rethinking Rape Law: International and Comparative Perspectives* (Abingdon: Routledge-Cavendish, 2010); Durham R, Lawson R, Lord A and Baird D, 'Seeing Is Believing: The Northumbria Court Observation Panel Report on 30 Rape Trials 2015–2016' (Newcastle-Upon-Tyne: Office of the Police and Crime Commissioner for Northumbria, 2016).
[91] Hoyano L, 'Cross-examination of Sexual Assault Complainants on Previous Sexual Behaviour: Views From the Barristers' Row' [2019] *Criminal Law Review* 77. [92] McGlynn (2017).

prosecutions for rape,[93] especially as it is known that women with racialised heritage suffer disproportionate levels of sexual violence compared to white women.[94]

While much feminist debate regarding how criminal law is constructed focuses on sexual offences, the feminist judgments project has highlighted how patriarchal constructions of the female role can also be found in other areas of criminal law, such as in relation to an ethic of care. For example, Cobb argues that the decisions in relation to omissions liability (particularly in cases of manslaughter) reflect assumptions about dependency and care-giving that 'dictate which care-giving relationships are appropriately recognised by the criminal law, shape the terms of the duties imposed on those relationships, and justify sanctions for those who fail to meet those standards'.[95] The same might be said of offences involving cruelty to, or neglect of, children, for which women are prosecuted at a disproportionate rate.[96]

Debate about the ability of the law to legitimise women's claims is ongoing. Even feminist judges might find it difficult to apply legal rules from a different perspective both because of a desire to conform to established legal norms and to appear credible. This is a significant barrier to the ability of the law to develop in a less gendered way. The opportunity in terms of both topic and space to apply feminist perspectives to law, along with personal commitment and encouragement/support, are required if the law is to be applied in a way that is less subservient to the dominant male hegemony.[97]

The criminal law is not only constructed from a primarily male point of view, but also from a white point of view. Using law in this way is part of a process of 'racial formation'.[98] The clearest example of a criminal law which has been constructed in a way that disproportionately affects people from BAME (primarily black) populations is the doctrine of joint enterprise (aka complicity). This doctrine allows two or more people to be convicted of the same offence arising out of the same incident, even if each took different roles and had different levels of involvement.[99] It is often used to prosecute suspected gang related violence, which develops and perpetuates stereotypes about gang membership and behaviour. Suspected gang related violence has been mobilised by the criminology of the dangerous 'other' and has reinforced myths surrounding black criminality. Data about young black

---

[93] Hudson (2003). Note that the terms 'black' and 'women' are equally important to black women, but different relational situations might bring one or other term more to the forefront of importance.

[94] See, e.g., Amnesty International, 'Maze of injustice. The failure to protect Indigenous women from sexual violence in the USA' (New York: Amnesty International USA, 2007); Topping A, 'Abuse of Asian girls missed because of focus on white victims, says report' *The Guardian*, 10 September 2013. For discussion about intersections of race, gender and sexual violence, see Decker M, Holliday C, Hameeduddin Z et al, '"You Do Not Think of Me as a Human Being": Race and Gender Inequities Intersect to Discourage Police Reporting of Violence against Women' (2019) 96 *Journal of Urban Health* 772–783. For a discussion about black men's experiences as victims of (racialised) sexual violence, see, e.g., Curry T, 'Expendables for Whom: Terry Crews and the Erasure of Black Male Victims of Sexual Assault and Rape' (2019) 42(3) *Women's Studies in Communication* 28.

[95] Cobb N, 'R v Stone and Dobinson. Commentary' in Hunter, McGlynn and Rackley (2010: 230).

[96] Ministry of Justice, *Statistics on Women and the Criminal Justice System 2017* (2018g). Available at: <https://assets.publishing.service.gov.uk/government/uploads/system/uploads/attachment_data/file/759770/women-criminal-justice-system-2017.pdf> (accessed 26 October 2020).

[97] Hunter R, 'More than Just a Different Face? Judicial Diversity and Decision-making' (2015) 68 *Current Legal Problems* 119–141. See further Hunter R, 'The Power of Feminist Judgments?' (2012) 20(2) *Feminist Legal Studies* 135–148.

[98] Davis and Ernst (2019: 763).

[99] For an explanation of this doctrine, see ch 12 of Child J and Ormerod D, *Smith, Hogan, & Ormerod's Essentials of Criminal Law* 3rd edn (Oxford: OUP, 2019). For critical analysis of the doctrine see, for example, Krebs B, 'Joint Criminal Enterprise' (2010) 73 *The Modern Law Review* 578–604; Hulley S, Crewe B and Wright S, 'Making Sense of "Joint Enterprise" for Murder: Legal Legitimacy or Instrumental Acquiescence?' (2019) 59(6) *British Journal of Criminology* 1328.

men comprises nearly 80% of information on police databases about suspected gangs,[100] serving to reproduce racialised entities to be policed,[101] with the use of algorithms adding to this process.[102] As an additional result of stereotyping, people who are not white are disproportionately prosecuted for alleged joint enterprise offences. Furthermore, reference to gang-type behaviour is much more likely to be made in the prosecution of non-white joint enterprise defendants than white joint enterprise defendants even though most fruitful prosecutions for offences of serious violence are of white people.[103] One study found that, in joint enterprise cases sampled where ethnicity was known, approximately two thirds of prosecutions were of people from non-white populations, and more than 40% were of black people.[104] According to charity and campaign group, Joint Enterprise: Not Guilty by Association,[105] 80% of people convicted under joint enterprise laws are from BAME communities. It seems that 'black people are serving time under joint enterprise at 11 times their presence in the population as a whole.'[106]

In 2016, the law on joint enterprise changed, moving the mental element required for successful prosecution from *foresight* about what co-defendants might do towards *knowledge* of what co-defendants might do.[107] This makes it harder to convict defendants under the law of joint enterprise. It was hoped that many of those convicted under the old law might successfully appeal their convictions and perhaps redress some of the imbalance in joint enterprise law for the 'hundreds of BAME individuals who have been unjustly convicted under its aegis'.[108] However, the courts have set an extremely high threshold just to hear an appeal, let alone for it to succeed.[109] As of mid-2020 there had been only one successful appeal since the change in the law, and that was by a white man.[110] Therefore, despite the change in the law, members of non-white communities continue to be treated unequally as a result of stereotypes perpetuated by this legal doctrine. The construction of criminal law in this way affects how the police operate: how they make their decisions about which areas are in need of surveillance, who should be stopped, arrested and have their case put forward for prosecution by the CPS. We discuss this further in the rest of this chapter.

---

[100] Williams P and Clarke B, 'The Black Criminal Other as an Object of Social Control' (2018) 7 *Social Sciences* 234.

[101] Owusu-Bempah, Akwasi 'Race and Policing in Historical Context: Dehumanization and the Policing of Black People in the 21st Century' (2017). Owusu-Bempah, Abenaa 'Defendant Participation in the Criminal Process.

[102] Huq A, 'Racial Equity in Algorithmic Criminal Justice' (2019) 68(6) *Duke Law Journal* 1043–1135.

[103] Williams P and Clarke B, 'Dangerous Associations: Joint Enterprise, Gangs and Racism' (London: Centre for Crime and Justice Studies, 2016).

[104] Jacobson J, Kirby A and Hunter G, 'Joint Enterprise: Righting A Wrong Turn?' (London: Prison Reform Trust, 2016).

[105] See <http://www.jointenterprise.co.uk> (accessed 26 October 2020).

[106] Stopes H, 'How do 11 people go to jail for one murder?' *The Guardian*, 9 March 2018.

[107] See *R v Jogee* [2016] UKSC 8. Again, space precludes detailed analysis of the judgment, but see Parsons S, 'Joint Enterprise Murder: R v Jogee' (2016) 80(3) *Journal of Criminal Law* 173–176.

[108] Bridges L, 'Lammy Review: will it change outcomes in the criminal justice system?' (2018) 59(3) *Race & Class* 80–90 at 83.

[109] See *R v Johnson and Others* [2016] EWCA Crim 1613. For analysis see Stark F, 'The Taming of Jogee?' (2017) 76(1) *Cambridge Law Journal* 4–7.

[110] *R v Crilly* [2018] EWCA Crim 168. For analysis see Krebs B, 'Joint Enterprise, Murder and Substantial Injustice: The First Successful Appeal Post-Jogee: R v Crilly [2018] EWCA Crim 168' (2018) 82(3) *Journal of Criminal Law* 209–211; and see <https://www.thejusticegap.com/joint-enterprise-exposes-all-that-is-wrong-with-our-justice-system-2/> (accessed 26 October 2020). Also Carvalho H, 'Joint Enterprise, Hostility and the Construction of Dangerous Belonging' in Pratt J and Anderson J (eds), *Criminal Justice, Risk and the Revolt against Uncertainty* (London: Palgrave Macmillan, 2020).

10.4 Inequality manifested through policing

Measures that disproportionately criminalise and punish people from racialised groups serve to reinforce a sense of being othered, ill protected and intrusively surveilled. As Faulkner and Burnett argue:

> It is important that people should think of themselves, and that the police should think of them, as part of a community that the police exists to serve, and not as being excluded from it, or as being in some way 'on the other side'. There should, in particular be no sense that religious or minority ethnic groups are not part of the same community, or that there is a separate 'criminal class'.[111]

But in 2019, only 6.9.% of police officers were from BAME backgrounds although 14% of the population is from a non-white background, with black female officers represented at even lower levels.[112] The extent of representation of different ethnic groups also varies by role and police force area with black and Asian officers being most represented in the lower ranks (e.g. amongst PCSOs).[113] As discussed in chapter 2, unequal levels of representation are likely to hinder police forces in understanding and building links with diverse communities, as well as symbolising structural inequalities and an unequal relationship between citizens and the state.

We know that police behaviour is influenced by their perceptions of dangerousness, stereotyped populations and risk across society. We also know that it is important that the police are trusted by the communities that they serve, for both detection and management of crime and the protection of the public, but this trust is often lacking.[114] We further know that policing activities are imbued with assumptions about race, class and gender. Predominantly black neighbourhoods tend to be over-policed but under-protected; the reverse of predominantly white neighbourhoods, with their ubiquitous privatised security measures (section 10.2.2).[115] This means that many crimes by white people in predominantly white neighbourhoods occur privately, and are less likely to be detected by the public police. More coercive policing in diverse and economically deprived neighbourhoods often pays little respect to notions of dignity for the residents or to the potential for institutional racism of focusing coercive police practices such as stop and search in these neighbourhoods (chapter 2). The control of marginal groups by the police goes deeper than the proclivities of individual officers, it is also:

> a product of either the wider social environment within which police operate and/or carelessly applied or deliberately unexamined aspects of policy and practice that produce ethnically based variation in experiences of policing as a by-product of other activities. Ethnic disproportionality is therefore predicted not only by bias and stereotyping but also by the fact that people from minority groups are affected by much wider processes of exclusion and are therefore more likely to be placed into marginal social categories [and locations] that draw attention from the police.[116]

---

[111] Faulkner and Burnett (2011: 106).

[112] Home Office. *Ethnicity facts and figures: Police workforce* (2018b) available at: <https://www.ethnicity-facts-figures.service.gov.uk/workforce-and-business/workforce-diversity/police-workforce/latest> (accessed 26 October 2020).

[113] Hales G, *Perspectives on policing: A diversity uplift? Police workforce and ethnicity trends* (London: The Police Foundation, 2020). The forces employing the most black and Asian police officers include especially the Metropolitan Police in London, but also British Transport Police, Greater Manchester Police, Leicestershire Police, West Midlands Police, West Yorkshire Police and Thames Valley Police.   [114] See section 2.5.3.

[115] Hudson (2003).

[116] Bradford et al, *Stop and Search and Police Legitimacy* (Abingdon: Routledge, 2017) p 82.

Consequently, those residents are unlikely to turn to the police for help when needed, which exacerbates feelings of un-belonging.[117] Indeed, the police's presence in these neighbourhoods often stirs up tensions and resentment. For example, research into 'gaunt, depressing estates' in inner London found that 'the police themselves would not enter them unless in company . . . the sense of anger directed towards the police by local street youth was palpable. . .'.[118] Who can be surprised about that anger, and mistrust in the police, when we read about this incident that occurred as we finalise this chapter (autumn 2020): a black teenager, bleeding from a racist attack, asked a police officer for protection. Instead of getting the medical help the boy requested, the officer searched him: 'Instead of being treated as victim, he was viewed as suspect. That attitude stems from a mindset of seeing black young teenagers as problem. It took one of Gerard's white friends to ask another police officer to call the ambulance.'[119]

The collective memory of the police also plays a role in the way they carry out their community duties (chapter 2).[120] For example, following the 2011 riots in London and elsewhere, young people in Tottenham, an area of London which has a lengthy history of tense relations between the black community and the police dating back to the Broadwater Farm riots of 1985,[121] have 'been labelled "feral rats" . . . and portrayed as "passive participants" . . . and "delinquents".'[122] Cop culture accordingly generates anxieties and stereotypes, both conscious and implicit, which manifest themselves in the way the police deal with different ethnic groups, both as suspects and victims. In the 1980s and 1990s, black people in particular were stereotyped as being linked to criminality. Fitzgerald and Sibbitt (1997: 41) quote one officer saying: 'The Japanese and the Chinese, culturally speaking, are very respectful. With black people we often prepare ourselves for the abuse in advance, or the knives (which is again a cultural thing).' However, growing concern about terrorist threats from 2001 onwards resulted in stereotyping about, and greater attention being paid to, South Asian communities too.[123] We cited, in chapter 2, one example of an officer with specialist responsibility for giving race and diversity lessons to recruits telling a public meeting in Cumbria that any sightings of young Asian men in an area of the Lake District should be reported to the police.[124] In this context, counter terrorism measures which led to the disproportionate policing of young Asian men, were felt to be 'excessive forms of regulation that were having a detrimental impact on community relations'.[125]

In 2012, the government announced Operation Nexus, whereby the police and immigration services work together to check status and gather information about foreign nationals. This not only perpetuated stereotypes already embedded in cop culture, but also 'having the police explicitly perform immigration control, underscores their role in

---

[117] Parmar (2019a).
[118] Hallsworth (2006: 303–307). This is a historic tendency. See for example, Keith M, *Race, Riots and Policing* (London: UCL Press, 1993) p 130.
[119] Gayle D, 'Injured boy "stopped and searched" by Met officer he asked for help' *The Guardian*, 1 July 2020.
[120] For a discussion of how young people may be provoked by the insensitive use of police powers into defiant gestures which in turn reinforce negative police perceptions of youth see Loader (1996: 153), and Hallsworth (2006: 306–307).
[121] Bridges L, 'Four Days in August: The UK Riots' (2012) 54(1) *Race & Class* 1–12.
[122] Elster J, 'Youth Voices in Post-English Riots Tottenham: The Role of Reflexivity in Negotiating Negative Representations' (2020) *Sociological Review*. See Newburn et al, '"The Biggest Gang"? Police and People in the 2011 England Riots' (2016) 28(2) *Policing and Society* 205–222 for a similar discussion regarding Toxteth and Brixton.
[123] Parmar A, 'Stop and Search in London: Counter-terrorist or Counter-productive?' (2011) 21(4) *Policing and Society* 369–382.
[124] Quoted in Equality and Human Rights Commission (2008: 19).
[125] Mythen and Kamruzzaman in Quirk, Seddon and Smith (2010: 225).

exclusion of those deemed undesirable'.[126] It also underscores who is constructed as a suitable enemy in need of policing, particularly in relation to suspected terror related activities. The by-product of measures that linked narratives of migration, criminalisation and terrorism means that, to the police, migrants and minority ethnic citizens are conflated, and inherently suspect because they appear similar. In turn, this allows 'nationality to act as a proxy for race, enabling frequent nationality checks for low-level offending to be carried out for visible minorities in particular, while being framed as ostensibly race neutral'.[127] You don't have to be a genius to work out that not many white people were arrested as a result of the notorious Home Office-sponsored vans that had this on their sides in 2013: 'In the UK illegally? . . . Go home or face arrest. 106 arrests last week in your area.'[128] The connections between difference, fear and risk thus continue to feed into notions of criminality, which is particularly concerning in light of Brexit politics that combine anti-immigrant and criminalising discourses.[129]

10.4.1 Inequality in pre-arrest decision-making

The criminal justice system is constructed against racialised youths through, for example, macro-level politics, prejudice during trials and—perhaps the most well-known factor—disproportionate use of stop and search.[130] This disproportionality is all the more troubling given that, as noted in chapter 2, though the police believe stop and search powers are important crime-fighting tools, research suggests otherwise.[131]

As we set out in chapter 2, although more white people are subjected to stop and search than non-white people, as one would expect given that the majority of the population in England and Wales is white, people who are of black and/or Asian heritage are greatly *overrepresented* in those searched. That is, when the proportion of people from different ethnic groups who are stopped and searched are compared to census estimates of the proportion of people who are ordinarily resident in the area where the stop occurred, ethnic minorities are disproportionately affected (see chapter 2, Table 2.2). People from all non-white populations are three times more likely, and black people six times more likely, to be stopped than white people.[132] Stop and search rates generally dropped after 2013 (chapter 2, Table 2.1), but its use has become increasingly concentrated on drug offences. *Disproportionate* use of stop and search powers has increased, but the rate at which drugs are found does not support the increased stop rate: proportionately more drugs are found as a result of stopping white people than non-white people, leading Shiner et al to conclude: 'Rates of stop and search appear to be more sensitive to deprivation and inequality than crime. The concentration of stop and search in deprived boroughs cannot be explained by patterns of drug use, including cannabis use.'[133] Furthermore, black people are more likely to be arrested and prosecuted for drug related offending, while white people are more likely to be offered an out of court disposal (see section 7.4.1).[134]

---

[126] Parmar (2019a: 4).   [127] Parmar (2019a: 5).
[128] See, e.g., Saul, *The Independent*, 9 October 2013. The stunt was stopped when the Advertising Standards Authority ruled the slogans to be misleading.   [129] Virdee and McGeever (2018).
[130] Irwin-Rogers K, 'Racism and Racial Discrimination in the Criminal Justice System: Exploring the Experiences and Views of Men Serving Sentences of Imprisonment' (2018) 2(2) *Justice, Power and Resistance* 243–266.
[131] Tiratelli M, Quinton P and Bradford B, 'Does Stop and Search Deter Crime? Evidence From Ten Years of London-wide Data' (2018) 58(5) *British Journal of Criminology* 1212–1231.
[132] The Lammy Review (2017).
[133] Shiner M, Carre Z, Delsol R and Eastwood N, *The Colour of Injustice: 'Race', drugs and law enforcement in England and Wales* (2018) p 9, available at: <http://www.stop-watch.org/uploads/documents/The_Colour_of_Injustice.pdf> (accessed 26 October 2020).   [134] Shiner et al (2018).

The most frequent type of 'search' is actually stop and account (see chapter 2), for which figures were published for the first time in 2008. Here black people were nearly two and a half times more likely to be asked to account for themselves than white people.[135] It is not possible to obtain up-to-date national statistics on this issue because the requirement for police forces to record stop and account was removed in 2011 following implementation of the Crime and Security Act 2010. But we do have statistics on s.60 stop and search powers:[136] black people are 40 times more likely to be stop-searched than white people.[137] Section 60 has been declared compatible with the ECHR,[138] even though it tends to conflate issues relating to gang violence and young black men in the criminal process.

What are the reasons for this ethno-racial disproportionality in stop and search practices? We mentioned some of these in chapter 2. First, citizens and their individual characteristics (including their race/ethnicity) become subject to overt prejudice, as well as stereotyping and/or implicit bias linked to police cultural norms, the nature of the job (e.g. its sometimes fast-paced nature), and the unpredictable situations in which the police have wide discretion; and police forces have proven reluctant at best, or unwilling at worst, to implement training on unconscious bias.[139] Second, stop and search activities tend to focus on areas with higher levels of crime and disorder, socio-economic disadvantage and higher proportions of non-UK born residents. Ethnic minorities are therefore more 'available' to be stopped and searched by the police because of location and also because of their routine activities, e.g. due to their lifestyle or their job.[140]

Writing this chapter in the summer of 2020, when the Black Lives Matter movement is highlighting the racialised nature of a wide range of police practices, we must consider radical solutions such as eliminating the use of stop and search altogether. However, this is unlikely to happen given the growing politicisation of crime and disorder since the late 1970s, in which successive political parties have come to rely on appearing tough on crime—most recently, violent crime like knife crime—through coercive policing tactics such as stop and search.[141] A compromise would be to:

- carefully delineate, in-keeping with it being used less over the last 10 years than before, the circumstances and kinds of crime for which it may be used;[142]
- improve training (e.g. about the meaning of 'reasonable suspicion' and how to treat citizens in a procedurally just fashion, based on dignity and respect and forms of bias);
- improve regulation (e.g. through citizen panels scrutinising stop and search practices or better recording of stops).

---

[135] Ministry of Justice (2008d: 26).

[136] Section 60 Criminal Justice and Public Order Act 1994 (s.60) allows police to stop-search people in defined areas and at defined times when they have good reason to believe it necessary in relation to serous violence and/or offensive weapons.

[137] Townsend M, 'Black people "40 times more likely" to be stopped and searched in UK' *The Guardian*, 4 May 2019. [138] *Roberts* [2015] UKSC 79. Discussed in section 2.4.

[139] See Bradford et al (2017), based on their analysis, inter alia, of 28,300 respondents to crime surveys in 2008–11.

[140] This was seen as the most important explanation by MVA and Miller (2000) in earlier research that did not find evidence of disproportionality. But this was done in just five police divisions which were, doubtless, heavily policed in part because of perceptions of their crime problems related to their ethnic mix.

[141] In March 2019, the police were given greater powers to stop and search without 'reasonable suspicion' in order to supposedly tackle growing knife crime, even though research suggests this would not be effective. See <https://www.theguardian.com/uk-news/2019/mar/31/police-given-more-stop-and-search-powers-to-tackle-knife> (accessed 26 October 2020). [142] Bradford et al (2017: 214).

Some of these elements of training and regulation were incorporated into the College of Policing's Best Use of Stop and Search Scheme, which began in 2014.[143] This is part of a broader discussion about the regulation of all police powers, particularly 'when things go wrong' (chapter 11). But we also know from the research available about stop and search, and about recruitment, retention and promotion of people from BAME populations in the police, that the police still have much work to do to challenge the racial prejudice of individual officers and the ways in which these attitudes and behaviours, along with police policies and processes, lead cumulatively to unfair experiences and outcomes for racialised citizens. As if to exemplify this, black and Asian people were twice as likely as white people to be fined by police during the 2020 Covid-19 pandemic.[144]

While racialised people are over policed, women are often under-protected by the police. Security is distributed and managed in society according to male ideas of what constitutes threat and risk, so women's safety is regarded as a matter of individual responsibility,[145] even though many women 'experience high and multiple levels of inequality'.[146] For example, in rape cases women have been responsibilised and thus blamed based on the clothes they wear, and where they go and at what time. But women are at greater danger in their homes and with people that they know, than on the street or at the hands of strangers.[147] Despite this, policing and the justice system as a whole has for decades failed to respond appropriately to domestic abuse suffered by women in particular.

From a legalistic point of view, the use of arrest for domestic abuse should be no different to its use for any other crime. Domestic abuse is assault, and there is no specific set of offences designed solely for physical domestic abuse (which may reflect some of the issues raised in section 10.3), and this might influence when the police think it is right to act.[148] Section 76 of the Serious Crime Act 2015 attempted to address some non-physically violent behaviour in abusive relationships by creating the offence of controlling or coercive behaviour in an intimate or family relationship.[149] England was the first country to implement legislation of this nature following campaigns by the grassroots organisation, Women's Aid. In the year to end March 2019, police recorded 17,616 offences of coercive control and, in the year ending December 2018, 97% of defendants prosecuted for coercive and controlling behaviour were male.[150] One study found that 95% of coercive control

---

[143] <https://www.college.police.uk/What-we-do/Support/uniformed-policing-faculty/stop-and-search/Pages/Best-Use-of-Stop-Search-Scheme.aspx> (accessed 26 October 2020). See also: the stop and search experiments done by NACRO in London in the 1990s, which sought to train the police on concepts like 'reasonable suspicion' discussed in ch 2. NACRO, *Policing Local Communities: The Tottenham Experiment* (London: NACRO, 1997). And also the training and reporting requirements that emerged from the Macpherson Inquiry and its wounding critique of the stop and search practices of the police, though these received a mixed response and did not last. See Foster et al (2005: 29–30).

[144] Dodd V, 'Met police twice as likely to fine black people over lockdown breaches—research' *The Guardian*, 3 June 2020. [145] Hudson (2003).

[146] Martin D and Wilcox P, 'Women, Welfare and the Carceral State' in Squires and Lea (2012: 161).

[147] Hudson (2003).

[148] Birdsall N, Kirby S and McManus M, 'Police–victim Engagement in Building a Victim Empowerment Approach to Intimate Partner Violence Cases' (2017) 18(1) *Police Practice and Research* 75–86. Scotland has recently enacted a specific offence relating to abusive behaviour in relation to a partner or ex-partner, which includes both physical and psychological violence (BBC News, *New domestic abuse law 'could change Scotland'* (2018) <https://www.bbc.co.uk/news/uk-scotland-42890990> (accessed 26 October 2020)).

[149] Previously, similar types of offending behaviour might have been prosecuted as harassment, but those offences did not specifically address the issue of setting boundaries of acceptable behaviour and power dynamics in intimate relationships.

[150] Office for National Statistics, *Domestic abuse in England and Wales: year ending November 2019* (ONS, 2019).

victims were female.[151] It seems clear that this is one instance where Parliament changed the law to recognise how inadequacies in male-centred offences have disproportionately affected women, and some important success has followed. In 2019, a murder conviction was overturned because the court accepted that the jury had not heard sufficient evidence about the defendant being coercively controlled by her former husband.[152] The harm caused by coercive control goes wide and is often indirect.[153] However, changes to the law are not fully reflected in changes to police practice: the new offence appears to be under-used, and the police still tend to be more reactive to allegations of domestic abuse where physical violence is present.[154]

Whether it is a relatively minor common assault, psychological harm or a very serious GBH or attempted murder depends—as with any other type of assault—on the seriousness of the injuries inflicted, if any, and the intent of the violent partner. Normally, one would expect these factors (including the strength of the evidence), along perhaps with the wishes of the victim, to determine whether or not the suspect is arrested. However, until the early 1990s domestic abuse was hardly treated as a criminal problem at all, except in the most severe cases. So the police generally arrested only when they both anticipated a successful prosecution and perceived the injuries and/or danger to the victim as grave. The police were reluctant to arrest where the victim was ambivalent, but also when they anticipated them changing their mind.[155] This created a vicious circle, insofar as many women lost confidence in the police and so were reluctant to call them, or were easily persuaded to withdraw their complaints because they expected the police to do little or nothing. In 2000 the UK Government produced a near-mandatory arrest policy (sometimes known as a 'pro-arrest' policy), following earlier largely ineffective measures,[156] and the passing of the Domestic Violence, Crime and Victims Act in 2004 was designed to signal to the police that they should take domestic abuse more seriously.

Risk aversion encourages operational officers to comply with positive arrest policies, even in cases where arrest is seen as counter-productive, contrary to the victim's wishes and interests, and unlikely to result in a prosecution. Pearson and Rowe document one such case in which the police were called to a domestic disturbance which had ended by the time they arrived and in which the victim made it clear that she would not provide a statement. They arrested her partner nonetheless and took him to police custody, knowing full well that the case would be NFA'd without the victim's statement and this is precisely what happened.[157] Indeed, this sense of risk aversion caused some officers in their study

---

[151] Barlow C, Walklate S, Johnson K, Humphreys L and Kirby S, *Police responses to coercive control* (2018) N8 Policing Research Partnership. See also Myhill A, 'Measuring Coercive Control: What Can We Learn From National Population Surveys?' (2015) 21(3) *Violence Against Women* 355–375.

[152] *Challen* [2019] EWCA Crim 916.

[153] There is a strong link between womens' offending, abuse and coercive relationships (Prison Reform Trust, '"There's a reason we're in trouble" Domestic abuse as a driver to women's offending' (2017) online at: <http://www.prisonreformtrust.org.uk/Portals/0/Documents/Domestic_abuse_report_final_lo.pdf> (accessed 26 October 2020).

[154] Barlow C, Johnson K, Walklate S and Humphreys L, 'Putting Coercive Control into Practice: Problems and Possibilities' (2020) 60(1) *British Journal of Criminology* 160–179; Robinson A, Pinchevsky G and Guthrie J, 'Under the Radar: Policing Non-violent Domestic Abuse in the US and UK' (2016) 40(3) *International Journal of Comparative and Applied Criminal Justice* 195–208. See also Robinson A, Pinchevsky G and Guthrie J, 'A Small Constellation: Risk Factors Informing Police Perceptions of Domestic Abuse' (2018) 28(2) *Policing and Society* 189–204.   [155] Edwards (1989).

[156] Home Office: Domestic Violence (Circular 19/2000) paras 3 and 4. On earlier measures see Domestic Violence (Circular 66/90) (London: Home Office, 1990), evaluated in Hoyle and Sanders (2000); Wright S, 'Policing Domestic Violence: A Nottingham Case Study' (1998) 20 *Journal of Social Welfare and Family Law* 397. The US findings are similar. For a review of English and American research see Paradine K and Wilkinson J, *Protection and Accountability: The Reporting, Investigation and Prosecution of Domestic Violence Cases* (London: HMIC and HMCPSI, 2004).   [157] Pearson and Rowe (2020: 143).

to interpret positive arrest policies as mandatory arrest policies, meaning that they had to make an arrest in all incidents involving domestic abuse. There is obviously a danger here of the pendulum having swung too far in favour of arrest, resulting in net reductions in overall freedom, even if one only takes victims' interests into account. However, a recent study by Myhill showed that whilst the presumptive arrest policy was found to be more salient in police work towards domestic abuse incidents,[158] officers nevertheless continued to apply traditional methods or the 'craft' work of policing and discretion to sometimes circumvent such policies and keep them in the background of their work. At times this meant incidents were shaped to suggest that no crime had occurred to avoid arresting suspects and having to book them into police custody. Pearson and Rowe similarly document a minority of cases in which domestic incidents were 'cuffed' (i.e. not recorded as a crime) as a work around of positive arrest policies,[159] thereby illustrating the power of discretion and its infusion into all that the police do, even for the most stringent of policies. The overall domestic abuse arrest rate averaged 38% of abuse-related recorded crime in the year ending March 2018.[160] But arrest is not necessarily the best outcome in all circumstances. Arrest appears to modestly reduce re-victimisation, but so does simple police attendance at the incident, and the value of arrest over attendance and referral advice to partner agencies is not clearly established.[161] Furthermore, powers of arrest are used disproportionately; women are three times more likely to be arrested than men when accused of domestic abuse, even though rates of reported incidents with female perpetrators are much lower than for male counterparts.[162] Police continue to focus their risk assessments on a narrow range of factors that tend to lead to action primarily in cases that involve a risk of significant physical violence.[163]

To further address concerns about policing domestic abuse, specialist police officers and training for police officers have been introduced alongside Independent Domestic Violence Advocates (IDVAs).[164] Police forces assess risk when incidents of domestic abuse are reported through the 'Domestic Abuse, Stalking and Harassment and Honour Based Violence'[165] matrix. However, the matrix pays insufficient attention to victims' own assessment of their level of risk and need, and assumes that they are acting under free will. Furthermore, the risk assessment factors were initially designed to deal with homicide, so a number of high harm level factors need to be present before a situation will meet the threshold of being considered high risk, limiting its ability to identify recidivism.

---

[158] Myhill A, 'Renegotiating Domestic Violence: Police Attitudes and Decisions Concerning Arrest' (2019) 29(1) *Policing and Society* 52–68.

[159] Pearson and Rowe (2020: 144).

[160] Office for National Statistics, *Domestic Abuse in England Wales: year ending March 2018* (2018b) available at: <https://www.ons.gov.uk/peoplepopulationandcommunity/crimeandjustice/bulletins/domesticabuseinenglandandwales/yearendingmarch2018> (accessed 27 October 2020).

[161] Vigurs C, Wire J, Myhill A and Gough D, *Police Initial Responses to Domestic Abuse A systematic review* (College of Policing, 2016) available at: <https://www.college.police.uk/News/College-news/Documents/Police_initial_responses_to_domestic_abuse.pdf> (accessed 27 October 2020). Also see American research indicating that women tend to suffer more, in a variety of ways, as a result of mandatory arrest policies: Sherman L and Harris H, 'Increased Death Rates of Domestic Violence Victims From Arresting vs. Warning Suspects in the Milwaukee Domestic Violence Experiment (MilDVE)' (2015) 11 *Journal of Experimental Criminology* 1.

[162] Hester M, '*Who Does What to Whom? Gender and Domestic Violence Perpetrators*' (Bristol: University of Bristol in association with the Northern Rock Foundation, 2009).

[163] Robinson, Pinchevsky and Guthrie (2018).

[164] Westmarland N, Johnson K and McGlynn C, 'Under the Radar: The Widespread Use of 'Out of Court Resolutions' in Policing Domestic Violence and Abuse in the United Kingdom' (2018) 58(1) *British Journal of Criminology* 1–16.

[165] Richards L, *DASH (2009): saving lives through early risk identification, intervention and prevention* (2009). Retrieved from <http://www.dashrischecklist.co.uk/> (accessed 27 October 2020).

These issues are compounded by frequent failures to take note of vital details and evidence during investigations.[166] In 2014 many forces still appeared to be committed to dealing appropriately with domestic abuse on paper alone. This was due to weak leadership, poor oversight and mismatched priorities according to HMIC, which called for urgent action.[167] Although there had been some improvement by 2015, there were still areas of weakness in relation to the way the police responded to and supported victims of domestic abuse.[168] In a particularly dramatic example, the police were found to have taken inadequate steps to address complaints of domestic abuse following the murder of Laura Stuart in August 2017: she reported concerns about her ex-partner's behaviour 18 times prior to her death, but the police failed to arrest or interview her eventual killer. The police's domestic abuse policy had not been complied with.[169]

As with all crime, alternatives to arrest exist in the form of out of court disposals and restorative justice (chapters 7 and 12), and are widely used in all police forces. This sometimes results in a downgrading of domestic abuse cases:

> [t]erms such as 'words of advice given' or 'verbal apology made' chime with pre- and early 1990s approaches, seeing domestic abuse as a private and non-serious matter that police officers can deal with without the need to progress through the formal criminal justice system. Police discretion was a problem in early studies of domestic abuse and continues to be a concern that is documented in more recent research.[170]

In the last edition of this book, the government was credited for establishing and maintaining a high priority for domestic violence, setting up specialist domestic abuse courts and creating a network of independent domestic abuse advisors to help victims negotiate the criminal justice process. The percentage of convictions secured for domestic abuse prosecutions ending in conviction rose to 76% in 2017/18.[171] However, prosecutions seem to be mostly limited to allegations, or where there is a risk, of serious physical violence because of the way the (often male) police filter what they regard as worthy of out of court disposal, arrest and prosecution. The strongest cases tend to make it through the door of the court, leaving many victims at risk of increasingly frequent psychological and physical violence.[172] Once there, prosecutors tended to routinely summons reluctant victims, effectively forcing their attendance at court. Thus victims of domestic abuse—usually women—were at the mercy of police and prosecutorial discretion that does not necessarily cater to their gender, race, age, ability and relationship specific needs. However, 'victimless prosecutions', relying on the provisions of the Criminal Justice Act 2003 which relaxed the prohibition on the use of hearsay (second hand) evidence, allow statements to be read out rather than requiring the witness to attend court, and these seem to be increasing in domestic abuse cases.[173]

---

[166] Birdsall, Kirby and McManus (2017).
[167] HMIC, *Everyone's Business: Improving the Police Response to Domestic Abuse* (London: HMIC, 2014).
[168] HMIC, *Increasingly Everyone's Business: A Progress Report on the Police Response to Domestic Abuse* (London: HMIC, 2015).
[169] See <https://policeconduct.gov.uk/news/changes-made-north-wales-police-policy-domestic-abuse-incidents-following-laura-stuart> (accessed 27 October 2020). For general discussion see Westmarland et al (2018).
[170] Westmarland et al (2018: 12). [171] ONS (2018).
[172] Bland M and Ariel B, 'Targeting Escalation in Reported Domestic Abuse: Evidence From 36,000 Callouts' (2015) 25(1) *International Criminal Justice Review* 30–53.
[173] Porter A, 'Prosecuting Domestic Abuse in England and Wales: Crown Prosecution Service "Working Practice" and New Public Managerialism' (2018) 28(4) *Social & Legal Studies* 493–516.

The Domestic Abuse Bill which, at the time of writing (summer 2020), is awaiting second reading in the House of Lords is an encouraging development. It will:

- put the new Designate Domestic Abuse Commissioner on a statutory footing;[174]
- create a statutory definition of domestic abuse encompassing a range of behaviours beyond physical violence;
- create new CPMs (chapter 1) in the form of Domestic Abuse Protection Notices and Domestic Abuse Protection Orders;
- create a duty for local authorities to provide support in refuges and other safe accommodation spaces;
- prevent cross-examination of victims by perpetrators;
- strengthen the ability of victims of domestic abuse to access special measures in civil courts (chapter 9).

Some of the measures will place pre-existing common law measures on a statutory footing and bring together provisions that are currently fragmented across statutes such as the Offences Against the Person Act 1861 and the Youth Justice and Criminal Evidence Act 1999. But the Bill has also been criticised for failing to address the significant funding cuts of the austerity years to local authorities that will undermine the reality of service provisions, and for failing to properly understand and address the needs of migrant women.[175] How far these provisions, and those that allow for increased use of hearsay evidence, will ultimately benefit victims in light of the police response to earlier initiatives remains to be seen.

10.4.2 Inequality in arrest and post arrest detention

Being black, particularly when also young, poor and/or living in 'rough' areas, makes one more liable to being arrested:

> . . . in 2014, when compared to their representation in the general population, BAME young males were 1.35 times more likely to be arrested than young white males . . . But these overall figures mask even higher rates of disproportional arrests for particular groups and crimes. Thus, young black males were 2.77 times more likely to be arrested than young white males, while for adult black men the likelihood of arrest was 3.28 times higher than for adult white men. . . . Young black females were also arrested for robbery at five times the rate for young white females.[176]

Moreover, the evidence against ethnic minority arrestees is, on average, significantly weaker than against white arrestees. In one study, for violent offences there was enough evidence to charge in 45% of white cases but only 37% and 17% respectively in cases involving black and Asian suspects, while for public order offences the corresponding figures were 84% (whites) 65% (blacks) and 64% (Asians).[177] Macpherson's Official Inquiry into the failure to apprehend the murderers of black London teenager Stephen Lawrence concluded that the Metropolitan Police embodies 'institutional racism', explaining why being young and black increases the probability that one will attract police suspicion—and that ethnic

---

[174] The role was created in 2019: <https://www.gov.uk/government/publications/domestic-abuse-bill-2020-factsheets/domestic-abuse-commissioner-factsheet> (accessed 27 October 2020).

[175] Warner C, 'Draft Domestic Abuse Bill: Progress or pitfall?' *Counsel Magazine*, May 2019; Grierson J, 'Domestic abuse bill fails to protect children and migrant women—charities' *The Guardian*, 3 March 2020.

[176] Bridges (2018: 81). This is consistent with most research over the last 40 years. See, e.g., Stevens and Willis (1979: 41), who found that black people were particularly liable to be arrested for preparatory and public order offences where little objective evidence is needed.

[177] Phillips and Brown (1998: 45).

minority victims are less likely than white victims to have their cases 'solved' by arrest.[178] The extent to which this takes place is a matter of debate.[179]

Less is known about what happens to members of racialised groups once actually in police custody, save that once arrested, black detainees of Afro-Caribbean origin are (proportionately) more frequently strip searched than any other group,[180] and that arrestees from BAME populations more frequently request independent legal advice at the police station than other racial groups[181] (though they are less trusting of that advice).[182] Non-white suspects in police custody less frequently feel they have been treated with dignity (in the sense of being treated as a person of equal worth), with this being mediated by less trust in police accountability mechanisms (in that if they were to make a complaint they were less likely to feel that this would be dealt with appropriately).[183] Black people also have lower levels of confidence in the police than white or Asian people. This may explain their greater reliance on the right to silence at the police station, leading to a disproportionate risk of being penalised at later stages in the criminal process because adverse inferences can be drawn from that silence.[184]

In relation to police bail decisions (chapters 4 and 7), Bucke and Brown found that black (though not Asian) suspects were detained disproportionately often, suspects charged with violent offences were less likely to be granted bail than other suspects, and the use of conditions varied greatly from station to station.[185] While this research is now dated, it seems that, as usual, the freedom of the most socially marginalised—in this case, black suspects—is valued less than that of others in the criminal justice system. However, in light of the recent changes to pre-charge bail (see sections 4.2.4 and 7.3.2), this is an area that requires sustained and more up-to-date research.

We also know detainees of non-white heritage die at disproportionately high rates while in police custody, or as a result of contact with the police, relative to numbers in the general population. Young black men, if acting erratically, are stereotyped as likely to be involved in violence and even dangerous, as mad or bad, despite frequent failure to properly assess (mental) health needs. The result is the over- and disproportionate use of force and weaponry against BAME detainees.[186] This results in the disproportionate killing of black men, both in and out of custody, of which Jean Charles de Menezes, Mark Duggan and Sean Rigg (chapter 4) are just a few examples that highlight the serious consequences of racial stereotyping by the police, and further damage the core values of justice and democracy. Notably, officers who behave in a racist way tend to be individualised (the so-called 'bad apple' theory), in contrast to the tendency to pathologise black people as dangerous.[187]

---

[178] *The Stephen Lawrence Inquiry* (1999); Bowling B, *Violent Racism* (Oxford: OUP, 1998).

[179] Murder investigations post-Macpherson continue to have a racialised dimension (notwithstanding denials by the police that this is so): Foster (2008).

[180] Newburn T, Shiner M and Hayman S, 'Race, Crime and Injustice? Strip Search and the Treatment of Suspects in Custody' (2004) 44(5) *British Journal of Criminology* 677–694.

[181] Skinns L, '"I'm A Detainee; Get Me Out Of Here": Predictors of Access to Custodial Legal Advice in Public and Privatized Police Custody Areas in England and Wales' (2009) 49(3) *British Journal of Criminology* 399–417; Pleasence P, Kemp V and Balmer N, 'The Justice Lottery? Police Station Advice 25 years on From PACE' (2011) <http://discovery.ucl.ac.uk/1322366/> (accessed 27 October 2020).

[182] The Lammy Review (2017).

[183] Skinns L, Sorsby A and Rice L, '"Treat Them as a Human Being": Dignity in Police Detention and its Implications for "Good" Police Custody' (2020) 60(6) *British Journal of Criminology* 1667–1688.

[184] Owusu-Bempah, Abenaa *Defendant Participation in the Criminal Process* (Abingdon: Routledge, 2017b)

[185] Bucke and Brown (1997: ch 7). See Raine J and Willson M, 'Police Bail with Conditions' (1997) 37(4) *British Journal of Criminology* 593 and Brown D, Offending on Bail and Police Use of Conditional Bail (Home Office Research Findings no 72) (London: Home Office, 1998) for similar findings.

[186] Athwal H and Bourne J, *Dying for Justice* (London: Institute of Race Relations, 2015).

[187] Further examples of this individualisation vs. pathologising discourse are found in Davis and Ernst (2019).

There is a huge amount of data and discussion that cannot be summarised in a few pages, we give further examples in section 4.4, and yet there are still gaps in the evidence. But if you are in doubt, see the short summary by the Editor of the *Criminal Law Review* and former Law Commissioner.[188]

We have also discussed how digitalisation has been deployed as a tool to save money and increase efficiency (section 1.9.3), and one way that police forces are being encouraged to focus their resources is via the use of predictive policing algorithms. But we have seen that the working practices of the police generally remain stubbornly discriminatory, be it conscious or not. Algorithms that are created to predict crime are built by humans, and are reliant on the use of historic police data—in which racialised citizens may be already over-represented due to police practices—to predict future patterns. As such, pre-existing bias is incorporated into, justified and perpetuated by the system. Thus 'people from black, Asian and minority ethnic (BAME) communities are disproportionately more likely to be arrested, leading the program to assume, wrongly, that the areas in which they live or spend time are the areas where there is more crime.'[189] By filtering pre-existing biases through a machine, biased practices are legitimised. This then dilutes the need for officers to build trust in the community that is being policed.

We know comparatively little about the needs of women who are detained at the police station, despite the fact that the Ministry of Justice recognises that '[w]omen in the criminal justice system or at risk of offending often have acute and complex needs that present in different ways to men . . . The police, as a woman's first point of contact with the justice system, have a key role to play in helping women to take the first important steps to access support'.[190] We do not even know how many women are detained each year, for what, for how long and the kind of vulnerabilities they may exhibit whilst detained by the police. Some of this information is collected by individual police forces but it is not collated and made publicly available.[191] Nonetheless there is growing evidence that female and male suspects in police custody have different offence profiles; officers are more likely to see the arrests of females as routes to health and social support, and more frequently take no formal action.[192] However, the number of young women being charged for violent offences is rising. Although gender stereotypes persist in the policing of women suspected of violence, this does not necessarily mean more harsh nor more lenient treatment. Instead, the police tend to view women as in need of control as a result of 'inappropriate' behaviour—a persistence of 'mad' or 'bad' stereotyping when patriarchal gender roles are breached.[193] In one study of a public protest, the police threatened or used violence towards women

---

[188] Ormerod D, 'Racism in the Criminal Justice System' [2020] *Criminal Law Review* 659. Also see discussions in chs 2, 4 and 11, plus the recommended reading at the end of the chapter.

[189] Couchman H, *Policing by Machine. Predictive Policing and the Threat to our Rights* (London: Liberty, 2019) available at: <https://www.libertyhumanrights.org.uk/sites/default/files/LIB%2011%20Predictive%20Policing%20Report%20WEB.pdf> (accessed 28 October 2020).

[190] Ministry of Justice, *Managing Vulnerability: Women* (2018e) available at: <https://assets.publishing.service.gov.uk/government/uploads/system/uploads/attachment_data/file/721190/police-guidance-on-working-with-vulnerable-women-web.pdf> (accessed 28 October 2020).

[191] The same goes for similar statistics about the ethno-racial composition of the suspect populations: HMIC, *The welfare of vulnerable people in police custody* (2015). Online at: <https://www.justiceinspectorates.gov.uk/hmicfrs/wp-content/uploads/the-welfare-of-vulnerable-people-in-police-custody.pdf> (accessed 23 June 2020).

[192] Howard League for Penal Reform, *Arresting the entry of women into the criminal justice system* (2019). Online at: <https://howardleague.org/wp-content/uploads/2019/09/APPG-Arresting-the-entry-of-women-into-the-criminal-justice-system.pdf> (accessed 15 June 2020).

[193] Young S 'Policing "Uncontrollable Banshees": Factors Influencing Arrest Decision Making' (2015) 14(1) *Safer Communities* 183–192; Young S, 'Gender, Policing and Social Control: Examining Police Officers' Perceptions of and Responses to Young Women Depicted as Violent' (2015) SCCJR Briefing Paper, Briefing No. 01/2012.

in ways that regulated what are considered to be appropriate forms of femininity, thereby perpetuating gender stereotypes.[194]

The potentially gendered nature of the police custody experience is only officially recognised to a limited extent. PACE Code of Practice C instructs officers to have regard to the dignity of the detainee when removing clothing or providing access to washing facilities; provides for suspects to speak to an officer of the same sex 'about any matter concerning the detainee's personal needs relating to their health, hygiene and welfare that might affect or concern them whilst in custody'; includes the provision of sanitary products free of charge; and there is a women's pathway (since 2019) within Liaison and Diversion schemes.[195] But beyond this, there has been very little detailed attention to the ways in which gender might generate, or interact with other, complex needs or vulnerabilities in the police detention setting. Police staff still feel uncomfortable providing sanitary products, perhaps because of the lack of gender balance in police custody staffing and also because of police preferences for recognising all suspects' individual needs, rather than the particular needs of women.[196]

Yet, the evidence suggests women detainees are highly likely to have particular needs, involving complex and overlapping forms of vulnerability, recognising of course that this is a loaded term especially when used in the context of women (see section 10.6). A high proportion of the women who are arrested and detained in police and/or prison custody suffer from a mental health condition; are more likely to have been taken into care, abused or witnessed violence as a child; have dependent children; to have committed offences to support drug use of another; to be victims as well as offenders.[197] We shall see that many of these issues feed into sentencing, which we discuss later.

10.5 Inequality in charging and post charge decision-making

We saw in section 10.4.2 that racialised people are often arrested when there would be insufficient evidence to charge. But we also know from chapter 7 that the CPS charge and prosecution decisions depend on what information is received from the police. We further know that prosecution decisions tend to endorse the wishes of the arresting/investigating officers. Despite the fact that the CPS bucks the criminal justice trend of staff from BAME population underrepresentation,[198] the evidence that prosecutorial decisions reflect inequalities in policing is mixed. In relation to joint enterprise prosecutions (see section 10.3), there are:

> racist assumptions built into anti-gang enforcement practices and the institutional racism of the JE prosecutorial strategy. Thus, violent offending by groups was three-to-four times more likely to be described as 'gang related' where young black men were involved than if young white offenders were involved. Secondly, the prosecution introduced evidence indicating gang involvement in nearly 80% of trials involving young black or mixed race suspects and less than 40% of the time when young white males were on trial.[199]

---

[194] Monk H, Gilmore J and Jackson W, 'Gendering Pacification: Policing Women at Anti-fracking Protests' (2019) 122(1) *Feminist Review* 64–79.   [195] PACE Code C, 2018: para 9.3A and B.
[196] Hodgson J, Skinns L, Munro V and Dehaghani R (2018) *A pilot study of the treatment of female detainees in five areas*, presentation given to the National Custody Forum, co-hosted by the University of Warwick and the NPCC, May 2018. Note this was a small-scale study in just five police force areas.
[197] Scott D, McGilloway S and Donnelly M, 'The Mental Health Needs of Women Detained in Police Custody' (2009) 18(2) *Journal of Mental Health* 144–151; Ministry of Justice (2018e) *Managing Vulnerability: Women*.
[198] Bridges (2018).
[199] Squires P, 'Constructing the Dangerous, Black, Criminal "Other"' *British Society of Criminology Newsletter*, No. 79, Winter 2016; Krebs B, 'Mens Rea in Joint Enterprise: A Role for Endorsement?' (2015) 74(3) *Cambridge Law Journal* 480–504.

These findings lead the Centre for Crime and Justice Studies to state:

> prosecutors regularly rely on racial stereotypes in relation to black defendants, using a range of signifiers to direct juries to increase the likelihood of conviction of secondary parties. For example, prosecution teams were reported as being more likely to appropriate discourses of 'gang insignia' and music videos or lyrics, particularly 'hip hop' and 'rap' genres, as a way of building a JE case against BAME prisoners.[200]

On the other hand, the Lammy Review found that an equal proportion of crime in general across ethnicities are charged, and that CPS decision-making does not contribute significantly to ethnic disproportionality. However, the review made no attempt:

> to investigate qualitative differences in charging decisions across the various ethnic groups, which previous research has suggested may have an important impact on the ways in which cases are processed subsequently. Thus, if BAME cases tend to result in more serious charges than those of white defendants based on similar types of alleged criminal behaviour (e.g., charges of robbery rather than theft, or of drug possession with intent to supply instead of mere possession), this can influence at which of magistrates' court or the Crown Court (the latter having more punitive sentencing powers) cases will be tried, as well as the type and length of sentence imposed if there is a conviction. Seriousness of charge can also influence decisions on whether defendants are remanded in custody prior to charge.[201]

Once charged, black people are more likely to elect Crown court trial,[202] perhaps reflecting the distrust in the criminal process that flows from interaction with the police. Defendants from some racialised groups are more likely to enter not guilty pleas initially, which means they are less likely to benefit from the sentencing discount discussed in chapter 7, and they thereby suffer an indirect form of discrimination.[203]

There is less research on post arrest and charge decision-making in relation to female suspects and defendants.[204] In 2017, just under half of women arrested were prosecuted, compared to more than two thirds of arrested men. The Ministry of Justice says that the police should aim 'to divert a woman out of the justice system and into support services, where appropriate.'[205] Women are referred at a higher rate to liaison and diversion services following arrest, and are more likely than men to be referred to services for alcohol misuse or as a result of a mental health condition.[206]

Prosecution rates for summary non-motoring offences involving female defendants have, however, increased overall. The Ministry of Justice attributes this to a rise in the number of prosecutions for TV licence evasion, noting that prosecutions against women were more likely to be brought by agencies other than the police.[207] Women were more

---

[200] Williams and Clarke (2016). [201] Bridges (2018: 84).

[202] Field S and Thomas P (eds), *Justice and Efficiency? The Royal Commission on Criminal Justice* (London: Blackwell, 1994).

[203] Owusu-Bempah (2017); Ashworth A, *Sentencing and Criminal Justice* (Cambridge: CUP, 2015).

[204] Most research that studies women in the criminal justice process tends to focus on the process of sentencing. See Posey B, Kowalski M and Stohr M, 'Thirty Years of Scholarship in the *Women and Criminal Justice* Journal: Gender, Feminism, and Intersectionality' (2020) 30(1) *Women & Criminal Justice* 5–29. Hine reports that a Google scholar search reveals literature on the topics of 'female offending generally, but others group around the topics of female crime rates; the features or factors related to female offending; women given sentences of imprisonment; and community sentencing and women', but does not mention policing and prosecution strategy (Hine J, 'Women And Criminal Justice: Where Are We Now?' (2019) 15(1) *British Journal of Community Justice* 5–18).

[205] Ministry of Justice (2018e) *Managing Vulnerability: Women*.

[206] Ministry of Justice (2018d) *Statistics on Women and the Criminal Justice System 2017*.

[207] Ministry of Justice (2016) *Statistics on Women and the Criminal Justice System 2015* available at: <http://iapdeathsincustody.independent.gov.uk/wp-content/uploads/2016/12/women-and-the-criminal-justice-system-statistics-2015.pdf> (accessed 28 October 2020).

likely to be cautioned for indictable offences than men, and received 24% of all cautions in 2015.[208] However, the proportion of women prosecuted for indictable offences has also increased since 2010, so that the gap between the proportion of men and women prosecuted for these has decreased. Black women are treated disproportionality punitively—they are twice as likely to be prosecuted than their white counterparts.[209] Whether this is because the socio-economic circumstances of black women are more likely to place them in situations in which they are exposed to arrest and prosecution through disproportionate surveillance, because the offence patterns differ, or because of discriminatory charging practices alone, is not clear.

In 2017, only just over a quarter of defendants prosecuted were female but women were proportionately more likely to be convicted than men.[210] This could be because women are likely to be prosecuted as a last resort, where the evidence is very strong, or it could be because, once in the system, women suffer from discriminatory decision-making on the basis of stereotypes about female behaviour. We simply do not know.

10.6 Sentencing and incarceration

In 2017, 25% of the prison population in England and Wales of 86,413 were from a non-white background. The same was true of over 40% of young people in custody.[211] For drugs offences, the chances of imprisonment are around 240% higher for BAME offenders, compared to white offenders. Comparable concerns were recorded for black adult females.[212] There was a similar pattern of disproportionate sentencing practices following the 2011 riots mentioned in chapter 8.[213]

The fact that non-white people are overrepresented in prisons may be partially explained by, and is in stark contrast to, their underrepresentation in jobs in most institutions of criminal justice. Among magistrates, 12% declare themselves as BAME, which is not representative of the general population. In 2017 the first non-white judge (Justice Singh) was appointed to the Court of Appeal: a 2.56% BAME representation on Court of Appeal benches. Women are also underrepresented at the highest levels of the legal profession. In 2014, 19% of Crown court defendants were from BAME groups, compared to 6% of judges.[214] The difficulty of judges relating to the defendants before them is discussed in chapter 8. The makeup of judges affects the way justice is done; a more diverse judiciary has the potential to make law and its application more humanistic.[215]

As Holdaway puts it, '[i]t is not *either* structural factors *or* police discrimination that lead to high crime rates for black youth but both.'[216] As race, gender and social class in particular intersect, black males living in poor urban areas have borne the brunt of mass imprisonment.[217] Indeed, 'the imprisonment of large numbers of unemployed people

---

[208] Ibid. [209] Ministry of Justice (2018g) *Statistics on Women and the Criminal Justice System 2017*.
[210] Ministry of Justice (2018g) *Statistics on Women and the Criminal Justice System 2017*.
[211] Fekete L, 'Lammy Review: Without Racial Justice, Can There Be Trust?' (2018) 59(3) *Race & Class* 75–79 at p. 76. [212] The Lammy Review (2017); Bridges (2018).
[213] Murji K and Neal S, 'Riot: Race and Politics in the 2011 Disorders' (2011) 16(4) *Sociological Research Online* 216–220. [214] Owusu-Bempah, Abenaa (2017).
[215] Christie (1994). See further ch 9, esp. section 9.3 of racial bias among judges and juries in the Crown court.
[216] Holdaway S, *The Racialisation of British Policing* (Houndmills: MacMillan, 1996) p 96. However, the term 'high crime rates', in common use, relates to the recorded figures, which are a product of arrest practices as well as 'actual' crime. See pp 84–104 of Holdaway's book for a sophisticated discussion of race, crime and arrests; and also Bowling B and Phillips C, *Racism, Crime and Justice* (Harlow: Longman, 2002) ch 6.
[217] Hudson (2003).

has conveniently enabled the United States to reduce its official unemployment rate by between 30 and 40% since the beginning of the 1990s'.[218] Warehousing of such populations is made possible in all industrialised countries, the UK included, via the aggressive policing tactics employed in 'rough' neighbourhoods. Such state level 'ethno-racial division intensifies class decomposition at the bottom, facilitates the shift to workfare and escalates the rolling out of the penal state', while penalisation also 'refurbishes the meanings and workings of "race"'.[219]

Drawing a similarity with risk factors related to BAME group offending, Martin and Wilcox point out that '[i]nsecurity and poorly paid employment are key factors in women's offending.'[220] Female imprisonment rates are significantly lower than those for men. In the UK, the female prison population has sat at approximately 4,000 since 2013.[221] Women are, however treated somewhat differently in relation to sentencing compared to men of any ethnicity: they are paternalised (through ideas about what a woman 'should' be like) and infantilised (through stereotypical narratives of weakness e.g. through abuse, or mental illness). Women who are less likely to be able to fall into the infantilised victim role (including black, lesbian or even independent) women 'are likely to receive more penal treatment than those who fit the stereotypes of conventional, victimised femininity'[222]

Female offenders are also subject to strategies of responsibilisation that are exercised on other marginalised groups in order to try and nudge them towards the white, male, middle class rhetoric of what it means to be a useful (non-criminal) member of society. Through both community based sentences and civil preventative measures (see section 1.1.2), people are forced to take help that those in positions of power think they need. For example, Parenting Orders are disproportionately given to lone mothers.[223] Martin and Wilcox report that women have, through various community sentencing measures—especially those designed to re-socialise them—'taken on board the dominant discourse of being personally responsible' by exhibiting feelings of shame, feeling that they are dangerous or blaming themselves for making 'bad choices' (such as being in abusive relationships).[224] Multi-agency partnerships that are sometimes promoted as empowering women (such as by building confidence to avoid abusive relationships, for example) are in fact thin veils for coerced responsibilisation strategies.[225] None of this is to suggest that women should not be empowered and counselled to avoid situations that further the inequity they experience. But surely the re-socialising of perpetrators of domestic abuse (in whatever form) should be prioritised. Female victims should not be made to feel that their predicament is somehow self-induced, making them feel further disempowered and excluded from the rest of society.

We have seen that women who are 'othered' as a result of gendered, complex living conditions (including histories of abuse, violence and sexual violence) are more likely to be imprisoned than others.[226] These tend to be the very women who suffer from disproportionate levels of mental illness,[227] and the rate of self-harm by women in prison is

---

[218] Bell (2011: 134).   [219] Wacquant in Squires and Lea (2012: 244).
[220] Martin and Wilcox in Squires and Lea (2012: 153).
[221] Ministry of Justice (2018g) *Statistics on Women and the Criminal Justice System 2017*.
[222] Hudson (2003: 140).
[223] Katz I, Corlyon J, La Placa V and Hunter S, *The relationship between parenting and poverty* (York: Joseph Rowntree Foundation, 2007). These are orders that carry criminal sanctions and can be made on the parent of a young offender to try and ensure that the family keeps the child out of further trouble.
[224] Martin and Wilcox in Squires and Lea (2012: 164)—citing a report on multi-agency partnerships for women offenders.
[225] Ibid. See also Moore (2019).   [226] Martin and Wilcox in Squires and Lea (2012: 154).
[227] Ibid.

five times higher than for male counterparts.[228] Clearly, governments and prison services struggle to deal with the needs of women in prison. Women offenders who are more troubled (infantilisation) rather than troublesome (paternalisation) may, perversely, be sent to prison for crimes that male counterparts would not be imprisoned for in order to access the services available in prison,[229]—even though it is extremely difficult to access services in prison, especially as overcrowding has increased in recent years.[230] On the other hand, prison rehabilitative services do, to some extent, justify the continued existence of prisons.

In recognition of some of these issues, the Corston Report[231] recommended a different sentencing regime for women, using small, multifunctional custodial centres alongside specialist community centres to operate as diversion from prison. The report recommended that the personal and individual needs of women who (are at risk of) offend(ing) be given greater recognition in the criminal process. The Womens' Centres that were set up as a result were reported to be successful in reducing reoffending by women, but by 2017 the centres were cutting services as austerity measures cut their funding.[232] In light of general agreement that limited progress had been made since the Corston Report, the government announced plans to focus on community intervention for (would-be) female offenders instead of building five specialist prisons.[233] The strategy was designed to address the vulnerability faced by women, but funding levels were criticised because campaigners felt they would undermine the ability of centres to provide positive intervention.[234] Women continue to be sentenced to a comparatively high proportion of short custodial sentences for relatively minor offences, where they are less likely to achieve enhanced status (which can—to an extent—relieve some of the worst aspect of imprisonment), than men.[235]

The evidence is, therefore, that the inequalities exercised at the beginning of the criminal process continue right through to sentencing and imprisonment: '[m]any offenders have never felt either "integrated" or "settled"' as their experience represents merely an extension of pre-existing marginality.[236] Young, disadvantaged men from racialised populations are over-represented in prison as stereotypes that they are a dangerous or risky population persist. On the other hand, stereotypes that women are responsible for their predicament, or are in need of treatment, influence sentencers to perpetuate practices that continue to disempower them.

---

[228] Ministry of Justice (2018g) *Statistics on Women and the Criminal Justice System 2017*.

[229] Martin and Wilcox in Squires and Lea (2012: 164).

[230] Criminal Justice Alliance, *Crowded Out? The impact of prison overcrowding on rehabilitation* (2012) available at: <http://criminaljusticealliance.org/wp-content/uploads/2015/02/Crowded_Out_CriminalJusticeAlliance.pdf> (accessed 28 October 2020).

[231] Home Office, *The Corston Report: A Report by Baroness Jean Corston of a Review of Women with Particular Vulnerabilities in the Criminal Justice System* (2007) available at: <https://webarchive.nationalarchives.gov.uk/20130206102659/http://www.justice.gov.uk/publications/docs/corston-report-march-2007.pdf> (accessed 28 October 2020).

[232] Howard League for Penal Reform, *Is this the end of women's centres?* (2016) available at: <https://howardleague.org/news/isthistheendofwomenscentres/> (accessed 28 October 2020). See further, Annison J and Brayford J (eds), *Women and Criminal Justice: From the Corston Report to Transforming Rehabilitation* (Bristol: The Policy Press, 2015).

[233] Ministry of Justice, *Female offender strategy* (London: Ministry of Justice, 2018d).

[234] Deardon L, 'Government scraps proposed women's "community prisons" in new strategy to reduce female offending' *The Independent*, 26 June 2018.

[235] Hine (2019).

[236] Moore (2019: 204).

10.7 Inequality and victimisation

10.7.1 Disproportionate levels of criminality experienced by marginalised groups

As a result of inadequate protection in poor neighbourhoods, poor black people often experience high levels of victimisation.[237] As noted earlier, if people believe the police to be against them—whether or not this belief is justified—then they are far less likely to participate in community policing or to co-operate with the police by reporting a crime to them, whether as a victim or witness. This is important because of the huge overlap between the suspect population and the victim/witness population even though 'criminality is associated with a minority, victimhood is associated with the majority, justifying the so-called rebalancing of the criminal justice system in favour of the victim'.[238] Interviews following the 2011 riots with a sample of predominantly young, ethnically diverse, inner city respondents revealed a legacy of mistrust between them and the police. They experienced stop and search as discriminatory, rude and disrespectful in how it was carried out, an instrument of control, and symbolic of 'all that was wrong with the police'. One described the police as 'the biggest gang in town' against whom they could not win. This led them to be reluctant to report crimes to the police, even when they were in need.[239] Other studies in the UK and abroad have reached similar conclusions.[240]

10.7.2 Hate crime laws

As discussed in section 1.7, socio-economically disadvantaged sections of society are disproportionately victims of crime as much as they are disproportionately criminalised by the various agencies of criminal justice. The overlap between these two categories may explain why laws that go some way to protect marginalised social groups evolved hesitantly.[241] But we do now have laws that recognise certain groups in society as disproportionately victimised, and acknowledge that such victimisation is a result of their membership of a marginalised group. Limited space leads us to only highlight key points. Readers who wish to develop their understanding in this field are directed to the extensive research conducted by Walters[242] and Mason.[243]

Hate crime is a crime committed with a motive of hatred or that demonstrates hostility towards the victim based on a particular characteristic. Police forces and the CPS should

---

[237] Hudson (2003). [238] Bell (2011: 98). [239] Newburn et al (2018: 219–220).

[240] Sargeant E, Murphy K and Cherney A, 'Ethnicity, Trust and Cooperation with Police: Testing the Dominance of the Process-based Model' (2014) 11(4) *European Journal of Criminology* 500–524; Viki G, Culmer M, Eller A and Abrams D, 'Race and Willingness to Cooperate with the Police: The Roles of Quality of Contact, Attitudes Towards the Behaviour and Subjective Norms' (2006) 45(2) *British Journal of Social Psychology* 285–302; Fitzgerald et al (2002: 49, 88).

[241] Hudson (2003).

[242] Walters M, Owusu-Bempah, Abenaa and Wiedlitzka S 'Hate Crime and the "Justice Gap": The Case for Law Reform' (2018) 12 *Criminal Law Review* 961–986; Perry B, Perry J, Schweppe J and Walters M, 'Introduction. Understanding Hate Crime: Research, Policy and Practice (2015) 27(6) *Criminal Justice Policy Review* 571–576; Walters M, 'Conceptualizing "Hostility" for Hate Crime Law: Minding "the Minutiae" When Interpreting Section 28(1)(a) of the Crime and Disorder Act 1998' (2014) 34(1) *Oxford Journal of Legal Studies* 47–74.

[243] Mason G, 'Legislating Against Hate' in Hall N, Corb A, Giannasi P and Grieve J (eds), *Routledge International Handbook on Hate Crime* (Abdingon: Routledge, 2014); Mason G, Maher J, McCulloch J, Pickering S, Wickes R and McKay C, *Policing Hate Crime: Understanding Communities and Prejudice* (Abingdon: Routledge, 2017); Mason G, 'Violence as Hate Crime: The Emergence of a Discourse' in Stubbs J and Tomsen S (eds), *Australian Violence: Crime, Criminal Justice and Beyond* (Sydney: Federation Press, 2016) pp 125–141.

record 'hate crime' as such. Special categories of hate crime evolved as a result of the historical failure of the police and criminal justice process to provide adequate responses to crimes motivated by prejudice. In the same way as the police tend to avoid a victim centred approach to domestic violence (section 10.4.1), they also tended to disregard 'hate' and record victims' experiences as 'ordinary' crimes.[244] Furthermore, as a result of already poor relationships between the police and minority communities discussed earlier, hate crimes are often underreported.

Specific 'protected characteristics' are now incorporated into hate crime legislation, which has developed piecemeal between the 1980s and 2000s, including:

- Race (Crime and Disorder Act 1998 and Public Order Act 1986, as amended by Anti-terrorism Crime and Security Act 2001 to create specific religiously aggravated offences and apply the same sentencing duty to all offences where there is evidence of religious aggravation, and by the Protection of Freedoms Act 2012 to include racially or religiously aggravated stalking).
- Religion (Crime and Disorder Act 1998 and Public Order Act 1986).
- Sexual Orientation (Criminal Justice Act 1998 and Criminal Justice and Immigration Act 2008).
- Disability (Criminal Justice Act 2003).
- Transgender Identity (Criminal Justice Act 1998, Criminal Justice and Immigration Act 2008 and Legal Aid, Sentencing and Punishment of Offenders Act 2012).

As a result of this piecemeal development, not all hate crime offences operate in the same way. Racial or religious hatred attaches to certain specified offences—mainly assault and threatening behaviour in public places—and creates separate charges under the Crime and Disorder Act 1998, such as racially aggravated common assault. The prosecution is required to prove both the existence of the base crime (here, common assault) and the aggravated element (hostility). If the aggravated element is proved, the maximum sentencing powers for the base offence are increased. So, using the common assault example, the maximum penalty is usually six months imprisonment but racially aggravated common assault carries a maximum sentence of two years imprisonment.[245] Hostility is not defined in statute, and does not necessarily have to be the motive for the original offence.[246]

While the Crime and Disorder Act 1998 created a set of offences that are specifically connected to racial or religious hatred, hate crimes against people who are disabled, lesbian, gay, bisexual or trans (which are rarely reported and even more rarely prosecuted) engage s.146 Criminal Justice Act 2003 (to be amended by the Sentencing Bill 2020).[247] If that section is activated, the court must increase the sentences imposed on conviction to account for the aggravation related to one of the protected characteristics. The section will

---

[244] HMICFRS *Understanding the difference. The initial police response to hate crime* (2018) available at: <https://www.justiceinspectorates.gov.uk/hmicfrs/wp-content/uploads/understanding-the-difference-the-initial-police-response-to-hate-crime.pdf> (accessed 27 October 2020). See also Bell (2011).

[245] The leading case on sentencing procedure is *Kelly & Donnelly* [2001] 2 Cr App R (S), which states that the court should decide the sentence without aggravation, then increase the sentence to take the aggravated element into account.

[246] *McFarlane* (2002) EWHC 485; *Woods* (2002) EWHC 85. There are also offences of inciting racial hatred under s.17 Public Order Act 1986, and of stirring up hatred under s.29 Public Order Act 1986, as amended by Racial and Religious Hatred Act 2006. These sections have a particular relationship with freedom of expression under Arts 10 and 17 of the ECHR, which we do not have room to discuss here.

[247] Section 145 of the same statute increases sentences for racial or religious aggravation in offences to which ss.28–32 Crime and Disorder Act 1998 do not apply. An offence of inciting hatred based on hostility to sexual orientation of any description created under s.74 Criminal Justice and Immigration Act 2008.

be activated if, at the time of committing the offence, or immediately before or after doing so, the offender demonstrated, or is motivated by, hostility towards the victim based on one of the characteristics. The defendant must be put on notice of the potential finding of hostility and given a chance to challenge it.[248] If proved, the court must openly state the existence of the aggravating feature, which applied to all crimes, unlike the provisions of the Crime and Disorder Act 1998. Also unlike the provisions of the Crime and Disorder Act, there is no increase in the maximum penalty available, nor a specific label for the offence. There are two views that one could take about this—that it is better for rehabilitation and reintegration into society; or that it is not fair labelling and undermines a victim's vulnerability, and that hate crimes are so damaging to the fabric of society generally that they ought be labelled as such for deterrent and shaming value.

Reporting and prosecution rates in relation to hate crime motivated by characteristics other than racial or religious hatred are low, despite rises in incidents of disability,[249] homophobic,[250] and transgender hate crime.[251] A survey in 2000 found that 90% of people with a learning disability had experienced bullying and harassment.[252] While that appeared to have been greatly reduced by 2019, one in three people with a learning disability were still reporting bullying.[253] Research being conducted by Mason-Bish examines the harassment experienced by disabled women through non-consensual touching.[254] However, victims of hate crime may lack the confidence or the understanding that they have been a victim of hate crime in order to report it: for example in 2017/18, 7,226 disablist hate crimes were recorded, but official estimates totalled disability hate crimes to 52,000.[255] So the Law Commission was tasked to consider extending the aggravated offences found in the Crime and Disorder Act 1998 to include where hostility is demonstrated on the grounds of disability, sexual orientation or gender identity, and the stirring up of hatred offences under the Public Order Act 1986 to include stirring up hatred on the grounds of disability or gender identity.[256] The report recommended a larger scale review, and a review of 'the adequacy and parity of protection offered by the law relating to hate crime and to make recommendations for its reform' was commissioned, a consultation paper being published in 2020.[257]

In 2011/12, police recorded 43,748 crimes as hate crimes: around 1% of all recorded crimes. The proportions across the five protected groups were: race 82%; sexual orientation 10%; religion 4%; disability 4%; and transgender 1%.[258] By 2015–18 there were

---

[248] *Lester* 63 Cr App R (S) 29.

[249] Giordano C, 'Disability Hate Crimes rise by one-third in a year cross England and Wales' *The Independent*, 15 October 2018.

[250] Marsh S, Mohdin A and McIntyre N, 'Homophobic and transphobic hate crimes surge in England and Wales' *The Guardian*, 14 June 2019.

[251] Hunte B, 'Transgender hate crimes recorded by police go up 81%' *BBC News*, 27 June 2019.

[252] Mencap (2000) *Living in Fear*. For more recent research see, e.g., Ralph S et al, 'Disability Hate Crime' (2016) 43 *British Journal of Special Education* 215; Healy J, "It Spreads Like a Creeping Disease": Experiences of Victims of Disability Hate Crimes in Austerity Britain' (2020) 35 *Disability and Society* 176; Lindsey J, 'Protecting Vulnerable Adults from Abuse' (2020) 32 *Child and Family Law Quarterly* 157; Tyson J, 'Disablist Hate Crime: A Scar on the Conscience of the Criminal Justice System?' in Tapley J and Davies P, *Victimology: Research, Policy and Activism* (London: Palgrave Macmillan, 2020).

[253] See <https://www.mencap.org.uk/press-release/new-research-mencap-shows-bullying-people-learning-disability-leading-social> (accessed 27 October 2020).

[254] See <www.privateplacespublicspaces.blog> (accessed 27 October 2020).

[255] HM Government (2018). *Hate Crime, England and Wales, 2017/18*. London: Home Office; Giordano (2018).

[256] Law Commission, *Hate Crime: The Case For Extending The Existing Offences* LC213 (2014) available at: <http://www.lawcom.gov.uk/app/uploads/2015/03/cp213_hate_crime_amended.pdf> (accessed 27 October 2020).

[257] See <https://www.lawcom.gov.uk/project/hate-crime/> (accessed 27 October 2020).

[258] See <http://lawcommission.justice.gov.uk/docs/cp213_hate_crime_summary.pdf> (accessed 27 October 2020).

approximately 184,000 hate crime incidents each year: around 2% of all police recorded crime. Rather than a rise, hate crime had on one measure decreased by 40% in the 10 years to 2017/18,[259] although Home Office statistics using a different measure report a 29% rise in hate crime (largely in relation to disability or transgender hate crimes) in 2016/17.[260] Although self reporting suggests much more incidence of hate crime than the police record, this is true of all crime. There does appear to be a general rise in reported incidents of hate crime, be that because policing has improved, people are more willing to come forward, or because actual incidents have increased. Hate crime almost certainly spiked following the result of the EU membership referendum in 2016, and following incidents motivated by terrorism in 2017.[261] These rises may indicate that society is increasingly fragmented.

In 2017/18, 13% of police recorded hate crime was referred for prosecution. This was a much lower percentage than a few years earlier, but a similar number of offences were prosecuted (14,151).[262] This reflects the rapid rise in reporting of hate crime, but the high attrition rate—which happens with many offences—is a concern. Attrition is because of a lack of evidence, lack of victim support for further action, or because the suspect was never identified.[263] The majority of prosecutions are those through which hostility on the basis of race has been demonstrated, while offences demonstrative of hostility based on disability or transgender status are least likely to result in prosecution.[264] The CPS blame their falling hate crime prosecution rate on a lack of police referrals,[265] but crimes motivated by, or demonstrative of, hate are more likely to be prosecuted than violence not motivated in such a way.[266] This does not necessarily mean that there has not been a fall in referrals to the CPS, but does show that the data held about hate crime is not clear and it remains difficult to reconcile different data sets.

There is no legislation in relation to gender and age. The CPS feels that crime with misogynistic undertones is sufficiently protected by the government strategy on ending violence against women and girls (see further chapter 12).[267] But this misses non-violent crime. In the meantime, Muslim women in particular suffer from hostile street harassment that hinders their ability to participate fully in society.[268] While there are no specific legal provisions in relation to crimes motivated by, or demonstrative of, hostility towards a victim's age, sentencing guidelines (see section 7.8) do invite courts to view the age of a victim as something that could increase vulnerability, and therefore aggravate the offence, leading to the imposition of a harsher sentence.

The CPS obtains convictions in a high proportion of all hate crime prosecutions—nearly 85% in 2017/18.[269] A similarly high conviction rate is obtained in relation to prosecuted

---

[259] Allen G and Zayed Y, *Hate Crime Statistics* (2019) House of Commons Briefing Paper No 08537 <https://researchbriefings.parliament.uk/ResearchBriefing/Summary/CBP-8537#fullreport> (accessed 27 October 2020).

[260] O'Neill A, *Hate Crime, England and Wales, 2016/17* Statistical Bulletin 17/17 (2017) <https://assets.publishing.service.gov.uk/government/uploads/system/uploads/attachment_data/file/652136/hate-crime-1617-hosb1717.pdf> (accessed 27 October 2020).   [261] O'Neill (2017); Allen and Zayed (2019).

[262] CPS, *Hate Crime Report 2017–2018* (2018b) <https://www.cps.gov.uk/sites/default/files/documents/publications/cps-hate-crime-report-2018.pdf#page=22> (accessed 27 October 2020).

[263] Allen and Zayed (2019).   [264] CPS *Hate Crime Report 2017–2018* (2018b); Allen and Zayed (2019).
[265] Ibid.   [266] Allen and Zayed (2019).

[267] See HM Government, *Ending Violence against Women and Girls Strategy 2016–2020* <https://assets.publishing.service.gov.uk/government/uploads/system/uploads/attachment_data/file/522166/VAWG_Strategy_FINAL_PUBLICATION_MASTER_vRB.PDF> (accessed 27 October 2020).

[268] Mason-Bish H and Zempi I, 'Misogyny, Racism, and Islamophobia: Street Harassment at the Intersections' (2019) 14(5) *Feminist Criminology* 540–559. The authors call for further intersectional research on hate crime.

[269] CPS *Hate Crime Report 2017–2018* (2018b).

crimes against older people—83.6%. The majority of those convictions (75%) were as a result of guilty pleas, which the CPS says 'indicates the quality of our casework and the strength of evidence remains high'.[270] That is, of course, one explanation for the high conviction rate. Another explanation is that, as discussed in chapter 7 in relation to other offences that are relatively unthreatening to powerful societal interests, prosecution is reserved only for strong cases, with prosecuting agencies being risk averse in relation to hate crime prosecution.

Hate crime has significant effects on both individual victims and on society as whole. Stirring up hatred perpetuates and encourages prejudice and discrimination, and victims of hate crime are more likely to suffer emotional and psychological impact after a crime than victims of non-hate crime.[271] But damage can be caused by hate crime legislation constructed on narrow grounds. One danger is to assume that people who fall within the categories of protected characteristics are vulnerable, which could perpetuate social models of vulnerability and historic categories of oppression, and construct rigid norms about categories of hate.[272] It could be argued that sentencing provisions that take into account the vulnerability of a victim are sufficiently broad to encapsulate circumstances when vulnerable victims have been targeted, but also to avoid categorising particular groups of people simply by virtue of a particular characteristic. However, the meaning and value attached to the term 'vulnerability' is contested,[273] and current constructions tend to perpetuate the status quo about who is regarded as vulnerable in the criminal process—often to the exclusion of defendants.[274]

10.8 Rights and belonging: How far can 'rights' take us?

In 2009, the then Shadow Home Secretary said: 'It's time we spent a bit more time worrying about the wrongs in our society, and a bit less about the rights of those who are disrupting it'.[275] But the groups who experience both of these things (wrongs and disrupted rights) often overlap, and 'where societies are characterized by radical diversity and gross inequality, democratic processes need to be underpinned by a strong commitment to human rights'.[276] Article 14 of the European Convention on Human Rights provides that public bodies must not behave in a discriminatory way. It is designed to protect people from discrimination on the basis of 'sex, race, colour, language, religion, political or other opinion, national or social origin, association with a national minority, property, birth or other status'. But Article 14 does not allow an action for discrimination alone; any action for discrimination must be attached to one of the fundamental rights protected by the Human Rights Act 1998, such as the right to liberty or the right to a fair trial. As discussed in chapter 1, human rights laws often provide little more than a safety net of protection for people. That is not to say that we would be better off without them, but 'human rights only protect and constrain when dignity is grossly undermined'.[277] It follows that human

---

[270] Ibid; 23.   [271] Allen and Zayed (2019); Tyson in Tapley and Davies (2020).
[272] Mason in Hall et al (2014).
[273] See Fineman M, 'The Vulnerable Subject and the Responsive State' (2010) 60 *Emory Law Journal*; Fineman M, 'Vulnerability and Social Justice' (2019) *Valparaiso University Law Review* 53.
[274] See, in relation to special measures and constructions of vulnerability, Fairclough S, 'Speaking Up For Injustice: Reconsidering the Provision of Special Measures Through the Lens of Equality' [2018] *Criminal Law Review* 4–19 and, on policing, Dehaghani R, 'Interrogating Vulnerability: Reframing the Vulnerable Suspect in Police Custody' (2020) *Social and Legal Studies* 417–440.
[275] Chris Grayling, cited in Bell (2011: 122).   [276] Hudson in Quirk, Seddon and Smith (2010: 303).
[277] Sanders A, 'Reconciling the Apparently Different Goals of Criminal Justice and Regulation; The "Freedom" Perspective' in Quirk, Seddon and Smith (2010: 64).

rights laws do little to protect marginalised populations from the frequent subtle (and not-so-subtle) disdain they often encounter from the police and other institutions of criminal justice. Those experiences reinforce any pre-existing sense of inequity and stress the power imbalances inherent in an unequal society. When persistent, these encounters can be destructive, but it is difficult to attach rudeness to a particular human right to make it actionable in the European Court of Human Rights. Even when it can be done, actions under the Human Rights Act 1998 must first exhaust all domestic remedies, will take a long time to process through the system, are expensive to bring and difficult to prove. Although the Commissioner for Human Rights, and the European Commission against Racism and Intolerance, have both recognised incidents when police forces have acted in a racially discriminatory way when detaining people, they also point to the problem of securing evidence in support of an allegation of such discrimination.[278]

Another problem is, as Hudson argues, 'law based on the notion of equal rights cannot remedy gender inequalities . . . if "equality" is taken to mean treating cases alike, women have to prove their "alikeness" before they can be treated equally'.[279] In *Opuz v Turkey*,[281] the European court accepted that there was an element of discrimination involved in failing to adequately protect women from domestic violence. In *Michael v Chief Constable of South Wales*,[281] counsel argued that the police have to protect victims of domestic violence in a non-discriminatory way, but the claim was largely dismissed save in relation to an Article 2 claim (see section 1.6.2 and 12.3.1). The case has not yet reached the European Court of Human Rights, but the case law on domestic abuse and human rights to date is inadequate.[282]

Hudson's point can be said of any socially disadvantaged group; for black people to be treated as white, they would need to prove their alikeness, and for poor people to be treated equally to rich, they would need to prove their alikeness. All of these factors do no more than encourage conformity to a dominant model of what it means to be a responsible citizen. In a similar vein, uncritical reliance on human rights discourse can be problematic because human rights are themselves bound in dominant ideas about what rights should convey and to whom:

> In the face of a security/rights dichotomy in which heightened military responses in the name of security prompted by fear, terror and crisis subordinates rights concerns, and confronted with discourses of responsibility and community in place of individual rights, rights have at least at the national level lost some of their energy and promise.[283]

The remaining potential for human rights to make better provision for marginalised groups is well illustrated in Brems' collection of rewritten ECtHR judgments,[284] which tackle issues involving children, gender, religious minorities, sexual minorities, disability and cultural minorities. Chaib illustrates how the ECtHR could, in relation to religious minorities, frame issues of necessity with greater nuance so that individual rights are protected,[285] while Burbergs advocates for a broader understand of 'community' in relation

---

[278] Murdoch J and Roche R, *The European Convention on Human Rights and Policing* (Council of Europe, 2013). [279] Hudson (2003: 117).
[280] (2009) Application no. 33401/02.   [281] [2015] UKSC 2.
[282] Burton M, 'R v Dhaliwal. Commentary' in Hunter, McGlynn and Rackley (2010); McQuigg R, 'Domestic Violence as a Human Rights Issue: Rumor v. Italy' (2016) 26(4) *The European Journal of International Law* 1009–1025.
[283] Sohki-Bulley B, *Governing (Through) Rights* (London: Bloomsbury Professional, 2016) p 4.
[284] Brems E (ed), *Diversity and European Human Rights: Rewriting Judgments of the ECHR* (Cambridge: CUP, 2013). See further, Brems E and Desmet E, *Integrated Human Rights in Practice. Rewriting Human Rights Decisions* (Cheltenham: Elgar, 2017).
[285] Chaib S, 'Suku Phull v France Rewritten From a Procedural Justice Perspective: Taking Religious Minorities Seriously' in Brems (2013: 218–240).

to Art 8 and disability healthcare.[286] Kavey, however, counsels against overreliance on the privacy element of Art 8 as an indirect method of marginalising minority sexual groups away from the public sphere.[287] All the authors in the collection demonstrate the transformative potential of human rights in relation to marginalised groups that could flow from a change in culture and application.

An approach that could be of use is 'cosmopolitan justice', which promotes the idea that everyone has rights, and:

> must be responded to without violence, however different, however incomprehensible, however fearsome and threatening they seem and an understanding that justice is owed to strangers as well as to those with whom we feel a sense of community.[288]

We recognise that 'community' is a loaded term and that society is made up of diverse overlapping networks (chapter 2). Each 'community' will have its own set of unique relations with the police that are likely to vary over time. Those who live in communities that suffer from endemic socio-economic marginalisation are likely to have a very different sense of community to those in wealthier communities that have better housing, higher levels of educational attainment and lower levels of police surveillance.[289] Thus 'broad statements referring to "community safety" or "community wellbeing" are often used by government officials without proper explication as to whose safety and wellbeing is being targeted'.[290] Community is, nonetheless, important in the context of criminal justice because situations can 'become dangerous if members of particular groups are collectively seen as "not belonging" or as potentially dangerous'.[291] Prime examples of this can be seen in the prosecution and conviction of innocent Irish people during the 'Troubles', with concerns about the impact of more recent anti-terrorism provisions on the sense of community felt by South Asian, Middle Eastern and Muslim communities.

As we discussed in chapter 2, a minority of prejudiced or aggressive officers can do immense damage to police-community relations.[292] A sense of collective injustice is reinforced when the subject of racist policing becomes high public-profile, as through the focus on police use of (lethal) force both in England, the US and elsewhere, through simmering tensions about stop and search practices and the policing of protest, the Stephen Lawrence Inquiry, or the broadcasting of The Secret Policeman. As we said in chapter 2, the 'pervasive and deeply entrenched' sense that police officers have about the 'suspiciousness' of people of black and Asian heritage[293] needs to be addressed. Any sense of 'not belonging' as a result of police attitudes and behaviour has implications for reported crime rates and policing, and for the criminal process through jury trial and judicial case management in which assumptions are made about 'suitable enemies'. Perhaps, recognising the

---

[286] Burbergs M, 'Rewriting Kolanis v UK. The Right to Community Living' in Brems (2013: 382–398).

[287] Kavey M, 'The Public Faces of Privacy: Rewriting Lustig-Prean and Beckett v UK' in Brems (2013: 293–326). Sohki-Bulley B, *Governing (Through) Rights* (Oxford: Bloomsbury Professional, 2016) p 4 cautions against the way rights have become privileges 'afforded only to those who are visible within our society.'

[288] Hudson in Quirk, Seddon and Smith (2010: 303). Cosmopolitan justice is more usually associated with international law, and international criminal law, to examine unequal resource distortion across the globe. See, for example, Moellendorf M, *Cosmopolitan Justice* (Blouder: Westview Press, 2002); Bailliet C and Franko Aas K, *Cosmopolitan Justice and its Discontents* (Abingdon: Routledge, 2011); Caney S, 'Cosmopolitan Justice and Equalizing Opportunities' (2001) 32(1–2) *Metaphilosophy* 113–134. [289] Moore (2019).

[290] Walters M, Paterson J, McDonnell L and Brown R, 'Group Identity, Empathy and Shared Suffering: Understanding the "Community" Impacts of Anti-LGBT and Islamophobic Hate Crimes' (2019) *International Review of Victimology*. [291] Faulkner and Burnett (2011: 75).

[292] 'I've seen behaviour in the past that was absolutely atrocious... it only takes a couple of people to destroy all the good work': sergeant quoted by Fitzgerald (1999: ch 4).

[293] Fitzgerald M and Sibbitt R, *Ethnic monitoring in police forces: A beginning* (Home Office Research Study 173 (London: Home Office, 1997) p 66.

limited impact of human rights law, what we need are alternative ideas of 'public', 'social', and 'community' to create a broader, more inclusive and compassionate politics of belonging, and that politics of belonging might be used to address some of the inequality currently perpetuated in the criminal process. This way of encouraging democracy in diverse and unequal societies merits further consideration, for which we do not have space. [294]

10.9 Conclusion

The criminal process has long been used to discipline groups that are categorised, in dominant socio-political circles, as 'dangerous' or 'risky'. The British history of colonialism (followed by migration from the former colonies) has assisted in the translation of those discourses into racially discriminatory practices that have been further shaped by relatively recent heightened fears about terrorism. Furthermore, the historically gendered nature of western capitalist society means that the criminal process has also been infused with patriarchal ideas. It is about those inequalities that the most research exists, though there are gaps, particularly in relation to females in police custody. We need to know more about other marginalised and disadvantaged groups, such as neurodiverse citizens. We also need to better understand the intersections between these groups if we are to achieve more sophisticated understandings of our core values of democracy and justice, as well as how to make criminal justice work more effectively for them (part of the third core value of 'efficiency').

Inequality of some description infuses all stages of the criminal process, and is particularly visible in policing and sentencing. While everyone has at least some degree of agency and autonomy, disproportionate numbers of people from marginalised groups become stuck somewhere in between exclusion from, and inclusion in, society and full access to citizenship, and disruption to and compliance with social order. These issues undermine the democratic potential of criminal justice. Searching for practices that enable marginalised groups to participate more fully could achieve greater justice (albeit that it could be expensive i.e. at the expense of efficiency).[295] We need a shift in discourse away from a desire to manage 'dangerous', 'undeserving' or 'enemy' populations through the criminal justice system. Reliance 'too exclusively on criminal justice as the main instrument for preventing and reducing crime, or for maintaining public confidence' will fail.[296] Social inequality is better dealt with through social policy than through criminal justice policy because 'courts cannot function as instrumental tools for management without sacrificing their greatest strengths in the protection of values'.[297] Thus the freedom model outlined in chapter 1 is not only concerned with maximising freedom through the use of, and constraints on, legal powers; it is equally concerned with maximising freedom through social policy where doing so increases freedom more than would be achieved by seeking the same aims through legal policy. Resources are equally important: since they are limited, the most efficient ways of achieving those aims should be used in order to preserve resource for the whole range of social purposes. But efficiency is as much a long-term matter as it is short-term. And in the long-term, inequality costs money as well as stability, health and happiness. The three core values of justice (social as well as legal), democracy (including inclusiveness), and efficiency therefore can all be made to work together.

---

[294] We do think it important to note, however, that all of our ideals are dependent on our cultural and relational situations, which may mean that justice can only ever be aspirational and not attainable. See Hudson (2003).

[295] On the meaning of participation see Owusu-Bempah, Abenaa, 'The Interpretation and Application of the Right to Effective Participation'(2018) 22(4) *International Journal of Evidence and Proof* 321–341.

[296] Faulkner and Burnett (2011: 69).   [297] Christie (1994).

This is a particularly apt set of considerations, at the time of writing, given the calls to defund the police in the US in the wake of the death of George Floyd and global Black Lives Matter protests, and to divert resources to organisations that can do more to tackle the root causes of crime. Taking up these suggestions, however, involves confronting an 'emperors-got-no-clothes' type-fallacy about the limited role of the police in controlling crime. This may prove a step too far for the current government, in which the Home Secretary, like many of those who have gone before her, is wedded to the idea of the police controlling crime, no more no less, and in which the government also has a dreadful track record of addressing growing levels of poverty and inequality.[298] What is also needed is the political will to address ethno-racial and gender-based forms of inequality throughout society in education, employment, healthcare, the media, politics etc, the structural effects of which become writ large on the criminal justice process, as evidenced in this chapter. Yet, this will to act seems lacking. Instead, at the time of writing, yet another commission on racial inequality has been set up to explore the issues, rather than acting on the recommendations of the many commissions and reports exploring racial inequality in Britain that have gone before it.[299] These include the Lammy Review, the Angiolini Review the Home Office report into the Windrush Scandal etc. Poverty, inequality, ethno-racial and gender-based forms of inequality are all political choices, which can no longer be ignored by those in power, if they ever could be, if there is to be a fair, just and equitable criminal justice process.

A pluralist model of society that 'is based upon the idea that power in modern social orders is dispersed rather than centralised and that a variety of interests can be mobilised to influence then inform the political agenda' might be able to empower diverse interests to make changes in social order possible.[300] But the belief that opposing interests can be reconciled through negotiation and bargaining presents 'a highly idealized picture of the relationship between the regulated party and the regulator'.[301] Perhaps, however, it doesn't have to be that way, and participants should be able to raise and discuss concerns in their own terms rather than in confines of traditional legal process.[302] Listening and responding more to individual voices in the criminal process can prove a powerful tool to enable participation,[303] and may enable hitherto silenced voices and perspectives to better inform the criminal justice system. This has the potential to improve the democratic value of the criminal justice process, and thereby achieve greater justice. As Hudson says, 'a common perspective may be unattainable, but accommodation nonetheless has to be found.'[304] This is all the more urgent in light of increased inequality, and what that means for the next generation of society.

---

[298] Alston P, *Visit to the United Kingdom of Great Britain and Northern Ireland Report of the Special Rapporteur on extreme poverty and human rights* (2019) online at: <https://undocs.org/A/HRC/41/39/Add.1> (accessed 27 October 2020); Stroud P, *Measuring Poverty 2020* (Social Metrics Commission, 2020).

[299] Ormerod (2020).

[300] Whyte D, 'An Intoxicated Politics of Regulation' in Quirk, Seddon and Smith (2010).

[301] Ibid: 168.

[302] Knop and Riles provide an excellent example of the alternative discourses that can be opened up by moving away from traditional legal process in their discussion of the case of the Comfort Women (Knop K and Riles A, 'Space, Time and Historical Injustice: A Feminist Conflict-of-Laws Approach to the "Comfort Women" Settlement (December 16, 2016)' *Cornell Legal Studies Research Paper No. 16–45* (2017) 102(3) *Cornell Law Review*). The Comfort Women were forced into sexual slavery during the Second World War, and court cases regarding damages have continued into the second decade of the twenty-first century. Riles points out that some of the most productive ways for the victims of the Japanese army to feel that that their stories had been heard was not through the law but through the arts, demonstrating the importance and potential for inequality to be addressed outside of criminal process. (Welsh L, 'The Role of Law in Temporal Reasoning: An Interview with Annelise Riles' (2017) 25(1) *Feminist Legal Studies* 123–129).

[303] Kaiser K and Holtfreter K, 'An Integrated Theory of Specialized Court Programs: Using Procedural Justice and Therapeutic Jurisprudence to Promote Offender Compliance and Rehabilitation' (2016) 43(1) *Criminal Justice and Behavior* 45–62.

[304] Hudson in Quirk. Seddon and Smith (2010: 286).

Further reading

Bell E, *Criminal Justice and Neoliberalism* (London: Palgrave Macmillan, 2011).

Brems E and Desmet E, *Integrated Human Rights in Practice. Rewriting Human Rights Decisions* (Cheltenham: Elgar, 2017).

Dingwall G and Hillier T, *Blamestorming, Blamemongers and Scapegoats.* (Bristol: The Policy Press, 2016).

Hudson B, *Justice in the Risk Society* (California: Sage, 2003).

Hunter R, 'More than Just a Different Face? Judicial Diversity and Decision-making' (2015) 68(5) *Current Legal Problems* 119–141.

Hunter R, McGlynn C and Rackley E (eds), *Feminist Judgments: From Theory to Practice* (Oxford: Hart Publishing, 2010).

Irwin-Rogers K, 'Racism and Racial Discrimination in the Criminal Justice System: Exploring the Experiences and Views of Men Serving Sentences of Imprisonment' (2018) 2(2) *Justice, Power and Resistance* 243–266.

Khan O and Shaheen F (eds), *Minority Report. Race and Class in post-Brexit Britain.* (London: Runnymede Trust, 2017).

Lammy, D (2017) *The Lammy Review: An Independent Review into the Treatment of, and Outcomes for, Black, Asian and Minority Ethnic Individuals in the Criminal Justice System* (London: Lammy Review).

Ormerod D, 'Racism in the Criminal Justice System' (2020) *Criminal Law Review* 659–662.

Wacquant L, *Punishing the Poor. The Neoliberal Government of Social Insecurity.* (Durham, NC: Duke University Press, 2009).

Westmarland N, Johnson K and McGlynn C, 'Under the Radar: The Widespread Use of "Out of Court Resolutions" in Policing Domestic Violence and Abuse in the United Kingdom' (2018) 58(1) *British Journal of Criminology* 1–16.

11

When things go wrong in the criminal justice process

KEY ISSUES

- Things that can go wrong in the criminal justice process
- How criminal justice officials can be regulated and to held to account
- Organisational, legal and democratic regulatory and accountability mechanisms associated with the police, courts and CPS
- The importance of independence in most criminal justice regulation and accountability
- The limitations of regulation and accountability and the disadvantageous position of citizens in challenging things that go wrong in the face of powerful criminal justice officials

11.1 Introduction

In 1989, 96 people died in the crush on the Leppings Lane terrace, at the Hillsborough football stadium, with a further 400 left injured and traumatised. Within four months, a judicial inquiry found that the main reason for the disaster was police mismanagement of the crowd, though an investigation by the police complaints body of the era, the Police Complaints Authority and a subsequent criminal investigation, failed to establish liability. The 1990/91 Coroners' inquest returned a majority verdict of accidental death. This was unsuccessfully challenged in 1993 by bereaved families. A High Court judge looked again at the case in 1997/8, and decided there was no substantial new evidence to justify a public inquiry. In 2000, a private prosecution saw the acquittal of a senior officers' assistant and a hung jury on his superior. The trial judge ruled out a retrial. A decade later, the bereaved families persuaded the Labour government to appoint an Independent Panel to review the case. In 2012 this panel reversed all prior official and media narratives.[1] In particular, it challenged the misinformation promulgated by the police via the *Sun* newspaper at the time of the disaster that blamed ticketless and drunken Liverpool fans. Subsequently, the High Court quashed the previous inquest's verdict of 'accidental death' and a new inquest decided in 2016 that the 96 victims were 'unlawfully killed'. Six police officers were then charged with perverting the course of justice and manslaughter, though the match commander on the day of the disaster, David Duckenfield, who was tried twice for the latter offence, was eventually acquitted in November 2019.[2]

---

[1] *Report of the Hillsborough Independent Panel* (London: The Stationery Office, 2012).
[2] *The Independent,* 10 November 2019. See generally, Scraton P, 'The Hillsborough Independent Panel and the UK State: An alternative route to "truth", "apology" and "justice"' in Carlen P and Ayres Franca L (eds), *Justice Alternatives* (Abingdon: Routledge, 2019).

INTRODUCTION

This case highlights many of the forms of accountability that are the focus this chapter and their limitations as a form of redress for citizens who are wronged during their encounters with the criminal justice system. Over the course of nearly 30 years, nine routes of redress were used to hold the police and other organisations to account for the Hillsborough disaster. These included judicial inquiries, police complaints processes, criminal investigations, civil litigation used by families and South Yorkshire Police officers to seek financial compensation, Coroners' inquests, appeals processes, judicial review (though this was not granted), private prosecutions and an Independent Panel. Campaigning by the Hillsborough Family Support Group also shows the importance of citizen-initiated forms of accountability and the role of technology and the media in enabling their voices to be heard by criminal justice officials and politicians. Hillsborough also illustrates the gravity and the severity of the consequences of things going wrong in the criminal justice process. Not only were large numbers of people killed or injured due to the failures of South Yorkshire Police in particular, but victims of the Hillsborough disaster, their families and wider society remain unconvinced that justice has been served. Things going wrong in the criminal justice process and failures to effectively challenge them therefore have the potential to shake the foundations of the criminal justice process, the trust that citizens place in it and indeed in other public institutions, and the basis on which consent to the exercise of state power rests.[3]

The Hillsborough disaster also highlights some of the things that can go wrong in the criminal justice process, and who might be involved in making and remedying mistakes. Though far from exhaustive, these mistakes might involve:

- incivility, e.g. where criminal justice officials are rude, impolite or disrespectful to citizens;
- harm to or deaths of citizens, e.g. where the police use of force is unnecessary, disproportionate or excessive or where criminal justice officials are negligent or fail to act when citizens they are interacting with are at risk of harm or death;
- corruption or abuse of powers, e.g. where citizens are wrongfully arrested or detained, denied legal advice, subjected to verballing or coerced into sexual relations with undercover police officers;
- miscarriages of justice, e.g. when the police fail to investigate crimes appropriately and citizens are then wrongfully accused and convicted and/or those who are responsible remain at large and continue to offend;
- discrimination, which may be either individual or institutional and is linked to protected characteristics such as race, ethnicity, religion, gender, sexuality, and also to social class.[4]

The police, prosecutors, juries, judges, solicitors and barristers, and a range of private sector personnel are all potentially implicated in making such mistakes during their encounters with citizens. For example, in police detention, civilian detention officers employed by private security companies work alongside police officers and access to custodial legal advice is facilitated by CDS Direct which is contracted out to the private sector. As Rowe notes,[5] accountability is more complex where the private sector are contracted by the

---

[3] Tyler T and Huo Y. *Trust in the Law: Encouraging public cooperation with the police and the courts* (New York: Russell Sage 2002). [4] See ch 10.
[5] Rowe M, *Policing the Police* (Bristol: Policy Press, 2020) pp 61–62. Concerns about the role of private security staff in police custody led the Home Affairs Committee to recommend that the IPCC should be able to investigate these staff, in the same way that they would investigate those employed by the police. Whilst this recommendation was welcomed by organisations such as G4S, it was not adopted into legislation and, instead, companies incorporated this requirement into their local contracts with individual police forces.

public sector to provide frontline duties and also where practitioners from multiple organisations attempt to work in a joined up fashion, as has become increasingly commonplace since the late 1990s.[6] Ultimately, it makes it hard to deduce where the metaphorical buck stops. Partnership working in criminal justice requires a similarly joined up approach to regulation and accountability; this is lacking, as we shall see in relation to the work of the inspectorates, complaints bodies (e.g. the Independent Office of Police Conduct (IOPC)) and Coroners' Inquests. Cases and complaints can therefore fall between the cracks of different criminal justice organisations and their corresponding accountability bodies.

This disastrous situation arises from the power afforded to criminal justice institutions, and austerity-led pressures to process citizens ever faster through the criminal justice system. As this book shows, criminal justice officials shape who enters the criminal justice process and how their cases progress, if at all, from arrest to conviction and sentence. For example, the police have huge discretion to decide who to stop-search and arrest and, once arrested and detained, they play a key role in shaping the outcome of criminal investigations—e.g. based on how they interview suspects, what other evidence they collect and when and how this evidence is disclosed to lawyers.[7] Citizens suspected of wrongdoing—even when those allegations prove to be unfounded—are therefore at a disadvantage relative to these powerful criminal justice officials, including when they seek redress for malpractice through regulatory and accountability mechanisms.[8] And this is so for some citizens more than others due to structural forms of disadvantages rooted in the intersection between race, ethnicity, class, gender, age, disability etc.[9] In relation to the police, Reiner calls this the 'riddle' of police accountability.[10] Paradoxically, 'as the monopolist of coercive resources, the police stand simultaneously as the guarantor of, and threat to, "citizen security"'.[11] Since many other criminal justice institutions also possess coercive resources, this riddle of accountability applies to them too.

This is all in spite of procedural rights and protections, including access to a lawyer, the right to silence, access to an interpreter or an appropriate adult, limitations on the length of time that someone may be detained by the police, requirements that police interviews are recorded, etc. These safeguards are often more limited in practice than they appear on paper: sometimes they get in the way of what criminal justice officials are trying to do. Also, we will see that not everyone knows they have been wronged, and, after the event, often do not know who to complain to, particularly if they have no legal advice. Even when a complaint is made, wronged citizens often have their word compared to that of powerful criminal justice officials, who generally close ranks to provide a single unified account at odds with that of the complainant. These criminal justice officials may also have the support of their trade union or a raft of lawyers on a scale that cannot be matched by ordinary citizens. Managerialism is also a powerful influence:

> The criminal justice process has exhibited a fading preoccupation with the principles and values of a coherent procedural system, while demonstrating far greater concern with the efficient management of criminalization. Efficiency is a key objective of contemporary criminal justice policy, alongside related concerns with austerity and cost-effectiveness, risk management, reductions in delay, and a more general productivity-driven managerialism.[12]

---

[6] Skinns L, *Police Custody: Governance, legitimacy and reform in the criminal justice process* (Cullompton: Willan, 2011) pp 164–167.   [7] See section 7.3.3.5.
[8] Schulenberg J, Chenier A, Buffone S and Wojciechowski C, 'An application of procedural justice to stakeholder perspectives: examining police legitimacy and public trust in police complaints systems' (2017) 27(7) *Policing and Society* 779–796.   [9] See ch 10.
[10] Reiner R, 'Who governs? Democracy, plutocracy, science and prophecy in policing' (2013) 13(2) *Criminology and Criminal Justice* 161–180.
[11] Loader I and Walker I, *Civilising Security* (Cambridge: CUP, 2005) pp 205.
[12] Hodgson J, *The Metamorphosis of Criminal Justice* (Oxford: OUP, 2020) p 72.

INTRODUCTION 521

A decade of austerity prioritised speed and efficiency above all else.[13] These external forces in combination with the powerful role played by criminal justice officials increase the likelihood of mistakes being made and things going wrong. Sometimes the effects are cumulative, slowly chipping away at the relationship between citizens—particularly, young black men—and criminal justice officials.[14] Incivilities and excessive use of force during police stop and search encounters can be seen in this light.[15] However, sometimes only one such encounter can have serious—and sometimes lethal—consequences for those involved. The murder by American police of George Floyd in May 2020 was an example, but British deaths in and out of custody are equally shameful (see section 4.4).

So accountability in the criminal justice process is complex. Even the terms of the debate are complex. For example, though regulation and accountability are often used interchangeably they are not the same thing. One way of distinguishing them is to see regulation as having a preventative forward-looking quality to it; whilst accountability is retrospective, only becoming possible after something has gone wrong in the criminal justice process.[16] Regulation is about rules and standards and the control exerted by political institutions, which are used to 'steer the flow of events and behaviour',[17] so that certain pre-defined outcomes are met.[18] Accountability, by contrast is a requirement to account for, or explain, conduct.[19] While explanation is valuable, guiding or directing future practices is more effective. But this distinction is not clear cut. Whilst regulation is about preventing events from happening, 'this may draw from, or be combined with, responding to events that have already occurred'.[20] Or vice versa, whilst accountability is about demanding explanations when something untoward has already happened, this may be combined with trying to prevent something of this kind happening again in the future. For example, the police complaints body, the IOPC, is on the surface an accountability body, which requires the police to explain, for example, a death in police custody. However, as discussed in this chapter, they often make recommendations for practice following an investigation, which has a regulatory effect.

We can also think of accountability in terms of the structures and institutions that are involved in trying to regulate or seek explanations from criminal justice officials. That is, we can think of it in terms of who is controlling or inviting explanations from criminal justice officials. As such, we can divide the institutional architecture of criminal justice regulation and accountability into three categories. First, it may be democratic in character emphasising the links between criminal justice officials, citizens and democratically elected individuals at the local and national level. Second, there are the more organisational and administrative forms of regulation and accountability, which may be either internal to criminal justice organisations or external to them. Third, there are the accountability and regulatory mechanisms which emphasise the links between the criminal justice officials,

---

[13] See section 1.9.1.

[14] Lerman A and Weaver V, *Arresting Citizenship: The Democratic Consequences of American Crime Control* (Chicago: University of Chicago Press, 2014).

[15] Fagan J, 'Dignity is the new legitimacy' in Dolovich S and Natapoff A (eds), *New Criminal Justice Thinking* (New York: NYUP, 2017); Tyler T, Fagan J and Geller A, 'Street Stops and Police Legitimacy' (2014) 11 *Journal of Empirical Legal Studies* 751–785.

[16] Seddon, T. (2010) 'Rethinking prison inspection: Regulating institutions of Confinement' in Quirk, Seddon and Smith (2010: 261–282).

[17] Braithwaite J, Makkai T and Braithwaite V, *Regulating Aged Care: Ritualism and the new pyramid* (Cheltenham: Edward Elgar, 2007) p 3.

[18] Black J, 'Critical reflections on regulation' (2002) 27 *Australian Journal of Legal Philosophy* 1–35.

[19] Chan J, 'Governing police practice: limits of the new accountability' (1999) 50 *British Journal of Sociology* 251–270. [20] Quirk, Seddon and Smith (2010: 264).

he law and legal institutions like the courts and sentencers. In what follows, we categorise the criminal justice regulatory and accountability apparatus according to this schema.

Neither regulation nor accountability necessarily provide redress for citizens who have been wronged. Redress can be compensation, prosecution, disciplining or (for defendants) acquittal. All these function in part to create accountability and to regulate but they tend to be blunt instruments, and are probably less effective than mechanisms designed primarily for regulatory and accountability purposes.

The effectiveness of regulation and accountability can only be assessed in relation to the proper purpose of the criminal justice system. Criminal justice should balance the 'core values' of justice, democracy and efficiency,[21] but in practice justice and democracy are subordinated to efficiency in the practices of the police, the CPS and the courts.[22] This is reflected not only in the kind of things that can go wrong in the criminal justice process, but also in the functioning of the organisations that are used to regulate and hold criminal justice officials to account for their actions. Criminal justice organisations largely regulate themselves. Indeed, self-regulation of the police is often seen as underpinning independent and impartial law enforcement.[23] But self-regulation makes wrongdoing hard to challenge. Add this to the limited value of safeguards discussed earlier, a guilty plea system driven by austerity and managerialism, and cultural practices that turn on the presumption of guilt not innocence. The result is accountability and regulatory practices stacked in favour of criminal justice officials and organisations, a failure highlighted all too well by the Hillsborough disaster. These failures are particularly stark for the more marginalised sections of society, particularly minority ethnic citizens, who tend to mistrust 'the system' as a whole.[24]

11.2 Democratic regulation and accountability

11.2.1 The police and politicians: The rise of Police and Crime Commissioners

Since 2011, one of the most obvious faces of democratic regulation and accountability of criminal justice is Police and Crime Commissioners (PCCs), who were introduced to reduce the democratic deficit,[25] though, as discussed shortly, this has spectacularly failed given the low turn-outs at PCC elections. Criminal justice institutions such as the police should be held accountable to, and regulated by, democratic institutions. However, this poses a 'democratic dilemma'.[26] Can the police be answerable to, yet independent from, government and party-political influences?

At the heart of the democratic dilemma is the doctrine of 'constabulary independence'. Police independence from governmental control underpinned the 'New Police' in nineteenth-century England.[27] The principle gained ground over the next 100 years. In 1930, *Fisher v Oldham* established the principle of 'constabulary independence':[28] Officers were

---

[21] See section 1.10.   [22] See chs 4, 8 and 9.
[23] Smith G, Seddon T and Quirk H, 'Regulation and criminal justice: Exploring the connections and disconnections' in Quirk, Seddon and Smith (2010: 1–24).
[24] The Lammy Review (2017).
[25] Crawford C, 'The English and Welsh experiment in democratic governance of policing through Police and Crime Commissioners: a misconceived venture or a good idea, badly implemented?' in Ross J and Delpeuch, T (eds), *Comparing the Democratic Governance of Police Intelligence: New Models of Participation and Expertise in the United States and Europe* (Northampton, MA: Edward Elgar, 2016).
[26] Bayley D and Stenning P, *Governing the Police Experience in Six Democracies* (New York: Routledge, 2016) p 2.   [27] Ibid, pp 45–46.
[28] *Fisher v Oldham* (1930) 2 KB 364.

regarded as independent in performing their duties, and not subject to instruction from elected or other authorities. This was consolidated when Lord Denning ruled that the police were accountable to 'the law and to the law alone' and free from political or partisan interests.[29] This idea subsequently extended to protect the autonomy of chief constables' policy-making as well as the discretion of police officers.

Between 1964 and 2011, the doctrine of constabulary independence was embodied, at least in theory, in a 'tripartite system' of accountability involving three poles: the chief constable, police authority (local councillors and independent members) and the Home Secretary. These arrangements were replaced in 2011 by local PCCs.[30] This 'quadpartite system',[31] embodies a relationship between the PCC and chief constable, with a more minor role being played by citizens who elect PCCs and a Police and Crime Panel that scrutinises PCC decision-making. From November 2012, PCCs have been elected every four years in each of the 43 police forces in England and Wales. They:

- hire and fire senior officers (accountability);
- draw up, in conjunction with the police, strategic plans setting out crime and policing priorities (regulation);
- set police budgets and ensure delivery of the strategic plan against this budget (regulation).

These roles suggest PCCs to be primarily regulatory, with an emphasis on the crime control agenda of the police,[32] and not necessarily concerned with miscarriages of justice or righting wrongs. Hence, the Prime Minister at the time they were introduced described PCCs as 'law and order champions: one person who sets the budgets, sets the priorities, hires and fires the chief constable, bangs heads together to get things done ... If you want more tough policing, you can get it'.[33] However, it is important not to over-state the extent to which control was ceded to local political officials through these arrangements, given the importance of national level organisations such as the inspectorates and the IOPC, and political agendas such as those associated with austerity from 2010 onwards, meaning that these arrangements can be seen as part of a broader system of 'rule at a distance' (see also section 11.3.7.2).[34]

What PCCs are not supposed to do is involve themselves in operational policing matters and are to focus on strategic matters instead. In new public management speak, the relationship between the PCC and the Chief Officer is akin to the 'Chairman' of a Board and the 'CEO'.[35] However, the line between strategic and operational matters

---

[29] *R v Metropolitan Commissioner, ex parte Blackburn* [1968] 2 WLR 894. However, this was subject to withering criticism such as by Lustgarten (*The Governance of the Police*. London: Sweet & Maxwell, 1986) as it suggests that police decisions over the use of public resources are above democratic scrutiny. Hence, later the Patten Commission on Policing suggested that 'operational responsibility' not 'operational independence' was a better way of conceptualising police freedom from government and political influence: Independent Commission on Policing in Northern Ireland, *A New Beginning: Policing in Northern Ireland—the Report of the Independent Commission on Policing in Northern Ireland (Patten Report)* (Belfast: Independent Commission on Policing in Northern Ireland, 1999). [30] Police Reform and Social Responsibility Act 2011.
[31] Raine J and Keasey P, 'From Police Authorities to Police and Crime Commissioners: Might policing become more publicly accountable?' (2012) 1(2) *International Journal of Emergency Services* 122–34.
[32] Crawford (2016). [33] Cameron D (2012: 5), cited in Bowling et al (2019: 249).
[34] Jones T and Lister S, 'Localism and police governance in England & Wales: Exploring continuity and change' (2019) 16(5) *European Journal of Criminology* 552–572.
[35] Chapman C, An Independent Review of the Police Disciplinary System in England and Wales (2014) pp 5–6. Online at: <https://assets.publishing.service.gov.uk/government/uploads/system/uploads/attachment_data/file/385911/An_Independent_Review_of_the_Police_Disciplinary_System_-_Report_-_Final....pdf> (accessed 1 September 2020).

is ambiguous,[36] leaving scope for political interference in police decision-making and practice, and the erosion of constabulary independence.[37] Of the 41 PCCs elected in the 2012 election, 29 had a party political affiliation with this figure increasing to 37 of 40 in 2016.[38] But PCCs are not a form of civilian oversight, rather political oversight, based on party political agendas, in which constituents are represented by one person, largely a white male with a policing or criminal justice background, elected on a low turnout.[39] Relationships between PCCs and chief officers are complex, fraught, and sometimes break down,[40] thereby undermining their success as an accountability mechanism, as is also the case in other jurisdictions with similar arrangements such as Australia, New Zealand, India and Canada.[41] Given that PCCs are simultaneously responsible for both holding chief officers to account and sacking them, chief officers may feel beholden to them and unwilling to question their authority.[42] There is also a risk of instability in police leadership roles,[43] if chief officers leave before being pushed out, and there can also be damage to police force and PCC reputations and legitimacy where tensions between PCCs and chief officers spill over into acrimonious and public spats.[44] Therefore, as a form of democratic accountability, PCCs are of questionable value.

11.2.2 New forms of accountability in criminal justice settings

11.2.2.1 Police- and citizen-initiated recordings, and social media

On 2 March 1991 a white man, George Holliday, video-recorded an incident outside his house. A black man, Rodney King, was being Tasered, stomped on and repeatedly beaten (56 times in total) by four police officers. Nineteen other officers watched. Both Holliday and King's brother tried to report the incident to the police to no avail. The 90 second film, aired nationally and internationally, finally gave credibility to allegations of wrongdoing by the Los Angeles Police Department (LAPD), as King's beating was one of a series of

---

[36] For example, if a PCC decided that a police force should focus on public reassurance, then this necessarily impacts on operational policing, especially in the context of finite resources, as resources would have to be diverted into funding more visible patrols, for example, and away from other policing tasks. See Lister S, 'The New Politics of the Police: Police and Crime Commissioners and the "Operational Independence" of the Police' (2013) 7(3) *Policing: A Journal of Policy and Practice* 239–247; Wells H, 'Grey areas and fine lines: negotiating operational independence in the era of the police and crime commissioner' (2015) 14(4) *Safer Communities* 193–202.

[37] Given the concentration of power into the hands of one individual and given PCCs role in assessing performance against policing priorities, PCCs 'go against the spirit if not the wording of Lord Denning's judgement'. See Lister (2013: 243).

[38] Mawby R and Smith K, 'Civilian oversight of the police in England and Wales: The election of Police and Crime Commissioners in 2012 and 2016' (2017) 19(1) *International Journal of Police Science and Management* 23–30. However, in 2012 at least, these party political affiliations were not always reflected in the manifesto priorities of PCCs, instead making generic pledges such as to reduce and prevent crime and protect the public. See Raine J, 'Electocracy with accountabilities? The novel governance model of police and crime commissioners' in Rowe M and Lister S (eds), *Accountability of Policing* (London: Routledge, 2015) pp 111–131.

[39] The turnout for the PCC elections was 15% in 2012 and 26% in 2016, being boosted by local elections held at the same time. See Mawby and Smith (2017).

[40] Wells (2015).   [41] Bayley and Stenning (2016: 59–63).

[42] Cooper S, 'Police and Crime Commissioners: a corrosive exercise of power which destabilises police accountability?' (2020) 4 *Criminal Law Review* 291–305.   [43] Ibid.

[44] In 2016, the PCC of Surrey, Kevin Hurley, publicly criticised the former Chief Constable of Surrey Police, Lynne Owens shortly after she became Director General of the National Crime Agency, claiming he had been planning to sack her due to his concerns about Surrey Police's handling of vulnerable victims. See here: <https://www.theguardian.com/uk-news/2016/feb/02/surrey-crime-commissioner-kevin-hurley-under-fire-criticising-lynne-owens-nca-chief> (accessed 1 May 2020).

incidents, as later discovered by the Christopher Commission.[45] There was serious rioting following King's beating which sent a message to those in 'authority' that the black and Hispanic residents of LA wanted to be 'treated right' by the police.[46]

The historically low visibility of police work out on the streets beyond the gaze of supervisors or inside police detention has become increasingly open to challenge through technological changes that facilitate new ways of recording and sharing details of police–citizen interactions. These can be citizen-initiated, as in the Rodney King case—and so much easier now we have smartphones with cameras, 24-hour news channels in search of newsworthy stories and easy access to social media and the Internet. This citizen journalism is referred to as 'sousveillance' or the 'synopticon', meaning a kind of surveillance from below in which the masses try to match the gaze of the powerful and to counter top-down panopticon-like surveillance by the state. This citizen-initiated surveillance of the police exposes police work to a 'new visibility'.[47] Challenges can also be police-initiated, for example, in the recording of all calls to the police, CCTV (and often audio-visual recording) in police custody, audio-visual recording of suspect interviews, satellite tracking of police vehicles, and body-worn cameras, the use of which was originally intended to enhance police accountability.[48]

How effective are recordings of police–citizen interactions in holding the police to account and regulating future police practices? Police recordings may be unavailable, missing or overlooked, as was the case during the original Independent Police Complaints Commission (IPCC) investigation into the death of Sean Rigg (see chapter 4). Citizen recordings may be publicly dismissed by the police for their lack of context and their inability to tell the whole story, or they may be prevented (e.g. by police blocking the view of those filming), confiscated or destroyed by the police,[49] or citizens may be too afraid or indifferent about the issues to even make the recordings in the first place.[50] Both types of recordings also still require interpretation,[51] which depends in part on who the audience is and the 'type' of victim.[52]

Yet 'a picture [and increasingly a video] is worth a thousand words'.[53] It can demand an explanation of police actions, as in the death of Ian Tomlinson, in which citizen-created videos of his death led to an IPCC investigation and an inquiry by the Home Affairs Committee of the House of Commons into the policing of the G20 demonstrations,[54] and/or changes to police practices. Citizen-made recordings are also increasingly being harnessed by campaigning organisations and activists to gather support for reform campaigns

---

[45] Christopher W, *The Christopher Commission Report* (1991) online at: <https://www.hrw.org/legacy/reports98/police/uspo73.htm> (accessed 2 September 2020).

[46] Skolnick J and Fyfe J, *Above the Law* (New York: Free Press, 1993) pp 1–14.

[47] Thompson J, 'The New Visibility' (2005) 22 *Theory, Culture and Society* 31–51; Goldsmith A, 'Policing's New Visibility' (2010) 50(5) *British Journal of Criminology*, 50(5), 914–934 at 931.

[48] Lum C, Stoltz M, Koper C and Scherer J, 'Research on body-worn cameras: What we know, what we need to know' (2019) 18(1) *Criminology & Public Policy* 93–118. As seen in ch 5, however, the value of body-worn cameras is not straightforward: Brucato B, 'Policing Made Visible: Mobile Technologies and the Importance of Point of View' (2015) 13(3/4) *Surveillance & Society* 455–473; Sandhu A, '"I'm glad that was on camera": a case study of police officers' perceptions of cameras' (2019) 29(2) *Policing and Society* 223–235; Haggerty K and Sandhu A, 'Policing on Camera' (2017) 21 *Theoretical Criminology* 78.

[49] Wall T and Linnemann T, 'Staring Down the State: Police Power, Visual Economies, and the "War on Cameras"' (2014) 10(2) *Crime, Media, Culture* 133–149.

[50] Farmer A, Sun I and Starks B, 'Willingness to Record Police-Public Encounters: The Impact of Race and Social and Legal Consciousness' (2015) 5(4) *Race and Justice* 356–377.

[51] See, e.g., Brucato (2015); Reilly P, 'Every little helps? YouTube, sousveillance and the "anti-Tesco" riot in Stokes Croft' (2015) 17(5) *New Media and Society* 755–771.

[52] Rowe (2020: 114).   [53] Rowe (2020).   [54] Goldsmith (2010).

and to challenge dominant police narratives (see section 11.2.4). Fear of citizen-initiated recordings may also deter police malpractice or at least the *appearance* of malpractice in the first place,[55] as has been found to be the case for coercion/illegitimate violence.[56] So neither police, nor citizen-initiated, recordings are systematic forms of regulation and accountability. But—unusually—they do advance all three 'core values' in partly democratising the relationship between police and citizens, enhancing the potential for justice to be done, and doing all this in a reasonably resource-efficient way. They also afford citizens slightly more power in their attempts to hold the police to account than has hitherto been the case.

11.2.2.2 Courtroom cameras

Audio-visual recording and broadcasting of courtroom proceedings, like recordings of the police, and other forms of digitalisation, are part of a broader technological turn in criminal justice. But they offer a more limited form of accountability, a form of transparency in which the public can see justice—or at least parts of justice—being done.[57] Since 2009, cameras have been increasingly allowed to film different courtroom stages and different aspects of trials, judgments, sentencing and appeals,[58] though jurisdictions such as the US, New Zealand and Scotland have been doing this for longer.[59] Victims, witnesses, jurors or other court staff are not filmed or broadcast. Members of the public are allowed to sit in magistrates' courts, Crown courts and the Court of Appeal, as are the media,[60] though they do so infrequently, especially in the lower courts.[61]

But transparency—and therefore accountability—is limited as choices inevitably have to be made about what is filmed and broadcast.[62] And, like police recordings, courtroom recordings are framed by cultural and institutional assumptions,[63] and consumed, interpreted and made sense of by the public in varied ways. For example, a sustained and uninterrupted talking-head shot of a judge for the duration of a summing-up speech encourages a perception of that judge as 'unaccountable and out-of-touch' reducing public trust in them and the criminal justice system.[64] So courtroom recordings create only an 'illusion of power' for citizens and tend to provide insights into court proceedings for existing not new audiences, making them more of an old not new form of visibility and accountability. They may even have a corrupting influence on victims, witnesses and jury members, and thus on the possibilities of a fair trial,[65] particularly where cases become widely reported in a sensationalist fashion during the course of the trial.[66] This 'transparency paradox'[67] has been a long-held reason for objecting to the televising of criminal trials in England and Wales, and partly explains why it remains limited.

---

[55] Sandhu A, 'Camera-friendly Policing: How the Police Respond to Cameras and Photographers' (2016) 14(1) *Surveillance and Society* 78–89.

[56] Brown G, 'The Blue Line on Thin Ice: Police Use of Force Modifications in the Era of Cameraphones and YouTube' (2016) 56(2) *British Journal of Criminology* 293–312.

[57] Moore S, Clayton A and Murphy H, 'Seeing justice done: Courtroom filming and the deceptions of transparency' (2021) 17(1) *Crime, Media, Culture* 127–144; Moran L, 'Visible Justice: YouTube and the UK Supreme Court' (2016) 5 *Annual Review of Interdisciplinary Justice Research* 223–263.

[58] Ibid. See also The Crown Court (Recording and Broadcasting) Order 2020.

[59] Garcia-Blanco I and Bennett L, 'Between a "media circus" and "seeing justice being done": Metajournalistic discourse and the transparency of justice in the debate on filming trials in British newspapers' (2021) 22(1) *Journalism* 176–195.

[60] <https://www.gov.uk/guidance/hmcts-whos-who-magistrates-court> (accessed 1 July 2020).

[61] See Chamberlain, P, Keppel-Palmer, M, Reardon, S, and Smith, T., (2019). 'It is criminal: The state of magistrates' court reporting in England and Wales'. *Journalism*, doi:10.1177/1464884919868049

[62] Moore et al (2019). [63] Moran (2016). [64] Moore et al (2019: 15). [65] Moran (2016).

[66] Garcia-Blanco and Bennett (2018). [67] Moran (2016: 234).

11.2.3 Voluntary sector monitoring bodies: The role of ICVs and ICVA

Another arena in which citizens are directly and actively involved in calling criminal justice institutions to account is as volunteers. They 'work throughout criminal justice: in police, court, prison, and community service delivery, oversight and campaigning, with a social benefit mandate'.[68] They include independent custody visitors (ICVs) in police custody, lay observers in court custody and Independent Monitoring Boards (IMBs) in prisons. The statutory aspects of the role stem from their membership of the UK National Preventative Mechanism (NPM), the primary role of which is to prevent torture and ill-treatment through independent monitoring in accordance with the Optional Protocol to the Convention Against Torture (OPCAT).[69] As discussed in section 11.3.7, the inspectorates are also members of, and play an important complementary role in, the UK NPM. Visits are made at any time, irrespective of whether a problem has been identified, so these are primarily regulatory bodies.

However, research into one ICV scheme showed the hold that the police had over it, such that the ICVs were trained and socialised into seeing police custody from a police perspective. As such, they could not provide effective regulatory challenge to police custody practices, particularly when also taking into account the power the police wielded over the custody block and any visitors to it, detainees or ICVs included.[70]

Whilst there are organisational impediments to the independent monitoring role played by ICVs and its effectiveness in regulating police practices, there are also examples of innovation and improved monitoring, such as in several police forces areas in 2019 and 2020.[71] Instead of ICVs visiting police custody and engaging in one-off conversations with a small number of detainees, 'enhanced visits' were introduced in which ICVs observed a detainee over a prolonged period, and also carried out a review of custody records for a sample of those detained during the ICV's visit. This more robust methodology gave ICVs a better understanding of police custody processes and enabled them to focus, for example, on particular vulnerable groups in custody such as children and young people and those with learning disabilities or mental health conditions. Though the pilot work 'strained expectations and relationships between ICV, OPCC and the police',[72] this also suggests that the new approach is helping to grow the independence of the ICV role.

11.2.4 Voluntary sector campaigning, activists and the academy

Voluntary local and national organisations (including the Howard League for Penal Reform, the Prison Reform Trust, Inquest, Just for Kids Law, Justice, Statewatch, Miscarriages of Justice UK and Liberty) also campaign and carry out advocacy work. However, their independence and critical edge is often at risk as many also bid to run services and/or are overly dependent on government funding due to the unpopular nature of the work they do.[73] Notably, the Criminal Justice Alliance, which represents a coalition

---

[68] Tomczak P and Buck G, 'The Criminal Justice Voluntary Sector: Concepts and an Agenda for an Emerging Field' (2019) 58(3) *Howard Journal of Crime and Justice* 276–297 at 278.

[69] <https://www.nationalpreventivemechanism.org.uk/monitoring/> (accessed 1 May 2020).

[70] Kendall J, 'Custody visiting: The watchdog that didn't bark' (2020) *Criminology and Criminal Justice* (online first); Kendall J, *Regulating Police Detention* (Bristol: Policy Press, 2018).

[71] <https://www.derbyshire.police.uk/news/derbyshire/news/news/forcewide/2020/june/royal-seal-of-approval-for-derbyshires-custody-monitoring-volunteers/> (accessed 1 July 2020).

[72] Fitzpatrick R and Thorne L, *Evaluation of the Independent Custody Evaluation Pilot*. (Confluence Partnership, 2020) p 22.

[73] Benson A and Hedge J, 'Criminal justice and the voluntary sector: a policy that does not compute' (2009) 77(1) *Criminal Justice Matters* 34–36; Mills et al, 'Exploring the relationship between the voluntary sector and the state in criminal justice' (2011) 2(2) *Voluntary Sector Review* 193–211; Neilson A, 'A crisis of identity: NACRO's bid to run a prison and what it means for the voluntary sector' (2009) 48(4) *Howard Journal of Criminal Justice* 401–110.

of 160 organisations interested in improving the criminal justice system,[74] is one of 16 designated bodies allowed to make 'super-complaints' about the police.[75] These concern 'systemic issues which are not otherwise dealt with by the existing complaints systems'.[76] Since their inception, the details of three such complaints have been published, though there were no details, at the time of writing, of stakeholder responses.[77]

The growing importance of the now global Black Lives Matter (BLM) movement also illustrates citizen-led attempts to hold criminal justice institutions to account for racialised forms of malpractice. It emerged in 2013 from racialised police practices in the US,[78] which came to a head following the death of unarmed 17-year-old African American, Trayvon Martin, shot by a white man, George Zimmerman, who was acquitted of his murder in 2012. However, any form of ill-treatment may be the subject of citizen-led counter-surveillance and activism through dissenting Tweets or posts and even revenge by meme,[79] all of which may be broadcast widely via social media. Though offering an individualised approach to what are largely institutional and structural problems, it also illustrates the power of social media to mobilise large sections of the population.[80] Media outlets have also been used by families of those who have been wrongfully accused to raise concerns about miscarriages of justice, as was the case for Sam Hallam,[81] as well as to organise protests, petitions and vigils concerned with securing the release of wrongfully convicted suspects. The uncontrolled nature of this form of citizen journalism and activism, however, means that in some cases it can spread misinformation as much as the right information.[82] These forms of dissent to criminal justice practices can also be short lived, not to mention there being issues of information overload and indeed saturation as people's newsfeeds become filled with similar stories, which risks de-sensitising the very groups that these media stories seek to mobilise. As such, citizen journalism and activism needs to be scrutinised in as critical a fashion as police and courtroom camera footage.

Some academics are also activists who use their research to hold criminal justice institutions to account and to advocate for criminal justice reform.[83] The most striking example is Phil Scraton, an academic whose long campaign for justice for the Hillsborough victims (the tragedy with which we began this chapter) drew on his research over many years. His standing was recognised when he was appointed to lead the Independent Inquiry.[84] Then there are collaborations 'where practitioners, such as victim advocates or non-profit workers, are included in the research design, implementation, and ideally, co-authorship of the final products' of academic research projects.[85] Students too hold criminal justice

---

[74] <http://criminaljusticealliance.org/> (accessed 1 May 2020).
[75] <https://www.gov.uk/government/publications/police-super-complaints-designated-bodies/designated-bodies> (accessed 1 May 2020).
[76] <https://www.gov.uk/guidance/police-super-complaints> (accessed 1 May 2020).
[77] <https://www.gov.uk/government/collections/police-super-complaints> (accessed 1 May 2020).
[78] Ince J, Rojas F and Davis C, 'The social media response to Black Lives Matter: how Twitter users interact with Black Lives Matter through hashtag use' (2017) 40(11) *Ethnic and Racial Studies* 1814–1830.
[79] The 'Casually pepper spray everything cop' meme is an example of this form of revenge on the police. See: <https://knowyourmeme.com/memes/casually-pepper-spray-everything-cop> (accessed 1 May 2020); Bayerl P and Stoynov L, 'Revenge by photoshop: Memefying police acts in the public dialogue about injustice' (2016) 8(6) *New Media & Society* 1006–1026.
[80] Logan J and Oakley D, 'Black lives and policing: The larger context of ghettoization' (2017) 39(8) *Journal of Urban Affairs* 1031–1046; Ince et al (2017).
[81] <https://www.theguardian.com/uk/2012/may/16/community-campaign-justice-sam-hallam> (accessed 1 May 2020).
[82] Poyser S, Nurse A and Milne R, *Miscarriages of Justice* (Bristol: Palgrave Macmillan, 2018) p 121.
[83] Belknap J, 'Presidential address: Activist criminology: Criminologists' responsibility to advocate for social and legal justice' (2015) 53(1) *Criminology* 1–22.
[84] *Report of the Hillsborough Independent Panel* (2012).   [85] Belknap (2015: 15).

institutions to account, for example, through Innocence Projects or clinical legal education, which involve law students doing unpaid work investigating cases to assist with a complaint to the police or an appeal in a criminal case. This type of academic engagement has increased exponentially as legal aid has been cut,[86] though its impact is primarily at the individual level and of limited capacity.[87]

11.2.5 Royal commissions, public inquiries and independent inquiries

Historically, Royal Commissions have been an important public avenue of accountability and regulation, being used to look at widespread and systemic issues and to propose reforms. For example, the Royal Commission on Criminal Procedure in 1981, fuelled by concern about the treatment of vulnerable suspects in the *Maxwell Confait* case, resulted in the introduction of the Police and Criminal Evidence Act 1984 (see chapter 1). Whilst it was far from benign in its intentions and effects, it was the first significant attempt to set out police powers and suspects' procedural rights. The Royal Commission on Criminal Justice in 1993 that followed was less significant as a regulatory mechanism and emphasised 'efficiency' at the expense of 'democracy' and 'justice'.[88] Since then, there have been no other Royal Commissions, though in 2019 one was announced to review and improve the efficiency and effectiveness of the criminal justice process. What a missed opportunity this is likely to be for objectively scrutinising criminal justice processes and their effects on citizens!

Whilst Royal Commissions have dwindled, Public inquiries have grown in number and frequency.[89] They ask three main questions: 1) What happened? 2) Why did it happen and who is to blame? 3) What can be done to prevent this happening again? Those with a broad criminal justice remit have been used for example to scrutinise the Grenfell Tower fire in 2017; the practices, culture and ethics of the British press circa 2007 (Leveson); the investigation of the murder of Stephen Lawrence in 1993 (Macpherson); the 1981 riots in Brixton, London (Scarman). But government ministers decide whether or not to establish an inquiry. And they have the power to hire and fire panel members, frame the terms of reference, restrict disclosure of documentation or public access to inquiry reports, and to terminate the inquiry.[90] The inquiry into the infamous 'undercover policing' scandal (see chapter 6) illustrates another problem: obstruction by the police. Established in 2015, by May 2020 it had still not heard any evidence in public due to the number of applications submitted by the police to keep police identities secret.[91] Inquiries are therefore sometimes seen as 'blatant lies, half-truths, evasions, legal sophistries, ideological appeals and

---

[86] Drummond O and McKeever G, *Access to Justice through University Law Clinics* (2015: Ulster University Law School).

[87] For discussion, see Thomas L, Vaughan S, Malkani B and Lynch T (eds), *Reimagining Clinical Legal Education* (Oxford: Hart Publishing, 2018).

[88] Young R and Sanders A, 'The Royal Commission on Criminal Justice: A confidence trick?' (1994) 15 *Oxford Journal of Legal Studies* 435.

[89] Though their roots stretch back to the seventeenth century, public inquiries were first formally introduced by Tribunals of Inquiry (Evidence) Act 1921, though are now regulated by the Inquiries Act 2005. Sixty-nine public inquiries were launched between 1970 and 2017, compared to only 19 in the previous 30 years <https://www.instituteforgovernment.org.uk/explainers/public-inquiries> (accessed 1 May 2020).

[90] Inquiries Act 2005. See Watkin Jones P and Griffin N, 'Public Inquiries: Getting at the Truth' *Law Gazette*, 22 June 2015. Online at: <https://www.lawgazette.co.uk/practice-points/public-inquiries-getting-at-the-truth/5049449.article> (accessed 1 May 2020).

[91] *The Guardian*, 10 May 2018 and 7 October 2020.

credible factual objections',[92] as well as a 'political tactic' used to affirm the legitimacy of institutions,[93] and to present the 'views from above'.[94]

By contrast, Independent Inquiries, like the Hillsborough Inquiry, have been established due to the failings of public inquiries or when a public inquiry is not held at all. The methodology used in the inquiry to seek disclosure of documents on public interest grounds has since been adapted and used in other independent inquiries such as the independent panel scrutinising the deaths of mothers and babies at Furness General Hospital in 2015.[95] Though the government still retains the right to veto such independent inquiries and though they are funded and supported administratively by state officials, their independently determined constitution, scope, terms of reference and operation, is unparalleled by public inquiries. As public inquiries became increasingly politicised and thus questioned as an accountability and regulatory tool, as demonstrated at the time of writing by large numbers of Conservative MPs voting against the implementation of recommendations from the Grenfell Tower Public Inquiry,[96] independent inquiries offer at least a glimmer of hope for ordinary citizens to be able to hold powerful institutions to account when things go wrong.

11.3 Organisational regulation and accountability

11.3.1 Complaints bodies

Most bureaucracies and public agencies maintain some form of grievance procedure for handling complaints by citizens about shoddy treatment, as is therefore the case for criminal justice agencies. Complaints may be initially dealt with by the agency that the complaint relates to, before being referred to an external independent party for further consideration and for a review of the internal handling of the complaint. The Crown Prosecution Service, for example, has a three stage process for dealing with complaints made by citizens about matters of service (e.g. treatment, misinformation, delays with dealing with complaints),[97] rather than legal issues.[98] Complaints bodies for other parts of the criminal justice process similarly operate a multi-stage process of internal then external investigation. For example, complaints may be made about judges', magistrates' or coroners' behaviour, language or conduct to the Judicial Conduct Investigations Office or local advisory committees to magistrates' courts, or eventually to the Judicial Appointments and Conduct Ombudsman if citizens are dissatisfied with the initial response. Similarly, citizens who wish to complain about their legal advisor must first complain to the legal service provider; then, if they are still dissatisfied and have also waited eight weeks in which to receive a response,

---

[92] Cohen S, *States of Denial: Knowing About Atrocities and Suffering* (Cambridge: Polity Press, 2001) p 114.
[93] Burton F and Carlen P, *Official Discourse: On Discourse Analysis, Government Publications, Ideology and the State* (London: Routledge, 1979) p 48. [94] Scraton (2019: 122).
[95] Other key Independent Inquiries with a criminal justice focus include investigations into child sexual exploitation in Rotherham from 1997–2013 (Jay); child sexual abuse involving MPs, local councils and church organisations (Butler-Sloss, then Woolf, Lowell Goddard, and at the time of writing, Jay); Jimmy Savile child sex abuse from the 1950s-80s (Smith).
[96] <https://www.theguardian.com/commentisfree/2020/sep/09/grenfell-tory-mps-inquiry-betray-recommendations> (accessed 9 September 2020).
[97] Any complaints relating to the Code of Practice for Victims of Crime (the Victims' Code) are referred to the Parliamentary and Health Service Ombudsmen. See chs 7 and 12.
[98] This dividing line between legal and service issues is far from easy to discern. <https://www.cps.gov.uk/independent-assessor-complaints> (accessed 10 July 2020).

they may contact the Legal Ombudsman. Complaints about lawyers breaching their code of conduct or being dishonest may also be directed to the relevant professional body: the Solicitors Regulation Authority[99] or the Bar Standards Board.[100]

The current police complaints body is the Independent Office for Police Conduct (IOPC). Its predecessors were the Independent Police Complaints Commission (2004–2018), the Police Complaints Authority (1986–2004), and the Police Complaints Board (1976–1985), with the 1964 Police Act first introducing the requirement that all complaints against the police be recorded and investigated. This procession of one organisation being replaced by another, each with the same role, tells us something about the (lack of) success of, and confidence in, the police complaints system. However, many of the critical issues that have dogged police complaints processes apply to other criminal justice complaints bodies. For example, the issue of independence, where criminal justice institutions play some role in investigating themselves—as is the case for the CPS, judges, magistrates and lawyers—is a common concern for all. Indeed, the importance but also impossibilities of independence permeate criminal justice and all its accountability and regulatory mechanisms.[101]

Bear in mind the impact that police malpractice may have on the complainant. These experiences can be visceral, painful, terrifying, unfair, undignified, not to mention life-altering and sometimes lethal. In 2008, Nicola Dennis was grabbed from her doorway and held face-down at gunpoint on a pavement with her hands bound behind her back for over 15 minutes by the police. 'I thought I was going to die', she said in a subsequent investigation of the incident.[102] Konstacja Duff's forced strip search and removal of clothes in police custody was experienced as undignified and traumatising.[103] During the strip search, she said that she was pinned to the floor and her clothes were cut off. She was then placed in a paper suit which revealed her breasts as it did not close properly and she said that she was 'paraded' through the custody area by the police and left on the floor in another cell.[104] She was subsequently diagnosed with PTSD.[105] The police complaints processes made it worse: for example, in the case of Konstacja Duff, the IPCC found there to be no wrongdoing, though they did recommend 'words of advice' be given to the officers involved; and the custody officer who authorised the strip search was exonerated.[106]

11.3.2 A potted history of the police complaints system

In the early iterations of this police complaints process, the police were left to entirely investigate themselves which served only to undermine the transparency and legitimacy of this

---

[99] See <https://www.sra.org.uk/consumers/problems/report-solicitor> (accessed 10 July 2020).

[100] See <https://www.barstandardsboard.org.uk/for-the-public/reporting-concerns.html#:~:text=If%20you%20have%20a%20concern,with%20the%20barrister%20directly%20first> (accessed 10 July 2020).

[101] Savage S, 'Thinking Independence: Calling the Police to Account through the Independent Investigation of Police Complaints' (2013) 53(1) *British Journal of Criminology* 94–112.

[102] Legal Action June 2008, p 4. See *R (Dennis) v IPCC* [2008] EWHC 1158 (Admin).

[103] She was arrested by the police in North London in 2013, after she went to the aid of a 15-year old boy who had been stopped by the police, to whom she attempted to give a card containing information about his rights. She was arrested and taken to Stoke Newington Police Station, where she was charged with assaulting and obstructing police officers, but was later found not guilty by a magistrate. After refusing to give her name and lying limp outside the police station, she was forcibly taken to a cell by female officers, whilst male officers waited outside. This was justified on the grounds that it was unclear what risk she posed to herself, an explanation later accepted by a disciplinary panel. See: <https://www.bbc.co.uk/news/uk-england-nottinghamshire-45439954> (accessed 1 May 2020).

[104] <https://www.theguardian.com/uk-news/2018/aug/23/met-custody-sergeant-faces-possible-dismissal-over-2013-strip-search-of-academic> (accessed 27 July 2020).

[105] <https://www.theguardian.com/uk-news/2018/aug/29/academic-konstancja-duff-passive-resistance-before-met-strip-search> (accessed 27 July 2020).   [106] Ibid.

process.[107] By the 1990s, public confidence was low, and falling. In 1996, more people did not trust the police to investigate themselves (40%) than did trust them (37%). Moreover, the percentage believing the PCA to be independent and impartial was 39% and 37% respectively.[108] Even the Police Federation's survey, conducted in 1997, produced similar results.[109] The lack of confidence was particularly marked in black communities, especially in the wake of the Stephen Lawrence scandal, with Macpherson therefore recommending the introduction of fully independent investigation of police complaints.[110] A drop in cases of complaints was mirrored by a rise in civil actions: the civil courts were filling a gap that the complaints system should fill.[111] The European Committee for the Prevention of Torture and Inhuman or Degrading Treatment or Punishment criticised the fact that 'the police themselves maintain a firm grip upon the handling of complaints against them.'[112] The Committee's view was based, in part, on its examination of Metropolitan Police files in which the police had settled cases where suspects were injured in police custody but there had been no prosecutions or disciplinary proceedings. We cannot make an independent assessment of whether the Committee's conclusions were justified, for the government censored these sections.[113] In *Khan*[114] an unlawful bugging was held to breach the ECHR Art 8. Under Art 13 everyone has a right to seek an effective remedy against allegedly unlawful actions. The English police complaints system did not provide this, according to the ECtHR, because of its lack of independence.

The momentum was unstoppable and the IPCC was created.[115] This was a civilian body with a staff of around 80 investigators, plus administrators, case workers and lawyers. The police still investigated the majority of (relatively minor) complaints themselves, but medium-serious cases were supervised by the IPCC, more serious ones were 'managed' by the IPCC, and the most serious were investigated by the IPCC itself. Conduct leading to death or serious injury was investigated by the IPCC whether or not there was a complaint.[116] However, criticisms of the IPCC continued. Rather than being an independent body, it remained reliant to a significant extent on police forces' professional standards departments to investigate complaints. Even when supervised by the IPCC there were concerns that these investigations could become distorted by the priorities of the police force under investigation rather than the interests of the complainant.[117] Moreover, 33% of the supposedly independent investigators for the IPCC were former police officers,

---

[107] For a detailed account see Smith G, *On the Wrong Side of the Law: Complaints against the Metropolitan Police 1829–1964* (London: Palgrave Macmillan, 2020).

[108] Police Complaints Authority, Annual Report, 1995/6 (London: SO, 1996). See also Maguire M and Corbett C, A Study of the Police Complaints System (London: HMSO, 1991) pp 147–8, and Waters I and Brown K, 'Police Complaints and the Complainants' Experience' (2000) 40 *British Journal of Criminology* 617. Both studies found that the majority of complainants were dissatisfied.

[109] House of Commons, *Home Affairs Select Committee, Police Disciplinary and Complaints Procedure*, 1st Report (HC 258–1, 1998), p 194. All these surveys are discussed in Harrison J and Cuneen M, *An Independent Police Complaints Commission* (London: Liberty, 2000).

[110] Sir William Macpherson of Cluny, *The Stephen Lawrence Inquiry* (Cm 4262-I) (London: SO, 1999). This was also found by the PCA's surveys.

[111] Dixon B and Smith G, 'Laying Down the Law: The Police, the Courts and Legal Accountability' (1998) 26 *International Journal of Sociology of Law* 419.

[112] Quoted in Harrison and Cuneen (2000: 1). [113] *The Guardian*, 13 January 2000.

[114] *Khan (Sultan) v United Kingdom* [2000] Crim LR 684.

[115] For a discussion of this history of 'scandal and reform' see Smith G, 'A Most Enduring Problem: Police Complaints Reform in England and Wales' (2006) 35 *Journal of Social Policy* 121.

[116] Police Reform Act 2002 (PRA), Part 2. The more general role of the IPCC is discussed at the end of this section. For a detailed account of the powers, structure and work of the IPCC see Harrison et al, *Police Misconduct: Legal Remedies* 4th edn (London: LAG, 2005) ch 4.

[117] Maguire and Corbett (1991).

leading to concerns about shared cultural priorities that further distorted the handling of investigations. The IPCC also lacked resources and teeth. As noted in a 2013 Home Affairs Committee report:

> Compared with the might of the 43 police forces in England and Wales, the IPCC is woefully underequipped and hamstrung in achieving its original objectives. It has neither the powers nor the resources that it needs to get to the truth when the integrity of the police is in doubt. Smaller even than the Professional Standards Department of the Metropolitan Police, the Commission is not even first among equals, yet it is meant to be the backstop of the system. It lacks the investigative resources necessary to get to the truth; police forces are too often left to investigate themselves; and the voice of the IPCC does not have binding authority. (p 4)[118]

The IPCC was also implicated in the mishandling of a number of high profile deaths following police contact, including John Charles de Menezes in 2005, where the IPCC were prevented from investigating by the Metropolitan Police;[119] Ian Tomlinson in 2009, where there were delays with starting an IPCC investigation into his death and in removing the City of London Police from the investigation;[120] Mark Duggan in 2011, in which the IPCC wrongly informed the media that Mr Duggan fired at the police before being fatally shot by the police.[121]

Criticisms of the IPCC continued throughout the 2010s,[122] eventually culminating in a government announcement to replace the IPCC with the IOPC.[123] Its Director General is appointed by the Queen and directly answerable to Parliament.[124] The IOPC have also for the first time been given the power to initiate investigations themselves, without a police referral, and to investigate the service the police provides to citizens and to increase the timeliness of investigations.[125] After only two years of existence at the time of writing, it is unclear at this stage whether *plus ça change et plus c'est la meme chose* with regards the IOPC. Yet, the independence of the IOPC remains of concern. An FOI request made to the IOPC in 2019 revealed that 28% of operational staff had a police background either as a former police officer or former civilian member of staff or both, with this figure going up to 40% for Operations Managers and Senior Investigators.[126] Given the newness of the IOPC and thus the lack of academic research specifically on it (as opposed to its predecessors), we cannot fully assess its impact, so discussion will inevitably rely on inferences drawn from prior research.

---

[118] House of Commons (2013) *Independent Police Complaints Commission*. Online at: <https://www.parliament.uk/business/committees/committees-a-z/commons-select/home-affairs-committee/news/130201-ipcc-report-published/> (accessed 13 July 2020).

[119] Smith G, 'Citizen oversight of independent police services: Bifurcated accountability, regulation creep, and lesson learning' (2009c) 3 *Regulation & Governance* 421–441.   [120] Ibid.

[121] <https://www.bbc.co.uk/news/uk-england-london-25776826> (accessed 14 July 2020).

[122] Drew Smith S, *An independent review of the governance arrangements of the Independent Police Complaints Commission* (2015) online at: <https://www.gov.uk/government/publications/governance-of-the-independent-police-complaints-commission> (accessed 14 July 2020).

[123] <https://www.opendemocracy.net/en/opendemocracyuk/ipccfail-police-complaints-watchdogs-decade-of-failure/> and <https://www.gov.uk/government/news/home-secretary-announces-reforms-to-ipcc> (accessed 14 July 2020).

[124] Policing and Crime Act 2017. Online at: <https://policeconduct.gov.uk/sites/default/files/Documents/Who-we-are/Our-Policies/IOPC_HomeOffice_Framework_Agreement.pdf> (accessed 14 July 2020).

[125] IOPC, Statutory guidance on the police complaints system (2020a) online at: <https://policeconduct.gov.uk/complaints-reviews-and-appeals/statutory-guidance> (accessed 14 July 2020), pp 6–7.

[126] <https://www.whatdotheyknow.com/request/ex_police_officers_employed_at_t> (accessed 14 July 2020).

11.3.3 The police complaints process

There are three main ways in which citizens' complaints may be addressed. First, their allegation may be treated informally and therefore will not be formally recorded by the police. These informal complaints are unknown in terms of their content or scale, which is problematic judging by the 36% of these non-recorded complaints that were appealed to the IOPC in 2018/19.[127] Though this changed in 2020 such that all complaints must be recorded,[128] at the time of writing there are no statistics available to assess this change to police practices. These informal complaints are dealt with by managers or professional standards departments and judged in relation to police force codes of conduct and of performance, which vary force by force,[129] and ethical standards that were introduced at the national level in 2014 and are often incorporated into local force policies.[130] Second, police complaints may be formally recorded and subject to a 'local resolution' (see section 11.3.5). The majority of recorded allegations are handled in this fashion. Third, a complaint may be referred to the IOPC (this happened in 52% of complaints in 2018/19 see later) who choose one of three investigatory routes (two of which involve the police investigating themselves), with a variety of different outcomes available at the end of this up to and including disciplinary or criminal proceedings.[131] When someone dies during or following police contact (and for the latter, where the police contact is relevant to their death), this must be reported to, and subject to, an independent investigation by the IOPC.[132] This will be discussed in the section on legal forms of accountability and regulation, alongside inquests conducted by coroners.

So, in spite of changes to the names and governance structures, the basic process for investigating police complaints has remained the same over the last sixty years, with the relevant police force investigating the *majority* of complaints made. These investigations are usually carried out by internal professional standards departments or sometimes supervisors in the relevant police force. The IOPC only investigate complaints considered to be 'serious and sensitive':

- serious corruption or serious assault;
- misconduct by police officers or staff—for example, possible criminal offences or serious injuries;
- where contact with the police may have caused or contributed to death or serious injury.[133]

---

[127] IOPC, *Police complaints statistics for England and Wales 2018/19* (2019a) online at: <https://policeconduct.gov.uk/research-and-learning/statistics/complaints-statistics> p 14 (accessed 15 July 2020).

[128] IOPC, *Guidance on capturing data about police complaints* (2020b) online at: <https://policeconduct.gov.uk/sites/default/files/Documents/statutoryguidance/Guidance_on_capturing_data_about_police_complaints.pdf> para 3.1–3.3 (accessed 27 July 2020).

[129] Chapman C, *An Independent Review of the Police Disciplinary System in England and Wales* (2014) online at: <https://assets.publishing.service.gov.uk/government/uploads/system/uploads/attachment_data/file/385911/An_Independent_Review_of_the_Police_Disciplinary_System_-_Report_-_Final....pdf>, para 3.3 (accessed 17 July 2020).

[130] College of Policing, *Code of Ethics: A Code of Practice for the Principles and Standards of Professional Behaviour for the Policing Profession of England and Wales* (2014) online at: <https://www.college.police.uk/What-we-do/Ethics/Documents/Code_of_Ethics.pdf> (accessed 17 July 2020).

[131] Disciplinary matters are dealt with under The Police (Conduct, Complaints and Misconduct and Appeal Tribunal) (Amendment) Regulations 2017.

[132] Article 2 of the ECHR (the right to life). See *Edwards v UK* 46477/99 [2002] ECHR 303; *Anguelova v Bulgaria* (2004) 38 EHRR 31; *Jasinskis v Latvia* (2010) ECHR 1. The only exception to this requirement is for deaths which are classed as 'apparent suicides', which are largely investigated locally or by the force in question.

[133] <https://www.policeconduct.gov.uk/investigations/what-we-investigate-and-next-steps> (accessed 14 July 2020).

Police forces can also make voluntary referrals to the IOPC. 'This may be, for example, because the complaint ... could have a significant impact on public confidence, or the confidence of particular communities, or the appropriate authority otherwise feels there is a need for independent involvement in the investigation.'[134] Alternatively, the IOPC may initiate an investigation themselves, e.g., when an incident comes to their attention directly.[135] When cases are referred or come to the attention of IOPC, they decide whether and what type of investigation to pursue of the following three options:

- Independent—the IOPC investigate the matter using their own investigators;
- Directed—the IOPC direct and control the investigation using police resources;
- Local—the police force professional standards department investigates, with no involvement from the IOPC.

At the end of the investigation, the IOPC may hear a police force's view about what should happen, but they make the final decision about whether misconduct meetings or gross misconduct hearings are necessary, albeit that the relevant force is left to carry out such disciplinary action.[136] The outcomes of this disciplinary action may be written warnings, final written warnings, reductions of rank or dismissal without notice. Further outcomes include referral of the case to the CPS for possible prosecution. For more minor matters, a force may decide to take non-disciplinary action such as by providing or encouraging reflection, learning or training, aimed either at individual officers or the organisation as a whole, or changes to policies, procedures and training where there may be wider lessons to be learned. Sometimes a combination of these outcomes may be necessary, for example, misconduct hearings *and* a criminal prosecution, with the former being delayed where it might interfere with the latter.[137] Complainants who are dissatisfied with the way their complaint has been handled may request a review of their case that, depending on its nature, may be completed either by the relevant local policing body or by the IOPC.[138] These are the only circumstances in which the IOPC would scrutinise the investigations of complaints by police forces.

Prior research suggests that local and directed investigations are frequently of limited value. Active day-to-day direction of investigations (e.g. formally directing investigators to pursue particular lines of enquiry) by pre-IOPC bodies was limited.[139] Even if all the investigation of all cases were directed in the required fashion, and even if that supervision were not so inadequate, the notion of investigation by the police would still be fundamentally flawed. This is because the IOPC (like its predecessors) is in a similar position to that of the CPS. None of these bodies assesses the facts of the incidents complained of, except in independent investigations. What they assess are reports of the facts, compiled by investigators whose job is to present a case. Since those investigators are police officers, the case they are generally predisposed to present will be that there is insufficient evidence to proceed. For although investigating officers are investigating alleged wrongdoing by other officers, much of this wrongdoing is part of everyday policing, is consistent with police working rules and will have been engaged in by themselves and/or their close colleagues. Arguably, the police psychologically neutralise the apparently deviant nature of their rule-breaking by using 'techniques of neutralisation' common to all occupational and

---

[134] IOPC (2020a: para 9.31).
[135] IOPC (2020a: para 9.36). As noted in 11.2.2.1 citizen recordings of their interactions with the police may encourage the IOPC to initiate an investigation.
[136] IOPC (2020a). [137] Ibid, para 17.31; p 126. [138] Ibid, paras 18.2, 18.5–18.7.
[139] Corbett and Maguire (1991).

cultural groups.[140] These techniques include 'condemning the condemners' and 'denying the victim', i.e., either blaming the complainant or disputing a crucial alleged fact about the complainant's injuries or loss. Such techniques enable the police to shrug off most complaints with a clear conscience.[141] Investigating officers, in other words, are steeped in 'cop culture' (see section 2.1.4), and see policing and rule-breaking through the eyes of that culture. Therefore, just as cases against ordinary suspects can be constructed to justify prosecution, cases against police officers and police staff suspected of wrongdoing can be constructed to justify no further action. The failure of the complaints process in notorious cases such as *Police Complaints Board, ex p Madden* (1983) and the 'Confait Affair'[142] provides further evidence that an investigative process, in which the police investigate themselves, is intrinsically faulty.

11.3.4 Complaints statistics: explaining low substantiation

As noted earlier, the majority of police complaints do not result in a referral to and investigation requested by the IOPC. Most result in a local resolution. Indeed, for the first time since 2008/9, in 2018/19, more formally recorded allegations were resolved locally than were investigated locally or through a directed investigation (48% compared to 40% of allegations).[143] The IOPC note that this may be due to changes to the legislation in 2012/13 which removed the requirement for complainants to consent to local resolution being used to deal with their complaint.[144] They go on to say that this change in approach 'allowed complaint handlers to address complaints in a way that reflected their seriousness'.[145] It is perhaps more accurate to say that this change allowed complaint handlers'—not complainants'—assessment of the seriousness of the allegation to inform the outcome of the complaint, with or without the complainants' support. Removal of complainants' consent to participate in local resolution underscores the already powerful role of criminal justice officials to determine the outcome of accountability processes (see section 11.3.5).[146]

The first set of statistics (2018/19) relating to the IOPC show:

- There were 31,097 complaints and 58,478 allegations formally recorded by police forces in England and Wales in 2018/19 (each complaint made can comprise multiple allegations). As shown in Table 11.1, since 2001/2 (i.e. shortly before the IPCC was introduced in 2004), these complaints grew, reaching a peak in 2014/15 and have been declining since then.

---

[140] Box S and Russell K, 'The Politics of Discreditability: Disarming Complaints Against the Police' (1975) 23 *Sociological Review* 315.

[141] For a more recent discussion of these techniques of neutralisation as employed by the Thai police see Prateeppornnarong D and Young R, 'A critique of the internal complaints system of the Thai police' (2019) 29(1) *Policing and Society* 18–35. In addition, the Thai police were also found to use 'illicit inducements in the form of bribes and corrupt favours' (p 32).

[142] See Baxter J and Koffman L, 'The Confait Inheritance – Forgotten Lessons?' [1983] *Cambrian Law Review* 14.

[143] See section 11.3.5. Only details of local or directed IOPC investigations appear in IOPC (2019a) statistics for 2018/19, because independent investigations relating to deaths or serious injuries appear in a different set of statistics, which are discussed in section 11.4.6.

[144] IOPC (2019a: 18). [145] Ibid.

[146] Schulenberg et al (2017); Prenzler T, Mihinjac, M and Porter L, 'Reconciling stakeholder interests in police complaints and discipline systems' (2013) 14(2) *Police Practice and Research* 155–168.

Table 11.1 Complaint cases recorded 2001/02–2018/19

	2001/02	2002/03	2003/04	2004/05
Total recorded in year	16,654	15,248	15,885	22,898
% annual change	-12	-8	4	44
	2005/06	2006/07	2007/08	2008/09
Total recorded in year	26,268	29,322	29,350	31,747
% annual change	15	12	0	8
	2009/10	2010/11	2011/12	2012/13
Total recorded in year	34,310	33,099	30,143	30,365
% annual change	8	-4	-9	1
	2013/14	2014/15	2015/16	2016/17
Total recorded in year	34,863	37,105	34,247	34,103
% annual change	15	6	-8	0
	2017/18	2018/19		
Total recorded in year	31,671	31,097		
% annual change	-7	-2		

- The most common allegation made in 2018/19 was 'Other neglect or failure in duty' (41%),[147] followed by 'all other categories' (29%),[148] and incivility, impoliteness and intolerance (12%).[149]
- This works out as an allegation rate of 264 allegations per 1,000 employees of police organisations, though this ranges from 93 per 1,000 in West Midlands Police to 465 per 1,000 in Devon and Cornwall Police.

This variation between police forces does not necessarily reflect differences in levels of complaints, rather it could simply be a difference in recording practices, in spite of guidance about which allegations should and should not be recorded.[150] Until 2020, police forces were not required to keep a note of informal complaints that do not need to be formally recorded, according to IOPC guidance. Forces like West Midlands Police that have low rates of recorded allegations per 1,000 staff could simply be formally recording fewer allegations than forces like Devon and Cornwall. Much in the way that crime statistics are shaped by police recording practices,[151] the same can be said of police complaints statistics. Similarly, much in the way that there is 'dark figure' of crimes that go unreported and unrecorded, the same is likely for police complaints. This means that what was is

---

[147] According to IOPC (2017: 15–16) guidance on the recording of complaints, this includes allegations with regard to 'a lack of conscientiousness and diligence concerning the performance of duties. This may include failure to record or investigate matters and keep interested parties informed. It includes failure to comply with orders, instructions, or force policy.'

[148] IOPC guidance does not offer a clear definition of what this includes presumably because it is too difficult to specify the broad range of police malpractice that it encompasses.

[149] This includes allegations of abusive, offensive or rude language or behaviour, but not harassment.

[150] IOPC (2020b).

[151] Maguire M and McVie S, 'Criminal data and criminal statistics: A critical reflection' in Liebling et al (eds), *The Oxford Handbook of Criminology* (Oxford: OUP, 2017).

reported and recorded in police complaints figures is likely to be only the 'tip of the iceberg', with people not making complaints to the police because they regard their complaint as not serious enough, because they lack confidence in themselves or in the complaints system, which is especially likely for minority ethnic groups, or perhaps because there is not enough support and assistance available to help people to make their complaint.[152]

Of the recorded allegations that were investigated (as opposed to resolved locally), 10% (n=2262) resulted in disciplinary or criminal proceedings. The likelihood of this was greater for more serious allegations such as those relating to sexual conduct, sexual assault, corruption, and malpractice. Where recorded allegations did not lead to criminal or disciplinary proceedings, only 12% of these remaining allegations (n=2360) were upheld.

In sum, an unknown proportion of allegations pass from being made by citizens to being formally recorded by the police. If allegations are recorded, the majority—48% in 2018/19—will be resolved locally. If they are formally recorded and investigated either locally or through a directed investigation after a referral to the IOPC (which was the case for 40% of allegations in 2018/19), there is a slim chance (10–12%) that this will result in consequences for the relevant police officers or police staff, either through the allegation being upheld, disciplinary action or prosecution. If we take these figures as a proportion of *all* allegations made, the rate of substantiation is even lower at 3.9% for disciplinary or criminal proceedings and 4% for allegations being upheld. When compared to the figures cited in the last edition of this book, the proportion of prosecution and disciplinary proceedings pursued has increased from 0.3% in 2008/9 to 3.9% in 2018/19 whilst the proportion of allegations being upheld has slightly increased from 3.6% in 2008/9 to 4% in 2018/19.[153] Nonetheless, at current levels, they remain objectively low. Indeed, this may explain the relatively large number of complainants who appeal decisions reached in local or directed IOPC investigations and whose appeal is upheld. In 2018/19, there were 1,310 such appeals of which 38% were upheld.[154]

There are many reasons for the low rate of substantiation of complaints. First, there is the process of case construction, denial of harm, stereotyping and discrediting of complainants, discussed earlier. Second, there is the closing of ranks by police officers who might have witnessed the events complained of and the inherent difficulty that people mistreated in police custody have in finding independent witnesses. 'Cop culture', in other words, creates evidential problems. Police officer collusion has been a major concern for over a decade. For example, concerns were raised following the death of Mark Duggan in 2011, where the officers involved were noted by the coroner as having been left in a room together before giving their statements to the IPCC.[155] The IOPC has since published statutory guidance which states that 'once the key policing witnesses have been identified they should be instructed not to speak (or otherwise communicate) about the incident with each other, or any other potential witnesses, both before and after they have given their

---

[152] Smith G, 'Why Don't More People Complain against the Police?' (2009b) 6(3) *European Journal of Criminology* 249–266 at 253.

[153] The figures cited here from the Fourth Edition of the book are for the number of prosecution/disciplinary proceedings and complaints being substantiated as a proportion of all complaints as oppose to all allegations. As noted in the 2018/19 figures a single complaint can contain multiple allegations so complaints and allegations are not the same thing.

[154] IOPC (2019a: 40). The number of appeals of IOPC investigation has declined by 54% from 2,426 in 2014/15 to 1,310 in 2018/19 and the proportion upheld has remained more or less the same at around 38–41%. It is unfortunate that these figures are not broken down by type of investigation to explore for example whether local (i.e. more police-dominated) investigations are upheld at a higher rate than directed investigations.

[155] Angiolini E, *Report of the Independent Review of Deaths and Serious Incidents in Police Custody* (2017) online at: <https://www.gov.uk/government/publications/deaths-and-serious-incidents-in-police-custody> (accessed 17 July 2020), para 10.20.

accounts.'[156] The only exception to this is if police officer or public safety is at risk and, if so, a record must be made of this communication. This statutory guidance is accompanied by College of Policing guidance from 2020 which states that 'officers and staff should not confer with others before making their accounts' given the importance of police witnesses they should 'individually record their honestly held recollection of the circumstances'.[157] This lengthy history of conferring and collusion, and the need to spell out that it is wrong, shows its ingrained nature. The 'blue wall of silence' runs deep in police culture and inhibits honest police officers from speaking out.[158]

In the past, officers under investigation often took early retirement or resigned for 'medical' reasons to avoid discipline or criminal charges. This is a form of plea bargain. Like all plea bargaining, the interests of the victim are set aside: from the police force's point of view the problem is dealt with easily, speedily and without publicity that would question why the malpractice occurred and what was being done to prevent recurrence, while the officers concerned lose their jobs but protect their record and pension rights. Now, though, a police officer may still be disciplined even after leaving the police service.[159]

As with other new arrangements, such as those relating to conferring between police officers, we do not yet know what the effects of this are, and whether it will improve the extent to which police officers are properly held to account for their actions through IOPC investigations and/or disciplinary proceedings. But the rule of law requires that the police (along with all other arms of government) should be accountable to 'the law'. Historically, the reality, in the context of the police complaints process, clearly falls well short of the rhetoric, given the small proportion of complaints that are upheld or lead to disciplinary proceedings. Given also the failures of other mechanisms of redress discussed throughout this chapter (e.g. civil action, private prosecutions or inquests in cases where people die during or following contact), these injustices compound themselves over time, and this amounts to the condoning of malpractice, which in turn allows yet more malpractice to flourish unpunished.

11.3.5 **Local resolution**

A past source of dissatisfaction among complainants was that complaints were 'all or nothing' events regardless of the seriousness of the incident.[160] Many just want an apology and a recognition of how they felt about their treatment by the police, or perhaps the opportunity for managers to be made aware of individual officers' malpractice so that lessons can be learned and the organisation reformed.[161] PACE therefore introduced the 'informal resolution' of complaints if this was the wish of both chief officer and complainant, and if the matter was insufficiently serious for it to be dealt with through disciplinary proceedings even if proven.[162] There is no requirement that the officer complained of, or the complainant, give consent for the use of this procedure.[163]

---

[156] IOPC, *Statutory guidance to the police force on achieving best evidence in death and serious injury matters* (2019b) online at: <https://www.policeconduct.gov.uk/sites/default/files/Documents/statutoryguidance/statutory-guidance-section-22-guidance.pdf> (accessed 17 July 2020), paras 20 and 21.

[157] College of Policing, *Post-incident procedures following death or serious injury* (2020) online at: <https://www.app.college.police.uk/app-content/death-or-serious-injury/?s#post-incident-management> (accessed 17 July 2020).

[158] Rowe (2020: 52); Maguire and Corbett (1991); Loveday (1989: 29). Better still, watch the BBC 'Line of Duty' series!

[159] Police (Conduct, Complaints and Misconduct and Appeal Tribunal) (Amendment) Regulations 2017.

[160] Brown D, *Police Complaints Procedure* (Home Office Research Study no 93) (London: HMSO, 1987).

[161] Ibid; Holmberg L, 'In service of the truth? An evaluation of the Danish Independent Police Complaints Authority' (2019) 16(5) *European Journal of Criminology* 592–611.

[162] PACE, s.85 has now been replaced by s.69 of the Police Act 1996, but there has been no material change.

[163] IOPC (2019b: 18).

This 'local resolution', consists of a meeting between the 'appointed officer' (handling the case on behalf of the police service) and the complainant, in which they discuss the nature of the complaint and what the complainant would see as an appropriate and realistic outcome, with an action plan being written to reflect these discussions.[164] This is followed by a meeting between the appointed officer and the officer complained against (at which the complainant's views are conveyed, and the police officer given a chance to respond). The emphasis during local resolutions is on organisational and individual learning rather than disciplinary or criminal sanctions as information collected during the local resolution cannot be used in subsequent disciplinary or criminal proceedings should the need arise. Some police forces have begun to use mediation between the complainant and the relevant police officer as part of their action plan for resolving complaints locally (see section on restorative justice later), but in the majority of cases, a local resolution will 'involve an explanation, giving the complainant information and an account from the officer complained about'.[165] It might also involve an apology from the relevant force and monitoring of and training for the individual officer or changes to police training or policies.

In theory, then, local resolutions provide a relatively legitimate route of redress in that it gives complainants a voice in the complaints process by discussing their complaint with the 'appointed officer', as well as being more timely than if the complaint were locally investigated following a referral to the IOPC (72 days compared to 158 days on average according to the 2018/19 figures).[166] However, local resolutions are contentious, with one study finding that 51% of complainants were dissatisfied.[167] At a time when complaints are going down, the growing number of appeals of local resolutions either to chief officers (up by 18% between 2017/18 and 2018/19, of which 16% were upheld) or the IOPC (up by 50% between 2017/18 and 2018/19, of which 67% were upheld) also suggests that this process does not work in the best interests of the complainant.[168]

In reality, informal resolution is more popular with police services than it is with either complainants or the officers complained against. Many complainants are 'nudged' into it, or even presented with a fait accompli.[169] Hill et al, who were allowed to observe what went on, found that in 42% of cases complainants were dissuaded from opting for a formal investigation by the police stressing how long this would take and how little would be achieved,[170] while in another 29% of cases informal resolution was presented as the only option. Moreover, the potential of informal resolution to achieve disciplinary or educative ends was exaggerated. The following explanation given by an appointed officer to a complainant is fairly typical of the salesmanship the researchers observed:

> You know, realistically, going down a formal route, you're looking at eight or nine months before you get a result. The result in all likelihood is going to be exactly the same, he'd

---

[164] IOPC (2014). [165] IOPC (2014: 6). [166] IOPC (2019b: 6).

[167] May et al, *From Informal to Local Resolution: Assessing Changes to the Handling of Low-level Police Complaints* (London: Police Foundation/IPCC, 2007b) p 23. On other jurisdictions see Prenzler et al (2017: 162–163).

[168] IOPC (2019a: 13–15). An appeal against a local resolution outcome may be lodged where it relates to the actions and decisions of an individual officer rather than to the decisions about how a police force is run, which in IOPC-speak is known as 'Direction and Control'.

[169] Corbett C, 'Complaints Against the Police: The New Procedure of Informal Resolution' (1991) 2 *Policing and Society* 47; Maguire and Corbett (1991); Waters I and Brown K, 'Police Complaints and the Complainants' Experience' (2000) 40 *British Journal of Criminology* 617; May et al, *Local Resolution: The Views of Police Officers and Complainants* (London: IPCC, 2007a).

[170] Hill et al, *Introducing Restorative Justice to the Police Complaints System: Close Encounters of the Rare Kind* (Occasional Paper No 20) (Oxford: Centre for Criminological Research, 2003a) Also see Young et al, 'Informal Resolution of Complaints Against the Police: A Quasi-Experimental Test of Restorative Justice' (2005) 5 *Criminal Justice* 279 at pp 287–278.

[the officer] probably get advice. What I'm suggesting to you is that the informal resolution, it is informal because it's not a formal interview, [but] it is a formal discipline.[171]

This is misleading because local resolution involves no formal admission of guilt and is not noted on the officers' records. Indeed, Hill et al found that appointed officers spent much of the time in their meetings with officers complained against reassuring them that the matter would not be recorded on their personal files, that they did not necessarily agree with the complaint, and so forth.[172]

Many complainants are disappointed when they receive a letter from the police service announcing blandly that the matter is now regarded as closed, with no information provided about the officer's reaction to the complaint, and often no apology from either that officer or the police service itself. In other words, the process raises citizens' expectations of a conciliatory spirit, only to dash them. Over half of the complainants expressed an interest to Hill et al in meeting the officer complained against so that each could hear the other's point of view, but this was arranged only rarely. Informal resolution at best 'results in an indirect transmission of views from the complainant to the officer complained against (which is all that some complainants want); at worst it is a means of suppressing a dispute and of bringing premature, bureaucratic closure to an incident.'[173] The potential that informal resolution appears to offer for officers and complainants to come to understand each other's behaviour and views is rarely realised in practice, in part because of inadequate resourcing, training and support.[174]

11.3.6 An assessment of the key elements of the police complaints system

We have seen that, despite ostensibly major changes, the complaints system still allows scope for the police to follow their own informal norms when investigating complaints against them. This is partly because investigating deviance by anyone (including criminals) is intrinsically difficult and likely to fail in the majority of cases.[175] It is also because processes requiring articulate argument, polite persistence and so forth are difficult for most complainants to engage with given that they may be drawn from more marginal sections of society and may not have the necessary social and cultural capital or the self-confidence which would enable their complaint to succeed in the face of powerful organisations like the police.[176] For younger and minority ethnic citizens, they may not even complain in the first place due to a lack of understanding of the work of the IOPC or due to a loss of faith in the impartiality of the IOPC and in their ability to handle complaints and perhaps also in 'the system' as whole.[177]

11.3.6.1 Investigative powers

The IPCC was the first independent UK body to have powers of its own to investigate police complaints. Indeed, the IPCC had many of the same powers, when investigating the police, as they did when the police investigate crime, including surveillance powers of the type discussed in chapter 6. This meant that the shooting of Mr Menezes in 2005,

---

[171] Hill et al (2003b: 19). [172] Hill et al (2003b: 22– 24). [173] Young et al (2005: 290).
[174] May et al (2007a).
[175] See Goldsmith A, 'External Review and Self-Regulation' in Goldsmith A (ed), *Complaints Against the Police: the Trend to External Review* (Oxford: OUP, 1991); Walsh D, '20 years of Handling Police Complaints in Ireland: A Critical Assessment of the Supervisory Board Model' (2009) 29 *Legal Studies* 305.
[176] Smith (2009a); Box and Russell (1975).
[177] IOPC, *The Independent Office for Police Conduct: Public Perceptions Tracker, Summary of Research for 2018– 19* (2019c) online at:<https://www.policeconduct.gov.uk/research-and-learning/statistics/public-confi- dence-and-engagement> (accessed 21 July 2020). *The Lammy Review* (2017: 6).

and the alleged attempted cover-up of it by the Commissioner of the Metropolitan Police, was therefore investigated by the IPCC itself—not, as would have happened before, by another force under the supervision of an independent body. The introduction of the IOPC brought with it a further set of independent investigatory powers, namely, to determine *when* they conduct an investigation.

Even with these independent powers of investigation, problems remain for the IOPC, especially in a system which is neither police-dominated nor fully independent, but a mixture of the two (a model which is also found in other jurisdictions such as Denver, Denmark, Israel, Ireland, Kansas City, Kenya, New York City, Ontario and the Philippines).[178] First, complaints bodies will only ever be able to investigate a tiny minority of all alleged wrongdoing, with independent investigations being reserved for only the most serious and significant cases (the resource problem is addressed in section 11.3.6.3). Second, independent investigation by 'civilian' investigators or civilian review boards are not a panacea. The difficulties include obstruction of investigators by the police, civilian investigators over-identifying with the problems of the police, the creation of cumbersome procedures to protect officers from the new outside body and a lack of understanding of policing on the part of civilians.[179] This last problem both impedes investigators in finding out what really happened, as officers can erect smokescreens more easily and pull the wool over the eyes of novices, and could lead to lack of understanding of why certain malpractice takes place, reducing the possibility of effective punishment and prevention measures.[180] This is certainly the impression given by the way the IPCC handled the de Menezes affair and many others since, such as the death of Ian Tomlinson.[181] It is also said that civilians who have not experienced 'the street' could not easily tell the difference between an officer 'trying honestly to do his job, but perhaps making mistakes', and a truly deviant officer 'who should not be in uniform'.[182] Many of the problems can be summed up as those of breaking into police culture, which, as we saw in chapter 2 and earlier, is very powerful. Nonetheless, where 'external' involvement in investigation is more than merely supervisory its impact can be considerable.[183]

11.3.6.2 Independence, impartiality, fairness and legitimacy

As the foregoing discussion illustrates independence in police complaints has been an enduring issue and one that is also relevant to other criminal justice complaints processes of the kind noted at the start of section 11.2 and indeed to all criminal justice accountability and regulation.[184] The importance of independence in police complaints processes has been increasingly emphasised at the European level and internationally. As Smith notes:

> Originally associated with English-speaking jurisdictions, what are variously referred to as independent, external, civilian or citizen complaints mechanisms thrive as a rapidly developing area of police policy. Cycles of reform at the national level, punctuated by scandals,

---

[178] Savage (2013); Prenzler et al (2013); Schulenberg et al (2017); Holmberg (2019); Kempe R, 'Civilian oversight of the police: The case of Kenya' (2019) 93(3) *The Police Journal* 202–228.

[179] For good surveys, see Loveday (1989) and McMahon M, 'Police Accountability: The Situation of Complaints in Toronto' (1988) 12 *Contemporary Crises* 301. Also see Goldsmith A and Farson S, 'Complaints against the Police in Canada: A New Approach' [1987] *Criminal Law Review* 615; Goldsmith (ed) (1991); Harrison and Cuneen (2000); and Prenzler T, 'Civilian Oversight of Police: A Test of Capture Theory' (2000) 40 *British Journal of Criminology* 659.

[180] Bayley D, 'Getting Serious about Police Brutality' in P Stenning (ed), *Accountability for Criminal Justice* (Toronto: University of Toronto Press, 1995).

[181] For a good general discussion, focusing especially on the de Menezes affair, see Smith (2009b).

[182] Maguire (undated) (quoting police officers).

[183] Goldsmith (ed) (1991). Disputed by Bayley (1995). [184] Savage (2013).

enquiries and legislative intervention . . . have contributed to a growing police complaints discourse and discernible waves of reform on the international stage . . . .[185]

Inadequate and insufficiently independent investigations into deaths at the hands of the police violate the ECHR Art 2 right to life.[186] Independence in police complaints processes is also integral to constitutional and organisational legitimacy where the former confers a mandate to use state sanctioned force.[187]

Yet this principle of independence, or perhaps this rhetoric, is compromised by the way police complaints processes work in practice. This is more obviously the case in police-dominated complaints systems and/or in authoritarian countries.[188] However, this argument still holds true for complaints systems in countries such as Britain; Nicola Dennis (see section 11.3.1) was so disgusted by the IPCC's decision that the officer who caused her to fear for her life merely deserved 'words of advice' (this was a supervised investigation) that she took the IPCC to court. The judge agreed with her.[189] This was no isolated case. A review of dozens of cases found the IPCC:

> failing to order proper inquiries; accepting police evidence without challenge; failing to disclose documents to complainants; misunderstanding the law; and rejecting complaints on weak grounds . . . failure to interview witnesses, failure even to interview the police officers involved, failure to collect CCTV footage (eventually retrieved in one case by the complainant's mother) and failure to gather medical evidence of alleged assault.[190]

One complaint, for example, was that an officer committed perjury. The magistrates believed this, saying the officer's evidence was 'not credible' but the IPCC did not. Complainants who had been paid compensation by the police had still not had their complaints upheld by the IPCC. For example, a man who was shot in the shoulder and held for a week on suspicion of terrorism because of faulty police information was simply told the police should have apologised. In that raid, all the 11 occupants of the house were taken to a police station even though only two were formally arrested. The IPCC accepted that three were assaulted by the police but made no disciplinary recommendations.[191] Sean Rigg died after being put in a police station 'cage', with CCTV cameras mysteriously not working, yet the IPCC put out a press statement that incorrectly accepted the police story, and justified waiting eight months before interviewing the police because 'there was nothing to suggest wrongdoing'.[192] The subsequent Coroners' Inquest into his death reached strikingly different conclusions, for example, even about the time of his death, in part because it took a more independent view of what happened. Such were the discrepancies between the two investigations into Mr Rigg's death, it prompted an independent review of the original IPCC investigation.[193] In 2008, 100 members of the Police Action Lawyers Group withdrew their backing for the IPCC, and two of the group's representatives resigned from the IPCC's advisory board in protest at its deference to the police.[194]

---

[185] Smith G, 'Oversight of the police and residual complaints dilemmas: independence, effectiveness and accountability deficits in the United Kingdom' (2013) 14(2) *Police Practice and Research* 92–103.

[186] *Ramsahai v The Netherlands* (2007), Application no 52391/99, 15 May 2007 judgment. Similarly, see Aston P, *Report of the Special Rapporteur on Extrajudicial, Summary or Arbitrary Executions*, UN Human Rights Council (2010) p 22.

[187] Torrible C, 'Reconceptualising the police complaints process as a site of contested legitimacy claims' (2018) 28(4) *Policing and Society* 464–479.

[188] Prateeppornnarong and Young (2019).   [189] *R (Dennis) v IPCC* [2008] EWHC 1158 (Admin).

[190] *The Guardian*, 25 February 2008.   [191] *The Guardian*, 14 February 2007.

[192] *The Guardian*, 22 August 2009. See also section 4.4.

[193] Baker D, *Deaths After Police Contact: Constructing Accountability in the 21st Century* (London: Palgrave Macmillan, 2016) p 8.   [194] *Legal Action*, June 2008, p 4.

A former Commissioner stated he 'could no longer support an organisation producing the worst of all outcomes—timidity towards police accountability and redress for complainants, combined with a drawn-out bureaucratic approach ...'[195]

It is unlikely that the IOPC will beef up its independence because of the intrinsic difficulties of the 'independent' role of operational staff in complaints bodies such as the IOPC discussed earlier. Yet independence, along with fairness, timeliness and the opportunity for their complaint to be upheld are what citizens want most from police complaints processes.[196] Perhaps the only solution therefore is a model similar to the one in Northern Ireland where all police complaints are independently investigated by the Police Ombudsman for Northern Ireland, hence its reputation as the 'Rolls Royce' of the police complaints world.[197] Though the Northern Irish complaints process is still far from perfect—for example, it was found to have a large proportion of staff from a police background in a 2011 review—the far reaching extent of its independence is thought to be at the root of higher levels of satisfaction amongst complainants.[198] Provided this independent role were also supplemented by the pursuit of a 'distinctive organisational culture' emphasising civilian values, this would hopefully limit the likelihood of civilian staff becoming socialised and imbued with police values.[199] An independent complaints body of this kind, though, would take significant resources which, after a decade of austerity, may not be forthcoming.

11.3.6.3 Resources

Limited resources held back the PCA, which had to decline to supervise 70–80% of the cases referred to it by the police.[200] While the IPCC was far better funded, it remained grossly under-resourced.[201] This was partly because of its success in encouraging more complaints and appeals, and the need to investigate more deaths and near-deaths as a result of European Court rulings.[202] But the IOPC's workforce increased by only 5% from 980 in 2016/17 (of which 88% of the workforce were white) to 1,030 in 2018/19 (of which 82% were white, thereby suggesting a greater increase in the white not non-white workforce).[203] So it is doubtful that it will be able to tackle the delays and investigative failures of its predecessor. However, legislative reforms introduced in 2020 include a stated intention for 'a more efficient system for dealing with police misconduct, making the investigation processes simpler and therefore quicker, including a requirement to provide an explanation where investigations take longer than 12 months'.[204] How these changes impact on practice remains to be seen.

---

[195] Crawley J, 'The Worst of All Outcomes' *Society Guardian*, 8 April 2009.

[196] Schulenberg et al (2017); Smith (2009a).   [197] Savage (2013: 94).   [198] Prenzler et al (2013).

[199] Savage S, 'Seeking "Civilianness": Police Complaints and the Civilian Control Model of Oversight' (2012) 53(5) *British Journal of Criminology* 886–904 at 903.

[200] Maguire and Corbett (1991: 12).

[201] House of Commons (2013); Public Accounts Committee, *Independent Police Complaints Commission* (HC335) (London: TSO, 2009) (also available as the Fifteenth Report of Session 2008–09 from the Committee's website).

[202] IPCC, *Building on Experience* ('Stocktake Consultation') (London: IPCC, 2008).

[203] IPCC, *Annual report and statement of accounts* (2017) pp 88–89 online at: <https://policeconduct.gov.uk/who-we-are/accountability-and-performance/annual-report-and-plans> (accessed 21 July 2020). IOPC staff diversity information 2018–19, online at: <https://policeconduct.gov.uk/who-we-are/accountability-and-performance/annual-report-and-plans> (accessed 21 July 2020).

[204] <https://policeconduct.gov.uk/news/legislative-reforms-signal-new-direction-police-complaints-system> (accessed 21 July 2020).

11.3.6.4 'Self-regulation'

There will never be sufficient resources for the IOPC to investigate all complaints or even to supervise them. The police will inevitably continue to investigate most themselves. It is common for complaints about professions to be investigated by those professions. However, the police are not like doctors and lawyers. First, while self-regulation is by no means ever perfect, the record of police complaints investigation and the rate at which they are substantiated is particularly lamentable (although not just in the UK). Second, the police have uniquely coercive powers, giving them greater opportunity for malpractice of a kind that carries very serious consequences for the individual citizen. Third, there is usually some element of choice on the part of people using doctors, lawyers, accountants and so forth, which is not true of suspects. Citizens cannot choose their police officers or control when they come into contact with them.

Finally, the police have a greater ability to hide malpractice than other professions because of their greater power and their capacity to choose the time, place and manner of their interaction with citizens. The IOPC, like its predecessors, receives reports of police investigations. Police 'case constructions' continue. A test of the IOPC is how far it is prepared to challenge these constructions in public. In all these respects the IOPC has the power and right to do this, and the new powers to investigate without a referral and the statutory guidance aimed at preventing key police witnesses from conferring are a good sign, though the low substantiation and discipline rates are not.

11.3.6.5 The rights of complainants

These have improved, but there is still some way to go. Despite non-police 'access points' for complainants—they may make their complaint directly to the IOPC via telephone, email or in writing—the initial assessment of the information provided and first contact that complainant has about their complaint is with a police officer from the relevant force. Complainants may find this disconcerting or even intimidating. Perhaps someone else— an IOPC member, for example—should do this.

During police-force led investigations of complaints (without a referral to the IOPC) which lead to a local resolution (i.e. most complaints), the complainant does not have a right to request that the IOPC intervene. In their FAQs for complainants, the IOPC say:

> [W]e cannot intervene in the progress of an investigation or instruct the police force to change the person in charge of investigating your complaint. If you have any requests, comments or criticisms about an ongoing police investigation, contact either the investigator looking into your complaint or someone else at the police force you complained to.[205]

But once this type of investigation, or indeed any other kind of investigation, is concluded, complainants do have a right to a review. This can be requested if a complainant is dissatisfied either with the outcome of an investigation or the way it was handled and when assessing these requests for a review the relevant review body examines whether the response to a case was 'reasonable and proportionate'.[206] Until the right to review replaced the right to appeal (in February 2020), appeals could be made against findings, discipline decisions, and (non-) disclosure, but not against decisions not to uphold (substantiate) a complaint or send the file to the CPS. We have seen that though the appeal rate is low, many appeals are successful, at around 38–41% for example for appeals of IPCC local or

---

[205] IOPC, *Frequently asked questions* (February 2020) (2020c) online at: <https://www.policeconduct.gov.uk/sites/default/files/Documents/Complaint_forms/IOPC_Complaints_FAQs_2020.pdf> (accessed 22 July 2020).

[206] <https://policeconduct.gov.uk/complaints-reviews-and-appeals/reviews-and-appeals> (accessed 22 July 2020).

directed investigations between 2014/15 and 2018/19.[207] Whether the new review process will have a similar success rate remains to be seen.

A major criticism of the old system was a presumption against disclosure to the complainant of documents found or produced in the course of the investigation. The presumption is now in favour of disclosure.[208] However, disclosure of witness statements is not a straightforward matter, particularly where a prosecution is possible. In *R (Green) v PCA*[209] the complainant sought witness statements in a case that could lead to the prosecution of the officers complained about in an incident in which a police officer knocked over the complainant in a police car and was charged with driving without due care and attention. The risk that the complainant might tailor his evidence to fit that of other witnesses was found to be too great to allow disclosure. However, these problems do not apply to disclosure of provisional findings and the final report in managed or directed investigations. Complainants have a right to be informed by the IOPC of:

- the progress of the investigation;
- any provisional findings of the investigation;
- whether an investigation report has been submitted;
- the action (if any) that is taken in respect of the matters dealt with in any such report;
- the outcome of any such action.[210]

Statutory Guidance of the IOPC also encourages transparency for the complainant by making the final report of their investigation available, subject to some exceptions such as information in it being of relevance to future criminal proceeding or to national security concerns.[211]

Complainants used to be excluded from misconduct hearings, but public hearings were introduced, with a few exceptions, from 2014.[212] The decision about whether a misconduct hearing takes place rests with the IOPC, with the IOPC also presenting cases against officers in hearings where there is a disagreement between the IOPC and the relevant police force.[213] This should increase justice and the appearance of justice.

11.3.6.6 Mediation and the injection of restorative values

Some forces have begun to use mediation during local resolution processes due to the presumed benefits of giving complainants—who mostly 'belong to disenfranchised parts of society'—a voice in both the specific proceedings and, by extension, 'debates about policing and public security'.[214] However, the research is dated. Young et al (2005) evaluated an initiative by Thames Valley Police in which complainants were offered the chance to meet the officer complained about in the presence of a facilitator trained in such restorative justice principles as promoting 'active listening', ensuring full exchange of views and

---

[207] See section 11.3.4 and IOPC (2019a: 40).   [208] Police Reform Act (PRA) 2002, s.20 and Sch 3.
[209] [2004] UKHL 6.
[210] PRA 2002. IOPC, *Making information available* (2019d) online at: <https://www.policeconduct.gov.uk/sites/default/files/Documents/Who-we-are/Our-Policies/iopc_making_information_available_march2019.pdf> p 1 (accessed 22 July 2020).   [211] IOPC (2020a: paras 11.16–21, 14.3).
[212] Readings D, *Police misconduct hearings* (2019) online at: <https://www.judiciary.uk/wp-content/uploads/2019/06/readings-2019-police-misconduct-hearings.pdf> (accessed 22 July 2020).
[213] IOPC, *IOPC independent investigations: Information for police officers, staff and their representatives* (2020d) online at: <https://www.policeconduct.gov.uk/sites/default/files/Documents/info-for-police/independent-investigations-information-for-police-officers-staff-and-their-representatives_IOPC_2020.pdf> p 9 (accessed 22 July 2020).   [214] Holmberg (2019: 608).

achieving a focus on harm and its repair. Of the 49 cases handled by a special Conflict Resolution Team, in 47 the complainants were offered a face-to-face meeting of this kind, and in 22 cases both police officer and complainant agreed. Where the offer was rejected indirect mediation was offered instead and mostly taken up.

The extent to which this was productive depended on the ability of those parties to think and behave in a restorative (rather than argumentative or aggressive) manner. Complainants expressed more satisfaction, and more positive attitudes towards the officer complained against, than a matched group of complainants who experienced a non-restorative process in a neighbouring force area. There was also a tendency for officers who had experienced a restorative meeting to learn or benefit directly from hearing the complainant's perspective, with one officer saying that he would no longer think about things with a 'blinkered policeman's attitude [but] think about how it affects other people'.[215] Local resolutions are ostensibly aimed at helping police forces and officers to learn from unhappy encounters and be more open about problems and failings. But so far neither complainants nor officers generally feel this is the usual result (May et al, 2007b).

11.3.6.7 Learning lessons and police reform: justice, democracy and efficiency

On the surface, the IOPC (and its predecessors) are primarily accountability (not regulatory) bodies. Alongside police forces, it receives complaints from the public and then investigates them, requiring police officers to retrospectively explain or account for their actions. The outcomes of these accountability processes might be an apology or explanation to the complainant, for example, or, more rarely, a misconduct hearing or criminal prosecution. However, in the interests of the legitimacy of the IOPC and the police forces they investigate and also in the interests of the 'core values' of justice, democracy and efficiency at the centre of this book, its regulatory potential must also be considered. This is rooted in the recommendations the IOPC is able to make based on its investigations and 'thematic work' not only for individual officers, but also for police policies and procedures and police organisations as a whole. So, in response to growing concerns about racial disparities in the use of police powers, the IOPC announced a thematic focus on race and discrimination in its investigatory work. This will involve 'independently investigating more cases where racial discrimination may be a factor in order to develop a body of evidence to identify systemic issues which should be addressed'.[216]

These regulatory and forward looking aspects of the work of the IOPC provide a possible platform for police reform, as long as it is not starved of resources (in the misguided and short-term pursuit of 'efficiency'). How recommendations made by the IOPC are adopted into police policies and practices, if at all, is likely to be contentious, however. The IOPC seems to be as much feared and loathed by the police as its predecessors. Similar issues dog the implementation and impact of recommendations made by the main criminal justice inspectorates (see section 11.3.7). Given the growing focus of the IOPC on public confidence—a crucial test of democracy—in what they do,[217] there is hope for this regulatory potential in the future. If so, there is also hope for a more just approach to the use of police powers, in which the goods and ills of police work are more evenly distributed between different

---

[215] Young et al (2005: 307).

[216] <https://www.policeconduct.gov.uk/news/iopc-announces-thematic-focus-race-discrimination-investigations> (accessed 27 July 2020).

[217] A three-year plan to improve public confidence was first announced in 2018. See here: <https://www.policeconduct.gov.uk/news/iopc-launches-first-three-year-plan-improve-public-confidence-policing> (accessed 27 July 2020).

members of society.[218] At the time of writing in 2020, when the police institution is facing yet another crisis connected once again to its treatment of minority groups,[219] this additional tool in the box for reforming the police is more essential than ever.

11.3.7 Inspectorates, performance data and managerialism

11.3.7.1 The role of the inspectorates

Criminal justice inspectorates, whose reports we have referred to frequently, are more self-evidently regulatory bodies than the complaints bodies. They are 'essentially preventative ... [aiming] ... to report on, and monitor the operation of, public services to improve performance and maintain appropriate standards'. There are four criminal justice inspectorates: Her Majesty's Inspectorate of Constabularies, Fire and Rescue Services (HMICFRS); Her Majesty's Crown Prosecution Service Inspectorate (HMCPSI); Her Majesty's Inspectorate of Prisons (HMIP); and Her Majesty's Inspectorate of Probation (HMIPr). A fifth inspectorate, Her Majesty's Inspectorate of Court Administration, was abolished in 2011. They are expensive, costing circa £30m per annum.[220]

Broadly speaking each of the inspectorates' roles is to conduct independent and evidence-based inspections of the work of the police, CPS, probation, prisons and other places of detention,[221] from which the inspectorates make recommendations, challenge poor performance, drive improvements, particularly linked to efficiency and effectiveness, and build public confidence in the organisations that they inspect.[222] Of the four inspectorates only one of them deviates from a narrow focus on efficiency and effectiveness. HMIP is the only inspectorate to focus on the rights and interests of criminal justice populations, emphasising the safety of prisoners, respect for human dignity, engagement in meaningful activities and preparation for resettlement, drawing on international human rights frameworks. Together these foci form the basis of their routine inspection work (e.g. PEEL assessments of the police focus on efficiency and effectiveness), in which they employ a variety of methodologies including organisational data, observation and interviews,[223] though some of these inspections are also thematic. For example, in 2020, HMICFRS published a thematic inspection on collaboration between police forces, and HMCPSI published a report on CPS responses to Covid.[224]

Though the inspectors are not regulatory bodies that can enforce compliance, criminal justice agencies generally feel obliged to act on their recommendations in the interests of

---

[218] Bowling B, 'Fair and Effective Policing Methods: Towards "GoodEnough" Policing' (2007) 8(S1) *Journal of Scandinavian Studies in Criminology and Crime Prevention* 17–32; Hough M, *Good Policing: Trust, Legitimacy and Authority* (Bristol: Policy Press, 2020).

[219] Skinns L, 'The police in England: an institution in crisis?' in Richards et al (eds), *Institutional Crisis in 21st Century Britain* (London: Palgrave Macmillan, 2014).

[220] See National Audit Office, *Inspection: A comparative study* (2015) online at: <https://www.nao.org.uk/wp-content/uploads/2015/02/Inspection-a-comparative-study.pdf> (accessed 24 July 2020).

[221] HMIP inspects and reports on conditions for and treatment of those in prison, young offender institutions, secure training centres, immigration detention facilities, police and court custody suites, customs custody facilities and military detention.   [222] National Audit Office (2015).

[223] Shute S, 'On The Outside Looking In: Reflections on the Role of Inspection in Driving Up Quality in the Criminal Justice System' (2013) 76(3) *Modern Law Review* 494–528.

[224] HMCIFRS, *The Hard Yards: Police to police collaboration* (2020a) online at: <https://www.justiceinspectorates.gov.uk/hmicfrs/wp-content/uploads/peel-spotlight-report-the-hard-yards-police-to-police-collaboration.pdf> (accessed 22 July 2020). HMCPSI, *CPS Responses to Covid-19* (2020) online at: <https://www.justiceinspectorates.gov.uk/hmcpsi/inspections/cps-response-to-covid-19-16-march-to-8-may-2020/> (accessed 22 July 2020).

maintaining public confidence. Through dialogue, constructive criticism, follow-up work and re-visits,[225] pressure can also be applied by the inspectorates to encourage compliance. Nonetheless, criminal justice organisations and officials are powerful entities—for instance, individual police forces have sometimes been described as 'fiefdoms' lead by powerful and increasingly politicised chief constables[226]—enabling them to resist attempts to force reforms on them. This is all the more likely where inspection reports are read as chastisement and criticism, leading to pressure points, conflict, defensiveness and the displacement of blame to others.[227] Therefore, compliance depends heavily on relationships between the inspectorates and the organisations they inspect, as well as with Parliament to whom the inspectorates report.[228] But there is no systematic measurement and evaluation of compliance with the recommendations of the inspectorates.[229]

11.3.7.2 Performance monitoring, micro-management and managerialism

The inspectorates are part of the architecture of control over criminal justice agencies, through which data is collected and performance is monitored particularly around central planks of managerialism such as efficiency, effectiveness, value for money, etc. This enables comparison and ranking of individual criminal justice agencies in relation to each other. The information is published on inspectorate websites so citizens can make such comparisons too.[230]

Some chief inspectors use their public role to assert their independence, defend the work of the inspectorates and to challenge and criticise government officials and ministers in relation to criminal justice matters.[231] Once again the issue of independence (as is the case with the role of the IOPC) is critical to the functioning of the work of the inspectorates, with Shute encouraging us to see this in relation to the inspectorates as primarily independence of judgement (rather than financial, political or operational independence), meaning an unwillingness to be a 'mouthpiece of others' and not being afraid 'to criticise government policies when it believes these are compromising the efficient, effective, or fair delivery of the services it inspects or eroding proper standards'.[232]

But government departments influence the work of inspectorates through levers such as the appointment and length of tenure of chief inspectors and the setting of budgets.[233]

---

[225] National Audit Office (2015). Inspectorates vary in the nature of this follow-up work with HMCPSI using regular follow-up processes whilst ICI Borders and Immigration use none and rely on Home Office information instead.

[226] Johnston L, Button M and Williamson T, 'Police, governance and the Private Finance Initiative' (2008) 18(3) *Policing and Society* 225–244.

[227] English L, 'The impact of an independent inspectorate on penal governance, performance and accountability: Pressure points and conflict "in the pursuit of an ideal of perfection"' (2013) 24(7–8) *Critical Perspectives on Accounting* 532–549.

[228] Owers (2010), for example, notes that human dignity, safety, decency, activity and settlement, i.e., the rights and interests of criminal justice populations are a focus of HMIP inspections, including in their work inspecting police custody facilities. See Owers A, 'The regulation of criminal justice: Inspectorates, ombudsmen and inquiries' in Quirk, Seddon and Smith (2010: 242).

[229] National Audit Office (2015: paras 2.18–2.20); Shute, (2013).

[230] For example, on the front page of the website for HMICFRS, you are invited to 'Find your police force' and when you do you can then look at facts and figures about the force, including its performance in its latest PEEL assessment.

[231] Hardwick N, 'Inspecting the Prison' in Jewkes Y, Bennett J and Crewe B (eds), *Handbook on Prisons* 2nd edn (Abingdon: Routledge, 2016). [232] Shute (2013: 514).

[233] House of Commons Committee of Public Accounts, *Inspection in Home Affairs and Justice*, online at: <https://www.parliament.uk/business/committees/committees-a-z/commons-select/public-accounts-committee/news/report-comparing-inspectorates/> (accessed 24 July 2020). See also National Audit Office (2015: paras 3.2–3.7).

They 'steer' criminal justice agencies from afar whilst letting criminal justice officials do the hard work of 'rowing' at the local level.[234] Much of this steering focuses on efficiency and effectiveness not the other core values of justice and democracy. The work of the HMICFRS, for example, provides 'limited scope to consider structural or institutional concerns about the impact of policing on marginalised, disadvantaged and socially excluded populations' that were discussed in chapter 10.[235] And HMIP does not ask fundamental questions about whether prisoners need to be in prison at all.[236] The inspectorates are therefore primarily a mechanism through which managerialist concerns about efficiency and cost-effectiveness come to be prioritised. Yet this managerialist focus 'can limit experimentation, favour "outputs" over "outcomes", skew practice to fit performance indicators, limit the discretion of field staff, and diminish an agency's real effectiveness in order to maximise the practices that are most easily measurable'.[237] Basically, what gets measured gets done. Human rights, selective law enforcement and all the other elements of 'justice' and 'democracy' are measured much less (and are harder to measure) and so take lower priority.

11.3.7.3 Joint inspections: The case of police custody

Following the UK signing up to the Optional Protocol to the UN Convention Against Torture (OPCAT) in 2003, these obligations were put into practice through the preventative inspection work carried out by the National Preventative Mechanism (NPM), which was formally designated in 2009. HMIC did not previously do this work as it was beyond its core remit. Yet, police custody is a place in which international human rights bodies may be particularly concerned about matters such as safeguarding, due process rights, treatment, conditions, healthcare, suicide prevention, etc.[238] In England and Wales the NPM is coordinated by HMIP but the day-to-day inspection work takes place in multi-organisational teams including HMICFRS, HMIP, the CQC and the ICVA (ICVA is discussed in section 11.2.3). Collectively they 'regularly' inspect in police custody facilities—circa 10 per annum—through a mixture of announced and unannounced visits, with the aim of preventing torture and other cruel, inhuman or degrading treatment or punishment.[239] Each of the 43 police forces of England and Wales should be inspected at least once every six years. The five main set of criteria used in these inspections are:

1. Leadership, accountability and partnerships, which includes an examination of performance management and governance structures.
2. Pre-custody: first point of contact, which includes issues of diversion and transportation to police custody, hospital etc. and the sharing of information about risk.

---

[234] Osborne D and Gaebler T, *Reinventing Government: How the Entrepreneurial Spirit is Transforming the Public Sector* (Reading, MA: Addison-Wesley, 1992) p 146. Given the focus on prisoner experiences, Bennett (2014) rejects the idea that HMIP inspections are managerialist at least compared to performance indicators and other tools of prison audit culture. See Bennett J, 'Resisting the Audit Explosion: The Art of Prison Inspection' (2014) 53(5) *Howard Journal* 449–467.

[235] Rowe (2020: 34). Similarly, HMIP have also been seen to perpetuate not challenge societal inequalities. See Bennett (2014). The same can be said of HMIP's role in the inspection immigration removal centres. See Bhui H, 'Can Inspection Produce Meaningful Change in Immigration Detention?' (2016) *Global Detention Project Working Paper No. 12*. Online at: <https://www.globaldetentionproject.org/wp-content/uploads/2016/05/bhui_gdp_working_paper_may_2016.pdf> (accessed 24 July 2020).

[236] Bhui (2016). Such matters become all the more critical in relation to immigration removal centres, where someone's detention will not have been determined through a lengthy legal and ostensibly fair process.

[237] Garland D, *The Culture of Control* (Oxford: OUP, 2001) p 189.   [238] Owers (2010: 19).

[239] For a full list of all the police custody inspections conducted see here: <https://www.justiceinspectorates.gov.uk/hmicfrs/our-work/article/criminal-justice-joint-inspection/joint-inspection-of-police-custody-facilities/> (accessed 22 July 2020).

3. In the custody suite: booking in, individual needs and legal rights including consideration of rights to legal advice, intimation, fitness for interview, interpretation, complaints, bail and release under investigation; consideration of treatment and respect for detainees; and the recognition of diverse needs and potential risks.
4. In the custody cell: safeguarding and healthcare, which includes the physical conditions of custody facility, access to health and mental healthcare, appropriate adults and consideration of the use of force.
5. Release and transfer from custody, which includes consideration of the operation of virtual court, the paperwork used to transfer people to prison or court and pre-release risk assessments.[240]

These joint inspections, along with academic research,[241] reveal many issues of concern, including 'an aversion to risk which has meant some detainees being denied items of basic dignity such as toilet paper or blankets, poor physical conditions in some places, and inconsistent healthcare provision'.[242] From the perspective of regulation, ensuring that the inspections impact on police practices and detainee experiences is a further area of ongoing concern, with no guarantees of compliance by police forces with the recommendations from these joint inspections.[243] This is partly because of the gap between human rights principles (in conventions, case law and the standards used to guide monitoring and inspections) and day-to-day practices in police custody settings.[244] For example, terms like torture, cruel, inhuman or degrading are not common place in the data collected by criminal justice institutions, who tend instead to refer to assault, bullying and harassment.[245] And the idea of 'regular' visits by HMIP and HMICFRS is not straightforward: frequency, intensity and quality of visits are equally important.[246]

11.4 Legal regulatory and accountability mechanisms

11.4.1 Trial remedies

One of the great dilemmas of any system of criminal justice is what to do about evidence obtained in the course of rule-breaking by police and other officials.[247] The crime control position is that the only sensible test of evidence is its probative value—i.e. its usefulness in securing a conviction. If evidence is obtained wrongly, the officials responsible should be dealt with and the wronged defendant should be compensated, in proceedings designed for those purposes. Excluding probative and reliable evidence at trial (that is, the use of

---

[240] HMIC, *Expectations for police custody: Criteria for assessing the treatment of and conditions for detainees in police custody* (2018) online at: <https://www.justiceinspectorates.gov.uk/hmiprisons/wp-content/uploads/sites/4/2018/05/Police-Expectations-2018.pdf> (accessed 24 July 2020).
[241] Skinns L, Sorsby A and Rice L, '"Treat them as a human being": dignity in police detention and its implications for "good" police custody' (2020) *British Journal of Criminology* 1667–1688.
[242] Owers (2010: 272).
[243] Hardwick N and Murray R, 'Regularity of OPCAT visits by NPMs in Europe' (2019) 25(1) *Australian Journal of Human Rights* 66–90.
[244] van Zyl Smit D, 'Humanising Imprisonment: A European project?' (2006) 12(2) *European Journal on Criminal Policy and Research* 107–120.
[245] Laing J and Murray R, 'Measuring the incidence of Article 3 ECHR violations in Places of Detention in the UK: Implications for the National Preventive Mechanism' (2017) *European Human Rights Law Review* 564–588.
[246] Hardwick and Murray (2019).
[247] The literature on this topic is enormous and only a brief outline is given here. For detailed discussions see, for instance: Choo A, *Evidence* 5th edn (Oxford: OUP, 2018); Giannoulopoulos D, *Improperly Obtained Evidence in Anglo-American and Continental Law* (Oxford: Hart, 2019).

an 'exclusionary rule')—or, worse, halting the trial altogether—so that a guilty person walks free, punishes the innocent public along with the guilty police. The purpose of the criminal trial is to establish whether guilt has been proved beyond reasonable doubt, not to provide a system of 'trial remedies'. Legal niceties should not obstruct the search for the truth.

The due process position is that the best way of deterring future breaches of the rules is by preventing the police from benefiting from them. Moreover, in so far as due process protections have value in themselves as ethical standards, a system which accepts evidence secured in breach of those standards is tainted. If citizens are to respect the law, the criminal justice system has to set an example. The crime control adherent argues that the ends justify the means. The due process adherent argues that the means themselves must have moral integrity, regardless of what ends are being pursued, and that trial remedies are one way of securing that.

There are several problems with both positions. For instance, both make assumptions about the value of all these remedies and controls without a firm factual basis for those assumptions. What discredits the criminal justice system more: ignoring apparently reliable evidence and allowing the apparently guilty to go free, or using illegally obtained evidence and, by doing so, condoning illegal police behaviour which may not be subject to any other sanction? And how valuable are trial remedies as protections? They provide no comfort for suspects who are not tried; that is, who are not charged or who plead guilty or who may have suffered greatly through having had their home unlawfully searched, being interrogated roughly or being denied access to legal advice.

Advocates of crime control and due process do share some common ground. If a minor rule were breached (for example, refreshments to a suspect held in cells being provided 10 minutes late) even the most ardent due process adherent would not advocate that all evidence secured thereafter should be excluded. And in the second edition of this book we confidently stated that no civilised systems would countenance the use of evidence secured through torture, no matter how reliable it might be. However, until the House of Lords overruled it, that is precisely what the Court of Appeal did endorse.[248] It seems that the limits to civilisation are unpredictable but there are no systems in democratic societies which use absolute all-embracing inclusionary or exclusionary rules. In weighing up the core values of justice, democracy and efficiency, the value or otherwise of the remedies discussed in this chapter should be assessed, along with the loss of confidence people would have in the system in the event either of condoning police rule-breaking or of acquittals stemming from the rejection of reliable evidence. Weight would also have to be given to the nature of the suspects' rights that the police had infringed, since some rights (such as the right of access to a lawyer) are so fundamental that even relatively minor infringements of them pose a fundamental threat to justice.[249] This would be so even if the general populace would prefer evidence obtained through such an infringement to be admitted at trial, since one of the purposes of a system of democratically established rights is to defend the interests of unpopular minorities against the preferences of the majority.

Historically, the common law position on exclusion was at the crime control end of the spectrum. In *Sang*[250] (where evidence was obtained by an agent provocateur) it was

---

[248] *A v Secretary of State for the Home Department (No 2)* [2005] UKHL 71, briefly discussed later.

[249] See *R v Samuel* [1988] QB 615 at 630, though the police appear to have been given more leeway to breach this provision in some contexts following *Ibrahim and Others v the United Kingdom* [2016] ECHR 750 and *Beuze v Belgium* [2018] ECHR 92. For discussion see Celiksoy E, 'Overruling "the Salduz Doctrine" in Beuze v Belgium: The ECtHR's further retreat from the Salduz principles on the right to access to lawyer' (2019) 10(4) *New Journal of European Criminal Law* 342–362.

[250] [1980] AC 402. For a concise modern history of the pre- and post-PACE situation, see Ormerod D and Birch D, 'The Evolution of the Discretionary Exclusion of Evidence' [2004] *Criminal Law Review* 767. Also, Sharpe (1998): ch 2 on the common law, and ch 3 on the background to the 1984 legislation.

held that judges had no general discretion to exclude non-confession evidence (e.g. fingerprints) simply because of the duplicitous or oppressive way in which it was obtained. However, confession evidence was treated differently, because of the peculiar difficulty of reconciling confession-inducing questioning with the right of silence.

When PACE was drafted, the government intended largely to re-enact common law rules on these issues. Section 76(2) requires the exclusion of confession evidence obtained oppressively or in conditions making it likely to be unreliable. Section 82(3) provides that nothing '... in this Part of this Act shall prejudice any power of a court to exclude evidence ... at its discretion' and s.78 allows judges to exclude, at their discretion, *any* evidence obtained 'unfairly' regardless of its reliability or probative value. In addition to these statutory provisions, we must consider the common law abuse of process doctrine under which prosecutions can be halted entirely.

The way 'unfairness' is interpreted by the judges, and how they use their discretion, tells us where on the due process/crime control spectrum we're moving and how the core values of justice, democracy and efficiency are balanced. Interpretation also must comply with the ECHR (Art 6, the right to a fair trial). Key principles that guide judicial decision-making are:

Reliability: Evidence which is unreliable will be excluded. Evaluating reliability is, however, not at all straightforward, and some court evaluations here are based implicitly on the other principles set out in this list. A pure crime control approach would adopt this principle alone.

Disciplinary: Sometimes evidence is excluded to discipline the police if the court considered that the police behaved especially badly or oppressively. Use of this principle in relation to all rule-breaking would be a hallmark of a pure due process approach.

Voluntarism: In keeping with the due process origins of English law (in theory, although not in practice), evidence obtained through compulsion used to be excluded, but is no longer. For example, interrogation is imposed, not requested (see chapters 4 and 5).[251]

Judicial integrity: Evidence should be excluded if this best preserves the moral integrity of the legal system and/or public confidence in it, and included if this best fulfils that aim. This effects some kind of compromise between due process and crime control positions, but such compromises tend to result in inconsistency from case to case. Thus, is integrity eroded more by a minor deviation from the rules which was motivated by dishonesty on the part of the police, or by a major deviation from the rules which was the result of honest error by the police? We shall see that this principle is articulated usually in relation to abuse of process.[252]

Protective: The essence of this principle is that where a defendant has been disadvantaged by a breach of the rules, the evidence obtained should be excluded. This could be seen as a variant on the 'judicial integrity' principle, in that it preserves moral integrity by preventing the system from profiting from a breach. This principle has the merit of effecting a principled compromise between due process and crime control positions, although as we shall see, in practice it has been misused by the courts.

11.4.1.1 PACE, s.76: oppression and reliability

We saw in chapter 5 that 'oppression' and 'unreliability' are slippery concepts. It is clear from that discussion that not all law-breaking, such as denial of access to legal advice, is oppressive.[253] Not knowing just what behaviour will, and will not, be excluded under this

---

[251] For full discussion about the circumstances, and ways, in which suspects and defendants are effectively compelled to participate see Qwusu-Bempah (2017), esp. ch 4.

[252] The use of evidence obtained by torture has been held to undermine the principle; *A and others v Secretary of State for the Home Department (No 2)* [2005] UKHL 71.

[253] *Parker* [1995] Crim LR 233.

heading limits its value as a deterrent to malpractice.[254] Circumstances 'likely' to render confession evidence 'unreliable' is similarly vague, and of similarly limited value as a deterrent. In *W*, for example, a confession made by a 13-year-old was held to be 'reliable'. Yet her 'appropriate adult' was her mother, who was psychotic at the time and therefore not capable of protecting or supporting her daughter.[255] Since anything which is excludable under s.76 is also, as we shall see, excludable under s.78, most defence lawyers argue both points.[256] There is therefore little case law to clarify the exact scope of s.76.

Judicial interpretation of s.76 focuses on police intentions rather than the effects of their behaviour on suspects even though s.76 was intended to protect suspects. In *Miller*[257] a paranoid schizophrenic was questioned at length. This produced hallucinations and delusions, along with a confession. The Court of Appeal held that the fact that the defendant experienced the interrogation as oppressive did not make it so in law, for this was not the intention of the police and would not have been the result in normal circumstances. This was small comfort to Miller. The decision ignored the fact that few suspects experience custodial interrogation as normal, that the application of pressure is a natural police interrogation tactic, and that many more suspects are 'vulnerable' than are ever officially recognised as such, as we saw in chapter 5. However, the 'reliability' rule should cater for such cases, and the Court of Appeal has frequently held that confessions by vulnerable suspects with very low IQs should be excluded on this basis.[258]

Since the courts only apply s.76 when the police are at fault, suspects who behave unreliably or feel oppressed because of their custodial circumstances do not benefit from this exclusionary provision, even though (as we saw in chapter 5) it is the police who determine what those custodial circumstances are. Thus in *Wahab*[259] the defendant and members of his family were arrested for drugs offences. Wahab asked his solicitor to negotiate with the police the release of his family in exchange for a confession. The responses of the police and solicitor were non-committal, but Wahab confessed anyway. He asked for the confession to be excluded on the ground that it was unreliable as it was made to secure his family's release. The Court of Appeal held not simply that the judge was right to regard it as reliable, as many factors could have led him to confess, but also that since the inducement to confess (release of his family) was self-induced, reliability was irrelevant—although, had his relatives been wrongly arrested, this would have been taken into account. Another major limitation on the potential power of s.76 to increase freedom or due process is the refusal of UK courts to adopt the 'fruit of the poisoned tree' doctrine under which evidence obtained as a result of oppressively obtained confessions is no more admissible than the confessions themselves.[260]

---

[254] However, the due process rationale of the rule was underlined in *Mushtaq* [2005] 1 WLR 1513, where the House of Lords held that, regardless of the ruling of the trial judge, if a jury considers a confession to have been obtained through oppression they should disregard it—even if they believe it to be true.

[255] [1994] Crim LR 130. See section 4.2.1 for discussion of vulnerable suspects and the 'appropriate adult'.

[256] See, for example, *McPhee v The Queen* [2016] UKPC 29, which was a decision based on similar principles of Commonwealth law, and in which the court discussed principles of unreliability alongside more general unfairness.   [257] [1986] 1 WLR 1191.

[258] See, e.g., the 'Tottenham Three' case: *Re Raghip, Silcott and Braithwaite* (1991) *The Times*, 9 December; *Sylvester* [2002] EWCA Crim 1327. The Privy Council accepted that Fetal Alcohol Spectrum Disorders could result in people making unreliable confessions (*Pora* [2015] UKPC 9). Campaigners for Brendan Dassey—made famous by the series, *Making a Murderer*, also argue that his confession is likely to be unreliable as a result of low IQ but this has not yet found favour with the American judicial system.

[259] [2003] 1 Cr App R 15.

[260] Indeed, s.76(4)(a) provides that exclusion does not affect the admissibility 'of any facts discovered as a result of the confession', though the prosecutor is not allowed to say that it was a confession which led to the discovery of such evidence—the 'fruit'. See Mirfield P, 'Successive Confessions and the Poisonous Tree' [1996] *Criminal Law Review* 554. Note that exclusion of collateral evidence can always be considered under s.78.

11.4.1.2 PACE, s.78: fairness

Section 78(1) provides that:

> ... the court may refuse to allow evidence ... if it appears to the court that, having regard to all the circumstances in which the evidence was obtained, the admission of the evidence would have such an adverse effect on the fairness of the proceedings that the court ought not to admit it.

Whereas s.76 applies to confession evidence alone, s.78 applies to all evidence. Unlike in relation to s.76, there is no rigid standard of proof applied to the exercise of s.78.[261] The test is one of 'fairness' and if the court is satisfied of this it must then exercise discretion (unlike s.76 where exclusion is mandatory if the 'oppression' or 'reliability' tests are satisfied). The decision not to adopt a hard and fast rule, combined with the sheer volume and diversity of unfair police practices, has resulted in a flood of reported appellate cases on exclusion. There is no consistent pattern in the deluge of appellate decisions (though see examples in section 5.5.1.2), so: 'The notion of fairness ... can refer to a multitude of aspects and merely furnishes an excuse for achieving whatever result is wanted without rigorous justification.'[262] We noted in chapter 5 that the Court of Appeal rarely interferes with trial judges' rulings about fairness. In Zuckerman's study, few, if any, of the judges interviewed articulated the principles discussed in section 11.4.1. One said that if his colleagues 'were asked about these principles they would not know what you were talking about'.[263] The appeal courts acknowledge that there are no absolute principles: s.78 does not require judges to use simple discretion but to exercise judgement in weighing all of the factors in cases.[264] All that is clear is that a pure 'disciplinary' rule is disallowed, for a court which automatically excluded evidence obtained in breach of legal rules would not be exercising discretion properly.[265] What principles seem to predominate?

Two contrasting cases illustrate the view often taken by the courts, as in s.76 cases, that the motivation of the police, rather than the effect of the unfair behaviour on the defendant, is most important. In *Alladice*,[266] the police delayed access to legal advice under s.58. They thought that they were entitled to do this but the Court of Appeal decision in *Samuel*[267] intervened, making what they thought was lawful into an unlawful act. The confession evidence secured in the absence of a solicitor was held admissible due, in part, to what the Court of Appeal regarded as their good faith. In *Mason*,[268] by contrast, the police deliberately deceived the defendant (D) and his solicitor, saying that they had found D's fingerprints on an item when in fact they had not. D confessed. It was held that the confession should have been excluded, even though the police lies were not characterised as unlawful. However, only rarely is it held that behaviour which does not breach PACE or other legislation such as RIPA (see chapter 6) should be excluded, trickery which does

---

[261] *Misick v The Queen* [2015] 1 WLR 3215 PC. See Keane A and McKeowon P, *The Modern Law of Evidence* (Oxford: OUP, 2018) ch 3 for discussion.

[262] Zuckerman A, 'Illegally Obtained Evidence: Discretion as a Guardian of Legitimacy' [1987] *Current Legal Problems* 55.

[263] Hunter M, 'Judicial Discretion: s 78 in Practice' [1994] *Criminal Law Review* 558 at 562.

[264] *Misick* [2015] 1 WLR 3215 PC.

[265] Consider this rejection of the due process position by the then Lord Chief Justice: 'the object of a judge in considering the application of s.78 is not to discipline or punish police officers or custom officers ...' (*Hughes* [1994] 1 WLR 876 at 879). Similarly strong statements were made in *Chalkley and Jeffries* [1998] 2 All ER 155. Most recently the courts indicated, in *Warren v Att General for Jersey* [2012] 1 AC 22, that a balancing act between the gravity of police misconduct and seriousness of the offence must be performed, and the court was critical of earlier decisions which seemed to discipline the police (e.g. *Grant* [2005] EWCA Crim 1089).

[266] (1988) 87 Cr App Rep 380. Similarly see *Marsh* (later).

[267] [1988] QB 615.   [268] [1987] 3 All ER 481.

not involve lying is not regarded as unfair per se, and where it is only defendants (not their lawyers) who are deceived the courts are far less sympathetic.[269] And, reflecting the increased profile of victims, in *Attorney-General's Reference No 3 of 1999*,[270] Lord Steyn said, by way of justifying the use of evidence that would not have been obtained were it not for prior illegal action by the police: 'There must be fairness to all sides . . . the position of the accused, the victim and his or her family, and the public.'[271]

More recently, the courts have relied on the principle of public interest to justify the admission of evidence even where there has been grave misconduct on the part of the police. In *King*,[272] the police bugged a cell to obtain evidence. The court, in ruling the evidence admissible, prioritised the issue of reliability over the breach of rules; because the police had not directly engaged with the suspect, the evidence was considered reliable and this factor trumped any wrongdoing on the part of the police. In *McKee*,[273] the court indicated that evidence obtained as a result of breached procedures as well as through breached laws is prima facie admissible. In *Warren*[274] the police knew that they were acting utterly unlawfully, including through an interference with the usually sacrosanct right to legal professional privilege. Although the court accepted that there had been grave misconduct on the part of the police, the judges allowed the case to proceed, and rely on the illegally obtained evidence. Because the police had not attempted to conceal their illegal behaviour from the court, coupled with the seriousness of the offence (professional drug importation), the defendants were said to still have a fair trial.

In the 1990s some judgments adopted a 'significant breach' test,[275] but the cases cited above show that the courts then moved away from it. Its merit was that it enabled judges to exercise discretion on the basis of the objective significance of the law in question. This is more certain and fairer than tests that require subjective judgements and a guess as to what defendants would have done had they been allowed by the police to exercise their rights. However, what amounts to a substantial breach is itself a matter of subjective interpretation. One might have thought that any breach of the ECHR would be 'significant'—that is what makes something a 'human right'. However, this is not the view of the courts, as regards the 'right to privacy' (Art 8) at any rate. Thus, as in *King*, confessions recorded illegally and covertly, for example, have not been excluded.[276] And in *Abdurahman* the police interrogated without arrest, caution or access to legal advice. These breaches were so substantial that the ECtHR decided they were contrary to the Art 6 right to a fair trial. But the conviction was upheld because the Court of Appeal considered the conviction to be safe.[277] On the other hand, in *Miller* a man was stopped while suspected of driving while

---

[269] See, e.g., *Maclean and Kosten* [1993] Crim LR 687; *Bailey and Smith* (1993) 97 Cr App Rep 365; and *Looseley* [2001] UKHL 53. See ch 6 for discussion of a variety of deceptive covert policing tactics that have been held to be fair. For further cases following the reasoning of *Alladice*, see *Mason* [2002] 2 Cr App R 38 and *Gill* [2003] EWCA Crim 2256.

[270] [2001] 2 AC 91.

[271] At p 118. See Grevling (1997) on the consideration of interests other than those of the defendant in s.78 cases. The idea that victims, or some notion of their rights, should influence trial outcomes is bizarre, yet increasingly used to promote crime control measures. See Jackson J, 'Justice for All: Putting Victims at the Heart of Criminal Justice?' (2003) 30 *Journal of Law and Society* 309 and ch 12.

[272] [2012] EWCA Crim 805.   [273] *Public Prosecution Service v McKee* [2013] UKSC 32.
[274] *Warren v Att General for Jersey* [2012] 1 AC 22.   [275] See, e.g., *Oransaye* [1993] Crim LR 772.
[276] *Mason* [2002], followed in *Button* [2005] Crim LR 571. Endorsed in *Khan v UK* [2001] 31 EHRR 45 and in *PG v UK* [2002] Crim LR 308 by the ECtHR. See ch 6 for discussion of covert policing. See generally, Ormerod D, 'ECHR and the Exclusion of Evidence: Trial Remedies for Art 8 Breaches?' [2003] *Criminal Law Review* 61. Failure to caution before questioning—undoubtedly a 'significant breach'—was regarded as irrelevant in *Senior and Senior* (2004), *Shillibier* [2006] EWCA Crim 793 and *Rehman* (2006). See criticism in Crim LR [2007] 102.

[277] [2019] EWCA Crim 2239; discussed at Crim LR [2020] 453.

drugged. The police knew he had learning difficulties and required an 'appropriate' adult'. They did not call one, and Miller was convicted of refusing to consent to a blood test. It was accepted that had he had an appropriate adult he might have been persuaded to agree to a test, and so the Divisional Court decided that the evidence that he refused should have been excluded.[278] The last edition of this book posited that the significant breach principle would be the most effective way of reducing miscarriages of justice and that, otherwise, implicit encouragement will be given to the culture of police malpractice. To us, the most powerful argument for excluding evidence, whatever the motives of the police, is that this is the only way of ensuring that suspects do not suffer from the wrongs done to them by the police. Ironically, it seems the courts can't decide!

11.4.1.3 Halting criminal prosecutions: the abuse of process doctrine

It has long been a principle of common law that trials could be halted by the judge if malpractice by police officers or prosecutors made the trial an 'abuse of process'.[279] Traditionally, it has been reserved for the most deplorable behaviour. Thus, in two major cases in the 1990s, where the defendants were effectively kidnapped unlawfully by the police and security services and brought to the UK against their will, the doctrine was invoked, and charges were dismissed on appeal. This was despite the reliability of the evidence against them not being in doubt. In *Mullen* [1999] the Court of Appeal said that the unlawful deportation of the defendant was:

> a blatant and extremely serious failure to adhere to the rule of law . . . the need to discourage such conduct on the part of those who are responsible for criminal prosecutions is a matter of public policy to which . . . very considerable weight must be attached.[280]

The application of the 'disciplinary' principle in this judgment is more apparent than real, as the Court held that judges must exercise a 'discretionary balance' (as with PACE, s.78). This applies the 'judicial integrity' principle, as in the notorious case concerning the suspected 'September 11' terrorists against whom there was evidence allegedly obtained in another country by torture;[281] and in a case where solicitor–client confidentiality was breached by unlawful police bugging of a police station exercise yard.[282] In these three cases it was eventually decided that the 'balance' should be exercised in the defendants' favour. But this last case has since been much criticised and the vagueness and unpredictability of this principle has led the 'balance' to come down against defendants in other cases where—in our opinion—officials behaved almost as reprehensibly.[283] There appears to have been a move away from stopping cases for abuse of process. In *Maxwell*, it was said that the doctrine should apply only when the accused cannot have a fair trial or where it would offend the court's sense of propriety to be asked to try the accused.[284] But there are a number of cases where the court appears to have a high threshold in terms of when its sense of propriety will be offended, and *Crawley* confirmed that the doctrine should be

---

[278] *Miller v DPP* [2018] EWHC 262 (Admin).
[279] For the background, see Choo A, 'Halting Criminal Prosecutions: The Abuse of Process Doctrine Re-visited' [1995] *Criminal Law Review* 864.
[280] The invocation of the 'rule of law' here follows the House of Lords' judgment in *Horseferry Road Magistrates Court, ex p Bennett* [1994] 1 AC 42. For discussion of the rule of law in this context see Sanders A and Young R, 'The Rule of Law, Due Process and Pre-Trial Criminal Justice' (1994) 47 *Current Legal Problems* 125.
[281] *A and others v Secretary of State for the Home Department (No 2)* [2005] UKHL 71.
[282] *Grant* [2005] 2 Cr App R 28.
[283] For a defence of the judicial integrity principle see Ashworth A, 'Testing Fidelity to Legal Values: Official Involvement and Criminal Justice' (2000) 63 *Modern Law Review* 633.
[284] *Maxwell* [2011] 1 WLR 1837.

applied only as a last resort[285]—that is, extreme situations involving agents provocateurs, destruction of evidence etc.[286] Sometimes courts halt cases where prosecutors cause unjustifiable delay,[287] although they balance this against creating a perverse incentive for the defence to cause delay[288] even though there is no evidence that this would actually occur, and it assumes that the defendant has no interest in having their case resolved quickly. In *S(D) and S(T)* the Court of Appeal indicated that decisions about whether there has been an abuse of process should be subject to the same sort of balancing act as when the courts consider applications to exclude evidence under s.78.[289] Finding coherent and constant principles is therefore impossible. The inconsistency of the case law shows that the judiciary does not always accept the need to discourage blatant and extremely serious failures to adhere to the rule of law. Is it right to convict citizens following trials tainted by such gross failures? Has not the verdict been deprived of all moral and condemnatory force by the illegal behaviour of the very officials charged with upholding the law?

11.4.1.4 The need for reform

We have seen that decisions on s.78 and abuse of process are generally crime control-based, the reliability principle usually outweighing the other principles except in cases of gross misconduct:

- judges often assert on tenuous grounds that evidence is sufficiently reliable to be put to the jury without the help of expert witness testimony;[290]
- what is 'gross' depends on a multitude of factors, not least the attitudes of the particular judges in the case—as was seen earlier in *Warren*;[291]
- violation of the ECHR is often regarded by the ECtHR as well as UK courts as insufficiently 'gross' to warrant exclusion of evidence.[292]

The UK is increasingly out of step with other democracies. For example, the lack of care for rights as such (the 'justice' core value) is likely to send 'shivers down the spine' of mainstream US lawyers.[293] A major inquiry now needs to decide: what principles should govern trial remedies; the extent to which those principles should apply equally in different situations (e.g. interrogation, covert policing, identification, retention of scientific evidence); whether particular weight should be given to breaches of the ECHR; whether s.78-type remedies and abuse of process, which are currently hopelessly blurred, should be merged.

---

[285] *Crawley* [2014] EWCA Crim 1028.

[286] Martin S, 'Lost and Destroyed Evidence: The Search for a Principled Approach to Abuse of Process' (2005) 9 *International Journal of Evidence and Proof* 158; Ormerod D and Roberts A, 'The trouble with *Teixeira*: developing a principled approach to entrapment' (2002) 6 *International Journal of Evidence and Proof* 38. See *Latif and Shazad* [1996] 1 All ER 353, *Looseley* (2001) and *R v Syed* [2018] EWCA Crim 2809. But in *Moon* [2004] the clear entrapment was held to be an abuse of process and the Court of Appeal said that proceedings should have been halted. For discussions of entrapment see Ormerod D, 'Recent Developments in Entrapment' [2006] 65 *Covert Policing Review* 65–67, which was applied in *Moore and Burrows* [2013] EWCA Crim 85, and Hill D, McLeod S and Tanyi A, 'The Concept of Entrapment' (2018) 12 *Criminal Law and Philosophy* 539.

[287] *Boardman* [2015] EWCA Crim 175.   [288] *R et al* [2016] 1 WLR 1872.

[289] *R v S(D) and S(T)* [2015] EWCA Crim 662; *Abdurahman* Crim LR [2020] 453 is an example, where the seriousness of the case (terrorism) seemed to outweigh the seriousness of the breach. The same type of reasoning was also applied in *Warren v Att General for Jersey* [2012] 1 AC 22.

[290] As in, for example identification cases (see, e.g., *Phillips* [2020] Crim LR 940, plus commentary, pp 941–944).

[291] [2012] 1 AC 22.   [292] *Ibrahim v United Kingdom* (2015) 61 EHRR 9.

[293] Giannoulopoulos D, *Improperly Obtained Evidence in Anglo-American and Continental Law* (Oxford: Hart, 2019), p 150.

These evaluations need to take into account not just formal legal principles and matters of 'internal' legal logic, but also the reality of the criminal justice process:

- the shift in policing tactics from reactive to proactive policing, which means that s.78 cases increasingly concern covert operations, surveillance, bugging, the use of informers and so forth; informers, for example, are even less trustworthy than the police, and when the police are undercover the scope for malpractice is at its height;[294]
- social media that, for example, make identification processes less reliable than ever;[295]
- whether or not a legal advisor or appropriate adult actually protected a defendant who was denied a particular right is more important than their presence when the malpractice occurred; that knowing one's rights and having the confidence to exercise them in coercive situations are not the same thing.

This should all be done alongside an appraisal of the degree of protection and remedial possibilities provided by other remedies discussed in this chapter—for although, arguably, an effective complaints system would provide a better remedy against malpractice than the exclusion of evidence, if there is no such alternative, exclusion of evidence is better than nothing.

11.4.2 Appeals from the magistrates' court

11.4.2.1 Rehearings in the Crown court

The rights of appeal in the English system differ according to whether the defendant was convicted in the magistrates' court or the Crown court.[296] Partly as a result of historical accident, and partly due to the unsatisfactory nature of summary justice (chapter 8), magistrates' courts convictions are subject to more extensive forms of appellate review. Unless the appeal is out of time, no leave (i.e. permission) is required for an appeal from this court to the Crown court, though the Criminal Procedure Rules (CrPR) require the appellant to summarise the issues to be dealt with on appeal. The appeal takes the form of a complete rehearing of the case before a professional judge and two or more magistrates who took no part in the original trial.[297] The grounds for appeal are unrestricted and fresh evidence will be admitted. This form of appellate review is not as generous or effective as might at first appear, however.

To begin with, an automatic right of appeal against conviction to the Crown court does not arise if the defendant pleaded guilty.[298] This automatically excludes around three-quarters of all defendants tried in the lower courts. Many may be aggrieved by the circumstances of the police investigation, the conduct of the prosecution or the behaviour of the magistrates' court itself, yet have felt themselves to have had little option but to

---

[294] Loftus B 'Normalizing covert surveillance: the subterranean world of policing' (2019) 70 *British Journal of Sociology* 2070–2091.

[295] Roberts A, 'The Frailties of Human Memory and the Accused's Right to Accurate Procedures' [2019] *Criminal Law Review* 911.

[296] For a comprehensive account see Taylor P (ed), *Taylor on Criminal Appeals* 2nd edn (Oxford: OUP, 2012).

[297] Senior Courts Act 1981, s.74; Part 34 of the Criminal Procedure Rules, available at: <http://www.justice.gov.uk/courts/procedure-rules/criminal/rulesmenu-2015#Anchor10> (accessed 29 July 2020).

[298] Magistrates' Courts Act 1980, s.108; *Crown Court at Birmingham, ex p Sharma* [1988] Crim L R 741. In these circumstances, the would-be appellant must make a prima facie case to the Crown court that the plea was equivocal. If the plea is found to be equivocal or involuntary, the Court must remit the case back to the magistrates' court so that a full trial can take place there (*Crown Court at Huntingdon, ex p Jordan* [1981] QB 857).

plead guilty (see chapter 7). The Court of Appeal insists, for example, that while defendants who plead guilty as a result of a charge bargain may face difficult choices between unpalatable alternatives, that is no ground for arguing that the plea of guilty was not freely made.[299] Not surprisingly, few defendants convicted on a guilty plea in the magistrates' courts mount successful challenges.[300] Here the system prioritises the core value of efficiency. Nobles and Schiff note, '[t]here were 390,344 convictions following guilty pleas in the Magistrates' Court in 2016. If 16.7% of these were appealed this would generate over 65,080 appeals!'[301] There are far fewer appeals than this: in 2018, the Crown courts received 8,240 appeals from magistrates' courts,[302] falling to 7,831 in 2019.[303] Given that the system is already creaking at the seams, there is a public interest in keeping avenues of appeal to a minimum. But this reflects the ideology of triviality that permeates magistrates' court cases (chapter 8), and the system's preference for efficiency as a result. In doing so, it ignores the problems of the pressures placed on defendants to plead guilty as soon as possible (chapters 7 and 8).

An appeal to the Crown court must be commenced within 15 days of the conclusion of the proceedings in the magistrates' courts.[304] Defendants who were legally aided[305] in the magistrates' courts will receive preliminary advice, at public expense, on whether they have grounds (i.e. reasons) for appeal, and this will cover preparing the notice of appeal. Those who were not legally aided may be able to ask for further advice under the 'advice and assistance' scheme but only if six months have elapsed since the original legally aided advice was received—taking it beyond the usual time limit—and there is something new to discuss. In all cases, however, a grant of full legal aid for appellate proceedings is subject to the application of a merits test[306] and a means test which takes into account income, savings and family circumstances.[307] If an appellant cannot obtain legal aid funding for assistance with an appeal, they might choose to pay privately or be unrepresented. For example, in one review over 90% of adult appellants were represented on appeal to the Crown court but more than half of that 90% were represented through private funding.[308] A financial deterrent remains in place in that a recovery of costs order can be made at the termination of the case—i.e. an unsuccessful appellant may be made to pay any of the prosecutor's costs that the court considers reasonable and just for the defendant to pay.[309] This also provides prosecutors with a mechanism to deter appeals, by indicating what costs might be as costs will already have been discussed in the magistrates' court on conviction. If the appellant

---

[299] *Herbert* (1991) 94 Cr App Rep 230.

[300] Only 35 appeals to the Crown court were remitted to the magistrates' courts in 1996: Mattinson J, *Criminal Appeals England and Wales, 1995 and 1996* (Research and Statistical Bulletin 3/98) (London: Home Office, 1998) table 4. More recent figures are not available.

[301] Nobles R and Schiff D, 'The Supervision of Guilty Pleas by the Court of Appeal of England and Wales—Workable Relationships and Tragic Choices' (2020) *Criminal Law Forum* (online).

[302] Sturge G, *Court statistics for England and Wales* House of Commons Briefing Paper CBP 8372 (London: House of Commons Library, 2019).

[303] Ministry of Justice, *Criminal Court statistics* (quarterly): January to March (tables) (London: Ministry of Justice, 2020b).

[304] Rule 34.2(2) of the Criminal Procedure Rules. Rule 34.2(3) allows an applicant to seek an extension of this time limit, but there is no right to an oral hearing or to reasons for a refusal to grant an extension: *Crown Court at Croydon, ex p Smith* (1983) 77 Cr App Rep 277.

[305] The terminology 'legal aid' was dropped in the wake of the Access to Justice Act 1999, which saw the replacement of the Legal Aid Board with the Legal Services Commission, but it is retained here for the sake of convenience.

[306] Access to Justice Act 1999, s.12(2). The merits test is discussed in ch 8.

[307] See <https://www.gov.uk/guidance/criminal-legal-aid-means-testing> (accessed 29 July 2020).

[308] Jacobson J, *By mistakes we learn? A review of criminal appeals against sentence*. Project Report (London: Transform Justice, 2013).

[309] Access to Justice 1999, s.17(2); Criminal Practice Directions XI Costs (2014), para 3.1.

is successful but has paid privately, they will only be able to receive their costs at legal aid rates, and will almost undoubtedly be insufficiently reimbursed for legal fees. Thus, even defendants who were right to appeal their convictions still have to pay to clear their name. This deterrent to people of poor or moderate means increases the inequality experienced at earlier stages of the system (chapter 10).

The rehearing lasts, on average, about an hour, compared with just over eight hours for a normal Crown court trial.[310] While this data is rather old, there is nothing to suggest that this has changed in recent years. The absence of a jury is one obvious factor lying behind this speed. Another is likely to be the lack of enthusiasm of legally aided lawyers to argue the case as fully as they perhaps should. Given that they are paid a fixed fee for this work, economics dictate that the faster they can dispose of the matter the better.[311] Fee cuts make 'working on appeals one of the worst paid aspects of their work'.[312] Moreover, this type of work is routinely allocated to inexperienced barristers, preparation on both sides tends to be minimal and prosecution disclosure of fresh evidence is almost unknown.[313] Where the appellant is unrepresented, there is no legally qualified court clerk to offer any help (unlike in the magistrates' court) and no duty solicitor (or barrister) scheme either. Imagine a layperson trying to counter the arguments of a prosecution barrister in an oak panelled courtroom presided over by a bewigged judge.

A further off-putting feature of these appeals is the wide power of the Crown court to vary decisions appealed or make any other order, including harsher sentences.[314] This is 'intended as a deterrent to frivolous appeals'.[315] But the system is organised around the principle of penalising defendants for resisting conviction (as expressed through sentence discounts for those pleading guilty), so prospective appellant's fears are understandable. The uncertainty of outcome and the possibility of being punished (in effect) for appealing, plus delay, expense, a reluctance to face the ordeal of a rehearing, and a wish for finality, surely dissuades many from taking matters further, and could be the cause of about 20% of those who do decide to challenge their convictions later abandoning their appeals.[316] Jacobson points to three main barriers to appealing: lack of access to good quality legal advice and representation, defendants' general resistance to the idea of appealing and the complexity of the appeals system.[317]

From 2010–19, the success rate for this type of appeal has been between 44 and 50%, with just under 2,000 appellants a year overturning their convictions and a similar number having their sentence reduced. These figures raise doubts about the quality of justice in the magistrates' courts. However, there is virtually no research into the adequacy of Crown court appellate review, or the kinds of cases that it rehears. Nearly all of the literature in this area concerns itself with the more glamorous matter of appeals to the Court of Appeal following trials on indictment. Yet the Crown court hears many thousand more appeals than the Court of Appeal each year.[318] Most of these are motoring cases.[319] We suspect that relatively wealthy 'white collar defendants' are responsible for a substantial

---

[310] Judicial and Court Statistics 2008, Cm 7697 (London: Ministry of Justice, 2009a).
[311] Nation D, 'He Can Always Appeal' (1992) 156 *Justice of the Peace* 521.   [312] Jacobson (2013: 1).
[313] Pattenden (1996: 242).
[314] Senior Courts Act 1981, s.48(4). Any new sentence must be within the sentencing limits which apply to the magistrates' court.   [315] Pattenden (1996: 219).
[316] Ministry of Justice, *Criminal Court statistics* (quarterly) (2020). This is not always allowed if the appeal has begun, or is about to begin: *Munden v Southampton Crown Court* [2005] EWHC 2512 (Admin).
[317] Jacobson (2013).
[318] MoJ (2009a) table 1.7 (Court of Appeal figures) and table 6.10 (Crown court figures). See further Naughton (2007) ch 2.   [319] Mattinson (1998) table 6.

proportion of appeals to the Crown court, which is why so few appeals are legally aided. It is also unclear—and research is needed—whether the Single Justice Procedure, which allows more people to be convicted of relatively minor offences in their absence and without even the presentational elements of due process (chapter 8) increases the success rate of appeals, though defendants who are convicted in their absence may also apply to have their conviction set aside if they can show that they were unaware that the proceedings were happening.[320]

Section 11 of the Criminal Appeal Act 1995 permits the Criminal Cases Review Commission (CCRC) (see later) to refer suspect convictions produced by the magistrates' courts—regardless of whether the defendant pleaded guilty or not. Recent research indicated that more than 20% of applications to the CCRC involve a defendant who has pleaded guilty.[321] This is a due process safety net and recognises that miscarriages of justice should be seen to be undone not only in high profile cases (such as the Birmingham Six, which originated in the Crown court) but also in situations of low visibility. Whether the CCRC provides effective redress for low-level miscarriages of justice will be examined later in this chapter.

11.4.2.2 Appeals by way of case stated to the High Court

An appeal lies to the Divisional Court where it is claimed that a "'conviction, order, determination or other proceeding" by the magistrates' court was in excess of jurisdiction or wrong in law'.[322] For example, it would be wrong in law for the magistrates to convict when they had heard no evidence to support such a decision. Since a full record of proceedings is not kept in the magistrates' court, the clerk to the justices is required to state the details of the case including the question(s) for determination by the Divisional Court. The latter court hears only legal argument and no evidence.

In principle this procedure gives defendants convicted of relatively trivial crimes access to the senior judiciary, thus allowing high quality supervision of some aspects of summary justice, not only determining the case in question but also creating precedents for the future. But applicants must ask magistrates' courts to state the case within 21 days of the final determination of it;[323] the justices may refuse to state cases when they consider applications 'frivolous';[324] and the court may require prospective appellants to enter into means-related recognisances to pay costs ultimately awarded against them.[325] Moreover, the right to appeal by way of rehearing in the Crown court is extinguished once an application has been made under the case stated procedure.[326] Legal aid is available for this type of appeal, subject to the usual merits test (but not the means test)[327] and the court may make a defence costs order at the end of the case depending on an appellant's means.[328] In 2019,

---

[320] Part 37, Criminal Procedure Rules; ss.14, 16E and 142 Magistrates' Courts Act 1980.

[321] Horne J, 'A Plea of Convenience: An Examination of the Guilty Pleas in England & Wales' PhD thesis, University of Warwick (2016). See further Nobles and Schiff (2020) and Hoyle C and Sato M, *Reasons to Doubt: Wrongful Convictions and the Criminal Cases Review Commission* (Oxford: OUP, 2019). A significant number of such applications concern defendants convicted of immigration reared offences where issues surrounding asylum were not correctly identified and relate to Crown court cases. See Holiday Y, Guild E and Mitsilegas V, *The Court of Appeal and the Criminalisation of Refugees* (London: QMUL and Birmingham: CCRC, 2018) and Sato M., Hoyle C and Speechley N-E , 'Wrongful convictions of refugees and asylum seekers: responses by the Criminal Cases Review Commission' (2017) 2 *Criminal Law Review* 106–122.

[322] Magistrates' Courts Act 1980, s.111; Senior Courts Act 1981, s.28; Criminal Procedure Rules, Part 35.

[323] Magistrates' Courts Act 1980, s.111(2).   [324] Magistrates' Courts Act 1980, s.111(5).

[325] Magistrates' Courts Act 1980, s.114; *Newcastle-upon-Tyne Justices, ex p Skinner* [1987] 1 All ER 349.

[326] Magistrates' Courts Act 1980, s.111(4).   [327] Access to Justice Act 1999, s.12(2)(b).

[328] AJA 1999, s.17(2).

the High Court received 39 appeals from the magistrates' courts by way of case stated and determined 31; 18 appeals of this nature were allowed (another one was withdrawn).[329] 2019 is only the second year since 2003 that the High Court has received less than 50 applications for case stated.

The court itself is usually made up of two High Court judges. If the appellant persuades *both* judges that an error of law has occurred[330] it is open to the Divisional Court to order a retrial in the magistrates' court although this should not be done if a rehearing would be oppressive (e.g. where a fair trial was no longer possible) or inappropriate (e.g. the offence in question is trivial).[331]

The prosecution has the same right to appeal as does the defence: an exception to the usual rule that the prosecution cannot appeal against an acquittal.[332] The Divisional Court may dispose of the case in various ways, including remitting the case to the magistrates' court with a direction to convict. It appears that the appellate courts do not regard the concept of 'jury equity' (see chapter 9) as having any application in the magistrates' courts.

11.4.2.3 Judicial review

While space prevents a detailed discussion of accountability through judicial review, applications for judicial review provide an alternative way of mounting a challenge (by either the prosecution or the defence) to a magistrates' court decision (including acquittal[333] or conviction) in the Divisional Court.[334] The purpose of such an action is to obtain a ruling that the proceedings in the lower court were tainted by illegality and to secure an appropriate remedy. An unreasonable refusal to 'state a case' can also be the subject of a judicial review action.[335] A number of procedural hurdles face the potential judicial review applicant. The application must be initiated 'promptly'—and in any event within three months of the time at which the grounds for judicial review arose.[336] Civil legal aid is available to help with the costs of mounting a judicial review application but this is subject to both a means and merits test. Permission to apply must always be obtained from the Divisional Court and in practice most applicants are denied this and are thus weeded out of the system. Of the 2,092 cases that reached permission stage in 2019, only 434 were granted permission to proceed at the first stage of review by a single High Court judge, though a further 87 were granted permission at an oral permission hearing before the full court. Only 1% of all cases lodged that reached a final hearing in 2019 were found in favour of the claimant.[337] It is not known how many successful applications result in the overturning of a conviction, as many of the cases reported in the statistics will not relate to criminal

---

[329] Ministry of Justice, Royal Courts of Justice Annual Tables – 2019 (2020b); table 3.30, online at: <https://www.gov.uk/government/organisations/ministry-of-justice/about/statistics> (accessed 29 July 2020).

[330] *Flannagan v Shaw* [1920] 3 KB 96.

[331] *Griffith v Jenkins* [1992] 1 All ER 65. Where the Divisional Court decision entails the innocence of the appellant the conviction will usually be quashed forthwith: Pattenden (1996: 224).

[332] For an example, see *DPP v P* [2007] EWHC (Admin). Since provisions of the CJA 2003 were enacted in 2005, the prosecution have also been able to ask for permission to appeal an acquittal in serious cases, but the procedure for making such a request is strict and it is seldom used (around six cases since 2005; William Dunlop, Mario Celaire, Wendell Baker, Gary Dobson, Russell Bishop and Michael Weir).

[333] It is easier for the prosecution to challenge an acquittal by way of case stated rather than judicial review, however, as case law suggests that the latter will not result in the quashing of an acquittal unless the trial itself was a nullity: *R v Hendon Justices ex parte DPP* [1994] QB 167.

[334] Senior Courts Act 1981, ss.29–31 and Civil Procedure Rules, Part 54.

[335] *Sunworld Ltd v Hammersmith and Fulham LBC* [2000] 2 All ER 837.

[336] Civil Procedure Rules 54.5.

[337] Ministry of Justice, *Civil Justice Statistics Main Tables Oct-Dec 2019* (2020a) table 2.2 <https://www.gov.uk/government/organisations/ministry-of-justice/about/statistics> (accessed 29 July 2020).

cases at all. The Divisional Court is supposed to grant permission if, on a quick perusal of the material presented, it thinks that it discloses what might on further consideration turn out to be an arguable case in favour of granting the relief sought.[338] However the Court often applies a more stringent test in order to ensure that judicial workloads remain 'manageable'.[339] There is no appeal against a decision by the full Court to refuse permission. Furthermore, the remedies available through this procedure are discretionary. This means that a convicted person may 'win' the argument but be denied a remedy because of some perceived broader interest of fairness or due administration of justice.[340] If it does quash a conviction, the Divisional Court can remit the case to the magistrates' court with directions on how to reconsider it, which might be by way of retrial.[341]

Better information about the social consequences of the present arrangements would further strengthen the case for reform. Research is needed to uncover the factors influencing decisions concerning whether or not to appeal, how people experience the appeal procedures in practice, and whether some social groups (e.g. ethnically marginalised populations, women, the young, the poor) encounter greater difficulties than others in pursuing an appeal. Above all, light needs to be shed on the impact of appeal processes and decisions on the quality of magistrates' justice.

11.4.3 Appeals from the Crown court to the Court of Appeal

An appeal lies to the Court of Appeal from the Crown court only on the ground that the conviction was 'unsafe'. Those convicted on indictment do not have the right to a rehearing. Instead, the Court of Appeal's role is essentially that of *reviewing* the fairness of the Crown court proceedings or, exceptionally, the accuracy of the result produced by the trial.

11.4.3.1 Applications for leave to appeal

Leave to appeal must be sought (normally within 28 days of conviction).[342] Most applications for leave are determined by a single High Court judge.[343] If an application for leave is refused, it may be renewed to the full Court of Appeal which will consider the matter afresh. The test to be applied when determining leave is whether the appeal seems 'reasonably arguable'.[344] These various preliminary filters are supposed to weed out 'weak' appeals. As we shall now see, however, 'weakness' may be the product of the legal and social processes through which an appeal is funnelled rather than an objective quality.

Financial considerations: legal aid and costs

It is standard for a representation order (legal aid) to be granted for trials on indictment. This also covers the cost of counsel advising on the prospect of a successful appeal against

---

[338] *IRC, ex p National Federation of Self-Employed and Small Businesses Ltd* [1982] AC 617.

[339] See Le Sueur A and Sunkin M, 'Applications for Judicial Review: The Requirement of Leave' [1992] *Public Law* 102, and the discussion by Harlow C and Rawlings R, *Law and Administration* 2nd edn (London: Butterworths, 1997) pp 530–536.

[340] E.g. *Peterborough Justices, ex p Dowler* [1996] 2 Cr App Rep 561.

[341] *R v Hereford Magistrates' Court, ex p Rowlands* [1998] QB 110.

[342] See Criminal Appeal Act 1968, s.18, sub-section 3 of which empowers the Court of Appeal to extend the time allowed for seeking leave to appeal.

[343] Section 31 of the Criminal Appeal Act 1968 enables a single judge to exercise various Court of Appeal powers. Leave is not required in the rare cases which are certified as suitable for appeal by the trial judge under the power given by s.1(2)(b). The Court of Appeal has actively discouraged trial judges from using this power: Pattenden (1996: 95–96).

[344] Auld (2001: 637), para 73.

conviction.[345] If counsel advises that there are, or may be, grounds for appeal, then legal aid also funds the professional drafting of these grounds. Alternatively, if counsel's initial advice is that there are no grounds for appeal, then the initial representation order is effectively terminated and the appellant must either pay for legal assistance privately, find a lawyer willing to act either under the more limited 'advice and assistance scheme'[346] or for free (pro bono), or try to pursue an appeal unassisted. Initial advice from counsel that grounds for appeal do not exist can thus operate as a filter, since many convicted persons may be deterred from pursuing an appeal if denied access to legal assistance.[347] Recent, though currently unpublished, research indicates that many lawyers are reluctant to provide advice in many so-called 'second opinion' cases because funding rates are very poor while the cases tend to be very complex.[348]

Once the application for leave is lodged, the Registrar of the Court of Appeal will usually refer the matter to a single judge but may bypass that stage and refer the matter to the full court. Single judges normally determine leave applications on the papers. Counsel can request an oral hearing but the Registrar will grant legal aid for this purpose 'only in very rare circumstances'.[349] If counsel are allowed to argue the application before the single judge, the expectation is that they will do so privately funded or pro bono.[350] This again privileges the rich and the lucky. The single judge can grant or refuse leave, or refer the matter to the full Court of Appeal.[351] Whenever a case is referred to the full Court of Appeal (whether by the Registrar or by the single judge) a representation order is almost invariably granted to cover the preparation and presentation of the appeal.[352] But if the single judge refuses leave to appeal, the applicant is given just 14 days in which to renew their application to the full court, except in special circumstances.[353] Legal aid is not granted to cover the legal costs of this, though it will be granted for the next stage if leave is granted. Counsel must therefore be prepared to undertake the work privately or on a pro bono basis. Since the rich can afford the legal costs involved regardless of the strength or weakness of the particular case, the legal aid rules once again breach the due process principle of equality of access to justice.

Unsuccessful appellants may be ordered to pay whatever costs the Court of Appeal considers 'just and reasonable'[354] and a recovery of defence costs order 'shall' also be made except in specified circumstances.[355] An explicit warning that unsuccessful appellants may have costs awarded against them is included in the standard form used to initiate

---

[345] Access to Justice Act 1999, s.26.   [346] This scheme is discussed in section 11.4.2.1.

[347] In one study, approximately half of the prisoners who did not appeal gave as one of their reasons the fact that a lawyer had advised them not to do so: Plotnikoff J and Woolfson R, *Information and Advice for Prisoners about Grounds for Appeal and the Appeals Process* (Royal Commission on Criminal Justice, Research Study no 18) (London: HMSO, 1993b) p 78.

[348] See ongoing research being conducted: <https://legalaidandrepresentatives.wordpress.com/> or <https://ccrc.gov.uk/research-at-the-ccrc/ongoing-research-at-the-ccrc/> (both accessed 29 July 2020).

[349] HMCTS, *Guide to Commencing Proceedings in the Court of Appeal Criminal Division* (London: HMCTS, 2018) online at: <https://assets.publishing.service.gov.uk/government/uploads/system/uploads/attachment_data/file/727918/Guide-to-proceedings-in-Court-of-Appeal-Criminal-Division-0818.pdf> (accessed 29 July 2020).   [350] HMCTS (2018).

[351] It is also possible for the judge to granted limited leave—i.e. only allow certain parts of an application to appeal to progress to the full court: *R v Hyde* [2016] EWCA Crim 1031.

[352] HMCTS (2018: A14-1).   [353] HMCTS (2018: A15-2).

[354] Prosecution of Offences Act 1985, s.18(2).

[355] Criminal Defence Service (Recovery of Defence Costs Orders) (Amendment) Regulations 2008 (SI 2008/2430), reg.4, amending Criminal Defence Service (Recovery of Defence Costs Orders) Regulations 2001. Youths, those on benefits, and those with few assets are the main exceptions.

an application for leave to appeal.[356] All this might be defensible if the filters in operation succeeded in weeding out only unarguable cases but, as we shall see, this is not so.

As with legal aid generally, claims made for work done or costs incurred may be reduced or even refused if considered unreasonable.[357] In one study, between a quarter and a third of solicitors and barristers complained that they had lost money because of these rules. It was claimed by 20% of solicitors that they no longer bothered to charge for work done in the 28 days following conviction.[358] It generally takes much longer than 28 days to find the fresh evidence or argument usually needed to win leave to appeal, and legal aid (if available at all) covers relatively little of this work.[359] More recent ongoing research suggests that many providers have simply stopped offering publicly funded or pro bono legal services in relation to appeal cases, that the lawyers who still do appeals work often do so at a loss for their firms, that the work is demoralising because of the complexity and bureaucratic barriers involved, and that the Legal Aid Agency is seen as a significant barrier to the work because its decisions about what are considered reasonable costs are often irrational.[360]

The guidelines prepared by the Court of Appeal require solicitors to address the issue of appeal without waiting for a request for advice from their clients. 'Immediately following the conclusion of the case, the legal representatives should see the defendant and counsel should express orally his [sic] final view as to the prospects of a successful appeal . . .'[361] Where the advice is positive, counsel must draft and send signed grounds of appeal to the defence solicitor 'as soon as possible'.[362] The defence solicitor must then notify the client, and lodge the appeal papers with the Registrar at the Court of Appeal.[363]

Bottoms and McClean reported that many of the convicted persons they interviewed saw the appeals process 'as a somewhat remote affair, a lawyer's procedure where they essentially had to rely on the professionals'.[364] This heavy reliance on counsel has drawbacks, especially as many become increasingly unwilling to provide a second opinion in a potential appeal case. Counsel are particularly unlikely to advise that errors by lawyers might provide grounds for appeal, which probably accounts for the low number of appeals drafted by counsel which assert this compared with those drafted by convicted persons themselves.[365] A further hurdle is that, when providing a second opinion, lawyers are now obliged to consult with the trial lawyers to ascertain their view about the prospective appellants' assertions.[366] Legal advice, when offered at all, is predominantly against appealing, or overestimates the risks involved, deterring all but the most committed of convicted persons from taking any further action.

[356] Form NG, pursuant to CrPR 39.3(1), (2) available from Ministry of Justice website.
[357] Criminal Defence Service (Funding) Order 2007, Sch 4, para 1.
[358] Plotnikoff and Woolfson (1993b: 83).
[359] The Angela Cannings case provides an example of some of these difficulties. See Cannings A, with Lloyd Davies M, *Against All Odds: A Mother's Fight to Prove her Innocence* (London: Time Warner Books, 2006) p 223.
[360] See <https://legalaidandrepresentatives.wordpress.com/> or <https://ccrc.gov.uk/research-at-the-ccrc/ongoing-research-at-the-ccrc/> (accessed 29 July 2020). Reporting anticipated for 2021.
[361] HMCTS (2018: A1–1). [362] Ibid. [363] CrimPR 39.2.
[364] Bottoms A and McClean J, *Defendants in the Criminal Process* (London: Routledge & Kegan Paul, 1976) p 178.
[365] Pattenden (1996: 105–106). In 55 of 160 CCRC case files reviewed for one ongoing study, the applicant's primary complaint was that they had been poorly represented by trial counsel (See <https://legalaidandrepresentatives.wordpress.com/> or <https://ccrc.gov.uk/research-at-the-ccrc/ongoing-research-at-the-ccrc/> (accessed 29 July 2020)).
[366] *R v Achogbuo* [2014] EWCA Crim 657; *R v McCook* [2014] EWCA Crim 734; *R v Lee* [2014] EWCA Crim 2928; *R v Grant-Murray and others* [2017] EWCA Crim 1228.

Temporal factors: time limits, delays and the loss of time 'rules'

The four-week time limit for lodging an appeal causes difficulties for some appellants, especially those that do not receive legal advice (as they are supposed to) after their trial ends in conviction. Those wrongfully convicted are often in shock at the conclusion of the trial, are not told or do not understand the time limit, and understandably lack confidence in their legal representatives. The limit can be waived if a reasoned application is lodged at the same time as the application for leave to appeal,[367] but this is unlikely unless the proposed appeal has obvious merit. Historically, the Court of Appeal has been unsympathetic to applicants who have tried to excuse their failure to meet the 28-day deadline by reference to financial difficulties.[368]

Sometimes the common law is 'clarified' in such a way that convictions based on the old understanding of the law were wrongful. This was just the situation in *Jogee*[369] (chapter 10) but the Court of Appeal was swift to add that out of time appeals based on a change in the law will not be readily granted. In fact the appellant must demonstrate 'substantial injustice' due to a change in the law; simply being the victim of a potential wrongful conviction is not considered enough.[370] This has proved to be a substantial barrier to appeals based on a change in the law.[371] The 14-day limit for seeking to overturn a single judge's refusal to grant leave to appeal is even less likely to be extended. Generally, it is clear that the Court of Appeal places great weight on the value of finality when considering requests for out-of-time appeals, particularly when those requests originate from those seen as morally undeserving.[372]

The incentive to appeal is much reduced for those imprisoned citizens who are due to be released before the appeal can be heard.[373] Delays in hearing cases will therefore be one determinant of the overall level of appeals. In 2017, the average waiting time for an appeal against conviction to be heard was 11.7 months.[374] The expedition required by the appellant in initiating appeals is not similarly required of judges. This is not the fault of

---

[367] CrimPR 36.4 and 39.3(1)(e)(ii); *R v Wilson* [2016] EWCA Crim 65.

[368] *Moore* (1923) 17 Cr App Rep 155; *Cullum* (1942) 28 Cr App Rep 150.

[369] *Jogee, Ruddock v The Queen* [2016] UKSC 8.

[370] *R v Johnson & Ors* [2016] EWCA Crim 1613. See further *R v Ordu* [2017] EWCA Crim 4 and Mrs Justice Cheema-Grubb DBE (2018) Criminal Bar Association Winter Conference Keynote Speech (London: CBA). For an only just out of time application, see *Ramsden* [1972] Crim LR 547. For discussion of the post-Criminal Appeal Act 1995 case law on this point see Kerrigan K, 'Unlocking the Human Rights Floodgates' [2000] *Criminal Law Review* 71 at 76–77 and, for the CCRC implications, Cooper S, 'Appeals, Referrals and Substantial Injustice' [2009] *Criminal Law Review* 152.

[371] Sir Richard Buxton, 'Joint Enterprise: Jogee, Substantial Injustice and the Court of Appeal' (2017) 2 *Criminal Law Review* 123; Krebs B, 'Joint Enterprise, Murder and Substantial Injustice: The First Successful Appeal Post-Jogee: R v Crilly [2018] EWCA Crim 168' (2018) 82(3) *Journal of Criminal Law* 209–211; Leggett Z, 'The Test for "Substantial Injustice" After Jogee and Johnson: R v Towers and Another [2019] EWCA 198 (Crim)' (2019) 83(5) *Journal of Criminal Law* 420–424.

[372] For example, *Richardson* [1999] Crim LR 563 where the Court refused an application for leave to appeal out of time even though it conceded that the delay was not the applicant's fault and that his conviction was undoubtedly 'unsafe'. For discussion, see Roberts S, 'Fresh Evidence and Factual Innocence in the Criminal Division of the Court of Appeal' (2017a) 81(4) *Journal of Criminal Law* 303–327; Roberts S, 'Post-Conviction Review in England and Wales: Perpetuating and Rectifying Miscarriages of Justice' in Lennon G, King C and McCartney C (eds), *Counter-terrorism, Constitutionalism and Miscarriages of Justice: A Festschrift for Professor Clive Walker* (London Hart Publishing, 2019) pp 249–267.

[373] 11% of those deciding not to appeal gave this as one of their reasons in the study by Plotnikoff and Woolfson (1993b: 104).

[374] HM Courts and Tribunals Judiciary, *Court of Appeal (Criminal Division) Annual Report 2016–17* (2017) <https://www.judiciary.uk/wp-content/uploads/2018/08/coa-criminal-div-2016-17-2.pdf> (accessed 29 July 2020).

the judges, with their 'crushing' case load,[375] but of government in not providing adequate resources. Judges sometimes appear to cut corners to minimise delay. Lord Justice Auld observed that provisional notes made by judges allotted to give judgment, whilst speeding up the processing of cases, 'often suggests to those in the court that they have made their mind up before hearing argument in the matter'.[376] Malleson argues that it is difficult to 'overturn' the preliminary view constructed by the court before it even hears the appeal. The court 'decides cases in hours which have occupied the trial courts for days, weeks or even months.'[377]

The loss of time 'rule', under which the Court of Appeal may order that some or all of the time spent appealing will not count towards a sentence of imprisonment, is also off-putting.[378] This is a classic crime control device aimed at deterring prisoners from exercising their 'right' of appeal. Changes in the 1960s which removed some of the disincentives to appealing and made it easier for convictions to be quashed, resulted in a quadrupling of applications to the Court of Appeal. The Lord Chief Justice responded by announcing that in future single judges hearing applications for leave deemed 'frivolous' could, and should, order loss of time.[379] The number of applications was instantly halved and remained at the lower figure of around 6,000 a year for several years. In *Gray*, the court said that 'the only means the court has of discouraging unmeritorious applications which waste precious time and resources is by using the powers given to us by Parliament in the Criminal Appeal Act 1968 and the Prosecution of Offences Act 1985'.[380] This seem to have had an effect; since 2016, the number of applications received has dropped to a new low of 4,580 in 2019.[381] The single judge can invite the court to consider a loss of time order if the applicant seeks to renew a refusal of leave. An appellant cannot merely rely on an advocate's advice that grounds of appeal exist to avoid a loss of time order being made, as this is not considered to be a sufficient answer to the question about the merits of an appeal.[382]

Applicants are asked for their representations as to why a loss of time direction should not be made.[383] The form on which appeals must be lodged (Form NG) spells out the loss of time provisions and requires appellants in custody to confirm by signature that they appreciate their significance. These deterrent messages make it still more unlikely that convicted persons whose lawyers advise against an appeal (or fail to give any advice at all) will pursue the matter. Denied legal aid, and faced with the potent threat of loss of time, the prospect of launching an appeal is not enticing. While loss of time orders are rare, their use and the length of time lost has crept up in the last 10 years.[384] There seems little

---

[375] Pattenden (1996: 56). The case load has been added to in recent years because the government increased prosecution appeal rights: the CJA 2003 granted the prosecution (but not the defence) the right of interlocutory appeal to the Court of Appeal against rulings by a trial judge (e.g. regarding the admissibility of evidence), but at the price (s.58(8)) that if the appeal fails an acquittal will necessarily follow: *R v Y* [2008] EWCA Crim 10 (where the introduction of this provision was described [19] as a 'significant shift of rights towards the Crown as against an individual' – see commentary by Ormerod to the case report at [2008] Crim LR 466). See also *R v O, J and S* [2008] EWCA Crim 463; [2008] Crim LR 892 (where it is noted that by that time there had already been 60 reported cases concerning this type of prosecution appeal).

[376] Auld (2001: 644, para 85).

[377] Malleson K, 'Decision-making in the Court of Appeal: The Burden of Proof in an Inquisitorial Process' (1997) *International Journal of Evidence and Proof* 175 at 186.

[378] Criminal Appeal Act 1968, s.29.

[379] Practice Note [1970] 1 WLR 663. Recently reaffirmed in *Kuimba* [2005] All ER (D) 110.

[380] *R v Gray & Ors* [2014] EWCA Crim 2372.

[381] Ministry of Justice, *Royal Courts of Justice Annual Tables – 2019* (London: MoJ, 2020b).

[382] *R v Gray and Others* [2014] EWCA Crim 2372. See also *R v Hart and Others* [2006] EWCA Crim 3239 [43].

[383] HMCTS (2018: A16-4).

[384] 2 Hare Court, *The Court Of Appeal Threatens More Loss Of Time Orders For Hopeless Appeals* (2015) online at: <https://www.2harecourt.com/training-and-knowledge/the-court-of-appeal-threatens-more-loss-of-time-orders-for-hopeless-appeals/> (accessed 29 July 2020).

prospect of getting rid of the loss of time rules. They chime with the managerial ethos that has become so prominent within the courts and a challenge to them on the basis that they infringe the ECHR has failed.[385]

Appeal rates in context

In 2019, 15% of applicants were granted leave by a single judge. Between 2016 and 2019, around 700–800 of the approximate 2,500 applicants who were refused initial leave to appeal renewed their application to the full court, which granted around 300.[386] Thus the vast majority of those subjected to this double-filter are weeded out. The success rate in terms of grant of leave of those who have their applications referred directly to the full court is, as one would expect, higher. But such applicants have only won the right to have their appeal heard. Most of those whose appeals are actually heard by the court fail to overturn their convictions.

The number of successful appeals against Crown court convictions is proportionately very low. The Court of Appeal proudly observed that in the year to September 2008 'less than 1% of [Crown court] convictions result in successful appeals. This clearly demonstrates good reason for confidence in the criminal justice system...'.[387] Roberts found a similarly very low success rate when focusing on appeals which related to the use of fresh evidence.[388] In 2019, 77 of 204 appeals against conviction were allowed, and only 24 of those resulted in a retrial being ordered.[389] So, of over 1,000 initial applications to appeal, only 77 were successful. The statistics need to be understood as the product of the dominant value of finality as woven into appellate law and procedure. Walker observed a relatively short-lived rise in applications to the Court of Appeal and 'quashings around the time of the major Irish miscarriage of justice cases' in the early 1990s.[390] Thus it seems that the Court of Appeal became more sensitive to due process values when public concern about miscarriages of justice was at its height, but that this has since waned.

Those who reach the court are not necessarily the appellants with the strongest cases. As Malleson notes, serious offences attracting long custodial sentences, relatively rare in the Crown court, are the staple diet of the Court of Appeal.[391] Since more run of the mill cases are allocated to less experienced Crown court judges—under whom miscarriages of justice might be expected to occur more frequently—it appears that the system operates so as to exclude the majority of potential appeals: 'The appeal process can be likened to an obstacle race: only the determined, strong and well prepared will reach the end—and they are likely to be found in the higher reaches of the offence and sentence scale' (Malleson 1991: 328). The true function of the various filters within the appeal system is not so much to weed out weak appeals as to deter all but the most committed from challenging their conviction.[392] The strength of this commitment will depend as much on such factors as

---

[385] *Monnell and Morris v United Kingdom* (1987) 10 EHRR 205.

[386] See Ministry of Justice, *Royal Courts of Justice Annual Tables – 2019* (London: MoJ, 2020b).

[387] Court of Appeal Criminal Division, *Review of the Legal Year 2007/2008*, para 1.7 (available from <http://www.hmcourts-service.gov.uk/cms/1497.htm> – accessed 5 January 2010).

[388] Roberts S, 'Fresh Evidence and Factual Innocence in the Criminal Division of the Court of Appeal' (2017a) 81(4) *Journal of Criminal Law* 303–327. For critique and an alternative analysis, see Dargue P, 'The Safety of Convictions in the Court of Appeal: Fresh Evidence in the Criminal Division through an Empirical Lens' (2019) 83(6) *Journal of Criminal Law* 433–449.

[389] Ministry of Justice, *Royal Courts of Justice Annual Tables – 2019* (London: MoJ, 2020b) Table 3.8.

[390] Walker C, 'The Judiciary' in Walker C and Starmer K (eds), *Miscarriages of Justice* (London: Blackstone, 1999c) p 221.

[391] Malleson K, 'Miscarriages of Justice and the Accessibility of the Court of Appeal' [1991] *Criminal Law Review* 323 at 325. This is confirmed by more recent statistics: Mattinson (1998: table 14).

[392] A further appeal lies (with leave) to the Supreme Court but only in the rare cases where the Court of Appeal is prepared to certify that a point of law of general public importance is involved.

the availability of legal advice and legal aid, the quality of legal advice, sentence length, and the fear of loss of time, as on the merits of the case or the intensity of grievance nursed.

11.4.3.2 The grounds for appeal

It is self-evident that the narrower the grounds for appeal, the harder it is to obtain leave to challenge a conviction. In understanding why relatively few of those convicted in the Crown court challenge their convictions it is therefore crucial to examine the grounds on which people may appeal.

Fairness and reliability: the meaning of an unsafe conviction

The Criminal Appeal Act 1995 replaced the provisions of s.2 Criminal Appeal Act 1968 and substituted for the three earlier grounds of appeal the single ground that the Court of Appeal thinks the conviction 'is unsafe'. But unsafe in what sense? The Act does not say. One possible interpretation was that the 1995 Act required the Court to dismiss an appeal if in no doubt that an appellant was guilty of the offence committed, regardless of any procedural errors or malpractice associated with the prosecution and trial. This apparent shift towards crime control was not acknowledged in Parliament during the passing of the legislation, however. In *Chalkley and Jeffries*[393] the Court of Appeal interpreted s.2 as meaning that the court could not overturn a reliable guilty verdict however unfair the trial might have been. In doing so the appellate judges were acknowledging that their existing practice was predominantly based on crime control values. The Court of Appeal has consistently championed the value of finality over that of procedural fairness.[394] Nonetheless, an interpretation of the Criminal Appeal Act which ruled out *any* possibility of quashing a factually reliable conviction, even when the trial had been tainted by blatant unfairness, would mark a break with the past and threaten the legitimacy of the courts. The Court of Appeal then changed tack by revisiting the question of whether abuse of process rendered a conviction 'unsafe'. It determined that the intention of Parliament had been to restate the existing practice of the court. On that basis it concluded that 'unsafe' did (or at least, could) include a conviction achieved through an abuse of process.[395]

This is one area in which the growing influence of the human rights perspective can be detected.[396] Article 6 of the European Convention secures to an accused the right to a 'fair' trial. If unfairness at a trial could not lead in itself to the quashing of a conviction, the Court of Appeal would arguably be failing to protect a fundamental human right. The denial of a fair trial and the failure of the appellate courts to cure this defect could then lead to an adverse finding against the UK by the European Court of Human Rights.

This is exactly what occurred in *Condron v UK*: 'the question whether or not the rights of the defence guaranteed to an accused under Art 6 of the Convention were secured in any given case cannot be assimilated to a finding that his conviction was safe in the absence of any enquiry into the issue of fairness'.[397] Acknowledging that ruling, the Court of Appeal in *Davis, Johnson and Rowe*[398] subsequently accepted that a conviction 'may be unsafe even where there is no doubt about guilt but the trial process has been "vitiated

---

[393] [1998] 2 All ER 155. This case is also examined in ch 3 (arrest) and in ch 11 (in discussing exclusion of evidence).

[394] See generally Malleson K, 'Appeals against Conviction and the Principle of Finality' (1994) 21 *Journal of Law and Society* 151; Roberts S, 'Reviewing the Function of Criminal Appeals in England and Wales' (2017b) 1 *Institute of Law Journal* 3–27.

[395] *Mullen* [1999] 2 Cr App Rep 143.

[396] For a review of the relevant case law, see Emmerson et al, *Human Rights and Criminal Justice* 2nd edn (London: Sweet & Maxwell, 2007) paras 17–25–17–41.

[397] (2001) 31 EHRR 1.   [398] [2001] 1 Cr App R 8 [56].

by serious unfairness or significant legal misdirection." ' The use of the word 'may' in this formulation is crucial. The court went on to note that 'the effect of any unfairness upon the safety of the conviction will vary according to its nature and degree' and rejected the argument that a breach of Art 6 would inexorably lead to a conviction being quashed. In short, the court's view is that only when *it* takes the view that serious procedural unfairness has occurred may otherwise reliable convictions become 'unsafe'.[399] Even then, the court will take into account the countervailing 'principle' that those reliably but unfairly convicted of grave crimes should have their convictions upheld on appeal.[400] That judicial wiggle room is valued by the appeal courts is also evident from *Togher*:[401] (i) 'if it would be right to stop a prosecution on the basis that it was an abuse of process, this Court would be *most unlikely* to conclude that if there was a conviction despite this fact, the conviction should not be set aside'; (ii) 'we consider that if a defendant has been denied a fair trial it will *almost be inevitable* that the conviction will be regarded as unsafe' [our emphasis]. This judicial vacillation for several years over such an important matter is deplorable. So is Parliament's failure to spell out what an 'unsafe' conviction might be. Parliament failed in its duty to state the law clearly. If Parliament and the courts are worried about the effect on public confidence (AKA, the populist media) of 'letting the guilty go free' they can always order retrials more.[402]

Unfortunately the ECtHR takes ECHR rights no more seriously, and allows domestic courts a wide margin of appreciation in relation to the Art 6 right to a fair trial.[403] Convictions may now be based solely on evidence presumed inadmissible until the Criminal Justice Act 2003 was enacted so long as the judge has considered 'counterbalancing principles' and has conducted an 'overall examination' of the fairness of the proceedings.[404] One difficulty the ECtHR has is that the Convention itself merely requires an effective remedy (Art 13) for a breach of one of its rights, while s.8 of the Human Rights Act 1998 confers discretion on the Court of Appeal to grant such relief or remedy as it considers just and appropriate.[405] Thus, one technique for upholding a conviction obtained through proceedings tainted by unfairness is for the court to claim that it has removed the taint through its own examination of the evidence. *Togher* celebrates this power while subsequent cases appear to broaden the circumstances in which it may be used.[406] The difficulty here, of course, is that the Court of Appeal is likely to be influenced by its awareness that the jury arrived at a guilty verdict, and by its knowledge of matters that may have been kept from the jury precisely because they were thought more prejudicial than probative (such as previous convictions). While the relatively open-ended nature of the powers available to the criminal courts in determining whether to uphold reliable but unfairly

---

[399] See also *R v Caley-Knowles; R v Jones (Iorwerth)* [2007] 1 Cr App R 13 (holding that a wrongful direction to a jury to convict does not necessarily render the conviction unsafe). This position was restated in *Brown* [2015] EWCA Crim 1328, which relied on the principles stated in *McInnes v HM Advocate* [2010] UKSC 7 that: 'The trial will be adjudged unfair if, but only if, the appeal court concludes that the non-disclosure gave rise to a real risk of prejudice to the defence. This in turn depends upon whether the appeal court regards the non-disclosure as having denied the defence the real possibility of securing a different outcome.'

[400] *Alfrey* [2005] EWCA Crim 3232.   [401] [2001] 3 All ER 463.

[402] For a range of discussions see Nobles R and Schiff D, *Understanding Miscarriages of Justice* (Oxford: OUP, 2000) ch 3 and their 'Due Process and Dirty Harry Dilemmas: Criminal Appeals and the Human Rights Act' (2001) 64 Modern Law Review 911, at p 922; Spencer (2007: 837).

[403] *Ibrahim v United Kingdom* (2015) 61 EHRR 9.

[404] *Al-Khawaja and Tahery v UK* (Application nos 26766/05 and 22228/06) (2011); *Ibrahim* [2012] EWCA Crim 837. For discussion, see Biral M, 'The Right to Examine or Have Examined Witnesses as a *Minimum* Right for a Fair Trial' (2014) 22(4) European Journal of Crime, Criminal Law and Criminal Justice 331–350.

[405] See further Dennis I, 'Fair Trials and Safe Convictions' (2003) 56 Current Legal Problems 211.

[406] Taylor and Ormerod (2004) at p 276 et seq. See, for example, *Steele & Ors* [2006] EWCA Crim 195 [37].

obtained convictions may enable them to do substantive justice (as they see it), the result is an unstable and unpredictable body of appellate case law.[407] This offends rule of law ideals, making it difficult for defence lawyers and others to judge when an appeal is worthwhile.

Reviewing 'mistakes' by juries: lurking doubts

Another basis on which a conviction might be regarded as 'unsafe' is where, despite the lack of any procedural error or unfairness, the jury is thought to have reached the wrong conclusion. It was not until the Criminal Appeal Act 1907 that convicted persons were given the opportunity to appeal on the basis that a factual mistake about their guilt had been made by a jury. The court chose to interpret its powers in the narrowest possible way. Prior to the mid-1960s, it refused to overturn the verdict of the jury unless it was one which no reasonable jury could have arrived at.[408] The crime control value of finality was clearly paramount.

This stance had a certain logic to it given that the Court of Appeal was not set up to rehear cases. Whereas the jury sees the witnesses and exhibits, and hears oral evidence, the Court of Appeal usually does no more than review the conduct of the trial as recorded in writing at the time. The jury might thus appear to be in a better position to assess the issue of guilt.[409] And to overturn jury verdicts on a frequent basis would call into question the assumption that trial procedures routinely produce correct verdicts, and that the job of deciding guilt properly lies with the jury, thus draining confidence in criminal justice.[410] On the other hand a concern with protecting the innocent might justify giving the benefit of any appellate doubt about guilt to a convicted person. The 1907 Act embodied the latter approach.[411] But the Court of Appeal preferred to act as if it had been given narrower powers, so Parliament tried again by passing the Criminal Appeal Act 1966. This directed it to quash convictions which were 'unsafe or unsatisfactory'. At first it seemed that the court took heed, introducing this 'lurking doubt' test:[412]

> the court must in the end ask itself a subjective question, whether we are content to let the matter stand as it is, or whether there is not some lurking doubt in our minds which makes us wonder whether an injustice has been done.

It was simply asserted in this case that the jury had come to the wrong verdict. At first blush it would seem that the lurking doubt test hoisted the value of avoiding wrongful convictions above that of finality. But whatever its rhetorical significance, it was crime control business as usual for the Court of Appeal thereafter: 'the application of the "lurking doubt" concept requires reasoned analysis of the evidence or the trial process, or both, which leads to the inexorable conclusion that the conviction is unsafe.'[413] So the doctrine is

---

[407] Roberts in Lennon et al (2014: 249–267).

[408] The fact that members of the court thought that they themselves would have returned a different verdict was, according to the judgment in *Hopkins-Husson* (1949) 34 Cr App Rep 47, 'no ground for refusing to accept the verdict of the jury, which is the constitutional method of trial in this country'. For further discussion, see Farrell A and Givelber D, 'Liberation Reconsidered: Understanding Why Judges And Juries Disagree About Guilt' (2010) 100(4) *Journal of Criminal Law and Criminology* 1549–1586.

[409] Appearances can be deceptive though. Just as in the interrogation context (see section 5.5) assessments of reliability based on mode of speech, appearance or behaviour are likely to be flawed, reflecting misconceptions about how liars present themselves. See McEwan J, *The Verdict of the Court* (Oxford: Hart, 2003) pp 104–114.

[410] See further Nobles and Schiff (2006: 252). Similar arguments no doubt influence the Court of Appeal in its discouragement of appeals on the basis that a judge has made a mistake of fact (e.g. in determining whether a confession was obtained by oppression and thus should not be heard by the jury): Pattenden R, 'The Standards of Review for Mistake of Fact in the Court of Appeal, Criminal Division' [2009] *Criminal Law Review* 15.

[411] Pattenden (1996: 141).   [412] *Cooper* [1969] 1 QB 267 at 271.

[413] *Pope* [2012] EWCA Crim 2241

only used on an exceptional basis,[414] with Dargue recording that, in a study of murder and rape cases between 2010 and 2016, 'lurking doubt' claims were successful in just three out of 30 cases.[415] Overall, fewer than one conviction per year is quashed on this basis, making it of little practical use to would-be appellants.[416]

The admission of fresh evidence at appeal

When the Court of Appeal was set up in 1907 it was given the power to go beyond merely reviewing the papers relating to the original trial. Under s.9 it could order the production of any document, exhibit or other thing connected with the proceedings and order that witnesses attend for examination either before the court or a commissioner appointed by the court. Parliament's intention was to allow the court ample power to reopen a case and get at the truth. The Court of Appeal interpreted these powers restrictively and nearly always refused to admit new evidence on appeal. Most notably, the court imposed a requirement that the evidence which an appellant wished to call must not have been available (in the sense that it could have been produced with reasonable diligence) at the trial.[417] Parliament responded in 1964 by introducing a new power allowing the court to order a retrial after the admission on appeal of fresh evidence.[418] But the court's restrictive approach to the reception of fresh evidence was maintained.[419] So Parliament tried again. It imposed a duty on the court to admit credible evidence which would have been admissible at trial whenever there was a reasonable explanation for the failure to adduce it earlier.[420] In practice, however, the court remained reluctant to step outside what it conceived to be its limited review function by admitting fresh evidence. Where the failure to adduce evidence at the original trial was attributable to a mistake on the part of the defendant's lawyers, the court rarely permitted that evidence to be heard on appeal.[421]

The court has occasionally received new evidence of matters arising subsequent to the trial. As such evidence, by definition, could not have been adduced at trial, its reception amounts to an implicit acknowledgement that the court's function goes beyond reviewing the propriety of what happened in the lower courts. But the grudging nature of the court's stance in this regard belies any commitment to protecting the innocent from wrongful conviction. Witnesses who wish to retract their trial testimony are not welcomed by the court as converts to the pursuit of truth and justice. As a judgment in 1990 put it: 'the mere fact that a prosecution witness chooses to come forward after the trial to assert that his evidence at trial was perjured will rarely provide a basis for permitting him to give evidence or for interfering with the conviction.'[422]

---

[414] Nobles R and Schiff D, 'After Ten Years: An Investment in Justice?' in Naughton M (ed), *The Criminal Cases Review Commission. Hope for the Innocent?* (Basingstoke: Palgrave Macmillan, 2012) pp 151–166.

[415] Dargue P, 'The Safety of Convictions in the Court of Appeal: Fresh Evidence in the Criminal Division through an Empirical Lens' (2019) 83(6) *Journal of Criminal Law* 433–449.

[416] Malleson (1993: 24); Pattenden (1996: 146–147); Roberts S, 'The Royal Commission on Criminal Justice and Factual Innocence: Remedying Wrongful Convictions in the Court of Appeal' (2004) 1(2) *Justice Journal* 86.

[417] Pattenden (1996: 130–132).   [418] Criminal Appeal Act 1964, s.1.   [419] Pattenden (1996: 137).

[420] Criminal Appeal Act 1966, s.5. The fresh evidence provisions were subsequently re-enacted in the Criminal Appeal Act 1968, s.23.

[421] The current position on 'incompetence cases' is that there must be conduct or failure by counsel which can be criticised and which resulted in the subsequent conviction being unsafe: *Grey* [2005] EWCA Crim 1413 [62]. See further the infamous case of Luke Dougherty, discussed at length in ch 2 of the *Report of the Departmental Committee on Evidence of Identification in Criminal Cases*, HCP 338 (1976).

[422] Turner cited in Malleson (1993: 10).

New evidence is sometimes allowed in serious cases if the evidence of innocence is overwhelming.[423] Taking the 'shaken baby' syndrome cases as an example, it is difficult to avoid the conclusion that what chiefly influences the court in these matters is whether it is likely to attract criticism for failing to reopen a case that aroused public concern.[424] Otherwise, the value of finality dominates its thinking and the inaccuracy of the original verdict is of subsidiary concern. This is illustrated more recently by *Nunn*.[425] This involved post-conviction disclosure of material that was not capable of forensic examination at the time of the original offence, but later expertise meant that it could subsequently be analysed. Much fresh evidence is achieved through later examination of case-related documents or exhibits, but the police refused to disclose the material when the defence asked for it. When this case went to the Supreme Court, it was an opportunity for the courts to balance the pre- and post-disclosure regimes, especially given that we know from our discussion in earlier chapters (7 and 8 in particular), that pre-trial disclosure is far from comprehensive and/or reliable. The Supreme Court, however, continued to take a narrow approach to post-conviction disclosure, making it more difficult for the potentially wrongfully convicted to access materials that could lead to a fresh evidence appeal. The effect of *Nunn*:

> . . . is that the State only need consider requests to access exhibits (using 'sensible judgement'), if there is a 'real prospect' that it will cast doubt on the safety of the conviction. Because of this discretion, even supposing material has been correctly retained and stored, getting access to it then is a lottery. Not only is permission required of the investigating force, who may not be motivated to facilitate the re-opening of a case they consider closed (with an assumed concomitant criticism of their initial investigation), but decisions are made on a piecemeal basis, sometimes even exhibit by exhibit . . . The post-conviction disclosure regime inhibits the ability of investigators to inquire into potential miscarriages of justice, leaving appellants unable to secure leave to appeal.[426]

Research in 2016 showed that 14% of Court of Appeal applications and cases raised fresh evidence.[427] The success rate for these appeals was, at 7% (of the 42 cases), lower than in an earlier study in 2002, and lower than it had been in 1990 (35%).[428] So the limited impact of fresh evidence does not stem from the specific judicial powers but rather reflects judicial working rules: deference to jury verdicts, and devotion to the principle of finality. However, when full court hearings of fresh evidence are considered (excluding initially refused applications), the chances of success on this ground improve greatly.[429]

---

[423] One such unusual case was *Cannings* [2004] 1 All ER 725. The death of a baby was attributed to 'shaken baby' syndrome, but there were no visible injuries to back up the medical theory that the baby must have suffered non-accidental injury because it was statistically highly improbable that the causes of death could have been medical. The fresh evidence that led to the child's mother's conviction being quashed was new medical thinking rejecting this statistical approach.

[424] See the discussion of the case law in Pattenden (1996: 135).

[425] *R (on the application of Nunn) v Chief Constable of Suffolk Police (Justice and Others Intervening)* [2014] UKSC 37.

[426] McCartney C and Shorter L, 'Exacerbating injustice: Post-conviction disclosure in England and Wales' (2019) 59 *International Journal of Law, Crime and Justice* 1–10 at 7–9.

[427] Roberts S, 'Fresh Evidence and Factual Innocence in the Criminal Division of the Court of Appeal' (2017a) 81(4) *Journal of Criminal Law* 303–327. [428] Roberts (2004).

[429] Dargue studied 472 cases between 2010 and 2016, and found that fresh evidence was raised in 130 cases. Fifty-nine of those 130 cases were successful appeals (45%) (though it should be noted that a not insignificant proportion of these cases were referrals form the CCRC, which skews the statistics somewhat given that the Court of Appeal must accept a CCRC reference). Dargue critiques Robert's analysis on the basis that she considered applications that were refused permission as well as full appeals, while Dargue's initial analysis was limited to rape and murder cases in which permission had been granted. See Dargue P, 'The Safety of Convictions in the Court of Appeal: Fresh Evidence in the Criminal Division through an Empirical Lens' (2019) 83(6) *Journal of Criminal Law* 433–449.

Once fresh evidence has been admitted, the Court of Appeal should assess the impact of the new evidence for itself, but *may* test its provisional view by posing the hypothetical question of whether that evidence, if presented at the original trial, might reasonably have affected the jury's decision to convict.[430] While the court has made clear that failure to raise an issue at trial does not automatically prevent it being received on appeal,[431] the court makes a clear distinction between matters that have not been raised and matters that could have been raised but were not pursued at the time. So, in *Foy*,[432] the court was critical of the practice of 'expert shopping' in which an alternative, more favourable, expert opinion had been sought. It seems that only where there has been a breakthrough in expert opinion, or some new information, will fresh evidence of this nature be admissible.[433] One problem with this is that history teaches us that experts do make mistakes, and sometimes serious ones, as the case of Angela Cannings—who was wrongfully convicted of murdering her two infant sons in 2002, on the basis of medical expert evidence—demonstrates. Here, again, we see the court giving priority to principles of finality and jury deference.

We saw earlier that the Court of Appeal is reluctant to admit fresh evidence of innocence on the basis that jury trial is the proper place for hearing and weighing evidence. This works against appellants' interests. But if fresh evidence is admitted, how a jury might have reacted to that evidence becomes, at best, a matter to which the court may have regard. This also works against appellants' interests. Whereas a jury at a retrial would not know of the quashed conviction, of the defendant's previous convictions and so forth, the Court of Appeal is privy to such prejudicial material. Given the court's historical stance of rarely ordering retrials in fresh evidence cases, the next best option from an appellant's point of view is for the judges to put themselves in an imaginary jury's shoes. Instead the judges have decided that they will decide the matter from their own point of view. It seems that the jury's role of determining guilt or innocence is regarded as constitutionally sacrosanct only when that works against the interests of appellants. But does it matter all that much whether the Court of Appeal evaluates fresh evidence from its own, or from a jury's, point of view? In legal theory, it should, but in reality it probably does not. Given that the Court of Appeal is privy to much prejudicial information, if it is set upon upholding a conviction it can easily justify this whichever test it applies. One only has to read appellate judgments to discover how easy it is to manipulate the relevant tests in order to arrive at a desired result.[434] Perhaps the only way to persuade the judiciary of the need for more due process is to demonstrate that miscarriages of justice remain a frequent occurrence. This brings us to the subject of post-appeal review.

11.4.4 Post-appeal: The Criminal Cases Review Commission

11.4.4.1 References by the Home Secretary to the Court of Appeal (prior to 1997)

Prior to 1997, unsuccessful appellants' next avenue to seek a review of their case was through the Home Secretary, who had the power to reopen a case. On average, the Home Office (Division C3) received 700–800 requests each year to reopen cases in this way, but agreed

---

[430] *Pendleton* [2002] 1 WLR 72. The 'jury impact test' was held to be equally applicable to 'fresh argument' cases: *Poole and Mills* [2003] EWCA Crim 1753 [64].

[431] *R v Erskine; R v Williams* [2009] EWCA Crim 1425.

[432] *R v Foy* [2020] EWCA Crim 270.

[433] Thomas M, '"Expert Shopping": Appeals Adducing Fresh Evidence in Diminished Responsibility Cases: R v Foy [2020] EWCA Crim 270' (2020) 84(3) *Journal of Criminal Law* 249–254.

[434] See further Nobles R and Schiff D, 'The Criminal Cases Review Commission: Establishing a Workable Relationship with the Court of Appeal' [2005] *Criminal Law Review* 173 at pp 186–188.

to only seven cases per annum.[435] Legal aid was not available for the preparation of petitions and, in consequence, many were ill-conceived or poorly presented. They were considered by a small number of legally unqualified Home Office officials without the resources to investigate. Occasionally the police were asked to re-examine evidence but critics argued that the police were more likely to cover up their own wrongdoing than root it out.[436] The Home Office was reluctant to refer many cases to the Court of Appeal for fear of being seen as interfering with the judicial function, and it had conflicting roles, since it was responsible for the police and the maintenance of law and order. The few cases it referred to were those in which there was fresh evidence or some other new consideration of substance that had yet to be put before the court.[437] External support and publicity was also important.[438] The Guildford Four secured the endorsement of a number of high profile 'worthies',[439] the Birmingham Six did not.

Lord Denning terminated the civil action brought by the 'Birmingham Six' against the police for assault, viewing the prospect of the police committing perjury and using violence and threats to extract involuntary confessions as an 'appalling vista'.[440] Evidently it was more important to him that the criminal justice system preserve its good name (even if undeserved) than that possibly innocent persons were given the chance to regain theirs. The Home Office did, years later, remit the case to the Court of Appeal, which said:

> As has happened before in references by the Home Secretary to this court under s.17 of the Criminal Appeal Act 1968, the longer this hearing has gone on the more convinced this court has become that the verdict of the jury was correct. We have no doubt that these convictions were both safe and satisfactory.[441]

This was a criticism of the referral not only in the particular case but other 'hopeless' references.[442] The 'Birmingham Six' remained in prison another three years. Only after a further reference from the Home Secretary were their convictions finally quashed, by which time they had collectively lost 96 years of freedom.

11.4.4.2 The Criminal Cases Review Commission in action

The overly-cautious approach of both the Court of Appeal and Home Office led to repeated calls for reform over a period of some 25 years. Many miscarriages of justice, like the Birmingham Six, had initially not been recognised as such by either. So in 1993 the Runciman Commission recommended that a 'Criminal Cases Review Authority' should be established. Relying on the police to re-investigate, not being subject to appeal, and having no power to make any recommendation to the Court of Appeal as to outcome, the proposed body looked very similar to the process it was to replace. The Runciman Commission's conservative blueprint was enacted more or less as it stood in the Criminal Appeal Act 1995 as the Criminal Cases Review Commission (CCRC). Whilst the CCRC is fiercely protective of its independence,[443] its ability to remain, and be seen as, independent of the Ministry of Justice in light of changes to Commissioner pay and tenure

---

[435] RCCJ (1993: 181).
[436] Mansfield M and Taylor N, 'Post-Conviction Procedures' in Walker C and Starmer K (eds), *Justice in Error* (London: Blackstone Press, 1993) p 164. [437] RCCJ (1993: 181–182).
[438] Home Affairs Committee, Report on Miscarriages of Justice (HC 421) (1981–82) para 10.
[439] Mansfield and Taylor (1993: 166).
[440] *McIlkenny v Chief Constable of the West Midlands* [1980] 2 WLR 689 at 706.
[441] Quoted by Rozenberg J, 'Miscarriages of Justice' in Stockdale E and Casale S (eds), *Criminal Justice Under Stress* (London: Blackstone, 1992) p 104. [442] Rozenberg (1992: 104).
[443] See CCRC, CCRC complains to IPSO about *The Times* article on the independence of the Commission (2020) available at: <https://ccrc.gov.uk/ccrc-complains-to-ipso-about-times-article-on-the-independence-of-the-commission/> (accessed 29 July 2020).<https://ccrc.gov.uk/ccrc-complains-to-ipso-about-times-article-on-the-independence-of-the-commission/> (accessed 29 July 2020).

(as a result of budgetary constraints) has been 'undoubtedly tested.'[444] The court in *Warner* decided that the CCRC remains operationally and constitutionally independent, despite Commissioners being appointed on the recommendation of the Prime Minister in a process managed by the Ministry of Justice.

The CCRC refers cases based on challenges to sentences as well as to convictions. Since 2012, the CCRC has received around 1,500 applications for review per year. This is a big increase over previous years, reflecting the ever-increasing prison population and the creation of an Easy Read application form designed to improve accessibility, a prison outreach programme and advertising.[445] This is vital in light of reduced access to legal aid (discussed later).

The CCRC's latest annual report records that between 1997 'and 31st March 2020 we referred 692 cases to the appeal courts at an average rate of around 30 cases per year. . . . Of the cases referred that had been decided by the appeal courts, 450 appeals succeeded and 207 failed.'[446] When the last edition of this book was written, the average referral rate was 35 cases a year. The CCRC referral rate seems to be dropping as a result of deference to the Court of Appeal and, some argue, insufficient interest in protecting the innocent.[447] The CCRC responded by analysing why its referral rate dropped.[448] That analysis concluded that criticism from the Court of Appeal and a drop in the CCRC's success rate may influence their referral pattern (i.e. they are more hesitant about referrals), but also identified changing work pressures. Consequently the CCRC designed an action plan to better identify miscarriages of justice, but it is too soon to see if this has been successful. Currently, the CCRC is referring more cases than the Home Office used to, but the vast majority of applications (around 97%) still do not result in a referral.

The CCRC in practice

The Commission may only refer cases in the restricted circumstances set out in s.13 of the Criminal Appeal Act 1995. It must consider that there is a 'real possibility' that the appellate court will not uphold the conviction or sentence.[449] The framework within which

---

[444] *Warner R v Secretary of State for Justice* [2020] EWHC 1894 (Admin) at 81.

[445] See <https://legalaidandrepresentatives.wordpress.com/findings/> (accessed 29 July 2020).

[446] CCRC (2020) Annual Report and Accounts 2019/20 (HC 521) (London: TSO): 14. By mid-2020, the CCRC has completed reviews of approx. 25,000 applications since 1997 (<https://ccrc.gov.uk/case-statistics/> (accessed 29 July 2020)).

[447] Robins J, 'Downward trend in number of miscarriage of justice cases being referred continues for third year' *The Justice Gap*, 22 July 2019; Allison E, Hattenstone S and Bowcott O, 'Miscarriages of justice body is not fit for purpose, lawyers say' *The Guardian*, 30 May 2018; Hoyle and Sato (2019); Quirk H, 'Identifying miscarriages of justice: why innocence in the UK is not the answer'(2007) 70(5) *Modern Law Review*.759–777; Naughton M, 'The Westminster Commission inquiry on the ability of the Criminal Cases Review Commission to deal effectively with miscarriages of justice: Please forgive me, but I won't be holding my breath.' *The Justice Gap* (2019); Naughton M, 'The Criminal Cases Review Commission: Innocence versus safety and the integrity of the criminal justice system' (2012) 58 *Criminal Law Quarterly* 207; Naughton M, 'Appeals Against Wrongful Convictions' in Corteen K, Morley S, Taylor P and Turner J (eds), *A Companion to Crime, Harm and Victimisation* (Bristol: Policy Press, 2016).

[448] Berlin S, *Criminal Cases Review Commission* (2018) <https://s3-eu-west-2.amazonaws.com/ccrc-prod-storage-1jdn5d1f6iq1l/uploads/2018/06/CCRC_REFERRAL_RATE_-_ANALYSIS.pdf> (accessed 29 July 2020).

[449] There is a difference between referral rates for cases going back to Crown court (i.e. summary cases: 1.9%) and cases being referred to the Court of Appeal (i.e. jury trial: 3.7%), which is hard to explain. The CCRC seems to exercise discretion by declining to refer cases back to the Crown court unless it considers that the applicant is actually innocent or the original conviction is tainted by a substantial breach of due process: Kerrigan K, 'Miscarriage of justice in the magistrates court: the forgotten power of the CCRC' (2006) *Criminal Law Review* 124. The existence of such discretion has been recognised in the context of referrals back to the Court of Appeal: *Smith (Wallace Duncan)* [2004] EWCA Crim 631 [29]. The 'one test fits all' approach of the Criminal Appeal Act 1995 is indicative of the scant attention paid by Parliament to the possibility of summary miscarriages of justice and how best to guard against or remedy them. So far the evidence suggests that the CCRC is making only a tiny contribution to this objective.

appeals will be heard following a CCRC referral is no different from the legal framework governing the initial appeal.[450] It follows that the CCRC is obliged to take into account the narrow way in which the Court of Appeal interprets its own powers[451] and equally obliged to take into account the fact that a Crown court must conduct a full rehearing once a case has been referred back to it.

The 'real possibility' test requires the CCRC to apply the same criteria to the merits of appeals from the Crown court as does the Court of Appeal. So it is not surprising that the CCRC mirrors the Court of Appeal's practice of weeding out most putative appellants. Moreover, applicants must already have exhausted their appeal rights, and the Commission must consider that the case involves some argument or evidence not previously put forward at the trial or the appeal stage.[452] The condition that appeal avenues must be exhausted does not apply if the Commission considers there are 'exceptional circumstances' justifying the making of a referral.[453] Recent research suggests that the CCRC has taken a particularly restrictive approach to the exceptional circumstances test while also placing greater reliance on applicants themselves—many of who are not legally represented—to identify what those circumstances might be.[454] Once referred, the appeal may be argued on any ground identified by the CCRC, and any other ground with leave of the Court of Appeal.[455] In cases where the CCRC refers on narrow grounds only, the court can, by refusing leave to expand those grounds, greatly restrict the ambit of an appeal. Where this happens it becomes impossible for appellants to put their cases holistically, thus reducing the likelihood that the conviction will be found unsafe.[456] This can be a particular problem when new 'second opinion' lawyers have been instructed: in general, every ground that an appellant wishes to argue should be lodged at the point of application.[457]

Generally, then, it is clear that the CCRC provides a means by which the applicant may be allowed to bring further appeals but only when there is something new and legally relevant to say. This is no different from the position that previously obtained under the old Home Office referral route. Without fresh evidence or new legal arguments the applicant to the CCRC is almost doomed to fail. Applicants who simply assert that the jury 'got it wrong' or that the CCRC should refer the case on the basis of a 'lurking doubt' make little headway.[458] The court must keep in mind 'alongside the safety of convictions, the public and private interests in an orderly, as well as just, system that secures finality of decisions'.[459] So the court departs from its own previous reasoning only in exceptional circumstances.

No provision for legal aid was made in the legislation setting up the CCRC. The limited state-funded assistance that was available was wholly inadequate given the complexities

---

[450] Criminal Appeal Act 1995, s.9(1).

[451] As confirmed by *Criminal Cases Review Commission, ex p Pearson* [1999] 3 All ER 498.

[452] Criminal Appeal Act 1995, s.13(1)(b) and (c).

[453] Criminal Appeal Act 1995, s.13(2). An example would be where an applicant has not exhausted appeal rights but the CCRC has already decided to refer a related case involving a co-defendant: CCRC, Annual Report 1999–2000, p 8.

[454] Hodgson J, Horne J and Soubise L, The Criminal Cases Review Commission Last resort or first appeal? (Criminal Justice Centre, University of Warwick, 2018).

[455] See s.14 of the Criminal Appeal Act 1995. The leave requirement was added by s.315 of the Criminal Justice Act 2003.

[456] Eady D, 'The Failure of the CCRC to Live Up to its Stated Values?: The case of Michael Attwooll and John Roden' in Naughton M (ed), *The Criminal Cases Review Commission* (London: Palgrave Macmillan, 2012).

[457] *James* [2018] EWCA Crim 285.

[458] See further Malleson (1995); Eady (2012: 74); Nobles R and Schiff D, 'After Ten Years: An Investment in Justice?' in Naughton (2012).

[459] *Poole and Mills* [2003] EWCA Crim 1753 [61].

involved in applying to the CCRC.[460] The results were predictable. After opening for new business, the CCRC was deluged with hopeless applications submitted by non-legally represented applicants—after only two years in full operation the CCRC had a backlog of cases which it estimated would take it between three and four years to clear.[461] This prompted the CCRC to proclaim through its literature the virtues of legal representation. It wanted lawyers to take on some of the investigative work that the CCRC would otherwise have to do; filter out hopeless applications; and make it easier for the Commission to grasp quickly the essential issues in those applications it receives. The Legal Aid Agency (LAA) now funds lawyers to conduct an 'initial screening' of a case, not normally exceeding two hours, but in practice the limit does not stop the solicitor getting paid if more time is spent on this stage.[462] The lawyer should reject the case and cease work immediately it becomes apparent that there will be no 'sufficient benefit' to the client to justify even this limited amount of public funding.[463] It will be easier to satisfy this test when the solicitor confines the investigation and advice to whether there was some procedural error at trial rather than looking into the much broader question of whether evidence can be found of actual innocence.[464]

If the case survives initial screening then further work can be undertaken at public expense, but only by repeatedly applying to the LAA, and the fees claimed can be reduced on 'audit'. Also, lawyers often complain that the LAA acts unreliably when determining claims, so they waste time preparing to defend themselves against the possibility of reduced costs, and another layer of bureaucracy and uncertainty is added to their work. And firms are not paid for appeals work until the CCRC either closes the case or refers it to the Court of Appeal.[465] Nonetheless, this scheme is more generous than previously, though funding rates were cut by 8.75% in 2014. Rates of representation have oscillated as these schemes have waxed and waned, but (after rising considerably) by 2020 they were back to the low levels reported when the CCRC first opened (c. 10%).[466] Thus most applicants to the CCRC are unrepresented, because the pay for lawyers is low, unreliable and late. As one lawyer put it:

> It is so badly paid and with the very low rates generally for crime, senior practitioners cannot spend time doing this work, not least travelling to see the clients [in prison]. The need to keep one's head above water drives senior solicitors to do work that pays, as opposed to work that does not, and unfortunately miscarriage work is regarded by many as at the bottom of the pile, purely because of finances.[467]

Things have only got worse for lawyers since this research was conducted. In 2019, one lawyer who was asked how legal aid cuts have affected CCRC casework said: 'Less likely to take on; overall profitability of criminal legal aid work is so low now, and these applications almost inevitably entail pro bono work, it is often simply not financially viable', while

---

[460] See Taylor with Mansfield (1999) and the second edition of this book at pp 652–653.
[461] CCRC, Annual Report 1998–99, p 12.
[462] Bird S, 'The Inadequacy of Legal Aid' in Naughton (2012) p 140.
[463] Bird (2012: 136). The sufficient benefit test is set out in sections 3.10 and 3.11, Part A, Standard Crime Contract. Guidance on 'second opinion' cases is found in section 11.6 and on the CCRC in sections 11.19 and 11.20 Part B, Standard Crime Contract, produced by the Legal Aid Agency. See <https://www.gov.uk/government/publications/standard-crime-contract-2017> (accessed 29 July 2020).
[464] Bird (2012: 146–147).   [465] Bird (2012).
[466] CCRC (2020) Annual Report and Accounts 2019/20 (HC 521) (London: TSO). For the situation 10–15 years earlier, see Hodgson J and Horne J, *The Extent and Impact of Legal Representation on Applications to the Criminal Cases Review Commission* (CCRC) (Warwick: Warwick University, 2008).
[467] Ewen Smith, a partner with 30 years' experience, quoted in Arkinstall J, 'Unappealing Work: The Practical Difficulties Facing Solicitors Engaged in Criminal Appeal Cases' (2004) 1(2) *Justice Journal* 95.

another reported: 'The uncertainty over funding has led many practitioners to become sceptical before agreeing to undertake such work.'[468]

The CCRC position is that good legal representation helps expedite its work, but does not increase the chances of a referral being made. Independent research suggests a more nuanced picture. In 2001–2007 unrepresented applicants had a 2.1% chance of having their case referred to the Court of Appeal compared with a 7.6% chance for represented applicants,[469] although this might be partly because lawyers try to take on strong cases where public funding is more assured. That legal representation *often* improves the chances of success seems incontrovertible. And legally represented applicants have a greater chance of having their case considered for full review (as opposed to being screened out at an early stage for ineligibility) than those who are not legally represented, and that alone might increase the chances of the case being referred.[470] However, the quality of legally-aided appeal work has been criticised, much as other legally-aided work has been. Some solicitors do little more than add their name to the 'client's' application form, proving reluctant thereafter to engage with the process of case review, with some lacking even a basic understanding of the CCRC's role.[471] Not many lawyers are able or willing to do as Glyn Maddox did when he worked on what was effectively a pro bono basis for 12 years in helping Paul Blackburn overturn his conviction (in May 2005) for which the latter had spent almost a quarter of century in prison.[472] Many lawyers who undertake this work run the appeals department (including CCRC cases) at a loss, subsidising it from Crown court or privately paid work.[473]

Initial impressions of the CCRC in its infancy were generally positive, suggesting that its low referral rate was not attributable to faulty investigative practices.[474] There are a number of welcome features of CCRC case-handling when compared with what went before. Cases considered prima facie eligible, and which raise significant new evidence or argument, are reviewed with care,[475] although some case review managers are no doubt more thorough and proactive than others.[476] The CCRC assembles the primary materials (exhibits, court transcripts and so forth), obtains fresh evidence and expert advice, and interviews witnesses (often doing this itself in more recent years, rather than relying on the police to do this).

---

[468] See *Headline Summary Report: Criminal Cases Review Commission: Legal Aid and Legal Representatives. Stage Three: Survey Of Representatives* <https://legalaidandrepresentatives.files.wordpress.com/2020/10/stage3_summary_v4.pdf> (accessed 29 July 2020).

[469] Hodgson and Horne (2008).

[470] See Hodgson and Horne (2008) and ongoing research being conducted: <https://legalaidandrepresentatives.wordpress.com/> or <https://ccrc.gov.uk/research-at-the-ccrc/ongoing-research-at-the-ccrc/> (both accessed 29 July 2020).

[471] Maddox G and Tan G, 'Applicant Solicitors: Friends or Foes?' in Naughton (2012) at pp 126–128; Hodgson and Horne (2008: 15); *Memorandum submitted by The Miscarriages of Justice Organisation (MOJO) to Select Committee on Home Affairs*, December 2003 (available from <http://www.publications.parliament.uk/>) p 2. The CCRC agrees about poor standards (Evidence given to Select Committee on Home Affairs on 27 January 2004, Q50–Q56), as does the Criminal Appeals Lawyers Association (Arkinstall (2004: 101–102)).

[472] Maddox and Tan (2012).

[473] See ongoing research being conducted: <https://legalaidandrepresentatives.wordpress.com/> or <https://ccrc.gov.uk/research-at-the-ccrc/ongoing-research-at-the-ccrc/> (both accessed 29 July 2020).

[474] See James et al, 'The Criminal Cases Review Commission: Economy, Effectiveness and Justice' [2000] *Criminal Law Review* 140.

[475] One indication of this is that in some 15% of the referred cases examined in depth by Hodgson and Horne (2008: para 6.5), none of the issues on which referral was based had been identified by either the applicant or the applicant's solicitor.

[476] Maddox and Tan (2009: 123–124); Hoyle and Sato (2019).

Criticisms and problems remain, however. All of the external investigating officers appointed by the Commission so far have been police officers.[477] A risk averse, defensive approach is taken in many investigations, with CCRC staff all too aware of the possibility of dissatisfied applicants (perhaps especially those with lawyers) launching proceedings for judicial review.[478] And investigation is a challenge: the CCRC's power to obtain materials from any public body is of decreasing value as more bodies become privatised (e.g. telecommunication companies and the Forensic Science Service). In addition, the CCRC is not included among the agencies which can make use of existing mechanisms for international co-operation and mutual assistance in criminal justice: 'In one recent case we estimate that the absence of such powers delayed completion of the review by almost two years'.[479] CCRC case review managers rarely visit prisoners or meet with their representatives, and are insufficiently open about the investigative steps they are taking, leaving applicants unsure whether they should be seeking themselves to make certain inquiries before evidence is lost or the trail goes cold.[480]

The CCRC has an overall 'success' rate of 67% in cases referred between 2011 and 2017.[481] Rather than this being 'a strong vindication of the Commission's judgment',[482] the CCRC is arguably applying a more demanding test than the civil standard of proof, also known as the 51% test.[483] The 'real possibility' test denotes a contingency which 'is more than an outside chance or a bare possibility, but which may be less than a probability or a likelihood or a racing certainty'.[484] Since a probability or likelihood can be thought of as anything more than an even chance, this judicial formulation suggests that the CCRC should take a less restrictive approach and allow its success rate to fall from 70% to, say, 30%. At this lower level the cases concerned would on average have a 'more than an outside chance', and 'less than a probability' of success. While this new policy would result in a higher proportion of failed cases, it should also mean that many more miscarriages of justice could be brought to light. It does seem, then, that the CCRC is excessively cautious in its referral decision-making.[485] There is little prospect that the CCRC will change its ways, however. The second Chair of the CCRC commented that while a 98% success rate would be cause for concern, a 70% success rate confirms 'that we are applying the test in a way that is reasonable . . . '[486] There has as yet been no independent scrutiny of the correctness

---

[477] CCRC, *Annual Report 2006–2007*, p 14 (more recent annual reports are silent on this issue). See further Hoyle and Sato (2019).

[478] Hoyle and Sato (2019). Judicial review is the only way of challenging a CCRC decision through the legal process, though the CCRC also has an extensive complaints procedure.

[479] CCRC (2005: 34).

[480] *Memorandum submitted by the Criminal Appeal Lawyers Association to the Select Committee on Home Affairs*, January 2004 (available from <http://www.publications.parliament.uk/>). See also Maddox and Tan (2009: 121–123). The concerns were raised again in ongoing research; <https://legalaidandrepresentatives.wordpress.com/> or <https://ccrc.gov.uk/research-at-the-ccrc/ongoing-research-at-the-ccrc/> (both accessed 29 July 2020). [481] Roberts in Lennon et al (2019: 249–267).

[482] Dennis I, Editorial [2003] *Criminal Law Review* 663.

[483] It is difficult to be certain about this absent independent scrutiny of the strength of cases both referred and not referred. As the CCRC has (correctly) pointed out, the fact that it has a 70% 'success rate' does not mean that it only refers cases that are 70% likely to succeed: Justice Committee (2009) p 25. Some cases referred with a lower chance of success will be 'balanced out' by others with a higher chance.

[484] *Criminal Cases Review Commission, ex p Pearson* [2000] 1 Cr App R 149.

[485] As Green (2012: 51–52) notes, the Court of Appeal is inconsistent and is sometimes more flexible in its reception of fresh arguments and evidence (even if they could have been presented at the initial trial) than the CCRC seems to believe. See also Newby M, 'Historical Abuse Cases: Why They Expose the Inadequacy of the Real Possibility Test', and Malone C, 'Only the Freshest Will Do' both in Naughton (2012).

[486] *Examination of Witnesses before the Select Committee on Home Affairs on 27 January 2004*, Q27.

of decisions not to refer cases to the Court of Appeal, however (beyond the occasional judicial review case), and the CCRC is not subject to external inspection in the way that most criminal justice agencies are. The 'fairness' core value demands that the Commission push at the boundaries of the real possibility test, and the court be more inclined to be receptive to fresh evidence and less deferential to the jury and the principle of finality.[487]

The effect of inadequate resources

The capacity of the CCRC to investigate cases is limited by lack of adequate resources. From the outset the CCRC did not have enough case workers in post to process the case load in a thorough and timely manner. A considerable backlog of cases built up and the Home Office, after initially rejecting calls to increase the number of case workers, eventually agreed to fund 50, which still fell short of what the CCRC felt it needed.[488]

By 31 March 2009, following successive budgetary squeezes, freezing of recruitment and stingy pay settlements which left staff 'angry and dispirited',[489] the figure had fallen to 44.[490] The CCRC expressed a need to recruit more case review managers in its most recent annual report,[491] especially following significant criticism about reviewers' workloads and a critical *Panorama* documentary.[492] Despite recent changes to working methods that boosted efficiency, there are still significant delays. The 2020 Annual Report indicated that 83% of cases were closed within 12 months of receiving the application, which met their target—especially for those in custody. But many of those cases are likely to have been 'no appeal' cases that were quickly and easily rejected (40% of applications per year).[493] Further, the delay experienced by any particular applicant may range from a few months to several years. The CCRC aims to complete reviews within two years in complex cases, but 5.2% of cases took more than two years to review at the last count.[494]

We need to consider the implications of the CCRC backlog for the patterns of application and referrals. Those serving shorter prison sentences (or the lawyers they approach) may think the game not worth the candle.[495] From their point of view, what matters most is how quickly the conviction can be quashed. Thus, to the delays within the CCRC must be added judicial delays on receipt of referrals. In 2017, average waiting times in respect of all appeals against conviction disposed of by the full court was 11.7 months. The average delay for appeals referred by the CCRC will presumably have been somewhat longer given that the Court of Appeal considers these cases 'to be notoriously complex'.[496] The CCRC affords priority to 'in-custody' cases over 'at-liberty' cases.[497] Even so, those sentenced to terms of imprisonment of less than five years with cases of any complexity are unlikely to see the CCRC as of much relevance. By the time they have exhausted their normal appeal rights, secured a referral from the CCRC, and had their referred case heard, they are likely

---

[487] See Hoyle and Sato (2019: 337).
[488] CCRC, *Annual Reports 1999–2000*, p 5 and 1998–99, p 12.
[489] CCRC, *Annual Report and Accounts 2007/08*, p 4.   [490] CCRC (2009a: 16).
[491] CCRC (2020) *Annual Report and Accounts 2019/20* (HC 521) (London: TSO).
[492] BBC, *Last Chance for Justice*. BBC 2, 5 June 2018. The CCRC's responses to the programme can be found on their website: <https://ccrc.gov.uk/ccrc-answers-to-panorama-questions/> (accessed 29 July 2020).
[493] Hodgson et al (2018); CCRC (2020) Annual Report and Accounts 2019/20 (HC 521) (London: TSO).
[494] CCRC, *Annual Report and Accounts 2019/20* (HC 521) (London: TSO, 2020).
[495] Arkinstall (2004: 96).
[496] Court of Appeal Criminal Division, *Review of the Legal Year 2007/2008*, para 1.3 (statistic) and para 7.2 (quote). Giving evidence before the Select Committee on Home Affairs on 27 January 2004 the Chair of the CCRC estimated the average length of time between referral and hearing to be 'around a year to 18 months' (Q30).
[497] CCRC (2009: 73). Other influential factors are the age or health of applicants or witnesses, and the possibility of deterioration of evidence (ibid).

to be at liberty again anyway. If a prisoner is due to be released before a fresh appeal is likely to be heard the incentive to pursue the matter is much reduced. While some will still want to 'clear their names', those with previous convictions of a similar type will presumably not see much point in doing this. Further, the priority given by the CCRC to in-custody cases means that those wrongfully convicted in the magistrates' courts receive from the CCRC least attention of all.

Our overall assessment is that, on the pattern to date, the CCRC, just like the Home Office before it, is dealing mainly in high-profile cases involving those sentenced to long periods of imprisonment. And it continues to be cautious in its decision-making concerning referrals to the Court of Appeal. As a result, the criticisms previously directed at the Home Office are increasingly being directed at the CCRC.[498]

11.4.4.3 The response of the Court of Appeal to the new referral process

In the late 1980s miscarriages of justice were rarely out of the headlines. Of the 38 appellants involved in cases referred back to the Court of Appeal by the Home Office in 1989–91, 37 had their convictions quashed.[499] This was both a cause and an effect of the Court of Appeal's greater willingness in more recent times to contemplate 'appalling vistas' of police and prosecution malpractice. The strongly worded judgment in *Judith Ward*[500] in which the Court of Appeal laid down clear rules governing the prosecution duty to disclose, is one example of this. The development of due process principles in cases such as this and *Edwards*[501] showed that the judiciary was no longer blind to the possibility of systematic malpractice by the police and prosecution agencies. Has this greater readiness to act on referrals carried on under the new system?

The initial signs were, on the whole, encouraging. In the very first case referred, the Court of Appeal acknowledged that 'the Criminal Cases Review Commission is a necessary and welcome body, without whose work the injustice in this case might never have been identified'[502]—even though this injustice could not be adequately remedied as Mr Mattan was hanged in 1952. The presiding judge in the Court of Appeal added his stamp of approval: 'It is essential to the health and proper functioning of a modern democracy that the citizen accused of crime should be fairly tried and adequately protected against the risk and consequences of wrongful conviction.'[503] Although the CCRC does not have the power to make any recommendation to the appellate courts, its Statement of Reasons for making the reference have been cited in judgments 'and have clearly been of material

---

[498] Concern at the inadequacies of the CCRC led to the creation of the 'Innocence Network', made up of projects (usually housed in universities) devoted to publicising, investigating and remedying the wrongful conviction of the innocent. See further Naughton M and McCartney C, 'The Innocence Network UK' (2005) 7(2) *Legal Ethics* 150. The value of such projects is debated by Quirk H, 'Identifying Miscarriages of Justice: Why Innocence in the UK is Not the Answer' (2007) 70(5) *Modern Law Review* 759 and Roberts S and Weathered L, 'Assisting the Factually Innocent: the Contradictions and Compatibility of Innocence Projects and the Criminal Cases Review Commission' (2009) 29(1) *Oxford Journal of Legal Studies* 43. The formal umbrella organisation for Innocence Projects in the UK was formally disbanded in 2014, though some universities still run their own innocence style projects. The only UK based Innocence Project affiliated with the US Innocence Project is run in Greenwich. See Robins J, 'University innocence projects: where are they now?' *The Guardian*, 27 April 2016.
[499] Two of these were ordered to be retried and were subsequently acquitted: see RCCJ (1993: 181).
[500] [1993] 1 WLR 619.
[501] [1991] 2 All ER 266. The Court of Appeal here ruled that the prosecution had a duty to disclose a police officer's disciplinary record to the defence if it is in issue. It also said that the defence could put before the jury the fact that police witnesses in the case had previously been disbelieved by juries in earlier trials.
[502] *Mattan*, *The Times*, 5 March 1998.
[503] *Criminal Cases Review Commission, ex p Pearson* [1999] 3 All ER 498.

assistance in many of the appeals'.[504] Similarly, the Court of Appeal stated its appreciation for the rigorous and prompt way the CCRC carried out investigations requested by the judiciary.[505]

In some cases, however, the Court of Appeal has implicitly or expressly criticised the CCRC decision to refer: for example, when a man had been dead for 75 years. The court was 'troubled that this conviction was referred at all' noting that there 'are no issues of exceptional notoriety, and therefore public interest . . . '.[506] As Nobles and Schiff (2005: 176) put it, 'the continuing work of the CCRC represents a significant ongoing threat to the Court of Appeal's ability to manage its role within the criminal justice system.' Tensions are bound to arise as the two bodies seek to develop a workable relationship.[507] It is implausible to think that the CCRC has been unaffected by judicial criticism; one of the CCRC's ex-Commissioners has written of the 'bruising outcome' of referrals that irked the judiciary.[508] While the CCRC does not accept that it is 'deeply worried' about its relationship with the Court of Appeal,[509] the CCRC is concerned about being criticised by the Court of Appeal, and this concern feeds into internal guidance notes used when reviewing cases.[510] We know that the CCRC tends to exercise excessive caution in referring cases, but has occasionally tested the boundaries of the court's willingness to reopen cases by, e.g. referring cases where the law has developed since the time of the original trial, presumably with a view to testing whether convictions can become vulnerable in the light of more modern standards of due process.[511] The Court of Appeal has sent out contradictory signals on this[512] and a number of other points.[513]

The CCRC is bound to take notice of such signals given that it may only refer convictions where it considers there is a real possibility that the court will quash them. Thus one might expect the referral rate to increase as the Court of Appeal lays down clearer norms in this area. But perhaps this is to expect too much. We argued earlier that it is relatively easy for appellate judges to manipulate legal resources (such as the *Pendleton* test) to arrive at the decision they instinctively favour. Just like the rest of us, judges are torn between due process and crime control values, with some more towards the crime control end of the

---

[504] CCRC, *Annual Report 1999–2000*, p 18.

[505] E.g. *Azam & Ors* [2006] EWCA Crim 161 [60]; Court of Appeal Criminal Division, Review of the Legal Year 2006/2007, para 4.7.

[506] *Knighton* [2002] EWCA Crim 2227 at para 73. The case is discussed more fully by Nobles and Schiff (2005a: 179–181). See also *R v Gore (deceased)* [2007] EWCA Crim 2789 [42].

[507] See also Zellick (2005) (replying to Nobles and Schiff (2005a)) and Nobles R and Schiff D, 'A Reply to Graham Zellick' [2005] *Criminal Law Review* 951.

[508] Elks L, *Righting Miscarriages of Justice? Ten Years of the Criminal Cases Review Commission* (London: Justice, 2008) p 110.

[509] CCRC (2018) *Answers to Panorama Questions*, online at: <https://ccrc.gov.uk/ccrc-answers-to-panorama-questions/> (accessed 29 July 2020).

[510] Hoyle and Sato (2019). [510] Memorandum submitted by MOJO.

[511] See James et al (2000: 143–144) for discussion of this line of referrals.

[512] See, e.g., *Kansal (No 2)* [2001] 2 Cr App R 30. More recent decisions have emphasised that the court must focus on the safety of the conviction, albeit with a view to what modern standards of fairness require and imply: *Hussain* [2005] EWCA Crim 31 and *Steele & Ors* [2006] EWCA Crim 195. The House of Lords has ruled that the Human Rights Act 1998 does not have retrospective application: *Lambert* [2001] 3 WLR 206, *Kansal* [2001] 3 WLR 107 and *Benjafield* [2003] 1 AC 1099.

[513] See, generally, Zellick (2005). The CCRC's ability to refer cases where a development in the law subsequent to conviction put that conviction in doubt was disliked by the Court of Appeal (*R v Cottrell and Fletcher* [2008] 1 Cr App R 7), which regained control over its ability to decide whether to entertain such appeals by the insertion of s.16C into the Criminal Appeal Act 1995 by s.42 of the Criminal Justice and Immigration Act 2008. See Nobles R and Schiff D, 'Absurd Asymmetry' (2008) 71(3) *Modern Law Review* 464, and Cooper (2009) for critique, and *R v Rowe* [2008] EWCA Crim 2712 [21] for discussion on the difference between a 'change of law' and a 'declaration of previously undefined law'.

spectrum than others, and all prone to being swayed one way or another by the particular facts of cases. Further incoherence is generated by what the second Chairman of the CCRC described as the 'occasionally uneven' quality of the court's work.[514] For example, the judges may not be specialists in criminal law, or the court's case law may be 'conflicting, unclear, or underdeveloped'.[515]

The more one examines appellate judgments the less one expects to find clear norms that are consistently applied. Consider again the case law vacillation over such crucial jurisdictional points as whether a reliable conviction can nevertheless be so tainted by unfairness as to be unsafe. The difficulty of the CCRC's position then becomes evident. If the Court of Appeal continues to tack between the poles of due process and crime control, the CCRC will have no choice but to follow queasily in its wake.

11.4.5 Civil claims

11.4.5.1 Causes of action

Earlier chapters showed that numerous statutes have defined a large number of police powers and rights for suspects. But, typically, no specific enforcement mechanisms or civil remedies accompany these provisions. Section 67(10) of PACE, for example, provides that a failure on the part of a police officer to comply with any of their provisions 'shall not of itself render him liable to any criminal or civil proceedings'.[516] People whose ECHR rights are infringed (e.g. Art 6 rights to a fair trial as a result of improper interrogation, or Art 8 rights to privacy as a result of an illegal bugging or house search) may sue and be compensated.[517] But unless a breach of legislation or a code of practice also breaches the ECHR, claimants must make such use as they can of existing tortious remedies, developed many years before police forces and modern investigative techniques were created. We look here at the main torts which might be used by people suspected or accused of crime and victims of crime for whom there were improprieties in the police investigation.[518] We also explore how the introduction of the Human Rights Act has provided a new avenue for suing the police where tort law has historically failed. It is also worth noting that in civil claims against the police a number of torts may be considered in one case, e.g. false imprisonment *and* malicious prosecution.[519]

(a) *False imprisonment:* This is sometimes known as wrongful arrest, unlawful arrest or false arrest. For example, in 2018, in *Parker v the Chief Constable of Essex Police*,[520] Michael Barrymore (real name Michael Parker) had been unlawfully arrested and falsely imprisoned because the arresting officer did not personally have grounds to believe that his arrest was necessary as the officer who was due to make the arrest had been delayed. False imprisonment can arise not just as a result of arrest and detention in the police station, but also during 'voluntary' questioning, or stop and search. For example, one complainant was awarded damages after attending a voluntary interview at a police station which led to his arrest, which he successfully claimed was unreasonable and unnecessary.[521] See also section 2.4.3.

---

[514] See also Elks (2008) e.g. at p 185.
[515] Zellick (2005: 938–939). For an example of such a referral see *Kennedy* [2005] EWCA Crim 685.
[516] PACE, s.67(8) made a breach of its Codes of Practice a disciplinary offence, but this was repealed in 1996.
[517] HRA 1998, ss.7 and 8.
[518] For details of all the torts discussed here see: Harrison et al (2005).
[519] For example, *Rowlands v Chief Constable of Merseyside Police* [2006] EWCA Civ 1773.
[520] [2018] EWCA 2788 (Civ).
[521] *Richardson v Chief Constable of the West Midlands* [2011] EWHC 773 (QB); [2011] 2 Cr App R 1; [2011] 3 WLUK 919 (QBD (Birmingham)).

(b) *Trespass:* If the police enter property without lawful authority, an action for trespass may follow. This can occur when an arrest warrant is invalid or based on inaccurate information, or in the purported exercising of other police powers, such as search and/or seizure of property (see chapter 6). In *Keegan v Chief Constable of Merseyside Police*,[522] for example, the claim for damages following a botched attempt to execute a search warrant at an address where the suspect no longer, if ever, lived, initially failed because the police actions, though mistaken due to false information having been provided by the accused, were viewed as lawful. However, this case later succeeded under Art 8 at the ECtHR, where it was argued that the complainants right to a home and private life had been breached by police failures to properly establish a link between the suspect and the address searched under warrant.[523]

(c) *Assault and intimidation:* Anything in excess of 'reasonable' and 'necessary' force in the purported exercise of a police officer's lawful powers is potentially grounds for civil action.[524] This use of force may be seen as 'unnecessary' where there were no reasonable grounds for arrest and it may be seen as 'unreasonable' where unapproved forms of force are used. These considerations may arise during any part of someone's arrest and detention, including, for example, whilst taking fingerprints. For example, force was seen as 'unreasonable' in *Adorian v MPC*, where a man subsequently conditionally discharged for obstructing the police suffered, in the course of arrest, multiple head, leg and hip fractures: 'a class of injury associated with head-on car crashes or falls from a significant height'.[525] But it is 'reasonable', for example, to allow a dog to inflict 'very nasty' injuries on a fleeing drink-drive suspect.[526] The threat of an unlawful act (for example, unreasonable use of force) is intimidation.[527] This may also occur if the police try to secure a confession through threats.

(d) *Malicious prosecution and malicious process:* If a prosecution is initiated both without prima facie evidence and maliciously, the defendant may sue for malicious prosecution. Few cases are successful, for courts give prosecutors considerable latitude in determining that there was prima facie evidence, and proving the subjective state of mind of 'malice' is intrinsically difficult; an example is a man acquitted of rape who lost his case even though major elements of the stories told by the people who claimed to be raped were demonstrably false.[528] However, another claimant was successful when evidence of murder was fabricated against him by a senior officer, which deceived the CPS into prosecuting him, even though the officer genuinely believed that the claimant was guilty.[529]

Convincing judges that the police act wrongly, even though the use of prosecution to cover up their own misdeeds is a well-known police tactic,[530] is very difficult. In the infamous *Alder* case (see chapter 4), two men had a fight. One later died in police custody. Mr Paul tried to break up the initial fight and later came forward as a voluntary witness. The police arrested and prosecuted him for murder. When it was established that the blow he

---

[522] [2003] EWCA Civ 936. [523] *Keegan v United Kingdom* [2006] ECHR 764; (2007) 44 EHRR 33.
[524] See s.117 of PACE. [525] [2009] EWCA Civ 18 per Sedley LJ.
[526] *Roberts v CC Kent* [2008] EWCA Civ 1588.
[527] See, e.g., *Allen v Metropolitan Police Comr* [1980] Crim LR 441.
[528] *Moulton v Chief Constable of the West Midlands* [2010] EWCA Civ 524.
[529] *Rees and Ors v Met Police Commissioner* [2018] EWCA Civ 1587. This case also shows that the police are liable, despite statutory charging, if (as is usual) the CPS based its actions solely on the file submitted to it by the police.
[530] Smith G, 'Actions for Damages against the Police and the Attitudes of Claimants' (2003) 13 *Policing and Society* 413. Also see ch 7 and several of the cases in section 11.4.5.3.

allegedly struck was unconnected with Mr Alder's death the charge was changed to GBH, and subsequently the case was discontinued. Mr Paul claimed that the police prosecuted him maliciously, to divert attention from their own contribution to Mr Alder's death. The claim failed initially as the trial judge removed the issue from the jury. Mr Paul successfully appealed against this ruling and a retrial was ordered. At the retrial an eight-strong jury decided unanimously that it was 'more likely than not that the police charged [Mr Paul] with causing GBH with intent to deflect potential criticism of the circumstances of Mr Alder's death' and seven of them concluded that the initial arrest was similarly motivated. Mr Paul was awarded £30,500.[531]

'Malicious process'—such as securing a search warrant maliciously—is similar, and negligence is not enough.[532] In both actions the prosecution has to have been resolved in the defendant's favour either through discontinuance or acquittal.[533] This is an application of the crime control principle that the end justifies the means. No matter how malicious a prosecution might have been, a person has no remedy if convicted.

(e) *Wrongful conviction:* Statutory compensation for wrongful conviction is normally only available where the conviction is overturned 'on the ground that a new or newly discovered fact shows beyond reasonable doubt that there has been a miscarriage of justice'.[534] It can take many years for compensation to be settled—in the very rare cases where claims are successful—leaving victims of miscarriages of justice virtually penniless in the meantime. An example of a successful claimant is George Lewis who was arrested by the infamous West Midlands Police Serious Crime Squad in 1987. He was head-butted, punched, racially abused and threatened with a syringe unless he signed blank sheets of interview notes. Police officers said he confessed in the car. He was convicted of armed robbery and spent over five years in jail until the Court of Appeal ordered a retrial (which the CPS abandoned). Eventually, in 1998, he received £200,000 compensation.[535] An exceptional case was that of Colin Stagg who spent a year in custody awaiting trial for the murder of Rachel Nickell. He received £706,000 from a discretionary government scheme even though he was not convicted (the actual killer, Robert Napper, was eventually convicted),[536] partly because, in the words of the judge at his trial, the police engaged in 'a blatant attempt to incriminate [him] by positive and deceptive conduct of the grossest kind'.[537] The discretionary scheme was scrapped bringing it into line with most other countries,[538] leaving those outside the statutory scheme

---

[531] *Paul v CC Humberside* [2004] EWCA Civ 308. See <http://news.bbc.co.uk/1/hi/england/humber/4656112.stm> (accessed 5 January 2010).

[532] See the search warrant case of *Keegan v Chief Constable of Merseyside Police* [2003] 1 WLR 2187.

[533] See, for example, *Martin v Watson* [1996] AC 74.

[534] CJA 1988, s.133, as amended (restrictively) by s.61 of the Criminal Justice and Immigration Act 2008. The interpretation of these provisions is not straightforward: Roberts S, 'Unsafe Convictions: Defining and Compensating Miscarriages of Justice' (2003) *Modern Law Review* 441. See also *R (Mullen) v Home Secretary* [2004] UKHL 18; *R (Allen) v Justice Secretary* [2008] EWCA Civ 808; *R (Adams) v Secretary of State for Justice* [2012] 1 AC 48, [2011] UKSC 18. See discussion in Hoyle C, 'Compensating Injustice: The Perils of the Innocence Discourse' in Hunter et al (eds), *The Integrity of Criminal Process: From Theory to Practice* (Oxford: Hart, 2016) and Quirk H, 'Compensation for Miscarriages of Justice: Degrees of Innocence' (2020) 79(1) *Cambridge Law Journal* 4–7.

[535] *The Guardian*, 20 January 1998.   [536] *The Guardian*, 19 December 2008.

[537] *The Guardian*, 14 August 2008. The scheme is discussed in *R (Niazi and Ors) v Home Secretary* [2008] EWCA Civ 755.

[538] Heard C and Fair H, 'Pre-trial detention and its over-use: evidence from ten countries' Project Report (London: Institute for Crime and Justice Policy Research, 2019). Online at: <https://eprints.bbk.ac.uk/30084/1/pre-trial%20detention%20final.pdf> (accessed 10 September 2020).

with no remedy other than to sue for compensation in the civil courts.[539] In some cases, though, no amount of compensation could cover the tragic loss of life that can accompany such cases, such as that of Sarah Reed who took her own life whilst on remand and without adequate mental healthcare in HMP Holloway in 2016.[540]

(f) *Breach of statutory duty:* This arises where no other remedy is available. However, it is unclear whether this action is possible in respect of all or even any breaches of PACE, and it certainly does not apply to rights found in the codes of practice only (such as the right to be informed of one's rights in s.56 of PACE) as the latter are not statutes. In *Cullen v Chief Constable of the RUC*[541] the police in Northern Ireland breached the equivalent of s.58 PACE by not giving reasons for denying a suspect in custody access to legal advice. The House of Lords held that as the denial was justified, no real harm was done, so the action failed, but left the door open for similar claims.

A further set of claims also arise in relation to the police's public duty to preserve the peace and protect the public by investigating and suppressing crime. For some time, this avenue of liability was unavailable. However, recent case law has paved the way for a growing obligation by the police to a private duty of care, primarily towards victims and potential victims of serious crime such as domestic homicide, trial witnesses murdered by the accused and sexual violence.[542] This 'collision course' of tort and human rights claims is of growing importance to actions against the police. It is against this backdrop that the eventual victory under the HRA of the victims of the notorious 'black cab rapist' John Worboys can be seen (see chapters 1 and 12).[543]

11.4.5.2 Rights but what remedies?

Just as the biggest obstacle in the way of prosecuting the police is that much malpractice which would be criminal if done by 'normal' people is not criminal when done by the police, the same is true of suing the police. Civil action is limited in respect of much of the subject matter of this book, such as the right to legal advice, not to be kept incommunicado and to be informed of one's rights; and the duties of the police to interrogate in accordance with Code of Practice C. These provisions are at the centre of the 'balance' struck by the Royal Commission on Criminal Procedure (Philips Commission): a quid pro quo for increasing police powers (regarding stop-search and pre-charge detention, for example). It was supposedly because these safeguards were so powerful that the right of silence had to go (see section 5.3). Loss of reputation can be compensated by suing for libel. Homeless travellers can be ejected from one's holiday cottage, development land or empty office block and sued for the owner's loss of amenity. But there is no such remedy if one is isolated from a lawyer and/or induced into a false confession through lies or deception.[544] The human rights perspective says little about the inadequate protection of the rights of suspects except in extreme cases. And, despite the John Worboys case (earlier) the ECHR has barely increased the remedies available.

This raises an important point about what purpose or purposes civil litigation serves. The Worboys case illustrates its potential as both an accountability tool and mechanism

---

[539] See <http://business.timesonline.co.uk/tol/business/law/article4619822.ece> (accessed 5 January 2010).
[540] See <https://www.inquest.org.uk/sarah-reed-inquest-conclusions> (accessed 10 September 2020).
[541] *Cullen v Chief Constable of the RUC* [2003] 1 WLR 1763.
[542] See especially *Robinson v Chief Constable of West Yorkshire* [2018] UKSC 4. For a discussion of earlier cases see Conaghan J, 'Investigating rape: human rights and police accountability' (2017) 37 *Legal Studies* 54–77. Also see ch 12.
[543] *DSD v Commissioner of Police for the Metropolis* [2018] UKSC 11.
[544] Sanders A, 'Rights, Remedies and the Police and Criminal Evidence Act' [1988b] *Criminal Law Review* 802.

for restitution in which individual complainants are able to seek financial compensation and answers about their treatment by the police. It may also have regulatory properties too, certainly if changes to police policies and practices are forthcoming, with the chances of this happening on a national scale being more likely where civil litigation receives widespread public attention. Where that is not the case, though, judicial review may be a more effective way of influencing organisational reform.[545] Where these regulatory aspects of civil litigation are more limited is in relation to deterring or controlling malpractice. Since torts are not crimes, punishment and deterrence are not the main objectives, so 'damages' are awarded simply to compensate for loss. But since torts are wrongs, it is sometimes possible to award 'punitive' or 'exemplary' damages. In the classic American Ford Pinto case huge punitive damages were awarded against Ford because it knew that the Pinto car had a dangerous design fault, but calculated that it would be cheaper to pay the occasional fatal damages claim than to change the design.[546] Punitive damages can be awarded against public bodies in relation to 'oppressive, arbitrary or unconstitutional action by the servants of government'[547] where 'the official acted intentionally or maliciously . . . with a reckless disregard for its legality'.[548] This is to punish and deter, but when the police lose an action it is not the individual officers who pay the damages but the police organisation, thereby blunting the deterrent effects of punitive damages. Moreover, the Court of Appeal sets limits to what juries could award, further blunting this regulatory tool.[549]

11.4.5.3 Pursuing civil actions

Having the right to sue does not mean that one is always able to sue. The first problem is establishing a case on the balance of probabilities (the civil standard of proof), when it is usually just one person's word against another's. Evidence of previous malpractice by the officers concerned can assist. But it is hard to obtain because the main way in which malpractice can be demonstrated is the flawed complaints system, which means that complaints do not necessarily lead to disciplinary action or prosecution of the police officers involved (see section 11.2 and the case of Leon Briggs discussed in 11.4.6.1). The second problem is that many people cannot afford the cost of a lawyer, and suspects are disproportionately drawn from the poorest sections of society. Legal aid is, in principle, available for those who cannot afford to sue. However, the means test has been steadily tightened up over the last 25 years, making an ever smaller proportion of the population eligible for legal aid. After the introduction of LASPO, and the Jackson Review and subsequent reform of 'no win no fee arrangements', the availability of legal aid depends on the cost/benefit ratio being satisfied, meaning that damages received must exceed the costs incurred,[550] and on the case thus being unsuitable for a conditional fee agreement (CFA).[551] However, many civil actions against the police *are* suitable for CFAs, which then rules out the possibility of legal aid, yet at the same time if the complainant signs a CFA they still have to pay their

---

[545] Rowe (2020: 56).
[546] See <http://www.calbaptist.edu/dskubik/pinto.htm> (accessed 5 January 2010).
[547] *Rookes v Barnard* [1964]. Now also see *Holden v Chief Constable of Lancashire* [1987].
[548] Cane P, *Tort Law and Economic Interests* (Oxford: OUP, 1996) p 301.
[549] *Thompson v Metropolitan Police Comr,* [1997] 2 All ER 762. For detailed discussion see Dixon and Smith (1998). These limits continue to be applied, as in *Rees v Met Police Commissioner* [2019] EWHC 2339 (QB) (the continuation of the *Rees* case cited earlier).
[550] This need not be the case where there is a wider public interest in the case, in which case the LAA considers whether the costs are proportionate to this public interest. On the whole, though, action against the police can involve relatively small sums of money, meaning that the cost-benefit ratio criteria may not be met.
[551] McGhie F, 'Overcoming the public funding hurdles' *Legal Action*, March 2015, online at: <https://www.lag.org.uk/article/202710/overcoming-the-public-funding-hurdles> (accessed 10 September 2020).

solicitors fees whether or not they are fully recovered from the police. It is therefore a high risk strategy.

Victims of improper police treatment are caught between a 'rock and a hard place'. The low level of damages awarded in actions against the police precludes many from accessing legal aid. Having to pay solicitor fees themselves, if they have the resources to do so, is very risky, given that if they lose they will also have to also pay the police's legal costs. Whilst a CFA is possible, again, due to the low level of any payout they may receive, they will end up having to pay their solicitors' fees regardless of the amount they are awarded in damages, meaning that they still potentially end up out of pocket. Clearly this is going to make civil action against the police off-putting to all but those who can afford the financial risk. Instead, such complainants may have to put their faith in the police complaints process which, as discussed earlier rarely produces satisfactory results. Moreover, the police complaints process may not produce the sense of satisfaction and vindication that civil litigants experience in actions against the police.[552]

How does this work in practice? 'Starting points' for non-punitive damages were set out (in the late 1990s)[553] at £500 (or £842.26 for claims made after 2013) for each hour of unlawful detention on a reducing scale. Presumably, then, a wrongful stop-search or arrest which did not lead to police station detention would attract far less than this. Such a brief detention, even if accompanied by an assault not causing injury, would not attract significant damages even if a claim of assault was upheld, so legal aid would generally not be provided. Malicious prosecution attracts higher sums because the suffering is drawn-out while fighting one's case.

Serious malpractice can attract significant damages. In *Hsu* the Court of Appeal decided that each plaintiff should receive £20,000 in non-punitive damages. Opinions on whether that was sufficient compensation for the degrading and unlawful actions of the police might legitimately differ. But it is hard for us to understand the psychological impact of such treatment if we have not experienced it ourselves. It is also important to note that the complainants' behaviour either historically or at the time of the incident they are complaining about can influence the amount awarded, with those who have multiple prior contacts with the police on the whole being awarded less in damages.[554]

Most cases are settled out of court. The plaintiff generally accepts a lower level of damages but avoids the delay involved in pursuing court proceedings and the risk of losing. However, the opportunity that a public court hearing would have provided for bringing police officers to account is lost. When police forces settle they avoid the shame of a public hearing and adjudication and do not admit liability. Thus most civil actions do little to punish, deter or genuinely compensate for the suffering. Take Leslie Burnett, who in 1988 was stopped by two officers who said they saw him tampering with a car. He was kicked, stamped and racially abused. At the police station: 'They all came to look at me like I was an exhibit in a zoo . . . and laughing.' Charged with assaulting the police, he was acquitted. In 1991 the Metropolitan Police settled out-of-court, awarding him £40,000 plus costs. But the police did not admit liability nor apologise to him. Mr Burnett said: 'I feel very bitter. . . . I see the officers in the street and they laugh at me. Why are they still in the police?'[555]

Since 1988 history has repeated itself several times. Babar Ahmad was arrested in 2003 for suspected terrorism. A civil jury awarded £60,000 to compensate him for being punched, stamped on, kicked and strangled. Yet the officer who did this remained in

---

[552] Smith G, 'Actions for damages against the police and attitudes of claimants' (2003) 13(4) *Policing & Society* 413–422.　　[553] *Hsu and Thompson* [1997] 2 All ER 762.
[554] As in *Rees v Met Police Commissioner* [2019] EWHC 2339 (QB).　　[555] *The Guardian*, 2 July 1991.

the police and continued to attract complaints of racist assault and was (unsuccessfully) prosecuted in 2009.[556] In the infamous Stephen Lawrence case, Duwayne Brooks was one of the victims but was treated by the police as a suspect. He was arrested for the murder of his friend simply because (a) he was there; and (b) he was black. He was then repeatedly charged with offences, all of which failed in court. The police finally agreed to settle the case for £100,000 in 2006—13 years after the initial assault.[557] Not by coincidence, Francisco Borg is another black man who, with a friend, was attacked by a gang in 1997, and asked the police for help. Instead, he was sprayed with CS gas, arrested and prosecuted. After the police dropped the charges Mr Borg began civil proceedings. The police gave him £40,000 in an out-of-court settlement in 2003, after the arresting officer admitted giving 'incorrect information'. Like Burnett, he remained aggrieved at the police attitude.[558]

Overall, tens or even hundreds of millions of pounds have been paid to victims of malpractice over the last 30 years. For example, in the 17 years from 1991 to 2008, the Metropolitan Police alone paid out some £30m.[559] No figures are available for the English and Welsh police as a whole, which is in itself scandalous and has lead academics to make FOIs in order to access these data. Table 12.3 presents data from such an FOI. For the 25 police forces that responded, it shows an overall downward trend in the claims made and claims substantiated between 2012 and 2017 and also in the amount of money offered as compensation as a result. This may be due to growing restrictions placed on legal aid and on 'no-win no-fee' cases following the Jackson Review in 2009 discussed earlier,[560] both of which mean greater financial risks involved for citizens that pursue claims against the police. Had this FOI included data from all 43 forces this suggests that roughly £6.9 million may have been paid out each year in civil actions brought by citizens, despite all of the obstacles strewn in the path of those wanting to sue the police.

From the due process viewpoint a growth in successful civil actions represents justice, and no more need be said. But the crime control perspective suggests the money could be better spent on more positive aspects of policing. The crime control adherent would first act, as the Court of Appeal did in *Hsu*, to reduce the amount of money paid out.

Table 12.3 Successful civil actions against 25 police forces in England and Wales 2012–17

	2012	2013	2014	2015	2016	2017
Actions resulting in substantiated claims	1212 (40%)	1042 (34%)	1070 (38%)	927 (35%)	952 (38%)	709 (29%)
No. of cases	3043	3043	2808	2653	2524	2447
Amount paid	£3,719,559	£4,783,633	£4,512,365	£4,317,038	£3,584,838	£2,9743,23

Adapted from Rowe (2020) and based on an FOI submitted to all police forces in England and Wales

---

[556] *The Guardian*, 4 November 2009.   [557] *The Guardian*, 10 March 2006.
[558] *The Guardian*, 24 April 2003. Claimants are generally more concerned that their grievances get an airing, and that the police recognise their mistakes and put measures in place to reduce the risk of recurrence, than to secure large amounts of money in compensation: Smith (2003).
[559] See Metropolitan Police Commissioner, *Annual Reports*.   [560] Rowe (2020: 53-58).

And, second, insist that the police complaints system is normally used first on the questionable assumption that under the IOPC it is less biased than its predecessors.[561]

For us, the answer is to tackle the problem at source by reducing the amount of malpractice so that there are fewer victims and less money paid out. This means creating organisational structures and cultures which discourage malpractice. For cases like Leslie Burnett's seem to have done little either to change police behaviour or to protect the freedom of people like him. Clearly civil actions do not succeed well in deterring malpractice, otherwise the number and value of civil claims would be going down significantly and not due to changes in access to legal aid to pursue those cases.

11.4.6 Death during or following contact with CJ institutions

11.4.6.1 Investigating deaths during or following police contact: The role of the IOPC[562]

In 2018/19, there were 276 deaths during or following police contact of which 42 were road traffic fatalities, three were fatal police shootings, 16 were deaths in or following police custody, including when arrested, detained or being taken to a medical facility (see also section 4.4), 63 were apparent suicides in the two days following police custody or where police custody was implicated in someone's suicide at a later point, and 152 were other deaths following police contact,[563] including for example after the police were contacted because someone was missing or because there were concerns about their mental health.[564] As noted in section 11.2.2, when someone dies during or following police contact, Art 2 of the ECHR is engaged.[565] This obliges the state not to take life, except in very limited and defined circumstances, and to take reasonable steps to protect life where there is a real and immediate risk. This means, for example, that where there is an indication that a death may be the result of police action, or failure to act, Art 2 requires that there is an independent and effective investigation to determine the circumstances and causes of the death. Indeed, in 2018/19, the vast majority of deaths during or following police contact were independently investigated by the IOPC, which aside from being in accordance with Art 2 requirements, is appropriate to their seriousness and the level of concern they generate for family members and the wider public.

---

[561] Discretion is retained to by-pass the complaints system: Legal Services Commission, *Funding Code Amendments 2005*. This followed a proposal on these lines in a Consultation Paper: *Legal Services Commission, A New Focus for Civil Legal Aid* (London: LSC, 2004) paras 4.7–4.10. See <http://www.legalservices.gov.uk/civil/guidance/funding_code.asp> (accessed 15 December 2009).

[562] Whilst we focus here primarily on the accountability mechanisms that arise when someone dies during or following police contact, there are also various regulatory mechanisms that should also be engaged to ensure that deaths are prevented in the first place. For deaths in police custody, for example, these include Code C of the PACE Codes of Practice and The College of Policing's Authorised Professional Practice, which both offer guidance on matters critical to preventing deaths in custody, including on risk assessment, healthcare provision, support for vulnerable detainees and the use of bail conditions. HMICFRS/HMIP also inspect police custody around a similar range of issues and will flag failings where they see them which, if addressed by police forces, should also help to prevent deaths in or following police custody. In 2014, a concordat was also signed between HMICFRS/HMIP, the College of Policing and the IPPC (now the IOPC) to share and promote best practice, which therefore reflects a growing regulatory not just accountability role for the IOPC too when it comes to deaths during and following police contact. See <https://www.policeconduct.gov.uk/sites/default/files/Documents/Who-we-are/Our-Policies/concordat_HMIC_COP_IPCC.pdf> (accessed 22 July 2020).

[563] These figures only include deaths in this category that involved an independent investigation by the IOPC.

[564] IOPC (2019e) *Deaths during or following police contact: Statistics for England and Wales 2018/19*. Online at: <https://www.policeconduct.gov.uk/sites/default/files/Documents/statistics/deaths_during_following_police_contact_201819.pdf> (accessed 25 August 2020).

[565] *Edwards v UK* 46477/99 [2002] ECHR 303. See also *Anguelova v Bulgaria* (2004) 38 EHRR 31 and *Jasinskis v Latvia* (2010) ECHR 1.

The one exception to this in 2018/19 was apparent suicides following police contact, the majority of which (48) were locally investigated by the relevant police force, with six being independently investigated and nine being referred back to relevant forces by the IOPC to make their own decision about how to proceed.[566] This more limited independent investigation of apparent suicides is perhaps because decisions about who should investigate such cases of deaths after police contact are not as clear-cut as for deaths during police contact. For starters, the links between someone's suicide and their contact with the police may not always be made and it may also be unclear whether prior police contact was a relevant factor in someone's death, especially if it fell outside the 48 hour window after contact. So the figures of apparent suicides after police contact may not be reliable, and may fluctuate according to political pressures, not just actual deaths.[567]

Independent investigation does not guarantee an outcome that family members consider to be just: the IOPC can only recommend disciplinary action be taken and refer cases to the CPS, leaving decisions about what happens next to the relevant police force and the CPS. The flaws in this process were highlighted by the recent case of Leon Briggs who died following restraint in a police cell whilst he was in the midst of a mental health crisis. His case was independently investigated and the IOPC referred the case to the CPS and recommended that disciplinary proceedings take place. However, the CPS decided not to prosecute the six officers involved. A misconduct tribunal collapsed in 2020, the blame for which was attributed to the IOPC by the police, and vice versa. After seven years of waiting, this situation reportedly left Mr Briggs' family 'devastated and outraged'. They lost faith in the IOPC and were fearful that the failures of the accountability process sent a message to police officers that they may act with impunity.[568]

The shifting of blame from one organisation to another, causing accountability mechanisms to fail, also arises where many agencies are involved in the lead up to someone's death. For example, though the police were largely found responsible for Sean Rigg's death in a police station in 2008 (see section 4.4), his mental health team were also implicated. Moreover, after he collapsed in police custody, the Forensic Medical Examiner failed to stay with him whilst he was in cardiac arrest.[569] Since police, medical and mental health practitioners each have their own set of accountability mechanisms, scrutiny of inter-organisational factors is discouraged and the factors that may be at the root of someone's death during or following police contact are not considered in the round. Coroners take a broader look at the circumstances of someone's death, and may make recommendations for future practice, but they have few powers to enforce these recommendations and therefore to ensure that others do not suffer similar lethal consequences of the actions of the police and other parties in the future (see next). In sum, though the police and other criminal justice practitioners increasingly work in conjunction with a range of other practitioners and organisations, including in incidents which lead to the most tragic and abhorrent deaths of citizens, this is not mirrored by correspondingly joined up approaches to accountability. This leads to inadequate explanations of what went wrong, and inadequate redress.

---

[566] IOPC (2019e: 4).
[567] Phillips et al, 'Non-custodial deaths: Missing, ignored or unimportant?' (2019) 19(2) *Criminology and Criminal Justice* 160–178.
[568] See <https://www.bbc.co.uk/news/uk-england-beds-bucks-herts-51587151> (accessed 22 July 2020).
[569] Baker D, *Deaths After Police Contact Constructing Accountability in the 21st Century* (London: Palgrave McMillan, 2017) pp 3–4.

11.4.6.2 Coronial processes

A death during or following contact with criminal justice organisations such as the police must also be referred to the coroner, who must then engage a pathologist so that a post-mortem may be carried out, a cause of death established and a public inquest must be opened typically involving a jury if the death happened *in* state custody.[570] Such inquests address the circumstances not just the means by which someone died through an inquisitorial fact finding process rather than via adversarial ascription of guilt: 'Their role is to establish who died, when and where they died, and how they died'.[571] As the Hillsborough case mentioned at the start of this chapter demonstrates, however, inquests can be far from neutral fact-finding exercises, they can be politically and emotionally charged with far-reaching consequences for those directly affected, but also for wider society and citizens' views of the legitimacy of criminal justice accountability mechanisms.

The ECHR has led to the scope of inquests being widened. Coroners now place emphasis on the circumstances of someone's death, including potentially systemic issues, and frequently use narrative verdicts (i.e. lengthier statement of findings) rather than short-form verdicts, or determinations, as they are now supposed to be known.[572] However, narrative determinations discourage lessons being learned, because they are lumped together in the 'unclassified category', which prevents meaningful statistical analysis of what these inquests collectively show.[573] At the same time, the detail enables the development of an official narrative of the circumstances of someone's death which may provide clarity and accuracy in complex cases, and which may enable a sense of closure for families.[574]

Though coroners' inquests are largely an accountability mechanism, a recent additional Art 2-related development has placed growing emphasis on the regulatory aspects of inquests, at least in theory. From 2013, the Chief Coroner directed coroners to mandatorily write a report to prevent future deaths (PFD) if a coroner had concerns that further deaths may arise. This report is then shared with the relevant authority who should, in theory, share it with relevant parts of their own organisation. There is also a requirement that this relevant authority—for example, chief police officers—must respond to the report within 56 days. However, there are no penalties for not responding to the report and the relevant authorities may simply acknowledge the report within the required timeframe rather than focusing on the quality of their response or on taking action in-line with the reports' recommendations. There are also often lengthy delays between a death and the publication of a PFD report and, furthermore, limited opportunity for the sharing of learning from reports across a range of criminal justice institutions (police, probation prisons), where there may be comparable but also inter-agency lessons to be learned.[575]

---

[570] ECHR, Art 2; Coroners and Justice Act 2009 s.1(2).

[571] Baker D, Deaths after police contact in England and Wales: the effects of Article 2 of the European Convention on Human Rights on coronial practice (2016) 12(2) *International Journal of Law in Context* 162–177 at 164.

[572] Ibid. Unclassified conclusions of inquests of which narrative verdicts are a part increased from 0.7% of all conclusions to inquests in 1995 to 20% in 2019. Indeed, this growth in unclassified conclusions is a key contributing factor to the increase in all conclusions. See: MOJ (2019a) *Coroner Statistics Annual 2019, England and Wales and Coroners statistics 2019: England and Wales* (statistical tables). Online at: <https://www.gov.uk/government/statistics/coroners-statistics-2019> (accessed 26 August 2020). [573] Baker (2016).

[574] Baker D, 'Using narrative to construct accountability in cases of death after police contact' (2019) 52(1) *Australian and New Zealand Journal of Criminology* 60–75.

[575] For a discussion of the importance of recommendations revolving around the need for collaboration and information sharing, particularly in cases of apparent suicide following police contact see: Chidgey K, Procter N, Baker A and Grech C, 'Suicide deaths following police contact: A review of coronial inquest findings' (2020) *Death Studies* 1–9.

In part, this is because this is not the purpose of the PFD reports, but also because they are published online, without a searchable database,[576] though plans were announced in 2020 to make recommendations in PFD reports more digestible and enforceable.[577] Regardless, since PFD reports were introduced there has not been a corresponding decrease in deaths, for example, during or following police contact, as might be expected were coroners' recommendations being put into practice.[578]

A further major area of concern has been about whether families have a voice in the inquest and can participate on equal terms with the criminal justice organisations being held to account. The latter are generally legally represented, but grieving families have to negotiate a complex, bureaucratic process in the hope of securing a legal aid lawyer. This stark contrast was noted by families during the first inquest into the Hillsborough disaster mentioned at the start of the chapter:[579]

> 'Police interests were well represented but the families – 43 of them – were represented by only one barrister, which we had to fund ourselves.' Family member

> 'For the first inquests, some families paid for one member of Counsel. We could not be included in this, so my brother was not represented. I, along with my partner, attended the inquest independently on a few occasions but felt really excluded as when the families went into a private room with the barrister, we were not privy to these conversations as we were not a paying client. We had no input into the first inquests whatsoever.' Debbie Matthews, sister of Brian Matthews[580]

In spite of Hillsborough, recommendations in the 2017 Angiolini review into *Deaths and Serious Incidents in Police Custody*, and campaigning work by charities such as Inquest[581] for automatic non-means-tested funding for legal representation during inquests, a 2019 government review concluded that the situation should remain largely unchanged.[582] This underscores the point made in the introduction to this chapter about the disadvantageous position of often times already disadvantaged citizens—by dint of structural forms of inequality—relative to powerful criminal justice organisations asked to account for their actions. This is so even when a citizen's family member has died after contact with the criminal justice system and whilst they seek to understand what happened.

---

[576] PFD reports for police-related deaths can be found here: <https://www.judiciary.uk/subject/police-related-deaths/> (accessed 26 August 2020).

[577] Kempen K, 'A summary review of talk given by the Deputy Chief Coroner at the IAP Keeping Safe Conference' ICVA Newsletter, 28 February 2020.

[578] Baker (2017).

[579] At the time of writing, the parents of Zane Gbangbola have once again raised the importance of the availability of legal aid for all families during inquests, as without one they felt they were unable to properly challenge the circumstances of their 7-year-old son's death and whether it was due to carbon monoxide poisoning, as claimed by the authorities, or hydrogen cyanide due to the dumping of landfill gas. See here: <https://www.truthaboutzane.com/#> (accessed 30 October 2020).

[580] Jones J, 'The patronising disposition of unaccountable power' A report to ensure the pain and suffering of the Hillsborough families is not repeated (2017) pp 37–39. Online at: <https://assets.publishing.service.gov.uk/government/uploads/system/uploads/attachment_data/file/656130/6_3860_HO_Hillsborough_Report_2017_FINAL_updated.pdf> (accessed 26 August 2020).

[581] See <https://www.inquest.org.uk/legal-aid-for-inquests> (accessed 26 August 2020).

[582] MOJ, Final report: Review of legal aid for inquests (2019g) p 11. Online at: <https://assets.publishing.service.gov.uk/government/uploads/system/uploads/attachment_data/file/777034/review-of-legal-aid-for-inquests.pdf> (accessed 26 August 2020).

11.5 Conclusion

In this chapter we considered the kind of things that can go wrong in the criminal justice process and evaluated the institutional architecture used to regulate the actions and effects of criminal justice officials and to hold them to account. We considered democratic mechanisms, including Police and Crime Commissioners, and the recording of police impropriety by citizens on smartphones. This 'new visibility' was compared with the more limited transparency arising from the carefully managed footage shared with the public from courtroom cameras, and highlights the growing importance of citizen participation in criminal justice accountability and regulation, which we also considered in relation to citizens' roles as volunteer Independent Custody Visitors, for example. We noted the role of the voluntary sector too, whose work can be both regulatory and aimed at holding criminal justice officials to account, e.g. trying to prevent miscarriages of justice and free prisoners who say they are innocent. We lastly considered the lack of Royal Commissions since the 1980s/1990s but the corresponding increase in independent panels that have become a more effective route of publicly addressing wrongdoing.

In the section on organisational accountability we considered the two-stage process for dealing with complaints about criminal justice officials, particularly police officers. The large majority of complaints are still investigated by the police force to whom the complaint relates, if these complaints are formally recorded at all. Only a minority are subject to independent investigation by the IOPC, but even then the police backgrounds of IOPC investigators and managers raises questions about just how independent these investigations are. We also explored the complementary role played by the five criminal justice inspectorates, only one of which monitors and inspects human rights-based issues whilst the remainder focus on efficiency and effectiveness. Since what gets measured gets done the inspectorates indirectly encourage a manageralist focus amongst the organisations that they inspect, i.e. a focus on speedy justice rather than the principles of justice. Like the IOPC, all the inspectorates face major challenges in maintaining their independence either from the organisations they inspect or the politicians that oversee them, and in directing changes to criminal justice policies and practices.

Lastly, we examined the major legal mechanisms used to regulate and hold criminal justice officials to account. This includes trial remedies for the few cases not disposed of by way of guilty pleas. Excluding evidence on the basis of oppression, unreliability, unfairness, abuse of process etc. has a limited regulatory effect on police and prosecutors, in part because the courts tend to base their decisions on the intentions, not the effects, of police actions and because much of the case law is inconsistent and incoherent. We also examined the complexity of the appellate process from the magistrates' and Crown courts. The appellate process is bureaucratic and cumbersome, and therefore difficult and intimidating. With legal aid not guaranteed and potentially carrying the risk of having to pay the prosecution costs, if the appeal fails, this deters all but the wealthy. It is not that the weakest cases are weeded out by the appellate process, rather people with the weakest will and weakest bank balance. Nor is the CCRC a major challenger, as it tends to defer to existing systems and processes. Civil litigation fares no better as an accountability tool and means of seeking financial compensation. Tort-based claims are often unavailable (e.g. if one is denied legal advice in custody), hard to substantiate, with limited punitive effect on the individual officers involved (as compensation is paid by the police force, not them) and unrealistic for most because of the potential costs. Deaths in custody remain a scandal despite improvements in inquests and IOPC investigations.

Bringing all this together in one chapter demonstrates the complexity of accountability and regulation in the criminal justice process. This is a challenge for citizens navigating this process, and sometimes a solution, particularly where some avenues of redress fail. This is illustrated by the Hillsborough tragedy, where justice was only possible because there *were* multiple and partly overlapping forms of redress. Similarly, the police were held to account in the Worboys case through campaigning, combined with civil litigation. Along with the power granted to criminal justice officials, which means they are both a guarantor of, and threat to citizens' well-being and security, this represents a second riddle of accountability. The complexity and multiple and overlapping layers of criminal justice regulation and accountability can bamboozle and thwart, but when a path can be navigated and different forms of regulation and accountability are brought together, at least a few citizens manage to secure something resembling justice. That this is necessary at all shows the power of criminal justice officials relative to citizens, who are largely left to regulate themselves.

One topic has been missing from this chapter: the prosecution of criminal justice officials. In practice that largely means police officers (and prison officers, who are outside the scope of this book). Earlier editions of the book had a section on this but there are so few prosecutions that we dropped it. The most obvious candidates for prosecution are officers causing the death of suspects in custody. But as we discuss in chapter 5 (section 5.4) hardly any are prosecuted, let alone convicted. Even the officers who shot Mr de Menezes' dead, mistaking this Brazilian citizen behaving normally for an Asian terrorist, were not prosecuted. The Met police were convicted, but just for health and safety crimes.[583] Nor was being illegally killed held to be a violation of his right to life.[584] This says it all about how society views police who kill and those who they kill.

But the main reason why most malpractice and (civil) lawbreaking is not prosecuted is because it is not criminal. This might seem like a *non sequitur*. After all, there are lots of things that many of us would like to be defined as criminal but which are not. But take the experience of Girma Belay, a 52-year-old refugee, for example. His home was raided, guns were pointed at him, he was stripped naked, and held in custody for six days. When he was released without charge an officer told him 'Sorry mate—wrong place, wrong time.' We are told 'Mr Belay is a shattered man. Tortured by flashbacks and gripped by fear . . .'.[585] What the police did to him was as devastating as if he had been the victim of a street gang. In an age when it is a crime to steal food when you're hungry, to swear at the police, or to daub graffiti on a building, it seems that government has no great wish to hold the police to account.

Were a better balance being struck between the values of justice, democracy and efficiency, as opposed to justice and democracy being subordinated to efficiency, perhaps fewer things would go wrong in the first place and there would be greater opportunities for accountability when they do. The 'efficient' guilty plea system prevents the accounts of the defence and the prosecution being compared in court, prevents clarification of inconsistencies and reduces the opportunity for trial remedies. The generally limited financial means and socio-cultural capital of users of the criminal justice system also puts them at a disadvantage when it comes to navigating its complexities and that of its regulatory and accountability mechanisms. And bodies like the IOPC and CCRC are starved of resources in the name of efficiency, making them pick and choose who they will try and help, and frequently reaching conclusions when too much time has passed for that to be of much value—which is a completely inefficient way of providing redress for victims of malpractice and wrongful conviction. As a result, citizen-initiated video-recordings and the use of various forms of media offer the greatest hope of levelling the playing field, at least to some extent, and enabling citizens to have a greater role in regulating and holding criminal justice institutions to account.

---

[583] *The Guardian*, 30 March 2016.   [584] *Da Silva v UK* (2016) 63 EHRR 12.
[585] *The Guardian*, 4 August 2005.

Further reading

Giannoulopoulos D, *Improperly Obtained Evidence in Anglo-American and Continental Law* (Oxford: Hart, 2019).

Hoyle C and Sato M, *Reasons to Doubt: Wrongful Convictions and the Criminal Cases Review Commission* (Oxford: OUP, 2019).

Jacobson J, *By mistakes we learn? A review of criminal appeals against sentence*. Project Report (London: Transform Justice, 2013).

Naughton M, 'Appeals Against Wrongful Convictions' in Corteen K, Morley S, Taylor P and Turner J (eds), *A Companion to Crime, Harm and Victimisation* (Bristol: Policy Press, 2016).

Nobles R and Schiff D, 'The Supervision of Guilty Pleas by the Court of Appeal of England and Wales—Workable Relationships and Tragic Choices (2020) *Criminal Law Forum* (online).

Roberts S, 'Post-Conviction Review in England and Wales: Perpetuating and Rectifying Miscarriages of Justice' in Lennon G, King C and McCartney C (ed), *Counter-terrorism, Constitutionalism and Miscarriages of Justice: A Festschrift for Professor Clive Walker* (London: Hart Publishing, 2018) pp 249–267.

Rowe M, *Policing the Police: Challenges of democracy and accountability* (Bristol: Policy Press, 2020).

Savage S, 'Thinking Independence: Calling the Police to Account through the Independent Investigation of Police Complaints' (2013) 53(1) *British Journal of Criminology* 94–112.

Shute S, 'On The Outside Looking In: Reflections on the Role of Inspection in Driving Up Quality in the Criminal Justice System' (2013) 76(3) *Modern Law Review* 494–528.

12

Victims, the accused and the future of criminal justice

KEY ISSUES

- How developments in criminal justice have affected suspects' rights (especially 'proactive' policing)
- Different types of victims' 'rights'
- Do and should victims have (legally) enforceable rights? If so, in relation to what matters?
- Enhancing victims' rights (especially those of vulnerable victims) without eroding defendants' rights
- Concluding thoughts on the future of criminal justice and how focus on 'core values' and the 'freedom' perspective can make it more fair and more effective

12.1 Introduction

In this book we have tried to show that in criminal justice trade-offs cannot be avoided. One of the main trade-offs is that in the course of catching and convicting more criminals, one will catch and convict more innocent people too. Another is that the system cannot always do what victims want, especially if different victims ask for different things, without prejudicing other important values such as equality of treatment. Criminal justice rules and policies reflect the natural ambivalence most of us feel when faced with uncomfortable reality, but unwillingness to accept this lesson fully has led to many rules and policies being unworkable.

This is not to say that due process-based rules, for example, are necessarily unworkable, nor that they are continually broken. The police probably stick to most of the rules most of the time. However, most of the time, the rules enable the police to do their job without difficulty. The problem arises when they get in the way. Due process rules are unworkable in the sense that, in those circumstances, the police have the incentive and the opportunity to break them with little fear of negative consequences. The same is true of procedures for taking account of victims.

The working rules of the law enforcement bureaucracies are not in harmony either with those legal rules which are due process-based or with those which seek to give effect to the interests of victims. And so we have a significant (but unquantifiable) level of rule-breaking by law enforcement agencies, some of which leads to (legally speaking) wrongful conviction, and much of which leads to unnecessary and unpleasant pre-charge detention. But many legal rules are inspired by crime control ideology, so we also have a significant (and also unquantifiable) level of wrongful conviction which is a product of the police following the legal rules, just as much unpleasant pre-charge detention, unequal treatment of different classes, racialised groups and sexes and even deaths in custody are perfectly lawful. The same is true of victims: sometimes what they want is ignored in defiance of applicable policies, and sometimes what they want is ignored in accordance with applicable policies. The criminal justice system encompasses largely crime control-oriented rules and even more profoundly crime control-oriented policies and practices. It follows that, overall, the criminal justice system is not due process or freedom oriented. The core value of 'efficiency' is generally prioritised over 'justice' and 'democracy'. Several important consequences flow from this, which we shall briefly survey in this final chapter.

12.2 Taking suspects' rights seriously

We saw in chapters 3 to 6 that, over the course of the twentieth century the police station became the central site of police investigation. Not only have interrogation-based confessions become steadily more central to the prosecution case, but other investigative procedures take place in, begin from, or are authorised in the police station by the police. PACE and subsequent developments legitimised and facilitated these evolving processes. Take the initiation of prosecutions: arrest and charge (which entail initial detention) have now almost entirely supplanted the use of report and summons (which does not) for all but the most minor offences; and the police themselves are increasingly disposing of cases by warnings, cautions and out of court disposals (OOCDs) (see section 7.4.4). Furthermore, much police power is used to further policies and strategies such as pre-empting protests, gathering information, disciplining 'suspect populations' and so forth, whereby there is no intention of prosecuting. There is nothing new in this, nor in police station detention being used as part of these tactics, but the legitimisation of all this has probably increased its scale, such that around half of all arrests do not result in any further action. A core crime control value is trust in the police. Trends in criminal justice show that policy-makers do generally have blind faith in them, and these trends intensified over the first two decades of this century.

Against our argument, one might contend that the police are closely regulated and that the system is 'in balance'. After all, everything that takes place in the station is regulated by custody officers, records, time limits, recordings (in the case of interrogations), special safeguards where suspects are vulnerable (such as appropriate adults, healthcare practitioners and so forth) and access to free legal advice for all. There are guarantees of proper treatment and freedom from coercion and violence. The CPS protects defendants by dropping weak cases. And technological developments such as body-worn cameras reduce the number of times the rhetorical question 'Are you doubting the word of a police officer?' decides who is believed. None of this works perfectly, but one might still argue that these protections operate satisfactorily most of the time. Most suspects who do not secure legal advice, for example, choose not to seek it and come to no harm as a result of not securing it. While there is some truth in these counter-arguments they are flawed.

First, they ignore wider developments that have circumvented the PACE regime. For while PACE made some policing controllable in the station, much policing has moved back outside, bringing in its wake several of the old problems and many new ones. Thus the practices of stop and account, stop-search and other forms of 'informal interviewing' (both inside and outside the station) enable the police to sidestep the controls now associated with formal interrogation. Moreover, many people who might otherwise have been forced to 'confess' are now simply tricked into committing crime while informers and undercover officers or surveillance devices look on. Surveillance generally has exploded as digital technology has made it so much easier and cheaper over time. And many OOCDs and warnings are administered outside the station by front-line officers free of any effective supervision.

Second, the police mainly regulate themselves: the officer carrying out the stop-search fills in the stop-search form, the police investigate complaints against themselves, and so forth. Self-regulation only works when it is in the interest of the organisation to secure compliance (see chapter 11). This is not, in the main, the case with the police. Effective regulation requires that power be dispersed—which, in the case of the police station, would mean giving defence solicitors, say, many more rights over the police than they have at present.[1] As it is, there is less accountability with each new development, creating more scope for malpractice and corruption.

Body-worn video (BWV) had been thought to solve much of this: since front-line officers are supposed to be issued BWV standardly, contested encounters should be automatically filmed. However, its usage should be 'incident-specific', proportionate and necessary to the situation.[2] Not only is it not 'on' all the time, but the officers themselves decide when and whether to turn it on (and off).[3] Moreover, the frame of view points out to suspects and victims, so what the police are doing is not necessarily recorded.[4] So not only can the footage be misleading but its apparent objectivity can lead to other evidence—that could change a court's understanding of an incident—being disregarded, as even the official 'police watchdog' has stated.[5]

The move to proactive and pre-emptive policing and on-street dispositions shows the resourcefulness of the government and its agencies to achieve the same goals as before but to find new ways of doing so when legal rules get in the way. But the police are neither structured nor sufficiently culturally attuned to make effective use of crime intelligence and scientific data to the extent required by the 'intelligence-led' model.[6] Moreover, the institutionally racist assumptions that structure policing and criminal justice also structures the artificial intelligence (AI), leading to subjective targeting. In a classic 'damned with faint praise' attempt at AI's defence, the former director of the Office of Science and Technology at the US National Institute of Justice said: 'There's no question that you can have biases within data but there are some ways to detect that bias mathematically,... These tools allow officers to make real decisions with, in my view, much less bias than they otherwise might.'[7]

---

[1] Sanders A, 'Can Coercive Powers be Effectively Controlled or Regulated?' in Cape E and Young R (eds), *Regulating Policing* (Oxford: Hart, 2008); Shearing C and Froestad J, 'Nodal Governance and the Zwelethemba Model' in Quirk et al (eds), *Regulation and Criminal Justice* (Cambridge: CUP, 2010).

[2] College of Policing, *Body-Worn Video* (2014). For use in relation to suspects, see ch 5.

[3] For discussion of the problems arising see Taylor E, 'Lights, Camera, Redaction... police body-worn cameras: autonomy, discretion and accountability' (2016) 14 *Surveillance and Society* 128.

[4] Adams I and Mastracci S, 'Visibility is a trap: the ethics of police body-worn cameras and control' (2017) 39 *Administrative Theory and Praxis* 313.

[5] IPCC, *IPCC Position Statement on Body Worn Video* (2016). The IPCC was the body that investigated serious complaints against the police until it was replaced by the IOPC (see ch 11). For a general discussion see Bowling B and Shruti I, 'Automated Policing: The Case of Body-Worn Video (2019) 15 *International Journal of Law in Context* 140.

[6] Maguire M and John T, *Intelligence, Surveillance and Informants: Integrated Approaches* (Police Research Series Paper 64) (London: Home Office, 1995); Barton A and Evans R, *Proactive Policing on Merseyside* (Police Research Series Paper No 105) (London: Home Office, 1999); on 'crime analysis' see Cope N, 'Intelligence Led Policing or Policing Led Intelligence?' (2004) 44 *British Journal of Criminology* 188; on police failings in collating simple information, particularly in relation to the murders of Jessica Chapman and Holly Wells, see Gill P, 'Policing in Ignorance?' (2004) 58 *Criminal Justice Matters* 14.

[7] Baraniuk C, 'Caught Before the Act' *New Scientist*, 11 March 2015.

However, proactive policing can only supplement, not supplant, reactive policing.[8] To organise a police force solely around 'targeted' crime and not to react to serious 'non-targeted' offending is unthinkable. Serious crimes will always be committed without the police's prior knowledge, thus calling for an investigative reaction. The police have to have some powers if there is to be a reasonable conviction rate without unreasonable expenditure of resources. However, their powers have been massively increased in defiance of two of the three 'core values': at the same time as proactive policing was developing in order to counteract the effect of PACE on police 'success' rates, the government virtually abolished the right to silence, sidelined legal advice (e.g. by making it more inaccessible through cuts to legal aid budgets) and reduced the need to intimidate to secure confessions, because silence became equally incriminating (chapter 5). A main plank of the so-called 'balanced' system was removed.

There are no remedies available to suspects who suffer from many of these rules being broken, and the remedies that are available are deeply flawed. Unfairly and illegally obtained evidence is frequently used at trial (chapter 11). And we know from chapters 7 to 9 that trials are rare anyway, for a host of reasons that have only a tenuous link with factual guilt and innocence. Further, the main reason why so many people do as the police tell them on the street, or refuse legal advice and make incriminating statements, is that they experience policing—especially in the station—as coercive, frightening and humiliating. Suspects make coerced choices without the police having to be overtly threatening or hostile. This crime control-based system subjects the police to the rule of law only in a minimalist and largely rhetorical manner.[9] The Human Rights Act, and the ECHR generally, has made little difference, acting only as the lowest of safety nets. As for the CPS acting as a safeguard, if the objective is to protect suspects and defendants would it not be better to put more resources into funding defence lawyers, into strengthening the defence side of the adversarial system?

A different challenge to our view of the system as primarily crime control oriented comes from Ericson and Haggerty, who argue that criminal justice has been completely transformed.[10] This rests on a wider argument that developed societies are becoming ever more obsessed with 'risk' (chapter 10). Institutions and individuals increasingly expect 'security', and the more breaches of that security there are, the more that (unfulfillable) demand swells. Risk assessment and risk management, based on progressively expanding information, have therefore become key tools in the attempt to increase security. The police are one of the key providers of information, particularly as their information-gathering powers increase. Hence the growth of powers to secure surveillance and other types of information, such as keeping DNA records of around a million arrested people who have not even been prosecuted.[11] BWV is another way of keeping mass information on suspects as well as offenders through facial recognition technology.[12]

Then there is a ratcheting effect: according to the government's own human genetics commission many people are arrested simply in order to justify taking a DNA sample.[13] So powers are created to take samples, then other powers are stretched in order to facilitate

---

[8] See, for example, Heaton R, 'Intelligence-Led Policing and Volume Crime Reduction' (2009) 3 *Policing* 292.
[9] See further Sanders A and Young R, 'The Rule of Law, Due Process and Pre-Trial Criminal Justice' (1994b) 47 *Current Legal Problems* 125.
[10] Ericson R and Haggerty K, *Policing the Risk Society* (Oxford: Clarendon Press, 1997).
[11] Keeping these records indefinitely is contrary to Art 8 of the ECHR: *Marper v UK* [2008] ECHR 1581. See ch 6. [12] Bowling and Shruti (2019).
[13] Human Genetics Commission [HGC], *Nothing to Hide, Nothing to Fear?* (London: HGC, 2009) See *The Guardian*, 24 November 2009.

taking as many samples as possible. Other examples include 'public protection' (MAPPA) monitoring of people who have been acquitted,[14] registration requirements and other forms of surveillance of sex offenders and 'foreign students', the accumulation of information on people subject to civil preventative measures (CPMs) (see chapter 1), and powers to freeze the funds of suspected terrorists (who have never been even charged with offences remotely connected with terrorism).[15] It is sometimes claimed that developments like this represent a shift in focus from 'post-crime' (that is, dealing with crimes that have been committed) to 'pre-crime' (that is, crime prevention and apprehension of crime at the planning stage).[16]

These developments are common to many western societies.[17] We can infer from this that the structural roots of these changes go deeper than the particular political or legislative fads of any one moment. Other agencies such as local authorities—not only the police—are increasing their information-gathering and surveillance powers and sharing information with each other. This results in government-by-information (or 'governmentality', as it is characterised by Foucault and his followers).[18] This disperses state power more widely than had been the case in earlier times.

Whilst these analyses accurately describe current developments up to a point, their 'either/or-ism' (crime control or surveillance control, state power or dispersed power, pre-crime or post-crime) is unnecessary. These processes are consistent with our argument that the system increasingly prioritises the core value of 'efficiency' over 'justice' and 'democracy'. As some crime control techniques, such as coercive interrogation methods, become more difficult to use—because there are some due process developments, and some of them are effective to some extent—surveillance techniques and scientific methods develop to fill the gap. Risk analysis does not displace crime control, but rather shores it up. The two go hand-in-hand. Further, as criminal methods become more sophisticated, so the methods of detecting it have to develop accordingly. Old methods are not replaced; they are supplemented by new ones so that a 'menu' of detection methods is available to cover increasingly varied needs.

Take terrorism legislation. The first edition of this book (1994) hardly mentioned it, as we actually believed that it could be, as the government claimed, 'temporary'. It became evident in the late 1990s that this was not true, so we did discuss it in the second edition. By the time that edition was published, in 2000, the conflict in Northern Ireland looked like it was going to be concluded peacefully, and we wondered whether we had been right the first time. How naive we were. Not only have new targets of this legislation been found, but the provisions have got much tougher and many of them have found their way into

---

[14] Such as Barry George who was acquitted of the murder of Jill Dando. His MAPPA order required him to keep the police informed of his address and movements. He challenged this in court (*The Guardian*, 30 November 2009) but left the UK as: 'I was hounded out of this country, It became impossible for me to walk anywhere as the police were following me everywhere. They had me under surveillance. It felt very claustrophobic. I was stopped and searched dozens of times. It was always public and it was humiliating.' (*Daily Mirror* 14 July 2013). MAPPA arrangements are set out at <https://www.gov.uk/government/publications/multi-agency-public-protection-arrangements-mappa--3> (accessed 24 July 2020).

[15] Sanctions and Anti-Money Laundering Act 2018.

[16] McCulloch J and Pickering S, 'Pre-Crime and Counter-Terrorism Imagining Future Crime in the "War on Terror"' (2009) 49 *British Journal of Criminology* 628; McCulloch J and Wilson D, *Pre-crime: Preemption, Precaution and the Future* (Routledge, London, 2016). For example, the HGC (2009) argues that the DNA database creates 'pre-suspects'.

[17] See, for example, Fijnaut C and Marx G (eds), *Undercover: Police Surveillance in Comparative Perspective* (The Hague: Kluwer, 1996); Marx G, *Windows into the Soul: Surveillance and Society in an Age of High Technology* (Chicago: U of Chicago Press, 2016).

[18] See, e.g., Foucault M, *The Government of Self and Others: Lectures at the Collège de France 1982–1983* (F Gros, ed; G Burchell, trans) (Basingstoke: Palgrave Macmillan, 2010).

'normal' criminal justice processes (such as extended detention periods). We have seen that terrorists, many more innocent people suspected of terrorism, and people like journalists and tourists innocently photographing public buildings who are no more likely to be terrorists than anyone else[19] are the subject of the most heavy-handed crime control methods *and* the most sophisticated covert policing methods alongside border authority surveillance (chapter 10). It would not be so bad if this Orwellian surveillance-control combination provided a safeguard against innocent people being detained for days. It doesn't. It doesn't even stop some of them being abused, and occasionally even being shot dead, as in the tragic case of Jean Charles De Menezes.[20] For counter-terrorism law is not a product of a rational policy cycle, but is part of a 'policy spiral': 'a policy which lacks clear initial purpose or subsequent direction, progression, control and reflection.'[21]

As we have seen, AI systems are not neutral, and so risk analysis in general is not a neutral process. By targeting high-crime social groups as well as high-risk individuals it draws on the 'knowledge' the criminal justice system has generated about marginalised sections of society that is a product of skewed thinking in the first place. In other words, risk analysis reproduces existing patterns instead of reconceptualising them, in order better to control or punish marginalised groups (chapter 10).[22] Proactive policing would have to increase hugely before reactive policing was so diminished that crime control truly gave way to surveillance control. And the powers acquired by local authorities and regulatory agencies do not challenge or weaken police power but add to it. The information-gathering process is greater than the sum of its parts. This is all part of the neo-liberal approach to government in general that we saw in chapter 1 now underpins most criminal justice processes. For example, the Criminal Procedure Rules not only diluted the adversarialism of criminal justice, but transformed it into a managerialist process.[23]

It is possible to envisage a different kind of system altogether. Without compulsory detention for all suspected offences except the most serious, the police would have to investigate more thoroughly before arrest. This would be less intrusive and therefore less eroding of freedom. Interviews could be conducted at home, work or anywhere suspects felt most comfortable. Most suspects would be happy to wait for a legal advisor or supporter to arrive in those circumstances. Covert methods and searches would be allowed, but would be better controlled—by, for example, the judiciary or a multidisciplinary body of part-time lay people on Parole Board lines. The police could be obliged to disclose their case to suspects and their advisors so that they knew what allegations they were answering and so that advisors did not have to barter their clients' rights. This system would lead to fewer confessions, fewer convictions and, on the face of it, greater expenditure of police resources (although the improvement in police-community relations it could lead to would increase public co-operation which should counterbalance, to an unknown extent, what the police lose in effectiveness). It is true that there would be fewer convictions of

---

[19] See, e.g., *The Independent*, 4 December 2009.

[20] *The Independent*, 2 November 2007. See also ch 10.

[21] Walker C, 'Counter-terrorism and counter-extremism: the UK policy spirals' (2018) *Public Law* 725. Another way of describing this is 'mission creep': see Cornford A, 'Terrorist precursor offences: evaluating the law in practice' (2020) *Criminal Law Review* 663, who also discusses the 'chilling effect' on suspect communities of such laws.

[22] See, in relation to 'crime analysis' for example, Innes et al, 'The Appliance of Science?: The Theory and Practice of Crime Intelligence Analysis' (2005) 45 *British Journal of Criminology* 39.

[23] Johnston E, 'The adversarial defence lawyer: myths, disclosure and efficiency - a contemporary analysis of the role in the era of the Criminal Procedure Rules' (2020) 24 *Evidence and Proof*. 35. Also see McEwan J 'Truth, efficiency and co-operation in modern criminal justice' (2013) 66 *Current Legal Problems* 203. The CrPR were first introduced in the mid 2000s and have been updated several times, including in 2014, 2015 and in 2020. Each update has reaffirmed that the criminal process is expected to adopt a more managerialist stance.

the guilty. But there would also be fewer convictions of the innocent, as well as less coercion of all suspects, whether guilty or not. Also, the latitude currently given to the police allows discretion to be exercised in unfairly discriminatory ways in terms of racialised group, socio-economic group, age and gender. Our ideal system would prioritise justice and democracy, with the aim of increasing freedom. The current system does not and cannot. To pretend otherwise is to delude ourselves.

12.3 Taking victims' rights seriously

This chapter has been concerned so far with the erosion of the freedom of suspects and defendants. We should be equally concerned with the freedom of victims. It is justifiable to reduce freedom for suspects if this leads to more freedom for victims, to the extent of a net gain in freedom. It is not possible to be sure about whether this has happened over the last 20 years or so, but it seems unlikely. As we saw in chapters 1 and 10, victims and offenders are not distinct groups. There is considerable overlap between them.[24] Further, what victims want most is not increased punishment or even detection, but some confidence that it will not happen again.[25] The kind of detection, prosecution and conviction methods detailed in this book create resentment and marginalisation on the part of suspects, offenders, their families and their communities. One result is stigmatisation and the enhancement of anti-authority attitudes that deintegrate rather than reintegrate, and that leads to more crime, not less. Time after time, newspaper stories report victims of wrongful arrest, for example, who say that they had not been in trouble before and had always respected the police, but do so no longer.[26] The reconviction rate is very high. In other words, taking freedom away from suspects and offenders in order to increase conviction rates does little to benefit victims. Restorative processes, which are less coercive and aim to reintegrate, are used increasingly, but they still only nibble away at the edges of conventional justice processes, and their effect on re-conviction rates is typically small.[27]

It could be argued that crime control methods do at least lead to relatively high arrest and prosecution rates, without which people would commit even more offences. Indeed one of the (unlawful) reasons for mass stop-search is precisely to intimidate suspect populations and deter them from offending. But this argument also ignores the point that members of the public (especially victims) are the main sources of information about the identity of offenders. In other words, crime control methods lead to relatively few arrests and prosecutions in relation to crimes of any seriousness. What are the most upsetting offences that occur frequently? There are sex offences, which have particular detection and conviction difficulties which no amount of police powers will ever be able to do much about (as we shall see, police resourcing—which was hugely cut from 2010–2020—is far more important); street robberies, where victims can often give descriptions and where the detection rate is reasonably high; and burglaries, where offenders are rarely seen in the act, and which usually remain undetected. Changes to police powers make very little difference to the detection and conviction rates of any of these offences.

---

[24] Drake D and Henley A, '"Victims" Versus "Offenders" in British Political Discourse: The Construction of a False Dichotomy' (2014) 53(2) *The Howard Journal* 141–157.

[25] Wedlock E and Tapley J, *What works in supporting victims of crime* (2016), available from <https://victimscommissioner.org.uk/> (accessed 29 September 2020).

[26] Type the phrase 'used to respect the police' plus the word 'arrest' into Google and you'll see what we mean.

[27] van Dijk J, 'Victim-centred restorative justice' (2013) 3 Restorative Justice 42; Hall (2018) ch 5; also see section 7.4.2.

Even if crime control methods do not reduce crime, they might at least ease the fears and assuage the anger of victims. Again, however, this wrongly assumes that victims and offenders are different people. Do crime control systems have the interests of victims at heart? We cast doubt on this in chapter 1, because in an adversarial system the two parties are the state and the suspect/defendant—so victims have no rights in 'their' cases. In one shocking example a 15-year-old female victim of sex abuse was arrested and held in cells for 20 hours against her will to ensure she would testify against the defendant.[28]

There are other ways in which the interests of the state and those of victims often do not coincide—e.g. plea bargaining, which is driven by the desire to conserve resources and to secure convictions in what might be weak cases. Some victims may benefit: they are saved from giving evidence and are guaranteed at least some kind of 'result', but many do not see it this way. In some of the most distressing and dangerous offences of all, that is, domestic violence and sexual offences, plea bargaining is both most rife and potentially most upsetting to victims. We should also remember that some weak (and indeed some strong) cases are mounted against innocent people. Just as due process-oriented systems do not help victims when guilty people are acquitted, equally, crime control-oriented systems do not help victims when innocent people are convicted. Pressure to plea bargain reduces the capacity of innocent (as well as guilty) people to contest guilt.

Also, crime control systems ill-serve victims of crime about which the state cares little: those dealt with by non-police agencies (see section 7.5). The Code of Practice for Victims of Crime, discussed at section 12.3.2, now applies to most law enforcement agencies. This is a major advance on previously, when non-police agencies (e.g. HSE, Environment Agency) were not included. However, victims of these crimes have less extensive rights than others.[29] The only reason for this can be that, as is clear throughout this book, victims of 'crimes of the powerful' are simply regarded as less important than 'normal' victims. In keeping with this further marginalisation of the already marginalised, this section will focus on victims dealt with by police and CPS.

The 'victim movement' has become increasingly influential. The political parties now compete with each other for the mythical 'victims' vote', and heed must also be paid to various international obligations.[30] The idea of 'victims' rights' has become increasingly important, both in substance and in rhetoric: a crime control approach may not be synonymous with increased rights for victims, but crime control policies are often (spuriously) justified in this way.[31] Four types of right can be identified.

---

[28] Norfolk A, 'Justice lets down a 15-year-old sex victim', *The Times*, 5 March 2014. See Hoyano L, 'Reforming the adversarial trial for vulnerable witnesses and defendants' [2015] *Criminal Law Review* 107.

[29] 'Duties on other service providers' are set out in the Code, ch 5. On victims of environmental crime and the problem of individualisation, for example, see Hall M, *Victims of Environmental Crime* (London: Routledge, 2013); Davies P, 'Environmental crime, victimisation and the ideal victim' in Duggan M, *Revisiting the Ideal Victim* (Bristol: Policy Press, 2018). And, on victims of corporate crime and other 'crimes of the powerful' see Walklate S (ed), *Handbook of Victims and Victimology* (London: Routledge, 2018) (chapters by Whyte and by Rothe and Kauzlarich) and Boukli A and Kotze J (eds), *Zemiology: reconnecting crime and social harm* (Cham, Switzerland: Palgrave Macmillan, 2018).

[30] See for example van Dijk J and Goenhuijsen M, 'A glass half full, or half empty? On the implementation of the EU's Victims Directive regarding police reception and specialized support' in Walklate S (ed), Handbook of Victims and Victimology (London; Routledge, 2018).

[31] Discussed briefly in ch 1. For a brief history of these developments, see Hall M, Victims of Crime: Construction, Governance and Policy (Palgrave Macmillan, 2018) ch 1 and 2.; Jackson J, 'Justice for All: Putting Victims at the Heart of Criminal Justice?' (2003) 30 *Journal of Law and Society* 309; and, Roach K, *Due Process and Victims' Rights: The New Law and Politics of Criminal Justice* (Toronto: University of Toronto Press, 2016). Braun K, *Victim Participation Rights: Variation across criminal justice systems* (London: Palgrave Macmillan, 2019) ch 1, 2.

12.3.1 'Substantive rights'

A person or organisation can be sued for negligence by someone who suffers reasonably foreseeable loss or harm because of failure to carry out a duty to that person. Whether the police have duties to particular victims of crime depends on whether it is 'fair, just and reasonable' to impose such a duty. The tort of negligence in general is a huge topic, and the circumstances under which it applies to the police–victim relationship demands far more discussion than we have space for. What follows is therefore an extremely simplified account.

Until recently the police appeared to enjoy a substantial degree of immunity from negligence claims where they failed to protect victims from the criminal acts of third parties.[32] Then it was held in *Robinson* that the normal principles of negligence liability apply to the police; this means that while police actions can breach the duty of care, omissions that allow harm to be done by a third party will rarely do so. However, in this case D injured V in the course of escaping arrest. Since the officers were negligent in trying to apprehend him whilst V was just 1m away, the chain of events that led to V's injury had been initiated by the police, who therefore breached their duty of care to V.[33] But human rights are not part of the law of tort. In chapters 1, 7 and 11 we mentioned the case of *Commissioner of Police of the Metropolis v DSD*. In this case notorious rapist, John Worboys, committed numerous offences including at least one (and probably a series of) rapes. The police did little to investigate a series of sexual assaults over many years. Had the police investigation been better, he could have been arrested before many of these offences were committed. Two of his victims used ss.7 and 8 of the HRA to successfully claim compensation from the Metropolitan Police for breach of their positive obligations to potential victims under ECHR Art 3.[34] While this affirms liability for omissions under the HRA, and it need not be proven that better policing would have definitely prevented the crimes, the threshold is unclear: there were repeated and protracted police failures in relation to very serious crimes in this case, and lesser failures would probably not have led to liability.[35]

What happens when suspects die at the hands of the police, and their loved ones wish to sue? In chapters 4 and 11 we discussed the scandal of deaths following police contact. Those discussions concerned criminal acts by officers causing death. In police custody most deaths arise from alcohol or drugs in particular and sometimes, though less often, from self-harm. It is now well-established that the police owe a duty of care to suspects in custody who die in such circumstances.[36] As a result, the police now assess the risk to suspects. While this should lead to fewer deaths, the risk cannot be eliminated. In *Orange v Chief Constable of the West Yorkshire Police*[37] a suspect hanged himself, but as the police

---

[32] *Michael v Chief Constable of South Wales* [2015] UKSC 2, for example, upheld the belief that there was no breach of the police duty of care to individuals harmed by third parties simply because of 'organisational defects or fault on the part of an individual' (at [114]). Whether this upheld 'police immunity' or not, became irrelevant in the light of *Robinson* (see next).

[33] *Robinson v Chief Constable of West Yorkshire* [2018] UKSC 4. See Commentary by Arnell in *Juridical Review* [2018] 128. For a pre-*Robinson* discussion (but where the critique of the 'omissions rule' is still valid) see Tofaris and Steel in [2016] 75 *Cambridge Law Journal* 128.

[34] [2018] UKSC 11. This followed several earlier ECtHR judgements. Whether the SC was right to state that merely (serious) operational failures, as distinct from systemic failings, should give rise to liability is questionable: see Levy's discussion in *Public Law* [2019] 251.

[35] Sikand M and Profumo L, 'Minding the gap: where does tortious liability for public authorities end and human rights liability begin? [2019] *Journal of Personal Iinjury Law* 44. Note that compensation given under the HRA is much lower than it is for tortious breaches.

[36] See, for example, *Reeves v Commissioner of Police of the Metropolis* [2000] 1 AC 360.

[37] [2002] QB 347.

were not aware that he was a suicide risk, and the risk assessment that they carried out was negative, their failure to take further precautions was held not to breach their duty of care. The fact that, as we saw in chapter 4, custodial conditions are so coercive that *everyone* should be seen as vulnerable to varying degrees, has escaped the courts' attention. Earlier chapters also commented on fatal shootings, such as Jean Charles de Menezes, in the wake of the July 2005 bombings, Mark Duggan and Harry Stanley. These tragedies are covered by both the tort of negligence and ECHR Art 2. There is no doubt about whether a duty is owed, the issue always being whether it was discharged negligently or without lawful justification. The ECtHR has said that deprivations of life must be subject to the most careful scrutiny, and that any use of force by the police or anyone else is unlawful unless absolutely necessary.[38] However, the use of force by agents of the state based on an honest and reasonable belief in its necessity to protect their own lives have been held not amount to a breach of Art 2.[39] It thus seems that only the most gross errors would violate Art 2.

Although this discussion has concerned how far the tort of negligence and the ECHR can be used to create or enforce the rights of victims in relation to the police or prosecution, some victims suffer from the deliberate, as well as negligent, actions of those agencies. Two types of example have been discussed in this book. First where a prosecution agency decides not to prosecute (this is discussed in chapter 7 and in section 12.3.3). Second, there is non- or selective enforcement. In the *ITF* case[40] (mentioned in section 7.2.2) a company was the victim of breaches of the peace. The police devoted only limited resources to the problem, leading to financial losses for the company. No rights were conceded to the victims, in recognition of the almost infinite resources that would be required to satisfy all victims of crime. The core value of (police) 'effectiveness' rightly helps to shape the developing law on substantive rights, but in all of these issues except the last, 'justice' and 'democracy' are given too little weight.

12.3.2 'Service rights': the Code of Practice for Victims of Crime

We introduced the Victims' Charter and the idea of 'service rights' in chapter 1. The Victims' Charter was first introduced in 1990, revised in 1996, and told victims that they are entitled to 'proper' services. This was replaced by a more robust Code of Practice in 2006, substantially revised in 2015,[41] with oversight from the Victims' Commissioner.[42]

One of the most important service rights is the offer of appropriate support. That is, general support requiring the police to put victims in touch with Victim Support, an independent (but government-funded) charity; and (where applicable) support prior to court proceedings, including pre-trial court visits. Other important rights are to be provided with appropriate facilities in court and to be given information about their cases

---

[38] The ECtHR decided in *Da Silva v United Kingdom* (2016) 63 EHRR 12 that UK arrangements for civil and criminal actions in the de Menezes case met Art 2 requirements. No decision was made by about whether the police had a lawful excuse for shooting de Menezes dead, and the negligence claim was settled out of court.
[39] *Davis* [2016] EWHC 38. See also, for example, *Bubbins v UK* [2005] ECHR 159 for a scandalous lethal police operation that was held to be lawful. See Foster S and Leigh G, 'Self-defence and the right to life; the use of lethal or potentially lethal force, UK domestic law, the common law and article 2 ECHR' (2016) 4 *European Human Rights Law Review* 398.   [40] *Chief Constable of Sussex, ex p ITF Ltd* [1999] 1 All ER 129.
[41] See <https://www.gov.uk/government/publications/the-code-of-practice-for-victims-of-crime> (accessed 29 September 2020). Chs 2 and 3 of the Code cover adult and child victims respectively.
[42] The role is actually 'to champion the interests of victims of crime and witnesses': <https://victimscommissioner.org.uk/> (accessed 29 September 2020). Also, in 2019 the first Domestic Abuse Commissioner was appointed: <https://publicappointments.cabinetoffice.gov.uk/appointment/designate-commissioner-for-domestic-abuse/> (accessed 29 September 2020). See also ch 10.

by agencies such as the police and the CPS. Because victims have no standing, they have traditionally had no right to know what was happening in 'their' cases and would, for example, sometimes find themselves bumping into the alleged offender because the latter is let out on bail, has had the case dropped or been given a non-custodial sentence.

In the mid 1990s, in selected police areas, victims in cases where someone had been charged would be asked whether they wanted information about 'their' cases. About two-thirds of victims who were asked did want this information, but many victims did not get all that they wanted, and many wanted to know not just *what* happened, but *why*. If a decision is unpalatable, the more that one is told, the more one wants to discuss and challenge it so that it can at least be *understood*. In other words, giving victims a 'right to know' raises expectations which, in many cases, are dashed; and we know that a clear explanation helps provide closure and restores dignity.[43] Moreover, in most cases no-one is charged. Failure to identify or charge a suspect can be upsetting—an understatement in a murder case like that of Stephen Lawrence, whose family were denied information, given misinformation, and then given unhelpful information about the investigation into the murder of their son.[44] This cannot be justified from a freedom perspective, as this is a form of 'secondary victimisation' which erodes freedom.[45]

The Code attempts to meet some of these problems by requiring the police and CPS witness care units (WCUs) and liaison units (WLUs) to provide information to victims— e.g. whether a suspect has been arrested (and, if so, what happened subsequently), bailed, charged etc; to explain the reasons for decisions (including offering to meet victims in particularly serious cases); and to provide care while victims and witnesses are in court. But performance is poor. The Crown Prosecution Service Inspectorate (HMCPSI) found that CPS resources are too stretched to, for example, properly discuss and explain decisions and processes in many cases.[46] And in over 40% of cases sampled in 2018, prosecutors failed to notify WLUs of prosecution decisions triggering the need to send letters. In most of these cases either no letter was sent to victims, or it was sent late/was of poor quality. Overall, less than 25% of the letters that were sent were of the expected quality: in particular, nearly half lacked empathy; and less than half of the letters that required legal explanations were readily comprehensible to non-lawyers.[47] These problems had all been identified previously.[48] There is a structural problem here: victims become frustrated when information is provided by different agencies, but the experimental 'one stop shops' of the 1990s were equally frustrating as the information-givers could not explain anything beyond what they were told to provide (which is one reason why WLUs, which convey information about decisions taken by prosecutors, perform badly). However, while the CPS may be right to prioritise actual prosecutions the CPS seems to be failing badly. Successive surveys of victims show, for example, that over half of victims are not offered pre-trial court visits, and 14% of victims whose cases go to the CPS are overall dissatisfied with the way the CPS

---

[43] Sanders et al, 'Victim Impact Statements: Don't Work, Can't Work' [2001] *Criminal Law Review* 447. Later research similarly found frustration that requests to be kept informed were not fulfilled: see, e.g., Graham et al, *Testaments of Harm: a Qualitative Evaluation of the Victim Personal Statements Scheme* (London: National Centre for Social Research, 2004) and discussion in section 12.3.4. See, for examples of explanations having positive effects, Iliadis M and Flynn A, 'Providing a Check on Prosecutorial Decision-making: An Analysis of the Victims' Right to Review Reform' (2018) 58 *British Journal of Criminology* 550.

[44] See Macpherson of Cluny, Sir W, *The Stephen Lawrence Inquiry* (Cm 4262-I) (London: SO, 1999).

[45] On 'secondary victimisation' see, e.g., Wolhuter L et al, *Victimology: Victimisation and Victim's Rights* (Abingdon: Routledge, 2009); Barkworth J and Murphy K, 'System contact and procedural justice policing: Improving quality of life outcomes for victims of crime' (2016) 22 *International Review of Victimology* 105.

[46] HMCPSI, *Communicating with* victims (2016b).

[47] HMCPSI, *Victim Liaison Units: Letters sent to the public by the CPS* (London: HMCPSI, 2018) pp 15–19.

[48] E.g. HMCPSI (2016).

keep them informed.[49] But it is not only a question of resources. To say that mutual displays of affection by prosecution and defence lawyers in front of the parents of a murdered child, for example, indicates lack of empathy would be a gross understatement.[50] Cultural, as well as legal, change is needed.

No rights in any real sense are provided, because these provisions (like those of the Charter before it) are not enforceable in the courts. Like many rights of suspects, there is no proper remedy for people who are deprived of this type of entitlement:[51] breaches of the Code should be referred initially to the service provider(s) concerned, and if that does not lead to a satisfactory result, the case can then be referred to the Parliamentary Ombudsman. The CPS can offer 'consolatory' (not compensatory) payments where complaints are justified.[52] This seems to herald the creation of a new class of 'semi-right'. Victim-oriented pressure groups have been competing for rights for decades, and consolation prizes hardly meet their demands. Nor does the treatment of complaints by the CPS, which has been found to be often poor.[53] Though other agencies (e.g. police, courts) are equally at fault: 'There is a gap between the handling of complaints as described by criminal justice agencies, and how victims feel they have been treated. . . . Changes in policy are not enough; agencies should ensure there are changes to practice.'[54]

Enhanced entitlements are available to victims of the most serious crimes, those who are persistently targeted, and those who are vulnerable or intimidated (and any others, at the discretion of the service provider) (Code, ch 1). These entitlements include speedier information about the progress of the case but the CPS performs badly here too in all the ways identified earlier.[55] In fact in 2015 it was found that in 95.7% of CPS letters to victims of domestic abuse no details of sources of support were provided.[56] Vulnerable victims are also considered for 'special measures', discussed briefly in chapter 9 and to be discussed next.

12.3.3 Vulnerable victims and witnesses

It was recognised decades ago that child victims of crime were less likely to have 'their' cases prosecuted, and more likely to suffer secondary victimisation, than adult victims. Children were often afraid to report crimes, were frequently not believed, had difficulty explaining or remembering exactly what happened, and could be made to appear untruthful or confused in court. Police officers and prosecutors were therefore reluctant to prosecute, and these children suffered greatly under cross-examination if there was a prosecution.[57] Once this was documented by research, and became a matter of public scandal because of revelations of widespread sexual abuse, court procedures were amended to facilitate prosecutions. The government established the Pigot Committee in 1988,[58] and interim measures were put in place.

People with learning disabilities and mental health conditions suffer from similar problems, so it made no sense to prevent them from being helped in the way children were

---

[49] CPS, *Victim and witness satisfaction survey* (2015b) p 12 and Fig 3.22 respectively.
[50] Erez E et al, 'From Cinderella to consumer: how crime victims can go to the ball' in Tapley J and Davies P (eds), *Victimology: Research, policy and activism* (London: Palgrave Macmillan, 2020).
[51] The lack of remedies for many 'rights' is discussed in ch 11. See also Hall (2018).
[52] <https://www.cps.gov.uk/crown-prosecution-service-complaints-consolatory-payments-guidance> (accessed 21 August 2020). [53] HMCPSI (2018) pp 31–38.
[54] Newlove B, *Review of Complaints and Resolution for Victims of Crime* (London: Office of the Commissioner for Victims and Witnesses, 2015) p 6.
[55] HMCPSI (2018) para 5.17. [56] HMCPSI (2016) para 1.5.
[57] Morgan J and Zedner L, *Child Victims* (Oxford: Clarendon Press, 1992).
[58] Pigot Judge T, *Report of the Advisory Group on Video-Recorded Evidence* (London: HMSO, 1989).

helped.[59] Sadly, what makes these groups of people vulnerable in the criminal justice system also makes them especially vulnerable to crime.[60] Some of the most exploited groups in society were receiving less protection than other victims. At the same time, concern was developing about witnesses being intimidated by defendants and their friends or family in some cases.[61] A Home Office working party therefore made wide-ranging proposals to support all these vulnerable and intimidated witnesses.[62] Many of these were enacted in 1999 and then added to subsequently, including in the Victims' Code.[63] But numerous police, prosecution and court procedures (and the attitudes and culture which lie behind them) which are not laid down in the law also needed to be changed. There is positive change, but it is slow and has not gone far enough.[64] We do not attempt here to discuss all these changes in detail, but it is important to provide a brief overview.[65]

The first problem that vulnerable victims face is whether or not to report the offence. Sometimes reluctance to report stems from the fact that their 'authority figures' (parents, teachers, carers) are the abusers or are close to the abusers. This is a structural feature of vulnerability about which little, regrettably, can be done. But traditionally some reluctance has been because of fear at how the police and courts would treat their complaint. For example, the police used often to be dismissive of crimes that may have been objectively minor but which were traumatic for the victims.[66] These fears were, and remain, justified in many cases, regarding all types of vulnerable people: those with learning disabilities and mental health conditions, and victims of sexual assault and domestic violence.[67] The position is equally unsatisfactory in the courts.[68] And if victims fear being humiliated in court they

---

[59] This was noted by Pigot (1989). See also Sanders et al, *Victims with Learning Disabilities* (Oxford: Centre for Criminological Research, 1997) summarised in Home Office Research Findings no 44 (London: Home Office, 1997).

[60] Again noted by Pigot (1989). Also see, for example, Williams C, *Invisible Victims: Crime and Abuse Against People with Learning Disabilities* (Bristol: Norah Fry Research Centre, 1995); Jones et al, 'Prevalence and risk of violence against children with disabilities' (2012) 380 *The Lancet* 899; Ellison L, 'Responding to the needs of victims with psychosocial disabilities: challenges to equality of access to justice' [2015] *Criminal Law Review* 28; Ralph et al, 'Disability hate crime' (2016) 43 *British Journal of Special Education* 215; Healy J, '"It spreads like a creeping disease": experiences of victims of disability hate crimes in austerity Britain' (2020) 35 *Disability and Society* 176; Lindsey J, 'Protecting vulnerable adults from abuse' (2020) 32 *Children and Family Law Quarterly* 157; Tyson J, 'Disablist hate crime: a scar on the conscience of the criminal justice system?' in Tapley and Davies (2020). See also section 10.7.2

[61] Maynard W, *Witness Intimidation: Strategies for Prevention* (PRG Crime Detection and Prevention Series Paper 55) (London: Home Office, 1994); Tarling et al, *Victim and Witness Intimidation: Findings from the British Crime Survey* (Home Office Research Findings No 124) (London: Home Office, 2000).

[62] Home Office, *Speaking Up for Justice* (London: Home Office, 1998b). We have referred to vulnerability throughout this book, and refer readers to section 10.7.2, esp. footnote 274.

[63] Youth Justice and Criminal Evidence Act (YJCE) 1999 (Part II); CJA 2003; Domestic Violence, Crime and Victims Act 2004. Victims' Code, 2015, ch 1. Much of this legislation is exceptionally and unnecessarily complex. Also see Ellison L, *The Adversarial Process and the Vulnerable Witness* (Oxford: OUP, 2001).

[64] On judges and lawyers see Henderson E, 'Taking control of cross-examination;' [2016] *Criminal Law Review* 181.

[65] See Drew S and Gibbs L, 'Identifying and accommodating vulnerable people in court' (2019) 10 *Archbold Review* 7 for a useful short discussion; Kirchengast T, *Victims and the Criminal Trial* (Palgrave Macmillan, 2016) esp. ch 4.   [66] Sanders et al (1997).

[67] Ellison L, 'Responding to the needs of victims with psychosocial disabilities: challenges to equality of access to justice' [2015] *Criminal Law Review* 28; HMCPSI and HMIC, *Joint Inspection on Young Victims and Witnesses* (2012); Domestic abuse is discussed in ch 10. Also see, for example, Belur J, 'Is Policing Domestic Violence Institutionally Racist? A Case Study of South Asian Women' (2008) 18(4) *Policing and Society* 426; on sexual offences, see later in this section.

[68] See, for example, Ellison L, 'The Use and Abuse of Psychiatric Evidence in Rape Trials' (2009) 13(1) *International Journal of Evidence & Proof* 28; Ellison (2015).

will frequently not report the matter at all. Even when they do, they often seek to withdraw their complaint or choose not to give evidence in court, often causing the case to collapse.

The police need to show vulnerable witnesses care and respect, but first they need to identify witnesses as vulnerable. Then they need to interview them in ways that elicit the best evidence without distorting their recollections or intimidating them. Further, compared with other witnesses, vulnerable witnesses tend to have greater difficulties in telling a traumatic story of victimisation several times. The police should adopt 'cognitive interviewing' techniques, but skill is needed both to identify mild cases of vulnerability and to use these techniques. In the past, the police were poor in both respects, and training and resources were inadequate.[69] However, the introduction of Ministry of Justice guidance in 2011 on Achieving Best Evidence (known by the acronym, ABE) sought to improve the interviewing of child victims and witnesses, then later, all vulnerable victims and witnesses and,[70] in some cases defendants, though it is yet to be used with child suspects.[71]

The next stage is the prosecution decision. The two tests discussed in ch 7 are applied here as in all cases. Because of the difficulties of these cases, many fall at the 'evidential' hurdle. It is not suggested by government (or us) that the tests should change. Instead, full and prompt investigation by the police is needed so that fewer cases are evidentially weak,[72] and the police need to inform the CPS of the problems which the vulnerability in question could cause. For there are ways of mitigating vulnerabilities so that evidence can be better presented in court, reducing the prospects of acquittal and thus feeding back to the prosecution decision, making a negative decision both less justifiable and less likely. A particularly important example is pre-court familiarisation (in the form of visits, videos and so forth), which reduces the fear many witnesses, particularly vulnerable witnesses, have of giving evidence. But even when witnesses are identified as vulnerable, the police often do not tell the CPS, and neither agency is good at seeking the views of witnesses on whether they want this type of help. The police and the CPS are supposed to carry out 'needs assessments', for example, but less than half of all victims recall being assessed;[73] while it may not always have been apparent that their needs were being assessed, and memories can be faulty, in one survey in 23% of applicable cases needs were not recorded on case files.[74] Police and the CPS are supposed to meet in difficult cases to discuss strategy. This used to be rare, but 'ground rules hearings' are now more common (chapter 9).[75]

---

[69] See Keenan et al, 'Interviewing Allegedly Abused Children with a View to Criminal Prosecution' [1999] *Criminal Law Review* 863. Interviewing is guided by Ministry of Justice, *Achieving best evidence in criminal proceedings* (2011). See also Burton et al, 'Implementing Special Measures for Vulnerable and Intimidated Witnesses: The Problem of Identification' (2006b) *Criminal Law Review* 229; HMCPSI/HMICA/HMIC (2009) 2.5–2.9 for similar findings (nearly 40% of vulnerable and intimidated witnesses not identified as such); O'Mahoney B et al, 'The early identification of vulnerable witnesses prior to an investigative interview' (2011) 13 *British Journal of Forensic Practice* 114; Wedlock and Tapley (2016).

[70] MOJ (2011a) Achieving best evidence in criminal proceedings: Guidance on interviewing victims and witnesses, and guidance on using special measures. Online at: <https://www.cps.gov.uk/sites/default/files/documents/legal_guidance/best_evidence_in_criminal_proceedings.pdf> (accessed 25 September 2020).

[71] See, for example, Gooch K and von Berg P, 'What Happens in the Beginning, Matters in the End: Achieving Best Evidence with Child Suspects in the Police Station' *Youth Justice*. (2019) 19(2) 85–101

[72] See, for example, Ellison L, 'Promoting Effective Case-building in Rape Cases: A Comparative Perspective' [2007] *Criminal Law Review* 691.

[73] CPS, Victim and witness satisfaction survey (2015b) p 51.

[74] HMIC, Witness for the prosecution: Identifying victim and witness vulnerability in criminal case files (2015), p 8.

[75] For the situation in the first decade of special measures see HMCPSI/HMICA/HMIC (2009) paras 3.1–3.2. Ground rules hearings are provided for in the Criminal Practice Directions 2015 (Consolidated para 3E) following encouragement by the court in *Lubemba* (2014) EWCA Crim 2064. Discussed in ch 9 and in Cooper P and Mattison M, 'Intermediaries, vulnerable people and the quality of evidence: an international comparison of three versions of the English intermediary model' (2017) 21 *Evidence and Proof* 351.

Support for witnesses is seen by police and prosecutors primarily in terms of the 'special measures' in court provided in the legislation. These are discussed in chapter 9 and include judges and barristers removing wigs and gowns, screening off the defendant from the sight of the witness, providing interpreters and communication aids (important not only for people who have difficulty with English but also for some people with learning disabilities who have difficulty speaking at all), and giving evidence via CCTV from a room outside the courtroom. Assessments are made in each case of which, if any, of these special measures would help the particular witness (because each vulnerability and every way of alleviating it is different) so that preparation and, where necessary, application to the court can be made in good time. Where appropriate, interviews should have been audio-visually recorded in advance and played in court, but this depends on proper identification at the start. And the decision was finally taken in 2020 that cross-examination can be done in advance and audio-visually recorded, 20 years after it was legislated.[76] The CJA 2003 extended most special measures to any witness who the judge or magistrate believes would benefit from them, which is a welcome recognition that *anyone* can be vulnerable in an artificial and intimidating situation like a court. Special measures are not automatically available for those who request them, except for most child witnesses for whom CCTV and the admission of prior recorded evidence in chief is automatic. But it is rare for applications to be rejected (Cooper and Roberts, 2005), and there is no doubt that this whole raft of measures has gone a substantial way to meeting the less-intractable problems of vulnerable witnesses.[77]

Finally, there are the actual procedures in court. There is the potential in all types of case for witnesses to find cross-examination, and sometimes questioning from the judge, upsetting and challenging. This can ruin an otherwise strong case as well as weak cases. It is sometimes hard to know whether testimony lacks credibility because it really is untrue or mistaken, or because questioning unfairly tripped up or confused the witness. In an adversarial system it is essential that the defence be allowed to test prosecution evidence, and if there is reasonable doubt about its strength, there should be an acquittal. Drawing the line between what is robustly fair and what is viciously destructive of the character of the witness is often difficult. Judges have the power to stop oppressive cross-examination,[78] and are encouraged to use this power more since the use of ground rules hearings increased. But victims will not be helped if convictions are quashed on the ground that judges did not give defence counsel full opportunities to cross-examine (see section 9.4.2). One possibility is for judges or intermediaries to 'translate' intimidating or convoluted questioning for witnesses, but the problem can only really be alleviated through changing the culture of the Bar, which is a long-term and indeterminate prospect.

The nature of the adversarial system puts limits on how far secondary victimisation of victims in the witness box can be reduced, as trashing, trapping and tripping is all part of proving and disproving cases.[79] Further, there remains too little understanding of the

---

[76] See <https://www.legislation.gov.uk/ukpga/1999/23/section/28> (accessed 29 September 2020) (implementing YJCE, ss.28). For a practical guide to the process see <https://www.criminalbar.com/wp-content/uploads/2020/08/s.28-FAQs-August-20-v1.11.pdf> (accessed 27 August 2020). See discussion in ch 9.

[77] Burton et al (2006b); Hamlyn et al, *Are Special Measures Working? Evidence from Surveys of Vulnerable and Intimidated Witnesses* (Home Office Research Study 283) (London: Home Office, 2004); HMCPSI/HMICA/HMIC (2009). However, for a note of caution regarding giving evidence through a live link see Mulcahy L, 'The Unbearable Lightness of Being? Shifts Towards the Virtual Trial' (2008) 35 *Journal of Law and Society* 464.

[78] *Milton Brown* [1998] 2 Cr App Rep 364. They rarely do this. See for example, Davis et al (1999).

[79] McBarnet D, 'Victim in the Witness Box – Confronting Victimology's Stereotype' (1983) 7 *Contemporary Crises* 293; Ellison (2001a).

variety of types of vulnerability and the ways in which vulnerabilities—particularly learning disabilities—are manifested. This means that often witnesses are thought, wrongly, to lack credibility[80] but there is little in this programme of action to deal with this problem. Police officers and prosecutors are supposed to seek the views of vulnerable victims and witnesses about the help they want or need. Whilst in the past they did this inadequately or not at all in many cases, perhaps because they wrongly believed that these victims and witnesses could not evaluate their own needs or express their wishes coherently, the 2011 ABE guidance put more pressure on the police and the CPS to assess the needs of vulnerable victims and witnesses and to put special measures in place.[81] Thus the use of special measures has gone up, leading to a much better deal for many of these witnesses, but many others still do not get what they want and need: for example, in one survey, between 16% and 22% wanted, but were not offered, screens, video-links, pre-recording of their testimony and/or the public gallery being emptied.[82]

For victims of sexual offences, in particular, aggressive and humiliating questioning in court has been a major cause of attrition—that is, acquittals and, further back down the line, withdrawals and decisions not to report.[83] For these victims, and those of certain other crimes, there are provisions to prevent defendants cross-examining in person[84] and to prevent certain types of evidence (on the witnesses' sexual history in particular) being elicited.[85] But while lack of consent, which is often impossible to prove,[86] remained an element in most sexual offences, the rate of acquittals and secondary victimisation of witnesses in court was inevitably higher than in most other offences. Changes to the definition of sexual offences in 2003 offered some hope of improvement.[87] But substantial difficulties remain (see discussion in section 10.3).

We should not fool ourselves into thinking that legal solutions can ever completely solve the problems faced by vulnerable victims. That is not because of a lack of will on the part of government or criminal justice agencies, or (primarily) a lack of resources. The fact is that vulnerable victims are in structurally weak positions in society. That is what makes them vulnerable. Social and cultural change might alleviate this for the victims of sexual offences and domestic violence, but not for those who are older or mentally vulnerable. People with very low actual or mental ages, for example, simply have less comprehension than other people. There comes a point when a witness has to be regarded as not competent to give evidence or, in some cases, not competent to give evidence on matters of detail or in relation to forgotten events. The legislation since 1999 tries to deal with this problem more intelligently than the law used to do, by providing for 'intermediaries' to 'translate' questioning for witnesses who cannot cope and by a 'competence' test of 'understanding'. As a result, many people with learning disabilities understand what is being asked when put in simple terms,[88] and judges and lawyers are getting better at this.[89] However, the

---

[80] Sanders et al (1997).   [81] Hamlyn et al (2004); Burton et al (2006a).
[82] CPS, Victim and witness satisfaction survey (2015b) fig 3.17; Also see Ellison (2015).
[83] Kelly et al, *A Gap or a Chasm? Attrition in Reported Rape Cases* (Home Office Research Study 293) (London: Home Office, 2005). See also ch 10.
[84] YJCE, s.35. There are also provisions giving judges discretion to prohibit cross-examination in person in any other case: ss.36 and 37.   [85] YJCE, s.41.
[86] Harris J and Grace S, *A Question of Evidence? Investigating and Prosecuting Rape in the 1990s* (Home Office Research Study 196) (London: Home Office, 1999); HMCPSI and HMIC, *A Report on the Joint Inspection into the Investigation and Prosecution of Cases Involving Allegations of Rape* (London: HMCPSI, 2002). See also discussion in ch 10.
[87] Sexual Offences Act 2003. See McEwan J, 'Proving Consent in Sexual Cases: Legislative Change and Cultural Evolution' (2005) 9 *Evidence and Proof* 1.
[88] Plotnikoff J and Woolfson R, *Intermediaries in the Criminal Justice System* (Bristol: Policy Press, 2015).
[89] Henderson E, 'Taking control of cross-examination' [2016] *Criminal Law Review* 181.

principles underlying the training they receive to do this have been said to be almost arbitrary; without being grounded in scientific understanding of the huge range of cognitive difficulties involved, court questioning will continue to obstruct the ability of vulnerable witnesses to give their best evidence.[90] And '[i]t is striking how little research has been conducted into the completeness, accuracy and coherence of the evidence that intermediaries facilitate.'[91]

It may be tempting in future to allow witnesses who understand very little of what is happening to give evidence, but this would be a further attenuation of the already-eroded rights of suspects and defendants. Along with further restrictions on cross-examination and the method of cross-examination to help vulnerable witnesses, this would harm the prospects of acquittal of innocent defendants. It hardly needs to be said that not all alleged victims and witnesses, whether vulnerable or not, tell the truth;[92] not all are correct in their beliefs and recollections; and some defendants are innocent even when victims tell the truth if, for example, a defence is proved or there is a lack of mens rea. But in an era of crime control-mindedness this could all be forgotten or brushed aside.

There would be no need for trials at all if we automatically accepted what victims and other witnesses said. We may soon reach the point when vindication of more victims' cases will only be achievable by failing to vindicate defence cases. This is the classic dilemma running through this book. The government deserves to be congratulated, in this respect at least, for not falling into this trap in the main. Most of these measures for vulnerable witnesses, legislative and otherwise, attempt to put vulnerable witnesses on a level playing field with other witnesses without eroding significant rights of defendants. However, the statutory provisions allowing defendants an intermediary when giving evidence are still not in force.[93] Case law has provided that entitlement,[94] but the government has tried to restrict access, with the connivance of the Court of Appeal.[95] And vulnerable defendants still have greater hurdles to surmount than do vulnerable victims to access other special measures. This blatant discrimination against defendants by comparison with victims is a clear breach of ECHR Art 6, the Equality Act 2010 and various UN Conventions.[96] Whether it is driven by the wish to obstruct fair trials for defendants or to save money is not clear. It's probably both.

---

[90] Cooper P et al, 'One step forward and two steps back? The "20 Principles" for questioning vulnerable witnesses and the lack of an evidence-based approach' (2018) 22 *Evidence and Proof* 392.

[91] Cooper P and Mattison M, 'Intermediaries, vulnerable people and the quality of evidence: an international comparison of three versions of the English intermediary model' (2017) 21 *Evidence and Proof* 351 at 367.

[92] See, e.g., Burnett R (ed), *Wrongful Allegations of Sexual and Child Abuse* (Oxford: OUP, 2016). A particularly unusual example was that of a teenager who claimed that she had been raped in a park by a tramp. A young man was later arrested on a minor charge and his DNA sample matched the one taken from the young woman. When the police questioned her again, because the man's description did not match that of the 'tramp', she admitted that she had had consensual sex with him. She was later jailed for six months: *The Guardian*, 27 September 2000. 'Nick's' case (see ch 1) is a more recent and even more serious example.

[93] Section 104 Coroners and Justice Act 2009, drafted to insert ss.33BA and 33BB into the YJCEA 1999, is not yet in force. This was criticised by the body appointed by government to propose law reforms: Law Commission, *Unfitness to plead* (2016) para 2.31–2.37; 2.62–2.69.

[94] *Walls* [2011] EWCA Crim 443; *OP v Secretary of State for Justice* [2015] 1 Cr App R 7.

[95] *Rashid* [2017] 1 WLR 2449, applying Criminal Practice Directions [2015] EWCA Crim 1567 consolidated Amendment No. 1 to the Criminal Practice Directions 2015 [2016] EWCA Crim 97 [CPD 2015]. For the latest changes see amendments to the CPD 2015: <https://www.justice.gov.uk/courts/procedure-rules/criminal/docs/2015/crim-practice-directions-I-general-matters-2015.pdf>, discussed in <https://www.icca.ac.uk/intermediaries-for-defendants/> (both accessed 29 September 2020). See also *R v Biddle* [2019] EWCA Crim 86.

[96] *SC v UK* [2005] Crim LR 130; Hoyano L and Rafferty A, 'Rationing Defence Intermediaries under the April 2016 CPD' [2017] *Criminal Law Review* 93; Fairclough S, 'Speaking up for injustice: reconsidering the provision of special measures through the lens of equality' [2018] *Criminal Law Review* 4.

12.3.4 Procedural rights

These are rights to be *involved* in one's case. Different legal systems provide a variety of ways of being involved, such as by providing information to the prosecutor or court through a 'victim personal statement' (VPS) as in some common law systems; by being a secondary party of some kind to the case as in many civil law systems;[97] or by being fully involved as in restorative processes.[98] This chapter will be primarily concerned with England and Wales where, traditionally, victims have not been involved at all.

Involvement can, in principle, take various forms—an opportunity to discuss, to be consulted, or to actually participate in decision-making. Whatever type of involvement is provided, it can take place at one or more of various stages of the criminal process: in particular, the decision to prosecute, bail/remand decisions, decisions to reduce or drop charges, sentencing and early release from prison. As with service rights, the freedom perspective is concerned to reduce secondary victimisation. So if being involved achieves this, without any loss of freedom to suspects or defendants, it is to be encouraged. In this section we consider two main types of participation.

12.3.4.1 Prosecution decisions

As we saw in chapter 1, challenging prosecution decisions used to be difficult. This was addressed partially in the original Victims' Charter, but case law[99] and the EU Victims' Directive[100] led to the Victims' Right to Review scheme in 2016. This is a two-stage process, internal to the CPS. The first stage is a local review. Complainants who are dissatisfied by the result can seek further review from a central CPS unit. It applies to initial prosecution decisions and the dropping of charges.

In 2018/19 out of 94,727 decisions that could have been challenged, there were appeals in just 2% of cases (1,930), of which 11% (205) were upheld.[101] It is hard to know what to make of such a low success rate. If in most cases the CPS diligently applies the provisions of the Code, to 'take account' of victims' interests and views, and correctly applies the rest of the Code, then the success rate should be low. On the other hand, the CPS is assessing its own decisions, so a sceptic would not anticipate much success anyway; and this is certainly the feeling of many victims using the scheme and that of their support workers.[102]

We do not know if most victims in the 94,522 cases where there was no challenge or where the challenge was unsuccessful feel better now. But it is unlikely. For the HMCPSI (2018) found that a high proportion of local responses are late, lack empathy, have errors and/or contain jargon that few complainants would understand. For example, one cited 'legal doctrine of recent possession', while a domestic abuse case cited lack of injuries for not prosecuting even though the case manager noted serious injuries in the file. Some

---

[97] Several common law and civil law systems are overviewed in Braun (2019) (see ch 7 for a focus on Germany); and Kirchengast (2016). Also see Gohler J, 'Victim rights in civil law jurisdictions' in Brown et al, *The Oxford Handbook of Criminal Process* (New York: OUP, 2019).

[98] For good discussions see Strang H, *Repair or Revenge: Victims and Restorative Justice* (Oxford: OUP, 2002); Dignan J, *Understanding Victims and Restorative Justice* (Maidenhead: Open UP, 2005); Strang et al, 'Victim evaluations of face-to-face restorative justice conferences: A quasi-experimental analysis (2006) 62 *Journal of Social Issues* 281; Bolivar D et al (eds), *Victims and restorative justice* (Oxford: Routledge, 2017).

[99] *Killick* [2011] EWCA Crim 1608.

[100] The EU Victims' Directive 2012/29/EU, adopted by the UK in 2012.

[101] See<https://www.cps.gov.uk/sites/default/files/documents/publications/Victims-Right-to-Review-Data-2018–19.pdf> (accessed 29 September 2020). The scheme is set out in the Victims' Code (p 23), which also refers to a National Police Chiefs Council right to review scheme.

[102] Iliadis M and Flynn A, 'Providing a Check on Prosecutorial Decision-making: An Analysis of the Victims' Right to Review Reform' (2018) 58 *British Journal of Criminology* 550.

even mixed up the name of the victim with that of the defendant.[103] A survey of victims regarding general CPS performance found that one-third were dissatisfied in general, but they were especially unhappy with 'right to review'; and even though 70% of victims in cases where the original charges were dropped considered this unfair, only 10% of these requested a review. It was too complicated for half those who did not,[104] and other research found that many do not know about it.[105]

Recent cases give some more insight. In one, a police officer chased a moped, whose driver was suspected of theft. The moped crashed, killing the driver. The CPS did not prosecute for causing death by dangerous driving. This was unsuccessfully challenged by the family of the deceased. A subsequent judicial review succeeded as the reviewing lawyer failed to consider the case thoroughly and failed to adequately explain his decision. The court stressed that in only cases with exceptional failings, such as here, would applications for judicial review of prosecution decisions be successful.[106] Sadly, exceptional failings by the police and the CPS are all too common. For example, a victim of sexual assault was dissatisfied with the decision from the local review and applied for a second stage review. She asked for that review to be delayed while she sought legal advice before making further representations. However, the (unfavourable) review took place before she could do that. Again, a judicial review was successful, but only because of the particular exceptional circumstances of the case.[107] And a victim of trafficking was not 'trafficked enough' for the police until she successfully had their decision not to investigate reversed. Then the CPS decided not to prosecute. The courts reversed that CPS decision too. But this took six years from the time the Home Office recognised the complainant as a victim of trafficking.[108] On the other hand, there are clear benefits for the few victims who are successful (and some of these cases ended in conviction), but also for victims who are at least helped to understand decisions they do not like. Being told, for example, that deciding against prosecution does not mean that they are disbelieved reduces secondary victimisation.[109] But you might ask why we need an elaborate review scheme in order to help victims understand the reasons for decisions in their cases—they could simply just have a conversation together.

These cases seem to confirm HMCPSI's finding that the quality of internal reviews is poor. They do not indicate a general willingness by courts to allow CPS decision-making to be generally opened up to scrutiny nor do they tackle fundamental problems. Earlier and in chapter 10 we noted the inadequate response by the police as well as the CPS to sexual and domestic abuse. The development of substantive rights to compensation for inadequate police action in such cases discussed earlier is an advance. But this does not yet seem to have prompted major changes, and is unlikely to do so. An investigation into rape in London concluded that inadequate action is primarily because of lack of resources in the 'austerity' years leading, for example, to the London CPS Unit being described as 'broken'.[110] And nationally: 'The violence against women and girls (VAWG) sector has faced disproportionate cuts in funding compared to other parts of the voluntary and community sector.'[111] A disproportionately high suicide rate for victims of these crimes is one of the tragic consequences.[112]

---

[103] HMCPSI (2018) paras 6.25, 6.28 and 6.31 respectively.
[104] CPS, *Victim and witness satisfaction survey* (2015b), p 11.   [105] Iliadis and Flynn (2018).
[106] *Torpey* [2019] Crim LR 985.   [107] *FNM* [2020] Crim LR 874.
[108] Taylor D, 'Judges quash decision not to prosecute diplomat over alleged trafficking' *The Guardian*, 9 July 2020.
[109] Iliadis and Flynn (2018).
[110] Angiolini E, *Report of the Independent Review into the Investigation and Prosecution of Rape in London* (2015).
[111] All-Party Parliamentary Group on Domestic and Sexual Violence, *The Changing Landscape of Domestic and Sexual Violence Services* (Bristol: Women's Aid Federation of England, 2015) p 6.
[112] Munro V and Aitken R, 'Adding insult to injury? The criminal law's response to domestic abuse-related suicide in England and Wales' [2018] *Criminal Law Review* 732.

Police and prosecution resources to investigate these crimes were slashed between 2010 and 2020 (the era of austerity) even while investigation (of sexual assaults in particular, because of complex evidence issues around social media) has become more complex. One response of the police was to classify as few alleged sexual assaults as possible as crimes to reduce how bad 'the figures' would look. A report from 2014 found that:

> The national rate of under-recording of sexual offences (including rapes) as crimes was 26 per cent, and the national rate of incorrect decisions to no-crime rapes was 20 per cent. In the case of rape no-crime decisions, in 22 per cent of cases there was no evidence that the police informed the complainant of their decision. These are wholly unacceptable failings.[113]

Yet matters then got worse. The prosecution and conviction rate for sexual assaults went down: from 5,000 and nearly 3,000 respectively in 2016/17, to 2,102 and 1,439 respectively in 2019/20. In that same three-year period the police referred 40% fewer cases to the CPS for prosecution.[114] The extent to which this reflects inadequate police investigation, overly strict evidential requirements by the CPS, and/or other reasons is not known. The historic high conviction rate as a proportion of prosecutions—but low conviction rate as a proportion of recorded offences—suggests that the CPS is reluctant to prosecute weak sexual assault cases. This was challenged by a recent report, which considered the starving of resources to the police in the 'austerity' years to be a major factor.[115] But this limited vindication of CPS decision-making has itself been criticised.[116]

It would be ironic if the CPS is too risk-averse, in light of its willingness, discussed in chapter 7, to often pursue other types of weak cases when this furthers broader police and prosecution policies. An attempted court challenge to the alleged risk-averse policy failed.[117] If the police fail to investigate large numbers of cases thoroughly—whether due to how priorities are ordered, negligence or inadequate resources—then there will be insufficient evidence to forward those cases to the CPS or, if they are forwarded, to prosecute them. Reviewing these decisions individually is virtually pointless: it is the quality of investigation and resourcing that is at issue, which no 'right to review' scheme can unravel. And the HMCPSI found that staff working in WLUs often worked weekends to try and keep up with caseloads because of under resourcing,[118] so the problem extends to all types of crime victim.[119] Hall's view that: 'The victims' right to review was therefore a hugely significant change in practice' giving victims 'a form of locus standi'[120] therefore greatly overstates the improvements in the system for victims. Once again, resource constraints undermine the core values of justice and democracy.

For anti-social behaviour there is a related innovation. Most anti-social behaviour comes to the notice of the agencies responsible for dealing with it (principally local police forces, housing associations and local government authorities) through reporting by people and groups affected, e.g. individuals, local businesses, tenants associations, etc. If these people

---

[113] Her Majesty's Inspectorate of Constabulary (2014). *Crime-Recording: Making the Victim Count* (London: HMIC), p 19.' [114] *The Guardian*, 30 July 2020.
[115] HMCPSI, *2019 Rape Inspection* (HMCPSI, 2019, Publication No CP001:1267)
[116] Deardon L, 'Government must reject "poor" watchdog report on falling rape prosecutions, women's groups say' *The Independent*, 30 January 2020.
[117] Deardon L, 'High Court refuses permission for legal challenge over falling rape prosecutions' *The Independent*, 17 March 2020. [118] HMCPSI (2018) e.g. para 6.21.
[119] 'The CPS faces a huge challenge in trying to improve the quality of its service to victims.... The CPS needs to be realistic about what is achievable given the ongoing financial constraints.' HMCPSI (2016) para 1.12.
[120] HMCPSI (2018) p 165.

or groups are dissatisfied with the official response they can apply to their local council Community Safety Partnership for it to be reviewed. This is the 'community trigger'.[121] But it has to cause 'harassment, alarm or distress' and have been the subject of several reports made soon after the behaviour concerned,[122] as the aim is to target persistent behaviour, not isolated incidents. We do not know how well this works, but commentators are sceptical. As with the right to review CPS decisions, government claims to put victims at the centre of decision-making are greatly overblown.[123]

12.3.4.2 Victim personal statements (VPS) and sentencing decisions

In the USA, where the victims' movement took off earlier than in the UK, involvement began to take the form of making a VPS to police or probation officers, who relayed the information provided by the victim to the court and/or the prosecutor. In England and Wales the 1996 Victims' Charter included a requirement that the police and the CPS take the interests of victims 'into account', and announced experimental VPS schemes in the same areas as the 'right to know' schemes. VPS is now nationwide and provided for in the Code (pp 21–22 and 28). The VPS supplements the original witness statement with another statement (written or recorded) detailing the medical, psychological, financial and emotional harm caused by the crime. Unlike in some American states,[124] only facts are sought, not opinions about what victims think should happen to the offender (Code, ch 2A, para 1.12). This is, in other words, not a consultative process.

Victims' interests are to be taken into account but not, it seems, their views about what is in their interests. Sanders et al (2001) found that a large minority of victims who opted to make a VPS were disappointed. Many who said, at the start of their case, that they were pleased that they participated, said at the end that they no longer felt this way. Thus one victim observed: 'I think it's all a gimmick. It achieves nothing. I took the victim impact statement very seriously and I'd suffered a very serious attack but I doubt that anyone even looked at it. It clearly didn't influence anything . . . a totally useless outcome.'[125] But Erez claims on the basis of her research that VPS is good for victims, because it 'empowers' them by making them visible to criminal justice officials who can thus no longer ignore their interests.[126]

---

[121] Anti-social Behaviour, Crime and Policing Act 2014 ss.104–105 and Sch 4. Anti-social behaviour legislation is briefly discussed in ch 1.

[122] Sections 104 and 105.

[123] Brown K, 'The community trigger for anti-social behaviour: protecting victims or raising unrealistic expectations?' [2015] *Criminal Law Review* 488; Heap V, 'Putting victims first? A critique of coalition anti-social behaviour policy' (2016) 36 *Critical Social Policy* 246. For the latest government guidance (July 2020) see <https://www.gov.uk/guidance/anti-social-behaviour-asb-case-review-also-known-as-the-community-trigger> (accessed 29 September 2020).

[124] For examples of the way this works even in capital punishment cases where juries, who in some states decide whether to order the death penalty, can be influenced by emotive appeals from victims' families, see Sebba L, 'Sentencing and the Victim: The Aftermath of *Payne*' (1994) 3 *International Review of Victimology* 141; Myers et al, 'The heterogeneity of victim impact statements: A content analysis of capital trial sentencing penalty phase transcripts' (2018) 24 *Psychology, Public Policy, and Law* 474. For a discussion of the use of victim impact statements in several jurisdictions, including the UK and the USA, see Booth T, *Accommodating Justice: Victim impact statements in the sentencing process* (Alexandria: Federation Press, 2015).

[125] Hoyle et al, *Evaluation of the 'One Stop Shop' and Victim Statement Pilot Projects* (London: Home Office, 1998) p 32.

[126] Erez E, 'Who's Afraid of the Big Bad Victim? Victim Impact Statements as Victim Empowerment *and* Enhancement of Justice' [1999] *Criminal Law Review* 545. The research by Erez and Hoyle, Sanders et al is now quite old, but the mixed findings and controversies continue. A report on a Scottish scheme, for example, takes a middle path: Chalmers et al, 'Victim Impact Statements: Can Work, Do Work (For Those who Bother to Make Them)' [2007] *Criminal Law Review* 360. Also see, for example, Booth (2015).

Erez argues that this has two beneficial consequences. First, she claims that participation is cathartic. Her findings and those of Sanders et al are reconcilable in that for some victims they are cathartic; but Sanders et al found this was so more at first than at the end of the case. Whether, on balance, they produce a net cathartic benefit is hard to say, but the question is not so much whether they 'work' in this way; they 'work', but 'for whom and under which conditions'?[127] Second, Erez claims that VPS can influence decisions.[128] She is here referring to sentencing only. Sanders et al (2001) found that VPS, in the Victims' Charter schemes at any rate, had virtually no effect on sentencing or on any of the pre-trial stages: a prosecutor observed 'You don't see impact statements having much of an impact',[129] and a judge referred to their 'PR value'[130] thus implying that they had no other utility. Again, there is little contradiction here, as Erez concedes that most research, including her own, found the effect to be slight.

This partly explains why VPS is so unsatisfactory for so many victims. They expect VPS to make a difference, and when it does not they are disappointed. Victims remain ignored even if not forgotten. Sanders et al found that few prosecutors, judges or magistrates were willing to take any notice of a VPS even though they almost universally subscribed to the rhetoric of victims' rights. And for decades, in both the UK and the USA a large number of impact statements used neither to be read nor put in the prosecution file.[131] This still seems to be a problem: in a recent UK survey, of those who made a VPS (many said they were not offered the opportunity) over half said they did not know if it had been used; and of those who did know, half said it wasn't.[132] The Victims' Commissioners' surveys found similar results; indeed, between 2014 and 2019 the proportion of victims offered the opportunity to do a VPS fell, and of those who did a VPS the proportion who believed it had been taken into account also fell (to less than 50%).[133] Being treated like this hardly restores the self-respect of victims or reduces their secondary victimisation. The victims' movement complaint was that victims were used by the system: their witness statements were taken and then they were ignored. And now under the VPS scheme? Two statements are taken (witness and personal), and then they are both frequently ignored. Hardly a revolutionary change. As Erez herself complains, the limited use of VPS represents a compromise between supporters and opponents of victims' rights, 'maintaining the time-honoured tradition of excluding victims from criminal justice with a thin veneer of being part of it'.[134] We do not regard this as empowerment.

Despite these findings, VPS schemes have been introduced nationwide. The statement is taken, by the police, at the same time as the witness statement. But since victims cannot express opinions, VPS have to be edited where appropriate, reducing victims' voice, and continuing to 'sideline' them. As the Victims' Commissioner said in a report on the

---

[127] Lens et al, 'Delivering a VIS: Emotionally effective or counter-productive?' (2015) 12 *European Journal of Criminology* 17.

[128] Many writers object to VPS precisely for this reason. See, for example, Ashworth A, 'Victim's Rights, Defendant's Rights, and Criminal Procedure' in Crawford A and Goodey J (eds), *Integrating a Victim Perspective within Criminal Justice* (London: Routledge, 2019); Sarat A, 'Vengeance, Victims and the Identities of Law' (1997) 6 *Social and Legal Studies* 163. The issue has not gone away: Moffett L, 'Victim Personal Statements in Managing Victims' Voices in Sentencing in Northern Ireland: Taking a More Procedural Justice Approach' (2017) 68 *Northern Ireland Law Quarterly* 555.

[129] Morgan R and Sanders A, *The Uses of Victim Statements* (London: Home Office, 1999) p 22.

[130] Ibid: p 7.

[131] Henley et al, 'The Reactions of Prosecutors and Judges to Victim Impact Statements' (1994) 3 *International Review of Victimology* 83; HMCPSI/HMICA/HMIC (2009: para 2.33).

[132] CPS, *Victim and witness satisfaction survey* (2015b), p 50.

[133] Newlove B, *The silenced victim: a review of the victim personal statement* (2015); Victims' Commissioner, *Victim personal statements 2018/19* (2019b). Both available at <https://victimscommissioner.org.uk/> (accessed 29 September 2020).

[134] Erez and Rogers (1999: 234–235).

experiences of victims and the VPS scheme as a whole: 'Despite the intentions to provide victims with the right to "voice" the impact of a crime—they are largely being denied this opportunity. . . . It is not enough to give victims a voice—this voice has to be heard.'[135]

In one sense there is no stopping the trend towards the provision of victim information to criminal justice officials and the courts. This is partly because, in the political sphere, no-one dares argue against 'victims' rights'. It is also because sentencing legitimately takes account of harm done (including emotional and psychological harm). Criminal courts have been receiving, and sometimes even seeking, such information in cases concerning serious sexual offences, robbery and violence for decades. However, statement schemes are not the best way of involving victims and of ensuring that relevant information is transmitted. In a CPS report discussing the results of a survey of victims the recommendations for reform aimed at increasing victim satisfaction listed a wide range of proposed enhancements to existing measures—but VPS was not mentioned. VPS was doubtless considered to add little or nothing for most victims.[136] Similarly, a review of evidence from research on 'what works' in supporting victims concluded that what victims most want (and need, if distress and secondary victimisation is to be reduced) is effective and timely information and two-way communication: participation in proceedings, whether through VPS schemes or otherwise, did not get a mention.[137]

There are more effective ways of taking account of victims' interests, reducing secondary victimisation and enhancing justice without undermining the rights of the accused. Civil law jurisdictions, international processes and restorative procedures provide models.[138] Indeed, there has been significant investment in the latter, with Police and Crime Commissioners (PCCs) being given a dedicated budget of £23 million in 2013 to build capacity for providing restorative justice to victims, though these funds have since 2016 been subsumed into PCC budgets for victims.[139] Even with this investment, recent research has shown that restorative justice tends to be seen by those delivering it as an 'optional extra', rather than as integral to the services provided to victims by the police.[140] Anything more meaningful would be more expensive than statement schemes and would also require us to rethink the role of victims in adversarial processes. For a crime control system that only pays lip service to the interests of victims, this is not even on the agenda. The penalty that will be paid is that, as victims continue to be dissatisfied, their concerns will be hijacked by populist politicians to justify ever greater incursions on the liberties and rights of suspects, defendants and prisoners.[141]

It is evident that there is no clear policy about how influential, if at all, victims should be. Many different ways of trying to put victims at 'the centre' of criminal justice have been

---

[135] Newlove B, *The silenced victim: a review of the victim personal statement* (2015) p 6. The title says it all.
[136] CPS, *Victim and witness satisfaction survey* (2015b) pp 67–69.
[137] Wedlock and Tapley (2016).
[138] See, for example, Sanders et al (2001) and Braun (2019), especially ch 9; and Doak J, 'Enriching Trial Justice for Crime Victims in Common Law Systems: Lessons from Transitional Environments' [2015] 21 *International Review of Victimology* 139.
[139] Restorative Justice Council, *A guide to restorative justice for Police and Crime Commissioner Candidates* (2016) online at: <https://restorativejustice.org.uk/sites/default/files/resources/files/RJC%20-%20guide%20for%20Police%20and%20Crime%20Commissioner%20candidates.pdf> (accessed 25 September 2020).
[140] Banwell-Moore R, *Restorative justice: understanding the enablers and barriers to victim participation in England and Wales*, unpublished PhD thesis, University of Sheffield (2020).
[141] See Elias R, *Victims Still: The Political Manipulation of Crime Victims* (London: Sage, 1993) and Sarat (1997). See also Roach (2016) for an insightful analysis of punitive and non-punitive (i.e. restorative) victims' rights models.

proposed over recent years.[142] But doing this would give victims a role in decision-making. No-one has yet worked out how to reconcile this with protecting the rights of suspects and defendants and ensuring a reasonable level of consistency.[143] A less dramatic solution is to provide victims with the right to legal representation. But if available free, even for just serious crimes, it would be hugely expensive; if it were not free, it would be unaffordable to all but the middle and upper classes; and the actual role of the lawyer is unclear. Nonetheless, there is a strong case for something on these lines for sexual and domestic violence in particular, as in some other jurisdictions.[144] It has been recommended for Northern Ireland[145] and the same arguments apply to the rest of the UK. 'Victim advocates', which we do have in the UK for sexual and domestic violence (see section 8.6), are not lawyers and have a more limited role, but provide a model that can be built on.[146]

Decisions about prosecution, bail, plea bargaining, discontinuance, sentence and release from prison are all now to be made with varying degrees of input from, and discussion with, those relatively few victims who wish to be involved. The new Code does not shed any light on how much notice agencies should take of victims. It is up to them.[147] The opportunity to provide for procedural rights on a consistent basis was not taken, and the formalistic distinction between 'service' and 'procedural' rights fails to recognise the interconnection between the two.[148] One consequence of the non-participatory ways in which victims are involved in criminal justice is that many experience courts (the Crown court at any rate) as 'structured mayhem'—in other words, as chaotic, other-worldly and often frightening.[149]

12.4 Rhetoric and reality: managing the gap

It is sometimes rhetorically said that it is better that 10 guilty people should escape justice rather than one innocent person be wrongly convicted. In addition to proclaiming the greater importance of acquitting the guilty than convicting the innocent, and recognising

---

[142] See, for example: Erez et al, 'From Cinderella to consumer: how crime victims can go to the ball' in Tapley and Davies (2020); and Dearing A, *Justice for Victims of Crime: Human dignity as the foundation of criminal justice in Europe* (Cham: Springer, 2017); Pemberton A and Reynaers S, 'The controversial nature of victim participation: The case of the victim impact statements' in Erez E, Kilchling M and Wemmers J (eds), *Therapeutic Jurisprudence and Victim Participation in Criminal Justice: International perspectives* (Durham, NC: Carolina Academic Press, 2011).

[143] For thoughtful discussions see Manikis M, 'Conceptualising the victim within criminal justice processes in the common law tradition' in Brown et al (2019); Moffett (2017); van der Merwe A and Skelton A, 'Victims' mitigating views in sentencing decisions: a comparative analysis' (2015) 35 *Oxford Journal of Legal Studies* 355.

[144] See, e.g., Braun (2019: ch 8).

[145] Gillen Review, *Report into the law and procedures in serious sexual offences in Northern Ireland: Part 1, Final Report* (2019) <https://www.justice-ni.gov.uk/sites/default/files/publications/justice/gillen-report-may-2019.pdf> i.

[146] Victims' Commissioner, *Victim Advocates* (2019a); Burman M and Brooks-Hay O, 'Feminist Framings of Victim Advocacy in Criminal Justice Contexts' in Tapley and Davies (2020).

[147] That judges may take VPS into account in sentencing, and are therefore evidence and subject to potential cross-examination, was confirmed in *Perkins* [2013] 2 Cr App R (S) 72, and the Criminal Practice Directions. However, when victims claimed they suffered great psychological harm from the crimes they suffered the judges accepted this without the defendants having any effective way of countering the claims (*Chall* [2019] EWCA Crim 865).

[148] This distinction is attributable to Ashworth A, 'Victim Impact Statements and Sentencing' [1993] *Criminal Law Review* 498. However, in addition to having to add to these two categories, as we do in this chapter, the apparently clear distinction is not, on further investigation, so clear-cut: Sanders et al (2001).

[149] Jacobson J, Hunter G and Kirby A, *Structured Mayhem: Personal Experiences of the Crown Court* (London: Criminal Justice Alliance, 2015). And see Kirby A, 'Effectively Engaging Victims, Witnesses and Defendants in the Criminal Courts' [2017] *Criminal Law Review* 949. See also ch 9.

the trade-off between the two, the fact that the number stated is 10, rather than 10,000, also recognises that we do not insist upon absolute certainty in the courtroom. And nor could we. Statistically, it follows that some convicted defendants will in fact be innocent. The system is not, and never will be, perfect.

The real problem with this rhetoric is that it does not adequately characterise the reality, or even the rules, of the criminal justice system. There is a gap between the rhetoric of the system as a whole (largely due process), the rules (displaying a mixture of values) and the reality (largely crime control). We say that the rhetoric is *largely* due process-oriented, for governments increasingly favour crime control rhetoric, rules and reality. This is usually dressed up in the language of caring for victims and 'the law-abiding majority': for example, by the Home Office seeking to 'rebalance the criminal justice system'[150] and the then Prime Minister stating ominously in 2005 that the 'rules of the game are changing'. Occasionally there is a little more honesty, as when the then-Secretary of State for Justice introduced the then-new Victims' Code: 'From today they [victims] will have more help than ever before to help bring offenders to justice . . .'.[151] Victims need to be treated well so that they will be more likely to co-operate.

The idea that victims should have the same rights as the accused (for example, to be protected and heard) is seductive. But the reason why accused people have these rights is because they stand to lose their liberty wrongly if they are deprived of them. The victim is not in the same position. This is why the freedom perspective gives some, but less, weight to the interests of victims than those of the accused. The new victim-centred rhetoric is therefore flawed, but it is also deceitful because it disguises the crime control drift.

This process could continue until we have a totalitarian 'police state', at least so far as the poor, youths, protesters, and other 'problem populations' identified in chapter 10 are concerned, but this is unlikely as it would be too politically dangerous. Within all the major political parties, there is sufficient attachment to the rhetoric and substance of due process to rule out the possibility of introducing an undiluted and naked system of crime control. There is also an ideological reason. By arguing that the criminal justice system has become too heavily tipped towards the interests of suspects, the government has chosen to lock itself into the discourse of 'balance' in which more crime control can be justified by reference to bits and pieces of due process. In this sense, due process is for crime control. But it also means that some genuine due process safeguards are sure to be retained, since one cannot create the appearance of due process if there is no substance to such safeguards.[152] Finally, the Human Rights Act 1998 and ECHR will ensure that there is an irreducible minimum of due process safeguards, at least for as long as they exist or remain applicable in England and Wales.

We have seen that the gap between rhetoric and reality is a little smaller when we consider the plight of victims. For vulnerable victims, there are real improvements. But most victims have 'rights' which are totally unenforceable, limited access to 'consolatory' payments from agencies that treat them badly, and less compensation from the Criminal Injuries Compensation Scheme (it was cut by £50m pa in 2012).[153] The 'rights' of victims

---

[150] *Justice for All* (2002) Cm 5563, para 0.3.
[151] See <https://www.gov.uk/government/news/victims-put-first-in-the-criminal-justice-system> (published December 2013) (accessed 9 September 2020).
[152] In this, we follow Thompson E P, *Whigs and Hunters* (London: Allen Lane, 1975) pp 259–265. See further Cole D, ' "An Unqualified Human Good": E.P. Thompson and the Rule of Law' (2001) 28(2) *Journal of Law and Society* 177.
[153] Hansard, 13 November 2012, volume 553; Miers D, 'Offender and state compensation for victims of crime: Two decades of development and change' (2014) 20 *International Review of Victimology* 145; Hall (2018: ch 5).

are therefore even flimsier than many of the rights of suspects and defendants. Indeed, government decided to expand the VPS scheme despite research evidence showing that it is often of limited value and perhaps unhelpful to as many victims as it is helpful. A Scottish evaluation produced more positive results than the English one, but still found that victims overwhelmingly sought improvements to the information they get about their cases in preference to involvement in decisions.[154] And a report commissioned by the Victims' Commissioner concluded that 'the key things that support victims are timely and accurate information; effective methods of communication with victims, both in delivering information and listening to victims' needs; multi-agency partnerships across the statutory and voluntary sectors and providing a range of services that are accessible and flexible . . .'.[155] In other words, service rights are more highly valued by victims than are procedural rights, but the latter are more headline grabbing so this is where the money and publicity are centred.

As Hall (2018) states, and as we have seen, victims are primarily supported as 'de facto prosecution witnesses' (to secure convictions) rather than 'as victims' whose needs will sometimes be primarily emotional and financial rather than conviction-oriented. The sex abuse victim who was locked up to ensure that she would testify against the defendant (see section 3 of this chapter) is a shocking example. But this is indicative of a wider problem: fewer than half of all vulnerable victims and witnesses feel they have sufficient support before giving evidence and similar numbers report being offered no follow-up care at all. And 7% of victims feel they were treated disrespectfully at some point, more by the police than any other agency.[156]

This all adds weight to the argument in this book that the UK has a system far more aligned to 'crime control' than 'due process' values (and favouring the 'efficiency' core value over the other core values). Crime control systems make use of the rhetoric of the rights of the victim, but do not provide the reality.[157] For real victims' rights would cost a lot and get in the way of crime control aims almost as much as do the rights of defendants. For victims, just as much as innocent suspects and defendants, want the *right people* to be convicted—which is not the same as wanting the *criminal population* to be controlled (the crime control objective)—and treating victims as criminals is self-defeating.

The powers of police and prosecution are therefore available to be used both for and against both suspects/defendants and victims—or without a care for either group. It may appear surprising that the crime control system serves victims as badly as it serves defendants until we remember that prosecution (in the minority of cases that get that far) requires the presentation of a case. All cases are constructions, and become the property of the side that built it. Cases often become far removed from the facts that provided their initial impetus and therefore, not infrequently, as far removed from anything the victim recognises as from anything the defendant recognises.

Thus while official rhetoric argues that the system is unbalanced in favour of 'offenders' and against victims, in reality, suspects/defendants/offenders and complainants/witnesses/victims are in a similar position, because the search for truth (whoever's version that might be) is subordinated to other priorities. Members of the public, whatever role they happen

---

[154] Chalmers et al (2007).   [155] Wedlock and Tapley (2016: 25).

[156] CPS, *Victim and witness satisfaction survey* (2015b) p 12–13, Satisfaction levels for non-vulnerable victims and witnesses are higher than for vulnerable people, but not greatly so.

[157] See McCullagh C, 'Respectable victims and safe solutions: the hidden politics of victimology' (2017) 68 *Northern Ireland Law Quarterly* 539 for an excellent discussion primarily concerned with Ireland but with general applicability.

currently to be occupying, have no significant leverage on the agencies and officials about what should happen, when, and to whom. Contrary to government rhetoric, most victims are more concerned that the system should protect them and help prevent future reoffending—in our terms, to increase the sum total of freedom—than to be punitive per se.[158] By restricting genuine victim participation in most cases the criminal justice system is exclusionary to both the accused and the victim, missing opportunities to enhance freedom.[159] It is therefore not surprising to find that surveys have consistently found that victim and witness satisfaction is highest with Victim Support and court witness services[160]—for, unlike the police, CPS and courts, these are the only agencies whose sole aim is to serve victims. The other agencies, rightly, have other objectives too. Nonetheless, the inadequate protection provided to the least powerful groups in society leads to distress, injury and death.

The criminal justice system will continue to represent a site of struggle and conflict. Many skirmishes will result in victories for due process (as where evidence is excluded on the ground of unfairness), even some battles may be temporarily won (as with the creation of court and police station duty solicitor schemes), only for ground to be taken back again (as with the restricted right of silence sidelining legal advice in many cases, and the formalisation of plea bargaining). The Court of Appeal sometimes quashes convictions to express its disapproval of police malpractice even though there is reliable evidence of guilt, some police officers behave ethically and advocate progressive reforms, and some defence lawyers provide an outstanding service to their clients, often at great emotional and financial cost to themselves. But these events and people tend to occur in high-profile contexts (as with the dramatic freeing of the 'Birmingham Six', Angela Cannings and Colin Stagg), creating an appearance of far more due process than is really the case. So the war will continue. Crime control cannot be imposed by an open show of naked force, since its ideological justification is that it increases real freedom and liberty, but nor are we asked to give our *informed* consent to it. Instead we are presented with a picture of a system—neatly balancing due process rights, crime control powers and the rights of victims—which is a gross distortion of reality. The 'democracy' core value is thus undermined.

Part of this distortion is achieved by judges and legislators proclaiming the virtues of due process at the same time as they are acting on crime control instincts. For example, the case law on exclusion provides the judges with a wide scope as to which precedents to follow, which tests to apply and which decisions to reach. The open texture of the law means that, and on this point we follow McBarnet (1981: 166), 'judges can both uphold, even eulogise, the rhetoric yet simultaneously deny its applicability . . . ' Thus the protections introduced by PACE and the Codes of Practice are used against suspects, so that when a solicitor is present, this is usually judged to be sufficient protection to condone rule-breaking such as failure to caution, record questioning properly and so forth. Similarly, in examining the Court of Appeal's powers, we saw how malpractice by police or prosecution agencies might be critcised but the conviction upheld. The use of rhetoric bearing little relation to reality is not confined to English governments and courts. The ECtHR is equally guilty. For example, we saw in chapter 8 that according to the ECtHR the bail decision has to be based on evidence (not speculation) and it has to be proven beyond reasonable doubt that someone is likely to breach bail. This is plainly ridiculous. Bail decisions

---

[158] Myers et al (2018).

[159] Sanders A, 'Victim Participation in an Exclusionary Criminal Justice System' in Hoyle C and Young R (eds), *New Visions of Crime Victims* (Oxford: Hart, 2002). Braun (2019).

[160] E.g. HMCPSI/HMICA/HMIC (2009: ch 5). This is an old survey as the Coalition government that took power in 2010 stopped regular surveys, and at the time of writing they have not re-started. Finding out what works for victims is low on the 'austerity' government's list of priorities.

in reality have to be based on risk and prediction (that is, *intelligent* speculation). This is a probabilistic, and not evidence-based, process and we doubt that anyone in the ECtHR believes otherwise.

The uneven distribution of due process protections across society is as worrying as their general erosion. At various points in this book, we have seen that disadvantaged sections of society are disproportionately at the receiving end of state power. 'We' are taken in by the ideological self-portrait of criminal justice because we have so little experience of the system and have no incentive to question its operation. It does not threaten 'our' interests, but appears to serve them. Ask people who regularly come into contact with the system, whether as victims or offenders, and they will have a different story to tell. We saw that this led to so much dissatisfaction with the police complaints system that radical reform was attempted, but this disaffection—bordering on disbelief in the rule of law—can be seen in many other criminal justice contexts (such as stop-search) where no change is on the cards: 'defendants' marginalization and passive acceptance are likely to have roots much deeper than the way the criminal justice system operates' but 'victims' and 'suspects'/'defendants' overlap, so we need a 'cultural shift towards a justice system which more actively and effectively engages with its lay participants, and which recognizes that treating people in a bullying, arrogant or condescending manner is simply unacceptable'.[161]

Widespread disbelief in the rule of law is hardly surprising, for when we look at the rule of law another gap between rhetoric and reality is revealed. As we argue elsewhere,[162] two vital elements of the rule of law are equality before the law (as between citizens in different communities and as between citizens and officials) and the accountability of state officials to the courts. We have seen that, despite the rhetoric, neither of these conditions apply in many situations. The gap is managed, however, because they *appear* to apply. For example, anyone can ask anyone else a question without requiring an answer. Whether on the street or in the station, this is held to apply equally to police officers as to citizens. But treating people *the same* in this way is not treating them *equally*. By ignoring the power which police officers exert over citizens, whether unstated (as often happens on the street) or overt (as in the station), the citizen is not treated equally and the police are not made subject to legal control—'consent' searches of people's homes, for example, are not subject to the restrictions, such as they are, of PACE. Moreover, because some communities are disadvantaged by comparison with others in the way this type of power is exercised, people are treated unequally in an *institutionalised* manner, thus further violating the rule of law. And the relative lack of accountability of enforcement agencies—police, CPS and non-police agencies—means that they almost never have to account for this or its effects, violating the rule of law yet further.

We cannot expect, and nor would we advocate, the adoption of either a consistent crime control philosophy and all that goes with it, nor the adoption of the due process model and all that that would imply. Unfortunately, the freedom approach which we advocate is also unlikely to materialise unless politicians take a lead in raising the debate as distinct from raising their opinion poll ratings. Looked at in this way, the prospects for an open, rational and fair system of justice are bleak.

Our negative tone might be criticised on the grounds that the English system is, for all its faults, the best in the world. It probably is better than most, and undoubtedly better

---

[161] Jacobson et al, *Inside Crown Court: Personal experiences and questions of legitimacy* (Bristol: Policy Press 2015) pp 207, 208.
[162] See Sanders and Young (1994b) in relation to police practices.

than some. This is as it should be, as we are still one of the wealthiest societies in the world. We ought to be able to afford the best justice and the best victim support. But victims, as well as suspects, are too frequently treated shamefully: 'Victims who have seen themselves transformed from Cinderella status to centre stage may find themselves once more retreating to the wings.... [leading] to the disenfranchisement of most victims.'[163] And if we are as civilised as we would like to think, we should aspire to have the best system. The argument of this book is that the system neither achieves, nor aspires to achieve, such a high standard. The due process and crime control models help us understand the tensions within the system as it stands. But they cannot help us make out a persuasive argument for a transformation of that system.

We have seen that human rights—while valuable for jurisdictions with an even worse record than that of the UK—provide only a basic floor of protections here. For example, the police still retain virtual immunity for deaths in police custody.[164] Some victims—of illegal eviction from their homes, pollution, unsafe work conditions, failure to pay minimum wages, domestic abuse, sexual assault, police violence and neglect—are less important than others. These victims are disproportionately from the most marginalised, poor and powerless sections of society.[165] The same 'austerity' measures that cause police and the CPS to operate with one hand tied behind their backs and thereby fail these people (as well as failing witnesses and victims in court) restrict what police and local agencies are able to do in response to, for example, complaints about anti-social behaviour and illegal evictions.[166] Or take the crime of paying less than the minimum wage: 'The office of the director of labour market enforcement said in its 2018 strategy that the average employer could expect an inspection by the HMRC's minimum wage team about once every 500 years.'[167] Just 3.6% of fly-tipping and pollution complaints lead to penalties, so not surprisingly pollution is rife (water firms discharged raw sewage into England's rivers 200,000 times in 2019).[168]

Human rights do not protect the individuals and communities suffering from all of this structural discrimination. Nor do they protect society as a whole from mass surveillance, so justice and democracy are undermined.[169] We need a new language in which to express our aspirations, and the language of freedom and its core values seems to us to provide a vocabulary most likely to persuade the various entrenched interest groups of the need for change. It is time to set the primary goal of the criminal justice system as the promotion of freedom of all citizens and social groups alike.

---

[163] Mawby R, 'Victim Support in England and Wales: The End of an Era?' (2016) 22 *International Review of Victimology* 203 at 217.

[164] Field S, 'The Corporate Manslaughter and Corporate Homicide Act 2007 and human rights - Part 2: has universal legal protection of the right to life been advanced in a custodial setting?' (2019) 30 *International Company and Commercial Law Review* 415.

[165] See Hall (2018: ch 1) for discussion of the 'construction' of crime victims.

[166] Demetriou S, 'From the ASBO to the injunction: a qualitative review of the anti-social behaviour legislation post-2014' [2019] *Public Law* 343 at 355. On illegal evictions see Wall T, 'No place like home: illegal evictions in "shadow" sector soar in lockdown' *The Guardian*, 23 August 2020. On the effects of CPS cuts see, e.g., HMCPSI (2016b) *Communicating with victims* para 1.8–9.

[167] Bland A, 'Priti Patel criticised over comments on Leicester's sweatshops' *The Guardian*, 12 July 2020.

[168] See reports by Laville and Laville and McIntyre in *The Guardian*, 1 and 21 July 2020.

[169] Hirst P, 'Mass surveillance in the age of terror: bulk powers in the Investigatory Powers Act 2016' (2019) 4 *European Human Rights Law Review* 403.

Further reading

Ashworth A and Zedner L, *Preventive Justice* (Oxford: OUP, 2014).

Boukli A and Kotze J (eds) *Zemiology: Reconnecting Crime and Social Harm* (Cham, Switzerland: Palgrave Macmillan, 2018).

Doak J, 'Enriching Trial Justice for Crime Victims in Common Law Systems: Lessons from Transitional Environments' [2015] 21 *International Review of Victimology* 139.

Hall M, *Victims of Crime: Construction, Governance and Policy* (Basingstoke: Palgrave Macmillan, 2018).

Hoyano L, 'Reforming the adversarial trial for vulnerable witnesses and defendants' [2015] *Criminal Law Review* 107.

M. Iliadis et al, 'Improving Justice Responses for Victims of Intimate Partner Violence: Examining the Merits of the Provision of Independent Legal Representation' (2021 45(1)) *International Journal of Comparative and Applied Criminal Justice*, 105–114.

McCulloch J and Wilson D, *Pre-crime: Preemption, Precaution and the Future* (London: Routledge, 2016).

Moffett L, 'Victim Personal Statements in Managing Victims' Voices in Sentencing in Northern Ireland: Taking a More Procedural Justice Approach' (2017) 68 *Northern Ireland Law Quarterly* 555.

Munro V and Aitken R, 'Adding insult to injury? The criminal law's response to domestic abuse-related suicide in England and Wales' [2018] *Criminal Law Review* 732.

Walklate S (ed), *Handbook of Victims and Victimology* (London; Routledge, 2018).

Bibliography

Abbot C (2009) *Enforcing Pollution Control Regulation* (Oxford: Hart).

Adams C (1995) *Balance in Pre-Trial Criminal Justice* (unpublished PhD thesis, LSE, 1995).

Adams I and Mastracci S (2017) 'Visibility is a trap: the ethics of police body-worn cameras and control' 39 ATP 313.

Adams-Quackenbush N, Vrij A, Horselenberg R, Satchell L and Van Koppen P (2020) 'Articulating guilt? The influence of guilt presumption on interviewer and interviewee behaviour', *Current Psychology*.

Adisa O (2018) *Access to Justice: Assessing the impact of the Magistrates' Court Closures in Suffolk* (Ipswich: Suffolk Institute for Social and Economic Research).

Adu-Boyake K (2002) 'Private Security and Retail Crime Prevention' (Unpublished MSc Dissertation, University of Portsmouth).

Agozino B (1997, republished 2018) *Black Women and the Criminal Justice System: Towards the decolonisation of victimisation* (Abingdon: Routledge Revivals).

Ainsworth P (2002) *Psychology and Policing* (Cullompton: Willan).

Airs J and Shaw A (1999) *Jury excusal and deferral, Research Findings No 102* (London: Home Office).

Akdeniz Y (2001) 'Regulation of Investigatory Powers Act 2000: Part 1: bigbrother. gov.uk: state surveillance in the age of information and rights' Criminal Law Review 73.

Alge D (2013a) 'Negotiated Plea Agreements in Cases of Serious and Complex Fraud in England and Wales: A New Conceptualisation of Plea Bargaining?' 19(1) European Journal of Current Legal Issues.

Alge D (2013b) 'The Effectiveness of Incentives to Reduce the Risk of Moral Hazard in the Defence Barrister's Role in Plea Bargaining' 16(1) Legal Ethics 162–181.

Ali A, Ghosh S, Strydom A and Hassiotis A (2016) 'Prisoners with intellectual disabilities and detention status. Findings from a UK cross sectional study of prisons.' 53–54 Research in Developmental Disabilities 189–197.

Allen G and Kirk-Wade E (2020) *Terrorism in Great Britain: The statistics.* House of Commons Briefing Paper CBP7613 (London: House of Commons).

Allen G and Zayed Y (2019) *Hate Crime Statistics.* Briefing Paper Number 08537 (London: House of Commons).

Allen J, Edmonds S, Patterson A and Smith D (2006) *Policing and the Criminal Justice System—public confidence and perceptions: findings from the 2004/05 British Crime Survey* (Home Office Online Report 07/06) (London: Home Office).

Allen R (2016) *The Sentencing Council for England and Wales: Brake or accelerator on the use of prison?* (London: Transform Justice).

Allen G, Audickas L, Loft P and Bellis A (2019) *Knife Crime in England and Wales.* House of Commons Briefing Paper SN4304 (London: House of Commons Library).

All-party Parliamentary Group on Domestic and Sexual Violence (2015) *The Changing Landscape of Domestic and Sexual Violence Services* (Bristol: Women's Aid Federation of England).

Almås I, Cappelen A and Tungodden B (2019) *Cutthroat Capitalism Versus Cuddly Socialism: Are Americans More Meritocratic and Efficiency-Seeking than Scandinavians?* Discussion Paper No. 4/2019 (Bergen: NHH Dept. of Economics).

ALSCHULER A (1995) 'The all-white American jury' 145 New Law Journal 1005.

ALSTON P (2019) *Visit to the United Kingdom of Great Britain and Northern Ireland Report of the Special Rapporteur on extreme poverty and human rights*. UN General Assembly A/HRC/41/39/Add.1 (Geneva: Office of the United Nations High Commissioner for Human Rights).

AMADI J (2008) *Piloting PNDs on 10–15 year Olds*. Ministry of Justice Research Series 19/08 (London: MOJ).

AMEY P, HALE C and UGLOW S (1996) *Development and evaluation of a crime management model* (Police Research Series Paper 18, London: Home Office).

AMNESTY INTERNATIONAL (2000) *Deaths in Police Custody: Lack of Police Accountability* (London: AI).

AMNESTY INTERNATIONAL (2007) *Maze of injustice. The failure to protect Indigenous women from sexual violence in the USA* (New York, Amnesty International USA).

AMNESTY INTERNATIONAL (2020) *Policing the Pandemic* (Online at: https://www.amnesty.org).

AMOS M (2007) 'The Impact of the Human Rights Act on the United Kingdom's performance before the European Court of Human Rights' Public Law 655.

ANGIOLINI E (2015) *Report of the Independent Review into the Investigation and Prosecution of Rape in London* (London: TSO).

ANGIOLINI E (2017) *Report of the Independent Review of Deaths and Serious Incidents in Police Custody* (London: TSO).

ANNISON J and BRAYFORD J (eds) (2015) *Women and criminal justice: From the Corston Report to Transforming Rehabilitation* (Bristol: The Policy Press).

ARANELLA P (1996) 'Rethinking the Functions of Criminal Procedure' reprinted in WASSERSTROM S and SNYDER C, *A Criminal Procedure Anthology* (Cincinnati: Anderson).

ARCE R (1995) 'Evidence Evaluation in Jury Decision-Making' in BULL R and CARSON D (eds), *Handbook of Psychology in Legal Contexts* (Chichester: Wiley).

ARIEL B, SUTHERLAND A and HENSTOCK D (2018) 'Wearing Body Cameras Increases Assaults Against Officers and Does Not Reduce Police Use of Force: Results from a Multi-Site Experiment' 13(6) European Journal of Criminology 744–755.

ARKINSTALL J (2004) 'Unappealing work: the practical difficulties facing solicitors engaged in criminal appeal cases' 1(2) Justice Journal 95.

ASHWORTH A (1978) 'A threadbare principle' Criminal Law Review 385.

ASHWORTH A (1979) 'Prosecution and Procedure in Criminal Justice' Criminal Law Review 490.

ASHWORTH A (1987a) 'Defining Offences Without Harm' in SMITH P (ed), *Criminal Law: Essays in Honour of J C Smith* (London: Butterworths).

ASHWORTH A (1987b) 'Public Order and the Principles of English Criminal Law' Criminal Law Review 153.

ASHWORTH A (1987c) 'The "Public Interest" Element in Prosecutions' Criminal Law Review 595.

ASHWORTH A (1993a) 'Plea, Venue and Discontinuance' Criminal Law Review 830.

ASHWORTH A (1993b) 'Victim impact statements and sentencing' Criminal Law Review 498.

ASHWORTH A (1996a) 'Crime, Community and Creeping Consequentialism' Criminal Law Review 220.

ASHWORTH A (1996b) 'Legal Aid, Human Rights and Criminal Justice' in YOUNG R and WALL D (eds), *Access to Criminal Justice* (London: Blackstone).

ASHWORTH A (1997) 'Defining Criminal Offences without Harm' in SMITH P (ed), *Criminal Law: Essays in Honour of J C Smith* (London: Butterworths).

ASHWORTH A (1998) 'Should the police be allowed to use deceptive practices?' 114 Law Quarterly Review 108.

ASHWORTH A (1999) 'Article 6 and the Fairness of Trials' Criminal Law Review 261.

ASHWORTH A (2000a) 'Testing Fidelity to Legal Values: Official Involvement and Criminal Justice' 63 Modern Law Review 633.

ASHWORTH A (2000b) 'Victim's rights, defendant's rights, and criminal procedure' in CRAWFORD A and GOODEY J (eds), *Integrating a Victim Perspective within Criminal Justice* (Aldershot: Ashgate).

ASHWORTH A (2001) 'Criminal Proceedings after the Human Rights Act: The First Year' Criminal Law Review 855.

ASHWORTH A (2002a) 'Re-drawing the boundaries of entrapment' Criminal Law Review 161.

ASHWORTH A (2002b) 'Responsibilities, Rights and Restorative Justice' 42(3) British Journal of Criminology 578.

ASHWORTH A (2004) 'Criminal Justice Reform: Principles, Human Rights and Public Protection' Criminal Law Review 516.

ASHWORTH A (2006) 'Sentencing' in MAGUIRE M, MORGAN R and REINER R (eds), *The Oxford Handbook of Criminology* 4th edn (Oxford: Clarendon Press).

ASHWORTH A (2007) 'Bail; human rights' Criminal Law Review 63.

ASHWORTH A (2015) *Sentencing and Criminal Justice* (Cambridge: CUP).

ASHWORTH A (2019) 'Victim's Rights, Defendant's Rights, and Criminal Procedure' in CRAWFORD A and GOODEY J (eds), *Integrating a Victim Perspective within Criminal Justice* (London: Routledge)

ASHWORTH A and BLAKE M (1996) 'The Presumption of Innocence in English Criminal Law' Criminal Law Review 306.

ASHWORTH A and FIONDA J (1994) 'The New Code for Crown Prosecutors: Prosecution, Accountability and the Public Interest' Criminal Law Review 894.

ASHWORTH A and REDMAYNE M (2005) *The Criminal Process* 3rd edn (Oxford: OUP).

ASHWORTH A and ZEDNER L, (2014) *Preventive Justice* (Oxford: OUP).

ASHWORTH A, GENDERS E, MANSFIELD G, PEAY J and PLAYER E (1984) *Sentencing in the Crown Court* (Occasional Paper no 10) (Oxford: Oxford Centre for Criminological Research).

ASPDEN K (2007) *Nationality: Wog: The Hounding of David Oluwale.* (London: Vintage Books)

ASTON P (2010) *Report of the Special Rapporteur on Extrajudicial, Summary or Arbitrary Executions.* UN Human Rights Council (Geneva: OHCHR).

ASTOR H (1986) 'The Unrepresented Defendant Revisited: A Consideration of the Role of the Clerk in Magistrates' Courts' 13(2) Journal of Law & Society 225–239.

ATHWAL H and BOURNE, J (eds) (2015) *Dying for Justice* (London: Institute for Race Relations).

ATKINSON R (2020) 'The new legal aid settlement is an insult' *The Times*, 5 March.

ATTORNEY-GENERAL (2003) *Review of the Role and Practices of the CPS in Cases Arising from a Death in Police Custody* (London: TSO).

ATTORNEY-GENERAL (2005) *The review of infant death cases: addendum to report on shaken baby syndrome* (London: Attorney-General's Office).

ATTORNEY-GENERAL (2018) *Review of the efficiency and effectiveness of disclosure in the criminal justice system* (Online: Attorney General's Office).

AUBREY-JOHNSON K and LAMBE S (2019) *Youth Justice Law and Practice* (London: Legal Acton Group).

AUDIT COMMISSION (1993) *Helping with enquiries: tackling crime effectively* (London: HMSO).

AULD LJ (2001) *Review of the Criminal Courts of England and Wales*: Report (London: The Stationery Office).

AUSTIN R (2007) 'The new powers of arrest' Criminal Law Review 459.

AYRES I and BRAITHWAITE J (1992) *Responsive Regulation: Transcending the deregulation debate* (New York: OUP).

AYRES M and MURRAY L (2005) *Arrests for Recorded Crime (Notifiable Offences) and* the Operation of Certain Police Powers under PACE: England and Wales, 2004/05. Home Office Statistical Bulletin 21/05 (London: Home Office).

AZZOPARDI J (2002) 'Disclosure at the Police Station, the Right of Silence, and *DPP v Ara*' Criminal Law Review 295–300.

BACH COMMISSION (2017) *The Right to Justice* (London; Fabian Society).

BACHE J (2019) 'Magistrates' Association comment on the Single Justice Procedure' (London: Magistrates' Association).

BACHMAIER L (2018) 'The European Court of Human Rights on negotiated justice and coercion' 26 EJCCLCJ 236.

BACON M (2014) 'Police culture and the new policing context' in Fleming J (ed), *The Future of Policing* (Abingdon: Routledge).

BACON M (2016) *Taking Care of Business: Police Detectives, Drug Law Enforcement and Proactive Investigation* (Oxford: OUP).

BAGGULEY P and HUSSAIN Y (2008) *Riotous Citizens* (Aldershot: Ashgate).

BAILIN A (2008)'The Last Cold War Statute' Criminal Law Review 625.

BAILLIET C and FRANKO AAS K (2011) *Cosmopolitan Justice and its Discontents* (Abingdon: Routledge).

BAIRD V, LORD A, LAWSON R and DURHAM R (2018) *Special Domestic Violence Courts—How Special are they?* (Northumbria: Soroptimists North of England and the Northumbria Court Observers Panel).

BAKER D (2016a) *Deaths After Police Contact: Constructing Accountability in the 21st Century* (London: Palgrave Macmillan).

BAKER D (2016b) 'Deaths after police contact in England and Wales: the effects of Article 2 of the European Convention on Human Rights on coronial practice' 12(2) IJLC 162–177.

BAKER D (2019) 'Using narrative to construct accountability in cases of death after police contact' 52(1) Australia and New Zealand Journal of Criminology 60–75.

BAKER D and PILLINGER C (2020) 'These people are vulnerable, they aren't criminals': Mental health, the use of force and deaths after police contact in England' 93(1) The Police Journal 65–81.

BAKER E (1998) 'Taking European Criminal Law Seriously' Crim LR 361.

BAKSI C, 'Charging powers passed from CPS to police' *Law Society Gazette* 9 May 2011.

BAKSI C 'Jeffrey report highlights criminal advocacy flaws' *Law Society Gazette* 12 May 2014; 3.

BAKSI C, 'Speeding up cases 'risks miscarriages'' *Law Society Gazette*, 29 November 2014; 3.

BALBUS I (1973) *The Dialectics of Legal Repression* (New York: Russell Sage).

BALDWIN J (1985) *Pre-Trial Justice* (Oxford: Basil Blackwell).

BALDWIN J (1992) *Preparing the Record of Taped Interview* (Royal Commission on Criminal Justice Research Study no 2) (London: HMSO).

BALDWIN J (1993a) 'Police Interview Techniques: Establishing Truth or Proof?' 33 BJ Crim 325.

BALDWIN J (1993b) 'Power and Police Interviews' 143 New Law Journal 1194.

BALDWIN J (1993c) *The Role of Legal Representatives at the Police Station* (Royal Commission on Criminal Justice Research Study no 3) (London: HMSO).

BALDWIN J (1997) 'Understanding Judge Ordered and Directed Acquittals in the Crown Court' Criminal Law Review 536.

BALDWIN J and BEDWARD J (1991) 'Summarising Tape Recordings of Police Interviews' Criminal Law Review 671.

BALDWIN J and FEENEY F (1986) 'Defence Disclosure in the Magistrates' Courts' 49 Modern Law Review 593.

BALDWIN J and HUNT A (1998) 'Prosecutors Advising in Police Stations' Criminal Law Review 521.

BALDWIN J and MCCONVILLE M (1977a) *Negotiated Justice* (London: Martin Robertson).

BALDWIN J and MCCONVILLE M (1977b) 'Patterns of Involvement Amongst Lawyers in Contested Trials in the Crown Court' 127 New Law Journal 1040.

BALDWIN J and MCCONVILLE M (1978a) 'Allegations Against Lawyers' Criminal Law Review 744.

BALDWIN J and MCCONVILLE M (1978b) 'The Influence of the Sentencing Discount in Inducing Guilty Pleas' in BALDWIN J and BOTTOMLEY A (eds), *Criminal Justice: Selected Readings* (Oxford: Martin Robertson).

BALDWIN J and MCCONVILLE M (1979) *Jury Trials* (Oxford: OUP).

BALDWIN J and MOLONEY T (1992) *Supervision of Police Investigation in Serious Criminal Cases* (Royal Commission on Criminal Justice Research Study no 4) (London: HMSO).

BALDWIN J and MULVANEY A (1987) 'Advance Disclosure in the Magistrates' Courts: How useful are the prosecution summaries?' Criminal Law Review 805.

BALDWIN J (1993) 'Police interview techniques: Establishing truth or proof?' 33(3) British Journal of Criminology 325–352.

BALDWIN J (1993b) 'Power and Police Interviews' 143 New Law Journal 1194 at 1195.

BALDWIN J (1993c) *The Role of Legal Representatives at the Police Station* (Royal Commission on Criminal Justice Research Study no 3) (London: HMSO, 1993c).

BALDWIN R (2004) 'The New Punitive Regulation' 67 Modern Law Review 351.

BALDWIN R (2005a) 'Is Better Regulation Smarter Regulation?' Public Law 485.

BALDWIN R (2005b) *Regulation in Question* (London: LSE).

BALDWIN R and BLACK J (2008) 'Really Responsive Regulation' 71 Modern Law Review 59.

BALL C (2000) 'A significant move towards restorative justice, or a recipe for unintended consequences?' Criminal Law Review 211.

BALL C, MCCORMAC K and STONE N (2001) *Young Offenders: Law, Policy and Practice* 2nd edn (London: Sweet & Maxwell).

BALL K and WEBSTER F (eds) (2003) *The Intensification of Surveillance* (London: Pluto Press).

BALLARDIE C and IGANSKI P (2001) 'Juvenile Informers' in BILLINGSLEY R, NEMITZ T and BEAN P (eds), *Informers: Policing, Policy, Practice* (Cullompton: Willan).

BANKOWSKI Z, HUTTON N and MCMANUS J (1987) *Lay Justice?* (Edinburgh: T & T Clark).

BANTON M (1964) *The Policeman in the Community* (London: Tavistock).

BANWELL-MOORE R (2020) *Restorative justice: understanding the enablers and barriers to victim participation in England and Wales* (unpublished PhD thesis, University of Sheffield).

BAR STANDARDS BOARD (2018) *Handbook* 3rd edn (London: BSB).

BARAK G (ed) (2015) *Routledge International Handbook of Crimes of the Powerful* (Abingdon: Routledge).

BARANIUK C (2015) 'Caught Before the Act' *New Scientist*, 11 March

BARCLAY G and TAVARES C (1999) *Information on the criminal justice system in England and Wales*. Digest 4 (London: Home Office).

BARKWORTH J and MURPHY K (2016) 'System contact and procedural justice policing: Improving quality of life outcomes for victims of crime' 22 International Review of Victimology 105.

BARLOW C, JOHNSON K, WALKLATE S and HUMPHREYS L (2020) 'Putting Coercive Control into Practice: Problems and Possibilities' 60(1) British Journal of Criminology 160–179;

BARLOW C, WALKLATE S, JOHNSON K, HUMPHREYS L and KIRBY S (2018) *Police responses to coercive control* (Leeds: N8 Policing Research Partnership).

BARNARD C and HARE I (2000) 'Police Discretion and the Rule of Law: European

Community Rights Versus Civil Rights' 63 Modern Law Review 581.

Barton A and Evans R (1999) *Proactive Policing on Merseyside*. Police Research Series Paper No 105 (London: Home Office).

Barton S (2016) 'Rare jail term for former officer who falsified evidence in sexual assault case' (Online: Hodge Jones and Allen Solicitors Ltd).

Bates E (2009) 'Anti-terrorism Control Orders: Liberty and Security Still in the Balance' 29 Legal Studies 99.

Bath C, Bharda B, Jacobson J and May T (2015) *There to help: Ensuring provision of appropriate adults for mentally vulnerable adults detained or interviewed by police* (London: NAAN).

Bath C (2019) *There to Help 2: Ensuring provision of appropriate adults for vulnerable adults detained or interviewed by police—An update on progress 2013/14 to 2017/18* (London: NAAN).

Baxter J and Koffman L (1983) 'The Confait Inheritance – Forgotten Lessons?' Cambrian Law Review 14.

Bayerl P and Stoynov L (2016) 'Revenge by photoshop: Memefying police acts in the public dialogue about injustice' 8(6) New Media & Society 1006–1026.

Bayley D (1994) *Police for the Future* (Oxford: OUP).

Bayley D (1995) 'Getting serious about police brutality' in P Stenning (ed), *Accountability for Criminal Justice* (Toronto: University of Toronto Press).

Bayley D and Stenning P (2016) *Governing the Police Experience in Six Democracies* (NYC: Routledge).

Bean P (2001) *Drugs and Crime* (Cullompton: Willan).

Bean P (2008) *Drugs and Crime*, 3rd edn (Cullompton: Willan).

Bean P and Billingsley R (2001) 'Drugs, crime and informers' in Billingsley R, Nemitz T and Bean P (eds), *Informers: Policing, Policy, Practice* (Cullompton: Willan).

Bean P and Nemitz T (1994) *Out of Depth and Out of Sight* (Loughborough: University of Loughborough, Midlands Centre for Criminology).

Bearchell J (2010) 'UK police interviews with suspects: a short modern history' in Adler J and Gray J (eds), *Forensic Psychology. Concepts, Debates and Practice* (Cullompton: Willan Publishing) 58–71.

Beetham D (1991) *The Legitimation of Power (Issues in Political Theory)* (London: Palgrave Macmillan)

Belknap J (2015) 'Presidential address: Activist criminology: Criminologists' responsibility to advocate for social and legal justice' 53(1) Criminology 1–22.

Bell B and Dadomo C (2006) 'Magistrates' Courts and the 2003 Reforms of the Criminal Justice System' 14(4) EJCCLCJ 339.

Bell E (2011) *Criminal Justice and Neoliberalism* (London: Palgrave Macmillan).

Belur J (2008) 'Is policing domestic violence institutionally racist? A case study of South Asian women' 18(4) Policing and Society 426.

Bennett J (2014) 'Resisting the Audit Explosion: The Art of Prison Inspection' 53(5) HJCJ 449–467.

Bennetto J (2009) *Police and racism: What has been achieved 10 years after the Stephen Lawrence Inquiry Report?* (London: Equality and Human Rights Commission).

Benson A and Hedge J (2009) 'Criminal justice and the voluntary sector: a policy that does not compute' 77(1) Criminal Justice Matters 34–36.

Benson M and Simpson S (2015) *Understanding White Collar Crime: An Opportunity Perspective*, 2nd edn (London: Routledge).

Berlin I (2002) *Liberty* (edited by Hardy H) (Oxford: OUP).

Berlin S (2018) *Criminal Cases Review Commission* (Online at: https://s3-eu-west-2.amazonaws.com/ccrc-prod-storage-1jdn5d1f6iq1l/uploads/2018/06/CCRC_REFERRAL_RATE_-_ANALYSIS.pdf).

BERLINS M (2008) 'Jury's Out on the Net Generation' *The Guardian*, 10 November.

BERRY J (2009) *Reducing Bureaucracy in Policing*: Interim Report (London: Home Office).

BEST D and KEFAS A (2004) *The role of alcohol in police-related deaths: analysis of deaths in custody (category 3) between 2000 and 2001* (London: Police Complaints Authority).

BEVAN G. HOLLAND T and PARTINGTON M (1994) *Organising Cost-Effective Access to Justice* (London: Social Market Foundation).

BEVAN M (2019) *Children and young people in police custody* (PhD thesis, LSE, 2019).

BHATT MURPHY (SOLICITORS), INQUEST and LIBERTY (2002) *Response to consultation paper on Attorney General's review of the role and practices of the CPS in cases of deaths in custody*.

BHUI H (2016) *Can Inspection Produce Meaningful Change in Immigration Detention?* Global Detention Project Working Paper No 12 (Geneva: GDP).

BILLINGSLEY R (2001) 'Informers' careers: motivations and change' in BILLINGSLEY R, NEMITZ T and BEAN P (eds), *Informers: Policing, Policy, Practice* (Cullompton: Willan).

BILLINGSLEY R (2009) *Covert Human Intelligence Sources; The 'unlovely face of police work'* (Hampshire: Waterside Press).

BILLINGSLEY R, NEMITZ T and BEAN P (eds), (2001) *Informers: Policing, Policy, Practice* (Cullompton: Willan).

BIRAL M (2014) 'The Right to Examine or Have Examined Witnesses as a Minimum Right for a Fair Trial' European Journal of Crime' 22(4) CLCJ 331–350.

BIRCH D (1989) 'The PACE Hots Up: Confessions and Confusions Under the 1984 Act' Criminal Law Review 95.

BIRCH D (1994) 'Excluding evidence from entrapment: What is a fair cop?' Current Legal Problems 73.

BIRCH D (1999) 'Suffering in Silence' Criminal Law Review 769.

BIRCH D (2000) 'A Better Deal for Vulnerable Witnesses?' Criminal Law Review 223.

BIRCH D (2002) 'Rethinking sexual history evidence: proposals for fairer trials' Criminal Law Review 53.

BIRCH D (2004) 'Hearsay: Same Old Story, Same Old Song' Criminal Law Review 556.

BIRD S (2012) 'The Inadequacy of Legal Aid' in NAUGHTON M (ed), *The Criminal Cases Review Commission: Hope for the Innocent?* (London: Palgrave Macmillan).

BIRDSALL N, KIRBY S and MCMANUS M (2017) 'Police–victim engagement in building a victim empowerment approach to intimate partner violence cases' 18(1) Police Practice and Research 75–86.

BISGROVE M and WEEKES M (2014) 'Deferred Prosecution Agreements' Criminal Law Review 416.

BLACK J (2002) 'Critical reflections on regulation' 27 Australian Journal of Legal Philosophy 1–35.

BLACKSTOCK J, CAPE E, HODGSON J, ORGORDOVA A and SPRONKEN A (2014) *Inside Police Custody: An Empirical Account of Suspects' Rights in Four Jurisdictions* (Cambridge: Intersentia).

BLAKE C (2000) 'Legal Aid: Past, Present and Future' *Legal Action*, Jan, p 6.

BLAKE M and ASHWORTH A (1998) 'Some Ethical Issues in Prosecuting and Defending Criminal Cases' Criminal Law Review 16.

BLAKE M and ASHWORTH A (2004) 'Ethics and the Criminal Defence Lawyer' 7(2) Legal Ethics 167.

BLAKE N (1985) 'Picketing, Justice and the Law' in FINE B and MILLAR R (eds), *Policing the Miners' Strike* (London: Lawrence and Wishart).

BLAKEBOROUGH L and PIERPOINT H (2007) *Conditional Cautions: An examination of the early implementation of the scheme*, MoJ Research Summary (London: MOJ).

BLAND L (1992) 'The Case of the Yorkshire Ripper: Mad, Bad, Beast or Male?' in RADFORD J and RUSSELL D (eds),

Femicide: The Politics of Woman Killing (New York: Twayne Publishing).

BLAND M and ARIEL B (2015) 'Targeting Escalation in Reported Domestic Abuse: Evidence From 36,000 Callouts' 25(1) International Criminal Justice Review 30–53.

BLAND N, MILLER J and QUINTON P (2000) *Upping the PACE? An evaluation of the recommendations of the Stephen Lawrence Inquiry on stops and searches* (Police Research Series Paper 128) (London: Home Office).

BLOCK B, CORBETT C and PEAY J (1993a) *Ordered and Directed Acquittals in the Crown Court*, (Royal Commission on Criminal Justice, Research Study no 15) (London: HMSO).

BLOCK B, CORBETT C and PEAY J (1993b) 'Ordered and Directed Acquittals in the Crown Court: A Time of Change?' Criminal Law Review 95.

BLOM-COOPER L (2018) *Unreasoned Verdict* (Oxford: Hart Publishing).

BLOWE K (2019) 'British police spied on grieving black families for decades' *The Guardian*, 25 October.

BOHLANDER M (1992) ' "... By a jury of his peers" – The issue of multi-racial juries in a poly-ethnic society' XIV(1) Liverpool Law Review 67.

BOLIVAR D et al (eds) (2017) *Victims and Restorative Justice* (Oxford: Routledge).

BONINO S and KAOULLAS G (2015) 'Preventing Political Violence in Britain: An Evaluation of over Forty Years of Undercover Policing of Political Groups Involved in Protest' 38 Studies in Conflict and Terrorism 10.

BONNER D (2007) *Executive Measures, Terrorism and National Security: Have the Rules of the Game Changed?* (Aldershot: Ashgate).

BOOTH T (2015) *Accommodating Justice: Victim impact statements in the sentencing process* (Alexandria: Federation Press).

BOTTOMLEY A (1987) 'Sentencing reform and the structuring of pre-trial discretion' in WASIK M and PEASE K (eds), *Sentencing Reform* (Manchester: MUP).

BOTTOMS A and MCCLEAN J (1976) *Defendants in the Criminal Process* (London: Routledge).

BOTTOMS A and TANKEBE B (2012) 'Beyond procedural justice: A dialogic approach to legitimacy in criminal justice' 102(1) Journal of Criminal Law and Criminology 119–170.

BOUKLI A and KOTZE J (eds) (2018) *Zemiology: Reconnecting crime and social harm* (Cham, Switzerland: Palgrave Macmillan).

BOWLING B (1998) *Violent Racism* (Oxford: Clarendon).

BOWLING B (2007) 'Fair and Effective Policing Methods: Towards "Good Enough" Policing' 8(S1) Journal of Scandinavian Studies in Criminology and Crime Prevention 17–32.

BOWLING B and MARKS E (2017) 'The Rise and Fall of Suspicionless Searches' 28(1) King's Law Journal 62–88.

BOWLING B, PARMAR A and PHILLIPS P (2008) 'Policing ethnic minority communities' in NEWBURN T (ed), *Handbook of Policing* 2nd edn (Cullompton: Willan).

BOWLING B and PHILLIPS C (2002) *Racism, Crime and Justice* (Harlow: Longman).

BOWLING B and PHILLIPS C (2007) 'Disproportionate and Discriminatory: Reviewing the Evidence on Police Stop and Search' 70(6) Modern Law Review 936.

BOWLING B and PHILLIPS P (2003) 'Policing ethnic minority communities' in NEWBURN T (ed), *Handbook of Policing* (Cullompton: Willan).

BOWLING B, REINER, R and SHEPTYCKI J (2019) *The Politics of the Police* 5th edn (Oxford; OUP).

BOWLING B and SHRUTI I (2019) 'Automated Policing: The Case of Body-Worn Video' 15 International Journal of Law in Context 140.

BOX S (1983) *Power, Crime and Mystification* (London: Tavistock).

Box S and Russell K (1975) 'The Politics of Discreditability: Disarming Complaints Against the Police' 23 Sociological Review 315.

Bradbury S and Feist A (2005) *The Use of Forensic Science in Volume Crime Investigation: A Review of the Research Literature* (Home Office Online Report 43/05) (London: Home Office).

Bradford B, Jackson J and Stanko E (2009) 'Contact and Confidence: Revisiting the Impact of Public Encounters with the Police' 19(1) *Policing and Society*.

Bradford B (2017) *Stop and Search and Police Legitimacy* (London: Routledge).

Braithwaite J (1989) *Crime, Shame and Reintegration* (Cambridge: CUP).

Braithwaite J (2000) 'The New Regulatory State and the Transformation of Criminology' 40 British Journal of Criminology 222.

Braithwaite J (2002) 'Setting Standards for Restorative Justice' 42(3) British Journal of Criminology 563–577

Braithwaite J (2002) *Restorative Justice and Responsive Regulation* (Oxford: OUP).

Braithwaite J, Makkai T and Braithwaite V (2007) *Regulating Aged Care: Ritualism and the new pyramid* (Cheltenham: Edward Elgar).

Brand S and Price R (2000) *The Economic and Social Costs of Crime* (Home Office Research Study 217) (London: Home Office).

Brants C and Field S (1995) 'Discretion and Accountability in Prosecution' in Harding C, Fennell P, Jorg N and Swart B (eds), *Criminal Justice in Europe: A Comparative Study* (Oxford: Clarendon).

Braun K (2019) *Victim Participation Rights: Variation across criminal justice systems* (Basingstoke: Palgrave).

Brayne S (2020) *Predict and Surveil* (Oxford: OUP).

Bredar J (1992) 'Moving Up the Day of Reckoning: strategies for attacking the "cracked trials" problem' Criminal Law Review 153.

Brems E (ed) (2013) *Diversity and European Human Rights: Rewriting Judgments of the ECHR* (Cambridge: CUP).

Brems E and Desmet, E (2017) *Integrated Human Rights in Practice. Rewriting Human Rights Decisions* (Cheltenham: Elgar).

Brereton D (1997) 'How Different are Rape Trials? A Comparison of the Cross-Examination of Complainants in Rape and Assault Trials' 37 British Journal of Criminology 242.

Brewis B (2016) 'The Interpretation of s. 41 of the Youth Justice and Criminal Evidence Act 1999 and the Impact of R v A (No 2) ([2002] 1 AC 45) Armando Andrade v R [2015] EWCA Crim 1722' 3 Journal of Criminal Law 169.

Bridges L (1992a) 'The Fixed Fees Battle' *Legal Action*, November, p 7.

Bridges L (1992b) 'The professionalisation of criminal justice' *Legal Action*, August, p 7.

Bridges L (1993) 'The Right to Jury Trial: How the Royal Commission Got it Wrong' 143 New Law Journal 1542.

Bridges L (1996) 'The Reform of Criminal Legal Aid' in Young R and Wall D (eds), (1996) *Access to Criminal Justice* (London: Blackstone).

Bridges L (1999) 'False Starts and Unrealistic Expectations' *Legal Action*, October, p 6.

Bridges L (2000) 'Taking Liberties' *Legal Action*, July, p 6.

Bridges L and Bunyan T (1983) 'Britain's new urban policing strategy – the Police and Criminal Evidence Bill in context' 10 Journal of Law and Society 85.

Bridges L and Cape E (2008) *CDS Direct: Flying in the Face of the Evidence* (London: CCJS, Kings College, London).

Bridges L and Choongh S (1998) *Improving Police Station Legal Advice* (London: Law Society).

Bridges L, Cape E, Abubaker A and Bennett C (2000a) *Quality in Criminal Defence Services* (London: Legal Services Commission).

Bridges L, Cape E, Fenn P, Mitchell A, Moorhead R and Sherr A (2007) *Evaluation of the Public Defender Service in England and Wales* (London: Legal Services Commission)

Bridges L, Choongh S and Mcconville M (2000) *Quality in Criminal Defence Services* (London: Legal Services Commission).

Bridges L, Choongh S and McConville M (2000) *Ethnic Minority Defendants and the Right to Elect Jury Trial* (London: Commission for Racial Equality).

Bridges L (2012) 'Four days in August: the UK riots' 54(1) *Race & Class* 1–12.

Bridges L (2018) 'Lammy Review: will it change outcomes in the criminal justice system?' 59(3) *Race & Class* 80–90.

Bridges L, Shiner M, Delsol R and Gill K (2011) Stop Watch Statement on Police Stop and Account, Chapter 5. (Online at https://www.stop-watch.org/uploads/documents/Stop Watch_Statement_on_Police_Stop_and_Account_-_21Dec11-_FINAL_(2).pdf (accessed 29 August 2020)).

Brink B and Stone C (1988) 'Defendants who do not ask for Bail' Criminal Law Review 152.

Britton N (2000) 'Examining police/black relations: what's in a story' 23(4) Ethnic and Racial Studies, 696.

Britton N (2000a) 'Race and Policing: A Study of Police Custody' 40(4) British Journal of Criminology 639.

Brodeur J-P (2010) *The Policing Web* (Oxford: OUP).

Brodin S (2016) 'The British Experience with Hearsay Reform: A Cautionary Tale' 84(4) Fordham Law Review.

Brogden M (1985) 'Stopping the People' in Baxter J and Koffman L (eds), *Police: The Constitution and the Community* (Abingdon: Professional Books).

Brogden M (1991) *On the Mersey Beat* (Oxford: OUP).

Brogden M and Brogden A (1984) 'From Henry III to Liverpool 8' 12 *International Journal of the Sociology of Law*.

Brookman F and Pierpoint H (2003) 'Access to legal advice for young suspects and remand prisoners' 42(5) Howard JCJ 452.

Brown A (2004)'Anti-Social Behaviour, Crime Control and Social Control' 43 Howard Journal of Criminal Justice 203.

Brown D (1987) *Police Complaints Procedure* (Home Office Research Study no 93) (London: HMSO).

Brown D (1989) *Detention at the Police Station under the Police and Criminal Evidence Act 1984* (Home Office Research Study no 104) (London: HMSO).

Brown D (1997) *PACE Ten Years On: A Review of the Research* (Home Office Research Study no 155) (London: HMSO).

Brown D (1998) *Offending on Bail and Police Use of Conditional Bail* (Research Findings no 72) (London: Home Office).

Brown D and Daus C (2015) The influence of police officers' decision-making style and anger control on responses to work scenarios 4(3) Journal of Applied Research in Memory and Cognition 294–302.

Brown D and Ellis T (1994) *Policing Low Level Disorder: Police use of section 5 of the Public Order Act 1986* (Home Office Research Study no 135) (London: Home Office).

Brown D, Ellis T and Larcombe K (1992) *Changing the Code: Police Detention under the Revised PACE Codes of Practice* (Home Office Research Study no 129) (London: HMSO).

Brown D, Turner J, and Weisser B (eds) (2019) *The Oxford Handbook of Criminal Process* (Oxford: OUP).

Brown G (2016) 'The Blue Line on Thin Ice: Police Use of Force Modifications in the Era of Cameraphones and YouTube' 56(2) British Journal of Criminology 293–312.

Brown J (2020) *Why is Police Bail Being Reviewed Again?* (London: House of Commons Library)

Brown K (2015) 'The community trigger for anti-social behaviour: protecting victims or raising unrealistic expectations?' Criminal Law Review 488.

Brown K (2017) 'The Hyper-Regulation of Public Space: The Use and Abuse of Public Spaces Protection Orders in England and Wales' 37(3) Legal Studies 543–568.

Brown K (2020) 'Punitive reform and the cultural life of punishment: moving from the ASBO to its successors' 22 Punishment & Society 90–107.

Brown M (2001) 'Race, Science and the Construction of Native Criminality in Colonial India' 5(3) Theoretical Criminology 345–368.

Brown R and Payne S (2007) *Process Evaluation of Salford Community Justice Initiative* (London: Ministry of Justice).

Brown S (1991) *Magistrates at Work* (Milton Keynes: Open UP).

Browning S (2019) *Women in Parliament and Government*. Briefing Paper. HC 01250 (London: House of Commons)

Brownlee I (2004) 'The statutory charging scheme in England and Wales: towards a unified prosecution system?' Criminal Law Review 896.

Brownlee I (2007) 'Conditional cautions and fair trial rights in England and Wales: form versus substance in the diversionary agenda?' Criminal Law Review 129.

Brucato B (2015) 'Policing Made Visible: Mobile Technologies and the Importance of Point of View' 13(3/4) Surveillance & Society 455–473.

Bryan I (1997) *Interrogation and Confession* (Aldershot: Dartmouth).

Bucke T and Brown D (1997) *In Police Custody: Police Powers and Suspects' Rights Under the Revised PACE Codes of Practice* (Home Office Research Findings no 59) (London: Home Office).

Bucke T (1997) *Ethnicity and Contacts with the Police: Latest Findings from the British Crime Survey* (Home Office Research Findings no 59) (London: Home Office).

Bucke T and James Z (1998) *Trespass and Protest: Policing under the Criminal Justice and Public Order Act 1994* (London: Home Office).

Bucke T, Street R and Brown D (2000) *The right of silence: the impact of the Criminal Justice and Public Order Act 1994* (Home Office Research Study no 199) (London: Home Office).

Bull R (2020) 'PEACE-ful Interviewing/Interrogation' in Shigemasu K, Kuwano S, Sato T and Matsuzawa T (eds), *Diversity in Harmony—Insights from Psychology* (Chichester: Wiley).

Bullock S (2008) *Police Service Strength* (Home Office Statistical Bulletin 08/08) (London: Home Office).

Burbergs M (2013) 'Rewriting Kolanis v UK. The right to community living' Brems E (ed), *Diversity and European Human Rights: Rewriting Judgments of the ECHR* (Cambridge: CUP).

Burman M and Brooks-Hay O (2020) 'Feminist Framings of Victim Advocacy in Criminal Justice Contexts' in Tapley J and Davies P (eds), *Victimology: Research, policy and activism* (London: Palgrave Macmillan).

Burnett R (ed) (2016) *Wrongful Allegations of Sexual and Child Abuse* (Oxford: OUP).

Burney E (1979) *Magistrate, Court and Community* (London: Hutchinson).

Burney E (2003) 'Using the Law on Racially Aggravated Offences' Criminal Law Review 28.

Burney E and Rose G (2002) *Racist Offences—How is the Law Working?* Home Office Research Study 244 (London: Home Office).

Burns R (2004) 'The Distinctiveness of Trial Narrative' in Duff A, Farmer L, Marshall S and Tadros V (eds), *The Trial on Trial: Truth and Due Process* (Oxford: Hart).

Burrow J (2000) 'Bail and the Human Rights Act 1998' 150 New Law Journal 677.

Burrows J, Henderson P and Morgan P (1994) *Improving Bail Decisions: the bail process project, phase 1* (Research and Planning Unit Paper 90) (London: Home Office).

Burrows J, Hopkins M, Hubbard R, Robinson A, Speed M and Tilley N (2005) *Understanding the attrition process in volume crime investigations*, Home Office Research Study 295 (London: Home Office).

Burton F and Carlen P (1979) *Official Discourse: On Discourse Analysis, Government Publications, Ideology and the State* (London: Routledge).

Burton M (2001) 'Reviewing CPS decisions not to prosecute' Criminal Law Review 374.

Burton M (2008) *Legal Responses to Domestic Violence* (Abingdon: Routledge-Cavendish).

Burton M (2009) 'Failing to Protect: Victims' Rights and Police Liability' 72(2) Modern Law Review 283.

Burton M (2010) 'R v Dhaliwal. Commentary' in Hunter R, McGlynn C and Rackley E (eds), *Feminist Judgments. From Theory to Practice* (Oxford: Hart).

Burton M, Evans R and Sanders A (2006a) *Are Special Measures for Vulnerable and Intimidated Witnesses Working? Evidence From the Criminal Justice Agencies* (Home Office Online Report No 01/06) (London: Home Office).

Burton M, Evans R and Sanders A (2006b) 'Implementing Special Measures for Vulnerable and Intimidated Witnesses: the Problem of Identification' Criminal Law Review 229.

Butler G (1999) *Inquiry into CPS Decision-Making in Relation to Deaths in Custody and Related Matters* (London: SO).

Butler S (1983) *Acquittal Rates* (Home Office Research and Planning Unit Paper 16) (London: HMSO).

Button M (2007) *Security Officers and Policing: Powers, Culture and Control in the Governance of Private Space* (Aldershot: Ashgate).

Button M (2020) 'The "New" Private Security Industry, the Private Policing of Cyberspace and the Regulatory Questions' 36(1) Journal of Contemporary Criminal Justice 39–55.

Buxton R (1990) 'Challenging and Discharging Jurors' Criminal Law Review 225.

Buxton R (2017) 'Joint Enterprise: Jogee, Substantial Injustice and the Court of Appeal' 2 Criminal Law Review 123.

Buzawa E and Buzawa C (1993) 'The Impact of Arrest on Domestic Assault' 36 American Behavioural Scientist 558.

Callan K (1997) *Kevin Callan's Story* (London: Little, Brown and Company).

Cameron N (1980) 'Bail Act 1976: Two Inconsistencies and an Imaginary Offence' 130 New Law Journal 382.

Cammiss S (2006) '"I will in a moment give you the full history": Mode of Trial, Prosecutorial Control and Partial Accounts' Criminal Law Review 38.

Cammiss S and Stride C (2008) 'Modelling Mode of Trial' 48(4) British Journal of Criminology 482.

Campbell A (2011) *The Fingerprint Inquiry Report* (Edinburgh, Scotland: APS Group Scotland).

Campbell D (2009) 'The Threat of Terror and the Plausibility of Positivism' Public Law 501.

Campbell J (2010) 'Neoliberalism's penal and debtor states: A rejoinder to Loïc Wacquant' 14(1) Theoretical Criminology 59–73.

Campbell L, Ashworth A and Redmayne M (2019) *The Criminal Process*, 5th edn (Oxford: OUP).

Campbell S (2002) *A review of anti-social behaviour orders* (Home Office Research Study 236) (London: Home Office).

Campbell T (2006) *Rights: A Critical Introduction* (London: Routledge).

Campeau H (2019) 'Institutional myths and generational boundaries: cultural inertia in the police organisation' 29(1) Policing and Society 69–84.

Cane P (1996) *Tort Law and Economic Interests* (Oxford: OUP).

Caney S (2001) 'Cosmopolitan Justice and Equalizing Opportunities' 32(1–2) Metaphilosophy 113–134.

CANNINGS A, with LLOYD DAVIES M (2006) *Against All Odds: A mother's fight to prove her innocence* (London: Time Warner Books).

CAOLAN E (2007) 'Reciprocity and rights under the European arrest warrant regime' 123 Law Quarterly Review 197.

CAPE E (1997) 'Sidelining Defence Lawyers: Police Station Advice After *Condron*' 1 International Journal of Evidence and Policy 386.

CAPE E (1999) 'Detention Without Charge: What Does "Sufficient Evidence To Charge" Mean?' Criminal Law Review 874.

CAPE E (2002) 'Incompetent police station advice and the exclusion of evidence' Criminal Law Review 471.

CAPE E (2003) 'The Revised PACE Codes of Practice: A Further Step Towards Inquisitorialism' Criminal Law Review 355.

CAPE E (2004) 'The rise (and fall?) of a criminal defence profession' Criminal Law Review 401.

CAPE E (2006a) *Police Station Advice: Advising on Silence*. Criminal Practitioners' Newsletter No 63, special edition (London: Law Society).

CAPE E (2006b) 'Police Station Law and Practice Update' *Legal Action*, April, p 10.

CAPE E (2006c) *Defending Suspects at Police Stations*, 5th edn (London: LAG).

CAPE E (2007) 'Modernising Police Powers – Again?' Criminal Law Review 934

CAPE E (2008a) 'Legal Aid Spending: Looking the other way' *Legal Action*, July, p 8.

CAPE E (2008b) 'Then and Now: twenty-one years of re-balancing' in CAPE E and YOUNG R (eds), *Regulating Policing: The PACE Act 1984, Past Present and Future* (Oxford: Hart).

CAPE E (2013) 'The counter-terrorism provisions of the Protection of Freedoms Act 2012: Preventing misuse or a case of smoke and mirrors?' Criminal Law Review 385–399.

CAPE E (2013) 'The Protection of Freedoms Act 2012: The Retention and Use of Biometric Data Provisions' Criminal Law Review 23–37.

CAPE E (2017) 'The Police Bail Provisions of the Policing and Crime Act 2017' Criminal Law Review 587–600

CAPE E, HARDCASTLE M and PAUL S (2020) *Defending Suspects at Police Stations* (London: LAG).

CAPE E and MOORHEAD R (2005) *Demand Induced Supply? Identifying Cost Drivers in Criminal Defence Work* (London: Legal Services Research Centre).

CAPE E and SMITH T (2016) *The practice of pre-trial detention in England and Wales: Research report* (Bristol: University of the West of England).

CAPE E and YOUNG R (eds) (1998) *Regulating Policing* (Oxford: Hart).

CARLEN P (1974) 'Remedial Routines for the Maintenance of Control in Magistrates' Courts' BJ Law & Soc 101.

CARLEN P (1976) *Magistrates' Justice* (London: Martin Robertson, 1976).

CARLEN P (1996) *Jigsaw: A political criminology of youth homelessness* (Buckingham: Open UP).

CARLISLE A (2009) *Fourth Report of the Independent reviewer pursuant to Section 14 of the PTA 2005* (London: SO).

CARLISLE, LORD (2005) *Report on the operation in 2004 of the Terrorism Act 2000* (London: TSO).

CARNS T and KRUSE J (1981) 'A Re-Evaluation of Alaska's Plea Bargaining Ban' 8 Alaska Law Review 27.

CARSON W (1970) 'White-Collar Crime and the Enforcement of Factory Legislation' 10 British Journal of Criminology 383.

CARTER E (2013) *Analysing Police Interviews: Laughter, Confessions and the Tape* (London: Bloomsbury)

CARTER I (1999) *A Measure of Freedom* (Oxford: OUP).

CARTER, LORD (2006) *Legal Aid: A Market-Based Approach to Reform* (London: Ministry of Justice).

CARTER, LORD (2007) *Securing the Future: Proposals for the efficient and sustainable use of custody in England and Wales* (London: Ministry of Justice).

CARVALHO H (2020) 'Joint Enterprise, Hostility and the Construction of Dangerous Belonging' in PRATT J and ANDERSON J (eds), *Criminal Justice, Risk and the Revolt against Uncertainty* (London: Palgrave Macmillan).

CASE S (2018) *Youth Justice: A critical introduction* (London: Routledge).

CASHMORE E (2001) 'The experiences of ethnic minority police officers in Britain: under-recruitment and racial profiling in a performance culture' 24(4) Ethnic and Racial Studies 642.

CASHMORE E and MCLAUGHLIN E (eds) (1991) *Out of Order?* (London: Routledge).

CAVADINO M (1997) 'A Vindication of the Rights of Psychiatric Patients' 24 Journal of Law and Society 235.

CAVADINO P and GIBSON B (1993) *Bail: The Law, Best Practice and the Debate* (Winchester: Waterside Press).

CAVENEY N, SCOTT P, WILLIAMS S and HOWE-WALSH L (2019) 'Police Reform, Austerity and "Cop Culture": time to change the record?' 30(10) Policing and Society 1210–1255.

CCRC (2005) *Annual Report and Accounts 2004–2005* (HC 115) (London: TSO).

CCRC (2009) *Annual Report and Accounts 2008/09* (HC 857) (London: TSO).

CCRC (2016) *Annual Report and Accounts 2015/2016* (HC 244) (London: TSO).

CCRC (2020) *Annual Report and Accounts 2019/20* (HC 521) (London: TSO).

CELIKSOY E (2019) 'Overruling "the Salduz Doctrine" in Beuze v Belgium: The ECtHR's further retreat from the Salduz principles on the right to access to lawyer' 10(4) New Journal of European Criminal Law 342–362.

CENTRE FOR JUSTICE INNOVATION (2014) *The case for dedicated domestic violence courts* (London: CJI).

CENTRE FOR JUSTICE INNOVATION (2015) *Problem-solving courts: An evidence review* (London: CJI).

CENTRE FOR SOCIAL JUSTICE (2013) *Something's got to Give. The state of Britain's voluntary and community sector* (London: Centre for Social Justice).

CENTREX (2004) *Practical Guide to Investigative Interviewing* (Bramshill: Centrex).

CHADWICK D and WESSON C (2020) '"Blocked at every level": criminal justice system professionals' experiences of including people with intellectual disabilities within a targeted magistrates' court' (forthcoming) Journal of Intellectual Disabilities and Offending Behaviour.

CHAIB S (2013) 'Suku Phull v France rewritten from a procedural justice perspective: Taking religious minorities seriously' in BREMS E (ed), *Diversity and European Human Rights: Rewriting Judgments of the ECHR* (Cambridge: CUP).

CHAKRABORTI N (2007) 'Policing Muslim Communities' in ROWE M (ed), *Policing Beyond Macpherson* (Cullompton: Willan).

CHALMERS J, (2014) '"Frenzied Law Making": Overcriminalization by Numbers' 67 Current Legal Problems 483–502.

CHALMERS J, DUFF P and LEVERICK F (2007) 'Victim impact statements: Can work, do work (for those who bother to make them)' Criminal Law Review 360.

CHALMERS J, LEVERICK F and SHAW A, (2015) 'Is Formal Criminalisation Really on the Rise? Evidence from the 1950s' Crim LR 177–191.

CHAMBERLAIN P, KEPPEL-PALMER M, REARDON S, and SMITH T (2019). 'It's criminal: The state of magistrates' court reporting in England and Wales.' Journalism August 1–17.

CHAN J (1996) 'Changing Police Culture' 36 British Journal of Criminology 109.

CHAN J (1997) *Changing Police Culture: Policing in a Multicultural Society* (Cambridge: CUP).

CHAN J (1999) 'Governing police practice: limits of the new accountability' 50 British Journal of Sociology 251–270.

CHAPMAN C (2014) *An Independent Review of the Police Disciplinary System in England and Wales* (London: TSO)

CHARLDORP T (2020) 'Reconstructing Suspects' Stories in Various Police Record Styles' in MASON M and ROCK F (eds), *The Discourse of Police Interviews* (Chicago: Chicago UP).

CHARMAN S (2017) *Police Socialisation, Identity and Culture: Becoming blue* (Basingstoke: Palgrave Macmillan).

CHERRYMAN J and BULL R (1996) 'Investigative Interviewing' in LEISHMAN F, LOVEDAY B and SAVAGE S (eds), *Core Issues in Policing* (Harlow: Longman).

CHIDGEY K, PROCTER N, BAKER A and GRECH C (2020) 'Suicide deaths following police contact: A review of coronial inquest findings' *Death Studies* 1–9.

CHIEF SURVEILLANCE COMMISSIONER (2005) *Annual Report 2004–5* (HC 444) (London).

CHIEF SURVEILLANCE COMMISSIONER (2009) *Annual Report 2008–9* (HC 704) (London).

CHILCOT SIR JOHN (2008) *Privy Council Review of Intercept as Evidence* (Cm 7324).

CHILD J and ORMEROD D (2019) *Smith, Hogan, & Ormerod's Essentials of Criminal Law*, 3rd edn (Oxford: OUP).

CHILDS M (1999) 'Medical Manslaughter and Corporate Liability' 19 Legal Studies 316.

CHOO A (1995) 'Halting criminal prosecutions: the abuse of process doctrine re-visited' Criminal Law Review 864.

CHOO A (2008) *Abuse of Process and Judicial Stays of Criminal Proceedings*, 2nd edn (Oxford: OUP).

CHOO A (2018) *Evidence*, 5th edn (Oxford: OUP).

CHOO A and NASH S (1999) 'What's the matter with s.78?' Criminal Law Review 929.

CHOO A and NASH S (2007) 'Improperly obtained evidence in the Commonwealth: lessons for England and Wales?' 11 International Journal of Evidence and Policy 75.

CHOONGH S (1997) *Policing as Social Discipline* (Oxford: Clarendon).

CHOONGH S (1998) 'Policing the Dross: A Social Disciplinary Model of Policing' 38 British Journal of Criminology 623.

CHOUDHURY T and FENWICK H (2011) *The Impact of Counter-terrorism Measures on Muslim Communities* (London: Equality and Human Rights Commission).

CHOUDRY S and HERRING J (2006a) 'Righting Domestic Violence' International Journal of Law, Policy and Family 95.

CHOUDRY S and HERRING J (2006b) 'Domestic violence and the Human Rights Act 1998: a new means of legal intervention?' Public Law 752.

CHRISTIE N (1994) *Crime Control as Industry* (Abingdon: Routledge).

CHRISTOPHER W, (1991) *The Christopher Commission Report* (Online at: https://www.hrw.org/legacy/reports98/police/uspo73.htm).

CLANCY A, HOUGH M, AUST R and KERSHAW C (2001) *Crime, Policing and Justice: the experience of ethnic minorities, Findings from the 2000 British Crime Survey* (Home Office Research Study 223) (London: Home Office).

CLARE I and GUDJONSSON G (1993) *Devising and Piloting an Experimental Version of the Notice to Detained Persons* (Royal Commission on Criminal Justice, Research Study no 7) (London: HMSO).

CLARK D (2007) 'Covert Surveillance and Informer Handling' in NEWBURN T, WILLIAMSON T and WRIGHT A (eds), *Handbook of Criminal Investigation* (Cullompton: Willan).

CLARK D (2004) *Bevan and Lidstone's The Investigation of Crime* (London: LexisNexis).

CLARK R (2001) 'Informers and Corruption' in BILLINGSLEY R, NEMITZ T and BEAN P (eds), *Informers: Policing, Policy, Practice* (Cullompton: Willan).

CLARKE A (1999) 'Safety or Supervision? The Unified Ground of Appeal and its Consequences in the Law of Abuse of Process and Exclusion of Evidence' Criminal Law Review 108.

CLARKE A, MORAN-ELLIS J and SLENEY J (2002) *Attitudes to Date Rape and Relationship Rape: A Qualitative Study* (London: Sentencing Advisory Panel).

CLARKE C and MILNE R (2001) *National Evaluation of the PEACE Investigative Interviewing Scheme, Police Research Award Scheme Report No: PRAS/149* (London: Home Office).

CLARKE M (2000) *Regulation: The Social Control of Business Between Law and Politics* (Basingstoke: Macmillan).

CLARKE R and HOUGH M (1984) *Crime and Police Effectiveness* (Home Office Research Study no 79) (London: HMSO).

CLARKE C and MILNE R (2016) 'England and Wales' in WALSH D, OXBURGH G, REDLICH A and MYKLEBUST T (eds), *International Developments and Practices in Investigative Interviewing and Interrogation: Volume 2: Suspects* (Abingdon: Routledge).

CLARKSON C (1996) 'Kicking corporate bodies and damning their souls' 59 Modern Law Review 557.

CLARKSON C (2005) 'Corporate Manslaughter: Yet More Government Proposals' Criminal Law Review 677.

CLARKSON C, CRETNEY A, DAVIS G and SHEPHERD J (1994) 'Assaults: the relationship between seriousness, criminalisation and punishment' Criminal Law Review 4.

CLAYMAN S and SKINNS L (2012) 'To Snitch or Not to Snitch? An Exploratory Study of the Factors Affecting Active Youth Co-operation with the Police' 22(2) Policing and Society 1–21.

CLAYTON R and TOMLINSON H (1988) 'Arrest and Reasonable Grounds for Suspicion' *Law Society Gazette*, 7 September.

CLEMENTS L (2005) 'Winners and Losers' 32(1) Journal of Law and Society 34.

COBB N (2010) 'R v Stone and Dobinson. Commentary' in HUNTER R, McGLYNN C and RACKLEY E (eds), *Feminist Judgments. From Theory to Practice* (Oxford: Hart).

COBLEY C (2003) 'Prosecuting Cases of Suspected "Shaken Baby Syndrome" – A Review of Current Issues' Criminal Law Review 93.

COEN M and DOAK J (2017) 'Embedding Explained Jury Verdicts in the English Criminal Trial' 37 Legal Studies 786.

COHEN S (1985) *Visions of Social Control* (Cambridge, Polity Press).

COHEN S (2001) *States of Denial: Knowing About Atrocities and Suffering* (Cambridge: Polity Press).

COLE D (2001) ' "An Unqualified Human Good": E.P. Thompson and the Rule of Law' 28(2) Journal of Law and Society 177.

COLEMAN R (2004) *Reclaiming the Streets: Surveillance, Social Control and the City* (Cullompton: Willan).

COLES D and MURPHY F (1999) 'O'Brien: Another Death in Police Custody' *Legal Action*, Nov, p 6.

COLLEGE OF POLICING (2014) *Body-Worn Video* (London: College of Policing).

COLLEGE OF POLICING (2014) *Code of Ethics: A Code of Practice for the Principles and Standards of Professional Behaviour for the Policing Profession of England and Wales* (London: College of Policing).

COLLEGE OF POLICING (2016) *Pre-charge bail: the possible implications of research* (London: College of Policing).

COLLEGE OF POLICING (2020) *Authorised Professional Practice guidance – Stop and search: transparent* (Online at: https://www.app.college.police.uk/app-content/stop-and-search/transparent/#using-body-worn-video-to-record-information).

COLLEGE OF POLICING (2020) *Post-incident procedures following death or serious injury.* (London: College of Policing).

COLLISON M (1995) *Police, Drugs and Community* (London: Free Association Books).

CONAGHAN J (2017) Investigating rape: human rights and police accountability, 37 Legal Studies 54–77.

COOK D (2006) *Criminal and Social Justice* (London: Sage).

COOK D, BURTON M, ROBINSON A and VALLELY C (2004) *Evaluation of Specialist Domestic Violence Courts and Fast Track Systems* (London: CPS).

COOPER D (2005) 'Pigot Unfulfilled: Video-recorded Cross-Examination under section 28 of the Youth Justice and Criminal Evidence Act 1999' Criminal Law Review 456.

COOPER D and ROBERTS P (2005) 'Monitoring Success: Special Measures under the YJCE 1999' 9 International Journal of Evidence and Policy 269.

COOPER D and ROBERTS P (2005) *Special Measures for Vulnerable and Intimidated Witnesses: An Analysis of CPS Monitoring Data* (London: CPS).

COOPER P and MATTISON M (2017) 'Intermediaries, vulnerable people and the quality of evidence: an international comparison of three versions of the English intermediary model' International Journal of Evidence and Policy 21: 351

COOPER P and MURPHY J (1997) 'Ethical approaches for police officers when working with informants in the development of criminal intelligence in the UK' 26 Journal of Social Policy 1.

COOPER P et al (2018) 'One step forward and two steps back? The "20 Principles" for questioning vulnerable witnesses and the lack of an evidence-based approach' International Journal of Evidence and Policy 22: 392.

COOPER S (2006) 'Legal advice and pre-trial silence - unreasonable developments' 10 International Journal of Evidence and Policy 60.

COOPER S (2009) 'Appeals, Referrals and Substantial Injustice' Criminal Law Review 152.

COOPER S (2020) 'Police and Crime Commissioners: a corrosive exercise of power which destabilises police accountability?' 4 Criminal Law Review 291–305.

COOPER V and WHYTE D (2017) *The Violence of Austerity* (London: Pluto Press).

COPE N (2004) 'Intelligence Led Policing or Policing Led Intelligence?' 44 Brtitish Journal of Criminology 188.

COPLEY C (2003) 'Prosecuting Cases of Suspected "Shaken Baby Syndrome" – A Review of Current Issues' Criminal Law Review 93.

COPPEN J (2008) 'PACE: A View from the Custody Suite', in CAPE E and YOUNG R (eds), *Regulating Policing* (Oxford: Hart).

CORBETT C (1991) 'Complaints Against the Police: The New Procedure of Informal Resolution' (1991) 2 Policing and Society 47.

CORKER D and YOUNG D (2002) *Abuse of Process and Fairness in Criminal Proceedings* (London: Butterworths).

CORKER D, TOMBS G and CHISHOLM T (2009) 'SS 71 and 72 of SOCPA: Whither the common law?' Criminal Law Review 261.

CORNFORD A (2020) 'Terrorist precursor offences: evaluating the law in practice' Criminal Law Review 663.

CORNISH W (1968) *The Jury* (London: Penguin).

COSTIGAN R and STONE R (2017) *Civil Liberties and Human Rights*, 11th edn (Oxford: OUP).

COSTIGAN R (2007) 'Identification from CCTV: The Risk of Injustice' Crim LR 591.

COUCHMAN H (2019) *Policing by Machine. Predictive Policing and the Threat to our Rights* (London: Liberty).

COUNCIL OF EUROPE (1985) *The Position of the Victim in the Framework of Criminal Law and Procedure* (Strasbourg: Council of Europe).

COUNCIL OF EUROPE, PARLIAMENTARY ASSEMBLY (2009) *Allegations of politically-motivated abuses of the criminal justice system in Council of Europe member states* (Strasbourg: Council of Europe).

Courts and Tribunals Judiciary (2017) *Court of Appeal (Criminal Division) Annual Report 2016–17* (London: Ministry of Justice).

Courts and Tribunals Judiciary (2018) 'Crown Court Compendium Part 2: Sentencing' (London: Judicial College).

Courts and Tribunals Judiciary (2018) *Judicial Diversity Statistics 2018.* (London: Ministry of Justice).

Cowan D and Lomax D (2003) 'Policing unauthorised camping' 30 Journal of Law and Society 283.

Cowan D and Marsh A (2001) 'There's Regulatory Crime and then there's Landlord Crime: From Rachmanites to Partners' 64 Modern Law Review 831.

Cox B (1975) *Civil Liberties in Britain* (Harmondsworth: Penguin).

Craig P (1997) 'Formal and Substantive Conceptions of the Rule of Law: An Analytical Framework' Public Law 467.

Crawford A (1997) *The Local Governance of Crime* (Oxford: Clarendon).

Crawford A (2007) 'Reassurance Policing: Feeling is Believing' in Henry A and Smith D (eds), *Transformations of Policing* (Aldershot: Ashgate).

Crawford A (2008a) 'Dispersal Powers and the Symbolic Role of Anti-Social Behaviour Legislation' 71(5) Modern Law Review 753.

Crawford A (2008b) 'Plural Policing in the UK: policing beyond the police' in Newburn T (ed), *Handbook of Policing* 2nd edn (Cullompton: Willan).

Crawford A and Lister S (2007) *The Use and Impact of Dispersal Orders* (London: Policy Press).

Crawford A and Newburn T (2003) *Youth Offending and Restorative Justice* (Cullompton: Willan).

Crawford A (2006) 'Networked governance and the post-regulatory state? Steering, rowing and anchoring the provision of policing and security', Theoretical Criminology, 10(4), pp. 449–479.

Crawford C (2016) 'The English and Welsh experiment in democratic governance of policing through Police and Crime Commissioners: a misconceived venture or a good idea, badly implemented?' in Ross J and Delpeuch T (eds), *Comparing the Democratic Governance of Police Intelligence: New Models of Participation and Expertise in the United States and Europe* (Northampton, MA: Edward Elgar).

Crawley J (2009) 'The worst of all outcomes' Society Guardian 8 April.

Cretney A and Davis G (1995) *Punishing Violence* (London: Routledge).

Cretney A, Davis G, Clarkson C and Shepherd J (1994) 'Criminalising assault: the failure of the "offence against society" model' 34 British Journal of Criminology 15.

Cribb J, Disney R and Sibieta L (2014) *The public sector workforce: past, present and future* IFS Briefing Note BN145. (London: Institute for Fiscal Studies).

Criminal Justice Alliance (2012) *Crowded Out? The impact of prison overcrowding on rehabilitation* (London: CJA).

Criminal Justice Joint Inspection (2016) *Delivering justice in a digital age* (London: HMCPSI and HMIC).

Criminal Justice Joint Inspection (2017) *Making it Fair: The Disclosure of Unused Material in Volume Crown court Cases* (London: HMCPSI and HMIC).

Criminal Law Revision Committee (1972) *Eleventh Report (General)* Cmnd 4991 (London: HMSO).

Crisp D and Moxon D (1994) *Case Screening by the CPS* (Home Office Research Study no 137) (London: Home Office).

Crisp D, Whittaker C and Harris J (1995) *Public Interest Case Assessment Schemes* (Home Office Research Study no 138) (London: Home Office).

Critchley S and Benasconi R (2002) *The Cambridge Companion to Levinas* (Cambridge: CUP).

Croall H (1988) 'Mistakes, Accidents and Someone Else's Fault: The Trading

Offender in Court' 15 Journal of Law and Society 293.

CROSBY K (2012) 'Controlling Devlin's jury: what the jury thinks, and what the jury sees online' Criminal Law Review 15

CROSBY K (2015) 'Juror Punishment, Juror Guidance and the CJC Act 2015' Criminal Law Review 578.

CROWN PROSECUTION SERVICE (1998) Discontinuance Survey (November) (unpublished: cited in *Criminal Justice System, Narrowing the Justice Gap*, 2002 (London: TSO)).

CROWN PROSECUTION SERVICE (2003) *Guidance on Prosecuting Cases of Racial and Religious Crime* (London: CPS).

CROWN PROSECUTION SERVICE (2007) *The Director's Guidance on Charging*, 3rd edn (London: CPS).

CROWN PROSECUTION SERVICE (2008a) *Special Domestic Violence Courts Review 2007-8* (London: CPS).

CROWN PROSECUTION SERVICE (2008b) *Violence against women report 2007-8* (London: CPS).

CROWN PROSECUTION SERVICE (2008c) *Guidance on Prosecuting Cases of Domestic Violence* (London: CPS).

CROWN PROSECUTION SERVICE (2013a) *Adult Conditional Cautions (Director's Guidance)* (London: CPS).

CROWN PROSECUTION SERVICE (2013b) *Code for Crown Prosecutors* (London: CPS).

CROWN PROSECUTION SERVICE (2013c) *Hate crime and crimes against older people report 2011-2012* (London: CPS).

CROWN PROSECUTION SERVICE (2015a) *Transforming Summary Justice* (London: CPS).

CROWN PROSECUTION SERVICE (2015b) *Victim and witness satisfaction survey* (London: CPS).

CROWN PROSECUTION SERVICE (2017) *Annual Review and Accounts 2016-2017* (London: TSO).

CROWN PROSECUTION SERVICE (2018a) *CPS publishes outcome of sexual offences review* (London: CPS).

CROWN PROSECUTION SERVICE (2018b) *Hate Crime Report 2017-2018* (London: CPS).

CROWN PROSECUTION SERVICE (2018d) *Key Measures 2017-2018* (London: CPS).

CROWN PROSECUTION SERVICE (2018d) *Rape and serious sexual offence prosecutions— Assessment of disclosure of unused material ahead of trial* (London: CPS).

CROWN PROSECUTION SERVICE (2019a) *Allocation of cases and Sending to the Crown Court* (London: CPS).

CROWN PROSECUTION SERVICE (2019b) *Annual Report and Accounts 2018-19* HC 2286 (London: TSO).

CROWN PROSECUTION SERVICE (2019d) *Bail—legal guidance* (London: CPS).

CROWN PROSECUTION SERVICE (2019e) *Feedback & Complaints: How to give feedback or make a complaint to the Crown Prosecution Service* (London: CPS).

CROWN PROSECUTION SERVICE (2020) *Assisted Suicide* (London: CPS)

CROWN PROSECUTION SERVICE and ASSOCIATION OF CHIEF POLICE OFFICERS (2004) *No Witness, No Justice Pilot Evaluation* (London: CPS and ACPO).

CROWN PROSECUTION SERVICE and INDEPENDENT POLICE COMPLAINTS COMMISSION (2005) *Protocol between the Crown Prosecution Service Casework Directorate and the Independent Police Complaints Commission* (London: TSO).

CROWN PROSECUTION SERVICE, DEPT. FOR EDUCATION, DEPT. OF HEALTH, WELSH ASSEMBLY GOVERNMENT, (2011) *Achieving Best Evidence: Guidance on interviewing victims and witnesses, and guidance on using special measures*, (London: Ministry of Justice).

CUNNINGHAM S (2005) 'The unique nature of prosecutions in cases of fatal road traffic collisions' Criminal Law Review 834.

CURRY T (2019) 'Expendables for Whom: Terry Crews and the Erasure of Black Male Victims of Sexual Assault and Rape' 42(3) Women's Studies in Communication 28.

CUSHING K (2014) 'Diversion from Prosecution for Young People in England

and Wales – Reconsidering the Mandatory Admission Criteria' 14 Youth Justice 140.

DALY G and PATTENDEN R (2005) 'Racial Bias and the English Criminal Trial Jury' 64(3) Cambridge Law Journal 678.

DALY K (2015) 'What Is Restorative Justice? Fresh Answers to a Vexed Question' 11(1) Victims & Offenders 1–21.

DAMASKA M (1973) 'Evidentiary Barriers to Conviction and Two Models of Criminal Procedure: A Comparative Study' 121 University of Pennsylvania Law Review 506.

DAMASKA M (1986) *The Faces of Justice and State Authority* (New Haven: Yale).

DANDO C, WILCOX R and MILNE R (2008) 'The cognitive interview: Inexperienced police officers' perceptions of their witness interviewing behaviour' 13 Legal and Criminological Psychology 59.

DANDO C, WILCOX R, MILNE R and HENRY L (2009) 'A Modified Cognitive Interview Procedure for Frontline Police Investigators' 23 Applied Cognitive Psychology 698.

DANEWID I (2019) 'The fire this time: Grenfell, racial capitalism and the urbanisation of empire' 26(1) European Journal of International Relations.

DARBYSHIRE P (1984) *The Magistrates' Clerk* (Chichester: Barry Rose).

DARBYSHIRE P (1990) 'Notes of a Lawyer Juror' 140 New Law Journal 1264.

DARBYSHIRE P (1991) 'The Lamp That Shows That Freedom Lives – Is it Worth the Candle?' Criminal Law Review 740.

DARBYSHIRE P (1997a) 'An Essay on the Importance and Neglect of the Magistracy' Criminal Law Review 627.

DARBYSHIRE P (1997b) 'For the New Lord Chancellor: Some Causes for Concern About Magistrates' Criminal Law Review 861.

DARBYSHIRE P (1997c) 'Previous Misconduct and Magistrates' Courts—Some Tales from the Real World' Criminal Law Review 105.

DARBYSHIRE P (1997d) 'Strengthening the Argument in Favour of the Defendant's Right to Elect' Criminal Law Review 911.

DARBYSHIRE P (2011) *Sitting in Judgment: the working lives of judges* (London: Hart).

DARBYSHIRE P (2014) 'Judicial case management in ten Crown courts' Crim Criminal Law Review 30–50.

DARBYSHIRE P (2017) *Darbyshire on the English Legal System*, 12th edn (London: Sweet and Maxwell).

DARBYSHIRE P and THOMAS C (2008) 'Exposing Jury Myths-Letters to the Editor' Criminal Law Review 888.

DARBYSHIRE P, with research by MAUGHAN A and STEWART A (2001) 'What Can We Learn from Published Jury Research? Findings for the Criminal Courts Review' Criminal Law Review 970.

DARGUE P (2019) 'The Safety of Convictions in the Court of Appeal: Fresh Evidence in the Criminal Division through an Empirical Lens' 83(6) Journal of Criminal Law 433–449.

DARGUE P (2020) 'An analysis of disclosure failings in murder appeals against conviction 2006–2018' Criminal Law Review 707.

DAVID G, RAWLS A and TRAINUM J (2018) 'Playing the Interrogation Game: Rapport, Coercion, and Confessions in Police Interrogations' 41 Symbolic Interaction 3–24.

DAVIES G (1996) 'Mistaken Identification: where law meets psychology head on' 35 Howard Journal of Criminal Justice 232.

DAVIES P (2015) 'Victims: continuing to carry the burden of justice.' *British Society of Criminology Newsletter*, 76 (Summer).

DAVIES P (2018) 'Environmental crime, victimisation and the ideal victim' in DUGGAN M, *Revisiting the Ideal Victim* (Bristol: Policy Press).

DAVIS A and ERNST R (2019) 'Racial Gaslighting' 7(4) Politics, Groups and Identities 761–774.

DAVIS G, HOYANO L, KEENAN C, MAITLAND L and MORGAN R (1999) *Assessment of the admissibility and sufficiency of evidence in child abuse prosecutions* (London: Home Office).

DAW R (1994) 'A Response' Criminal Law Review 904.

DAYAN C (2011) *The Law is a White Dog: How Legal Rituals Make and Unmake Persons* (New Jersey: Princeton UP).

DE MAS S (2003) 'Protecting the Legal Rights of the Travelling Citizen: Easier Said than Done' Criminal Law Review 865.

DE SCHUTTER O and RINGELHEIM J (2008) 'Ethnic Profiling: A Rising Challenge for European Human Rights Law' 71(3) Modern Law Review 358.

DE THAN C and ELVIN J (2019) 'Private prosecution: a useful constitutional safeguard or potentially dangerous historical anomaly?' Criminal Law Review 656.

DEARDON L (2018) 'Government scraps proposed women's 'community prisons' in new strategy to reduce female offending' *The Independent*, 26 June.

DEARING A (2017) *Justice for victims of crime: human dignity as the foundation of criminal justice in Europe* (Cham: Springer).

DECKER M, HOLLIDAY C, HAMEEDUDDIN Z, SHAH R, MILLER J, DANTZLER J and GOODMARK L, (2019) '"You Do Not Think of Me as a Human Being": Race and Gender Inequities Intersect to Discourage Police Reporting of Violence against Women' 96 Journal of Urban Health 772–783.

DEHAGHANI R (2016) 'Exploring the Implementation of the Appropriate Adult Safeguard in Police Custody' 55(4) Howard Journal of Criminal Justice 396–413.

DEHAGHANI R (2017) 'Automatic authorisation: an exploration of the decision to detain in police custody' Criminal Law Review 187.

DEHAGHANI R (2019) *Vulnerability in Police Custody* (Abingdon: Routledge).

DEHAGHANI R (2020) 'Interrogating vulnerability: reframing the vulnerable suspect in police custody' 24(4) Social and Legal Studies 417–440.

DEHAGHANI R and NEWMAN D (2019) 'Can – and should – lawyers be considered 'appropriate' appropriate adults?' 58(1) Howard Journal of Criminal Justice 3–24.

DELL S (1971) *Silent in Court* (London: Bell).

DEMBOUR M-B (2006) *Who Believes in Human Rights?* (Cambridge: CUP).

DEMETRIOU S (2019) 'From the ASBO to the injunction: a qualitative review of the anti-social behaviour legislation post 2014' Public Law 343–361.

DEMETRIOU S (2020) 'Crime and anti-social behaviour in England and Wales: an empirical evaluation of the ASBO's successor' 40 Legal Studies 458–476.

DEMPSEY M (2007) 'Towards a feminist state: what does 'effective' prosecution of domestic violence mean?' 70 Modern Law Review 908.

DEMPSEY M (2009) *Prosecuting Domestic Violence* (Oxford: OUP).

DENNIS I (1993) 'Miscarriages of Justice and the Law of Confessions' Public Law 291.

DENNIS I (2003) 'Fair Trials and Safe Convictions' (2003) 56 Current Legal Problems 211.

DENNIS I (2003a) 'Editorial' Criminal Law Review.

DENNIS I (2003b) 'Fair Trials and Safe Convictions' 56Current Legal Problems 211.

DENNIS I (2005) 'Reverse Onuses and the Presumption of Innocence: In Search of Principle' Criminal Law Review 901.

DENNIS I (2006) 'Convicting the guilty: outcomes, process and the Court of Appeal' Criminal Law Review 955.

DENNIS, I (2017) *The Law of Evidence* (London: Sweet and Maxwell).

DENNIS I (2018) 'Prosecution disclosure: are the problems insoluble?' Criminal Law Review 829.

DEPARTMENT FOR BUSINESS ENTERPRISE & REGULATORY REFORM (2007) *Statutory Code of Practice for Regulators* (London: DBERR).

DEPARTMENT FOR CONSTITUTIONAL AFFAIRS (2005a) *Judicial Statistics: England and Wales for the year 2004*, Cm 6565 (London: TSO).

DEPARTMENT FOR CONSTITUTIONAL AFFAIRS (2005b) *Jury Research and Impropriety, Response to Consultation*, CP 04/05 (London: DCA).

DEPARTMENT FOR CONSTITUTIONAL AFFAIRS (2006a) *Review of the Implementation of the Human Rights Act* (London: DCA).

DEPARTMENT FOR CONSTITUTIONAL AFFAIRS (2006b) *Delivering Simple, Speedy, Summary Justice* (London: DCA).

DEPARTMENTAL COMMITTEE ON FRAUD TRIALS (1986) *Report* (London: HMSO).

DEPARTMENTAL COMMITTEE ON LEGAL AID IN CRIMINAL PROCEEDINGS (1966) *Report* (Cmnd 2934) (London: HMSO).

DEVLIN A and DEVLIN T (1998) *Anybody's Nightmare* (East Harling: Taverner Publications).

DHAMI M (2002) 'Do Bail Information Schemes Really Affect Bail Decisions?' 41 Howard Journal of Criminal Justice 245.

DHAMI M (2004) 'Conditional Bail Decision Making in the Magistrates' Court' 43 Howard Journal of Criminal Justice 27.

DHAMI M and MANDEL R (2013) 'How do defendants choose their trial court? Evidence for a heuristic processing account' 8(5) Judgment and Decision Making 552–560.

DI FEDERICO G (1998) 'Prosecutorial Independence and the democratic requirement of accountability in Italy' 38 British Journal of Criminology 371.

DICKSON B (2007) 'The processing of appeals in the House of Lords' Law Quarterly Review 571.

DICKSON B (2013) *Human Rights and the United Kingdom Supreme Court* (Oxford: OUP).

DIGNAN J (1992) 'Repairing the damage: can reparation be made to work in the service of diversion?' 32(4) British Journal of Criminology 453.

DIGNAN J (2005) *Understanding Victims and Restorative Justice* (Maidenhead: Open UP).

DIGNAN J and CAVADINO M (1996) 'Towards a Framework for Conceptualising and Evaluating Models of Criminal Justice from a Victim's Perspective' 4 International Review of Victimology 153.

DIGNAN J and WHYNNE A (1997) 'A Microcosm of the Local Community? Reflections on the Composition of the Magistracy in a Petty Sessional Division in the North Midlands' 37 British Journal of Criminology 184.

DINE J (1993) 'European Community Criminal Law?' Criminal Law Review 246.

DINGWALL G and HARDING C (1998) *Diversion in the Criminal Process* (London: Sweet & Maxwell).

DINGWALL G and HILLIER T (2016) *Blamestorming, Blamemongers and Scapegoats* (Bristol: The Policy Press).

DIXON B and SMITH G (1998) 'Laying Down the Law: The Police, the Courts and Legal Accountability' 26 IJ Soc of Law 419.

DIXON et al, 'Safeguarding the Rights of Suspects in Police Custody' (1990a) 1 Policing and Society 118.

DIXON D (1991) 'Common Sense, Legal Advice, and the Right of Silence' PL 233.

DIXON D (1997) *Law in Policing* (Oxford: Clarendon).

DIXON D (2005) 'Regulating police interrogation' in WILLIAMSON T (ed), *Investigative Interviewing: Rights, Research Regulation* (Cullompton: Willan).

DIXON D (2006) '"A Window into the Interviewing Process?" The Audio-visual Recording of Police Interrogation in New South Wales, Australia' 16(4) Policing & Society 323.

DIXON D, BOTTOMLEY A, COLEMAN C, GILL M and WALL D (1989) 'Reality and Rules in the Construction and Regulation of Police Suspicion' 17 IJ Sociology of Law 185.

DIXON D, COLEMAN C and BOTTOMLEY K (1990b) 'Consent and the Legal Regulation of Policing' 17 JLS 345.

DOAK J (2003) 'The victim and the criminal process: an analysis of recent trends in regional and international tribunals' 23 LS 1.

DOAK J (2005) 'Victims' rights in criminal trials: prospects for participation' 32 JLS 294.

DOAK J (2008) *Victims' Rights, Human Rights and Criminal Justice: Reconceiving the Role of Third Parties* (Oxford: Hart).

DOAK J (2015) 'Enriching Trial Justice for Crime Victims in Common Law Systems: Lessons from Transitional Environments' 21 Int Review Vict 139.

DOAK J and MCGOURLAY C (2012) *Evidence in Context* (Abingdon: Routledge).

DOCKING M and BUCKE T (2006) *Confidence in the police complaints system: a survey of the general population* (London: IPCC).

DOHERTY M and EAST R (1985) 'Bail Decisions in Magistrates' Courts' 25 BJ Crim 251.

DOCKING M, GRACE K and BUCKE T (2008) *Police Custody as a "Place of Safety": Examining the use of s 136 of the MHA 1983* (London: IPCC).

DONAGHY R (2009) *One Death Too Many* (Department for Work and Pensions, Cm 7657) (Norwich: TSO).

DONOGHUE J (2014) 'Reforming the Role of Magistrates: Implications for Summary Justice in England and Wales' 77 MLR 928

DORAN S (1989) 'Descent to Avernus' 139 NLJ 1147.

DORAN S (1991) 'Alternative Defences: the "invisible" burden on the trial judge' Crim LR 878.

DORAN S (2000) 'The Necessarily Expanding Role of the Criminal Trial Judge' in DORAN S and JACKSON J (eds), *The Judicial Role in Criminal Proceedings* (Oxford: Hart).

DORAN S and GLENN R (2000) *Lay Involvement in Adjudication: Review of the Criminal Justice System in Northern Ireland* (Criminal Justice Review Research Report no 11) (Belfast: SO).

DORAN S and JACKSON J (1997) 'The Case for Jury Waiver' Crim LR 155.

DORLING D, GORDON D, HILLYARD P, PANTAZIS C, PEMBERTON S and TOMBS S (2008) *Criminal obsessions: Why harm matters more than crime* (London: Centre for Crime and Justice Studies).

DORN N, MIRJI K and SOUTH N (1992) *Traffickers: Drug markets and law enforcement* (London: Routledge).

DOUZINAS C (2007) 'Left or Rights?' 34 JLS 617.

DRAKE D and HENLEY A (2014) '"Victims" Versus "Offenders" in British Political Discourse: The Construction of a False Dichotomy' Howard JCJ 53: 141.

DRAKE K, BULL R and BOON J (2008) 'Interrogative suggestibility, self-esteem, and the influence of negative life events' 13 Legal and Criminological Psychology 299.

DRAKE D and HENLEY A (2014) "Victims" Versus "Offenders" in British Political Discourse: The Construction of a False Dichotomy' 53(2) Howard JCJ 141–157.

DREW S and GIBBS L (2019) 'Identifying and accommodating vulnerable people in court' 10 Archbold Review 7.

DREW SMITH S (2015) *An independent review of the governance arrangements of the Independent Police Complaints Commission.* (London: TSO).

DROR I and CHARLTON D (2006) 'Why Experts make Errors' 56 J Forensic Identification 600.

DRUMMOND O and MCKEEVER G (2015) *Access to Justice through University Law Clinics* (Ulster: Ulster University Law School).

DUFF P (1998) 'Crime Control, Due Process and "The Case for the Prosecution"' 38 BJ Crim 611.

DUFF P and FINDLAY M (1983) 'Jury vetting – The jury under attack' 3 LS 159.

DUFF P and HUTTON N (eds) (1999) *Criminal Justice in Scotland* (Aldershot: Dartmouth).

DUFF R and MARSHALL S (2006) 'How Offensive Can You Get?' in VON HIRSCH A and SIMESTER A (eds), *Incivilities: Regulating Offensive Behaviour* (Oxford: Hart Publishing).

Duff R, Farmer L, Marshall S and Tadros V (eds) (2004) *The Trial on Trial* (Oxford: Hart).

Duff R (2013) 'Towards a Modest Legal Moralism' 8 Criminal Law and Philosophy 217–235.

Dunnighan C and Norris C (1996) 'A risky business: the recruitment and running of informers by English police officers' 19 Police Studies 1.

Durham R, Lawson R, Lord A and Baird QC, V (2016) *Seeing Is Believing: The Northumbria Court Observation Panel Report on 30 Rape Trials 2015–2016.* (Newcastle-Upon-Tyne: Office of the Police and Crime Commissioner for Northumbria).

Durston G (2005) 'Previous (In)Consistent Statements after the Criminal Justice Act 2003' Crim LR 206.

Dworkin R (1981) 'Principle, Policy, Procedure' in Tapper C (ed), *Crime, Proof and Punishment* (London: Butterworths).

Eady D (2012) 'The Failure of the CCRC to Live Up to its Stated Values?: The case of Michael Attwooll and John Roden' in Naughton M (ed), *The Criminal Cases Review Commission: Hope for the Innocent?* (London: Palgrave Macmillan).

East R (1985) 'Jury Packing: A Thing of the Past?' 48 MLR 518.

East R (1987) 'Police Brutality: Lessons of the Holloway Road Assault' 137 NLJ 1010.

East R and Thomas P (1985) 'Freedom of Movement: *Moss v McLachlan*' 12 JLS 77.

Easton S (1998a) 'Legal Advice, Common Sense and the Right of Silence' 2 IJ E&P 109.

Easton S (1998b) *The Case for the Right to Silence* (Aldershot: Ashgate).

Easton S and Piper C (2016) *Sentencing and Punishment. The Quest for Justice.* (Oxford: OUP).

Eaton M (1987) 'The Question of Bail' in Carlen P and Worrall A (eds), *Gender, Crime and Justice* (Milton Keynes: Open UP).

Edwards I (2001) 'Victim participation in sentencing: the problems of incoherence' 40 Howard JCJ 39.

Edwards I (2002) 'The place of victims' preferences in the sentencing of "their" offenders' Crim LR 689.

Edwards I (2004) 'An Ambiguous Participant: The Crime Victim and Criminal Justice Decision Making' 44 BJ Crim 967.

Edwards J (1984) *The Attorney General, Politics and the Public Interest* (London: Sweet & Maxwell).

Edwards S (1989) *Policing Domestic Violence* (London: Sage).

Edwards T (2008) 'The Role of Defence Lawyers in a Re-Balanced System' in Cape E and Young R (eds), *Regulating Policing* (Oxford: Hart).

Eijk G (2020) 'Exclusion through Risk-Based Justice: Analysing Combinations of Risk Assessment from Pretrial Detention to Release' BJ Crim, online first.

Ekblom P and Heal K (1982) *The police response to calls from the public* (Research and Planning Unit Paper no 9) (London: Home Office).

Elias R (1993) *Victims Still: The Political Manipulation of Crime Victims* (London: Sage).

Elks L (2008) *Righting Miscarriages of Justice? Ten Years of the Criminal Cases Review Commission* (London: Justice).

Elliman S (1990) 'Independent Information for the CPS' 140 NLJ 812.

Ellison L (1998) 'Cross-Examination in Rape Trials' Crim LR 605.

Ellison L (2001a) *The Adversarial Process and the Vulnerable Witness* (Oxford: OUP).

Ellison L (2001b) 'The Mosaic Art? Cross-examination and the Vulnerable Witness' 21 LS 353.

Ellison L (2002a) 'Cross-examination and the Intermediary: Bridging the Language Divide?' Crim LR 114.

Ellison L (2002b) 'Prosecuting Domestic Violence Without Victim Participation' 56 MLR 834.

ELLISON L (2003) 'Responding to Victim Withdrawal in Domestic Violence Prosecutions' Crim LR 760.

ELLISON L (2007) 'Promoting effective case-building in rape cases: A comparative perspective' Crim LR 691.

ELLISON L (2009) 'The Use and Abuse of Psychiatric Evidence in Rape Trials' 13 IJE &P 28.

ELLISON L (2015) 'Responding to the needs of victims with psychosocial disabilities: challenges to equality of access to justice' Crim LR 28.

ELLISON L (2019) 'Credibility in Context: Jury Education and Intimate Partner Rape' E&P 263

ELLISON L and MUNRO V (2009a) 'Reacting to Rape' 49(2) BJ Crim 202.

ELLISON L and MUNRO V (2009b) 'Of "normal sex" and "real rape": exploring the use of socio-sexual scripts in (mock) jury deliberation' 18(3) SLS 291.

ELLISON L and MUNRO V (2009c) 'Turning mirrors in windows? Assessing the impact of (mock) juror education in rape trials' 49(3) BJ Crim 363.

ELLISON L and MUNRO V (2010) 'Getting to (not) guilty: examining jurors' deliberative processes in, and beyond, the context of a mock rape trial' 30(1) LS 74–97.

ELLISON L and MUNRO V (2013) 'Better the Devil You Know? "Real Rape" Stereotypes and the Relevance of a Previous Relationship in (Mock) Juror Deliberations' 17 IJ E&P 433.

ELLISON M and MORGAN A (2015) *Review of Possible Miscarriages of justice- Impact of Undisclosed Undercover Police Activity on the Safety of Convictions Report to the Attorney General* HC 291 (London: TSO).

ELSTER J (2020) 'Youth voices in post-English riots Tottenham: The role of reflexivity in negotiating negative representations' 68(6) Sociological Review 1386–1402.

EMMERSON B, ASHWORTH A and MACDONALD A (2007) *Human Rights and Criminal Justice*, 2nd edn (London: Sweet & Maxwell).

EMMERSON B, ASHWORTH A, MACDONALD A and SUMMERS M (2012) *Human Rights and Criminal Justice*, 3rd edn (London: Sweet & Maxwell).

ENGLISH L M (2013) 'The impact of an independent inspectorate on penal governance, performance and accountability: Pressure points and conflict "in the pursuit of an ideal of perfection"' 24 (7–8) Critical Perspectives on Accounting 532–549.

ENVIRONMENT AGENCY (2018) *Environment Agency enforcement and sanctions policy* (Bristol: Environment Agency).

EQUALITY and HUMAN RIGHTS COMMISSION (2009) *Police and Racism: What has been Achieved 10 Years after the Stephen Lawrence Inquiry Report?* (London: Equality and Human Rights Commission).

EQUALITY and HUMAN RIGHTS COMMISSION (2010) *Stop and Think: A Critical Review of the Use of Stop and Search Powers in England and Wales* (London: Equality and Human Rights Commission).

EREZ E (1994) 'Victim participation in sentencing: and the debate goes on' 3 Int Rev Victimology 17.

EREZ E (1999) 'Who's Afraid of the Big Bad Victim? Victim Impact Statements as Victim Empowerment *and* Enhancement of Justice' Crim LR 545.

EREZ E and ROGERS L (1999) 'The Effects of Victim Impact Statements on Criminal Justice Outcomes' 39 BJ Crim 216.

EREZ E et al (2020) 'From Cinderella to consumer: how crime victims can go to the ball' in TAPLEY J and DAVIES P, *Victimology: Research, policy and activism* (Basingstoke: Palgrave Macmillan).

ERICSON R (1981) *Making Crime: A Study of Detective Work* (London: Butterworths).

ERICSON R (1982) *Reproducing Order: A Study of Police Patrol Work* (Toronto: University of Toronto Press).

ERICSON R (1994) 'The Royal Commission on Criminal Justice System Surveillance' in MCCONVILLE M and BRIDGES L (eds),

Criminal Justice in Crisis (Aldershot: Edward Elgar).

Ericson R and Haggerty K (1997) Policing the Risk Society (Oxford: Clarendon).

Ericson R and Haggerty K (1999) 'Governing the Young' in Smandych R (ed), Governable Places: Readings on governmentality and crime control (Aldershot: Ashgate).

Erin C and Ost S (eds) (2007) The criminal justice system and healthcare (Oxford: OUP).

European Court of Human Rights (2018) Guide on Article 6 of the European Convention on Human Rights (Strasbourg: Council of Europe).

European Court of Human Rights (2020) Factsheet—Derogation in time of emergency (Strasbourg: Council of Europe).

Evans M and Morgan R (1992) 'The European Convention for the Prevention of Torture: Operational Practice' 41 ICLQ 590.

Evans R (1991) 'Police Cautioning and the Young Adult Offender' Crim LR 598.

Evans R (1993a) 'Comparing Young Adult and Juvenile Cautioning in the Metropolitan Police District' Crim LR 572.

Evans R (1993b) The Conduct of Police Interviews with Juveniles (Royal Commission on Criminal Justice Research Study no 8) (London: HMSO).

Evans R (1994) 'Cautioning: Counting the cost of retrenchment' Crim LR 566.

Evans R (1996) 'Is a police caution amenable to judicial review?' Crim LR 104.

Evans R and Ellis R (1997) Police Cautioning in the 1990s (Home Office Research Findings no 52) (London: HMSO).

Evans R and Ferguson T (1991) Comparing Different Juvenile Cautioning Systems in One Police Force Area (Report to the Home Office Research and Planning Unit).

Evans R and Lewis P (2013) Undercover: The True Story of Britain's Secret Police (London: Faber and Faber).

Evans R and Puech K (2001) 'Reprimands and warnings: populist punitiveness or restorative justice?' Crim LR 794.

Evans R and Wilkinson C (1990) 'Variation in Police Cautioning Policy and Practice in England and Wales' 29 Howard JCJ 155.

Ewing K and Tham J-C (2008) 'The Continuing Futility of the Human Rights Act' PL 668.

Fagan J (2017) 'Dignity is the new legitimacy' in Dolovich S and Natapoff A (eds), New Criminal Justice Thinking (New York: New York UP).

Fair Trials International (2013) Pre Trial Detention in France (France: Open Society Foundation. Local Experts Group).

Fairclough S (2017) '"It doesn't happen . . . and I've never thought it was necessary for it to happen": Barriers to vulnerable defendants giving evidence by live link in Crown Court trials' 21(3) IJ E&P 209.

Fairclough S (2018) 'Speaking up for Injustice: Reconsidering the provision of special measures through the lens of equality' Crim LR 4–19.

Farmer A K, Sun I Y and Starks B C (2015) 'Willingness to Record Police-Public Encounters: The Impact of Race and Social and Legal Consciousness' 5(4) Race and Justice 356–377.

Farrell A and Givelber D (2010) 'Liberation Reconsidered: Understanding Why Judges and Juries Disagree About Guilt' 100(4) JCLC 1549–1586.

Farrugia L and Gabbert F (2019) 'The "appropriate adult": What they do and what they should do in police interviews with mentally disordered suspects' 29(3) Criminal Behaviour Mental Health 134–141.

Farrugia L and Gabbert F (2020)' Vulnerable suspects in police interviews: exploring current practice in England and Wales' 17 Jo Investigative Psychol and Offender Profiling 17–30.

Faulkner D (1996) Darkness and Light: Justice, Crime and Management for Today (London: Howard League).

Faulkner D (2010) Criminal justice and government at a time of austerity. Criminal Justice Alliance Discussion Paper (London: CJA).

FAULKNER D and BURNETT R (2011) *Where Next for Criminal Justice?* (Bristol: The Policy Press).

FEELEY M and SIMON J (1994) 'Actuarial Justice: The Emerging New Criminal Law' in NELKEN D (ed), *The Futures of Criminology* (London: Sage).

FEILZER M and HOOD R (2004) *Differences or Discrimination?* (London: Youth Justice Board).

FEKETE L (2018) 'Lammy Review: without racial justice, can there be trust?' 59(3) Race & Class 75–79.

FELDMAN D (2002) *Civil Liberties and Human Rights in England and Wales*, 2nd edn (Oxford: OUP).

FELDMAN D (2006) 'Human rights, terrorism and risk: the roles of politicians and judges' PL 364.

FENNER S, GUDJONSSON G and CLARE I (2002) 'Understanding of the police caution (England and Wales) Among Suspects in Police Detention' 12 Jo Community & Applied Social Psychology 83.

FENWICK H (1993) 'Confessions, Recording Rules, and Miscarriages of Justice: A Mistaken Emphasis?' Crim LR 174.

FENWICK H (1995) 'Rights of victims in the criminal justice system' Crim LR 843.

FENWICK H (1997) 'Charge Bargaining and Sentence Discount: the Victim's Perspective' 5 Int R Victimology 23.

FENWICK H (2002) 'The Anti-Terrorism, Crime and Security Act 2001: A Proportionate Response to September 11?' 65(5) MLR 724.

FENWICK H (2017) 'Terrorism and the control orders/TPIMs saga' (2017) PL 609.

FERRAGINA E and ARRIGONI A (2017) 'The Rise and Fall of Social Capital: Requiem for a Theory?' 15(3) Political Studies Review 355–367.

FIELD S (1993) 'Defining Interviews under PACE' 13 LS 254.

FIELD S (2007) 'Practice cultures and the "new" youth justice in England and Wales' 47 CJ Criminology 311.

FIELD S (2008) 'Early intervention and the "new" youth justice' Crim LR 177.

FIELD S (2019) 'The Corporate Manslaughter and Corporate Homicide Act 2007 and human rights - Part 2: has universal legal protection of the right to life been advanced in a custodial setting?' 30 Int Company and Commercial LR 415.

FIELD S and JORG N (1991) 'Corporate Liability and Manslaughter: Should we be going Dutch?' Crim LR 156.

FIELD S and THOMAS P (eds) (1994) *Justice and Efficiency? The Royal Commission on Criminal Justice* (London: Blackwell).

FIELDING N (1985) *Community Policing* (Oxford: Clarendon).

FIELDING N (1988) *Joining Forces* (London: Routledge).

FIELDING N (2006) *Courting Violence: Offences against the Person Cases in Court* (Oxford: OUP).

FIELDING N (2018) *Professionalising the Police: The Unfulfilled Promise of Police Training* (Oxford: OUP).

FIELDING N, BRAUN S and HIEKE G (2020) *Video Enabled Justice Evaluation.* (Guildford: University of Surrey).

FIJNAUT C and MARX G (eds) (1996) *Undercover: Police Surveillance In Comparative Perspective* (The Hague: Kluwer).

FINCH E and MUNRO V (2006) 'Breaking Boundaries?: Sexual Consent in the Jury Room' LS 303.

FINCH E and MUNRO V (2007) 'The Demon Drink and the Demonised Woman: Socio-Sexual Stereotypes and Responsibility Attribution in Rape Trials Involving Intoxicants' SLS 591.

FINCH E and MUNRO V (2008) 'Lifting the Veil: The Use of Focus Groups and Trial Simulations in Legal Research' JLS 30.

FINE B and MILLAR R (eds), (1985) *Policing the Miners' Strike* (London: Lawrence and Wishart).

Fineman M (2010) 'The Vulnerable Subject and the Responsive State' 60 Emory Law Journal.

Fineman M (2019) 'Vulnerability and Social Justice' 53 Valparaiso Uni LR 53.

Fisher G (2000) 'Plea Bargaining's Triumph' 109 Yale LJ 857.

Fisher H (1977) *Report of an Inquiry into the Circumstances leading to the Trial of Three Persons on Charges arising out of the Death of Maxwell Confait and the Fire at 27 Doggett Road, London SE6* (HCP 90) (London: HMSO).

Fisher J (2005) 'Intercept evidence' *Counsel*, September issue, p 9.

Fiti R, Perry D, Giraud W and Ayres M (2008) *Statistical Bulletin: Motoring Offences and Breath Test Statistics England and Wales 2006* (London: Ministry of Justice).

Fitzgerald M (1993) *Ethnic Minorities and the Criminal Justice System* (Royal Commission on Criminal Justice, Research Study no 20) (London: HMSO).

Fitzgerald M (1999) *Stop and Search: Final Report* (London: Metropolitan Police).

Fitzgerald M and Sibbitt R (1997) *Ethnic monitoring in police forces: a beginning* (Home Office Research Study 173) (London: Home Office).

Fitzgerald M, Hough M, Joseph I and Quereshi T (2002) *Policing for London* (Cullompton, Willan).

Fitzpatrick B (2009) 'Immunity from the law' in Billingsley R (ed), *Covert Human Intelligence Sources; The 'unlovely face of police work'* (Hampshire: Waterside Press).

Fitzpatrick B, Seago P, Walker C and Wall D (2000) 'New Courts Management and the Professionalisation of Summary Justice in England and Wales' 11 Criminal Law Forum 1.

Fitzpatrick R and Thorne L (2020) *Evaluation of the Independent Custody Evaluation Pilot* (Unpublished report: Confluence Partnership).

Flacks S (2018) 'The stop and search of minors: A "vital police tool"?' 18(3) Criminology and Criminal Justice 364–384.

Flacks S (2020) 'Law, necropolitics and the stop and search of young people' 24(2) Theoretical Criminology 387–405.

Flanagan R (2008) *The Review of Policing: Final Report* (London: HMIC).

Flint J and Hunter C (2011) 'Governing by civil order: towards new frameworks of support, coercion and sanction?' in Quirk H, Seddon T and Smith G (eds), *Regulation and Criminal Justice* (Cambridge: CUP).

Flood-Page C and Mackie A (1998) *Sentencing Practice: an examination of decisions in magistrates' courts and the Crown Court in the mid-1990s* (Home Office Research Study no 180) (London: Home Office).

Flood-Page C, Campbell S, Harrington V and Miller J (2000) *Youth Crime: Findings from the 1998/99 Youth Lifestyles Survey* (Home Office Research Study 209) (London: Home Office).

Forensic Science Regulator (2016) *Annual Report* (London: FSR).

Forensic Science Regulator, (2020) *Annual Report 17 November 2018–16 November 2019* (London: FSR).

Forensic Science Service (1996) *Using Forensic Science effectively: A joint project by ACPO and the FSS* (Birmingham: Forensic Science Service).

Forensic Science Service (2005) *Annual Report, 2004–5* (London: SO).

Forster S (2009) 'Control Orders: Borders to the Freedom of Movement or Moving the Borders of Freedom?' in Wade M and Maljevic A (eds), *A War on Terror? The European Stance on a New Threat, Changing Laws and Human Rights Implications* (New York: Springer).

Forum Against Islamphobia and Racism, Al-Khoei Foundation and the Muslim College (2004) *Counter-Terrorism Powers: Reconciling Security and Liberty in an Open Society: Discussion Paper – A Muslim*

Response (London: FAIR) (online at http://www.fairuk.org/policy.htm).

FOSTER J (2003) 'Police Cultures' in NEWBURN T (ed), *The Handbook of Policing* (Cullompton: Willan).

FOSTER J (2008) '"It might have been incompetent, but it wasn't racist": murder detectives' perceptions of the Lawrence Inquiry and its impact on homicide investigation in London' 18(2) Policing and Society 89.

FOSTER J, NEWBURN T and SOUHAMI A (2005) *Assessing the Impact of the Stephen Lawrence Inquiry*, Home Office Research Study 294 (London: Home Office).

FOSTER S and LEIGH G (2016) 'Self-defence and the right to life; the use of lethal or potentially lethal force, UK domestic law, the common law and article 2 ECHR' 4 EHRLR 398.

FOUCAULT M (1977) *Discipline and Punish* (London: Allen Lane).

FOUCAULT M (1979) *The History of Sexuality* vol 1 (London: Allen Lane).

FOUCAULT M (2010) *The Government of Self and Others: Lectures at the Collège de France 1982–1983* (F Gros, ed; G Burchell, trans) (Palgrave Macmillan: Basingstoke)

FOUZDER M (2018) 'Criminal legal aid fragility putting rights at risk—MPs' *Law Society Gazette*, 26 July.

FOUZDER, M (2018) 'LAA relaxes "ghost" solicitor rule' *Law Society Gazette*, 2 July.

FOUZDER M (2020) 'Legal aid fees: MoJ offer to receive resounding "no"' *Law Society Gazette*, 20 March.

FOUZDER M (2018) 'MoJ goes on hiring spree to strengthen Public Defender Service' (online at: https://www.lawgazette.co.uk/practice/moj-goes-on-hiring-spree-to-strengthen-public-defender-service/5067311.article).

FOX D, DHAMI M and MANTLE G (2006) 'Restorative final warnings: Policy and practice' 45 Howard Jo 129.

FRANK N and LOMBNESS M (1988) *Controlling Corporate Illegality* (Cincinnati: Anderson).

FRANKEL M (1975) 'The Search for the Truth: An Umpireal View' 123 U Penn LR 1031.

FREEDMAN L (2005) *The Official History of the Falklands Campaign* (2 Vols) (London: Routledge).

FREEMAN M (1981) 'The Jury on Trial' CLP 65.

FULLER L (1978) 'The Forms and Limits of Adjudication' 92 Harv LR 353.

FUSSEY P and MURRAY D (2019) *Independent Report on the London Metropolitan Police Service's Trial of Live Facial Recognition Technology* (Colchester, University of Essex)

GALANTER M (1983) 'Mega-Law and Mega-Lawyering in the Contemporary United States' in DINGWALL R and LEWIS P (eds), *The Sociology of the Professions* (London: Macmillan).

GALLIGAN D (1987) 'Regulating Pre-Trial Decisions', in DENNIS I (ed), *Criminal Law and Justice* (London: Sweet & Maxwell).

GALLIGAN D and SANDLER D (2004) 'Implementing Human Rights' in HALLIDAY S and SCHMIDT P (eds), *Human Rights Brought Home* (Oxford: Hart).

GARCIA-BLANCO I and BENNETT L (2021) 'Between a "media circus" and "seeing justice being done": Metajournalistic discourse and the transparency of justice in the debate on filming trials in British newspapers' 22(1) Journalism 176–195.

GARLAND D (1990) *Punishment and Modern Society* (Oxford: Clarendon Press).

GARLAND D (1996) 'The Limits of the Sovereign State: Strategies of Crime Control in Contemporary Society' 36 BJ Crim 445.

GARLAND D (1999) '"Governmentality" and the Problem of Crime' in SMANDYCH R (ed), *Governable Places: Readings on governmentality and crime control* (Aldershot: Ashgate).

GARLAND D (2001) *The Culture of Control* (Oxford: OUP).

GARSIDE R, GRIMSHAW R, FORD M and MILLS H (2019) *UK Justice Policy Review* Vol 8 (London: Centre for Crime and Justice Studies).

GASKARTH J (2011) 'Entangling Alliances? The UK's Complicity in Torture in the Global War on Terrorism' 87(4) *International Affairs* 945–964.

GASTIL J. DEESS, P. WEISER, P and SIMMONS C (2010) *The Jury and Democracy: How Jury Deliberation Promotes Civic Engagement and Political Participation* (Oxford: OUP).

GEARTY C (2005) '11 September 2001, Counter-terrorism, and the Human Rights Act' 32 Jo Law and Society 18.

GEARTY C (2006) *Can Human Rights Survive?* (Cambridge: CUP).

GELLES M, McFADDEN R, BORUM R and VOSSEKUIL B (2005) 'Al-Qaeda-related subjects: a law enforcement perspective' in WILLIAMSON T (ed), *Investigative Interviewing: Rights, Research, Regulation* (Cullompton: Willan).

GELSTHORPE L and GILLER H (1990) 'More Justice for Juveniles' Crim LR 153.

GEMMILL R and MORGAN-GILES R (1981) *Arrest, Charge and Summons: Arrest Practice and Resource Implications* (Royal Commission on Criminal Procedure, Research Study no 9) (London: HMSO).

GENDERS E (1999) 'Reform of the Offences Against the Person Act: Lessons from the Law in Action' Crim LR 689.

GIANNOULOPOULOS D (2019) *Improperly Obtained Evidence in Anglo-American and Continental Law* (Oxford: Hart).

GIBBS P (2017) *Defendants on video— Conveyor belt justice or a revolution in access?* (London: Transform Justice).

GIBBS P and KIRBY A (2014) *Judged by peers? The diversity of lay magistrates in England and Wales.* Working Paper. Institute for Criminal Policy Research (London: Birkbeck, University of London).

GILCHRIST E and BLISSETT J (2002) 'Magistrates' Attitudes to Domestic Violence and Sentencing Options' 41 Howard Journal 348.

GILL O (1976) 'Urban stereotypes and delinquent incidents' 16 BJ Crim 312.

GILL P (2000) *Rounding up the usual suspects? Developments in contemporary law enforcement intelligence* (Aldershot: Ashgate).

GILL P (2004) 'Policing in Ignorance?' 58 Criminal Justice Matters 14.

GILLEN REVIEW (2019) *Report into the law and procedures in serious sexual offences in Northern Ireland* (https://www.justice-ni.gov.uk/sites/default/files/publications/justice/gillen-report-may-2019.pdf).

GILLESPIE A (2005) 'Reprimanding juveniles and the right to due process' 68 MLR 1006.

GILLESPIE A (2009) 'Juvenile Informers' in BILLINGSLEY R (ed), *Covert Human Intelligence Sources: The 'unlovely face of police work'* (Hampshire: Waterside Press).

GILLESPIE A (2020) 'Juvenile informers: Is it appropriate to use children as Covert Human Intelligence Sources?' 79(3) Cam LJ 459–489.

GLAZEBROOK P (2002) 'A better way of convicting businesses of avoidable deaths and injuries?' 61 Cam LJ 405.

GLEESON E and GRACE K (2009) *Police Complaints: Statistics for England and Wales 2007/08, IPCC Research and Statistics Series: Paper 12* (London: IPCC).

GLIDEWELL I (1998) *Review of the Crown Prosecution Service: A Report* (Cm 3960) (London: HMSO).

GOBERT J (1989) 'The Peremptory Challenge – An Obituary' Crim LR 528.

GOBERT J (1997) *Justice, Democracy and the Jury* (Aldershot: Dartmouth).

GOBERT J (2008) 'The Corporate Manslaughter and Corporate Homicide Act 2007' 71 MLR 413.

GOBERT J and PUNCH M (2003) *Rethinking Corporate Crime* (London: Butterworths).

GOHLER J (2019) 'Victim rights in civil law jurisdictions' in BROWN D et al, *The Oxford Handbook of Criminal Process* (New York: OUP).

GOLDING B and SAVAGE S (2008) 'Leadership and Performance management' NEWBURN T (ed), *The Handbook of Policing*, 2nd edn (Cullompton: Willan).

GOLDSMITH A (1990) 'Taking Police Culture Seriously: Police Discretion and the Limits of the Law' 1 Policing and Society 91.

GOLDSMITH A (1991) 'External Review and Self-Regulation' in GOLDSMITH A (ed), *Complaints Against the Police: the Trend to External Review* (Oxford: OUP).

GOLDSMITH A and FARSON S (1987) 'Complaints against the Police in Canada: A New Approach' Crim LR 615.

GOLDSMITH A (2010) 'Policing's New Visibility' 50(5) BJ Crim 914–993.

GOLDSMITH C (2008) 'Cameras, Cops and Contracts: What Anti-social Behaviour Management Feels like to Young People' in SQUIRES P (ed), *ASBO Nation: The Criminalisation of Nuisance* (Bristol: The Policy Press).

GOOCH K and von BERG P (2019) 'What Happens in the Beginning, Matters in the End: Achieving Best Evidence with Child Suspects in the Police Station' 19 Youth Justice 85.

GOODMAN-DELAHUNTY J, DHAMI M and MARTSCHUK N (2014) 'Interviewing high value detainees: Securing cooperation and disclosures' 28 App Cog Psych 883–897.

GOOLD B (2004) *CCTV and Policing: Public Area Surveillance and Police Practices in Britain* (Oxford: OUP).

GORDON J (1992) 'Juries as Judges of the Law' 108 LQR 272.

GORDON P (1985) *Policing Immigration: Britain's Internal Controls* (London: Pluto Press).

GORDON P (1987) 'Community Policing: Towards the Local Police State' in SCRATON P (ed), *Law Order and the Authoritarian State* (Milton Keynes: Open UP).

GORIELY T (1996) 'The Development of Criminal Legal Aid in England and Wales' in YOUNG R and WALL D (eds), *Access to Criminal Justice: Legal Aid, Lawyers and the Defence of Liberty* (Oxford: Blackstone Press).

GORIELY T (2003) 'Evaluating the Scottish Public Defence Solicitors' Office' 30 JLS 84.

GORIELY T, MCCRONE P, DUFF P, KNAPP M, HENRY A, TATA C, LANCASTER B and SHERR A (2001) *The Public Defence Solicitors' Office in Edinburgh: An Independent Evaluation* (Edinburgh, Scottish Executive Central Research Unit).

GOTTFRIED E and CHRISTOPHER S (2017) 'Mental Disorders Among Criminal Offenders: A Review of the Literature' 23(3) Journal of Correctional Health Care 336–346.

GRACE S (1995) *Policing Domestic Violence in the 1990s* (Home Office Research Study no 139) (London: Home Office).

GRACE S (2014) '"Swift, Simple, Effective Justice?" Identifying the Aims of Penalty Notices for Disorder and Whether these have been Realised in Practice' 53(1) The Howard Journal 69–82.

GRACE S (2020) *Policing the coronavirus lockdown: The limits of on-the-spot fines* (online: BSC Policing Network Blog).

GRAHAM J, WOODFIELD K, TIBBLE M and KITCHEN S (2004) *Testaments of harm: a qualitative evaluation of the Victim Personal Statements Scheme* (London: National Centre for Social Research).

GRANTHAM R (2016) 'Investigative Interviewing in New Zealand' 1(1) iIIRG Bulletin 10.

GRAY A, FENN P and RICKMAN N (1996) 'Controlling Lawyers' Costs through Standard Fees: An Economic Analysis' in YOUNG R and WALL D (eds), *Access to Criminal Justice* (London: Blackstone).

GRAY J (2015) 'What constitutes a "reasonable belief" in consent to sex? A thematic analysis' 21(3) Journal of Sexual Aggression 357–353.

GRAY P (2005) 'The politics of risk and young offenders' experiences of social exclusion and restorative justice' 45(6) BJ Crim 938.

GREEN A (2008) *Power, Resistance, Knowledge: The epistemology of policing* (Sheffield: Midwinter & Oliphant).

GREEN A (2009) 'Challenging the Refusal to Investigate Evidence Neglected by Trial Lawyers' in NAUGHTON M (ed), *The Criminal Cases Review Commission* (London: Palgrave Macmillan).

GREEN A (2012) 'The Problem with Fresh Evidence' in NAUGHTON M and TAN G (eds), *Innocence Network UK (INUK) Symposium on the Reform of the Criminal Cases Review Commission* (INUK: online)

GREEN P (1990) *The Enemy Without: Policing and Class Consciousness in the Miners' Strike* (Milton Keynes: Open UP).

GREER S (1990) 'The Right to Silence: A Review of the Current Debate' 53 MLR 719.

GREER S (1994) 'Miscarriages of Criminal Justice Reconsidered' 57 MLR 58.

GREER S (1995) 'Towards a sociological model of the police informant' 46 BJ Sociol 509.

GREER S (1995) *Supergrasses* (Oxford: OUP).

GREER S (2001) 'Where the grass is greener? Supergrasses in comparative perspective' in BILLINGSLEY R, NEMITZ T and BEAN P (eds), *Informers: Policing, Policy, Practice* (Cullompton: Willan).

GREER S (2005) 'Protocol 14 and the Future of the European Court of Human Rights' PL 83.

GREER S (2006) *The European Convention on Human Rights: Achievements, Problems and Prospects* (Cambridge: CUP).

GREER S (2008) 'Human rights and the struggle against terrorism in the United Kingdom' 2 EHRLR 163.

GREER C and MCLAUGHLIN E (2012) '"This is not Justice": Ian Tomlinson, Institutional Failure and the Press Politics of Outrage' 52(2) BJ Crim.

GREGORY J (1976) *Crown Court or Magistrates' Court?* (Office of Population Censuses and Surveys) (London: HMSO).

GREGORY J and LEES S (1996) 'Attrition in rape and sexual assault cases' 36 BJ Crim 1.

GREIG-MIDLANE J (2019) 'An institutional perspective of neighbourhood policing reform in austerity era England and Wales' 21(4) International Journal of Police Science & Management 230–243.

GREVLING K (1997) 'Fairness and the exclusion of evidence' 113 LQR 667.

GRIFFITH J (1997) *The Politics of the Judiciary*, 5th edn (London: Fontana).

GRIFFITHS B and MURPHY A (2001) 'Managing anonymous informants through Crimestoppers' in BILLINGSLEY R, NEMITZ T and BEAN P (eds), *Informers: Policing, Policy, Practice* (Cullompton: Willan).

GRIFFITHS D and SANDERS A (2013) The road to the dock: prosecution decision-making in medical manslaughter cases. in SANDERS A and GRIFFITHS D (eds), *Bioethics, Medicine and the Criminal Law: Medicine, Crime and Society vol. 2* (Cambridge: CUP).

GRIMSHAW R and FORD M (2018) Young people, violence and knives- revisiting the evidence and policy discussion, Centre for Crime and Justice Studies, UK Justice Policy Review Focus (online at: https://www.crimeandjustice.org.uk/sites/crimeandjustice.org.uk/files/Knife%20crime.%20November.pdf).

GROSSKURTH A (1992) 'With Science on their Side' *Legal Action*, May, p 7.

GUDJONSSON G (2003) *The Psychology of Interrogations and Confessions: A Handbook* (Chichester: Wiley).

GUDJONSSON G (2007) 'Investigative Interviewing' in NEWBURN et al (eds), *Handbook of Criminal Investigation* (Cullompton: Willan).

GUDJONSSON G (2017) 'Memory distrust syndrome, confabulation and false confession' 87 Cortex 156–165.

GUDJONSSON G and MACKEITH J (1990) 'A Proven Case of False Confession: Psychological Aspects of the Coerced-compliant Type' 30 Med Sci Law 187.

GUDJONSSON G, SIGURDSSON J, SIGURDARDOTTIR A, STEINTHORSSON H and SIGURDARDOTTIR V (2014) 'The Role of Memory Distrust in Cases of Internalised

False Confession' 28 Appl Cognit Psy chol 336–348.

GUS JOHN PARTNERSHIP (2003) *Race for Justice: a review of CPS decision making for possible racial bias at each stage of the prosecution process* (London: CPS).

HAGGERTY K and SANDHU A (2017) 'Policing on Camera' 21 Theoretical Criminology 78.

HAIL-JARES K, LOWREY-KINBERG B, DUNN K and GOULD J (2018) 'False Rape Allegations: Do they Lead to a Wrongful Conviction Following the Indictment of an Innocent Defendant?' 37(2) Justice Quarterly 281–303.

HAIN P (1976) *Mistaken Identity* (London: Quartet).

HAINES F (1997) *Corporate Regulation: Beyond 'Punish or Persuade'* (Oxford: Clarendon).

HAKKANEN H, ASK K, KEBBELL M, ALISON L and Anders Granhag P (2009) 'Police Officers' Views of Effective Interview Tactics with Suspects: The Effects of Weight of Case Evidence and Discomfort with Ambiguity' 23 Appl Cog Psych 468.

HALES G (2020) *Perspectives on Policing: A diversity uplift? Police workforce and ethnicity trends* (London: The Police Foundation).

HALL A (1990) 'Police Complaints: Time for a Change' *Legal Action*, August, p 7.

HALL J (2020) The Terrorism Acts in 2018 (online at https://terrorismlegislationreviewer.independent.gov.uk/wp-content/uploads/2020/03/Terrorism-Acts-in-2018-Report-1.pdf).

HALL M (2013) *Victims of Environmental Crime* (London: Routledge).

HALL M (2018) *Victims of Crime: Construction, Governance and Policy* (Basingstoke: Palgrave Macmillan).

HALL S, CRITCHER C, JEFFERSON T, CLARKE J and ROBERTS B (1978) *Policing the Crisis* (London: Macmillan).

HALLIDAY J (2001) *Making Punishments Work: Report of a Review of the Sentencing Framework for England and Wales* (London: Home Office).

HALLIGAN-DAVIS G, and SPICER K (2004) *Piloting 'on the spot' penalties for disorder: final results from a one-year pilot, Findings 257* (London: Home Office).

HALLSWORTH S (2005) *Street Crime* (Cullompton: Willan).

HALLSWORTH S (2006) 'Racial Targeting and Social Control: Looking behind the Police' 14 Crit Crim 293–311.

HAMLYN B, PHELPS A, TURTLE J and SATTAR G (2004) *Are Special Measures Working? Evidence from Surveys of Vulnerable and Intimidated Witnesses* (Home Office Research Study 283) (London: Home Office).

HAMPTON P (2005) *Reducing Administrative Burdens: Effective Inspection and Enforcement* (HM Treasury, London: SO).

HANLON G and JACKSON J (1999) 'Last Orders at the Bar? Competition, Choice and Justice for All. The Impact of Solicitor-Advocacy' 19(4) OJLS 555.

HANNAN M, HEARNDEN I, Grace K and Bucke T (2011) *Deaths in or following police custody: examination of the cases 1998/09–2008/09* (London: HMIC).

HARCOURT B (2010) 'Neoliberal Penality: A Brief Genealogy' 14 Theoretical Criminology 74.

HARDING C, FENNELL P, JORG N and SWART B (1995) *Criminal Justice in Europe: A Comparative Study* (Oxford: Clarendon).

HARDWICK N (2016) 'Inspecting the Prison' in JEWKES Y, BENNETT J AND CREWE B (eds), *Handbook on Prisons*, 2nd edn (Abingdon, Routledge).

HARDWICK N and MURRAY R (2019) 'Regularity of OPCAT visits by NPMs in Europe' 25(1) Aus JHR 66–90.

HARFIELD C (2009) 'Regulation of CHIS' in BILLINGSLEY R (ed), *Covert Human Intelligence Sources: The 'unlovely face of police work'* (Hampshire: Waterside Press).

HARFIELD C (2012) 'Police Informers and Professional Ethics' 31 Criminal Justice Ethics 2 73–95.

HARFIELD C and HARFIELD K (2018) *Covert Investigation* (Oxford: OUP).

Hargreaves J (2018) 'Police Stop and Search Within British Muslim Communities: Evidence for the Crime Survey 2006–11' 58(6) BJ Crim 1281–1302.

Hargreaves J, Cooper J, Woods E and McKee C (2016) *Police Workforce, England and Wales, 31 March* Home Office Statistical Bulletin 05/16 (London: Home Office).

Hargreaves J, Linehan C and McKee C (2017) *Police Powers and Procedures, England and Wales, Year ending 31 March 2016* (London: Home Office).

Harlow C and Rawlings R (1997) *Law and Administration*, 2nd edn (London: Butterworths).

Harris D, O'Boyle M and Warbrick C (1995) *Law of the European Convention on Human Rights* (London: Butterworths).

Harris J and Grace S (1999) *A question of evidence? Investigating and prosecuting rape in the 1990s, Home Office Research Study 196* (London: Home Office).

Harrison J and Cuneen M (2000) *An Independent Police Complaints Commission* (London: Liberty).

Harrison J, Cragg S and Williams H (2005) *Police Misconduct: Legal Remedies*, 4th edn (London: LAG).

Hart H (1961) *The Concept of Law* (Oxford: Clarendon).

Hartless J, Ditton J, Nair G and Phillips S (1995) 'More Sinned Against than Sinning: A Study of Young Teenagers' Experience of Crime' 35 BJ Crim 114.

Hartwig M, Anders Granhag P and Vrij A (2005) 'Police Interrogation from a Social Psychology Perspective' 15(4) Policing & Society 379.

Harvey D (2005) *A Brief History of Neoliberalism* (Oxford: OUP).

Harvey D (2014) 'The Googling Juror: The Fate of the Jury Trial in the Digital Paradigm' NZ L Rev 203

Hastie R, Penrod S and Pennington N (1983) *Inside the Jury* (Cambridge, Mass: Harvard UP).

Havis S and Best D (2004) *Stop and Search Complaints: A Police Complaints Authority Study* (London: Police Complaints Authority).

Hawkins K (1983) 'Bargain and Bluff' 5 L Pol Q 8.

Hawkins K (1984) *Environment and Enforcement* (Oxford: OUP).

Hawkins K (1990) 'Compliance Strategy, Prosecution Policy, and Aunt Sally: A Comment on Pearce and Tombs' 30 BJ Crim 444.

Hawkins K (2002) *Law as Last Resort* (Oxford: OUP).

Haworth K (2018) 'Tapes, transcripts and trials: The routine contamination of police interview evidence' 22(4) IJ E&P 428–450.

Hayes M (1981) 'Where Now the Right to Bail?' Crim LR 20.

Healy J (2020) '"It spreads like a creeping disease": experiences of victims of disability hate crimes in austerity Britain' 35 Disability and Society 176.

Heap V (2016) Putting victims first? A critique of coalition anti-social behaviour policy' 36 Critical Social Policy 246.

Heard C and Fair H (2019) Pre-trial detention and its over-use: evidence from ten countries. Institute for Crime and Justice Policy Research, London, UK (online at: https://eprints.bbk.ac.uk/30084/1/pre-trial%20detention%20final.pdf).

Heaton R (2000) 'The prospects for intelligence-led policing' 9 Policing and Society 337.

Heaton R (2009) 'Intelligence-Led Policing and Volume Crime Reduction' 3 Policing 292.

Heaton-Armstrong A and Wolchover D (2007) 'Woeful Neglect' 157 NLJ 624.

Heaton-Armstrong A, Shepherd E, Gudjonsson G and Wolchover D (eds) (2006) *Witness Testimony* (Oxford: OUP).

Heaton-Armstrong I (1986) 'The Verdict of the Court . . . and its Clerk?' 150 JP 340.

Hedderman C and Moxon D (1992) *Magistrates' court or Crown Court? Mode of trial decisions and sentencing* (Home Office Research Study no 125) (London: HMSO).

HEFFERNAN L (2009) 'DNA and Fingerprint Retention; *S and Marper v UK*' 34(3) Europ LR 491.

HEIDE S and CHAN T (2018) 'Deaths in police custody' 57 Journal of Forensic and Legal Medicine 109–114.

HELM R (2019a) 'Conviction by consent? Vulnerability, autonomy, and conviction by guilty plea' 83(2) JCrim L 161–172.

HELM R (2019b) 'Constrained Waiver of Trial Rights? Incentives to Plead Guilty and the Right to a Fair Trial' 46(3) JLS 423–447.

HENDERSON E (2016) 'Taking control of cross-examination' Crim LR 181.

HENDRY J and KING C (2017) 'Expediency, Legitimacy, and the Rule of Law: A Systems Perspective on Civil/Criminal Procedural Hybrids' 11 Criminal Law and Philosophy 733–757.

HENHAM R (1999) 'Bargain Justice or Justice Denied? Sentence Discounts and the Criminal Process' 63 MLR 515.

HENHAM R (2000) 'Reconciling Process and Policy: Sentence Discounts in the Magistrates' Courts' Crim LR 436.

HENHAM R (2002) 'Further Evidence on the Significance of Plea in the Crown Court' 41 Howard Journal 151.

HENKEL L and COFFMAN J (2004) 'Memory Distortions in Coerced False Confessions: A Source Monitoring Framework Analysis' 18 Appl Cognit Psychol 567–588.

HENLEY M, DAVIS R and SMITH B (1994) 'The reactions of prosecutors and judges to victim impact statements' 3 Int Rev Victimology 83.

HER MAJESTY'S CHIEF INSPECTOR OF PRISONS (2019) *Annual Report for 2018–19 HC 2469* (London: House of Commons).

HER MAJESTY'S COURT and TRIBUNAL SERVICE (2018) *Guide to Commencing Proceedings in the Court of Appeal Criminal Division* (London: HMCTS).

HER MAJESTY'S COURTS and TRIBUNAL SERVICE and MINISTRY OF JUSTICE (2019) *Experimental statistics on Failure to Appear warrants in the magistrates' courts* (London: Ministry of Justice).

HER MAJESTY'S COURTS and TRIBUNALS JUDICIARY (2017) Court of Appeal (Criminal Division) Annual Report 2016–17 (Online at: https://www.judiciary.uk/wp-content/uploads/2018/08/coa-criminal-div-2016-17-2.pdf).

HER MAJESTY'S COURTS and TRIBUNALS JUDICIARY (2018) *Judicial Diversity Statistics* (London: Ministry of Justice).

HER MAJESTY'S CROWN PROSECUTION SERVICE INSPECTORATE (1999a) *Evaluation of Lay Review and Lay Presentation* (London: HMCPSI).

HER MAJESTY'S CROWN PROSECUTION SERVICE INSPECTORATE (1999b) *Review of adverse cases* (London, HMCPSI).

HER MAJESTY'S CROWN PROSECUTION SERVICE INSPECTORATE (2000) *Thematic Review of the Disclosure of Unused Material* (London: HMCPSI).

HER MAJESTY'S CROWN PROSECUTION SERVICE INSPECTORATE (2002) *Report on the Thematic Review of Casework Having a Minority Ethnic Dimension* (April). (London: HMCPSI).

HER MAJESTY'S CROWN PROSECUTION SERVICE INSPECTORATE (2002a) *Review of HQ casework* (London: HMCPSI).

HER MAJESTY'S CROWN PROSECUTION SERVICE INSPECTORATE (2002b) *Report on the Thematic Review of Casework Having a Minority Ethnic Dimension* (April) (London: HMCPSI).

HER MAJESTY'S CROWN PROSECUTION SERVICE INSPECTORATE (2003), *Thematic review of attrition in the prosecution process* (London: HMCPSI).

HER MAJESTY'S CROWN PROSECUTION SERVICE INSPECTORATE (2004a) *Violence at Home* (London: HMCPSI).

HER MAJESTY'S CROWN PROSECUTION SERVICE INSPECTORATE (2004b) *A follow-up review of cases with an ethnic minority dimension* (London: HMCPSI).

HER MAJESTY'S CROWN PROSECUTION SERVICE INSPECTORATE (2007) *Discontinuance-Thematic Review* (London: HMCPSI).

HER MAJESTY'S CROWN PROSECUTION SERVICE INSPECTORATE(2008a) *Disclosure—Thematic Review* (London: HMCPSI).

HER MAJESTY'S CROWN PROSECUTION SERVICE INSPECTORATE (2008b) *File Management and Organisation: An Audit of CPS Performance* (London: HMCPSI).

HMCPSI (2009) *Report of the thematic review of the quality of prosecution advocacy and case presentation* (London: HMCPSI).

HER MAJESTY'S CROWN PROSECUTION SERVICE INSPECTORATE (2015) *Thematic review of the CPS advocacy strategy and progress against the recommendations of the follow-up report of the quality of prosecution advocacy and case presentation* (London: HMCPSI).

HER MAJESTY'S CROWN PROSECUTION SERVICE INSPECTORATE (2016a) *Better Case Management. A Snapshot* (London: HMCPSI).

HER MAJESTY'S CROWN PROSECUTION SERVICE INSPECTORATE (2016b) *Communicating with victims* (London: HMCPSI).

HER MAJESTY'S CROWN PROSECUTION SERVICE INSPECTORATE (2017) *Business as usual? A follow-up review of the effectiveness of the Crown Prosecution Service contribution to the Transforming Summary Justice Initiative. Publication No. CP001:1219* (London: HMCPSI).

HER MAJESTY'S CROWN PROSECUTION SERVICE INSPECTORATE (2018) *Victim Liaison Units: Letters sent to the public by the CPS* (London: HMCPSI).

HER MAJESTY'S CROWN PROSECUTION SERVICE INSPECTORATE (2019) *Rape Inspection Publication No CP001:1267* (London: HMCPSI).

HER MAJESTY'S CROWN PROSECUTION SERVICE INSPECTORATE (2020) *Disclosure of Unused Material in the Crown Court* (London: HMCPSI).

HMCPSI and HMIC (2002) *Report on the Joint Inspection into the Investigation and Prosecution of cases Involving Allegations of Rape* (London: HMCPSI).

HMCPSI and HMIC (2004) *Violence at Home: The Investigation and Prosecution of Cases Involving Domestic Violence* (London: HMCPSI).

HMCPSI and HMIC (2007) *Without consent: Report on the joint inspection into the investigation and prosecution of cases involving allegations of rape* (London: HMCPSI).

HMCPSI and HMIC (2008) *Joint Thematic Review of the New Charging Arrangements* (London: HMCPSI).

HMCPSI and HMIC (2012) *Joint Inspection on Young Victims and Witnesses* (London: HMCPSI).

HMCPSI, HMICA and HMIC (2009) *Report of a Joint Thematic Review of Victim and Witness Experiences in the Criminal Justice System* (London: HMCPSI).

HER MAJESTY'S GOVERNMENT (2016) *Ending Violence against Women and Girls Strategy 2016–2020* (London: Home Office).

HER MAJESTY'S GOVERNMENT (2018) *Hate Crime, England and Wales, 2017/18* (London: Home Office).

HMIC (2011) *Adapting to Austerity* (London: HMIC).

HMIC (2014) *Crime-Recording: Making the Victim Count* (London: HMIC).

HMIC (2014) *Everyone's Business: Improving the Police Response to Domestic Abuse* (London: HMIC).

HMIC (2015) *Increasingly Everyone's Business: A Progress Report on the Police Response to Domestic Abuse* (London: HMIC).

HMIC (2015) *The welfare of vulnerable people in police custody* (London: HMIC).

HMIC (2015) *Witness for the prosecution: Identifying victim and witness vulnerability in criminal case files* (London: HMIC)

HMIC and HMCPSI (2007) *Justice in policing: A joint thematic review of the handling of cases involving an allegation of a criminal offence by a person serving with the police* (London: HMIC).

HER MAJESTY'S INSPECTORATE OF CONSTABULARY and FIRE and RESCUE SERVICES (2013) Stop and Search Powers: Are the police using them effectively and fairly? (HMIC: London) (Online at https://www.justiceinspectorates.gov.uk/hmicfrs/media/stop-and-search-powers-20130709.pdf).

HER MAJESTY'S INSPECTORATE OF CONSTABULARY and FIRE and RESCUE SERVICES (2018) *Understanding the difference. The initial police response to hate crime* (London: HMICFRS).

HER MAJESTY'S INSPECTORATE OF CONSTABULARY and FIRE and RESCUE SERVICES (2020a) *The Hard Yards: Police to police collaboration* (London: HMICFRS).

HER MAJESTY'S INSPECTORATE OF CONSTABULARY and FIRE and RESCUE SERVICES (2020b) PEEL spotlight report: Diverging under pressure (HMCFRS: London).

HER MAJESTY'S INSPECTORATE OF PRISONS (2000) *Unjust Deserts* (December) (HMPI: London).

HER MAJESTY'S INSPECTORATE OF PRISONS (2012) *Remand prisoners: A thematic review* (HMPI: London).

HER MAJESTY'S INSPECTORATE OF PRISONS and HMIC (2009) *Report on an inspection visit to police custody suites in Cambridgeshire Constabulary* (London: HMIP and HMIC).

HER MAJESTY'S PRISON SERVICE (2013) *Order 6101 Bail Information Scheme* (London: Ministry of Justice).

HERBERT A (2003) 'Mode of Trial and Magistrates' Sentencing Powers: Will increased powers inevitably lead to a reduction in the committal rate?' Crim LR 314.

HERBERT A (2004) 'Mode of Trial and the Influence of Local Justice' 43 Howard Jo 65.

HERBERT P (1995) 'Racism, impartiality and juries' 145 NLJ 1138.

HESTER M (2009) *Who Does What to Whom? Gender and Domestic Violence Perpetrators* (Bristol: University of Bristol in association with the Northern Rock Foundation).

HESTER M and WESTMARLAND N (2005) *Tackling Domestic Violence: effective interventions and approaches*, Home Office Research Study 290 (London: Home Office).

HESTER M, HANMER J, COULSON S, MORAHAN A and RAZAK A (2003) *Domestic Violence: making it through the criminal justice system* (Sunderland: University of Sunderland).

HEWITT S (2010) *Snitch! A History of the Modern Intelligence Informer* (London: Continuum Books).

HICKMAN T (2005) 'Between Human Rights and the Rule of Law: Indefinite Detention and the Derogation Model of Constitutionalism' 68(4) MLR 655.

HICKMAN T (2008) 'The courts and politics after the Human Rights Act: a comment' PL 84.

HILL D, MCLEOD S and TANYI A (2018) 'The concept of entrapment' 12 Crim Law and Phil 539.

HILL R, COOPER K, HOYLE C and YOUNG R (2003a) *Introducing Restorative Justice to the Police Complaints System: Close Encounters of the Rare Kind*, Occasional Paper No 20 (Oxford: Centre for Criminological Research).

HILL R, COOPER K, YOUNG R and HOYLE C (2003b) *Meeting Expectations: The Application of Restorative Justice to the Police Complaints Process*, Occasional Paper No 21 (Oxford: Centre for Criminological Research).

HILLIARD B (1987) 'Holloway Road – Unfinished Business' 137 NLJ 1035.

HILLSBOROUGH INDEPENDENT PANEL (2012) *The Report of the Hillsborough Independent Panel* (London: The Stationery Office).

HILLYARD P (1987) 'The Normalization of Special Powers: from Northern Ireland to Britain' in SCRATON P (ed), *Law, Order and the Authoritarian State* (Milton Keynes: Open UP).

HILLYARD P (1993) *Suspect Community* (London: Pluto Press).

HILLYARD P and GORDON D (1999) 'Arresting statistics: the drift to informal justice in England and Wales' 26 JLS 502.

HILLYARD P (1993) *Suspect Community* (London: Pluto Press).

HILLYARD P, PANTAZIS C, TOMBS S and GORDON D (eds) (2004) *Beyond Criminology: Taking Harm Seriously* (London: Pluto Press).

HILSON C (1993) 'Discretion to Prosecute and Judicial Review' Crim LR 739.

HILTON N, HARRIS G and RICE M (2007) 'The Effect of Arrest on Wife Assault Recidivism: Controlling for Pre-Arrest Risk' 34(10) Criminal Justice and Behaviour 1334.

HINE J (2019) 'Women and Criminal Justice: Where Are We Now?' 15(1) British Journal of Community Justice 5–18

HIRST P (2019) 'Mass surveillance in the age of terror: bulk powers in the Investigatory Powers Act 2016' 4 EHRLR 403.

HMCPSI (2020) CPS Responses to Covid-19 (online at: https://www.justiceinspectorates.gov.uk/hmcpsi/inspections/cps-response-to-covid-19-16-march-to-8-may-2020/).

HMIC (2015) *The welfare of vulnerable people in police custody* (Online: HM Inspectorate of Constabulary)

HMIC (2015) Witness for the prosecution: Identifying victim and witness vulnerability in criminal case files (online at: https://www.justiceinspectorates.gov.uk/hmicfrs/publications/vulnerability-in-criminal-case-files/).

HMIC (2018) Expectations for police custody: Criteria for assessing the treatment of and conditions for detainees in police custody (online at: https://www.justiceinspectorates.gov.uk/hmiprisons/wp-content/uploads/sites/4/2018/05/Police-Expectations-2018.pdf).

HMICFRS (2016) *Report on an unannounced inspection visit to police custody suites in Lancashire 31 May–10 June 2016 by HM Inspectorate of Prisons and HM Inspectorate of Constabulary* (Online: HMICFRS).

HMICFRS (2019) *Report on an unannounced inspection visit to police custody suites in the Metropolitan Police Service, 8–20 July 2018* (Online: HMICFRS).

HMICFRS (2020) *Sussex Police—Joint Inspection Report—February 2020* (Online: HMICFRS).

HMIP and HMIC (2009) *Report on an inspection visit to police custody suites in Cambridgeshire Constabulary*, 24–26 November 2008 (online at: https://www.justiceinspectorates.gov.uk/hmicfrs/media/cambridgeshire-custody-suites-joint-inspection-20080229.pdf).

HOARE J and FLATLEY J (2008) *Drug Misuse Declared: Findings from the 2007/08 British Crime Survey* (London: Home Office).

HOBBS D (1988) *Doing the Business* (Oxford: OUP).

HOBBS D, HADFIELD P, LISTER S and WINLOW S (2003) *Bouncers: Violence and Governance in the Night-time Economy* (Oxford: OUP).

HODGSON J (1992) 'Tipping the Scales of Justice: The Suspect's Right to Legal Advice' Crim LR 854.

HODGSON J (1994) 'Adding Injury to Injustice: the Suspect at the Police Station' 21 JLS 85.

HODGSON J (1997) 'Vulnerable Suspects and the Appropriate Adult' Crim LR 785.

HODGSON J (2001) 'The police, the prosecutor and the juge d'instruction' 41 BJ Crim 342.

HODGSON J (2002) 'Hierarchy, Bureaucracy and Ideology in French Criminal Justice' 29 JLS 227.

HODGSON J (2003) 'Codified Criminal Procedure and Human Rights: Some Observations on the French Experience' Crim LR 165.

HODGSON J (2005) *French Criminal Justice* (Oxford: Hart).

HODGSON J (2020) *The Metamorphosis of Criminal Justice* (Oxford: OUP).

HODGSON J and HORNE J (2008) *The extent and impact of legal representation on applications to the Criminal Cases Review Commission (CCRC)* (Warwick: Warwick University).

HODGSON J, HORNE J and SOUBISE L (2018) *The Criminal Cases Review Commission*

Last resort or first appeal? (Warwick: Criminal Justice Centre, University of Warwick).

HODGSON J and TADROS V (2013) 'The Impossibility of Defining Terrorism' 16(3) NCLR 494–526.

HOFMEYR K (2006) 'The problem of private entrapment' Crim LR 319.

HOLDAWAY S (1983) *Inside the British Police* (Oxford: Blackwell).

HOLDAWAY S (1996) *The Racialisation of British Policing* (Houndmills: Macmillan).

HOLDAWAY S (2003) 'Final warning: Appearance and Reality' 4 Criminal Justice 355.

HOLDAWAY S and O'NEILL M (2007) 'Where has all the racism gone? Views of racism within constabularies after Macpherson' 30(3) Ethnic and Racial Studies 397.

HOLIDAY Y, GUILD E and MITSILEGAS V (2018) *The Court of Appeal and the Criminalisation of Refugees* (London: QMUL and Birmingham).

HOLMBERG L (2019) 'In service of the truth? An evaluation of the Danish Independent Police Complaints Authority' 16(5) European Journal of Criminology 592–611.

HOME AFFAIRS COMMITTEE (1981–82) *Report on Miscarriages of Justice* (HC 421) (London: TSO).

HOME AFFAIRS COMMITTEE (1998–99) *The Work of the Criminal Cases Review Commission* (HC 569) (London: TSO).

HOME AFFAIRS COMMITTEE (2007–2008) *Policing in the 21st Century, Seventh Report* (HC 364-I) (London: TSO).

HOME AFFAIRS COMMITTEE (2015) *Hate crime and its violent consequences inquiry* (HC 609) (London: TSO).

HOME AFFAIRS SELECT COMMITTEE (2008) *Policing in the 21st Century* HC 364-I, Seventh Report (2007–2008) (London: HMSO).

HOME OFFICE (1972) *Report of the Commission to Consider Legal Procedures to Deal with Terrorist Activities in Northern Ireland* (Cmnd 5185) (London: HMSO).

HOME OFFICE (1986) *Criminal Justice, Plans for Legislation* (Cmnd 9658) (London: Home Office).

HOME OFFICE (1986) *Report of the Departmental Committee on Fraud Trials* (London: HMSO).

HOME OFFICE (1990) *Domestic Violence (Circular 66/90)* (London: Home Office)

HOME OFFICE (1992a) *Guide to Interviewing* (London: HMSO).

HOME OFFICE (1992b) *Costs of the Criminal Justice System 1992, vol 1* (London: Home Office).

HOME OFFICE (1997a) *Review of Delay in the Criminal Justice System* (Narey Report) (London: Home Office).

HOME OFFICE (1997b) *Statistics on the Operation of Prevention of Terrorism Legislation* (HO Stat Bull, 4/97) (London: Home Office).

HOME OFFICE (1998a) *Juries in Serious Fraud Trials* (London: Home Office Communication Directorate).

HOME OFFICE (1998b) *Speaking up for Justice, Report of the Interdepartmental Working Group on the treatment of Vulnerable or Intimidated Witnesses in the Criminal Justice System* (London: Home Office).

HOME OFFICE (1999) *Statistics on Race and the Criminal Justice System 1998* (London: Home Office).

HOME OFFICE (2001a) *Achieving best evidence in criminal proceedings: Guidance for vulnerable and intimidated witnesses, including children* (London: Home Office).

HOME OFFICE (2001b) *Statistics on the Operation of Prevention of Terrorism Legislation* (Statistical Bulletin 16/01) (London: Home Office).

HOME OFFICE (2002) *Justice for All* (Cm 5563) (London: TSO).

HOME OFFICE (2003a) *Making a Victim Personal Statement* (London: Home Office).

HOME OFFICE (2003b) *Safety and Justice: The Government's Proposals on Domestic Violence* (Cm 5847) (London: TSO).

HOME OFFICE (2004) *An evaluation of the phased implementation of the recording of police stops* (London: Home Office).

HOME OFFICE (2004a) *Building Communities, Beating Crime—A better police service for the 21st Century* (Cm 6360) (London: TSO).

HOME OFFICE (2004b) *Modernising Police Powers to Meet Community Needs—A Consultation Paper* (London: Home Office).

HOME OFFICE (2004c) *National Policing Plan 2005–2008: Safer, Stronger Communities* (London: Home Office).

HOME OFFICE (2004d) *An evaluation of the phased implementation of the recording of police stops* (London: Home Office).

HOME OFFICE (2005a) *Stop & Search Manual* (London: Home Office).

HOME OFFICE (2005b) *Criminal Statistics England and Wales 2004* (Home Office Statistical Bulletin 19/05) (London: Home Office).

HOME OFFICE (2007) *The Corston Report: A Report by Baroness Jean Corston of a Review of Women with Particular Vulnerabilities in the Criminal Justice System* (London: Home Office).

HOME OFFICE (2008) *PACE Review: Government proposals in response to the Review of the Police and Criminal Evidence Act 1984* (Policing Powers and Protection Unit) (London: Home Office).

HOME OFFICE (2009a) *Statistics on Terrorism Arrests and Outcomes Great Britain, 11 September 2001 to 31 March 2008, Statistical Bulletin 04/09* (London: Home Office).

HOME OFFICE (2009b) *Regulation of Investigatory Powers Act 2000: Consolidating Orders and Codes of Practice, A Public Consultation* (London: Home Office).

HOME OFFICE (2009c) *Crime in England and Wales: Quarterly Update to December 2008 (Statistical Bulletin 06/09)* (London: Home Office).

HOME OFFICE (2012) *Police Powers to Prosecute Strengthened* (London: Home Office).

HOME OFFICE (2014) Best Use of Stop and Search Scheme (online at https://assets.publishing.service.gov.uk/government/uploads/system/uploads/attachment_data/file/346922/Best_Use_of_Stop_and_Search_Scheme_v3.0_v2.pdf).

HOME OFFICE (2015) *The Strategic Policing Requirement* (London: Home Office).

HOME OFFICE (2016) *Do initiatives involving substantial increases in stop and search reduce crime? Assessing the impact of Operation BLUNT 2* (London: Home Office).

HOME OFFICE (2017a) *Anti-social Behaviour, Crime and Policing Act 2014: Reform of Anti-social Behaviour Powers—Statutory Guidance for Frontline Professionals* (London: Home Office)

HOME OFFICE (2017b) *Police officer misconduct, unsatisfactory performance and attendance management procedures* (London: Home Office).

HOME OFFICE (2018a) *Covert Human Intelligence Sources: Revised Code of Practice* (CHIS Code) (London: Home Office).

HOME OFFICE (2018b) *Ethnicity facts and figures: Police workforce* (London: Home Office).

HOME OFFICE (2018c) *Operation of police powers under the Terrorism Act 2000 and subsequent legislation: Arrests, outcomes, and stop and search, Great Britain, quarterly update to December 2017 Statistical Bulletin 05/18* (London: Home Office).

HOME OFFICE (2018d) *Police powers and procedures, England and Wales, year ending 31 March 2018*, (London: Home Office, 2018).

HOME OFFICE (2019a) *Crime Outcomes in England and Wales: year ending March 2019*, (Statistical Bulletin 12/19) (London: Home Office).

HOME OFFICE (2019b) *Operation of Police powers under the Terrorism Act 2000 and subsequent legislation, year ending March 2019* (London: Home Office).

Home Office (2019c) *Police Powers and Procedures, England and Wales, year ending 31 March 2019* (London: Home Office).

Home Office (2019d) Police powers and procedures, England and Wales, October (London: Home Office). (Available at https://assets.publishing.service.gov.uk/government/uploads/system/uploads/attachment_data/file/841408/police-powers-procedures-mar19-hosb2519.pdf).

Home Office (2019e) *Police Use of Force Statistics, England and Wales, April 2018 to March 2019* (London: Home Office).

Home Office (2020a) *Arrests September 2020* (online at: https://www.ethnicity-facts-figures.service.gov.uk/crime-justice-and-the-law/policing/number-of-arrests/latest).

Home Office (2020b) *Interviewing Suspects* (London: Home Office).

Home Office (2020c) *Operation of police powers under the Terrorism Act 2000 and subsequent legislation*, Bulletin 15/20 (London: Home Office).

Home Office (2020d) *Police Powers: Pre-charge Bail Government consultation* (London: Home Office).

Home Office, APCC, and NPCC (2019) *Forensics Review: Review of the provision of forensic science to the criminal justice system in England and Wales* (London: Home Office).

Honess T and Matthews G (2012) 'Admitting Evidence of a Defendant's Previous Convictions (PCE) and its impact on juror deliberations in relation to juror processing style and juror concerns over the fairness of introducing PCE' 17(2) *Legal and Criminological Psychology* 360–379.

Honess T, Levi M and Charman E (1998) 'Juror Competence in Processing Complex Information: Implications from a Simulation of the Maxwell Trial' Crim LR 763.

Hood C (1991) 'A Public Management for all Seasons?' 69(1) *Public Administration* 3–19.

Hood C, James O, Jones G, Scott C and Travers T (1999) *Regulation Inside Government* (Oxford: OUP).

Hood R (1992) *Race and Sentencing* (Oxford: OUP).

Hood R and Shute S (2000) *The Parole System at Work* (Home Office Research Study no 202) (London: Home Office).

Hood R, Shute S and Seemungal F (2003) *Ethnic Minorities in the Criminal Courts: Perceptions of Fairness and Equality of Treatment Research Series no. 2/03* (London: DCA).

Hooker B (2000) 'Rule-Consequentialists' in LaFollette H (ed), *The Blackwell Guide to Ethical Theory* (Oxford: Blackwell).

Hopkins K, Uhrig N and Colahan M (2016) *Associations between ethnic background and being sentenced to prison in the Crown court in England and Wales in 2015* (London: Ministry of Justice).

Hopkins M and Sparrow P (2006) 'Sobering up: Arrest referral and brief intervention for alcohol users in the custody suite' 6(4) *Criminology & Criminal Justice* 389.

Horne J (2016) *A Plea of Convenience: An Examination of the Guilty Pleas in England & Wales*, PhD thesis, University of Warwick.

Horowitz I, Keer N, Park E and Gockel C (2006) 'Chaos in The Courtroom Reconsidered: Emotional Bias and Juror Nullification' 30 *Law and Human Behaviour* 163.

Hough M (2012) 'Researching trust in the police and trust in justice: a UK perspective' 22(3) *Policing and Society* 332–345.

Hough M (2020) *Good Policing: Trust, Legitimacy and Authority* (Bristol: Policy Press).

Hough M and Mayhew P (1985) *Taking Account of Crime* (Home Office Research Study no 111) (London: HMSO).

Hough M, Jacobson J and Millie A (2003) *The Decision to Imprison: Sentencing and the Prison Population* (London: Prison Reform Trust).

House of Commons (2009) *Report of the Interception of Communications Commissioner for 2008* (HC 901) (London: TSO).

House of Commons (2013) *Independent Police Complaints Commission* (London: TSO).

House of Commons (2016) *Role of the magistracy within the criminal justice system* (London: TSO).

House of Commons Committee of Public Accounts (2015) *Inspection in Home Affairs and Justice.* (London: TSO).

House of Commons Home Affairs Committee (2016) *Role of the magistracy within the criminal justice system* (HC 165) (London: TSO).

House of Commons Home Affairs Select Committee (1998) *Police Disciplinary and Complaints Procedure, 1st Report* (HC 258-1). (London: TSO).

House of Commons Justice Committee (2018) *Criminal Legal Aid* (HC 1069) (London: TSO).

House of Lords Science and Technology Committee (2019) *Forensic science and the criminal justice system: A blueprint for change* (HL Paper 333) (London: TSO).

Howard League for Penal Reform (1993) *The Dynamics of Justice* (Report of the Working Party on Criminal Justice Administration) (London: Howard League).

Howard League for Penal Reform (2016) *Is this the end of women's centres?* (London: Howard League).

Howard League for Penal Reform (2019) *Arresting the entry of women into the criminal justice system* (London: Howard League).

Howes L (2020) 'Interpreted investigative interviews under the PEACE interview model: police interviewers' perceptions of challenges and suggested solutions' 21(4) Police Practice and Research 333–350.

Hoyano L (2014) 'What is balanced on the Scales of Justice? In search of the Essence of the Right to a Fair Trial' Crim LR 4.

Hoyano L (2015) 'Reforming the adversarial trial for vulnerable witnesses and defendants' Crim LR 107.

Hoyano L (2019) 'Cross-examination of sexual assault complainants on previous sexual behaviour: views from the barristers' row' Crim LR 77.

Hoyano A, Hoyano L, Davis G and Goldie S (1997) 'A Study of the Impact of the Revised Code for Crown Prosecutors' Crim LR 556.

Hoyano L and Rafferty A (2017) 'Rationing Defence Intermediaries under the April 2016 CPD' Crim LR 93.

Hoyle C (1988) *Negotiating Domestic Violence* (Oxford: Clarendon).

Hoyle C (2012) 'Feminism, Victimology and Domestic Violence' in Walklate, S (ed) *Handbook of Victims and Victimology* (Abingdon: Routledge).

Hoyle C (2016) 'Compensating Injustice: The Perils of the Innocence Discourse' in Hunter et al (eds), *The Integrity of Criminal Process: From Theory to Practice* (Oxford: Hart).

Hoyle C and Sanders A (2000) 'Domestic violence: From victim choice to victim empowerment' 40 BJ Crim 14.

Hoyle C and Sato M (2019) *Reasons to Doubt. Wrongful Convictions and the Criminal Cases Review Commission* (Oxford: OUP).

Hoyle C, Cape E, Morgan R and Sanders A (1998) *Evaluation of the 'One Stop Shop' and Victim Statement Pilot Projects* (London: Home Office).

Hucklesby A (1992) 'The Problem with Bail Bandits' 142 NLJ 558.

Hucklesby A (1994) 'The Use and Abuse of Conditional Bail' 33 Howard JCJ 258.

Hucklesby A (1996) 'Bail or Jail? The Practical Operation of the Bail Act 1976' 23 JLS 213.

Hucklesby A (1997a) 'Court Culture: An Explanation of Variations in the Use of Bail by Magistrates Courts' 36 Howard JCJ 129.

Hucklesby A (1997b) 'Remand Decision Makers' Crim LR 269.

HUCKLESBY A (2001) 'Police Bail and the Use of Conditions' 1(4) Criminal Justice 441.

HUCKLESBY A (2004) 'Not necessarily a trip to the police station' Crim LR 803.

HUCKLESBY A (2013) *Pre-charge bail: an investigation of its use in two police forces. Briefing Paper* (Leeds: University of Leeds).

HUCKLESBY A and LISTER S (eds) (2017) *The Private Sector and Criminal Justice* (London: Palgrave).

HUCKLESBY A and MARSHALL E (2000) 'Tackling offending on bail' 39(2) Howard JCJ 150.

HUDSON B (2000) 'Punishing the Poor: Dilemmas of Justice and Difference' in HEFFERNAN W and KLEINIG J (eds), *From Social Justice to Criminal Justice: Poverty and the Administration of Criminal Law* (Oxford: OUP).

HUDSON B (2002) 'Restorative Justice and Gendered Violence: Diversion or Effective Justice?' 42 BJ Crim 616.

HUDSON B (2003) *Justice in the Risk Society* (London: Sage).

HUDSON B (2011) 'Regulating democracy: justice, citizenship and inequality in Brazil' in QUIRK, H, SEDDON T and SMITH G (eds), *Regulation and Criminal Justice* (Cambridge: CUP).

HUGHES G (2007) *The Politics of Crime and Community* (London: Palgrave Macmillan).

HUGHES G, PILKINGTON A and LEISTAN R (1998) 'Diversion in a Culture of Severity' 37 Howard JCJ 16.

HULLEY S, CREWE B and WRIGHT S (2019) 'Making Sense of "Joint Enterprise" for Murder: Legal Legitimacy or Instrumental Acquiescence?' 59(6) BJ Crim 1328–1346.

HUMAN GENETICS COMMISSION (2009) *Nothing to Hide, Nothing to Fear?* (London: HGC).

HUNGERFORD-WELCH P (2017) 'Better Case Management' *Counsel Magazine*, October.

HUNTER M (1994) 'Judicial discretion: s 78 in practice' Crim LR 558.

HUNTER R (2012) 'The Power of Feminist Judgments?' 20(2) Feminist Legal Studies 135–148.

HUNTER R (2015) 'More than Just a Different Face? Judicial Diversity and Decision-making' 68 CLP 119–141.

HUNTER R, MCGLYNN C and RACKLEY E (eds) (2010) *Feminist Judgments: From Theory to Practice* (Oxford: Hart Publishing).

HUQ A (2019) 'Racial equity in algoritic criminal justice' 68(6) Duke Law Journal 1043–1135.

HUTTER B (1988) *The Reasonable Arm of the Law?* (Oxford: OUP).

HYLAND K and WALKER C (2014) 'Undercover policing and underwhelming laws' Crim LR 555.

HYNES S (2008) 'Fixed Fees, best value tendering and the CDS' March, *Legal Action*, p 6.

HYNES S and ROBINS J (2009) *The Justice Gap-whatever happened to legal aid?* (London: LAG).

ILIADIS M and FLYNN A (2018) 'Providing a Check on Prosecutorial Decision-making: An Analysis of the Victims' Right to Review Reform' 58 BJ Crim 550.

INCE J, ROJAS F and DAVIS C (2017) 'The social media response to Black Lives Matter: how Twitter users interact with Black Lives Matter through hashtag use' 40(11) Ethnic and Racial Studies 1814–1830.

INDEPENDENT OFFICE FOR POLICE CONDUCT (2019a) *Police complaints statistics for England and Wales 2018/19* (Sale: IOPC).

INDEPENDENT OFFICE FOR POLICE CONDUCT (2018b) Police Complaints: Statistics for England and Wales 2017/18 (London: IOPC) (nline at: https://policeconduct.gov.uk/sites/default/files/Documents/statistics/complaints_statistics_2017_18.pdf).

INDEPENDENT OFFICE FOR POLICE CONDUCT (2019c) *The Independent Office for Police Conduct: Public Perceptions Tracker, Summary of Research for 2018–19.* (Sale: IOPC).

Independent Office for Police Conduct (2019d), *Making information available.* (Sale: IOPC).

Independent Office for Police Conduct (2020a) *Statutory guidance on the police complaints system* (Sale: IOPC).

Independent Office for Police Conduct (2020b) *Guidance on capturing data about police complaints* (Sale: IOPC).

Independent Office for Police Conduct (2020c) *Frequently asked questions (February 2020).* (Sale: IOPC).

Independent Office for Police Conduct (2020d) *IOPC independent investigations: Information for police officers, staff and their representatives* (Sale: IOPC).

Independent Police Complaints Commission (IPCC) (2008a), *Building on Experience* ('Stocktake Consultation') (London: IPCC).

Independent Police Complaints Commission (IPCC) (2008b) *Near Misses in Police Custody: A Collaborative Study with Forensic Medical Examiners in London.* (London: IPCC).

Independent Police Complaints Commission (IPCC) (2009a) *Annual Report and Statement of Accounts 2008/9: incorporating our report on deaths during or following police contact* (London: IPCC).

Independent Police Complaints Commission (IPCC) (2009b) *Police complaints and discipline, 2008/9* (London: IPCC).

Independent Police Complaints Commission (IPCC) (2016) *IPCC Position Statement on Body Worn Video* (London: IPCC).

Information Commissioner's Office (2020) *Mobile phone data extraction by police forces in England and Wales: Investigation Report* (London: ICO).

Innes M (2000) '"Professionalising" the role of the police informant' 9 Policing and Society 357.

Innes M (2003) *Investigating Murder: Detective Work and the Police Response to Criminal Homicide* (Oxford: OUP).

Innes M, Fielding N and Cope N (2005) 'The Appliance of Science?: The Theory and Practice of Crime Intelligence analysis' 45 BJ Crim 39.

Innes M, Roberts C, Lowe T and Innes H (2020) *Neighbourhood Policing* (Oxford: OUP).

Inquest (2000) *Death in Police Custody: Report on Harry Stanley* (London: Inquest).

Institute for Government (2019) *Criminal courts - 10 Key Facts* (London: Institute for Government).

Institute of Fiscal Studies (2015) *IFS Green Budget 2015* (London: IFS).

Intelligence and Security Committee of Parliament (2018) *Detainee Mistreatment and Rendition: 2001–2010* (London: TSO).

Interception of Communications Commissioner (2009) *Report of the Interception of Communications Commissioner for 2008* (HC 901).

Investigatory Powers Commissioner's Office (2018) *Annual Report 2018* (HC 67) (London: IPCO).

IOPC (2019) *Deaths during or following police contact* (Online: IOPC).

IOPC (2019a) *Police complaints statistics for England and Wales 2018/19* (online at: https://policeconduct.gov.uk/research-and-learning/statistics/complaints-statistics).

IOPC (2019b) *Statutory guidance to the police force on achieving best evidence in death and serious injury matters* (online at: https://www.policeconduct.gov.uk/sites/default/files/Documents/statutoryguidance/statutory-guidance-section-22-guidance.pdf).

IOPC (2019c) *The Independent Office for Police Conduct: Public Perceptions Tracker, Summary of Research for 2018–19* (online at: https://www.policeconduct.gov.uk/research-and-learning/statistics/public-confidence-and-engagement).

IOPC (2019d) *Deaths during or following police contact: Statistics for England and Wales 2018/19* (online at: https://www.

policeconduct.gov.uk/sites/default/files/ Documents/statistics/deaths_during_ following_police_contact_201819.pdf).

IOPC (2020a) *Statutory guidance on the police complaints system* (online at: https://policeconduct.gov.uk/ complaints-reviews-and-appeals/ statutory-guidance).

IOPC (2020b) *Guidance on capturing data about police complaints* (online at: https:// policeconduct.gov.uk/sites/default/files/ Documents/statutoryguidance/Guidance_ on_capturing_data_about_police_ complaints.pdf).

IOPC (2020c) *Frequently asked questions* (February 2020) (online at: https://www. policeconduct.gov.uk/sites/default/files/ Documents/Complaint_forms/IOPC_ Complaints_FAQs_2020.pdf).

IPCC (2006) *Report, dated 27th February 2006, of the Review into the events leading up to and following the death of Christopher Alder on 1st April 1998* (London: IPCC).

IPCC (2008) *Building on Experience* ('Stocktake Consultation') (London: IPCC).

IPCC (2008) *Near Misses in Police Custody: A Collaborative Study with Forensic Medical Examiners in London* (London: IPCC).

IPCC (2017) *Annual report and statement of accounts* (online at: https://policeconduct. gov.uk/who-we-are/accountability-and-performance/annual-report-and-plans).

IPSOS MORI (2016) *Public Confidence in the Police Complaints System 2016 report prepared for the Independent Police Complaints Commission* (London: Ipsos MORI).

IRVING B (1980) *Police Interrogation: A Study of Current Practice* (Royal Commission on Criminal Procedure Research Paper no 2) (London: HMSO).

IRVING B and DUNNIGHAN C (1993) *Human Factors in the Quality Control of CID Investigations* (Royal Commission on Criminal Justice, Research Study no 21) (London: HMSO).

IRVING B and MCKENZIE I (1989) *Police Interrogation: The Effects of the Police and Criminal Evidence Act 1984* (London: Police Foundation).

IRWIN-ROGERS K (2018) 'Racism and racial discrimination in the criminal justice system: Exploring the experiences and views of men serving sentences of imprisonment' 2(2) Justice, Power and Resistance 243–266.

JACKSON J (1993) 'Trial Procedures' in WALKER C and STARMER K (eds), *Justice in Error* (London: Blackstone).

JACKSON J (1995) 'Evidence: Legal Perspective' in BULL R and CARSON D (eds), *Handbook of Psychology in Legal Contexts* (Chichester: Wiley).

JACKSON J (1996) 'Judicial Responsibility in Criminal Proceedings' 49 CLP 59.

JACKSON J (2001) 'Silence and proof: extending the boundaries of criminal proceedings in the UK' 5 IJ E&P 145.

JACKSON J (2003) 'Justice for all: Putting victims at the heart of criminal justice?' 30 JLS 309.

JACKSON J (2008) 'Police and Prosecutors after PACE: The Road from Case Construction to Case Disposal' in CAPE E and YOUNG R (eds), *Regulating Policing* (Oxford: Hart).

JACKSON J (2013) 'Justice, Security and the Right to a Fair Trial: Is the Use of Secret Evidence Ever Fair?' PL 720–736.

JACKSON J and DORAN S (1992) 'Diplock and the Presumption Against Jury Trial: a critique' Crim LR 755.

JACKSON J and DORAN S (1995) *Judge without Jury* (Oxford: OUP).

JACKSON J and DORAN S (1997) 'Judge and Jury: Towards a New Division of Labour in Criminal Trials' 60 MLR 759.

JACKSON J, HUQ A, BRADFORD B and TYLER T (2013) 'Monopolizing force?: police legitimacy and public attitudes towards the acceptability of violence' Psychology, Public Policy and Law 13–14

JACOBSON J (2008) *No One Knows: Police Responses to Suspects with Learning Disabilities and Learning Difficulties* (London: Prison Reform Trust).

JACOBSON J (2013) *By Mistakes We Learn? A review of criminal appeals against sentence. Project Report.* (London: Transform Justice)

JACOBSON J, HUNTER G and KIRBY A (2015) *Structured Mayhem: Personal Experiences of the Crown Court* (London: Criminal Justice Alliance).

JACOBSON J, HUNTER G and KIRBY A (2015) *Inside Crown Court* (Bristol: Policy Press).

JACOBSON J, KIRBY A and HUNTER G (2016) *Joint Enterprise: Righting A Wrong Turn?* (London: Prison Reform Trust).

JACONELLI J (2002) *Open Justice: A Critique of the Public Trial* (Oxford: OUP).

JAMES A, TAYLOR N and WALKER C (2000) 'The Criminal Cases Review Commission: Economy, Effectiveness and Justice' Crim LR 140.

JEFFERSON T and GRIMSHAW R (1984) *Controlling the Constable: Police Accountability in England and Wales* (London: Muller)

JEFFERSON T and WALKER M (1992) 'Ethnic Minorities in the Criminal Justice System' Crim LR 83.

JEHLE J and WADE M (eds) (2006) *Coping with Overloaded Criminal Justice Systems: The Rise of Prosecutorial Power Across Europe* (Berlin: Springer).

JENNINGS W, STOKER G and WARREN I (2019) 'Brexit and public opinion: cities and towns- the geography of discontent'. *Brexit and Public Opinion.* (London: Kings College).

JEORY T (2016) Austerity and class divide likely factors behind Brexit vote, major survey suggests. *The Independent*, 29 June

JEREMY D (2008) 'The prosecutor's rock and hard place' Crim LR 925.

JOHNSON A (2008) '"From where we're sat . . .": Negotiating narrative transformation through interaction in police interviews with suspects' 28(3) Text & Talk 327–349.

JOHNSON A (2014) 'Foucault. Critical theory of the police in a neoliberal age' 61(141) Theoria 5–29.

JOHNSTON E (2020) 'The adversarial defence lawyer: Myths, disclosure and efficiency—A contemporary analysis of the role in the era of the Criminal Procedure Rules'24(1) IJ E&P 35–58.

JOHNSTON L, BUTTON M and WILLIAMSON T (2008) 'Police, governance and the Private Finance Initiative' 18(3) Policing and Society 225–244.

JONES C (1994) *Expert Witnesses* (Oxford: OUP).

JONES C and VAGG J (2007) *Criminal Justice in Hong Kong* (Abingdon: Routledge).

JONES D (2020) 'The Potential Impacts of Pandemic Policing on Police Legitimacy: Planning Past the COVID-19 Crisis' 14(3) *Policing: A Journal of Policy and Practice* 579–586.

JONES J (2007) 'Persons With Intellectual Disabilities in the Criminal Justice System: Review of Issues' 51(6) Int J of Offender Therapy and Comp Criminol 723–733.

JONES J (2017) 'The patronising disposition of unaccountable power' A report to ensure the pain and suffering of the Hillsborough families is not repeated (online at: https://assets.publishing.service.gov.uk/government/uploads/system/uploads/attachment_data/file/656130/6_3860_HO_Hillsborough_Report_2017_FINAL_updated.pdf).

JONES L et al (2012) 'Prevalence and risk of violence against children with disabilities' 38 *The Lancet* 899.

JONES S (2008) 'Partners in Crime: A study of the relationship between female offenders and their co-defendants' 8(2) Criminology & Criminal Justice 147.

JONES T (2003) 'The governance and accountability of policing' in NEWBURN T (ed), *The Handbook of Policing* (Cullompton: Willan).

JONES T (2008) 'The accountability of policing' in NEWBURN T (ed), *The Handbook of Policing* 2nd edn (Cullompton: Willan).

JONES T and LISTER S (2019) 'Localism and police governance in England & Wales: Exploring continuity and change' 16(5) EurJ Crim 552–572.

JONES T and NEWBURN T (2002) 'The Transformation of Policing? Understanding Current Trends in Policing Systems' 42(1) BJ Crim 129.

JONES T and NEWBURN T (2012) 'The Convergence of US and UK Crime Control Policy: Exploring Substance and Process' in NEWBURN T and SPARKS R (eds), *Criminal Justice and Political Cultures* (Devon: Willan Publishing).

JONES T, NEWBURN T and SMITH D (1996) 'Policing and the Idea of Democracy' 36 BJ Crim 182.

JORG N, FIELD S and BRANTS C (1995) 'Are Inquisitorial and Adversarial Systems Converging?' in HARDING C, FENNELL P, JORG N and SWART B (eds), *Criminal Justice in Europe* (Oxford: Clarendon).

JOYCE R and XU X (2019) *Inequalities in the twenty-first century. Introducing the IFS Deaton Review* (London: IFS).

JUDICIAL COLLEGE (2018) Crown Court Compendium, Part 1. Jury and Trial Management and Summing Up (online at: https://www.judiciary.uk/wp-content/uploads/2018/06/crown-court-compendium-pt1-jury-and-trial-management-and-summing-up-june-2018-1.pdf).

JULIAN R (2007) 'Judicial Perspectives on the conduct of serious fraud trials' Crim LR 751.

JULIAN R (2008) 'Judicial Perspectives in Serious Fraud Cases' Crim LR 764.

JUSTICE (1994) *Unreliable Evidence? Confessions and the Safety of Convictions* (London: Justice)

JUSTICE (2001) *Public Defenders: Learning from the US Experience* (London: Justice).

JUSTICE (2018) *Preventing Digital Exclusion from Online Justice* (London: Justice).

JUSTICE COMMITTEE (2013) *Transforming Legal Aid: evidence taken by the Committee.* (HC91) (London: TSO).

KAISER K and HOLTFRETER K (2016) 'An integrated theory of specialized court programs: Using procedural justice and therapeutic jurisprudence to promote offender compliance and rehabilitation' 43(1) Criminal Justice and Behavior 45–62.

KALUNTA-KRUMPTON A (1998) 'The Prosecution and Defence of Black Defendants in Drug Trials' 38 BJ Crim 561.

KALVEN H and ZEISEL H (1966) *The American Jury* (Boston: Little, Brown).

KASSIN S (2008) 'Confession Evidence: Commonsense Myths and Misconceptions' 35(10) Criminal Justice and Behavior 1309.

KASSIN S (2012) 'Why Confessions Trump Innocence' 67(6) American Psychologist 431–445

KASSIN S (2018) Why SCOTUS Should Examine the Case of "Making a Murderer's" Brendan Dassey (online at: https://www.apa.org/news/press/op-eds/scotus-brendan-dassey).

KATZ I, CORLYON J, LA PLACA V and Hunter S (2007) *The relationship between parenting and poverty* (York: Joseph Rowntree Foundation).

KAVEY M (2013) 'The public faces of privacy: Rewriting Lustig-Prean and Beckett v UK' in BREMS E (ed), *Diversity and European Human Rights: Rewriting Judgments of the ECHR* (Cambridge: CUP).

KAYE T (1991) *'Unsafe and Unsatisfactory?' Report of the Independent Inquiry into the Working Practices of the West Midlands Police Serious Crime Squad* (London: Civil Liberties Trust).

KEANE A and MCKEOWN P (2019) 'Time to abandon "beyond reasonable doubt" and "sure": the case for a new direction on the criminal standard and how it should be used' Crim LR 505.

KEANE A and MCKEOWN P (2020) *The Modern Law of Evidence* (Oxford: OUP).

KEBBELL M and GILCHRIST E (2004) 'Eliciting evidence from eyewitnesses in court' in ADLER J (ed), *Forensic Psychology: Concepts, Debates and Practice* (Cullompton: Willan).

KEBBELL M, ALISON L and HURREN E (2008) 'Sex Offenders' Perceptions of the effectiveness and fairness of humanity, dominance, and displaying an understanding of cognitive distortions in police interviews: a vignette study' 14(5) Psychology, Crime and Law 435.

Keenan C, Davis G, Hoyano L and Maitland L (1999) 'Interviewing Allegedly Abused Children with a View to Criminal Prosecution' Crim LR 863.

Keith M (1993) *Race, Riots and Policing* (London: UCL Press).

Kellough G and Wortley S (2002) 'Remand for Plea: Bail Decisions and Plea bargaining as Commensurate Decisions' 42 BJ Crim 186.

Kelly L, Lovett J and Regan L (2005) *A Gap or a Chasm?: Attrition in Reported Rape Cases, Home Office Research Study 293* (London: Home Office).

Kemp C, Norris C and Fielding N (1992) 'Legal Manoeuvres in Police Handling of Disputes' in Farrington D and Walklate S (eds), *Offenders and Victims, Theory and Policy* (London: British Society of Criminology).

Kemp V (2008) *A scoping study adopting a 'whole-systems' approach to the processing of cases in the Youth Courts* (London: Legal Services Research Centre).

Kemp V (2010) *Transforming legal aid: access to criminal defence services* (London: Legal Services Commission).

Kemp V (2013) '"No time for a solicitor": Implications for delays on the take up of legal advice' Crim LR 184–202.

Kemp V (2018) *Effective Police Station Legal Advice Country Report 2: England and Wales* (Online: University of Nottingham).

Kemp V (2020a) 'Digital legal rights: Exploring detainees' understanding of their right to have a lawyer and potential barriers to accessing legal advice' Crim LR 129–147.

Kemp V (2020b) 'Authorising and Reviewing Detention: PACE Safeguards in a Digital Age' Crim LR 569–584.

Kemp V and Balmer N (2008) *Criminal Defence Services: Users' Perspectives, Research Paper No. 21* (London: Legal Services Research Centre).

Kemp V, Pleasence P and Balmer N (2012) 'Whose time is it anyway? Factors associated with duration in police custody' Crim LR 736–752.

Kempe R (2020) 'Civilian oversight of the police: The case of Kenya' 93(3) *The Police Journal* 202–228.

Kempen K (2020) A summary review of talk given by the Deputy Chief Coroner at the IAP Keeping Safe Conference, *ICVA Newsletter*, 28 February.

Kempen K (2020) *ICVA update 1/5/20*, Weekly email update.

Kendall J (2018) *Regulating Police Detention* (Bristol: Police Press).

Kendall J (2020) 'Custody visiting: The watchdog that didn't bark' Criminology and Criminal Justice (online first).

Kerrigan K (2000) 'Unlocking the Human Rights Floodgates' Crim LR 71.

Kerrigan K (2006) 'Miscarriage of Justice in the Magistrates' Court: The Forgotten Power of the Criminal Cases Review Commission' Crim LR 124.

Kershaw C, Nicholas S and Walker A (2008) *Crime in England and Wales, 2007/8* (Home Office Statistical Bulletin 07/08) (London: Home Office).

Kessler A (2005) 'Our Inquisitorial Tradition: Equity Procedure, Due Process, and the Search for an Alternative to the Adversarial' 90 Cornell L Rev 1181.

Khan O and Shaheen F (eds) (2017) *Minority Report. Race and Class in post-Brexit Britain* (London: Runnymede Trust).

Kibble N (2000) 'The sexual history provisions' Crim LR 274.

Kibble N (2005) 'Judicial Perspectives on the Operation of s.41 and the Relevance and Admissibility of Prior Sexual History: Four Scenarios' Crim LR 190.

King M (1981) *The Framework of Criminal Justice* (London: Croom Helm).

KING M and MAY C (1985) *Black Magistrates* (London: Cobden Trust).

KIRBY A (2017) 'Effectively Engaging Victims, Witnesses and Defendants in the Criminal Courts' Crim LR 949.

KIRCHENGAST T (2016) *Victims and the criminal trial* (Basingstoke: Palgrave Macmillan).

KIRK D (2013) 'Editorial: The Jury's Out' 173 Journal of Criminal Law.

KNIGHT M (1970) *Criminal Appeals* (London: Stevens).

KNOP K and RILES A (2017) 'Space, Time and Historical Injustice: A Feminist Conflict-of-Laws Approach to the "Comfort Women" Settlement (December 16, 2016).' Cornell Legal Studies Research Paper No. 16–45, 102(3) Cornell L Rev.

KOFFMANN L 'Holding Parents to Account: Tough on Children, Tough on the Causes of Children' (2008) 35(1) J Law and Society 113.

KREBS B (2010) 'Joint Criminal Enterprise' 73 MLR 578–604.

KREBS B (2015) 'Mens rea in joint enterprise: a role for endorsement?' 74(3) Cam LJ 480–504.

KREBS B (2018) 'Joint Enterprise, Murder and Substantial Injustice: The First Successful Appeal Post-Jogee: R v Crilly [2018] EWCA Crim 168' 82(3) JCL 209–211.

KYD S, ELLIOT T and WALTERS M (2017) *Clarkson and Keating: Criminal Law* 9th edn (London: Sweet and Maxwell).

LACEY N (1994) 'Government as Manager, Citizen as Consumer: The Case of the Criminal Justice Act 1991' 57 MLR 534.

LACEY N (2007) 'Legal Constructions of Crime' in MAGUIRE M, MORGAN R and REINER R (eds), *Oxford Handbook of Criminology* 4th edn (Oxford: OUP).

LACEY N, WELLS C and QUICK O (2003) *Reconstructing Criminal Law* 3rd edn (London: LexisNexis).

LAING J (1995) 'The Mentally Disordered Suspect at the Police Station' Crim LR 371.

LAING J and MURRAY R (2017) 'Measuring the incidence of Article 3 ECHR violations in Places of Detention in the UK: Implications for the National Preventive Mechanism' EHRLR 564–588.

LAMMY D (2017) *The Lammy Review: An independent review into the treatment of, and outcomes for, Black, Asian and Minority Ethnic individuals in the Criminal Justice System* (London: HM Govt).

LANGBEIN J (1978) 'The Criminal Trial Before Lawyers' 45 U Ch LR 263.

LARCOMBE W (2002) 'The `Ideal' Victim v Successful Rape Complainants: Not What You Might Expect' 10(2) Feminist Legal Studies 131–148.

LARKIN P (2007) 'The criminalisation of social security law; towards a punitive welfare state?' 34 JLS 295.

LASSITER G, WARE L, RATCLIFF J and IRVIN C (2009) 'Evidence of the camera perspective bias in authentic videotaped interrogations' 14(1) Legal and Criminological Psychology 157.

LAW COMMISSION (1994a) *Binding Over* (Report No 222) (London: HMSO).

LAW COMMISSION (1994b) *Involuntary Manslaughter* (Report no 135) (London: HMSO).

LAW COMMISSION (1996a) *Evidence in Criminal Proceedings: Previous Misconduct of a Defendant, Consultation Paper no 141* (London: HMSO).

LAW COMMISSION (1996b) *Involuntary Manslaughter* (Report no 237) (London: HMSO).

LAW COMMISSION (1998) *Consents to Prosecution* (HC 1085) (Report no 255) (London: SO).

LAW COMMISSION (1999) *Bail and the Human Rights Act 1998* (Report no 269) (London: Law Commission).

LAW COMMISSION (2009) *Expert Evidence in Criminal Proceedings* (Consultation Paper No 325) (London: TSO).

LAW COMMISSION (2009) *The Admissibility of Expert Evidence in Criminal*

Proceedings (Consultation Paper No 190) (London: TSO).

LAW COMMISSION (2011) *Expert Evidence in Criminal Proceedings in England and Wales* (HC 829) (London: TSO).

LAW COMMISSION (2014) *Hate Crime: The Case For Extending The Existing Offences* LC213 (London: TSO).

LAW COMMISSION (2016) *Unfitness to plead* London: TSO).

LAW COMMISSION (2018) *Search Warrants* (Consultation Paper 235) (London: HMSO).

LAW COMMISSION (2020) *Search Warrants* HC 852 (London: HMSO).

LAW SOCIETY (2019a) *Criminal Justice System in Crisis. Parliamentary Briefing* (London: The Law Society).

LAW SOCIETY (2019b) *Influencing For Impact: The Need For Gender Equality In The Legal Profession* (London: The Law Society).

LAW SOCIETY (2019c) *Release under investigation: September 2019.* (London: The Law Society).

LAW SOCIETY (2020a) *Coronavirus (Covid-19) interview protocol.* (online at: https://www.lawsociety.org.uk/support-services/advice/articles/coronavirus-covid-19-interview-protocol/).

LAW SOCIETY (2020b) *Criminal legal aid review: latest proposals are insufficient* (London: The Law Society).

LAWRENCE F (1999) *Punishing Hate: bias crimes under American law* (Cambridge, Mass.: Harvard UP).

LAYCOCK G and TARLING R (1985) 'Police Force Cautioning: Policy and Practice' 24 Howard JCJ 81.

LE SUEUR A and SUNKIN M (1992) 'Applications for Judicial Review: The Requirement of Leave' PL 102.

LEA S, LANVERS U and SHAW S (2003) 'Attrition in Rape Cases' 43 BJ Crim 583.

LEA J and HALLSWORTH S (2013) 'Bringing the state back in: Understanding neoliberal security' in SQUIRES P and LEA J (eds), *Criminalisation and Advanced Marginality: Critically exploring the wok of Loic Wacquant* (Bristol: Policy Press).

LEE M (1998) *Youth, Crime, and Police Work* (Basingstoke: Macmillan).

LEE R (2005) 'Resources, Rights and Environmental Regulation' 32 JLS 111.

LEGAL SERVICES COMMISSION (2002) *Public Defender Service: first year of operation* (London: LSC).

LEGAL SERVICES COMMISSION (2004) A New Focus for Civil Legal Aid (London: LSC).

LEGAL SERVICES COMMISSION (2007) *Best Value Tendering of Criminal Defence Services* (London: LSC).

LEGAL SERVICES COMMISSION (2009) *Best Value Tendering for CDS Contracts 2010 – Consultation Paper* (London: LSC).

LEGGETT J, GOODMAN W and DINANI S (2007) 'People with learning disabilities' experiences of being interviewed by the police' 135 British Journal of Learning Disabilities 168.

LEGGETT Z (2019) 'The Test for "Substantial Injustice" After Jogee and Johnson: R v Towers and Another [2019] EWCA 198 (Crim)' 83(5) JCL 420–424.

LEIGH A, JOHNSON G and INGRAM A (1998) *Deaths in Police Custody: Learning the Lessons* (Home Office Police Research Series, Paper 26).

LEIGH L (2006) 'Lurking doubt and the safety of convictions' Crim LR 809.

LEIGH L (2007) '"The seamless web?" Diversion from the criminal process and judicial review' 70 MLR 654.

LEIGH L and ZEDNER L (1992) *A Report on the Administration of Criminal Justice in the Pre-Trial phase in England and Germany* (Royal Commission on Criminal Justice, Research Study no 1) (London: HMSO).

LENG R (1993) *The Right to Silence in Police Interrogation: A Study of Some of the Issues Underlying the Debate* (Royal Commission on Criminal Justice Research Study no 10) (London: HMSO).

LENG R (2001) 'Silence pre-trial, reasonable expectation and the normative distortion of fact-finding' 5 IJ E&P 240.

LENG R and TAYLOR R (1996) *Blackstone's Guide to the Criminal Procedure and Investigations Act 1996* (London: Blackstone).

LENG R, TAYLOR R and WASIK M (1998) *Blackstone's Guide to the Crime and Disorder Act 1998* (London: Blackstone).

LENNON G (2015) 'Precautionary Tales: suspicionless counter-terrorism stop and search' 15(1) CCJ 44–62.

LENS K et al (2015) 'Delivering a VIS: Emotionally effective or counter-productive?' 12 EurJ Crim 17.

LEO R (1994) 'Police Interrogation and Social Control' 3 Social and Legal Studies 93.

LEO R (2008) *Police Interrogation and American Justice* (Cambridge MA: Harvard UP).

LEO R (2020) 'Structural Police Deception in American Police Interrogation: A Closer Look at Minimization and Maximization' Interrogation Confession and Truth: Comparative Studies in Criminal Procedure 183–207.

LERMAN A and WEAVER V (2014) *Arresting Citizenship: The Democratic Consequences of American Crime Control* (Chicago: University of Chicago Press).

LEVESLEY T and MARTIN A (2005) *Police Attitudes to and use of CCTV* (Home Office Online Report 09/05) (London: Home Office).

LEVESON, LORD (2015) *Leveson's Review of Efficiency in Criminal Proceedings* (London: HMSO).

LEVESON, LORD (undated) 'Consistency and Confidence' *Counsel Magazine* (online).

LEVI M (2002) 'Economic Crime' in MCCONVILLE M and WILSON G (eds), *The Handbook of the Criminal Justice Process* (Oxford: OUP).

LEVI M and BURROWS J (2008) 'Measuring the impact of fraud in the UK' 48 BJ Crim 293.

LEVITAS R (2005) *The Inclusive Society?: Social Exclusion and New Labour*, 2nd edn (Basingstoke: Palgrave Macmillan).

LEWIS C, BROOKS G, BUTTON M, SHEPHERD D and WAKEFIELD A (2014) 'Evaluating the case for greater use of private prosecutions in England and Wales for fraud offences' 42(1) IJLCJ 3–15.

LEWIS H and MAIR G (1989) *Bail and Probation Work II: the use of London Bail Hostels for Bailees* (Home Office Research and Planning Unit Paper no 50) (London: Home Office).

LEWIS J (2007) 'The European Ceiling on Human Rights' PL 720.

LEWIS P (1997) 'The CPS and Acquittals by Judge: Finding the Balance' Crim LR 653.

LEWIS R (2004) 'Making Justice Work: Effective Legal Interventions for Domestic Violence' 44 BJ Crim 204.

LEXIS NEXIS (2016) '(Direct) Access All Areas: Is the Bar making the most of direct access?' 8 June (online).

LIBERTY (2009) *Home Office Consultation on the Regulation of Investigatory Powers Act 2000: Consolidating Orders and Codes of Practice* (London: Liberty).

LIBERTY (2009) Mobile Fingerprint Scanners Bring a Dangerous New Front to the Hostile Environment (London: Liberty) (Online at https://www.libertyhumanrights.org.uk/issue/mobile-fingerprint-scanners-bring-a-dangerous-new-front-to-the-hostile-environment/) (Accessed 31 August 2020).

LIDSTONE K (1984) 'Magistrates, the police and search warrants' Crim LR 449.

LIGHTOWLERS C and QUIRK H (2015) 'The 2011 English "Riots": Prosecutorial Zeal and Judicial Abandon' 55(1) BJ Crim 65–85.

LINDON G and ROE S (2017) *Deaths in police custody: A review of the international evidence* (London: Home Office).

LINDSEY J (2020) 'Protecting vulnerable adults from abuse' 32 CFLQ 157.

LIPPERT R (2014) 'Neo-Liberalism, Police, and the Governance of Little Urban Things' 18 Foucault Studies 49–65.

LIPPKE R (2017) 'A limited defence of what some will regard as entrapment' 23 Legal Theory 283.

LISTER S (2013) 'The New Politics of the Police: Police and Crime Commissioners and the "Operational Independence" of the Police' 7(3) Policing: A Journal of Policy and Practice 239–247.

LISTER S, SEDDON T, WINCUP E, BARRETT S and TRAYNOR P (2008) *Street Policing of Problem Drug Users* (York: Joseph Rowntree Foundation).

LITTLECHILD B (1995) 'Reassessing the Role of the "Appropriate Adult"' Crim LR 540.

LIVINGSTONE S and MURRAY R (2004) 'The Effectiveness of National Human Rights Institutions' in HALLIDAY S and SCHMIDT P (eds), *Human Rights Brought Home* (Oxford: Hart).

LLOYD-BOSTOCK S (2000) The Effects of Hearing About the Defendant's Previous Criminal Record: A Simulation Study' Crim LR 734.

LLOYD-BOSTOCK S (2007) 'The Jubilee Line Jurors: does their experience strengthen the argument for judge-only trial in long and complex fraud cases?' Crim LR 255.

LOADER I (1996) *Youth Policing and Democracy* (Basingstoke: Macmillan Press).

LOADER I (2020) *Revisiting the Police Mission* (London: Police Foundation) (online at: https://www.cgi-group.co.uk/sites/default/files/2020-04/the-police-foundation-strategic-policing.pdf).

LOADER I and MULCAHY A (2000) 'The power of legitimate naming: Part II – making sense of the elite police voice' 41(3) BJ Crim 252.

LOADER I and MULCAHY A (2001) 'The power of legitimate naming: Part I – Chief Constables as social commentators in post-war England' 41(1) BJ Crim 41.

LOADER I and MULCAHY A (2003) *Policing and the Condition of England: Memory, Politics and Culture* (Oxford: OUP).

LOADER I and WALKER I (2005) *Civilising Security* (Cambridge: CUP).

LOADER I and WALKER N (2001) 'Policing as a Public Good: Reconstituting the Connections between Policing and the State' 5(1) Theoretical Criminology 9–35.

LOFTUS B (2009) *Police Culture in a Changing World* (Oxford: OUP).

LOFTUS B (2019) 'Normalizing covert surveillance: the subterranean world of policing' 70 Br J Sociol 2070–2091.

LOFTUS B, GOOLD B and MACGIOLLASHUI S (2016) 'From a Visible Spectacle to an Invisible Presence: The Working Culture of Covert Policing' 56(4) BJ Crim 629–645.

LOFTUS E (2019) 'Eyewitness testimony' 33 Appl Cog Psychol 498–503.

LOGAN J and OAKLEY D (2017) 'Black lives and policing: The larger context of ghettoization' 39(8) Journal of Urban Affairs 1031–1046.

LONG J (2008) 'Keeping PACE? Some Front Line Policing Perspectives' in CAPE E and YOUNG R (eds), *Regulating Policing* (Oxford: Hart).

LONG L and JOSEPH-SALISBURY R (2019) 'Black mixed-race men's perceptions and experiences of the police' 42(2) Ethnic and Racial Studies 198–215.

LORD CHANCELLOR'S DEPARTMENT (LCD) (1992) *A New Framework for Local Justice* (Cm 1829) (London: LCD).

LOVEDAY B (1989) 'Recent developments in police complaints procedure' Local Gov Studies May/June 25.

LUDWIG A and FRASER J (2014) 'Effective use of forensic science in volume crime investigation: Identifying recurring themes in the literature' 54 Science and Justice 1 pp 81–88.

LUM C, STOLTZ M, KOPER C and SCHERER J (2019) 'Research on body-worn cameras: What we know, what we need to know' 18(1) Criminology & Public Policy 93–118.

LUNA E and WADE M (eds) (2012) *The Prosecutor in Transnational Perspective* (Oxford: OUP).

LUNDRIGAN S, DHAMI M and MUELLER-JOHNSON K (2016) 'Predicting verdicts using pre-trial attitudes and standard of proof' 21 Legal and Criminological Psychology 95–110.

LUSTGARTEN L (1986) *The Governance of the Police*. (London: Sweet & Maxwell).

LUSTGARTEN L (2003) 'The Future of Stop and Search' Crim LR 603.

LUSTGARTEN L (2006) 'Human Rights: Where Do We Go From Here?' 69(5) MLR 843.

LYNCH-WOOD G and WILLIAMSON D (2007) 'The social licence as a form of regulation for small and medium enterprises' 34 JLS 321.

LYNCH-WOOD G and WILLIAMSON D (2010) 'Regulatory compliance: organisational capacities & regulatory strategies for environmental protection' in QUIRK H, SEDDON T and SMITH G (eds), *Regulation and Criminal Justice* (Cambridge: CUP).

LYON D (2001) *Surveillance Society: Monitoring Everyday Life* (Buckingham: Open UP).

LYON D (2007) *Surveillance Studies: An Overview* (Cambridge: Polity Press).

LYON D (2018) *The Culture of Surveillance: Watching as a Way of Life* (Cambridge: Polity Press).

MACDONALD S (2006) 'A Suicidal Woman, Roaming Pigs and A Noisy Trampolinist: Refining the ASBOs definition of Anti-Social Behaviour' 69 MLR 183.

MACDONALD S and TELFORD M (2007) 'The use of ASBOS against young people in England and Wales: Lessons from Scotland' 27(4) Legal Studies 604.

MACK J (1976) 'Full-time Major Criminals and the Courts' 39 MLR 241.

MACPHERSON OF CLUNY, SIR W (1999) *The Stephen Lawrence Inquiry* (Cm 4262-I) (London: SO).

MACRORY R (2006a) *Regulatory Justice: Sanctioning in a post-Hampton world, Consultation Document* (London: Cabinet Office).

MACRORY R (2006b) *Regulatory Justice: Making Sanctions Effective* (London: Cabinet Office).

MADDOX G and TAN G (2012) 'Applicant Solicitors: Friends or Foes?' in M Naughton (ed) *The Criminal Cases Review Commission: Hope for the Innocent?* (London: Palgrave Macmillan).

MADGE N (2006) 'Summing Up - a judge's perspective' Crim LR 817.

MADOOD T (2003) 'Muslims and the Politics of Difference' Political Quarterly 100.

MAGUIRE M (1988) 'Effects of the PACE provisions on Detention and Questioning' 28(1) BJ Crim 19.

MAGUIRE M (2000) 'Policing by risks and targets: Some dimensions and implications of intelligence-led crime control' (2000) 9(4) Policing and Society 315–336.

MAGUIRE M (2002) 'Regulating the Police Station: The case of the Police and Criminal Evidence Act 1984' in MCCONVILLE M and WILSON G (eds), *The Handbook of the Criminal Justice Process* (Oxford: OUP).

MAGUIRE M and CORBETT C (1991) *A Study of the Police Complaints System* (London: HMSO).

MAGUIRE M and JOHN T (1995) *Intelligence, surveillance and informants: integrated approaches* (Police Research Series Paper 64) (London: Home Office).

MAGUIRE M and MCVIE S (2017) 'Criminal data and criminal statistics: A critical reflection' in Liebling A et al (eds), *The Oxford Handbook of Criminology* (Oxford: OUP).

MAGUIRE M and NORRIS C (1992) *The Conduct and Supervision of Criminal Investigations* (Royal Commission on Criminal Justice, Research Study no 5) (London: HMSO).

MAGUIRE M, MORGAN R and REINER R (eds) (2007) *Oxford Handbook of Criminology*, 4th edn (Oxford: OUP).

MAIMAN R (2004) ' "We've Had to Raise Our Game": Liberty's Litigation Strategy under the Human Rights Act 1998' in HALLIDAY S and SCHMIDT P (eds), *Human Rights Brought Home* (Oxford: Hart).

MAIR G and LLOYD C (1996) 'Policy and Progress in the Development of Bail Schemes in England and Wales' in PATERSON F (ed), *Understanding Bail in Britain* (Edinburgh: Scottish Office).

MAKEPEACE A (2008) 'Pumping up the volume to make legal aid profitable' Law Society Gazette (25 January).

Malik K (2020) That Clayton Barnes is still not a citizen shows the ongoing cruelty of 'hostile environment' *The Guardian*, 28 June.

Malleson K (1991) 'Miscarriages of Justice and the Accessibility of the Court of Appeal' Crim LR 323.

Malleson K (1993) *Review of the Appeal Process* (Royal Commission on Criminal Justice, Research Study no 17) (London: HMSO).

Malleson K (1994) 'Appeals against Conviction and the Principle of Finality' 21 JLS 151.

Malleson K (1995) 'The Criminal Cases Review Commission: How Will It Work?' Crim LR 929.

Malleson K (1997) 'Decision-making in the Court of Appeal: The Burden of Proof in an Inquisitorial Process' IJ E&P 175.

Malleson K and Roberts S (2002) 'Streamlining and Clarifying the Appellate Process' Crim LR 272.

Malone C (2012) 'Only the Freshest Will Do' in Naughton M (ed) *The Criminal Cases Review Commission: Hope for the Innocent?* (London: Palgrave Macmillan).

Manikis M (2012) 'Recognizing Victims' Role and Rights during Plea Bargaining: A Fair Deal for Victims of Crime' 58 CLQ 411.

Manikis M (2019) 'Conceptualising the Victim Within Criminal Justice Processes in the Common Law Tradition' in Brown D et al (eds), *The Oxford Handbook of Criminal Process* (New York: OUP).

Mansfield M and Taylor N (1993) 'Post-Conviction Procedures' in Walker C and Starmer K (eds), *Justice in Error* (London: Blackstone).

Mares H (2002) 'Balancing Public Interest And A Fair Trial In Police Informer Privilege: A Critical Australian Perspective' 6 IJ E&P 94.

Mark R (1973) *Minority Verdict* The 1973 Dimbleby Lecture (London: BBC).

Marks S (1995) 'Civil Liberties at the Margin: the UK Derogation and the European Court of Human Rights' 15 OJLS 68.

Marsh L (2016) 'Leveson's Narrow Pursuit of Justice: Efficiency and Outcomes in the Criminal Process' 54 CLWR

Marshall G (1978) 'Police Accountability Revisited' in Butler D and Halsey A (eds), *Policy and Politics* (London: Macmillan).

Martin D and Wilcox P (2012) 'Women, Welfare and the Carceral State' in Squires P and Lea J (eds), *Criminalisation and Advanced Marginality: Critically Exploring the Work of Loic Wacquant* (Bristiol: The Policy Press).

Martin S (2005) 'Lost and Destroyed Evidence: The Search for a Principled Approach to Abuse of Process' 9 IJE&P 158.

Marx G (1988) *Undercover: Police Surveillance in America* (Berkeley: UCLA Press).

Marx G (1992) 'Under-the-covers Undercover Investigation: Some Reflections on the States' Use of Sex and Deception in Law Enforcement' 11 Criminal Justice Ethics 1.

Marx G (2016) *Windows into the Soul: Surveillance and Society in an Age of High Technology* (Chicago: U of Chicago Press).

Mason G (2014) 'Legislating Against Hate' in Hall N, Corb A, Giannasi P and Grieve J (eds), *Routledge International Handbook on Hate Crime* (Abingdon: Routledge).

Mason G (2016) 'Violence as Hate Crime: The Emergence of a Discourse' in Stubbs J and Tomsen S (eds), *Australian Violence: Crime, Criminal Justice and Beyond* (Sydney: Federation Press).

Mason G, Maher J, McCulloch J, Pickering S, Wickes R and McKay C (2017) *Policing Hate Crime: Understanding Communities and Prejudice* (Abingdon: Routledge).

Mason-Bish H and Zempi I (2019) 'Misogyny, Racism, and Islamophobia: Street Harassment at the Intersections' 14(5) Feminist Criminology 540–559.

Masschaele J (2008) *Jury, State, and Society in Medieval England* (New York: Palgrave Macmillan).

MATRAVERS M (2004) '"More Than Just Illogical": Truth and Jury Nullification' in DUFF A, FARMER L, MARSHALL S and TADROS V (eds), *The Trial on Trial: Truth and Due Process* (Oxford: Hart).

MATRIX KNOWLEDGE GROUP (2008) *Dedicated Drug Court Pilots; A process report* (London: Ministry of Justice).

MATTHEWS R, HANCOCK L and BRIGGS D (2004) *Jurors' perceptions, understanding, confidence and satisfaction in the jury system: a study in six courts*, Online Report 05/04 (London: Home Office).

MATTINSON J (1998) *Criminal Appeals England and Wales, 1995 and 1996* (Research and Statistical Bulletin 3/98) (London: Home Office).

MAWBY R (2016) 'Victim Support in England and Wales: The End of an Era?' 22 International Review of Victimology 203.

MAWBY R and SMITH K (2017) 'Civilian Oversight of the Police in England and Wales: The Election of Police and Crime Commissioners in 2012 and 2016' 19(1) IJPSM 23–30.

MAXWELL G and MORRIS A (2002) 'The Role of Shame, Guilt, and Remorse in Restorative Justice Processes for Young People' in WEITEKAMP E and KERNER H (eds), *Restorative Justice: Theoretical Foundations* (Devon: Willan Publishing).

MAY R (1998) 'Jury Selection in the United States: Are There Lessons to be Learned?' Crim LR 270.

MAY SIR J (1992–3) *Report of the inquiry into the circumstances surrounding the convictions arising out of the bomb attacks in Guildford and Woolwich in 1974, Second Report* (1992–3 HC 296).

MAY T, HOUGH M, HERRINGTON V and WARBURTON H (2007a), *Local resolution: the views of police officers and complainants* (London: IPCC).

MAY T, HOUGH M, HERRINGTON V and WARBURTON H (2007b) *From Informal to Local Resolution: Assessing changes to the handling of low-level police complaints* (London: Police Foundation/IPCC).

MAY T, WARBURTON H, TURNBULL P and HOUGH M (2002) *Times They are a Changing: Policing of Cannabis* (York: YPS).

MAYNARD W (1994) *Witness Intimidation: Strategies for Prevention, PRG Crime Detection and Prevention Series Paper 55* (London: Home Office).

MCARA L and MCVIE S (2005) 'The Usual Suspects: Street Life, Young People and the Police' 5 Criminal Justice 5.

MCARA L and MCVIE S (2007) 'Youth Justice? The Impact of System Contact on Patterns of Desistance from Offending' 4 European Jo Criminology 315.

MCBARNET D (1981) 'Magistrates' Courts and the Ideology of Justice' 8(2) JLS 181–197.

MCBARNET D (1983a) *Conviction* (London: Macmillan).

MCBARNET D (1983b) 'Victim in the Witness Box – Confronting Victimology's Stereotype' 7 Contemporary Crises 293.

MCBRIDE J (2018) *Human rights and criminal procedure: the case law of the European Court of Human Rights* (Strasbourg: Council of Europe).

MCCABE S and PURVES R (1972a) *By-passing the Jury* (Oxford: Basil Blackwell).

MCCABE S and PURVES R (1972b) *The Jury at Work* (Oxford: Basil Blackwell).

MCCABE S and PURVES R (1974) *The Shadow Jury at Work* (Oxford: Basil Blackwell).

MCCAHILL M (2002) *The Surveillance Web: The Rise of Visual Surveillance in an English City* (Cullompton: Willan).

MCCARTNEY C (2006a) 'The DNA Expansion Programme and Criminal Investigation' 46(2) BJ Crim 175.

MCCARTNEY C (2006b) *Forensic Identification and Criminal Justice* (Cullompton: Willan).

MCCARTNEY C and SHORTER L (2019) 'Exacerbating Injustice: Post-conviction Disclosure in England and Wales International Journal of Law' (59) Crime and Justice 1–10.

McCartney C and Wortley N (2018) 'Under the Covers: Covert Policing and Intimate Relationships' Crim LR 137.

McColgan A (2000) *Women Under the Law: The False Promise of Human Rights* (London: Longman).

McConville M (1991) 'Shadowing the Jury' 141 NLJ 1588.

McConville M (1992) 'Videotaping Interrogations: Police Behaviour On and Off Camera' Crim LR 532.

McConville M (1993) *Corroboration and Confessions: The Impact of a Rule Requiring that no Conviction can be Sustained on the Basis of Confession Evidence Alone* (Royal Commission on Criminal Justice Research Study no 13) (London: HMSO).

McConville M (1998) 'Plea Bargaining: Ethics and Politics' 25 JLS 562.

McConville M (2002) 'Plea Bargaining' in McConville M and Wilson G (eds), *The Handbook of the Criminal Justice Process* (Oxford: OUP).

McConville M and Baldwin J (1981) *Courts, Prosecution and Conviction* (Oxford: OUP).

McConville M and Baldwin J (1982) 'The Role of Interrogation in Crime Discovery and Conviction' 22 BJ Crim 165.

McConville M and Bridges L (1993) 'Pleading Guilty Whilst Maintaining Innocence' 143 NLJ 160.

McConville M and Bridges L (eds), (1994) *Criminal Justice in Crisis* (Aldershot: Edward Elgar).

McConville M and Hodgson J (1993) *Custodial Legal Advice and the Right to Silence* (Royal Commission on Criminal Justice Research Study no 16) (London: HMSO).

McConville M and Marsh L (2014) *Criminal Judges: Legitimacy, Courts and State-Induced Guilty Pleas in Britain* (London: Edward Elgar).

McConville M and Marsh L (2020) *The Myth of Judicial Independence* (Oxford: OUP).

McConville M and Mirsky C (1998) 'The State, the Legal Profession, and the Defence of the Poor' 15 JLS 342.

McConville M and Mirsky M (2005) *Jury Trials and Plea Bargaining: A True History* (Oxford: Hart).

McConville M and Morrell P (1983) 'Recording the Interrogation: Have the Police got it Taped?' Crim LR 158.

McConville M and Sanders A (1992) 'Weak Cases and the CPS' LS Gaz, 12.

McConville M and Shepherd D (1992) *Watching Police, Watching Communities* (London: Routledge).

McConville M and Wilson G (eds) (2002) *The Handbook of the Criminal Justice Process* (Oxford: OUP).

McConville M, Hodgson J, Bridges L and Pavlovic A (1994) *Standing Accused* (Oxford: Clarendon).

McConville M, Sanders A and Leng R (1991) *The Case for the Prosecution* (London: Routledge).

McCullagh C (2017) 'Respectable Victims and Safe Solutions: The Hidden Politics of Victimology' 68 NILQ 539.

McCulloch J and Pickering S (2009) 'Pre-Crime and Counter-Terrorism: Imagining Future Crime in the "War on Terror"' 49 BJ Crim 628.

McCulloch J and Wilson D (2016) *Pre-crime: Preemption, Precaution and the Future* (Routledge, London).

McEldowney J (1979) 'Stand by for the Crown – An Historical Analysis' Crim LR 272.

McEwan J (1989) 'Documentary Hearsay Evidence – Refuge for the Vulnerable Witness?' Crim LR 629.

McEwan J (2003) *The Verdict of the Court* (Oxford: Hart).

McEwan J (2004) 'The Adversarial and Inquisitorial Models of Criminal Trial' in Duff A, Farmer L, Marshall S and Tadros V (eds), *The Trial on Trial* (Oxford: Hart).

McEwan J (2005) 'Proving Consent in Sexual Cases: Legislative Change and Cultural Evolution' 9 IJ E&P 1.

McEwan J (2013) 'Truth, Efficiency and Co-operation in Modern Criminal Justice' 66 CLP 203.

McEwan J, Redmayne M and Tinsley Y (2002) 'Evidence, Jury Trials and Witness Protection—The Auld review of the English Criminal Courts' (2002) 6 IJ E&P 163.

McGhie F (2015) Overcoming the public funding hurdles, *Legal Action*, March 2015 (online at: https://www.lag.org.uk/article/202710/overcoming-the-public-funding-hurdles).

McGlynn C (2010) 'R v A (No 2)' in Hunter R, McGlynn C and Rackley E (eds) *Feminist Judgments. From Theory to Practice* (Oxford: Hart).

McGlynn C (2017) 'Rape Trials and Sexual History Evidence: Reforming the Law on Third-Party Evidence' JCL 81(5) 367–392.

McGlynn C and Munro V (eds) (2010) *Rethinking Rape Law: International and Comparative Perspectives* (Abingdon: Routledge-Cavendish).

McGlynn C, Westmarland N and Johnson K (2018) 'Under the Radar: The Widespread Use of "Out of Court Resolutions" in Policing Domestic Violence and Abuse in the United Kingdom' 58(1) BJ Crim 1–16.

McGuiness T (2016) *Pre-charge bail. House of Commons Library Number 7469* (London: House of Commons).

McGuinness T (2016) *Changes to Criminal Legal Aid. House of Commons Briefing Paper No 6628* (London: House of Commons).

McIvor G (1996) 'The Impact of Bail Services in Scotland' in Paterson F (ed), *Understanding Bail in Britain* (Edinburgh: Scottish Office).

McKay S (2018) *Blackstone's Guide to the Investigatory Powers Act 2016* (Oxford: OUP).

McKeever G (1999) 'Detecting, Prosecuting and Punishing Benefit Fraud: The Social Security Administration (Fraud) Act 1997' 62 MLR 261.

McKenzie I, Morgan R and Reiner R (1990) 'Helping the Police with their Enquiries' Crim LR 22.

McKinnon C (2006) *Are Women Human?* (Harvard: Harvard UP).

McLaughlin E (2007) *The New Policing* (London: Sage).

McLaughlin E and Murji K (1995) 'The End of Public Policing? Police Reform and "the New Managerialism" ' in Noaks L, Levi M and Maguire M (eds), *Contemporary Issues in Criminology* (Cardiff: University of Wales Press).

McLaughlin H (1990) 'Court Clerks: Advisers or Decision-Makers?' 30 BJ Crim 358.

McMahon M (1988) 'Police Accountability: The Situation of Complaints in Toronto' 12 Contemporary Crises 301.

McQuigg R (2016) 'Domestic Violence as a Human Rights Issue: Rumor v. Italy' 26(4) European Journal of International Law 1009–1025.

Medford S, Gudjonsson G and Pearse J (2003) 'The Efficacy of the Appropriate Adult Safeguard During Police Interviewing' 8 LCP 253.

Meehan A (1993) 'Internal Police Records and the Control of Juveniles' 33 BJ Crim 504.

Memon A, Vrij A and Bull R (2003) *Psychology and Law: Truthfulness, Accuracy and Credibility of Victims, Witnesses and Suspects*, 2nd edn (Chichester: John Wiley).

Memon H (2013) 'Video Identification of Suspects' 7 Policing 3.

Menkes D and Bendelow G (2014) 'Diagnosing Vulnerability and "Dangerousness": Police Use of Section 136 in England and Wales' 13(2) Journal of Public Mental Health 70–82.

Metropolitan Police Authority (2007) *Counter-Terrorism: the London Debate* (London: MPA).

Mhlanga B (1999) *Race and the CPS* (London: SO).

Middleton D (2005) 'The Legal and Regulatory Response to Solicitors Involved in Serious Fraud' 45 BJ Crim 810.

Mika H and Zehr H (2017) 'Fundamental Concepts of Restorative Justice' Restorative Justice 73–81.

Miller J, Bland N and Quinton P (2000) *The Impact of Stops and Searches on Crime and the Community* (Police Research Series Paper 127) (London: Home Office).

Miller J, Quinton P, Alexandrou B, Packham D (2020) 'Can Police Training Reduce Ethnic/Racial Disparities in Stop and Search? Evidence from a Multisite UK Trial' Criminology and Public Policy (online first).

Miller S (1999) *Gender and Community Policing: Walking the Talk* (Boston MA: North Eastern UP).

Millington T and Williams S (2007) *The Proceeds of Crime* (Oxford: OUP).

Mills A, Meek R and Gojkovic D (2011) 'Exploring the Relationship Between the Voluntary Sector and the State in Criminal Justice' 2(2) *Voluntary Sector Review* 193–211.

Milne R and Bull R (1999) *Investigative Interviewing: Psychology and Practice* (Chichester: Wiley).

Ministry of Justice (2008) *Statistics on Race and the Criminal Justice System 2006/7* (London: MoJ).

Ministry of Justice (2008b) *Criminal Statistics England and Wales, 2007* (London: MoJ).

Ministry of Justice (2008c) *Arrests for Recorded Crime (Notifiable Offences) and the Operation of Certain Police Powers under PACE England and Wales 2006/07* (London: MoJ).

Ministry of Justice (2008d) *Statistics on Race and the Criminal Justice System 2006/7* (London: MoJ).

Ministry of Justice (2009) *Statistics on Race and the Criminal Justice System, 2007/8* (London: MoJ).

Ministry of Justice (2009a) *Judicial and Court Statistics 2008*, Cm 7697 (London: MoJ).

Ministry of Justice (2009b) *Statistics on Race and the Criminal Justice System, 2007/8* (London: MoJ).

Ministry of Justice (2009c) *Legal Aid: Funding Reforms, Consultation Paper 18/09* (London: MoJ).

Ministry of Justice (2009d) *Crown Court means testing: Response to consultation CP(R) 06/09* (London: MoJ).

Ministry of Justice (2009e) *Sentencing Statistics 2007 England and Wales* (London: MoJ).

Ministry of Justice (2010) *Breaking the Cycle: Effective Punishment, Rehabilitation and Sentencing of Offenders* (London: MoJ).

Ministry of Justice (2011a) *Achieving best evidence in criminal proceedings: Guidance on interviewing victims and witnesses, and guidance on using special measures* (London: MoJ).

Ministry of Justice (2011b) *Statistics on Race and the Criminal Justice System 2010* (London: MoJ).

Ministry of Justice (2012) *Swift and Sure Justice: The Government's Plans for Reform of the Criminal Justice System* CM 8388 (London: MoJ).

Ministry of Justice (2013) *Code of Practice for Adult Conditional Cautions* (London: MoJ).

Ministry of Justice (2014) *Independent criminal advocacy in England and Wales: Jeffrey Review final report* (London: MoJ).

Ministry of Justice (2015a) *Code of Practice for Victims of Crime* (London: MoJ).

Ministry of Justice (2015b) *Simple Cautions for Adult Offenders* (London: MoJ).

Ministry of Justice (2016) *Statistics on Women and the Criminal Justice System 2015* (London: MoJ).

Ministry of Justice (2017a) *Justice Statistics quarterly, England and Wales, April 2016 to March 2017 (provisional)* (London: MoJ).

MINISTRY OF JUSTICE (2017b) *Criminal court statistics (quarterly): July to September 2017* (London: MoJ).

MINISTRY OF JUSTICE (2018a) *Criminal Court Statistics (annual)* (London: MoJ).

MINISTRY OF JUSTICE (2018b) *Criminal Court Statistics Quarterly, December* (London: MoJ).

MINISTRY OF JUSTICE (2018c) *Criminal Justice Statistics: Overview tables* (London: MoJ).

MINISTRY OF JUSTICE (2018d) *Female offender strategy* (London: MoJ).

MINISTRY OF JUSTICE (2018e) *Managing Vulnerability: Women* (London: MoJ).

MINISTRY OF JUSTICE (2018f) *Statistics on Race and the Criminal Justice System* (online at: https://assets.publishing.service.gov.uk/government/uploads/system/uploads/attachment_data/file/849200/statistics-on-race-and-the-cjs-2018.pdf).

MINISTRY OF JUSTICE (2018g) *Statistics on Women and the Criminal Justice System 2017* (London: MoJ).

MINISTRY OF JUSTICE (2019a) *Coroner Statistics Annual 2019, England and Wales and Coroners statistics 2019: England and Wales (statistical tables)* (Online at: https://www.gov.uk/government/statistics/coroners-statistics-2019).

MINISTRY OF JUSTICE (2019b) *Criminal court statistics quarterly, England and Wales, January to March 2019* (London: MoJ).

MINISTRY OF JUSTICE (2019c) *Criminal court statistics quarterly, England and Wales, April to June 2019* (London: MoJ).

MINISTRY OF JUSTICE (2019d) *Criminal court statistics quarterly, England and Wales, October to December 2019* (London: MoJ).

MINISTRY OF JUSTICE (2019e) *Criminal Court Statistics. Overview Tables September 2019* (London: MoJ).

MINISTRY OF JUSTICE (2019f) *Crown Court Plea Tool. Criminal court statistics quarterly: October to December 2019* (London: MoJ).

MINISTRY OF JUSTICE (2019g) *Final report: Review of legal aid for inquests* (online at: https://assets.publishing.service.gov.uk/government/uploads/system/uploads/attachment_data/file/777034/review-of-legal-aid-for-inquests.pdf).

MINISTRY OF JUSTICE (2019h) *Statistics on Race and the Criminal Justice System 2018* (London: MoJ).

MINISTRY OF JUSTICE (2020a) *Civil Justice Statistics Main Tables Oct-Dec 2019; table 2.2* (London: MoJ).

MINISTRY OF JUSTICE (2020b) *Criminal Court statistics (quarterly): January to March (tables)* (London: MoJ).

MINISTRY OF JUSTICE (2020b) *Royal Courts of Justice Annual Tables – 2019* (London: MoJ).

MINISTRY OF JUSTICE (2020c) *Criminal Legal Aid Review: An accelerated package of measures amending the criminal legal aid fee schemes* (London: MoJ).

MINISTRY OF JUSTICE and ATTORNEY GENERAL'S OFFICE (2017) *Limiting the use of complainants' sexual history in sex cases*, CM 8547 (London, TSO).

MIRFIELD P (1996) 'Successive Confessions and the Poisonous Tree' Crim LR 554.

MIRFIELD P (1997) *Silence, Confessions and Improperly Obtained Evidence* (Oxford: OUP).

MIRFIELD P (2009) 'Character and Credibility' Crim LR 135.

MITSILEGAS V (2017) 'European Criminal Law After Brexit' 28 Criminal Law Forum 219–250.

MODOOD T (2003) 'Muslims and the Politics of Difference' Political Quarterly 100.

MOECKLI D (2007) 'Stop and Search Under the Terrorism Act 2000: A Comment on *R (Gillan)* v *Commissioner of Police for the Metropolis*' 70 MLR 654.

MOELLENDORF M (2002) *Cosmopolitan Justice* (Blouder: Westview Press).

MOFFETT L (2017) 'Victim Personal Statements in Managing Victims' Voices in Sentencing in Northern Ireland: Taking a More Procedural Justice Approach' 68 NILQ 555.

Monk H, Gilmore J and Jackson W (2019) 'Gendering Pacification: Policing Women at Anti-fracking Protests' 122(1) Feminist Review 64–79.

Montgomery J (1998) 'The Criminal Standard of Proof' 148 NLJ 582.

Moody S and Tombs J (1982) *Prosecution in the Public Interest* (Edinburgh: Scottish Academic Press).

Moody S and Tombs J (1983) 'Plea Negotiations in Scotland' Crim LR 297.

Mooney J and Young J (2000) 'Policing Ethnic Minorities: Stop and Search in North London' in Marlow A and Loveday B (eds), *After Macpherson: Policing after the Stephen Lawrence Inquiry* (Lyme Regis: Russell House).

Moore R (2019) 'The Enigmas of Rehabilitation and Resettlement: Forms of Capital, Desistance and the Contextualisation of Carceral-Community Offender Transitions' 58(2) Howard Journal 202–219.

Moore S (2008) 'Street Life, Neighbourhood Policing and "the Community" in Squires P (ed) *ASBO nation: The criminalisation of nuisance* (Bristol: Policy Press).

Moore S, Clayton A and Murphy H (2021) 'Seeing Justice Done: Courtroom Filming and the Deceptions of Transparency' Crime, Media, 17(1) *Crime, Media, Culture* 127–144.

Moorhead R (2004) 'Legal Aid and the Decline of Private Practice: Blue Murder or Toxic Job?' 11(3) IJ of the Legal Profession 160.

Moran L (2016) 'Visible Justice: YouTube and the UK Supreme Court' 5 Annual Review of Interdisciplinary Justice Research 223–263.

Morgan Harris Burrows LLP (2009) *Research into the impact of bad character provisions on the courts*, Ministry of Justice Research Series 5/09 (London: MOJ).

Morgan J and Zedner L (1992) *Child Victims* (Oxford: Clarendon).

Morgan P and Henderson P (1998) *Remand Decisions and Offending on Bail* (Home Office Research Study no 184) (London: Home Office).

Morgan R (2002) 'Magistrates: The Future According to Auld' 29 JLS 308.

Morgan R and Jones S (1992) 'Bail or Jail?' in Stockdale E and Casale S (eds), *Criminal Justice Under Stress* (London: Blackstone).

Morgan R and Newburn T (1997) *The Future of Policing* (Oxford: OUP).

Morgan R and Sanders A (1999) *The Uses of Victim Statements* (London: Home Office).

Morgan R, Reiner R and McKenzie I, *Police Powers and Policy: A Study of the Work of Custody Officers* (report to ESRC) (unpublished).

Morison J and Leith P (1992) *The Barrister's World* (Milton Keynes: Open UP).

Morrison G (2018) 'Admissibility of Forensic Voice Comparison Testimony in England and Wales' Crim LR 20.

Moston S and Engelberg T (1993) 'Police Questioning Techniques in Tape Recorded Interviews with Criminal Suspects' 3 Policing and Society 223.

Moston S and Engelberg T (2011) 'The Effects of Evidence on the Outcome of Interviews with Criminal Suspects' 12 Police Pract Res 518–26.

Moston S and Stephenson G (1993) *The Questioning and Interviewing of Suspects Outside the Police Station* (Royal Commission on Criminal Justice Research Study no 22) (London: HMSO).

Moston S, Stephenson G and Williamson T (1992) 'The Effects of Case Characteristics on Suspect Behaviour During Police Questioning' 92 BJ Crim 23.

Moston S and Williamson T (1990) 'The Extent of Silence in Police Interviews' in Greer S and Morgan R (eds), *The Right to Silence Debate* (Bristol: University of Bristol).

Mountford L and Hannibal M (2007) 'Simplier, Speedier Justice for All?' 158 Sols Journal 1294.

Moxon D (1988) *Sentencing Practice in the Crown Court* (Home Office Research Study no 103) (London: HMSO).

Mueller-Johnson K, Dhami M and Lundrigan S (2018) 'Effects of Judicial Instructions and Juror Characteristics on Interpretations of Beyond Reasonable Doubt' 24 Psychology, Crime and Law 117–133.

Mulcahy A (1994) 'The Justifications of Justice: Legal Practitioners' Accounts of Negotiated Case Settlements in Magistrates' Courts' 34 BJ Crim 411.

Mulcahy A, Brownlee I and Walker C (1993) *An Evaluation of Pre-Trial Reviews in Leeds and Bradford Magistrates' Courts* 33 Home Office Research Bulletin 10. (London: TSO).

Mulcahy L (2008) 'The Unbearable Lightness of Being? Shifts Towards the Virtual Trial' 35 JLS 464.

Mulcahy L (2010) *Legal Architecture: Justice, Due Process and the Place of Law* (Abingdon: Routledge).

Mulcahy L (2013) 'Putting the Defendant in their Place: Why Do We Still Use the Dock in Criminal Proceedings?' 53(6) BJ Crim 1139–1156.

Mulcahy L and Rowden E (2020) *The Democratic Courthouse: A Modern History of Design, ue Process and Dignity* (Abingdon: Routledge).

Mulcahy L, Rowden E and Teeder W (2020) *Exploring the Case for Virtual Jury Trials during the COVID-19 crisis* (University of Cardiff, University of Oxford, Oxford Brookes University).

Mullock A (2009) 'Prosecutors Making (Bad) Law?' 17 MedLR 290.

Munday R (1993) 'Jury Trial, Continental Style' 13 LS 204.

Munday R (1995) 'What Do the French Think of heir Jury?' 15 LS 65.

Munday R (1996) 'Inferences from Silence and European Human Rights Law' Crim LR 370.

Munday R (2005) 'What Constitutes "Other Reprehensible Behaviour" under the Bad Character Provisions of the Criminal Justice Act 2003?' Crim LR 24.

Mungham G and Bankowski Z (1976) 'The Jury in the Legal System' in Carlen P (ed), *The Sociology of Law* (Keele: University of Keele).

Munro V (2008) 'Of Rights and Rhetoric: Discourses of Degradation and Exploitation in the Context of Sex Trafficking' 35 JLS 240.

Munro V (2018) *The impact of the use of pre-recorded evidence on juror decision-making: an evidence review* (Edinburgh: Scottish Government (Crime and Justice)).

Munro V and Aitken R (2018) 'Adding Insult to Injury? The Criminal Law's Response to Domestic Abuse-related Suicide in England and Wales' Crim LR 732.

Murdoch J and Roche R (2013) *The European Convention on Human Rights and Policing* (Strasbourg: Council of Europe).

Murji K and Neal S (2011) 'Riot: Race and Politics in the 2011 Disorders' 16(4) Sociological Research Online 216–220.

Murray K, McVie S, Farren D, Herlitz L, Hough M and Norris P (2020) 'Procedural Justice, Compliance with the Law and Police Stop-and-search: A Study of young people in England and Scotland' *Policing and Society* (online first).

Murray R (2018) 'Police Body Camera interviews are taking us back to a dark age' (online at: https://mintedlaw.wordpress.com/2018/03/23/police-body-camera-interviews-are-taking-us-back-to-a-dark-age/).

MVA and Miller J (2000) *Profiling Populations Available for Stops and Searches* (Police Research Series Paper 131).

Myers B et al (2018) 'The Heterogeneity of Victim Impact Statements: A Content Analysis of Capital Trial Sentencing Penalty Phase Transcripts' 25 Psychology, Public Policy, and Law 474.

Myhill A (2015) 'Measuring Coercive Control: What Can We Learn From National Population Surveys?' 21(3) Violence Against Women 355–375.

MYHILL A (2019) 'Renegotiating Domestic Violence: Police Attitudes and Decisions Concerning Arrest' 29(1) Policing and Society 52–68.

MYTHEN G and KAMRUZZAMAN P (2011) 'Counter-terrorism and Community Relations: Anticipatory Risk, Regulation and Justice' in QUIRK H, SEDDON T and SMITH G (eds), *Regulation and Criminal Justice* (Cambridge: CUP).

MYTHEN G, WALKLATE S and KHAN T (2009) ' "I'm a Muslim, but I'm not a Terrorist": Victimization, Risky Identities and the Performance of Safety' 49(6) BJ Crim 736.

NACRO (1997) *Policing Local Communities: The Tottenham Experiment* (London: NACRO).

NASH M (2010) 'The Art of Deception—UK Public Protection Policy and the Criminal Justice "Crisis" of 2006' 38(3) IJLCJ 79.

NASH R and WADE K (2009) 'Innocent but Proven Guilty: Eliciting Internalised False Confessions Using Doctored Video Evidence' 23 Appl Cog Psychol 624.

NATION D (1992) 'He Can Always Appeal' 156 JP 521.

NATIONAL AUDIT OFFICE (2000) *Criminal Justice: Working Together HC 29 Session 1999-2000 executive summary* (London: TSO).

NATIONAL AUDIT OFFICE (2009) *The Procurement of Legal Aid in England and Wales by the Legal Services Commission HC 29 2009-10* (London: TSO).

NATIONAL AUDIT OFFICE (2015) *Inspection: A comparative study* (London: TSO).

NATIONAL POLICING IMPROVEMENT AGENCY (2018) Policing Improvement Agency, *Practice Advice on Stop and Search in Relation to Terrorism* (London: NPIA).

NAUGHTON M (2005a) 'Miscarriages of Justice and the Government of the Criminal Justice System: An Alternative Perspective on the Production and Deployment of Counter-Discourse' 13 Critical Criminology 211.

NAUGHTON M (2005b) 'Redefining Miscarriages of Justice' 45 BJ Crim 165.

NAUGHTON M (2007) *Rethinking Miscarriages of Justice* (Houndmills: Palgrave Macmillan).

NAUGHTON M (ed) (2009) *The Criminal Cases Review Commission* (Houndmills: Palgrave Macmillan).

NAUGHTON M (2009) 'The Importance of Innocence for the Criminal Justice System' in NAUGHTON M (ed), *The Criminal Cases Review Commission* (Houndmills: Palgrave Macmillan).

NAUGHTON M (2012) 'The Criminal Cases Review Commission: Innocence versus Safety and the Integrity of the Criminal Justice System' 58 CLQ 207.

NAUGHTON M (2013) *The Innocent and the Criminal Justice System: A Sociological Analysis of Miscarriages of Justice* (Basingstoke: Palgrave Macmillan).

NAUGHTON M (2016) 'Appeals Against Wrongful Convictions' in CORTEEN K, MORLEY S, TAYLOR P and TURNER J (eds), *A Companion to Crime, Harm and Victimisation* (Bristol: Policy Press).

NAUGHTON M (2019) 'The Westminster Commission inquiry on the Ability of the Criminal Cases Review Commission to Deal Effectively with Miscarriages of Justice: Please Forgive Me, but I won't be Holding My Breath' *The Justice Gap*, online.

NAUGHTON M and MCCARTNEY C (2005) 'The Innocence Network UK' 7(2) Legal Ethics 150.

NEILSON A (2009) 'A Crisis of Identity: NACRO's Bid to Run a Prison and What it Means for the Voluntary Sector' 48(4) Howard JCJ 401–410.

NELKEN D (1983) *The Limits of the Legal Process* (London: Academic Press).

NEMITZ T and BEAN P (1994) 'The Use of the Appropriate Adult Scheme' 34 Med Sci and the Law 161.

NEWBURN T (1999) *Understanding and preventing police corruption* (Police Research Series Paper 110 (London: Home Office).

NEWBURN T (2006) 'Contrasts in Intolerance: Cultures of Control in the USA and Britain' in NEWBURN T and ROCK P (eds),

The Politics of Crime Control: Essays in Honour of David Downes (Oxford: Clarendon Press).

Newburn T (ed) (2008) *Handbook of Policing*, 2nd edn (Cullompton: Willan).

Newburn T (2015) 'The 2011 England Riots in Recent Historical Perspective' 55(1) BJ Crim 39–64.

Newburn T (2016) 'Social Disadvantage, Crime, and Punishment' in Dean H and Platt L (eds), *Social Advantage and Disadvantage* (Oxford: OUP).

Newburn T, Diski R, Cooper K, Deacon R, Burch A and Grant M (2016) '"The Biggest Gang"? Police and People in the 2011 England Riots' 28(2) Policing and Society 205–222.

Newburn T and Elliott J (1998) *Policing Anti-drug Strategies: tackling drugs together 3 years on* (London: Home Office Police Research Group).

Newburn T and Hayman S (2001) *Policing, Surveillance and Social Control* (Cullompton: Willan).

Newburn T, Jones T and Blaustein J (2018) 'Framing the 2011 England Riots: Understanding the Political and Policy Response' 57(3) Howard Journal 339–362.

Newburn T, Shiner M and Hayman S (2004) 'Race, Crime and Injustice? Strip-search and the Treatment of Suspects in Custody' 44(5) BJ Crim 677.

Newburn T, Williamson T and Wright (eds) (2007) *A Handbook of Criminal Investigation* (Cullompton: Willan).

Newby M (2012) 'Historical Abuse Cases: Why They Expose the Inadequacy of the Real Possibility Test' in Naughton M (ed), *The Criminal Cases Review Commission* (London: Palgrave Macmillan).

Newlove B (2015) *Review of Complaints and Resolution for Victims of Crime* (London: Office of the Commissioner for Victims and Witnesses).

Newman D (2013) *Legal Aid Lawyers and the Quest for Justice* (Oxford: Hart Publishing).

Newman D and Welsh L (2019) 'The Practices of Modern Criminal Defence Lawyers: Alienation and its Implications for Access to Justice' 48(1–2) CLWR 64–89.

Newton T (1998) 'The Place of Ethics in Investigative Interviewing by Police Officers' 37 Howard JCJ 52.

Neyland D (2009) 'Surveillance, Accountability and Organisational Failure: The Story of Jean Charles de Menezes' in Goold B and Neyland D (eds), *New Directions in Surveillance and Privacy* (Cullompton: Willan).

Neyroud P (2018) *Out of Court Disposals Managed by the Police: A Review of the Evidence* (CUP).

Neyroud P and Beckley A (2001) 'Regulating Informers: The Regulation of Investigatory Powers Act, Covert Policing and Human Rights' in Billingsley R, Nemitz T and Bean P (eds), *Informers: Policing, Policy, Practice* (Cullompton: Willan).

Ng W and Skinns L (2021), 'A Formal Interview Tool in an Informal Setting? An Exploratory Study of the Use of Body-Worn Video at the Scene of an Alleged Crime' *Criminal Law Review*, June.

Nicol D (2006) 'Law and Politics after the Human Rights Act' PL 722.

Nicolson D and Reid K (1996) 'Arrest for Breach of the Peace and the European Convention on Human Rights' Crim LR 764.

Nijhar P (2009) *Law and Imperialism. Criminality and Constitution in Colonial India and Victorian England* (Abingdon: Routledge).

Nixon J and Hunter C (2009) 'Disciplining Women: Anti-social Behaviour and the Governance of Conduct' in Millie A (ed), *Securing Respect* (Bristol: Policy Press).

Nixon J and Parr S (2006) 'Anti-social Behaviour: Voices From the Front Line' in Flint J (ed), *Housing, Urban Governance and Anti-Social Behaviour* (Bristol: Policy Press).

Nobles R and Schiff D (1995) 'Miscarriages of Justice: A Systems Approach' 58 MLR 299.

Nobles R and Schiff D (1996) 'Criminal Appeal Act 1995: The Semantics of Jurisdiction' 59 MLR 573.

Nobles R and Schiff D (1997) 'The Never Ending Story: Disguising Tragic Choices in Criminal Justice' 60 MLR 293.

Nobles R and Schiff D (2000) *Understanding Miscarriages of Justice* (Oxford: OUP).

Nobles R and Schiff D (2001) 'Due Process and Dirty Harry Dilemmas: Criminal Appeals and the Human Rights Act' 64 MLR 911.

Nobles R and Schiff D (2001a) 'Due Process and Dirty Harry Dilemmas: Criminal Appeals and the Human Rights Act' 64 MLR 911.

Nobles R and Schiff D (2001b) 'The Criminal Cases Review Commission: Reporting Success?' 64 MLR 280.

Nobles R and Schiff D (2002) 'The Right to Appeal and Workable Systems of Justice' 65(5) MLR 676.

Nobles R and Schiff D (2004) 'A Story of Miscarriage: Law in the Media' 31 JLS 221.

Nobles R and Schiff D (2005) 'A Reply to Graham Zellick' Crim LR 951.

Nobles R and Schiff D (2005) 'The Criminal Cases Review Commission: Establishing a Workable Relationship with the Court of Appeal' Crim LR 173.

Nobles R and Schiff D (2005b) 'A Reply to Graham Zellick' Crim LR 951.

Nobles R and Schiff D (2006) 'Theorising the Criminal Trial and Criminal Appeal: Finality, Truth and Rights' in Duff A, Farmer L, Marshall S and Tadros V (eds), *The Trial on Trial Vol 2: Judgment and Calling to Account* (Oxford: Hart).

Nobles R and Schiff D (2008) 'Absurd Aysmmetry' 71(3) MLR 464.

Nobles R and Schiff D (2012) After Ten Years: An Investment in Justice? In Naughton M (ed), *The Criminal Cases Review Commission. Hope for the Innocent?* (Basingstoke: Palgrave Macmillan).

Nobles R and Schiff D (2018) 'Criminal Justice Unhinged: The Challenge of Guilty Pleas' 39 OJLS 100.

Nobles R and Schiff D (2020) 'The Supervision of Guilty Pleas by the Court of Appeal of England and Wales—Workable Relationships and Tragic Choices' 31 Crim Law Forum 513–552.

Norman J (2009) 'Seen and Not Heard: Young People's Perceptions of the Police' 3(4) Policing: A Journal of Policy and Practice.

Norrie A (1993) *Crime, Reason and History* (London: Weidenfeld and Nicolson).

Norrie A (1998) ' "Simulacra of Morality?" Beyond the Ideal/Actual Antinomies of Criminal Justice' in Duff A (ed), *Criminal Law: Principle and Critique* (New York: CUP).

Norris C (2003) 'From Personal to Digital: CCTV, the Panopticon, and the Technological Mediation of Suspicion and Social Control' in Lyon D (ed), *Surveillance as Social Sorting: Privacy, Risk and Digital Discrimination* (London: Routledge).

Norris C and Dunnighan C (2000) 'Subterranean Blues: Conflict as an Unintended Consequence of the Police Use of Informers' 9 Policing and Society 385.

Norris C, Fielding N, Kemp C and Fielding J (1992) 'Black and Blue: An Analysis of the Influence of Race on Being Stopped by the Police' 43 BJ Sociology 207.

Norris C, Moran J and Armstrong G (eds) (1999) *Surveillance, CCTV and Social Control* (Aldershot: Ashgate).

Nuffield Council on Bioethics report (2007) *The forensic use of bioinformation: ethical issues* (London: Nuffield Council on Bioethics).

O'Brien M (2008) *The Death of Justice* (Talybont: Y Lolfa Cyf).

O'Brien D and Epp J (2000), 'Salaried Defenders and the Access to Justice Act 1999' 63 MLR 394.

O'Donnell I and Edgar K (1998) 'Routine Victimisation in Prisons' 37 Howard Journal 266.

O'Connell M (2005) 'Confessions in police custody' Sept, *Counsel*, 12.

O'Connor P (1990) 'The Court of Appeal: Re-Trials and Tribulations' Crim LR 615.

O'Connor P (1993) 'Prosecution Disclosure: Principle, Practice and Justice' in Walker C and Starmer K (eds), *Justice in Error* (London: Blackstone).

O'Floinn M and Ormerod D (2012) 'Social Networking Material as Criminal Evidence' Crim LR 486.

O'Loan N (2007) *Statement by the Police Ombudsman for Northern Ireland on her investigation into the circumstances surrounding the death of Raymond McCord Junior and related matters* (Belfast).

O'Mahoney B et al (2011) 'The Early Identification of Vulnerable Witnesses Prior to an Investigative Interview' 13 British Journal of Forensic Practice 114.

O'Mahoney D and Doak J (2004) 'Restorative Justice – is More Better? The Experience of Police-led Restorative Cautioning Pilots in Northern Ireland' 43(5) Howard Journal 484.

O'Mahony P (1992) 'The Kerry Babies Case: Towards a Social Psychological Analysis' 13 Irish Jo Psychology 223.

O'Neill A (2017) *Hate Crime, England and Wales, 2016/17*. Statistical Bulletin 17/17 (London: Home Office).

O'Neill M (2019) *Police Community Support Officers* (Oxford: OUP).

O'Neill M and Loftus B (2013) 'Policing and the Surveillance of the Marginal: Everyday Contexts of Social Control' 17(4) Theoretical Criminology 437–454.

O'Sullivan H and Ormerod D (2017) 'Time for a Code: Reform of Sentencing Law in England and Wales' 19 Eur JL Reform 285.

Office for Criminal Justice Reform (2007) *Working Together to Cut Crime and Deliver Justice: Criminal Justice System Business Plan 2009-2010* (London: TSO).

Office for National Statistics (2018a) *Crime in England and Wales: year ending September 2017* (London: ONS).

Office for National Statistics (2018b) *Domestic Abuse in England Wales: year ending March 2018* (London: ONS).

Office for National Statistics (2019) *Domestic abuse in England and Wales: year ending November 2019* (London: ONS).

Ohrn H and Nyberg C, 'Searching for truth or confirmation?' (undated) 2(1) iIIRG Bulletin 11.

Ormerod D (2001) 'Sounds Familiar: Voice Identification Evidence' Crim LR 595.

Ormerod D (2002) 'Sounding Out Expert Voice Identification' Crim LR 771.

Ormerod D (2003) 'ECHR and the Exclusion of Evidence: Trial Remedies for Article 8 Breaches' Crim LR 61.

Ormerod D (2006) 'Recent Developments in Entrapment' 65 Covert Policing Review 65–67.

Ormerod D (2008) 'Editorial' Crim LR 337.

Ormerod D (2020) 'Racism in the Criminal Justice System' Crim LR 659.

Ormerod D and Birch D (2004) 'The Evolution of the Discretionary Exclusion of Evidence' Crim LR 767.

Ormerod D and McKay S (2004) 'Telephone Intercepts and Their Admissibility' Crim LR 15.

Ormerod D and Perry D (eds) (2020) *Blackstone's Criminal Practice 2021* (Oxford: OUP).

Ormerod D and Roberts A (2002) 'The Trouble with *Teixeira*: Developing a Principled Approach to Entrapment' 6 IJ E&P 38.

Ormerod D and Roberts A (2003) 'The Police Reform Act 2002 – Increasing Centralisation, Maintaining Confidence and Contracting Out Crime Control' Crim LR 141.

Ormerod D and Taylor R (2008) 'The Corporate Manslaughter and Corporate Homicide Act 2007' Crim LR 589.

Ormston R, Chalmers J, Leverick F, Munro V and Murray L (2019) *Scottish Jury Research: Findings from a Large Scale Mock Jury Study* (Edinburgh: Scottish Government).

Osborne D and Gaebler T (1992) *Reinventing Government: How the Entrepreneurial Spirit is*

Transforming the Public Sector (Reading, MA: Addison-Wesley).

Ovey C (1998) 'The European Convention on Human Rights and the Criminal Lawyer: An Introduction' Crim LR 4.

Owers A (2010) 'The Regulation of Criminal Justice: Inspectorates, Ombudsmen and Inquiries. Regulation and Criminal Justice' in Quirk H, Seddon T and Smith G (eds), *Regulation and Criminal Justice: Innovations in Policy and Research* (Cambridge: CUP).

Owusu-Bempah Akwasi (2017) 'Race and Policing in Historical Context: Dehumanization and the Policing of Black People in the 21st Century.' Theoretical Criminology 21.

Owusu-Bempah Abenaa (2017) *Defendant Participation in the Criminal Process* (Abingdon: Routledge).

Owusu-Bempah Abenaa (2018) 'The Interpretation and Application of the Right to Effective Participation' 22(4) IJ E&P 321–341.

Oxburgh G and Dando C (2011) 'Psychology and Interviewing: What Direction Now in our Quest for Reliable Information?' 13 British Journal of Forensic Practice 135–147.

Oxburgh G, Ost J, Morris P and Cherryman J (2014) 'The Impact of Question Type and Empathy on Police Interviews with Suspects of Homicide, Filicide and Child Sexual Abuse' 21(6) *Psychiatry, Psychology and Law* 903–917.

Oxford T (1991) 'Spotting a Liar' Police Review 328.

Ozin P, Norton H and Spivey P (2006) *PACE—A Practical Guide* (Oxford: OUP).

PA Consulting (2004) *No Witness, No Justice—National Victim and Witness Care Project*: Interim Evaluation Report.

Packer H (1968) *The Limits of the Criminal Sanction* (Stanford: Stanford UP).

Padfield N (1993) 'The Right to Bail: a Canadian Perspective' Crim LR 510.

Padfield N (1996) 'Bailing and Sentencing the Dangerous' in Walker N (ed), *Dangerous People* (London: Blackstone).

Padfield N (2003) *Text and Materials on the Criminal Justice Process* 3rd edn (London: LexisNexis).

Palmer C (1996) 'Still Vulnerable After All These Years' Crim LR 633.

Palmer K, Oates W and Portney P (1995) 'Tightening Environmental Standards: The Benefit-Cost or the No-Cost Paradigm?' 9 Journal of Economic Perspectives 119.

Palmer P and Steele J (2008) 'Police Shootings and the Role of Tort' 71 MLR 801.

Panatzis C and Gordon D (1997) 'Television Licence Evasion and the Criminalisation of Female Poverty' 36 Howard JCJ 170.

Pantazis C and Pemberton S (2009) 'From the "Old" to the "New" Suspect Community: Examining the Impacts of Recent UK Counter-Terrorist Legislation' 49(5) BJ Crim 646.

Paradine K and Wilkinson J (2004) Protection and Accountability: The Reporting, Investigation and Prosecution of Domestic Violence Cases (London: HMIC and HMCPSI).

Parker H, Casburn M and Turnbull D (1981) *Receiving Juvenile Justice* (Oxford: Basil Blackwell).

Parliamentary Joint Committee on Human Rights (2004) *Deaths in Custody*, HC 137 session 2003–4.

Parmar A (2011) 'Stop and Search in London: Counter-terrorist or Counter-productive?' Policing and Society, 21:4, 369–382

Parmar A (2016) 'Race, Ethnicity and Criminal Justice: Refocusing the Criminological Gaze' in Bosworth M, Hoyle C and Zedner L (eds), *Changing Contours of Criminal Justice* (Oxford: OUP).

Parmar A (2018) 'Policing Belonging: Race and Nation in the UK' in Bosworth M, Parmar A and Vazquez Y (eds) *Race, Criminal Justice and Migration Control* (Oxford: OUP).

Parmar A (2019a) 'Arresting (non) Citizenship: The Policing Migration Nexus of Nationality, Race and Criminalization' Theoretical Criminology 1–22.

PARMAR A (2019b) 'Policing Migration and Racial Technologies' 59(4) BJ Crim 398–957.

PARRY L (2006) 'Protecting the Juvenile Suspect: What is the Appropriate Adult Supposed To Do?' 18 CFLQ 373.

PARSON S (2016) 'Joint Enterprise Murder: R v Jogee' 80(3) JCL 173–176.

PATERSON F and WHITTAKER C (1994) *Operating Bail* (Edinburgh: Scottish Office).

PATRICK R (2011). '"A Nod and a Wink": Do "Gaming Practices" Provide an Insight into the Organisational Nature of Police Corruption?' 84(3) Police Journal 199–221.

PATTENDEN R (1991) 'Should Confessions be Corroborated?' 107 LQR 319.

PATTENDEN R (1992) 'Evidence of Previous Malpractice by Police Witnesses and *R v Edwards*' Crim LR 549.

PATTENDEN R (1995) 'Inferences from Silence' Crim LR 602.

PATTENDEN R (1996) *English Criminal Appeals 1844–1994* (Oxford: Clarendon Press).

PATTENDEN R (1998) 'Silence: Lord Taylor's Legacy' 2 IJ E&P 141.

PATTENDEN R and SKINNS L (2010) 'Choice, Privacy and Publicly Funded Legal Advice at the Police Station' 73(3) MLR 349–70.

PATTEN C (1999) *A New Beginning: Policing in Northern Ireland—the Report of the Independent Commission on Policing in Northern Ireland* (Belfast: Independent Commission on Policing in Northern Ireland).

PATTENDEN R (2009) 'The Standards of Review for Mistake of Fact in the Court of Appeal, Criminal Division' Crim LR 15.

PEACH C (2006) 'Islam, Ethnicity and South Asian Religions in the London 2001 Census' 31 *Trans Inst Br Geogr NS* 353–370.

PEARCE F and TOMBS S (1990) 'Ideology, Hegemony and Empiricism: Compliance Theories of Regulation' 30 BJ Crim 423.

PEARCE F and TOMBS S (1997) 'Hazards, Law and Class: Contextualising the Regulation of Corporate Crime' 6 Social and Legal Studies 79.

PEARSE J and GUDJONSSON G (1996) 'Police Interviewing Techniques at Two South London Police Stations' 3 Psychology, Crime & Law 763.

PEARSON G and ROWE M (2020) *Police Street Powers and Criminal Justice* (London: Bloomsbury).

PEARSON G, ROWE M and TURNER L (2018) 'Policy, Practicalities and PACE S 24: The Subsuming of the Necessity Criteria in Arrest Decision Making by Frontline Police Officers' 45(2) JLS 282–308.

PEAY J and PLAYER E (2018) 'Pleading Guilty: Why Vulnerability Matters' 81 MLR 929.

PEMBERTON A and REYNAERS S (2011) 'The Controversial Nature of Victim Participation: The Case of the Victim Impact Statements' in EREZ E, KILCHLING M and WEMMERS J (eds), *Therapeutic Jurisprudence and Victim Participation in Criminal Justice: International perspectives* (Durham, NC: Carolina Academic Press).

PEMBERTON S (2008) 'Demystifying Deaths in Police Custody: Challenging State Talk' 17 SLS 237.

PEPIN S, LIPSCOME S and ZAYED, Y (2017) *Provision of Legal Aid. House of Commons Debate Pack* CDP 207–0239 (London)

PERCY-SMITH J and HILLYARD P (1985) 'Miners in the Arms of the Law: A Statistical Analysis' 12 JLS 345.

PERRY B, PERRY J, SCHWEPPE J and WALTERS M (2015) 'Introduction. Understanding Hate Crime: Research, Policy and Practice' 27(6) Criminal Justice Policy Review 571–576.

PETERSON J, SKEEM J, KENNEALY P, BRAY B and ZVONKOVIC A (2014). 'How Often and How Consistently Do Symptoms Directly Precede Criminal Behaviour Among Offenders With Mental Illness?' 38 Law and Human Behavior 439–449.

PHILLIPS C and BOWLING B (2007) 'Racism, Ethnicity, Crime, and Criminal Justice' in MAGUIRE M, MORGAN R and REINER R (eds), *Oxford Handbook of Criminology*, 4th edn (Oxford: OUP).

PHILLIPS C and BROWN C (1998) *Entry into the criminal justice system: a survey of arrests and their outcomes* (Home Office Research Study 185) (London: Home Office).

PHILLIPS J, GELSTHORPE L and PADFIELD N (2019) 'Non-custodial Deaths: Missing, Ignored or Unimportant?' 19(2) Criminology and Criminal Justice 160–178.

PHILLIPS M, MCAULIFF B, KOVERA M and CUTLER B (1999) 'Double-Blind Photoarray Administration as a Safeguard Against Investigator Bias' 84 J Applied Psychology 940.

PHILLIPS S and VERANO S (2008) 'Police Criminal Charging Decisions: An Examination of Post-arrest Decision-making' 36(4) Journal of Criminal Justice 307–315.

PHILLIPSON G (2007) 'Bills of Rights as a Threat to Human Rights: The Alleged "Crisis of Legalism"' PL 217.

PIERPOINT H (2001) 'The Performance of Volunteer Appropriate Adults' 40 Howard JCJ 255.

PIERPOINT H (2006) 'Reconstructing the Role of the Appropriate Adult in England and Wales' 6(2) Criminology & Criminal Justice 225.

PIERPOINT H (2008) 'Quickening the PACE? The Use of Volunteers as Appropriate Adults in England and Wales' 18 Policing and Society 397.

PIGOT JUDGE T (1989) *Report of the Advisory Group on Video-Recorded Evidence* (London: HMSO).

PILIAVIN I and BRIAR S (1964) 'Police Encounters with Juveniles' 70 AJ Sociology 206.

PIVATY A (2020) *Criminal Defence at Police Stations: A Comparative and Empirical Study* (Abingdon: Routledge).

PIZA E, WELSH B, FARRINGTON D and THOMAS A (2019) 'CCTV Surveillance for Crime Prevention: A 40-year Systematic Review with Meta-analysis' 18(1) Criminology and Public Policy 135–159.

PLAYER E (1989) 'Women and Crime in the City' in DOWNES D (ed), *Crime and the City* (Basingstoke: Macmillan).

PLAYER E (2007) 'Remanding Women in Custody: Concerns for Human Rights' 70(3) MLR 402.

PLEASENCE P, KEMP V and BALMER N (2011) 'The Justice Lottery? Police Station Advice 25 Years on From PACE' Crim LR 3–18.

PLOTNIKOFF J and WOOLFSON R (1993a) *From Committal to Trial: Delay at the Crown Court* (London: Law Society).

PLOTNIKOFF J and WOOLFSON R (1993b) *Information and Advice for Prisoners about Grounds for Appeal and the Appeals Process* (Royal Commission on Criminal Justice, Research Study no 18) (London: HMSO).

PLOTNIKOFF J and WOOLFSON R (1998) *Witness Care in Magistrates' Courts and the Youth Court* (Home Office Research Findings no 68) (London: Home Office).

PLOTNIKOFF J and WOOLFSON R (2001) '*A Fair Balance*'? Evaluation of the Operation of Disclosure Law (Home Office: London).

PLOTNIKOFF J and WOOLFSON R (2005) *Review of the effectiveness of specialist courts in other jurisdictions* (London: Department for Constitutional Affairs).

PLOTNIKOFF J and WOOLFSON R (2008) 'Making the Best Use of the Intermediary Special Measure at Trial' Crim LR 91.

PLOTNIKOFF J and WOOLFSON R (2015) *Intermediaries in the Criminal Justice System* (Bristol: Policy Press).

POLICE COMPLAINTS AUTHORITY (PCA) (1996) *Annual Report, 1995/6* (London: SO).

POLLARD C (1994) 'A Case for Disclosure' Crim LR 42.

POLLARD C (1996) 'Public Safety, Accountability and the Courts' Crim LR 152.

PONTING C (1985) *The Right to Know, The Inside Story of the Belgrano Affair* (London: Sphere).

PORTER A (2019) 'Prosecuting Domestic Abuse in England and Wales: Crown Prosecution Service "Working Practice" and New Public Managerialism' 28(4) SLS 493–516.

PORTER M and van der LINDE C (1995) 'Green and Competitive: Ending the Stalemate' 73 Harv BRev 120.

Posey B, Kowalski M and Stohr M (2020) 'Thirty Years of Scholarship in the *Women and Criminal Justice* Journal: Gender, Feminism, and Intersectionality' 30(1) Women & Criminal Justice 5–29.

Povey D and Smith K (eds) (2009) *Police Powers and Procedures, England and Wales 2007/08* (Home Office Statistical Bulletin 7/09) (London: Home Office).

Powell, A (2019) *Unemployment by Ethnic Background. Briefing Paper.* HC 6385

Powell-Smith A (2020) Stop and account: how is this little-known police practice being used? (online at: https://missingnumbers.org/stop-and-account/).

Poyser S, Nurse A and Milne R (2018) *Miscarriages of Justice* (Bristol, Palgrave Macmillan).

Prateeppornnarong D and Young R (2019) 'A Critique of the Internal Complaints System of the Thai Police' 29(1) Policing and Society 18–35.

Pratt J (2017) 'Risk Control, Rights and Legitimacy in the Limited Liability State' 57 BJ Crim 1322–1339.

Pratt J and Bray K (1985) 'Bail Hostels – Alternatives to Custody?' 25 BJ Crim 160.

Prenzler T (2000) 'Civilian Oversight of Police: A Test of Capture Theory' 40 BJ Crim 659.

Prenzler T, Mihinjac M and Porter L (2013) 'Reconciling Stakeholder Interests in Police Complaints and Discipline Systems' 14(2) Police Practice and Research 155–168.

Prime J, White S, Liriano S and Patel K (2001) *Criminal careers of those born between 1953 and 1978*, Home Office Statistical Bulletin 4/01 (London: Home Office).

Prison Reform Trust (2017) *'There's a reason we're in trouble' Domestic abuse as a driver to women's offending* (London: Prison Reform Trust).

Public Accounts Committee (2009) Independent Police Complaints Commission (HC335) (London: TSO).

Purshouse J (2017) 'Article 8 and the Retention of Non-conviction DNA and Fingerprint Data in England and Wales' Crim LR 253

Purshouse J (2020) '"Paedophile Hunters", Criminal Procedure, and Fundamental Human Rights' 47 JLS 384–411.

Putnam R (2015) *Our Kids* (New York: Simon and Schuster).

Quick O (2006) ' Prosecuting "Gross" Medical Negligence: Manslaughter, Discretion and the CPS' 33 JLS 421.

Quinn K (2004) 'Jury Bias and the European Convention on Human Rights: A Well-kept Secret?' Crim LR 998.

Quinn K and Jackson J (2007) 'Of Rights and Roles: Police Interviews with Young Suspects in Northern Ireland' 47 BJ Crim 234.

Quinton P (2003) *An Evaluation of the New Police Misconduct Procedures* (Home Office Online Report 10/03).

Quinton P, Bland N and Miller J (2000) *Police Stops, Decision-making and Practice* (Police Research Series Paper 130) (London: Home Office).

Quirk H (2006) 'The Significance of Culture in Criminal Procedure Reform: Why the Revised Disclosure Scheme Cannot Work' 10 IJ E&P 42.

Quirk H (2007) 'Identifying Miscarriages of Justice: Why Innocence in the UK is Not the Answer' 70(5) MLR 759.

Quirk H (2013) 'Twenty Years On, the Right of Silence and Legal Advice: The Spiralling Costs of an Unfair Exchange' 64(4) NILQ 465–483.

Quirk H (2016) *The Rise and Fall of the Right to Silence* (Abingdon: Routledge).

Quirk H (2019) 'The Case for Restoring the Right of Silence' in Child J and Duff R (eds), *Criminal Law Reform Now. Proposals and Critique* (Oxford: Hart).

Quirk H (2020) 'Compensation for Miscarriages of Justice: Degrees of Innocence' 79(1) Cam LJ 4–7.

Raifeartaigh U (1997) 'Reconciling Bail Law with the Presumption of Innocence' 17 OJLS 1.

Raine J and Keasey P (2012) 'From Police Authorities to Police and Crime Commissioners: Might policing become more publicly accountable?' 1(2) International Journal of Emergency Services 122–34.

Raine J and Willson M (1995) 'Just Bail at the Police Station?' 22(4) JLS 571.

Raine J and Willson M (1996) 'The Imposition of Conditions in Bail Decisions' 35 Howard JCJ 256.

Raine J and Willson M (1997) 'Police Bail with Conditions' 37(4) BJ Crim 593.

Raine J (2015) 'Electocracy with Accountabilities? The Novel Governance Model of Police and Crime Commissioners' in Rowe M and Lister S (eds), *Accountability of Policing* (Abingdon: Routledge).

Ralph S, Capewell C and Bonnett E (2016) 'Disability Hate Crime: Persecuted for Difference' 43 British Journal of Special Education 215–232.

Ratcliffe J (2016) *Intelligence-led Policing* 2nd edn (London: Routledge).

Ratcliffe P, Gudjonsson G, Heaton-Armstrong A and Wolchover D (2016) *Witness Testimony in Sexual Cases: Evidential, Investigative and Scientific Perspectives* (Oxford: OUP).

Rawley A and Caddy B (2007) *Damilola Taylor: An independent review of forensic examination of evidence by the Forensic Science Service* (London: Home Office).

Rawnsley A (2010) *The End of the Party* (London: Penguin).

Rayner J (2009) 'Duty Calls' *Law Society Gazette*, 1 October, 11.

Readings D (2019) 'Police Misconduct Hearings' 1 Tribunals Edition 2.

Redlich A, Yan S, Norris R and Bushway S (2018) 'The Influence of Confessions on Guilty Pleas and Plea Discounts' 24(2) Psychology, Public Policy, and Law 147–157.

Redmayne M (1995) 'Doubts and Burdens: DNA Evidence, Probability and the Courts' Crim LR 464.

Redmayne M (1997) 'Process Gains and Process Values: the CPIA 1996' 60 MLR 79.

Redmayne M (1998) 'The DNA Database: Civil Liberty and Evidentiary Issues' Crim LR 437.

Redmayne M (2001) *Expert Evidence and Criminal Justice* (Oxford: OUP).

Redmayne M (2002a) 'Appeals to Reason' 65 MLR 19.

Redmayne M (2002b) 'The Relevance of Bad Character' 61 CLJ 684.

Redmayne M (2004) 'Disclosure and its Discontents' Crim LR 441.

Redmayne M (2006) 'Theorising Jury Reform' in Duff A, Farmer L, Marshall S and Tadros V (eds), *The Trial on Trial: judgment and calling to account* (Oxford: Hart).

Redmayne M (2007) 'Rethinking the Privilege Against Self-Incrimination' 27(2) OJLS 209.

Redmayne M (2009) 'Book Review of *Evidence of Bad Character* and *Hearsay Evidence in Criminal Proceedings* by J Spencer' 48 Howard JCJ 108.

Redmond D (2005) 'License to Live?' 155 (7182) NLJ 962.

Reilly P (2015) 'Every Little Helps? YouTube, Sousveillance and the 'anti-Tesco' Riot in Stokes Croft' 17(5) New Media and Society 755–771.

Reiner R and Spencer J (eds) (1993) *Accountable Policing* (London: IPPR).

Reiner R (1985) *The Politics of the Police* (Oxford: OUP).

Reiner R (2006) 'Beyond Risk: A Lament for Social Democratic Criminology' in Newburn T and Rock P (eds), *The Politics of Crime Control: Essays in Honour of David Downes* (Oxford: Clarendon Press).

Reiner R (2007) 'Success or Statistics? New Labour and Crime Control' 67 Criminal Justice Matters 4.

Reiner R (2013) 'Who Governs? Democracy, Plutocracy, Science and Prophecy in Policing' 13(2) Criminology and Criminal Justice 161–180.

REKRUT-LAPA T and LAPA A (2014) 'Health Needs of Detainees in Police Custody in England and Wales: Literature Review' 27 Journal of Forensic and Legal Medicine 69–75.

RENFIGO A, SLOCUM L and CHILLAR V (2019) 'From Impressions to Intentions: Direct and Indirect Effects of Police Contact on Willingness to Report Crimes to Law Enforcement' 56(3) Journal of Research in Crime and Delinquency.

RESTORATIVE JUSTICE COUNCIL (2016) *A guide to restorative justice for Police and Crime Commissioner Candidates* (Norwich: RCJ).

RICE L (2020) 'Junior Partners or Equal Partners? Civilian Investigators and the Blurred Boundaries of Police Detective Work' 30(8) Policing and Society.

RICHARDSON G, with OGUS A, and BURROWS P (1983) *Policing Pollution: A Study of Regulation and Enforcement* (Oxford: Clarendon).

RILEY D and VENNARD J (1988) *Triable-Either-Way Cases: Crown Court or Magistrates' Court? (Home Office Research Study, no 98)* (London: HMSO).

ROACH K (1999a) 'Four Models of the Criminal Process' 89 JCLC 671.

ROACH K (1999b) *Due Process and Victims' Rights: The New Law and Politics of Criminal Justice* (Toronto: University of Toronto Press).

ROBBINS I (2006) 'Privatization of Corrections: A Violation of U.S. Domestic Law, International Human Rights, and Good Sense' 13(3) Human Rights Brief 12–16.

ROBERTS A (2004) 'The Problems of Mistaken Identification: Some Observations on Process' 8 IJ E&P 100.

ROBERTS A (2008) 'Drawing on Expertise: Legal Decision Making and the Reception of Expert Evidence' Crim LR 443.

ROBERTS A (2009) 'Eyewitness Identification Evidence: Procedural Developments and the Ends of Adjudicative Advocacy' 6(2) International Commentary on Evidence 3.

ROBERTS A (2019) 'The Frailties of Human Memory and the Accused's Right to Accurate Procedures' Crim LR 911.

ROBERTS D (1993) 'Questioning the Suspect: the Solicitor's Role' Crim LR 369.

ROBERTS J and BRADFORD B (2015) 'Sentence Reductions for a Guilty Plea in England and Wales: Exploring New Empirical Trends' 12(2) Journal of Empirical Legal Studies 187–210.

ROBERTS J and ASHWORTH A (2016) 'The Evolution of Sentencing Policy and Practice in England and Wales, 2003–2015' 45 Crime and Justice 307–358.

ROBERTS J and HOUGH M (2009) *Public opinion and the jury: an international literature review*, Ministry of Justice Research Series 1/09 (London: MoJ).

ROBERTS K (2009) 'Investigative Interviewing and Islamic Extremism: The Case of Public Safety Interviews' (undated) 2(1) iIIRG Bulletin 30.

ROBERTS P (1994) 'Science in the Criminal Process' 14 OJLS 469.

ROBERTS P (1996) 'What Price a Free Market in Forensic Science?' 36 BJ Crim 37.

ROBERTS P (2002) 'Science, Experts and Criminal Justice' in MCCONVILLE M and WILSON G (eds), *Handbook of the Criminal Justice Process* (Oxford: OUP).

ROBERTS P (2008) 'Comparative Criminal Justice Goes Global' 28 Ox J of Legal Studies 369.

ROBERTS P and WILLMORE C (1993) *The Role of Forensic Science Evidence in Criminal Proceedings* (Royal Commission on Criminal Justice Research Study no 11) (London: HMSO).

ROBERTS P and ZUCKERMAN A (2004) *Criminal Evidence* (Oxford: OUP).

ROBERTS R (2015) *Criminal Justice in Times of Austerity* (London: Centre for Crime and Justice Studies).

ROBERTS S (2003) 'Unsafe Convictions: Defining and Compensating Miscarriages of Justice' MLR 441.

ROBERTS S (2004) 'The Royal Commission on Criminal Justice and Factual Innocence:

Roberts S, Remedying Wrongful Convictions in the Court of Appeal' 1(2) Justice Journal 86.

Roberts S (2017a) 'Fresh Evidence and Factual Innocence in the Criminal Division of the Court of Appeal' 81(4) Journal of Criminal Law 303–327.

Roberts S (2017b) 'Reviewing the Function of Criminal Appeals in England and Wales' 1 Institute of Law Journal 3–27.

Roberts S (2018) 'Post-Conviction Review in England and Wales: Perpetuating and Rectifying Miscarriages of Justice' in Lennon G, King C and McCartney C (eds), Counter-terrorism, Constitutionalism and Miscarriages of Justice: A Festschrift for Professor Clive Walker (London: Hart Publishing).

Roberts S and Weathered L (2009) 'Assisting the Factually Innocent: the Contradictions and Compatibility of Innocence Projects and the Criminal Cases Review Commission' 29(1) OJLS 43.

Robertshaw P (1998) Summary Justice (London: Cassell).

Robertson G (1994) 'Entrapment Evidence: Manna From Heaven, or Fruit of the Poisoned Tree?' Crim LR 805.

Robins J (2018) Guilty Until Proven Innocent (Hull: Biteback Publishing).

Robins J (2019) 'Downward trend in number of miscarriage of justice cases being referred continues for third year' The Justice Gap, 22 July.

Robinson A, Pinchevsky G and Guthrie J (2018) 'A Small Constellation: Risk Factors Informing Police Perceptions of Domestic Abuse' 28(2) Policing and Society 189–204.

Robson J (2017) 'A Fair Hearing? The Use of Voice Identification Parades in Criminal Investigations in England and Wales' Crim LR 36.

Rock P (1993) The Social World of an English Crown Court (Oxford: Clarendon).

Rock P (2004) Constructing Victims' Rights (Oxford: OUP).

Rock P (2014) 'Victims' Rights' in Vanfraechem I, Pemberton A and Mukwiza Ndahinda F (eds), Justice for Victims: Perspectives on Rights, Transition and Reconciliation (Abingdon: Routledge).

Rogers J (2006) 'Restructuring the Exercise of Prosecutorial Discretion in England and Wales' 26 OJLS 775.

Rogers J (2020) 'Private Prosecutions and Safeguards' Crim LR 769.

Rose D (1996) In the Name of the Law: The Collapse of Criminal Justice (London: Jonathan Cape).

Ross J (2019) 'Betrayal by Bosses: Undercover Policing and the Problem of "Upstream Defection" by Rogue Principals', in Brown D, Turner J and Weisser B (eds), The Oxford Handbook of Criminal Process (Oxford: OUP).

Roulin M and Ternes M (2019) 'Is it Time to Kill the Detection Wizard? Emotional Intelligence Does not Facilitate Deception Detection' 137 Jan Personality and Individual Differences 131–138.

Rowden E (2013) 'Virtual Courts and Putting "Summary" Back into "Summary Justice": Merely Brief, or Unjust?' In Simon J, Temple N and Tobe R (eds), Architecture and Justice: Judicial Matters in the Public Realm (Farnham, Surrey: Ashgate).

Rowe M (2007) 'Rendering Visible the Invisible: Police Discretion, Professionalism and Decision-making' 17(3) Policing & Society 279.

Rowe M (2020). Policing the Police (Bristol: Policy Press).

Rowe M, Pearson G and Turner E (2018) 'Body-Worn Cameras and the Law of Unintended Consequences: Some Questions Arising from Emergent Practices' 12(1) Policing 83–90.

Royal Commission on Criminal Justice (RCCJ) (1993) Report (Cm 2263) (London: HMSO).

Royal Commission on Criminal Procedure (RCCP) (1981) Cmd 3297. The Investigation and Prosecution of Criminal Offences in England and Wales: The Law and Procedure (Cmnd 8092–1) (London: HMSO).

Rozenberg J (1987) *The Case for the Crown* (Wellingborough: Equation).

Rozenberg J (1992) 'Miscarriages of Justice' in Stockdale E and Casale S (eds), *Criminal Justice Under Stress* (London: Blackstone).

Rozenberg J (1994) *The Search for Justice* (London: Hodder & Stoughton).

Rumney P (2006) 'False Allegations of Rape' 65(1) Cam LJ 128.

Ryder M (2008) 'RIPA Reviewed' Archbold News 4.

Sagana A, Saverland M and Merckelbach H (2017) 'Witnesses' Failure to Detect Covert Manipulations in their Written Statements' 14 Journal of Investigative Psychology and Offender Profiling 3.

Salerno J, Peter-Hagene L and Sanchez J (2016) 'Expressing Anger Increases Male Jurors' Influence, but Decreases Female Jurors' Influence, during Mock Jury Deliberations' 28 Jury Expert 29.

Samuels A (1997) 'Custody Time Limits' Crim LR 260.

Sanders A (1977) 'Does Professional Crime Pay? – A Critical Comment on Mack' 40 MLR 553.

Sanders A (1985a) 'Class Bias in Prosecutions' 24 Howard JCJ 76.

Sanders A (1985b) 'Prosecution Decisions and the Attorney-General's Guidelines' Crim LR 4.

Sanders A (1986) 'Arrest, Charge and Prosecution' 6 LS 257.

Sanders A (1987) 'Constructing the Case for the Prosecution' 14 JLS 229.

Sanders A (1988a) 'Personal Violence and Public Order' 16 IJ Sociology of Law 359.

Sanders A (1988b) 'Rights, Remedies and the Police and Criminal Evidence Act' Crim LR 802.

Sanders A (1988c) 'The Limits to Diversion from Prosecution' 28 BJ Crim 513.

Sanders A (1990) 'Access to a Solicitor and s 78 PACE' *Law Society Gazette*, 31 October, p 17.

Sanders A (1996) 'Access to Justice in the Police Station: An Elusive Dream?' in Young R and Wall D (eds), *Access to Criminal Justice* (London: Blackstone).

Sanders A (ed) (1997) *Victims with Learning Difficulties* (Oxford: University of Oxford Centre for Criminological Research).

Sanders A (1998) 'What Principles Underlie Criminal Justice Policy in the 1990s?' 18 OJLS 533.

Sanders A (1999) *Taking Account of Victims in the Criminal Justice System* (Edinburgh: Scottish Office).

Sanders A (2001) *Community Justice: Modernising the Magistracy in England and Wales* (London: IPPR).

Sanders A (2002a) 'Core Values, the Magistracy and the Auld Report' 29 JLS 324.

Sanders A (2002b) 'Victim Participation in an Exclusionary Criminal Justice System' in Hoyle C and Young R (eds), *New Visions of Crime Victims* (Oxford: Hart).

Sanders A (2008) 'Can Coercive Powers be Effectively Controlled or Regulated?' in Cape E and Young R (eds), *Regulating Policing* (Oxford: Hart).

Sanders A (2011) 'Reconciling the Apparently Different Goals of Criminal Justice and Regulation: The "Freedom" Perspective' in Quirk H, Smith G and Seddon T (eds), *Regulation and Criminal Justice: Innovations in Policy and Research* (Cambridge: CUP).

Sanders A (2016) 'The CPS 30 Years On' Crim LR 82.

Sanders A (2018) 'The CPS, Policy-making and Assisted Dying: Towards a "Freedom" Approach' in Child J and Duff A (eds), *Criminal Law Reform Now: Proposals & critique* (Oxford: Hart).

Sanders A and Bridges L (1990) 'Access to Legal Advice and Police Malpractice' Crim LR 494.

Sanders A and Bridges L (1999) 'The Right to Legal Advice', in Walker C and Starmer K (eds), *Miscarriages of Justice* (London: Blackstone).

SANDERS A, BRIDGES L, MULVANEY A and CROZIER G (1989) *Advice and Assistance at Police Stations and the 24 Hour Duty Solicitor Scheme* (London: Lord Chancellor's Department).

SANDERS A, CREATON J, BIRD S and WEBER L (1997) *Victims with Learning Disabilities* (Oxford: Centre for Criminological Research).

SANDERS A, HOYLE C, MORGAN R and CAPE E (2001) 'Victim Impact Statements: Don't Work, Can't Work' Crim LR 447.

SANDERS A and JONES I (2012) 'The Victim in Court' in WALKLATE S (ed), *Handbook of Victims and Victimology* (Devon: Willan Publishing).

SANDERS A and YOUNG R (1994) 'The Rule of Law, Due Process and Pre-Trial Criminal Justice' 47 CLP 125.

SANDERS A and YOUNG R (2008) 'Police Powers' in NEWBURN T (ed), *Handbook of Policing*, 2nd edn (Cullompton: Willan).

SANDFORD S (2002) 'Levinas, Feminism and the Feminine' in CRITCHLEY S and BENASCONI R *the Cambridge Companion to Levinas* (Cambridge: CUP).

SANDHU A (2016) 'Camera-friendly Policing: How the Police Respond to Cameras and Photographers' 14(1) Surveillance and Society 78–89.

SANDHU A (2019) '"I'm Glad That Was on Camera": A Case Study of Police Officers' Perceptions of Cameras' 29(2) Policing and Society 223–235.

SANDHU K (2018) 'Working Class in Britain? You Must be White' *New Internationalist*, 16 March.

SARAT A (1997) 'Vengeance, Victims and the Identities of Law' 6 SLS 163.

SARGEANT E, MURPHY K and CHERNEY A (2014) 'Ethnicity, Trust and Cooperation with Police: Testing the Dominance of the Process-based Model' 11(4) European Journal of Criminology 500–524.

SATO M, HOYLE C and SPEECHLEY N-E (2017) 'Wrongful Convictions of Refugees and Asylum Seekers: Responses by the Criminal Cases Review Commission' Crim LR 106.

SAVAGE S (2012) 'Seeking "Civilianness": Police Complaints and the Civilian Control Model of Oversight' 53(5) BJ Crim 886–904.

SAVAGE S (2013) 'Thinking Independence: Calling the Police to Account through the Independent Investigation of Police Complaints' 53(1) BJ Crim 94–112.

SAVAGE S and CHARMAN S (1996) 'Managing Change', in LEISHMAN F, LOVEDAY B and SAVAGE S (eds), *Core Issues in Policing* (Harlow: Longman).

SCARMAN SIR L (1981) *The Brixton Disorders: 10–12 April 1981* (Cmnd 8427) (London: HMSO).

SCHNEIDER J and SCHNEIDER P (2008) 'The Anthropology of Crime and Criminalization' 37 Annu. Rev. Anthropol 351–373.

SCHOLLUM M (2017) 'Bringing PEACE to the United States' (Nov) The Police Chief 3.

SCHULENBERG J, CHENIER A, BUFFONE S and WOJCIECHOWSKI C (2017) 'An Application of Procedural Justice to Stakeholder Perspectives: Examining Police Legitimacy and Public Trust in Police Complaints Systems' 27(7) Policing and Society 779–796.

SCHULHOFER S (1992) 'Plea Bargaining as Disaster' 101 Yale LJ 1979.

SCHWARTZ J (1997) 'Relativism, Reflective Equilibrium, and Justice' 17 LS 128.

SCOTT D, MCGILLOWAY S and Donnelly M (2009) 'The Mental Health Needs of Women Detained in Police Custody' 18(2) Journal of Mental Health 144–151.

SCOTT R and STUNTZ W (1992) 'A Reply: Imperfect Bargains, Imperfect Trials and Innocent Defendants' 101 Yale LJ 2011.

SCRATON P (2019) 'The Hillsborough Independent Panel and the UK State: An Alternative Route to "Truth", "Apology" and "Justice"' in CARLEN P and AYRES FRANCA L (eds), *Justice Alternatives* (Abingdon: Routledge).

SCRATON P and CHADWICK K (1987) *In the Arms of the Law: Coroners' Inquests and Deaths in Custody* (London: Pluto).

SEAGO P, WALKER C and WALL D (2000) 'The Development of the Professional Magistracy in England and Wales' Crim LR 631.

SEBBA L (1994) 'Sentencing and the Victim: The Aftermath of *Payne*' 3 Int Rev Victimology 141.

SEBBA L (1996) *Third Parties: Victims and the Criminal Justice System* (Columbus: Ohio State UP).

SEDDON T (2010) 'Rethinking Prison Inspection: Regulating Institutions of Confinement' in Seddon T, Quirk H and Smith G (eds), *Regulation and Criminal Justice: Innovations in Policy and Research* (Cambridge: CUP).

SEKAR S (2009) 'The Failure of the Review of the Possible Wrongful Convictions Caused by Michael Heath' in NAUGHTON M (ed), *The Criminal Cases Review Commission* (London: Palgrave Macmillan).

SEKAR S (2012) *The Cardiff Five: Innocent Beyond Any Doubt* (Hook: Waterside Press).

SENTENCING COUNCIL (2016) *Allocation Guideline* (London: Sentencing Council).

SENTENCING COUNCIL (2017) *Reduction in Sentence for a Guilty Plea* (London: Sentencing Council).

SHAFER B and WIEGAND O (2006) 'It's Good to Talk – Speaking Rights and the Jury' in DUFF A, FARMER L, MARSHALL S and TADROS V (eds), *The Trial on Trial: Judgment and Calling to Account* (Oxford: Hart).

SHAPLAND J (2016) 'Forgiveness and Restorative Justice: Is It Necessary? Is It Helpful?' 5(1) OJLR 94–112.

SHAPLAND J and HOBBS R (1989) 'Policing Priorities on the Ground' in MORGAN R and SMITH D (eds), *Coming to Terms with Policing* (London: Routledge).

SHAPLAND J, ATKINSON A, ATKINSON H, DIGNAN J, EDWARDS L, HIBBRERT J, HOWES M, JOHNSON J, ROBINSON G and SORSBY A (2008) *Does restorative justice affect reconviction?* MoJ Research Series 10/08, (London: MOJ).

SHAPLAND J, WILLMORE J and DUFF P (1985) *Victims in the Criminal Justice System* (Aldershot: Gower).

SHARP D and ATHERTON S (2007) 'To Serve and Protect? The Experiences of Policing in the Community of Young People From Black and other Ethnic Minority Groups' 47(5) BJ Crim 746.

SHARPE S (1994) 'Covert Police Operations and the Discretionary Exclusion of Evidence' Crim LR 793.

SHARPE S (1996) 'Covert Policing: A Comparative View' 25 Anglo-Am LR 163.

SHARPE S (1998) *Judicial Discretion and Criminal Investigation* (London: Sweet & Maxwell).

SHARPE S (1999) 'HRA 1998: Article 6 and the Disclosure of Evidence in Criminal Trials' Crim LR 273.

SHARPE S (2000) *Search and Surveillance: The movement from evidence to information* (Aldershot: Ashgate).

SHAW H and COLES D (2007) *Unlocking the Truth: Families' Experiences of the Investigation of Deaths in Custody* (London: Inquest).

SHEARING C and FROESTAD J (2010) 'Nodal Governance and the Zwelethemba Model in H QUIRK, T SEDDON AND G SMITH (eds), *Regulation and Criminal Justice: Innovations in Policy and Research*, 103–133. (Cambridge: CUP).

SHEPHERD E (2007) *Investigative Interviewing: The Conversation Management Approach* (Oxford: OUP).

SHEPHERD E and GRIFFITHS A (2021) *Investigative Interviewing: The Conversation Management Approach* (Oxford: OUP (forthcoming)).

SHEPHERD E and MILNE R (1999) 'Full and Faithful: Ensuring Quality Practice and Integrity of Outcome in Witness Interviews' in HEATON-ARMSTRONG A, SHEPHERD E and WOLCHOVER D (eds), *Analysing Witness Testimony* (London: Blackstone).

SHERMAN L and HARRIS H (2015) 'Increased Death Rates of Domestic Violence

Victims From Arresting vs. Warning Suspects in the Milwaukee Domestic Violence Experiment (MilDVE)' 11 J Exp Criminol 1.

Sherwood M (2007) *After Abolition: Briton and the Slave Trade since 1807* (London: I.B. Tauris).

Shiner M (2006) *National Implementation of the Recording of Police Stops* (London: Home Office).

Shiner M, Carre Z, Delsol R and Eastwood N (2018) *The Colour of Injustice: 'Race', drugs and law enforcement in England and Wales* (London: LSE and STOPWATCH).

Shute S (2013) 'On The Outside Looking In: Reflections on the Role of Inspection in Driving Up Quality in the Criminal Justice System' 76(3) MLR 494–528.

Shute S, Hood R and Seemungal F (2005) *A Fair Hearing? Ethnic Minorities in the Criminal Courts* (Cullompton: Willan).

Sigler J (1974) 'Public Prosecution in England and Wales' Crim LR 642.

Sigurdsson J and Gudjonsson G (1996) 'Psychological Characteristics of "False Confessors": A Study Among Icelandic Prison Inmate and Juvenile Offenders' 20 Personality and Individual Differences 321.

Sikand M and Profumo L (2019) 'Minding the Gap: Where Does Tortious Liability for Public Authorities End and Human Rights Liability Begin?' JPIL 44

Silvestri A (ed) (2012) *Critical Reflections: Social and Criminal Justice in the First Year of Coalition Government* (London: Centre for Crime and Justice Studies).

Silvestri M (2017) 'Police Culture and Gender: Revisiting the "Cult of Masculinity"' 11 Policing 289.

Simester A and Von Hirsch A (ed) (2006) *Incivilities: Regulating Offensive Behaviour* (Oxford: Hart).

Simon D (1992) *Homicide: A Year on the Killing Streets* (London: Hodder & Stoughton).

Simon J (2007) *Governing Through Crime* (Oxford: OUP).

Sisson S (1999) *Cautions, Court Proceedings, and Sentencing: England and Wales, 1998* (London: Home Office).

Skinns L (2009a) '" Let's Get it Over With": Early Findings on Factors Affecting Detainees' Access to Custodial Legal Advice' 19(1) Policing & Society 58.

Skinns L (2009b) '"I'm a Detainee; Get me Out of Here"' 49(3) BJ Crim 399.

Skinns L (2010) '"Stop the Clock": Predictors of Detention Without Charge in Police Custody Areas' 10(3) Criminology and Criminal Justice 303–320.

Skinns L (2011) *Police Custody: Governance, Legitimacy and Reform in the Criminal Justice Process* (Cullompton: Willan).

Skinns L (2014) 'The Police in England: An Institution in Crisis?' in Richards D et al (eds), *Institutional Crisis in 21st Century Britain* (London: Palgrave Macmillan).

Skinns L (2019) *Police Powers and Citizens' Rights*, (Abingdon: Routledge).

Skinns L (2020) '"Seeing the light": material conditions and detainee dignity inside police detention' All Souls Seminar Series, Centre for Criminology, University of Oxford, 23 January.

Skinns L, Sorsby A and Rice L (2020) '"Treat Them as a Human Being": Dignity in Police Detention and its Implications for "Good" Police Custody' BJ Crim 1667–1688.

Skinns L, Sprawson A, Sorsby A, Smith R and Wooff A (2017) 'Police Custody Delivery in the Twenty-first Century in England and Wales: Current Arrangements and their Implications for Patterns of Policing' 4(3) European Journal of Policing Studies 325.

Skinns L and Wooff A (2020) 'Pain in Police Detention: A Critical Point in the "Penal Painscape"?' 31(3) Policing and Society 245–262.

Skogan W (1990) *The Police and Public in England and Wales: A British Crime Survey Report, Home Office Research Study 117* (London: HMSO).

Skogan W (1994) *Contacts between Police and Public—Findings from the 1992 British Crime Survey (Home Office Research Study no 134)* (London: Home Office).

Skolnick J (1966) *Justice Without Trial: Law Enforcement in a Democratic Society* (New York: John Wiley and Sons).

Skolnick J and Fyfe J (1993) *Above the Law* (New York: Free Press).

Skyrme T (1994) *History of the Justices of the Peace* (Chichester: Barry Rose).

Slapper G (1993) 'Corporate Manslaughter' 2 SLS 423.

Slapper G (1999) *Blood in the Bank: Social and Legal Aspects of Death at Work* (Aldershot: Ashgate).

Slapper G and Tombs S (1999) *Corporate Crime* (Harlow: Longman).

Smart C (1989) *Feminism and the Power of Law.* (London: Routledge).

Smethurst A and Collins K (2019) 'Mock Jury Perceptions of Vulnerable Defendants Assisted in Court by Intermediaries – Are Juror's Expectations Violated?' 15(1) Applied Psychology in Criminal Justice 23–40.

Smith D (1991) 'Origins of Black Hostility to the Police' 2 Policing and Society 6.

Smith D (1997a) 'Case Construction and the Goals of Criminal Process' 37 BJ Crim 319.

Smith D (1997b) 'Ethnic Origins, Crime and Criminal Justice' in Maguire M, Morgan R and Reiner R (eds), *Oxford Handbook of Criminology* 2nd edn (Oxford: Clarendon).

Smith D and Gray J (1983) *Police and People in London* vol 4 (Policy Studies Institute) (Aldershot: Gower).

Smith E (2017) 'Victims in the Witness Stand: Socio-Cultural and Psychological Challenges in Eliciting Victim Testimony' in Tibori-Szabó K and Hirst M (eds), *Victim Participation in International Criminal Justice* (The Hague: T.M.C. Asser Press).

Smith G (1997) 'The DPP and Prosecutions of Police Officers' 147 NLJ 6804.

Smith G (1999a) 'Double Trouble' 149 NLJ 1223.

Smith G (1999b) 'The Butler Report: An Opportunity Missed?' 149 NLJ 20 August.

Smith G (2001) 'Police Complaints and Criminal Prosecutions' 64 MLR 372.

Smith G (2003) 'Actions for Damages Against the Police and the Attitudes of Claimants' 13 Policing and Society 413.

Smith G (2004) 'Rethinking Police Complaints' 44 BJ Crim 15.

Smith G (2005) 'Comment on *Brooks v Commissioner of the Police of the Metropolis*' 69 Jo Criminal Law 4.

Smith G (2006) 'A Most Enduring Problem: Police Complaints Reform in England and Wales' 35 Jo Social Policy 121.

Smith G (2009a) 'European complaints' April, *Legal Action*, p 38.

Smith G (2009b) 'Why Don't More People Complain against the Police?' 6(3) European Journal of Criminology 249–266.

Smith G (2009c) 'Citizen Oversight of Independent Police Services: Bifurcated Accountability, Regulation Creep and Lesson Learning' 3 Regulation & Governance 422.

Smith G (2013) 'Oversight of the Police and Residual Complaints Dilemmas: Independence, Effectiveness and Accountability Deficits in the United Kingdom' 14(2) Police Practice and Research 92–103.

Smith G (2020) *On the Wrong Side of the Law: Complaints against the Metropolitan Police 1829–1964* (London: Palgrave Macmillan).

Smith G, Seddon T and Quirk H (2010) 'Regulation and Criminal Justice: Exploring the Connections and Disconnections' in Quirk H, Seddon T and Smith G (eds), *Regulation and Criminal Justice: Innovations in Policy and Research* (Cambridge: CUP).

Smith J (1995) 'The Criminal Appeal Act 1995: (1) Appeals against Conviction' Crim LR 920.

Smith O (2018) *Rape Trials in England and Wales* (London: Palgrave).

Smith O and Skinner T (2017) 'How Rape Myths Are Used and Challenged in Rape and Sexual Assault Trials' 26(4) SLS 441–466.

Smith R (1991) 'Resolving the Legal Aid Crisis' (1991) *Law Society Gazette*, 27 February, p 17.

Smith R (2017) *Diversion in Youth Justice* (Abingdon: Routledge).

Smith T (2013) 'The "Quiet Revolution" in Criminal Defence: How the Zealous Advocate Slipped into the Shadow' 20(1) International Journal of the Legal Profession 111–137.

Smith T (2018) 'The "Near Miss" of Liam Allan: Critical Problems in Police Disclosure, Investigation Culture, and the Resourcing of Criminal Justice' Crim LR 711.

Smith T and Cape E (2017) 'The Rise and Decline of Criminal Legal Aid in England and Wales' in Flynn A and Hodgson J (eds), *Access to Justice and Legal Aid: Comparative Perspectives on Unmet Legal Need.* (Oxford: Hart).

Snider L (1991) 'The Regulatory Dance: Understanding Reform Process in Corporate Crime' 19 IJ Soc of Law 209.

Snider L (1993) *Bad Business: Corporate Crime in Canada* (Toronto: University of Toronto Press).

Snoussi D and Mompelat L (2019) '*We Are Ghosts' Race, Class and Institutional Prejudice* (London: Runnymede Trust).

Softley P (1980) *Police Interrogation: An Observational Study in Four Police Stations* (Royal Commission on Criminal Procedure Research Study no 4) (London: HMSO).

Sohki-Bulley, B (2016) *Governing (Through) Rights* (Oxford: Bloomsbury Professional)

Sommerlad H (2001) ' "I've Lost the Plot": An Everyday Story of the "Political" Legal Aid Lawyer' 28 JLS 335.

Sommers S and Ellsworth P (2003) 'How Much Do We Really Know About Race and Juries? A Review of the Social Science Theory and Research' Chicago-Kent Law Review 997.

Sommers S and Marotta S (2014) 'Racial Disparities in Legal Outcomes: On Policing, Charging Decisions, and Criminal Trial Proceedings' 1(1) Policy Insights from the Behavioral and Brain Sciences 103–111.

Sosa K (2012) *Proceed with Caution: Use of Out-of-Court Disposals in England & Wales* (London: Policy Exchange).

Soubise, L (2017) 'Prosecuting in the Magistrates' Courts in a Time of Austerity' Crim LR 847.

Soukara S, Bull R, Vrij A and Turner M (2009) 'A Study of What Really Happens in Police Interviews of Suspects' 15(6) Psychology, Crime and Law 493.

Southgate P (1986) *Police-Public Encounters* (Home Office Research Study 90) (London: Home Office).

Southgate P and Ekblom P (1984) *Contacts Between Police and Public* (Home Office Research Study no 77) (London: HMSO).

Spalek B, Lambert R and Haqq Baker A (2009) 'Minority Muslim Communities and Criminal Justice: Stigmatized UK Faith Identities Post 9/11 and 7/7' in Bhui H, *Race & Criminal Justice* (London: Sage).

Spencer J (1991) 'Judicial Review of Criminal Proceedings' Crim LR 259.

Spencer J (2006) *Evidence of Bad Character* (Oxford: Hart).

Spencer J (2007) 'Quashing Convictions for Procedural Irregularities' Crim LR 835.

Spencer J (2008) 'Quashing Convictions for Procedural Irregularities' Cam LJ 227.

Spencer J (2014) *Hearsay Evidence in Criminal Proceedings*, 2nd Edn (Oxford: Hart Publishing).

Spencer J (2016) *Evidence of Bad Character*, 3rd Edn (Oxford: Hart Publishing).

Spicker P (2011) *How Social Security Works: An introduction to benefits in Britain* (Bristol: Policy Press).

Sprack J and Sprack M (2019) *A Practical Approach to Criminal Procedure*, 16th edn (Oxford: OUP).

SQUIRES D (2006) 'The Problem of Entrapment' 26(2) OJLS 351.

SQUIRES P (2012) 'Neoliberal, Brutish and Short? Cities, Inequalities and Violences' in SQUIRES P and LEA J (eds) *Criminalisation and Advanced Marginality: Critically Exploring the Work of Loic Wacquant* (Bristol: Policy Press).

SQUIRES P (ed) (2008) *ASBO Nation: The Criminalisation of Nuisance* (Bristol: Policy Press).

SQUIRES P 'Constructing the dangerous, black, criminal "other"' British Society of Criminology Newsletter, No. 79.

STARK F (2017) 'The Taming of Jogee?' 76(1) Cam LJ 4–7.

STEDMAN JONES D (2012) *Masters of the Universe: Hayek, Friedman, and the Birth of Neoliberal Politics* (New Jersey: Princeton UP).

STEFFENSMEIER D. PAINTER-DAVIS N and ULMER J (2016) 'Intersectionality of Race, Ethnicity, Gender and Ade on Criminal Punishment' 60(4) Sociological Perspectives 810–833.

STENSON K (2000) 'Crime Control, Social Policy and Liberalism', in LEWIS G et al (eds), *Rethinking Social Policy* (Milton Keynes: Open UP).

STENSON K (2012) 'The State, Sovereignty and Advanced Marginality in the City' in SQUIRES P and LEA J (eds) *Criminalisation and Advanced Marginality: Critically Exploring the Work of Loic Wacquant* (Bristol: Policy Press).

STENSON K and EDWARDS A (2004) 'Policy Transfer in Local Crime Control: Beyond Naïve Emulation' in NEWBURN T and SPARKS R (eds), *Criminal Justice and Political Cultures* (Cullompton: Willan).

STENSON K and WADDINGTON P (2007) 'Macpherson, Police Stops and Institutionalised Racism' in ROWE M (ed), *Policing Beyond Macpherson* (Cullompton: Willan).

STEPHEN F and TATA C with the assistance of SWEENEY L, FAZIO G and CHRISTIE A (2007) *Impact of the Introduction of Fixed Fee Payments into Summary Criminal Legal Aid: Report of an independent study* (Edinburgh: Scottish Executive).

STEPHEN F, FAZIO G and TATA C (2008) 'Incentives, Criminal Defence Lawyers and Plea Bargaining' 28(3) International Review of Law and Economics 212.

STEPHENSON G (1990) 'Should Collaborative Testimony be Permitted in Courts of Law?' Crim LR 302.

STEPHENSON G (1992) *The Psychology of Criminal Justice* (Oxford: Blackwell).

STEVENS P and WILLIS CF (1979) *Race, Crime and Arrests* (HORS no 58) (London: HMSO).

STOCKDALE R and WALKER C (1999) 'Forensic Evidence' in WALKER C and STARMER K (eds), *Miscarriages of Justice* (London: Blackstone).

STONE C (1988) *Bail Information for the Crown Prosecution Service* (New York: VERA Institute of Justice).

STONE R (2013) *The Law of Entry, Search and Seizure* (Oxford: OUP).

STONE V and PETTIGREW N (2000) *The Views of the Public on Stops and Searches* (Police Research Series Paper 129) (London: Home Office).

STONEMAN M-J, JACKSON L, DUNNETT S and COOKE L (2019) 'Variation in Detainee Risk Assessment Within Police Custody Across England and Wales' 29(8) Policing and Society 951–967.

STOTT C, LIVINGSTONE A and HOGGETT J (2008) 'Policing Football Crowds in England and Wales: A Model of Good Practice?' 18 (3) Policing and Society 258.

STRANG H (2002) *Repair or Revenge: Victims and Restorative Justice* (Oxford: OUP).

STRANG H and BRAITHWAITE J (eds) (2000) *Restorative Justice: Philosophy to Practice* (Ashgate: Dartmouth)

STRANG H et al (2006) 'Victim Evaluations of Face-to-Face Restorative Justice Conferences: A Quasi-experimental Analysis' 62 Journal of Social Issues 281.

STRICKLAND P (2015) *Bail Accommodation and Support Service. House of Commons Briefing Paper Number 05774* (London: House of Commons).

STRIDBECK U (2020) 'Coerced-Reactive Confessions: The Case of Thomas Quick' 20 Journal of Forensic Psychology Research and Practice 305–322.

STROUD P (2020) *Measuring Poverty 2020* (London: Social Metrics Commission).

STUBBS J (2007) 'Beyond Apology? Domestic Violence and Critical Questions for RJ' 7 Criminology and Criminal Justice 169.

STURGE G (2018) *UK Prison Population Statistics*, House of Commons Briefing Paper Number CBP-04334 (London: House of Commons).

STURGE G (2019) *Court statistics for England and Wales*, House of Commons Briefing Paper CBP 8372 (London: House of Commons Library).

SUKUMAR D, HODGSON J and WADE K (2016) 'Behind Closed Doors: Live Observations of Current Police Station Disclosure Practices and Lawyer-Client Consultations' Crim LR 12.

SUKUMAR D, HODGSON J and WADE K (2016) 'How the Timing of Police Evidence Disclosure Impacts Custodial Legal Advice' 20(3) IJ E&P 200–216.

SUKUMAR D, WADE K and HODGSON J (2016) 'Strategic Disclosure of Evidence: Perspectives From Psychology and Law' 22(3) Psychology, Public Policy, and Law 306–313.

SUNSTEIN C (2002) *Risk and Reason: Safety, Law and the Environment* (Cambridge: CUP).

TADDIA M (2014) 'Solicitor-Advocates: Raising the Bar' *Law Society Gazette*, 22 September.

TAGUE P (2000) 'Economic Incentives in Representing Publicly-Funded Criminal Defendants in England's Crown Court' 23 Fordham International Law Review 1128.

TAGUE P (2006) 'Tactical Reasons for Recommending Trials Rather than Guilty Pleas in Crown Court' Crim LR 23.

TAGUE P (2008) 'Barristers' Selfish Incentives in Counselling Clients' Crim LR 3.

TAIT D and GOODMAN-DELAHUNTY J (2017) 'The Effect of Deliberation on Jury Verdicts' in TAIT D and GOODMAN-DELAHUNTY J (eds), *Juries, Science and Popular Culture in the Age of Terror* (London: Palgrave Macmillan).

TAK P (ed) (2005) *Tasks and Powers of the Prosecution Services in the EU Member States* (2 vols) (Nijmegen: Wolf).

TALBOT J (2010) 'Prisoners' Voices: Experiences of the Criminal Justice System by Prisoners With Learning Disabilities' 15(3) Tizard Learning Disability Review 33–41.

TANKEBE, J, REISIG M and WANG X (2016) 'A Multidimensional Model Of Police Legitimacy: A Cross-Cultural Assessment' 40 Law and Human Behavior 11–22.

TAPPER C (2004) 'Evidence of Bad Character' Crim LR 533.

TARLING R, DOWDS L and BUDD T (2000) *Victim and witness intimidation: Findings from the British Crime Survey, HO Research Findings No 124* (London: Home Office).

TATA C (1999) 'Comparing Legal Aid Spending' in REGAN F, PATERSON A, GORIELY T and FLEMING D (eds), *The Transformation of Legal Aid* (Oxford: OUP).

TATA C (2019) '"Ritual Individualization": Creative Genius at Sentencing, Mitigation and Conviction' 46(1) JLS 112–140.

TATA C (2020) *Sentencing: A Social Process* (London: Palgrave Macmillan).

TATA C and GORMLEY J (2016) *Sentencing and Plea Bargaining: Guilty Pleas versus Trial Verdicts* in: Oxford Handbooks Online (Oxford: OUP).

TATA C and STEPHEN F (2006) 'Do Changes to the Structure of Legal Aid Remuneration Make a Real Difference to Criminal Case Outcomes?' Crim LR 722.

TATA C, GORIELY T, MCCRONE P, DUFF P, KNAPP M, HENRY A, LANCASTER B and SHERR A (2004) 'Does Mode of Delivery Make a Difference to Criminal Case Outcomes and Clients' Satisfaction?

The Public Defence Solicitor Experiment' Crim LR 120.

Taylor C (2005) 'Advance Disclosure and the Culture of the Investigator' 33 IJ Sociology of Law 118.

Taylor C (2006) *Criminal Investigation and Pre-Trial Disclosure in the United Kingdom: How Detectives Put Together a Case* (Lampeter: Edwin Mellen Press).

Taylor E (2016) 'Lights, Camera, Redaction . . . Police Body-worn Cameras: Autonomy, Discretion and Accountability' 14 Surveillance and Society 128.

Taylor N and Denyer R (2014) 'Judicial Management of Juror Impropriety' 78(1) JCL 43–64.

Taylor N and Ormerod D (2004) 'Mind the Gaps: Safety, Fairness and Moral Legitimacy' Crim LR 266.

Taylor P (ed) (2012) *Taylor on Criminal Appeals*, 2nd edn (Oxford: OUP).

Taylor R, Leng R and Wasik M (2004) *Blackstone's Guide to the Criminal Justice Act 2003* (Oxford: OUP).

Taylor R with Mansfield M (1999) 'Post-conviction Procedures' in Walker C and Starmer K (eds), *Miscarriages of Justice* (London: Blackstone).

Taylor R, Wasik M and Leng R (2004) *Blackstone's Guide to the Criminal Justice Act 2003* (Oxford: OUP).

Taylor W (2005) Review of Police Disciplinary Arrangements (London: Home Office).

Temkin J (2000) 'Prosecuting and Defending Rape: Perspectives from the Bar' (2000) 27 JLS 219.

Temkin J (2003) 'Sexual History Evidence – Beware the Backlash' Crim LR 217.

Temkin J and Krahe B (2008) *Sexual Assault and the Justice Gap* (Oxford: Hart).

Terry M, Johnson S and Thompson P (2010) *Virtual Court pilot Outcome evaluation*, (London: MoJ).

The Fingerprint Inquiry (2011) *The Fingerprint Inquiry Report* (Edinburgh: APS Group).

The Secret Barrister (2018) *Stories of the Law and How It's Broken* (London: Macmillan).

Thomas C (2008) 'Exposing the Myths of Jury Service' Crim LR 415.

Thomas C with Bulmer N (2007) *Diversity and Fairness in the Jury System*, Ministry of Justice Research Series 2/07 (London: MoJ).

Thomas L, Vaughan S, Malkani B and Lynch T (eds) (2018) *Reimagining Clinical Legal Education* (Oxford: Hart Publishing).

Thomas M (2020) '"Expert Shopping": Appeals Adducing Fresh Evidence in Diminished Responsibility Cases: R v Foy [2020] EWCA Crim 270' 84(3) JCL 249–254.

Thomas, C (2010) *Are Juries Fair? Ministry of Justice Research Series 1/10* (London: MoJ).

Thomas, C (2013) 'Avoiding the Perfect Storm of Juror Contempt' Crim LR 6.

Thomas C (2017) *2016 UK Judicial Attitude Survey* (London: UCL Judicial Institute).

Thomas C (2017) 'Ethnicity and the Fairness of Jury Trials in England and Wales 2006–2014' 11 Crim LR 860–876.

Thomas C (2020) 'The 21st Century Jury: Contempt, Bias and the Impact of Jury Service' Crim LR 987–1011.

Thompson E (1975) *Whigs and Hunters* (London: Allen Lane).

Thompson F (1981) 'Social Control in Victorian Britain' 34(2) Economic History Review 189–208

Thompson J (2005) 'The New Visibility' 22 Theory, Culture and Society 31–51.

Thompson T (2000) *Bloggs 19* (London: Time Warner).

Thornton J (2019) 'The Way in Which Fee Reductions Influence Legal Aid Criminal Defence Lawyer Work: Insights from a Qualitative Study' 46(4) JLS.

Thornton J (2020) 'Is Publicly Funded Criminal Defence Sustainable? Legal Aid Cuts, Morale, Recruitment and Retention in the English Criminal Law Professions' Legal Studies 40(2) *Legal Studies* 230.

THORNTON P (1993) 'Miscarriages of Justice: A Lost Opportunity' Crim LR 926.

TILLEY N (2016) 'Intelligence-led Policing and the Disruption of Organized Crime: Motifs, Methods and Morals' in DELPEUCH T and Ross J (eds), *Comparing the Democratic Governance of Police Intelligence* (Northampton, MA: Edward Elgar).

TILLEY N and FORD A (1996) *Forensic Science and Crime Investigation* (Crime Prevention and Detection Series Paper 73) (London: Home Office).

TILLEY N, ROBINSON A and BURROWS J (2007) 'The Investigation of High-volume Crime' in NEWBURN T, WILLIAMSON T and WRIGHT A (eds), *Handbook of Criminal Investigation* (Cullompton: Willan).

TINSLEY Y (2001a) 'Even Better Than the Real Thing? The Case for Reform of Identification Procedures' 5 IJ E & P 235.

TINSLEY Y (2001b) 'Juror Decision-Making: A Look Inside the Jury Room' Selected Papers from the British Criminology Conference, vol 4,

TIRATELLI M, QUINTON P and BRADFORD B (2018) 'Does Stop and Search Deter Crime? Evidence From Ten Years of London-wide Data' 58(5) BJ Crim 1212–1231.

TOMBS S (1995) 'Law, Resistance and Reform: Regulating Safety Crimes in the UK' 4 Social and Legal Studies 343.

TOMBS S and WHYTE D (2007) *Safety Crimes* (Cullompton: Willan).

TOMBS S and WHYTE D (2008) *A Crisis of Enforcement: The decriminalisation of death and injury at work* (Centre for Crime and Justice Studies Briefing no 6, Kings College London).

TOMCZAK P and BUCK G (2019) 'The Criminal Justice Voluntary Sector: Concepts and an Agenda for an Emerging Field' 58(3) Howard JCJ 276–297.

TOMKINS A (2002) 'Legislating Against Terror: the ACTS Act 2001' PL 205.

TONEY R (2001) 'Disclosure of Evidence and Legal Assistance at Custodial Interrogation: What Does the ECHR Require?' 5 IJ E&P 39.

TONRY M (2004) *Punishment and Politics: Evidence and Emulation in the making of English crime control policy* (Cullompton: Willan).

TONRY M (2014) 'Why Crime Rates Are Falling throughout the Western World' 43(1) Crime and Justice.

TORRIBLE C (2018) 'Reconceptualising the Police Complaints Process as a Site of Contested Legitimacy Claims' 28(4) Policing and Society 464–479.

TOWNEND J (2020) 'Covid-19, the UK's Coronavirus Act and emergency "remote" court hearings: what does it mean for open justice?' *The Justice Gap*, 30 March.

TOWNSHEND C (1993) *Making the Peace: Public Order and Public Security in Modern Britain* (Oxford: OUP).

TRANSFORM JUSTICE (2018) *Presumed Innocent but Behind Bars—is Remand overused in England and Wales?* (London: Transform Justice).

TRANSFORM JUSTICE (2019) *The Right to Know You Are Accused of a Crime* (London: Transform Justice).

TULLY B and MORGAN D (1997) 'Fair warning?' 29 September, *Police Review*, p 24.

TULLY G (2016) *Annual Report 2016* (Birmingham: Forensic Science Regulator).

TYLER T (1990) *Why People Obey the Law* (New Haven: Yale University Press).

TYLER T (2003) 'Procedural Justice, Legitimacy, and the Effective Rule of Law' 30 Crime and Justice 283–357.

TYLER T (ed) (2007) *Legitimacy and Criminal Justice: An International Perspective* (New York: Russel Sage Foundation).

TYLER T, FAGAN J and GELLER A (2014) 'Street Stops and Police Legitimacy' 11 Journal of Empirical Legal Studies 751–785.

TYLER T and HUO Y (2002) *Trust in the Law: Encouraging Public Cooperation with the Police and the Courts* (New York: Russell Sage).

TYSON J (2020) 'Disablist Hate Crime: A Scar on the Conscience of the Criminal Justice

System?' in Tapley J and Davies P (eds), *Victimology: Research, policy and activism* (London: Palgrave Macmillan).

Uglow S (2002) *Criminal Justice*, 2nd edn (London: Sweet and Maxwell).

Valentine T and Heaton P (1999) 'An Evaluation of the Fairness of Police Line-ups and Video Identifications' 13 *Applied Cognitive Psychology* 59.

Vallano J, Evans J, Schreiber Compo N and Kieckhaefer J M (2015), 'Rapport-Building During Witness and Suspect Interviews: A Survey of Law Enforcement' 29 Appl. Cognit. Psychol 369–380.

van Charldorp T (2020) 'Reconstructing Suspects' Stories in Various Police Record Styles' in Mason M and Rock F (eds) *The Discourse of Police Interviews.* (Chicago: Chicago UP).

Van Der Merwe A and Skelton A (2015) 'Victims' Mitigating Views in Sentencing Decisions: A Comparative Analysis' 35 OJLS 355.

van Dijk J (2000) 'Implications of the International Crime Victims Survey for a Victim Perspective' in Crawford A and Goodey J (eds), *Integrating a Victim Perspective within Criminal Justice* (Aldershot: Ashgate).

van Dijk J (2013) 'Victim-centred Restorative Justice' 3 Restorative Justice 42.

van Dijk J and Groenhuijsen M (2018) 'A Glass Half Full, or Half Empty? On the Implementation of the EU's Victims Directive Regarding Police Reception and Specialized Support' in Walklate S (ed), *Handbook of Victims and Victimology* (London: Routledge).

Van Slyke S, Benson M and Cullen F (eds) (2016) *The Oxford Handbook of White Collar Crime* (Oxford: OUP).

Van Zyl Smit D (2006) 'Humanising Imprisonment: A European Project?' 12(2) European Journal on Criminal Policy and Research 107–120.

Vander Becken T and Kilchling M (eds) (2000) *The Role of the Public Prosecutor in European Criminal Justice Systems* (Brussels: KVAB).

Vanderhallen M, Vervaeke G and Holmber V (2011) 'Witness and Suspect Perception of Working Alliance and Interviewing Style' 8 Journal of Investigative Psychology and Offender Profiling 2.

Vennard J (1981) *Contested Trials in Magistrates' Courts* (Home Office Research Study no 71) (London: HMSO).

Vennard J (1985) 'The Outcome of Contested Trials' in Moxon D (ed), *Managing Criminal Justice* (London: HMSO).

Vennard J and Riley D (1988) 'The Use of Peremptory Challenge and Stand By of Jurors and Their Relationship to Final Outcome' Crim LR 731.

Vennard J, Davis G, Baldwin J and Pearce J (2004) *Ethnic minority magistrates' experience of the role and of the court environment* DCA Research Report 3/2004 (London: DCA).

Victims' Commissioner (2019a) *Victim Advocates* (London: Office of the Commissioner for Victims and Witnesses).

Victims' Commissioner (2019b) *Victim personal statements 2018/19* (London: Office of the Commissioner for Victims and Witnesses).

Vigurs C, Wire J, Myhill A and Gough D (2016) *Police Initial Responses to Domestic Abuse: A systematic review* (College of Policing).

Viki G, Culmer M, Eller A and Abrams D (2006) 'Race and Willingness to Cooperate with the Police: the Roles of Quality of Contact, Attitudes Towards the Behaviour and Subjective Norms' 45(2) British Journal of Social Psychology 285–302.

Virdee A and McGeever B (2018) 'Racism, Crisis, Brexit' 41(10) Ethnic and Racial Studies 1802–1819.

Virgo G (2008) 'Terrorism: Possession of Articles' Cam LJ 236.

Vogel M (2007) *Coercion to Compromise: Plea Bargaining, the Courts and the Making of Political Authority* (Oxford: OUP).

Vogler R (1982) 'Magistrates and Civil Disorder' (November) LAG Bull 12.

Vogler R (1991) *Reading the Riot Act* (Milton Keynes: Open UP).

Vogler R (2016) *A World View of Criminal Justice* (Oxford: Routledge).

Vogt G and Wadham J (2003) *Deaths in Police Custody: Redress and Remedies* (London: Civil Liberties Trust).

von Hirsch A and Roberts J (2004) 'Legislating Sentencing Principles' Crim LR 639.

von Hirsch A, Bottoms A, Burney E and Wilkstrom P-O (1999) *Criminal Deterrence and Sentence Severity* (Oxford: Hart).

Vrij A (2008a) *Detecting Lies and Deceit*, 2nd edn (Chichester: Wiley).

Vrij A (2008b) 'Nonverbal Dominance Versus Verbal Accuracy in Lie Detection: A Plea To Change Police Practice' 35(10) Criminal Justice and Behavior 1323.

Vrij A (2011) 'Editorial: Interrogation Techniques, Information-gathering and (False) Confessions' 16(2) Legal and Criminological Psychology.

Vrij A, Granhag P and Porter S (2010) 'Pitfalls and Opportunities in Nonverbal and Verbal Lie Detection' 11(3) Psychological Science in the Public Interest 89–121.

Wacquant L (2009) *Punishing the Poor: The Neoliberal Government of Social Insecurity* (Durham: Duke UP).

Wacquant L (2012) 'The Wedding of Workfare and Prisonfare in the 21st Century: Responses to Critics and Commentators' in Squires P and Lea J (eds), *Criminalisation and Advanced Marginality. Critically Exploring the Work of Loic Wacquant* (Bristol: Policy Press).

Waddington D (2007) *Policing Public Disorder* (Cullompton: Willan).

Waddington P (1991) *The Strong Arm of the Law* (Oxford: Clarendon).

Waddington P (1994) *Liberty and Order* (London: UCL Press).

Waddington P (1998) 'Controlling Protest in Contemporary Historical and Comparative Perspective' in della Porta D and Reiter H (eds), *Policing Protest: The Control of Mass Demonstrations in Western Democracies* (Minneapolis: University of Minnesota Press).

Waddington P (1999a) 'Police (Canteen) Sub-Culture: An Appreciation' 39 BJ Crim 286.

Waddington P (1999b) *Policing Citizens* (London: UCL Press).

Waddington P, Stenson K and Don D (2004) 'In Proportion: Race, and Police Stop and Search' 44(6) BJ Crim 889.

Waddington P and Wright M (2008) 'Police Use of Force, Firearms and Riot Control' in Newburn T (ed), *Handbook of Policing*, 2nd edn (Cullompton: Willan).

Wade K (2009) 'Innocent but Proven Guilty: Eliciting Internalised False Confessions Using Doctored Video Evidence' 23 Appl. Cognit. Psychol. 624.

Wade M and Jehle J (eds) (2008) 'Prosecution and Diversion within Criminal Justice Systems within Europe' 14 (2, 3) Special Issue, European Jo Crim Policy and Research.

Wadham J, Mountfield H and Edmundson A (2007) *Blackstone's Guide to the Human Rights Act 1998*, 4th edn (Oxford: OUP).

Wake R, Simpson C, Homes A and Ballantyne J (2007*) Public perceptions of the police complaints system* (London: IPCC).

Wakefield A (2003) *Selling Security* (Cullompton: Willan).

Walker C (1999a) 'Miscarriages of Justice in Principle and Practice' in Walker C and Starmer K (eds), *Miscarriages of Justice* (London: Blackstone).

Walker C (1999b) 'The Agenda of Miscarriages of Justice' in Walker C and Starmer K (eds), *Miscarriages of Justice* (London: Blackstone).

Walker C (1999c) 'The Judiciary' in Walker C and Starmer K (eds), *Miscarriages of Justice* (London: Blackstone).

Walker C (2002a) *Blackstone's Guide to the Anti-Terrorism Legislation* (Oxford: OUP).

Walker C (2002b) 'Miscarriages of Justice' in McConville M and Wilson G (eds),

The Handbook of the Criminal Justice Process (Oxford: OUP).

WALKER C (2004) 'Terrorism and Criminal Justice – Past, Present and Future' Crim LR 311.

WALKER C (2007) 'The Treatment of Foreign Terror Suspects' 70 MLR 427.

WALKER C (2008) '"Know Thine Enemy as Thyself": Discerning Friend from Foe Under Anti-terrorism Laws' 32(1) Melbourne Univ LR 275–301.

WALKER C (2008) 'Post-charge Questioning of Suspects' Crim LR 509.

WALKER C (2009) *Blackstone's Guide to the Anti-Terrorism Legislation*, 2nd edn (Oxford: OUP).

WALKER C (2014) *Blackstone's Guide to the Anti-Terrorism Legislation*, 3rd edn (Oxford: OUP).

WALKER C (2016) 'Post-charge Questioning in UK Terrorism Cases: Straining the Adversarial Process' 20(5) IJHR 649–665.

WALKER C (2018) 'Counter-terrorism and Counter-extremism: The UK Policy Spirals' PL 725.

WALKER C and HORNE A (2012) 'The Terrorism Prevention and Investigation Measures Act 2011: One Thing but Not Much the Other?' May Crim LR 421–438.

WALKER C and MCGUINNESS M (2002) 'Commercial Risk, Political Violence and Policing the City of London' in CRAWFORD A (ed), *Crime and Insecurity: The Governance of Safety in Europe* (Cullompton: Willan).

WALKER C and STOCKDALE E (1995) 'Forensic Science and Miscarriages of Justice' 54 Cam LJ 69.

WALKER C and WALL D (1997) 'Imprisoning the Poor: TV Licence Evaders and the Criminal Justice System' Crim LR 173.

WALKLATE S (ed) (2018) *Handbook of Victims and Victimology* (London: Routledge).

WALKLEY J (1988) *Police Interrogation: A Handbook for Investigators* (London: Police Review Publishing Company).

WALL D (1996) 'Keyholders to Criminal Justice' in YOUNG R and WALL D (eds), *Access to Criminal Justice* (London: Blackstone).

WALL T and LINNEMANN T (2014) 'Staring Down the State: Police Power, Visual Economies, and the "War on Cameras"' 10(2) Crime, Media, Culture 133–149.

WALSH D (2009) '20 Years of Handling Police Complaints in Ireland: A Critical Assessment of the Supervisory Board Model' 29 Legal Studies 305.

WALSH D and BULL R (2010) 'Interviewing Suspects of Fraud: An In-Depth Analysis of Interviewing Skills' 38(1–2) Journal of Psychiatry & Law 99–135.

WALSH D and BULL R (2012) 'Examining Rapport in Investigative Interviews with Suspects: Does its Building and Maintenance Work?' 27 J Police Crim Psych 73–84.

WALSH D and BULL R (2015) 'Interviewing Suspects: Examining the Association Between Skills, Questioning, Evidence Disclosure, and Interview Outcomes' 21(7) Psychology, Crime & Law 661–680.

WALSH D and MILNE R (2007) 'Giving P.E.A.C.E. A Chance: A Study of DWP's Investigators' Perceptions of their Interviewing Practices' 85 Public Administration 525.

WALSH D and MILNE R (2008) 'Keeping the Peace? A Study of Investigative Practice in the Public Sector' 13 Legal and Criminological Psychology 39.

WALSH D, MILNE B and BULL R (2016) 'One Way or Another? Criminal Investigators' Beliefs Regarding the Disclosure of Evidence in Interviews with Suspects in England and Wales' 31(2) J Police Crim Psych 127.

WALSH D, OXBURGH G, REDLICH A and MYKLEBUST T (2016) *International Developments and Practices in Investigative Interviewing and Interrogation Vol. 1: Victims and Witnesses* (London: Routledge).

WALTERS M (2014) *Hate Crime and Restorative Justice: Exploring Causes, Repairing Harms* (Oxford: OUP).

WALTERS M (2014) 'Conceptualizing "Hostility" for Hate Crime Law: Minding "the Minutiae" when Interpreting section 28(1)(a) of the Crime and Disorder Act 1998' 34(1) OJLS 47–74.

WALTERS M (2018) '"Better in My Day": Judges' Verdict on Advocacy Standards' *Law Society Gazette*, 27 June

WALTERS M, OWUSU-BEMPAH A and WIEDLITZKA S (2018) 'Hate Crime and the "Justice Gap": The Case for Law Reform' 12 Crim LR 961–986.

WALTERS M, PATERSON J, MCDONNELL L and BROWN R (2019) 'Group Identity, Empathy and Shared Suffering: Understanding the "Community" Impacts of anti-LGBT and Islamophobic Hate Crimes' International Review of Victimology.

WARBURTON H, MAY T and HOUGH M (2003) *Opposite Sides of the Same Coin: Police Perspectives on Informally Resolved Complaints* (London: The Police Foundation).

WARBURTON H, MAY T and HOUGH M (2005) 'Looking the Other Way: The Impact of Reclassifying Cannabis on Police Warnings, Arrests and Informal Action in England and Wales' 45 BJ Crim 113.

WARD J (2015) 'Transforming 'Summary Justice' Through Police-led Prosecution and 'Virtual Courts'' (2015) 55 BJ Crim 341

WARD J (2016) *Transforming Summary Justice: Modernisation in the Lower Criminal Courts.* (London. Routledge)

WARNER C (2019) Draft Domestic Abuse Bill: Progress or pitfall? *Counsel Magazine*, May.

WASIK M (1996) 'Magistrates: Knowledge of Previous Convictions' Crim LR 851.

WASIK M and TAYLOR R (1995) *Blackstone's Guide to the Criminal Justice and Public Order Act 1994* (London: Blackstone).

WATERS I and BROWN K (2000) 'Police Complaints and the Complainants' Experience' 40 BJ Crim 617.

WATKIN JONES P and GRIFFIN N (2015) Public Inquiries: Getting at the Truth, Law Gazette, 22 June 2015.

WATSON C, WEISS K and POUNCEY C (2010) 'False Confessions, Expert Testimony, and Admissibility' 38 Journal of the American Academy of Psychiatry and the Law 174–86.

WATSON S (2000) 'Foucault and Social Policy' in LEWIS G et al (eds), *Rethinking Social Policy* (Milton Keynes, Open UP).

WEATHERITT M (1980) The Prosecution System: Survey of Prosecuting Solicitors' Departments (Royal Commission on Criminal Procedure, Research Study no 11) (London: HMSO).

WEDLOCK E and TAPLEY J (2016) *What works in supporting victims of crime* (London: Office of the Commissioner for Victims and Witnesses).

WEISSELBERG C (2008) 'Mourning Miranda' 96 Calif LR 1519.

WELLS C (2001) *Corporations and Criminal Responsibility*, 2nd edn (Oxford: OUP).

WELLS C (2004) 'The Impact of Feminist Thinking on Criminal Law and Justice: Contradiction, Complexity, Conviction and Connection' Crim LR 503.

WELLS C (2006) 'Corporate Manslaughter: Why Does Reform Matter?' 122 South African LJ 646.

WELLS C (2017) *Abuse of Process*, 3rd edn (Oxford: OUP).

WELLS G, KOVERA M, DOUGLASS A, BREWER N, MEISSNER C and WIXTED J (2020) 'Policy and Procedure Recommendations for the Collection and Preservation of Eyewitness Identification Evidence' 44(1) Law and Human Behaviour 3–36.

WELLS G, OLSON E and CHARMAN S (2003) 'Distorted Retrospective Eyewitness Reports as Functions of Feedback and Delay' 9 J Experimental Psychology: Applied 42.

WELLS H (2015) 'Grey Areas and Fine Lines: Negotiating Operational Independence in the Era of the Police and Crime Commissioner' 14(4) Safer Communities 193–202.

WELSH L (2013) 'Are Magistrates' Courts Really a 'Law Free Zone'? Participant Observation and Specialist Use of

Language' 13 Papers from the British Criminology Conference 3–16.

WELSH L (2016) 'Magistrates, Managerialism and Marginalisation: Neoliberalism and Access to Justice' Doctoral thesis (PhD), University of Kent.

WELSH L (2017) 'The Effects of Changes to Legal Aid on Lawyers' Professional Identity' 44(4) JLS 559–585.

WELSH L (2017) 'The Role of Law in Temporal Reasoning: An Interview with Annelise Riles' 25(1) Feminist Legal Studies 123–129.

WELSH L (2018) 'The plight of the unrepresented defendant' *The Justice Gap*, 9 May.

WELSH L and HOWARD M (2019) 'Standardisation and the Production of Justice in Summary Criminal Courts: A Post Human Analysis' 28(6) SLS 774–793.

WEST R (1999) *Caring for Justice* (New York: NYUP).

WESTERA N and KEBBELL M (2014) 'Investigative Interviewing in Suspected Sex Offences' in BULL R (eds), *Investigative Interviewing* (NYC: Springer).

WESTMARLAND L (2005) 'Police Ethics and Integrity: Breaking the Blue Code of Silence' 15 Policing & Society 145.

WESTMARLAND L (2008) 'Police Cultures' in NEWBURN T (ed), *The Handbook of Policing*, 2nd edn (Cullompton: Willan).

WESTMARLAND L (2013) '"Snitches get Stitches": US Homicide Detectives' Ethics and Morals in Action' 23(3) Policing and Society 311–327.

WESTMARLAND N, JOHNSON K and McGLYNN C (2018) 'Under the Radar: The Widespread Use of "Out of Court Resolutions" in Policing Domestic Violence and Abuse in the United Kingdom' 58(1) BJ Crim 1–16.

WEYEMBERGH A (2017) 'Consequences of Brexit for European Union Criminal Law' 8(3) New Journal of European Criminal Law 284–299.

WHITE A (2014) 'Post-crisis Policing and Public–Private Partnerships: The Case of Lincolnshire Police and G4S' 54(6) BJ Crim 1002–1022.

WHITE A and GILL M (2013) 'The Transformation of Policing: From Ratios to Rationalities' 53(1) BJ Crim 74–93.

WHITE K and BRODY S (1980) 'The Use of Bail Hostels' Crim LR 420.

WHITE R (1985) *The Administration of Justice* (Oxford: Basil Blackwell).

WHITE R (2006) 'Investigators and Prosecutors or, Desperately Seeking Scotland: Re-formulation of the "Philips Principle"' 69 MLR 143.

WHITFIELD J (2007) 'The Historical Context: Policing and Black People in Post-war Britain' in ROWE M (ed), *Policing Beyond Macpherson* (Cullompton: Willan).

WHYTE D (2007/8) 'Gordon Brown's Charter for Corporate Criminal' 70 Criminal Justice Matters 31.

WHYTE D (2011) 'An Intoxicated Politics of Regulation' in QUIRK H, SEDDON T and SMITH G (eds), *Regulation and Criminal Justice* (Cambridge: CUP).

WIEDLITZKA S, WELSH L and CLARKE A (2020) *Criminal Cases Review Commission: Legal Aid and Legal Representatives. Stage Three: Survey Of Representatives* (Brighton: University of Sussex).

WILCOX A and YOUNG R (2006) *Understanding the Interests of Justice* (London: Legal Services Commission).

WILCOX A and YOUNG R (2007) 'How Green was Thames Valley?: Policing the Image of Restorative Justice Cautions' 17(2) Policing and Society 141.

WILCOX A, YOUNG R and HOYLE C (2004) *Two-year resanctioning study: a comparison of restorative and traditional cautions.* Home Office Online Report 57/04 (London: Home Office).

WILDING B (2008) 'Tipping the Scales of Justice?: A Review of the Impact of PACE on the Police, Due Process and the Search for the Truth 1984-2006' in CAPE E and YOUNG R (eds), *Regulating Policing* (Oxford: Hart).

WILKINS G and ADDICOT C (2000) Operation of Certain Police Powers Under PACE, Statistical Bulletin 9/00 (London: Home Office).

WILKINSON P (2001) *Terrorism versus Democracy* (London: Frank Cass).

WILLIAMS C (1995) *Invisible Victims: Crime and Abuse Against People with Learning Disabilities* (Bristol: Norah Fry Research Centre).

WILLIAMS G (1979) 'The Authentication of Statements to the Police' Crim LR 6.

WILLIAMS G (1985) 'Letting off the Guilty and Prosecuting the Innocent' Crim LR 115.

WILLIAMS J (2000) 'The CDA: Conflicting Roles for the Appropriate Adult' Crim LR 911.

WILLIAMS P and CLARKE B (2016) *Dangerous associations: Joint enterprise, gangs and racism* (London: Centre for Crime and Justice Studies).

WILLIAMS P and CLARKE B (2018) 'The Black Criminal Other as an Object of Social Control' 7 Soc. Sci. 234.

WILLIAMS R and JOHNSON P (2008) *Genetic Policing: The Use of DNA in Criminal Investigations* (Cullompton: Willan).

WILLIAMS W (2020) *Windrush Lessons Learned Review* HC 93 (London: Home Office).

WILLIAMSON T (1994) 'Reflections on Current Police Practice' in MORGAN D and STEPHENSON G (eds), *Suspicion and Silence* (London: Blackstone).

WILLIAMSON T and BAGSHAW P (2001) 'The Ethics of Informer Handling' in BILLINGSLEY R, NEMITZ T and BEAN P (eds), *Informers: Policing, Policy, Practice* (Cullompton: Willan).

WILLIS C (1983) *The Use, Effectiveness and Impact of Police Stop and Search Powers* (Home Office Research and Planning Unit Paper no 15) (London: Home Office).

WILLMOTT D, BODUSZEK D and BOOTH N (2017) 'The English Jury on Trial' 82 Custodial Review 12–14.

WINDLE J, MOYLE L and COOMBER R (2020) '"Vulnerable" Kids Going Country: Children and Young People's Involvement in County Lines Drug Dealing' 20(1–2) Youth Justice 64–78.

WINDLESHAM LORD (1988) 'Punishment and Prevention: The Inappropriate Prisoners' Crim LR 140.

WINTER J (2002. 'The Truth Will Out? The Role of Judicial Advocacy and Gender in Verdict Construction' 11(3) SLS 343–367.

WOLCHOVER D (1989) 'Guilt and the Silent Suspect' 139 NLJ

WOLCHOVER D (1989) 'Should Judges Sum up on the Facts?' Crim LR 781.

WOLHUTER L, OLLEY N and DENHAM D (2009) *Victimology: Victimisation and Victim's Rights* (Abingdon: Routledge).

WONNACOTT C (1999) 'The Counterfeit Contract – Reform, Pretence and Muddled Principles in the New Referral Order' 11 CFLQ 209.

WOOD J (1999) 'Appendix – Extracts from the Transcript of the Trial of the Birmingham six, Lancaster, June 1975' in WALKER C and STARMER K (eds), *Miscarriages of Justice* (London: Blackstone).

WOODMAN C, (2018) *Spycops in context: A brief history of political policing in Britain* (London: Centre for Crime and Justice Studies).

WOODY W and FORREST K (2020) *Understanding Police Interrogation: Confessions and Consequences* (New York: NYUP).

WOOLF (1991) *Prison Disturbances April 1990, Report of an Inquiry by The Rt Hon Lord Justice Woolf (Parts I and II) and His Honour Judge Stephen Tumim (Part II)* (Cm 1456) (London: HMSO).

WOOLF (2000) *Unjust Deserts: A thematic review of the Chief Inspector of Prisons of the treatment and conditions for unsentenced prisoners in England and Wales* (London: Home Office).

WORTHERN T (2008) 'The Hearsay Provisions of the Criminal Justice Act 2003: So Far, Not So Good?' Crim LR 431.

WRIGHT F (2007) 'Criminal Liability of Directors and Senior Managers for Deaths at Work' Crim LR 949.

WRIGHT S (1998) 'Policing Domestic Violence: A Nottingham Case Study' 20 JSWFL 397.

WYNER R (2003) *From the Inside: Dispatches from a Women's Prison* (London: Aurum Press).

YJB (2019) *Youth Justice Statistics 2017/18 England and Wales* (London: HMSO).

YOUNG H (2002) Securing Fair Treatment: An Examination of the Diversion of Mentally Disordered Offenders from Police Custody, Unpublished PhD (Birmingham University).

YOUNG J (1994) *Policing the Streets—Stops and Search in North London* (London: Islington Council).

YOUNG J (1999) 'The Politics of the Human Rights Act' 26(1) JLS 27.

YOUNG J (2002) 'Searching for a New Criminology of Everyday Life: A Review of the "Culture of Control" by David Garland' 42 BJ Crim 228.

YOUNG M (1991) *An Inside Job* (Oxford: OUP).

YOUNG R (1987) *The Sandwell Mediation and Reparation Scheme* (Birmingham: West Midlands Probation Service).

YOUNG R (1993) 'The Merits of Legal Aid in the Magistrates' Courts' Crim LR 336.

YOUNG R (1996) 'Will Widgery Do?' in YOUNG R and WALL D (eds), *Access to Criminal Justice* (London: Blackstone).

YOUNG R (2000) 'Integrating a Multi-Victim Perspective into Criminal Justice Through Restorative Justice Conferences' in CRAWFORD A and GOODEY J (eds), *Integrating a Victim Perspective within Criminal Justice* (Aldershot: Ashgate).

YOUNG R (2002) 'Testing the Limits of Restorative Justice: The Case of Corporate Victims' in HOYLE C and YOUNG R (eds), *New Visions of Crime Victims* (Oxford: Hart).

YOUNG R (2003) 'Review of Henham R, Sentence Discounts and the Criminal Process' 7 2) Edinburgh LR 267.

YOUNG R (2008) 'Street Policing after PACE: The Drift to Summary Justice' in CAPE E and YOUNG R (eds), *Regulating Policing* (Oxford: Hart)

YOUNG R (2010) 'Ethnic Profiling and Summary Justice - An Ominous Silence' in SVEINSSON K (ed), *Ethnic Profiling: The Use of 'Race' in UK Law Enforcement* (London: Runnymede Trust).

YOUNG R (2013) 'Exploring the Boundaries of the Criminal Courtroom Workgroup' 42(3) Common Law World Review 203–239.

YOUNG R and GOOLD B (1999) 'Restorative Police Cautioning in Aylesbury' Crim LR 126.

YOUNG R, HOYLE C, COOPER K and HILL R (2005) 'Informal Resolution of Complaints Against the Police: A Quasi-Experimental Test of Restorative Justice' 5 Criminal Justice 279.

YOUNG R, MOLONEY T and SANDERS A (1992) In the Interests of Justice? (Birmingham: Birmingham University).

YOUNG R and SANDERS A (1994) 'The Royal Commission on Criminal Justice: A Confidence Trick?' 15 OJLS 435.

YOUNG R and SANDERS A (2004) 'The Ethics of Prosecution Lawyers' 7(2) Legal Ethics 190.

YOUNG R and WALL D (eds) (1996a) *Access to Criminal Justice* (London: Blackstone).

YOUNG R and WALL D (1996b) 'Criminal Justice, Legal Aid and the Defence of Liberty' in YOUNG R and WALL D (eds) *Access to Criminal Justice* (London: Blackstone).

YOUNG R and WILCOX A (2007) 'The Merits of Legal Aid in the Magistrates' Courts Revisited' Crim LR 109.

YOUNG S (2012) *Gender, Policing and Social Control: Examining Police Officers' Perceptions of and Responses to Young Women Depicted as Violent*, SCCJR Briefing Paper, Briefing No. 01/2012 (The Scottish Centre for Crime and Justice Research).

YOUNG S (2015) 'Policing "Uncontrollable Banshees": Factors Influencing Arrest

Decision Making' 14(4) Safer Communities 183–19.

YOUNG W, CAMERON N and TINSLEY Y (1999) *Juries in Criminal Trials: A Summary of the Research Findings, Preliminary Paper 37, Vol 2* (Wellington, New Zealand: Law Commission).

ZANDER M (1974) 'Are Too Many Professional Criminals Avoiding Conviction?' 37 MLR 28.

ZANDER M (1979) 'Operation of the Bail Act in London Magistrates' Courts' 129 NLJ 108.

ZANDER M (1991) 'What the Annual Statistics Tell Us About Pleas and Acquittals' Crim LR 252.

ZANDER M (1993) 'The "Innocent" (?) Who Plead Guilty' 143 NLJ 85.

ZANDER M (2000) 'The Criminal Standard of Proof – How Sure is Sure?' 150 NLJ 1517.

ZANDER M (2003) *Cases and Materials on the English Legal System*, 9th edn (London: Butterworths).

ZANDER M (2005) *The Police and Criminal Evidence Act 1984*, 5th edn (London: Sweet & Maxwell).

ZANDER M (2007) *Cases and Materials on the English Legal System* (Oxford: OUP).

ZANDER M (2014) 'Is the Criminal Bar Doomed?' Criminal Law and Justice Weekly 178 JPN 295

ZANDER M and HENDERSON P (1993) *The Crown Court Study, Royal Commission on Criminal Justice Research Study no 19* (London: HMSO).

ZEDNER L (2007) 'Pre-Crime and Post-Criminology?' 11 Theoretical Criminology 261.

ZELLICK G (2005) 'The Criminal Cases Review Commission and the Court of Appeal: The Commission's Perspective' Crim LR 937.

ZUCKERMAN A (1987) 'Illegally Obtained Evidence: Discretion as a Guardian of Legitimacy' CLP 55.

ZUCKERMAN A (1990) 'The Weakness of the PACE Special Procedure for Protecting Confidential Material' [1990] Crim LR 472.

ZUCKERMAN A (2014) 'No Justice Without Lawyers—The Myth of an Inquisitorial Solution' 33 CJQ 355.

Index

A
Abuses of power
  arrest
    remedies, 152–154
    use for unofficial purposes, 117
  complaints against the police
    complaints bodies, 530–531
    complaints statistics, 536–539
    continuing self-regulation, 545
    funding and resources, 544
    history of police complaints system, 531–533
    independence, impartiality, fairness and legitimacy, 542–544
    investigative powers, 541–542
    'local resolution' procedure, 539–541
    platform for police reform, 547–548
    police complaints process, 534–536
    rights of complainants, 545–546
    use of mediation, 546–547
  covert policing, 307, 318–319
  deaths in custody
    coronial process, 594–595
    role of the IOPC, 592–593
  democratic regulation and accountability
    courtroom cameras, 526
    police- and citizen-initiated recordings, and social media, 524–526
    Police and Crime Commissioners, 522–524
    role of ICVs and ICVA, 527
    royal commissions, public inquiries and independent inquiries, 529–530
    voluntary sector campaigning, activists and the academy, 527–529
  entry, search and seizure, 318–320

  fabricated evidence, 335–336
  informers, 301–304
  inspectorates
    performance monitoring, micro-management and managerialism, 549–550
    preventative inspection work, 550–551
    role as regulatory bodies, 548–549
  questioning of suspects
    'sidelining' legal advice, 221–224
  role of human rights, 31–33
  stop and search
    giving and recording reasons, 87–91
    monitoring records, 91–93
    remedies, 94–97
  summary proceedings, 429–430
Abuses of process
  inquisitorial approaches, 13–14
  prosecutions, 326
  trial remedies
    exclusion of evidence, 551–553
    fairness, 555–557
    halting of proceedings, 557–558
    need for reform, 558–559
    oppression and reliability, 553–554
Accountability
  appeals from Crown court to Court of Appeal
    applications for leave to appeal, 564–570
    grounds for appeal, 570–575
  appeals from magistrates' courts
    case stated to the High Court, 562–563
    judicial review, 563–564
    rehearings in the Crown court, 559–562
  complaints against the police
    complaints bodies, 530–531
    complaints statistics, 536–539

  continuing self-regulation, 545
  funding and resources, 544
  history of police complaints system, 531–533
  independence, impartiality, fairness and legitimacy, 542–544
  investigative powers, 541–542
  'local resolution' procedure, 539–541
  platform for police reform, 547–548
  police complaints process, 534–536
  rights of complainants, 545–546
  use of mediation, 546–547
  Crown Prosecution Service (CPS), 355–356
  democratic regulation and accountability
    courtroom cameras, 526
    police- and citizen-initiated recordings, and social media, 524–526
    Police and Crime Commissioners, 522–524
    role of ICVs and ICVA, 527
    royal commissions, public inquiries and independent inquiries, 529–530
    voluntary sector campaigning, activists and the academy, 527–529
  example of Hillsborough disaster, 518–519
  inspectorates
    performance monitoring, micro-management and managerialism, 549–550
    preventative inspection work, 550–551
    role as regulatory bodies, 548–549
  key issues, 275
  legal regulatory and accountability mechanisms

Accountability (contd.)
  exclusion of evidence, 551–553
  fairness, 555–557
  halting of proceedings, 557–558
  need for reform, 558–559
  oppression and reliability, 553–554
  magistrates' courts, 417
  overview, 275–277
  problems with covert policing, 308–309
Acquittals
  crime control and due process compared, 20–22
  directed and ordered acquittals, 433–436
  judicial interventions, 447–451
  overview of process, 4
  quality and fairness of summary justice, 422–424
'Actuarial justice', 40
Administrative offences, 2
Advanced marginality theory, 486–487
Adversarial system
  bail decision-making process, 410–411
  Crown court trials, 432
  impact of numerous guilty pleas, 357
  inquisitorial theories compared, 11–14
  problems of jury comprehension, 475–476
  procedure and evidence, 454
  right to legal advice, 193
  taking suspects' rights seriously, 602
Adverse inferences
  conflating silence with guilt, 224
  right of silence, 214–217, 458
Anti-social behaviour orders (ASBOs)
  hybrid offences, 5–6
  standard of proof, 10
Appeals
  bail, 415
  from Crown Court to Court of Appeal
    applications for leave to appeal, 564–570
    grounds for appeal, 570–575
    jury bias, 437–438
  from magistrates' courts
    case stated to the High Court, 562–563
    judicial review, 563–564
  rehearings in the Crown court, 559–562
  overview of process, 3–4
Appropriate adults
  detention at police stations, 161–162
  questioning of suspects, 235–238, 268
Arrest
  discretionary powers
    discriminatory policing, 144–148
    impact on the public, 148–151
    practical requirement for reasonable suspicion, 131–133
  English approach to crime control and due process, 22–23
  inequality manifested through policing
    arrest and post arrest detention, 500–503
    pre-arrest decision-making, 494–500
  key issues, 110
  legal basis
    breaches of the peace, 124–128
    citizen's arrest, 129–131
    summary arrests, 119–121
    terrorism, 121–124
    with warrant, 119
  meaning and scope, 110–113
  models of justice contrasted
    crime control, 115
    due process, 115
    freedom, 115
  percentage of arrests by ethnicity, t 3.1
  place of arrest, 116–117
  purposes
    ostensible purposes, 113–115
    unofficial purposes, 117–118
  searches without consent
    after arrest without warrant, 285–286
    to make an arrest without warrant, 285
  'social disciplinary model', 21–22
  street policing in context, 55–56
  unofficial purposes, 117–118
  working rules
    demeanour, 136–138
    desires of victim, 139–141
    organisational factors, 141–143
  previous convictions, 138–139
  public order offences, 133–136
  rule of law, 143–144
  wrongful arrest, 152–154
Assault
  stop and search, 94
Attorney-General's Guidelines for Prosecution, 327
Austerity justice
  budget cuts, 43–46
  impact of economic downturn in 2008, 42–43

B
Bad faith
  prosecutions, 326
  questioning of suspects, 244
Bail
  appeals, 415
  conditional bail, 408–409
  criteria for withholding
    failure to answer, 407
    further offences, 406–407
    obstruction of justice, 406
    overview, 406
  decision-making process
    adversarial theories, 410–411
    breaches of bail, 413–414
    relevant information, 411–413
    variations between courts, 409–410
    wrongful denial of bail, 414–415
  inequality manifested through policing, 501
  models of justice contrasted, 403–405
  police bail, 165
  presumption in favour, 416–417
  presumption of innocence, 405
  questioning of suspects
    discretionary powers, 247–248
    manipulation of custodial conditions, 246–247
  time limits on remand, 415–416
'Beyond reasonable doubt', 9–10
Body-worn video (BWV), 601
Breaches of statutory duty, 588
Breaches of the peace
  arrest powers, 124–128
  standard of proof, 10
British Crime Survey

'stop and account', 82
stop and search, 72
Burden of proof
   Crown court trials, 458
   elements of particular offences, 466
   general principles, 9–10

C
Case management, 373
Cautioning
   government policy, 342
   rates, 343–346
   release from detention, 165
   right of silence, 214
CCTV
   arrest powers, 132
   deaths in custody, 184
   detention at police stations, 208
   impact of managerialism, 41
   stop and search, 58
   use for surveillance, 275, 294–295
Charge bargaining
   Crown court practice
      defendants' perceptions, 378
      judicial supervision, 378–379
      role of defence barrister, 374–376
      role of prosecuting counsel, 376–378
   legal advice, 372–373
   overview, 370
   role of CPS, 370–372
Charges
   charging and post charge decision-making, 503–505
   detention without charge
      'helping with inquiries', 166–167
      time limits - non-terrorists, 167–170
Children
   arrest, 120
   citizen's arrests, 130
   out-of-court disposals, 324
   youth courts *see* **Youth courts**
Citizens' powers
   arrest, 129–131
   stop and search, 83–84
Civil claims
   blurring of boundaries with crime, 5–6
   causes of action, 585–588
   covert policing, 307
   effectiveness, 588–589
   successful actions against police 2012–17 t, 12.3
   underlying difficulties, 589–592
   use of negligence claims, 607–608
Civil preventive measures (CPM), 5–6
Class discrimination
   arrest, 110, 144–148
   composition of juries, 440–441
   creating 'dangerous classes' and 'suitable enemies', 482
   high levels of victimisation
      hate crime laws, 508–512
      marginalised groups, 508
   sentencing and incarceration, 506
Community policing
   inequality and victimisation, 508
   stop and search, 56, 106
Community resolution, 346–348
Complaints against the police
   cases recorded 2001/2–2018/19, t 11.1
   complaints bodies, 530–531
   complaints statistics, 536–539
   continuing self-regulation, 545
   deaths in custody, 181, 592–593
   funding and resources, 544
   history of police complaints system, 531–533
   independence, impartiality, fairness and legitimacy, 542–544
   investigative powers, 541–542
   'local resolution' procedure, 539–541
   platform for police reform, 547–548
   police complaints process, 534–536
   rights of complainants, 545–546
   use of mediation, 546–547
Conditional bail
   detention without charge, 165
   general principles, 408–409
Confessions
   acceptance of crime control approach, 271
   false confessions
      coerced confessions, 266–268
      corroboration, 269–271
      effect of new regime, 265–266
      suggestibility, 268–269
   police tactics
      best interests approach, 251
      confrontational approach, 252–253
      deception techniques, 250–251
      persuasive questioning, 249
      softly softly approach, 251–252
      tape recordings, 230
Constabulary independence, 325–327
Control orders, 171–172
Convictions
   crime control and due process compared, 20–22
   difficulty in fraud cases, 475–476
   judicial interventions, 447–451
   majority verdicts, 444–447
   quality and fairness of summary justice, 422–424
   wrongful conviction, 587–588
Cop culture
   arrest, 133, 144, 150, 157
   complaints process, 536, 538
   inequalities in policing, 493
   stop and search, 60–63, 107
Corroboration
   applications for search, 287
   false confessions, 269–271
   identification evidence, 283
Court of Appeal
   applications for leave to appeal, 564–570
   grounds for appeal, 570–575
   overview of process, 3
   response to CCRC, 583–585
   retrials, 448
Courts
   courtroom cameras, 526
   digitalisation, 46
   overview of civil process, 5
   overview of criminal process, 3
Covert policing
   advantages and disadvantages, 308–310
   covert human intelligence sources (CHISs)
      informers, 299–304
      legal regulation, 298–299
      policing strategies, 297–298

Covert policing (contd.)
  undercover police officers, 304–306
  interception of communications, 295–297
  key issues, 275
  meaning and scope, 293–295
  overview, 275–277
  remedies, 318
  surveillance
    directed surveillance, 308
    general principles, 306–307
    intrusive surveillance, 307–308
    property interference, 307
COVID-19
  arrest powers, 118
  availability of legal advice, 198
  black and Asian people, 496
  derogation of human rights, 27
  detention without charge, 169
  identification of suspects, 163
  impact on inequality, 479
  jury trials, 432, 476–477
  live link court facilities, 46
  penalty notices for disorder, 348–349
  questioning outside of police station, 225–226
  remand in custody, 332
  role of the inspectorates, 548
  street policing in context, 55
Crime control approach
  arrest
    models of justice, 115
    no requirement for reasonable suspicion, 131
    official purpose, 120, 133
  bail, 403–404, 416–417
  CPS objectives, 356
  creation of 'dangerous classes', 482
  decisions on s.78 and abuse of process, 558
  detention at police stations
    central issue to criminal justice, 209
    detention without charge, 177–178
    overview, 155–156
  effect of inequality, 481, 516
  English approach, 22–24
  goals, 20–22
  human rights constraints, 24
  impact of managerialism, 41
  jury trials, 431–432
  law of arrest, 151
  legal rules and their effect, *f*

2.1
marginal groups, 492, 508
Police and Crime Commissioners (PCCs), 523
procedure and evidence, 455
processes of exclusion and colonialism, 482–483
prosecutions, 329
questioning of suspects
  changing practices, 210–211
  conclusions, 271–273
  importance to the police, 211–213
reconfiguration of criminal law and criminal justice, 1–2
role of justices' clerks, 402–403
sentence discount principle, 384
social justice, 46
stop and search
  competing demands of crime control versus liberty, 108–109
  desirability of 'firming up' the law, 108
  impact of stop-search powers, 97–102
summary proceedings, 429
taking suspects' rights seriously, 603
taking victims' rights seriously, 605–606
trial remedies, 551–553
underlying principles, 18–19
Crime pre-emption
  effect of recent shift towards preventive orders, 11
  expansion of criminal liability, 6–7
  impact of managerialism, 41
  new approach, 1–2
  social justice, 46
  taking suspects' rights seriously, 601
Criminal Cases Review Commission
  CCRC in practice, 577–582
  effect of inadequate resources, 582–583
  establishment, 576–577
  response of Court of Appeal, 583–585
Criminal justice
  accountability
    democratic regulation and accountability, 522–530
    inspectorates, 548–551
    legal regulatory and ac-

countability mechanisms, 551–559
  organisational regulation and accountability, 530–548
adversarial and inquisitorial approaches compared, 11–14
approach to guilt and innocence
  burden of proof, 9–10
  overview, 8–9
  standard of proof, 10–11
austerity justice
  budget cuts, 43–46
  impact of economic downturn in 2008, 42–43
complaints against the police
  complaints bodies, 530–531
  complaints statistics, 536–539
  continuing self-regulation, 545
  funding and resources, 544
  history of police complaints system, 531–533
  independence, impartiality, fairness and legitimacy, 542–544
  investigative powers, 541–542
  'local resolution' procedure, 539–541
  platform for police reform, 547–548
  police complaints process, 534–536
  rights of complainants, 545–546
  use of mediation, 546–547
conflict between rights of accused persons and victims, 622–627
crime control and due process
  conflicting value systems, 17–18
  English approach, 22–24
  goals, 20–22
  digitalisation, 46–48
  freedom approach, 38–39
how things can go wrong
  concluding remarks, 596
  overview, 518–522
  role of democratic regulation and accountability, 522–530
  role of organisational regulation and accountability, 530–548
human rights approach
  balancing process, 24–25

INDEX

derogation of rights, 27
inadequate guidance for judiciary, 28–29
maximalist alternative and margin of appreciation, 29–30
minimalist safety net, 27–28
problems with conflicting rights, 30–31
problems with individualistic remedies, 31–33
qualification of rights, 26
vagueness and inconsistency, 25–26
key issues, 1
managerialism, 39–42
nature and structure, 1–2
recent trends
 approach to victims, 33–38
 measurement of crime, 17
 Philips Commission, 14–15
 Runciman Commission, 15–16
 value choices about goals, 17–18
social justice approach, 48–50
structure of English process
 civil and criminal matters distinguished, 5–6
 law and behaviour distinguished, 6–8
 overview, 2–4
Crown courts
appeals from magistrates' courts, 559–562
appeals to Court of Appeal
 applications for leave to appeal, 564–570
 grounds for appeal, 570–575
bail appeals, 415
charge bargaining
 defendants' perceptions, 378
 judicial supervision, 378–379
 role of defence barrister, 374–376
 role of prosecuting counsel, 376–378
guilty pleas
 avoiding the Crown court, 369
 pressures to avoid, 369
mode of trial hearings in magistrates' courts, 424–428
overview of process, 3

trial by judge and jury
 composition of jury, 436–444
 directed and ordered acquittals, 433–436
 evaluation of jury's performance, 466–467
 examination of witnesses, 463–464
 hearsay evidence, 462–463
 identification evidence, 462
 judicial interventions, 447–451
 judicial summings up, 451–454
 key battleground for the due process and crime control models, 431–433
 key issues, 431
 majority verdicts, 444–447
 narrowing of jury's domain, 474–477
 need for research into real jury decision-making, 477
 previous convictions, 458–462
 procedure and evidence, 454–456
 right to silence, 457–458
 structure of offences, 464–466
Crown Prosecution Service (CPS)
case construction and evidential sufficiency
 duty to review cases, 332–335
 fabricated evidence, 335–336
 interrogation and witness evidence, 336
 non-disclosure of evidence, 338–342
 scientific evidence, 337
 summaries of interviews, 336–337
charge bargaining, 370–372
discretionary powers
 constabulary independence, 325–327
 legality and opportunity systems contrasted, 324–325
history and origins, 322–323
organisation, 355–356
public interest test
 flexible concept, 342–343
 strategies with mode of trial, 427–428

Curfews, 5, 51, 171, 409, 416
Custody officers
informing suspects of rights, 158–159
police bail, 165
powers and duties, 156–158
right to legal advice, 194
Runciman Commission, 208
vulnerable persons, 160–165
working rules for prosecution, 329–332

D
Deaths in custody
causes, 184–187
coronial process, 594–595
defined, 182
overview, 158, 181–188
right to life (Art 2, 184, 184–187
role of IOPC, 181, 592–593
statistics, 182–184
use of negligence claims, 607–608
use of restraint by police, 162
vulnerable suspects, 160
Deception techniques, 250–251
Derogation of rights, 27
Detention at police stations see also **Questioning of suspects**
central issue to criminal justice, 207–209
deaths in custody, 181–188
detainees held for more than 24 hours, *t 4.1*
detention without charge
experience of detention, 177–181
'helping with inquiries', 166–167
purposes, 173–177
time limits - non-terrorists, 167–170
time limits - terrorists, 170–173
inequality manifested through policing, 500–503
key issues, 155
legal advice
 arrangements prior to PACE, 188–189
 erosion of safeguard, 204–207
 human rights, 189–190
 lawyers' attitudes and practice, 198–207
 PACE, 189–192
 police attitudes and practices, 194–198

Detention at police stations (contd.)
  police ploys, t 4.3
  requests and consultation rates, t 4.2
  take-up by suspects, 192–194
  manipulation of custodial conditions, 246–247
  overview, 155–156
  powers and duties of custody officer
    informing suspects of rights, 158–159
    overview, 156–158
    police bail, 165
    vulnerable persons, 160–165
  preventative inspection work, 550–551
  'social disciplinary model', 21–22
Digitalisation, 43, 46–48, 342, 435, 502
  police- and citizen-initiated recordings, and social media, 526
Diplock courts, 474–475
Directed acquittals, 433–436
Disclosure rules
  case construction by CPS and non-disclosure, 338–342
  Crown court trials, 456–457
  jury vetting, 439
Discretionary powers
  arrest
    impact on the public, 148–151
    practical requirement for reasonable suspicion, 131–133
  bail, 247–248
  prosecutions
    constabulary independence, 325–327
    legality and opportunity systems contrasted, 324–325
  stop and search, 56–59
Discrimination see also **Inequality**
  arrest
    key issues, 110
    race, class and gender, 144–148
  composition of juries, 436, 440–443
  detention at police stations
    deaths in custody, 185–186
    strip searches, 179

  difficulty with civil claims, 590–591
  processes of exclusion and colonialism, 482–484
  right to elect trial, 428
  sentence discount principle, 360
  stop and search, 84–86
Disorder see **Public order**
DNA evidence
  National DNA Database (NDNAD), 310–311
  ratcheting effect, 602–603
  usefulness, 266
Dock identification, 280
Domestic violence
  arrest, 110
  impact of feminist writers, 7
  inequality manifested through policing, 496–500
  mode of trial hearings in magistrates' courts, 428
  specialist magistrates, 428–429
Due process see also **Human rights**
  adversarial and inquisitorial approaches compared, 13–14
  arrest
    models of justice, 115
    official purpose, 115–117
    requirement for genuine need, 120
  bail, 405
  benefits for victims, 33–35
  centrality of legal aid, 392–393
  complaints against the police, 542–544
  CPS objectives, 356
  discretion of prosecution agencies, 326
  English approach, 22–24
  freedom approach, 39
  goals, 20–22
  human rights
    derogation of rights, 27
    inadequate guidance for judiciary, 28–29
  impact of numerous guilty pleas, 357
  jury bias, 438
  jury selection, 443–444
  legal rules and their effect, f 2.1
  problems with conflicting rights, 30
  questioning of suspects
    changing practices, 210–211
    conclusions, 271–273

  right of silence, 214
  right to legal advice, 189–190
  role of justices' clerks, 401–403
  sentence discount principle, 382–386
  social construction of criminal law, 488–489
  summary proceedings, 429
  trial remedies, 555–557
  undercover police officers, 305
  underlying principles, 19–20
  wrongful arrest, 152

E
Early administrative hearings, 403
Enforcement
  overview of process, 2–3
  procedural justice and police legitimacy, 37–38
Entry powers
  case studies, 292–293
  with consent, 291–292
  human rights protections, 283–284
  key issues, 275
  overview, 275–277
  without consent
    after arrest without warrant, 285–286
    to make an arrest without warrant, 285
    other circumstances with warrant, 286–289
Environment Agency
  enforcement body, 2
  prosecutions, 352–353
  taking victims' rights seriously, 606
Equality and Human Rights Commission, 32, 89, 93
Evidence see also **Adverse inferences; Confessions**
  admission of fresh evidence at appeal, 573–575
  adversarial and inquisitorial approaches compared, 11–14
  case construction and evidential sufficiency
    duty to review cases, 332–335
    fabricated evidence, 335–336
    interrogation and witness evidence, 336
    non-disclosure of evidence, 338–342
    scientific evidence, 337
    summaries of interviews, 336–337

INDEX

covert policing
  advantages and disadvantages, 308–310
  covert human intelligence sources (CHISs), 297–306
  interception of communications, 295–297
  key issues, 275
  meaning and scope, 293–295
  overview, 275–277
  surveillance, 306–308
directed and ordered acquittals, 433
DNA evidence
  National DNA Database (NDNAD), 310–311
  ratcheting effect, 602–603
  usefulness, 266
exclusion of evidence, 551–553
importance of police questioning, 211–212
informers
  dangers arising, 301–304
  usefulness, 299–301
judicial summings up, 452–453
key rules, 462–464
non-interrogative techniques, 320
scientific evidence
  case construction, 337
  importance, 312
  key issues, 275
  meaning and scope, 310–311
  overview, 275–277
  problems of proof, 318
  regulation, 315–318
  underlying problems, 313–315
sufficiency for prosecutions
  police working rules, 329–332
  'realistic prospect' test, 328–329
witness identification
  classic problem of policing, 277
  dock identification, 280
  eyewitness identification, 280
  eyewitness reliability, 280
  key issues, 275
  overview, 275–277
  PACE, 281
  questioning of suspects, 277–279
  reliability, 280

  underlying problems, 282–283
  wrongful arrest, 152
Eyewitness identification, 280

F

Fabrication of evidence, 335–336
Fact bargains, 379–380
Fairness *see* Due process
False confessions
  coerced confessions, 266–268
  corroboration, 269–271
  effect of new regime, 265–266
  suggestibility, 268–269
False imprisonment, 585
Feminist perspectives
  ability of the law to legitimise women's claims, 490
  impact of patriarchal constructions of the female role, 490
  impact on criminal law, 7
  raising awareness of domestic violence, 7
  rape myths, 489
Fingerprint evidence, 178–179
Forensic evidence, 311–312
Freedom approach
  arrest
    key issues, 110
    models of justice, 115
    working rules, 144
  cautioning, 343
  centrality of legal aid, 392–393
  cop culture, 62
  CPS objectives, 356
  detention at police stations, 155–156
  general principles, 38–39
  judicial interventions in jury trials, 450
  role of justices' clerks, 403
  stop and search
    competing demands of crime control versus liberty, 108–109
    typical effects, 102–105
Freedom of association (Art 11)
  qualified right, 26
  stop and search, 96
Fundamental rights *see* Human rights

G

Gender bias *see* Sex discrimination
Government policies

  abolition of right to elect trial, 427–428
  approach to inequality, 516
  attempts to abolish jury trial, 475–476
  austerity justice
    budget cuts, 43–46
    impact of economic downturn in 2008, 42–43
  cautioning, 342
  'constabulary independence', 522
  directed and ordered acquittals, 435–436
  factors influencing stop and search, 59
  importance of police questioning, 211
  managerialism, 39–42
  neighbourhood policing, 108
  recent trends in criminal justice, 14–18
  rejection of Law Commission proposals on scientific evidence, 315
  role conflict of CPS, 333
  social justice approach, 48–49
Guilty pleas
  fact bargains, 379–380
  impact of discretion and current practice, 386–388
  influencing factors, 357
  mass production, 356–357
  miscarriages of justice, 380–381
  powers and pressures
    avoiding the Crown court, 369
  sentence discount principle
    crime control approach, 384
    due process, 489–491
    human rights, 383–384
    indications and bargains, 365–368
    managerialism, 384
    rationale, 360–361
    remarks from judiciary, 361
    role of defence lawyers, 362–365
    Sentencing Guidelines Council, 359–360
    sparing victims, 384–386
    statutory basis, 358–359

H

'Hard' evidence, 320
Hearsay evidence, 423
  Crown court trials, 462–463
  hybrid offences, 6

'Helping with inquiries', 166–167
HM Revenue and Customs, 324
Homicide
  criteria for withholding bail, 416
  deaths in custody *see* **Deaths in custody**
Human rights
  approach to criminal justice
    balancing process, 24–25
    derogation of rights, 27
    inadequate guidance for judiciary, 28–29
    maximalist alternative and margin of appreciation, 29–30
    minimalist safety net, 27–28
    problems with conflicting rights, 30–31
    problems with individualistic remedies, 31–33
    qualification of rights, 26
    vagueness and inconsistency, 25–26
  arrest
    breaches of the peace, 126
    degrading treatment, 149–150
    interference with rights, 120
    requirement for reasonable suspicion, 131–133
    terrorism, 121–124
    wrongful arrest, 153
  bail
    presumption of innocence, 405
    right to liberty and security (Art 5), 417
  burden of proof, 9–10
  centrality of legal aid, 392–393
  control orders, 171
  detainees held for more than 24 hours, 169
  detention at police stations
    central issue to criminal justice, 209
    deaths in custody, 184
    general approach, 158
    terrorist suspects, 171
    entry, search and seizure, 283–284
    examination of witnesses, 463–464
    freedom of association (Art 11)
    qualified right, 26

  stop and search, 96
  hearsay evidence, 463
  inadequacy of laws based upon equal rights, 512–515
  jury bias, 436
  jury selection, 443–444
  privacy (Art 8)
    detention at police stations, 209
    entry, search and seizure, 283–284
    intrusive surveillance, 340
    key issues, 275
    overview, 275–277
    qualified right, 26
    use of scientific evidence, 317
  prohibition of torture or inhuman or degrading treatment or punishment (Art 3)
    absolute right, 26
    detention at police stations, 158, 209
    failure of system, 32
    wrongful arrest, 148–149
  questioning of suspects
    conclusions, 271
    presumption of innocence, 210
    right of silence, 214
  right to liberty and security (Art 5)
    bail, 417
    detainees held for more than 24 hours, 169
    terrorist suspects, 171
  right to life (Art 2)
    deaths in custody, 184
    privacy versus protection dilemma, 209
    taking victims' rights seriously, 608
  sentence discount principle, 383–384
  stop and search, 71, 74, 76
  taking victims' rights seriously, 608
  undercover police officers, 305
  use of scientific evidence, 317
Hybrid offences
  blurring of boundaries with crime, 5–6
  examples, 6

I
ID parades
  fabricated evidence, 335
  PACE, 281

  underlying problems, 282
Identification evidence
  classic problem of policing, 277
  Crown court trials, 462
  dock identification, 280
  eyewitness identification, 280
  eyewitness reliability, 280
  key issues, 275
  overview, 275–277
  PACE, 281
  questioning of suspects, 277–279
  rejection of unreliable evidence, 462
  reliability, 280
  underlying problems, 282–283
Independent custody visitors (ICVs), 527
Independent inquiries, 529–530
Independent Office for Police Conduct (IOPC)
  complaints statistics, 536–539
  current police complaints body, 531–533
  deaths in custody, 181, 184, 592–593
  failures, 520
  funding and resources, 544
  history of police complaints system, 531
  independence, impartiality, fairness and legitimacy, 542–544
  investigative powers, 541–542
  platform for police reform, 547–548
  police complaints process, 531
  rights of complainants, 545–546
  unlawful arrests, 149
Inducements to talk, 242–243
Industrial action
  arrest powers, 125–126
Inequality *see also* **Discrimination**
  access to justice, 50
  advanced marginality theory, 486–487
  creating 'dangerous classes' and 'suitable enemies', 482
  disclosure of evidence, 456
  high levels of victimisation
    hate crime laws, 508–512
    marginalised groups, 508
  impact on all stages of the criminal process, 515–516

inadequacy of laws based
upon equal rights, 512–
515
jury trials, 474
key issues, 479
overview, 480–481
police practices
arrest and post arrest
detention, 500–503
charging and post charge
decision-making, 503–
505
pre-arrest decision-making, 494–500
race discrimination, 492–
494
problem with the discretion, 396
processes of exclusion and
colonialism, 482–484
rise of risk society, 485–486
sentencing and incarceration, 505–507
significant trends in twenty-
first century, 479–480
social construction of criminal law, 487–491
Informal questioning, 253–258
Informers
dangers arising, 301–304
usefulness, 299–301
Inquisitorial systems, 11–14
Inspectorates
performance monitoring,
micro-management and
managerialism, 549–
550
preventative inspection
work, 550–551
role as regulatory bodies, 548–549
Interception of communications, 295–297
Interrogation see **Questioning of suspects**
Intimate searches and samples, 179–180
Intimation, 158–159
Investigation of crime
investigative interviewing, 258–262
purposes of arrest, 120
Investigatory Powers Commissioner, 294, 297–298,
308

J
Judicial review
appeals from magistrates'
courts, 563–564
victims' entitlement, 4

wrongful arrest, 152
Judiciary
Crown court trials
directed and ordered
acquittals, 433–436
judicial interventions, 447–451
judicial summings
up, 451–454
majority verdicts, 444–447
procedure and evidence, 454–456
disagreement with verdict, 468–469
jury selection, 438
sentence discount principle
indications and bargains, 365–368
supervision of charge bargaining, 378–379
Juries
absence in magistrates'
courts, 417–418
composition, 436–444
Crown court trials
directed and ordered
acquittals, 433–436
examination of witnesses, 463–464
hearsay evidence, 462–463
identification evidence, 462
judicial interventions, 447–451
judicial summings
up, 451–454
key battleground for the
due process and crime
control models, 431–
433
majority verdicts, 444–447
previous convictions, 458–
462
procedure and evidence, 454–456
right to silence, 457–458
structure of offences, 464–
466
evaluation of performance
absence of reasons, 466–
467
changing values, 474
disagreements with verdict, 468–471
general impressions, 467–
468
shadow juries, 471–473
key issues, 431
mode of trial hearings in magistrates'
courts, 424–428

narrowing of jury's domain, 474–477
need for research into real
jury decision-making,
477
rape myths, 488
vetting, 439
Justices' clerks, 401–403

K
'Kettling', 127, 151

L
Lawyers see also **Legal advice**
charge bargaining
case management, 373
role of defence barrister, 374–376
role of prosecuting counsel, 376–378
Criminal Defence Service, 204–207
disagreement with verdict, 469
gender bias, 487
justices' clerks, 401–403
legal advice for detained
suspects
para-legals and trainees, 199
quality of assistance, 201–
204
telephone advice, 200–201
unavailability and contact
time, 198
seizure of items subject to
legal privilege, 290
solicitors' duty scheme, 192
special advocates, 171
Legal advice
charge bargaining, 374–376
detention at police stations
arrangements prior to
PACE, 188–189
erosion of safeguard,
204–207
human rights, 189–190
lawyers' attitudes and
practice, 198–207
PACE, 189–192
police attitudes and practices, 194–198
police ploys, t 4.3
requests and consultation
rates, t 4.2
take-up by suspects, 192–
194
impact of budget cuts, 45
informing suspects of
rights, 158–159
justices' clerks, 401–403

Legal advice (contd.)
  overview of process, 4
  questioning of suspects, 221–224
  seizure of items subject to legal privilege, 290
Legal aid
  civil claims, 589–590
  reform proposals, 393
  summary proceedings
    costs to public purse, 396–397
    means test, 393–394
    merits test, 394–396
    quality of work, 397–401
Legal rules *see* **Rule of law**
Legal Services Commission, 204
Legality system of prosecution, 324–325

M

Macpherson Report, 62, 68, 71–72, 81, 95, 98
Magistrates' courts
  appeals from
    case stated to the High Court, 562–563
    judicial review, 563–564
    rehearings in the Crown court, 559–562
  guilty pleas
    avoiding the Crown court, 369
    key issues, 389
  overview of process, 3
  proceedings in selected years, t 8.1
  search warrants, 285–9
  summary proceedings
    bail, 403–417
    justices' clerks, 401–403
    legal aid, 392–401
    obstacles to justice, 429–430
    overview, 389–392
    quality and fairness of justice, 417–428
    specialist magistrates, 428–429
Malicious prosecution, 586–587
Malpractice *see* **Abuse of powers**
Managerialism
  distortion of crime control model, 33
  factors influencing stop and search, 59
  inspectorates, 549–550
  overview, 39–42

  sentence discount principle, 384
Margin of appreciation, 29–30
Measurement of crime
  recent trends, 17
Miscarriages of justice
  Criminal Cases Review Commission
    CCRC in practice, 577–582
    effect of inadequate resources, 582–583
    establishment, 576–577
    response of Court of Appeal, 583–585
  detention of vulnerable suspects at police stations, 160
  disagreements with verdict, 468–471
  fabrication of evidence, 335–336
  guilty pleas, 380–381
  judicial summings up, 452
  jury bias, 437–438
  post-appeal
    Criminal Cases Review Commission, 576–585
    Home Secretary references to the Court of Appeal (pre-1997), 575–576
  problems with scientific evidence, 314
  recent trends, 14–15
  right to legal advice, 193
  role of human rights, 30
  role of justice system, 3–4
  summary proceedings, 429–430
  types of wrongful conviction, 4
  wrongful denial of bail, 414–415
Mock juries, 471–473
Mode of trial proceedings, 424–428
Models of justice contrasted
  crime control, 115
  due process, 115
  freedom, 115

N

Necessity principle
  arrest, 120, 134, 143
  detention at police stations, 173
'Neo-liberalism', 39–42
'New penology', 40
No further action (NFA), 331
Non-arrestable offences, 119–121

O

Offences
  arrestable and non-arrestable offences, 119–121
  elements to be proved, 464–466
Opportunity systems of prosecution, 324–325
Oppression
  questioning of suspects, 244–245
  trial remedies, 553–554
Ordered acquittals, 433–436
Out of court disposals (OOCDs)
  cautioning, 342
  community resolution and restorative justice, 346–348
  penalty notices for disorder, 348–350
  police working rules, 350–351
  taking suspects' rights seriously, 600

P

PACE
  arrestable and non-arrestable offences, 120
  breaches of statutory duty, 588
  detention at police stations
    custody officers, 157–158
    'helping with inquiries', 166–167
    informing suspects of rights, 158–159
    overview, 155–156
    purposes, 173–177
    time limits - non-terrorists, 167–170
    vulnerable persons, 160–165
  fairness, 555–557
  identification evidence, 281
  'local resolution' procedure for police complaints, 539
  oppression and reliability, 553–554
  questioning of suspects
    cautioning, 226–227
    false confessions, 265–266
    general control of interrogation, 210–211
    informal questioning, 253–258
    investigative interviewing, 260–261
    recording of interviews, 231–235

requirements for formal interview, 228–231
right to legal advice, 235
right to remain silent, 214
right to legal advice
  delaying access, 190–191
  notification of right and provision of advice, 191–192
  statutory provisions, 189–190
stop and search
  giving and recording reasons, 87–91
  individualised suspicion of a specific offence, 78–80
  inhibitory effect, 107
  monitoring of search records, 92
  Philips Commission's proposals, 63–64
  reasonable suspicion, 64–73
  role of legal rules, 59–60
  targeted offences, 73–80
Penalty notices for disorder
  public interest test, 348–350
  release from detention, 165
Peremptory jury challenges, 439, 439–440
Philips Commission
  arrest
    changing police practices, 153
    disruption of life, 112
  blueprint for new system, 14–15
  detention at police stations purposes, 174
  false confessions, 265
  police interviews, 231–232
  prosecution of weak cases, 329
  recommendations for Chief Crown Prosecutor, 355
  stop and search
    constraints and controls, 87
    four new types of rule, 63–64
    monitoring of search records, 91
Phone tapping, 338
Pleas
  fact bargains, 379–380
  impact of discretion and current practice, 386–388
  miscarriages of justice, 380–381
  powers and pressures, 369
  sentence discount principle

crime control approach, 384
due process, 489–491
human rights, 383–384
indications and bargains, 365–368
managerialism, 384
rationale, 360–361
remarks from judiciary, 361
role of defence lawyers, 362–365
Sentencing Guidelines Council, 359–360
sparing victims, 384–386
statutory basis, 358–359
Police
advanced marginality theory, 486–487
arrest
  discretionary powers, 131–133
  key issues, 110
  legal basis, 119–131
  meaning and scope, 110–113
  models of justice contrasted, 115
  ostensible purposes, 113–115
  place of arrest, 116–117
  remedies for abuse of powers, 152–154
  unofficial purposes, 117–118
breaches of statutory duty, 588
cautioning, 343–346
civil claims against
  causes of action, 585–588
  effectiveness, 588–589
  successful actions against police 2012–17, t 12.3
  underlying difficulties, 589–592
complaints against the police
  complaints bodies, 530–531
  complaints statistics, 536–539
  continuing self-regulation, 545
  funding and resources, 544
  history of police complaints system, 531–533
  independence, impartiality, fairness and legitimacy, 542–544
  investigative powers, 541–542
  'local resolution' procedure, 539–541

platform for police reform, 547–548
rights of complainants, 545–546
use of mediation, 546–547
covert activities
  advantages and disadvantages, 308–310
  covert human intelligence sources (CHISs), 297–306
  interception of communications, 295–297
  meaning and scope, 293–295
  overview, 275–277
  surveillance, 306–308
deaths in custody
  coronial process, 594–595
  role of the IOPC, 592–593
democratic regulation and accountability
  police- and citizen-initiated recordings, and social media, 524–526
  Police and Crime Commissioners, 522–524
detention of suspects
  central issue to criminal justice, 207–209
  death in custody, 181–188
  detention without charge, 167–173
  key issues, 155
  legal advice, 188–207
  overview, 155–156
  powers and duties of custody officer, 156–165
disagreement with verdict, 469
freedom approach, 38
impact of managerialism, 39–42
inequality manifested through policing
  arrest and post arrest detention, 500–503
  charging and post charge decision-making, 503–505
  pre-arrest decision-making, 494–500
  race discrimination, 492–494
informers
  dangers arising, 301–304
  usefulness, 299–301
legal rules and their effect, *f 2.1*
National Decision Model, *f 7.1*

Police (contd.)
  organisational regulation and accountability, 534–536
  overview of process, 2
  penalty notices for disorder, 348–350
  prosecutions
    constabulary independence, 325–327
    history and origins, 322–323
    legality and opportunity systems contrasted, 324–325
    public interest test, 342–351
    'realistic prospect' test, 328–329
    working rules, 329–332
  questioning of suspects
    confessions, 265–271
    control of police powers, 225–240
    from due process to crime control, 210–211
    importance to the police, 211–213
    key issues, 210
    police tactics, 241–262
    right to remain silent, 214–225
  stop and search see **Stop and search**
  street policing in context, 54–56
  taking suspects' rights seriously, 600–605
Police and Crime Commissioners (PCCs), 522–524
Police bail, 165
Police Community Support Officers (PCSOs)
  changed forms of policing, 58
  informal questioning of suspects, 226
  stop and search, 83
Pre-trial reviews
  abolition by Criminal Procedure Rules, 432
  charge bargaining, 373
  role of justices' clerks, 403
Presumption of innocence
  bail, 405
  effect on reverse burden, 9
  fundamental principle of police questioning, 210
Previous convictions
  arrest, 138–139
  Crown court trials, 458–462
Privacy (Art 8)
  detention at police stations, 209
  entry, search and seizure, 283–284
  intrusive surveillance, 340
  key issues, 275
  overview, 275–277
  qualified right, 26
  use of scientific evidence, 317
Private policing
  citizen's arrest, 129–131
  stop and search, 83–84
Private prosecutions
  history and origins, 322
  lack of constraints, 327–328
Privilege
  admission of evidence, 556
  covert policing, 307
  legal advice, 161, 222
  seizure of items subject to legal privilege, 290
  self-incrimination, 214
Proceeds of crime, 5–6
Prohibition of torture or inhuman or degrading treatment or punishment (Art 3)
  absolute right, 26
  detention at police stations
    general approach, 158
    privacy versus protection dilemma, 209
  failure of system, 32
  wrongful arrest, 148–149
Proof
  burden of proof, 9–10
  civil claims, 589
  Crown court trials, 458
  elements of particular offences, 466
  scientific evidence, 318
  standard of proof, 10–11
Prosecutions
  case construction and evidential sufficiency
    duty to review cases, 332–335
    fabricated evidence, 335–336
    interrogation and witness evidence, 336
    non-disclosure of evidence, 338–342
    scientific evidence, 337
    summaries of interviews, 336–337
  discretionary powers
    constabulary independence, 325–327
    legality and opportunity systems contrasted, 324–325
  evidential sufficiency
    police working rules, 329–332
  history and origins, 322–323
  inequality manifested through policing, 503–505
  key issues, 322
  malicious prosecution, 586–587
  non-police agencies, 351–355
  organisation of CPS, 355–356
  overview of process, 2–3
  Police National Decision Model, *f* 7.1
  private prosecutions
    lack of constraints, 327–328
  procedural rights for victims, 616–619
  public interest test
    cautioning, 343–346
    community resolution and restorative justice, 346–348
    flexible concept, 342–343
    penalty notices for disorder, 348–350
Public inquiries, 529–530
Public interest immunity, 303
Public interest test
  cautioning, 343–346
  community resolution and restorative justice, 346–348
  flexible concept, 342–343
  penalty notices for disorder, 348–350
Public order offences
  arrest
    discretionary powers, 132
    legal basis, 127–128
    official purpose, 133
    working rules, 133–144
  conditional bail, 408
  inequality in arrest and post arrest detention, 500
  summary proceedings, 426

Q
Qualified rights, 26
Questioning of suspects *see also* **Detention at police stations**
  control of police powers
    conditions and facilities, 240–241
    formalities, 228–231
    place of interview, 272–275
    recording of interviews, 231–235
    termination of interviews, 238–240

INDEX

vulnerable persons, 235–238
crime control approach, 271–273
due process to crime control, 210–211
importance to the police, 211–213
key issues, 210
police tactics
  effectiveness, 262–265
  inducements to talk, 242–243
  informal questioning, 253–258
  investigative interviewing, 258–262
  legal restraints, 241–242
  no decision to be made, 249
  oppression, 244–245
  provision of expert knowledge, 248–249
  traditional approaches, 246–253
  unfair interrogation, 243–244
  unreliable evidence, 245
purpose of arrest, 115
right of silence
  adverse inferences, 214–217
  cautioning, 214
  conflating silence with guilt, 224
  consequences of refusal to co-operate, 217–218
  continuing debates, 224–225
  disclosure rules, 218–219
  legal advice, 221–224
  statistical trends, 219–220
  use of right, t 5.1
witness identification, 277–279

R
Racial discrimination
arrest, 144–148
  key issues, 110
  arrest and post arrest detention, 500–503
  charging and post charge decision-making, 503–505
  composition of juries, 436, 440–443
  deaths in custody, 184–187
  detention at police stations
    deaths in custody, 185–186
    strip searches, 179

difficulty with civil claims, 590–591
inequality manifested through policing, 492–494
processes of exclusion and colonialism, 482–484
right to elect trial, 428
sentence discount principle, 360
sentencing and incarceration, 505–506
stop and search, 84–86, 494–496
'Realistic prospect' test, 328–329
Reasonable suspicion
arrest
  impact on the public, 148–151
  no requirement, 131
  practical requirement for reasonable suspicion, 131–133
  working rules, 133–144
control orders, 172
stop and search
  difficult concept, 64–67
  extra powers, 73–77
  individualised suspicion of a specific offence, 78–80
  working assumptions and working rules, 68–73
Records
custody officers, 158
police interviews, 231–235
Rehabilitation of offenders, 42–43
Remedies
civil claims
  causes of action, 585–588
  effectiveness, 588–589
  successful actions against police 2012-17, t 12.3
  underlying difficulties, 589–592
covert policing, 318
deaths in custody
  coronial process, 594–595
  role of the IOPC, 592–593
human rights approach, 31–33
stop and search, 94–97
taking suspects' rights seriously, 602
trial remedies
  exclusion of evidence, 551–553
  fairness, 555–557
  halting of proceedings, 557–558
  need for reform, 558–559

oppression and reliability, 553–554
use of negligence claims, 607–608
wrongful arrest, 110, 152–154
Restorative justice
community resolution, 346–348
complaints against the police, 546–547
multi-victim perspective, 134
Reverse burden of proof
elements of particular offences, 466
general principles, 9–10
Right of silence
adverse inferences, 214–217
cautioning, 215
changing values, 474
conflating silence with guilt, 224
consequences of refusal to co-operate, 217–218
continuing debates, 224–225
disclosure rules, 218–219
legal advice, 221–224
statistical trends, 219–220
trial by judge and jury, 457–458
use of right, t 5.1
vulnerable persons, 189–190
Right to liberty and security (Art 5)
bail, 417
detention at police stations
  detainees held for more than 24 hours, 169
  terrorist suspects, 171
Right to life (Art 2
absolute right, 26
detention at police stations
  deaths in custody, 184
  privacy versus protection dilemma, 209
  taking victims' rights seriously, 608
Risk society
effect of inequality, 481, 485–486
impact of managerialism, 40
taking suspects' rights seriously, 602
Royal commissions, 529–530
Rule of law
arrest, 143–144
detention of terrorists, 170
freedom of police to detain suspects, 209
judicial fairness, 417
prosecution policies, 325
questioning of suspects, 241–242

Rule of law (*contd.*)
   rationale for police conduct, 38
Runciman Commission
   Criminal Cases Review Commission, 576
   detention at police stations, 207, 208
   evaluation of jury's performance, 468
   judicial interventions, 449
   origins and establishment, 15–16
   police interviews, 258
   research into real jury decision-making, 477
   right of silence, 225
   sentence discount principle, 366, 384

S
Scientific evidence
   case construction, 337
   importance, 312
   key issues, 275
   meaning and scope, 310–311
   overview, 275–277
   problems of proof, 318
   regulation, 315–318
   underlying problems, 313–315
Search powers *see also* **Seizure**; **Stop and search**
   case studies, 292–293
   with consent, 291–292
   human rights protections, 283–284
   key issues, 275
   overview, 275–277
   without consent
      after arrest without warrant, 285–286
      to make an arrest without warrant, 285
      other circumstances with warrant, 286–289
Seizure
   case studies, 292–293
   with consent, 291–292
   human rights protections, 283–284
   key issues, 275
   overview, 275–277
   without consent
      excluded material, 290
      items subject to legal privilege, 290
      special procedure material, 290–291
      wide powers, 289–290
Sentence discount principle
   guilty pleas
      due process, 382–383
      human rights, 383–384
      indications and bargains, 365–368
      remarks from judiciary, 361
      role of defence lawyers, 362–365
      sparing victims, 384–386
   human rights, 383–384
   indications and bargains, 365–368
   judiciary
      indications and bargains, 365–368
   pleas
      due process, 382–383
      human rights, 383–384
      indications and bargains, 365–368
      remarks from judiciary, 361
      role of defence lawyers, 362–365
      sparing victims, 384–386
   problems arising, 382–383
   Runciman Commission, 366, 384
   victims, 384–386
Sentencing
   charge bargaining
      Crown court practice, 373–379
      legal advice, 372–373
      overview, 370
      role of CPS, 370–372
   co-operation at police station, 247–248
   discount principle
      avoiding the Crown court, 369
      crime control approach, 384
      due process, 489–491
      human rights, 383–384
      indications and bargains, 365–368
      managerialism, 384
      rationale, 360–361
      remarks from judiciary, 361
      role of defence lawyers, 362–365
   Sentencing Guidelines Council, 359–360
      sparing victims, 384–386
      statutory basis, 358–359
   fact bargains, 379–380
   impact of discretion and current practice, 386–388
   inequality, 505–507
   powers and pressures
      avoiding the Crown court, 369
   victim personal statements (VPS), 619–622
Sex discrimination
   arrest, 144–148
   lawyers, 487
   police custody experience, 526
   prosecutions, 505
   rape myths, 473
   sentencing and incarceration, 506–507
   stop and search, 61–62
Shadow juries, 471–473
Silence *see* **Right to remain silent**, 189–190
'Social disciplinary model', 21–22
Social justice, 48–50
'Soft' evidence, 320
Special advocates, 171
Special procedure material, 290–291
Standard of proof
   civil claims, 589
   general principles, 10–11
   scientific evidence, 318
Stop and search
   allied powers, 77–78
   citizen's stop-search, 83–84
   complaints process, 538
   constraints and controls
      challenging a questionable search, 94–97
      giving and recording reasons, 87–91
      monitoring of search records, 91–93
      Philips Commission, 87
   cop culture, 60–63
   desirability of 'firming up' the law, 108
   English approach to crime control and due process, 23
   ethnic groups stopped and searched in England and Wales 2018/19, *t* 2.2
   factors influencing discretion
      changed forms of policing, 58
      interpretational latitude, 58
      organisational, 59
      personal, 57
      political/managerial pressures, 59
      procedural, 58
      societal pressures, 59

working assumptions and working rules, 57–58
impact of stop-search powers
  crime control, 97–102
  police-community relations, 105–106
  undermining of freedom, 102–105
inequality manifested through policing, 494–496
key issues, 53
overview, 53–54
PACE
  giving and recording reasons, 87–91
  individualised suspicion of a specific offence, 78–80
  inhibitory effect, 107
  monitoring of search records, 92
  Philips Commission's proposals, 63–64
  reasonable suspicion, 64–73
  targeted offences, 73–80
police working assumptions, 107–108
racial discrimination, 84–86
recorded stop-searches, t 2.1
rise of 'stop and account', 80–83
role of legal rules, 59–60
street policing in context, 54–56
taking suspects' rights seriously, 601
Strikes
arrest powers, 125–126
Strip searches, 177–178
Summary arrest, 119–121
Summary proceedings
justices' clerks, 401–403
key issues, 389
legal aid
  costs to public purse, 396–397
  means test, 393–394
  merits test, 394–396
  quality of work, 397–401
  reform proposals, 393
models of justice contrasted, 403–405
obstacles to justice, 429–430
overview, 389–392
quality and fairness of justice
  absence of jury, 417–418
  acquittals and convictions, 422–424
  mode of trial, 424–428
  role of magistrates, 418–422

specialist magistrates, 428–429
Summings up, 451–454
Supergrasses, 300
Surveillance
directed surveillance, 308
general principles, 306–307
intrusive surveillance, 307–308
property interference, 307
Suspects
detention at police stations
  central issue to criminal justice, 207–209
  death in custody, 181–188
  detention without charge, 167–173
  key issues, 155
  legal advice, 188–207
  overview, 155–156
  powers and duties of custody officer, 156–165
English approach to crime control and due process, 22–23
questioning by police
  confessions, 265–271
  control of police powers, 225–240
  from due process to crime control, 210–211
  importance to the police, 211–213
  key issues, 210
  police tactics, 241–262
  right to remain silent, 214–225
social justice approach, 48
taking suspects' rights seriously, 600–605

T
Tape recordings
case construction by CPS, 336
police interviews, 231–235
Telephone tapping, 338
Terrorism
arrest
  key issues, 110
  police powers, 121–124
composition of jury, 441
derogation of rights, 27
detention at police stations
  experience of detention, 180–181
  informing suspects of rights, 159
  time limits, 170–173
hybrid offences, 6
impact of human rights, 28

increase in police powers, 16
response to human rights, 9–10
risk management techniques, 2
standard of proof, 10
stop and search, 74–75
taking suspects' rights seriously, 603–604
Time limits
detention at police stations
  non-terrorists, 167–170
  terrorist suspects, 170–173
remand in custody, 415–416
Torts *see* **Civil actions**
Transparency
key issues, 275
overview, 275–277
problems with covert policing, 308–309
Trespass
civil claims, 586
covert policing, 307
Trials
courtroom cameras, 526
judge and jury
  composition of jury, 436–444
  directed and ordered acquittals, 433–436
  disclosure rules, 456–457
  evaluation of jury's performance, 466–467
  examination of witnesses, 463–464
  hearsay evidence, 462–463
  identification evidence, 462
  judicial interventions, 447–451
  judicial summings up, 451–454
  key battleground for the due process and crime control models, 431–433
  key issues, 431
  majority verdicts, 444–447
  narrowing of jury's domain, 474–477
  need for research into real jury decision-making, 477
  previous convictions, 458–462
  procedure and evidence, 454–456
  right to silence, 457–458
  structure of offences, 464–466
  rule-breaking by police and other officials.

Trials (contd.)
   exclusion of evidence, 551–553
   fairness, 555–557
   halting of proceedings, 557–558
   need for reform, 558–559
   oppression and reliability, 553–554
   summary proceedings in magistrates' courts
      bail, 403–417
      justices' clerks, 401–403
      legal aid, 392–401
      overview, 389–392
'Truth-discovery', 12

U
Undercover police officers, 304–306
Unreliable evidence
   questioning of suspects, 245
   scientific evidence, 318
   trial remedies, 553–554
   witness identification, 280

V
Vehicle stops
   reasonable suspicion, 66
   reasonable suspicion not required, 73–74
Victims
   bail conditions, 165
   community resolution and restorative justice, 346–348
   conflict with the rights of accused persons, 622–627
   CPS objectives, 356
   desire to arrest offender, 139–141
   difficulty with civil claims, 590
   directed and ordered acquittals, 435
   entitlement to judicial review, 4
   failure of human rights, 30
   freedom approach, 38–39
   impact of recent changes, 33–38
   key issues, 599
   sentence discount principle, 384–386
   significance of Stephen Lawrence case, 37
   specialist magistrates, 428–429
   taking victims' rights seriously
      Code of Practice for Victims of Crime, 609–610
      erosion of freedoms, 605–606
      procedural rights, 616–622
      use of negligence claims and the ECHR, 607–608
      Victims' Charter, 608–609
      vulnerable victims and witnesses, 610–615
   victim personal statements (VPS), 619–622
   working rules, 599–600
Vulnerable persons
   arrest
      preventative powers, 120
      for self-protection, 120
   cross examination of witnesses, 450
   detention at police stations, 160–165, 188, 208
   directed and ordered acquittals, 435
   failure of human rights, 28, 30
   questioning of suspects, 235–238, 268
   social justice approach, 49
   victims and witnesses, 610–615

W
Warrants
   arrest, 119
   entry, search and seizure, 285–289
   interception of communications, 296
Witnesses
   bail conditions, 165
   case construction by CPS, 336
   criteria for withholding bail, 406
   directed and ordered acquittals, 435
   examination at Crown court, 463–464
   identification evidence
      classic problem of policing, 277
      dock identification, 280
      eyewitness identification, 280
      key issues, 275
      PACE, 281
      questioning of suspects, 277–279
      reliability, 280
      underlying problems, 282–283
   judicial summings up, 452–453
   vulnerable victims and witnesses, 610–615

Y
Youth courts
   'either way' cases, 424
   liberal approach, 425
   presiding magistrates, 418
   sentencing discounts, 360
   structure of English process, 3
   summary proceedings, 389

Z
'Zero tolerance', 56, 59